People, Places, and Times
Readings in Canadian Social History
Volume 2: Post-Confederation

Cynthia R. Comacchio
Wilfrid Laurier University

Elizabeth Jane Errington
Royal Military College / Queen's University

THOMSON
_____*_____
NELSON

Australia   Canada   Mexico   Singapore   Spain   United Kingdom   United States

THOMSON

NELSON

People, Places, and Times: Readings in Canadian Social
History, Volume 2: Post-Confederation

by Cynthia R. Comacchio and Elizabeth Jane Errington

**Associate Vice President,
Editorial Director:**
Evelyn Veitch

Executive Editor:
Anne Williams

Marketing Manager:
Laura Armstrong

Developmental Editors:
Mike Thompson, Colleen Shea

Photo Researcher:
Cynthia Howard

Permissions Coordinator:
Cynthia Howard

Senior Production Editor:
Bob Kohlmeier

Copy Editor:
Sarah Robertson

Proofreader:
Sheila Wawanash

Indexer:
Dennis A. Mills

Production Coordinator:
Ferial Suleman

Design Director:
Ken Phipps

Interior Design:
Katherine Strain

Cover Design:
Peter Papayanakis

Cover Images:
Erik Christensen Photo (top and
bottom); Harry McLorinan/The
Globe and Mail (middle)

Compositor:
Carol Magee

Printer:
The P. A. Hutchison Company

**Library and Archives Canada
Cataloguing in Publication**

People, places and times : readings
in Canadian social history / [edited
by] Cynthia R. Comacchio and
Elizabeth Jane Errington.

Includes bibliographical references
and index.
Contents: v. 1. Pre-Confederation
— v. 2. Post-Confederation.
ISBN 0-17-640617-4 (v. 2)

1. Canada—Social conditions—
Textbooks. 2. Canada—History—
Textbooks. I. Comacchio, Cynthia
R., 1957– II. Errington, Jane, 1951–

HN103.P45 2006   971
C2005-902346-5

CONTENTS

PREFACE ... xi

INTRODUCTION ... xv

Post-Confederation Timeline ... xvii

Maps of Canada in 1867 and in the 21st Century ... xix

Topic 1
Aboriginal Peoples: Communities and Conditions of Life ... 1

Context ... 3

    References/Further Reading ... 4

Illustration 1.1 ... 5

Articles ... 5

Article 1.1
Nicole St-Onge
Memories of Métis Women of Saint-Eustache, Manitoba, 1910–1980 ... 6

Article 1.2
Hugh Shewell
"Bitterness Behind Every Smiling Face": Community Development and Canada's First Nations,
    1954–1968 ... 20

Document 1.1
Interview with Solomon Johnston, Mistawasis First Nation ... 38

Document 1.2
Margaret Ecker Francis
Strange Women in Our Midst: The First Canadians ... 41

Topic 2
Industrial Canada: Socioeconomic Transformation, Class, and Labour ... 45

Context ... 47

    References/Further Reading ... 48

Illustration 2.1 ... 49

Articles ... 49

Article 2.1
Jeremy L. Stein
Dislocations: Changing Experiences of Time and Space in an Industrialising Nineteenth-Century
    Ontario Town ... 50

Article 2.2
Miriam Wright
Young Men and Technology: Government Attempts to Create a "Modern" Fisheries Workforce in Newfoundland, 1949–70 ... 63

Document 2.1
Report of Commission to Enquire into the Necessity of a New Brunswick Factory Act ... 75

Document 2.2
Interview with Mrs. Jill Halpenny ... 78

Document 2.3
The Canadian UAW-CIO Win the Peace Plan ... 79

Topic 3
Governing Modernity: Social Science, Social Reform, and the State ... 83

Context ... 85

   References/Further Reading ... 86

Illustration 3.1 ... 87

Articles ... 87

Article 3.1
Alan Hunt
Measuring Morals: The Beginnings of the Social Survey Movement in Canada, 1913–1917 ... 88

Article 3.2
Sean Purdy
Industrial Efficiency, Social Order and Moral Purity: Housing Reform Thought in English Canada, 1900–1950 ... 106

Document 3.1
J. S. Woodsworth
The Seamy Side or Social Pathology ... 123

Document 3.2
Drink (Editorial in *Calgary Eye Opener*) ... 129

Document 3.3
A Juvenile Court Probation Officer ... 130
As the Twig Is Bent: What Are We Doing to Keep Children from the Reformatory? ... 130

Topic 4
Citizens and Nation: Race, Ethnicity, and Immigration ... 133

Context ... 135

   References/Further Reading ... 137

Illustration 4.1 ... 137

Articles ... 138

Article 4.1
Elizabeth Beaton
An African-American Community in Cape Breton, 1901–1904 ... 139

Article 4.2
Kerry Badgley
"As Long as He Is an Immigrant from the United Kingdom": Deception, Ethnic Bias and
    Milestone Commemoration in the Department of Citizenship and Immigration,
    1953–1965 ... 158

Document 4.1
J. T. M. Anderson
Immigrant Communities ... 170

Document 4.2
James Jenkins
Editorials in *The Dawn of Tomorrow* ... 174

Topic 5
Public and Private Worlds: Women, Men, and Family ... 179

Context ... 181

    References/Further Reading ... 182

Illustration 5.1 ... 183

Articles ... 183

Article 5.1
Magda Fahrni
The Romance of Reunion: Montreal War Veterans Return to Family Life, 1944–1949 ... 184

Article 5.2
Robert A. J. McDonald
"He Thought He Was the Boss of Everything": Masculinity and Power in a Vancouver Family ... 200

Document 5.1
Ruby Cress
Letters from the 1950s ... 216

Document 5.2
Claire Drainie Taylor
Swift Current ... 221

Topic 6
Regulating Sexuality: The Moral, the "Normal," and the Deviant ... 227

Context ... 229

    References/Further Reading ... 230

Illustration 6.1 ... 231

Articles ... 231

Article 6.1
Catherine Gidney
Under the President's Gaze: Sexuality and Morality at a Canadian University During the Second
     World War ... 232

Article 6.2
Valerie J. Korinek
"Don't Let Your Girlfriends Ruin Your Marriage": Lesbian Imagery in *Chatelaine* Magazine,
     1950–1969 ... 245

Document 6.1
Percy E. Ryberg, MD
On Sex Education ... 265

Document 6.2
Anglican Synod of Ontario
Recommendations Re the Protection of Girl Life ... 267

Document 6.3
Basic Education (Editorial in *Toronto Star*) ... 271

Topic 7
Age Matters: Youth and the Elderly ... 273

Context ... 275

     References/Further Reading ... 276

Illustration 7.1 ... 277

Articles ... 277

Article 7.1
Linda Ambrose
Cartoons and Commissions: Advice to Junior Farmers in Postwar Ontario ... 278

Article 7.2
Megan J. Davies
Renovating the Canadian Old Age Home: The Evolution of Residential Care Facilities in B.C.,
     1930–1960 ... 294

Document 7.1
Speech of the Hon. Sir Richard Cartwright on Old Age Pensions ... 308

Document 7.2
Minister Discusses Old-Age Pensions ... 310

Document 7.3
Toronto's First Teenage Club ... 311

Topic 8
Modernizing Institutions: Church and School ... 313

Context ... *315*

References/Further Reading ... *316*

Illustration 8.1 ... *317*

Articles ... *317*

Article 8.1
Cynthia Comacchio
Inventing the Extracurriculum: High School Culture in Interwar Ontario ... 318

Article 8.2
Heidi Macdonald
Doing More with Less: The Sisters of St. Martha (PEI) Diminish the Impact of the
   Great Depression ... 334

Document 8.1
The Women's Canadian Club of St. John, N.B.
A Suggested Programme for Empire Day Celebration 1915 in the Schools of
   New Brunswick ... 354

Document 8.2
Excerpts from *Fact and Fancy* ... 358

Document 8.3
H. H. Draper
"My First Day of School" and "My Primary School Teacher" ... 362

Document 8.4
Excerpts from *The Boy's Own Book* ... 364

Document 8.5
"Students' Council Notes" from *En Avant* ... 367

Topic 9
Medium and Message: Popular Culture, Mass Media, and National Identity ... 369

Context ... *371*

References/Further Reading ... *372*

Illustration 9.1 ... *373*

Articles ... *373*

Article 9.1
Neil Sutherland
Popular Media in the Culture of English-Canadian Children in the Twentieth Century ... 374

Article 9.2
Ryan Edwardson
The Many Lives of Captain Canuck: Nationalism, Culture, and the Creation of a Canadian Comic
    Book Superhero ... 393

Document 9.1
Harry J. Boyle
Excerpt from *With a Pinch of Sin* ... 404

Document 9.2
Massey Commission
The National Gallery ... 407

Document 9.3
Ontario Secondary School Teachers' Federation
Our Culture: Canadian or American? ... 410

Topic 10
The Playing Fields: Sport and Recreation ... 413

Context ... 415

> *References/Further Reading* ... 416

Illustration 10.1 ... 417

Articles ... 417

Article 10.1
Robert S. Kossuth and Kevin B. Wamsley
Cycles of Manhood: Pedaling Respectability in Ontario's Forest City ... 418

Article 10.2
Michael A. Robidoux
Imagining a Canadian Identity through Sport: A Historical Interpretation of Lacrosse
    and Hockey ... 434

Document 10.1
Excerpts from *Freedom to Play* ... 445

Document 10.2
Newspaper Coverage of Hockey ... 448

Topic 11
Nature and Society: Tourism, Conservation, and Environmental Issues ... 457

Context ... 459

> *References/Further Reading* ... 460

Illustration 11.1 ... 461

Articles ... 461

Article 11.1
Lynda Jessup
The Group of Seven and the Tourist Landscape in Western Canada, or The More Things
 Change ... 462

Article 11.2
John Sandlos
From the Outside Looking In: Aesthetics, Politics, and Wildlife Conservation in the
 Canadian North ... 483

Document 11.1
James White
The Work of the Commission of Conservation ... 504

Document 11.2
William Clark Bethune
Conservation of Game ... 507

Topic 12
Postmodern Canada: Contemporary Social Issues ... 509

Context ... 511

 References/Further Reading ... 513

Illustration 12.1 ... 514

Articles ... 514

Article 12.1
Peter Li
The Place of Immigrants: The Politics of Difference in Territorial and Social Space ... 515

Article 12.2
Will Straw
In and Around Canadian Music ... 525

Document 12.1
Secrétariat à la politique linguistique
Living in French in Quebec ... 533

Document 12.2
I Am Canadian (Joe's Rant) ... 536

Document 12.3
A Rant for the Record Books ... 537

CANADIAN HISTORY WEBSITES ... 541

COPYRIGHT ACKNOWLEDGMENTS ... 543

INDEX ... 547

PREFACE

When we first began to think about compiling a two-volume reader on the social history of Canada, the project was at once exciting and rather daunting. The basic premise of the volumes was clear: to offer students a selection of articles and documents that explored the lives, experiences, and concerns of "ordinary" people, or of those — such as women, Native peoples, children, and immigrants — whom scholars in the past have often discounted or even overlooked. The readers also intended to introduce students to some of the major approaches and key questions that Canadian social historians are currently confronting and working with. But the social history of Canada is immense, in space and time and inhabitants. The nation, and the colonies that existed before Confederation, not only span a continent, but they also were and are "home" to an almost unimaginable variety of peoples. Moreover, as social history itself has become, in many ways, part of the mainstream of Canadian history, there is now a rich and diverse literature that makes choosing articles a difficult task. *People, Places, and Times* presents a small selection of this burgeoning history — one intended to introduce students to both the practice of social history in Canada and some of the tools historians use in their explorations.

There was any number of ways to organize the two readers. Most introductory courses in Canadian history taught in universities use Confederation as the primary dividing line. The assumption, both implicitly and often explicitly, is that the creation of the nation is the most significant event in Canada's history. But 1867 is a political marker and it has much less significance for anthologies that emphasize society and culture. Many of the social, economic, and political processes and concerns that shaped the lives of Aboriginal peoples and colonists before Confederation continued to influence many Canadians' lives well into the 20th century. And yet social historians do not ignore the political. Scholars often examine social developments in relation to the growth of governments and residents' expectations of the state, whether it was imperial, colonial, or national. What seem to be strictly political events and debates were also occasions for individuals and groups who were not officially part of the process to assert their own identity, as well as opportunities for social and economic views to be presented and contested. The choice of the creation of the nation as a reference point for these readers is one that, we hope, will also make these volumes broadly useful in university and college classrooms.

At the same time, the articles included in *People, Places, and Times* do reflect the fact that a large part of what is now Canada — like the North and large parts of the West (including British Columbia) — remained colonies, first of Great Britain and then the central Canadian government, until well into the 20th century. Although the first of July was an occasion for celebration for the so-called fathers of Confederation and their supporters, it had little impact on the day-to-day lives and concerns of most of its new citizens. Of far greater influence on colonists' and Canadians' lives, and on how they saw themselves and the world around them, were the larger economic and social structures of their societies. In very broad terms, *People, Places, and Times* reflects quite different economic and social worlds. Volume 1 is concerned with life in colonies that were predominantly preindustrial and rural, existing in what many historians now term the premodern world. Whether in the French empire in North America in the 17th and 18th centuries, or in British North America in the 19th century, the family was the basic social and economic unit. There was often little distinction between work and home, between the private and the public. This premodern or traditional socioeconomic order persisted in some places in the new nation into the 20th century; in parts of Canada, imperial ideas and assumptions about social structures and relationships among colonists continued to affect the lives of First Nations people, women, and missionaries (to name but a few).

As the topics covered in Volume 2 illustrate, Canadians were not only building a nation after 1867, they were becoming "modern." New technologies — railways, the telegraph, the telephone — were helping to stitch together the disparate parts of the young Dominion; they were also propelling a growing number of Canadians into an urban and industrial world that increasingly turned to the state for guidance and assistance. Although family continued to be the most important institution in Canadians' lives, there were now appearing increasing distinctions between work and home, work and play, public and private. This transformation was already well under way in some towns and cities in the more established colonies of British America before 1867. But as the 19th century came to a close, the new economy was transforming social and political institutions across Canada and having a marked impact on more and more residents' lives.

The materials selected for *People, Places, and Times* reflect some of the issues and themes that have preoccupied social historians since this field of inquiry emerged in the late 1960s. Social historians try to understand the past from "the bottom up" in order to capture the voices and experiences of people in their everyday worlds. Forty years ago, such histories were decidedly at odds with what most practising historians thought was important: the triumphant story of Canada's passage from colony to nation; its rapid social, economic, and political progress; and the stories of the "great men" who guided first the colonies and then Canada. But contemporary social movements and concerns about, for example, the place of women in the workplace and society at large, or First Nations' determination to maintain their culture and land, encouraged Canadians to look to the past to understand their present. At the same time, the growing number of students entering universities began to demand that their courses of studies be "relevant" to their world. At first glance, women, workers, First Nations, Black Canadians, students, and a host of others did not seem to have a history, for their stories were not part of the grand sagas that scholars were telling about politicians and diplomats and generals — by and large white, privileged men. Yet they clearly were there, in time, space, and history, and were instrumental in settling, developing, and sustaining this land.

Many young Canadian scholars turned to the innovative work of social and cultural historians in Great Britain, Europe, and the United States for ideas and models about how to reclaim the histories of peoples who had left little in the way of written records, the traditional mainstay of the historian's evidence. Social historians discovered a wealth of new sources and evidence in land, tax, and probate records; census manuscripts; and church registers. Also telling stories of people who had been lost, neglected, or barely touched upon were police reports; stories and advertisements in newspapers and magazines; court reports; company, union, and institutional records; and, more recently, physical artifacts and material culture, including furniture, archaeological evidence, and photographs. The more traditional sources — official documents and diaries, letters, and personal papers — were also approached with new tools, often borrowed from other disciplines such as the social sciences and literary criticism.

In many ways, social history is now coming of age and, as is reflected in the offerings here, scholars have often gone beyond the need to locate previously "invisible" colonists and Canadians to trying to tease out how individuals and communities saw themselves and interacted with each other and the wider world. Social historians are also concerned about how "big" issues — war, famine, migration, elections, political controversy, and economic and social transformation — affected both individuals and the shape and internal dynamics of the fundamental social institutions: the family, the church, the school, and the workplace. This means asking new questions of the sources and finding new ways to analyze often patchy, disparate, and seemingly disconnected material. Today, scholars are also concerned about how understandings of class, race, gender, age, religion, and culture have shaped colonists' and Canadians' experiences and identities. They explore how the meanings of these categories were contingent and mutable, changing over time and dependent on specific places and circumstances. Postmodernist scholars have illustrated how, by deconstructing the language of the texts that are our evidence, we can acquire a sense of how social and personal identities were understood and lived. What did it mean to be "manly," for example, for members of the early 19th-century colonial elite? Was this conceptualization different for members of a Baptist congregation at the turn of the century? How were women of these two groups, separated by class and time as well as by gender, socialized to certain ideals of femininity?

Organization of the Text

People, Places, and Times reflects what might be considered both classic social history, which entails recovering the voices and lives of neglected and often marginalized actors, and some of the more recent developments in the field that pursue matters of identity and representation. Each volume has twelve topics that have been chosen to reflect either a central issue in the history of the period or a theme that illustrates one of the main categories in social history. Each topic includes a brief contextual introduction, two articles about the subject under consideration, and a number of illustrations and document excerpts from the period. The topics are organized in rough chronological order, although the stories told in the articles often weave in and out in time and space. The articles have been chosen to reflect some of the most important and often new work in specific subject areas. They also illustrate the diverse sources and approaches that social historians employ as they try to tickle out people's lives and experiences. The illustrations and document excerpts supplement the topic under consideration, or expand the purview of the discussion by suggesting different aspects or viewpoints than those examined in the articles. Suggested questions on the articles, illustrations, and documents will help to encourage critical reading, textual analysis, and group discussion, all three of which are integral to the historian's training. Finally, the short list of additional readings is intended to help students situate the issue historically and to pursue further research.

It is hoped that the two volumes of *People, Places, and Times* will, individually and together, constitute a starting point for students' introduction to the infinitely interesting social history of Canada. Practical constraints must obviously limit the number of topics that can be covered, and the articles and documents that can be included. We have only started to address the key question "whose history is it, anyway?" It seems needless to say that there remains much to be uncovered, discovered, and recovered about the histories of Canadians, and that there is a wide scope for much more historical "digging." What is heartening in the face of this challenge is the simple truth that, as we investigate new topics, revise existing interpretations, and reopen old debates, we recapture important parts of our collective past while coming a little closer to understanding how these inform social issues in the Canada of our own times.

Acknowledgments

The authors and the publisher wish to thank the following people who reviewed the manuscript during development and provided suggestions for improvement: Robin Anderson, University College of the Fraser Valley; Geoffrey Booth, Laurentian University at Georgian College; Terry Crowley, University of Guelph; Graeme Decarie, Concordia University; Ross Fair, Ryerson University; Anne Gagnon, University College of the Cariboo; Alan Gordon,

University of Guelph; Jacqueline Gresko, Douglas College; James Hull, Okanagan University College; Bruce Muirhead, Lakehead University; Steve Penfold, University of Toronto; Adele Perry, University of Manitoba; Gillian Poulter, Acadia University; David Quiring, University of Saskatchewan; Paige Raibmon, Simon Fraser University; and Catharine Wilson, University of Guelph.

INTRODUCTION

This collection of readings and documents is concerned with the interwoven themes, issues, and topics that have constituted the development of Canadian society since the birth of the nation-state in 1867. A number of historical strands make themselves visible in these studies. The first of these is the concept of "nation-building," the foremost objective of the newborn Dominion of Canada, a fledgling nation-state stitched together from the disparate pieces that made up British North America in the mid-19th century. Initially a none-too-eager marriage of two nations, English- and French-speaking, Protestant and Catholic, Canada was conceived within a grand vision of a future territory "from sea unto sea." The earliest nation-building project entailed taking in the more reluctant of the Atlantic colonies as well as the "Great Northwest" and British Columbia, each bringing with them their different traditions and their diverse societies of Aboriginal peoples, the First Nations that were given no part in the design of Confederation.

Nation-building did not end with territorial expansion, a feat that was accomplished before the dawn of the 20th century. What remained an encompassing and ongoing project was the creation of a national identity that, despite frequent reminders from Quebec about the two-nations covenant, continued to emphasize the British, English-speaking, Protestant values of its largest social group. Nation-building meant resettling Aboriginal communities to make way for European immigrants and the reproduction of English Canada on the western plains; the "Canadianization" of the newcomers through voluntary and state campaigns; the consequent expansion of the state for this purpose; and all manner of regulatory measures, informal and inscribed in law, to ensure that the native-born and recently arrived alike understood and embraced certain prescribed concepts of citizenship.

The second major theme or trend reflected in the topics considered here is that of modernization. By the time of Confederation, the modernizing processes of industrialization and urbanization were making themselves felt. The turn of the century would see their intensification, in conjunction with the arrival of the first significant wave of "new Canadians," many from such nontraditional sources (that is to say, not British or American) as Eastern Europe and the Mediterranean. Their decision to leave their native lands for one in every sense "new" was shaped in no small part by the promotional campaigns and homesteading policies of the federal government. Also enthusiastically supporting both nation-building and industrialization, and consequently the goals of Sir John A. Macdonald's National Policy of 1879, were the entrepreneurs and investors who needed cheap labour and an expanded domestic market.

The negative repercussions of ambitious nation-building and rapid modernization were far from the minds of those Canadians who put their faith in Sir Wilfrid Laurier's optimistic prophecy that the 20th century would be "filled by Canada." Even among the number (mostly of the English-speaking, Protestant, urban, middle-class sector of "British" Canadians) who were concerned enough about possible ill effects to organize into reformist organizations under the social gospel umbrella, there was much faith in the capacity of modern science to identify social problems — at times more imagined than real — and to remedy them as well. Traditional

Christian principles, helped along by the developing social sciences, became the key to social regeneration, to the realization of the ideal modern Canada. In their attempts to carry out their plans for this "new Jerusalem," the modern state also took shape, which brings us to another of the historic trends of the post-Confederation period. State formation was both a modern and a modernizing process. Those who clamoured for attention to the social problems of the day insisted that only the state could deal with them effectively and efficiently. In this manner, the bureaucracy of the state developed, gradually giving rise to what was termed "the modern welfare state" in the wake of World War II.

The developing relationship between society and state, which belongs to both nation-building and modernization, necessarily brought about a more active role for the state in the everyday lives of "ordinary" Canadians. Alongside this development, and in its support, ideals of modern citizenship took shape. These ideals, for all the rhetoric of science and modernity, held tenaciously to traditional constructions of class, gender, race, religious, regional, and age distinctions, to name the most obvious. For the better part of the 20th century, the model Canadian was invariably white, middle-class, Anglo-Protestant, and male. Those to whom this classification did not apply were expected to strive toward some happy semblance. By finding ways to regulate schooling, labour, public health, child-rearing, domestic relations, sexuality, and even leisure, every Canadian — and especially those who aspired to become Canadian — was either an ideal modern citizen in the making or simply "deviant."

Finally, and in keeping with the original aims of the pioneering social historians of some forty years ago, the formation of identity (both individual and collective) is also an important theme, in its complex interrelations with social class, race, region, language, religion, and gender, and in the different duties and privileges defined by age. All of these serve as a means to locate individuals and groups in society and to confer upon them a certain status, position, and role that define the individual's relations with fellow citizens and, taken as a whole, the national identity. In Canada, the meanings of these identifying categories are further complicated by the larger question of what it means to be Canadian, especially in view of the French and British historical connections and the geographic proximity and cultural similarities of a socially and economically powerful United States. Nation-building, state formation, social organization, and even self-development ultimately impinge on this vast question of identity.

The essays in this volume are meant to illustrate current sociohistorical approaches to a select number of subjects. Of the vast number that were considered for inclusion, we eventually decided to narrow the field — with only a few exceptions — to those published within the last ten years; not readily available to students outside of the scholarly journals; and, again for the most part, to those written by scholars who are beginning to make their mark in the small community that is the Canadian historical profession. The illustrations and documents that make up the primary source material included here were chosen to offer a sense of what, and how, the actual historical actors thought about some of the events and issues of their day, and also to demonstrate the kinds of evidence that historians employ in their study of past societies. Students of Canadian social history will see that there is much potential for further development of the topics discussed in this volume, and that the topics themselves encourage the pursuit of diverse others. I hope that these essays, organized thematically but chosen with a view to regional representation and chronological development, will introduce beginners to the lively historiography currently available, enrich the historical understanding of those who are more familiar with the subject area, and — most important — inspire new generations to take up the infinite challenges and the infinite array of subjects that are implied in the category of "social history."

Post-Confederation Timeline

1867
The British North America Act unites Ontario, Quebec, Nova Scotia, and New Brunswick to form the Dominion of Canada. Sir John A. Macdonald becomes the first prime minister.

1870
The Red River Rebellion, under Métis leader Louis Riel, results in the creation of the province of Manitoba.
The Northwest Territories joins Confederation.

1871
The first Dominion census enumerates a population of 3,689,257.
British Columbia joins Confederation.
The federal government and First Nations in the west sign the first of the numbered treaties.

1872
The Trades Union Act, legalizing worker organization, is passed by the Macdonald government.
The Dominion Lands Act is passed to encourage western settlement.

1873
Prince Edward Island joins Confederation.

1874
Alexander Graham Bell invents the telephone in Brantford, Ontario.

1875
The Supreme Court of Canada is established.
Jennifer Trout becomes the first woman licensed to practise medicine in Canada.
Grace Lockhart becomes the first Canadian woman to receive a bachelor's degree.

1876
The Indian Act defines the special status and land regulations of Aboriginal peoples on reserves across the nation.
Dr. Emily Stowe founds the Toronto Women's Literary Club, Canada's first suffrage group.

1882
The Royal Society of Canada is established.

1885
The North-West Rebellion, led by Louis Riel, is unsuccessful. Riel is found guilty of treason and executed in Regina.
The driving in of the last spike at Craigellachie in British Columbia marks the completion of the Canadian Pacific Railway.

1893
The National Council of Women of Canada is formed.

1896
Gold is discovered in the Yukon, leading to the Klondike gold rush of 1897–98.

1901
Guglielmo Marconi receives the world's first radio transmission at Signal Hill in St. John's, Newfoundland.

1902
Canada's first movie theatre opens in Vancouver.

1905
Saskatchewan and Alberta join Confederation.

1907
The Asiatic Exclusion League is established in British Columbia. Anti-Asian riots take place in Vancouver's Chinatown.

1909
The first flight in Canada is made by John McCurdy's *Silver Dart*.

1914
World War I begins. The Borden government passes the War Measures Act.

1916
Prohibition of alcohol, one of the main reform planks of women's organizations since the late 19th century, comes into effect in Alberta.

1917
A "temporary" income tax is introduced to raise money for the war effort.
The government introduces conscription, which divides the nation along English–French lines.
In Halifax harbour, the largest man-made explosion to date kills 2,000 people and injures 9,000.

1918
World War I ends. Of the more than 600,000 Canadians who fought in Europe, 60,000 were killed and 173,000 were wounded.
The Statistics Act, creating the Dominion Bureau of Statistics, is passed.
The Spanish Flu of 1918–19 kills some 50,000 Canadians.

1919
The Winnipeg General Strike takes place.

1920
Women become eligible to sit in the House of Commons.

1921
Frederick Banting and Charles Best discover insulin.
Agnes Macphail becomes the first woman elected to Canada's Parliament.

1923
The Chinese Immigration Act of 1923 comes into effect. Under the act, all Chinese, with the exception of businessmen, diplomats, students, and those applying under "special circumstances," are prohibited from entering Canada.

1927
The Canada Pension Act is introduced by the King government.
The Dominion Day celebration is marked by Canada's first cross-country radio broadcast.

1929
The British Privy Council reverses the Supreme Court of Canada decision in the Persons Case by ruling that women are eligible to be senators.

1930
Cairine Wilson becomes Canada's first female senator.

1932
An Act of Parliament creates the Canadian Radio Broadcasting Commission, forerunner of the Canadian Broadcasting Corporation (est. 1936).

1934
The Dionne Quintuplets are born in Corbeil, Ontario.

1935
The "On to Ottawa Trek," a protest by unemployed men, ends in a riot in Regina.

1937
Prime Minister Mackenzie King establishes the Royal Commission on Dominion-Provincial Relations (Rowell-Sirois Commission) to investigate the issue of jurisdiction over social welfare.
Trans-Canada Airlines is created by an act of Parliament to provide air service across Canada.

1939
The National Film Act creates the National Film Board, with film producer John Grierson as its first director.
George VI and Queen Elizabeth begin the first royal tour of Canada.
Canada declares war on Germany.

1940
Quebec women get the vote in provincial elections.
Conscription is introduced, but is restricted to homeland defence.
The Unemployment Insurance Act is passed.

1941

The federal government passes legislation permitting the enlistment of women in the army. The Canadian Women's Army Corps (CWAC) is formed.

1942

The federal government announces that all people of Japanese origin in coastal British Columbia will be relocated to the province's interior.

A plebiscite is held on the issue of conscription; English Canada votes in favour of — and French Canada against — letting the King government out of its pledge to avoid it.

1944

The Family Allowance Act is passed.

1945

Canada becomes a founding member of the United Nations.

Victory in Japan [V-J] Day marks the end of the World War II. Over a million Canadians fought; 42,000 were killed.

In Ottawa, the defection of Soviet embassy clerk Igor Gouzenko reveals a Soviet spy ring in Canada; the Cold War begins.

1946

The Canadian Citizenship Act, which creates a Canadian citizenship separate from the British, is passed.

1949

Newfoundland becomes Canada's tenth province.

1951

The Report of the Royal Commission on the Arts, Letters and Sciences (Massey Report) is released.

The Indian Act of Canada is revised, excluding Aboriginal women who marry non-Aboriginal men from receiving federal government benefits.

1952

Vincent Massey, who chaired the Massey Commission, becomes Canada's first native-born governor general.

The first CBC television station goes on the air.

1957

Ellen Louks Fairclough becomes the first woman to be appointed to Canada's federal cabinet.

1960

Liberal Jean Lesage becomes premier of Quebec, heralding the "Quiet Revolution."

Prime Minister John Diefenbaker introduces the Canadian Bill of Rights.

1964

Canadians are issued social insurance cards for the first time.

1965

Canada's official flag is unveiled.

1966

The Canada and Quebec Pension Plans begin operation.

The CBC becomes the first Canadian television network to broadcast in colour.

1967

The Order of Canada is created.

Expo 67 opens in Montreal.

1968

Canada's medicare system comes into effect.

1969

The Official Languages Act is passed. Under the act, government services must be provided to citizens in English or French.

1970

The kidnapping of a British diplomat and the murder of a Quebec cabinet minister by the Front de libération du Québec (FLQ), a radical separatist organization, leads to the October Crisis and the first peacetime imposition of the 1914 War Measures Act.

The Royal Commission on the Status of Women (Bird Commission) reports to Parliament.

1980

Jeanne Sauvé becomes the first woman Speaker of the House of Commons.

Bone cancer survivor and amputee Terry Fox begins his "Marathon of Hope" run across Canada to raise money for cancer research.

Quebec rejects separation in the first sovereignty referendum.

"O Canada" becomes Canada's official national anthem.

1982

Canada's new Constitution (the Canada Act) and the Charter of Rights and Freedoms are enacted.

Dominion Day is renamed Canada Day.

1983

Bertha Wilson is appointed Canada's first female Supreme Court justice.

Jeanne Sauvé becomes Canada's first female governor general.

1988

Prime Minister Brian Mulroney officially apologizes for the internment of Japanese Canadians during World War II.

1989

The Canada–U.S. Free Trade Agreement comes into effect.

Audrey McLaughlin replaces Ed Broadbent as NDP leader, becoming the first female head of a major party in Canadian history.

An anti-feminist gunman murders fourteen women at the University of Montreal's École Polytechnique before killing himself.

1990

The Bloc Québécois Party, Canada's first federal separatist party, is established.

Manitoba and Newfoundland fail to ratify the Meech Lake Accord.

1992

Dr. Roberta Bondar becomes the first Canadian woman in space.

The Newfoundland cod fishery is closed down for two years.

The Charlottetown Accord is rejected in a national referendum.

1993

Prince Edward Island's Catherine Callbeck becomes the first female premier in Canadian history.

Kim Campbell becomes Canada's first female prime minister.

1994

The North American Free Trade Agreement (NAFTA) between Canada, the United States, and Mexico comes into effect.

Hockey is made Canada's official winter sport; lacrosse becomes the official summer sport.

1995

The "no" side wins a narrow victory in the second Quebec referendum.

1998

The federal government formally apologizes for the past mistreatment of First Nations.

1999

Nunavut is created on April 1; Paul Okalik becomes its first premier.

Adrienne Clarkson becomes Canada's second female governor general.

Beverley McLachlin becomes the first female chief justice of the Supreme Court.

Bill C-23 extends full benefits and obligations — excluding the right to marry — to persons in same-sex relationships.

2000

Canada's population reaches 30,750,000.

Canada in 1867

Canada in the 21st Century

Topic 1

Aboriginal Peoples:

Communities and Conditions of Life

Main street of the village on the reserve of the Kamloops band of the Shuswap, 1940; British Columbia Archives, D-03879.

CONTEXT

The past invariably informs much of what unfolds in the present. Nowhere is this more evident than in the history of Canada's Aboriginal peoples. Whether the issue is self-government, education, or still-unsettled land claims, such matters now in the news have roots stretching back several centuries. Many of the ideas and policies of the colonial societies and their governments, both informal and official, were consolidated after Confederation through such important legislation as the Indian Act of 1876 and its various 20th-century amendments. Effectively making all "Indians" wards of the federal government, that legislation defined a long-lasting relationship premised on a racially defined subordination of the lands' first inhabitants.

The articles in this section suggest how methods borrowed from cultural anthropology, archaeology, and ethnology (the latter, when combined with historical analysis, is referred to as ethnohistory) can enrich our historical understanding of communities that left little in the way of written documents, the historian's traditional evidence. As government bureaucracies expanded, a great many records about Native peoples were generated from the perspective of those in power. While useful to historians, such records only rarely allow for Native voices to come through. Oral tradition served Aboriginal peoples as the principal means of passing on their stories and preserving the record of their past. Social scientists have long used this form of testimony to examine societies, but historians have tended to be wary of an approach that leaves much to the potentially faulty medium of human memory. With the growing interest in social history that developed during the 1960s, interdisciplinary methods were increasingly put to effective use. Such seminal studies as those of Bruce Trigger (1985) and Julie Cruikshank (1990), which reconstruct elements of the Native past by means of material culture and memory, demonstrated the value of these forms of analysis as applied to marginalized, nonliterate societies. Especially in the past fifteen years or so, historical studies that combine oral history with more conventional documentary analysis have gone far to recover the Aboriginal side of the story in a manner that considers both the means and effects of their subjugation while also showing how they attempted, if often unsuccessfully, to advocate for their own rights in a severely unbalanced relationship.

This subjugation of Aboriginal communities, already impoverished and weakened by the declining buffalo hunt that was their mainstay, was central to the federal government's aim of transforming the West and achieving the vision of a Dominion "from sea unto sea." Intended by the Macdonald Conservative government to clear the way for settlement and agricultural production by Euro-Canadians and a select group of European immigrants, the Indian Act and the "numbered treaties" that were signed in the 1870s moved Natives to government-designated reserves where they could be contained and supervised. Although they were promised the supplies and training that would have enabled them to become productive agricultural settlers, the government's policies made this aim impossible to achieve. As Sarah Carter (1999) has demonstrated, provisions and equipment were inadequate, and stringent regulations, most notably certain "pass laws," prevented Natives from leaving the reserves to sell goods at market. At best, only a bare subsistence level of agriculture was supported. When Natives failed to measure up to expectations that did not take into account how poorly their conversion to a farming economy and lifestyle was managed, they were castigated for what was perceived as a racially determined inability to settle. The outcome, as material and health conditions on the reserves deteriorated rapidly and communities became demoralized, simply confirmed the suspicions of Indian agents, and doubtless many others, that Native men were incapable of providing for their families and that Native women were dissolute, immoral, and somehow responsible for their deplorable situation. A number of Métis people — children of mixed Native–white marriages — combined forces with some Aboriginal tribes to protest the trampling of their rights in the Saskatchewan River territory. Led by Louis Riel, who had organized a similar protest in Red River in 1869, the North-West Rebellion of 1885 was resolutely crushed by the government, assisted by the newly laid Canadian Pacific Railway that carried militia from Central Canada and the newly established North-West Mounted Police.

The policies of successive governments profoundly changed the Aboriginals' way of life, their culture, their community organization, and their relations with other Canadians, as well as with those in authority, whether Indian agents, police, clergy, or health, education, and welfare professionals; in short, it affected every facet of their history. The arrival of white women among the new settlers also effectively ended the practice of intermarriage according to the "custom of the country" that had existed since the early fur trade years. Previously upheld in Canadian courts, the validity of these mixed marriages was negated in 1886, when it was decided that the "cohabitation of a civilized man and a savage woman" was not legal marriage. Children were thereby disentitled from their fathers' estates, and were most often consigned to live in poverty with their mothers on the reserve, where, according to the strictures of the Indian Act, neither they nor their mothers could enjoy any of the advantages of being "status Indians." Native men and the children of their mixed marriages, on the other hand, retained their status.

Government initiatives and the prejudices of the wider society were supported by an educational system that became the key to "reforming" Aboriginal peoples for the purposes of their white "superiors." As J. R. Miller (1991, 1996) has shown, although the treaties promised schools on the reserves, as desired by Native communities, residential schools — many at a considerable distance — were believed to be the best antidote to "deficient" Aboriginal homes. Indian Act amendments in 1895 made attendance compulsory, authorizing justices or Indian agents to commit Native children under the age of sixteen to industrial schools or boarding schools. The residential school system broke up families and nearly destroyed the generational process of cultural transmission that ensured the continuation of the community's language, customs, and historical knowledge. For the better part of a century, the residential schools also exposed many Native children to neglect and emotional, physical, and sexual abuse. Growing public concern, along with the enfranchisement and increasing politicization and organization of First Nations after 1960, led to the systematic closing of the schools during the 1970s and an official apology by the Government of Canada in 1996. As with the land claims that date back to the late 19th-century treaties, the court cases concerning the horrors of the residential schools make both of these persistent contemporary issues, all the while underlining their historical basis.

REFERENCES/FURTHER READING

Barman, Jean, and Marie Battiste, eds. *First Nations Education in Canada: The Circle Unfolds*. Vancouver: University of British Columbia Press, 1995.

Brownlie, Robin. *A Fatherly Eye: Indian Agents, Government Power, and Aboriginal Resistance in Ontario, 1918–1939*. Toronto: University of Toronto Press, 2003.

Carter, Sarah. *Aboriginal People and Colonizers of Western Canada to 1900*. Toronto: University of Toronto Press, 1999.

———. *Capturing Women: The Manipulation of Cultural Imagery in Canada's Prairie West*. Montreal and Kingston: McGill-Queen's University Press, 1997.

———. *Lost Harvests: Prairie Indian Reserve Farmers and Government Policy*. Montreal and Kingston: McGill-Queen's University Press, 1990.

Cruikshank, Julie. *Life Lived Like a Story: Life Stories of Three Yukon Native Elders*. Vancouver: University of British Columbia Press, 1990.

Dickason, Olive. *Canada's First Nations: A History of Founding Peoples from Earliest Times*. Toronto: Oxford University Press, 1997.

Lux, Maureen. *Medicine That Walks: Disease, Medicine, and Canadian Plains Native People, 1880–1940.* Toronto: University of Toronto Press, 2001.

Miller, J. R. *Shingwauk's Vision: A History of Native Residential Schools.* Toronto: University of Toronto Press, 1996.

———. *Skyscrapers Hide the Heavens: A History of Indian–White Relations in Canada.* Toronto: University of Toronto Press, 1991.

Neylan, Susan. *The Heavens Are Changing: Nineteenth-Century Protestant Missions and Tsimshian Christianity.* Montreal and Kingston: McGill-Queen's University Press, 2004.

Trigger, Bruce. *Natives and Newcomers: Canada's "Heroic Age" Revisited.* Montreal and Kingston: McGill-Queen's University Press, 1985.

ILLUSTRATION 1.1 (P. 1)

Located in southern British Columbia, at the confluence of the North and South Thompson rivers, Kamloops was first inhabited by Natives of the Shuswap tribe of the Salish Nation. The first non-Native settlement in southern British Columbia was the trading post of Fort Kamloops, built in 1812, and taken over by the Hudson's Bay Company in 1821 when it amalgamated with the North West Company.

Issue to Consider

*   A town's main street usually says much about its socioeconomic condition. What do the buildings shown in Illustration 1.1 suggest about the Shuswap community in 1940?

ARTICLES

In this section, Nicole St-Onge uses family histories to contextualize the memories of the Métis women whose stories, as recounted in their own words, are the heart of her discussion. Hugh Shewell's approach to post–World War II community development projects is more conventional in his reliance on government documents, but he also uses interviews with Indian Affairs employees who, unlike the policymakers, were directly involved in these projects, mediating between the government and the Aboriginal communities, for better and worse.

Article 1.1

Nicole St-Onge

Memories of Métis Women of Saint-Eustache, Manitoba, 1910–1980[1]

Issues to Consider

- Based on her analysis of her subjects' experiences, what does St-Onge contend is "the reality of the rural hierarchy"? How did gender and race intersect with class to define the status of rural labourers?
- In so many ways, these women's stories counter the period's gender constructions regarding ideal womanhood, as well as middle-class ideals about a protected and dependent childhood. How do their personal histories serve as a counter-narrative to prevailing assumptions, and even our own, about early 20th-century women and children?
- St-Onge relies on a sample of twenty interviews conducted over two years with nine Métis women. What is especially striking about their stories as a group? What arguments can be made for and against the representativeness of this sample? What are the strengths and weaknesses of the oral history approach?
- How did family, school, and church serve to define these women's choices?
- What more would you like to know about these women's lives? What would you ask them?

INTRODUCTORY COMMENTS

In an article entitled "Hired Men: Ontario Agricultural Wage Labour in Historical Perspective"[2] Joy Parr wrote the following, telling, words:

> Scholars too have claimed that from the beginnings of the province, agriculturalists' desire for independence combined with the rigorous seasonality of rural work to determine that "no hierarchical labour organization would persist in Canadian agriculture."[3] Yet in each successive generation from the settlement phase onward, rural wage labourers have been essential to the functioning of the province's persistent and unmistakably hierarchical agricultural system. Through two centuries of clearing, tilling, seeding, and harvesting, the relationships between land and labour and capital and labour have changed, but the reality of the rural hierarchy has been as enduring as the season.[4]

The "rural hierarchy" examined by Parr for Ontario also existed and endured in the Prairie region of Canada. Census data available since 1891 reveal that hired men, over the age of fourteen, were always an important component of farm labour on the Prairie; they represented 13% (6,000) of all rural workers in 1891, 19.4% (84,000) in 1931 and 14.1% (46,000) in 1951.[5] Yet, standard histories of North American agriculture have had difficulty probing beyond the positivist myth that surround the "Family Farm." Few studies discuss in any detail the existence of

Source: Nicole St-Onge, "Memories of Métis Women of Saint-Eustache, Manitoba, 1910–1980," *Oral History Forum* 19/20 (1999/2000): 90–111.

an impoverished underclass of rural wage workers. Even oral history projects dealing with rural inhabitants have tended to be celebratory; charting the progress of a community since its pioneering days without much regard or analysis to the price paid by some individuals for this "success." Or, other rural oral history projects have been apocalyptic lamenting the demise of the Family Farm again without much regard for the consequences of this economic and social restructuration for people other than the owners of farms or the businesses that service them.[6]

What is missing in many of the previous studies is an analysis of the "other." Those non-proprietors who had a crucial role in the creation and the maintenance of a rural economy that has endured, albeit with many changes and crises, till today. To progress, agricultural studies, especially those with an oral history component, must go beyond the public discourse and critically examine the life experiences of a rural proletariat that has, in the Prairie region, existed for well over a hundred years. Even the official statistics quoted above do not yield a clear picture since only "males over the age of fourteen" are counted. The participation of children and women in the wage labour rural economy is invisible with this type of counting. Yet, the narratives of eight women presented below clearly indicate that the paid labour of women and children was an important component of 20th-century agriculture practices. Beyond this, the narratives also show that ethnic and racial identities, in this case Métis, played a role in the perpetuation of a rural labouring class. These women, and their families, are part of a much broader social category, composed of impoverished agrarian wage labourers, that spans the interior of North America. The Métis women discussed below have more in common with the Mexican and Chicano migrant workers of the USA than with their farm-owning neighbours. These *Métisses*, their parents, grandparents and, in some cases, their children, like their southern counterparts, have been caught in a rural agrarian hierarchy that has them firmly at the bottom of the social scale by economic and racial means.

THE HISTORICAL SETTING

The village of Saint-Eustache is situated near the heartland of the territory occupied by the White Horse Plains Métis. It is an offshoot of the older, nearby settlements of Baie Saint-Paul, Saint-François-Xavier and, a bit further to the east, Saint-Charles. The Assiniboine River which runs to the north of the village was one of the main tributaries used by natives and by white traders for transportation and trade from Red River to the Qu'Appelle Valley and westward. Company employees and others associated with the fur trade began early on to congregate along its shores and those of its tributaries. There are signs of occupation along the wooded banks from the early 1800s. The White Horse Plains Métis, besides working for the fur companies as tripmen or freighters, were heavily involved in buffalo hunting throughout the 19th century.

Saint-Eustache itself was established at the end of the 19th century. Its very first occupants were former residents of the Baie Saint-Paul settlement trying to escape repeated flooding of the Assiniboine river. Though its size has varied over the years Saint-Eustache has had an average population of about five hundred people of either Métis or French Canadian origin. The village has always known certain ethnic divisions that reflect themselves in the settlement pattern. Until recently, impoverished Métis families congregated in what was derisively called *Fort Rouge*. This was a small agglomeration situated on the eastern fringes of the village on the "wrong" side of the Coulee du Moulin. The core of the village contained a mixture of slightly better off Métis and some French Canadian families. The well-to-do farmers, enviously called les habitants by the Fort Rouge residents, had their land holdings all around Saint-Eustache but were perceived as residing largely to the west of the village.

THE MÉTIS FAMILIES

With some exceptions, discussed below, the majority of the Métis families living in and around Saint-Eustache during the first half of the 20th century originated from the Saint-François-Xavier settlement. They left their parish lots in the 1870s and the 1880s; part of a much larger movement that saw hundreds of members of these old fur trade families resettle in the Northwest, namely in the Qu'Appelle Lake settlement, the Fort Ellice area and, some, in the Batoche area of present day Saskatchewan.[7] Some family branches chose a more nearby Manitoba relocation, such as Saint-Eustache, Saint-Laurent and Oak Point.[8] For the Saint-Eustache area this last group appears to have been made up mostly of the more impoverished elements of the White Horse Plains Métis. Surveys such as those conducted by the Hudson's Bay Company in 1835 and by ecclesiastical authorities during the 1868 Red River colony famine show these families to have had few horses, oxen or cultivated acres. They were part of a socio-economic class described by Gerhard Ens as largely composed of "tripmen" who survived the long prairie winters mostly on advances provided by the HBC for the next canoeing or freighting season.[9]

Once settled in the Saint-Eustache the Métis families became differentiated into two groups: the "village" Métis and the "Fort Rouge" Métis. Both groups saw themselves, and were perceived, as being "Métis" but the former group was considered by the community at large and by its members as slightly better off economically and, generally, socially more acceptable. An analysis of the family backgrounds of women respondents from both these groups is made further in this paper in an attempt to understand how this cleavage occurred and how it perpetuated itself.

THE NARRATORS

Twenty interviews were conducted in Saint-Eustache, Manitoba, between 1992 and 1994. Nine were with Métis women, eight of which had been born in Saint-Eustache and had spent the bulk of their lives there. The ninth was with a woman also born in the village but whose family had migrated in the 1910s, along with several others, to take up homesteads in the San Clara, Manitoba, region. The eight women whose narratives were examined for this article are, in alphabetical order, Alma Richard née Branconnier (b. 1911), Bertha McKay née Carrière (b. 1910), Imelda St-Cyr née Larocque (b. 1924), Irene Ducharme née Lécuyer (b. 1915), Virginie St-Cyr née McKay (b. 1914), Graziela Piché née Paul (b. 1917), Marianne McKay née St-Cyr (b. 1911), Victoria McKay née St-Cyr (b. 1912).

FAMILY BACKGROUNDS

Four interviews were made with women from the village Métis families. Though the life stories of all four echo each other the origin of one, Bertha Carrière, differs from the rest slightly.

The Carrière clan originates from the Saint-Norbert settlement along the Red River. At some point Bertha Carrière's great-grandfather, Daniel Sn, left Saint-Norbert to take up land in Saint-Charles. After the 1870 transfer he claimed and was recognised as the occupant of lot 33, 98 acres, for which he received a land patent in 1882. At some point the family moved to Saint-Eustache and, in the 1916 Tax Assessment Roles for the municipality of Cartier, the grandfather, Daniel Jn, was listed as a "farmer owner resident" in ward six (Saint-Eustache area) owning three horses, four cows, eight pigs and cultivating 10 of 112 acres of land. His son,

Bertha's father William Carriére, owned 110 acres also in ward six and he cultivated 50 of these. This family differs from the other Métis families of the community by having no direct link with Saint-François-Xavier and by being part of the 19th century Red River Métis elite. However, this relative affluence would not carry over to Bertha's generation. None of the brothers and sisters married into the French Canadian farming families of the area and most of the family's wealth was lost during the 1930s depression. In 1937 Bertha Carrière would marry Donald McKay, a Fort Rouge Métis. Her life would then resemble that of other impoverished Métis women of the area.

The other three village respondents, Graziela Paul, Irene Lécuyer and Alma Branconnier, all come from old Saint-François-Xavier families. However, Irene Lécuyer's great-grandfather and grandfather had spent several years in Assumption, North Dakota, and the families of several great uncles and aunts still reside there. None of the men appear to have worked under contract for the HBC and no river lots are listed as being occupied by them after 1870. Though the Paul and Branconnier paternal ancestors are listed as having cultivated land, cattle, horses and carts in the 1835 Survey, none of the paternal grandparents had river lots patented in their name after 1870. By 1916 the fathers of Graziela and Irene are listed as labourers, the first as a squatter on his father-in-law's land and the second as occupying land designated as a Road Allowance. Eventually Irene Lécuyer's mother, a schoolteacher from France, would buy twenty acres thus easing family poverty. Only Jean-Baptiste Branconnier is listed in 1916 as the owner-occupant of four acres but none of it was labelled "cultivated" and no farm animals are noted.

Again with the exception of Bertha Carrière the village respondents describe their fathers as having been agricultural labourers and winter wood cutters. Irene Lécuyer notes:

> Il travaillait comme tous les autres. Il avait pas d'éducation. Il travaillait chez les farmers. On avait un peu d'animaux. Il faisait du foin. Ça vendait du foin, ça vendait du bois ...

> He worked like the others. He had no education. He worked for the farmers. We had some animals. He made hay. He sold hay. He sold wood.[10]

Alma Branconnier's voice still rings with indignation, decades later, when recounting her father's last winter job:

> Oui à la journée un peu partout. Il était travaillant boy! Quatre journées avant qu'il meurt il fardochait pour Fretton. Tu te rappelles quand ils avaient la terre ... sur le bord du chemin. Il a été déraciner un arbre. Y a fait un trou plus gros que la table ... à quatre pattes ... le 20 février. Le lendemain y a attrapé une pneumonie. La dernière souche qui a déterré. A cette heure c'est easy y'ont toutes des engins!

> Yes, he worked days everywhere. He was a worker boy! Four days before he died he was removing stumps for Fretton. You remember when they had the land ... near the road. He uprooted a tree. There was a hole as big as the table ... on his hands and knees ... February 20. The next day he caught pneumonia. The last stump he ever uprooted. Now it is easy. They have the machines. [...] [11]

The four respondents from the Fort Rouge area of Saint-Eustache are all members of the two large clans, the McKay and the St-Cyr, that settled there. Both these families have links to the Athabasca region of the Northwest. Virginie McKay's maternal great-great-grandfather, Ignace McKay, worked as a guide and steersman in that area. His daughter, Justine, became the first wife of Jean-Baptiste St-Cyr, the descendant of an old Athabasca Métis family. All the St-Cyrs living in the Saint-Eustache area today are the descendants of either this union or of Jean-Baptiste's second union with Flavie Larocque of Saint-François-Xavier. The two St-Cyr sisters interviewed, Marie-Anne and Victoria, are the daughters of Elzear St-Cyr whose parents were the above-mentioned Jean-Baptiste St-Cyr and his second wife, Flavie Larocque. In the 1835 census Ignace McKay, the occupant of lot 81 in Saint François-Xavier, owned three cattle and farmed four acres. His son, Pierre McKay Sn, Virginie's great-grandfather, claimed lot 5 in Baie Saint-Paul but did not receive a patent. However, by 1916 he would be listed in the tax assessment rolls as the owner occupant of thirty-three acres, none of it cleared, covering what is now called Fort Rouge. Family lore recalls that when Pierre Sn came to Saint-Eustache "he took out a one sixty [acres]." He and his son Pierre McKay Jn parcelled out small plots to the other members of the extended family (both McKay and St-Cyr). The fourth woman interviewed was Imelda Larocque, daughter of Daniel Larocque, of Saint-François-Xavier, and Eleonore McKay, the daughter of Pierre McKay Sn. Interestingly, Imelda Larocque married Alex St-Cyr whose grandmother, Flavie Larocque, was in fact Imelda's father's aunt. This is but one example of the complex web of kinship ties that exist in the Fort Rouge families.

When discussing the economic activities of the parents of the Fort Rouge respondents it is immediately apparent that life was difficult even though all three (counting the two sisters as one) had some small acreage. Imelda Laroque never knew her father, who died when she was six. She was the youngest of eight children and her mother was able to support those still living at home by working as a house cleaner and cook in nearby farms. Imelda comments that what got them through the winter was her mother's "beautiful garden and great canning." Her two sisters-in-law, Marie-Anne and Victoria St-Cyr, comment that their father was a labourer and a hunter.

> *Ah mon doux seigneur, il faisait toutes sortes d'affaires. On avais-tu de la misère. Ya longtemps. Il travaillait ... la chasse aux lièvres, les rats d'eau, les canards. [worked for wages?] Ah ben il travaillait à gâges pour les Chabot eux autres, les stooks[12] ... il stookait, il faisait des gâges comme ça. [in winter?] Y avait pas d'ouvrage, pans toute. Il faisait la chasse. Y a tué assez des lièvres, on mangeait de la graisse pis de la galette pour déjeuner. Ça faisait dur y'a longtemps!*

> Oh my god, he did all sorts of things. We had hard times. Long ago. He worked ... hunted rabbits, muskrats, ducks ... He worked for wages for the Chabot, them, the stooks ... he stooked. He got money like that. In winter he had no work, nothing. He hunted. He killed enough rabbits, we ate lard and bannock for breakfast. It was hard long ago![13]

In some ways Virginie McKay perhaps had the most difficult of childhoods being one of three daughters of an unwed mother, Adeline Marie McKay, the daughter of Pierre McKay Jn. Her mother worked "in the fields" most of her life.

> *Combien de fois que Freddie [Beaudin] a engagé ma mère ... Même a fesait l'ouvrage des hommes ... avec Marianna ... C'était une petite mais dem aussi c'était une travaillante! Ça travaillait tout le temps ensemble. Des fois ça ramassait les racines. Ben foullait que ça travaille avec la hache pour couper les racines. Ah ben y'ont tu fait de l'ouvrage je suppose. Pis ça stookait, ça prenait des jobs ... je me rappelle ça passait en wagon ... ça emmenait leur lunchs, ça mangeait la-bas. Ça en faisait encore. Des fois ça travaillait tard le soir. C'éait a la fraîcheur hein. Ça stookait. Ça prenait ça à l'acre.*

> How many times Freddie Beaudin hired my mom ... She even did men's work ... with Marianna ... she was small but damn she was a worker! They worked all the time together. Sometimes they would gather the roots (i.e., clear fields). Well, they had to work with an axe. Well, they did a lot of work I suppose. They also stooked, they would take contracts ... I remember they would go in a wagon ... they would bring their lunches, ate there. Then they would work some more. They worked till late at night. It was cool then. They stooked. They took it by the acre.[14]

However, living with her mother and two sisters in their grandfather's house offered some compensation. Though not a farmer, Pierre McKay Jn did spend a lot of time growing a large garden and taking care of several fruit trees that produced large "blue" plums. He also had chickens, turkeys, horses and a milk cow. Perhaps this lifestyle was financed by the selling off of parcels of land. Such actions might explain the latent animosity members of the St-Cyr family express towards Virginie McKay. They had been obliged to buy their lots from Pierre McKay Sn and Jn.

CHILDHOOD AND ADOLESCENCE

The socio-economic status of the parents do not appear to differ greatly in the narrators' different descriptions. It becomes a question of degrees of poverty. However, childhood experiences between the village and Fort Rouge women do. What becomes immediately apparent is the marked differences in the degree of formal education received by both sets of women.

Bertha Carrière comments that she went to school to age fourteen. In her last year, grade seven, she went to school in the morning and stayed at home "to help" in the afternoon. When asked why she stopped Bertha associates herself to the French Canadian farm children.

[all stopped at 14?] *La plupart arrêtait, oui. Ils savaient pas qu'est ce que c'était être instruite dans ce temps là. C'était tout des fermiers. Pis y avait besoin des enfants pour travailler. Chez nous y avait rien que deux garçons, le plus vieux et le plus jeune. Le reste c'était toutes des filles, huit. Y fallait qu'on remplace les garçons. On travaillait dans les champs ...*

Most stopped, yes. They did not know what it was to be educated back then. They were all farmers. They needed the children to work. Us, there were only two boys, the oldest and the youngest. The rest were all girls, eight. We had to replace the boys. We worked in the fields.[15]

Irene Lécuyer also stopped school at age fourteen, part way through grade eight, to help at home and later on to work in farmers fields.

The other two village women spent much less time in the schoolroom then their counterparts. Graziela Paul attended school sporadically till age thirteen. She had to stay home to take care of her younger sibling while her mother worked as a cook in the Saint-Eustache convent where thirty-five novitiates and "several" nuns resided. When she was thirteen her parents sent her to the nearby Elie convent as a working boarder. She worked there till she was eighteen in exchange for room, board, clothes and minimal schooling.

Jai été a l'école, quand j'ai rentré au couvent, quand j'avais la chance, a peu près une heure par jour. Il fallait que je travaille parce que les soeurs gardaient des pensionnaires. Y avait a peu près une quarantaine de pensionnaires, tout ben, plus. Il fallait que je lave la vaisselle, nettoyer la cuisine, aider faire la cuisine, même des fois le lavage, toute sortes d'affaires ... Y payaient pas. C'était juste pour ma nourriture pis man linge. Pour à rien ... Pis les habitants il fallait qui donnent de la viande pour payer pour leurs enfants pour mettre au couvent après l'école. Y en a qui donnait la 'moqué' d'un cochon, quelque chose comme ça. Ça fait que nous autres on prenait la viande puis on faisait de la saucisse, toutes sortes d'affaires. Je regrette pas le couvent parce que j'ai appris à canner, j'ai appris à coudre, j'ai appris à faire toutes sorte d'affaires.

I went to school, when I went to the convent, when I had the chance, maybe one hour a day. I had to work because the nuns kept boarders. There were maybe forty borders, maybe more. I had to wash the dishes, clean the kitchen, help with the cooking, sometimes do the washing, all sorts of things ... they did not pay. It was just for my food and my clothes. For nothing ...

and the farmers, they had to give meat to pay for their children's board after school. Some gave half a pig, something like that. That meant that we had to take the meat and make sausages, all sorts of things. I don't regret my convent days because I learned to can, I learned to sew, I learned all sorts of things.[16]

Alma Branconnier went to school only till the age of twelve. After that she was placed on the farm of a French Canadian farmer, Raymond Senecal, to help in the house and barnyard for two dollars a month. Her father came and collected the money every month. She states frankly that she did not like school but that she cried the first few days of working on the farm. Asked why she was put to work so young she responds frankly:

[parents needed money?] *I guess. Quand t'a six enfants pis un homme et une femme autour de la table. Rien que un homme qui travaille pour une piastre par jour. On était huit pour manger!*

I guess. When you have six children and a man and a woman around the table. And only one man working for one dollar a day. We were eight who had to eat![17]

Alma continued to give her wages to her father up until her marriage. She notes she felt obligated to contribute especially after the death of her mother from birth complications when Alma was seventeen.

All four women from the village finished at least the equivalent of grade six. Though none express much enthusiasm for their convent education there is little overt hostility. It was a far different experience for the Fort Rouge women.

The two sisters, Marie-Anne and Victoria St-Cyr, only attended school till grade three. Poverty seemed to have been the number one obstacle to pursuing an education. Marie-Anne stated simply that there were not enough winter clothes for all the children. Victoria also blamed the racist attitudes of the French Canadian farm kids.

J'ai arrêté au grade trois. J'a pas appris grand chose ... On avait de la misère pour le linge, le manger, les sandwichs, des affaires de même ... On venait pas a l'école tous les jours; à pied, au bout là-bas à peu près un mille, un petit brin plus. Je te dis quand t'est pas bien habillé, pis alter a l'école ... [laughed at you?] Oui, les petits canayens c'est assez haïssable ... Je m'en rappelle le frère à Pascal, Joe-Louis, lui tout avait de la misère pour les sandwichs, hein, pis y avait des choutièmes, mashait ça les choutièmes, pis s'avait de l'air la couleur de beurre. Il faisait des sandwichs avec ça, pis les p'tits canayens s'en vient, "Avec cossai t'a beurré à matin?" "Du beurre!" C'était des choutièmes! Je te le dis il étaient "vinienes," les Rivard pis les Lachance. On a mangé de la galette pis de la graisse ... il fallait bien. On avait rien que ça.

I stopped in grade three. I did not learn much ... we had trouble for clothing, food, sandwiches, stuff like that ... We did not go to school every day; on foot, a mile away. I tell you when you are not dressed ... and going to school, the French Canadians were hurtful ... I remember Pascal's brother, Joe-Louis, he had problems with the sandwiches, eh, and they had turnips, he mashed those turnips up. They were the colour of butter. He made sandwiches with that. The little French Canadians would come "with what did you butter today?" "Butter!" It was turnips! I tell you they were mean the Rivard and the Lachance. We ate bannock and lard. That is all we had.[18]

Their sister-in-law, Imelda Larocque, went to school till grade four. All three, along with most of their siblings and spouses, are in fact functionally illiterate.

The fourth Fort Rouge resident, Virginie McKay, went to school up until grade eight. As noted above she was the daughter of a single mother but her maternal grandfather, Pierre McKay Jn, was somewhat better off than the other residents of Fort Rouge. She comments she finished grade eight but did not continue because grade nine and ten were given in the convent of Elie and there was not enough money to send her. Unlike the others, Virginie did not work for farmers after leaving school but rather worked as a cook in the Mayfair Hotel in Portage La Prairie. Despite having completed what education was given in Saint-Eustache she, like the other Fort Rouge residents, felt bitterness towards the French Canadian segment of the population.

> Ben, avant t'étais Métis pis c'était toute. T'étais rien, t'étais Métis. Encore ben pire nous autres, on était des bâtards. C'est ça que la soeur disait, la soeur Wilfried aussi là. Ça fait que ... Moi je ne me suis pas laissé là, je me débattais toujours, ben ...

> Well, before, you were Métis and that was all. You were nothing. You were Métis. It was worst for us because we were bastards. That is what the sister said, sister Wilfried also. Therefore ... me, I never stayed there, I always struggled, so ...[19]

EARLY ADULTHOOD

All four village women had parallel experiences after leaving school. They worked for farmers either in their homes or in the barns milking cows. Bertha McKay also worked for a time as a cleaner and nurse's aid at the Saint-Boniface Hospital. Alma Branconnier, as noted above, started working for farmers at the age of twelve. Both Graziela Paul and Irene Lécuyer also worked for farmers. Irene Lécuyer is the only one of the four who began to work directly in the fields harvesting cucumbers and other vegetables. Graziela Paul continued the type of work she had known in the Elie convent with the added responsibilities of the milk cows:

> J'ai parti de là, j'avais à peu près 18 ans ... j'ai parti pour aller travailler pour les habitants, après ça ... j'ai travaillé pour Gros Pouce Lachance. J'ai travaillé là pour un an à 35 cents par jour. [in the fields?] Dans la maison, pis 14 enfants. Je to dis dans les couches, pis faire le pain tous les 2 jours, c'est de l'ouvrage. Là j'ai parti pour travailler pour Dave Bremner. J'avais un p'tit brin plus cher là. Il me donnait cinq piastres par mois ... C'était de l'ouvrage ... parce que y avait les hommes de Crépaud [Bremner] qui travaillaient là. Il fallait les nourrir hein! Ça fait qu'on avait le déjeuner pour les hommes, après ça on faisait le déjeuner pour les enfants ... foulait qu'on tire à peu près 20 vaches avec la p'tite fille. Pis en plus séparer ça, c'était de l'ouvrage.

> I left there when I was about 18 ... I left to work for the farmers, afterwards ... I worked for Gros Pouce Lachance. I worked there a year for 35 cents a day. In the house, and 14 children. I tell you we had diapers, and making bread every two days, it was work. Then I left to go work for Dave Bremner. I had a bit more there. He gave me five dollars a month ... it was work ... because there were Crepaud's men who worked there. We had to feed them eh! So we had breakfast for the men, after we made breakfast for the children ... then we had to milk about 10 cows, with the little girl. Then we had to separate it, it was work.[20]

Neither Bertha Carrière or Irene Lécuyer mention handing money over to their parents but the other two are very clear over the fact of seeing little of their salaries till their marriage. Graziela Paul commented:

> Cet argent là allait toute à mes parents pour les faire vivre. J'ai jamais gardé de l'argent sur moi ... je leur donnais de l'argent pour acheter des groceries, toute ça.

> That money there all went to my parents to make them live. I never kept money on me ... I gave them the money so they could buy groceries, all that.[21]

Reactions vary between the four women when discussions centre on pre-marital socializing. Bertha Carrière talks about the fun she had in the local dance hall in Baie St-Paul.

> *On allait aux danses. Y avait des halls. On avait du fun … c'était du monde par icitte qui faisait la musique. Si on voulait danser un square dance, on leur disait de jouer un square. Alexandre Hamelin gardait le Hall … pis, c'était tin bon danseur … Y avait tout le temps ben du monde … On marchait. On restait à la farme chez Carignan là. On marchait, on dansait toute la nuite, on marchait pour s'en venir. On travaillait le lendemain toute la journée … Ils vous laissaient pas dormir … Toutes les jeunes de St-Eustache se rencontraient là.*

> We went to the dances. There were halls. We had fun … it was people from around here that made the music. If we wanted a square dance we told them to play a square. Alexandre Hamelin kept the hall … and he was a good dancer … there was always lots of people … We walked. We were staying at the Carignan farm there. We walked, we danced all night, and we walked home … We worked all day … They would not let us sleep. All the young people in St-Eustache met there.[22]

Graziela Paul comments that before she married she never went out. They socialized at home. She only started to go to dances after her marriage. Irene Lécuyer notes they were only allowed to go to house parties and dance there before her marriage. Alma Branconnier remembers she only went out at night when her father was away working:

> [went out?] *Nul part! J'avais plus de mère. Mon défunt père était trop marabout. À 10 h il disait "c'est le temps de dire le chapelet." Il fallait ben que ça sort les gars là. On avait pas le droit d'aller roder sur le chemin ben don … c'était rien que les buggys. Temps en temps j'allais prendre des rides en buggys … quand qu'il était pas!*

> No where! I had lost my mother. My deceased father was too grumpy. At 10 p.m. he would say "It's time for the rosary." They had to get out those boys there. We were not allowed to go wander on the road or else … it was just buggies. From time to time I would go for rides on the buggies … when he was not there!"[23]

All four women married in their early twenties except for Bertha Carrière who married when she was twenty-seven. The first three married Saint-Eustache Métis men, labourers they had known for years. Bertha married, to the disapproval of her parents, Donald McKay of Fort Rouge who was a farm hand. The Fort Rouge women also married in their early twenties with the exception of Imelda Larocque who married at sixteen. They married their Fort Rouge counterparts, men with little or no formal education. Though the village women marked the marriage ceremony with a family dinner and dance or a two day trip to Winnipeg, the weddings in Fort Rouge were much more humble affairs. For example, Victoria St-Cyr married Pascal McKay in September 1937 at 7h30 in the morning. She comments on the lack of money:

> *Pas d'argent pour faire des noces. Pas d'argent pour traiter le gars qui nous a drivé seulement … Le curé a demandé à Pascal à la confession "As-tu de l'argent pour payer pour ton mariage?" Y a donné dix piastres. Y avait rien d'autres chases. [célébrations?] Un déjeuner chez ma mère. Tu sais ce qu'on a mange? Les patates réchauffées, la galette pis la graisse! C'est ça notre noces. Le déjeuner.*

> No money for the wedding. No money to pay the guy who drove us even … The priest asked Pascal at confession "do you have money to pay for your marriage?" He gave him ten dollars. That is all he had. We had breakfast at my mother's. You know what we ate? Reheated potatoes, bannock and lard! That was my wedding. Breakfast.[24]

ADULTHOOD/MARRIED LIFE

All eight women married in the Depression era and their descriptions of their married lives reflect those times. There is no great difference in their accounts of their working lives after marriage. All describe precarious lives marked with hardship. Bertha McKay moved to Fort Rouge after her marriage and her life resembled those of the other women from there. The three women remaining in Saint-Eustache combined working for wages with the demands of raising families. Graziela Paul comments that after their marriage they rented rooms "here and there" in the village and worked in the fields. She worked for thirty-five cents a day and her husband for fifty cents a day. She adds that they were able to get by because she managed to plant a large garden and do enough canning for the winter. Alma Branconnier also worked in the fields most of her adult life. The first few years she spent her summers hand weeding the vegetable fields:

> Pour Laurent Chabot, 10 cents de l'heure. Avec Joe Pagée et Joe Lécuyer. Les crimes d'hommes. Ça piochait en avant. Pis nous autres, à quatre pattes en arrière. T'aurais du voir nos genoux. C'était toute rouge!

> For Laurent Chabot, 10 cents an hour. With Joe Pagée and Joe Lécuyer. Those damn men. They hoed in front. And us, on our hands and knees in the back You should have seen our knees. They were all red![25]

The five married women from Fort Rouge, including Bertha Carrière, also worked in the fields for French Canadian farmers most of their adult lives. When one compares their life histories again it becomes a question of differences of degrees of poverty. Victoria St-Cyr comments that for the first few years after their marriage, she and her husband lived in a small one room log cabin. This is not unusual for the times within the Métis population in general of the village but what is surprising is that her "shack," as she calls it, had no floor:

> On a resté sur mon père, un mois. Après ça on s'est fait un petit shack … Pis on a battu sur le terrain de mon père. On a resté deux ans pas de plancher. Rien que la terre. Pas d'argent pour acheter un plancher … On était ben. On avait des cartons, des tapis, hein!

> We stayed at my father's perhaps a month. After that we made ourselves a little shack … and we cut hay on my father's land. We stayed two years without a floor. Only dirt. No money to buy a floor … We were O.K. We had cardboard, carpet, eh![26]

She and the other women worked in the sugar beet fields in the summer and helped the men "stooking" during the grain harvest. The only work they appear not to have done was wood cutting and field clearing in the winter, something all the husbands appear to have done at some time or another.

Differences become apparent between the two groups of women later on in their lives, after the Second World War. The three women still residing in the village eventually acquired a milk cow and some barnyard animals. Both Alma Branconnier and Irene Lécuyer eventually sold milk for ten cents a quart, butter twenty-five cents a pound and eggs ten cents a dozen. They also raised pigs and salted their own pork. This gave them an extra source of revenue and allowed them to cut down substantially on the cost of feeding their growing family. Their husbands acquired horse teams and worked clearing land for farmers with "stoneboats" or found employment in the Pine Falls lumber industry as freighters. The only woman to keep a milk cow in Fort Rouge was Imelda Larocque, who took her animal with her when she worked in the fields so that it could feed on discards:

On partait du chemin icitte jusqu'à l'autre coulée là-bas à genoux. Dans les rang pour nettoyer. On l'ôtait … c'était les betteraves. On laisait rien qu'une betterave. On garrochait les autres. On amenait notre vache. [why?] Bien pour avoir le lait pour les enfants.

We would start at the road here and go to the other coulee there. We removed … they were beets. We left only one beet. We would throw the others. We would bring our cow. So the children would have milk."[27]

PERCEPTION OF SELF

All eight women see themselves as Métis and believe to varying degrees that they suffered because of their ethnic identity. They also see a clear distinction between themselves and their French Canadian neighbours in term of social status and material wealth. Bertha Carrière, a woman whose lifestyle in her youth resembled most that of the French Canadians of the village and parish, still noted differences:

Pis à l'autre bout par là c'était pareil … ils se mélangeaient pas avec le monde du village. [who?] Nous autres on les appelait les Canayens. On était pas assez high class. Y onvaient plus d'argent. Y onvaient des grosses farms. Y pouvaient acheter des grosses machines pour travailler.

At the other end it was the same … they did not mix with the people of the village. We called them the Canadians. We were not high class enough. They had more money. They had big farms. They could buy big machinery to work.[28]

The economic difference translated into a social one. Irene Lécuyer remembers feeling left out of social life of the parish:

Y [a parish priest for forty years] était pour les riches. It was so insulting. Y allait rencontrer les riches. Les pauvres y en faisait pas de cas. Dans ce temps là y avait les dames de Sainte-Anne puis les enfants de Marie. Bien les enfants de Marie c'était rien que les enfants des riches. It's true. Oui c'est vrai! Tout le monde peut le dire ça. Toute la paroisse peut le dire si ils veulent dire la vérité; ils vont le dire.

He [priest] was only for the rich. It was so insulting. He would only go meet the rich. The poor were of no matter. In those days there were the Ladies of Sainte-Anne and the Children of Mary. Well the Children of Mary was only for the children of the rich. It's true! Yes, it's true! Everybody can say it. The whole parish can say it if they want to say the truth. They will say it.[29]

The most bitter comments towards the French Canadian farmers came from the residents of Fort Rouge. When asked if there was a difference between the Métis and the French Canadians Imelda Larocque replied indignantly:

Ah oui! They say it's dead but it's not! Je sais que toutes les dos blancs y ont fait leur … In raison qui ont l'argent, c'est a cause qui ont gardé les Métis travailler pis les payer moins … comme 25 cents de l'heure. Eux autres comment d'argent que ça faisaient? You're always under … Oui. Des fois, je m'en rappelle 4 heures, 5 heures le matin on partait pour travailler dans les champs.

Oh yes! They say it's dead but it's not! I know all the "white backs" [French Canadians], they made … the reason they have money, it is because they kept the Métis working and they paid them less … like 25 cents an hour. Them, how much money they made? You're always under … Yes, I remember 4 o'clock, 5 o'clock in the morning we would leave to work in the fields.[30]

When asked if there were "differences" between Métis families living in the village proper and those residing in Fort Rouge responses varied depending on place of residence and, in general, were more cautious. The women born in Fort Rouge avoided the question or simply commented, as Imelda Larocque does, that "it was all the same." The village-born women were more forthright in their opinions. Graziela Paul emphatically denied having relations in Fort Rouge, adding:

> Je me suis jamais occupé de personne. J'ai toujours rien que gardé mes enfants. J'ai jamais badré personne, jamais!

> I never meddled with people. I always only took care of my children. I never bothered anyone, never![31]

Irene Lécuyer comments, when asked if she was considered poor, that only the farmers were rich. When asked if she was as poor as the Fort Rouge residents she declares:

> On était pas a ce rang là. Oh non … entre les fermiers et les gens pauvres. [still considered Métis?] Oh yah!

> We were not at that level. Oh no … between the farmers and the poor people. [Still Métis?] Oh yes! [32]

Bertha Carrière comments that she saw no difference between the two groups but finished with the telling comment:

> [Difference between the two?] Non. Mais ils se mélangeaient pas comme là cet'heure. Avant ça ils se mélangeaient pas comme la cett' heure … Pis à l'autre bout par là c'était pareil … ils se mélangeaient pas avec le monde du village …

> [Differences] No, but they did not mix like they do today. Before they did not mix like that. At the other end it was the same … they did not mix.[33]

CONCLUDING REMARKS

Joy Parr writes that, in the 1930s, "five times as many temporary as annual wage-paying farm jobs were offered in Ontario … half of all seasonal engagements being of female harvest hands."[34] This situation was reflected in the Prairie region. What differs between the two regions, at least for the Saint-Eustache area, is that in the West paid farm labour became a transgenerational occurrence performed by a population perceived as being of distinct ethnic or racial origin.

The eight women whose narratives were examined in this paper all come from old fur trading era families with a history of at least partial involvement in a wage labour economy. Their paternal ancestors worked as tripmen and freighters coupled with bison-hunting activities for the Saint-François-Xavier families. After 1870, they increasingly hired on as agricultural workers. For reasons still hotly debated by historians[35] these Métis families, with the possible exception of the Carrière family, did not hold on to their river lots and engage in full-time farming. Whatever the reasons, the 20th century saw this population become increasingly poor and have fewer and fewer opportunities outside the farming wage economy.

These Métis families continued to practice a form of mixed economy. They worked seasonally for cash, clearing land, weeding, and stooking the grain harvest. All the while they maintained a small acreage where a garden could grow and occasionally a cow pastured. When associated with small game hunting, they could thus see to the immediate food needs of the family. Though these plots provided them with a modicum of security, they also tied them to the countryside and to seasonal, poorly paid, field labour. Certainly for the Fort Rouge families, linguistic and educational barriers along with an awareness of latent racism kept them away from urban areas where the possibility of better jobs existed. Several times in the interviews, Fort Rouge narrators expressed their fear and distrust at the idea of having abandoned or sold their plots and moved to Winnipeg or even a smaller city such as Portage La Prairie to look for better working conditions.

The generation of women interviewed appear to have been the first to be involved on a regular basis in the wage labour economy. Some did have mothers who worked for money but it appears to have been the result of exceptional circumstances such as widowhood or being a single mother. None mention their grandmothers working for money outside the home. This growth in female employment might easily be explained by the increasing demands of the farming economy linked to the decreasing possibilities for lucrative employment for Métis men as the fur trade receded and the bison herds disappeared. All the eight women interviewed indicate that the wages of their husbands, and often when they were younger their fathers, were not enough to maintain a household. Had Saint-Eustache farmers[36] followed Prairie-wide trends and adopted more highly mechanized and intensive grain growing practices after the First World War this rural wage labouring class might well have disappeared. But, early on, farmers in the area became involved in dairying and, increasingly, in growing sugar beets, potatoes, cucumbers and other "stoop crops." These crops required intensive manual intervention throughout the growing season and their harvests were difficult to mechanize, thus ensuring a steady demand for cheap seasonal workers. It was work women could do and, given the circumstances in Saint-Eustache, work Métis women had to do. […]

As soon as possible the narrators, and their male counterparts, left school, or were taken out by their needy families, to work in the fields. Thus they perpetuated the cycle of a marginalised existence predicated on a complete dependence on the French Canadian farming families for work. This dependence was not mutual since farmers could bring in other labourers such as Indians from the Sandy Bay reserve or, more recently, migrant workers from Mexico. With greater access to education, the children of the village women interviewed moved out of agrarian wage labour. It took another generation before a significant number of Fort Rouge Métis stopped working in the fields. Even to this day, seasonal farm work is a fact of life for several of the interviewed Fort Rouge women's grandchildren.

NOTES

1. I would like to thank the Manitoba Heritage Federation Inc. and the University of Ottawa for their financial support during fieldwork in Saint-Eustache. I would also like to thank Philip A. Beaudin for his help in creating phonetic transcription of the interviews.
2. J. Parr, "Hired Men: Ontario Agricultural Wage Labour in Historical Perspective," *Labour/Le Travail*, 15 (Spring 1985): 91–103.
3. H. Clare Pentland, *Labour and Capital in Canada 1650–1860* (Toronto 1981), 59, cited in ibid., p. 91.
4. Parr, "Hired," 91–92.
5. Recalculated from M. C. Urquhart and K. A. H. Buckley, *Historical Statistics of Canada* (Toronto 1965), 355.
6. Lu Ann Jones and Nancy Grey Osterud, "Breaking New Ground: Oral History and Agricultural History," *The Journal of American History*, 76 (September 1989): 553.
7. Marcel Giraud, *Le Métis Canadien: son role dans l'histoire des provinces de l'Ouest* (Paris 1945), 1137.
8. Giraud, *Le Métis Canadien*, 1137.
9. Gerhard J. Ens, *Homeland to Hinterland: The Changing Worlds of the Red River Métis in the Nineteenth Century* (Toronto 1996), 136.

10. Irene Lécuyer, transcript (phonetic transcription), 4.
11. Alma Branconnier, transcript (phonetic transcription), 5.
12. Stooks: an old English word used to describe a group of sheaves set upright in a field to allow the grain to dry.
13. Marie-Anne St-Cyr, transcript (phonetic transcription), 3.
14. Virginie McKay, transcript (phonetic transcription), 6.
15. Bertha Carrière, transcript (phonetic transcription), 13.
16. Graziela Paul, transcript (phonetic transcription), 16.
17. Alma Branconnier, 7.
18. Victoria St-Cyr, transcript (phonetic transcription), 5.
19. Virginie McKay, 24.
20. Graziela Paul, 19.
21. Graziela Paul, 21.
22. Bertha Carrière, 16.
23. Alma Branconnier, 8.
24. Victoria St-Cyr, 15–16.
25. Alma Branconnier, 15.
26. Victoria St-Cyr, 16–17.
27. Imelda Larocque, transcript (phonetic transcription), 42.
28. Bertha Carrière, 29.
29. Irene Lécuyer, 13.
30. Imelda Larocque, 41.
31. Graziela Paul, 43.
32. Irene Lécuyer, 18.
33. Bertha Carrière, 28.
34. Parr, "Hired," 102.
35. Nicole St-Onge, "Thomas Flanagan: Métis Lands in Manitoba," *Revue d'histoire de l'Amérique Française*, 46, 3 (Hiver 1993): 521–523.
36. In fact, all the Portage La Prairie region.

Article 1.2

Hugh Shewell

"Bitterness Behind Every Smiling Face": Community Development and Canada's First Nations, 1954–1968

Issues to Consider

- Shewell's introductory comments refer to a paradox inherent in British colonial policy regarding Native peoples in the early 19th century. What is this paradox and what explains its continued importance during the 20th century?
- In what ways is "assimilation" synonymous with "disappearance" where attitudes and policies toward Native peoples are concerned? If both pre- and post-Confederation governments were aiming for assimilation, what were the notable changes after the 1876 Indian Act?
- What explains the widespread Euro-Canadian perception of Aboriginals as a "dependent" people?
- Why was the government unable to look to other approaches despite a near-century of failure "to solve Indian dependency and the question of their assimilation"?
- By the late 1950s, the new policy was "integration." How was integration different from assimilation?
- What role was defined for Natives in the community development projects of the 1960s? Did they fulfill that role as planned? What was ultimately accomplished?
- What do the interviews with the key players, especially Walter Rudnicki and Jerry Gambill, offer? Are there other voices that would make an impact in this story?

From the early nineteenth century, when settlement in Canada began to accelerate, the pressure to acquire Indian lands similarly intensified. Consequently, the British colonial office was obliged to develop new policies to recognize the encroachment of European civilization on Indian societies.[1] To appease Christian missions and English humanitarian organizations, colonial policy in Canada sought to protect and "civilize" Indians, in the belief that their survival lay in Christianization and the acquisition of European culture.[2] Paradoxically, the protection of Indians was seen to lie in their assimilation into the dominant, non-Native society.[3] Implicit in British colonial policy were questions about the status and place of Indians in Canada, as well as their relationship with the Euro-Canadian society and its institutions. It is these questions that continue to inform Canadian Indian policy to this day, although the goal of absolute assimilation — or disappearance — has largely, though not entirely, dissipated.[4]

Until Confederation, the emphasis of colonial policy had remained on the protection and 'gradual civilization' of Indians. After 1867 and the passage of the Indian Act in 1876, however, successive federal administrations attempted to subjugate them and effect their assimilation into the mainstream population.[5] For almost a century Ottawa implemented various unsuccessful strategies to this end. Despite this continuous failure, the assimilation policy

Source: Hugh Shewell, "Bitterness Behind Every Smiling Face: Community Development and Canada's First Nations, 1954–1968," *Canadian Historical Review* 83, no. 1 (2002): 58–84.

endured, supported by the ideological biases of politicians, administrators, and the general public that Indians were overly dependent on the state and that their independence could only be accomplished if they were dispersed into Canadian society as self-sufficient individuals.

The dependency of Indians was the outcome of European economic expansion and of federal policies that excluded and marginalized them. This article is a study of a modern — that is, apparently progressive — attempt by the federal government to solve Indian dependency and the question of their assimilation. The implementation of a community development program in 1965 resulted from the failure of previous strategies, the federal government's concern that Indians were too dependent on social assistance as a source of support, and the belief that the provinces must become involved in assisting Indians to full citizenship.[6] Archival and secondary sources form the basis of the research, although interviews and correspondence with some of the actors are included. The position and arguments are focused on the federal perspective, and the provincial perspective, though considered, remains a subject for further research.

It was clear by the mid-1940s that strategies to assimilate Indians had failed. The situation of the First Nations was also a national disgrace and an international embarrassment. An article in the *Economist* stated: "Canadian Indian policy has done little beyond save the Indian from extinction ... [O]n the whole, conditions on Indian reservations ... have remained ... in the category of slums."[7] By 1944 political levels of the federal government were considering a new approach to Indian assimilation: to extend the full rights of citizenship gradually to Indian persons.[8] The government determined that it would play a positive role in Indian communities, a determination that corresponded with new Canadian policies to extend social rights of citizenship and implement welfare state measures. The federal government also wanted the provinces to extend their services to Indian reserves as a way of fostering citizenship and of ensuring that all Canadians were treated alike. It hoped also to transfer to the provinces some of the costs of Indian administration.

The 1948 report of the joint Parliamentary Committee on the Indian Act confirmed this approach. The committee recommended that aspects of Indian administration be accomplished with federal–provincial cooperation to bring about the economic assimilation of Indians "into the body politic of Canada." In discussing social services, the committee noted that they were "dealt with under provincial ... powers. However, it should be possible to arrive at such financial arrangements as might bring Indians within ... provincial legislation, in order that there be mutual and co-ordinated assistance to facilitate the Indians to become ... citizens proud of Canada and of the provinces in which they reside."[9] This recommendation crystallized Indian policy direction after the Second World War. Assimilation remained the objective, but the extension of rights of citizenship, including social services, was to be a key strategy in achieving that end. In 1949 the Indian Affairs Branch was transferred from the Department of Mines and Resources to the new Department of Citizenship and Immigration. The transfer was a symbolic declaration by the federal government that Indian policy was to be proactive in elevating Indians to full citizenship. It also meant that no longer would Indians be the afterthought of a department whose primary interest was land and resource exploitation, an interest too often contrary to the protection of Indian rights. Instead, the government would enhance the civil and social rights of Indians and welcome them into the Canadian mainstream. The Indian Act of 1951 helped to set this new tone, although its principal features remained in line with the original act of 1876. While it eliminated more coercive elements of the old act and removed the ban on cultural practices, it did not change the objective of assimilation.[10]

By the late 1950s the term "assimilation" was replaced by "integration," although little change in policy direction had occurred.[11] Testifying at the joint Parliamentary Committee on Indian Affairs in 1961, H. M. Jones, the director of Indian Affairs, stated, "We have been using the word integration. It seems to fit ... with the feeling that the future of the Indians is to become ... citizens of the country but still retain their culture and background ... I heard some experts argue ... the difference between assimilation and integration. They had me ... confused. Presently ... I think the Indians are ... more happy with the word integration than with ... assimilation."[12] Although this testimony implied the recognition of cultural pluralism in Canada, Jones also meant that if integration was more palatable to the Indians, then so be it — let assimilation be termed integration.

Integration was less coercive than assimilation, relying more on ideological persuasion than on mandatory measures. Thus, James S. Frideres argues that integration implied not the actual integration into society, but the reproduction of Indian consent to the social order through regulation and control. Indian policy was successful if Indians consented or deferred to their domination and implicitly accepted the state as the agent of the economic and social order. Indian behaviour and aspirations could be controlled through programs and services that diverted them and promised them full equality. In this sense, integration meant deference to and domination by the institutional structures of the state.[13]

From 1948 to 1963 the Indian Affairs Branch concentrated on improving its methods of welfare provision and on finding ways of encouraging the provinces to extend their welfare services to Indian communities. These latter efforts were largely unsuccessful, mainly because the provinces, though "sympathetic in the abstract," had neither the financial nor the professional resources to do so and because the branch administration was not adept in establishing cooperation with them.[14] The branch director for most of this period, H. M. Jones, a retired army colonel, struggled to maintain direction and seemed unable to implement worthwhile ideas. He resented criticism of the branch, and his administration remained isolated from the larger public service to the extent that other public servants thought Indian Affairs an anachronism, referring to it as "Colonel Jones' lost battalion."[15] Dr George F. Davidson, as deputy minister of welfare (in the Department of Health and Welfare) and later as deputy minister in Citizenship and Immigration, dealt with Jones frequently. Jones, he recalled, was "a frozen-faced, military type. His impersonal presence was what impressed you most ... You felt ... little warmth or humanity in him, although there was more than appeared ... But he acted more as a stern father in ... Indian Affairs than he did as a humanitarian ... You wouldn't slap Hubert Jones on the back."[16]

Nevertheless, his administration was involved in some initiatives that were important antecedents to the Community Development Program (CDP). During the 1950s, one solution proposed to ameliorate the social and economic conditions of Indian communities was leadership training. Such training, it was argued, would develop a base of leadership through which band councils could identify and solve community problems. A good example was the Social Leadership Program implemented in 1954 to train leaders to tackle social problems. The program was also intended as a stopgap, pending the extension of provincial services onto the reserves.[17] However, Jessa Chupik-Hall, in her account of these and similar programs, concludes that they were not effective in resolving the complexity of the problems they were created to address.[18]

Another initiative was the branch's association with the Indian-Eskimo Association of Canada. The IEA, a largely non-Native, national voluntary organization, sought to promote understanding by non-Natives of Native peoples in Canada. In 1961 the IEA's executive director was John Melling, who had been deputy director of the Department of Adult Education and Extra-Mural Studies at the University of Leeds.[19] Under Melling's leadership, the IEA set out to educate the Canadian community to the "Indian Problem" and to involve it in its solution. Melling's work eventually took him to many of Canada's northern reserves and their adjacent non-Native communities. On his return from one such trip in 1961, he delivered a speech to the Women's Canadian Historical Society in Toronto in which he criticized the federal government and its implicit support of the exploitation of Indian peoples. The Toronto *Globe and Mail* reported him as saying: "Although those in Ottawa express belief in equality for … native Canadian peoples, by the time their policies reach new municipalities in the north they appear as zoning regulations to keep Indian and Eskimo Canadians separate from white people; they find themselves underwriting policies of business firms in the north which forbid fraternizing; and, although Ottawa officials believe housing for both Indian and Eskimo people is … inadequate, the Government's … policies reflect established patterns based on inequality." Noting that Indians were a completely subjugated people as a result of contact with European culture, Melling concluded by stating, "There is extreme bitterness behind every smiling Indian face … and it is justified."[20]

This report angered the deputy minister of the Department of Northern Affairs and National Resources, R. Gordon Robertson, who wrote sharply to Melling condemning his remarks. "You would appear to be attributing to us motives which are false," he complained. Referring to Melling's statement about zoning regulations, he stated: "You no doubt have in mind that in many northern communities there are sharp physical distinctions which reflect income levels just as there are in any southern Canadian community. In the north … income lines happen to coincide with ethnic lines, but there are enough exceptions to this pattern to dispose of any charges of segregation." Robertson copied his letter to Jones and to Clare Clark, president of the IEA. Melling immediately made apologies to Jones and Robertson. His final words to Robertson summed up the conflict between the two organizations. "Government and IEA are engaged in most difficult work," he wrote. "Their ways of approach, though they should be complementary, cannot, in a number of respects, be quite the same."[21] Today, Robertson recalls little of the incident, but remembered the relations with the IEA as "characterized by mutual respect and harmonious professional and personal relations before and after the correspondence … cited. That does not mean constant identity of viewpoint."[22]

What importance can be attributed to the relationship between Indian Affairs and IEA and to this incident? A department as insular and steeped in organizational culture as Indian Affairs, which thought itself to be expert in "advancing" Indians in Canada, would inevitably condemn criticism aimed at what it thought it did best. The IEA experience foreshadowed the dangers for newcomers and outsiders who were seen by veteran insiders as "knowing the answers." To Jones and many of his subordinates, community education, development, and even leadership training were potentially subversive to the Indian administration, which was about Indian management, not emancipation.[23]

The initiatives so far described occurred within the overall context of branch efforts to develop policy to foster the extension of provincial services to Indian reserves and to overcome what H. B. Hawthorn described as "discrimination in … service provision to Indian people."[24] Generally, the provinces remained reluctant to treat Indians as citizens of their respective jurisdictions, did not uniformly extend their franchise, and did not extend their social services to them.[25] Although federal income security programs were available to Indians, provincial social assistance and services such as child welfare were not. Historically, the federal government had always provided assistance on the reserves. During the postwar Joint Parliamentary Committee hearings, however, the Canadian Welfare Council had recommended the extension of provincial services to Indian reserves. Thus, during the 1950s, the branch attempted to ally with the CWC's influential Public Welfare Division, whose membership was mainly senior provincial and municipal welfare administrators. Through close contact with these administrators, it was thought that provincial jurisdictions might soften to the idea of extending their services.[26]

Meanwhile, there were important developments in Ontario. The 1954 report *Civil Liberties and Rights of Indians in Ontario* had spurred the Ontario government to extend its welfare programs — including child welfare — culminating in 1959 with an amendment to the General Welfare Assistance Act that granted bands quasi-municipal status to administer social assistance on the reserves.[27] The GWA initiative impelled the branch to develop a policy for the extension of services that would encourage all the provinces to follow Ontario's lead. In the spring of 1960 Ellen Fairclough, the minister of citizenship and immigration, announced to the House that the federal government was prepared to negotiate and to contribute to the funding of the extension of provincial services. Few provinces, however, showed any interest.[28]

In late 1963 the outgoing Conservative government of John Diefenbaker commissioned H. B. Hawthorn, an anthropologist at the University of British Columbia, to develop a comprehensive database of Canada's Indians and to make recommendations about future policy and programs for the branch. The report of 1966 provided three explanations for this lack of progress. First, it agreed with the branch's assessment that the provincial systems were overloaded and that reserves would find it difficult to accommodate the municipal–private sector mix of service delivery. In addition, the provinces were simply discriminatory in their treatment of Indians. Second, the federal government shouldered some blame for its historical claim of exclusive responsibility for Indians. The provinces could not be expected to warm to the extension of their services when the branch remained vague in its policy intent, uninformed about the problems it wanted solved, and retained a negative view of welfare. Finally, there was no groundswell of demand from Indian communities for provincial services. Although Hawthorn acknowledged the preference Indians held for a direct relationship with the Crown and their distrust of the provinces, he concluded that the extension of provincial services to Indian communities would be a good thing and that Indians should be induced to demand them. But in Ontario the experience of provincial social assistance was already uneven. Many bands did not wish to participate for political or cultural reasons. Others couldn't afford to because Ottawa required them to pay all or a portion of their relief costs. The various forms of cost sharing available to provincial jurisdictions did not apply to Indians.[29]

By 1963 the branch was stagnant, unable to secure provincial involvement or to find solutions to Indian poverty and escalating welfare costs.[30] Sally M. Weaver describes the branch as fraught with contradictions that were embodied within Jones himself. While he had some vision of advancing Indian citizenship, his rigid personality, strict adherence to the Indian Act, and paternalistic ideas prevented the branch from seeking creative solutions.[31] Hawthorn identified the branch's isolation from the internal politics of the public service as a decisive factor in its inability to carry its policies forward. It resulted in the branch failing "to carve out for itself that minimum position of power and influence in the federal government which was a prerequisite for the successful implementation of a progressive Indian policy."[32] Only a change in government would produce that prerequisite.

In 1963 conditions in Indian communities were shameful. The welfare dependency rate of 36 per cent was over ten times the national average. In the fiscal years 1961/2 and 1962/3, total welfare expenditures had risen 5 per cent. The average age of Indian mortality was nearly half that of the non-Indian population and was attributable mainly to preventable diseases. Public health, housing, and sanitation were deplorable. Commenting on these data, the branch's senior administrative clerk remarked in a memo, "it is feared that the scale of relief assistance available to Indians is a serious contributing factor in these appalling statistics."[33]

The election of the Liberals in 1963 represented a turning point in Canadian Indian policy. Prime Minister Pearson was determined to introduce an era of cooperation between

Ottawa and the provinces, and this goal included the advancement of Indian citizenship within each province. A new, senior administration was appointed to develop and implement policies that would achieve this fundamental objective. Besides Guy Favreau, the new minister of citizenship and immigration, a new deputy, Claude Isbister, was appointed in 1964. R. F. Battle, the chief of the Economic Development Division, was promoted to branch director. Walter Rudnicki, a social worker formerly with the Arctic division of Northern Affairs and Natural Resources, became the chief of the Welfare Division. Finally, a new Federal–Provincial Relations Division was created to funnel policy initiatives that involved the provinces.[34]

Neither Favreau nor Isbister had any knowledge of First Nations' peoples, but both wanted to energize the branch and advance Indian policy. Battle knew that the branch had floundered and wanted to explore ideas for new programs.[35] Isbister regarded him highly.[36] Rudnicki had an excellent reputation for his community work among the Inuit and, it was thought, would bring new ideas to the Welfare Division, where spending was second only to the Education Division.

The branch was an oppressive bureaucracy. "It was a military environment," Rudnicki recalled. "Indians used to come to the Department totally submissive ... their hats in hand, heads bowed low. They looked ... terrorized."[37] By 1964 the atmosphere had changed. The new administration had decided that community development would form the basis of Indian policy in Canada. Isbister remembered meeting with his senior officials to discuss "what were we going to do, and what were our objectives ... and what Bob Battle and others were saying was that community development was the best game in town." Isbister had moved into a department, he said, "where senior officials had not been ... purposeful." When community development was proposed, he recalled, "I remember saying, okay, that's what we try to do. I gave that as much backing as I could from the position I had." Isbister knew about community development from his knowledge of similar United Nations programs and had a reputation for being "constructively minded" when he was an assistant deputy minister at the Department of Finance.[38] According to Cunningham, Favreau and Isbister were critical to the CDP's approval. "Favreau was in favour of community development ... and went to bat for the Program at the Cabinet table. With Favreau's support, the other Ministers approved the cabinet submission and the CDP. Whereas Favreau ... sold the CDP at the political level, Isbister's support was key within the bureaucracy ... [H]is support was essential to selling the CDP to the bureaucrats while implementing it within their midst."[39]

Rudnicki prepared the proposal for Cabinet. To make it acceptable, he knew he had to appeal to the objectives of reducing welfare dependency and promoting self-sufficiency. Simultaneously, it had to appeal to principles of Indian equality and citizenship. Rudnicki recalled, "If I just came forth with a community development program I didn't think it would get ... far, but if I linked it to ... things I knew some ... ministers were concerned about like self-sufficiency and ... dependency problems ... reducing welfare costs, and all that ... [I knew that it would get approved]. I didn't think it through in ... today's concepts, it was the sixties concepts and the politics of the day."[40] The sixties concepts of community development were influenced by two models. The first, the adult education model from England, was based on learning and communication theories. Implemented in British colonies to foster leadership and to promote social and economic development, it had also been applied in areas such as London's East End, notably Toynbee Hall. Rudnicki was informed by this model and by one of its chief practitioners and theorists, Dr T. R. Batten of the University of London. The model centred on developing indigenous leadership to organize the community around key issues. Batten was interested in how communities acquire and use knowledge to their advantage. This development required an understanding of effective agency and of what constituted a community. The second model was American. It was less developed and it focused on community mobilization and confrontation with authority in response to poverty and other issues in America's inner cities. The community action model became the central strategy of the US War on Poverty and was popularized among American academics by the activist Saul Alinsky.[41]

Rudnicki liked Batten's advice, training material, and papers. Of social change, Batten wrote: "We study community development to learn how to influence people for the 'better.' To do this we need to know something about people's beliefs, values, and customs, and their attitudes and relationships to each other. One of the ... difficulties is that we ... often disagree about what is 'better.' "[42] Ironically, despite the democratic principles inherent in community development, Indians were not consulted or involved in the development of the proposal.[43] This omission was also true for the front-line bureaucracy at Indian Affairs whose role would be critical to the CDP's implementation, and it may have been fatal.

Rudnicki's proposal was submitted to Cabinet in February 1964. Leaving the definition of community development vague, the emphasis was on what would happen to Indians and to government expenditures as a *result* of community development. In essence, the CDP was to be a federal funding and cost-sharing initiative with the provinces to encourage them to accept more responsibility for Indian communities, particularly for welfare services. Urgent measures were needed, it was argued, to bring Indian peoples into the twentieth century. "Experience in the under-developed areas of the world and ... trends in Canadian public opinion support a community development approach as one effective way of achieving this aim." In the proposal, the branch argued that community development would maximize the use of material and human resources available in Indian communities and each province. The effect of this "would be to step up mobilisation of Indian initiative and to ... promote self-sufficiency. One of its ... results would be to accelerate transfer to Indian communities of responsibility and authority for the management of their affairs." Thus, the program would provide a framework for coordinating existing health, education, welfare, and economic development services on the reserves and, ultimately, "reduce costs in such palliative areas as welfare assistance."[44] Just how or why this change would occur was not fully explained.[45] The argument, however, was that increased autonomy and direction over their own affairs, coupled with links to provincial infrastructures, would lead First Nations to greater self-sufficiency and reduced welfare dependency. According to Rudnicki, the idea that welfare dependency would decrease was based on the premise that community development would restore pride to the First Nations and would help them move outwards both in working to improve their communities and in getting jobs in the mainstream society.[46]

The effectiveness of the CDP would be measured by the reduction of per capita Indian welfare costs to the same level as non-Indians. The proposal appealed to Cabinet for its promise of two outcomes: first, the projected saving in welfare expenditure and, second, the objective of integrating Indian and provincial welfare services. These developments, it was surmised, would lead to the integration of Indian communities with provincial and municipal levels of society.[47] Kris Uppal, a former regional CDP official for Indian Affairs, stated that Rudnicki "tried to establish a model in which community development would be inversely proportional to welfare payments — if ... community development ... increases, then welfare decreases."[48] However, a senior clerk who reviewed the proposal recalled his scepticism. "That was one of the things about Rudnicki. He started off with a ... theoretical premise and he built this ... submission all on a supposing so and so ... on a theory without ... basis."[49] Nevertheless, Rudnicki, convinced these outcomes would occur, also recommended replacing the Welfare Division with a Social Programs Division, anticipating that the branch would no longer administer social assistance.[50]

Cabinet approved the program in late May 1964 and the branch immediately planned its first year of operation in 1965.[51] This outline included hiring and training twenty-five community development officers and seven supervisors for the regions, as well as developing the criteria for the selection and approval of communities where the program would likely be effective.[52] In

January 1965 the Treasury Board approved the branch's request to make direct grants to the provinces and to individual bands. This financing would enable the bands to plan and implement community-based projects and would assist the provinces in extending their services.[53] Shortly after, the branch issued a document that provided guidelines for assessing requests for grants from the regions and from the band councils. It described how, and under what conditions, Indian Affairs would flow funds directly to the bands. The guidelines identified three fundable, inoffensive activities that would be considered "community development": the development of administrative and physical infrastructure, the implementation of non-profit socioeconomic improvement projects, and the provision of cultural or recreational programs.[54]

What was contentious was the process by which these activities would be developed. Two new procedures stood out: direct Indian involvement in decision-making, and the circumvention of lines of authority. Rudnicki recalled the latter's subversive nature. "I arranged things regionally so that community development workers ... reported directly to me [in Ottawa]. People fought that ... but I insisted on it." As for the Indians, because Rudnicki wanted them to be able to circumvent the authority of the local agent, he proposed a national Indian organization. This suggestion was rejected as too political by the old guard. They countered with the idea of regional and national Indian advisory committees that would occasionally counsel the department on what it should be doing. Rudnicki agreed because, "once you start bringing people into advisory meetings ... then they can meet afterwards in hotel rooms and start sharing experiences and get other kinds of information."[55] The advisory committees were approved.

The attempt to have the provinces become more active in Indian communities was a failure. A federal–provincial conference in October 1964 resulted in agreement on the role of the provinces in community development and on a general approach to the extension of their services. According to newspaper reports of the conference, the extension of welfare services was to occur in two stages: province by province and with the agreement of each band. Provincial services would not be imposed on the bands, and existing federal welfare services would continue to meet appropriate provincial standards.[56] Only Ontario took full advantage of the agreement. The other provinces did not extend their social assistance services, although some — notably the three Prairie provinces — were already involved in community development with Indian communities. A booklet published by the Indian-Eskimo Association identified four provinces that had established community development services for their Native communities: Manitoba (1958), Ontario (1962), Alberta (1963), and Saskatchewan (1964).[57] According to Hawthorn, the provinces distinguished between the extension of community development programs and the extension of social assistance, the former being proactive and publicly palatable, the latter palliative and less popular.[58]

Isbister recalled that getting the provinces involved "was like hammering sand." He remembered going to many meetings with them and "talking about [the extension of services], listening to their hard luck stories about their budgets and ... problems, and about federal responsibilities. You'd go to a lot of effort. The waves would come up and nothing to be seen the next morning!"[59] C. N. C. Roberts, a senior branch clerk who hadn't favoured the CDP, was sympathetic to the provinces. "I think they realized what a can of worms they would be getting into. Ottawa was ... glossing over so much of it. They realized ... it was going to cost an awful lot of money."[60]

Hawthorn's assessment of the provincial positions, while more even-handed, was not flattering. The report could find no legal or jurisdictional reasons for the provinces not to extend their welfare services. "No less important for the conduct of intergovernmental relations than possible outbreaks of intergovernmental vituperation," the report noted, "is the deep-seated legacy of historical assumptions as to the respective roles of federal and provincial governments in providing services for Indian communities."[61] Noting that the federal government was offering almost 100 per cent payment for community development *and* welfare services, the provinces' stubborn refusal to extend services puzzled the Hawthorn team. However, provincial acquiescence was predicated on the federal government surrendering its constitutional jurisdiction over Indians, something it would not do.[62] Even when a generous Indian funding formula called CAP II had been incorporated into the Canada Assistance Plan (1966), the provinces did not take up the offer.[63]

The First Nations were third-party on-lookers. They played no direct role in the development of the CDP or in the federal–provincial conference of 1964. In the case of Ontario, they had been consulted, but were not signatories to any agreements. Nationally, First Nations could have clamoured for or firmly supported direct provincial involvement in their affairs, but there was scant evidence that any did, a fact confirmed by Hawthorn.[64] The response of Indian organizations and bands to the recommendations of the Joint Committee of the Senate and the House of Commons on Indian Affairs (1959–61) had already revealed hostility to integration. In fact, there was among many a desire to maintain their direct, exclusive relationship with Ottawa in all matters.[65]

Obviously these problems hindered the CDP's effectiveness in achieving its broader objectives concerning the provincial extension of services. Nevertheless, the CDP had important outcomes. One, especially, resulted from the recruitment and training of the community development officers and the implementation of the program in the field. The CDOs were recruited through nation-wide advertising and interviewing. Rudnicki and his supporters were not interested in hiring apologists for the branch. "These community development workers were intended to be the spearhead of giving Indian people back their 'heads' ... so that they could start challenging what ... we were doing." The workers were to create scope for challenges and to encourage less submission from Indians and greater expression of their anger. What the program required were community development officers whose commitment would be "something tantamount to a kamikaze pilot ... and being prepared to be fired."[66]

The interviews tested the commitment Rudnicki felt was necessary to make the program effective. Loyalty to the First Nations was paramount. "People were ... carefully selected in the first instance by trying to assess their ... value systems," Rudnicki remembered. A situation requiring a moral choice was posed to each candidate. They were then told that they had been placed on a reserve and were building trust with the community. Rudnicki continued:

> A mountie comes to see you one day. He says, "Look, I've been told there's a still on this reserve, and I'm not sure where to look but I think you probably know, so tell me. I won't turn you in or anything. Just give me the information and we'll knock off this still and arrest the people concerned." What do you do? People who answered, "Well, I'd have to tell the mountie," their interview ceased right there! They had to be totally identified with the people they were with, for bad or for worse. They weren't going to become spies or manipulators, even if it was a question of breaking the law."[67]

Groups of twenty to thirty officers were hired in the initial and subsequent phases of the program. Besides the CDOs, branch personnel — particularly Indian agents — were included in each training module, as were many Indians hired as community development assistants. Among the latter was George Manuel, who later was chief of the Assembly of First Nations. The assistants were paid about $400 or $500 a month less than the officers.[68] The mix of personnel set up an explosive but creative dynamic. They were all brought to Ottawa and other locations for training and deployment to the field.

Initially, two-week sensitivity training modules were planned, but because the sessions were intense the modules were extended to three months. Dr Farrell Toombs, a psychologist and an associate professor at the University of Toronto, led the sessions. A follower of Carl Rogers, he used a humanist, "person-centred" approach to therapy. Rogerian therapy became a popular tool in encounter groups — the method Toombs employed in training the community development officers.[69] Toombs was well respected by Isbister, who described him as "a treasure." Manuel also thought highly of Toombs. "In the three months he worked with us ... he impressed me as a person with a high degree of humanity. If there is any one man outside the Indian community who has inspired human development within our community it is Farrell Toombs."[70]

Some sessions were held in a leased seminary in Ottawa. It had a windowed rotunda on the third floor that was ideal for the training format. "There was no agenda," Rudnicki recalled, "no curriculum. People sat around in a big circle with Farrell sitting there in the midst of them. And they just talked for three months. I ... just dropped in now and then. I'm not sure of everything that happened but I know there were fist fights, and there were people who dissolved into tears."[71] Jerry Gambill, among the first CDOs, described the focus of the groups. "In today's terminology," he said, "it would be personal empowerment done on a Rogerian foundation." There was a reason why Rogerian methods were linked to Batten's ideas about community development. "If the rationale of the program was for people to develop themselves and take control of their own affairs, then the catalyst to do this had to be people who were prepared to do that for themselves." Gambill described his first group session and how it set the tone for a process that would instil in the participants a will to reclaim personal power and to overcome an oppressive system:

> We came in and sat down and here was Farrell at the head of the circle. We sat there for perhaps two hours, and no one said a word, everyone waiting for *the* power to do something! Farrell wasn't prepared to play the role. When he did begin, he did so by ... revealing himself to these strangers ... in a way which would encourage them to take risks with each other. So he began this ... autobiography — which had to do with his relationship with his wife who was schizophrenic and quite ... ill. He, a psychiatrist at the University of Toronto having to care for his wife and her ... behaviour. So, it was very personal. It began to take off from there.
>
> This was a mixed group of Indian Agents and community development people. Some of the Indian people just took off in this atmosphere — they seized the power ... and just released years of frustration. The Indian Affairs types are shocked by this outburst. These people ... have the temerity to question what they dedicated their lives to. They wanted order to be restored — they had come there to learn about community development, they were not learning anything, and they were demanding that Farrell teach them what he had been hired to do! So this ... just kept going. Then people began to realise that they could control such things as ... coffee breaks, and what hour they would begin the course, and what they would do, whether they'd take a day off, and so forth! During the course of this, external events were taking place. There'd be some blockade somewhere, some outrage, some Indian person making a demand, or whatever. And people reacting to that and saying, "Well, we should be responding to this, we should be doing something." And then, as Indian Affairs — because all these people were on the payroll — as Indian Affairs did administrative things that affected the lives of the participants — well, someone was getting docked pay, or someone was not getting time off to see their sick wife — then the group would begin to rally around that cause. "Well, if he's not going to get his pay then I'm not going to take mine, and we're all going on strike." So here's this group becoming extremely unruly.[72]

Gambill also described how the participants divided into two groups, those who flourished in the open structure and went "through a personal liberation and empowerment," and those, mainly bureaucrats, who thought the whole process a waste of time and money. This split foreshadowed the conflict that would occur between the old guard and the CDOs once the program was under way. Gambill thought many of the agents had decided that community development was a form of social manipulation through which they could get Indians to do what they wanted them to do.[73] The sessions aroused years of repressed anger towards Indian Affairs and Canada's treatment of First Nations. Nearly all the CDOs completed their training fully opposed to the Indian management practices of the federal government.[74]

Once in the field, the CDOs practised community work in different ways. There were those who did nothing, those who appeared to do nothing, and those who almost immediately took action.[75] Robert Cunningham shows how, in some communities, little was accomplished. Reporting a personal communication with Rudnicki, he wrote, "In some communities CDOs initiated little ... social change — finding themselves part of the ... bureaucracy rather than as the Agents charged with changing it. Other CDOs became coopted by the system and ... felt as though they could not afford to be fired."[76]

Appearing to do nothing for at least three months — an approach recommended to the CDOs during training — was Gambill's strategy. "I was just finding out all kinds of things and asking ... questions ... You know, kind of diagnosing what was going on there."[77] In this approach, however, the seeds of potential disruption were sowed. It was for some CDOs the most effective method and led to "change and conflict the likes of which had not been seen on most reserves in anyone's memory."[78] According to Rudnicki, it was the method employed by the successful CDOs and involved getting to know people informally, building trust, and challenging their assumptions or fears about change and the authority of Indian Affairs. In effect, it was a way to empower them.[79]

Manuel was interested in quick, direct action. He and the CDO Tony Karch were assigned to the Cowichan Reserve on Vancouver Island. Using a community survey, they identified one issue, inadequate housing. Manuel cultivated the leadership of a band member, Abraham Joe. A committee was established and decided that the best way to get new housing was to embarrass Indian Affairs locally and nationally. The committee then invited the press to view Cowichan housing conditions and to witness, first hand, Third World conditions in Canada. The story ran nationally, forcing the new minister, Arthur Laing, to deliver a substantial housing program at Cowichan.[80] Manuel and Karch went on to educate band members in effective politics, introduced adult education to reduce illiteracy and promote academic abilities, and trained band members in community problem-solving skills.[81]

Many of the CDOs inspired confidence within the reserve communities and encouraged levels of self-determination that subverted existing policies or found alternatives to restrictive practices. The effect of these interventions was to raise resistance and hostility in the old guard field administration.[82] Gambill, for example, was assigned to Akwesasne (St. Regis Agency). He later discovered that he had always been viewed with suspicion. While he was developing community relationships and consulting with the agent about the reserve and its issues, it transpired that the agent — who believed Gambill had "gone Indian"— the priest, and the local RCMP officer all worked to discredit him in the eyes of the people. Gambill tried to work with all community factions, but finally looked to the traditional longhouse people. "As far as I could see," he said, "these were the ... solid people of the community in terms of real community interest, and ... having the character and strength, the kind of thing a community builds on."[83]

Pressured by the senior administration to disassociate from the longhouse, Gambill was fired when he didn't heed warnings and accept the "offer" of an alternative post. True to his commitment, and the wishes of strong community elements, he refused to leave. Gambill's resilience caused a rift in the community between the Indian Affairs's apologists and the traditional members of the longhouse. His case was finally taken up by the CBC national television program *This Hour Has Seven Days*, but the upshot of all this attention is unclear. Gambill remained at Akwesasne for several more years, though not under the auspices of the CDP or of Indian Affairs.[84]

For many of the regions and their agents, these and other examples created so much unrest that a crisis of confidence occurred between the field and Ottawa. Rudnicki recollected that "at headquarters I was under the gun. 'Walt, look we didn't want revolution, we want evolution.' I was dubbed a bad administrator because I didn't ... control all this. Which was okay. I considered the program a success."[85] Rudnicki was soon deposed and transferred to another section of the branch. He was replaced by Wilf Churchman, formerly director of development, who changed key elements of the CDP and returned to standard lines of reporting through the field rather than directly to Ottawa.[86] By 1968 the CDP as originally conceived had ended. Ironically, aspects were replaced by leadership training, while the inoffensive projects resurfaced as make-work programs using redirected social assistance entitlements.[87]

Various explanations account for the demise of the CDP. All include the internal uproar the program had created. In describing the CDOs as "mainly ... college students or graduates," Helen Buckley writes that the "young *animateurs* were critical of the conditions on the reserves and ... thought they had a mandate to stir things up, so there were clashes with the authorities in the ... course of doing their job. Much ... publicity was generated and ... the Department called it quits." Weaver and Cunningham make similar observations, while Manuel and Posluns cite the words of Gerry Piper, a CDO who resigned in frustration: "One doesn't tell a group of battle-scarred, dedicated, overworked and underpaid old vets that their work has been in vain, especially when the group-doing-the-telling is relatively new to the battlefield. Nor does one tell the underworked and overpaid, pension-calculating civil servant that he's about to lose his soft touch. That is political naiveté beyond comprehension."[88]

These explanations lend support to Lipsky's analysis of street-level bureaucrats, those in the field who are hardened to their work, are bitterly proud of doing things a certain way, and believe that only they understand the client population. Students of Lipsky also observed that street-level bureaucrats experience a sense of "illusory freedom," thinking they are more in control of their organization than is the case. They resist changes that alter service delivery or that require a different relationship with the service recipients. With respect to the CDP, the policy was presented not only in written but in human form, the CDOs! Thus, the agents' resistance had to be overt and vociferous. Had it not been so, then the illusory freedom they experienced in managing First Nations peoples would have been eroded and their role as agents of state oppression exposed. Such a truth was simply not tolerable, to them as career civil servants, or to the government.[89]

Cunningham argues that the CDP's real threat to the bureaucracy was the end of the reproduction of First Nations' consent and deference to the Canadian state. The structural processes of the Indian Affairs bureaucracy had evolved over time so that the local agents had little control over policy, but nearly absolute control over its administration. They controlled Indians collectively and individually, but never earned an authentic trust with them, only a grudging obedience. Their allegiance was to Ottawa, not to the community. Additionally, the agents' jobs were rigidly defined and endlessly routine, with no room for creativity. Conversely, the CDOs were *of*, but not *in*, the bureaucracy. They were trained to distrust and to act outside the system. Their allegiance was to the community, and they had to earn its trust. It was their job, implicitly or explicitly, to assist Indian people to wrest control from the agents and to take control of their own affairs. The CDOs' jobs were open-ended, fluid, and creative. Not surprisingly, the agents and the CDOs were bound to come into conflict: one dedicated to maintaining the status quo, the other to destroying it and liberating First Nations from post-colonial rule.[90]

Some attribute the program's demise to its failure to fulfil its economic promises. Buckley argues that the CDP was too focused on process and decision-making and that, despite its short life, it demonstrated how the federal government had opted too quickly for the community development approach when "more sensible solutions" could have been found. The problem was unemployment, and community development — a Third World approach to a problem in a First World country — was not going to solve it. Of prairie First Nations, Buckley writes that they "had been able to support themselves as long as there was work that matched their qualifications and employers willing to hire them. They had been made destitute by changes in the world beyond the reserve and by the Department's failure to see that they got educated, trained, and hired, or that they got access to capital for farming or business." By focusing on community development, the branch had resorted to old views about the "backwardness" of First Nations and, in its timid community projects, had reaffirmed its and the larger society's "devotion to the principle that solutions must not occasion hardship for employers or loss of investment in resource industries."[91]

Manuel and Posluns made somewhat the same argument before Buckley, but were supportive of the CDP. The need for jobs was important, but other community needs — housing, schools, infrastructure — were equally urgent. Almost anything an Indian community was going to propose, including jobs, would cost a lot of money. The government was simply not prepared to pay. "What happened to the Community Development program at ... Cowichan," they wrote, "is not really any different from what happened at ... other reserves across Canada. There was no money for economic development." With reference to the Hawthorn Report, Manuel and Posluns opined that community development could not succeed without a firm basis in economic development, but that economic development without community control would be "only another form of imperial conquest."[92]

Their reference to the Hawthorn Report is significant. Although Buckley and Weaver note its importance at the time, neither argues the *connection* between it and the ultimate demise of the CDP.[93] The program was in trouble before the report's release, but the report no doubt drove the final nail into the CDP coffin and, in doing so, also drove a few into its own. Hawthorn supported community development as a means of developing local government *and* he advanced the principle of Citizens Plus: that Indians retain their unique status and rights while taking their place as full and equal citizens in Canada. Although the idea of community development was not problematic to Indian Affairs — it could be used to get people to do what was wanted of them — the reality that it could be used to foster more emphasis on "Plus" than on "Citizens" certainly figured into the government's shelving of Hawthorn in 1968. Arguably, the confluence of the recommendation that Indians be "citizens plus" with the turmoil produced by the CDP contributed to the Liberal government's wariness of Indians exercising special rights. Rudnicki had crafted the CDP so that one led to the other, so both had to go. Ironically, Rudnicki rejected the Hawthorn Report when he was in the Privy Council Office because he thought, probably correctly, that it still invested too much power in Indian Affairs.[94]

The underlying principle that Rudnicki had followed in designing the CDP was the devolution of authority to the bands. At the time, he had not understood that devolution was "a two-edged sword." "Devolution could be returning to people their sovereignty, or [it] could be working towards final termination," he stated. "That's what it turned out to be ... a termination issue, coming under provincial jurisdiction."[95] Rudnicki thought the community development initiative was really about integration at a macro level. Postwar Indian policy had focused on the gradual termination of the special protection of First Nations. Every time the branch modified programs such as social assistance or education, associated with national organizations, or conferred with the provinces, it had attempted to move First Nations towards the termination of the constitutional relationship between them and Canada.[96]

In retrospect, Rudnicki thought the CDP released two conflicting forces. The first was devolution leading to termination. In this case, community development was intended to provide the inner strength to Indians to reach out to Canada and become part of it. Thus, integration would be realized as they accepted more responsibility for the management of their own affairs, which was really their administration of Indian Affairs for the government. Devolution would inevitably lead to the construction of a replica bureaucracy on the reserves, whether or not the provinces extended their services.[97] In fact, this was one recommendation of the Hawthorn Report that did, in effect, become policy and remains a dominant theme to the present day.[98]

The second outcome of the CDP was that it catalyzed a new relationship between Indian Affairs and First Nations. The National and Regional Indian Advisory Committees, the consultation process that occurred around the 1969 white paper on Indian policy, and other processes contributed to a new, politicized interface between Indian leaders and the federal government. The program did not itself politicize First Nations, but it provided avenues of attack and exposed the weaknesses of Indian Affairs in ways that had not been previously available. First Nations learned how to make effective demands on the system and to extract more from it than before.[99] Of this legacy, Manuel and Posluns wrote: "Whatever happened to the program, the experience it had given to people, and the knowledge that they had gained from that experience, could not be taken away ... On every reserve where the Community Development program had a measure of success, people had a new measure of their own individual and collective capacities, and a new yardstick by which to measure would-be friends."[100] Despite diluting the program's political punch, the branch could not return to former times. The program had given voice to First Nations and that voice would not be silenced.

Where did the CDP fail? It failed in two areas that remain evident today. First, from the federal standpoint, it did not resolve the question of the provincial extension of services. Ontario remains the only province to have fully extended its welfare services. The only movement by the other provinces has been in child welfare. Since 1989 several tripartite agreements have been formulated permitting First Nations to deliver their own child welfare programs in accordance with provincial statutes and standards. That they must accommodate alien standards remains a sore point. Many would like the federal government to pass child welfare legislation applicable to reserves, while others would prefer the jurisdictional right to do it themselves.[101]

Second, the CDP failed to resolve the important question of the status of First Nations within Canada. While it helped the movement towards self-government, more than thirty years later their status remains unchanged, though their undefined rights have been entrenched in the constitution. Alan Cairns, a contributing author to the 1966 Hawthorn Report and an expert on the Canadian Constitution, recently revisited this question by advocating a return to the principle of Citizens Plus. Cairns rejects concepts of nationhood and third order government advocated by the 1996 *Report of the Royal Commission on Aboriginal Peoples*, the 1983 report *Indian Self-Government in Canada*, as well as a significant body of literature that propounds similar ideas.[102] He argues that the Citizens Plus solution — guaranteeing equal citizenship, special rights, and a modicum of self-government — is the only viable one in light of the numbers of Indians in urban settings, the changing demographics of First Nations communities, their interdependence with Canada, and the ability of a federal system to accommodate such an arrangement.[103]

Cairns's ideas are compelling but now seem ahistorical, despite his acknowledgment of all that has transpired in Canada–First Nations relations since 1966, including the powerful Aboriginal movement towards self-government. The main problems with his discussion are the lack of recognition of the full diversity of Indian voice and academic thought, the seeming inattention to the politics and discourse of decolonization, and the implicit acceptance of the idea that the only post-colonial solution lies within the political framework of the existing colonial order. Taiaiake Alfred, a Mohawk scholar from Kahnawake Territory, develops a different stance. He attacks sovereignty as a European construct, "an exclusionary concept rooted in an adversarial and coercive Western notion of power." He argues that there is no moral justification for state sovereignty, or for indigenous leaders to seek sovereignty or to deal with state leaders to determine what level of self-government will be acceptable. To do so simply reinforces the hegemony of the state and encourages indigenous leaders "to re-frame and moderate their nationhood demands to accept the *fait accompli* of colonization, to collaborate in the development of a 'solution' that does not challenge the fundamental imperial lie." The goal is to create a post-colonial relationship which does not entail a European cultural superiority and which promotes a "mutually respectful stance." Before it is even possible to move ahead to co-existence, however, the task and process of decolonization must first continue. Alfred concludes that we "need to convince others to join us in challenging the state's oppression of indigenous peoples ... All actions in this effort ... must be ... guided by four principles. First, undermine the intellectual premises of colonialism. Second, act on the moral imperative for change. Third, do not cooperate with colonialism. Fourth, and last, resist further injustice."[104]

ACKNOWLEDGMENTS

The author would like to acknowledge the helpful comments of the *CHR* referees in the preparation of this article.

NOTES

1. John L. Tobias, "Protection, Civilization, Assimilation: An Outline History of Canada's Indian Policy," *Western Canadian Journal of Anthropology* 6, 2 (1976): 13–30, reprinted in A. L. Getty and Antoine S. Lussier, eds., *As Long as the Sun Shines and Water Flows: A Reader in Canadian Native Studies* (Vancouver: UBC Press 1983), 40. The term "Indian" in this article refers to those peoples defined and registered as Indian under the Canadian Indian Act (RSC 1988). Indians in Canada usually refer to themselves according to their specific cultural and tribal nationhood or, generically, as First Nations peoples.

2. Roger Gibbins and J. Rick Ponting, "Historical Overview and Background," in J. Rick Ponting, ed., *Arduous Journey: Canadian Indians and Decolonization* (Toronto: McClelland & Stewart 1986), 25; Tobias, "Protection," 40–1.

3. J. Rick Ponting and Roger Gibbins, *Out of Irrelevance: A Socio-Political Introduction to Indian Affairs in Canada* (Scarborough: Butterworths 1980), 12, cited in Robert Cunningham, "Community Development at the Department of Indian Affairs in the 1960s: Much Ado about Nothing" (MA thesis, University of Saskatchewan 1997), 30–1.

4. Alan C. Cairns, *Citizens Plus: Aboriginal Peoples and the Canadian State* (Vancouver: UBC Press 2000), 77–9.

5. Tobias, "Protection," 43–5.

6. Sally M. Weaver, *Making Canadian Indian Policy: The Hidden Agenda, 1968–1970* (Toronto: University of Toronto Press 1981), 20, 24–8.

7. "The Canadian Indian" in the *Economist*, reprinted in the *Montreal Gazette*, 28 July 1944, cited in Hugh Shewell, "Origins of Contemporary Indian Social Welfare in the Canadian Liberal State: An Historical Case Study in Social Policy, 1873–1965" (PhD dissertation, University of Toronto 1995), 385.

8. Transcript of speech by Minister of Mines and Resources T. A. Crerar at the Convention of Indians, Ottawa, 7 June 1944, cited in Hugh Shewell, "Jules Sioui and Indian Political Radicalism in Canada, 1943–1944," *Journal of Canadian Studies* 34, 3 (1999): 232.

9. Canada, Special Joint Committee of the Senate and the House of Commons Appointed to Examine and Consider the Indian Act, *Minutes of Proceedings and Evidence*, Fourth Report, 22 June 1948 (Ottawa: King's Printer 1948), 189–90.

10. James S. Frideres, *Aboriginal Peoples in Canada: Contemporary Conflicts*, 5th ed. (Scarborough: Prentice Hall/Allyn and Bacon Canada 1998), 17; J. R., Miller, *Skyscrapers Hide the Heavens: A History of Indian–White Relations in Canada*, rev. ed. (Toronto: University of Toronto Press 1991), 221–2; Tobias, "Protection," 52–3.

11. Gibbins and Ponting, "Historical Overview and Background," 26.
12. Canada, Twenty-Fourth Parliament — Fourth Session, Joint Committee of the Senate and the House of Commons on Indian Affairs, *Minutes of Proceedings and Evidence*, No. 8 (Ottawa: Queen's Printer 1961), 291.
13. Frideres, *Aboriginal Peoples in Canada*, 226–7, cited in Cunningham, "Community Development at the Department of Indian Affairs," 32–3.
14. H. B. Hawthorn, ed., *A Survey of the Contemporary Indians of Canada: A Report on Economic, Political, Educational Needs and Policies*, vol. 1 (Ottawa: Indian Affairs Branch, Department of Indian Affairs and Northern Development 1966), 312–42, 386–403; Shewell, "Origins," 562, 582.
15. Weaver, *Making Canadian Indian Policy*, 46.
16. Dr George F. Davidson, personal interview, Dec. 1992, cited in Shewell, "Origins," 634, n. 52.
17. Margaret Payne, "Indians Train for Leadership" (June 1962), in Canada, Department of Citizenship and Immigration, Canadian Citizenship Branch, *Citizenship Projects among Indians* (Ottawa: Queen's Printer 1965), 10, 12–13; "Leadership Development among Indians" (1964), no author, in *Citizenship Projects*, 16–17; Canada, Department of Citizenship and Immigration, Indian Affairs Branch, *The Indian in Transition* (Ottawa 1962), 25; NA, RG 10, CR series, vol. 8463, file 1/23-21, pt 1, "Indian Social Leaders," paper prepared by P. F. Grant, 6 May 1953, 3–4.
18. Jessa Chupik-Hall, "'Good Families Do Not Just Happen': Indigenous People and Child Welfare Services in Canada" (MA thesis, Trent University 2001), 52–5, 63.
19. NA, RG 10, CR series, vol. 8591, file 1/1-10-18, pt 2, various correspondence; letter, Mrs W. H. Clark, chair, National Commission on the Indian Canadian, to Jones, 28 April 1958; D. L. Jackson to J. H. Gordon, Director of Welfare Division, 22 May 1958; Canada, *Citizenship Projects*, 4.
20. *Globe and Mail*, 17 Oct. 1961.
21. NA, RG 10, CR series, vol. 8591, file 1/1-10-18, pt 5, Robertson to Melling, 19 Oct. 1961; Melling to Jones, 23 Oct. 1961; Melling to Robertson, 23 Oct. 1961.
22. Robertson, personal correspondence to author, 13 Nov. 2000.
23. Hawthorn, ed., *Contemporary Indians of Canada*, 367–70; Frank Cassidy, "Approaches to Welfare Reform in Indian Communities," in Frank Cassidy and Shirley B. Seward, eds., *Alternatives to Social Assistance in Indian Communities* (Halifax: Institute for Research on Public Policy 1991), 9; Frideres, *Aboriginal Peoples in Canada*, 227.
24. Hawthorn, ed., *Contemporary Indians of Canada*, 391.
25. Ibid., 346; Weaver, *Making Canadian Indian Policy*, 45.
26. Shewell, "Origins," 582–3, 591.
27. Ibid., 566, 606, 618, and n. 26.
28. Ibid., 599, n. 124, 622–7, 646–7, n. 75; NA, RG 10, CR series, vol. 6923, file 1/29-1, pt 4. "Memorandum to Cabinet," 10 Aug. 1959.
29. Hawthorn, *Contemporary Indians of Canada*, 319, 323–4, 331–4, 338–9. Hawthorn assembled a team of social and political scientists, legal experts, social workers, and educators to work on and write the report. See Sally M. Weaver, "The Hawthorn Report: Its Use in the Making of Canadian Indian Policy," in Noel Dyck and James B. Waldram, eds., *Anthropology, Public Policy, and Native Peoples in Canada* (Montreal and Kingston: McGill-Queen's University Press 1993).
30. Weaver, "The Hawthorn Report," 76–7.
31. Weaver, *Making Canadian Indian Policy*, 44–7.
32. H. B. Hawthorn, ed., "The Politics of Indian Affairs," abridged from chapter 17, *Contemporary Indians of Canada*, in Getty and Lussier, *As Long as the Sun Shines*, 173.
33. Canada, Department of Citizenship and Immigration, Indian Affairs Branch, "The Big Picture," Statement Prepared by Walter Rudnicki for Federal–Provincial Conference on Poverty, Nov. 1965, cited in Weaver, *Making Canadian Indian Policy*, 26–7; NA, RG 10, CR series, vols. 6924, 6925, file 1/29-1, pts 5 and 9, Jones to Davidson, 30 Nov. 1960; and C. N. C. Roberts, document to file, "Consolidation Sheet," 10 June 1963; vol. 6925, file 1/29-1, pt 9, "Request to Treasury Board for 'Adoption of provincial or local municipal welfare rates and regulations for Indians,'" no date, about 18 Dec. 1963.
34. Shewell, "Origins," 677–80; Weaver, *Making Canadian Indian Policy*, 28.
35. Weaver, "The Hawthorn Report," 76–8.
36. Claude Isbister interview, April 1993, cited in Shewell, "Origins," 680, n. 131.
37. Walter Rudnicki interview, May 1993, cited in ibid., 681.
38. Isbister interview, 680, n. 131; Tom Kent, *A Public Purpose* (Montreal and Kingston: McGill-Queen's University Press 1988), 238.

39. Cunningham, "Community Development at the Department of Indian Affairs," 58.

40. Rudnicki interview, 682, 696.

41. NA, RG 10, CR series, vol. 8193, file 1/29-6, pt 1, "Community Development Course," and Dr T. R. Batten, University of London Institute of Education, to Rudnicki, 6 Feb. 1964; Peter Marris and Martin Rein, *Dilemmas of Social Reform: Poverty and Community Action in the United States*, 2nd ed. (Chicago: University of Chicago Press 1973).

42. NA, RG 10, CR series, vol. 8193, file 1/29-6, pt 1, "Community Development Course."

43. Cunningham, "Community Development at the Department of Indian Affairs," 54, 61.

44. NA, RG 10, CR series, vol. 8193, file 1/29-6, pt 3, Memorandum to Cabinet, "Community Development, Indian Affairs Branch," items 3, 4, and 5, Feb. 1964.

45. Cunningham, "Community Development at the Department of Indian Affairs," 60; Shewell, "Origins," 698

46. Rudnicki interview, 699, n. 169.

47. NA, RG 10, CR series, vol. 8193, file 1/29-6, pt 3, Memorandum, "Community Development," items 7, 8, and 9.

48. K. D. Uppal, personal communication 1994, cited in Cunningham, "Community Development at the Department of Indian Affairs," 60.

49. Interview with former senior administrative clerk, Indian Affairs Branch, May 1993.

50. NA, RG 10, CR series, vol. 8193, file 1/29-6, pt 3, Memorandum, "Community Development," item 9 (c).

51. Ibid., "Details of Request to the Honourable the Treasury Board," 12 Jan. 1965; vol. 6925, file 1/29-1, pt 10, "Details of Request to the Honourable the Treasury Board," 16 June 1964; Weaver, *Making Canadian Indian Policy*, 27, n. 15.

52. NA, RG 10, CR series, vol. 6925, file 1/29-6, pt 3, Isbister to R. G. McNeill, chairman, Civil Service Commission, 1 June 1964; Battle, Circular No. 117 to Indian Commissioner for B.C., Regional Supervisors, *Re: Introduction of Community Development Program*, 8 Jan. 1965.

53. Ibid., Mackenzie to Isbister, 18 and 19 Jan. 1965; Treasury Board Minutes No. 635419, 19 Jan. 1965, and No. 635420, 4 Feb. 1965.

54. Ibid., "Report on Grants to Band Councils," 1 April 1965.

55. Rudnicki interview, cited in Cunningham, "Community Development at the Department of Indian Affairs."

56. *Globe and Mail*, 31 Oct. 1964; *Ottawa Citizen*, 30 Oct. 1964.

57. E. R. McEwen, Community Development Services for Canadian Indian and Métis Communities (Toronto: Indian-Eskimo Association of Canada 1968), 16–17.

58. Hawthorn, *Contemporary Indians of Canada*, 355.

59. Isbister interview, cited in Shewell, "Origins," 719.

60. Roberts interview, cited ibid.

61. Hawthorn, *Contemporary Indians of Canada*, 348.

62. Weaver, *Making Canadian Indian Policy*, 22; Hawthorn, *Contemporary Indians of Canada*, 344–58, 386–403.

63. Hugh Shewell and Annabella Spagnut, "The First Nations of Canada: Social Welfare and the Quest for Self-Government," in John Dixon and Robert P. Scheurell, eds., *Social Welfare with Indigenous Peoples* (London: Routledge 1995), 23.

64. Hawthorn, "The Politics of Indian Affairs," 177–8.

65. Shewell, "Origins," 652–7, 662–5.

66. Rudnicki interview, May 1993.

67. Ibid. Similar accounts are found in Cunningham, "Community Development at the Department of Indian Affairs," 63; and in Peter McFarlane, *Brotherhood to Nationhood: George Manuel and the Making of the Modern Indian Movement* (Toronto: Between the Lines 1993), 75.

68. George Manuel and Michael Posluns, *The Fourth World: An Indian Reality* (Toronto: Collier-Macmillan 1974), 130.

69. Cunningham, "Community Development at the Department of Indian Affairs," 64; Brian Thorne, *Carl Rogers* (London: Sage 1992). Some accounts describe Toombs as a psychiatrist. See Manuel and Posluns, *The Fourth World*, 135.

70. Isbister interview, April 1993; Manuel and Posluns, *The Fourth World*, 130.

71. Rudnicki interview, May 1993.

72. Jerry Gambill interview, May 1993. Manuel describes similar sessions held at Laval University in Quebec City. See Manuel and Posluns, *The Fourth World*, 130–3.

73. Gambill, personal communication 1994, cited in Cunningham, "Community Development at the Department of Indian Affairs," 66.

74. Weaver, *Making Canadian Indian Policy*, 28.

75. Cunningham, "Community Development at the Department of Indian Affairs," 67–8.
76. Rudnicki, personal communication, 1994, cited ibid.
77. Gambill, personal communication to Rob Cunningham, 1994, cited ibid., 67.
78. Cunningham, "Community Development at the Department of Indian Affairs," 67.
79. Rudnicki, personal communication to Rob Cunningham, 1994, cited ibid., 67.
80. McFarlane, *Brotherhood to Nationhood*, 79–82.
81. Manuel and Posluns, *The Fourth World*, 148; McFarlane, *Brotherhood to Nationhood*, 82–3.
82. Weaver, *Making Canadian Indian Policy*, 28.
83. Gambill, personal communication, 1994, cited in Cunningham, "Community Development at the Department of Indian Affairs," 70. The factions to which Gambill refers were not identified. Generally, the longhouse people were protective of Mohawk cultural practices, adhered to traditional forms of government, and resisted Indian Affairs interference. Other factions adhered to band government defined by the Indian Act and were more accepting of federal programs and the dominant culture.
84. Cunningham, "Community Development at the Department of Indian Affairs," 72–3.
85. Rudnicki interview, May 1993. Rudnicki makes a similar comment in Cunningham, "Community Development at the Department of Indian Affairs," 69.
86. Cunningham, "Community Development at the Department of Indian Affairs," 73.
87. Manuel and Posluns, *The Fourth World*, 155; Weaver, *Making Canadian Indian Policy*, 28–9; Hugh Shewell, "The Use of Social Assistance for Employment Creation on Indian Reserves: An Appraisal," in Cassidy and Seward, eds., *Alternatives to Social Assistance*, 19–24.
88. Helen Buckley, *From Wooden Ploughs to Welfare: Why Indian Policy Failed in the Prairie Provinces* (Montreal and Kingston: McGill-Queen's University Press 1992), 102–3; Weaver, *Making Canadian Indian Policy*, 28–9; Cunningham, "Community Development at the Department of Indian Affairs," 73–5; Gerry Piper, cited in Manuel and Posluns, *The Fourth World*, 152.
89. M. Lipsky, *Street-Level Bureaucracy* (New York: Russell Sage 1980); Richard Weatherley, *Reforming Special Education: Policy Implementation from State Level to Street Level* (Cambridge: MIT Press 1979), cited in Christopher Ham and Michael Hill, *The Policy Process in the Modern Capitalist State* (Brighton: Wheatsheaf Books 1984), 136–42. The overall analysis is derived from Ham and Hill, *The Policy Process*, 139–40.
90. Cunningham, "Community Development at the Department of Indian Affairs," 83–8.
91. Buckley, *From Wooden Ploughs to Welfare*, 102–3.
92. Manuel and Posluns, *The Fourth World*, 150–1.
93. Buckley, *From Wooden Ploughs to Welfare*, 103–4; Weaver, *Making Canadian Indian Policy*, 24; Weaver, "The Hawthorn Report and Indian Policy," 80–1.
94. Weaver, "The Hawthorn Report," 84–9.
95. Rudnicki interview, cited in Shewell, "Origins," 699.
96. Shewell, "Origins," 699, 720–1.
97. Rudnicki interview, cited ibid., 721.
98. Hawthorn, *Contemporary Indians of Canada*, 285, 310; NA, RG 10, CR series, vol. 8620, file 1/1-15-13, "An Historical Review of Indian Affairs Policies and Some New Directions for the Future," notes for an address by Mr. R. F. Battle to the Trinity College Conference on the Canadian Indian, 22 Jan. 1966, 8.
99. Buckley, *From Wooden Ploughs to Welfare*, 103; Cunningham, "Community Development at the Department of Indian Affairs," 88–9.
100. Manuel and Posluns, *The Fourth World*, 155.
101. Shewell and Spagnut, "The First Nations of Canada," 29–32.
102. Canada, *Report of the Royal Commission on Aboriginal Peoples* (Ottawa: Canada Communication Group Publishing 1996), cited in Alan C. Cairns, *Citizens Plus*, chap. 4, 136–42; "Indian Self-Government in Canada," *Minutes and Proceedings of the Special Committee on Indian Self-Government*, No. 40, 12 and 20 Oct. 1983, cited in Cairns, *Citizens Plus*, 175–88.
103. Cairns, *Citizens Plus*, see chap. 5.
104. Taiaiake Alfred, *Peace, Power, Righteousness: An Indigenous Manifesto* (Toronto: Oxford University Press 1999), 59, 60, 63, 144–5.

Document 1.1

Interview with Solomon Johnston, Mistawasis First Nation

Born in what would become Saskatchewan, three years after the Riel Rebellion took place in that territory in 1885, Solomon Johnston was a Cree and a member of the Mistawasis First Nation, located near the town of Leask. The band, originally the Sak-kaw-wen-o-wak, took the new name to honour Chief Mistawasis, whose story Johnston recounts in this interview, relying on the oral tradition of his people. In 1876, recognizing that buffalo hunting could no longer sustain his people, Mistawasis signed Treaty No. 6 at Fort Carlton, where a monument commemorates the chief. As Johnston tells the story, he also refused to take part in the Riel Rebellion.

Issues to Consider

- What comes through in the personal details of Johnston's life, in regard to his character, the work that he did to support himself and his family, life on the reserves, and his community's values and aspirations?
- What were some of the promises made to the Natives under the treaties? Were these promises kept, according to Johnston?
- The Queen mentioned several times is Queen Victoria, who reigned during the time of the treaties and under whose authority the federal government negotiated them. How is she depicted? Why do you think the Natives felt this way about the Queen?
- What does Johnston tell us about the schooling of Native children?
- What does he tell us about the oral tradition concerning Chief Mistawasis and his band's participation in the Riel Rebellion? What does the Chief's declaration about the Queen signify?

Mitawasis' oldest son was married to Starblanket's daughter. Their son's name was We yah te kaw pay o, and that was my mother's first husband. My mother was Starblanket's daughter. They got married and We yah te kaw pay o died about 1883 or 1884. Then my mother married my dad. My dad and Mistawasis were first cousins. We were very poor, but we had a few ponies. I've seen times when we didn't have any flour, but there was a flour mill in the area. They used to give us the bran and we ate that. We had a lot of vegetables such as potatoes and turnips, so we didn't starve.

When I became 16 years old, the Indians were starting small farms. I began farming with my brother in law. Together we had three ponies and three oxen. The first year we farmed ten acres of oats and eight of wheat. That summer we were told that oxen would be available from the Indian Affairs Board and the following fall there would be an agency set up with a blacksmith, a farm instructor, a superintendent and interpreters. The farm instructor's name was Mackenzie.

Source: "Our Elders: Interviews with Saskatchewan Elders," Saskatchewan Indian Cultural Centre, http://www.sicc.sk.ca/cgi-bin/sicc/epage.pl?39.

My brother in law and I got ourselves going by the sale of cord wood to the agency, and by hauling pole wood. The money we made went into what cattle we could afford and we moved from my brother in law's homestead to a place four miles south. I was a bachelor there for a while, but I always had company in the winter time. In winter we would haul hay and wood to Leask where there were a lot of white people and settlers that would buy it, for anywhere between $8 and $10 a load. I made a good living out of this. I never had to buy meat as I had enough cattle that I could slaughter and have dried meat all winter. My parents taught me this way of life. I never had to beg for food.

In the summertime, I used to take my wheat to Shellbrook. We had good crops that graded number one or number two. Once I took in ten seamless bags of number one wheat, two bushels to the bag. Each bag of wheat could be exchanged at the mill for one bag of flour. At one time the mill manager in Shellbrook told me my wheat was so good that the Queen herself would be proud to use it. Other men knew I had this good wheat too, Joe Dreaver and Norman Fraser. I usually had plenty of flour for my own use so I would give some flour to my relations that needed it.

In the winter, I hunted. I used to kill lots of muskrats and lynx. When I went on these hunting trips, I used to go alone; I left my family at home to look after the house. I had a good hunting dog who was very smart. People tried to buy it from me but I wouldn't sell it. People used to ask me how I killed so many coyotes but it wasn't hard for me. There were lots around on the prairie, and these used to follow each other around, leaving many tracks. I would bait my traps, set it on one of these trails and cover it with snow. Then I would go out on the trapline on horseback, and ride back and forth on each side and around the trap. Coyotes are very smart and curious, and there were a lot of wild horses roaming around then. The coyotes would investigate the tracks around the traps and, sooner or later, get caught. I was not a good trapper. I just fooled them. I had to out-think those coyotes. With this method I caught 23 coyotes one winter. The prize was $12 to $17 a pelt and I got many coyotes each winter.

For lynx, I used my hunting dog, who would chase them up a tree, making it easy for me to shoot them. Lynx pelts brought me $20 a pelt and sometimes more. I also trapped muskrats in winter. It didn't matter how deep the muskrat lodge was, my dog could find it and begin digging in the snow. My hunting dog helped a lot.

I farmed a little in the spring, and during the summer I would break some land. Where I used to farm there was six or seven, maybe ten, acres broken that they used as a sports ground. This was 1895 or 1896. Eventually, I broke all that land, about 39 acres, with oxen in about two or three years. When I came back to this sports ground after one winter, someone else was there, so I didn't bother this land anymore. Instead, I farmed a little way from there. I bought this land from Jacob, my brother in law, who was ill then.

This was the exact spot where they had signed their first treaty, and where they first camped, right on my quarter of land. By the road you can see Mistawasis' first house, and you can still see the medicine tree. I thought I wouldn't cover them so that people could see this for a long time.

Over there, near the bush, stood the first Indian village built during the treaty and for two or three years after. This was the village where Mistawasis and his people lived; it was called the King's House. After World War I they built another house about half a mile east with the help of Indian Affairs. They had been told that they could not live like animals without flooring in their houses, and were given lumber to build houses like the white man's.

There were a lot of promises made about the treaties. If Indians wanted to go anywhere, they could travel free on the train. Today we pay if we want to travel. But I guess we don't pay as much. If any matter became too troublesome we were promised to be able to go and see the Queen, without paying. Mistawasis, Starblanket, O'Soup and Kew-Sta-Howe went once. They got as far as Ottawa, but once there, they were either tricked or discouraged into turning back. The Queen had said that if anyone was harassing us regarding treaties, to come to her, and that she was able to do anything, but that she was not God.

Chief Piapot was the one that broke the ticket on the train; he had four wives, and one was a beautiful young girl. A young boy had his eye on that one, the Chief's wife, and I guess she liked him too. They took off together on the train, and when the Chief found out, he was very hurt. He went to the Indian agent and asked that free tickets on the train cease. He said that any criminal could use the train to escape and never be found. I say Piapot was wrong to do this. He was only one man, and the Queen had said that no man with two legs could break the treaty.

The Queen did not buy any of the minerals underground, and said that someone else may come along and just take the land over without asking us, so we had better make the treaty with her, and this we did. She knew that the Indians were going to be treated poorly. She made the treaty because she wanted to own Canada. She still owns it, but I have never received any nets or the ammunition promised. We were also promised cattle, which we got. They were branded "I.D." (Indian Department). I never wanted anything to do with these cattle, but some people did. My dad did. When they killed one, they had to ask permission. If they did not, they got into trouble, they were called the "King's cattle." This is the time when Indians were treated like kids. When they asked for something they never got it. If they needed anything, they were told to write a letter about it. The only answer to these letters was always "we will look into it." Many of these things ended not so long ago. We were told that anything was possible in the white man's way of living, even for an Indian to be trained as a lawyer. Indian Affairs built some schools in Battleford and Regina which were called "Industrial Schools." There you could train as a carpenter, blacksmith, tailor or other things. Even women were taught the white man's way of living. We who went to that school were good carpenters, those like the deceased Jacob Badger, Andrew Akesim, and Solomon Bayer. The teachers only taught us enough so that we could just begin to read. The older girls taught us in the evening but during the day we cut wood, picked stones, all the worst jobs. We didn't learn anything; we didn't know anything. I read only a little now. The only thing I know is how to survive and my dad taught me that, my dad and the old people. [...]

Across the road, about 100 yards from my field, is where the medicine sticks were. This is where the Indians were living when trouble came at the time Louis Riel started the war. They were informed that they would be told by a policeman as soon as anything happened. At this time we had a Presbyterian minister in the area named McKay. He was a missionary and spoke good Cree. Around the afternoon of March 26, a policeman rode in and right away the Indians knew there was a war. McKay went to the church and then returned. All the Indians gathered at Chief Mistawasis' house. McKay told them there had been a battle, the first shots were fired at Duck Lake. The mounted police asked the Indians what they were going to do, and the Indians replied that they would move out immediately. First they wanted to send two messengers to Sandy Lake and two to Muskeg Lake to tell them there was a war. The Indians knew the Sandy Lake and Muskeg Bands would be ready to go as they wanted to maintain their treaty with the Queen. It hadn't been even 20 years since they signed the treaty. "We will flee from the war. We will not fight the Queen, and we will not fight for her either. We will go our own way." [...]

Long ago, Indians lived better lives. They looked after each other, were sensitive to one another and respected each other. When they talked, they never said "God," only when they worshipped did they use that word. They had faith in Him only.

Document 1.2

Margaret Ecker Francis

Strange Women in Our Midst: The First Canadians

Chatelaine magazine began publication in 1928 and soon became the most popular all-Canadian magazine read by Canadian women. Although aimed primarily at middle-class housewives, the magazine did not shy away from discussing contentious matters. This article about Native women considers their prospects, especially those of the younger generation, shortly after World War II.

Issues to Consider

- If we were to employ discourse analysis in reading this piece, we would deconstruct the writing by paying close attention to the tone, to the choice of words used (including metaphor and other types of imagery), and especially to how the subject is represented or portrayed as a result. What do you think is Francis's intention in writing this piece? Is it an antiracist commentary? Are there internal contradictions?
- What view are we given of Natives in general and women in particular? What does this view suggest about prevailing constructions of gender and race at the time of Francis's writing? What does the choice of title suggest?
- The women who figure centrally in St-Onge's essay were born during the Great War years and would have been middle-aged at the time of Francis's writing. Do you think their stories might differ from those of these young women, because of their age, experience, and time? Are there similarities in the lives of the so-called strange women of this piece and the Métis women of St-Onge's study?

Some day, perhaps, a writer of the Indian race will pen one of the greatest of Canadian novels. The setting will be a small community somewhere along the St. Lawrence, or the rocky shore of Georgian Bay, or the northern tundra of Saskatchewan, or a fishing village lashed by the Pacific.

This will be a psychological novel, a tale of emotions and instincts in conflict with environment.

The chief character? A young Indian woman. She will be attractive, intelligent, perhaps trained for a job. But her mind will be like a stunted jack pine, misshapen and distorted by the hostile winds that blow upon it, yet, like a tree, with a beauty of its own through these buffetings.

Without a doubt, tragedy will be the tone of the novel, because this young woman will stand as a symbol of thousands of her own race, caught in the conflict of two cultures.

A modern Canada will have given her a fair education. She has had an opportunity to observe the habits of the white race. From young girls her own age she caught a love of pretty clothes, the desire to be as wholesome and attractive as they.

But even though she learned these lessons well, the heroine of this unwritten book remains an outsider. No one can quite overlook her misfortune of having in her veins the blood of the first Canadians.

Source: Margaret Ecker Francis, "Strange Women in Our Midst: The First Canadians," *Chatelaine* 20, no. 8 (August 1947): 24–25, 51.

The girl returns to her own village, and this time she's in conflict with her own people. While she has struggled to become a modern Canadian woman, they have fought to cling to their old way of life with its tribal customs and traditions. The girl wants none of them, for in the white town these very things have branded her a person apart.

She would like to work, to use the training she has received. But in most parts of Canada the only jobs open to her are housework, being a maid in a third-rate hotel or a waitress in an east-end café. If she is trained as a nurse or teacher, she can teach only in Indian schools or nurse in Indian hospitals. Even those positions are hard to get. If she has stenographic training, few white employers are interested in her services.

Perhaps she does succeed in finding a niche for herself, but then as she grows older her thoughts turn toward marriage, a home and children. And once more there is conflict.

There's the theme — the framework for a growing Canadian problem. It's a problem that government agents across the country, and Indian leaders themselves, say is more widespread than the white population knows. Indeed, it's a fair guess that until the recent newspaper reports from Ottawa, where Indian affairs have been aired and tribal briefs presented to the Government, the general public had little knowledge of the modern life of our First Canadians. Yet they number some 126,000 souls; they are domiciled on some 2,200 reserves. Because of their separate community pattern they have remained outside the line of march of Canadian life. And in that fact lies a story of heartbreak and frustration for thousands of young Indians.

Most of us would prefer not to examine it too closely. There's more romantic attraction in the old picture of Indians living in tepees and liking it; of Indian women preferring their dress of beaded doeskin to a sleek little suit and a smart hat.

But the English girls who married Indian soldiers overseas and came back to live on the reserves have opened a few people's eyes. Abroad, Indian soldiers were accepted in most cases without question, and they behaved themselves with dignity. It was a shock to their brides to discover that in their own land they were not accepted.

In Calgary the other day an English girl, married to an Indian, bought some wine for a birthday celebration. To her horror, she was arrested, tried and fined, and the purchases confiscated. It was explained to her that she was not a free human being, as she had imagined, but an Indian, without citizenship and without the privileges British people take for granted.

On any Indian reserve in Canada, one could come face to face with the problems of Indian women. But it was in a community on Vancouver Island that I talked to 75-year-old Catharine, her face seamed with some deep inherent sadness, and to 20-year-old Gladys, her face sullen with hostility against white people who denied her goat's hair clothing. True, some of them could knit sheep's wool into the heavy sweaters for which this community was famous. But most of the younger women found even this tiresome, she said. The arts and customs of other times were dying out and Catharine obviously mourned their passing. She also resented, it appeared, the desire of some of the younger people to live like their white neighbors.

That would mean Gladys, who has tried and failed. "Education," one government agent had told me, "is the hope of the Indian women." But after meeting Gladys, one could not resist the question — was not, perhaps, the price of this education too high?

An increasing number of girls are going into the higher grades of school. Family allowances help. At school, along with their regular studies, the girls are taught nutrition. They are bright, and do particularly well in sewing and art classes. More and more of them are finishing high school, taking business courses, attending normal school and entering hospital training. But what then?

Gladys matriculated at the head of her class. After a business course she went to the city. Because she looked "too Indian," white employers turned her down. For the same reason, decent boardinghouses closed the doors in her face.

Reluctantly Gladys went back to the reserve, to join the family in the rickety cottage. She managed to get a part-time job in a lawyer's office in the nearby village, but she isn't too pleased to meet white people these days.

Crossly, she shooed the chickens away from the door which she opened only part way when I knocked. She was a squat girl, but her clothes were neat and her hair done becomingly.

Yes, she liked her job, she said. "The older women of my family worked like slaves. My work is easier." But she was obviously discontented. As she talked she looked apprehensively over her shoulder into the untidy room, which was such a far cry from the home of a white-collar girl in the city. Then a man's voice called out to her roughly.

"I'm sorry," she said. "My father doesn't wish me to talk to you."

When I had told J. Coleman, B.C. Inspector of Indian Agencies, about Gladys, he said, "Her case was probably typical. Any Indian girl with ambition is up against the heartbreak of racial prejudice. More and more of them want to train for careers, but when they do it's difficult for them to find jobs, places to live, or friends."

But Mr. Coleman's faith in the Indians of Canada is great.

"Many of them are superior to people of our white communities," he said. "But it's the whites that are the problem. If white people would recognize the virtues of the Indians it would speed up their assimilation. After all, many of our most brilliant Canadians have Indian blood in their veins. It proves that the Indians can be absorbed into the population through marriage, and that alone is the solution to our Indian problem."

When that happens there will no longer be Gladys, torn between two cultures, her roots in the primitive past and her mind tuned to the civilization of today and tomorrow.

Topic 2

Industrial Canada: Socioeconomic Transformation, Class, and Labour

A mother weaving beside her children, Cap-à-l'Aigle, Quebec, circa 1910;
photograph by Edith M. Small, National Library and Archives Canada,
PA-040744.

CONTEXT

The years between the last quarter of the 19th century and the outbreak of World War I in 1914 brought intensive, transformative socioeconomic change to the young Dominion. A predominantly family-based agrarian economy, in which men, women, and children all played distinct but interdependent productive roles, changed into one that featured mechanized factory production. Industry grew and cities expanded as the labour market responded to rural out-migration and immigration from overseas. By 1900, there were 70,000 factories in Canada; 60 percent of the labour force was nonagricultural. During the so-called second industrial revolution that began with the new century, hundreds of smaller "manufactories" merged into the large corporations characteristic of modern capitalism. Industrial capitalism also brought about some reconfiguration of ideas about skill, gender, and family. Men left the home to work, while women remained there in charge of household and children. Underpinning this "male breadwinner family" model, the ideology of gender-defined "separate spheres" became the most powerful factor restricting women's access to paid labour.

Industry's impact on private lives was matched by its influence on public policy, not only through the political clout of industrial capitalists, but also through social reform campaigns supporting protective legislation, especially regarding working women and children, as will be discussed in Topic 3. In 1889, the Conservative government of Sir John A. Macdonald received the report of the Royal Commission on the Relations of Capital and Labour, instigated precisely for the purpose of examining the social side effects of the industrialization that was already proceeding apace. The commissioners summarized their findings in language that starkly reveals their sense of the intensity of the changes taking place in Canada: "In acquiring the industry at one bound," they contended, "we have become possessed just as quickly of the evils which accompany the factory town and which in other lands were the creatures of gradual growth."

If such "evils" appeared the universal outcome of "modernization," to borrow a sociological term that identifies the hand-in-hand processes of industrialization and urbanization, historians have revealed a picture of change over time that allows for some continuities, for ways in which new rhythms of work and everyday life can be seen to have coexisted with older preindustrial ones. The transformation was neither quick — despite the connotations of "industrial revolution"— nor uniform and consistent. Its effects varied across and within regions and even within provinces, as well as within the working class, for whom skill level, gender, race, age, and location all made a difference in how they ultimately fared. Ontario and Quebec emerged as the industrial heartland of the new age; the Atlantic provinces, despite promising beginnings, soon fell behind; British Columbia would provide the necessary resources culled from mine and forest; and the Prairies, as Macdonald's National Policy of 1879 envisioned it, would be the agricultural breadbasket of the nation. From the start, one of the fundamental, lasting consequences of industrialization was its regional character, reinforcing geographic and historical differences to map the country into distinct sectors, materially, politically, and culturally.

Industrialization transformed social relations alongside those of production, creating more visible boundaries between classes with the emergence of an urban proletariat. The mechanization of production wore away at the skill levels, hence the social status, of some craftsmen. It also drew increasingly from a burgeoning supply of unskilled, "cheap" labour — a significant proportion of which, during the early years, consisted of underpaid women and children. Like the new order itself, the workers' response to these changes was anything but universal. As workers became increasingly class-conscious, they were motivated to organize into trade unions structured mostly along a traditional craft basis, which meant that they excluded all but the skilled. The Trades and Labor Congress was founded in 1883 to bring together all Canadian unions. By 1902, the conservative American Federation of Labor dominated the Canadian union movement. The American predominance would prove hard to shake.

The history of labour and class formation, together with the sociocultural as well as economic repercussions of the industrial revolution, was among the first subjects to be explored when social history began to take shape during the turbulent 1960s. With the New Left making its presence felt in university student movements and among faculty in Western Europe and North America, it is not surprising that class formation and class relations should have sparked interest. The 1970s marked the beginnings of an impassioned pursuit of related subjects in their Canadian historical context, as witnessed in the inauguration of a dedicated scholarly journal, *Labour/Le Travail* (initially *Labour/Le Travailleur*), in 1976, and the appearance of seminal works by Irving Abella, David Bercuson, Desmond Morton, and Terry Copp, among others. Most of these works focused on labour organization, chronological development, and policy. By the early 1980s, a new generation of historians approached the more expansive subject of working-class history, often within a framework of empirical Marxism. Much inspired by the path-breaking work of English historian Edward P. Thompson, and by such American historians as Herbert Gutman and David Montgomery, they sought to understand how the culture of the Canadian working class contributed to its development as a social group conscious of its position in industrial society and looking to collective action to improve that position.

Ethnicity and "race" were early recognized as influential factors in the formation of class and the development of class consciousness. Within short order, historians of women began to look at how gender conventions, specifically the die-hard biological conceptualization of women's primary roles as wives and mothers, restricted their employment opportunities and ultimately decreed the type of work they performed, their remuneration for it, and their status in the labour force. As Document 2.1 indicates, social reformers advocated protective legislation, in place by the 1880s, that regulated work hours and conditions to preserve the physical and moral health of future mothers. Gender as well as class and ethnic background differentiated both work and private life, but, as revealed in studies that consider how these identities are socially constructed, economic necessity made the boundaries between the public and the private less rigid than the notion of separate spheres for women and men might allow. Despite the fact that the majority of male workers did not earn enough to support their families on their wages alone until after World War II, the work of women was consistently gender-defined, undervalued, and underpaid. Children, too, were gradually removed from the factories and mines. Yet some poor families so needed the wages of women and children that employers were able to get around the law through the "putting out" system that demanded long hours by women and children for even lower wages, but in the supposed comfort of their own homes.

REFERENCES/FURTHER READING

Abella, Irving. *Nationalism, Communism and Canadian Labour: The CIO, the Communist Party, and the Canadian Congress of Labour 1935–1956.* Toronto: University of Toronto Press, 1973.

Avery, Donald. *Dangerous Foreigners: European Immigrant Workers and Labour Radicalism in Canada, 1896–1932.* Toronto: McClelland and Stewart, 1979.

Bercuson, David. *Fools and Wise Men: The Rise and Fall of One Big Union.* Toronto: McGraw-Hill Ryerson, 1978.

Cook, Ramsay, and Robert Craig Brown. *Canada 1896–1921: A Nation Transformed.* Toronto: McClelland and Stewart, 1974.

Copp, T. *The Anatomy of Poverty: The Condition of the Working Class in Montreal, 1897–1929.* Toronto: McClelland and Stewart, 1974.

Frager, Ruth. *Sweatshop Strife: Class, Ethnicity, and Gender in the Jewish Labour Movement of Toronto, 1900–1939.* Toronto: University of Toronto Press, 1992.

Gutman, Herbert. *Work, Culture, and Society in Industrializing America: Essays in American Working-Class and Social History.* New York: Knopf, 1976.

Kealey, Gregory S. *Toronto Workers Respond to Industrial Capitalism, 1867–1892.* Toronto: University of Toronto Press, 1980.

Kealey, Linda. *Enlisting Women for the Cause: Women, Labour, and the Left in Canada, 1890–1920.* Toronto: University of Toronto Press, 1998.

Montgomery, David. *Beyond Equality: Labor and the Radical Republicans: 1862–1872.* New York: Knopf, 1967.

Palmer, Bryan. *A Culture in Conflict: Skilled Workers and Industrial Capitalism in Hamilton, Ontario, 1860–1914.* Montreal and Kingston: McGill-Queen's University Press, 1979.

Parr, Joy. *The Gender of Breadwinners: Women, Men, and Change in Two Industrial Towns, 1880–1950.* Toronto: University of Toronto Press, 1990.

Sangster, Joan. *Earning Respect: The Lives of Working Women in Small-Town Ontario, 1920–1960.* Toronto: University of Toronto Press, 1995.

Thompson, Edward P. *The Making of the English Working Class.* London: Gollancz, 1964.

Wright, Miriam. *A Fishery for Modern Times: Industrialization of the Newfoundland Fishery, 1934–1968.* Toronto: University of Toronto Press, 2001.

ILLUSTRATION 2.1 (P. 45)

Issue to Consider

- What does this pre–World War I photograph suggest about the condition of many working-class families during the early 20th century? What does it suggest about the gap between the view that women should be housewives and mothers exclusively and the real lives of many women (including those with very young children)?

ARTICLES

In sociological terms, the expansion of industry and its parallel process of urbanization are known as modernization. Although the term implies progress, social historians have paid critical attention to the ways in which the late 19th-/early 20th-century mechanization of production, alongside the growth of transportation and communication networks, profoundly changed both the nature of work and the rhythms of life. Jeremy L. Stein presents a case study of how these changes were manifested in the Eastern Ontario town of Cornwall, highlighting the day-to-day repercussions of the process as they affected that town's residents. As he indicates, the results were ambivalent: what can be said for certain is that, across the nation, where industry proceeded, few aspects of life remained untouched. Another important area within working-class history that has recently developed, as exemplified by Miriam Wright's article, concerns the interplay of class, gender, and regional culture in the relationship between workers and the expanding modern state.

Article 2.1

Jeremy L. Stein

Dislocations: Changing Experiences of Time and Space in an Industrialising Nineteenth-Century Ontario Town

Issues to Consider

- Why does Stein use the concept of dislocation to discuss the sociocultural impact of industrialization in Cornwall? What were some of the specific changes taking place in Cornwall in the latter half of the 19th century? Were they unique to the town or common to all industrializing Canadian urban centres?
- Why must change almost inevitably focus on technology?
- Stein uses the term "social vignette" to describe each of the three parts into which his article is divided. What does he mean by this term? Is his approach to his subject effective? What else might historians want to know about the subject?
- The primary sources that Stein relies on are generally print media — local newspapers and other published contemporary writings. What are some of the strengths and weaknesses of using media as a historical source?
- What other sources might historians use to examine a topic as complex as sociocultural change as experienced by "ordinary" people in their everyday lives?

The consequence of advances in transport and communications for the way human experiences of time and space have changed historically is widely recognised (Castells 1989; Falk and Abler 1980; Janelle 1968). Responses to these changes in Europe and North America during the nineteenth and twentieth centuries have been well documented by scholars but studies have tended to chart elite responses rather than the reactions of ordinary people (Harvey 1989, 1990; Kern 1983; Marvin 1988; Schivelbusch 1977). Such commentaries have also tended to fall into the trap of technological determinism: to assume, for example, that the changes described occurred and can be explained as a direct result of technological change, rather than being the product of complex historical circumstances shaped by broader social and economic processes, or allowing for time-lags between technological innovation and its social consequences. In a Canadian context little has been written on this subject, especially on the inter-relationships between past technological change, associated industrialisation and changing historical experiences of time and space.

This article briefly examines how ordinary Canadians' experiences of time and space changed during the nineteenth century in the context of an Ontario town undergoing industrialisation.[1] The changes documented coincided with and were a consequence of processes of industrialisation and technological change that originated in Europe and which swept over the

Source: Jeremy L. Stein, "Dislocations: Changing Experiences of Time and Space in an Industrialising Nineteenth-Century Ontario Town," *British Journal of Canadian Studies* 14, no. 1 (1999): 115–30.

province of Canada from the 1830s. Although these processes were universally experienced by Canadian cities they were experienced differently in different places. Hence I focus on one urban centre, the town of Cornwall in Eastern Ontario, located seventy miles west of Montreal on the north bank of the St Lawrence River. In 1850 Cornwall had a modest industrial base. The town, however, experienced considerable industrial expansion between the late-1860s and 1870s when several prominent Montreal industrialists established cotton mills there. During this time the town became a major textile manufacturing centre. Cornwall's population grew accordingly, rising from 1,915 in 1861 to 6,805 in 1891 (Canada 1860–1: 72; 1890–1: 42).

Cornwall's industrialisation was accompanied by, and interrelated with, processes of urbanisation and modernisation. For the general populace, one of the most noticeable set of changes these combined processes represented was the introduction of a range of new innovations, from steamboats to electric lighting systems. Consequently, although I do not wish to imply a causal or deterministic relationship between technological innovation and changing experiences of time and space, my discussion of the latter almost inevitably focuses on technology: on the introduction of a set of new technologies, and on how they were experienced; on how Cornwall's Town Council and the town's social elites debated the acquisition of technology (what I term the social reception of technology); and on technology's social consequences. By use of the term "technology" I mean both machines and knowledge about their functioning and operation, for technology is inseparable from its social organisation (Cardwell 1994; Rosenberg 1976). Instead of providing a detailed history of technological change, my intention is to focus on the social interpretation of technology; on how it was variably interpreted as it was viewed through different social lenses. Experience of technology was not limited to the wealthy. The effects of improved transport and communications, for example, would have been widely noticed: in the greater range and availability of consumer goods; in the speed of delivery of local produce to foreign markets; in greater access to news and the speed of its delivery; or, if not directly experienced, the purchase of new technologies by wealthy individuals, private firms or local authorities for communal purposes would have been generally witnessed.

This article is divided into three parts each intended as a social vignette detailing, in three separate social spaces, how citizens of Cornwall experienced time and space differently during the nineteenth century. The first part considers how improvements in transport and communications tightened Cornwall's external relationships to the outside world. The second part considers the advent of large-scale manufacturing in Cornwall and the experience of working in the town's textile mills. The third part considers the social reception of technology by Cornwall as a community, and focuses on the Council's purchase of a steam fire engine.

TIGHTENING THE TIME-SPACE NET: THE ANNIHILATION OF SPACE AND TIME

The middle decades of the nineteenth century saw the Province of Canada caught up in the prevailing wind of improvement that had swept over from Britain and the United States. The improving spirit was most conspicuous in the economic sphere. By 1848 there existed a fully operational and enlarged set of canals along the St Lawrence, and this, together with the introduction of steamship, railroad and telegraph services during the 1840s and 1850s, served to knit the fledgling province together and to integrate it more fully with its neighbours to the south and to the east. The spirit of improvement was particularly observable in the changing conditions of travel and communications in the nineteenth century: in the improved comfort of travel; in the regularity of steamship and rail services; in the frequency of the mails; and in reduced journey times (Ross 1991).

Consider for a moment the nature of travel along the St Lawrence during the nineteenth century. Visitors to Ontario in the early nineteenth century experienced the downstream journey from Kingston to Montreal as a set of journeys, alternating between stagecoaches and steamboats, for treacherous rapids prevented the continuous passage of steamboats. Charles Dickens, who journeyed from Kingston to Montreal in 1842, described these trips by stage-coach as "tedious" for "the roads are bad and the travelling slow" (Dickens 1989: 249–51). His journey, involving several portages by stagecoach, took over thirty hours to complete. Further evidence of travel in the Cornwall area in the early nineteenth century is provided by Jacob Pringle, County Court Judge, historian and lifetime resident of Cornwall (Pringle 1972). Pringle recalls the summer journey eastward from Cornwall to Montreal in 1830 lasting between twelve and thirteen hours, with the return journey taking a similar length of time. In winter, covered sleighs replaced stagecoaches, and in spring and fall strong wagons were used built to withstand the poor roads and the incessant mud. Pringle describes travelling during these two seasons as especially difficult and wearying. The journey could take twenty-four hours and involved steady ploughing through the mud, with passengers sometimes having to help the driver dig out the wheels of the wagon which had got stuck in a mud hole (pp. 108–9).

More spacious steamboats and improved steamboat technology gradually smoothed jour-neys along the St Lawrence. Steamboats had been introduced in 1809 and with successive improvements in speed, safety and design they steadily eased the journey between Kingston and Montreal (Glazebrook 1938: 67–8). One such innovation was the Ericsson screw propeller, introduced in the 1830s and 1840s, which displaced paddle wheels, thereby reducing the draught of steamboats and making navigable the gentler rapids of the St Lawrence (Ross 1991: 62–3). Steamboats obviated the need for long stagecoach rides between places, making trips faster and more comfortable. In places where the rapids were long and treacherous canals and railways replaced stagecoach routes. This was the case to the west of Cornwall where the Cornwall Canal, completed in 1842, was built to circumvent the Long Sault Rapids. Stages were still the common means of transport in winter, spring and fall until the completion of the Grand Trunk Railway between Toronto and Montreal in 1855–6, at which time stagecoaches "disappeared forever from this part of the country" (Pringle 1972: 109–10).

These changes and improvements did not go unnoticed by nineteenth-century travellers. Simple recourse to travel guides would have made the steady reduction in journey times apparent to the regular traveller. The *Disturnell Railroad, Steamboat and Telegraph Book for 1850*, for instance, records twenty-six hours as the usual steamboat passage from Montreal to Kingston (Disturnell 1850: 67). An equivalent guide three years later shows that twenty-four hours was sufficient for the journey (Disturnell 1853: 79).

Communications was another area in which change was observable and sometimes dra-matic. Cornwall was connected to the telegraph in 1847 and to the telephone in 1878. Combined these technologies inaugurated a phase of "time-space convergence" (Falk and Abler 1980; Janelle 1968). This concept describes the process by which, over time, places are drawn closer together as a consequence of improvements in transport and communications. The effect of this process was demonstrated in 1854 when Isabella Bird journeyed along the St Lawrence (Bird 1966). Having arrived in Cornwall she discovered that she had left her watch in Kingston. Bird was astonished when told that within only half an hour of telegraphing this news to Kingston her watch had been found. She described the event as "an instance of the way in which utilitarian essentials of a high state of civilisation are diffused throughout Canada" (p. 246), illustrating a common nineteenth-century association in Western ideologies of dominance between technology and notions of civilisation (Adas 1989).

A re-ordering of spatial relationships was accompanied by a re-ordering of time. One element of this was the greater precision by which time was measured. This is observable in Cornwall's Town Council Minutes which record payments to labourers employed on municipal public works projects. During the 1860s and 1870s the Council regularly paid labourers by the day, or in fractions of the day, with the records indicating the use of ever more precise units of time. In 1868, for example, the minimum amount of time paid for was a "quarter day" (Town Council Minutes[2] 25 October 1868). In 1871 John O'Brian was paid for "41 [and] 8½/10 days work" [sic], implying a ten-hour work day and a minimum unit of paid time of just half an hour (TCM, 14 August 1871). Furthermore, from 1873, the Council's payments to labourers are recorded in hours rather than as fractions of the day (TCM, 14 September 1873).

The re-ordering of time is also noticeable in the form of stricter work routines, a subject I return to later on in this article in my discussion of factory discipline in Cornwall's textile mills. In the 1860s and 1870s there appears to have been no single work routine within which all residents of the town of Cornwall operated. Instead, there were multiple, intersecting work routines. Labourers employed by the Town Council, as we have seen, worked a ten-hour day. Store clerks in this period put in a regular fourteen-hour day on weekdays, with an extra hour or two on Saturdays (*Cornwall Standard*, 12 August 1886). By the late 1880s this situation had changed somewhat. In 1889 the 1,400 employees of Cornwall's textile mills worked a strict eleven-hour day, this being the standard work routine for at least twenty per cent of the town's labour force (Royal Commission 1889: 1058, 1063). At first, this appears to imply that the other eighty per cent of Cornwall's labour force worked to different, possibly non-industrial work routines. But this ignores the effect Cornwall's textile mills had on the town's other establishments. This is demonstrated by the fact that several of Cornwall's institutions adjusted their work routines to suit the textile mills' work schedules. For example, in 1883, the town's Post Office curtailed its former practice of closing during the early evening to enable mill employees to collect their mail on their journey home (*Freeholder*, 16 February, 2 March 1883). Similarly, early closing arrangements in Cornwall's shops were successfully resisted during the 1870s and 1880s because mill employees were unable to shop during the day (*Freeholder*, 4, 14, 18 May 1883; *Reporter*, 9 December 1876; *Standard*, 12, 19 August 1886). The real significance of the work routine of Cornwall's textile mills thus lay in the effect it had on Cornwall's other work environments, inextricably binding them together, and reducing "the power of Cornwall's traditional institutions to set the order of urban activities" (Stein 1995: 287).

By far the most significant temporal change that occurred during the nineteenth century was the introduction of standard time. Systems of standard time were initially introduced on the North American railroads in the mid-nineteenth century to avoid accidents and the confusion of having multiple times along a rail route, each locality having a different astronomically accurate local time (Bartky 1989; Kern 1983; Stephens 1989). The first formal agreement between North American railway companies to establish a regional standard time occurred in New England in 1849 (Bartky 1989: 28). It took another thirty-four years before the continental North American railway network adopted the system of uniform time-keeping. This took place on 18 November 1883. The switch was clearly significant, inaugurating universal public time along the railroads, and being the basis of our current time zones. One commentator has described the introduction of standard time as "the most momentous development in the history of uniform public time since the invention of the mechanical clock in the fourteenth century" (Kern 1983: 11). While it is known that opposition to standard time erupted on the margins in the United States, where the discrepancy between local and standard time was most conspicuous, little is known of how the change was experienced in urban Canada (Bartky 1989: 50–2).

Contemporary newspapers show that the Grand Trunk was the last of the four lines serving Montreal to adopt the new system of measuring time. The railway adopted standard time at noon on 18 November 1883 (*Montreal Star*, 19 November 1883). To avoid the confusion of different local and railroad times many towns and cities across North America declared their civil time would match that of the railroads in their vicinity (Bartky 1989: 49–50). This was the case in Montreal and in neighbouring centres. Points east of the Eastern Standard Time zone had to retard their clocks, points west, to advance. Thus Montreal switched its clocks back six minutes when, at eight o'clock in the morning on 19 November 1883, the city adopted Eastern Standard Time (*Montreal Star*, 19 November 1883). Quebec City adopted the standard for civic purposes on the eighteenth and put its clock back fifteen minutes (*Ottawa Daily Citizen*, 19 November 1883). In Kingston the city's caretaker advanced the public clock by five minutes and fifty-five seconds at 12:30 p.m. on the nineteenth (*Kingston British Whig*, 17 November 1883). In Cornwall one of the city's newspaper editors reminded readers that if they wished "to be in time for the trains, and down to time in other respects [they] should put [their] watch or ... clock back five minutes and forty seconds" (*Freeholder*, 16 November 1883). Except for these news items, the adoption of standard time received limited comment in the press, and there was no identifiable public opposition to the change. But this does not imply that the change was insignificant, as Sir Sandford Fleming, the chief propagandist for standard time, realised in 1889, when he described its adoption as "a noiseless revolution ... effected throughout the United States and Canada" (Fleming 1889: 357). The change was symbolic of the increasing integration and interdependence of distant places and of the ascendancy of clock time. That it went largely unnoticed does not detract from this argument, for major social and economic transformations, especially in their early stages, do not always generate significant social comment. The adoption of standard time in urban central Canada was not experienced as a dramatic or sudden event. This was partly because the new system of time-keeping was steadily introduced on the North American continent over several decades, and because it easily co-existed with other local work routines.

The effects of all these changes and improvements was captured in the common mid-nineteenth-century phrase "the annihilation of space and time," which symbolised both the spirit of improvement of the age and the fact that the changes described could sometimes be not only dramatic and exciting but also bewildering (Ross 1991: 46–81). The historical record does not provide clear evidence to determine how widespread was this ideal of social and economic progress. The phrase captures the sense of disrupture and dislocation associated with rapid technological and social change. However, because changes were also experienced gradually and cumulatively (as in the case of reduced passage times) or noiselessly (as in the case of the adoption of standard time), I would argue that they were as often taken for granted by the vast majority of urban dwellers, who for lack of time or education, were unable to document their observations. We can speculate that a result of their urban experience was a greater willingness to accept the routineness of social, economic and technological change.

CORNWALL'S INDUSTRIALISATION

The combined effect of many of the changes discussed above was to tie Cornwall more closely than ever before to neighbouring settlements and to the outside world. These changes set the scene for Cornwall's industrialisation. Standard time, although not a necessary pre-condition for Cornwall's industrialisation, was a sign of Cornwall's increasing integration into national and international economic and political structures. Improved transport and communications was a more likely pre-condition for Cornwall's industrialisation. It made the town more accessible to outside investment. The advent of large-scale textile manufacturing in Cornwall after 1868 was in fact the product not of local capital, but of external investment by a group of Montreal industrialists. This, in turn, made the town's economic livelihood increasingly subject to external events.

Cornwall experienced considerable industrial expansion between 1868 and 1880 when Montreal industrialists established three textile companies, with their headquarters in Montreal, but with each company building substantial mills in Cornwall. Prior to this, the town's industrial base was modest. In 1850 Cornwall was described as "a neat, quiet, old-fashioned looking place … not a place of any great business" (Smith 1851: 388–9). An 1862 directory shows little change. The town in that year had several blacksmiths, saddlers and tanneries, and three manufacturing establishments making respectively carriages, shoes, and sashes and doors. In addition, the town had two flour mills, two tin-smiths and a foundry (National Archives of Canada 1862). These were all small-scale family enterprises performing custom work for a local market.

Prior to the construction of textile mills in Cornwall the town's largest industrial establishment was Andrew Hodge's grist mill. It was capitalised in 1871 at $41,000, with production in that year valued at $59,000. It employed five people. By comparison, the Cornwall Manufacturing Company, the first of the three textile companies to build mills in Cornwall, was capitalised at $390,000, employed 145 people, and produced goods to the value of $200,000 (Canada 1871). The second and third mills were built respectively in 1872 and 1880. As with the Cornwall Manufacturing Company these were massive structures, highly capitalised and employing large numbers of workers.

Manufacturing of this kind and on this scale was actively encouraged by Cornwall's Town Council. Cornwall's political representatives thereby sought to achieve economic stability and social advancement through industrial expansion. The Council, composed of the town's leading merchants and professionals, combined a set of beliefs about progress, a commitment to being self-built, and a strong sense of civic patriotism, what Elizabeth Bloomfield terms an "urban ethos" (Bloomfield 1983: 212). The Council agreed to grant tax exemptions and to pay substantial bonuses to persuade industrialists to establish mills in Cornwall (TCM, 9 February 1871). The Council also redrew Cornwall's political boundary enabling them to pay a bonus to the Cornwall Manufacturing Company (TCM, 19 February 1872). The company wished to locate its mill beside the Cornwall Canal on a stretch of land adjacent to, but beyond the jurisdiction of, the Town of Cornwall. This prevented the Council paying the company a bonus. Following a successful petition by the Council to the Lieutenant Governor of Ontario, permission was granted for the land in question to be annexed to the town, thereby allowing the bonus to be paid (Ontario Gazette, 9 March 1872). The Council's actions were strongly supported by Cornwall's social elites who voted substantially in favour of granting bonuses and tax exemptions to the proposed mills. This was partly self-interest, for it was believed that the mills, by providing hundreds of jobs, would pump substantial sums of money into the local economy, thus benefiting the town's merchants, as well as its property holders, through enhanced property values.

Cornwall's cotton mills represented a new industrial landscape. By virtue of their size and scale, their capitalisation, their number of employees, their type of ownership and system of management, they were innovative institutions, different from Cornwall's other industrial establishments. The cotton mills were particularly distinguishable by their intensified level of social discipline, characterised by strict systems of time-, work- and machine-discipline (Thompson 1967). For example, there was a strict eleven-hour work day. Work at the Canada Cotton and Stormont mills commenced at half-past six in the morning, with a break of an hour for lunch at midday, and then resumed until half-past six in the evening. On Saturdays employees worked until noon with the rest of the day considered a "half-holiday." In 1889 this was the standard routine for the 1,400 mill employees of Cornwall's cotton mills, a routine symbolised by the factory's clocks and bells (Royal Commission 1889: 1058, 1062–3, 1068). Time- and work-discipline is noticeable also in the supervision of mill employees and in the system of fines. A table of fines was posted up in every work room of the cotton mills. Fines were imposed for various offences: for lateness, bad or spoiled work, spitting, damage to company property or for negligence and absenteeism (pp. 1069–70). There was, in addition, the ultimate threat of dismissal. Workers also experienced forms of spatial discipline, being confined during work hours within the factory gates, and in the factory assigned to specific floors, work spaces and machines, where they were subject to the continuous surveillance of overseers who enforced work standards and work discipline (Foucault 1979; Stein 1995).

Workers' experience of technology in Cornwall's cotton mills also illustrates the Janus-like quality of technical innovation. On the one hand, technology brought social and economic improvements: the adoption of faster machinery had the potential to increase output and the amount of work performed in a given time. On the other hand, technology had its downside. Faster machines implied increased exploitation of the workforce by extraction of what Marx termed "relative surplus value" (Marx 1976: 447–8). Moreover, workers were increasingly subject to "machine-discipline," the notion of the machine's power to impose a work rhythm on human labourers (Prude 1983: 126–9). Although stoppages occurred and traditional methods of resistance were well practised in the integrated system of production utilised in cotton mills of the 1870s and 1880s, workers had limited control over the pace of their work. This had the additional consequence of increasing the risk to workers of industrial accidents. The Ontario factory inspectors' reports of the 1880s show a high incidence of accidents involving workers who caught limbs or fingers in the weaving and spinning machinery or in the drive mechanism connecting equipment on different floors of the mill (Stein 1992: 139–55). Another example of the double-edged nature of technology was the introduction of gas and electric lighting systems. Cornwall's cotton mills were the first institutions in Canada to install electric lighting systems, allowing work to be more easily conducted at night, but such systems, by allowing for an extension of the work day, had the disadvantage of further exploiting workers (Cornwall Freeholder, 30 March, 6 April 1883).

By the late nineteenth century the systems of time-, work- and machine-discipline discussed above were a common experience to the 1,400 employees who laboured in Cornwall's textile mills. Clearly the routine of the factory intersected with routines of work, rest and play in family and community life outside the factory gates, as Tamara Hareven discusses in her book Family Time and Industrial Time (Hareven 1982). In Cornwall, the nature of these intersecting routines is uncertain. It may be noted that Cornwall experienced a significant influx of French Canadians in the 1870s and 1880s. By 1881 the town was thirty per cent French-speaking (Canada 1880–1: 130–1, 262–3, 360–1). Many of these new residents worked in the town's textile mills, and possibly were directly recruited for that purpose. However, newspapers of the period do not record that this generation of factory workers had a different attitude to time than the English-speaking population, or that Catholic feast days came into conflict with industrial work rhythms.

THE SOCIAL RECEPTION OF TECHNOLOGY

Technology was also consumed and experienced on an institutional and communal scale. This included the acquisition by private institutions of new technology which sometimes became a subject of civic pride and an excuse for civic celebration. This was the case in April 1883 when the Canada Cotton Company installed electric lighting in their new weave shed, the first installation in Canada of Edison's incandescent electric lighting system. This was a public event, widely reported in the press, and an occasion for Cornwall's social elites to demonstrate that their community was progressive in matters of technology. Four hundred people from Ottawa and Montreal, including journalists and leading politicians and merchants, were jointly invited by the directors of the Canada Cotton Company and Hamilton's Edison Electric Light Company to view the display. Thomas Edison himself was among those present (Senior 1984: 231; *Freeholder*, 30 March, 6 April 1883; *Montreal Daily Star*, 4 April 1883). When the system was switched on 800 looms were simultaneously set in motion and above them 400 electric lights. The *Montreal Gazette* reported the noise as "indescribable" and the light as "brilliant" (*Montreal Gazette*, 4 April 1883). The *Ottawa Daily Citizen* described the scene as rivalling "the best lighted streets of the biggest cities of the Dominion" (*Ottawa Daily Citizen*, 5 April 1883). The only dissenting voice was Cornwall's *Freeholder* which, for party political reasons, described the Canada Cotton Mill's weave shed as an "unnecessary extravagance," and listed objections to the electric light, suggesting that "its too intense and flickering brilliancy" produced afflicting forms of ophthalmia among mill operatives, and "that electric light has had its day" (*Freeholder*, 2 March 1883). These reports illustrate the growing importance of the news media in the late nineteenth century for spreading knowledge about new technologies to a wider public and how social elites used technology for the purposes of urban boosterism. The differing interpretations also suggest possible fractures in Cornwall's social matrix, that not all elements of the town's social elites favoured considerable public expenditure on new and modern technology.

A second example of the "communal" consumption and reception of technology was the acquisition by Cornwall's Town Council of technology intended to improve the provision of urban services. During the 1870s and 1880s, the Council invested in a variety of technologies from fire-fighting equipment to street lighting and waterworks systems. Strictly speaking these were not "communal" decisions because only property holders could vote on these matters. Furthermore, because merchants rather than industrialists predominated on the Town Council, its decisions tended to reflect mercantile interests rather than those of the textile mills. Nevertheless, urban technology became a subject of widespread public debate both in the local press and in town meetings, which were open to all, irrespective of property ownership status. These debates surrounding the acquisition of new technologies indicate how technology was socially valued and the social groups responsible for driving technological change. The remainder of this article focuses on the events surrounding the Council's purchase in 1876 of a steam fire engine as it is a good illustration of the significance of new technology to an emerging nineteenth-century Canadian city.

The decision to purchase a steam fire engine was influenced by a wish to better protect Cornwall's central business district and its cotton mills from fire. Fires had destroyed the Cornwall Manufacturing Company's mill in 1870 and the Stormont mill in 1874 (Pringle 1972: 293–4). In the former case, it was only after the Council agreed to pay the company bonuses amounting to $12,000 and to grant it tax exemptions, that the company agreed to rebuild its mill (TCM, 9 February, 13 April, 7 December 1871, 8, 22 January 1872). These early mills most likely had their own fire protection systems so that Cornwall's fire brigade was a supplementary precaution, to be drawn upon, if and when necessary. Certainly when the mills were rebuilt, fire protection was an important element in their construction, probably at the insistence of fire insurance companies. An 1882 fire insurance map, showing the design of the Stormont mill when it was rebuilt in 1882, includes standpipes, a pump with a capacity of 1,500 gallons of water a minute, water tanks, sufficient hose, and automatic sprinklers. The establishment of a separate mill fire company was also proposed at this time (National Archives of Canada 1882). Nevertheless, the importance of Cornwall's cotton mills to the town's economic livelihood was still a powerful incentive for improving the town's fire-fighting resources. Population growth was another factor, as was the perception that if Cornwall was to attract further private investment it had to be seen to be progressive in protecting its existing industries from fire.

Cornwall's Town Council authorised the acquisition of a steam fire engine in May 1876 and appointed a special fire committee to oversee its purchase (TCM, 9 May 1876). The committee considered offers from two fire engine manufacturers, one from the Silsby Company of New York State, the other from a company based in Chatham, Ontario. Both companies offered to supply the Council with an engine, 300 feet of hose, hose reels and hose carts. The Committee initially recommended the more expensive Silsby engine because of its constant water pressure and because of its craned neck which allowed easy movement in confined spaces (TCM, 9 June 1876). However, events intervened. First, the necessary bylaw to ratify the fire committee's decision was defeated because of local protectionist sentiment which asserted that buying an American fire engine was an unpatriotic act (*Reporter*, 12 August 1876). Second, a fire, which broke out on the morning of 26 July, successfully demonstrated the effectiveness of the Chatham engine. By coincidence, the Chatham engine, brought to Cornwall by the Chatham Company as a demonstration model, was conveniently located at the canal wharf near to the scene of the fire. Two local engineers who managed to get the engine to work pumped water from the Canal onto the burning buildings and successfully prevented the fire from spreading. Thus, according to one local newspaper, the town's commercial sector was rescued from certain destruction (Pringle 1972: 142; *Reporter*, 5 August 1876; Senior 1984: 266–7). Shortly after the fire the Council received a petition signed by 287 Cornwall residents requesting that for the better protection of their property, the Chatham engine be purchased immediately. The Council soon obliged, purchasing from the Chatham Company a steam fire engine, 300 feet of hose and two hose carts for $3,450 (TCM, 7 August 1876).

The story of the steam fire engine illustrates several key points about technology. Firstly, the purchase of a steam fire engine was one of several measures taken to improve the town's ability to fight fires. Others included passing a set of bylaws to regulate the height of buildings and the storage of combustible materials, reorganising the management of the town's volunteer fire brigade, and standardising its response to fires (TCM, 13 October, 6 November 1876). These measures constituted a recognition that new technology was no guarantee of success and that its effectiveness depended on the efficient social organisation of those who used it.

Secondly, the example of the steam fire engine illustrates the limits of technological change. Although the steam fire engine was technically a communal investment, purchased out of public funds, not everyone would directly benefit from its acquisition. A direct consequence of the Council's decision to locate the fire engine in the Town Hall was that it could only be effective in the central part of town where Cornwall's textile mills, principal retail stores and its merchants were located. Properties on either side of this district could not be adequately protected because of insufficient hose and because no proximate water body existed in these areas from which to pump water onto a fire. This spatial bias is further evidence that Cornwall's retail merchants, a self-interested urban mercantile elite who dominated the Town Council, were the principal agitators for improved fire protection and not the town's industrialists. This indicates that support for technological change within the community had social limits. Purchasing a steam fire engine also had much to do with the wish of Cornwall's mercantile elite to demonstrate Cornwall's progressiveness as a community. Possession of sophisticated fire-fighting technology demonstrated the town's commitment to protecting its commercial and industrial property. This was especially important in a context where communities like Cornwall were competing to attract scarce investment capital.

Thirdly, Cornwall's experience of fighting fires, and events subsequent to the Council's purchase of the steam fire engine, show a tendency to "annihilate space and time." This accords well with Marx's observations in the 1850s, that within capitalist societies there was a tendency to overcome the barriers of time and space and to speed up the turnover time of capital (Marx 1973: 524–44, 620–37, 670–3). In David Harvey's more recent account of contemporary capitalism he identifies similar tendencies but suggests that they are common features of urban capitalist societies rather than of capitalism per se (Harvey 1989, 1990). These arguments and observations have been highly influential in a range of academic writings, aiding explanations of tremendous historical advances in global transport and communications, and highlighting their significance. But the emphasis in these writings has been upon advances in long-distance travel and communications, typically *between* cities, thereby neglecting similar processes in operation *within* cities.

Historically, fire-fighting has always been associated with a tendency to overcome the physical barriers of time and space. Speed is critical to effective fire-fighting. Hence the importance of swiftly sounding the alarm of fire and of a rapid response, ensuring that fire-fighters, water and equipment quickly reach the scene of a fire. Prior to the advent of modern technology, church bells were often used to warn a community of the outbreak of a fire, and most early North American communities had volunteer fire brigades and could organise water distribution by simple recourse to a bucket brigade (Baird 1986: 39; Blake 1956; Wade 1959). The modernisation of North American fire-fighting during the nineteenth century brought with it greater access to improved technology and the professionalisation of fire-fighting with improved management of its methods and resources (Monkkonen 1988: 89–110). These changes were partly a response to public demands to improve and speed up the fire-fighting process, and were often driven by the wish to better protect accumulated urban assets. Hence developments in fire-fighting should be considered in the context of general advances in urban communications, of improved urban service provision during the nineteenth century, and of growing social expectations in both these areas (Stein 1996; Tarr 1987; Tarr and Dupuy 1988). In late nineteenth- and early twentieth-century Canada demands to speed up the fire-fighting process often occurred in the aftermath of serious fires.[3] Frequently, telegraph boxes and telephones were installed to speed up the warning systems. In Cornwall, the steam fire engine, originally dragged by hand through the city's streets, was supplied with horses, and in winter with sleighs to speed up its despatch to a hypothetical scene of fire (*Freeholder*, 30 March 1883, 8 February 1884). These measures can be interpreted as common-sense responses recognising the importance, as stated above, of quickly sounding the alarm of a fire and of a rapid response. But the measures also illustrate increasing communal emphasis on the economic value of time and space. This was because newspaper editors and community leaders consistently identified "time" and "space" as critical problems that prevented improved fire protection. Time wasted in sounding the alarm, delays in reaching the fire, and problems of water supply and distribution, common subjects in the press reporting of fires at this time, all emphasised the importance of overcoming time and distance, and the possible financial consequences to the community if the problems were not adequately addressed. The solution was often seen to lie in technology, because growing expectations of its reliability, and a shared belief in its capacity to overcome the barriers of time and space, implied greater potential to save urban property.

CONCLUSIONS

Industrialisation in Cornwall, Ontario, involved a restructuring of the human experience of time and space. The most tangible evidence of this was the replacement of multiple local times by standard railroad time. The adoption of standard time was symbolic of Cornwall's increasing integration into national and international economic and political structures. That the change received limited social comment in central Canada's metropolitan press, and that there was no identifiable public opposition to it, may be explained by the length of time the new system of time-keeping took to be implemented on the North American continent. It also suggests that by the late nineteenth century clock time was already well established in Cornwall.

In other contexts change was more obvious and observable, no less so than in the field of transport and communications. During the early decades of the nineteenth century, travel along the St Lawrence became gradually more comfortable and less time-consuming. By mid-century, the telegraph, and then later the telephone, heralded a period of instantaneous communications. A consequence of improved transport and communications was considerable reductions in relative distances between places. Cornwall was thereby increasingly integrated with neighbouring settlements and the outside world. Although change was sometimes sudden and dramatic it was also experienced gradually over years and decades, as a steady accumulation of small-scale improvements. This was true of reduced journey times, which were directly discernible by the regular traveller and by others in the improved speed of delivery and availability of a range of economic goods. This example demonstrates how new ways of experiencing time and space were observable by all groups in the population.

Improved transport and communications was probably an important precondition for Cornwall's subsequent industrial expansion. In the late 1860s and 1870s, Cornwall's industrialisation brought with it new types of business organisation whose management systems were characterised by intensified levels of social discipline and surveillance in the workplace. Although these institutions co-existed with other kinds of industrial enterprise, by the late 1880s the new industrial disciplines of Cornwall's textile mills were the normal routine for a significant proportion of the town's workforce. These routines also affected the wider community, with several other of Cornwall's institutions adjusting their routines to suit the work schedules of the town's textile mills. Industrial rhythms and economic conceptions of time and space appear to have become dominant by the 1870s and 1880s, and were noticeable in contexts beyond the workplace, for example, in the process of fire-fighting. However, this dominance was never entirely complete. Industrial rhythms continued to intersect with other community, work and family routines. Moreover, although the "annihilation of space and time" is a recurring metaphor for the changes described in this article, it is uncertain how widespread this ideal of social and economic improvement was. The case of the steam fire engine suggests that this progressive ideal was largely limited to an urban mercantile elite who, for self-interest, wished to initiate technological and social change.

NOTES

1. For a more detailed investigation of Cornwall's industrialisation and for a discussion of social discipline in the town's textile mills see Stein (1992) and (1995). Further details of the modernisation of Cornwall's fire-fighting may be found in Stein (1996). What concerns me in this article is the variety of ways in which ordinary Canadians experienced time and space differently in a range of urban contexts during ongoing processes of industrialisation, urbanisation and modernisation in the nineteenth century.
2. Hereafter TCM.
3. See, for example, Armstrong (1978).

REFERENCES

Adas, M., *Machines as the Measure of Men: Science, Technology and Ideologies of Western Dominance* (Ithaca and London: Cornell University Press, 1989).

Armstrong, F. H., "The second great fire of Toronto, 19–20 April 1904," *Ontario History*, 70 (1978), 3–38.

Baird, D. M., *The Story of Fire-Fighting in Canada* (Erin, ON.: Boston Mills Press, 1986).

Bartky, L, "The adoption of standard time," *Technology and Culture*, 30:1 (January 1989), 25–56.

Bird, I. L., *The Englishwoman in America* (Toronto: University of Toronto Press, 1966).

Blake, N. M., *Water for the Cities: A History of the Urban Water Supply Problem in the United States* (Syracuse: Syracuse University Press, 1956).

Bloomfield, E., "Building the city on a foundation of factories: The 'industrial policy' in Berlin, Ontario, 1870–1914," *Ontario History*, 75:3 (September 1983), 207–43.

Cardwell, D., *The Fontana History of Technology* (London: Fontana Press, 1994).

Castells, M., *The Informational City: Information Technology, Economic Restructuring and the Urban-Regional Process* (Oxford: Blackwell, 1989).

Canada, *Census of Canada*, 1860–1, vol. 1.

———, *Census of Canada*, 1871, Cornwall, Schedule No. G., Return of industrial establishments, Microfilm (reel C10,006), Public Archives of Canada.

———, *Census of Canada*, 1880–1, vol. 1.

———, *Census of Canada*, 1890–1, vol. 1.

The Cornwall Freeholder, 16 February, 2, 30 March, 6 April, 4, 14, 18 May, 16 November 1883, 8 February 1884.

The Cornwall Reporter, 5, 12 August, 9 December 1876.

The Cornwall Standard, 12, 19 August 1886.

Corporation of the Town of Cornwall, *Town Council Minutes*, Simon Fraser Centennial Library, Cornwall, 25 October 1868, 9 February, 13 April, 14 August, 7 December 1871, 8, 22 January, 19 February 1872, 14 September 1873, 9 May, 9 June, 7 August, 13 October, 6 November 1876.

Dickens, C., *American Notes for General Circulation* (London: Penguin Books, 1989).

Disturnell's Railroad, Steamboat and Telegraph Book (New York: J. Disturnell, 1850).

Disturnell's Railway, Steamship and Telegraph Book (New York: J. Disturnell, March 1853).

Falk, T. and R. Abler, "Intercommunications, Distance and Geographical Theory," *Geografiska Annaler*, series B (1980), 59–67.

Fleming, S., "Time-reckoning for the twentieth century," *Annual Report ... Smithsonian Institution ... for the Year Ending June 30, 1886* (Washington, DC: Smithsonian Institution, 1889).

Foucault, M., *Discipline and Punish: The Birth of the Prison* (New York: Vintage Books, 1979).

Glazebrook, G. P. de T., *A History of Transportation in Canada* (Toronto: The Ryerson Press, 1938).

Hareven, T. K., *Family Time and Industrial Time: The Relationship Between the Family and Work in a New England Industrial Community* (Cambridge: Cambridge University Press, 1982).

Harvey, D., *The Condition of Postmodernity: An Enquiry into the Origins of Cultural Change* (Oxford and Cambridge, MA: Basil Blackwell, 1989).

———, "Between space and time: Reflections on the geographical imagination," *Annals of the Association of American Geographers*, 80:3 (1990), 418–34.

Janelle, D. G., "Central place development in a time-space framework," *The Professional Geographer*, 20 (1968), 5–10.

Kern, S., *The Culture of Time and Space 1880–1918* (Cambridge, MA: Harvard University Press, 1983).

The Kingston British Whig, 17 November 1883.

Marvin, C., *When Old Technologies Were New: Thinking About Electric Communication in the Late Nineteenth Century* (New York: Oxford University Press, 1988).

Marx, K., *Capital*, vol. 1 (London, 1976).

Monkkonen, E. H., *America Becomes Urban: The Development of US Cities and Towns 1780–1980* (Berkeley: University of California Press, 1988).

The Montreal Daily Star, 4 April 1883.

The Montreal Gazette, 4 April 1883.

The Montreal Star, 19 November 1883.

National Archives of Canada, National Manuscript Collection, negative no. 21,998. Map of Stormont, Dundas, Glengarry, Prescott and Russell Counties, 1862.

———, National Manuscript Collection, negative no. 9,380. C. E. Goad Fire Insurance Map, 1882.

The Ontario Gazette, 9 March 1872.

The Ottawa Daily Citizen, 5 April, 19 November 1883.

Pringle, J. F., *Lunenburgh or the Old Eastern District* (Cornwall, ON: Standard Printing House, 1890, repr. Belleville, ON: Mika Silk Screening Ltd., 1972).

Prude, J., *The Coming of Industrial Order: Town and Factory Life in Rural Massachusetts 1810–1860* (Cambridge: Cambridge University Press, 1983).

Rosenberg, N., *Perspectives on Technology* (Cambridge: Cambridge University Press, 1976).

Ross, E., *Full of Hope and Promise: The Canadas in 1841* (Montreal and Kingston: McGill-Queen's University Press, 1991).

Royal Commission on the Relations of Capital and Labor in Canada, Evidence — Ontario (Ottawa: Queen's Printer and Controller of Stationary, 1889).

Schivelbusch, W., *The Railway Journey: Trains and Travel in the 19th Century* (New York: Urizen Books, 1977).

Senior, E. K., *From Royal Township to Industrial City: Cornwall 1784–1984* (Belleville, ON: Mika Publishing Company, 1984).

Smith, W. H., *Canada: Past, Present and Future, Being an Historical, Geographical, Geological and Statistical Account of Canada West*, vol. 2 (Toronto: Thomas Maclear, 1851).

Stein, J., "Industrialising Cornwall: Time, space and the pace of change in a nineteenth-century Ontario town," unpublished MA thesis, Queen's University, 1992.

———, "Time, space and social discipline: Factory life in Cornwall, Ontario, 1867–1893, *Journal of Historical Geography*, 21:3 (1995), 278–99.

———, "Annihilating space and time: The modernisation of fire-fighting in late nineteenth-century Cornwall, Ontario," *Urban History Review/Revue d'histoire urbaine*, 24:2 (March 1996), 3–11.

Stephens, C., "'The most reliable time': William Bond, the New England railroads, and time-awareness in 19th-century America," *Technology and Culture*, 30:2 (January 1989), 1–24.

Tarr, J. A., "The city and the telegraph: Urban telecommunications in the pre-telephone era," *Journal of Urban History*, 14:1 (1987), 38–80.

Tarr, J. A., and G. Dupuy (eds.), *Technology and the Rise of the Networked City in Europe and America* (Philadelphia: Temple University Press, 1988).

Thompson, E. P., "Time, work-discipline, and industrial capitalism," *Past and Present*, 38 (December 1967), 56–97.

Wade, R. C., *The Urban Frontier: The Rise of Western Cities, 1790–1830* (Cambridge, MA: Harvard University Press, 1959).

Article 2.2
Miriam Wright

Young Men and Technology: Government Attempts to Create a "Modern" Fisheries Workforce in Newfoundland, 1949–70

Issues to Consider

- Wright contends that the "man of the sea" is a social construction dependent on a traditional gender ideology. How do we see this "gender ideology" operating in the response of Newfoundland men to the type of wage labour involved in the developing frozen fish industry?
- Why was it considered important for the state at its various levels to become involved in promoting the frozen fish industry, both in colonial Newfoundland and after the province joined Confederation in 1949?
- How does Wright support her argument that the state has "come to play a role in shaping and mediating gender relations" in the Newfoundland fishery?
- The majority of Wright's sources are government reports and other documents from the national and provincial archives. What other kinds of sources might be helpful to historians dealing, as Wright is, with social relations?
- In what ways is the transformation described by Wright in post–World War II Newfoundland both similar to and different from the changes described by Stein in late 19th-century Ontario?

Making one's living from the sea is an occupation around which whole mythologies have grown. Popularized through songs, stories, and pictures, the "man of the sea" is a romanticized vision of the people who actually make their living fishing. It is a particularly masculine stereotype, depicting a world fraught with danger, hardship, and inhabited by strong, risk-taking men who were socially isolated and resistant to change. Despite the pervasiveness of this image, the reality of gender relations in present and historic fisheries is far more complex, mediated as it is through social and economic relations of work and society. With the advent of heightened levels of state intervention in fishing economies in the second half of the 20th century, state institutions, policies, and practices have also come to play a role in shaping and mediating gender relations. [...]

To understand something of the historic gender relations in the fishery, we need to have a broader knowledge of the changes that were occurring in the economy, as well as an awareness of how a specific gender ideology was part of the fabric of the state's modernization plans. In the years following World War II, the Newfoundland fishing economy was transformed from a predominantly inshore, household-based, saltfish-producing enterprise into an industrialized economy dominated by vertically integrated frozen fish companies.[1] This transition was initially fueled by larger changes in capital, markets, and technology taking place at the international

Source: Miriam Wright, "Young Men and Technology: Government Attempts to Create a 'Modern' Fisheries Workforce in Newfoundland, 1949–70," *Labour/Le Travail* 42 (1998): 143–59.

level, particularly in the United States where quick freezing had been pioneered by large companies such as Birdseye (General Seafoods-General Foods), Booth Fisheries, and Gorton-Pew. In the post-war period, the United States became the primary market for frozen fish and Newfoundland was a major supplier. Early in this transition, the state became involved in supporting this new industry — first the Commission of Government that ruled Newfoundland from 1934 to 1949, then the Canadian federal government, as well as the new provincial administration headed by Premier Joseph Smallwood after Newfoundland joined Confederation. These various levels of the state were involved in financing and supporting this transformation, largely through loans to private frozen fish firms, vessel and gear development projects and through educational training programmes for people in the fishery. Although the state was not united in its methods of assisting the fishery,[2] both federal and provincial governments generally promoted the idea of a centralized, industrialized, and "modernized" fishery.

The state was far from gender-neutral in these interventions and played a role in mediating, and sometimes shaping, gender relations in the fishery. Although some authors have begun to look at the state and women in the fishery in this period,[3] relatively little is known about how the state perceived men and their place in the "modern" fishery. For our purposes, the male breadwinner ideology which [Ruth Roach] Pierson found in the Unemployment Insurance debates may have some relevance for a study of state economic policies and the Newfoundland fishery.[4] British historian Keith McClelland has associated the rise of this ideology with the growth of the industrial economy.[5] Although working class women were an integral part of the labour force from the beginning of the industrial revolution, middle class reformers and male working class trade unions began promoting the middle class domestic ideal in the latter years of the 19th century. Just as the model of the male as the sole family income-earner was a later development in the industrialization process in Britain and North America, this concept was a relatively recent development in Newfoundland. The male breadwinner ideology, which assumed the primacy of male labour, had not previously been a part of the gender relations in outport Newfoundland.

Historically, Newfoundland's gendered division of labour arose out of the needs of the inshore resident fishery and the production of dry salted-codfish known as "shore cure," a product highly valued in the markets of southern Europe.[6] In the Newfoundland inshore fishery, saltfish was produced through the efforts of the entire family. Men, for the most part, caught the fish using small boats and gear such as handlines and cod traps, while the shore crew (consisting of wives, daughters, sisters, and younger sons), would help split and salt the fish.[7] The women would then take the salted fish and spread them onto wooden fish flakes, or racks, to dry in the sun for a week or so until cured. The women tended the fish, taking it in each night, or during inclement weather. Besides curing the fish, women also provided the basic needs of the family by gardening, preserving food, and making clothing. As the transition to an industrialized fishery occurred, however, state planners and the policies they created suggested that women would have a minimal role in the economy and that men should shoulder a larger share of the responsibility for providing for the family. This paper will argue that the male breadwinner model, the dominant gender ideology of western culture (but not of Newfoundland outport culture at the time), was embedded in state economic policies for the Newfoundland fishery in the post–World War II period.

The state's plans for the transformation of the Newfoundland fishery workforce was tied to its plans for "modernizing" the fishery itself. Technology was seen as the key to improving the fishery and the introduction of offshore trawlers, "near-shore" longliners, new gear types, and electronic sounding equipment was part of the larger plan to industrialize the fishery. State planners, however, believed that the men who worked in the Newfoundland fishery needed to be transformed so they could be integrated into the new fishing economy. Fishers were expected to drop their older fishing methods, outlooks, and patterns of occupational pluralism and become "professional" harvesters and processors.

By the 1960s, government training programmes increasingly focused on encouraging young men to work on offshore trawlers. The intensification of offshore fishing by foreign countries in this period, and the demands of the government-funded frozen fish companies for greater quantities of fish, led the federal government to assist in the development of Canada's deepsea fleet. Despite state efforts, however, the difficult working conditions and poor remuneration for trawler crews ensured that the young men in question were reluctant to follow the career path the state encouraged them to take. Although the attempts to recruit young men as trawler crews were not entirely successful, this and the other examples of the government's mediating role helps illustrate the complexity of economy, state, and gender ideology all involved in the construction of a new fisheries workforce.

STATE PLANNERS' REACTIONS TO THE GENDERED DIVISION OF LABOUR IN THE HOUSEHOLD FISHERY

As government officials turned their attentions to the fishery in the 1940s and early 1950s, they began expressing dismay at the existing gender division of labour in the inshore fishery. For the most part, both federal and provincial planners found women's involvement in the household fishery to be anachronistic — a sign that the Newfoundland fishing economy was at a delayed state of development. A provincial Department of Fisheries official, H. C. Winsor, deplored the sight of the outport "woman of 30 who looks 60 with thick ankles, bent back and lined face."[8] The effects of the weather and physical labour, considered "rugged" in a man, were unseemly in a woman. A prevalent theme in the early discussions of the rural economy was the need to eradicate the dependence on female labour.

A federal Department of Fisheries employee, W. F. Doucet, who surveyed the province in 1952 as part of a team investigating the fishery, wondered at the lack of distinction between "public" and "private" in the inshore fishery. The foundation of the male breadwinner/female dependent gender ideology is the assumption that men and women inhabit separate spheres. Men belong to the public world of politics and commerce, while women inhabit the private realm of home and family. Doucet was struck, not only by the different division of labour in this economy, but also the unity of home and workplace. He remarked:

> In these and a few other settlements one is arrested by the cohesiveness of the family and the extent to which the fishery is a family endeavour. The stores, the flakes and the home are one unit. Men catch the fish and women make or cure it.[9]

The fact that Doucet would remark on the nature of the family fishery and women's role within it suggests that this society had a different set of expectations about the roles of men and women from his own. He noted:

> I was happy to see that in relatively few communities is this way of life accepted with passive resignation. Women are gradually "wisening up," probably a direct result of the radio and the movie projector, and are beginning to rebel against their enslavement to the fish flake. This may indicate the dawn of a new era.[10]

Doucet suggested that North American culture, through radio and movies, was leading women to aspire to more purely domestic pursuits. By becoming aware of North American social norms, where the male breadwinner/female dependent model was more dominant, women supposedly would wish to adopt the new culture. In expressing these views, the fisheries planners were trying to impose the hegemonic gender ideology of male breadwinner/female dependent on a society with different gender roles.

The issue of women's participation in the rural economy arose in the first major investigation into the Newfoundland fishery after Confederation. The *Report of the Newfoundland Fisheries Development Committee* of 1953, the work of a group of federal and provincial government representatives, recommended centralization of production through government-supported frozen fish and saltfish plants, the introduction of new technology, as well as small-scale community development.[11] In addition, the report suggested that in the "modern" fishery, men would be the primary breadwinners. The report applauded the removal of women from the fishery, saying it would "allow them to devote their time to their household duties and to live in an atmosphere of human dignity as wives and mothers."[12] Women, it was suggested, did not belong in the market economy and should leave to fulfil their "natural" roles as dependent wives and mothers. Conversely, men would have to take care of their women and not depend directly on their labour to produce fish for market.

Despite the assertions of these government officials, however, the gradual withdrawal of women from fish curing had more to do with economics than American movies. In the 1950s, the rise of the frozen fish industry meant that women's shore work was no longer required to the same extent. After women stopped making shore cure, however, few could afford to depend solely on the labour of their husbands. Many women moved into jobs at the frozen fish processing plants that were built on the island during this period. By the 1980s, women made up 50 per cent of the workforce in those plants, but remained for the most part in the lowest paying jobs in positions deemed "unskilled" such as packing and trimming.[13]

MALE BREADWINNER IDEOLOGY AND FISHERIES POLICIES

The belief of fisheries planners that women would leave the fishery was tied to their assumption that men would become the primary breadwinners for their families. This transformation of men into sole family income-earners, however, was tied to the broader plan to replace the saltfish industry with the frozen fish industry, and to replace the rural household system with the relations of production and consumption of an industrial society. This meant encouraging men to learn to operate the new technology of the modern fishery, as well as giving them skills to allow them to earn more money to make up for the loss of the economic activities of the other family members. Providing men with skills and technological training was considered crucial to enable them to increase their fishing efficiency, raise their productivity, and increase their incomes. With their higher incomes, fishing families could purchase items for their daily needs, rather than relying on the labour of all family members. "Professionalization" of fishers, meaning that men would become more specialized in their skills and activities so that they would spend more of their time fishing, was one of the major themes in the Newfoundland educational programmes. No longer would the fisher be a "jack-of-all-trades," as the Newfoundland Director of Fisheries Training described them, but the bearer of highly specialized technical knowledge.[14] Creating a new fisheries workforce, then, encompassed both the explicit needs of a modern, industrial society (a technologically-trained workforce) and the implicit belief that males, in their new roles as primary family breadwinners, would fulfil those needs.

Several fisheries income support programmes of the period reveal the inherent assumption that males were the main income-earners for the family. In 1957, a new Unemployment Insurance programme for fishers and other seasonal workers was created. For the first time, fishers, working either singly or in fishing crews, would receive benefits based on their sales of fresh or salted fish to registered buyers. The male breadwinner model which Pierson argued permeated earlier Unemployment Insurance debates was inherent in the new programme for fishers. Women were explicitly excluded from making contributions or receiving benefits if they were married to any member of the fishing crew.[15] If married women did work as members of the crew, their shares were attributed to their husbands. Since most fishing crews were comprised of family members, this effectively proscribed wives' direct involvement in fishing operations, either through working on the boat, or curing the catch on shore. Implied in this policy is the assumption that the labour, and the fruits thereof, belonged to the men, not the women. Men, according to the Unemployment Insurance programme, were workers and should be rewarded as such. Women should be discouraged from working, but if they did, their labour was considered property of the male head of household.

The male breadwinner model was further strengthened by the practice of issuing social benefits of various kinds based on the marital status of the fisher. Unemployment insurance benefits, for example, were slightly higher for those fishers with dependents than those who were single.[16] An emergency assistance programme for those experiencing a catch failure in the inshore fishery in 1965 also made similar distinctions. Fishers short of qualifying insurable weeks received a flat rate of $200 that winter if they were single and $350 if they were married.[17] Training programmes organized by the provincial Department of Fisheries in the 1950s and early 1960s, but partially funded through the federal Department of Labour, also provided separate daily allowances for single and married men while they were participating in the courses.[18] No such programmes of financial assistance were extended to the female members of the workforce.

TRAINING YOUNG MEN FOR THE MODERN FISHERY

Apart from income support initiatives, both federal and provincial governments were involved in establishing various technological training programmes. Technology has long been seen in western culture as a "masculine" domain, and male workers' attempts to control the introduction of new technology into the workforce has been a prevalent theme in recent studies of the gendered labour process.[19] Unlike some of the more traditional trades where workplace skills were transmitted from worker to worker or through experience, the skills needed to operate offshore vessels and processing plant machinery were new. There were some concerns, however, about the efficacy of educating older men, partly because of the relatively high illiteracy rate among outport fishers, and partly because of a presumed reluctance on the part of the fishers to try new methods.[20] W. C. MacKenzie, for example, complained about how the "deep-seated resistance to change" among the inshore fishers hampered efforts to decrease dependence on small boat fishing.[21] Young men, believed to be more adaptable to modern ways, became the focus of the fisheries training programmes. Pervasive was the idea that the new young men of the fisheries would have to be fundamentally different from their fathers. In fact, the planners believed that technical training in an institution would soon replace the "traditional" forms of fisheries knowledge passed down from fathers to sons.

Not only would they have to learn new skills, but the young men would have to adopt a "modern" spirit, a mind-set conducive to technological change. In 1954, Robert Hart, the chief supervisor of the Industrial Development Service in the federal Department of Fisheries, discussed the merits of training programmes. He argued, "I can think of no more worthy cause … than in preparing the minds of the young men in Newfoundland to cope with an advancing fisheries development programme."[22] Such a programme, he claimed, would only be effective if the courses helped "create a new concept in their minds," along with the practical skills they would gain.

This attitude can also be found in an earlier report written by federal Deputy Minister of Fisheries, Stewart Bates, for Nova Scotia. Bates declared that technical training was crucial to develop the "desired habits of mind."[23] The *Report of the Newfoundland Fisheries Development Committee* also contained references to the need to develop a progressive frame of mind, and specifically an "industrial discipline" among the workers.[24] Not only would the young men of the modern fishery workforce be capable, technically skilled breadwinners, they would also be accepting of North American values and way of life.

Although federal officials sometimes spoke about the need to educate the young men, it was Premier Joseph R. Smallwood who "adopted the cause." In 1962 he called a fisheries conference and invited fishers, plant owners, government officials, and others connected to the fishery. The fishers themselves talked mainly about their concerns for obtaining better prices, problems with securing bait, the lack of funds for improving their equipment, and the threat posed by foreign fishing trawlers. In his final address, Smallwood acknowledged these issues, yet chose to single out the problem of unemployed young men and declared it to be the single gravest crisis facing the Newfoundland fishery. "These young men," he told the crowd,

> around our outports today are the blood and brawn that built the British Empire. They can very quickly go to seed … if they are allowed to degenerate into cigarette smoking, loungers and loafers hanging around the rocks, living partly on the dole … without any real driving ambition to work.[25]

Just as Pierson found that unemployment was seen as a "man's" problem, Smallwood too was concerned that young men would not find their place in society as workers.

Smallwood believed that technology was the key to attracting young men to the fishery. "If they're going back into the fishery, that fishery has to be a far more up-to-date thing, a far more modern thing."[26] Smallwood was widely known for his ability to pull the rhetorical strings to political advantage, and his campaign for educating the young men in Newfoundland was partly related to his attempts to retrench popular support after some setbacks in the 1950s.[27] Nevertheless, significant is Smallwood's emphasis on the need to shape this valuable resource, the young men of Newfoundland, into the workforce of the future. Both the young men and the fishery needed to be transformed, introduced to the industrial age, and together they would build a new North American industrial society in Newfoundland.

The emphasis on young men and technology as the perfect partnership for the modern fishery was embodied in the College of Fisheries, Navigation, Marine Engineering and Electronics, which opened in St. John's in 1964. Of the five general streams of study offered, three were directly related to crewing or maintaining offshore fishing vessels — Nautical Science, Mechanical Engineering, and Electrical Engineering. The others included Naval Architecture, which provided training in shipbuilding and design, and the Department of Food Technology which organized in-plant training programmes for fish processing plant employees.

The overwhelming focus of the College of Fisheries, in its early years, however, was training young men to work as trawler crews. Trawler technology was considered essential for the development of the frozen fish industry in Newfoundland in the first fifteen years after Confederation. The frozen fish industry was relatively new to the province, with a half dozen small companies having been established during World War II. Through loan assistance from the provincial government these vertically integrated companies were able to expand their operations and build more frozen fish plants around the island. This made them, however, heavily dependent on trawlers to obtain a sufficient supply of fish to keep the plants operating at full capacity throughout the year.

Getting young men to join the trawler crews was an integral part of the company owners' plans to make their businesses viable. They always assumed, however, that the new trawler workforce would be male. In the pre-Confederation fishery, men had done most of the harvesting, with women only rarely going out on the water. Government and industry people alike assumed that this gender division of labour would continue into the modern era. Also, the unique workplace conditions of offshore trawler work meant that the people who worked together also had to live together during the voyages. The company owners wanted technologically-trained, physically strong workers, all of the same gender. Although in the years that followed, many women began fishing on inshore vessels, the offshore trawler work environments remained exclusively male.[28]

The College of Fisheries represented a new era — not only a new industrial fishery, but also a new way of acquiring knowledge and skills apart from the traditions of their fathers. It represented a break from the past and a panacea for the problems of the Newfoundland fishery. Knowledge would no longer be passed from father to son, but from technological expert to student within an institutional setting provided by the state. An unbounded faith in the ability of "technological man" to solve the problems of the world was behind this approach to industrializing the fishery. In the process, the young men would be moulded into technologically-trained, family breadwinners.

The enthusiasm with which various government planners greeted the opening of the college displayed the hope placed in this new direction. A scientist with the Fisheries Research Board, C. H. Castell, who was invited to attend the opening ceremonies, remarked how Smallwood had effectively orchestrated the event to put the young men front and centre.[29] Noting that Smallwood was a "past-master of a showman," Castell claimed the ceremony was replete with such dignitaries as members of the provincial cabinet, the Chief Justice, and members of the staff of the college sitting on the stage. The front rows of the hall were left empty.

> After some stirring music by a local choir of folk singers the 150 young men, dressed in their black sweaters, bright crests and gray trousers, marched in. They looked wonderful and behaved themselves well.[30]

According to Castell, Smallwood made a point of emphasizing that Newfoundland was taking a step into the future by training these young men in the latest fisheries technology. As Castell noted, however, the college was far from prepared for the new students at that point, with only a few instructors appointed or classes organized.

Smallwood's enthusiasm about the young men and technology, and the hopes for a better way of life, was echoed by other fisheries officials. Dr. D. L. Cooper, who was employed by the provincial Department of Fisheries, argued in a report for the Atlantic Rural Development Agency that:

> ... the hope of a bright future in the fishery lies in the young men, those still in school, those who will enter school, those young enough and with sufficient basic education to undergo a rigorous upgrading to the normal standard required for technical education in a profession that is developing with such speed.[31]

Likewise, an article in the federal fisheries publication, *Fisheries of Canada*, enthused about the presence of the young men at the College of Fisheries, and the promise they held for a highly developed fishery. "Among the students," the article claimed,

> are tomorrow's skippers and mates of the streamlined and efficient sea-going fishing vessels: the marine engineers who will operate engine rooms grown highly sophisticated in a world of advancing technology.[32]

The future would be a world of advancing technology, guided and controlled by the trained, knowledgeable young men building a better way of life. Implicit was the belief that these young men would no longer have to rely on the labour of their wives to make a living.

POLICY INTO PRACTICE: THE DIFFICULTIES OF SECURING OFFSHORE TRAWLER WORKERS

Translating those visions of the new industrial society and the men who would develop it into practice, however, proved to be a challenge. Young men did not flock to the trawler jobs as both government officials and company owners had expected. Amid all the enthusiasm about technology bringing with it a better life, those promoting the offshore fishery did not seem to realize the significance of the profound workplace changes. Unlike the inshore fishery, trawler crews went to sea for up to ten days at a time, where they were expected to operate the trawls, and to split and ice the catch. The work was tiring and dangerous, particularly on the older side trawlers that were in use by the companies in the 1960s. Living conditions were cramped, and unlike other industrial workers, the trawler crews could not go home after their shifts were finished. Most trawler workers would only see their families once or twice a month, when the ship made a one- or two-day stopover in port to unload the catch and obtain supplies. Stress on family life was considerable, as the spouses remaining at home were left with the task of caring for children or aging parents. The men working on the offshore trawlers had to live without daily contact with relatives and friends.[33]

Besides the difficult working conditions, until the mid-1970s, there were no guaranteed wages for trawler crews. At one level, the offshore fishery was industrialized, in that the trawlers were owned by vertically integrated fishing companies, which controlled the harvesting, processing, and marketing of fishery products. Yet, the company–crew relations had not yet made the transition to an industrial relationship. Vestiges of an older payment arrangement traditionally used in the Newfoundland Banks fishery, a deepsea, schooner/dory fishery which had declined by the mid-20th century, appeared in the new offshore trawler fishery. In the Banks fishery, as in the trawler fishery, the people who fished on these vessels received a share of the catch, rather than a guaranteed wage. Typically, the company which owned the boat received one share, the captain another, and the crew divided the remaining share. If the catch was poor, instead of taking home money, the crew might end up owing the company money for food. Instead of being considered company employees, the trawler workers were designated "co-adventurers." The term was ironic, however, as it implied the workers had some stake in the enterprise. Trawler workers did not have shares in the vessel or the company, and had very little control over their working lives. Factors such as the type, size, age, and condition of the vessel itself, as well as the skills of the captain, greatly affected the ability of the trawler crews to make a catch that would produce good returns. According to a study on working conditions in the offshore industry, trawler crews in the 1960s did not even have formal, signed contracts with vessel owners — they simply showed up at the port when it was time to embark on a fishing trip.[34] Despite the mythology of the fisherman as a risk-taker, the young men of Newfoundland, for the most part, were unwilling to take the kind of gamble that was offered by the large fishing companies. Clearly, the transition from a rural, household economy to an industrial economy was not smooth. The fact that young men for the most part resisted the government's attempts to recruit them indicates that transforming the social and economic relations of the fishery, and changing the way that men worked and lived, was not uncontested.

Indeed, working on a trawler was considered a job of last resort by young men in the 1960s and early 1970s, and the men showed it by the extremely high turnover rate for trawler crews, and the companies had difficulty in attracting and keeping workers. John Proskie, an economist with the federal Department of Fisheries, studied nine trawlers in 1966.[35] Of the nine vessels he studied, three were 120-foot trawlers and six were 130-foot trawlers. Most vessels sailed short-handed, as only 7.6 per cent of the trips for the 120-foot ships and 4.7 per cent of the trips for the 130-foot ships were made with a full crew of fourteen and sixteen respectively.

Indications of the high turnover rate can be found in the statistics relating to the total number of men employed on these vessels over the course of one year. The three 120-foot vessels which had positions for a total of 42 workers actually employed 84 different men in 1966. Likewise, the six 130-foot boats with positions available for 96 men employed 277 men. According to another study on working conditions in the offshore fishery, most of the men who worked on trawlers in the period from 1956–1968 only did so casually, or part-time.[36] The fact that jobs were plentiful in other parts of Canada at that time also contributed to the high turnover rate.

Not only did fisheries planners underestimate the young men's lack of enthusiasm for the jobs in the newly-industrialized sector of the fishery, the expected move of people from the inshore to the offshore fishery did not occur. In fact, there were indications that many of the men who did take jobs on the trawlers were most likely not sons of inshore fishers. No complete demographic study of trawler crews of the 1960s has been done, but evidence suggests that there may have been a connection between the 1960s trawler crews and the older Banks fishery. The Banks fishery was concentrated in a few communities such as Grand Bank, Burin, and Harbour Breton. Although they fished from schooners equipped with dories rather than from other trawlers, the men of the Banks fishery were accustomed to working on the high seas for weeks at a time. When the Banks fishery declined in the 1940s, many of the younger men of those communities left to obtain jobs in the offshore fishery of Nova Scotia. Others, however, remained and worked in the growing offshore fishery controlled by the frozen fish companies. A report from the Newfoundland Frozen Fish Trades Association on training of trawler crews claimed that many of their trawler workers were older men who had formerly worked in the Banks fishery.[37] As well, a survey done in 1967 found that the majority of trawler workers came from families where one or more male relatives had also worked on trawlers, suggesting that recruitment occurred through families and community ties.[38] If, as this preliminary evidence indicates, there was a connection between the Banks communities and the new offshore trawler fishery, this raises a number of questions about recruitment patterns and attachments to the offshore fishery. How many of the young men who went through the College of Fisheries programmes remained in the offshore sector, and for how long, as opposed to those with connections to the Banks fishery? Did a familiarity with an offshore fishery, albeit of a rather different kind, make for an easier transition to life on the trawlers? These and other questions about the impact of fisheries development on Newfoundland fishers remain.

One of the foundations of the industrial development project, the steady integration of Newfoundland men into the offshore fishery, was far from secure by the mid-1960s. Both government officials and frozen fish company owners became alarmed at the lack of interest on the part of young men in the offshore fishery. The labour shortage became more acute after the federal government introduced the Fisheries Development Act in 1966, which provided assistance on a greater scale for companies needing to acquire trawlers. In fact, increasing Canada's trawler fleet became a major emphasis of federal policy as a response to the growing numbers of foreign vessels fishing off the shores of Newfoundland and Nova Scotia. In an attempt to encourage young men to fill the deepsea fishery courses at the Newfoundland College of Fisheries, government and industry joined forces.[39] The provincial government quickly organized the Special Committee to Plan Emergency Action on Manpower Training for the Fishing Industry. This committee estimated the numbers of future workers needed in the industry and began organizing "crash courses" for trawler crews at the College of Fisheries. As well, the Newfoundland Frozen Fish Trades Association submitted formal briefs to both the Royal Commission on Education and Youth, and to the provincial government endorsing the "crash course" programme.[40] In fact, the frozen fish company owners suggested that training programmes be held in Burin because, as they said, "the young people of the south coast are ... traditionally deepsea minded." Several hundred young men went through the programme over the next few years.[41] Gradually the total number of trawlers increased from 36 vessels in 1963 employing 480 men to 64 vessels in 1972 employing 1300 men, yet high turnover rates for the trawler crews continued.[42]

The turning point for the offshore fishery came in the 1974–1975 season, when the newly-unionized trawler crews staged a strike for union recognition, and to overturn the "co-adventurer" status.[43] According to Leslie Harris, chair of the Board of Conciliation tasked with resolving this issue, fish landings had been declining as a result of intensive foreign fishing, exacerbating the problem of low earnings, when the earning of the trawler workers was dependent on the size of the catch.[44] Harris made the argument that trawler workers deserved to be treated in a similar manner to skilled labourers. He argued that trawler workers were akin to working class labourers, but without the comforts and security of a guaranteed wage. Harris also claimed that trawler work needed to be "professionalized," elevated to the level of a skilled tradesmen. With higher incomes that reflected the "skill" of the worker, and the danger and discomfort of deepsea fishing, the problem of encouraging young men to join the trawler fleets would be alleviated. The companies finally agreed to provide a degree of security in the incomes of trawler workers. Other workplace innovations were instituted, such as the improved safety and working conditions on the vessels. These changes, together with the shortage of work in other parts of the country, contributed to the gradual stabilization of the trawler crews for the offshore fishery.

Although the working conditions and remuneration of trawler workers improved, there was never a move to "professionalize," or recognize the "skills" of female processing plant workers. The move to improve incomes and working conditions of trawler workers was a gendered process, as ideas about skill and the needs of a family breadwinner were wound into it. The only major concession that female fish plant workers received was that in the early 1970s, the Newfoundland government rescinded the law which permitted female workers to be paid a lower minimum wage than males.

CONCLUSION

The transition from saltfish to frozen fish, from a household economy to something resembling a North American consumer industrial society forever altered the lives of the fishing people of Newfoundland. The expanding scale and scope of state intervention in the fishery in the post-war era also played a significant role in shaping the possibilities open to men and women. Fisheries planners brought with them their assumptions about gender roles inherent in the dominant gender ideologies of mainstream North American culture. In fact, they tried to create a new workforce, a new working class for the modernized Newfoundland fishery — a fishery characterized by centralized, vertically integrated frozen fish companies and the latest technological equipment for harvesting and processing. They envisioned the new fishery worker, first and foremost as male, the sole family breadwinner, trained in technological skills needed for the industrialized fishery. With his increased efficiency and productivity, the family breadwinner would presumably earn enough money so that his wife and children would no longer have to contribute to the production of saltfish for market.

The government fishery officials' plans for a new fishery workforce, however, did not go entirely as expected. The anticipated flood of young men into the offshore sector did not materialize. Only after wages stabilized and working conditions improved did working on a trawler appeal to people in Newfoundland. Visions of women being "freed" to follow domestic pursuits while their husbands laboured to bring home the family income never quite materialized either, as many women took jobs as trimmers and packers in the frozen fish processing plants. The legacy of state intervention and the gender ideology that was a part of it, however, has remained, and become embedded in the complex relationship of economy, society, and the Newfoundland fishery.

NOTES

1. Miriam Wright, "Newfoundland and Canada: The Evolution of Fisheries Development Policies, 1940–1966," PhD thesis, Memorial University of Newfoundland, 1997.

2. Ruth Roach Pierson, "Gender and the Unemployment Insurance Debates in Canada, 1934–1940," *Labour/Le Travail*, 25 (Spring 1990), 77–103.

3. Wright, "Newfoundland and Canada," chapters Three and Four. The provincial government provided direct assistance to private enterprise through loans from 1949 to 1966, whereas the federal government preferred more generalized support through public works projects, experimental gear and fishing programs, and educational training.

4. Patricia M. Connelly and Martha MacDonald, "State Policy, the Household and Women's Work in the Fishery," *Journal of Canadian Studies*, 26, 4 (1991–92), 18–32; Barbara Neis, "From 'Shipped Girls' to 'Brides of the State': The Transition from Familial to Social Patriarchy in the Newfoundland Fishing Industry," *Canadian Journal of Regional Science*, 16, 2 (1993), 185–211; Miriam Wright, "Women, Men and the Modern Fishery: Images of Gender in Government Plans for the Canadian Atlantic Fisheries," in C. McGrath, B. Neis, M. Porter, eds., *Their Lives and Times: Women in Newfoundland and Labrador* (St. John's 1995).

5. Keith McClelland, "Masculinity and the 'Representative Artisan' in Britain 1850–1880," in Michael Roper and John Tosh, eds., *Manful Assertions: Masculinities in Britain since 1800* (London 1991).

6. See Hilda Chaulk Murray, *More Than 50%: A Woman's Life in a Newfoundland Outport, 1900–1950* (St. John's 1979); Marilyn Porter, "'She Was Skipper of the Shore Crew': Notes on the History of the Sexual Division of Labour in Newfoundland," *Labour/Le Travail*, 15 (Spring 1985), 105–23.

7. These gender divisions were flexible, at times. Men sometimes helped with the shore work, while women very occasionally fished. Historically, women also worked as cooks on the Labrador schooners, vessels outfitted to fish in the summer months off the Labrador coast.

8. Provincial Archives of Newfoundland and Labrador (hereafter PANL), GN 34/2, file Newfoundland Fisheries Development Authority (hereafter NFDA) H. C. Winsor, H. C. Winsor to Edwin Burdell, 4 August 1958.

9. National Archives of Canada (hereafter NAC), RG 23, v. 1749, file 794-17-1 [4], W. F. Doucet to I. S. McArthur, Markets and Economics Service, 6 August 1952.

10. NAC, RG 23, v. 1749, file 794-17-1 [4], W. F. Doucet to I. S. McArthur, Markets and Economics Service, 6 August 1952.

11. Newfoundland and Canada, *Report of the Newfoundland Fisheries Development Committee* (St. John's 1953).

12. Newfoundland and Canada, *Report of the Newfoundland Fisheries Development Committee*, 102.

13. Susan Williams, *Our Lives Are at Stake: Women and the Fishery Crisis in Newfoundland and Labrador* (St. John's 1996); Fishery Research Group, *The Social Impact of Technological Change in Newfoundland's Deepsea Fishery* (St. John's 1986).

14. PANL, GN 66/2/C, file Annual and Periodic Reports on Progress of Fisheries Training Programme, "Fisheries Training Progress in Newfoundland" by R. H. Squires, 29 October 1956.

15. PANL, GN 34/2, file NFDA Unemployment Insurance, "Changes in Unemployment Insurance Regulations Applicable to Fishermen," Ottawa, November 1958.

16. NAC, RG 23, v. 1137, file 721-64-3 [4], "Fisherman's Handbook on Unemployment Insurance, First Edition," Ottawa: Unemployment Insurance Commission, no date.

17. PANL, GN 34/2, file 11/4/16.2 vol. 1, Federal Department of Fisheries Press Release, 15 January 1966.

18. PANL, GN 34/2, file 214/15 vol. l, Administrative Assistant to R. H. Squires, Director of Vocational Training, 1 April 1959.

19. See Ava Baron, ed., *Work Engendered: Toward a New History of American Labor* (Ithaca 1991).

20. PANL, GN 34/2, file 11/80/7, ARDA Study No. 1024 —"Education" by D. L. Cooper, 3 September 1964.

21. NAC, RG 23, v. 1751, file 794-17-1 [14], W. C. MacKenzie to Deputy Minister of Fisheries, no date.

22. NAC, RG 23, v. 1751, file 794-17-7 [1], Robert Hart, chief supervisor, Industrial Development Service, to Otto Young, Fisheries Research Board, 29 May 1954.

23. Stewart Bates, *The Report on the Canadian Atlantic Sea-Fishery* (Halifax 1944), 22.

24. Newfoundland and Canada, *Report of the Newfoundland Fisheries Development Committee*, 72.

25. PANL, MG 644, file 287, "Proceedings, Fisheries Convention, September 27, 1962," 4–5.

26. PANL, MG 644, file 287, "Proceedings, Fisheries Convention, September 27, 1962," 5.

27. In the 1950s, several of Smallwood's key cabinet ministers left politics in opposition to Smallwood's policies. Also, Smallwood's actions in decertifying the International Wood Workers of America union during the 1959 loggers' strike were the target of much criticism both within and outside the province. See Richard Gwyn, *Smallwood, the Unlikely Revolutionary* (Toronto 1972).

28. According to the Canada 1991 Census, women comprised 10 per cent of inshore fishers, but none of the off-shore trawler workers. The large factory freezer trawlers of the former Soviet Union, which began fishing in the waters off the coast of Newfoundland in the 1960s, did have female workers aboard.

29. NAC, RG 23, Accession 90-91/230, Box 10, file 711-29-7 [1], "Impressions of the Newfoundland School of Fisheries" by C. H. Castell, 5 March 1964.

30. NAC, RG 23, Accession 90-91/230, Box 10, file 711-29-7 [l], "Impressions of the Newfoundland School of Fisheries" by C. H. Castell, 5 March 1964.

31. PANL, GN 34/2, file 11/80/7, ARDA Study No. 1024, 3 September 1964.

32. *Fisheries of Canada*, 19, 9 (March 1967), 4.

33. Fisheries Research Group, *The Social Impact*, 171–204.

34. Fisheries Research Group, *The Social Impact*, 171–204.

35. *Fisheries of Canada*, 20, 8 (1968), 13–9.

36. Fisheries Research Group, *The Social Impact*, 171–204.

37. PANL, MG 644, file 340, "A Brief Concerning National Fisheries Development Program Submitted to the Federal-Provincial Conference on Fisheries Development by the Fisheries Council of Canada — Appendix I, The Frozen Fish Trades Association Limited, St. John's, Newfoundland," 20 January 1964.

38. Fisheries Research Group, *The Social Impact*, 174.

39. PANL, GN 34/2, file NFDA Manpower Training, W. F. Compton, President, College of Fisheries to E. Harvey, NFFTA, 19 February 1966.

40. Centre for Newfoundland Studies Archives, Memorial University of Newfoundland, J. R. Smallwood Papers, file 3.12.047, "Brief–Hon. J. R. Smallwood, Premier of Newfoundland — Manpower Requirements — Deepsea Trawlers and Shore Processing Plants," by E. A. Harvey, Frozen Fish Trades Association, February 1966; "Brief by the Frozen Fish Trades Association Limited to the Royal Commission on Education and Youth," 1 March 1966.

41. PANL, GN 34/2, file NFDA Fisheries College 1963–1970, Cyril Banikhin, Director of Administration, College of Fisheries to Ross Young, 19 March 1968.

42. Fisheries Research Group, *The Social Impact*, 171–204.

43. For background on the trawler strike, see David Macdonald, *Power Begins at the Cod End: The Newfoundland Trawlerman's Strike, 1974–75* (St. John's 1980).

44. Leslie Harris, *Report of the Conciliation Board appointed in the matter of the Fishing Industry (collective bargaining) Act and in the matter of a dispute between Newfoundland Fishery, Food and Allied Workers, Local 465 and B.C. Packers Ltd., Atlantic Fish, Division of Consolidated Foods Ltd., National Sea Products Ltd., Fishery Products Ltd., and Booth Fisheries* (St. John's 1974), 28–53.

Document 2.1

Report of Commission to Enquire into the Necessity of a New Brunswick Factory Act

Appointed to inspect factories and inquire into the need and possibilities for regulatory legislation to protect the health and safety of workers (especially women and children), the commission drafted a New Brunswick Factory Act ("An Act for the Protection of Persons Employed in Factories") that was presented to, and eventually passed by, the provincial legislature. One of the commissioners, Emma Fiske, was the first woman to serve on a commission of enquiry in New Brunswick. John Palmer, who served as chair of the commission, was an important industrialist and owner of a Fredericton shoe factory.

Issues to Consider

- How would you assess the commissioners' assertion in their cover letter to the lieutenant governor that they received no complaints from employees of the manufactories they visited?
- There was a general consensus among the business owners that legislation regulating factory labour would be harmful to their companies. What might be the reasons for this opinion? How might it actually be in their best interests, from the standpoint of production and profit, to support such legislation?
- What is the role defined for the government in this legislation? For the employer?
- What do official documents such as this, prepared by government-appointed commissioners for the specific task of informing legislation, tell us about the conditions of work and the life of the working class? What do such documents *not* tell us? What kind of documents would a historian want to have in order to fill out and balance official documents?

To His Honour the Honourable Jabez Bunting Snowball, D. C. L., L. L. D., Lieutenant-Governor-in-Council.

MAY IT PLEASE YOUR HONOUR:

Your Commissioners appointed to investigate as to the necessity of a Factory Act in the Province of New Brunswick, and to suggest Amendments to the Bill which was before the Legislature, during the session of 1904, beg to report:

That they have visited the several factories in Saint John, Campbellton, Newcastle, Chatham, Fredericton, Marysville, Woodstock, Saint Stephen and Moncton, and in such several places have examined and heard numerous witnesses.

Source: New Brunswick, Commission to Enquire into the Necessity of a Factory Act, *Report of Commissioners Appointed to Enquire into and Investigate as to the Necessity of a Factory Act in the Province of New Brunswick, New Brunswick, 1905* (King's Printer: Fredericton, N.B., 1906). Also available online at http://www.lib.unb.ca/Texts/NBHistory/Commissions/bin/read_commission.cgi?file=es38r0T&dir=ES38.

While they have found many of the factories in a very creditable condition, there are some, to which, in the opinion of your Commissioners, an improved condition would be beneficial, as to the protection of the health and safety (in case of fire) of the employees.

The weight of the testimony was that while there was no objection to a Factory Act, no absolute necessity existed for it at the present time.

Your Commissioners found no complaints from the employees as to their condition and all seemed well satisfied with their treatment by their several employers.

Your Commissioners found a feeling existing among some of the larger manufacturers that it would be unwise to pass legislation which might interfere with the investment of capital in manufactories, for the reason that in this Province these industries are in their infancy and should be encouraged, rather than impeded.

Your Commissioners have drafted a Factory Act, which they respectfully submit for Your Honour's consideration.

We have the honour to be, Sir,
Your Honour's most obedient servants,

JOHN PALMER, Chairman.
EMMA S. FISKE,
CHARLES MCDONALD,
MICHAEL J. KELLY,
KILGOUR SHIVES.

Dated this 1st day of March, 1905.

BILL. AN ACT FOR THE PROTECTION OF PERSONS EMPLOYED IN FACTORIES.

Be it enacted by the Lieutenant-Governor and Legislative Assembly as follows:

1. This Act shall be known as "The New Brunswick Factories' Act, 1905;" [...]
3. No child shall be employed in any factory, except in special cases authorized in writing by the Inspector.
4. The Lieutenant-Governor in Council may, from time to time, by Order in Council, notice of which shall be published in the Royal Gazette, prohibit the employment of girls under the age of 18 and boys, under the age of 16, in factories, the work of which is deemed by the Lieutenant-Governor in Council to be dangerous or unwholesome.
5. To employ in a factory any young girl or woman shall be deemed to be unlawful, and so that the health of such young girl or woman is likely to be permanently injured, if, in that factory, there is a contravention of the following provisions of this section, that is to say:
   (a) It shall not be lawful for a young girl or woman to be employed for more than ten hours in one day, nor more than sixty hours in one week, unless a different apportionment of the hours of labor per day has been made for the purpose of giving a shorter day's work on Saturday.

(b) In every factory the employer shall allow every young girl and woman therein employed not less than one hour at noon each day for meals, but such hour shall not be counted as part of the time herein limited as respects the employment of young girls and women.

6. Where any young girl or woman is employed on any day to a later hour than seven o'clock in the afternoon, she shall on every such day, and in addition to the hour for the noon-day meal hereinbefore provided for, be allowed not less than forty-five minutes for another or evening meal, between five and eight of the clock in the afternoon. [...]

11. (1) Every factory shall be kept in a cleanly state, and free from effluvia of any drain, privy or any other nuisance.

(2) A factory shall not be so overcrowded while work is carried on therein as to be injurious to the health of the persons employed therein, but shall contain 300 cubic feet of air space to each employee.

(3) Every factory shall be ventilated in such a manner as to render harmless, so far as is reasonably practicable, gases, vapors, dust or other impurities generated in the course of the manufacturing process or handicraft carried on therein that may be injurious to health.

(4) In every factory there shall be kept provided a sufficient number and description of privies, earth or water closets and urinals for the employees of such factory; such closets and urinals shall at all times be kept clean and well ventilated, and a separate set thereof shall be provided for the use of male and female employees, and shall have respectively separate approaches.

(5) A factory in which there is a contravention of this section, or of the regulations made for the enforcement of this section, shall be deemed to be kept unlawfully, and so that the health of any person employed therein is likely to be permanently injured, and the employer shall, because thereof, be deemed to be guilty of a contravention of the provisions of this Act. [...]

34. If a factory is not kept in conformity with this Act, the Court of Summary Jurisdiction, in addition to or instead of inflicting a fine or penalty or other punishment upon the employer, may order certain means to be adopted by the employer, within the time named by the Court, for the purpose of bringing his factory into conformity with this Act; the Court may also, upon application, enlarge the time so named; but if, after the expiration of the time named or enlarged by subsequent order, the order is not complied with, the employer shall be liable to a fine not exceeding $10 for every day that such non-compliance continues.

Document 2.2

Interview with Mrs. Jill Halpenny

In this excerpt from an interview, Mrs. Jill Halpenny discusses her experience of working at Eaton's in Toronto as a teenager during the Great War. Her widowed mother had emigrated from England just before the war; they settled in a basement apartment in Toronto. The war itself, as historians have remarked, was fought as much in the factories as in the trenches, making the home front integral to the war effort and accelerating the process of industrialization. The war also brought large numbers of Canadian women into the workforce.

Issues to Consider

- What does Mrs. Halpenny's recollection suggest about the experiences of women workers in the early 20th century and, more specifically, during the Great War?
- What arguments might an employer such as Eaton's use to justify the poor working conditions? Why would the predominantly female workforce comply?

I was sewing at Eaton's, making blouses. Summer we worked on winter clothes, and winter we worked on summer clothes. There was a big room with rows and rows of sewing machines, power machines. I was tucking blouses and sometimes making the sleeves. You never finished a garment up. Some days you'd be working on sleeves; another time you'd be working on the tucking machine, putting tucks in them; some would be working on collars. I remember my number yet: "1888"! They'd throw a bundle over to you. "Get that through. They're waiting for it in the store." We had to work hard. We worked piecework, and if we made five or six dollars a week, that was good. We didn't dare complain. We just rushed it through. We had a lady overseer. Nobody else bothered us. But if you weren't satisfactory, you were let out. I don't remember my being let out, only when it came a slack time, and then they would call you in again when they had more work. If you got a better job, well, you took the better job.

   You were kept busy. There was no coffee break or anything like that. We worked from eight o'clock till six, with an hour for lunch. At lunch, we sat where we worked, on benches, and we ate our lunch off them. We had to take our own tea, and it wasn't bags like it is now — it was loose. We took that with us and got some sugar and just had them scalded. Oh, we had to sit right by our own machines. That's all we had — no lunchroom.

Source: Reprinted from D. Read, ed., *The Great War and Canadian Society: An Oral History* (Toronto: New Hogtown Press, 1978), 168.

Document 2.3

The Canadian UAW-CIO Win the Peace Plan

The organization known today as the Canadian Auto Workers has a long and militant history in Canada, especially in Ontario, where the majority of the automobile manufacturing plants (mostly American-based) are located. In 1937, a major strike at the General Motors plant in Oshawa, Ontario, led to the establishment in Canada of the U.S.- based Congress of Industrial Organizations (CIO). Unlike the American Federation of Labor, which had advocated organization along craft lines, the CIO promoted a more radical industrial unionism that organized all workers in a particular industry. By World War II, the UAW-CIO was the largest union in Canada. In 1944, the Mackenzie King Liberal government passed legislation guaranteeing labour the right to organize and to bargain collectively. In 1946, a successful strike by 17,000 workers at the Ford plant in Windsor, Ontario, where the UAW-CIO demanded recognition, led to acceptance of the Rand Formula. Named after the appointed arbitrator, Mr. Justice Ivan Rand of the Supreme Court, the formula provided for compulsory "check-off" union dues for all plant employees whether or not they belonged to the union.

Issues to Consider

- This plan was prepared at a UAW-CIO convention during the final year of World War II. What was the UAW-CIO's stand on the war, and what did it suggest about workers' attitudes toward the war and their own participation in the war effort?
- Who were the authors of this plan? What was the plan's intended audience or readership?
- How did the UAW-CIO leadership envision the position of workers in the postwar period? What did it see as the ideal relationship between labour, capital, and the state?
- What specific goals did the UAW-CIO envision for its members in postwar Canada? What do these goals tell us about Canadian workers during this time?

(Approved unanimously by the District 26 Council, UAW-CIO Meeting of October 28–29, 1944, King Edward Hotel, Toronto)

The UAW-CIO expects that victory will bring industrial democracy — steady jobs at union wages, the 40 hour week, annual vacations with pay, guaranteed minimum yearly income, all-inclusive health insurance for the worker and his family, full recognition of labour unions and genuine labour partnership in industry and government.

The UAW-CIO understands that the conversion period will be difficult and stands ready to co-operate with the Ford Motor Company, General Motors, Chrysler Corporation, Massey-Harris Limited, De-Havilland Aircraft and all other employers of our industries and the government to accomplish the gigantic and complicated conversion problem in the shortest possible time, and to the satisfaction and benefit of all.

The UAW-CIO knows that war victory results from the unity of all, labour, management and government, working to back up our fighting services. We will win the peace, achieve an even greater position in the life of Canada for the auto-aircraft-agricultural industries, and contribute to the greater prosperity of the nation through co-operation between labour, the employers and government. This is the post-war path of the UAW-CIO.

Source: *The Canadian UAW-CIO Win the Peace Plan*, http://collections.ic.gc.ca/cau/archiveframe.html.

PLANNING FOR VICTORY

The immediate and fundamental task of the UAW-CIO, as it is of the entire Canadian nation, is to plan and work for an early and unconditional surrender of Fascist Germany and Japan. This great objective requires on the international field an increase to the utmost of unity and co-operation of all of the United Nations, and at home here in Canada an overall planned mobilization of forces of production.

Our union, the largest labour union in Canada, and a part of the biggest labour union in the world, has contributed its full quota towards the victory now within our grasp. The Canadian workers of the UAW-CIO auto, aircraft, and agricultural machinery plants, etc. have every reason to be proud of their war record, for ours is Canada's largest war-producing industry; 15,000 of our brothers and sisters serve in Canada's Armed Services; 51,000 UAW-CIO members are soldiers of production.

While we know that fierce fighting is still ahead to conquer the inner-fortresses Germany and Japan we glory in the undeniable fact that no power now can stop the complete victory of the United Nations. The plan for Canada for war has contributed greatly to this certain victory.

Now, without for a moment slackening our war effort, we can and indeed must look ahead and plan to win the peace.

PLANNING FOR PEACE

The peace plan applies the lessons we have learned at bitter cost during the war.

No. 1 lesson: Fascist aggressors can be wiped out only by the unity and action of all democratic, peace-loving nations. Peace, economic and social-prosperity expanding trade after this war can only be achieved through United Nations unity.

No. 2 lesson: Canada can produce nine million dollars worth of production a year when planning is effective. All Canadians able and willing can be usefully employed on jobs at decent wages and salaries in the peace which will follow this war.

The UAW-CIO is resolutely convinced that just as we will win the war … we can and will win the peace.

OUR INDUSTRY'S PEACE-TIME PLAN

The UAW-CIO, speaking in the name of labour, declares:

Peace must bring our industry a new and greater era of expansion and prosperity. In the stronger Canada which will arise in the post-war, the auto-aircraft-agricultural industries will occupy a very important place. The tasks will be to make hundreds of thousands of cars for Canadian families, trucks and busses for transportation and industry, tractors and labour-saving machinery for the farmers, and aircraft for commercial and private aviation.

Our post-war goal must be to build approximately 400,000 passenger cars and 100,000 trucks a year, twice the highest pre-war production. Such production, together with the doubling of tractor and agricultural machinery output and the building of post-war aircraft industry, would mean that we will solve the conversion of present war-production capacity.

During the war our industry has produced over two billion dollars worth of war vehicles. In the post-war years our industry can do as good a job, for need and the markets exist.

A tremendous back-log of purchasing power will buy our cars and trucks after the war. Hundreds of thousands of Canadian business men and families will need new cars and trucks. Before the war in Canada there was one motor vehicle for every 7.6 persons and in the U.S.A. one motor vehicle for every 3.9 persons. We believe that, after the war, Canada will catch up with the United States in this regard. Our peace slogan is: A car for every family; A car and a tractor for every farmer.

In addition to the enormous domestic market our industry has available great export markets in Europe, Russia and Asia. Our top pre-war auto-truck exports of 47 million dollars can be multiplied manyfold.

The UAW-CIO pledges its every effort to co-operate with the management and government to expand the purchasing power of the Canadian people and our domestic market, and to gain for Canada the largest possible share of the world export trade in autos, trucks, aircraft and agricultural machinery.

This, we declare in the name of our 51,000 members, is the peace plan to benefit labour, management and the nation, to guarantee steady jobs at union wages for our returning veterans and the workers now engaged in our plants on war production and to help build the new world of peace, economic prosperity and co-operation as agreed upon by the United Nations.

PLANNING FOR CONVERSION

The years following the war of 1914–1918 were marked by economic chaos which resulted from the unplanned demobilization of Canada's industry and manpower, and the failure of the victorious Allies to co-operate to win the peace. The UAW-CIO is convinced that this will not happen after this war, provided the United Nations co-operate to win the peace, provided we have co-operation in Canada to convert our war production to peacetime needs.

Conversion will not be a one-way street. Success depends upon labour-management-government responsibility and co-operation.

The UAW therefore proposes:

1. That the Hon. C. D. Howe, Minister of Reconstruction, convene as quickly as possible a Conversion Conference with representation of labour and management to lay down definite conversion plans for our industry.
2. That within the limits of the military situation, new plans of war output be agreed upon, and that all other productive capacity of our industry not needed for such war output be converted to peacetime production. We believe that at this stage of the war, as at the beginning, war and civilian production can proceed side by side. Toolroom facilities not needed for war to be immediately turned to peacetime tooling-up.

3. That a Reconstruction Joint Council representative of the government, management and the UAW-CIO be established and that joint labour-management-government councils be established regionally and in all plants.
4. Maintenance of labour standards during the conversion period.
5. Industry should now establish reserve funds to be paid to employees previously employed who may be temporarily unemployed during reconversion.

The UAW-CIO proposes that a minimum of $25.00 per week (inclusive of unemployment insurance benefits) be paid to all temporarily unemployed workers of our industry as suggested above.

We propose that every worker who may be temporarily laid off during conversion be entitled to two weeks' notice.

INDUSTRIAL DEMOCRACY IN THE PEACETIME

The UAW-CIO has complete faith in the ability of the Canadian people to win the peace, to build up a greater and more prosperous democracy, and to play their part in securing peace for ourselves, our children, and their children.

The old days of pre-1939 must give way to a new era of industrial democracy jobs, union wages, modern homes and a happy life for all who are able and willing to work.

Labour has a mighty responsibility and task in this regard. The UAW-CIO inasmuch as it is the largest union in our country has an especially important responsibility, and will meet it. The UAW-CIO with contractual relations with all the main employers and most of the smaller employers in our industries enters the battle to win the peace.

The UAW-CIO in the negotiation of the renewal of all existing collective agreements and in all new agreements stands ready to write into these agreements the basic principles of labour and management responsibility and mutual co-operation to win the peace, to make the post-war an era of industrial democracy and unity for the mutual benefit of labour and the employees and the nation.

Among these basic principles are the following:

1. Maintenance and improvement of the wage and labour standards achieved in our industry.
2. Full employment and a guaranteed annual income for all workers.
3. The 40 hour work week.
4. An annual vacation of two weeks with full pay.
5. Reinstatement of all returning veterans to a job.
6. Equal pay for equal work.
7. Full recognition of the UAW-CIO by management and government as the representative of the workers of the industry.
8. Labour partnership: Representation in the industry's Reconstruction Joint Council, establishment of labour management machinery and committees throughout the industry.
9. Full health and hospitalization insurance protection for the workers and their families.

Topic 3

Governing Modernity: Social Science, Social Reform, and the State

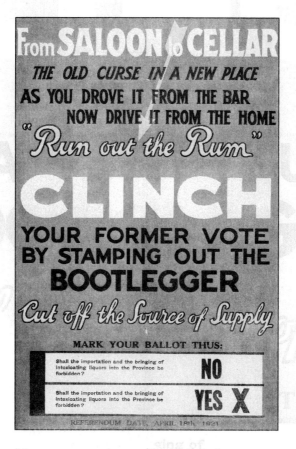

A temperance poster used in the Ontario
Referendum of 1921, http://www
.canadianheritage.com/reproductions/
20864.htm.

CONTEXT

As the material in Topic 2 demonstrates, by the last quarter of the 19th century changes in the nature of production and social organization were demanding certain adjustments on the part of Canadians. The broad social impact of these changes also fuelled public anxieties, especially within the middle class — mostly Protestant, of British background, and urban — about the potential for class unrest, racial degeneration, and a general disorder of the kind that sociologists classify as "anomie." These worried observers feared that industrialization, urbanization, and immigration, if left unregulated, might disrupt their comfortable neighbourhoods, and that they would be powerless to protect their families from what they invariably saw as negative influences. Within their circle, there was a pervasive sense of foreboding about the collapse of cherished social institutions and relations, including the family itself. The years of transformative structural change, therefore, were also years of growing public involvement in social and moral reform, much of it organized under the auspices of the social gospel movement. Espousing an activist Christianity, the social gospel was the response of the churches to the worst abuses of industrial capitalism in the interest of achieving a just and orderly "New Jerusalem." In Quebec, Pope Leo XIII's encyclical *Rerum Novarum* (*The New Order*, 1891), which condemned uncontrolled capitalism, sparked similar activities among Catholics.

The subject of social reform is among the most developed within the Canadian historical literature, in large part because it is so encompassing, both in the sense that it was a pervasive movement that consciously strove to reform virtually every aspect of private lives for the public good, and also because of its specific themes and issues. Historians interested in class, the role of women, gender, and race, immigration and other social policies, public health and family and child welfare, and ultimately the evolving role of the state, could explore each of these, through the medium of social reform. Also advantageous was the reformers' own proclivity for organization and documentation, and their attachment to the methods of social science, as Alan Hunt discusses in his contribution to this section. Earlier works tended to stay at the organizational level of social reform, and to examine reformist thought as reformers expressed it. While this approach permitted some glimpses into the urban underclass that was their focus, these glimpses were necessarily mediated through the moral judgments of their observers. The middle-class, primarily Anglo-Celtic and Protestant values and aspirations of the reformers, and their particular vision of nation-building, therefore, came to be fully explored. Much less was known, or could be known in any direct fashion, about the recipients of reform measures and how they were affected.

Emphasis on the "social control" aspects of reform thought and activity, however much the reformers themselves may have been striving toward that objective, leaves little historical space for agency on the part of the target group. But social historians are dedicated to the concept of agency, striving to understand the ways in which individuals and groups acted on their own behalf, as historical agents rather than mere passive subjects of more powerful social groups and state policies. Some modifications of Marxist theory, such as the concept of ideological hegemony formulated by the Italian Marxist Antonio Gramsci (1891–1937), were applied effectively to show that ruling classes do not need to use imposition: they can persuade their subjects of the benefits of their ideas and programs so that they will willingly accept them. This approach also allows for the "clientele" to make choices, to embrace what is appealing and modify or resist what is not. Giving due consideration to the give-and-take aspects of social relations, such persuasion is far more relational than the top-down social control approach.

The theories of French philosopher Michel Foucault (1926–1984) have had an enormous influence on the writing of social history, especially where reform and regulation are concerned. Foucault used discourse analysis, also called "deconstruction," to examine how particular traits are consistently ascribed to certain social groups, and how these groups are described or represented in certain ways such that language itself shapes or "constructs" social identities. By means of these discursive relations, reformers can identify certain social groups as innately in need of some form of supervision and regulation, which only they, with the help of state agencies, can properly carry out. So, for example, Topic 1 revealed the workings of racial and gender construction in regard to Aboriginal peoples, while Topic 2 discussed the ways in which constructions of class and gender came together to define a certain "ideal" worker.

Foucault also argued that social order and discipline are maintained by the modern state through the surveillance and regulation of private lives as conducted by its expanding bureaucracy and its institutions and agencies — the education, health, legal, and social work structures, for example. Middle-class women played a key role in the period's reform campaigns, both within their own organizations, such as the National Council of Women of Canada, and as significant components of other groups. The most influential of these was the Moral and Social Reform Council of Canada (1907), effectively the first national social work organization, which became the Social Service Council in 1913. The self-defined mandate of such groups was to guide Canadians safely through the turmoil of socioeconomic change, with their middle-class Christian values and institutions intact and reinforced. The period's focus on nation-building connected specific definitions of individual virtue with national stability, supplying further reason for public involvement in private lives. It was at this moment that social reform took on some of the methods of social science, which was itself assuming a more professional form in Canada.

The Great War renewed calls for the state to do something about the toll taken by modern industry and modern warfare, as witnessed in damaged health, broken families, juvenile delinquency, and the continuing prospects of social disorder. The war's horrendous casualties also focused attention on the population as a biological resource, legitimizing arguments about state intervention to counter those losses. The most important of these government initiatives was the Canadian Council on Child Welfare, established in 1921. It became the Council on Child and Family Welfare in 1929, indicating the more-inclusive mandate that was the legacy of the decade's family-centred reform debates and measures. The widespread suffering occasioned by the Great Depression, and the need for massive state as well as citizen involvement to conduct the war effort after 1939, would see one of the social gospel's key objectives gradually realized as steps were taken toward a modern welfare state that secured a "social minimum" for all of its citizens.

REFERENCES/FURTHER READING

Allen, Richard. *The Social Passion: Religion and Social Reform in Canada, 1914–1929*. Toronto: University of Toronto Press, 1971.

Burke, S. *Seeking the Highest Good: Social Service and Gender at the University of Toronto, 1888–1937*. Toronto: University of Toronto Press, 1997.

Campbell, Robert S. *Sit Down and Drink Your Beer: Regulating Vancouver's Beer Parlours, 1925–1954*. Toronto: University of Toronto Press, 2001.

Christie, Nancy, and Michael Gauvreau. *A Full-Orbed Christianity: The Protestant Churches and Social Welfare in Canada, 1900–1940*. Montreal and Kingston: McGill-Queen's University Press, 1996.

Cook, Sharon A. *"Through Sunshine and Shadow": The Women's Christian Temperance Union, Evangelicalism, and Reform in Ontario, 1874–1930*. Montreal and Kingston: McGill-Queen's University Press, 1995.

Foucault, Michel. *The Archaeology of Knowledge*. New York: Pantheon Books, 1972.

———. *Discipline and Punish: The Birth of the Prison*. New York: Pantheon Books, 1977.

Kealey, Linda, ed. *A Not Unreasonable Claim: Women and Reform in Canada, 1880s–1920s*. Toronto: Canadian Women's Educational Press, 1979.

Mills, Allen. *Fool for Christ: The Political Thought of J. S. Woodsworth*. Toronto: University of Toronto Press, 1991.

Shore, M. *The Science of Social Redemption: McGill, the Chicago School, and the Origins of Social Research in Canada*. Toronto: University of Toronto Press, 1987.

Strange, Carolyn. *Toronto's Girl Problem: The Perils and Pleasures of the City, 1880–1930*. Toronto: University of Toronto Press, 1995.

Valverde, Mariana. *The Age of Light, Soap and Water: Moral Reform in English Canada, 1885–1925*. Toronto: McClelland and Stewart, 1991.

ILLUSTRATION 3.1 (P. 83)

Ontario had been "dry" since the war years, thanks to earlier, successful temperance campaigns, and then to federal prohibition in 1917, as part of the war effort; federal prohibition was rescinded in 1918 after the Armistice.

Issue to Consider

*   Who is the particular target of the 1921 temperance campaign depicted in Illustration 3.1? What does this target suggest about previous campaigns? What does the reference to "the home" tell us?

ARTICLES

In this section, Alan Hunt and Sean Purdy use Foucauldian approaches to examine aspects of reform in early 20th-century Canada, and to reveal how social reform had a fundamentally moralistic basis that reflected the values of the Protestant middle class. Hunt's work outlines the vital union of social gospel and social science that underpinned reform initiatives, while Purdy's article reveals how reformers drew connections between the health of families, healthy homes, citizenship, and nation-building.

Article 3.1
Alan Hunt

Measuring Morals: The Beginnings of the Social Survey Movement in Canada, 1913–1917

Issues to Consider

- Hunt uses a "social construction" approach in his consideration of how social surveys became important tools to further reform and regulation. Why does he contend that the main question is not about the surveyors' motivations, but about how the surveys should be read (i.e., what historians should be able to see from a close textual analysis)? What does he argue are the principal reasons for the adoption of the survey method in reform campaigns?
- What does Hunt mean when he refers to "the problematization of the social realm"?
- What is the concept of "pastoral power"?
- Which sectors of the population were specifically "constructed" as social problems? What does this tell us about those doing the constructing? What were the remedies proposed?
- What connections does Hunt make between Canadian reform efforts and those of the Americans? What is historically valuable about understanding the American influence on Canadian efforts?
- Hunt's primary sources are the surveys that are the focus of his article. What other sources of the time might historians use to examine the topic of social and moral regulation?

In the early years of the twentieth century North America witnessed an upsurge of attempts to investigate the moral climate. Forms of investigation categorized as "surveys" were the main technique employed, and different forms of surveys were produced in Canada. To what extent can these surveys can be understood as attempts to measure morals? I offer a reading of the Canadian social survey movement, not by asking questions about reformers' motives, but rather by focusing on the way in which the surveys problematized Canadian social life through the construction of a network of dangers and evils generated by the interaction of urbanism and immigration.

Much of the attention focused on the formation of "the social" during the course of the nineteenth century has emphasized the key role of the emergent welfare state in constituting a network of fields through which it could act upon an aggregated population.[1] This line of argument is extended here by the contention that non-state bodies, such as the Canadian survey movement, played a key role in elaborating the elements, schematically represented by urbanism and immigration, that formed the core of the problematization of the social realm.

The Canadian social surveys can be understood through the lens of the idea of "pastoral power" as a form of power focused on ensuring, sustaining, and improving the well-being of the population through attending to the lives of each and every individual. The social survey project was a form of pastoral power that identified social problems in the form of troublesome populations and locations and sought to institute forms of regulation that addressed individuals for their own benefit and for the well-being of the whole.

Source: Alan Hunt, "Measuring Morals: The Beginnings of the Social Survey Movement in Canada, 1913–1917," *Histoire sociale/Social History* 35, no. 69 (2002): 171–94.

In Canada projects of moral reform had been initiated from the early days of settlement as a distinctively Protestant tradition. Traditionally these had taken the form of moral exhortation grounded in religious moral codes such as the Ten Commandments. With increasing religious pluralism and secularization, appeal to such unitary codes ceased to have the same effectiveness. The Canadian Presbyterians came increasingly under the influence of "social gospel" theology, which shifted the focus of attention from individual salvation to what may be called moral environmentalism.[2] The task of instilling piety, purity, and probity involved addressing the "social question," social and economic conditions under which the population lived. Between 1909 and 1911 the Presbyterian Board of Social Service and Evangelism undertook a study of "the city." The Board's report argued that the moral condition of the cities was a multidimensional problem having ethical, philanthropic, political, social, and moral aspects. The list of symptoms of immorality reveals the interconnections within a diverse range of moral and social conditions: drinking, gambling, Sabbath desecration, vice, alien races and tongues, housing, sanitation, education, and recreation. The environment of the masses, especially in the expanding urban areas, had to be improved if they were to be Christianized and Canadianized. As the Rev. James A. Macdonald, a leading progressive Presbyterian, expressed it: "The city is the strategic point in the warfare against evil, the storm centre is there; there the fiercest battle waged."[3]

The social gospel movement increasingly emphasized the link between evangelism and social service. The modern scientific investigative techniques of social surveys would discover the facts; these then needed to be presented to the Canadian public; this in turn would result in a changed climate and generate attitudes that would promote policies to eliminate the adverse socio-economic causes. Appropriate legislation would remove the evils from the community and foster harmonious social relations. The strongly moralistic nature of this project is revealed by the legislative programme adopted in 1913 that proposed: raising the age of sexual consent (seduction from 16 to 18 and carnal knowledge from 14 to 16); criminalizing employers who seduced female employees under 21; whipping men who procured girls for immoral purposes; making the prosecution of solicitation by both males and females easier; prohibiting gambling and betting on horse races; criminalizing obscene or blasphemous language in a public place; criminalizing living in adultery or fornication. The furtherance of this comprehensive project for the moralization of urban conditions was what spurred the collaboration between the Methodists and the Presbyterians to undertake a systematic programme of social surveys.

SOCIAL SURVEYS AND MORALS REPORTS

Between 1911 and 1915 a series of social surveys was conducted in major cities across Canada. The crucial year was 1913, during which surveys were conducted in Fort William, Hamilton, London, Port Arthur, Regina, Sydney, Winnipeg, and Vancouver. These surveys were carried out as a collaborative project between the "social gospel" wings of the Methodist and Presbyterian Churches. In 1907 the Presbyterian Rev. John G. Shearer[4] and the Methodist T. A. Moore set up the Moral and Social Reform Council of Canada, with Shearer as its secretary, as an umbrella organization to coordinate the moral reform efforts of the Protestant churches, organized labour, and other women's groups.[5] In addition to the overlapping organizations of the two denominations, they had each developed their own institutional apparatus, the Methodist Department of Temperance and Moral Reform and the Presbyterian Board of Social Service and Evangelism.[6] These two bodies collaborated to organize and carry out surveys coordinated by Walter A. Riddell and A. J. W. Myers. Riddell (1881–1963) is a significant figure; because he was working on his doctorate in sociology at Columbia University, he was regarded as having the relevant expertise to be put in charge in 1913 as Director of Social Surveys for the Methodist-Presbyterian survey project.

While most of the Canadian surveys were initiated by the Methodist-Presbyterian alliance, by far and away the most important and influential one was the Toronto survey, which came about by a different route.[7] In 1912 the Toronto Vigilance Committee called for measures to prevent young girls from becoming prostitutes. The Methodist-Presbyterian joint board and the Toronto Local Council of Women (TLCW) lobbied the Toronto municipal government to appoint a commission to investigate the "social evil" and the "white slave traffic." The municipal authorities equivocated, probably as a result of opposition from the police to the survey proposal. The project was galvanized by a lecture tour by William Coote, a leading figure of the British purity movement; he was the secretary of the National Vigilance Association and a dynamic orator from a radical working-class puritan tradition. His visit resulted in the establishment of a National Committee for the Suppression of the White Slave Trade in Canada, and by 1913 he had made "white slavery" a major national issue. Unable to secure timely municipal action, the TLCW established its own Survey Committee, and this was sufficient to precipitate the decision to establish an official commission.

THE SURVEY MOVEMENT IN THE UNITED STATES

To appreciate the differences between the Methodist-Presbyterian surveys and the Toronto survey, we must briefly explore parallel developments in the United States. The Toronto survey differs from the other Canadian surveys in that it was closely modelled on the American vice commissions that, starting in New York with the report of the Committee of Fifteen entitled *The Social Evil* (1902),[8] gathered momentum and were conducted in cities, large and small, between 1910 and 1917.[9] Surprisingly, these reports have not as yet received any sustained attention.[10] Their major characteristic is that they were discursively constructed from a mixture of two elements, traditional Protestant moral sermonizing against sin and immorality and primitive "social science" elements for the inscription of evil through statistical data and tables; in combination they formed a project of representing and intervening in the social in which sin and evil had become fused.

A second and parallel tradition in the United States consisted of social surveys that were strongly influenced in their methodology and construction by an incipient social science tradition. The most important embodiment of this tradition was the Pittsburgh Survey of 1906–1909. Resulting from the intellectual and organizational leadership of Paul U. Kellogg and financed by the Russell Sage Foundation, the survey produced results that were published in five substantial individually authored volumes.[11] After Pittsburgh, Kellogg, along with Shelby Harrison, promoted a social survey movement which produced many hundreds of studies in a similar style.[12] The debate on the significance of the survey movement in the United States has been almost exclusively focused on the question of its contribution to the emergence of sociology as an academic discipline.[13] Studies of the emergence of the social sciences in Canada have taken a similar stance, viewing Canadian sociology through the lens of the dual filiation to Britain and the United States.[14] This is not the place to enter that debate, save to note that it is conducted in conventional linear developmental terms and thus takes modern sociology for granted as its end point.

As a result there has been little interest in the conjunctural relationship between the social survey movement and moral regulation movements of the period. This issue is evidenced in one salient feature of the Pittsburgh survey that has gone unnoticed. Only a few years after the completion of Kellogg's Pittsburgh survey, the city had its own "vice commission" survey conducted by the city's Morals Efficiency Commission. This report made no mention at all of the large-scale earlier survey even though it had created much interest, positive and negative, in the city. In what was perhaps an indirect reference, Siebel's later report insisted that it relied upon personal inquiry by members of the commission rather than the "tales of paid professional investigators."[15] More generally, none of the vice commission reports referred to any "social survey" reports, and the latter occasionally made disparaging comments about the former.

At first sight it appears that there were two quite separate movements, the vice commissions and the social surveys, with neither acknowledging the existence of the other. Such an inference is too easy. While there were real differences, these were more of style than of substance. The social surveys were secular reform projects suspicious of the religious moralizing of the vice commission reports. Both types had an activist orientation intended to stimulate local community action. The Pittsburgh survey pioneered the presentation of findings by touring exhibitions; these used photographs and display boards which summarized the statistical data and were blazoned with reform slogans. It is significant that the Canadian social surveys also mounted such travelling exhibitions, and their displays and placards were identical in design to those used in Pittsburgh. The illustrations accompanying many of the published surveys are reproductions of exhibition placards which combine some simple slogan with a statistical representation. The surveyors could be taken as having formed the view that it was no longer sufficient to denounce sin; it was now necessary to find the means of disseminating representations of evil that underlined the social and individual harm caused. [...]

The two American variants of social investigations help in situating the distinguishing features of the Canadian surveys. The Toronto survey is firmly in the vice commission tradition; its primary target was commercialized vice to the extent that even the self-standing medical report was almost exclusively concerned, in a strongly moralistic view, with venereal diseases. In contrast, the Methodist-Presbyterian surveys directed their attention to socio-economic conditions; not all of them even mentioned prostitution and when they did the treatment was cursory.

OTHER CANADIAN SURVEYS

A number of other published reports do not fit the dual model identified above. One example is an inquiry conducted in 1910 by the Social Vice Commission of Winnipeg, chaired by Justice H. A. Robson and appointed by Winnipeg City Council.[16] The inquiry arose from charges made by D. John G. Shearer in the Toronto press. Shearer was the joint-secretary of the influential Board of Moral and Social Reform of Canada and a major figure in the social gospel wing of the Presbyterian Church. He charged that the Winnipeg authorities permitted segregated prostitution with 50 "houses" in operation, that the police made no serious attempt to enforce the laws against prostitution, and, more generally, that the whole matter was suggestive of graft.

The report managed to exonerate the city of the general charge of promoting vice, despite the finding that there did exist a policy of toleration and regulation within a restricted area and that the number of houses of vice had increased from 29 to 50. The commission's obvious reluctance to confront the police directly is evidenced by the conclusion that these conditions did not involve any corruption in the police authority even though the general conditions were a "reproach to any civilized community."[17]

To complete the account of the social survey reports, two other varieties should be noted. The first was further instance of the Methodist-Presbyterian collaboration to undertake "rural social surveys."[18] These surveys were preoccupied with the impact of rural depopulation upon church membership and participation (for example, in Huron County the population had fallen from 64,000 to 39,000 between 1875 and 1913). They were unflinching in their criticism of the passive role of the churches and their ministers, but nevertheless insisted that "the Church is the organization that is best qualified to lead in the rehabilitation of the countryside."[19] The Swan River survey also castigated those ministers who restricted their role to preaching and took no interest in such matters as scientific farming, education, or youth recreation. It urged the churches to provide healthy recreations to draw young men away from the pool-rooms.[20]

The final form of moral survey was a series of discrete reports dealing with Montreal; two such reports were private, while two others were conducted by a local "Committee of Sixteen." The two most ambitious of these concerned conditions in Montreal. The sub-title of Herbert Ames's study is A Sociological Study of a Portion of the City of Montreal.[21] It set out to conduct a "sociological" investigation into conditions in working-class Montreal, contrasting "above the hill" and "below the hill." However, there is little indication of method of study; Ames undertook "a house-to-house canvass," but there is no indication whether or not this formed the source of statistical tables reproduced. The most significant form of presentation is the inscription of data on street maps (for example, social composition by percentage of Franco- and Anglo-Canadians, average wages, and average family size, among other factors) to provide a spatial representation of social data. This work is located within the tradition of moral environmentalism as witnessed by the contention that outside privies posed a "danger to public health and morals"; while the health implications of sanitary provisions were well established, there was no attempt to disclose the moral danger.[22] [...]

READING THE CANADIAN SURVEYS

The Methodist-Presbyterian surveys provide an ideal opportunity through which to explore the question: How should we read social and morals surveys? We are not assisted by asking why the surveys were conducted. The documents themselves tell us little about the motivations that underlay the project. The motives were further complicated because the minutes and regular reports of the respective departments of the two churches assume the value of the project as a self-evident core element of the social gospel credo. It seems unlikely that they were intended to reproduce anything approaching the ambitious nature of the Pittsburgh survey.[23] The Canadian surveys were so different in scope, scale, and method that they cannot be regarded as attempts to imitate the surveys being conducted south of the border. It should be noted that all the reports were explicitly described as "preliminary"[24] but, as far as I have been able to establish, no plans were made for carrying out any fuller investigations.

The surveys are also interesting for what they do not say. They tell us surprisingly little about the methods adopted or how the expanded surveys should proceed. Like many reports of the period, they provide little information about sources or how the studies were undertaken. Some reproduce the reports of named municipal or provincial officials, and large portions of the texts give every appearance of being transcriptions of material provided by other unacknowledged officials. The London (Ontario) survey was the most explicit; two "investigators" were imported and 50 local members of the Men's Federation were involved in the survey.[25] While we have no reason to expect formal methodological statements of statistical sophistication, it should not be forgotten that the work of Booth, Rowntree, and others had been widely publicized.

Some surveys claimed that their inquiries manifested a desire for "civic self-analysis," which was a prominent theme in Pittsburgh-style investigations in the United States, but the Canadian surveys give little indication of any substantial local involvement. While in

Pittsburgh significant efforts had been undertaken to secure the involvement of a variety of local interests and representation, there is no corresponding evidence with respect to the Canadian surveys.[26] It is probable that the Methodist-Presbyterian alliance assumed that it itself "represented" the community or at least its respectable and nativist core. These absences make it possible to approach these documents as "texts" with a minimum of presuppositions. A description of their major features sets the scene for an analysis of the texts.

A DESCRIPTION OF THE CANADIAN SOCIAL SURVEYS

The published reports are by no means uniform in content, coverage, or style, but they do share a number of common features.

Introduction: The Regina and Vancouver reports are particularly interesting in that they carry identical introductions. The survey project was defined as one of "civic self-analysis," and this was contrasted with the "muck-raking" of American exposé politics (Riis, Steffens, and others).[27] It was recognized that the Pittsburgh survey "gave a strong impetus to the survey idea." The survey idea had much to offer Canada: "Indeed, it is likely that in time we shall be so impressed with the necessity of social investigation that each large city will have its bureau of social research making that continuous study which is the only basis for intelligent action for civic betterment."[28] Only the Regina survey, conducted by J. S. Woodsworth, and the Sydney survey, conducted by Bryce M. Stewart,[29] referred to the populist mode of presentation pioneered by the Pittsburgh survey; the potential role of "civic or social exhibitions" to present graphically, by means of maps, charts, pictures, and models, the conditions discovered was commended, but there is no evidence that such an exhibition was mounted.[30]

History: Some surveys start with a brief history of the city in question; this is gleaned from some other publication (for example, the Hamilton survey reproduced a history provided by a local newspaper which is almost exclusively a history of the designation of the township and the division and sub-division of lots).[31] Others provided details on the economic history of the city (for example, the Fort William report gave an account of the transition from the early fur trade to the modern granary economy).[32]

"The field": All reports used this term to designate their object of inquiry; it connotes a straightforward identification of the land area under investigation (so many acres) and in some cases both the area and the population size. There was an implicit concern with issues of social-economic progress. In a number of reports the advent of the telephone seems to have been regarded as an index of "modernity"; for example, in Port Arthur by 1913 there were 2,370 telephones of which 1,774 were private.[33]

Population: Population was generally given in aggregate, and particular attention was paid to ethnic origin, focusing on the proportions of English-speaking to non-English-speaking, the latter category being employed to designate "immigrants."[34] Something of the underlying concerns is revealed by the Fort William survey, which expressed concern about "the large number of Ruthenians" even though the statistics reveal only 63.[35] In the Port Arthur survey, illiteracy was reported as highest among southern Europeans, while Finns, Norwegians, and Swedes showed "strong desire to learn English"[36]

Economic life: Most reports gave details of major sources of employment. In the majority of cases there was specific concern with trade union organization. Unionization was referred to in a positive light; but an underlying concern about the links between labour and liquor interests is captured by the frequent inquiry about whether union locals met in premises selling alcohol and whether meetings were held on Sunday.

While unions were viewed positively, socialist propaganda was treated differentially: some reports treated socialism positively while others were more negative. The most explicit reference appears in the Hamilton survey, which noted that immigrants were being "embittered against Canada" because of low wages and poor housing and that "one can scarcely wonder that many of them accept the teachings of the Russian Socialist organizer who is working among them."[37] In contrast, the Port Arthur report provided a much more sympathetic treatment of socialism, arguing that, if socialists and labour were to unite, their future voting strength would be considerable. The influence of "social gospel" is evident in the argument that the "Socialist cause" had been held back because a "great number of Socialists are free thinkers," but that socialism should appeal especially to the Christian."[38]

Municipal administration: Most reports gave a formal statement of the administrative structure of the municipal government, such as the relationship between mayor, council, and officers, and in some cases some quantification of the tax base of city finances was provided.

Recreation: Here there is an interesting bifurcation. On one hand, recreations were viewed as a positive force, while on the other, recreations, particularly commercial recreations, were problematized. In the Port Arthur survey, popular social and cultural recreations were reported: "winter amusements" were listed as skating and snowshoeing; in summer there were football, baseball, boating, tennis, and golfing. Others, in line with American surveys' concern with the benefits of public recreational space, viewed parks and playgrounds as a key index of social progress.

The two particular forms of recreation that elicited concern were commercialized recreation (such as movie theatres and dance halls) and, almost universally, the drinking habits of the working population. The Vancouver survey focused on commercial recreation and expressed concern about theatres and movie-houses, noting that in one theatre the audience was 99 per cent male and had an "atmosphere of an antechamber to darker evils."[39] The pervasive temperance sentiments of the Methodist-Presbyterian alliance led to considerable attention being focused on bars and saloons. With respect to drinking establishments, there is evidence of some direct survey activity. It is significant that five of the surveys investigated the numbers frequenting either saloons or pool-rooms. The Hamilton survey attended to both; a survey was made on a designated evening of pool-rooms and bars. The report hastened to assure its readers that the investigators had remained "just long enough to make the required observations."[40] However, this was deemed long enough to ascertain the numbers present, whether or not they were "intoxicated," the number of minors and females, and the moral tone of the conversation (distinguishing between "decent," "obscene," and "blasphemous").[41]

Crime: Most reports carried details of data on arrests, summonses, or both (presumably supplied by the police). The problem of crime was exclusively constructed as a concern with the proportion of offences that could be attributed to alcohol. Thus, the Hamilton report calculated that, of 4,602 cases in 1912, 1,891 were liquor cases and a further 640 "may" have been due to drink. In Port Arthur the figures were 2,668 summonses and arrests, 1,692 being alcohol offences, mainly that of being drunk and incapable. Most reports presented an economic quantification of the drink problem in the form of a "Drink Account," a tactic that had been widely used in Woman's Christian Temperance Union (WCTU) campaigns in both the United States and Canada. The account calculated the revenue received from granting licences and wages to bartenders as credit; the debit was the money spent in bars as well as the cost of the arrest, detention, trial, and imprisonment of offenders. These figures always revealed a large "loss" to the community; for example, in London, Ontario, it amounted to $715,007 for the year 1912–1913.[42]

Housing: While there was common concern with overcrowding and poor sanitation in homes of the working-class and immigrants, little effort was made to quantify housing conditions. The reports relied on descriptive examples of overcrowded accommodation.

Health: All the reports provided detailed tables of mortality and infant mortality rates. Most carried lengthy but unanalysed lists of the causes of death. The only specific focus of attention in a number of reports was a concern with tuberculosis that "thrives in dark and unventilated homes."[43]

Prostitution: There is a sharp contrast in the attention devoted to "the social evil." While, as has been noted, prostitution formed the central concern of the Toronto report, only the Port Arthur and Fort William reports paid any attention to prostitution, and they carried identical text covering the "Twin Cities." Until recently prostitution had been openly tolerated. The usual pattern was the "bawdy house" with only a small number owned by one of the female inmates. The report noted a "hopeful outlook" arising from an unconfirmed report that one "inmate" had committed suicide by poison. Recently the police, particularly in Port Arthur, had adopted a policy for "eradicating this evil" and now claimed that only one such house remained. All inmates had been ordered to leave the bawdy houses. But the report stated that a more stubborn form of the social evil had arisen, in which prostitution was a "family affair" being known to parents or guardians. In the Vancouver report a brief mention in a section headed "political life" reported that the provincial government had failed to act against the "segregated district."

The Regina report reveals a significant feature about the construction of sexual morality: "There is no open prostitution. The police are vigilant. The blocks are pretty clean, but it is strongly suspected that one or two of the hotels are used as houses of assignation. Attention should be called to the number of young girls who are about the streets and cafes unaccompanied, between eleven and twelve at night."[44] This reveals that the term "social evil" was often a code for a concern with the regulation of female sexuality and more generally with the regulation of hetero-social space — the mixing of young people in the public spaces of urban areas.[45] This emerges with particular clarity in a contradiction evident in a hesitancy about the desirability of public parks, which was often accompanied by the insistence that they be better supervised or closed after dark. The London report expressed concern about Springbank Park because it was full of secluded and dark nooks and corners without adequate supervision."[46]

READING THE SOCIAL SURVEY MOVEMENT

It is practical to avoid asking about the "purposes" or "motives" of the Canadian social survey movement on the grounds that, while the texts disclose legitimatory discourses, there is rarely, if ever, any means of distinguishing between the announced motives and the "real motives" that may be suspected to lurk beneath the surface of the language deployed. Rather, I am concerned to track the way in which — to use Foucault's terminology — the surveys "problematized" Canadian social life in the early part of the twentieth century. "A problematization is a way in which experience is offered to thought in the form of a problem requiring attention."[47] The pursuit of the problematizations employed by the social surveyors requires two analytic steps.

First, it is necessary to explore the way in which "the social" domain that formed the object of inquiry of these reports was constructed. I use "social" not as some generic concept that is a simile for society as some unity or totality, typically designating everything that falls within the spatial boundaries of a nation state. Rather, "the social" involves those aspects of human life involved in relations with others that are perceived as being a field that is a potential or suitable object for purposive action or regulation.

Thus in early twentieth-century Canada only certain sectors or segments of the population were constructed as exhibiting the type of problems requiring organized action.[48] Concretely, "the social" referred to two segments, the troublesome poor of the cities and the "immigration flood." The former were viewed as posing a threat of disorder and contagion, moral and medical. Immigrants shared the dangers posed by the poor with the added dimension of their slow rate of "Canadianization," conceived as a question of language, namely the acquisition of English. Beneath this lay the evocative but illusive notion of "Canadianization," so deeply embedded in the common sense of the period that its content remained largely unspecified. It is significant that Canadianization functioned as a "floating" signifier: one employed, as occasion demanded, to designate a shifting set of troublesome or worrying attributes. Sometimes it referred to a specific construction of "Christianization," always distinguished in the first instance from Catholicism, but it also frequently articulated a concern about the religious diversity of the shifting profile of immigration. At other times Canadianization denoted a more dispersed set of social virtues of which the most prominent was the deeply ingrained trope of moral regulation discourses captured by the dichotomy between idleness and work. The charge of idleness was not so much a judgement about the work habits of the new immigrant working class, but rather a marker of cultural distance.

Secondly, problematization needs to be approached comparatively. This requires attention to both what was included and what was excluded in the survey reports and then to the way in which the "social problems" requiring attention were identified. The reports exhibit a shifting focus on a set of social problems of which the most important were urban poverty, rural depopulation, temperance, and prostitution. The targets of Canadian moral regulation discourses were more dispersed than those in the American vice commissions, whose major thrust was the intertwined problems of alcohol and vice. The presence of saloons provided the social space in which prostitution flourished, and the brothels generated the political alliance between liquor and vice interests. This is captured in the central preoccupation with "commercialized vice."

The dispersed targets of the Canadian social surveys were such that, while some explicitly addressed the issue of prostitution, others mentioned it only in passing, if at all.[49] The Canadian surveys were characterized by an assortment of themes which dealt broadly with urban social conditions addressed under a dispersed set of headings. These included housing, population, public health, religion, recreation, alcohol, and related topics. It is noticeable that for a centrally coordinated set of surveys they are remarkably different in their organization and sequence of topics, even though their treatment exhibits strong continuities. This attests both to the absence of any strategic plan or survey method and to the considerable local autonomy of the individual surveys.

QUANTIFYING THE SOCIAL AND THE MORAL

The Canadian surveys provide evidence of an emerging attempt to link "numbers" and "morals." The reports relied almost exclusively on data collected by other agencies. Little or no effort was made to undertake any work on the data so collected. Numbers were treated as if they spoke for themselves; it was assumed that it was sufficient to present some aggregate number for the readers to share the conclusions drawn by the compilers. This evident naivety goes hand in hand with acknowledgement of the British survey pioneers Charles Booth and Seebohm Rowntree and of Paul Kellogg and the Pittsburgh survey. The reformers were aware of the prestige of such studies, but, rather than employing the techniques of data collection, statistical procedures, and presentation, they seemed content to invoke that authority. The reformers seem to have believed that it was merely necessary to reproduce the data they collected in the appropriate form for the results to speak directly to their audience.

The most distinctive form of presentation, influenced by the Pittsburgh survey, involved mounting public exhibitions of the findings. These exhibitions relied on two specific tactics: the visual representation of numbers and the translation of data into slogans. The visual representation of quantitative data employed three main forms of presentation: the pie chart, the segmented circle which divided some population into segments represented as percentages of the total; bar charts, which similarly represented proportions as vertical blocks; and standard numerical tables quantifying such matters as population increases and mortality rates over time. A further feature was the occasional use of indicative numerical data, the most frequent illustration being the detailing of the number of telephones installed in businesses and private homes as an index of degree of modernization, although this term itself was not used.

The failure to interrogate the numbers collected or to make use of any more sophisticated statistical techniques is all the more strange in light of the fact that Walter A. Riddell had been brought back by Shearer and Moore from his sociology doctorate at Columbia University to direct the surveys. One possible explanation is that, as was frequently stressed in the reports, the surveys were only "preliminary," intended to identify topics for subsequent detailed surveys. It is more likely that it was taken for granted that numbers and facts spoke for themselves and that this assumption accounts for the primitive nature of these surveys.

Within this frame of reference, social judgements are primarily moral assertions. Thus, to quantify the number of people in saloons or pool-rooms on a single night, without inquiring whether the number might be rising or falling or whether it might be more or less than in some other city, only makes sense within the moral vision that deems it inherently bad for any number of people to be drinking alcohol. Yet the fact that it was thought necessary to provide numbers is evidence of the prestige of numbers which had been established within the recent past.[50] The function of the numbers and their visual representation served merely to confirm the implicit moral discourse that underlay the text.

The fate of the projected full surveys remains something of a mystery. It is not even certain that the Methodist-Presbyterian organizers regarded the Toronto survey as the first such full survey. Reference to the survey project became displaced by the planning for the Social Service Congress, held in Ottawa in March 1914, and did not reappear after that event. At the Congress, Riddell, the chief coordinator of the surveys, delivered an address in which he described the significance of the survey project: "In discovering and in presenting to the popular mind the collective sins of the community and in bringing the responsibility for these home to the common conscience, the Social Survey has made perhaps its largest contribution."[51] Only one other speaker mentioned the surveys, however, and then only in the most general terms. The majority of speeches delivered relied on simpler rhetorical forms that gave priority to moralizing discourses that asserted a normative judgement on the wrongness of the prevailing social conditions and then proceeded to propound a vision of what must be done to right that wrong. One rhetorical style did employ numbers in a way that remains common to the reforming impulse that is alive and well today; this technique involved numerical inflation. Dr. Charles Hastings, the Medical Officer of Health for Toronto, sought to demonstrate the importance of "social hygiene" measures to treat venereal diseases by wild inflation of the numbers affected; thus he claimed that 75 per cent of adult males contracted gonorrhea and 15 per cent syphilis.[52] The logic of such claims is that big numbers confirm a big problem.[53]

In his presentation Riddell stressed the preliminary nature of the eight surveys that had been completed and stated that a further four were to be conducted in the summer of 1914, but these seem never to have been carried out. It seems reasonable to assume that, as for so many other organizations, the portents of the coming world war transformed the social and political agenda. As a consequence the only substantial and lasting manifestation of the Canadian social survey movement was the Toronto Social Survey Commission of 1915.

THE TORONTO SOCIAL SURVEY

The Toronto survey was conducted after the first wave of Methodist-Presbyterian surveys. It exhibits both significant differences and continuities with the earlier surveys, but its relationship to its predecessors is by no means clear. As noted earlier it came about by a different route, being the only survey which resulted from the demands of a wider social movement than the Methodist-Presbyterian alliance, with important roles being played by the Council of Women, the WCTU, and local reform politicians.

Not only was the Toronto survey the fullest survey undertaken but it was also the most interesting in a number of respects. First, it was the most open of all the surveys in that its conclusions were not foregone. Its terms of reference were to investigate "the white slave traffic, existing vice and social disease."[54] The question of the existence of white slavery was a highly charged topic; in much contemporary coverage in press and pulpit the issue was presented in a distinctively nationalistic form, alleging that Canadian girls were being snared into prostitution and found themselves in the brothels of Chicago and other American cities. It was therefore of great significance that the Toronto survey concluded that "there has been no positive evidence secured of the existence in Toronto of a system of obtaining and retaining involuntary victims."[55]

Secondly, the Toronto report was the only one to provide an analysis of prostitution that took account of contemporary trends. The authors were surprised that "the number of houses of ill-fame appeared so small."[56] They explained the small number of brothels by the growth in the number of houses of assignation and the large number of individual prostitutes using their own accommodation. The report noted an even more recent development, the emergence of massage parlours.[57]

The report is significant in drawing attention to changes in the form of prostitution, from brothels to "self-employed" prostitutes. This led the authors to focus attention on "casual prostitution" and "charity girls."[58] Such immorality "invades offices, shops" and "lurks" in amusement parks, skating rinks, and dance halls. What was regarded as particularly significant was that those so engaged were "not a segregated and despised class."[59] As many commentators have noted, this move widens the scope of the moral regulation project to encompass the whole field of female sexual conduct. But there was a paradox in the report's treatment: it was attentive to the changing forms of sexual conduct of the young. This in turn led to a preoccupation with the wider field of the recreation of young working-class women. Yet, despite their self-proclaimed commitment to a scientific method, the authors made no attempt to quantify these changes. The decline in the number of brothels was merely asserted, as was the rise in the number of houses of assignation. There was no attention to whether there was more or less prostitution or to the number of massage parlours. Similarly, there was no interest in the spatial location of prostitution in the community.[60] These omissions stemmed not only from the lack of any rigorous or systematic mode of inquiry, but also from the radical change of focus to the broader field of inquiry of the "girl problem."[61] The report thus came to focus on the question of why young women became sexually promiscuous and resorted to prostitution. This issue had preoccupied the moral reform movement since the rise of organized opposition to prostitution in the latter part of the nineteenth century. The question was perplexing because it was framed within the long-established vision of female sexuality, which held that any sexual interest or activity outside marriage was regarded as inimical to the very nature of womanhood.

The Toronto report reworked the themes which had dominated the numerous American vice commission reports without adding significantly to them. The major figuration of the report was the "woman adrift" who lived independently, unsupported and unsupervised by family, community, or church; these absences or vacuums were seen as drawing the young woman into vice. It is important to note that it was her leisure rather than her work that was the major object of concern. The nature of her work stripped her of the modesty that was the primary protection against sexual vulnerability and preserved female chastity. This vulnerability was amplified by the pervasive discursive construction of female sexuality; while naturally innocent, women were viewed as inherently vain, attracted to finery and to the search for pleasures. This vision of femininity, when combined with the recognition that the city offered them only dreary low-paid jobs, rendered women as always in danger of corruption and seduction and thus as potential carriers of social and moral degeneration.

Thus the Toronto report addressed, as had many of the American vice commissions, the vexed problem of the low pay received by the majority of young urban working women. The Toronto report found that insufficient wages were a significant cause of the lapse into prostitution, but, while many of the American vice commissions engaged in detailed, if not necessarily systematic, empirical study of female wages, the Toronto survey merely pronounced that wages were too low. The authors drew back from a radical critique of employers. Low wages were, the report insisted, "not the only or indeed the chief cause."[62] The logic of this conclusion was that, since the majority of young women on low wages did not engage in prostitution, poor wages could not be the "cause" of the "fall" of those who did lapse. The report recommended a minimum wage law, but, as if to confirm that the problem was not just a matter of wages, it proposed that all large employers of young women should appoint someone to be responsible for the social and moral well-being of their employees.

Having thus addressed the economic dimension, the report devoted most of its attention to the recreational activities of young women. It reported on dance halls, skating rinks, movie houses, vaudeville, and other commercial entertainments. With respect to the dance halls, the report deplored the unregulated and unsupervised contact between young men and women and denounced "the free and promiscuous intercourse of the sexes in public dances." In a similar vein, skating rinks were condemned on the grounds that they "furnish opportunities for promiscuous acquaintance and are extensively used as rendezvous for immoral purposes." The conception of the proper relations between young men and women is revealed in the observation that "young girls enter into conversations with strangers at public rinks, and make free with young men to whom they have not been introduced."[63] Yet no detailed investigation was undertaken of youth recreation. The knowledge relied upon was the common-sense understandings of respectable society which "knew" that such things went on and that they were wrong.

PROBLEMATIZING THE SOCIAL, CONSTRUCTING PASTORAL POWER

How should the Canadian social surveys be understood? At first sight they could well be viewed as incomplete and insubstantial attempts to problematize the intersection of social and moral problems; moreover, the endeavour was abandoned as the Great War spread its shadow across the world and was never to be revived in the postwar period. It is important to avoid making unwarranted claims about the significance of this aborted project. Yet it had a significance that needs to be retrieved.

The proponents of the survey movement grasped the central importance of the necessity for society to seek to know itself and that the means to that end was to apply "science." Yet, in identifying the objective, they were unable to fulfil it because of the extent to which they were locked into a taken-for-granted knowledge of the very object, "society," which they sought to know. The best that they were able to achieve was to advance a classificatory scheme into which that knowledge was to be framed. Hence they produced a classificatory scheme which presumed a set of given boundaries between government, administration, economic conditions, social conditions, and moral conditions.

Furthermore, the goal that "society should know itself" was an activity that was discursively constructed so as to be undertaken by the voluntary organizations of moral reform. It is interesting to note that no calls were made on the state for official investigations to be conducted; indeed, there was very little discussion of the role of either federal or provincial institutions. The state seems to enter their conception of how local social problems were to be addressed as the legislative agency, to pass the laws that inquiry revealed as necessary. There are always problems in speculation about the explanation of absences, but it is probable that the religious origins of Canadian moral reform operated within the parameters of social gospel theology, which stressed that the church was centrally concerned not just with the spiritual domain, but with the social realm. I will return to this issue in arguing that the social survey project can best be understood as a form of pastoral power.

Nikolas Rose's description of moral technologies captures the techniques employed by the Canadian surveys:

> Figures, charts, maps, vivid descriptions of social explorers showed how coextensive were the topographies of class, occupation, morality, criminality and disease. Thus the space of the town became intelligible in new ways, in the spatial imagination produced by all those who thought that in order to govern relations between people more effectively one had first to inscribe them. One sees, in short, a multiplication of "laboratories of conduct" in which were performed a whole variety of ethical experiments on human beings.[64]

The Canadian surveys never succeeded in achieving the final stage described by Rose, however, in that they failed to generate the "laboratories of conduct." Why was this? In part it was because of the contingent circumstances of the outbreak of war, but more fatal was the reformers' emerging realization that, in the face of religious, cultural, and political diversity, their advocacy was impeded by their own narrow theological frame of reference within which these inquiries were undertaken.

Yet, in another sense, we should perhaps concede that the Canadian survey movement achieved the major elements of the necessary transformation. By the time Canada became immersed in the radically different preoccupations of war, the Methodist-Presbyterian alliance had already laid the basis for the break with theologically grounded moral regulation. The framework within which the surveys were undertaken was already well on the way to a shift to a model that today we would term "social work" and that reformers had begun to call "social service." This mutation is evidenced in the bewildering change of nomenclature of their organizational apparatus. The Presbyterian Church of Canada established a Department of Temperance and Other Moral and Social Reforms in 1907, which was quickly renamed the Board of Social and Moral Reform (1908); this became the Board of Moral and Social Reform and Evangelism in 1910 and finally the Board of Social Service and Evangelism in 1911. In a similar progression the Methodist Church of Canada's Department of Temperance, Prohibition and Moral Reform, established in 1902, changed to the Department of Social Service and Evangelism in 1914 and to the Department of Evangelism and Social Service in 1918.

This shift in the episteme of Canadian moral regulation was epitomized by the Social Service Congress of 1914. The sequence of sessions gave priority to "The Church" in the first, but this was followed by sessions on "Industrial Life and Labor," "Child Welfare," "The Problem of the City," "The Problem of the Country," "Commercialized Vice and the White Slave

Trade," "Immigration and the Humanization of Religion," "Political Purity," and finally "Temperance." The secularization was most clearly marked by the significant role given both in the agenda and on the platform to the "Trades and Labor Congress" and the "Dominion Grange and Farmers' Association." The policy statement adopted also reflected the new reconfiguration of the project of "social service." Its main elements established a commitment to a more equitable distribution of wealth, the abolition of poverty, protection of childhood, protection of the physical and moral health of women in industry, industrial accident compensation, conciliation and arbitration in labour disputes, proper housing, adequate care of dependent and defective persons, the reclamation of criminals, wholesome recreation, and the protection of society against contagious diseases.

These concerns constitute what Pierre Bourdieu has described as "preconstructed objects of inquiry" that are generated by self-evident and taken-for-granted "social problems." These more or less arbitrarily defined social categories, such as "youth" and "immigrants," are taken as natural objects. Bourdieu makes the point that "the preconstructed is everywhere"; the self-evident character of these objects of inquiry stems from the fit between objective structures and subjective categories formed within the prevailing cultural knowledge in a way that shields them from being questions. Thus these categories form the perspective that brings certain questions into focus, but excludes others. "Social science is always prone to receive from the social world it studies the *issues* that it poses about the world. Each society, at each moment, elaborates a body of *social problems* taken to be legitimate, worthy of being debated, of being made public."[65]

I suggest that we can best grasp the distinctive features of the categories which permeate the Canadian social surveys by viewing them through the lens of Michel Foucault's concept of "pastoral power." This concept first enters his work as a direct application of the Christian pastoral ministry which lays down a host of rules for individual conduct. Foucault then expands it by drawing on the metaphor at the heart of the Christian pastoral ideal, that of the shepherd and the flock. The shepherd takes care of the individuals within the flock to protect the flock as a whole.[66] He argues that the conception expanded its scope, moving beyond the religious sphere and playing an increasingly important role in civil society. "Pastoral power" is an "individualizing power": "[I]f the state is the political form of a centralized and centralizing power, let us call pastorship the individualizing power."[67] "Pastoral governance" became absorbed into governmental techniques during the eighteenth century and remains an important technique of regulation down to the present. Pastoral power is directed to ensuring, sustaining, and improving the lives of each and every one. Foucault was concerned with the aggregation of people, conceived as a population, by means of focusing on the care of individuals. Thus the growth of public health systems is pastoral in that caring for the health of individuals prevents the spread of contagious diseases to the population as a whole; pastoral power involves the use of techniques for the governance of others.

The social survey project was a form of pastoral power that identified social problems and, in particular, troublesome populations and sought to devise means of regulation that addressed individuals, both for their own sake and for the well-being of the whole. The language of pastoralism came easily to activists in the social gospel movement; the church as shepherd and the congregation as flock was a familiar imagery. But the social gospel effected a significant discursive shift. The "flock" was no longer the church congregation, but was the growing population outside the immediate reach of the church. To envisage how the working poor and the recently arrived immigrants, who made up an increasing proportion of the working poor, might be reached entailed a further significant shift. It was no longer the church as an institutional power with a natural right to govern, but rather the congregation of the church, led by its pastorate, that had to reach out to the working poor. Translated into social terms it was the respectable classes, whose respectability was confirmed by their participation in and through the church, that must attend to the needs of the working poor. [...]

The project of the social survey movement, partial and incomplete though it was, stands as testimony to the emergence of a new configuration of social power. The project of the surveys was committed to scientific modes of inquiry, but unable to realize their application. It was, as a result, unable to yield the specific forms of knowledge needed to inform the attempt to create a pastoral mode of governance by the respectable classes over the aggregated mass of the working poor.

NOTES

1. Thomas Osborne and Nikolas Rose, "In the Name of Society, or Three Theses on the History of Social Thought," *History of the Human Sciences*, vol. 10, no. 3 (1997), pp. 87–104; Mary Poovey, *Making a Social Body: British Cultural Formation, 1930–1864* (Chicago: University of Chicago Press, 1995).

2. The social gospel movement became a major influence on Canadian Protestantism during the last two decades of the nineteenth century. Richard Allen, "The Social Gospel and the Reform Tradition in Canada, 1890–1928," *Canadian Historical Review*, vol. 49, no. 4 (1968), pp. 381–399; Ramsay Cook, *The Regenerators: Social Criticism in Late Victorian English Canada* (Toronto: University of Toronto Press, 1985); Brian J. Fraser, *The Social Uplifters: Presbyterian Progressives and the Social Gospel in Canada, 1875–1915* (Waterloo: Wilfrid Laurier University Press, 1988).

3. Quoted in Fraser, *The Social Uplifters*, p. 80.

4. Shearer was a major moral reformer who had come to prominence in the temperance movement. He had been full-time secretary of the Lord's Day Alliance and had played a key role in securing the passage of the first federal Sunday Observance Act in 1906. In 1914 he became the General Secretary of the Social Service Council of Canada, where he continued to press for surveys employing social science methods.

5. The Council changed its name to the Social Service Council of Canada in 1914, a vivid illustration of the transformation of "moral reform" to "social work."

6. These bodies underwent a series of frequent name changes over the period under investigation, but since the nomenclature used here was in use in 1913, it will be retained for the purposes of this study.

7. Toronto Social Survey Commission, *Report of the Social Survey Commission, Toronto. Presented to the City Council, October Fourth, 1915* (Toronto: Carswell, 1915).

8. Committee of Fifteen, *The Social Evil: With Special Reference to Conditions Existing in the City of New York*, ed. Edwin R. A. Seligman (New York: G. P. Putnam's Sons, 1902).

9. I have identified 39 such reports, but it is likely that there were more. Many big cities carried out ambitious reports (Boston, Chicago, New York, Philadelphia), but so also did much smaller communities such as Elmira (New York), Grand Rapids (Michigan), and Paducah (Kentucky).

10. I have offered an overview of the American vice commissions in chapter 5 of Alan Hunt, *Governing Morals: A Social History of Moral Regulation* (Cambridge: Cambridge University Press, 1999); otherwise, there have only been studies of individual reports.

11. Elizabeth Beardsley Butler, *Women and the Trades: Pittsburgh, 1907–1908* (New York: Russell Sage Foundation, 1909); Margaret Byington, *Homestead: The Households of a Mill Town* (New York: Russell Sage Foundation, 1910); Crystal Eastman, *Work-Accidents and the Law: The Pittsburgh Survey* (New York: Russell Sage Foundation, 1910); John A. Fitch, *The Steel Workers* (New York: Russell Sage Foundation, 1910); and Paul U. Kellogg et al., *Wage-Earning Pittsburgh* (New York: Russell Sage Foundation, 1914).

12. Allen M. Eaton and Shelby M. Harrison, *A Bibliography of Social Surveys: Reports of Fact-Finding Studies Made as a Basis for Social Action* (New York: Russell Sage Foundation, 1930).

13. This debate is well represented by Maurine Greenwald and Margo Anderson, eds., *Pittsburgh Surveyed: Social Science and Social Reform in the Early Twentieth Century* (Pittsburgh: University of Pittsburgh Press, 1996); Martin Bulmer, Kevin Bales, and Kathryn K. Sklar, eds., *The Social Survey in Historical Perspective, 1880–1940* (Cambridge: Cambridge University Press, 1991).

14. For example, Marlene G. Shore emphasizes the significance of the Chicago School in *The Science of Social Redemption: McGill, the Chicago School, and the Origins of Social Research in Canada* (Toronto: University of Toronto Press, 1987). Theresa Richardson and Donald Fisher, eds., *Development of the Social Sciences in the United States and Canada: The Role of Philanthropy* (Stamford, Conn.: JAI Press, 1999), attach greater importance to the social services movement.

15. George Seibel, *Report and Recommendations of the Morals Efficiency Commission* (Pittsburgh: Morals Efficiency Commission, 1913), p. 1.

16. Justice H. A. Robson, *Judge Robson on Segregation or Toleration of Vice: Duties of Police Authorities, the Enforcement of Law: Report of the Social Vice Commission Winnipeg, January 11th, 1911* (Toronto: Moral and Social Reform Council of Canada, 1911).

17. Robson, *Judge Robson on Segregation or Toleration of Vice,* p. 12.

18. Rural surveys formed a significant component of the spread of the American social survey tradition and many dozens were published; detailed in Eaton and Harrison, *A Bibliography of Social Surveys.*

19. Cooperating Organizations of the Presbyterian and Methodist Churches, *The Rural Survey of County of Huron, Ontario* (n.p., 1914), p. 6.

20. Department of Social Service and Evangelism of the Methodist and Presbyterian Churches, *Swan River Valley, Manitoba: Report of a Rural Survey of the Agricultural, Education, Social and Religious Life* (n.p., 1914).

21. Herbert B. Ames, *The City Below the Hill: A Sociological Study of a Portion of the City of Montreal* (Montreal: Bishop Engraving and Printing Co., 1897).

22. Ibid., p. 31.

23. The only Canadian survey to refer explicitly to the Pittsburgh survey as part of the survey tradition was that of Sydney (Nova Scotia). Department of Temperance and Moral Reform of the Methodist Church and the Board of Social Service and Evangelism of the Presbyterian Church, *Report of a Preliminary and General Social Survey of Sydney, Nova Scotia* (n.p., 1913).

24. The Vancouver report is sub-titled "A Brief Investigation … Which Indicate the Need of an Intensive Social Survey, the Lines of Which Are Herein Suggested."

25. Presbyterian Committee on Religious Education, Methodist Department of Temperance and Moral Reform and the Presbyterian Board of Social Service and Evangelism, *The City of London, Ontario: Report of a Limited Survey of Educational, Social and Industrial Life* (London: Men's Federation of London, 1913).

26. An exception is the local investigators recruited to survey the drinking establishments in London, Ontario; it should be noted that the Men's Federation was a recently formed Methodist-Presbyterian organization.

27. Jacob Riis, *How the Other Half Lives* (New York: Charles Scribner's Sons, 1890); Lincoln Steffens, *The Shame of the Cities* (New York: Peter Smith, 1904).

28. Department of Temperance and Moral Reform of the Methodist Church and the Board of Social Service and Evangelism of the Presbyterian Church, *Report of a Preliminary and General Social Survey of Regina* (n.p., 1913), p. 4.

29. *Report of a Preliminary and General Social Survey of Sydney, Nova Scotia.*

30. The parallel "rural surveys" made use of travelling exhibitions which travelled around the small country towns (for example, the Huron County survey of 1914 and the Swan River Valley survey of 1914).

31. Department of Temperance and Moral Reform of the Methodist Church and the Board of Social Service and Evangelism of the Presbyterian Church, *Report of a Preliminary and General Social Survey of Hamilton* (n.p., 1913).

32. Department of Temperance and Moral Reform of the Methodist Church and the Board of Social Service and Evangelism of the Presbyterian Church, *Report of a Preliminary and General Social Survey of Fort William* (n.p., 1913).

33. Department of Temperance and Moral Reform of the Methodist Church and the Board of Social Service and Evangelism of the Presbyterian Church, *Report of a Preliminary and General Social Survey of Port Arthur* (n.p., 1913).

34. No survey gives any indication of the source of population statistics, but, since there is a general reliance on information provided by the city administration, it is likely that these are locally generated figures.

35. *Report of a Preliminary and General Social Survey of Fort William,* p. 8.

36. *Report of a Preliminary and General Social Survey of Port Arthur,* p. 7.

37. Department of Temperance and Moral Reform of the Methodist Church and the Board of Social Service and Evangelism of the Presbyterian Church, *Report of a Preliminary and General Social Survey of Hamilton* (n.p., 1913), p. 13.

38. *Report of a Preliminary and General Social Survey of Port Arthur,* p. 10.

39. Department of Temperance and Moral Reform of the Methodist Church and the Board of Social Service and Evangelism of the Presbyterian Church, *Vancouver, British Columbia: The Report of a Brief Investigation of Social Conditions in the City Which Indicate the Need of an Intensive Social Survey, the Lines of Which Are Herein Suggested* (n.p., n.d.), p. 12.

40. *Report of a Preliminary and General Social Survey of Hamilton*, p. 20.
41. A similar survey was conducted in London, Ontario, on Saturday, November 8, 1912, when the investigators found 561 men in bars (of whom 44 were under age and 195 intoxicated) and 12 women in side rooms. *The City of London, Ontario*, p. 67.
42. *The City of London, Ontario*, p. 71.
43. *Vancouver, British Columbia*, p. 16.
44. *Report of a Preliminary and General Social Survey of Regina*, p. 33.
45. Alan Hunt, "Regulating Heterosexual Space: Sexual Politics on the Early Twentieth Century," *Journal of Historical Sociology*, vol. 15, no. 1 (2002), pp. 1–34.
46. *The City of London, Ontario*, p. 11.
47. Nikolas Rose and Mariana Valverde, "Governed By Law?," *Social and Legal Studies*, vol. 7 (1998), p. 573.
48. In some respects the concept "the social" is similar to earlier usage in sociology of the "social problem" except that it refers to a troublesome social category rather than troublesome behaviour. For completeness the concept of "the social" requires the presence of another segment, namely, agents concerned and able to engage in organized action.
49. The Winnipeg inquiry, in response to Shearer's allegations of "tolerated vice," was exclusively concerned with the link between alcohol and prostitution. This focus was wedded to a concern, more distinctive of American Progressivism than Canadian reform discourses, with "graft" and police corruption. A lengthy session at the Social Service Congress, held in Ottawa in 1914, was devoted to "political purity" debating the corruption that was perceived as characterizing the party system. Social Service Congress, *Report of Addresses and Proceedings* (Toronto: Social Service Council of Canada, 1914). Prostitution was central to the Toronto survey and the Montreal reports and was a significant element in the reports on Fort William and Port Arthur.
50. It may also be assumed that an educated and concerned audience, which we can presume to be the audience reformers hoped would visit the public exhibition of the data, would be able to read the stylizations of numbers and that such an audience had come to expect numbers as confirmation of the seriousness and accuracy of the undertaking. See Patricia Cohen, *A Calculating People: The Spread of Numeracy in Early America* (Chicago: University of Chicago Press, 1982); Mary Poovey, *A History of the Modern Fact: Problems of Knowledge in the Sciences of Wealth and Society* (Chicago: University of Chicago Press, 1998).
51. W. A. Riddell, "The Value of the Social Survey" in *Social Service Congress*, p. 59.
52. Charles J. Hastings, "The Consequences of Prostitution and Suggested Remedies" in *Social Service Congress*, pp. 208–217.
53. Similar rhetorical tactics are found today among those who seek to focus attention on such issues as sexual harassment and AIDS by techniques that inflate the number of those affected.
54. *Report of the Social Survey Commission, Toronto*, p. 1.
55. Ibid., p. 15.
56. Ibid., p. 9.
57. The report concluded that massage parlours were houses of prostitution "and worse — the 'worse' standing for things abominable and unspeakable, things compared with which ordinary prostitution, as the word is commonly understood, is respectable. It is even impossible to give the details of the treatment given by the women professing to give only legitimate massage to men — transgresses the bounds of decency" (p. 17). This was the only observation concerning specific sexual practices — it may be inferred that what was so impossible to mention was oral sex.
58. The "charity girls" being those who engaged in sexual relations after participating in some form of heterosexual activity involving entertainment and "treats." See Kathy Peiss, "'Charity Girls' and City Pleasures: Historical Notes on Working Class Sexuality, 1880–1920" in Ann Snitow, Christine Stansell, and Sharon Thompson, eds., *Powers of Desire: The Politics of Sexuality* (New York: Monthly Review Press, 1983), pp. 51–73.
59. *Report of the Social Survey Commission, Toronto*, p. 13.
60. Only in the Vancouver report was there any attention paid to changes in the spatial distribution of prostitution; both prostitution and liquor were linked to the presence of an Asian immigrant quarter.
61. Carolyn Strange, "From Modern Babylon to a City Upon a Hill: The Toronto Social Survey Commission and the Search for Sexual Order in the City" in Roger Hall et al., eds., *Patterns of the Past: Interpreting Ontario's History* (Toronto: Dundurn, 1988), pp. 255–277, and *Toronto's Girl Problem: The Perils and Pleasures of the City, 1880–1930* (Toronto: University of Toronto Press, 1995).
62. *Report of the Social Survey Commission, Toronto*, p. 36.
63. Ibid., p. 56.

64. Nikolas Rose, *Powers of Freedom: Reframing Political Thought* (Cambridge: Cambridge University Press, 1999), pp. 104–105.

65. Pierre Bourdieu, "The Practice of Reflexive Sociology" in Pierre Bourdieu and Loïe Wacquant, eds., *An Invitation to Reflexive Sociology* (Chicago: University of Chicago Press, 1992), p. 236.

66. The concern for each and for all is captured in Foucault's essay "Omnes et Singulatim: Towards a Criticism of 'Political Reason'" in S. McMurrin, ed., *The Tanner on Human Values*, vol. 2 (Salt Lake City: University of Utah Press, 1981), pp. 223–254.

67. Michel Foucault, "Politics and Reason" in L. D. Kritzman, ed., *Politics, Philosophy, Culture: Interviews and Other Writings, 1977–1984* (New York: Routledge, 1988), p. 60.

Article 3.2

Sean Purdy

Industrial Efficiency, Social Order and Moral Purity: Housing Reform Thought in English Canada, 1900–1950

Issues to Consider

- Purdy argues that housing reform was premised on a doctrine of "community" meant to overcome class and racial differences. How did this become the chosen approach? What objectives did the reformers hope to realize by emphasizing community?
- Why was housing singled out as a pressing social problem early in the social gospel campaign? How did the material reality of working-class housing come to be framed in terms of the middle-class ideal of home?
- Why was the state seen as a necessary partner to voluntary efforts in "reforming" private homes, a situation that might be seen as paradoxical? What was the Commission of Conservation's role?
- Purdy notes the measure of moral judgment about the "slum dwellings" of the urban working class that existed alongside the Christian obligation for the affluent to assist the needy and the larger social reform impulse that this obligation encouraged. What was "moral" about this particular social problem?
- Like Hunt, Purdy discusses the social construction of class, race, the ideal home, and other key concepts. What does he discover about their interrelations?

In the Autumn of 1910, Henry Vivian, British M.P. for Birkenhead and prestigious housing reformer, visited numerous Canadian cities to present a series of "illustrated lectures" on city planning and housing reform. Vivian's graphic description of slums and dilapidated housing conditions in the Old World surprised few listeners. Tales of squalid hovels with overcrowded "inmates" breeding crime and moral degeneracy were commonly associated with European and, increasingly, American cities. What startled the sensitive scruples of Canada's social elite was Vivian's pointed depiction of widespread slum conditions in Canada. In a lecture in Ottawa, Vivian sternly noted that in most Canadian cities "less science and forethought are given to the care of human beings than a modern farmer gives to the raising of his pigs."[1]

Vivian was not the first person to raise concerns about housing conditions in Canada. Moral reformers in the late nineteenth century had isolated the inferior state of working-class housing as one of the key social ills of Canada's burgeoning industrial cities. Yet there was still a sense of unease about the nature of the problem and the need for intervention in 1910 since Canadian cities, it was widely believed, had avoided the acute social problems of urbanization characteristic of Europe and the United States. Moreover, the view that active intervention by concerned citizens and the state was needed to solve economic and social problems was still the

Source: Sean Purdy, "Industrial Efficiency, Social Order and Moral Purity: Housing Reform Thought in English Canada, 1900–1950," *Urban History Review* 25, no. 2 (1997): 30–40.

preserve of a few forward-minded intellectuals and labour movement activists. This all changed in the tumultuous years surrounding the First World War as the housing reform movement blossomed under the auspices of governments convinced of the necessity of solving the critical problems of poor housing conditions. Amidst widespread social unrest, governments were forced to act by establishing the first housing programs, setting the stage for the expanded social housing ventures which marked the post–Second World War era.

This paper traces the evolution of reform ideology in the housing sphere in the first half of the twentieth century by critically analyzing the ideas and practices of a number of key housing reformers and agencies. Premised on middle-class beliefs in the necessity of state intervention and the capacity of the trained expert to alleviate social conflict, the movement for housing betterment centred on a doctrine of "community" that ostensibly stood above labour and capital, aiming to harmonize social relations for the greater good of the nation. To this end, stress was placed on bettering the physical conditions of workers' dwellings in order to improve the productive capacity of the labour force. But the concentration on the physical quality of workers' homes was also tied to the wider ideological goal of strengthening the family — a cornerstone of the nation and the state in the estimation of reform-minded citizens.

The role housing reform could play as part of the larger project of securing social consent by stabilizing family structures and contributing to the construction of a distinct national identity constituted pivotal concerns in the discourse of the reform effort. Progressives aimed to extend state intervention in the housing sphere in order to allay the impact of industrialization and preserve class cooperation and social hierarchy. Yet without losing sight of this distinct regulatory thrust from above, it is also necessary to chart how housing experts and policy makers groped through the contradictions of urban society in a creative manner they themselves saw as more or less disinterested. As the Italian Marxist Antonio Gramsci insightfully put it: "The intellectuals are breaking loose from the dominant class in order to unite themselves to it more intimately."[2]

RESPONSES TO THE HOUSING PROBLEM BEFORE 1914

The "Housing Question" in Canada evolved out of the broader urban reform movement which emerged in the late nineteenth and early twentieth century.[3] Middle- and upper-class reformers attempted to come to terms with what they perceived as an alarming rise in urban poverty, child neglect and crime — all regarded as corrosive influences on the social order. In the first decade of the new century, the residues of nineteenth-century social thought were still evident, as housing reformers stressed individual responsibility and moral virtue as the fundamental traits of social and economic well-being. However, explanations of the urban crisis usually began to combine these moral imperatives with distinct consideration for efficient living conditions which spoke to the widespread apprehension about the effects of poverty on economic performance and social harmony.

Housing first became a major concern in Canadian urban centres due to the increasing dangers of contagious diseases and "immorality" which seemingly spread from the slums to more affluent neighbourhoods. Since infectious diseases could spread to the entire city there was a clear incentive for reformers to clean up the slums. As Paul Rutherford aptly notes: "Disease did not respect social standing."[4] Squalid housing conditions were an important impetus behind the emergence of the modern public health project around the turn of the century. While most public health ideas at the time incorporated elements of both schools of current medical thought — environmentalism and eugenics[5]— medical officials concentrated on the slum "environment," arguing that once these slovenly blots were removed the housing problem would vanish. In keeping with this ecological emphasis, dwelling inspections, building standards and sanitary regulations provided the early groundwork for public health activity.

But there was a pronounced interest in eradicating the moral failings of slum dwellers as well. J. J. Kelso, the founder of the Children's Aid Society and an early advocate of housing reform, applied the metaphor of disease to the moral degeneration of the urban environment itself, likening the slum to a rotting community, a "perfect labyrinth of hovels."[6] Social purity campaigns of the era and sensationalist critiques in newspapers and urban affairs journals were wedded to a traditional focus on moral depravity.[7] A 1906 editorial in the *Toronto Daily News* indicates the emphasis placed on public decency: "... the Ward [a slum] constitutes a constant menace to the physical and moral health of the city. It is an open sore from which flow fetid currents which cannot but be corrupting to the whole community."[8] The physical scarring of the city was linked explicitly to the slide into moral impurity, adding ideological ammunition to the reform crusaders' attempt to repair the social fabric of the city.

In the face of intense market competition, some manufacturers soon added their voice to the chorus of concern for the working-class housing problem. While partially couched in arguments about the moral consequences of substandard living conditions on workers, industrialists were more attentive to the threat to workplace efficiency that inadequate dwellings posed. Although they upbraided "rapacious landlords"[9] for raising the costs of housing and thereby increasing the pressure for wage increases, employers hinted that blame lay beyond the sole responsibility of unscrupulous individuals. Presaging the later obsession with instilling efficiency in all facets of life, they discerned that there was a direct link between the factories and the homes of workers, a relationship that needed to be reinforced. "It is the best class of philanthropy that which results in raising the condition of our citizens and thereby increasing their efficiency," *Industrial Canada*, the organ of the Canadian Manufacturers' Association (CMA), asserted in 1911.[10] Bettering the housing conditions of the working class also promised to offset the spectre of class conflict. Recognizing that by improving home environments a healthy, contented workforce could be generated, sections of the business community joined reformers in calling for action on the housing question.

Since the family was to many in the upper classes the very wellspring of community life, early reformers often isolated the physical and moral effects of substandard housing quality on family life as a prime motive for action. The home in reform discourse was more than merely a physical structure; it reflected a widely held set of ideas about society, the family and women. Declining birthrates, the transformation of industrial production and women's increasing participation in the wage labour force prompted early reformers to focus upon the threats to the "natural" role of women as mother and provider in the family home. Kelso echoed the sentiments of many in the reform community when he described the family home as the "foundation stone of the state."[11] The early domestic science movement aspired to fortify the mortar by applying rational techniques to living in order to reinforce the "proper" family form and enhance workplace efficiency. "Until women have learned the science of living and properly regulating the household expenditure in proportion to the income," one domestic scientist declared, "wage earners at least will be labouring under a disadvantage."[12] Improving housing aimed to ensure stable family arrangements free from the insidious influences of the city.

The responses of moral reformers, some far-sighted capitalists and even public health officials to the problem of working-class housing were usually based on superficial impressions gained from first-hand observations or lurid newspaper stories that exposed the racy underside of Canada's metropolises. The paucity of solid data on living conditions in the cities provoked observers to embark on detailed studies to ascertain the precise nature and extent of the problem.

In Montreal, wealthy manufacturer Herbert Ames published *The City Below the Hill* in 1897, a statistical examination of social conditions in Montreal's working-class west end. Ames's study charted incomes, rental costs, and housing density and types through survey and mapping techniques. Frequent comparisons to the European housing situation and the inclusion of model house plans reflected Ames's awareness of international conditions. In a vein characteristic of public health reform, he stressed the lack of proper sanitary facilities, insufficient sunlight and air, and constricted living space in working-class tenements which resulted in deficient public health and high mortality rates. Despite its limited precision, the study provided some hard data which reinforced the general impression that housing conditions were in need of substantial improvement.

Ames combined an essentially idealistic view of social reform with an empirical orientation on urban problems. He highlighted the necessity of "scientific knowledge," but advocated decidedly moderate philanthropic solutions based on his belief that the "business experience" of the upper classes should be rationally applied to urban problems.[13] Where many of his contemporaries trod a fine line between environmentalism and individualism, Ames grasped the centrality of wider social conditions in the causes of urban degradation. He refuted the argument that "drink, crime or voluntary idleness"[14] were the underlying factors behind urban misery. Still, moral regeneration loomed large in Ames's approach. He looked to the enlightened attitudes of philanthropists to solve the housing problem and disapproved of state intervention in the housing market. He shared the same concerns and assumptions of crusading journalists: the moral effects of overcrowding, the individual responsibility of tenants and landlords, and the essentially self-correcting tendencies of the economy. By providing minimal state assistance through sanitary regulations and the moral uplift of reform from above, Ames hoped to raise society as a whole: "Increase in ability to surround themselves with influences which improve the mind, morals and health of this part of the community means elevation for society from its foundations, whereby all above is also raised."[15]

Bridging the spiritually-based moralism of nineteenth-century social criticism and the scientific social analysis of the twentieth century was the Social Gospel Movement. Its primary reform component, the Social Service Congress of Canada, consisted of representatives from the Protestant churches, farm and labour groups, and the Woman's Christian Temperance Union. In the words of one of its spokespersons, it concentrated upon "the impressive fact that in this civilized and Christian country both civilization and Christianity are challenged by the economic, industrial and social conditions upon which the fabric of the state is erected."[16] The magnitude of social dislocation and the incapacity to achieve effective reform compelled a shift in emphasis to the wider social environment. In 1913 the Congress undertook comprehensive surveys of five urban and two rural areas throughout Canada. Attention was drawn in these studies to the problems of shoddy dwelling construction, inadequate sanitation and the attendant moral decay, conditions which were particularly marked in the industrial cities.[17] Social Gospellers' concern with social investigation demonstrates that the scientific bases of housing reform were beginning to overtake the individualistic and philanthropic inclination of early reformers, although they were still animated by traditional moral imperatives.[18]

For the majority of middle- and upper-class commentators, it was still convenient to attribute poverty and criminality to individual weaknesses rather than structural flaws in the economy and society. But, despite the limited restrictive solutions suggested to the housing problem, early housing reform responses should not be underestimated. The Victorian creed of the "inexorability of material and moral progress"[19] and faith in individualistic solutions were gradually eroding in the face of palpable threats of class conflict and the recognition of the increasingly interdependent nature of modern society. So threatening were these social dislocations that *Industrial Canada* cautioned that: "Out of the slums stalk the Socialist with his red flag, the Union agitator with the auctioneer's voice and the Anarchist with his torch."[20] In order to stave off such conflictual social relations, as well as the menace to family life posed by women's changing role and the dilution of the emerging national identity by immigrants, reformers appreciated that some form of sustained intervention was required.[21] The crucible of the First World War would accelerate the appeal of social scientific analysis, interacting neatly with a growing state prepared to intercede more directly in the housing question.

WAR AND SOCIETY: HOUSING REFORM FROM 1914–30

The drive for scientific approaches to urban difficulties began before the First World War but received a great boost during wartime as governments faced the exigencies of rapacious international economic and military competition. In the housing sphere, this was manifested in a heightened sense of urgency for state intervention, predicated on the belief that only a rational, state-supported approach to urban-industrial problems would offset the perils of economic crisis, labour strife, family dissolution and the dilution of "Canadian" citizenship. It was in this period of anxious reassessment of the country's social problems that the movement for housing improvement first blossomed. The years from the First World War through the early 1930s saw the establishment of a city planning profession with housing as a principal component and irregular but expanding government initiatives to improve national housing conditions.

The Commission of Conservation, 1909–21, was the first federal organization devoted to considering the afflictions generated by industrialization. It was commissioned in 1909 and charged with investigating the general field of natural and human resource conservation, collecting, interpreting and publicizing information, and advising on policy issues. The Town Planning Branch published a monthly bulletin, *Conservation of Life*, whose circulation reached 12,000 in 1917.[22] The Commission also extended its activities into the academy, inaugurating lecture courses at the University of Toronto and McGill University in 1919–20. The stress on extensive publicity and education echoed the contemporary belief that enlightened public opinion would ensure effective action. Indeed, an appreciative article in *Saturday Night* on the eve of the Commission's demise proclaimed that in the sphere of town planning it had "shouldered the burden of creating, so to speak, a national conscience."[23]

The Commission's public health branch was first appointed to deal with housing issues. This is indicative of the concern with the environmental health aspects of housing hardship — sanitation and disease prevention. Traditional medical advice focused on personal hygiene, community sanitation and health education mixed with a hereditarian strain which viewed the corruption of the social order as a result of the biological inferiority of certain persons, especially immigrants. But the rapid and erratic economic growth of the period also brought to the fore the pressing issues of anarchic urban development and failures of the residential construction industry to provide adequate quantities of affordable housing. The new profession of town or city planning sought to fill the gap by promising a more wholistic approach to land development and housing. The masthead of the *Journal of the Town Planning Institute of Canada* concisely defined the profession's function as "the scientific and orderly disposition of land and buildings in use and development with a view to obviating congestion and securing economic and social efficiency, health and well-being in urban and rural communities."[24] As Martin Daunton puts it, town planning strived to ameliorate the vagaries of unbridled free enterprise, introducing "order and discipline for the benefit of market forces by creating an agreed framework of debate for planners, developers, and politicians."[25]

Public interest in town planning culminated in a decision by the Commission to seek a full-time advisor on town planning. Successful petitions to hire British planning expert Thomas Adams came from the CMA, the Canadian Public Health Association, the Order of the Daughters of the Empire, the National Council of Women, the Board of Trade of Hamilton and numerous charities. Adams was a noted planner associated with the British Garden City

Movement.[26] He was a prodigious writer, editing and writing much of *Conservation of Life*, and altogether publishing 139 articles from 1914–21 and a major book, *Rural Planning and Development: A Study of Rural Conditions and Problems in Canada*, that drew national and international acclaim.[27] Under the auspices of the Commission, Adams assisted in the creation of national and local Civic Improvement Leagues and successfully promoted the establishment of a national town planning organization, the Town Planning Institute of Canada.[28] Most of the provincial planning legislation of the period was either written or aided by Adams; he worked as a consultant to the Ontario Housing Commission and was instrumental in planning designs for the Halifax Reconstruction Commission and the federal housing program of 1918.[29] The Commission, under Adams's guidance, played a central role in providing ideological legitimation for the emerging theory and practice of town planning and helped promulgate its merits to a wide network of reformers, academics and politicians.

The *efficiency movement*, exemplified in the sphere of production relations by scientific management guru Frederick Taylor, was alive and well in Canada in municipal government and social welfare reform and was central to Adams's views on the housing question. "This is an age in which 'efficiency' is a great catchword," A. G. Dalzell, a former assistant to Adams, outlined in a 1920 speech to real estate agents. "Industrial efficiency, commercial efficiency, national efficiency and personal efficiency are terms constantly before us."[30] The war provided a solid impetus for emphasizing efficient home life. "As a result of the past three years experience," Adams noted in 1918, "we have been made to see very clearly the extent to which the output of war industries and the production of food depends not only on the organization of labour but also on the conditions under which the labourer lives."[31] The Hydrostone scheme in Halifax was designed with this in mind: "To properly house the worker, to give him air space and light, pure water, and efficient means of transportation to his work, is merely exercising enlightened self-interest in the interests of our industries — for labour is the most costly and important factor in production, although it is frequently least considered."[32]

The ambitious post-war drive for social and economic reconstruction punctuated the reform community's trepidation over intensified social conflicts. The National Industrial Conference (1919) and the Royal Commission on Industrial Relations (1919) both highlighted poor dwelling conditions as one of the chief causes of the working-class upheaval and recommended immediate measures to tackle the problem. CMA President Thomas Rodens warned his fellow manufacturers about the urgency of housing reform in 1918, stressing "it was that condition that brought about the downfall of Russia, the indifference of the guiding class to these conditions."[33] By war's end, housing reform was no longer considered a local issue of concern only to the poor but rather was seen as a major obstacle to the advancement of a industrial nation.[34] In his initial report to the Housing Committee of the federal Cabinet in November 1918, Adams underscored the critical demand for state intervention in the housing sphere: "We cannot have these things [social peace] if we hold hard to antiquated notions regarding the license to use the rights of property to the injury of mankind. Property has duties as well as rights."[35] Co-partnership schemes, a model of housing provision in which private investors and tenants would buy shares in a housing company, employing the combined revenue to build houses, would encourage cooperation and dissuade "socialistic ideas."[36] Uppermost in Adams's mind was the belief that the contending classes could be brought together in a cooperative alliance for collective national preservation.

Recourse to nationalism proved to be a helpful means of blunting the bruising social conflicts of the war period. As a ruling myth, nationalism strived to eclipse other social divisions, especially class, by positing an overarching national identity. Along with immigration controls, social policies proved a particularly convenient means of shaping the contours of the "nation." Social policies worked to define the boundaries of the "national" working class by sanctioning a specific model of class structure — what constitutes a proper "citizen"— and by attempting to mould social relations within the nation — what constitutes the proper behaviour of these officially defined citizens.[37] The discourse of housing improvement, along with its counterparts in other areas of social policy, assisted in cultivating the popular fiction of Anglo-supremacy and spreading the racist message that "outsiders" were to blame for the country's problems.

The threat of "race suicide" loomed large in the outlook of housing reformers as it did in all the social improvement campaigns of the era.[38] It was believed that the miserable health of the working class, most visibly demonstrated in the high failure rates in military medical inspections and the large-scale "infiltration" of non-British immigrants, would jeopardize the future of the Anglo-Saxon "race." Neither was there disagreement that the physical, mental and moral state of the "race" faced grave danger unless speedy action was taken. W. Struthers, a prominent public health official, expressed reformers' concerns succinctly: "Poor housing conditions, lack of light and ventilation, uncleanliness, ignorance of proper care of the body and of the laws of health, unwholesome and improper food and drink, the prevalence of venereal and other diseases are rapidly producing a degenerate race."[39] Charles Hodgetts argued that temporary shacktowns on the margins of urban areas were becoming the "overcrowded permanent homes of a foreign population — hot beds of parasitic and communicable diseases and breeders of vice and inequity."[40] Such bigotry was extended to working-class British and American immigrants as well, revealing the new-found view that race degeneration stemmed partly from urban-industrial life. The distinguished psychiatrist C. K. Clarke regarded them as "failures at home, and are often so because of congenital defects. Their progeny may rise above their own level, but they never cease to suffer from their misfortunes of birth."[41] It was not the wretched housing conditions that immigrant workers had to endure that was isolated as the problem, but rather the immigrants themselves.

The construction of race was developed in relation to external economic and political pressures as well as internal conflicts. In an era of competing imperialisms, the menace posed by detrimental living conditions on economic and military capacity caused great apprehension among social commentators and policy makers. In an article entitled "Defective Children" Dr. Helen MacMurchy, a noted Ontario paediatrician and leading eugenicist, favourably cited British Prime Minister Lloyd George's admonition that "You cannot have an A1 army on a C3 population."[42] Detailing the impressive housing schemes in the German city of Ulm, Noulan Cauchon, future president of the Town Planning Institute of Canada, argued that Canada needed to meet the challenge of the enemy: "Such is the efficiency of the enemy whom we will have to fight industrially after the war and reveals one of the reasons why he can compete so successfully — wherein he has learned to live efficiently and cheaply."[43] The influence of "social imperialism,"[44] in which social reform ideas were thoroughly permeated with imperialist assumptions, was striking.

Since the home was regarded as the basic unit of social organization, it was chosen as the chief site in the battle for "Canadianization." Racial and ethnic assumptions intersected with the dominant views of woman's role as nurturer of the "race." Henry Vivian spoke to a receptive Calgary audience, contending that: "the future of our Empire, the future of our race depends upon the preservation of those conditions that make for the retention and the strength of that individuality, and upon that our future really exists. The individual home, the individual family, the individual brought up in home, and the association of home life — upon that all our success depends."[45] "There is no more sacred word in the English language than 'Home,'" Dr Charles Hastings, Toronto's Medical Officer of Health articulated, "and on the retaining of the sacredness and significance of our homes depends the future of our municipality and our Nation."[46]

Home life was to be improved through programs directed at regulating the domestic labour of working-class and immigrant women, focusing on child-raising and household work. To social imperialists, as Anna Davin has shown, "population was power"[47] so motherhood needed to be placed on a scientific basis to ensure the continuance of the Anglo-Saxon race and to bring unhealthy immigrants up to scratch. If Taylorism pledged to increase efficiency in the labour process, domestic science vowed to "modernize" daily home life. A properly kept, compact family home fitted with the increasingly common amenities of electric lighting, water, cooking appliances and indoor toilets offered a certain future, free from the vagaries of cramped, unsanitary lodgings.[48] It is likely that many reformers were motivated by genuine personal consideration for the casualties of industrial capitalism. But altruistic concerns were overshadowed by the vital effort to create a stable family unit comprised of fit and complacent workers which guaranteed the protection of the nation.

In tandem with the crude procedures of house inspections and condemnations, the emerging public health education project was utilized to instill the values of thriftiness, efficiency and "Canadianness." In 1911, housekeepers were hired by the Industrial Hygiene and Housing Division of the Toronto public health department to provide advice on "cleanliness, sanitation and Canadian methods of house keeping."[49] Speaking of the Ward, Toronto's "notorious" immigrant slum, Joseph Howes of the Bureau of Municipal Research recommended that since the "majority of the residents are usually foreigners, often not speaking our language, not fully understanding our laws, and frequently without the Anglo-Saxon ideas of sanitation," the reform effort should be concentrated on the "the process of education and Canadianization."[50] With this attitude in mind, Charles Hastings sent out women sanitary inspectors to go into immigrants' houses to "teach them how to clean up and keep clean their homes and environments … Many of these people, by reason of birth and environments, have neither the moral stamina or the intellect to rid themselves of their vices and shortcomings."[51] The process of racial "degeneration" was believed to be best tackled by "Canadianizing" housewives in order to equip families with the tools of citizenship needed to build a sound nation.

The favoured tenure choice in the project of protecting the sanctity of the family and nation was the single-family dwelling. All municipalities, Charles Hastings said, "must have a keen sense of the social and national significance of the term 'home' as being of one-family dwellings."[52] Reformers had a keen sense of the benefits of the single-family dwelling since it promised to uphold stable family life in a manner consistent with the market economy. The promotion of house plans drafted to rationalize and improve women's domestic labour served a similar purpose and was evident in the housing designs of the co-partnership and government-sponsored ventures of the period. The proper single-family dwelling included well-designed facilities for domestic labour and suitable moral content in design through clearly-defined thresholds between bedrooms and between houses to ensure privacy. The social gravity of atomized family and domestic life in bourgeois reform thought was striking.[53] Housing improvement advocates joined social workers and maternal feminists to intervene in family life in order to maintain the family unit and protect motherhood, domesticity, children and, by extension, the nation.

The housing innovations that women's organizations urged centred on women's "instinctive" role as mother and housewife. Mrs. Campbell MacIvor of the Women's Party petitioned the Ontario government in 1918 boldly contesting that: "Men have been telling us for years that women's place is in the home and now they have appointed a Housing Committee which is sitting up at the Parliament Buildings and there's not a woman on it."[54] Marjorie MacMurchy of the Canadian Reconstruction Association accentuated "the need for women's brains and experiences in planning homes."[55] The Ontario Woman Citizen's Association wrote to Ontario premier Hearst demanding a part to play in housing policy, contending that: "It seems only reasonable that those who are by nature and experience best qualified to advise on these points should be empowered to give other women the benefit of their wisdom at first hand."[56] The ideology of maternal feminism informed the political culture of the women's movement and their housing reform agenda as they aimed to extend the boundaries of women's sphere to the enlarged realm of "social housekeeper."

Despite the decline of the reform impulse in the 1920s, housing reformers could point to the First World War era as a catalyst which sparked the first comprehensive planning legislation, several co-partnership housing ventures and a national housing program. Moreover, the ideological and political precedents had been set for the recognition of the necessity of state intervention in housing provision. While some state involvement in the housing sphere was accepted, few of the intellectuals and philanthropists advocating housing progress saw the need to directly contradict the private market. The concept of the right to decent housing, whatever the fluctuations of the market, would have to await the crucial decade of the 1930s. Fewer still believed that capitalist society itself was responsible for the lack of decent shelter opportunities. It would take the most devastating economic crisis in the history of world capitalism and changing political conditions to advance beyond this limited outlook.

THE TRIUMPH OF THE PROFESSIONAL HOUSER: HOUSING REFORM IN THE 1930s–40s

Just as the economic and social uncertainty of the First World War motivated a push for scientific competency in housing analysis to supersede the impressionistic views of amateur reformers, so too did the stormy ordeal of the depression and Second World War years clinch the professional and scientific status of proponents of housing advancement. Reflecting wider developments in the social sciences, housing reformers found an attentive audience in government circles and universities founded academic positions in the field of urban studies. Throughout the 1930s–40s, there was a plethora of reports, commissions and surveys at all levels of government and academia dealing with the housing question. Wartime mobilization and the fear of economic depression and social unrest after the war precipitated significant legislative and regulatory interventions in housing and sustained ventures in government housing provision.[57] Much of the reform discourse was interwoven with social democratic viewpoints, embracing a conviction that governments should permanently intervene through technocratic planning within the capitalist system to ensure that decent housing was available to all people. But there were decidedly conventional solutions proposed to the question of women's role in the housing sphere and assumptions of moral respectability stood alongside deeper critiques of the system.

The 1930s marked a coming of age of the new social sciences as academics and policy makers were given renewed incentive to apply practical scientific knowledge to social problems because of the abject failure of governments to solve the economic crisis. Social scientists skilfully cultivated support from the civil service and business community, arguing that social science was able to meet the challenge of social and economic adversity and thereby thwart radical challenges to the system.[58] They forcefully asserted that "laissez-faire" policies were anachronistic in the context of a complex, interdependent industrial economy. A cooperative relationship between government, business and academia hinged on sensible intervention in the workings of the market was therefore deemed essential to remedy the crisis.

Social democracy found intellectual expression in the League for Social Reconstruction (LSR), an eclectic group of intellectuals associated with the Co-operative Commonwealth Federation (CCF). The LSR's platform combined redistributive economic policies under the rubric of technocratic central planning with social policies intended to deliver essential services for victims of the market economy. The League worried that the unchecked profit motive of monopoly capitalism rode roughshod over stable family life and overall social and economic progress.[59] The most renowned housing reformers of the era, Harry Cassidy, Leonard Marsh and Humphrey Carver, were all members of the LSR and theories of state-directed economic regeneration found a larger audience in liberal political circles.

The inclusion of a program for housing progress in the LSR's manifesto, *Social Planning for Canada*, attests to the importance housing was accorded in the grander schemes of social democratic modernization. Written by Humphrey Carver, a Toronto architect and later a key official in the Central Mortgage and Housing Corporation, it stuck to the LSR's general critique of the "unrestrained system of profit-making enterprise" in capitalism, encouraging the mass production of low-cost rental units for the working class to improve work habits and uplift family life. The capitalist, Carver chastized, "is ready enough to scrap obsolete machinery in his plant [but] is not interested in the domestic equipment of his employees."[60] The only solution was to reject the principles of "private profit" and "remunerative investment" by dispensing direct grants for public housing projects.[61] The existing building industry was to remain the chief instrument of this program, but if private contractors were found to be unwilling, nationalization of the building industry was threatened. The age-old problem of exorbitant land costs and speculation was to be dealt with in much the same way as Thomas Adams's proposals during the First World War: through a comprehensive system of urban and industrial planning, under the central coordination of a Federal Housing and Town Planning Authority. Unlike Adams, however, Carver was amenable to using the full power of an interventionist government to expropriate slum lands for public housing ventures.[62]

The concept of technical expertise was also fully extended to include the standardization of building production methods and materials. Carver recognized the obstacles that inefficient construction processes posed for proper dwelling conditions: "… it is necessary to apply to the design and construction of homes the same scientific rationalization that has been applied, for instance, to automobile plants; to reduce the costs of fabrication and assembly so that modern living conditions may become the normal possession of every householder."[63] In a 1948 study sponsored by CMHC, Carver suggested that governments should take an active role in the formation of a large-scale building industry to expedite standardization, reduce labour costs and generally smooth out the building labour process to allow cheap and competent dwelling construction.[64] Carver and his contemporaries spurned the predominant views on home ownership promotion espoused by liberal policy makers, but shared the opinion that dwelling forms should be refined through rationalized designs in order to facilitate mass production and consumption standards.[65]

The brutal misery of the 1930s induced governments to continue the tradition of civic surveys established by the Social Service Congress earlier in the century. Extensive studies of Halifax, Hamilton, Ottawa, Winnipeg, Montreal and Toronto in the early 1930s showed a proliferation of critical slum conditions and rampant social distress. The ground-breaking Toronto study, known as the Bruce Report, was considered a milestone in the movement for housing betterment. Written by University of Toronto professors Harry Cassidy and Eric Arthur, it utilized precise survey techniques and identified the heavily skewed distribution of income, high unemployment and anarchic land development as the main culprits of slum housing. A review of the Report by Leonard Marsh, a McGill economist who later gained fame as a key player in the government's post-war reconstruction plans, lauded the analytical depth of the study and its proposed solutions. Marsh explicitly emphasized the relation between income distribution, consumer demand for shelter and general patterns of economic development and endorsed the author's call for a National Housing Commission to oversee and implement reform measures.[66] In the depths of economic crisis, expert opinion reiterated once again that housing was a national concern.

The establishment of an informal housing advocacy group to follow up the recommendations of the Bruce Report speaks to public housers' recognition of the importance of merging grass roots activism with conventional lobbying to spur action on the public housing front. A drop-in housing centre was set up on the University of Toronto campus "to gain community interest and support" for public action in slum clearance, public housing and centralized planning. A number of Toronto academics, architects and reform-minded politicians used this forum to discuss and debate housing betterment and eventually the group organized two national conferences in 1939 which criticized the federal government's Dominion Housing Act (1938).

A sense of balanced community life, deep-seated trust in the efficacy of centralized intervention and citizen participation formed key planks of the public housers' platform. Carver believed that efficient community planning would "promote loyalty to local government, churches, recreation centres, institutions."[67] The Citizen's Planning and Housing Association (CPHA), formed during the war to promote subsidized rental housing in Toronto, endeavoured to elevate citizen participation in the reform process through continuous propaganda and lobbying of government officials. Regent Park North, the first full-fledged public housing project in Canada, was the successful conclusion of what Carver called the CPHA's "sustained evangelistic effort."[68] Despite their reservations about the eventual outcome of the project, the new breed of idealistic public housers, termed "Citizens in Action" by Albert Rose, a main backer of Regent Park, considered their exertions an eminently patriotic contribution to national democratic life.[69] Indeed, Harry Cassidy, who became Professor of Social Welfare at the University of California, Berkeley, and Humphrey Carver saw social welfare measures such as public housing as a bulwark against Fascism and class conflict.[70]

The necessity of dealing with the widespread slum conditions found in civic investigations brought out the crudely environmentalist streak in 1930–40s planning ideology. Direct slum elimination was bandied about by public health officials decades earlier, but the political will for comprehensive action was not yet paramount. The genuine social concerns of most planners differed from the routine insensitivity of government officials. Yet callous urban renewal strategies were the preferred initial course of action in public housers' strategy since they thought that the removal of slums would stimulate the development of public housing projects by freeing up cheap land for municipal housing authorities.[71] Furthermore, it was held that the elimination of slum dwellings would mitigate the pathology of slum areas. It would not do, Humphrey Carver contended, to simply renovate the affected area. Only slum elimination integrated with a comprehensive approach to city planning would suffice: "It is as unwise as ever it was to put new wine into old bottles; a repaired slum still remains a slum."[72] Analysis of slum areas was still confined to narrow sociological analyses of the "pathological imperative," a presumption which connected social "deviance," crime, physical degeneration of facilities and immorality to slum dwellers. The repressive aspects of the technocratic initiative thus went hand-in-glove with the creed that every citizen had a right to decent housing.

If the professional housers more or less clearly discerned class divisions in the housing question, they certainly retained restrictive views of women's proper social role, especially in the domestic sphere. In the name of the preservation and bolstering of the family, reformers paid particular attention to domestic architecture. Simplicity, efficiency and economy were the key words in the arrangement of the domestic environment as well as external housing form. As Carver put it in *Social Planning for Canada*, "the mechanization of household equipment and the economy of bedroom space to be cleaned would help to liberate the housewife from the monotonous servitude of domestic chores and allow her to develop family life in more fruitful directions."[73] Albert Rose seconded Carver's optimism, lauding the Regent Park scheme for raising "maternal efficiency."[74] It is noteworthy that when discussing the importance of making special provisions for "untypical families" in public housing, Eric Arthur, a Toronto architecture professor and member of the federal government's Subcommittee on Housing and Community Planning, referred to families with large numbers of children rather than other "untypical families" such as those led by sole support parents.[75] The proposed model of social relations within the home were still hinged on a strict notion of nuclear family life, delimiting individual aspirations, especially those of women. If women were mentioned at all outside the strict realm of family life it was to champion their skills as potential housing estate managers, which called for a combination of "social worker and business manager,"[76] pointing to the common judgment that women's "natural" home management skills should be applied to the community as a whole to ensure the smooth functioning of society. As Ruth Roach Pierson and Margaret Hobbs have demonstrated in their study of the Home Improvement Plan, instituted by the federal government in 1936 to "upgrade" housekeeping and dwelling forms, all but a small minority of socialist observers accepted assumptions of women's traditional role as nurturer of sturdy family life.[77]

A lecture series on town planning and housing instituted by the University of Toronto's School of Social Work in 1944 furnishes an illuminating glimpse of the accumulated experience of the 1930–40s housing reform movement. In a survey of Canada's housing policy history, Leonard Marsh, now Executive Secretary of the federal government's Committee of Reconstruction and author of the influential 1943 government study *Report on Social Security*[78] which provided the intellectual framework for the post-war Canadian welfare state, presented the most articulate expression of the attitude that sustained government commitment was necessary for superior shelter provision. Favourably quoting American houser Catherine Bauer on the progressive social vision of Marx, William Morris and Roosevelt's New Deal, Marsh, while no Marxist, insisted that "Housing cannot be regarded as an isolated or departmentalized field, but only as a basic part of the modern social environment, and also as a product of all the social forces at work."[79] While he separated economic needs and social criteria in the housing policy realm, he underscored the connection between employment, income distribution and decent shelter opportunities — all necessary for the collective vitality of the nation.

Eric Arthur similarly emphasized the need for a comprehensive and integrated public housing plan. Reflecting his personal knowledge and admiration of the New Deal housing projects in the United States, he suggested that public housing schemes should include community centres, health clinics and laundries under the close supervision of well-trained housing managers.[80] Public housing provision could only successfully proceed if it was integrated with detailed town planning and community infrastructure development. In contrast to early twentieth-century reform currents, the strict regulatory thrust was tempered by social democratic reformers' support for citizen participation and inclusive community development schemes.[81] Nevertheless, an attempt to instill in project dwellers a sense of middle-class morality and social order was evident. Arthur, while believing in the "goodness and decency" of low-income tenants, endorsed the view of an American public housing manager that tenants could not be entrusted to care for lawns in housing estates.[82] Combining confidence in the benefits of well-planned public dwelling provision with a clear accent on the regulation of inhabitants, wartime reform thought would presage the dominant thrust of post-war social housing practices.

The growth of the state bureaucracy in the Second World War era assured reformers that their special capabilities had an important place in modern society. By employing the methodological insights of the social sciences and recognizing the necessity of probing deeper into the system itself, they identified inequities of income distribution as one of the main causes of the lack of adequate shelter provision. Only a comprehensive policy of income maintenance and social policy measures within the parameters of a permanently interventionist government could hope to secure decent housing for all. Yet existing social divisions were tacitly sanctioned and by reducing essentially political questions to the technical exigencies of science, the common ideological conviction that there were technical solutions to profound social and economic problems was fortified.[83]

CONCLUSION

The uneven evolution of housing reform from the amateurish dabbling of philanthropic businessmen to the statistically-based inquiries of university trained economists spanned three crucial decades in the growth of the capitalist social order and the modern state. Despite operating strictly within the confines of capitalism, housing reformers nevertheless believed that their suggestions for social advancement transcended class boundaries, working for the greater benefit of the community. Oblivious to the contradiction in this formulation between an all-embracing "community" and a class-divided society, reformers believed that moderate amendments in the housing sphere were essential in the struggle for economic modernization and social harmony. To an anxious middle class in a time of political uncertainty, the push for industrial efficiency, moral righteousness and social stability pledged to ameliorate the urban crisis by providing suitable shelter for workers, striving to shape a stable and productive workforce. The scientific uplifting of home life on "Canadian" lines through various state-directed reform measures promised to check urban deterioration and reinforce the nation. In this way, housing reformers, in concert with the larger social reform effort, occupied a significant place in the project of nation-building by helping shape a healthy, productive and divided workforce.

ACKNOWLEDGMENTS

I wish to thank Adam Givertz, Bryan Palmer, conference participants, anonymous referees and the editors for helpful comments on earlier drafts of this paper and the Ontario Graduate Scholarship and the Social Science and Humanities Research Council Doctoral Fellowship for financial aid in researching and writing this paper.

NOTES

1. Paraphrase of Vivian's Speech in "The Urgency of the Housing Problem in the Province of Quebec," *Conservation of Life* (hereafter COL) (January 1919): 4.
2. Antonio Gramsci, "Some Aspects of the Sexual Question," in David Forgacs ed., *The Gramsci Reader* (London: Lawrence and Wishart 1988), 281, 296. See also David Harvey, "Labor, Capital, and Class Struggle Around the Built Environment in Advanced Capitalist Societies," in Kevin Cox ed., *Urbanization and Conflict in Market Societies* (Chicago: Maaroufa Press 1978), 23. On the complexity of the reform movement's response to urban problems, see Peter Hall, *Cities of Tomorrow: An Intellectual History of Urban Planning and Design in the Twentieth Century* (Oxford: Basil Blackwell 1988), 5, 44.
3. For a bibliography of housing reform literature in this early period, see J. David Hulchanski, *Canadian Town Planning, 1900–1930: A Historical Bibliography*, Volume II, Housing (Toronto: Centre for Urban and Community Studies, University of Toronto 1978).
4. Paul Rutherford, "Tomorrow's Metropolis: The Urban Reform Movement in Canada, 1880–1920," in G. Stelter and A. Artibise eds., *The Canadian City: Essays in Urban History* (Toronto: McClelland and Stewart 1977), 370–371. For the focus on sanitary conditions in the European housing reform movement, see Nicholas Bullock and James Reid, *The Movement for Housing Reform in Germany and France, 1840–1914* (Cambridge: Cambridge University Press 1985).

5. Alan Sears, "Immigration Controls as Social Policy: The Case of Canadian Medical Inspection, 1900–1920," *Studies in Political Economy*, No. 33 (Autumn 1990): 105–106, n.5.

6. J. J. Kelso, "Can Slums Be Abolished or Must We Continue to Pay the Penalty?" (Toronto, n.d.), in Paul Rutherford ed., *Saving the Canadian City: The First Phase 1880–1920, an Anthology of Early Articles on Urban Reform* (Toronto: University of Toronto Press 1974), 166. For the use of metaphors of disease to describe the city in Europe, see Hall, *Cities of Tomorrow*, 35.

7. Rutherford, "Tomorrow's Metropolis," 371. For an interpretation that stresses the "moulding of subjectivity" through moral reform, see Mariana Valverde, *The Age of Light, Soap and Water: Moral Reform in English Canada, 1885–1925* (Toronto: McClelland and Stewart 1991).

8. *Toronto Daily News*, 8 November 1906. See as well Maria, "Forced to Live with Crime and City Lands Are Vacant," *Toronto Globe*, 2 December 1906.

9. Thomas Roden, "The Housing of Workmen," *Industrial Canada* (March 1907): 654.

10. Ibid. (August 1911): 52.

11. Kelso, "Can Slums Be Abolished …?" 167.

12. "The Labor Question and Women's Work and Its Relation to 'Home Life'" in Ramsay Cook and Wendy Mitchinson eds., *The Proper Sphere, Women's Place in Canadian Society* (Toronto: Oxford University Press 1976), 153. For a thorough analysis consult Veronica Strong-Boag, *The New Day Recalled, Lives of Girls and Women in English Canada, 1919–1939* (Toronto: Copp Clark Pitman 1988), Chapter 4.

13. Herbert Ames, *The City Below the Hill* (1897; repr. Toronto: University of Toronto Press 1972), 114.

14. Ibid., 75.

15. Ibid., 37.

16. Quoted in R. C. Brown and Ramsay Cook, *Canada 1896–1921, A Nation Transformed* (Toronto: McClelland and Stewart 1974), 294. See also Richard Allen, *The Social Passion, Religion and Social Reform in Canada, 1914–1928* (Toronto: University of Toronto Press 1973). On the transition from religiously based morality to secularized social reform, see Ramsay Cook, *The Regenerators, Social Criticism in Late Victorian English Canada* (Toronto: University of Toronto Press 1985), 5, 169, 231.

17. Allen, *The Social Passion*, 12, 24.

18. For the more developed "crisis of intellectual authority" in the American case that eventually led to the dominance of secularized social science, see Thomas Haskell, *The Emergence of Professional Social Science* (Urbana: University of Illinois Press 1977), vi–viii, 234–255.

19. David Ward, "The Progressives and the Urban Question: British and American Responses to the Inner City Slums, 1880–1920," *Transactions, Institute of British Geographers* 9 (1984): 303.

20. *Industrial Canada* (May 1912): 3.

21. On this point, note Doug Owram, *The Government Generation, Canadian Intellectuals and the State, 1900–1945* (Toronto: University of Toronto Press 1986), 57.

22. "Report of the Committee on Press and Co-operating Organizations," *Commission of Conservation Annual Meeting* (1917) (hereafter *COC Annual Meeting*), 277.

23. "The Commission of Conservation," *Saturday Night* (January 1921): 9.

24. *Journal of the Town Planning Institute of Canada*, (June-August 1921): 1.

25. Martin Daunton, *House and Home in the Victorian City* (London: Edward Arnold 1983), 5. For Canada, see Walter Van Nus, "The Fate of City Beautiful Thought in Canada, 1893–1930," in Stelter and Artibise eds., *The Canadian City*; and Ian Gunton, "The Ideas and Policies of the Canadian Planning Profession, 1909–1931," in G. Stelter and A. Artibise eds., *The Usable Urban Past*, Carleton Library No. 119 (Toronto: Macmillan of Canada with the Institute of Canadian Studies, Carleton University 1979), 181.

26. Stelter and Artibise, "Conservation Planning," 24. Note also Michael Simpson, *Thomas Adams and the Modern Planning Movement* (London: Mansell 1985).

27. D. J. Hall, *Clifford Sifton*, Vol. 2 (Vancouver: University of British Columbia Press 1985), 258. For Adams's international reputation, see Stelter and Artibise, "Conservation Planning," 25.

28. On the Leagues, see Civic Improvement League, *Report of Preliminary Conference Held under the Auspices of the Commission of Conservation* (Ottawa: Commission of Conservation 1915); and *Civic Improvement, Report of a Conference Held in Co-operation with the Commission of Conservation* (Ottawa: Commission of Conservation 1916).

29. A perusal of the Annual Reports of the Commission and COL indicates that Adams had a vast sphere of influence. See also Oiva Saarinen, "The Influence of Thomas Adams and the British New Town Movement in the Planning of Canadian Resource Communities," in Stelter and Artibise, eds., *The Usable Urban Past*, 273.

30. *Town Planning and Conservation of Life* (hereafter *TPCL*) (July-September 1920): 66.

31. "The Housing Problem and Production," *COL* (July 1918): 49.

32. Adams, "Civic and Social Questions in Canada," *COL* (April-June 1916): 54–55. While this paper is not directly concerned with the responses of the "clients" of housing reform it is important to note that reform schemes were often resisted at some level by workers. In the Hydrostone case, for instance, some former residents of the area protested the reordering of the neighbourhood along top-down reform lines. See John Weaver, "Reconstruction of the Richmond District in Halifax: A Canadian Episode in Public Housing and Town Planning, 1918–1921," *Plan Canada* 6 (March 1976): 36–47. For a similar response in the case of the Toronto Housing Company scheme, see my article " 'This is not a company; it is a cause': Class, Gender and the Toronto Housing Company, 1912–1920," *Urban History Review* 21 (April 1993): 88–89.

33. Bacher, *Keeping to the Private Market*, 79–80.

34. See Susanni Magri and Christian Topalov, " 'Reconstruire': l'habitat populaire au lendemain de la première guerre mondiale, étude comparative France, Grande-Bretagne, Italie, Etats-Unie," *Archives Européeanes de sociologie* 29 (1988): 319–370.

35. "Civic and Social Questions in Canada," *COL* (April-June 1916): 55.

36. "Partner-Ownership Building Societies," *COL* (October 1919): 78, 72–79.

37. On these insights, see the pioneering work by Sears, pp. 91–92, and George Steinmetz, "Workers and the Welfare State in Imperial Germany," *International Labour and Working Class History* 40 (Fall 1991): 18–23. For a more detailed explication of this argument in the Canadian case, see Sean Purdy, "Building Homes, Building Citizens: Housing Reform and Nation Formation in Toronto, 1900–1920," *Canadian Historical Review* 79(3): 492–523.

38. Consult Carol Lee Bacchi, "Race Regeneration and Social Purity: A Study of the Social Attitudes of Canada's English-Speaking Suffragists," in J. M. Bumstead ed., *Interpreting Canada's Past*, Vol. 2, After Confederation (Toronto: Oxford University Press 1986), 192–207.

39. W. Struthers, "The Point of View in Medical Inspection of Schools," *Public Health Journal* 4/2 (1913), 67 cited in Sears, "Immigration Controls," 92.

40. Charles Hodgetts, "Unsanitary Housing," *COC Annual Meeting* (1911), 56.

41. C. K. Clarke, "The Defective Immigrant," *COL* (April 1919): 37. On immigrants, see as well Charles Hastings, "The Modern Conception of Public Health Administration," *COL* (October 1917): 90. Alan Sears explains why British immigrants were not spared the rancour of the social imperialists. See Sears, 92–93, 99, 107 n.5.

42. Helen MacMurchy, "Defective Children," *Social Welfare* (March 1919). On MacMurchy, see Angus McClaren, *Our Own Master Race: Eugenics in Canada, 1885–1945* (Toronto: McClelland and Stewart 1990), Chapter 2.

43. Public Archives of Canada (hereafter PAC), Cauchon Papers, MG30 C105, Vol. 1, Address to the Rotary Club of Hamilton, 2 August 1917. Admiration for Germany's brand of welfare capitalism was widespread before and during the war. The only caveat offered was that Germany was perhaps too rigid in the implementation of its measures. See Dr. Charles Hodgetts, "Comments," *Report of the First Canadian Housing and Town Planning Congress*, Winnipeg, 15–17 July 1912; PAC, MG28 1275, Vol. 16, Papers of the Canadian Institute of Planners, Report of an Address to the Calgary City Planning Commission, Henry Vivian, "Town Planning and Housing," 9 April 1912, p. 15.

44. See Sidney Jacobs, "Race, Empire and the Welfare State: Council Housing and Racism," *Critical Social Policy* (1984), 11.

45. NA, MG28 1275, Vol. 16, Papers of the Canadian Institute of Planners, Report of an Address to the Calgary City Planning Commission, "Town Planning and Housing," 9 April 1912, p. 15.

46. City of Toronto, Minutes of the City Council, *Report of the Board of Health 1918*, Appendix A, 711.

47. Anna Davin, "Imperialism and Motherhood," *History Workshop* 5 (1978): 10.

48. Suzanne Mackenzie, *Women and the Reproduction of Labour Power in the Industrial City: A Case Study*, Working Paper No. 23, (Brighton: Centre for Urban and Regional Studies, Sussex University 1980), 85.

49. MacDougall, *Activists and Advocates*, 79. Marilyn Barber has discovered that immigration literature intended for British domestic servants, while promoting Canada as a British country, also stressed that British women must "learn Canadian ways." Consult "Sunny Ontario for British Girls, 1900–1930," in Jean Burnet ed., *Looking into My Sister's Eyes: An Exploration in Women's History* (Toronto: Multicultural History Society of Ontario 1986), 63.

50. Joseph Howes, "Housing Needs in the Ward and their Relation to the General Housing Situation in Ontario," *Social Welfare* (October 1920): 15.

51. Charles Hastings, "The Modern Conception of Public Health Administration," *COL* (October 1917): 89, 90.

52. "Suggestions for the Housing Problems," *Industrial Canada* (August 1912): 66.

53. Daunlon, *House and Home*, 37. Nuclear family privacy is something Lizabeth Cohen has found American reformers sought to inculcate in working-class homes. Consult "Embellishing a Life of Labor: An Interpretation of the Material Culture of American Working-Class Homes, 1885–1915," *Journal of American Culture* (1980): 759.

54. *Toronto Daily News* 26 November 1918.

55. Review of "Better Houses for Canadians," *Toronto Daily News*, 17 May 1919.

56. Public Archives of Ontario (hereafter PAO), Sir William Hearst Papers, Correspondence, MU 1307, Ontario Woman Citizen's Association to Hearst, 16 December 1918.

57. For a comprehensive bibliography of reform literature and government housing studies and an outline of government legislation in the 1930–40s, see J. David Hulchanski, *Canadian Town Planning and Housing, 1930–1940: A Historical Bibliography* (Toronto: Centre for Urban and Community Studies, University of Toronto 1978) and *Canadian Town Planning and Housing, 1940–1950: A Historical Bibliography* (Toronto: Centre for Urban and Community Studies, University of Toronto 1979).

58. Barry Ferguson and Doug Owram, "Social Scientists and Public Policy from the 1920s through World War II," *Journal of Canadian Studies* 15 (Winter 1980–81): 3–17.

59. Michiel Horn, "Leonard Marsh and the Coming of the Welfare State in Canada," *Histoire Sociale/Social History* 9 (May 1976): 197–204.

60. Humphrey Carver, "A Housing Programme" in The Research Committee of the League For Social Reconstruction, *Social Planning for Canada* (1935; repr. Toronto: University of Toronto Press 1975), 451–452.

61. Ibid., 458. It is worthwhile noting here that key figures in the building materials and construction sectors supported public housing programmes, hoping that they would provide much-needed demand for their products. See John Bacher and David Hulchanski, "Keeping Warm and Dry: The Policy Response to the Struggle for Shelter Among Canada's Homeless, 1900–60," *Urban History Review* 16 (October 1987): 151.

62. Carver, "A Housing Programme," 461.

63. Ibid., 459. Also note E. G. Faludi, "Housing the Nation," *Canadian Forum* (November 1941): 242.

64. Humphrey Carver, *Houses for Canadians: A Study of Housing Problems in the Toronto Area* (Toronto: University of Toronto Press 1948), 61–63.

65. On this point, see John Belec, John Holmes, and Tod Rutherford, "The Rise of Fordism and the Transformation of Consumption Norms: Mass Consumption and Housing in Canada, 1930–1945," in Richard Harris and Geraldine Pratt eds., *Housing Tenure and Social Class* (Gavle: Institute for Building Research 1988), 227–228.

66. Leonard Marsh, Review of the "Report of the Lieutenant-Governor's Committee on Housing Conditions in Toronto," *Canadian Journal of Economics and Political Science* 1 (February 1935): 119–122.

67. Humphrey Carver, "Analysis of Planning and Housing," *Journal, Royal Architectural Institute of Canada* (September 1937): 195.

68. Ibid., 82.

69. On the development of Regent Park, see Albert Rose, *Regent Park, A Study in Slum Clearance* (Toronto: University of Toronto Press 1958).

70. Harry Cassidy, *Social Security and Reconstruction in Canada* (Toronto: The Ryerson Press, 1943), 3–6; Humphrey Carver, "The Architecture of Democracy," *Journal, Royal Architectural Institute of Canada* (October 1938): 221.

71. See Carver, "A Housing Programme," 460–461. This analysis is expounded in the American context by Marc Weiss, "The Origins and Legacy of Urban Renewal," in Pierre Clavel et al. eds., *Urban and Regional Planning in an Age of Austerity* (New York: Pergamon Press 1980), 54.

72. Carver, "A Housing Programme," 460. See also Harry Cassidy, *Social Security*, 59. On slum pathology, note Gerald Daly, "The British Roots of American Public Housing," *Journal of Urban History* 15 (August 1989): 417.

73. Carver, "A Housing Programme," 463. Carver also shared the same concerns of World War I era reformers over separating boys and girls in housing projects. See his "Analysis of Planning," 195.

74. Rose, *Regent Park*, 108.

75. Eric Arthur, "Housing for Canada," Lecture 16, in *Planning of Canadian Towns with Special Reference to Post-War Opportunities in Town Planning and Housing*, A Course of Lectures Arranged by the School of Architecture in the University of Toronto, Volume 5 (Toronto: School of Architecture, University of Toronto 1944), 14.

76. Carver, "A Housing Programme," 458.

77. Margaret Hobbs and Ruth Roach Pierson, "'A kitchen that wastes no steps …': Gender, Class and the Home Improvement Plan, 1936–1940," *Histoire Sociale/Social History* 41 (May 1988): 9–39.

78. Leonard Marsh, *Report on Social Security for Canada* (1943; repr. Toronto: University of Toronto Press 1975).

79. Leonard Marsh, "Industrialization and Urbanization in Canada with Their Implications for Housing," Lecture 3 in *Planning of Canadian Towns*, Volume 1, 11–12.

80. Eric Arthur, "Housing for Canada," Lecture 16, ibid., 1–16. These suggestions did not extend to communal facil-
    ities but were akin to the coin laundries and other facilities common in private apartment buildings. For the
    much more far-reaching design proposals of early feminists, see Dolores Hayden, *The Grand Domestic Revolution:
    A History of Feminist Designs in American Homes, Neighbourhoods and Cities* (Cambridge, MA, and London: MIT
    Press 1981).
81. For a contrasting view, see Charlotte Whitten, *The Dawn of Ampler Life* (Toronto: Macmillan 1943), which was
    a conservative response to Leonard Marsh's *Report on Social Security.* Historian Frank Underhill criticized the
    reform movement for its policy of "nice genteel agitation," placing his hopes for housing reform in a powerful
    labour party. "The Housing Fiasco in Canada," *Canadian Forum* (October 1937): 228.
82. Arthur, "Housing for Canada," 10. In fact, he seemed to sympathize with the manager's statement that "poison
    ivy, surrounded by barbed wire, would be a godsend" in maintaining lawns in the project. A glimpse of the
    social control aims of 1930s housing reformers is shown by Humphrey Carver's appreciative reference to the fact
    that a fellow CHPA member, Harold Clark, was the grandson of a close friend of the Cadbury family, famous for
    their ultra-paternalistic British company housing scheme, Bourneville Garden Village. See Carver,
    Compassionate Landscape, 86. For a satirical look at such corporate reform endeavours in Britain in the early
    twentieth century, see George Bernard Shaw's play *Major Barbara* in Lee Jacobus ed., *The Bedford Introduction of
    to Drama* (New York: St. Martin's Press 1989), 555–596. For a penetrating look at the top-down reform
    approach of Viennese social democrats in the housing sphere, see Helmut Gruber, *Red Vienna, Experiment in
    Working-Class Culture, 1919–1934* (Oxford: Oxford University Press 1991), 46–65, 146–179.
83. Magali Larson, "The Production of Expertise and the Constitution of Expert Power," in Thomas Haskell ed.,
    The Authority of Experts, Studies in History and Theory (Bloomington: University of Indiana Press 1984), 64.

Document 3.1
J. S. Woodsworth

The Seamy Side or Social Pathology

James Shaver Woodsworth (1874–1942) is the best known of the social gospel leaders in early 20th-century Canada. An ordained Methodist minister, a social democrat, and a pacifist, he worked closely with immigrants and workers at All People's Mission in Winnipeg's north end. His support of the working class led to his arrest in June 1919 on charges of seditious libel for editorials written during the Winnipeg General Strike (the case was subsequently dropped). He was elected to the House of Commons as a Manitoba Independent Labour Party representative (under the Progressive Party banner) from Winnipeg North Centre. In 1933, he helped to establish the Co-operative Commonwealth Federation, a social democratic precursor of the New Democratic Party. The excerpt below is from a book Woodsworth wrote about his experiences at All People's Mission.

Issues to Consider

- What does the term "social pathology" imply? Why would a minister and social reformer use medical terminology to describe urban problems?
- In the lengthy list of infractions reprinted from the *Telegram*, the most common charges are "drunk on street" (3,033), "breach of street by-law" (1,461), and "vagrancy" (640). What can we infer from the number of arrests in these related categories? Is there a direct link between number of arrests and actual level of criminality?
- In the *Telegram*'s list of perpetrator nationalities, the largest number of offenders are Canadian and English. What does this statistic tell us about the racial anxieties of the time?
- Woodsworth quotes a discussion of slums by J. J. Kelso, child welfare reformer and founder of the Children's Aid Society. How does Kelso characterize the slum situation? Do his views, and the language that he uses to express them, support the conclusions of Hunt and Purdy?
- In the excerpts from reports by Miss Charity Cook, the *Winnipeg Free Press*, and Lucy W. Brooking, the underlying moralism of the assessments of social problems is evident. What are the connections made? How do class, race, and gender figure in the equation?

And when Jesus drew nigh, he saw the city and wept over it.

– Luke

Source: J. S. Woodsworth, "The Seamy Side or Social Pathology," chap. 8 in *My Neighbor* (1911; repr., Toronto: University of Toronto Press, 1971), 131–53.

Winnipeg police statistics, 1910: Offences

Offence	Count	Offence	Count
Assault	14	Disorderly	423
Assault and battery	322	Discharge firearms	10
Assault occ. bodily harm	41	Driving motor while drunk	1
Attempted theft	–	Circulating obscene matter	3
Attempted murder	9	Defamatory libel	2
Attempted fraud	1	Driving at immoderate rate	7
Assaulting peace officer	18	Deserting employment	2
Abusive language	1	Drunk on railway duty	2
Attempted rape	1	Demanding money with intent to steal	6
Attempted burglary	3	Exhibiting immoral play	2
Aid and abet in theft	1	Executing valuable security by fraud	1
Aggravated assault	1	Escape from lawful custody	8
Attempted personation	1	Forgery and uttering	28
Attempted carnal knowledge	1	Forgery and attempting to utter	8
Aid and abet dog fight	1	Forgery	3
Attempted robbery	2	Fraud	46
Attempt to procure case seduction	2	Frequenting bawdy house	1
Attempted gross indecency	1	Harboring vicious dog	4
Attempted to engage in prize fight	2	Housebreaking with intent	1
Attempted shop-breaking	1	Housebreaking with theft	10
Burglary	1	Indecent assault	9
Bigamy	1	Inmate of bawdy house	56
Breach of health by-law	595	Inmate of disorderly house	3
Breach of street by-law	1,461	Indecent act	–
Breach of early closing by-law	160	Interdiction	1
Breach of license by-law	160	Incest	1
Breach of parks by-law	61	Inmate of opium joint	15
Breach of pound by-law	36	Interfering with railway signals	1
Breach of dairy by-law	35	In possession of stolen goods	1
Breach of bakery by-law	4	Keeping bawdy house	56
Breach of plumbing by-law	2	Keeping gaming house	13
Breach of militia by-law	2	Keeping opium joint	4
Breach of building by-law	75	Keeping resort for prostitutes	3
Breach of electric by-law	8	Murder	3
Breach of Lord's Day by-law	83	Material witnesses	4
Breach of various by-laws	234	Manslaughter	2
Carry revolver	30	Neglect to support children	1
Cruelty to animals	44	Neglect to support wife	2
Carnal knowledge girl under 14	18	Neglect of duty endangering life	2
Contribute to delin. of juvenile	1	Owning vicious dog	9
Challenge to prize fight	1	Obtaining money by false pretences	36
Cause explosion to endanger life	1	Obtaining credit by false pretences	7
Cause bodily harm by neglect of duty	4	Obtaining goods by false pretences	4
Drunk on street	3,033	Obtaining board by false pretences	1
Drunk and disorderly	397	Operating street car while drunk	1

Obstructing peace officer	8	Theft	422
Obstructing sanitary constable	1	Theft of post letters	2
Obstructing street railway constable	1	Theft from dwelling-house	4
Playing or looking on in gaming house	172	Theft from person	13
Pointing revolver	7	Trespass	9
Procuring	5	Throwing missile at street car	8
Perjury	2	Using threatening language	41
Refuse to pay wages	216	Using insulting language	19
Refuse to pay livery	13	Unlawfully selling cocaine	3
Rape	4	Unlawfully wounding	3
Receiving stolen goods	9	Using profanity on street	1
Riding on railway watchman's ticket	11	Vagrancy	640
Refusing to pay chimney sweep	5	Wilful damage	53
Robbery	13	Witnesses	9
Seduction	7	Wounding with intent	8
Shop-breaking and theft	11	Summary arrests	406
Selling of cigarettes to minors	1	Arrests on warrant	158
Supplying drugs for unlawful purposes	1		

Telegram, Jan. 10th, 1911

Nationalities represented in above

American	384	Italian	37
Austrian	16	Icelander	39
Assyrian	3	Indian	5
Africander	2	Jew	21
Australian	2	Norwegian	74
Bukowinian	13	New Zealander	6
Belgian	9	Newfoundlander	2
Bohemian	8	Polish	248
Canadian	1,343	Ruthenian	347
Chinamen	122	Russian	51
Dutch	28	Roumanian	16
English	1,092	Scotch	845
French-Canadian	151	Swede	118
French	35	Swiss	1
Finlander	8	Welsh	26
German	113		
Galician	43		
Greek	4	Total	6,024
Halfbreed	261		
Hungarian	11		
Irish	540		

Police Report

Slums result from three causes, lack of regulation and supervision on the part of the city, the greed of land-owners, and the necessities of the poor.

Webster's Dictionary says that the word "slum" is supposed to be a contraction of the word "asylum," and is a back street of a city, especially one filled with a poor, dirty and vicious population.

This is only a partial definition, for a street, so long as it is a street, can with a little effort be redeemed from the slum condition. No, the slum is something worse than a back street; it is a lane or alley, a series of lots about one hundred and fifty feet deep, with three or four houses, hovels or shacks erected, one behind the other, and entirely hidden from the view of the ordinary passerby. It is a place where stables, barns and sheds have been converted into residences, not for one, but often for two or three families, with none of the ordinary requirements of home life.

In earlier days, men were either passively allowed, or took permission, to erect rows of lath and plaster cottages on lanes not fifteen feet wide; yards were divided and subdivided until in some districts there is a perfect labyrinth of hovels, absolutely lacking in sanitary conveniences, and in various stages of dilapidation and decay. Such a thing as "repairs" is never dreamed of, for the rent can be obtained all the same, and to fix up looks like unnecessary extravagance. The household refuse, slops, dishwater, etc., are thrown outside the door to sow the diseases that daily attack the inmates, sending adults to the hospital and babies to the graveyard.

One could find in his heart some measure of sympathy and acquiescence if the hovels were built and owned by the poor themselves, but these places are owned by well-to-do citizens who sin against their city from avaricious motives, and live in luxury on the exorbitant rents imposed on the poor and comfortless occupants. J. J. Kelso, in *Can Slums Be Abolished?*

It is true not only of the world, but of this city, that one-half does not know how the other half lives; to thousands in Toronto a knowledge of conditions in the "Ward," so far as housing conditions are concerned, would come as a surprise and shock. The words of Rev. Benjamin Gregory, of Manchester, that "there is nothing in that city to compare with the housing conditions in Toronto," and the words of another, that "London itself does not present such conditions," should arouse the interest of worthy citizens and lead to serious inquiry. It is safe to say the worst conditions cannot be readily seen by the slum visitor, but even a general view of conditions must convince anyone of the criminal carelessness of any community which permits such conditions to exist, much more to continue.

Here is one instance: A dirty hovel, the floor of which is broken down toward the middle, so that it rests on the ground, and on the floor water stagnates for many months of the year. In it are three apartments bearing the semblance of rooms, and in these a family consisting of father, mother, four children, and a boarder manage to exist. The father has been out of work for months; the mother, soon to bear again the responsibility of motherhood, goes out daily to earn a partial support for the family by doing janitor work. In another case, in surroundings almost similar, we find the father has been ill for months, and the mother looks so — the wonder is that it could be otherwise. The eldest son, a mere child, is a criminal, returning regularly to the hands of the police, and this is what we might expect. In neither house referred to are there any sanitary conveniences. These two typical places to which we have referred can be called neither homes nor houses.

Then let anyone take a general view of the surroundings and be convinced that here is the festering sore of our city life. The lanes, alleyways and back yards are strewn with refuse, houses behind houses, and in the yards between unsightly piles of ramshackle out-houses that are supposed to provide sanitary conveniences — some of these reeking with filth and stench. Then let someone not already convinced walk through these surroundings when the rain has fallen and the hot sun beats down, and smell the smoke of their torment that ascends continually, and we would hear such a protest as would cause some action to be taken. We are told that in the midst of all this these poor people pay ten or twelve dollars per month for these miserable rambling hovels that would not sell for fifty dollars apiece. Rev. H. S. Magee, in *Christian Guardian*.

We are told that we have no slum district in Toronto and know nothing about the tenement house; but we do know that there is a great deal of overcrowding, and the effect on the children is something that we will realize better later on. I fear that Toronto is breeding a class of criminals that will keep it busy to take care of in the next few years, if nothing is done. The effect on children as regards their health is very bad. Our work is all among the poor, and only yesterday one of our workers went to a home where father, mother and five children were living in two rooms. One child was tubercular. They were sleeping four in one bed, and the sick child on a couch. These children sleep in the living-room. There was another case where a child was born in one of these homes. The mother was in an advanced stage of tuberculosis, and father, mother and four children slept in a room 10 ft. x 12 ft. The kitchen was a mite of a place only large enough for a stove, table and chairs. These people living in this huddled condition and with no precaution whatever taken against this disease, you can imagine what chance these children have …

Close to our mission there is a family of seven — three of these are grown-up girls — living in a tiny cottage, and they have a man boarder living with them. I don't know what chance there is for these girls, and next door to them is a family consisting of father, mother and two growing children. They have seventeen men boarders and only one accommodation.

I know of another case where a girl and boy were adopted — not brother and sister — and as there were a number of other children in this house, they occupied the same room until the boy was 19 and the girl 16 or 17, and to-day she is one of the most difficult problems we have in our mission. She is bold and brazen, no soft spot in her. But what else could you expect! She was reared where a blessing was asked at table, but I ask you what chance had she to grow up virtuously in a crowded place like that. I leave it to your own imagination how horrible the conditions are where the father or mother drink, or perhaps both, huddled in these close quarters? Is it not natural that we should find many children practising vice? Our hearts ache for them but we are helpless. We have one family not far from our mission where the woman drinks and is thoroughly immoral. She has a little boy about ten years of age threatened with tuberculosis. He was in the hospital and they said his only chance was good nourishment, the best of care and lots of fresh air, but in this place there is no possible ventilation. They live in two little rooms, and there are two or three women of disreputable character who have two other little boys. We come across so much of that kind of thing in our work, and yet people cannot believe that such a state of affairs exists in Toronto. Miss Charity Cook, *Conference Charities and Correction*, 1909. […]

In connection with the arrest yesterday of _____ , alias, _____ , of the underworld, charged with keeping a disorderly house, at 264 Main Street, a state of affairs was revealed that fortunately has never before been known in Winnipeg. Although the facts did not come out when the woman pleaded guilty and was fined $50 and costs with the option of three months in jail, it is stated that her place has been a regular "hang out" for messenger boys of all ages from 15 to 18 or 20, and that some of the boys were accustomed to spending nearly all their spare time at the place. The woman, it is stated, paid the boys trifling sums for running messages, washing dishes, sweeping floors and other work about the place, but allowed them to frequent her rooms any time they came around. Some of the boys who are on night duty have admitted that they spent most of their mornings and afternoons in the house "just for the fun of the thing." The woman is a confirmed drug fiend. _____ , arrested in connection with the same place, appeared in court in a terrible condition from the effects of morphine and a recent attack of pneumonia. Her case was adjourned. *Winnipeg Free Press*, Feb. 4th, 1910. [...]

In the good days to come, when we have Vigilance Committees looking after the morals of every lonely camp, and Morality Societies, such as have been organized in some few of our towns, to unearth the hidden strongholds of vice and to protect the weak and lift up the fallen, and bring them back to God again; when our Government at last recognizes and lifts the burden of its duty in protecting the feeble-minded as well as the insane; and especially in that Golden Age ahead, when no double standards of morality will be tolerated, we shall look back upon the early days of the poor, benighted twentieth century as to the darkness of the Middle Ages. But it will be remembered that even then Love Divine stirred in the hearts of men and women, causing them to make a noble fight against these evils, and for the purification and right development of the sources of humanity. So let us work and hope and trust, and "put a cheerful courage on," never for one moment forgetting that in the hearts of the defective, and even of the depraved, there is yet a chord that responds to the Divine touch:

> "In the mud and scum of things,
> There always, always something sings."

Lucy W. Brooking, Supt. The Haven

[....]
From the address of the President of the Canadian Conference of Charities and Correction, 1910:

There is no prospect of immediate profit in the problems with which this assemblage has set itself to deal, and yet surely it is eminently desirable even for the material welfare of the nation that once a year we should gather together and discuss the conditions of men who have fallen, of women who are unfortunate, of children who are homeless and helpless, putting to one side the moral and sentimental phase of the question — forgetting for the moment the claims of the bad and the unfortunate upon our attention or commiseration.

It is surely the fact that every neglected child for whom a good home is found, every law-breaker restored to a good citizenship, every practical effort to lessen the awful toll in human life that we now pay through excessive and avoidable infant mortality, or the three thousand consumptives' graves that are annually filled in this Province (Ontario), every movement to improve the conditions of the poor, to clean out the slums and bring the light of cleanliness and health to places dark with filth and disease, must ultimately conduce to our material prosperity as a people. [...]

Document 3.2

Drink (Editorial in *Calgary Eye Opener*)

The *Calgary Eye Opener* was founded by a Scottish emigrant, Bob Edwards (1864–1922), who arrived in the West in 1895 and established a number of small weekly newspapers. The satirical and darkly humorous *Eye Opener* originated in High River, Alberta, in 1902, but Edwards moved the paper to Calgary the following year. At its peak, its weekly circulation figure of 30,000 exceeded the population of Calgary, indicating a nationwide readership. With scathing wit, Edwards attacked such targets as the Canadian Pacific Railway, land speculators, the new breed of civil servants required by the expanding bureaucratic state, and — as this excerpt attests — the liquor interests. The paper folded with his death in 1922.

Issues to Consider

- What is the tone of this piece? Who is it directed to, who is it chastizing, and what do we learn about the writer from his views and the way in which he expresses himself?
- Since prohibition was in effect at this time, what is the problem? What does this problem tell us about the regulation of drinking at the time?
- What does Edwards find particularly offensive about the "uprising generation" and its drinking habits?
- What does he propose as the ideal remedy to the situation? How can beer be a viable alternative to "bone-dry prohibition"?

Our young men and women have caught the prevailing contempt and disregard of the law. And this has naturally extended to a breaking away from the moral and social code which was the backbone of the family life of our own days. Now, we are idly looking on and seeing far too many of our youngsters debauched. The Social Service League doesn't seem to care, so we suppose it is all right.

Liquor is common at private parties and at private and public dances, and no stranger in our schools. It is not a very pleasant sight to see a bright young girl take a slug of liquor with verve and aplomb, and then proceed to comment on its quality with an air evidently based on knowledge and experience.

We are told that if we reprobates of this passing generation would suffer ourselves to be deprived of our tipple, it would count to us for Grace and Holiness. It was all for the uprising generation. Let us look at the uprising generation: the bar has been abolished as an adjunct to the hotel and is now firmly established in bottle and flask in the bedroom, the dining-room, the office and the hip pocket. And the uprising generation are fast becoming steady patrons of this new kind of bar.

Those young folk really do not like the muck they drink, but it registers a kick and that's that. That many of them graduate from hootch to drugs is not to be doubted. We happen to know that the supply of hypodermic needles is not equal to the demand. And what about the next generation? Our pernicious reformers have much to answer for.

This state of affairs cannot continue. The remedy is absolute bone-dry prohibition or Beer only. Either one or the other, and the first-mentioned has already proved impossible. This leaves the Beer. The liquor traffic can be controlled by strategy alone. Merely forbidding the manufacture, importing, warehousing and retailing of spirituous liquors is just so much bunk. The strategy in this case is Beer and excellent strategy it is too, as any boozological Fool would tell you.

Source: Editorial, "Drink," *Calgary Eye Opener*, July 1, 1922, 3.

Document 3.3
A Juvenile Court Probation Officer

As the Twig Is Bent: What Are We Doing to Keep Children from the Reformatory?

The Juvenile Delinquents Act (1908) established specialized courts as well as institutions and treatment for those under the age of sixteen years who were charged with criminal offences, or with the "status offences" having to do with "immorality" or even poor family relations. The act cast juvenile offenders as misguided children who needed to be kept apart from adult criminals in order to straighten out under the guidance of specially trained police, judges, and probation officers. A number of the appointed judges were women, who were thought to be particularly suitable for dealing with children and young people. The following excerpt from *Chatelaine* magazine was written by an anonymous probation officer (possibly a woman, although the writing itself does not reveal the writer's sex).

Issues to Consider

- The probation officer begins by citing statistics, but without establishing whether they represent a rise or decline over time, or what proportion of the youth population they pertain to. As such, they are virtually meaningless. What reasons might there be to use numbers in this fashion?
- What particular instances of "delinquency" does the writer single out in discussing these numbers? Are these actions "criminal," or can they be classified under another label? What does the writer's granting of special significance to such actions suggest about those involved in defining and remedying delinquency?
- What does the writer see as both the root cause of juvenile delinquency and its most effective solution?

The latest complete tabulated returns, those of 1925, show that in that year there were 8,064 convictions against boys and 675 convictions against girls registered in Canadian criminal courts. [...] Some of the cases represent the bringing into the world of illegitimate babies, some of the figures stand for follies of unguarded youth that have filled the blood of children with infection, have crippled, destroyed and killed them. [...]

[...] statistics show that at the end of 1925 there were in detention in Canada 445 persons in industrial refuges for females, 403 in reformatories for females, 2,193 in reformatories for males, 2,602 in common jails and 2,345 in penitentiaries. This represents a tremendous waste of money and happiness. [...]

What are the practical steps? I would say [...] housing regulation, more generous assistance to enable dependent mothers to stay in their homes and take care of their children, the opening of schools and school-grounds as social centres, the exclusion of children under sixteen years of age from public dance halls, stiffening of regulations with regard to the supplying of minors with liquor, better administration of the "contributing to delinquency" laws.

Source: A Juvenile Court Probation Officer, "As the Twig Is Bent: What Are We Doing to Keep Children from the Reformatory?" *Chatelaine*, March 1928.

Next and fundamentally important, we must train and if necessary force parents to carry the responsibility of the support of the children they have invited into the world. Other countries have framed Lazy Husbands' Acts [...] to cope with this situation. They have statutes which make it possible to arrest the man who does not attempt to support his family. [...]

It would be feasible to enact a law by which the parents of children found guilty of misdemeanors would be automatically charged with failure to properly care for them and train them and the burden of proof would rest on the accused. Drastic? Yes. And such legislation would do more than any other one influence to reduce the number of juvenile offences. [...]

One report showed that a landlady, being able to rent all other space, slept with two children in the kitchen and had three other children using a bed under the stairs in the hall. If these rooms were large, sunny and clean this congestion would not be so bad, but it usually occurs in business districts where the dwellings are often ramshackle houses, crowded together, not worth repairing. Large blocks cut off much of the fresh air and constant traffic creates noise and dirt.

The crime-producing tendencies of such homes are obvious. The children escape as often as possible from their cramped quarters. They drift to the sidewalks, the gatherings under street lights, or to shops and dance halls, anywhere where they may find space and light, and if the weather is cold, warmth. They also find opportunity for mischief that sometimes degenerates into serious misdemeanor. [...]

Topic 4

Citizens and Nation:
Race, Ethnicity, and Immigration

"Coloured Colony," Athabasca Landing, Alberta; Canada, Dept. of the
Interior collection 1936, Library and Archives Canada PA-040745,
http://www.collectionscanada.ca.

CONTEXT

The social reformers encountered in Topic 3 were intent on making the "Canadianization" of the foreign-born a key initiative, regarding them as the most disturbing element within the urban working class as well as the new prairie settlements. Our contemporary attachment to multiculturalism (see Topic 12) obscures the fact that this late 20th-century notion has been projected back through time to suggest a tolerance of ethnic diversity that simply did not exist when the first wave of immigration, under the Liberal government (1896–1911) of Sir Wilfrid Laurier, was getting under way. During the opening two decades of the new century, roughly three million prospective Canadians arrived from other nations. Among these were some half-million immigrants from Asia and southern and central Europe. Canada's population, at 5.3 million in 1901, increased 43 percent by 1921. Recent immigrants made up 22 percent of that total. However much Canada needed them to fulfill plans for western agricultural development and an integrated national economy, the newcomers frequently faced hostility from their hosts. Contrary to the rhetoric about the "open door," as historians of race, immigration, and ethnicity in Canada have revealed, the approach to the newcomers is best summed up in the term "assimilation." What they meant by this actually translated to an "Anglo-conformity" reflecting the values and customs of the dominant class.

Historical work on race, ethnicity, and immigration follows from our historical record, then, in which immigration has played such a vital role. Immigration policy, in particular, as well as western settlement, are subjects of historical research of long standing. As with many other subjects considered in this collection, however, the more sociohistorical aspects began to be probed within the context of the social movements and ideas of the past forty years or so. It stood to reason that study of other marginalized groups, such as the working class and women, would encourage studies of how newcomers fared in Canada, especially considering the blurred lines marking out these various social groups and identities. The new activism of Aboriginals, the "distinct society" aims of Quebec, questions about bilingualism and biculturalism, and the renewed post–World War II immigration — especially that from "non-traditional" sources — as well as official multiculturalism, all served to inspire historical examination of the diverse themes and issues that compose this subject. During the 1970s and early 1980s, pioneering studies by such historians as Robert Harney and John Zucchi attempted to show how, over time, interaction with the host society meant that transplanted communities were neither representative of their original societies — where, obviously, history did not stop when they left — nor fully assimilated into their new culture. By choice and by circumstance, in view of their hosts' attitudes and policies, they remained "foreign" and identified primarily by race.

More recent studies have uncovered the constructed aspects of race, how these relate to gender and class, and how they justified certain regulatory approaches in the interests of nation-building. This approach is most revealing when the least "desirable" are considered, especially Asian immigrants and people of colour. As Topic 3 shows, the churches initiated evangelical, educational, and medical missions in immigrant neighbourhoods across Canada. The public school curriculum was redesigned to transmit "Canadian" morals, religious principles, and family values through children to their homes. In the summer of 1910, the University of Toronto set up the first of three downtown "settlement houses" modelled on London's famous Toynbee Hall and Chicago's Hull House. The settlements allowed social work students to combine their study of urban slums with social service. Their primary purpose was to train immigrants in the duties of citizenship, with special efforts extended to the children, who were identified as "Canadians in the making." Yet some groups, as Elizabeth Beaton demonstrates in her study of African-American workers in Nova Scotia, were simply considered "unassimilable," and few attempts were made to overcome the racism that created the "Coketowns" and

"Chinatowns" of urban centres. While few immigrants in the past could have escaped the social pressure to become Canadian, defined in English-speaking, white, preferably Protestant and middle-class terms, historians have also shown that these newcomers were not without agency. They built upon networks of family, kin, and neighbours to make their own way amid the challenges of the new environment, at a time when the state did little to assist their adjustment, relying on voluntary efforts, often denominational missionary societies intent on their "conversion." They wanted their children, hope of the future, to learn the English language and Canadian ways, but they managed, in their home life and through their cultural institutions, to instill in them also a respect for their own ethnic roots. All suspicions to the contrary, many of them established themselves, prospered, and became Canadian, though perhaps not in the ways that the purveyors of Anglo-conformity desired.

Some of these immigrants were sojourners, "target migrants" who intended to stay only long enough to improve their families' material situation in their countries of origin. The process of "chain migration," based on networks of family and kin, facilitated their quest for new opportunities. Kinship networks provided crucial assistance with employment, housing, child care, and finances; they could make all the difference between permanent settlement and the decision to return to whatever starting place was home. Those who had arrived earlier frequently took in boarders from their homeland, usually from their own kin or community, permitting women to contribute to the family economy without working outside the home. More than most working-class families, those of immigrants had to submerge individual ambitions to work together for their material welfare and success in the new land. For those deemed racially "undesirable," official immigration policy worked to thwart permanent settlement. After the railway boom of the late 19th century, Chinese and South Asian immigration was severely restricted through the imposition of a high "head tax" and other discriminatory measures. In the census of 1911, these immigrant communities were almost exclusively male. The Chinese Immigration Act of 1923 (also known as the Chinese Exclusion Act) prohibited the entry of Chinese women, thus the growth of the Chinese communities in Canada. Many families were broken up forever as a result; others would reconstitute only after World War II. The long history of anti-Asian feeling certainly laid the basis for the evacuation of Japanese-Canadians from British Columbia after the attack on Pearl Harbor in December 1941.

The communities that "Canadians" tended to classify as slums, as inescapable evidence of class- and race-defined urban pathology, were resources for mutual aid and solidarity that often gave their residents their only protection against the hostile society surrounding them. For their hosts, they represented only noise, dirt, congestion, and the potential for trouble signified by these "uncivilized" and "inferior" people from other lands. This was especially the case for those whom race made particularly visible, as Elizabeth Beaton details in her discussion of Nova Scotia's early 20th-century Black community. A number of African-Canadian communities began with the late 18th-century flight of the Loyalists from the American War of Independence, while others were started by those who escaped slavery on the "underground railroad" a century later. On the whole, Black immigrants have historically occupied the lowest rung of the racial pecking order; attempts to settle were often blocked outright, as in the case of a group of African-Americans from Oklahoma who tried to immigrate to the prairie west in 1911.

In the wake of the Second World War, the Holocaust, and international pressure from humanitarian groups to open the gates — largely closed by Depression and war, even to the extent of denying entrance to Jewish refugees from the Nazi horrors — Canadian immigration policy began a slow, incremental liberalization. Yet, if the 1951 Immigration Act of the Liberal Mackenzie King government permitted a wider entry, the "open door" remained more mythic than real. A noble attempt by the Conservative government of John Diefenbaker to ensure, in a Bill of Rights, that colour and ethnicity would not be barriers to Canadian citizenship meant that immigrants formerly at the bottom of the racial hierarchy began to be admitted in larger numbers during the 1960s. Finally, Liberal Prime Minister Pierre Elliott Trudeau framed an official multicultural policy in 1971, further reinforced by his successor, Conservative Brian Mulroney. By their labour and perseverance, immigrants have contributed tremendously to the attainment of our nation-building objectives. Until very recently, however, we have not been so eager to embrace the cultural diversity that they also brought to the nation.

REFERENCES/FURTHER READING

Abella, I., and H. Troper. *None Is Too Many: Canada and the Jews of Europe, 1933–1948*. Toronto: Lester & Orpen Dennys, 1982.

Anderson, Kay. *Vancouver's Chinatown: Racial Discourse in Canada, 1875–1980*. Montreal and Kingston: McGill-Queen's University Press, 1995.

Backhouse, Constance. *Colour-Coded: A Legal History of Racism in Canada, 1900–1950*. Toronto: Osgoode Society for Canadian Legal History and University of Toronto Press, 1999.

Bristow, P., D. Brand, L. Carty, A. P. Cooper, S. Hamilton, and A. Shadd. *"We're Rooted Here and They Can't Pull Us Up": Essays in African Canadian Women's History*. Toronto: University of Toronto Press, 1994.

Harney, R. *Gathering Place: Peoples and Neighbourhoods of Toronto, 1834–1945*. Toronto: Multicultural History Society of Ontario, 1985.

Iacovetta, Franca. *Such Hardworking People: Italian Immigrants in Postwar Toronto*. Montreal and Kingston: McGill-Queen's University Press, 1992.

Loewen, R. *Family, Church and Market: A Mennonite Community in the Old and the New Worlds*. Toronto: University of Toronto, 1993.

Patrias, Carmela. *Patriots and Proletarians: Politicizing Hungarian Immigrants in Interwar Canada*. Montreal and Kingston: McGill-Queen's University Press, 1994.

Petroff, L. *Sojourners and Settlers: The Macedonian Community in Toronto to 1940*. Toronto: University of Toronto Press, 1995.

Swyripa, F. *Wedded to the Cause: Ukrainian-Canadian Women and Ethnic Identity, 1891–1991*. Toronto: University of Toronto Press, 1993.

Walker, James W. St. G. *"Race," Rights and the Law in the Supreme Court of Canada: Historical Case Studies*. Waterloo: Osgoode Society for Canadian Legal History and Wilfrid Laurier University Press, 1997.

Ward, W. Peter. *White Canada Forever: Popular Attitudes and Public Policy Toward Orientals in British Columbia*, 2nd ed. Montreal and Kingston: McGill-Queen's University Press, 1990.

Winks, Robin W. *The Blacks in Canada: A History*. 2nd ed. Montreal and Kingston: McGill-Queen's University Press, 1997.

Zucchi, John. *Italians in Toronto: Development of a National Identity, 1875–1935*. Montreal and Kingston: McGill-Queen's University Press, 1988.

ILLUSTRATION 4.1 (P. 133)

In 1910–11, about one thousand African-American migrants from Oklahoma moved to the prairies, particularly Alberta, where they established several rural settlements around Edmonton. Many of these communities were abandoned or depopulated during the Great Depression and World War II as their residents left to seek work in the cities.

Issue to Consider

- Illustration 4.1 is a family photograph taken during the Great Depression in a part of the country that was hit particularly hard. What can we surmise about the "family story" of these people by looking closely at the photograph? What about their social position?

ARTICLES

As Elizabeth Beaton reveals in her discussion of the short-lived Nova Scotia communities of African-American workers, enticed to the province by entrepreneurs who needed their skill and labour, few attempts were made to assist their integration into the larger working-class white community because of the racial barriers that their colour represented. Unlike the earlier immigration with its large cohort of lone male sojourners, the postwar wave that is the focus of Kerry Badgley's essay was primarily a process of family relocation. Racial selectivity and economic expediency still shaped its regulations, as is evident in Badgley's description of the government's promotional scheme to locate the ideal millionth postwar immigrant.

Article 4.1
Elizabeth Beaton

An African-American Community in Cape Breton, 1901–1904

Issues to Consider

- Why was the Dominion Iron and Steel Company so eager to hire African-Americans, despite the racial prejudices of the time?
- What are some of the difficulties that Beaton cites about doing historical research on marginalized communities? What would be the ideal records for a topic such as this one?
- Beaton contends that the skill of Black workers gave them more status than the period's racism would ordinarily allow, but also that, ultimately, "the reality of racial and paternalistic attitudes" would undermine the entire group's experience. What examples does she give of the "paternalism" that was so bound up with the host society's constructions of race, and especially of "Blackness"?
- What explains public perceptions of Black women and domestic life? What does this indicate about the relationship between race, sexuality, and gender?
- How was Black working-class culture perceived by white Sydney residents? Were there differences in perception between white workers and the more affluent of the white community?

In Sydney, Nova Scotia, on 8 August 1902, preparations were well underway for celebrating the imminent coronation of Edward VII. Local businesses, large and small, would be represented by floats; veterans from the recently ended Boer War would march; all would be led by several prominent local bands. But the highlight of the parade was to be the miniature steel works on wheels drawn by six and four horse teams, presented by the Dominion Iron and Steel Company (DISCO). One local newspaper reported that: "The employees of the Steel Company will march over the bridge 1500 strong.... The employees have spent over $6000 in getting their feature in shape."[1] The parade took place the following day.

> The second division comprising the various floats of the Dominion Steel Co ... was headed by the Sydney Coronet Band and in it the people of Sydney had exhibited to them a steel plant in miniature, including the manufacture of coke. Lieutenant Collidge was in command and each department was under its own marshals. The following departments were represented ...: ore hoisting and shipping piers, the open hearth and blast furnaces, blooming mills, mechanical and electrical, foundry, pattern shop, transportation, warehouses and coke ovens.... An American gentleman viewing the Coronation parade from the veranda of the Sydney Hotel said he never in his life saw better.[2]

Aside from the irony of Sydney's biggest parade, honouring an English King, being commented upon by an American, what was noteworthy about this event? The answer is found in a remarkable photograph, taken that day, of an imposing seven-metre-high "miniature" blast

Source: Elizabeth Beaton, "An African-American Community in Cape Breton, 1901–1904," *Acadiensis* 24, no. 2 (Spring 1995): 65–97.

furnace riding on a flatbed. The flag-bedecked, bunting-wrapped replica, plainly an important part of the coronation spectacle, was "marshalled" by a group of black men, dressed in suits, who were clearly in charge. This scene was an anomaly, for, in the context of racial attitudes in early 20th century Sydney, black men would not normally be given such significant public responsibility. Who were these men?

These black men were among several hundred African-American skilled furnace men brought to Sydney to work at DISCO's blast furnaces during its foundation years. Small business people, including a barber and several tavern, restaurant and dance hall owners, came along with the steel workers.[3] They came with women and children and settled, for a brief period, in Sydney, in the Whitney Pier area, where they can be defined as a "community."

Any attempt to document the experience of this community of Blacks must, for the most part, be based on "outsider" depictions derived from steel company records and newspaper references, which provide, essentially, a white, male, authoritarian perspective. But "insider" portrayals are also available to a limited extent. For instance, in archival sources we find identifiable persons with names, families, homes, and with connections to community institutions. Also, through newspapers the Blacks told their own story of their hopes for their sojourn in Cape Breton and of their long journey back home to the United States.

Historically, the presence of African-Americans in Cape Breton from 1901 to 1904 was a result of the movement put in train by the transition of American Blacks from slavery to farm labourers to industrial workers, and the national and world-wide work migrations which were sparked by industrialization. These demographic shifts are well documented in a broad range of

Black steel workers marshalling a blast furnace "miniature" in coronation parade; photograph no. 91-602-2253, Beaton Institute, photographer unknown.

literature. African-American work migrations to Canada from the United States in the late 19th and early 20th centuries brought farmers to Central and Western Canada; others came north to work as sleeping car porters.[4] It is impossible to calculate exactly how many African-American men, women and children came to Cape Breton from the United States during the period 1901 to 1904. Several hundred men were in Sydney over the entire period; in all likelihood they were part of a migratory community experiencing the same constant movement all over North America typical of other foreign worker groups at DISCO. Such a pattern is implicit in the variety of arrival and departure dates found in the available records. The wives of the black steel workers probably accounted for a relatively small proportion of the migrants. At the same time, the description of a social occasion on Tupper Street in Cokeville in 1902 implies the presence of a significant number of unattached women in the African-American community.[5]

This study of the brief African-American experience in the Cape Breton steel industry presents perhaps the first documentation of the American Blacks, involving not only male workers, but also the women and children who accompanied them as part of an industrial work migration. A consideration of the experience of this group — their arrival, their accommodations, through to the evolution of their social life — can serve to suggest how the skilled status of the male members of the community, the blast furnace workers, was off-set by the realities of racial and paternalistic attitudes which affected the experience of the group as a whole.

That black men were hired for work in the blast furnace is in keeping with the recognized hierarchy of jobs in the work culture of steel making. The blast furnace, which produced molten iron from iron ore, coke and limestone, was the first step towards producing basic carbon steel. This part of steel making was considerably more dirty and dangerous than the steel-producing open hearth operation, which was the next stage in the process. The open hearth workers, by virtue of actually "making" the steel, were the highest ranking workers at the plant, along with the skilled craftsmen like the machinists, bricklayers and carpenters. The blast furnace tended to hire lower status local whites, foreigners or black workers, while the open hearth was reserved for white anglophone workers. This informal "policy" was ubiquitous in the North American steel industry until the 1960s.[6]

Blacks had worked in the American iron-making industry as early as 1842, when industrialist Joseph R. Anderson successfully employed slaves as puddlers, heaters and rollers at the Tredegar Iron Works, a foundry and rolling mill complex in Richmond, Virginia. By the end of the Civil War, over 2,000 slaves were labouring in numerous iron mills in Tennessee's Cumberland River Valley.[7] With the development of modern iron and steel works in the decade after the American Civil War, employers continued to hire these black iron workers, often seeking to use them as strike-breakers during labour disputes.[8] However, the recruitment of Blacks also reflected their abilities as iron workers; indeed, during the period from 1875 to the First World War, black iron workers were recognized as skilled.[9] At the Homestead Steel Works, for example, some Blacks rose rapidly to skilled positions.[10] By 1907, at the Homestead Steel Works, 17 per cent of the black workforce were identified as "skilled"; similarly 27 per cent of Pittsburgh's black iron and steel workers were skilled.[11]

Blacks from a variety of backgrounds have worked at the Sydney steel plant during its entire history. Most of the available information focuses on West Indian workers, the first reports of whom appeared in 1909, although some probably arrived earlier.[12] And migrant black workers from mainland Nova Scotia were undoubtedly at the plant from its beginnings and were also working in the coal industry.[13] Their exact numbers and dates of arrival are difficult to ascertain, but they probably followed the same work patterns as other rural Nova Scotia workers in the steel industry, travelling back and forth as work was available in industry or in their home communities. The present-day Nova Scotian Blacks are well integrated with the West Indians. Black steel workers from the United States are remembered in the oral tradition of the community, but have merited only passing mention in scholarly and popular studies.[14] On the whole, the American black steel workers remain something of an enigma, partly because there is no evidence of their descendants in present-day Sydney, but especially because many of them held unusual status as skilled workers in the early Sydney steel plant, a status not afforded other black steel workers until the 1960s.

Distinctions between "skilled" and "unskilled" are well recognized as the chief demarcations within the early 20th century working class in Canada, as elsewhere.[15] In the steel industry, the persistence of the recognized value of skilled workers confirmed the social distance between them and the industry's "yard" labourers. However, the work context of the early steel industry — steel or iron men, mechanics or tradesmen versus labourers or yard workers — had definitions that were often based more on the racial, ethnic or religious background of a worker than on knowledge or expertise. These distinctions, which were to carry through many years, were crystallized by the influx of immigrant workers.

In Sydney, as in other industrial towns, this class system within a class was signalled by the location of workers at the workplace, and by their rates of remuneration. Within the broader community, it was signalled by the type, quality and location of their dwelling places. Indeed, the development of Sydney as an industrial city was characterized by these differentiations, with each group — plant management, skilled workers and labourers — living in distinct communities. Whitney Pier, the district close by the dirtiest end of the coke- and steel-making processes, became known as the settlement area of "labourers" from all over the world. Ashby, located further away from the plant, but close enough for walking to work, housed management and many skilled workers.[16]

The process of importing foreign workers for the plant's start-up, whether skilled or labourers, was carried out under an agreement between Nova Scotia's government and DISCO.[17] Not only were the skilled workers invited by the steel company; their transportation was arranged, and they lived, at least initially, in accommodation provided by the company. That these workers often brought their families with them further proclaimed their "skilled" status. While white Americans were generally welcomed into the workforce, considerable debate surrounded the importation of Slavs, Italians and Blacks.[18] Such attitudes were reflected in Cape Breton newspapers which hailed the arrival of supervisory American workers, but portrayed other newcomers in a generally negative light, often referring to them as "labourers," even though they might have been brought in for their specific expertise. Nativist, and sometimes racist, sentiments were evident when foreigners were hired instead of local men. Thus, for example, a letter to the *Daily Post* editor in 1902 described black workers as "foul-mouthed ... niggers" who replaced good, "god-fearing" native workmen.[19] On another level, many local citizens subscribed to the notion, also founded in racism, that American Blacks were brought to work at the Sydney plant because black people could better stand the heat of the blast furnaces.

The recruitment of skilled workers from the United States was of particular importance because the Sydney plant represented an almost total transfer of American steel-making technology. Most of the construction engineers were American, as were the department managers at every level. These supervisory personnel stayed for brief periods of one or two years, after which they returned to the United States. Their comings and goings were avidly reported by local newspapers, as Sydney found itself in the company of other major steel cities in the United States.[20]

Networking between steel plant supervisory employees across the continent ensured that the hiring situation in the steel industry was well known. And incoming supervisors usually hired skilled workers from amongst their former colleagues or employees.[21] The first Superintendent of Furnaces at DISCO, Shiras MacGilvray, came from Pittsburgh. In the glow of the first iron cast in late 1900 and the anticipation of three more furnaces starting up in early 1901, MacGilvray noted in a letter to a foreman at Ferona, Nova Scotia, that there were local "labour problems" in terms of the lack of experienced workers.[22] He sent further letters to associates at steel plants in Pennsylvania, Ohio and New York State, seeking foremen and other experienced men. For instance, he wrote to W. W. McKeown of Leetonia, Ohio, in 1901, asking for a foreman and complaining that, "As we expected the labour here is poor … not having any experience in this work."[23] In July 1901, MacGilvray moved on to work for Carnegie Steel in Pittsburgh. He was immediately replaced by John H. Means, whose family was connected with the Means Fulton Iron Works in Birmingham. Means had turned down an offer of $12,000 from Empire Steel and Iron (Catassuaga, Pennsylvania) in favour of Dominion Iron and Steel.[24] Almost as soon as he took up his position with DISCO, Means began recruiting amongst his network of Alabama and Pennsylvania steelmen. He also brought in workers from Buffalo and Tonawanda and requested workers from Maryland.[25] Superintendent Means wrote to David Baker, DISCO General Superintendent, that "We are sadly in need of some competent men there [at the pig machine] to handle that part of the business."[26] Repeatedly he complained of the inexperience of the men working for him, particularly Newfoundlanders and Italians.[27]

It was Means who opened the door to African-American blast furnace workers at the Sydney plant. Already a mobile workforce, the black workers were prepared to respond to Means' suggestion that they travel to Cape Breton. Given the shortage of experienced furnace workers throughout the North American iron and steel industry at the time, it seems reasonable to surmise that Means was offering higher wages than the workers were currently receiving at American plants. Certainly, he was offering significantly better rates of pay than MacGilvray had offered in the previous months. For instance, a "keeper" was paid $2.25 per 12 hour day by MacGilvray, but was offered $2.75 by Means as of August 1901; a Hot Blast-Man under MacGilvray received $1.80 per day compared to Means' rate of $2.25; Means' 1st Helper got $2.20 compared to the previous rate of $1.70 per day. The highest rate, $3.00 per day, was for iron carriers.[28] These rates represented the most important jobs of the process of the blast furnace. Except for the "keeper," who was in charge of ensuring the correct amounts of raw materials, the skilled workers were found in the cast house, from where the operation was controlled. Labourers, paid considerably less, worked at the "back" of the furnace constantly "charging" layers of limestone, coal and iron ore into the top of the furnace.[29]

Means found the prospect of hiring black workers particularly attractive since he believed that they were more likely than their white counterparts to bring a large number of their fellow workers with them. This opinion he based on the argument that they would feel more comfortable and be safer in larger numbers.[30] Privately, however, Means expressed some reservations as to the length of time the Africans-Americans would stay, or even whether they would agree to come. On 10 August 1901, he wrote DISCO's General Superintendent that, "We had a wire from the South saying that men are very scarce, and that there may be some trouble getting them here, and even did they come, they were only expected to stay until winter, whereas the men you would probably bring [from Eastern Pennsylvania and Maryland] we might be able to hold right along."[31] In correspondence with transportation agents, Means mentioned another reservation: "I have not made up my mind definitely about this matter, as I fear the men will be unable to stand this climate."[32]

Means' recruitment of African-Americans from Birmingham, Pittsburgh and Colorado was based in a complex labour network, one which kept black steel workers in touch with each other wherever they went to work.[33] Except that it was racially-based, this networking was not unlike the communications between other industrial workers, considered to be the "most natural and most wide spread factor in mobilizing a workforce," significant evidence of which is found in archival records, both written and oral.[34] However, issues relating to working conditions would have been especially pertinent to the black workers since their history of being used as strike-breakers often prejudiced the attitudes of white workers against them in violent ways.[35] [...]

DISCO arranged the transportation of the black workers by informal tender in correspondence with several American railway or "road" agencies. In August and September, 1901, Means negotiated with the Merchants and Miners Transportation Company (Baltimore), the Central Georgia Railway Company (Birmingham), Southern Railroad (Birmingham) and "L and N" (Birmingham). These companies offered not only to transport the workers but also to act as agents in finding them. Means was prepared to take advantage of the competition amongst the carriers: "I think we should get a very favourable rate on these men."[36] The offer of transportation to the black workers was qualified with certain restrictions consisting of deduction by instalment or refund, with return fare based on six months' work. These limitations were not always clear in correspondence with the prospective employees, but Means made the arrangements very clear to General Superintendent Baker.

> In regard to the men in the South: The propositions I made these men after consulting with Mr. Moxham [General Manager of DISCO], was as follows:
>
> If they came up here and stayed until the middle of December we would give them transportation here and back. This was to bridge over our troubles until skilled workmen from Germany arrived. It took us some little while to work this movement up in the South on account of the delay in writing and getting answers.[37]

As a result of these efforts, on about 15 October 1901, 33 men and three women arrived in Sydney. The *Daily Post* announced the arrival of this group of "Coloured Furnace Men" as labourers, not skilled workmen, reporting that "Thirty colored labourers arrived from Pittsburgh [sic] last night to work about the furnaces of the steel company."[38] Their names, including reference to their wives, were posted in the DISCO Mailing Room as "coloured men from Alabama."[39] Bart Bryan, DISCO's time keeper, had the same list for deductions from pay for furnace shoes. The names appear again in orders relating to reimbursement for travel expenses, and in a note to a Sydney haberdasher requesting that work clothing be supplied to individual workers: "Please give Ike Kennedy 2 suits of heavy cheap underwear. Horton one pair of overalls and one suit heavy cheap underwear. Tom Cadenhead one pair overalls, charging same to my account. If you have not got these overalls, please get them for [me]."[40]

Concurrent with these arrangements for men, mainly from Alabama, a strategy to bring more black iron workers from Pennsylvania was implemented. As with the first group, Means insisted on getting only "good" experienced men. [...]

John Means had also written to Squire White in Pueblo, Colorado, informing him and his fellow workers of the jobs available, wages and transportation arrangements. He obviously believed that the arrival of the first lot of black workers would influence their decision to come: "I have 33 men and 3 women who will arrive here from North Birmingham tonight [or] tomorrow night. Mr. Hutton is with them. John Watts, Albert Martin, Will and quite a lot of the boys that you know.... In case you boys make up your minds to come here I think I can arrange your transportation."[41]

As Means explained to General Superintendent Baker, the pay increases promised the new workers were premised on the assumption that these skilled workers would increase the efficiency of the new No. 3 blast furnace.

> As to wages these men were to get; iron carriers $3.00 per day provided four men carried the iron; $2.50 if 5 men carried it; or $2.00 if we worked 7 as we do now. The sand cutters were to be paid $2.25 with 4 men to furnace, instead of six now at $2.00. Fallmen were to get $2.00

for two men in the fall instead of three, as we have now at, at $1.80. Scrappers were to be paid $1.60 as we pay them now. These men are all cast shed men, keepers, sand cutters and iron carriers, fall and scrap men.[42]

Clearly the high rate of pay was based on cutting the normal personnel per turn by almost half. The possibility of doing this in a new blast furnace was, at best, remote. Nevertheless, even experienced men, perhaps swayed by the overwhelming publicity about the new Cape Breton plant, which was promoting itself as the most modern in North America, apparently accepted the argument that such efficiency could be achieved.[43]

The incoming men were not informed that they were to be a stop-gap workforce until German workers arrived. Although they had been officially encouraged to stay as long as 18 months, they were not expected to stay longer than six. Yet, it is possible that Means did not expect or want the German workers, and that he preferred to have Southern Blacks at the furnace. Means saw the first 33 men as a "trial lot.... Should I be able to satisfy them with the place I am going South myself to move about 100 [men]."[44] A couple of months later, the *Daily Post* noted:

> J. H. Means, General Manager of the Dominion Coal and Iron Company [sic], Sydney, Cape Breton, has left on his return to Nova Scotia with three carloads of Tennessee and Alabama negroes who will go to work in the furnaces there. Mr. Means encountered some opposition to the deportation of the negroes, but finally got them. He took the wives and daughters along with the men. Mr. Means has already a number of negro hands at Sydney where the furnaces are located and it appears that their work has been satisfactory.[45]

The migration to Canada appeared to be closely watched by American newspapers. According to the *Bangor Daily News*, the same "three carloads" of black workers and their families, mentioned by the Sydney paper, travelled by way of the Pemaquid Line steamer to Mt. Desert Ferry, then on the Maine Central train to the border. Looking back in 1903, the Bangor reporter's recollection of the group was somewhat clouded by his stereotypical perceptions of Southern Blacks as musical, happy-go-lucky cotton workers who did not have enough sense to mind the cold:

> At the last end of the procession came a crowd of 250 colored people ranging in size from a baby in arms to old men barely able to walk. They were dressed in all kinds of fantastic garb, none which seemed sufficient to half warm a person and which made me shiver to look at. But they didn't seem to mind it at all. They laughed and joked with one another and to the other passengers and railroad men. They cared not for the cold, it didn't cause them the least worry, though it caused them to shiver and made the little ones cry from their suffering. Those who had musical instruments played upon them. Not sad and disheartening music, but the gayest of gay, rollicking jigs and that kind of stuff. They had been that way all the distance from Rockland, said the steam boat men ... To one who seemed a bit more intelligent than the others, the writer propounded the question, where they were heading. "Gwine, child'?" said he, "why, we're gwine to Sidney [sic], Cape Breton, to work in the steel mill and we's gwine to get big wages is we uns. It's gwine to be mighty sight nicer'n working in the cotton fields, so tis, honey." And then he was away and aboard the cars.[46]

More information was sought from a man who may have been Superintendent Means: "The white man who accompanied and apparently had charge of the party ... stated that they were going down to Sidney [sic] to work in the mills, and that they were to be paid good wages, and it was thought that they would be better off. That was as near as anyone learned at the time as to the wages they were going to receive."[47]

It is unclear whether these workers insisted on bringing their families to Cape Breton as a condition of their coming to work at the Sydney plant. But whatever the reasons, in the case of each group of Southern workers who came to Sydney, arrangements between the company, the workers and the transportation agencies included spouses.[48] Three of the men in the first group had brought their wives, although the company initially promised only that wives, washerwomen or cooks could be brought after the men were settled. And the inclusion of women in this first group was mentioned, perhaps as an enticement, to the Colorado workers when Superintendent Means noted in passing that "33 men and 3 women will arrive from North Birmingham tonight."[49]

The figures given by the Maine newspaper along the route suggest that several hundred persons were involved in this part of the migration alone. In contrast, a newspaper in Bath, Maine, reported 60 "negroes on their way to Sydney" on 20 December 1901.[50] It is possible that these were the male workers in the three railcars referred to earlier. Whether there were, as reported, actually 250 people in this group is uncertain and perhaps unlikely; it was probably an approximation. Although the precise number of migrants remains elusive, it is clear that the recruitment efforts had borne fruit and, by the beginning of 1902, significant numbers of workers had arrived in Sydney to take up the jobs they had been offered. These new recruits, some of them with families, required immediate accommodation.

The housing accommodation provided for the skilled black workers and their families gives the first real hint that, for DISCO'S management, as for the rest of the community, race superseded skill in determining the status accorded to black workers. Many scholarly studies on housing have identified a connection between housing and status, particularly when the status is based on race. Discriminatory housing policies and residential segregation, in turn, affected the inhabitants' position "as workers in the labour market by limiting and constraining their economic and political behaviour."[51] The experience of living in inadequate housing and being confined to undesirable areas was certainly not new to American Blacks who migrated north to find work.[52] However, the American Blacks had expected a different situation in Sydney. They and their families were given "[a]lluring promises of fine houses to live in, garden spots, cheap living and more."[53] Instead, their housing would consist of company "shacks" and other poorly outfitted dwellings. These shacks, which normally housed single men, became the quarters of both men and women in the case of the African-Americans. This was especially significant in a town where housing for skilled and semi-skilled workers of Anglo-Celtic background ranged from company hotels to hundreds of substantial and well-built double and single family dwellings in the Ashby area of Sydney.[54] The African-Americans, in contrast, lived in Whitney Pier, on the northeast side of the steel plant or coke ovens, close to its operations, in the area known at that time as "Cokeville" or "Cokovia." Cokeville was the designated area for foreign white workers of lower status, and was the least desirable area of Whitney Pier.[55] (See Plan of Sydney, 1902, showing Cokeville in Ward V [Whitney Pier].)

Shacks, or very basic bunk houses, were the most common shelter supplied by the steel company for unskilled workers.[56] Foreign skilled workers, including the Italians and Hungarians, also found accommodation in company shacks. These shacks could be found at several locations on the steel plant grounds or near the plant in Whitney Pier (see 1903 map indicating "Shackville").[57] Most were occupied by Italian workers.[58] After the completion of the construction of the steel plant, DISCO sold off some of the company-owned shacks.[59] In 1901, in a statement regarding health conditions in Whitney Pier, the steel company noted that it "had only a few men in the shacks."[60] But evidently the company held on to some of these structures, using them to house their African-American recruits later that year.[61] Thus, a 1902 newspaper report refers to "coloured shacks" or to "old Steel Company shacks," describing one such as a two storey building in which "coloured people of both sexes" lived, located "near the Steel Co.'s fence at the blooming mills."[62] By 1905, however, Poll Tax collectors expressed surprise at finding the "coloured quarters" in Cokeville occupied "not by negroes, but by Hungarians, Poles and Newfoundlanders."[63] Their description gave a picture of conditions in the shacks as they must have been for the black workers who arrived in 1901:

The conditions in some of these places are bad beyond description. Some of the houses are fairly clean, but the majority are exceedingly filthy. There is no sewage or water connection and the ventilation is foul. The beds are simply a big deal table about seven feet broad which runs down the whole length of the room. The men wrap themselves up in their blankets and lie on this shelf as close as they can pack. There is also in the room a stove, which the inmates seem to think it a point of humour to keep as hot as possible, and hanging from the ceiling, which is about ten feet high, are the spare clothes of the men. None of the beds are ever aired, for as soon as one shift is out of them, another is in.[64]

Nor had the Blacks permanently disappeared from the area, for these same buildings were the shacks with "mostly coloured tenants," which remained on the plant property between Railroad Street and the rolling mills and were documented on a 1907 Fire Insurance Atlas.[65] (See 1907 Goad's Fire Insurance Atlas.)

The steel company also built, or at least renovated, houses for the African-Americans. However, based on the incomplete records available, it would appear that the buildings designated for the use of the black workers and their families were substandard. One recorded problem was with regard to heating. On two occasions Superintendent Means asked the time keeper to fix the heating by rerouting the stove piping through the cellar and the unheated rooms in several houses. The obvious fire risk of this solution was not mentioned. Means also endeavoured to hurry the rehabilitation of alternate housing. His urgent tone implied that a commitment to proper housing was necessary if they were to retain the black workers, whose skills were critical to the operation of furnaces. He wrote to the DISCO time keeper:

I wish you would send a carpenter over to the houses occupied by the Niggers and have the stove pipes led through the rooms that have no fire in them so that they may be partially heated by the radiation.

Please get this done for me at once as it is important that I make these men as comfortable as possible. Also, please let me know what Mr. Baker thought of the scheme for the two big houses with the furnaces in the cellar.[66]

A few days later, a memo to General Superintendent Baker seemed to suggest that houses would be built by the company:

I beg to hand you herewith specification of a house that I would like to have for the Negroes and which I am sure would please most of white men with small families. This house possibly will cost here about $225 and will rent for $5.00 a month.[67]

It is unclear where the houses were to be located, or whether they were finally built. But it is probable that many African-Americans rented accommodation other than shacks, for it seems unlikely that several hundred men, women and children would live in shacks for their entire sojourn in Sydney.[68]

During that sojourn, the little Black community would establish their own working class culture, which white Sydney would, for the most part, perceive as negative and threatening. The social life of the African-Americans was most often depicted, in police reports and the local newspapers, in stories of violence between men, or between men and women. Black women were particularly singled out for charges of drunkenness, vagrancy and prostitution. The conditions of life for the newcomers, and their responses to them, in so far as they can be glimpsed in such reports, were typical of boom town societies across North America in the early 20th century. Sydney's response to the situation reflected middle class attitudes typical of North American industrial cities of the time.[69] The city, or at least the middle class sector of the city, aspired to be sophisticated and refined, and consciously tried to sustain that view of itself through its press. The inevitable gaps in that self-perception were blamed on the behaviour of working class immigrants, particularly those at the lower end of the social scale. In Sydney, blame for social disorder was most commonly placed on Blacks and Italians.[70] Newspaper reports of a shooting incident involving two African-American iron workers, which resulted in a death, demonstrated both police and press attitudes towards the Black community. Curiously, police attitudes seemed to be based on Southern American stereotypes not necessarily attributed to Blacks:

> Just before the arrival of the chief, the *Record* man asked Officer McDonald if he was going back home then. "No," replied the officer, "these fellows around here might start some of their Southern antics and attempt to lynch this man, and I am going to stay here and keep order." He ordered all those who were not immediate friends of the wounded man out of the room, all obeying promptly, without a show of objection.[71]

The press viewed this tragedy, which had occurred at a local dance hall, as further evidence of the undesirability of the Blacks, and implied that such incidents were to be expected.[72]

In their portrayal of life in "Shackville," local gossip columnists focused on squalor, violence and sexual immorality. Domestic disputes figured prominently in such reports. For example, on 27 September 1902, the *Daily Post* carried the story of "[a] coloured gentleman from Shackville" who

> related a tale of woe at the police station yesterday morning. The root of all his troubles he attributed to the inconstancy of his wife, who he said had other admirers calling upon her while he was away absent at work. The lady is at present in Truro while her admirer is at present in Sydney. The husband wishes to have him punished to the full extent of the law "just" he says to "to teach other young fellows who are guilty of similar offenses a lesson."[73]

In contrast, "Domestic Troubles at Shackville" detailed the experience of a woman who had moved out of her home and into another man's home, and was now asking for police protection from her husband.[74] Such reports about life in "Shackville" were juxtaposed against news items about the activities of Sydney's more "respectable" citizens, descriptions of piano recitals, dramatic productions, or the latest millinery additions to one of the town's fine stores.

In contrast to their "respectable" white middle class counterparts, black women, particularly unattached women, were regularly depicted as explicitly immoral or implicitly suspect. There is no evidence that domestic work, the most common employment for single black women in other cities, was an option for those who came to Sydney.[75] It is likely, therefore, that some did turn to prostitution as the surest means of making a living.[76] The presence of these women was a civic embarrassment:

> A shocking sight was witnessed at Cokeville about noon yesterday, three coloured women in a helpless state of intoxication were lying on the side walk of the principal street of that district. Passersby in order to avoid a shower of abuse turned their steps the other way. The coloured part of the population of Cokeville now predominate and judging by their actions of late will require strict police surveillance.[77]

In most news reports, the women's full names were not given. If a woman was identified at all, it was in reference to the man to whom she was related, or her first name was given in a joking tone. The exception was when there was an actual charge of prostitution, vagrancy or theft. In such cases reporters regularly used inflationary literary devices to further degrade the women. For example, women charged with vagrancy were often described as "ladies in their finery," a phrase which functioned euphemistically to identify prostitutes. Sadie Whallen, a "coloured beauty of Cokovia," was charged with relieving a Swedish sailor of his "roll."[78] It is likely that the "disorderly houses raided and wrecked" in 1902 in Whitney Pier housed at least some black prostitutes.[79] Newspaper articles provide little more than vague hints of the social conditions of African-American women in Sydney. Yet the women's experiences, as viewed through the prism of local newspaper reports, suggest that many black women who came to Sydney, especially, though not exclusively, those who might fall into the category of "camp followers," were at both the service and the mercy of their own men or of white men in authority.

Yet, there were more positive social interactions between black men and women which indicated a cohesiveness of community. These took place at Curry's dance hall, located on Tupper Street in Cokeville. It appeared that on each pay day (weekly) at the steel works, "the usual coloured ball was held in the coloured hall on Tupper Street."[80] The dances there offered an opportunity for men and women to meet and court in a situation that was removed from the critical view of white society.[81] We might not have known about this aspect of the Blacks' social life had it not been for a tragic incident, an altercation resulting in the death of 47 year old North Carolina native G. B. Scott, who was unmarried and lived in shack no. 4. He was a "sort of floor manager" at the dance hall. The fatal shot was fired by 46 year old James Brooks, who was himself critically wounded. A resident of shack no. 7, Brooks was married, with a family in Georgia. He was at the dance hall with "a lady friend."[82] Although the newspaper report of this tragedy depicts the African-Americans as "restless" and violent, it also hints at the emergence of a leisure culture. The social activities alluded to in this case had a material significance: they took place in a building recognized as a focus for the community. The men involved emerge as distinct individuals, who had lives outside the workplace, and "homes," however impermanent. They were members of a community which had begun to take root.

Religion formed the basis of another level of cohesion amongst the Blacks, and one which was more acceptable to the white community. Given the widely understood importance of Black spirituality throughout their entire North American history, it is not surprising to find that religion played a vital part in the lives of the American Blacks who came to Sydney.[83] In January 1902, shortly after the arrival of black workers and their families, an African Methodist Episcopal (AME) congregation was established in Sydney. Its organizer was Reverend John Coleman, who was "Presiding Elder of Missions among coloured people in the Maritime Provinces" for the AME. As such, he would be aware of black communities throughout the region, and would attend to those seeking the spiritual guidance of the AME.[84] A native of Holmes County, Mississippi, Coleman had trained in Theology at Victoria College at the University of Toronto, and was the author of "several works dealing with the condition and characteristics of his people."[85] Coleman initiated his public work in the black community by seeking out the white authority figures of Sydney and the steel company, to get their permission and blessing.[86] [...]

The AME used "shack 81" as its "Cape Breton mission headquarters," at least for a time.[87] It is believed that the AME church was located on Tupper Street; but it is possible that no actual "church" was ever built and that Tupper Street was simply the location of shack 81. Ultimately, however, the continuing success of the church would depend upon the support of its parishioners. In August 1904, the *Daily Record* reported that the Blacks had been without a preacher for the past three months, but that Rev. Coleman was seeking $1,200 to find and hire young men to "preach and teach the coloured children of which there were fifty in Sydney.... [A] considerable sum has already been subscribed by coloured people and white people in Sydney."[88] But by this time, the numbers of American Blacks had begun dwindling and there is no evidence that another clergyman was sent.

Schooling for black children, apparently the result of lobbying by the AME, and yet another signal of community formation, followed the same pattern of initial success and then a rapid decline in 1904. In early 1902, Rev. Coleman had reminded the City of its obligation to provide education for black children, pointing out that the wife of the AME preacher was already teaching on an informal basis: "There is no provision yet ... for educating the children, but until something is done in that direction, our people have secured the services of Mrs. Hill. There are quite a number of children there, and the matter is somewhat important."[89] Shortly thereafter, in September 1902, a school for the "Coloured Children," called Cokovia School, was opened by the City of Sydney. The *Daily Post* reported: "In addition to the ordinary schools it was found necessary to provide a school with a teacher of their own, for the coloured people residing at Cokeville, and this matter has been engaging the attention of the Board for some time with result that it will soon be established."[90] The school, located on Henry Street, had one classroom with 32 pupils taught by a Mrs. Selena Williams, a Nova Scotia Black.[91] In the city's 1902 annual report, the chairperson of the school board, Mayor Crowe, declared that the Cokovia School had the best record of attendance for the year, the pupils having attended an average of 74 of 84 days.[92] In the city's annual report for 1902, the salary for the Cokovia School teacher was recorded as $68.46; in 1903 her salary was $145.67 for teaching 34 pupils for 187 days. The "Coloured School" was still in operation in 1904, but by 1905 it had disappeared from the city's records.[93]

The virtual disappearance of the American Blacks from Sydney by the end of 1904 raises questions, especially since many of them had stayed longer than expected, and had begun to lay the foundations for a permanent community. Why did they leave? A variety of possibilities present themselves.

The Cape Breton climate is still cited in local lore as the main reason for the Blacks' departure. In early 1902 DISCO denied a report by an unidentified Halifax paper that "a large number of the first contingent and some of the second have returned to their homes for climatic reasons." DISCO spokesmen insisted that the "southern arrivals stand the climate very well … the coloured are no more migratory in their tendencies than the white employees of the company."[94]

For many black workers, as for other migrant workers, the reason for leaving was assuredly related to the availability of work. After the famous 1904 strike for union recognition, which began on 1 June and ended 23 July, American Blacks were among the many foreign workers who left Sydney. The *Daily Post*'s gossip column reported in late July:

> Many Italian workman [sic] who … were refused employment at the steel works, because of misconduct during the recent strike, left yesterday by the fast train for different parts of the United States. A number of coloured men who were employed at the furnaces since Mr. Means had charge of them left yesterday for Colorado where they expect to secure employment.[95]

It is possible that the departure of Superintendent Means from the steel plant resulted in the Blacks not having the protection and privilege of skilled status in their work, or jobs of any kind, for that matter.[96]

But substandard housing and inadequate wages for American black workers were the apparent causes of the largest group departure in late 1902. The story became news when Walter Griffin and his wife, part of the original group from Alabama in 1901, arrived at Bangor, Maine, on 13 January 1903, telling of having walked from Sydney as part of a group returning home to Alabama:

> According to the story of Walter Griggin [Griffin] and his wife who applied at the police station here today for shelter for 250 coloured people who are walking home from Sydney C.B. to Alabama, a jaunt of about 2900 miles. All are penniless, destitute and disappointed. The Griggins [Griffins] who were scantily clad and suffered from hunger and cold, told a pitiful story. They say that about one year ago, an agent came to their town in the South, hiring coloured people to work in the steel mills in Sydney and promising $2 a day.
>
> Alluring promises of fine houses to live in, garden spots, cheap living and more were held out to them, with the result, the Griggins [Griffins] say, about 100 men and their families, numbering 250 people in all went to Cape Breton last March. [sic]

What the Griggins [Griffins] said they found [was] not at all as promised them. They got no pay at all until they worked sixty days and then only $1.25 a day or even less. There had been considerable trouble between the negroes and mill owners which had resulted in many Italians being brought from Pittsburgh to take their places.

The entire colony, so the Griggins [Griffins] said, had decided to tramp back to Alabama and thought they could get there somehow and sometime. They said that the winter had been fearfully cold and they had suffered a great deal.

They think that the others are not a great way behind and that nearly the whole colony of 250 are on the way between Boston and Cape Breton. The local authorities have not yet decided what course to take.

A local steel company official when seen by a *Record* reporter last evening regarding the matter gave the report an emphatic denial. He declared that the coloured people imported from Alabama were all doing well. They were earning twice as much as they ever did before, and they were happy and contented.[97]

The story was denied by the steel company and mildly ridiculed by the Sydney paper. Yet, the experience of Walter Griffin and his wife gains credence when compared with earlier newspaper reports concerning a large number of Blacks travelling through Maine from Alabama to Sydney in December 1901.[98]

An interview with Walter Griffin as the group left Bangor revealed that they were leading a larger group who had left Sydney six months earlier, in August 1902.[99] They had worked on farms along the way in order to survive. Some of the party had died on the way and some were ill as a result of exposure. The Griffins' plan was to go to Bucksport, Maine, by train and then on to Boston on the steamer *Penobscot*. Their story about the group which followed was verified by railroad men between Bangor and Vanceboro on the Maine Central line, who "constantly hear reports of colored people tramping south."[100]

The depletion of Sydney's American Black community appeared to have continued until there was virtually no one left of the group. However, Sydney Directories show that a few stayed in Sydney. In 1907, Henry Bell, from the first group of arrivals in 1901, was a porter at the Sydney Hotel on the Esplanade in downtown Sydney; in 1914, he was "a shoeshine" on Victoria Road; his "home" was on Curry's Lane in Cokeville. A paper hanger named Henry Bell "roomed" on Curry's Lane in 1923.[101] According to oral tradition, he ran a drinking establishment on Curry's Lane for several years, beginning around 1910.[102] Another American Black, Colonel Jim Brooks, known as a "mulatto," operated a restaurant at 82 Tupper Street, near the coke ovens, for over 20 years. He was the James Brooks, mentioned earlier, who was wounded in the shoot-out with G. B. Scott in the Tupper Street dance hall. Reputedly, Brooks ran a tavern on Curry's Lane and carried a pistol on his hip.[103] Georgina Cambridge, one of the oldest members of the West Indian Black community, remembers Jim Brooks who, with his American wife, ran a restaurant, not a tavern, on Tupper Street. Mrs. Cambridge heard that he wore a gun, although she never saw it; she knew that he had been shot at a dance hall on Tupper Street.[104] These American Blacks probably stood out in local memory because of their businesses. It is notable that, in 1907 and afterward, neither was employed by DISCO. But one man from the original group, Isiah Robinson, was employed by DISCO in 1907; he had disappeared from the record by 1914.[105] The fact that a few Blacks stayed on may be less important than the disappearance of the group's institutions, their school and their church. In effect, the loss of these institutions meant the end of their community.

Why did the American Black community, with its backbone of skilled workers, and inherent potential for permanence found in its institutions, end as it did? It can, perhaps, be suggested that the solidarity that brought the American Blacks to Cape Breton also guided them away in response to their collective will. It was this same solidarity, founded on race, that empowered them to form, and briefly sustain, a community, establishing formal institutions for the practice of their religion, to educate their children and for the purpose of recreation.

Because the record is so vague, and almost totally dependent upon white, "official" documentation, we may never fully understand the complexities of the decisions made by this group. Certainly, there is potential for further research that might take us to the industrial towns and cities of the United States from whence they came and to which they probably returned. At the same time, limited as the sources are, they still serve to deepen our understanding of the recruitment and transportation of African-Americans to Sydney, and of their experiences both as workers and as part of the fabric of Sydney's boomtown society during the early years of the steel industry. The story of these black workers and their families in Sydney provides insights into the definition and importance of "skill" in the start-up years of Sydney's steel plant, as well as into the process of moving skilled workers from one place to another through complicated networks of work migration.

While the story of this migratory community is solidly grounded in American history, parallels can be found in the Canadian black experience. The American Blacks shared with Canadian Blacks, especially Nova Scotian Blacks, the realization of the importance of religion as the underpinning of community; religion, in turn, propelled the establishment of educational institutions for both black groups.[106] Parallel patterns can also be found with regard to employment opportunities and working conditions, although the American black workers appeared, initially, to be viewed and treated as "skilled," unlike other Blacks in industry at the time. James Walker noted that "blacks have been acceptable in Canada whenever they have provided a needed service to the local economy … [but] [a]cceptability did not necessarily imply equality."[107] Mobility, both in the search for jobs and in the escape from direct or indirect discrimination, is an ongoing characteristic of Blacks in Canada of every background. The most prominent example, of course, is the black Loyalists' departure from Nova Scotia to Sierra Leone in 1792. But, throughout their history, Blacks have migrated across Canada and across the border to the United States. Indeed, even as the Blacks were coming into Canada during the period 1901–1904, large numbers of young Blacks were leaving Canada to go to the United States where economic and educational opportunities were better.[108]

We can thank the people of Whitney Pier for holding this significant community of African-Americans in their collective memory for so long. Because of Whitney Pier's longstanding oral tradition and because of newly uncovered archival sources, the work and social life of the American Blacks who lived in Sydney from 1901 to 1904 can now be better understood. Through their participation in the industrial experience of the Atlantic region, these American black men, women and children have become part of Canadian history.

ACKNOWLEDGMENTS

I am indebted to Delphin Muise, Rusty Bittermann, Joy Mannette and Graham Reynolds for their helpful suggestions: also to Mary Keating for her ideas on Sydney's early schools; to Kate Curric of the Beaton Institute, University College of Cape Breton, for her able archival assistance and her editorial suggestions; to a group of steel workers who responded to the presentation of an earlier version of this paper, especially Frank Murphy and Wally MacKinnon.

NOTES

1. "Preparation for Big Celebration: Coronation of King Edward," *Daily Record* (Sydney), 8 August 1902, p. 5. Sydney's *Daily Record* showed several variations in its name over the years: *Daily Record, Sydney Record, Sydney Daily Record, The Record*; Sydney's *Daily Post* underwent similar name changes.

2. "Coronation," *Daily Post*, 11 August 1902, p. 1.

3. *Sydney Record*, 10 October 1902; Toby Morris papers, MG7, G2, Beaton Institute; also informal discussions with Frank Murphy, 1992–94, who recalled delivering the daily newspaper in the coke ovens in the 1920s.

4. Howard and Tamara Palmer, "The Black Experience in Alberta," in *Peoples of Alberta: Portraits of Cultural Diversity* (Saskatoon, 1985), pp. 365–93; Agnes Calliste, "Sleeping Car Porters in Canada: An Ethnically Submerged Split Labour Market," *Canadian Ethnic Studies*, XIX, 1 (1987), pp. 1–22; James Walker, *A History of Blacks in Canada* (Ottawa, 1980), pp. 67–9.

5. "Squabble at Dance Ends in Tragedy," *Sydney Record*, 10 October 1902, p. 1. This was not unusual, for Sydney was, in effect, part of the diaspora in which most of the American black women who travelled north between 1870 and 1910 were unmarried, separated or widowed. See Jacqueline Jones, *Labour of Love, Labour of Sorrow: Black Women, Work and Family from Slavery to the Present* (New York, 1986), pp. 155–6.

6. For documentation and discussion of the hierarchy of job locations, see John A, Fitch, *The Steel Workers* ([1910] Pittsburgh, 1989), Introduction by Roy Lubove, pp. 22–31, 148–9; Craig Heron, *Working in Steel: The Early Years in Canada, 1883–1935* (Toronto, 1988), pp. 76–8. These views are confirmed by research carried out by the Beaton Institute Steel Project; see, especially, interviews with steel workers, MG 14, 206, C and D. For early documentation of the dangers in the blast furnace, see L. A. Spring, *Non-Technical Chats about Steel and Iron* (New York, 1917). The retardation of up-to-date safety practices in the blast furnace may be related to the traditional status of its workers.

7. Dennis C. Dickerson, *Out of the Crucible: Black Steel Workers in Western Pennsylvania, 1875–1980* (Albany, 1986), p. 8.

8. Ibid., pp. 8–10; See also Herbert G. Gutman, *Work, Culture and Society in Industrializing America* (New York, 1977), pp. 121–3, 152.

9. Dickerson, *Out of the Crucible*, pp. 7–26.

10. Margaret Byington, *Homestead: The Households of a Milltown* ([1910] Pittsburgh, 1974), p. 14.

11. Dickerson, *Out of the Crucible*, p. 20.

12. Elizabeth Beaton, "Is Cape Breton a Caribbean Island? West Indian Black Immigration to Industrial Cape Breton," Report, Beaton Institute; Walker, *A History of Blacks in Canada*; Robin Winks, *Blacks in Canada: A History* (Montreal, 1971). Individual family histories have vague references to 1906–07 arrivals of single men.

13. Interview, Marion Reid, 1994 (transcript in Elizabeth Beaton Papers, MG12, 198, Beaton Institute); see also The HERO Collection, Dalhousie University Archives. Familiar Nova Scotian Black names are absent from the 1901 census, possibly because of the transient nature of this workforce.

14. Winks, *Blacks in Canada*, p. 300. As well as mentioning the African-Americans in Sydney, Winks hints that population increases in Hamilton and Windsor were due to the immigration of Blacks. See also Heron, *Working in Steel*, p. 12; Elizabeth Beaton and Mary Keating, *"From the Pier, Dear": Images of a Multicultural Community* (Sydney, 1993), pp. 13–14.

15. Harry Braverman, *Labor and Monopoly Capital: The Degradation of Work in the Twentieth Century* (New York, 1975); Bryan Palmer, *A Culture in Conflict: Skilled Workers and Industrial Capitalism in Hamilton, Ontario, 1860–1914* (Montreal, 1979); Greg Kealey and Bryan Palmer, *Dreaming of What Might Be: The Knights of Labour in Ontario, 1880–1900* (New York, 1982). Recent scholarly discussions, such as Heron, *Working in Steel*, pp. 52–4, have changed this view, acknowledging a broadened base of "skilled" knowledge, thus blurring definitional boundaries of the function and worth of workers.

16. See E. Beaton, "Industrialization, Urbanization and the Peopling of Whitney Pier," in "Housing, People and Place: A Case Study of Whitney Pier," Ph.D. thesis, forthcoming. Also Beaton and Keating, *"From the Pier, Dear."*

17. See Mary Jane Lipkin, "Reluctant Recruitment: Nova Scotia Immigration Policy, 1867–1914," M.A. thesis, Carleton University, 1982, pp. 57–8.

18. Lipkin, "Reluctant Recruitment," pp. 58–9. There is a large and well-known body of Canadian and American literature which deals with immigration policies and nativist attitudes regarding foreign workers. See Donald Avery, *Reluctant Hosts: Canada's Response to Immigrant Workers, 1896–1994* (Toronto, 1995); Howard Palmer and Jean Burnet, *Coming Canadians: An Introduction to a History of Canada's Peoples* (Toronto, 1988); Howard Palmer and Tamara Palmer, *Patterns of Prejudice: A History of Nativism in Alberta* (Toronto, 1982).

19. Letter to the Editor by D. W. S., "Steel and Native Labour," *Daily Record*, 14 April 1902. See also "Steel Co. and Home Labour," *Daily Record*, 11 April 1902.

20. "Presentation to J. W. Brophy," *Sydney Record*, 15 April 1904, referred to a farewell "do" at the Savoy Theatre for the American foreman of the blooming mill mechanical department who was leaving to work in Buffalo's Lackawanna plant after several years in Sydney; See also "Five Iron Workers Registered from New York Staying at the Bellevue," *Daily Record*, 7 January 1901.

21. This pattern is emphasized in a remarkable series of letterbooks from the DISCO Blast Furnace Department, which outline the experiences of a succession of furnace supervisory personnel. The importance of these letterbooks goes beyond elucidating the availability of jobs and the process of hiring, for the letterbooks also give the names of the hired personnel and insights into their personal situations. DISCO Furnaces Letterbooks, MG 14, 38, Beaton Institute (hereafter referred to as DISCO Letterbooks).

22. S. MacGilvray to W. G. Taylor (Ferona, Nova Scotia), 19 December 1900, DISCO Letterbooks. Taylor subsequently became foreman of the DISCO iron yard.

23. S. MacGilvray to W. W. McKeown, 22 April 1901, DISCO Letterbooks. Also MacGilvray to Andrew Graham (New York), 28 December 1900; E. L. Messler (Eliza Furnaces, Pittsburgh), 9 March 1901; Wm. Smith (Eliza Furnaces, Pittsburgh), 19 March 1901; Thomas Slater (Lorraine, Ohio), 13 April 1901; L. Grammer (Cleveland, Ohio), 14 April 1901; Means to McCrery (DISCO General Superintendent), 25 May 1901, DISCO Letterbooks.

24. MacGilvray to Means, 8 July 1901; Means to Sims, 31 July 1901, DISCO Letterbooks.

25. Means to H. O'Shea (Johnstown, Pa.), 26 July 1901; E. L. Penruddock (Care Foundry, Birmingham), 20 August 1901; W. H. Miller (General Foreman, DISCO), 31 August 1901, DISCO Letterbooks.

26. Means to Baker, 10 August 1901; See also Means to Bryan (DISCO Time Keeper), 21 August 1901, DISCO Letterbooks.

27. Means to Baker, 19 August 1901; to Bryan 21 August and 26 August 1901; to Baker, 27 August 1901, DISCO Letterbooks.

28. MacGilvray to Graham (New York), 28 December 1900; "Notice" posted by Means, 27 July 1901, DISCO Letterbooks.

29. The blast furnace operated continuously, smelting up to 400 tons of iron per day. Heated by blasts of hot air from several huge adjoining stoves, the raw iron ore dripped through red-hot coke and a reducing agent, limestone, in the 80-foot-high "salamander," or barrel, of the furnace. The "cast" of molten iron took place every four hours unto the sand troughs below and the waste, or "slag," fell into pits nearby.

30. Means to Thomas Goodwin (Woodward, Ala.), 30 August 1901, DISCO Letterbooks. Thomas Cozzolino's Autobiography (1935) tells of attacks made on black workers by white workers; Thomas Cozzolino Papers, MG I, vol. 1191 C. Public Archives of Nova Scotia, also available as a Report, Beaton Institute.

31. Means to Baker, 10 August 1901, DISCO Letterbooks.

32. Means to Turner, General Passenger Agent (Baltimore), 23 August 1901, DISCO Letterbooks.

33. Joe William Trotter, Black Milwaukee: The Making of an Industrial Proletariat, 1915–1945 (Urbana, 1985) argues that the black workers' experience "was shaped by ... racial realities and that the workers used Black institutions and various social and economic networks ... to resist second class citizenship," cited in Dickerson, Out of the Crucible, p. 5. See also David Brody, Steel Workers in America: The Nonunion Era ([1960] New York, 1969), p. 185.

34. Fitch, The Steel Workers, p. 143. For examples, see the range of documentation in the Ethnic Files, MG 7, Beaton Institute.

35. Stanley Lieberson, A Piece of the Pie: Blacks and White Immigrants since 1880 (Berkeley, 1980), pp. 102–4, discusses the practice of lynching Blacks who were strike-breakers; see also Gutman, "The Negro and the United Mine Workers of America," in Work, Culture and Society, p. 121.

36. Means to Baker, 28 September 1901, DISCO Letterbooks.

37. Means to Baker, 30 September 1901, DISCO Letterbooks. European workers came in at least two batches, both at approximately the same time as the American Blacks: "Iron Workers from Austria," Daily Record, 15 October 1901; "Austrian and German Workers for Sydney," Daily Record, 23 November 1901.

38. "Local News of Interest," Daily Post, 16 October 1901. There is no evidence that this group came from Pittsburgh.

39. Means to Mailing Clerk, 29 October 1901: Willis Capers, Jim Thomas, Will Davis, Ike Kennedy, Josh Jamison, John Watts, Jeff Bowers, Tom Cadenhead & wife, Joe Hill, Fred Barnes, Louis Fletcher, John Lewis, Simon Pearson, Rich Horton, Arch Drake, George Strong, Toney McCoy, Jim Scott, Chas Stewart, Albert Martin & wife, Walter Griffin & wife, Louis Massey, John Taylor, Ed Moore, John Mayfield, Wm. Bolden (Bowling?), Geo. Williams, Isiah Robinson, Henry Bell, George Newsome, Hugh McGlathery, John Watts.

40. Means to Bryan, 1 November 1901; "Meals in transit" [no date]; Means to Messrs. Blackie and Company (Sydney), 21 October 1901, DISCO Letterbooks.

41. Means to White, 14 October 1901, DISCO Letterbooks.

42. Means to Baker, 30 September 1901, DISCO Letterbooks.

43. For examples of this boosterism, see "Progress of Completion of the Sydney Steel Works," Halifax Herald, 31 August, 1901; "The Pivotal Point of the World Commerce: The Sydneys, Cape Breton, The Great Coal and Iron Centre at Tidewater," Halifax Herald, 31 August 1901; Waldon Fawcett, "Supplement" ("The Sydney Steel Works"), in Scientific American (April 1902).

44. Means to Jacob, 4 September 1901, DISCO Letterbooks.
45. *Daily Post*, 21 December 1901.
46. "Their Promised Land Was One of Despair: Sad Plight of 250 Alabama Negroes Who Came North in Search of Riches," *Bangor Daily News*, 13 January 1903, p. 10.
47. Ibid.
48. *Daily Post*, 21 December 1901; Telegram, Means to Jones ("L and N" Railway), 30 September 1901; "Meals in Transit" [no date]; Means to Strong, 29 August 1901; Telegram, Means to Strong, 29 August 1901, DISCO Letterbooks.
49. Means to White (Colorado), 14 October 1901, DISCO Letterbooks.
50. *Daily Post*, 21 December 1901.
51. Jose Ramon Sanchez, "Residual Work and Residual Shelter: Housing Puerto Rican Labour in New York City from World War II to 1983," in Rachel G. Bratt, Chester Hartman and Ann Meyerson, eds., *Critical Perspectives on Housing* (Philadelphia, 1986), p. 202. See also D. M. Smith, *Geography, Inequality and Society* (Cambridge, 1957); David Hummon, "House, Home and Identity in Contemporary American Culture," in Setha Low and Erve Chambers, eds., *Housing Culture and Design* (Philadelphia, 1989), pp. 207–28; James S. Duncan, *Housing and Identity: Cross-Cultural Perspectives* (London, 1981); David Harvey, *Social Justice and the City* (London, 1973).
52. Jones, *Labor of Love*, pp. 183–5, 262–3, documents the housing conditions in Chicago, of tenement buildings with small, congested, damp and often leaky rooms that were fire hazards and located in areas infested by rodents which carried disease. Byington, *Homestead*, pp. 50–2, and Dickerson, *Out of the Crucible*, pp. 55–60, describe rental conditions for Blacks in Homestead and other steel towns in Pennsylvania. Other examples are found in Litwack, *North of Slavery*, pp. 168–70; Brody, *Steelworkers in America*, p. 186; John Bodnar, *Steelton: Immigration and Industrialization, 1870–1940* ([1977] Pittsburgh, 1990), p. 6.
53. "Negroes Walking Back to Alabama: Ridiculous Story about Sydney Published in the Lewiston Journal, A Negro's Pitiful Tale Asserts that 250 Destitute Negroes Have Started to Walk from Sydney," *Sydney Daily Record*, 17 January 1903, p. 7.
54. See Beaton, "Housing a Boom Town Society," in "Housing, People and Place."
55. In more recent years the colloquial name for Cokeville has been "the Coke Ovens."
56. Ron Crawley, "Off to Sydney: Newfoundlanders Emigrate to Cape Breton, 1890–1914," *Acadiensis*, XVII, 2 (Spring 1988); Leo Jessome, "The Price Paid," Report, Beaton Institute.
57. Shacks were also used at steel company locations outside Sydney at Crawley's Creek, at the limestone quarry at George's River and at gravel quarries or water lines at Sydney River. It is likely that rents were paid as deductions from salary: such information is not presently available.
58. Informal interviews with Ron DiPenta, 1990–93. See also "Warehouse and Shack for 50 Italians Burned at George's River," *Daily Record*, 2 April 1903, p. 1. Company-owned shacks should not be confused with "shacks" operated by local entrepreneurs from 1900 (ca.) until the 1940s.
59. Descriptions of such accommodations are provided in advertisements placed in local newspapers by the DISCO Boarding House Department. For instance, in 1900, DISCO advertised a shack at Sydney River: "For Sale: furniture, sheets, blankets, mattresses, pillows, heating and cooking stoves … very cheap, and a shack building 160 feet by 40 feet." "For Sale," *Daily Record*, 14 August 1900. See also Cozzolino Autobiography (1935), p. 33.
60. "Board of Health," *Daily Record*, 1 May 1901, p. 8.
61. Other workers continued to use the shacks as well: "Strikers (mainly Italians) got notice to quit their shacks," *Sydney Record*, 2 March 1902.
62. "Squabble at Dance," *Sydney Record*, 10 October 1902, p. 1. Almost a year later the *Daily Record*, 9 July 1903, had a reference to John Mayfield, "a coloured man and his wife … near their home in the steel co. shacks," p. 8.
63. "Condition of the Coloured Shacks," *Daily Post*, 26 November 1905.
64. Ibid.
65. E. Goad, *Fire Insurance Atlas for Sydney* (1907), p. 14.
66. Means to Bart Bryan, 24 October 1901, DISCO Letterbooks.
67. Means to David Baker, 28 October 1901, DISCO Letterbooks.
68. *MacAlpine Directory* (Sydney), 1903, indicates that two of the first group, William Bowling and Hugh McGlathery, had private boarding accommodations; Isiah Robinson lived in a rented house. The Directory is not, of course, a dependable source in locating persons of lower (job or social) status.
69. Bodnar, "Maintaining the Social Order," in *Steelton*, p. 77, notes that concerns were raised by city leaders about Blacks whose "conduct and manners" were "distressing" and who, if they could not live in "respectable" houses, were urged "not to select a place so close to Front Street." See also A. F. Artibise, *Winnipeg: A Social History of*

Urban Growth (Montreal, 1975); Terry Copp, *Anatomy of Poverty: The Condition of the Working Class in Montreal, 1897–1929* (Toronto, 1974).

70. *Daily Record*, 19 February 1901: an Italian was charged for stabbing a woman at the shacks; 11 November 1901: a Negro was charged for drunkenness and wife beating; *Daily Post*, 27 October 1902: an Italian was accused of theft.

71. *Daily Record*, 10 October 1902.

72. Ibid.

73. *Daily Post*, 27 September 1902.

74. *Daily Post*, 3 October 1902. For a discussion of the relationship between black men and black women vis-à-vis racial solidarity between genders in the context of oppression, see bell hooks, "Representations: Feminism and Black Masculinity," in *Yearning: Race, Gender, and Cultural Politics* (Toronto, 1990), pp. 65–77.

75. On the other hand, the Canadian Immigration Department correspondence suggests that West Indian black women were welcomed to Sydney as domestics after 1910. Canadian Immigration Branch Records, file 810666, National Archives of Canada. The 1901 census shows that many single white women, mainly from rural Cape Breton, worked as domestics.

76. This is in keeping with recent studies of women's "alternative economies" in industrial society. For instance, Jones, *Labor of Love*, pp. 181–2, discusses some of the negative "incentives" for prostitution amongst black women: concentrations of civic crime and the inability of the woman to support herself by other means; Gutman, *The Black Family in Slavery and Freedom*, p. 636, in response to white observations of the 1880s that black women were "promiscuous" and prone to be involved in prostitution, suggests that the "weakened social position of women" and the fact that the courts offered little support for them may have accounted for their lifestyles. See also Marion Goldman, *Gold Diggers and Silver Miners: Prostitution and Social Life on the Comtstock Lode* (Ann Arbour, 1981); Richard Symanski, *The Immoral Landscape: Female Prostitution in Western Societies* (Toronto, 1981).

77. *Daily Post*, 22 September 1902.

78. *Daily Record*, 6 December 1901.

79. "Cokovia Crows Virtuous," *Daily Record*, 24 January 1902.

80. *Daily Post*, 10 October 1902.

81. Little attention has been paid to the dance hall in the study of working class leisure. Yet it might be compared, in terms of its separateness from authority, to the bar room as discussed by Roy Rosenszweig, *Eight Hours for What We Will: Work and Leisure in an Industrial City, 1870–1920* (Cambridge, 1983), pp. 40–5. Unlike most bar rooms, however, the dance hall allowed for the legitimate participation of women, and accommodated a range of community activities, including showers and weddings. Whitney Pier has a long tradition of dance halls which were usually ethnically exclusive; some were privately owned and some had connections with mutual benefit societies. For a discussion of dancing in Alberta's urban and rural communities, see Donald Wetherell with Irene Kmet, *Useful Pleasures: The Shaping of Leisure in Alberta, 1896–1945* (Regina, 1990), pp. 237–7.

82. Both men had arrived in Sydney on 16 December 1901. *Daily Post*, 10 October 1902.

83. For comments on the role of specific churches in black steel communities, see Dickerson, *Out of the Crucible*, pp. 65–8, 111, 114; Bodnar, *Steelton*, pp. 107–8; Leon Litwack, "The Gospel and the Primer," in *Been in the Storm So Long*, pp. 450–501. See also J. A. Mannette, "'Stark Remnants of Blackpast': Thinking of Gender, Ethnicity and Class in 1780s Nova Scotia," in *Alternate Routes 7* (1984); C. H. Long, *Significations: Sins, Symbols, and Images in the Interpretation of Religion* (Philadelphia, 1986); E. Beaton, "Religious Affiliation and Ethnic Identity of West Indians in Whitney Pier," *Canadian Ethnic Studies*, XX, 3 (1988).

84. The papers of the AME were not examined in this research, but attempts by the AME to start a congregation in Sydney in 1923, when most of the Blacks were West Indian, and either Anglican or Methodist, suggests that the AME was prepared to proselytize where it was not specifically invited. See "New Church to Be Erected at Whitney Pier," *Cape Breton Post*, 23 January 1923. Such a congregation did not organize; instead, an African Orthodox Church was built at that time.

85. "Coloured Congregation: African Church Regularly Organized by Rev. Coleman Near Steel Works Church Built in Spring," *Daily Record*, 24 January 1902. The historic importance of the AME Church to African Americans is outlined in Leon Litwack, "The Church and the Negro," in *North of Slavery: The Negro in the Free States, 1790–1860* (Chicago, 1961), pp. 187–213.

86. This procedure was in keeping with industrialists' "philanthropic" policies in dealing with workmen throughout North America and Britain. For instance, E. M. Bainbridge and G. B. Walker, "Dominion Coal Company Ltd., Report on Mines and Properties (1904)," recommended that in dealing with workmen, the company should "[w]ork with the clergy as much as possible, ... let them feel that in philanthropic work they

can always have the sympathy and support of the Company," Steel Papers, MG14, 13, 8A, Box 37, file 22, p. 24, Beaton Institute. See also Fitch, *The Steel Workers*, p. 224, which notes that steel workers felt that the clergy was "one of them" [management]; Bodnar, *Steelton*, pp. 6–9.

87. Ibid.

88. "Coloured Church," *Daily Post*, 31 August 1904.

89. "Coloured Congregation," *Daily Record*, 24 January 1902.

90. "The Schools of Sydney," *Daily Post*, 2 September 1902.

91. Selena Williams was born in Halifax County in 1872. After teaching in Whitney Pier, she taught in Quebec and in black communities on mainland Nova Scotia. She was married to a steel worker (American?) named Joseph Jefferson (date of marriage unknown). It is not clear how she was appointed to teach in Sydney, except that she was part of a "pool" of black Nova Scotia teachers who worked in black communities in the province. See Doris Evans and Gertrude Tynes, *Telling the Truth: Reflections, Segregated Schools of Nova Scotia* (Halifax, 1995), pp. 49–50.

92. *City of Sydney Annual Report*, 1902, McConnell Library, Sydney.

93. *City of Sydney Annual Reports*, 1902, 1903, 1904, 1905, McConnell Library, Sydney.

94. "Are Staying On," *Daily Record*, 2 January 1902, p. 1.

95. "Left Yesterday," *Daily Post*, 28 July 1904. Participation by immigrant workers in Canadian unions and strikes is discussed to a limited extent by Ron Crawley, "Class Conflict and the Establishment of the Sydney Steel Industry, 1899–1904," in Ken Donovan, ed., *The Island: New Perspectives on Cape Breton History, 1713–1990* (Fredericton, 1990), pp. 145–64; Palmer, *Culture in Conflict*; Heron, *Working in Steel*; Donald Avery, *"Dangerous Foreigners": European Immigrant Workers and Labour Radicalism in Canada, 1896–1932* (Toronto, 1979). There is almost no discussion of early black participation in union activities in the Canadian literature. However, in American labour history the issue is discussed in depth by Bernard Mandel, "Samuel Gompers and the Negro Worker 1886–1914," in August Meier and Elliott Rudwick, eds., *The Making of Black America: The Black Community in Modern America* (New York, 1969), pp. 75–93; Fitch, *The Steel Workers*; Dickerson, *Out of the Crucible*; Gutman, *Work, Culture and Society*; Brody, *Steelworkers in America*.

96. Means' departure was noted in the *Daily Record*, 8 February 1903. Means was succeeded by W. S. Hutton whom he had invited to the plant in 1901. Correspondence between E. Arnold (DISCO Chemist) and W. S. Hutton (Superintendent of Blast Furnaces), 5 March 1903, DISCO Letterbooks.

97. "Negroes Walking Back to Alabama," *Sydney Record*, 17 January 1903, p. 7.

98. Cited in "Sad Plight of 250 Alabama Negroes Who Came North," *Bangor Daily News*, 13 January 1903, p. 10. There is an apparent discrepancy in the dates of the group's arrival in Cape Breton, given the previous documentation of the arrival of a large group through Maine in December 1901.

99. "Griffin and Wife Will Leave Today," *Bangor Daily News*, 15 January, p. 5.

100. Ibid.

101. *MacAlpine Directory* (Sydney), 1907, 1914, 1923.

102. Joe Keller, interview (transcribed), MG7, G2, Beaton Institute.

103. *MacAlpine Directory* (Sydney), 1907, 1914, 1918, 1923, 1928. Brooks was also remembered by Joe Keller (transcription), MG 7, G2, Beaton Institute.

104. Georgina Cambridge, informal interviews, November 1995.

105. *MacAlpine Directory* (Sydney), 1903, 1907, 1914.

106. See Tynes and Evans, *Telling the Truth*; Pearleen Oliver, *A Brief History of the Coloured Baptists of Nova Scotia, 1782–1953* (Halifax, 1953); Frank Boyd, *McKerrow: A Brief History of Blacks in Nova Scotia* (Halifax, 1976); Beaton, "Religious Affiliation and Ethnic Identity"; Mannette, " 'Stark Remnants of Blackpast' "; James Walker, *The Black Identity in Nova Scotia: Community and Institutions in Historical Perspective* (Halifax, 1985). Also Donald E. Fairfax, "The Black Church and Youth"; Wayne Adams, "The Black Church and the Black Man"; Carolyn Homas, "The Black Church and the Black Woman"; Donald D. Skeir, "The African United Baptist Association and the Black Man in Nova Scotia," in Bridglal Pachai, ed., *Canadian Black Studies* (Halifax, 1979).

107. Walker, *History of Blacks in Canada*, pp. 81–2.

108. Ibid., p. 67.

Article 4.2

Kerry Badgley

"As Long as He Is an Immigrant from the United Kingdom": Deception, Ethnic Bias and Milestone Commemoration in the Department of Citizenship and Immigration, 1953–1965

Issues to Consider

- How did the original "public education" premise of commemorating the millionth immigrant change into a "public relations exercise"?
- How might immigration officials have justified upholding a "traditional" race-based construction of the ideal immigrant, especially since the scheme was supposed to promote ethnic tolerance and the value of immigration?
- What could explain why immigration officials became so fixated on the notion that a teenage boy would be the ideal immigrant? When they discussed the possibility of a female candidate, what were their primary criteria?
- Why, in Badgley's view, did government officials go to such lengths to conceal the "tricks" behind their plans to stage the welcoming of the millionth immigrant?
- Badgley proposes that immigration officials might have "misread" Canadian attitudes toward immigration, making their choice of a British immigrant potentially harmful. What kind of evidence do historians need to get a sense of public opinion?

In late 1953 it dawned on some officials in the Department of Citizenship and Immigration that, in the spring of 1954, Canada would receive its millionth post-war immigrant. To mark that event, they felt that a celebration was in order. Rather than carefully monitoring the number of immigrants arriving in Canada and selecting the person they believed to be the millionth, or randomly selecting an individual as he or she disembarked from plane or ship, these officials, not wishing to leave anything to chance, devised a plan rife with deception in order to ensure that the millionth immigrant would fulfil their criteria; that is, that the candidate be young, male, British and potentially successful.

The following paper focuses on this scheme and briefly describes subsequent attempts at milestone commemoration in the department. In so doing, it will be argued that, in committing this deception, the actions of these officials may have represented a misreading of public opinion regarding immigration, and even if it did not, the original goal of using milestone commemoration to show the public the benefits of immigration was lost. Valuable insights can be obtained in learning how an institution sees itself and wishes to be perceived. An analysis of

Source: Kerry Badgley, "As Long as He Is an Immigrant from the United Kingdom": Deception, Ethnic Bias and Milestone Commemoration in the Department of Citizenship and Immigration, 1953–1965," *Journal of Canadian Studies* 33, no. 3 (1998): 130–44.

self-perception may lead to a better understanding of how an institution actually functions; it has indeed, an impact on policy formulation. The work of Ian McKay, for example, on the state-directed cultivation of image in Nova Scotia points to the value of this sort of inquiry.[1] Finally, this paper hopes to stimulate further research into the public relations side of immigration policy — an aspect that has been all but ignored in scholarly writing.[2]

The period from the mid-1940s to the mid-1960s was an ambiguous one, as far as immigration policy was concerned. According to Freda Hawkins, much of this ambiguity stemmed from the failure to resolve what purpose or purposes immigration performed. Did immigration serve international political ends? Did it lead to needed population growth? Did it stimulate the economy? Did it fill gaps in the labour force? According to Hawkins, no clear answer to these questions emerged. Those who formulated immigration policy believed that it served all of these objectives, to varying degrees, but appeared reluctant to state definitively the extent to which immigration met these goals.[3]

Hawkins also argues that many Canadians were not particularly keen on the idea of letting certain ethnic groups into Canada. She cites as evidence some rather damning testimony of the Trades and Labour Congress and the Canadian Congress of Labour before the Senate's Standing Committee on Immigration and Labour, which was struck in 1946 and continued its investigations until 1953.[4] How representative these views were of mainstream perceptions is debatable. There is little doubt that there were nativistic and outright racist elements in Canadian society, a trend that continues to the present, but what percentage of Canadians actually held these beliefs? If anything, as Howard Palmer writes, the post-war era was a period during which economic prosperity and changing intellectual and social assumptions diminished nativism and prejudice, and helped pave the way for the growing acceptance of pluralism by the 1960s.[5] Discussing the 1940s, Donald Avery argues that, while Canadians remained wary about accepting large numbers of refugees, especially if they were Jewish, there were indications that the country was gradually discarding xenophobic and racist polities.[6] Canada may not have been an immigrant's paradise, and certainly there was tension between continued nativism by some and greater acceptance of ethnic diversity by others, but there were signs that attitudes towards non-British immigration were increasingly welcoming.

In the cases where nativistic or racist views persisted, one wonders whether state pronouncements on the subject actually helped encourage or reinforce these perceptions. Prime Minister Mackenzie King's statement on Canada's long-term immigration policy, announced in May 1947, is a case in point. In addition to standard nationalistic rhetoric about immigration being a matter of national prerogative and not a right, and about self-interested reasons for encouraging immigration to Canada, King noted: "Immigration must not distort the present character of the Canadian population. The restriction on Asiatic immigration must remain."[7] With these sorts of views being articulated by the country's leader, an examination of how the state tried to influence public opinion on immigration is in order.

Scarcely a year after the creation of the Department of Citizenship and Immigration in 1950,[8] Georges R. Benoit, chief of the Operations Division, pointed out to C. E. S. Smith,[9] director of the Immigration Branch, that the success of Canada's immigration policy depends, and will increasingly depend, upon enlightened public support.[10] Thus, it was vitally important from an operational perspective that every effort be made to explain the significance and value of immigration to Canada in all its aspects, demographic, economic and social. To this end, co-operation with the CBC and private broadcasters was encouraged, and the appointment of a public speaker to travel across the country promoting immigration was considered. Benoit wanted the Editorial and Information Division to map out a public information programme so that many misconceptions could be removed from the minds of many well-disposed but ill-informed people.[11]

It appears that these suggestions, for unknown reasons, were not acted upon. There are references to other attempts to educate Canadians about the benefits of a vigorous immigration policy. In 1953, partly in response to the good number of requests from Canadian individuals, schools and colleges, as well as from voluntary organizations engaged in citizenship promotion, the departmental Committee on Publications considered preparing a pamphlet which would outline the contribution of various ethnic groups to Canada. Without giving any reason for doing so, the committee decided not to approve the undertaking at the present time. Nor does it appear that the decision was reversed over the next few years.[12]

In late 1953, an opportunity arose for Benoit that was too good for him to pass up. It occurred to him that the millionth post-war immigrant was due to arrive in Canada in May 1954, and, in a memorandum to Smith, he argued that the event would provide an excellent opportunity to focus public attention on immigration and the social acceptance of immigrants.[13] As with his earlier suggestion, it appears that Benoit wished to use his division to promote more ethnic tolerance.

The day after this memorandum was drafted, however, brought events that would distort and eventually doom the celebration. Smith brought the proposal to the attention of Laval Fortier, the deputy minister, who thought that it would bring the department some favourable publicity. Believing that Fortier should be aware of the possible down-side of such an event, Smith then pointed out potential pitfalls. For instance, some journalists who were hostile to immigration might cast the event and the department in a negative light. Furthermore, there might be difficulty in selecting the suitable prospect. Fortier then suggested that the millionth immigrant should be a young Britisher.[14] Note the change in orientation: instead of informing the public of the value of immigration, the commemoration now was to be a public relations exercise — one emphasising the Britishness of immigration to Canada. More importantly, it is at this point that one sees for the first time the idea of pre-selecting the millionth immigrant.

The next step was to ask E. B. Reid, head of the Editorial and Information Division, what he thought of the idea. Aside from Reid's prediction that certain newspapers (especially *The Globe and Mail*) would criticise the government and claim that two million immigrants could have been accepted during the same period, he thought the idea was a sound one. He noted, however, that there were three potential dangers that would have to be considered:

1) the millionth immigrant may be an unstable character whose failure to become established … in Canada might prove a boomerang at a later date;

2) a sceptical press might want to know how the millionth immigrant was definitively established;

3) if a pre-selected immigrant was taken into the Department's confidence, he or she might state publicly at some future date that the whole thing was staged. This could prove embarrassing.

To ameliorate these concerns, the officer-in-charge of immigration in London might be able to notify Ottawa of three or four people who would be suitable candidates.

These people, Reid emphasised, should have good employment records in a trade for which there was a demand in Canada.

My choice would be a young married man and for photographic purposes it would be better if he were accompanied by his family. Of course, if the scheme was to work, it would be necessary to place a departmental official at the gangplank of the ship to whom the officer on board might point out the millionth immigrant. If the press was curious as to how we established that this particular person was the millionth, we will then be in a position to tell them that the 204th person down the gangplank was the millionth and this was the 204th. This will then appear to be spontaneous and certainly will come as a complete surprise to the immigrant concerned.[15]

Smith discussed the plan with Fortier, who suggested the person selected should be a boy between the age of 14–16. No reason was offered as to why this should be the case.[16]

The selection requirements for the ideal millionth immigrant were subsequently fleshed out in a confidential memorandum from Smith to L. G. Cumming, superintendent of Immigration in London, England. Not only should the candidate be male, British and between 14 and 16 years old, but he should also be the son of a man who has a good employment record in the United Kingdom and whose background would indicate that he would have a minimum of difficulty becoming established in and adjusting to living in Canada. As Smith wrote to the superintendent, "We have no choice as to whether the immigrant is English, Welsh, Irish (Northern Ireland) or Scotch [sic] as long as he is an immigrant from the United Kingdom."[17] Cumming believed that there would be no difficulty in finding a suitable candidate.[18]

It would be fair to state that, at this point in the scheme, a certain amount of paranoia set in among those involved, a condition that was to remain for the duration. In mid-January a relatively innocuous editorial appeared in the *Montreal Gazette*, which merely indicated that the millionth post-war immigrant would arrive in Canada in a few months, but that it was unlikely that anyone would know the identity of this person when the time came.[19] Upon seeing the article, Reid wrote to the director that, because of the attitude of the press, every effort should be made to create the appearance of plausibility when selecting the millionth immigrant. Reid feared that if the potential millionth was taken into the government's confidence, at some future date

> [he] could say quite casually and without any intention of creating a controversy that he was informed before he left England that he would be the millionth. In the hands of an unfriendly paper such as the *Globe and Mail*, we could be held up to considerable ridicule.[20]

Quite simply, this would not do.

One might assume that, at that point, with the complication of media interest, the risk of being discovered trying to pre-select a person had become so great that the plans should be dropped. Instead, Reid suggested that the millionth immigrant simply not be told that he had been selected, a suggestion that met with Smith's approval. Smith, in turn, passed the proposal up to Deputy Minister Fortier who, evidently, concurred. In late January 1954, Immigration officials in Ottawa asked Immigration personnel in London to forward a list of potential candidates, with instructions that none of these people was to be informed that they might be chosen. A short time later, Cumming sent the name of a 17-year-old boy whom he felt was eminently suitable for our purposes.[21]

At the same time, Howard R. Hight, officer-in-charge of the Belfast Immigration Office, submitted the name of another candidate who was sailing to Canada with his parents and 10 siblings. Hight felt that the Canadian media would find in this Irish boy considerable potential for a good human interest story. His father and mother had immigrated to Canada much earlier, but had returned to Ireland during the Depression. The family eventually realised that Canada offered the best opportunity for prosperity, so the father returned in advance of the family and secured employment.[22] Reid agreed that this boy might generate considerable positive publicity, particularly in view of the fact that everybody loves the Irish. Still, he was concerned about the family's chances in Canada, and suggested that someone from a regional office close to where the father had settled make a diplomatic investigation into the family circumstances, including the father. In fact, when it came time to investigate the family in

Belfast, a pretext was found. As Cumming noted to Smith, "In order to avoid any inkling of the real reason of this enquiry becoming known, we have simply asked that Parts 1 and 2 of Form OS8 [Application for Admission to Canada — the form in use at that time] be completed ... on the grounds that he [the candidate] is over 16 years of age."[23] The added advantage of having the form filled out was that it included a photograph of the applicant, which could be forwarded to Smith.

As with most closely guarded secrets, the news that Canada was anticipating its millionth post-war immigrant and that the event might be commemorated spread to certain individuals outside government circles. In late February Smith learned that a representative of KLM Airlines had called the Ottawa Immigration office. This official had mentioned that a company employee in Holland had heard that Canada was expecting its millionth immigrant and asked if the millionth could be brought into the country by that airline. In what was becoming increasingly characteristic truth-stretching, Smith replied that the department had "no idea who the millionth immigrant will be, but my thought would be that in view of the fact that most immigrants arrive by sea, the likelihood would be that the millionth would be reaching Canada in that way."[24]

At the same time officials in the United Kingdom continued to send OS8 forms of potential candidates to Ottawa. Editorial comments, pointing out the strengths and weaknesses of the candidate, often accompanied them. To cite but one example, when Cumming sent the director an application form for a 15-year-old boy, he observed that the candidate was employed as a plumber's apprentice, "which means that his education cannot be very complete." In subsequent correspondence it was learned that the boy had another strike against him — his father worked in the building trades, an occupation that was often negatively affected by seasonal changes.[25]

In the meantime, Cumming received a call from Major J. S. P. Armstrong, the agent-general for Ontario in London, who asked if anything could be done to ensure the selection of a British subject. Evidently, the London Daily Telegraph wished to write a feature story on the subject when the millionth immigrant arrived in Canada. Cumming proceeded to mislead Armstrong by informing him that he knew nothing officially about any pre-selection, although he imagined that the department would have in mind very much the ideas he had expressed. He also informed Armstrong that, for obvious reasons, no publicity could be made in advance of the event as any reference to a specific person as the millionth immigrant would throw discredit on any recognition that might be made of his arrival.[26]

By 15 March three names had been submitted as potential candidates, but all three were rejected by Ottawa officials for one reason or another. With time quickly running out (by the end of March the total number of post-war immigrants was expected to top the 980,000 mark), Smith asked Cumming to keep pressing all United Kingdom offices for further recommendations. Regarding the Telegraph's request, Smith replied that department officials were still in the process of deciding whether to take any newspapers into their confidence in advance. Pressure to do so was mounting, though. In fact, Smith had been approached by the Toronto Star Weekly and the Montreal Weekend Picture magazine. Both of these publications wanted to produce feature stories on the subject.[27]

By that time word of the millionth immigrant was becoming increasingly widespread. J. L. Whitehead of the Liverpool office of the Cunard Steamship Company wrote to his superior in Montreal, Arthur Randles, that the Belfast News-Letter had reported that the Canadian government contemplated a special ceremony to mark the event. Whitehead informed Randles that, due to Northern Irish press criticisms of conditions for immigrants to Canada (chiefly, that many who emigrated could not find work), the millionth immigrant should be English. Naturally, if at all possible he should come over on a Cunard ship. Randles forwarded a copy of

Whitehead's letter to Smith, who replied that the identity of the millionth immigrant and the steamship line that would carry him or her were as yet unknown; however, in view of the large number of British arriving, "there is every possibility that he or she may be a Britisher."[28]

Meanwhile, the search for the ideal millionth immigrant continued. Reid was informed in late March of a Scottish 16-year-old boy who seemed to fit the bill, and he asked W. A. McFaul, eastern district superintendent of Immigration stationed in Montreal, to make a routine call on his father, who had already come to Canada. Reid instructed McFaul that there was to be no intimation to the father that his son "is likely to be the millionth immigrant as we want to make it appear as something in the nature of 'the luck of the draw.'" By this time another likely candidate had been located in England, and Immigration officials were asked to make the same sort of inquiries about this boy and his family.[29]

Details of how such discreet inquiries were undertaken were provided in a very self-satisfied report written by F. Stafford, officer-in-charge of the Edmonton Citizenship and Immigration Office. Stafford interviewed the father of one of the prospective candidates, leading him to believe that "my interview was only to ascertain how he had been making out in Canada, how he liked the country, and his prospects for the future." Like most trusting souls, the father was extremely co-operative and furnished the information requested without hesitation. Stafford managed to gather considerable information about the man's family and did not appear to have any misgivings about the deceptive nature of his interview.[30]

As if department officials did not have their hands full enough worrying about the millionth immigrant, in early April Immigration Deputy Minister Laval Fortier informed Smith that he had received word of the imminent arrival of the 100,000th Dutch immigrant. Fortier did not want a large ceremony, but thought the event important enough to inform Smith that both the minister and himself would arrange to be present at the dockside when the 100,000th arrived.[31]

All the while that these events were taking place, Smith was forwarding the application forms and recommendations sent by the district officers to Reid, who wrote lengthy replies with his impressions of several potential immigrants. One candidate, although eminently suitable himself, was rejected because his family was far from being typical immigrants (the father was a clergyman). Another was rejected due to his relatively low level of education. Another was dismissed because his father planned to take up farming in Canada, a notoriously unpredictable occupation. Yet another candidate, who was scheduled to arrive one week after the ceremony commemorating the 100,000th Dutch immigrant, was rejected because to have the celebrations so close together would have been anti-climatic. All in all, Reid was far from satisfied with the candidates suggested by the London office, and he recommended that a very strongly worded letter go forward to Mr. Cumming "immediately asking him to make an immediate analysis of OS8s of persons sailing on either the *Franconia* on May 6 or the *Georgic* on April 24, and that we give him a little more freedom of choice." The matter was so urgent that Reid recommended that the criteria be widened so as to include anyone in the younger age bracket, either male or female. The message was dutifully relayed to the London office.[32]

Reid was being extraordinarily careful, but a decision had to be made and made soon. On 12 April he recommended to Smith that a 16-year-old boy from England be selected as the millionth immigrant. A Central District Immigration officer investigated the boy's older sister and brother-in-law, with whom the boy was to live, and found them representative of the better than average type working-class family, clean in appearance, well spoken, friendly and co-operative. Based on this assessment, Reid recommended that this boy be chosen as the millionth, provided that the London office did not come up with anyone better.[33] It appears that this individual was seriously considered, because a speech for the minister to deliver at the ceremony was drafted by the Editorial and Information Division that made specific reference to him.[34] Still searching for the ideal candidate, though, London and other United Kingdom offices continued to send names of potential individuals,[35] and the District offices continued to carry out investigations.[36]

If anything, the number of potential candidates made matters more complicated for Reid, who informed the deputy minister on 21 April that no final selection had been made yet, but that the field had been narrowed down to three.[37] In fact, by late April officials in Ottawa were becoming so desperate for an ideal candidate that they entertained the idea of having a young Danish woman as the millionth immigrant.[38]

By early May the millionth immigrant still had not been chosen, despite the influx of potential candidates and numerous discreet inquiries.[39] Reid reported to Fortier that of the 35 possible candidates that had been proposed most recently, all but eight had been discarded. These remaining candidates included two British women, one of whom was of striking appearance and very photogenic and the other, four and a half months pregnant, who although not beautiful, was reasonably, attractive. Despite this, Reid, for unknown reasons, dismissed everyone on the short list as not very hopeful. Undaunted, he asked for any instructions Fortier might have to remedy the situation.[40]

What transpired over the next few days is not recorded in the files, but on 10 May Cumming received a telegram from Smith consisting of four words: MILLIONTH IMMIGRANT WELCOME CANCELLED. The only subsequent reference to the planned commemoration in the archival files is a newspaper clipping in which Conservative Member of Parliament (MP) George Hees theorised that the planned celebrations — during which the millionth immigrant was to be given a house, it was alleged — had been called off because it was learned that he/she was coming to Canada at the recommendation of another immigrant who had made use of the air immigration scheme instituted by George Drew while he was premier of Ontario: "[R]ather than remind people that [Drew] by his imaginative scheme had brought a great many first class citizens to Canada, the Government apparently decided not to recognize the millionth arrival."[41] Aside from one question posed in the House of Commons by W. M. Hamilton, a Progressive Conservative MP, not much more was made of the scheme by the opposition. In his question, Hamilton asked the minister if the millionth immigrant had arrived and, if so, who she or he was. Harris replied that the millionth had already arrived, but no one seems to know who he or she might be. He also noted that the government had considered recognising the one millionth immigrant, "but we felt that this was a continuing policy and that it would perhaps not do any particular good if we recognised one more than another. We feel that they are all good, all desirable and all welcome."[42] It appears that interest in learning what actually happened quickly subsided, and the incident was forgotten.

The following year Reid oversaw a number of promotional projects aimed at attracting immigrants to Canada,[43] but it appears that events designed to inform and educate Canadians of the benefits of immigration were not in the department's plans for 1955.[44] In fact, over the next few years Immigration officials responsible for publicity and promotion apparently concentrated their efforts overseas in an attempt to encourage immigration to Canada.[45] The only reference to building support for immigration at home is a suggestion from the deputy chief of Operations that Canada might follow the Australian example and establish a good neighbour movement, making use of existing Citizenship Councils as a starting point.[46]

What happened? Had Reid become so terrified at the prospect of having the scheme discovered that he intentionally sabotaged the project? Had he set standards that were simply too high for mere mortals to attain? Had he wanted the plan to fail for moralistic reasons? Had the whole plan been unworkable? Answers to these questions probably never will be known. What is clear, however, is that Immigration officials did not learn any lessons about the hazards of planning milestone commemorations. The early 1960s witnessed a resurgence of such events, and the projects that were undertaken bear the hallmarks of the less-than-principled behaviour of officials in the early 1950s.

In late 1960 the officer-in-charge in Copenhagen received a telegram from the department's Information Branch that stated that "the minister was anxious that the two millionth immigrant scheduled to arrive [in] Canada [the] first fortnight [in] December be [a] Danish boy or girl thirteen to seventeen." Why the minister wished to have a Danish person as the two millionth is a mystery — there is no explanation in the files, nor does it appear that Canada needed to curry Denmark's favour in any way. This time, however, it seems that there was not to be any lengthy deliberations as to whom the candidate should be. The next day Copenhagen informed Ottawa that the David Toft family would be arriving on 5 December, and that a photograph and details of the family would be sent over shortly.[47] During the course of the next few days, officials in Copenhagen and Ottawa exchanged missives concerning members of the Toft family, with Ottawa wishing to learn as much as possible, for use in publicity material, about their background, hobbies and interests. Ottawa had no preference as to whether the son or the daughter was selected as the two millionth immigrant, but preferred the daughter if she was photogenic and articulate.[48] With the ideal candidate chosen, Georges Benoit, now the director of Immigration, reminded the deputy minister that the arrival of the two millionth immigrant would be underscored lightly. The minister or the prime minister might wish to send a telegram of congratulations, Benoit might meet the family at Quebec and a number of promotional gimmicks might be employed, but Benoit thought that it was better to be accused of under-playing than the opposite. That said, Benoit took the liberty of informing his contact at the National Film Board of Canada of the event.[49]

It appears that Immigration officials were a bit more honest about the two millionth immigrant than they had been about the one millionth, but not by much. Benoit informed the Office of the Premier of Quebec that Annette Toft would be, statistically, the two millionth, and on 25 November he told the editor of a Danish-language newspaper that the two millionth immigrant had already been selected. Even so, from the evidence it appears that Canadians were to believe that the decision was a random one.[50]

The event was a success. Eastern District Superintendent McFaul officially welcomed the family and read a telegram from the minister (another deception — the telegram had been written days earlier and had been put on the CN Telegraphs printer in telegram form). A number of federal and provincial officials, as well as representatives from private organizations, bestowed gifts and good wishes upon the Tofts, and the event was covered by CBC Radio and Television and by some daily newspapers. According to department officials, the Toft family members were uncontroversial but charming, thus making the event a public relations coup for the department.[51]

Further public relations efforts directed at Canadians were sporadic, as the department continued to direct most of its time and resources on attracting immigrants to Canada.[52] Departmental files make only one more reference to a milestone commemoration, this time to mark the arrival of the 100,000th immigrant of 1965. The person, again pre-selected, was, surprisingly enough, a young, photogenic Scottish woman.[53]

Why the fuss? Why did Canadian Immigration officials make such elaborate plans and resort to such deception to ensure that the millionth immigrant was of the right sort? To attempt to answer the question requires some speculation, as government files on the subject are sketchy regarding motives.

First, it must be allowed that there were certain segments of Canadian society that might have protested the commemoration of anything related to immigration or immigrants. Certainly, nativistic and racist groups would have been outraged if a member of an undesirable group was honoured. Yet one wonders how much impact such protestations would have had, especially in light of how relatively little media coverage and publicity these events actually received.[54] Moreover, even if Immigration officials had been honest and randomly selected the millionth immigrant, there was a more than better chance that he or she would have been British, given the number of immigrants from Britain arriving in Canada at that time as compared to immigrants from other countries.[55] Evidently, in their minds that risk was not worth taking.

The problem, arguably, was that Immigration officials had a vision of how the department should be perceived, and their decisions were made and actions taken within this context. Of course, the real context was one in which many immigrants experienced a wide range of problems after arriving in Canada, and in which, increasingly, immigrants were non-British. But Immigration officials virtually ignored these facts. They wanted to be perceived as bringing only the best and the brightest prospects to Canada, and they wanted to be associated, primarily, with British immigrants. The distortions and outright lies they resorted to, and the amount of energy and resources they expended, for something as relatively innocuous as a milestone commemoration reveal how deeply these views were held.

In addition, what the foregoing suggests is that Immigration officials misread Canadians' perceptions about immigration, or were condescending in their attitudes with respect to what immigrants Canadians would accept. Their efforts to educate Canadians on the need and desirability of accepting immigrants, while commendable, were tainted by their biases and actions. In fact, their efforts may have done more harm than good. By focusing on white, Western European immigrants (particularly British), there was no attempt to inform Canadians of the benefits of accepting immigrants from other parts of the world.[56] Arguably, their attitudes and decisions at that time were to have profound and often negative effects on attitudes towards non-traditional immigrants in the ensuing years.

NOTES

1. See his "Tartanism Triumphant: The Construction of Scottishness in Nova Scotia 1933–1954," *Acadiensis* XXI.2 (Spring 1992), and his *The Quest of the Folk: Antimodernism and Cultural Selection in Twentieth-Century Nova Scotia* (Montreal and Kingston: McGill-Queen's University Press, 1994).
2. Generally, immigration history falls into two main categories: studies that chronicle a community's experience and studies that analyse government policy, broadly conceived. For examples of the former, see Anna Reczynska, *For Bread and a Better Future: Emigration from Poland to Canada, 1918–1939* (Toronto: Multicultural History Society of Ontario, 1996); and Franca Iacovetta, *Such Hardworking People: Italian Immigrants in Postwar Toronto* (Montreal and Kingston: McGill-Queen's University Press, 1992). For examples of the latter, see Howard Adelman, Allan Borowski, Meyer Burstein and Lois Foster, eds., *Immigration and Refugee Policy: Australia and Canada Compared* (Toronto: University of Toronto Press, 1994); Freda Hawkins, *Canada and Immigration: Public Policy and Public Concern*, 2nd ed. (Kingston and Montreal: McGill-Queen's University Press, 1988); and Reg Whitaker, *Double Standard: The Secret History of Canadian Immigration* (Toronto: Lester & Orpen Dennys, 1987). For examples of attempts to combine these two categories, see Irving Abella and Harold Troper, *None Is Too Many: Canada and the Jews of Europe, 1933–1948* (Toronto: Lester & Orpen Dennys, 1982); D. C. Savage, "Keeping Professors Out: The Immigration Department and the Idea of Academic Freedom, 1945–90," *Dalhousie Review* 69.4 (Winter 1989–90); Angelika Sauer, "A Matter of Domestic Policy? Canadian Immigration Policy and the Admission of Germans, 1945–50," *Canadian Historical Review* LXXIVV.2 (June 1993).
3. Hawkins 71–72.
4. Ibid. 84–85.
5. Howard Palmer, *Reluctant Hosts: Anglo-Canadian Views of Multiculturalism in the Twentieth Century, Immigration in Canada: Historical Perspectives*, ed. Gerald Tulchinsky (Toronto: Copp Clark Longman Ltd., 1994) 312–13. Palmer also argues that the 1950s and 1960s witnessed growing tolerance towards established minority groups in

English-speaking Canada (315). It should be stressed that generalisations such as this must be approached with caution. According to polls conducted in the early 1950s, there were many Canadians who believed that Canada did not need any more immigrants, an attitude that changed little until the 1970s. Some polls, however, such as the one taken in May 1954, indicated that more Canadians (45.7%) believed immigration was a good thing than those (38.3%) who thought it not a good thing. Nancy Tienhaara, *Canadian Views on Immigration and Population: An Analysis of Post-War Gallup Polls* (Ottawa: Manpower and Immigration, 1974) 61. What the polls do not reveal, however, is the reason why a respondent would hold such a view. The motivation may have been economic, based on racist assumptions, ideological bias or other reasons. Furthermore, polls do not reveal the vehemence (or lack thereof) with which such views are held. Even the way in which a question is phrased partly determines the response. On some of the methodological problems associated with immigration polls, see Tienhaara 6–7. The point here is that if public opinion (or public perception) was changeable, Immigration officials did little to try to alter people's perceptions of immigration with the schemes that they devised.

6. Donald H. Avery, *Reluctant Host: Canada's Response to Immigrant Workers, 1896–1994* (Toronto: McClelland & Stewart, 1995) 146.

7. Cited in Hawkins 93.

8. The original Department of Citizenship and Immigration was created in 1950 and existed until 1966 (a department with a similar name was established in the 1990s). The department brought together several federal offices that were responsible for a wide range of social and cultural functions. Hawkins 95–101.

9. Charles Edward Stanfield Smith was a career civil servant. He served with the Soldier Settlement Board until 1923 when he was hired as an Immigration inspector. In 1938 he became immigration superintendent of the Western District and in 1944 was appointed commissioner of Immigration. In 1950 he was named director of Immigration and in 1958 was made an assistant to the deputy minister, a position he held until his death in 1962. National Archives of Canada (NA), RG 32 (Public Service Commission), Vol. 635, file 5-P-53 (Smith, C.E.S.) pts. 1 & 2.

10. As had been the case in the past, most of the department's promotional efforts were aimed at prospective immigrants to Canada rather that at Canadians themselves. See NA, RG 26 (Citizenship and Immigration), Vol. 78, file 1-18-5 (Canadian Information Abroad — Inter-Departmental Committee, pts. 1 & 2, and Vol. 92, file 3-5-1 (Publicity and Advertising, Immigration Branch), pts. 2 & 3 for examples of the department's efforts to attract immigrants.

11. NA, RG 76 (Immigration Branch), Vol. 908, file 572-15, pt. 1 (Publicity Regarding Implementation of Immigration Policy & Stimulation of Immigration — henceforth referred to as RG 76, Vol. 908), Chief, Operations Division to Acting Director, Immigration Branch, 15 November 1951.

12. NA, RG 26, Vol. 78 (Government Publications Committee — General), Committee Minutes, 13 February 1953, 26 June 1953.

13. RG 76, Vol. 908, Memorandum: Chief, Operations Division to Smith, 3 November 1953. Commemoration of immigration milestones had been undertaken prior to that time. The arrival of the 50,000th Displaced Person to be received by Canada was marked with a ceremony at Pier 21 in Halifax in 1949. It appears, however, that the celebration was small-scale. Unfortunately, government documents describing these early events do not appear to have survived. The example cited here comes from a photograph used to illustrate Trudy Duivenvoorden Mitic's article, "Gateway to Canada," *The Beaver* (February-March 1995): 13. The accompanying text, however, makes no mention of the event. Interestingly, the 50,000th DP happened to be photogenic eight-year-old Ausma Nevalds from Latvia. See also J. P. LeBlanc, "Pier 21 — Its Legacy ... Its Future," *Canadian Immigration Historical Society Bulletin* 19 (January 1995): 8–9.

14. RG 76, Vol. 908. Handwritten note, Smith to E. B. Reid, Editorial and Information Division, 4 November 1953.

15. Ibid., Reid to Smith, 5 November 1953.

16. Ibid., undated handwritten note by Smith.

17. Ibid., Memorandum: Smith to L. G. Cumming, Superintendent, London, 9 November 1953.

18. Ibid., Memorandum: Cumming to Smith, 28 December 1953 and Director to Superintendent, 6 January 1954.

19. *Montreal Gazette*, 12 January 1954: 2. The article also noted that Citizenship and Immigration Minister Walter Harris was taking a middle-of-the-road approach to immigration policy so as not to offend those who favoured restrictions on the number of people allowed into the country, and those who favoured increased immigration.

20. RG 76, Vol. 908, Reid to Smith, 12 January 1954.

21. Ibid., Smith to Fortier, 12 January 1954; Smith to Cumming, 28 January 1954; Cumming to Smith, 4 February 1954.

22. Ibid., Hight to Cumming, 4 February 1954.

23. Ibid., Reid to Smith, 23 February 1954; Cumming to Smith, 19 February 1954.

24. Ibid., Memorandum to Smith, 26 February 1954; Smith to H. R. Semmelink, Royal Dutch Airlines, 3 March 1954.

25. Ibid., Cumming to Smith, 2 March 1954. Smith, leaving nothing to chance, had ordered discrete inquiries about his father, who had already come to Canada, be made. Ibid., Reid to R. N. Munroe, Western District Superintendent, 11 March 1954.

26. Ibid., Cumming to Smith, 10 March 1954.

27. Ibid., Smith to Cumming, 15 March 1954. See also NA, RG 26, Vol. 92, File 3-5-4, (Publicity — Reception of Immigrants), pt. 1, Reid to Director, 15 March 1954, Smith to Deputy Minister, 15 March 1954.

28. RG 76, Vol. 908. J. L. Whitehead, Cunard Steamship Company, Liverpool, to A. Randles, Cunard, Montreal, 18 March 1954; Randles to Smith, 22 March 1954; Smith to Randles, 25 March 1954.

29. Ibid., Reid to McFaul, 26 March 1954; Cumming to Smith, 25 March 1954; Reid to W. R. Baskerville, Central District Superintendent of Immigration, 31 March 1954.

30. Ibid., F. Stafford to R. N. Munroe, District Superintendent Immigration, 23 March 1954. At least Stafford gave a favourable assessment of the father, whom he regarded as one of the best type of British immigrant. W. A. McFaul, of the Eastern District Immigration office, was somewhat less enthusiastic about the candidate he was asked to interview. McFaul to E. B. Reid, 5 April 1954. For another appraisal, see C. W. Desormeau to Baskerville, Central District Superintendent, 9 April 1954.

31. RG 26, Vol. 92, file 3-5-4, Fortier to Smith, 5 April 1954. In the same paragraph, Fortier mused about possible gifts to be given to the millionth immigrant, concluding that the nature of the gift would vary depending on who was selected. Fortier wished to know if officials had chosen a male, female, minor or adult. Smith's reply, if any, was not recorded. Fortier also wrote that the 100,000th Dutch immigrant was expected to arrive on 19 May 1954. Remarkably, on that very day, Jacoba Geradina Koosje Bol arrived and was hailed as the 100,000th immigrant. From the sparse information surrounding this event in the department's files, it seems that the Dutch Embassy in Canada was largely responsible for staging the event. According to one newspaper account, the skipper of a Holland America Line ship received word the night before docking at Montreal that Bol had been named the 100,000th. Bol was a photogenic 18-year-old woman who sailed to Canada with her family, and was described as pert and pretty in the newspaper story. Bol was greeted at the Montreal docks by Immigration Minister Walter Harris and Dutch Ambassador A. H. J. Lovink. *Montreal Gazette*, 20 May 1954: 12. Another newspaper noted that Bol arrived in Canada clutching a return ticket to the Netherlands, as she intended to look Canada over for three years before deciding whether or not she would stay. *The Globe and Mail*, 20 May 1954: 10.

32. RG 76, Vol. 908. Reid to Smith, 7 April 1954; Smith to Cumming, 8 April 1954; Reid to Smith, 12 April 1954.

33. Ibid., Reid to Smith, 12 April 1954.

34. RG 26, Vol. 92, file 3-5-4, Reid to Deputy Minister, 13 April 1954.

35. See, for example, RG 76, Vol. 908, Officer-in-Charge, Glasgow to Cumming, 14 April 1954; Officer-in-Charge, Belfast to Cumming, 14 April 1954; Cumming to Smith, 15 April 1954; Cumming to Reid, 21 April 1954. In this last correspondence, Cumming began to let Reid know of the frustrations he and his staff had endured, pointing out that they had searched through some 1,500 files in the London Central Registry for suitable candidates. In addition, the Glasgow office searched through roughly 1,000 files. Cumming to Reid, 23 April 1954.

36. Ibid., McFaul to Reid, 21 April 1954; Baskerville to Reid, 21 April 1954.

37. Ibid., Reid to Fortier, 21 April 1954.

38. Smith had actually called the Copenhagen Immigration office to see if they had any potential candidate. Ibid., Officer-in-Charge, Copenhagen to Smith, 29 April 1954.

39. Ibid., Baskerville to Smith, 4 May 1954; Officer-in-Charge, Sudbury, to Smith, 5 May 1954; Baskerville to Smith, 5 May 1954.

40. Ibid., Baskerville to Reid, 5 May 1954, Reid to Fortier, 6 May 1954.

41. Ibid., Telegram, Smith to Cumming, 10 May 1954; newspaper clipping, 9 June 1954. Hees was certain that the government knew the identity of the millionth immigrant. How and when he received his information is not known, but it appears that Hees was not interested in pursuing the matter, since he did not question Harris on the topic in the House of Commons. On Drew's scheme, see Nancy Kiefer, "Premier Drew and the British Air Migration Plan of 1974," unpublished MA research paper, Ontario Institute for Studies in Education, 1983.

42. House of Commons Debates, 24 May 1954: 5006–07.

43. Including one in which 22 NATO journalists toured Canada. RG 76, Vol. 908, Reid to Smith, 29 April 1955; Smith to Deputy Minister, 3 May 1955.

44. That said, a number of projects were developed to reach out to prospective immigrants. These included a planned radio broadcast in the United Kingdom entitled "Canada Hour" that was to be broadcast over the BBC. H. T. Peters, Immigration Branch to Smith, 2 May 1955; Smith to Reid, 5 May 1955. The idea never got beyond the planning stage.

45. RG 76, Vol. 909, file 572-15, pt. 2, Reid to Minister, 22 May 1959; Director of Immigration to Fortier, 8 June 1959; Director of Information to Director of Immigration, 9 July 1959; Fortier to Minister, 21 January 1960.

46. Ibid., Deputy Chief of Operations to Chief of Operations. The suggestion was that council secretaries, who would be paid by the department, would present to the councils the departmental policy and explanatory material. In return, an annual conference might be held so that council representatives could present their suggestions and criticisms and where officials of this department could reply.

47. Ibid., Telegram, Impress to Mapleleaf — Copenhagen, 15 November 1960; Telex, Mapleleaf to Imm Ottawa, 16 November 1960. The father, David Toft, was a dental technician who arrived in Canada in October 1960. He hoped to establish his own business in Calgary. Ibid., Department of Citizenship and Immigration Press Release, 29 November 1960.

48. Ibid., Telegram, Impress to Mapleleaf — Copenhagen, 16 November 1960. See also Ibid., Officer-in-Charge, Calgary to Benoit, 16 November 1960; Benoit to Deputy Minister, 17 November 1960; Benoit to Eastern District Superintendent — Montreal, 24 November 1960.

49. Ibid., Benoit to Deputy Minister, 17 November 1960. One gimmick thought of by Benoit was to have the Calgary Board of Trade present René Toft with a dog. Ibid., Benoit to Officer-in-Charge — Calgary, 25 November 1960.

50. Ibid., Benoit to A. Larue, Chef du Cabinet du Premier Ministre, 25 November 1960; Benoit to E. Melander, 25 November 1960. Benoit did not inform the editor that the person chosen was the statistical two millionth. The press release issued by the Department for Canadian consumption made no mention as to how officials knew that Toft was the two millionth. Ibid., Department of Citizenship and Immigration Press Release, 29 November 1960.

51. Ibid., McFaul to Director of Information, 6 December 1960; G. F. Davidson, Department of Citizenship and Immigration to W. E. Greaves, Canadian Embassy, Copenhagen, 22 December 1961. There was another deception: although the press release noted that David Toft planned to establish a business in Calgary, it appears that officials learned in late November 1960 that Toft intended to remain in Canada only if he was unsuccessful in obtaining American visas for himself and his family. RG 76, Vol. 909, Officer-in-Charge, Calgary to Director of Information, 23 November 1960. This, of course, was not mentioned in newspaper coverage of the event. In fact, the impression given in most press accounts was that the Toft family were enamoured of Canada. See, for example, *Toronto Daily Star*, 5 December 1960: 5. As with other newspapers that mentioned the event, the *Star* ducked the issue of how the Department had determined Toft was the two-millionth simply by noting that she had been named as such. Interestingly, on the same day the *Star* story appeared, *The Globe and Mail*, the newspaper Reid had feared during the planned millionth immigrant celebrations, ran a feature story with the headline "Jobs Scarce, Dreams Deflated, Immigrants Go Back to Europe," *The Globe and Mail*, 5 December 1960: 23. In fact, there was no mention of the two millionth immigrant in *The Globe and Mail*.

52. RG 76, Vol. 909. R. J. Curry to A/Deputy Chief of Operations, 28 February 1964.

53. RG 76, Vol. 909. Forthcoming Events — Canadian Service, undated document. The 100,000th, a Miss Elspeth Ann Whitley, arrived in Canada on 29 September 1965. According to a newspaper account of the event, Whitley was chosen by virtue of the fact that she made the 100,000th formal application for entry as a landed immigrant. Whitley, described as a beautiful, shy ballet student, was greeted by Prime Minister Lester Pearson, Immigration Minister John Nicholson and other dignitaries. *The Globe and Mail*, 30 September 1965: 5.

54. None of the newspapers consulted contained editorials — favourable or otherwise — regarding the events. In fact, the celebrations themselves were usually relegated to the back pages and bear the hallmarks of filler/human interest stories. Although one can never know what the response would have been if the millionth immigrant had been from Africa or Asia, it is reasonable to assume that the newspapers would have not covered the events any differently.

55. In 1954, for example, of the 154,227 immigrants who arrived in Canada, 49,974, (32.4%), listed British as their ethnic origin. M. C. Urquhart and K. A. H. Buckley eds., *Historical Statistics of Canada* (Toronto: Macmillan, 1965): 27, Series A 316–336.

56. That said, there were times when Immigration officials scored points for highlighting Canada's humanity, such as when Hungarian refugees were accepted in 1956. See Hawkins 114–17.

Document 4.1
J. T. M. Anderson

Immigrant Communities

James Thomas Milton Anderson (1878–1946) was an educator, writer, and politician who started his teaching career in Yorkton district Saskatchewan, and became inspector of schools in 1911. In 1918, the year *The Education of the New-Canadian* was published, he was appointed director of education for new Canadians. He became leader of the provincial Conservative Party in 1924 and served as premier of Saskatchewan from 1929 to 1934.

Issues to Consider
- Why does Anderson believe the education of immigrants to be, as the book's subtitle declares, "Canada's Greatest Educational Problem"?
- Anderson refers to Woodsworth, discussed in Topic 3, and his work with the immigrants of Winnipeg's north end. Does he share Woodsworth's perspective on their condition and what can be done about it?
- How does Anderson compare the "foreign" teacher with the "Canadian" teacher and the Canadian public school? What is the basis of his views?

Almost every city, town and village throughout Western Canada has its "Germantown." Foreigners of various nationalities have taken up their abodes in segregated areas, where rents are as a rule low and sanitary and housing conditions poor. They have their own churches and their own newspapers, and sometimes their own fraternal societies. Little English is spoken, and their ideas and customs remain foreign. Here are bits of Bohemia, Italy, Russia, Hungary, transferred to this side of the Atlantic and set down in our cities. Few assimilative agencies penetrate to these back streets. An occasional visit from a ward politician too often affords the only indication of interest in their presence. Were it not for the fact that their children are compelled to attend the public schools, where they obtain a knowledge of the English language, their presence might well give us cause for alarm. In a few centres large-hearted Canadian citizens have taken a direct interest in these people, and good results have been obtained. The All People's Mission, Winnipeg, has done much towards the work of assimilation, and too much credit cannot be given the earnest and self-sacrificing workers of that excellent institution. This Mission represents the effort of the Methodist Church to meet the special needs of the immigrant population of the city. It is supported by contributions from the city churches; by grants from the General Missionary Society and the Woman's Missionary Society; by special donations from individuals, churches, and societies, and by collections taken in the Mission meetings. Their aim, as outlined in Woodsworth's "Strangers within our Gates," is well worth the earnest consideration of all who are interested in interpreting Canadian life to our immigrant citizens. It runs thus: "Our aim is to bridge the gulf between our well-to-do, church-going Canadian citizens and the immigrant peoples, often alien in language, race, religion, and social life and ideals. Our policy is flexible, and is the practical working out of our watchwords:

Source: J. T. M. Anderson, "Immigrant Communities," chap. 2 in *The Education of the New-Canadian: A Treatise on Canada's Greatest Educational Problem* (London and Toronto: J. M. Dent and Sons, 1918), 26–29, 31–34, 36–38.

"1. First things first.
"2. Thy Kingdom come.
"3. Lord, open our eyes.
"4. Not to be ministered unto, but to minister.
"5. Supply real needs.
"6. Fill the vacant niche.
"7. Do it now.
"8. Stay with it.
"9. Prevention better than cure.
"10. Organized helpfulness."

Several institutions conducted under the auspices of the Presbyterian Church in Canada are doing most creditable work. The Robertson Institute, in Winnipeg, near All People's Mission, is an Evangelical Settlement House, ministering to representatives of fifteen nationalities, meeting their physical, social, intellectual, moral, and religious needs, and spreading an influence over two thousand persons of all ages, coming from over four hundred families. The same Church does similar work in St. Christopher House, Toronto, and Chalmers' House, Montreal. These are supported entirely by the Social Service Department of the Presbyterian Church in Canada.

In many cities the Y.M.C.A. is doing excellent work among the foreign citizens. In several places night schools are regularly conducted during the winter months. But much more needs to be done. This work of bettering conditions among the inhabitants of "Germantown," socially, morally, and intellectually, should be taken up more extensively. Why should our legislatures go on annually voting thousands of dollars for the maintenance and support of neglected children, while practically no organized efforts have been made to remove the causes which produce such children? It is quite true that economic and social conditions, arising from a heavy tide of immigration, have much to do with this problem, and it is also true that in the pioneer stages of a province's development such conditions are bound to exist to a greater or less degree; but every effort should be put forth by our provincial statesmen to see that the number of neglected children is reduced to a minimum. Is it not too often the case that an attempt is made to ease the public conscience by providing funds for the maintenance of these unfortunate children, while little or nothing is done to mitigate or remove the evil? [...]

Throughout the prairie provinces great stretches of land have been settled by immigrants from European countries. In many cases, as in the cities, they very seldom come into contact with Canadian influences. They, too, have their own churches and their own newspapers. The language of the home is German, Ruthenian, Hungarian, Bohemian, or Polish, as the case may be. In the villages where they trade they have their own merchants, speaking their own language. In these settlements there is but one force at work to Canadianize their children — the public school. Even here the teacher is very often one of their own nationality, who has an inadequate knowledge of our language, and a very vague idea of Canadian citizenship and all that it stands for. [...] The most conspicuous, perhaps, of these settlers who have made their homes apart from English-speaking people are the Ruthenians and German Mennonites. The Doukhobors, although fewer in number, may also be mentioned, especially those known as "community" members. Of these settlers the Ruthenians are slowly but surely becoming more and more anxious to have their children educated in the English language, and, despite the retarding influences of certain members of the clergy and a few nationalistic agitators, they are fast forging ahead, and their descendants will make a worthy contribution to our national structure. For the most part they are successful farmers, and many of them have become comparatively wealthy. In Manitoba large colonies are to be found at Gimli, Sifton, Starbuck,

Brokenhead, and in the Shoal Lake district. In Saskatchewan there are large settlements at Canora, Rosthern, and Vonda. In Alberta the largest settlement lies north-east from Edmonton, past Star and Pakan. There are not very many of these people in British Columbia. As will be shown later, the Ruthenians readily respond to sympathetic treatment, and many of them are becoming educated, while some are entering public life in various capacities.

The Mennonites of the West are found in Southern Manitoba, Southern Saskatchewan, and Alberta. In several sections they have retained their old customs, and little progress has been made, especially in the matter of education. The rising generation, however, is steadily showing signs of unrest, and we may confidently look forward to the time when these people will form a strong link in our imperial chain. In Saskatchewan colonies are found near Swift Current, Hague, and Rosthern, where assimilation has been retarded owing to the absence of state public schools.

The principle of communism prevails among the Doukhobors who have settled in the Western Provinces. Many, however, have become independent, and no longer recognize the authority of their former leader. Some have written in eulogistic terms of the beauty of this community life, but most Canadians will fail to approve of a people who favor a mode of life which absolutely denies a public school education to the children living in the community. We suspect the integrity and honor of a man who denounces the education of the young, who forbids parents to allow their children to attend the public schools, without making provision for their education elsewhere. Last year, at a night school in a Western town, there were in attendance two young Doukhobors, one a girl of fifteen and the other a boy of fourteen, who had never been a day at public school. The parents had been forbidden to send them to school, and this by the autocratic leader of the community. They were bright, but mentally-starved children, and as one witnessed their eagerness to learn to read and write English, he could not but feel that Canada has made a very serious mistake in allowing such a man to guide the destinies of so many of her future citizens. His policy, apparently, is to keep the people in ignorance, and all the while we, as Canadians, blindly turn our heads the other way and continue our dreams of nation-building. Let us have a thorough investigation of conditions among these people, and let us insist upon the state exercising its right to see that every one of these New-Canadians obtains what in free Canada should surely be one's birthright — a public school education!

A much more hopeful condition of affairs exists in what may be termed the "mixed" rural communities. Here are found Germans and Poles, Bohemians and Ruthenians, English and Americans, occupying adjoining sections. All their children attend the same public schools; they deal at the same village store, and they attend the same public gatherings. There must, obviously, be a common medium of communication, and that, of course, must be the English language. The remarkable progress that has been made by the people of such districts should warn our Dominion statesmen against the mistake that has been made in the past of allowing large colonies to be formed of people composed solely of one foreign nationality. [...]

Such progress largely depends upon the work done in the public schools. The following story of an energetic young teacher's experience in one of these mixed districts fully exemplifies the truth of this statement:

"I was the first teacher in this little prairie school, in the midst of a foreign settlement in which were represented half a dozen foreign nationalities — Swedish, Hungarian, German, Ruthenian, Polish, and Slovak. My feeling of aversion soon wore off, and I became intensely interested in teaching these children English. In a few days they were making use of English sentences, executing commands and playing games. At the same time filthy clothing was being discarded and the little girls began to appear in cleaner dresses. The boys soon made free use of towels, soap, and combs, and instead of the large 'chunks' of bread wrapped in filthy rags, there soon appeared neatly-parcelled lunches, with the bread carefully sliced. Thus the work went merrily on! The enrolment reached over sixty in three months, and at the end of this period each of the forty children, who, at the beginning of the term knew absolutely no English, could carry on a fluent conversation in the language of this country."

Then came a grand union picnic, held in connection with the six or seven schools in the vicinity. A large parade was held, and the pupils of this school won first prize for the best marching and general appearance. How proud those parents were! A great many New-Canadians saw the light that day!

After the summer vacation, the teacher referred to returned to the now beloved work with renewed vigor, and the fall term culminated in a grand concert on Christmas Eve. Over forty items appeared on the programme, and over forty children read, recited, took part in dialogues, or sang, and *every word used belonged to the English language*. It was quite interesting to listen to seven boys, each reciting a verse from "The Choice of Trades," and each boy belonging to a different nationality. At the conclusion of the programme a beautiful Christmas tree was robbed of its presents and many a little heart made glad. Then came the national anthem by these future citizens, and as they lustily sang, their more or less ignorant parents looked on with smiling faces.

Thus in about nine months these children obtained a good working knowledge of our language, were given an insight into the social side of Canadian life, and were started on the march upward.

This incident, not uncommon in the West, emphasizes the great need for enthusiastic, sympathetic, thoroughly qualified Canadian teachers in the schools attended by our New-Canadians. The unqualified, half-Canadianized "foreign" teacher cannot properly inculcate those ideas so essential in laying the foundation of true citizenship in Canada. Within a few miles of the school referred to above are foreign schools which have always been under such unqualified teachers, and, except for a barely noticeable ability to speak a little English, nothing of much value has been accomplished. After all, the mere teaching of children to *speak* our language is not the most important phase of this great educational problem!

Document 4.2
James Jenkins

Editorials in *The Dawn of Tomorrow*

The Dawn of Tomorrow was a weekly newspaper founded in London, Ontario, in 1923 by James and Christina Jenkins to serve the city's Black community, although it had a wider Ontario readership. It was the official organ of the Canadian League for the Advancement of Colored People, of which the Jenkinses were active members.

Issues to Consider
- In the first editorial ("Education"), the writer, James Jenkins, uses war imagery to describe what young people of his community are confronting. What is the point that he is making?
- Jenkins discusses a number of causes for the inferior educational status of the young besides the systemic racial discrimination that exists. What does he consider the most important of these "internal" causes?
- The second editorial ("Race Co-operation") ends with a parable about a drummer that could be read as racist in its depictions of the "hero." Discuss.
- In commenting on the out-migration of young "Colored" people due to racism in hiring practices, Jenkins is very careful in his phrasing and in his final request. This is not the same tone that he uses in the first editorial, in which he pleads with members of his own community. What do you think explains this difference in tone?
- Considering the discrimination that his community faces everywhere — in the schools, in the labour market, on the streets, and even in the military — why does Jenkins take the approach that he does in "100 Per Cent Canadians"?

EDUCATION (JULY 21, 1923)

We are finding out, to our regret, that 90 per cent of our boys and girls are not finishing the public schools. The number of boys and girls entering [and] finishing high schools and colleges are so small that we may consider that number a nonentity. This is indeed a very sad state of affairs. We find that the children of other races are being given the best education which the country affords. The public schools, high schools, technical schools, colleges and post graduate schools are crowded with them, and these are the boys and girls whom our children must compete with in the future. Can we expect them to win the race of life? Can we expect an army equipped with boomerangs and tomahawks to win against an army equipped with machine guns, aeroplanes and all of the modern inventions of war? Yet this is exactly what we are expecting. We are not encouraging our children to stay in school. In many instances we are taking them out of school as soon as the law allows us to do so in order that they may earn a few paltry dollars. How much better would it be to let the "family" shift for itself and to keep our children in school a few years longer? Would it not be far better for the children and for the race to forego a few suits of clothes, a few new dresses and hats, a few pleasures, and give the boys and girls a chance. I visited a certain city recently and while there I visited a mother who pointed with great pride to her son who had just finished dentistry. She also pointed with pride to her dress and to her husband's suit. "This," said she, "is my only dress, and that is Will's only suit, but the pain of sacrifice was nothing compared with the joy which we are experiencing since our boy has finished his course." Would to God we had more such mothers and fathers.

It is men and women with a vision like this mother and father had who are helping race building.

If you would ask me why our sisters and brothers in the republic south of us are forging ahead of us I would tell you they have found the only solution for the race problem i.e. EDUCATION. Parents have forgotten their own interests in contemplating the interests of their children, the interests of their posterity.

I have talked with mothers and fathers here about keeping their children in school. They have given me this answer: "What's the use when they can find no employment at which they may use their education." I have talked with white business men upon this subject and I have told them what our people think and say. They invariably answer me thus: "The limit to the opportunity of your boys and girls is set by your own people. If they are qualified any and all positions are opened to them." Who is right and who is wrong? I know not. But the burden of proof rests upon ourselves. So let us here highly resolve to educate our children, and when shall their education cease? Not until they have crossed over the river Jordan.

RACE CO-OPERATION (JULY 21, 1923)

I have often wondered if the mass of our people have given real thought to race co-operation, what it means, and the far reaching results if carried into operation.

We in Canada, especially, spout a good deal about co-operation and its benefits and we get together (I speak advisedly) and do nothing except blow off a lot of hot air.

We see the great need of co-operation, religiously, politically, commercially, etc., but self interest keeps us apart.

A race of people which has the power to do things, whose individual members have the qualifications for the making of scientific men, financial leaders, commercial organizers, inventors and big men in any walk of life, who can stand shoulder to shoulder with men in like profession of any other race, and whose individual members do not co-operate as a unit, never get anywhere.

Our interests all through the community, yes all through the country are intertwined so vitally that the success or failure of one member of our group is felt by all the other members.

Co-operation means support at all times to our boys and girls who are preparing themselves for professions, our lawyers, doctors, dentists, contractors, merchants and manufacturers.

One of the necessary elements, then, is race consciousness, pride in our race, pride in our men, who by their honesty, truthfulness and unselfishness are leaders and successful men; always boosting, and thereby acting as a unit for the advancement of the whole, breaking down opposition, stifling the mob spirit, and leading to a thorough recognition of our qualities as men and women, irrespective of race or color.

A story is told of a drummer, who on visiting a southern city was given a lift by a Colored bus driver by the name of Sam. Sam was famous for his dexterity in using his whip. Desiring to test the truthfulness of the reports of Sam's prowess, as they drove along something like the following took place between them.

"Sam, see that beetle crawling yonder?"

"Yes suh."

"Well, I bet you can't hit it with your whip."

Sam grinned, "crack" went his whip and the beetle was no more.

A little farther down the road, a butterfly fluttered about.

"Sam, you can't hit that butterfly."

"Crack" and the butterfly was completely annihilated by the end of Sam's twenty foot lash. A little farther down the road a sort of brownish bag was noticed hanging to the limb of a tree.

"Now Sam, another try."

Sam turned the whites of his eyes on the drummer and said, "No suh!"

"Why Sam, what's the matter?"

"Them's hornets sah and they're organized."

Sam knew that if he disturbed that nest, he would have the whole colony of hornets on him. Organized to defend their home and their lives and therefore he feared and respected them.

And so I say to the Colored people of the country, organize, get together on a basis that demands respect from all people. [...]

OUR YOUNG MEN PASS ON (AUGUST 4, 1923)

We have always looked upon the passing of our young men and young women from Canada to the United States and to other countries as one of the saddest aspects of the race. We have tried to examine the circumstances surrounding their leaving and we find that in nearly every case it is the highly ambitious and talented boys and girls who are leaving us; those who have been specially prepared for service through trades and technical school. They claim that for some reason, they can not find employment here in Canada for which they have prepared, nor can they find employment here in other fields which are remunerative.

The awkwardness of the situation is clearly illustrated in the passing of Stanley Drake, of London, Ont., to Detroit. A few years ago Mr. Drake finished a course in mechanical drawing in the technical school, London. On leaving the institution he was given a highly commendable letter by the principal and was sent to a certain business firm which was in need of a draftsman. The head of the firm read Mr. Drake's letter, conferred with his superintendent and then assured Stanley that he would be sent for within a few days. More than three years have elapsed and yet he has not heard from this firm. He tried another firm and then another, to be turned down each time. The best position which he could obtain was that of janitor, which he accepted. He filled this position with honor and credit, remaining in it until friends in Detroit interceded for him and secured him a better position. [...]

Canada, and especially the Colored people of Canada, can ill afford to lose such young men. It is our duty to see to it that conditions which make it necessary for such young men and women to leave are changed. We believe it is the duty of the business firms of our country to open the doors of opportunity to our boys and girls, whereby they will remain at home, and Canada will not be drained of her young manhood and womanhood and of her very best talent.

100 PER CENT CANADIANS (SEPTEMBER 1, 1923)

When the World-War first began some nine years ago, our boys were among the first to offer themselves for service with the Canadian forces. In some instances, not in all cases, they were told by the recruiting officers in charge that: "At present we are not enlisting foreigners." Even today it is not an uncommon thing to hear people who certainly ought to know better refer to us as foreigners. Therefore, for the benefit of the uninformed, we wish to state in no uncertain terms that we, the Colored people of the Dominion of Canada, are 100 per cent Canadians. We are Canadians, not by naturalization, nor by adoption, but we are Canadians by birth, by patriotism, by culture, and training and by a heritage of more than 200 years of unbroken, unblemished citizenship. We look with much pride and we feel with patriotism the fact that, excluding the Indian, our race has as long a period of occupancy upon Canadian soil as any other race of people, longer even by far than most races.

In the early days when Canada was in the making and when she was threatened by invasion from without, our forefathers bore arms in her defense. When she was menaced by rebellion from within, they were not lacking in their loyalty to Canada. And surely the part which our heroes played in the late World-War convinces the world of our loyalty to Canada and to Canadian ideals. It was our fathers who suffered and who blazed the way and helped to clear the forests, to build the railroads and bridges to build the cities and towns. When Canada suffered, they suffered with her and when she was prosperous they rejoiced in her prosperity. So by every natural and God-given right we are 100 per cent Canadians, and we resent any insinuation to the contrary. Any attempt to proscribe or to treat us otherwise than as full Canadian citizens is looked upon with disfavor, not only by our own race but by fair and broad minded men of all races. I remember during the war the school children of the city were giving a demonstration of their patriotism by drilling in pairs through the streets, waving flags, singing "We'll Never Let the Old Flag Fall." There was one Colored child in the drill, who by an over sight was left to drill alone. I also remember the editorial appearing in the London Advertiser the next day. It was the strongest condemnation of the over sight, of having the Colored child march alone, that is possible for the human mind to conceive. In a conversation with the editor a few days afterwards he informed me that he had more complimentary letters upon this editorial than upon any other subject upon which he had ever written.

We feel that in Canada race makes no distinction in citizenship, and that the white, the brown, the yellow and the black races must all march to a common ideal abreast, and we feel certain that because our ancestors came from Africa in the far distant past, our status as citizens should not be different from other citizens whose foreparents came from England, Ireland or France.

Topic 5

Public and Private Worlds: Women, Men, and Family

Model of Thorncrest Village, Etobicoke, Ontario, circa 1945; photograph by Gordon H. Jarrett, Thorncrest Homes Association Inc. fonds, City of Toronto Archives, http://ohqdigit.tpl.toronto.on.ca/.

CONTEXT

By the 1920s, as Topic 3 demonstrates, the confluence of a rising academic social science and public preoccupation with a modernity both enticing and terrifying resulted in an ever-lengthening list of "social problems" to be addressed by reform campaigns and, increasingly, by state intervention. It appeared to many Canadians that the very source of all public good — the family itself — was being undermined by the forces of modernization, now accelerated by war. Much of the fear about social degeneration had to do with the impression of "Canadians" that the expanding class of immigrants and workers was outpacing the "better stock," in the bluntly racist terms of the time, in having children. Canadian families needed the support of society and state to protect and further the well-being of their members, but the "other" families also required such assistance in order to become truly Canadian, as discussed in Topic 4. Always sensitive to socioeconomic change, families came to serve as barometers to gauge its nature, its impact on the nation, and what might be in store for the future. After the Great War, the state became actively involved in family-watching through such agencies as the Canadian Council on Child and Family Welfare (1920), intended to be a clearing-house for research on families and related policy initiatives. The latter were primarily directed at parental — especially maternal — education in the interests of making healthier, happier families for a more productive, orderly, and stable modern Canada. Families were the foremost concern of modern welfare state initiatives, as is witnessed in the first universal welfare payment — the family allowance, or baby bonus, allocated to mothers by the federal government in 1945. The 1950s, in fact, saw a revival of the Victorian cult of domesticity. Canadians, after decades of depression and war, married younger and had more children than they had since the century's beginning, initiating the baby boom that has shaped much of the nation's social history since World War II. The "sexual revolution" of the 1960s also transformed ideas, behaviour, and state policy in regard to gender, marriage, and family.

Where the history of private lives is concerned, much that historians long to know is out of reach because of the undocumented and behind-closed-doors nature of the subject. In the early years of this subfield of social history, during the 1970s, those who wanted to explore domestic relations in the past saw much promise in the then-new methods of computer-assisted quantitative analysis, at least in regard to matters that could reasonably be measured in numbers: birth, marriage, death and fertility rates; household size and composition; age at marriage and the birth of the first child; age of familial independence; the workings of inheritance systems; the rate and extent of youth out-migration, and so on. This method also allowed for at least some members of specific families or age cohorts to be tracked over time, perhaps over the course of two or more decennial censuses, permitting a sense of change as well as continuity in certain family patterns.

Although still important, the demographic approach has been built upon and filled out by historians interested in the life stages of families, how they fared at different points in the history of their individual members as well as in their collective family history. Another approach attempts to uncover familial dynamics, especially in the form of family strategies for inheritance, for schooling and the sharing of labour in the family economy (whether domestic labour or wage labour), and generally for improving the family's conditions and collective quality of life. The shaping influences of class, gender, race, age, and region have been explored capably in the recent historiography, especially in regard to the transition from an agrarian to an industrial family economy. As discussed in Topic 3, Michel Foucault's theories about discipline and surveillance, and his preferred discourse analysis, have also made a significant impact in the historical study of the intertwined relations of family, society, and state.

Family is so closely bound to women's historical role and status that, until very recently, few dared to question the assumed, exclusive, biologically based definition of woman-as-mother. The pioneering historians of women, many inspired by the second-wave feminism of the 1960s and 1970s, took up the challenge of writing women into the conventional male-centred historical narrative. Many of the early studies examined women in their own domain — in the organizations and movements, such as temperance and suffrage, that were very much the public extension of their private maternal role: hence the "maternal feminism" classification that is given to the ideas and programs of these late 19th-/early 20th-century women. Women's work, education, health, and domestic roles were also, obviously, crucial topics. By the 1990s, the application of contemporary feminist and critical theories to the study of women in the past led to a new interest in gender, a construct that connected biological sex — the physical attributes of femaleness and maleness — with certain ascribed social roles, at once defining both the norm, which was really more an ideal, and those who deviated from it. While we still lack a book-length Canadian study of the history of manliness as a social construct, historians recognize that "gender" is not a synonym for "women," that men, in sum, are gendered too and must consequently function as social beings within the confines of the prescribed manly role in any given historical setting.

The selections in this section, although not focused exclusively on women, nonetheless indicate a variety of ways in which ideals about domesticity have long constrained women's public roles. Through the better part of the 20th century, marriage and family were seen to be the true, biologically ordained feminine vocation, even as women were making greater inroads into higher education, the professions, and the working world generally. But these studies also show how men are confined by social understandings of what it means to be born male.

REFERENCES/FURTHER READING

Arnup, K. *Education for Motherhood: Advice for Mothers in 20th Century Canada.* Toronto: University of Toronto Press, 1994.

Baillargeon, D. *Making Do: Women, Family and Home in Montreal During the Great Depression.* Waterloo: Wilfrid Laurier University Press, 1999.

Bradbury, B. *Working Families: Age, Gender and Daily Survival in Industrializing Montreal.* Toronto: Oxford University Press, 1993.

Chambers, L. *Married Women and Property Law in Victorian Ontario.* Toronto: University of Toronto Press, 1997.

Christie, N. *Engendering the State: Family, Work and Welfare in Canada.* Toronto: University of Toronto Press, 2000.

Comacchio, C. R. *The Infinite Bonds of Family: Domesticity in Canada, 1850–1940.* Toronto: University of Toronto Press, 1999.

Gossage, P. *Families in Transition: Industry and Population in Nineteenth-Century Saint-Hyacinthe.* Montreal and Kingston: McGill-Queen's University Press, 1999.

Halpern, M. *And on That Farm He Had a Wife: Ontario Farm Women and Feminism, 1900–1970.* Montreal and Kingston: McGill-Queen's University Press, 2002.

Korinek, V. *Roughing It in the Suburbs: Reading Chatelaine Magazine in the Fifties and Sixties.* Toronto: University of Toronto Press, 2000.

Levesque, A. *Making and Breaking the Rules: Women in Quebec, 1919–1939.* Toronto: McClelland and Stewart, 1994.

Mitchinson, Wendy. *Giving Birth in Canada, 1900–1950.* Toronto: University of Toronto Press, 2002.

Morton, S. *Ideal Surroundings: Domestic Life in a Working-Class Suburb in the 1920s.* Toronto: University of Toronto Press, 1995.

Parr, J. *Domestic Goods: The Material, the Moral and the Economic in the Postwar Years.* Toronto: University of Toronto Press, 1999.

Snell, J. *In the Shadow of the Law: Divorce in Canada, 1900–1939.* Toronto: University of Toronto Press, 1993.

Strong-Boag, V. *The New Day Recalled: Lives of Girls and Women in English Canada, 1919–1939.* Toronto: Copp Clark Pittman, 1988.

ILLUSTRATION 5.1 (P. 179)

The post–World War II years were characterized by family formation and a renewed focus on domesticity after many years of postponing this vital step, as young people's "natural" progression through life was impeded by the world-historical events of depression and war. For the first time since the turn of the 20th century, age at marriage declined and, directly related, fertility and birth rates climbed, thus spawning the so-called baby boom. The prosperity of the times finally allowed for the male-breadwinner family ideal to be realized for more Canadians, and demand for housing, long curtailed, rose to the point that new suburbs became a boom industry. Illustration 5.1 appears to be a staged photograph with professional actors posing as an ideal family much captivated by the model of a new housing development planned for Etobicoke, a middle-class, largely British suburb that became part of the Municipality of Metropolitan Toronto in 1953.

Issue to Consider

- The fact that the photograph is likely staged does not detract from its value as a historical source. What do we learn about prevailing gender and family ideals and class-based aspirations by "reading" this photo? How does the "model" suburban village fit into this construct?

ARTICLES

Both articles in this section examine the construction of gender roles in relation to the family, especially in its idealized form. The returning soldiers of Magda Fahrni's piece share with the stern patriarch of Robert McDonald's essay a commitment to a certain "head of household" role that, while not easy to muster in and of itself in view of the historical pressures on men to be successful providers and dutiful citizen-soldiers, is nonetheless central to their self-worth, their sense of "normal" manliness, and their social status. As the authors reveal, the women in these stories are also subjected to gender constructions that identify them primarily in relation to men as their husbands, fathers, and brothers.

Article 5.1
Magda Fahrni

The Romance of Reunion: Montreal War Veterans Return to Family Life, 1944–1949

Issues to Consider

- Why does Fahrni use the word "romance" to describe the veterans' return to family life?
- How is marriage "constructed" at this time in Canadian society? How is the war seen to have affected it? What broader social implications do both marriage and the war's effects seem to hold for Canadians, judging by public opinion and the few state agencies and social workers directly involved with veterans' families?
- Within the context of "problem" families, how are women depicted? How are men portrayed?
- What solutions are proposed for dealing with the difficulties of reintegrating veterans into "normal" domestic life? What do the solutions tell us about social ideals and "family values" of the time?
- What role is the state looked upon to play within the private family in the post–World War II years? What does the state actually do, and how does this match the public's expectations?
- What kinds of primary sources does Fahrni rely on to consider this subject? What do historians need to be aware of in using sources of this nature?

> *"They return with new cells, old eyes,*
> *to their strange children and older wives."*
>
> – Earle Birney, "Young Veterans" (1945)[1]

This article is entitled "the romance of reunion" because the narratives of homecoming that were told during the last years of the Second World War and the first few years of peace included many of the elements of a literary romance. Like a romance, these war stories had young, valiant heroes and loyal, virtuous heroines who had suffered through a period of trial and tribulation. As in a romance, these heroes and heroines had vanquished evil and been vindicated by victory. These narratives of reunion, like romances, ended with the welcoming embrace between the returning hero and the girl he'd left behind. And, like romances, these stories had great popular appeal. "Integrating" myths, aimed at all classes and cultures, they were told in fiction and film, in song, in advertisements, and in magazine articles. They were also told in photographs: a couple embracing at a train station, or children on the knee of a father in uniform.[2]

Source: Magda Fahrni, "The Romance of Reunion: Montreal War Veterans Return to Family Life, 1944–1949," *Journal of the Canadian Historical Association* 9 (1998): 187–201.

Historians have also told this tale. V-E Day and V-J Day meant the return of the armed forces. North America settled down into domesticity, into the suburbs, into relative affluence. And, one is left to assume, everyone lived happily ever after. Recent historical literature has challenged assumptions of postwar prosperity, suburban homogeneity, and contented nuclear families. The fifties are beginning to look more complicated.[3] Historians of Canada have remained largely silent, however, about the period of transition in family life that was the late 1940s.

This paper, part of a larger project on the renegotiation of family in the wake of the Second World War, examines the reworking of relationships between, primarily male, war veterans and their families. The study focuses on Montreal, but its conclusions, I would suggest, apply more broadly. A city of at least three solitudes, French-Catholic, English-Protestant, and Jewish, Montreal provides an internal contrast of language, religion, and ethnicity. While Montreal itself was a particular, perhaps unique, juxtaposition of language and culture, the variety of relationships within the metropolis point to the possibilities elsewhere in the wake of the war. The conclusions drawn here underline the centrality of heterosexuality to the postwar renegotiation of relationships.[4] They also suggest the benefits to be gained from examining military and family histories as linked, rather than isolated, experiences.

The metaphor of reunion resonated even for those who did not themselves have loved ones overseas. Indeed, governments and communities, as well as individuals and families, participated in the romance with Canadian veterans. Some of the elements of romance no doubt rang true for many postwar families, and I am not trying to posit a simple dichotomy between the sentimental ideal and a more pedestrian reality. But the moment of reunion, while it may have been the ending to one story, was the beginning of another. Suffering from wounds, illness, "battle exhaustion," or anxiety about the future, veterans and their advocates looked to the family as an agent of postwar healing. Women, as wives, girlfriends, or mothers, were to ensure the "mental reestablishment of soldiers."[5] Yet veterans found that returning home was often difficult and that readjusting to civilian status and family life required considerable work. This gap between expectations and experience, aggravated by the fact that war had sometimes soured relationships, was harder to bear given the rhetorical force of the reunion narrative for soldiers and their families. The adjustment of male war veterans to family life in the late 1940s can be viewed through four different sets of relationships: those with prewar wives and girlfriends; those with war brides; those with sons and daughters; and those with parents.

WIVES AND GIRLFRIENDS

The romance of reunion emerged from the heightened idealization of the heterosexual family during the war. Men posted overseas, single and married, had had plenty of time in which to romanticize ideas of marriage and parenthood. Veterans were returning to start their own homes, while girls and women were assumed to be eagerly anticipating weddings and children now that the boys were back. As one married French-Canadian sergeant told his chaplain in September 1944, "J'ai bonne espoir que tout cela sera fini bientôt et que je pourrai enfin reprendre la vie tranquille que je menais avec ma chère épouse avant la guerre."[6]

Yet social service agencies, in Montreal and across the nation, discovered to their dismay that the soldiers' return produced "intimate and complex" domestic problems.[7] Veterans suffering from "shattered nerves" found it difficult to readjust to family life.[8] The fact that so many of these unions were "mariages éclairs"— whirlwind weddings that had taken place immediately before enlistment, during wartime leaves, or in the first flush of homecoming — was part of the problem. The usual strains of new relationships were exacerbated by problems of inadequate housing, lodging with in-laws, and the attendant lack of privacy. Yet even long-established relationships suffered from the strains of separation. Many husbands found wives changed by the time apart, imbued with a new sense of independence and self-sufficiency.[9] Other wives had suffered from loneliness and a lack of leisure activity while their husbands were away. Both parties had experienced serious problems of morale. Women were stretched thin by years of managing households and children alone, men by long periods of time away from home and family.[10]

Separation by time and distance meant that a great deal of weight had been placed on letters that crossed the Atlantic, with consequent problems of miscommunication. Wives and mothers worried about a lack of news from husbands and sons in action.[11] Military officials noted that the only thing as bad for soldiers' morale as discouraging news from home was no news from home. Women were encouraged to write frequently to their companions, to eschew complaints, and to fill letters with good news.[12] Not all couples wrote regularly to one another, however. Even among frequent correspondents, there was room for misinterpretation and for fretting over silences and omissions. The most potent source of worry had to do with infidelity. Wives and girlfriends worried about soldiers' references to women met overseas.[13] Friends and relatives took it upon themselves to keep soldiers and their partners informed of any misbehaviour, often without much evidence. As one young, unmarried sergeant overseas wrote to his Montreal priest in June 1944, "J'ai été les plus sincères avec R —— et il me semble avoir fait tous les sacrifices pour me la garder, on est si loin l'un de l'autre! Je ne comprends pas encore qui a bien pu lui mettre dans la tête que j'étais attaché de quelque façon que ce soit à une autre fille. *C'est parfaitement faux* et vous pouves me croire."[14] The morale of servicemen and of their families was adversely affected, the Artillery Branch of the Montreal Soldiers' Wives League noted, by "anonymous letters containing malicious information."[15]

Tales of wartime infidelity were common currency in 1940s Canada. Military Lotharios and ungrateful women who refused to wait for soldier-sweethearts had become stock characters in public discourse.[16] The enforced mobility of married men and the increased visibility of women living alone fuelled the narratives of unfaithfulness. Determining how often rumours of infidelity were founded was difficult enough then; any attempt by the historian to quantify infidelity in the past is foolhardy. It is likely that war, through spousal separation, increased geographic mobility, and new work opportunities for women (which provided a measure of independence as well as new possibilities for romantic partners) did hasten the breakdown of some relationships. War also seems to have provided an escape from those relationships that were already rocky: there is a great deal of evidence to indicate that unhappy home lives were one spur to military enlistment.[17] Although it is probably safe to assume that anxiety about infidelity was more common than actual instances of adultery, those instances that did come to light were enough to fuel a larger discourse of disloyalty.[18]

The public concern about infidelity was paralleled by policy-makers' more private negotiation of its consequences. Soldiers', and later veterans', personal lives were open to scrutiny in a way that those of most civilians were not. Candidates for military enlistment submitted their health, finances, and family relationships to examination by the various military bureaucracies; they were thoroughly "administered" citizens. At the same time, they had access to sources of state assistance that many civilians did not. Activities that had always taken place, then, came to the attention of state and private agencies more frequently during the war. The application process for dependents' allowances, in particular, uncovered "irregular" relationships such as common-law marriages, adulterous unions, and illegitimate children.[19] Social service agencies in Montreal and elsewhere, long used to dealing with the problems of unmarried mothers, now discovered the wives of soldiers giving birth to the children of men other than their husbands.[20] Frequently, women in such a situation attempted to place their children for adoption, often before their husbands returned or learned of the situation. Other wives came to the attention of family agencies because they were deliberately neglecting their illegitimate children out of "guilt and anxiety over the husband's reaction."[21] Wives' infidelity was attributed to loneliness, to "disreputable" leisure pursuits such as frequenting dance halls and beer parlours, and to retaliation for their husbands' own extramarital encounters overseas.[22]

The Dependents' Allowance Board (DAB) suspended allowances to wives on evidence of their sexual infidelity. It was, the Board's Chairman argued, "a general practice in welfare legislation to demand fidelity on the part of the wife in receipt of public funds."[23] Even questionable leisure activities, such as wives entertaining men in their homes, were cause for the DAB to assign the family to the supervision of a social agency. Part of the concern over disloyal and "immoral" wives was that they were perceived to be abdicating their "domestic responsibility."[24] The children of adulterous wives were sometimes removed to the care of relatives or institutions, particularly when wives were living with their new male companions.[25] If the wife promised to mend her ways, her children were allowed to remain in the home, and their dependents' allowances were increased in order to compensate for the loss of their mothers' allowance.[26]

The unfaithfulness of soldiers and their partners inspired considerable comment. Gossip played an important role in the public and private negotiation of disloyalty. In addition to affecting the relationships in question, gossip frequently had a tangible effect on wives' and children's material well-being. The DAB relied heavily on rumours and innuendo to pinpoint unfaithful husbands and especially wives. Neighbours and in-laws, in particular, took it upon themselves to inform the Board of sexual disloyalty.[27] The Board insisted that the allowances of unfaithful wives whose soldier-husbands were overseas were not suspended without prior investigation. In the case of wives whose husbands were posted in Canada, however, a husband's request was sufficient to have his wife's allowance suspended until allegations of her infidelity were disproven.[28] Moreover, private citizens used the dependents' allowance system as a means of condemning disloyalty. One Montreal woman whose husband was having an affair with the wife of a soldier, for instance, reported this "other woman" to the DAB in order to have her dependents' allowance cut off.[29] Such tattling reflected personal grudges, but also pointed to the larger question of who was perceived to be entitled to state support. In the minds of the public, like that of the DAB, the criterion for receiving military allowances was clearly loyalty: men's loyalty to their country, and women's loyalty to the men who were loyal to their country. As Nora Lea of the Canadian Welfare Council emphasized, the unfaithful wife who was not remorseful had "forfeited her right to consideration as the soldier's wife."[30]

Yet gossip concerning sexual infidelity occasioned a certain backlash. The Dependents' Allowance Board was criticised by representatives of some family agencies on a number of grounds, one of which was its reliance on gossip as sufficient evidence for withholding allowances.[31] When it did undertake to investigate claims of immorality and infidelity, these agencies charged, the DAB and affiliated public bodies used "Gestapo" and "bullying" techniques. Montreal agencies complained "that information secured in this way was not treated as confidential and that before the investigation was completed a large sized scandal was public property in the neighborhood."[32] A family agency elsewhere in Canada likewise accused the Department of Pensions and National Health of taking "a murky satisfaction in the sexual delinquencies of the soldiers' wives."[33] Furthermore, critics noted, the suspension of allowances harmed the soldiers' children as much as his wife by decreasing the family's income.[34] Married women pregnant with "illegitimate" children, moreover, were avoiding seeking medical care for fear that their allowances would be suspended.[35] Certain Montreal social agencies were accused of keeping wives' adultery a secret from the DAB so that allowances would not be withheld.[36] Others applied to the Board for the reinstatement of wives' allowances where they thought it warranted.[37]

Clearly, the reaction to women's infidelity was not monolithic. A concern for the morale of soldiers overseas, and a desire to preserve family units for the postwar period, meant that certain social agencies were willing to turn a blind eye, or at least a forgiving one, to sexual indiscretions. Some family agencies tried to prevent official reports from going to husbands overseas, particularly when wives appeared repentant. As one social worker explained, "Not that we wish to excuse them whatsoever, but we feel too, that if the matter could be kept quiet, we might be able to keep the family together for the sake of the husband who is Overseas."[38] Many social workers, including some employed by public bodies, agreed that "a definite family break could be avoided" if husbands were not informed of wives' illegitimate children until the couple had a change "to meet and talk things over."[39] At the very least, family agencies pleaded, wives should be given the opportunity to tell their husbands themselves rather than have them receive the news from the DAB.[40]

The DAB also professed concern for the soldiers' morale, but it took a different tack. Wives would "have greater peace of mind" if they confessed all, the Board argued, but regardless, husbands ought to be informed of wives' illegitimate children as soon as possible. As R. O. G. Bennett, Chairman, explained,

> Careful as one tries to be in covering up the situation, the chances are the man will get word at some future time and distressing as the news will be to him now, it is thought by the Board that it is better for him to know when he has time to think over things while away rather than to return home and find out later. It is the attitude of the Board that to be fair to the soldier overseas, he should be informed how things are going at home.[41]

The differing attitudes of the DAB and the private family agencies are interesting. At one level, this was a difference between those who formulated policy and those faced with implementing it. But there were other reasons for the contrasting approaches. Veterans of the First World War often filled key positions in federal departments such as the DAB and the Department of Veterans' Affairs.[42] The "clients" of the DAB were members of the armed forces and, in a sense, the Board was standing in for the absent husband and father, while social agencies were concerned with the needs of various family members.[43] Local agencies had roots in their communities that predated the war, and intended to continue serving their clients once peace was secured. Federal bodies such as the Dependents' Allowance Board and the Dependents' Board of Trustees (DBT), on the other hand, took their direction from Ottawa and were intended to function only "for the duration." It is worth noting that in the Quebec context, where enthusiasm for military enlistment was muted and opposition to conscription intense, the intervention of the DAB and the DBT in marital difficulties probably did little to improve French-Canadian families' opinions of the federal government.[44] [...]

Women's infidelity was interrogated to a far greater degree than men's. The occasional lapse of judgment by men far from loved ones was not ideal, but it was tolerated and perhaps even expected.[45] As Ruth Jamieson has shown for Britain, for the military bureaucracies, the sexual fidelity of a soldier's wife "was also taken to be an index of her commitment to the national interest."[46] The question of soldiers' own loyalty was slightly more ambiguous. Their loyalties to their families, to the nation, and to comrades-in-arms may have been reinforcing, but perhaps, as Susan Hartmann suggests, fidelity to fellow soldiers took precedence. The result, she argues, was that in the United States, "The sexual double standard was reinforced on the grounds that the horrors of war both excused male infidelity and required female faithfulness."[47] [...]

How, then, did postwar couples deal with relationships that were at the very least strained, and often fractured? Most married couples probably stuck it out. It is possible, as one social service agency argued, that the impact of their wives' infidelity on soldiers' morale was less than might be supposed. Certainly some soldiers, despite "rather desperate" first reactions, took the news of wives' infidelity in stride. The DAB claimed that a serviceman's reactions would "depend a good deal on their marital relationship before he enlisted, on his behaviour since they have parted, and on the point of view of his relatives and their influence upon him."[48] Some soldiers accepted their wives' "illegitimate" children as their own. One French-Canadian woman, for instance, gave birth to her eighth child during the war, a child fathered by someone other than her soldier-husband. The soldier and his wife were reconciled, however, and the family stayed together.[49] Soldiers could request that dependents' allowances be reinstated to their unfaithful wives and/or allocated to their wives' illegitimate children. The DAB would agree to these requests if the wife showed signs of changing her "immoral" ways, and if the soldier agreed to raise the children as his own.[50]

Evidence of formal or de facto postwar marital breakdown is substantial, however. Divorce, for instance, increased in Quebec in the immediate postwar period, particularly among servicemen's families. Petitions to the Dominion government from Montreal residents rose steadily through the war years and jumped sharply in the immediate postwar period.[51] Yet in a predominantly Catholic province with no divorce courts, where a divorce required the delay, expense, and notoriety involved in petitioning the Dominion government, legal divorce was but one form of marital dissolution. More common, especially for French Canadians, were legal separations of bed-and-board or informal separations. Catholic organisations warned Quebecers that civil divorce was not a valid way of dissolving Christian marriages, while even agencies that catered primarily to non-Catholic clients, such as Montreal's Society for the Protection of Women and Children, advised judicial separation rather than divorce in "cases of marital discord."[52] Some soldiers simply chose not to return to their relationships. Social service agencies noted the large number of wives abandoned by soldier-husbands; military enlistment was occasionally tantamount to desertion.[53] Some married Canadian soldiers formed second families in Europe and elected to stay with them: a precedent established during the First World War a generation earlier.[54] Meanwhile, soldiers who were unmarried but who had girlfriends or fiancées in Canada frequently came home with new wives, met overseas.

WAR BRIDES

Those who lived through the war were struck by the huge number of marriages hastily made in Canada and overseas. The explosion of marriages after September 1939 has been attributed by one historian of Britain to a "last-dance" mentality that saw sexual tension heightened by the excitement of war and a reckless and romantic attitude in the face of an unknown future.[55] In Canada, other factors no doubt forced the formalisation of relationships that might otherwise have remained unsolemnised: hopes of avoiding conscription, for instance, or the opportunity to allocate and receive dependents' allowances. The improved economic situation, moreover, meant that couples who had courted in the depths of the Depression could finally afford to establish their own households. For many Canadian soldiers, a "last-dance" attitude would result in marriages to women met in Europe, primarily England. The subsequent arrival in Canada of close to 45,000 "war brides" and their more than 21,000 children captured the public's attention and also encapsulates many of the peculiar difficulties of postwar marital adjustment.[56]

The immigration of British brides began midway through the war and was largely completed by 1947.[57] Those who settled in Montreal were probably the lucky ones, benefiting at least from a city with all kinds of amenities. Some arrived while their husbands were still fighting overseas; many came with young children.[58] Brides were greeted by spouses and by in-laws: the publicity accorded to these reunions was extensive. The photograph of "Jane-Margaret et son papa" that appeared in *La Presse* on 7 March 1946, for instance, depicted the reunion at Bonaventure Station of M. Bérubé, former member of the Fusiliers Mont-Royal, his English bride, and their one-year-old daughter, Jane-Margaret. Newspaper articles gushed about "heureuses Canadiennes," "nouvelles citoyennes du Canada": young English women who were being received with open arms and who would create comfortable homes for their veteran-husbands.[59]

In addition to the usual resources offered by an urban centre, English women found special provisions made for them, largely by the city's Anglo-Protestant community. CN Rail and Red Cross set up a canteen, a rest-area, and a nursery for British mothers and children arriving at Montreal's Bonaventure Station. The Acorn Club, established "to welcome and help in anyway possible all British brides arriving in Montreal," sent "a letter of welcome to every member two weeks after her arrival" in the city. Members of the Local Council of Women were requested to do everything in their power "to help the British war brides to become happy and useful Canadian citizens." The YWCA, meanwhile, offered to arrange French lessons for them.[60]

Not everyone was caught up in the romance of the British brides, however. Many French Canadians looked askance at these English women newly arrived on their soil. L'Association Catholique de la Jeunesse Canadienne Française (l'ACJC) argued that English women were morally unworthy of young French-Canadian men, despite their often superior education. French-Canadian families would not necessarily extend a warm welcome to these brides, the ACJC warned, and furthermore, would the children of these unions be French or English?[61]

War brides themselves found much to adjust to. Canadian observers were surprised by reports of unhappy British wives, and tended to attribute their discontent to Montreal's postwar housing crisis. The Victoria Rifles Ladies Association of Montreal felt it essential that the housing shortage be rectified so that "no Canadian or British bride will feel like returning home to mother just because we have failed to provide liveable homes for them."[62] Others blamed marital unhappiness on conflicts with in-laws. Montreal's Society for the Protection of Women and Children (SPWC) reported in 1945 and 1946 that it was seeing an increased number of cases involving "marriages contracted overseas by service personnel," including "numerous cases in which the War-bride is not accepted by the soldier's family." The SPWC noted "more or less acute marital difficulties related to "culture, religion and race," to the transition to urban living, and to situations where "the soldier has reverted to an attachment made prior to his departure for overseas service."[63] One woman's story captures war brides' frustrations with both housing and in-laws. The woman's husband, a veteran, worked the nightshift, and the couple and their two children lived with the husband's married sister. Not long after her arrival in the city, the woman wrote to the Montreal Soldiers' Wives League, "Please can you refer me how to find out about returning home. I have two children and am expecting another. We have one room here, and have been told that we must find another place. Whereas we can't — places are hard to get and I wish to return to England."[64]

Other war brides were also prepared to return home. Montreal service clubs such as the Oak Society for British War Wives perceived "this inability to settle down" to be widespread and problematic.[65] Newspapers noted that English wives were returning to the UK because they found Canadians cold and unfriendly.[66] Meanwhile, numerous instances of abandoned war brides were coming to the attention of social service agencies. A few women deserted by Canadian husbands overseas decided nonetheless to come to Canada.[67] The conclusions to some of these stories can be found in the *Statutes of Canada*: each year between 1945 and 1949 saw parliamentary divorces awarded to Montreal residents whose marriages had taken place in wartime England.[68] Yet as observers were quick to point out, those war brides who returned to Britain were the exception rather than the rule. *La Presse*, for instance, reported in November

1945 that only 29 of the 9,000 British war brides who had so far arrived in Canada had requested a return to England.[69] Many wartime romances no doubt took longer to unravel. But most war brides probably, as their French-Canadian neighbours would have said, "se débrouillaient."

CHILDREN

Many returning soldiers met their children for the first time, or encountered them after a separation of several years.[70] Wartime commentators had expressed considerable concern over Canada's temporarily fatherless children. Even worse was the prospect that this temporary state might become permanent. As the Association Catholique de la Jeunesse Canadienne Française worried, "Combien d'enfants ne connaîtront pas leur père et n'auront pas son aide pour se faire un avenir."[71] The nation-wide perception that juvenile delinquency was flourishing was rooted in anxiety over women's paid work and "latch-key" children. Were the children of employed mothers and enlisted fathers under proper supervision? Mothers were seen to be incapable of enforcing the strict discipline that was the purview of fathers. Members of the Montreal Soldiers' Wives League felt that soldiers' children were deprived of "the steadying hand of a father in their guidance and upbringing"; veterans' advocates worried that soldier-fathers would return home from overseas "to find incipient juvenile delinquency in the home."[72] The effect of fathers' absence on children's emotional and (hetero)sexual development was also a concern. Observers worried about daughters' "future adjustment to men and marriage." Sons, meanwhile, might become "overdependent" on their mothers as a result of being "thrown too much with women." "The boys who are raised during the war years," warned the Canadian Youth Commissioners, "must be safeguarded against becoming men who are 'tied to their mothers' apron strings.'"[73]

Commentators were aware that relations between returned soldiers and their children might be strained. A federal government brochure reminded veterans to "tenir compte de la croissance des enfants durant leur absense." Promoters of Volunteer Citizens' Committees noted that veterans were often strangers to their children. Veterans interviewed by Barry Broadfoot recounted the disappointment on the part of the children who had expected their returning fathers to be larger-than-life war heroes and who found instead only ordinary men.[74] Awkward relations between veterans and children affected veterans' relationships with their wives; likewise, strained marital relations affected children's perceptions of their soldier-fathers.[75] Children also suffered from the fall-out of marriages shattered by war; some children were taken into institutional or foster care after their servicemen-fathers returned and their parents' marriages disintegrated.[76]

Some idea of the pressure that both military service and the return to family life placed on men can be ascertained from the more extreme and tragic examples of veterans' difficulties with their children. La Presse, for instance, published a photograph of a battered infant in March 1947, under the caption "Le pitoyable enfant d'un ancien combattant aussi malheureux." A 39-year-old Montreal war veteran, Edmond O'Driscoll, had been charged with injuring his six-month-old daughter Maureen three time in three months, breaking her arms and fracturing her ribs and collarbone. O'Driscoll had undergone lengthy treatment at Ste. Anne's Military Hospital for a head wound and apparently was not always conscious of his actions. Perhaps, the newspaper suggested, the baby's injuries could be attributed to the fact that the six-foot veteran was not aware of his strength and held her too tightly. O'Driscoll was scheduled for a mental examination by the judge hearing the case. The journalist's sympathy was clearly extended to the former soldier as well as to his child.[77] Montreal's Society for the Protection of Women and Children, meanwhile, described two cases of incest involving

Second World War veterans and their daughters in its submission to the Royal Commission on the Criminal Law relating to Criminal Sexual Psychopaths in 1956.[78] Child-beating and incest were surely not the experience of most veterans. But such incidents do speak to the problematic nature of reunion and also to the ways in which veterans' troubles were framed in their communities.

PARENTS

Second World War veterans were "sons" as well as "lovers."[79] Married veterans and their wives were often depicted as the heroes and heroines of the postwar romance of reunion, but, in fact, most Canadian veterans were young and single.[80] Veterans were referred to in the popular press as "boys," often "our boys": in a sense, they were everyone's sons. Parents, and often siblings, were expected to contribute to the task of rehabilitation. The Department of Veterans' Affairs noted approvingly that Montreal parents were encouraging their sons to get "back to work."[81] The Jeunesse Ouvrière Catholique Féminine reminded families and friends that young working-class men were returning much changed by their military experiences, often nervous and irritable. Women were to help them to readjust by reintroducing them to good habits, notably religion.[82]

Yet while young soldiers were sons, they were often in the ambiguous position of allocating dependents' allowances to their parents and siblings.[83] This was not necessarily a new situation, given Montreal's history of child and teen labour and given the working-class background of many soldiers.[84] Parents of soldiers and veterans, used to relying on sons' earnings, had a clear sense of entitlement to state-administered allowances. As one woman reminded the Montreal Soldiers' Wives League in January 1946, "After all, I am a veteran's mother and entitled to my check...."[85] Moreover, parents across the country exhibited a marked preference for soldiers' and veterans' allowances over other forms of social welfare; military allowances were a source of pride rather than stigma.[86]

Those veterans who were young and unmarried but whose adolescence had ended abruptly with their period of service found the return to the nest frustrating after several years of absence and mobility. Montreal's severe postwar housing shortage meant that veterans frequently moved back into overcrowded parental homes. Friction ensued as parents were forced to adjust to their young sons' independence and resistance to parental authority.[87] With regard to female veterans, the Canadian Youth Commission thought it likely that "once the first pleasure of returning home is over, the standards of the parents will appear more rigid than ever and the advice and restrictions more irksome than before."[88] Readers of the daily press were exposed to grim examples of the difficulties of rehabilitation. For instance, 25-year-old Laurent Leduc, a Montreal navy veteran, was charged in February 1946 with knifing his father in the back in a fit of hysteria, and with attempting to attack his mother and sisters.[89]

Well-known Canadian psychiatrist Brock Chisholm noted that "Many people still speak of our soldiers as 'boys,'" but insisted that "It is very important that we should not regard our soldiers as boys but rather that we should see them clearly as they are — grown up responsible men."[90] War's function as a rite of passage was highlighted by the fact that these men often returned with new family responsibilities.[91] The transfer of assigned pay and dependents' allowances from mothers to new brides suggests one way in which the war transformed, and often strained, filial relationships. As soldiers and veterans transferred their allegiances and allowances from mothers to wives, mothers not only felt displaced, but suffered tangible consequences. Social service agencies noted the financial hardship caused to mothers by this switch, and by the fact that allowances to mothers were less than those to wives. Widowed mothers, in particular, often relied on their allowances to cover the costs of medical care.[92] Conflict was aggravated in situations where new brides were living with their in-laws. Housing shortages, the increased cost-of-living, fixed incomes, and perceptions of respectable living arrangements meant that families often doubled up, particularly while soldier-husbands were overseas. The General Secretary of Montreal's YWCA observed that in such situations, "Disagreements often start regarding allowances, discipline of children, etc., between mothers-in-law and wives, both of whom may be the official responsibility of the enlisted men."[93] The heroine of an advertisement for Castoria, a young mother living with her mother-in-law while her soldier-husband was overseas, presumably spoke to a receptive audience when she complained, "J'ai un emploi de guerre … et des ennuis avec belle-maman."[94]

Unfaithful spouses, unhappy war brides, unfamiliar children, and neglected parents were some of the darker elements of the postwar romance. As poststructuralist scholars argue, the telling of any story involves the suppression of other stories that might be told just as well; every narrative is built on omissions and exclusions.[95] The silences in the romance of reunion are important. Most obviously, this was a resolutely heterosexual narrative. Despite, or perhaps because of, the military bureaucracy's exposure to homosexual relationships between armed forces personnel during the war, such relationships received no sanction in the dominant discourse of postwar reunion.[96] Furthermore, sexual relationships were privileged over others. More soldiers had parents than had wives, for instance, but it was the reunion of the male soldier and his female companion that attracted the most public attention.

Moreover, such was the commitment of the narrative to heterosexuality and to "traditional" gender roles that female veterans fit uneasily into the conventional story. The returning military hero was depicted as male; women's role was to wait loyally at home. The Canadian public was assured that women veterans, like their male counterparts, were eagerly anticipating establishing homes and families of their own. As historian Ruth Pierson has shown, servicewomen's marriages to servicemen were given extensive publicity.[97] But it was difficult to reconcile the female veterans' wartime mobility, military experience, and (albeit limited) degree of sexual freedom with the romance of reunion. Certainly those unmarried service women discharged for pregnancy played little part in postwar romances.[98]

Narratives of reunion were also problematic given the anti-conscription, and sometimes antiwar, sentiment in Quebec. Indeed, the homecoming narratives coexisted uneasily with counter-narratives, such as those recorded by Pierre Vallières, of French-Canadian men "hidden in the woods, armed with their rifles," who had "mobilized their wives and children to organize resistance to the military police."[99] In this case, the North American military hero met his match in the French-Canadian antihero resisting the coercive power of the state and British imperialism. The reunion tales also tended to elide questions of class: the differing experiences of officers and rank-and-file servicemen, or the particular difficulties of working-class family economies. The romance of reunion was produced and narrated in Quebec, as it was elsewhere on the continent. But given the dynamic of French–English relations and the political economy of enlistment within the province, it also met with greater challenges than elsewhere.

This examination of "domestic demobilization" blends social and military history in an attempt to bridge the gap between accounts of Canadians in wartime and histories of families in Canada in the 1950s. The romance of postwar reunion had a certain timeless quality, harking back to a mythical golden age of Ulysses and Penelope, and was no doubt told in the wake of other military conflicts such as the First World War, a generation earlier. Indeed, the strength of the narrative can be attributed partly to its familiarity. But the length of the war, Canadians' "total war" effort, the extent to which women had taken on "men's jobs," the homosocial nature of life for many Canadians in wartime, and the legacy of the Depression, ensured that these heterosexual reunion narratives had a particular resonance in the late 1940s. Veterans faced other difficulties upon their return: securing employment, for instance, or finding a home despite Montreal's severe postwar housing shortage. Family strains were especially deeply felt, however, given that Canadian soldiers, like those pledging allegiance to other nations, had been encouraged to fight to preserve Home and Family, and given that the postwar years witnessed an intense pressure to rebuild households disrupted by war. Widespread evidence of troubled marriages and of women's sexual autonomy was, in part, what lay behind the push for conjugal domesticity in the postwar period. Many of the seemingly tranquil nuclear families of the 1950s clearly had unsettled histories.

ACKNOWLEDGMENTS

Earlier versions of this paper were presented to the York Women's History Group and the York Graduate History Conference in the spring of 1998. I would like to thank all those who offered suggestions for improvement, especially Bettina Bradbury. I would also like to thank Nancy Christie for helping me locate the records of the Dependents' Allowance Board, and the *Journal*'s anonymous referees for their comments. The financial support of the Social Sciences and Humanities Research Council of Canada is gratefully acknowledged.

NOTES

1. Earle Birney, "Young Veterans" in *Now Is Time* (Toronto, 1945), 55.
2. For reunion photographs, see *La Presse*, 30 avril 1945, p. 3; National Archives of Canada (NA), MG 28 I 311, Montreal Soldiers' Wives League (MSWL), Vol. 4, File 83, Clipping from *The Gazette*, 22 December 1943. On the romance in literature, see Northrop Frye, *The Secular Scripture: A Study of the Structure of Romance* (Cambridge, Mass., 1976). Kate Darian-Smith has argued that Australian women interviewed decades after the Second World War described their wartime experiences using the structure and language of "conventional romance narratives." See "Remembering Romance: Memory, Gender and World War II," in *Gender and War: Australians at War in the Twentieth Century*, Joy Damousi and Marilyn Lake, eds. (Cambridge, 1995), 117–29.
3. Susan Prentice, "Workers, Mothers, Reds: Toronto's Postwar Daycare Fight," *Studies in Political Economy* 30 (Autumn 1989): 115–41; Franca Iacovetta, *Such Hardworking People: Italian Immigrants in Postwar Toronto* (Montreal, 1992); Line Chamberland, "Remembering Lesbian Bars: Montreal 1955–1975," *Journal of Homosexuality* 25 No. 3 (1993): 231–61; Joanne Meyerowitz, ed., *Not June Cleaver: Women and Gender in Postwar America, 1945–1960* (Philadelphia, 1994). On postwar pressures for domesticity, conformity, and "normality," see Doug Owram, *Born at the Right Time: A History of the Baby Boom Generation* (Toronto, 1996); Veronica Strong-Boag, "Home Dreams: Women and the Suburban Experiment in Canada, 1945–1960," *Canadian Historical Review* 72 (December 1991): 471–504; Mona Gleason, "Psychology and the Construction of the 'Normal' Family in Postwar Canada, 1945–1960," *CHR* 78 (September 1997): 442–77; Mona Gleason, "Disciplining Children, Disciplining Parents: The Nature and Meaning of Advice to Canadian Parents, 1945–1955," *Histoire Sociale/Social History* 29 (May 1996): 187–210.
4. On "the constitution of heterosexual normality" in postwar English Canada, see Mary Louise Adams, *The Trouble with Normal: Postwar Youth and the Making of Heterosexuality* (Toronto, 1997).
5. NA, MG 28 I 311, MSWL, Vol. 3, File 64, Speech by Brock Chisholm, 13 November 1944: Women's Responsibility for Mental Reestablishment of Soldiers. On battle exhaustion, see Terry Copp and Bill McAndrew, *Battle Exhaustion: Soldiers and Psychiatrists in the Canadian Army, 1939–1945* (Montreal and Kingston, 1990).
6. "I am hopeful that all this will be over soon and that I will finally be able to take up the calm life I led with my dear wife before the war." Archives Nationales du Québec à Montréal (ANQM), P257, Mouvement des Travailleurs Chrétiens (MTC), Vol. 11, File, Cent Mariés – J. M., C. G. Sgt J. M. to Rév. Père Victor-M. Villeneuve, 11 septembre 1944. See also NA, MG 30 C 92, Marion Creelman Savage papers, Vol. 7. *Consumers' News* (June 1945): 7; (November/December 1945): 2.

7. NA, MG 30 C 92, Savage papers, Vol. 3, File, Council of Women, Montreal Local, 1948–51. 1947 Report of the Convener for the Welfare of Members of National Defence Services and their Dependents. See also, e.g., NA, MG 28 I 129, Montreal Society for the Protection of Women and Children (SPWC), Vol. 5, File, Minutes of Board Meetings, June 1943 to 22 March 1945. Minutes of Meeting of the Board of Directors of the SPWC, 20 September 1944.

8. NA, MG 28 V 86, Jewish Family Services of the Baron de Hirsch Institute (JFS), Vol. 12, File, Minutes of Meetings, Case and Adoption Committee, Jewish Child Welfare Bureau, 1944–48. Minutes of Meeting of Placement Committee, 28 March 1944; also Vol. 10, File, Minutes of Meetings of Case Committee, Family Welfare Department, 1944–45. Minutes, 28 October 1944.

9. NA, RG 36, Series 18, Dependents' Allowance Board (DAB), Vol. 12, File, Committees Local – General Correspondence. "Volunteer Citizens' Committees"; Marion V. Royce, *The Effect of the War on the Life of Women: A Study* (Geneva; Washington, 1945), 71; Canadian Youth Commission, *Youth, Marriage and the Family* (Toronto, 1948), 46.

10. On wives' loneliness, see Archives de l'Université de Montréal (UM), P16, Fonds de l'Action Catholique Canadienne (ACC), P16/R 219. R. P. Valère Massicotte, O.F.M. "La Déliquance juvenile et la guerre" (Montreal, 1944); NA, MG 28 I 311, MSWL, Vol. 5, File 25. Women's Auxiliary of the R.C.C.S., Annual Report, 1944. For a soldier-husband's perspective on "personal family trouble brought upon by discouragement and loneliness and war bastard that prey on soldier wifes [sic]," see NA, RG 36, Series 18, DAB, Vol. 29, File, Inadequacy of Allowances, Complaints, Etc. DAB 5-6, Vol. 3. Letter from C.E.N. to DAB, n.d.

11. NA, MG 28 I 311, MSEL, Vol. 5, File 25. Report of Victoria Rifles Ladies Association [1944–45?] regarding men's neglect in writing regularly to their wives and mothers.

12. Robert England, *Discharged: A Commentary on Civil Re-establishment of Veterans in Canada* (Toronto, 1943), 325; *La Presse*, 22 avril 1944.

13. NA, MG 28 I 10, Canadian Council on Social Development (CCSD), Vol. 134, File 600. Response to Questionnaire from Welfare Convener, Royal Montreal Regiment; NA, RG 36, Series 18, DAB, Vol. 29, File, Children of Unmarried Mothers, DAB 5-5. G. F. Thompson to DAB, 6 March 1943.

14. "I have been most sincere with R —— and feel that I have made every sacrifice to keep her, we are so far from one another! I still do not understand who could have put the idea in her head that I was somehow attached to another girl. *It's perfectly false* and you can believe me." Emphasis in the original. ANQM, P104, Jeunesse Ouvrière Catholique (JOC), Container 250, File, Militaires, Sgt. G. L. to R. P. Victor Villeneuve, juin 1944.

15. NA, MG 28 I 10, CCSD, Vol. 134, File 600. Response to questionnaire from MSWL, Artillery Branch, June 1942. See also NA, RG 36, Series 18, DAB, Vol. 28, File, Reports on Conferences and Inspections. DND Memorandum by Ruth Harvey, 16 December 1941.

16. See ANQM, P257, MTC, Vol. 24, File, Divers – Faits. Faits [n.d.]; ANQM, P104, JOC, Container 170, File, Divers (Amour - guerre - chomage). Forum populaire: "L'Amour est-il aveugle?"; *La Presse*, 15 août 1945, p. 18.

17. NA, MG 28 V 86, JFS, Vol. 10, File, Minutes of Meetings of Case Committee, Family Welfare Dept., 1946–47. Case of the T. family, 3 May 1946; NA, MG 28 I 10, CCSD, Vol. 134, File 600 (II). Response to questionnaire from David G. Stevenson, Children's Aid Society for the County of Ontario and the City of Oshawa, June 1942.

18. See NA, RG 36, Series 18, DAB, Vol. 50, File, Procedure 43. Gwyneth Howell to Ruth Harvey, 30 April 1948; Charles H. Young to R. O. G. Bennett, 20 October 1942. Young claimed that the number of unfaithful wives was "small compared with the total number of enlisted men," but noted that "nevertheless such problems loom very large to the local groups who have to deal with them."

19. NA, RG 36 Series 18, DAB, Vol. 36, File, Petitions of Unmarried Applicants, DAB 7-24-117. R. O. G. Bennett to Colonel Ralston, 8 August 1942; Memorandum to Deputy Adjutant-General from H. T. Cook, 21 October 1942.

20. See NA, MG 28 I 311, MSWL, Vol. 2, File 33, E. I. Smit to C. H. Young, 5 May 1943; J. F. Chisholm to Children's Service Association, 10 November 1943; NA, MG 28 I 129, SPWC, Vol. 5, File, Minutes of Board Meetings, 18 April 1945 to 15 January 1947. Executive Secretary's Report, Annual Meeting, 22 March 1946.

21. NA, RG 36, Series 18, DAB, Vol. 28, File, Reports on Conferences and Inspections. Children's Aid Society Meeting [Ottawa], 1 December 1941.

22. See, e.g., NA, RG 36, Series 18, DAB, Vol. 28, File, DAB 4-5, Vol. 4, General Correspondence with Welfare Agencies; NA, RG 38, Department of Veterans' Affairs, Vol. 184, File, Rehabilitation, Confidential Letters, Vol. 2. Counsellors' Reference Book, April 1945, "Collaboration of Social Welfare Agencies with Ex-Service Personnel and the DVA"; NA, MG 28 I 10, CCSD, Vol. 134, File 600. Responses to questionnaire, 1942; CYC, *Youth, Marriage, and the Family*, 44–45.

23. NA, RG 36 Series 18, DAB, Vol. 50, File, Procedure 43, Suspension of Allowances for Wife on Ground of Improper Conduct. R. O. G. Bennett to Charles H. Young, 27 October 1942. The Chairman added that "Even in needy Mothers' Allowance Regulations, where in most cases, the mother is a widow, the procedure is to declare her ineligible for a Government allowance is [sic] she has irregular relations with a man." It appears that mothers' allowances in other provinces were also cut off upon news of recipients' "illegitimate" pregnancies. See "Report on the Visit to the Montreal Agencies, March 29 and 30," by R. Harvey, DAB, 3 May 1943, in the same file.

24. NA, RG 36, Series 18, DAB, Vol. 50, File, Procedure 43. R. O. G. Bennett to Charles H. Young, 27 October 1942; R. O. G. Bennett to Miss R. Robertson, 3 December 1943.

25. NA, RG 36, Series 18, DAB, Vol. 50, File, Procedure 43. Memo re D.A.B. & C.W.C. by Nora Lea, 14 June 1941; Vol. 28, File, Montreal Welfare Department, DAB 4-7."Families referred by D.A.B. to the Bureau d'Assistance Sociale aux Families for supervision and re-education." 31 July 1944.

26. NA, RG 36, Series 18, DAB, Vol. 50, File, Procedure 43. R. O. G. Bennett to Charles H. Young, 27 October 1942.

27. See NA, MG 28 I 10, CCSD, Vol. 134, File 600 (II). Response to questionnaire from Local Superintendent, Children's Aid Society of Huron County, Goderich, 15 June 1942; NA, RG 36, Series 18, DAB, Col. 28, File, Report on Conferences and Inspections. DND, Memorandum by R. Harvey, 16 December 1941; File, DAB 4-3, Vol. 1, Investigations, Department of Pensions and National Health. K. M. Jackson to R. O. G. Bennett, 24 August 1945.

28. NA, RG 36, Series 18, DAB, Vol. 50, File, Procedure 43. R. O. G. Bennett to Charles H. Young, 27 October 1942.

29. NA, MG 28 V 86, JFS, Vol. 11, File, Minutes of Case Conferences: Family Welfare Department and Jewish Child Welfare Bureau, 1944–46. Case History to be presented at conference between Child Welfare Bureau and Family Welfare Department, 26 December 1944. See also NA, MG 28 I 10, CCSD, Vol. 134, File 600 (I). Response to questionnaire from Family Service Bureau, Hamilton.

30. NA, RG 36, Series 18, DAB, Vol. 50, File, Procedure 43. Memo re D.A.B. and C.W.C. by Nora Lea, 14 June 1941.

31. NA, RG 36, Series 18, DAB, Vol. 28, File, Report on Conferences and Inspections. DND, Memorandum by R. Harvey, 16 December 1941; Vol. 50, File, Procedure 43. Gwyneth Howell to Ruth Harvey, 30 April 1943.

32. NA, RG 36, Series 18, DAB, Vol. 28, File, DAB 4-7, Montreal Welfare Department. "Conference on Working Relationships Between the Dependents' Allowance Board and Protestant Welfare Agencies of Montreal," 15 October 1941.

33. NA, RG 36, Series 18, DAB, Vol. 28, File, DAB 4-5, Vol. 4, General Correspondence with Welfare Agencies. K. M. Jackson to Ruth Harvey, 16 November 1943.

34. NA, RG 36, Series 18, DAB, Vol. 28, File, Procedure 43. MCSA, Memorandum on Problems caused by Stoppage of Pay, or Reductions in Allowances paid to Dependents or Enlisted Men, October 1942; NA, MG 28 I 10, CCSD, Vol. 134, File 600. Response to questionnaire from G. B. Clarke, General Secretary, Family Welfare Association, Montreal, 12 June 1942.

35. NA, RG 36, Series 18, DAB, Vol. 28, File, Report on Conferences and Inspections. Children's Aid Society Meeting [Ottawa], 1 December 1941.

36. NA, RG 36, Series 18, DAB, Vol. 28, File, Montreal Welfare Department, DAB 4-7. R. O. G. Bennett to Charles Young [n.d. but 1941]; and "Conference on Working Relationships Between the Dependents' Allowance Board and Protestant Welfare Agencies of Montreal," 15 October 1941, for the Montreal SPWC's denial of these charges.

37. NA, MG 28 I 311, MSWL, Vol. 5, File 18. Report of Welfare Committee, Women's Division, Black Watch (R.H.R.) of Canada, 1942.

38. NA, RG 36, Series 18, DAB, Vol. 28, File, DAB 4-5, Vol. 4, General Correspondence with Welfare Agencies. Olive M. Snyder to R. O. G. Bennett, 3 May 1943.

39. NA, RG 36, Series 18, DAB, Vol. 28, File, Reports on Conferences and Inspections. Report on Canadian Conference of Social Workers, May 1944. See also NA, RG 36, Series 18, DAB, Vol. 29, File, Children of Unmarried Mothers, DAB 5-5. B.W. Heise to R. O. G. Bennett, 5 August 1942.

40. NA, RG 36, Series 18, DAB, Vol. 50, File, Procedure 43. F. N. Stapleford to Joseph E. Laycock, 24 June 1941; Vol. 28, File, DAB 4-5, Vol. 4, General Correspondence with Welfare Agencies. George F. Davidson to R. O. G. Bennett, 28 June 1944.

41. NA, RG 36, Series 18, DAB, Vol. 28, File, DAB 4-5, Vol. 4, General Correspondence with Welfare Agencies. R. O. G. Bennett to Olive M. Snyder, 28 May 1943.

42. England, *Discharged*, 78; Desmond Morton, *A Military History of Canada: From Champlain to the Gulf War*, 3rd ed. (Toronto, 1992), 176, 182.

43. NA, RG 36, Series 18, DAB, Vol. 50, File, Procedure 43. R. O. G. Bennett to Miss R. Robertson, 11 March 1944.

44. My thanks to Denyse Baillargeon for this observation.

45. See Susan Hartmann, "Prescription for Penelope: Literature on Women's Obligations to Returning World War II Veterans," *Women's Studies* 5 (1978): 230–31.

46. Ruth Jamieson, "The Man of Hobbes: Masculinity and Wartime Necessity," *Journal of Historical Sociology* 9 (March 1996): 33.

47. Hartmann, "Prescriptions for Penelope," 231, 236.

48. NA, MG 28 I 10, CCSD, Vol. 134, File 600, questionnaire. Service Men's Families, Morale and Security, 1942. Commissioner, Bureau of Child Protection, Saskatchewan, to Dr. George F. Davidson, 15 June 1942; NA, RG 36, Series 18, DAB, Vol. 28, File, DAB 4-5, Vol. 4, General Correspondence with Welfare Agencies. R. O. G. Bennett to Olive M. Snyder, 28 May 1943.

49. NA, RG 36 Series 18, DAB, Vol. 28, File, Montreal Welfare Department, DAB 4-7. "Families referred by D.A.B. to the Bureau d'Assistance Sociale aux Families for supervision and re-education," 31 July 1944.

50. NA, RG 36, Series 18, DAB, Vol. 29, File, Children of Unmarried Mothers, DAB 5-5. R. O. G. Bennett to F. G. Thompson, 14 April 1943; Vol. 28, File, DAB 4-5, Vol. 4, General Correspondence with Welfare Agencies. R. O. G. Bennett to Olive M. Snyder, 28 May 1943.

51. *La Presse*, 6 avril 1946, p. 32; CYC, *Youth, Marriage and the Family*, 52; NA, RG 36, Series 18, DAB, Vol. 36, File, Permission to Marry (Army) – DAB 7-24-102g, Vol. 1. Circular No. 103, 3 April 1944; *Statutes of Canada* 1944–45; 1945; 1946; 1947; 1948; 1949 (8 George VI – 13 George VI).

52. UM, P16, ACC, P16/H3/18/84. "Le Mariage Chrétien" (1946); NA, MG 28 I 29, SPWC, Vol. 6, File, SPWC Minutes, 19 February 1947 to 24 March 1950. Minutes of Meeting of Board of Directors, 19 October 1949. Approximately 20 percent of the parliamentary divorces awarded to Montreal couples between 1944 and 1946 went to couples where at least one of the partners had a French surname; clearly, French Canadians were under-represented. See *Statutes of Canada* 1944–45; 1945; 1946 (8 George VI – 10 George VI).

53. NA, MG 30 C 92, Savage Papers, Vol. 3, File, Council of Women, Montreal Local, 1948–51. Local Council of Women, Vancouver, BC, Annual Report of Convener of Armed Forces. See also David A. Kent, "'Gone for a Soldier': Family Breakdown and the Demography of Desertion in a London Parish, 1750–91," *Local Population Studies* 45 (1990): 27–42.

54. James Snell, *In the Shadow of the Law: Divorce in Canada 1900–1939* (Toronto, 1991).

55. Raynes Minns, *Bombers and Mash: The Domestic Front 1939–45* (London, 1980), 180.

56. For statistics on war brides and their children, see Desmond Morton, *1945: When Canada Won the War* (Ottawa: CHA Historical Booklet no. 54, 1995), 11. For the reminiscences of English war brides, see Joyce Hibbert, *The War Brides* (Toronto, 1978).

57. *La Presse* noted that the last boatload of war brides and children was expected to arrive in Halifax on 21 November 1946 and that after 30 November, dependents of Canadian soldiers wishing to come to Canada would have to pay their own way. Yet an article on 8 February 1947 observed that 400 Canadian soldiers had recently arrived in Halifax and that the ship's passengers included 26 war brides and their children. See *La Presse*, 3 octobre 1946, p. 4; 2 novembre 1946, p. 28; 8 février 1947, p. 35.

58. NA, MG 28 I 311, MSWL: Vol. 5, File 25. Annual Report of the Recording Secretary, Women's Auxiliary of the R.C.C.S. (Montreal) [1944]; Vol. 3, File 54. Canadian Red Cross Society, Quebec Provincial Division, Lists of Dependents (Army) Arriving from Britain for Montreal.

59. *La Presse*, 7 mars 1946, p. 4; 27 novembre 1944, p. 4; 27 mars 1944, p. 4; 2 novembre 1946, p. 63.

60. *La Presse*, 6 décembre 1944, p. 4; NA, MG 28 I 311, MSWL, Vol. 3, File 65. Mary Elder to all Auxiliary Presidents, 1 June 1945; NA, MG 30 C 92, Savage Papers, Vol. 3, File, Council of Women – National – 1940–1948. Marion D. Savage, National Convener, to Local Conveners, 13 October 1945; NA, MG 28 I 311, MSWL, Vol. 1, File 91. Association Meeting and Directors' Meeting, 12 October 1945.

61. ANQM, P104, JOC Container 240, File, Commission Canadienne de la Jeunesse. Mémoires soumis par le comité central de l'ACJC à la Commission Canadienne de la Jeunesse, 27–28 janvier 1945. See also UM, P16, ACC, P16/04/52, Commission Canadienne de la Jeunesse, Comité provincial du Québec, Mémoire sur la famille, for similar worries about the linguistic and religious problems posed by war brides.

62. NA, MG 28 I 311, MSWL, Vol. 5, File 25. Victoria Rifles Ladies Association, Report of Welfare Committee [1946?]. For more on British wives and the housing shortage, see NA, MG 28 I 311, MSWL: Vol. 1, File 91. Executive Meeting, 5 January 1945; Vol. 3, File 54. Chairman of Oak Society for British War Wives to MSWL, n.d.; Vol. 3, File 66. President of Royal Montreal Regiment Ladies Committee to Mrs. Wright, 19 November 1945.

63. NA, MG 28 I 129, SPWC: Vol. 6, File, Minutes, 19 February 1947 to 24 March 1950. Report of the Executive Secretary for the Year 1946; Vol. 5, File, Minutes of Board Meetings, 18 April 1945 to 15 January 1947. Executive Secretary's Report, Annual Meeting, 22 March 1946; also Minutes of Meeting of Board of Directors, 16 May 1945.

64. NA, MG 28 I 311, MSWL, Vol. 3, File 54. Mrs. V to MSWL, September 1945 and n.d.; also Canadian Red Cross Society, Quebec Provincial Division, List of Dependents (Army) who arrived in Montreal Ex. Vessels W933 and W934 on 29 August 1945.

65. NA, MG 28 I 311, MSWL, Vol. 3, File 54. Chairman of Oak Society for British War Wives to MSWL, n.d.

66. *La Presse*, 2 novembre 1946, p. 28. Barry Broadfoot's interviews with veterans also uncovered evidence of the poor reception given to some English wives and he notes that many returned to England after a very short time in Canada. See *The Veterans' Years: Coming Home from the War* (Vancouver; Toronto, 1985), 87, 134.

67. NA, MG 28 I 10, CCSD, Vol. 58: File, 489. K. M. Jackson to Monsieur L. Désilets, 25 février 1948; File 489A. Memorandum re: Wives of Canadian Servicemen Overseas Proceeding to Canada but either Widowed or Deserted, 1946; File 489A. Reverend S. A. Yeo to Miss Lillian Thompson, 4 December 1946.

68. *Statutes of Canada 1944–45; 1946; 1947; 1948; 1949 (8 George VI – 13 George VI)*. See also NA, MG 28 I 10, CCSD, Vol. 58, File 489A. Memorandum re: Wives of Canadian Servicemen Overseas Proceeding to Canada but either Widowed or Deserted, 1946.

69. *La Presse*, 28 novembre 1945, p. 4. See also comments by a representative of the Department of Immigration in NA, MG 28 I 311, MSWL, Vol. 5, File 18. MSWL Welfare Report, n.d.

70. On veterans and their children in the United States, see William M. Tuttle, Jr., *'Daddy's Gone to War': The Second World War in the Lives of America's Children* (New York; Oxford, 1993), esp. Ch. 12. See also the scattered examples in Neil Sutherland, *Growing up: Childhood in English Canada from the Great War to the Age of Television* (Toronto, 1997), e.g., p. 45.

71. ANQM, P104, JOC, Container 240, File, Commission Canadienne de la Jeunesse. Mémoires soumis par le comité central de l'ACJC à la Commission Canadienne de la Jeunesse, 27–28 janvier 1945, "Jeunesse et Famille."

72. NA, MG 28 I 311, MSWL, Vol. 3, File 65. Mrs. Ward C. Pitfield to David Munroe, 30 March 1945; England, *Discharged*, 326. There is a growing secondary literature on juvenile delinquency in twentieth-century Canada. See Jeff Keshen, "Wartime Jitters over Juveniles: Canada's Delinquency Scare and Its Consequences, 1939–1945," in *Age of Contention: Readings in Canadian Social History, 1900–1945* (Toronto, 1997). For a study that explores the gendered and sexualised nature of postwar delinquency discourses, see Mary Louise Adams, *The Trouble with Normal*, esp. Ch. 4.

73. CYC, *Youth, Marriage and Family*, 50–52.

74. *La Presse*, 12 juin 1945, "Le chemin du retour," p. 6; NA, RG 36, Series 18, DAB, Vol. 12, File, Committees Local – General Correspondence. Janet R. Keith, "Volunteer Citizens' Committees"; Broadfoot, *The Veterans' Years*, 94.

75. CYC, *Youth, Marriage and Family*, 50.

76. NA, MG 28 V 86, JFS, Vol. 12, File, Minutes of Meetings, Case and Adoption Committee, Jewish Child Welfare Bureau, 1944–1948. Minutes, Meeting of Placement Committee of JCWB, 28 March 1944. See also Sutherland, *Growing Up*, 83, 106.

77. *La Presse*, 5 mars 1947, p. 3.

78. McGill Archives, MG 2076, Montreal Council of Social Agencies, Container 14, File 244. SPWC, Summary of Representations to be made before the Royal Commission on the Criminal Law relating to Criminal Sexual Psychopaths, 30 January 1956.

79. D. H. Lawrence, *Sons and Lovers* (New York, 1913).

80. After the first year of war, during which the married unemployed enlisted in great numbers, the average soldier tended to be single. See NA, MG 28 I 311, MSWL, Vol. 5, File 24. MSWL to Mr. E. I. Smit, March 1942. See also England, *Discharged*, 152.

81. NA, RG 38, DVA, Vol. 193, File 65-47-A. Monthly Report on Activities, 1 August 1944. Robert England's massive rehabilitation manual, *Discharged*, was written to reassure servicemen and their parents (see p. 376).

82. ANQM, P104, JOC, Container 28, File, Bulletins des Chefs de la J.O.C.F. 1945–1946–1947. Bulletin mensuel J.O.C.F. Mars 1946."Le retour de nos vétérans."

83. NA, MG 28 I 311, Vol. 1, File 91. Executive Committee Meeting, 19 January 1940; NA, MG 28 V 86, JFS, Vol. 10, File, Minutes of Meetings of Case Committee, Family Welfare Department, 1944–45. Follow up, 9 May 1945.

84. On Montreal soldiers' class background, see ANQM, P104, JOC, Container 170, File, Organisation. Projet d'un service de soldat. Organisé par la J.O.C. et la L.O.C. 2e copie. On child and teen labour in mid-twentieth-century Montreal, see Dominique Marshall, *Aux origines sociales de l'État-providence: Families québécoises, obligation scolaire et allocations familliales 1940–1955* (Montreal, 1998).

85. NA, MG 28 I 311, MSWL, Vol. 2, File 33. Mrs. C to MSWL, January 1946. See also NA, RG 36, Series 18, DAB, Vol. 29, File, Mothers' Allowance, DAB. 5-1. C. W. Lundy to R. O. G. Bennett, 19 March 1942.

86. NA, RG 36, Series 18, DAB, Vol. 29, File, Mothers' Allowances, DAB 5-1. C. W. Lundy to R. O. G. Bennett, 26 July 1943.

87. *La Presse*, 5 novembre 1945, "Idéal à mettre à la portée de nos comnattants," p. 4; NAQM, P104, JOC, Container 216, File, Soldats (Service). Memarandum of the J.O.C. To the CANADIAN GOVERNMENT in Favour of Demobilized Young Men [n.d.]; CYC, *Youth, Marriage and the Family*, 43.

88. ANQM, P104, JOC, Container 58, File, Emissions Radiophoniques – Campagne des loisirs – 1946. 3ème émission. Semaine de propagande de la J.O.C. 16 au 23 juin 1946; CYC, *Youth, Marriage and the Family*, 62–63.

89. *La Presse*, 6 février 1946, "Accusé d'avoir tenté d'assassiner son père," p. 3.

90. NA, MG 28 I 311, MSWL, Vol. 3, File 64. Speech by Brock Chisholm, 13 November 1944: "Women's Responsibility for Mental Reestablishment of Soldiers." See also England, *Discharged*, 329–30.

91. NA, MG 29 I 311, MSWL, Vol. 2, File 33."Clothing Allowance for Discharged Officers," n.d.

92. NA, MG 28 I 311, MSWL, Vol. 2, File 33. Janet Bennett to MSWL, 23 May 1944; also Report of Sub Committee on Need of Soldiers' Widows and Widowed Mothers for Supplementary Grants, n.d. See also NA, MG 28 I 10, CCSD, Vol. 134, File 600. Response to questionnaire from H. P. Lyne, Kelvington Branch Canadian Legion, Kelvington, Saskatchewan, July 1942.

93. NA, RG 38, DVA, Vol. 193, File 65-47-A. Monthly Report on Activities, 2 February 1943; NA, MG 28 I 10, CCSD, Vol. 134, File 600. E. J. Verity to Director of Relief, Veteran Block, Regina, 10 July 1942; File 600 (2). Catherine Stuart Vance to Charles H. Young, 10 June 1942.

94. "I have a war job … and troubles with mother-in-law," *La Presse*, 7 avril 1945, p. 15.

95. For a well-known statement of this position, see Joan Wallach Scott, *Gender and the Politics of History* (New York, 1988).

96. On the homecomings of gay and lesbian veterans in the United States, see Allan Bérubé, *Coming Out Under Fire: The History of Gay Men and Women in World War Two* (New York, 1990), esp. Ch. 9. For Canada, see the fragmentary evidence in Gary Kinsman, *The Regulation of Desire: Homo and Hetero Sexualities*, 2nd ed., revised (Montreal, 1996), 154–57. For evidence of lesbian relationships in the Canadian navy, see Ruth Roach Pierson, " 'They're Still Women After All' ": The Second World War and Canadian Womanhood* (Toronto, 1986), 275 n. 83. For Australia, see Ruth Ford, "Lesbians and Loose Women: Female Sexuality and the Women's Services during World War II," in *Gender and War*, Damousi and Lake, eds., 81–104.

97. Pierson, " 'They're Still Women,' " 159–61, 184.

98. See NA, RG 38, DVA, Vol. 197, File, Rehabilitation, Statistics, Women's Division. Proceedings: Training Conferences on Women's Rehabilitation, 83–87. On the question of servicewomen's sexual respectability, see Pierson, " 'They're Still Women,' " Ch. 5; Ruth Ford, "Lesbians and Loose Women."

99. Pierre Vallières, *White Niggers of America*.

Article 5.2
Robert A. J. McDonald

"He Thought He Was the Boss of Everything": Masculinity and Power in a Vancouver Family[1]

Issues to Consider

- How does McDonald describe the class and ethnic aspects of Henry Bell-Irving's approach to fatherhood and family relations? Why, in his view, are these aspects complicated?
- In what ways does the author consider the Bell-Irving patriarch, and the family itself, representative or typical of Canadian fathers and Canadian families of the time? In what ways are they untypical?
- How does McDonald characterize Marie Bell-Irving and the marital relationship? Is his theory about her "uses" of ill health convincing?
- Where the historical subjects of gender and family role are concerned, McDonald asserts the importance of examining "the links between public role and private power" by stepping into the domestic realm. How does he go about this, in Bell-Irving's case? Where does private power make itself most felt in the family setting? How did the familial power of men differ from that of women?
- It is important for historians to examine gender in relational terms, as McDonald does. What can we learn about manliness by considering not only father/son relationships, but father/daughter and husband/wife relations as well? What can this kind of examination tell us about feminine gender roles?

Henry Bell-Irving, a Vancouver industrialist, was not pleased with his sons, especially the eldest. Enrolled at Loretto, a prestigious public school in Scotland, the boys were following in the footsteps of their father. The boys seemed not to be taking their education seriously, and Henry had had enough. In a November 1907 letter he told them that if they wanted "to become real men," then they should read and study his letter carefully: "keep it by you and act on it, and the sooner the better. I can only give the course, it is for you to steer it and go full steam ahead." One part of the message emphasized hard work and individual achievement and is a classic statement of the Victorian liberal values that were widely shared across the middle class of the time: "A man is the maker of his own fortune ... He is either self made or never made. By industry, application, and good use of leisure time, he may become almost anything he pleases ... Idleness and not work is a curse." The other part of the letter reflected the Bell-Irvings's status as a Scottish borderlands family of wealth, history, and education, and it was more upper- than middle-class in tone. A man must not only work hard but have character, Henry asserted: a measure of modesty allows you to "avoid contentiousness and contradictions and carping fault finding." Do all you can "to cultivate good manners," for manners "make the man and want of them the fellow."

Source: Robert A. J. McDonald, "'He Thought He Was the Boss of Everything': Masculinity and Power in a Vancouver Family," BC Studies, no. 132 (2001/02): 5–30.

Improve yourself "by studying the lives of men who have become great — learn how they succeeded, and *why* others have failed." In conclusion, "be a gentleman always — you were born gentlemen — educated and brought up as such … it now rests with you to remain so."[2]

The author of this paternal advice, Henry Ogle (H.O.) Bell-Irving, was one of the most influential businessmen to emerge in Vancouver, British Columbia, in its early years as a city. Bell-Irving arrived on the west coast in 1885 and died in the city at the age of seventy-four in 1931. Trained in Karlsruhe, Germany, as a civil engineer, H.O. had gained employment as a surveyor-engineer on the Rocky and Selkirk Mountain sections of the Canadian Pacific Railway line in 1882. Three years later, he quit the company and headed west to Granville, the Burrard Inlet lumber village that became the City of Vancouver in 1886. A restless young entrepreneur hoping to regain clear title to his father's estate at Milkbank in Dumfriesshire, near Lockerbie in the Scottish Lowlands, he correctly discerned that British Columbia's infant salmon-canning industry offered tremendous potential for making money. In the fall of 1890 he found among family and friends in Scotland the capital to consolidate nine west coast canneries, seven of which were on the Fraser River, into one corporation — the Anglo-British Columbia Packing Company Ltd. At the outset Anglo-BC Packers, which Bell-Irving managed through his agency company in Vancouver, was "the world's No. 1 producer of sockeye salmon." Through solid management the canning enterprise prospered, and Henry Bell-Irving's fortune grew. At his death he left an estate of $339,000 (net), placing it sixteenth among the top fifty Vancouver fortunes of the period. In addition, he had already given away a considerable, though undetermined, amount to help Britain and Canada fight the First World War, and to support the families of his ten children.[3] […]

Henry quickly established a family in the city, bringing from England a young bride named Marie Ysabel del Carmen Beattie, whom he had met in Switzerland a number of years earlier.[4] Bella, as she was known, arrived shortly before the new city burned to the ground on 13 June 1886, leaving her, one suspects, rather unimpressed with this raw and undeveloped place on the outer edge of empire. While raised at her family's country estate at St. Michael's near Torquay in Devon, England, Bella was born in Santiago, Cuba, where her wealthy family owned a sugar plantation. Bella's father was, like the Bell-Irvings, from the Scottish Lowlands, while her mother, born Marie Isabel Brooks, was partly of French ancestry but had been born in the West Indies, suggesting that the Brooks and Beattie families had a long-time connection with investment in the Americas. The union of Henry and Bella, then, was a marriage of two imperial business families that had participated actively in the expansion of capital and influence from Britain to far-off parts of the globe.[5] One of those far-off places was British Columbia.

The privileged background of the Bell-Irvings translated easily, and predictably, into a high-status lifestyle. Henry and Bella lived in large houses; had many servants; hired governesses and tutors to educate their children (and then sent them to elite schools); participated in status-defining rituals such as the round of afternoon visits known as "at homes"; belonged to the best clubs and the most prestigious charities; purchased Cadillacs; travelled frequently to Europe; and owned an island (Pasley Island, located near Vancouver at the entrance to Howe Sound), which H.O. had purchased in 1909 for the exclusive recreational use of his family.[6] For the Bell-Irvings, status and class blended into a coherent, and reinforcing, whole.

Being British in a city where 85 per cent of the population shared a British cultural background also legitimized the Bell-Irving family's social power. The family members were British by birth and metropolitan (rather than provincial) by outlook and lifestyle. Their reference points were London, Milkbank, and Torquay rather than Vancouver, at least until after the First World War. Britain remained their second home, and, for more than four years (starting in 1903), their first. They bought tweed suits, deerstalker caps, carpets, fabric, and furniture in London, even having the chintz covering on chairs reglazed in the Old Country.[7] At the outset of the Boer War the Bell-Irving children stood on the railway platform in Vancouver and sang "Soldiers of the Queen" to the first contingent of Boer War troops to leave from the west coast for South Africa (to the great amusement of the soldiers themselves).[8] As the eldest Bell-Irving daughter pointed out many years later, "in our generation we were not unhappy to be a colony of Britain."[9]

The family's British-centric view of the world is most evident in Henry Bell-Irving's unlimited enthusiasm for imperial federation. He moved back to England in October 1903 to be closer to his boys, who were in British schools, and to join Joseph Chamberlain's campaign for the creation of an imperial tariff and an end to British free trade. He fought to have the Dominion government support the imperial navy rather than create a Canadian one, and, in 1910, he organized a large public meeting in Vancouver to urge that Canada help Britain build Dreadnoughts. According to his obituary, Henry Bell-Irving was a "strong imperialist" and the "Father of Imperial Preference."[10] Yet H.O.'s enthusiasm for empire co-existed with an equally strong Scottish identity. For ceremonial occasions the Bell-Irving men wore tweed kilts and listened to the music of a Scottish pipe band, and the boys learned Scottish dancing and were sent to a Scottish public school.[11] Henry Bell-Irving was both a Briton and a Scot but not, in any discernible way, a Canadian.

Given his ethnocentrism and strong support for imperialism, Henry Ogle Bell-Irving's views on British Columbia's Asian population are hardly surprising. Imperialist ideology wed the values of Social Darwinism with those of British nationalism to create a sense of imperial duty, a belief in the need to carry British culture to the peoples of the world. H.O. shared that vision and its assumptions. As an employer of labour he played a major role in breaking the strikes of Fraser River sockeye salmon fishermen in 1893 and 1900. Typical of his class, he also espoused an open labour market in which wages could be regulated through immigration, including the

Mah Sing and Sam at Bell-Irving home on Seaton Street, circa 1902. Mah Sing is on the left, Sam is looking at the camera. The picture was taken to send to relatives in China—the books were intended to impress. Private, Elizabeth O'Kiely.

immigration of Chinese and Japanese labourers.[12] As a capitalist he viewed labour as an economic factor of production, asserting publicly in 1891 that the Chinese "are less trouble and less expense than whites. They are content with rough accommodation at the canneries ... I look upon them as steam engines or any other machine."[13] His rhetoric was class-based but betrayed a level of racism that cannot be explained by class interest alone. In a newspaper story (published in England) about the BC salmon-canning industry he argued that "no Britisher would prefer [the] employment of Chinamen if satisfactory white labour were obtainable."[14] Yet at home he and Bella developed a close, though paternalistic, relationship with their Chinese servants. Mah Sing, shown opposite with Sam, served the Bell-Irvings for many years.

The class position of the Bell-Irvings is complicated by the family's history, economic role, and geographic location. The Bell-Irvings claimed roots in the Scottish countryside that, by one account, reached back to the twelfth century, and the family's history as members of Scotland's landed gentry remained into the early 1900s an important component of H.O.'s identity.[15] Yet, while family history suggests that Henry Bell-Irving belonged to the lower reaches of Britain's aristocratic class, both Henry and Bella also came from families that were actively engaged in business and embraced capitalist values. Indeed, while H.O.'s "youthful ambition had been to make enough money to regain clear title to his father's estate in Scotland," he found the entrepreneurial climate of the New World more suited to his temperament and, in 1895, sold his equity in the family home at Milkbank to his cousin John Bell-Irving.[16] In British terms, then, Henry Bell-Irving is best viewed as a member of the middle class, though admittedly its upper portion. One British study also refers to the upper middle class as the bourgeoisie, and the two terms will be used interchangeably in this essay with regard to references to Britain.[17] But the Bell-Irvings also lived in Vancouver, where high status was based on achievement rather than ascription, and where, in lieu of a titled aristocracy or a landed gentry, wealthy business and professional families constituted an upper class. Thus, the language that best describes the class position of the Bell-Irving family (upper middle class or bourgeoisie on the one hand, upper class on the other) will depend, in part, on whether the perspective is from the Old World or the New World.[18]

* * *

So far I have defined the Bell-Irving family through the categories of class, race, and ethnicity, and I have emphasized what we know about the family as public figures. But the 1907 letter from H.O. to his sons hints at another perspective, one that takes us through the front door of the family home and into the private realm of domestic life. It is a world in which assumptions about the gender roles of men and women also played a crucial part in shaping family life. The concept of gender is simple enough: it states that how a man or a woman functions is not only a matter of biology, or sex, but also a product of history. A male is born a man, but his masculinity "is a human convention," something that is historical and must be viewed as fluid, variable, and contested.[19] An examination of gender forces us to look beyond the public realm as a site where men exercised influence and to explore the links between public role and private power. For, as British historians Michael Roper and John Tosh point out, we need to recognize that "men's power in history has resided in their masculinity, as well as in their material privilege and their manipulation of law and custom."[20] With this understanding of gender in mind, I would like to explore some of the ways in which masculinity was defined, and contested, within the Bell-Irving family. Making H.O. visible as a father and as a husband both complicates and enriches our understanding of his success as a businessman in early Vancouver.

Let us start by looking at H.O.'s relationship with the men in his family. Henry and Bella had ten children, six of them boys. Conventional wisdom prescribed that, in Victorian middle-class families, the men should participate in public affairs outside of the home while the women, less rational than their husbands but with a special capacity to nurture and educate, should prevail in the home. This separate-spheres ideology was followed closely in the Bell-Irving household — H.O. as the breadwinner and uncontested head of the family, Bella as mother and house manager — but only to a point, for, to begin with, Henry Ogle Bell-Irving actively managed the upbringing of his boys and was guided in doing so by his understanding of what it meant to be a man. On more than one occasion he expressed frustration that his two oldest sons, Henry Beattie and Richard, were not measuring up to this ideal. The 1907 letter is interesting in part because it defined, in somewhat contradictory terms, what he believed a "real man" to be. H.O. himself had succeeded both as a businessman and a gentleman, but the tension between the two ideals was less easily bridged by his family. None of his boys distinguished himself in business, as he had done, and, with the possible exception of Richard (the second son, who took over the family business), the gentlemanly ideal seems to have had greater force than the business ideal. The eldest son (Henry Beattie) was a superb cannery man but was constantly in debt and seems not to have had a good sense of how to manage money. As his financial resources diminished in the late 1920s he was unable to retreat from a lifestyle — complete with servants, parties, and private schools for his children — that he felt was appropriate to his own family's identity as "the Henry Bell-Irving Juniors."[21]

Part of the difficulty that the sons encountered as businessmen, I am suggesting, may have come from the mixed signals that their father left about what it meant to be "real men": self-made and hard-working businessmen on the one hand, and gentlemen on the other.[22] For, in sending all six sons, and his eldest grandson, to the prestigious British public school of Loretto, located near Edinburgh, H.O. chose for them an education that equated masculinity with the values of British society's upper strata. Through education at a "public" (i.e., a fee-based) school, young men were to develop "character," a concept that British historian J. A. Mangan has described as "a common synonym for manliness in the language of the period."[23] The concept of "character" incorporated antithetical values: on the one hand "the virtues of a young Christian gentleman (honesty, modesty, honour and a foundation of true religion)," on the other a "manly code" that was more explicitly masculine (success, aggression, and ruthlessness), though always marked by "victory within the rules, courtesy in triumph, compassion for the defeated."[24] Among the first-rank public schools in Britain in the last half of the nineteenth century, Loretto was famous for emphasizing the physical side of this equation and for stressing the role that athleticism played in the development of character: fresh air, cold baths, team sports, and rugged self-sufficiency.[25] Like Bell-Irving, Loretto's famous headmaster, H. H. Almond, also believed that athleticism forged character more powerfully than did "book learning."[26]

While taking on a specific class character at Loretto, this infatuation with athleticism was broadly shared by middle-class men in the United States and Canada, as well as in Britain, at the end of the century. As E. Anthony Rotundo says with regard to the United States, the body itself became a vital component of manhood: strength, appearance, and athletic skill mattered more than in previous centuries.[27] Reflecting this association of physical athleticism with manhood, H.O. kept himself in excellent shape and was a noted hunter and skater. He also climbed mountains and, each morning, lifted weighted dumbbells. Indeed, he was climbing Vancouver's North Shore mountains at the beginning of his seventy-fourth year and took a skating trip to Europe — during which he skated with the young skating sensation Sonja Henie — just months before his death. Loretto translated into class terms a commitment to athleticism and sports that was popular at the time and that was a key element of Henry Bell-Irving's definition of manhood.

The turn-of-the-century period was also one in which athleticism had become equated with war, which "was thought to breed a new, forceful manhood."[28] The link between athleticism and militarism reached its fullest expression in enthusiasm for empire, and H.O. was a most enthusiastic imperialist. It is not surprising, then, that he would choose to educate his sons in schools that saw as their mandate the training of imperial leaders. Military service was especially emphasized, with public school boys being "continually reminded of their patriotic duty, of their roles as military leaders," and of the close relationship between games like football and war.[29] H.O. would have agreed with another ardent imperialist in Canada, Montreal's David Ross McCord, that "war served a noble function in that it strengthened both individual manliness and national character."[30] Little wonder, then, that Henry Bell-Irving and his sons expressed their notions of masculinity in military terms.

They did so especially during the First World War. The Bell-Irvings greeted the outbreak of war with patriotic enthusiasm. By November 1914 five of the six boys had enlisted, and the sixth, a student at Loretto, did so in the middle of the war. All six gained commissions spread across the army, navy, and air force. They won numerous citations for bravery, were constantly being injured, and tragically lost one of their members within weeks of the war's end. H.O. contributed to the war effort in more material ways as well, especially in financially supporting the purchase of machine guns for the war effort.[31] The media loved the symbolism of the Bell-Irving family's war record, which it portrayed in highly gendered terms. An American journal spoke of H.O.'s sons as "splendid specimens of manhood," while the *London Daily Express* described them as "all red-blooded, red-haired and red-fibred, with grit marked all over them."[32] From London to Vancouver, H.O. Bell-Irving became known as "the father of a famous fighting family."[33]

H.O.'s pride as a father who had done his duty to God and country animated a family photograph taken in London in January 1918, the father surrounded by his sons, all in uniform. H.O. had used his considerable influence to have all six sons pulled from their military positions for the sake of the family reunion in London. The family's eldest daughter, Isabel, also worked in London at Lady Ridley's, a private hospital where the boys would go when injured, but it was the sons who most obviously spelled success for Bell-Irving as a father.[34]

The potential contradiction in Bell-Irving's understanding of manliness — emphasizing, as it did, a man's role as both the economic and social head of the family — became a very real contradiction in the mid-1920s when he had to choose which of his two eldest sons would succeed him as head of H. Bell-Irving and Company. Roper and Tosh have argued that "one of the most precarious moments in the reproduction of masculinity is the transfer of power to the succeeding generation, whether it be within the family from father to son, via apprenticeship in the case of skilled workers, or by 'palace revolutions' in business. The key question is whether the 'sons' take on the older generation's gender identity without question, or whether they mount a challenge, and if so, how."[35] In the Bell-Irving family, conflict pitted Henry Ogle against his eldest son, Henry Beattie, and came to a head over the issue of succession in the family business. When, in 1925, H.O. made the decision to pass on the presidency of H. Bell-Irving and Company to his second son rather than to his first, tensions that had been developing for years exploded. Particularly distressing to H.O. was the fact that others in the family sided with their brother, arguing that, as the eldest male, and following family tradition, Henry Jr. had the right to succeed his father. Yet the differences between father and son were not exclusively about control of the business, for Henry Beattie had been challenging his father's authority for years. "As a boy, a youth and a grown man Henry has continually countered me — personally and in business," H.O. wrote to Alan Duncan, his fifth son. "Time and again I have felt myself at the end of my tether … twice he has done his utmost to turn me out of the house I have taken a lifetime to build up — all the while receiving payment for which I was directly responsible."[36] The decision to hand over the business to Richard rather than to Henry Jr. was not sudden, he wrote on another occasion, "but the result of cumulative decisions stretching back twenty years."[37] Amid much acrimony, Henry Jr. finally resigned from the family firm in 1928 to join a rival company, Canadian Fish.[38]

At the core of the father's unease with his eldest son was the deep suspicion, evident as early as 1907 but confirmed by the latter's work record after the war, that Henry Jr. lacked "character" and, thus, did not live up to the standards of a gentleman. When H.O. had spoken of avoiding "contentiousness and contradictions and carping fault finding," he was talking especially to the eldest. He used similar language about his eldest son in the mid-twenties, describing him as conceited and arrogant, a man whose "dominating character" and "extreme self-assurance" made him unfit for the mantle of leadership. Richard, the second son, had learned how to obey, and "therefore can command," but not Henry, who had to be " 'Boss' or Nothing."[39] H.O. was especially upset when Henry Jr. tried to undermine his father's authority among other members of the family. In doing so, Bell-Irving wrote in his diary, his words betraying the influence of the public school ethos, "Henry [the son] was not playing the game."[40] In response to the accusation that it was he, Henry Ogle Bell-Irving, who was being disloyal to the family by denying the eldest son his rightful inheritance, H.O. shot back that loyalty was also due to family and friends in Britain "who were good enough 35 years ago to entrust me with their money."[41] It was the legacy of that initial investment that was now threatened. In a letter to the London directors of Anglo-BC Packers explaining his decision, H.O. wrote, "One of the Company's main sources of strength here [in Vancouver] is the splendid support given by our bankers based on the confidence they have in the character of the personnel of the firm";[42] his son's impulsive and unauthorized actions, and, by implication, his lack of character, threatened that confidence. After patiently observing his son for years Henry Ogle Bell-Irving felt that he had no choice: "I must do my duty."[43]

Bell-Irving's decision reveals much about his understanding of a man's role. Without question Henry Beattie, while very different from his father in his ability to manage money, and perhaps in his business judgement, shared with his father a strong personality. H.O. was notorious for his desire to control everyone and everything around him — according to one of his grandsons, "he was always directing things," "he thought that he was the boss of everything," "he was pretty hard on his children"[44] — and Henry Beattie similarly liked control. Yet the clash between father and son that profoundly divided the family was also, in important ways, the product of conflicting notions of masculinity, pitting the father in his role as custodian of family wealth, on the one hand, against the father as defender of family tradition, on the other.

* * *

This focus on relationships between the men in the Bell-Irving family, a male-centred perspective that is common in studies of masculinity, obscures the fact that looking at men's relationships with women is one of the most telling ways of exploring masculine power. In the words of Roper and Tosh, "masculinity (like femininity) is a relational construct, incomprehensible apart from the totality of gender relations."[45] Yet, uncovering the voice of women in such a male-dominated social world as that of the Bell-Irving family is not easy. The family has left a rich collection of company letters, cannery records, and business diaries but little evidence generated by women. My information about Bella and her eldest daughter, Isabel, comes almost entirely from interviews, in sharp contrast to the written records left by the men. We know virtually nothing about H.O.'s relationship with his three youngest daughters.

In many ways the Bell-Irvings were a typical business family of the late nineteenth century, a time when men and women were viewed as creatures with opposing qualities — the men "active, independent, rational, dominant," the women "pious, pure, submissive, domestic." In such families, boys mattered more than girls.[46] They certainly did among the Bell-Irvings. When listing family members in his diary, H.O. identified all the boys first, and then the girls, regardless of birth order. The priority given to the boys had special meaning for Isabel, the family's third child (born in 1889) and eldest daughter. Isabel was very close to her father, riding with him daily in Stanley Park and making the rose for his boutonnière every morning. Throughout the 1920s, when she lived with her husband, Ben Sweeny, in a house (owned by H.O.) next door to her parents, she served regularly as hostess (in place of her bed-ridden mother) at social functions in the family home. But the relationship between father and daughter was taxing for Isabel, a point conveyed emphatically by a story told by Isabel's daughter, Verité Purdy. On one occasion, Purdy recounts, H.O. berated Isabel for wearing lipstick, which he forbade his daughters to use. But the red on her lips was blood, not lipstick, from the lip that she had bitten, while tense, trying to please him. Purdy suggests that Isabel Sweeny was a very sad person during the interwar years, married to a man (Ben Sweeny, from an upper-class Vancouver family) who was incapable of making money and was looked down upon by H.O. for being unsuccessful, and lacking the appreciation of her demanding father. When Henry Bell-Irving learned that he was dying of cancer, he called together his five remaining sons (a sixth had been killed in the war) to tell them of his fate, leaving his eldest daughter — who was in house at the time but was not invited to hear the news — to learn of his illness by chance. Dealing with the death of their father was the business of the men in the family, not the women. Nor did H.O. make any special provision in his will for Isabel, who received much less from the estate than did her brothers.[47]

But it is H.O.'s marriage that best illustrates the link between public role and private power in the Bell-Irving household. Henry and Bella came from similar backgrounds, though Bella's family was undoubtedly wealthier than Henry's. Henry and Bella were probably very much in love when the marriage began, but we know almost nothing about how they viewed each other in the years that followed. More certain is the fact that, during the first decade of the marriage, H.O. sired children at a rate of one every fifteen months and that they had three more thereafter at longer intervals, for a total of ten. She appears to have lost at least one additional child through a miscarriage. We also know that Bella's health began to deteriorate before she had finished having children. A letter in H.O.'s business correspondence dated December 1898 reveals that Bella had been "very ill for the past six weeks" from bronchitis, pneumonia, "and other troubles" and hoped to travel to California for a long period of recuperation.[48] She had given birth to her ninth child earlier in the year. Six years later, when Bella was forty-two, she gave birth to Beatrice, her last. By then she was already suffering from rheumatoid arthritis and could barely walk. The condition continued to worsen. A photo taken in 1914 shows Bella walking with a cane, and, by the end of the war, when she was in her late fifties, she had become a permanent invalid.[49] She spent much of her remaining life, about twenty-five years, upstairs, attended by three nurses per day working in shifts.

In an era that viewed illness as a female weakness, and in a family where bourgeois values and upper-class social pretensions combined to emphasize the physical qualities of masculinity, Bella's disability evoked little sympathy from her husband. "Mother had a very strenuous life in many ways," her eldest daughter, Isabel, stated in an interview recorded in the 1970s; "I think she just wasn't strong enough for it, quite apart from having so many of us." At the same time, H.O.'s emphasis on athleticism and strong bodies left little room for illness or physical weakness. H.O.'s grandson, Henry Pybus Bell-Irving, states that "grandfather had an intense abhorrence of illness," a view shared by the family's oldest daughter, Isabel, who observed: "Daddy was never understanding of illness."[50]

Yet, within this very patriarchal family, Bella did have influence. Well educated, with a solid command of the French and Spanish languages, and an accomplished pianist, Bella was "used to being the belle of the ball, and it never occurred to her not to be."[51] From her bedroom she managed the home, designed the garden, commanded servants, arranged parties, and received visitors. Indeed, she is said to have known where every piece of linen in the house was to be found. Her style, like that of H.O., could be described as "starchy," and she was, in her later years, very much the "Grand Dame." Her imperious manner may have been influenced by the Beattie family's history as plantation owners in Cuba, where slavery persisted until 1880 and where Bella is said to have been "brought up not to raise a little finger; the servants did everything." When, as a child, Elizabeth O'Kiely visited her grandmother, Bella would be seated in a chair, nurses at her side. The young girl would approach, kiss Bella's arthritic hands, which were folded on her lap, and then back away and remain silent until spoken to by "Granny B-I." Polite conversation and caraway seed cake followed.

How Bella viewed her husband is unclear, but we do have enough evidence to speculate. At one level Bella was very supportive of H.O., for she shared with him a set of values and expectations that flowed from their overlapping class and ethnic backgrounds. For example, when her eldest son started working for the family as the manager of a northern cannery, Bella wrote him a letter that was similar in tone to the one H.O. wrote his sons in 1907. In it she praised her husband for "building up a great future for his sons" and urged Henry Jr. not to rest content until he had attained great things and become an important man.[52] At some point, however, the marriage of Henry and Bella seems to have evolved from a relationship based on love and respect to an arrangement held together by convention and duty. They became, to borrow a line, "yokemates without intimacy."[53] By the 1920s, H.O. "kept busy not staying at home."[54] He spent weekends at his retreat on Pasley Island, where Bella refused to go; skating at the Connaught Skating Club, which he had founded before the First World War; and, in the words of one grandson, "pissing off to Europe all the time," often with either Isabel or Beatrice, the eldest and youngest of his daughters, or with Sophia Merritt, one of several widows with whom he spent considerable time after the First World War. Bell-Irving was also fond of buying the widow Merritt very expensive hats.[55]

As for Bella, she got angry. She desperately wanted to outlive H.O., and even though he had always been the picture of athletic vigour and good health, while she was frail, may have had Parkinson's Disease as well as arthritis, and moved around in a wheel chair, she survived him by five years. Indeed, Bella is said to have stated at H.O.'s wake, with a twinkle in her eye: "I made it!" She especially resented having so many children, a point noted by several members of the family. When her youngest son, Aeneus, announced to her in 1934 that he and his wife had just had a baby girl, and that Bella was, once again, a grandmother, Bella showed little interest. "Tell me about the Quintuplets," she beseeched him, referring to the famous Dionne Quintuplets who had been born that same week; "I was silly," she continued, "I should have had you all in two litters [of five]," just like the Quintuplets.[56] [...]

* * *

Social space is never neutral, and an exploration of the gendered nature of domestic space provides a final opportunity to examine the relationship between masculinity and domesticity within the Bell-Irving family.[57] In particular, anyone who visited the Bell-Irving homes on Seaton Street (now West Pender Street), which they rented from 1897 to 1903, or on Harwood Street (called The Strands) in the fashionable West End, which they built in 1908 and resided in for more than twenty years, would have confronted incontrovertible evidence that H.O. Bell-Irving liked to hunt. How else can we interpret the turn-of-the-century photograph, located in a family album, of the drawing room at Seaton Street? H.O. organized major hunting expeditions up the coast and into the interior of British Columbia in search of trophy animals such as big-horned sheep, moose, caribou, elk, and grizzly bear. The trips would last from ten to forty days and cost between $750 and $3,000.[58] H.O. appears to have gone hunting alone, except for a guide and cook in his employ. Hunting was "closely bound up with the symbolism of imperialism" and, by the late nineteenth century, was believed to differentiate unambiguously "the virile from the 'effeminate' imperialist." Characterized by an elaborate code of behaviour, it also served as "the mark of the Imperial gentleman, distinguishing the sportsman from the butcher."[59] Henry Bell-Irving saw himself as both an imperial gentleman and a sportsman. He would not have viewed kindly any suggestion that he was a "butcher."

What gives particular significance to H.O.'s hunting prowess is the location of his trophies within the Bell-Irving homes. Animal trophies are "symbols of male potency,"[60] and their use as decoration asserts an unmistakable masculine presence in a room. For instance, British imperial historian John MacKenzie notes that billiard rooms, which are quintessential male preserves, asserted their "masculinity through the dark browns and green baize of its decoration and, above all, [through] the animal skins on the floor and the horns around its walls."[61] Known to the eldest daughter, Isabel, as "daddy's heads," the trophies in the drawing room of their Seaton Street home seem to overwhelm Bella [in a photograph taken around 1900]. This association of the drawing room with masculinity ran counter to the fashion of the time, when the drawing room and dining room were, symbolically, differentiated by gender, with richly textured fabrics and colours defining the drawing room as unmistakenly feminine, and dark woods and formal furnishings making the dining room unambiguously masculine.[62] Through the symbolism of the hunt H.O. defined the interior of the family's Seaton Street home as masculine space.

We know more about The Strands, which H.O. designed and constructed after the family returned from England. The Strands featured a large hall at the front of the house, with a dining room and a drawing room off the hall. Characterized by a very high ceiling and a second-floor balcony that looked down onto the hall, and from which bedrooms were connected, the hall featured a massive fireplace and a sprung floor for dancing. Unlike the drawing room at Seaton Street, the one at The Strands was more typically feminine. As such it contrasted sharply with the hall, which was more "rough-and-tumble" than pretty and provided a site for displaying H.O.'s animal heads. As O'Kiely notes, "Just inside the front door [of The Strands] stood a small, upright stuffed bear with a silver tray in hand for receiving visitors' calling cards. H.O.'s hunting trophies — moose, elk, caribou and mountain goat — gazed down from the walls overhead."[63] A photograph of the hall shows a large bearskin on the floor in front of the fireplace.[64]

At one level the hall at The Strands, the most important social space in the house, was a gender-neutral room where the sexes mixed easily, especially at dances that could attract as many as 150 family friends and acquaintances. Yet, while more gender-neutral than the dining and drawing rooms of The Strands, the hall also reflected the paternalistic heritage of masculine baronial halls in Scotland.[65] Indeed, the hall at The Strands was explicitly modelled after the large central hall at Milkbank, the Bell-Irvings' ancestral home in the Scottish Lowlands. It too featured a huge fireplace, a twenty-foot ceiling with a balcony halfway up leading to the bedrooms, and "the spoils of animals" on the walls and floor. In this sense the Vancouver house bore the unmistakable imprint of Henry Bell-Irving, who drew upon the deeply rooted class and ethnic influences of the Scottish countryside to make it his own. His wife's influence appears to have been limited to what their granddaughter called "Bella's drawing room," which, "with its soft silks, glazed chintz, and delicate French furniture, was the only part of the house with any pretensions to elegance."[66]

* * *

What, then, are we to make of this story of the domestic life of Henry Bell-Irving? At one level the conclusion is obvious: Bell-Irving acted as we might expect the head of a bourgeois family to have done in the late nineteenth and early twentieth centuries. He exercised the powers that were accorded to men by the prevailing gender assumptions of the time. He successfully fulfilled the masculine role of provider, making a great deal of money that allowed the Bell-Irving family to maintain its position atop Vancouver's social hierarchy. H.O.'s role within his family also corresponds to some of the generalizations now emerging in American and British literature about fatherhood in middle-class families before the First World War. The older notion that husbands and wives had influence only within their gender-specific separate spheres, and that fathers remained uninvolved in family matters such as the education of their children, has, according to one expert, been "laid to rest forever,"[67] and the fact that our journey into the Bell-Irving home revealed a father who cared deeply about the future of his sons should not surprise us. In addition, a recent study of parenthood and masculinity in the American north offers useful insights into the tension that existed between fathers and sons. The emphasis middle-class men placed on breadwinning meant that fathers felt increased pressure to steer their sons into jobs where they could succeed as men and, of course, bring credit to their fathers.[68] The result, says Stephen Frank in *Life with Father*, is that relations between fathers and sons were often less emotional and more conflict-laden than were those between fathers and daughters.[69] The foregoing study suggests that this may have been the case within the Bell-Irving family, where H.O.'s high expectations for the success of his sons led to a relationship that appears to have been more respectful than loving. Should we view Henry Bell-Irving, then, as a typical middle-class father of the Victorian and Edwardian eras in Canadian history?

In addition, should we see Henry Bell-Irving as exemplifying a trend within the middle class towards more equal partnerships between husbands and wives, each remaining within their separate spheres but increasingly sharing power and moral leadership within the family? Barbara Ehrenreich and Deidre English have noted that the patriarch was traditionally an elder male who had absolute authority over his family.[70] Such "father rule" characterized the pre-industrial family, writes John Tosh, because production took place within the household where family, servants, and apprentices lived and worked together under a single roof and where a pyramidal structure of authority, with the father at the top, made economic sense.[71] With industrialization and the separation (for men) of work from home, some measure of the patriarch's influence, especially in domestic affairs, was diminished. Indeed, there is now a considerable literature that explores both the erosion of men's power within the family in the industrial era and the feelings of insecurity that this erosion engendered for middle-class men.[72] A generally accepted view holds that the creation of specifically masculine spaces, such as the den or billiard room, within the middle-class home, and the emergence of big-game hunting as a fashionable sport,[73] can be seen as efforts by bourgeois men to shore up their increasingly threatened masculine identity.

However, I do not believe that Henry Bell-Irving felt his masculinity to be threatened or that he accepted the principle of sharing power with his family. Instead, he appears to have been a patriarch of the older, early nineteenth-century type identified by Ehrenreich and English as a husband, a father, and a head-of-family who was in control and who expected to be obeyed. The reason why Henry Bell-Irving embraced an increasingly threatened form of patriarchal power may be found at the intersection of his position within the Victorian bourgeoisie and his heritage as a member of the Lowland Scottish gentry. Thus, he did not just want his sons to be successful businessmen, he also wanted them to be gentlemen, and the tension created between these contrasting ideals divided H.O. from his family. In Henry Bell-Irving's case, then, class and ethnicity constructed a gender role that overlapped to some extent with middle-class trends but that remained distinctive. In that sense the Bell-Irving story underlines the now commonly accepted conclusion that gender is socially constructed and, being neither fixed nor singular, can display a remarkable diversity.[74]

The story of Henry Bell-Irving's relationship with his family suggests two other observations about the study of gender in Canada. First, Canadian studies of masculinity have focused upon the bottom and middle levels of the social hierarchy but almost never on the top.[75] Yet issues that were important to the Bell-Irvings, such as education, succession in the family business, and notions of manliness were very much a product of particular social circumstances in the upper echelons of Canada's, and Vancouver's, social hierarchy. The illumination of the complexities of gender construction in Canada's past will require studies from across the social spectrum, including the top. In addition, Bella's story offers interesting suggestions about how class both retarded and facilitated resistance to patriarchy. She shared her husband's goals for their sons, and one suspects that she similarly embraced the class and gender values that shaped their lives. Furthermore, Bella does not appear to have challenged the roles assigned to women by the domestic-spheres ideology. Yet the self-assurance that comes with social privilege also empowered her, later in life, to resist her husband's influence within the confines of the family home and to gain some independence from him. Such agency could take place, however, only within the limits imposed by H.O.'s continued role as family patriarch.

NOTES

1. In January 2001 this article was presented as the Seagram Lecture to the McGill Institute for Canadian Studies, and I would like first to thank Desmond Morton, the institute's director, for his invitation to work and study as the Seagram Chair at McGill. Several members of the Bell-Irving family have contributed to this study. Special appreciation is owed to the late Elizabeth O'Kiely, without whose generous support in providing access to family papers, photographs, and stories the essay could not have been written. Four other family members generously provided interviews: the Honourable H. P. Bell-Irving, Ian Bell-Irving, Verité Purdy, and Darg Bell-Irving. I also appreciate the various forms of research assistance provided by Jean Barman, Tina Loo, Carla Paterson, Annemarie Adams, and Brian Lewis.

2. Paragraph from letter written by Henry Bell-Irving to his sons at Loretto School, Scotland (14–25 November 1907?), City of Vancouver Archives (hereafter CVA), Bell-Irving Family Papers (hereafter BIFP), Add. MSS 1, vol. 86, Correspondence Outward.

3. For H. O. Bell-Irving's history, see *Vancouver Daily Province* (hereafter *Province*), 19 February 1931, 1–2; *Daily Colonist*, 21 February 1931, 4; G. S. Andrews, "The Bell-Irving Land Surveyors in British Columbia," *British Columbia Historical News* 12, 4 (Summer 1979): 11–16; and C. W. Parker, ed., *Who's Who in Western Canada*, vol. 1 (Vancouver: Canadian Press Association, 1911), 106. For the formation of the Anglo-British Columbia Packing Company Limited, see *Pacific Fisherman* (50th Anniversary Number) 50 (August 1952): 15; *Daily News-Advertiser* (hereafter *News-Advertiser*), 5 May 1891, 8; Henry Doyle, "Rise and Decline of the Pacific Salmon Fisheries," Special Collections Division, University of British Columbia Library, MS, vol. 1, pp. 191–92; and Dianne Newell, ed. and intro., *The Development of the Pacific Salmon-Canning Industry: A Grown Man's Game* (Montreal: McGill-Queen's University Press, 1989), 205–06. For Henry Bell-Irving's probated estate, see British Columbia Attorney-General, Estate Records, British Columbia Archives and Records Service (BCARS), BC Supreme Court, Vancouver Probates, GR1415, file 1931/16,148. Gifts to his children are documented in CVA, BIFP, Add. MSS 1, vol. 48, diary, 18 November 1916, and vol. 49, diary, 7 November 1917; H. Bell-Irving to Aeneus, 12 February 1925, CVA, BIFP, Add. MSS 1, Correspondence Outward; and CVA, BIFP, Add. MSS 1, vol. 65, diary, (?) October 1927, and vol. 70, diary, 15 November 1929.

4. Marie Isabel del Carmen Beattie (Bella) was born in 1862 in Santiago, Cuba, and died in 1936 in Vancouver. Her mother was Marie Isabel Brooks and her maternal grandmother was Rosa Despaigne of Bordeaux. Rosa Despaigne's family had interests in Saint Domingue in the West Indies. Richard Hudson Beattie, Bella's father, was also, like the Bell-Irvings, from the Scottish Lowlands but appears to have moved to Torquay, Devon, in 1883 (information from the "Brooks Family Tree," Elizabeth O'Kiely's private records, and P. J. Bottrill, Area Librarian, South Devon area, Torquay, to Robert McDonald, 19 August 1996).

5. Andrews, "The Bell-Irving Land Surveyors in British Columbia," 11–14; *The Bell-Irvings of BC* (Burnaby: Burnaby Art Gallery, 1980), in Special Collections Division, University of British Columbia Library, pamphlet collection, SPAM 9664; "Diamond Wedding Rejoicing at Whitehall," newspaper clipping, n.p., 14 November 1903, in CVA, BIFP, Add. MSS 1, vol. 77, scrapbook; and CVA, BIFP, Add. MSS 1, vol. 65, diary, 29 October 1927.

6. Information in this paragraph taken from a variety of newspaper and other sources. The upper stratum of Vancouver society, of which the Bell-Irvings were a part, is discussed in Robert A. J. McDonald, *Making Vancouver: Class, Status, and Social Boundaries, 1863–1913* (Vancouver: UBC Press, 1996), chap. 7. For Pasley

Island, see CVA, Add. MSS 54, Matthews Collection, Streets and Place Names File, "Pasley Island"; and H. Bell-Irving to Mr Sprott, 19 July 1910, CVA, BIFP, Add. MSS 1, vol. 87, Correspondence Outward.

7. Notes from Elizabeth O'Kiely's interview with Isabel Sweeny, circa early 1970s, Elizabeth O'Kiely, private collection (hereafter Isabel Sweeny Interview, notes), 16 and 22; H. Bell-Irving to Messrs. Goodel and Graham, Clothiers, London, 13 December 1888, CVA, BIFP, Add. MSS 1, vol. 82, Correspondence Outward; H. Bell-Irving to Peter Robinson Ltd., London, 5 January 1898, Add. MSS 1, vol. 83, Correspondence Outward; and CVA, BIFP, Add. MSS 1, vol. 53, diary, 3 February 1920.

8. Isabel Sweeny Interview, notes, 10.

9. Ibid., 9.

10. Quotations from *Colonist*, 21 February 1931, 4. See also *News-Advertiser*, 13 October 1903, 5; H. Bell-Irving to Mr. Congden, 15 July 1904, CVA, BIFP, Add. MSS 1, vol. 86, Correspondence Outward; H. Bell-Irving to Editor, *Dumfries and Gallowan Courier and Herald*, 13 January 1906, ibid., vol. 85, Correspondence Outward; H. Bell-Irving to Sir Charles [H. Tupper], 15 April 1909, ibid., vol. 86, Correspondence Outward; and H. Bell-Irving to Mr. [George?] Cowan, 12 February 1910, ibid., vol. 87, Correspondence Outward.

11. Isabel Sweeny Interview, notes, 21; H. Bell-Irving to W. L. McLennan, 5 January 1897, CVA, BIFP, Add. MSS 1, vol. 83, Correspondence Outward; and H. Bell-Irving to Piper James Begg, 10 April 1909, ibid., vol. 86, Correspondence Outward. For his view that Loretto provided "a sound practical English education," see H. Bell-Irving to Mr. [H. B.] Tristram, 8 January 1904, ibid., vol. 84, Correspondence Outward.

12. H. O. Bell-Irving, Chairman, Special Committee, Vancouver Board of Trade, to Secretary, V.B. of T., 1 October 1907, CVA, BIFP, Add. MSS 1, vol. 86, Correspondence Outward.

13. Geoff Meggs, *Salmon: The Decline of the British Columbia Fishery* (Vancouver: Douglas and McIntyre, 1991), 25.

14. "Colonial Onlooker" [H. B-I] to Editor, *The Western Morning News* (Plymouth, England), 6 January 1906, CVA, BIFP, Add. MSS 1, vol. 85, Correspondence Outward.

15. Reference to the family's twelfth-century roots is from the *Japan Mail*, 30 July 1904, in CVA, BIFP, Add. MSS 1, vol. 28, diary, May-December 1904. The Scottish history of the Beattie family (i.e., the family of Bella's father) is unknown.

16. Andrews, "The Bell-Irving Land Surveyors of British Columbia," 14 and "Unionist Campaign in Mid-Oxon," *Oxford Times*, 8 February [1904?], in O'Kiely, private collection.

17. Brian Lewis, *The Middlemost and the Milltowns: Bourgeois Culture and Politics in Early Industrial England* (Stanford: Stanford University Press, 2001), 1–2 and 432, n. 2.

18. This discussion of the class position of the Bell-Irvings within British society and Canadian society is informed by John Tosh, *A Man's Place: Masculinity and the Middle-Class Home in Victorian England* (New Haven: Yale University Press, 1999), 11–13 and 19–20; Harold Perkin, *The Rise of Professional Society: England Since 1880* (London: Routledge, 1989), 62–100; and Andrew C. Holman, *A Sense of Their Duty: Middle-Class Formation in Victorian Ontario Towns* (Montreal and Kingston: McGill-Queen's University Press, 2000), 3–49.

19. Quotation from E. Anthony Troper, *American Manhood: Transformations in Masculinity from the Revolution to the Modern Era* (New York: Basic, 1993), 1. Alice Kessler-Harris has defined gender as "the socially shaped cluster of attributes, expectations, and behaviors assigned to different sexes" ("Treating the Male as 'Other': Redefining the Parameters of Labor History," *Labor History* 34, 2-3 [Spring-Summer 1993]: 191). See also Joy Parr and Mark Rosenfeld, eds., *Gender and History in Canada* (Toronto: Copp Clark, 1996), 1.

20. Quotations from Michael Roper and John Tosh, "Historians and the Politics of Masculinity," in *Manful Assertions: Masculinities in Britain Since 1800*, ed. Michael Roper and John Tosh (London and New York: Routledge, 1991), 4 and 1.

21. From a letter of Henry Beattie Bell-Irving to Henry Ogle Bell-Irving, n.d., 1929, read to Robert McDonald by Ian Bell-Irving, 7 August 1997.

22. The problem of how to resolve the tension between aristocratic and bourgeois influences in families with ties to both the landed gentry and the upper middle class was not unique to the Bell-Irvings. Over the past twenty years British historians have debated the influence of industrialization on the structure of British society. One perspective, strongly expressed by Martin Wiener, emphasizes the "gentrification" of the bourgeoisie, another the "bourgeoisification" of the aristocracy, and a third some variety of plutocratic blending. Examples of this literature include, for the "gentrification" argument, Martin Wiener, *English Culture and the Decline of the Industrial Spirit, 1850–1980* (Cambridge: Cambridge University Press, 1981), and, for the "bourgeoisification" thesis, Robert Gray, "Bourgeois Hegemony in Victorian Britain," in Jonathan Bloomfield, ed., *Papers on Class, Hegemony and Party* (London: Lawrence and Wishart, 1977), 73–93. See also F. M. L. Thompson, "Aristocracy, Gentry, and the Middle Class in Britain, 1750–1850" in Adolf M. Birke and Lother Kettenacker, eds., *Middle Classes, Aristocracy and Monarchy* (München: K. G. Saur, 1989), 15–34; and Patricia Thane, "Aristocracy and

the Middle Class in Victorian England: The Problem of 'Gentrification,'" in ibid., 15–34 and 93–109. For a general comment on this debate, see Dror Wahrman, *Imagining the Middle Class: The Political Representation of Class in Britain, c. 1780–1840* (Cambridge: Cambridge University Press, 1995), 5.

23. J. A. Mangan, *Athleticism in the Victorian and Edwardian Public School: The Emergence and Consolidation of an Education Ideology* (Cambridge: Cambridge University Press, 1981), 45

24. Ibid., 135.

25. The philosophy of H. H. Almond, the headmaster at Loretto school from 1862 to 1903, is discussed in ibid., 48–58, 162–63, and 190–91; and in J. A. Mangan, *The Games Ethic and Imperialism: Aspects of the Diffusion of an Ideal* (New York: Viking, 1985), 24–28. Jean Barman has studied the dissemination of the public school ethos to British Columbia in *Growing Up British in British Columbia: Boys in Private Schools* (Vancouver: UBC Press, 1984).

26. Mangan, *Athleticism*, 49; and H. Bell-Irving to Mr. [H. B.] Tristram, 8 January 1904, CVA, BIFP, Add. MSS 1, vol. 84, Correspondence Outward. H. H. Almond was Loretto's headmaster from 1862 to 1903.

27. Rotundo, *American Manhood*, 6. See also p. 222.

28. Ibid., 240–41.

29. Quotations in this paragraph from Mangan, *Athleticism*, 56 and 191; see also Mangan, *The Games Ethic and Imperialism*, 21–43.

30. Donald A. Wright, "Remembering War in Imperial Canada: David Ross McCord and the McCord National Museum," *Fontanus* 9 (1996): 97.

31. Bell-Irving also joined with a group of leading Vancouver businessmen to form the Aero Club of British Columbia, an instrument for training RFC pilots, and he served as "the unofficial recruiting officer for the Royal Flying Corps in British Columbia." See Elizabeth O'Kiely, *Gentleman Air Ace: The Duncan Bell-Irving Story* (Madiera Park: Harbour, 1922), 34, 60–61, and 168.

32. Newspaper clipping, unnamed, 13 September 1916, CVA, BIFP, Add. MSS 1, vol. 79, scrapbook and *London Daily Express*, n.d. [November 1917–June 1918], ibid., vol. 50, diary.

33. So great was H.O.'s zeal that in August 1917 he brought down upon himself considerable criticism for labelling as "traitors" and "friends of the Kaiser" western Canadian Liberals who backed Sir Wilfrid Laurier in opposing conscription. See the *Vancouver Sun*, 13 August 1917; *Province*, 13 August 1917; and *News-Advertiser*, 14 August 1917, CVA, BIFP, Add. MSS 1, vol. 79, scrapbook. The quotation, cited in the *Province*, was from the speech used to introduce Bell-Irving to the pro-conscription rally.

34. See O'Kiely, *Gentleman Air Ace*. H. O. Bell-Irving had participated actively in the creation of a Scottish militia regiment in Vancouver in 1909 and 1910. See H. Bell-Irving to Lord Strathcona, 7 May 1909, CVA, BIFP, Add. MSS 1, vol. 86, Correspondence Outward; and Bernard McEvoy and Capt. A. H. Finlay, *History of the 72nd Canadian Infantry Battalion Seaforth Highlanders of Canada* (Vancouver: Cowan and Brookhouse, 1920), 1–2 and 6.

35. Roper and Tosh, *Manful Assertions*, 17.

36. H. Bell-Irving to Duncan Bell-Irving, 3 May 1928, CVA, BIFP, Add. MSS 1, vol. 89, Correspondence Outward.

37. H. Bell-Irving to John [Bell-Irving], 9 April 1928, ibid., vol. 89, Correspondence Outward.

38. CVA, BIFP, Add. MSS 1, vol. 66, diary, 3 May 1928, 7 May 1928, and 20 May 1928.

39. Quotations from Henry Bell-Irving to John [Bell-Irving], 9 April 1928, CVA, BIFP, Add. MSS 1, vol. 89, Correspondence Outward; H. Bell-Irving to Mr. Corbett, 24 January 1925, ibid., vol. 88, Correspondence Outward; and H. Bell-Irving to John [Bell-Irving], 13 August 1925, ibid., vol. 88, Correspondence Outward. See also CVA, BIFP, Add. MSS 1, vol. 62, diary, 6 July 1925, and 9 July 1925.

40. CVA, ibid., vol. 62, diary, 8 July 1925.

41. H. Bell-Irving to Duncan [Bell-Irving], 14 August 1925, CVA, BIFP, Add. MSS 1, vol. 88, Correspondence Outward.

42. H. Bell-Irving to Mr. Corbett, 24 January 1925, ibid., vol. 88, Correspondence Outward.

43. CVA, BIFP, Add. MSS 1, vol. 62, diary, 9 July 1925.

44. Henry Pybus Bell-Irving, interview with Robert McDonald, 18 June 1997.

45. Roper and Tosh, "Historians and the Politics of Masculinity," 2 (quotation) and 13. Several working-class historians are leading the way in exploring the place of women in the construction of masculinity. For the United States, see Kessler-Harris, "Treating the Male as 'Other'"; Elizabeth Faue, "Gender and the Reconstruction of Labor History: An Introduction," *Labor History* 34, 2–3 (Spring-Summer 1993): 169–77; and Ava Baron, "Gender and Labor History: Learning from the Past, Looking to the Future," in *Work Engendered: Toward a New History of American Labor*, ed. Ava Baron (Ithaca and London: Cornell University Press, 1991), 1–47. For Canada, see Suzanne Morton, *Ideal Surroundings: Domestic Life in a Working-Class Suburb in the 1920s* (Toronto: University of Toronto Press, 1995), esp., 108–56.

46. For instance, Henry James Sr., the clergyman and father of noted American writer Henry James Jr., was inter-
    ested only in the education of his boys because he "firmly believed that girls were moral by nature, whereas boys
    had to learn to be good." See Jean Strouse, *Alice James: A Biography* (Boston: Houghton Mifflin, 1980), xiii and
    45.

47. Interviews by Jean Barman and Robert McDonald with Elizabeth O'Kiely, 30 May 1997; and by McDonald with
    Verité Purdy at Courtney, British Columbia, 17 February 1998.

48. H. Bell-Irving to Mr. Smith, 21 December 1898, CVA, BIFP, Add. MSS 1, vol. 83, Correspondence Outward.

49. O'Kiely, *Gentleman Air Ace*, 18 (photograph) and 208.

50. Quotations from Henry Pybus Bell-Irving, interview with Robert McDonald, 18 June 1997; and Isabel Sweeny
    Interview, notes, 27. See also O'Kiely, *Gentleman Air Ace*, 170–71.

51. Elizabeth O'Kiely, interview with Jean Barman and Robert McDonald, 30 May 1997.

52. Raymond Eagle, *In the Service of the Crown: The Story of Budge and Nancy Bell-Irving* (Ottawa: Golden Dog,
    1998), 8.

53. Rotundo, *American Manhood*, p. 141.

54. Ian Bell-Irving, interview with Robert McDonald, 7 August 1997.

55. Sophia Merritt was the daughter of Sir Charles Hibbert and Lady Tupper, who had moved to Vancouver in
    1898, and the granddaughter of Sir Charles Tupper, a father of Confederation and, for a period in 1896, prime
    minister.

56. Darg Bell-Irving, interview with Robert McDonald, 17 August 2000.

57. The idea that all space is socially constructed, and that its use reflects structures of power within the commu-
    nity, is suggested in Susan G. Davis, *Parades and Power: Street Theatre in Nineteenth-Century Philadelphia*
    (Philadelphia: Temple University Press, 1986), 13–14.

58. Several of Henry Bell-Irving's hunting trips are documented in his business records. See correspondence from
    1 May 1897 to 29 June 1897 in CVA, BIFP, Add. MSS 1, vol. 83, Correspondence Outward; CVA, BIFP, Add.
    MSS 1, vol. 49, diary, 10 July 1917 to 8 October 1917; and ibid., vol. 64, diary, 12 August 1926 and 16 August
    1926.

59. John M. MacKenzie, "The Imperial Pioneer and Hunter and the British Masculine Stereotype in Late Victorian
    and Edwardian Times," in *Manliness and Morality: Middle-Class Masculinity in Britain and America, 1800–1940*,
    eds. J. A. Mangan and James Walvin (Manchester: Manchester University Press, 1987), 176–98 (quotations on
    pp. 180, 179, and 183). On masculinity and hunting, see also Morton, *Ideal Surroundings*, 127–28.

60. Tina Loo, "Of Moose and Men: Hunting for Masculinities in the Far West, 1880–1939," unpublished paper, 21.

61. MacKenzie, "The Imperial Pioneer and Hunter," 180–81.

62. For the differentiation of the dining room and the drawing room by gender, see Ian Gow, "The Dining Room,"
    and Juliet Kinchin, "The Drawing Room," in Annette Carruthers, ed., *The Scottish Home* (Edinburgh: National
    Museums of Scotland, 1996), 125–80; and Mark Girouard, *Life in the English Country House: A Social and
    Architectural History* (New Haven: Yale University Press, 1978), 205, 233, and 292.

63. O'Kiely, *Gentleman Air Ace*, 18–19.

64. Ibid., 19.

65. Girouard, *Life in the English Country House*, 288–92; and Annette Carruthers, "Studying the Scottish Home,"
    and David Jones, "The Hall and the Lobby," in Carruthers, *The Scottish Home*, 8, 28–33, and 116–20.

66. O'Kiely, *Gentleman Air Ace*, 19.

67. Robert L. Griswold, "Introduction to the Special Issue on Fatherhood," *Journal of Family History* 3, 24 (July
    1999): 252; and Tosh, *A Man's Place*, 77, 103, and 115.

68. Ibid., 3–4 and 115.

69. Stephen M. Frank, *Life with Father: Parenthood and Masculinity in the Nineteenth-Century American North*
    (Baltimore and London: Johns Hopkins University Press, 1998), 2–5 and 152–60.

70. Barbara Ehrenreich and Deidre English, *For Her Own Good: 150 Years of the Experts' Advice to Women* (London:
    Pluto, 1979), 6 and 10.

71. Tosh, *A Man's Place*, 3, 25, and 60–62.

72. For instance, see Cynthia Comacchio, "Bringing up Father: Defining a Modern Canadian Fatherhood,
    1900–1940," in Lori Chambers and Edgar-André Montigny, eds., *Family Matters: Papers in Post-Confederation
    Canadian Family History* (Toronto: Canadian Scholars' Press, 1998).

73. Loo, "Of Moose and Men"; Gail Bederman, *Manliness and Civilization: A Cultural History of Gender and Race in
    the United States, 1880–1917* (Chicago: University of Chicago Press, 1995), chap. 5; and MacKenzie, "The
    Imperial Pioneer and Hunter." The language of "class" employed in this paragraph is somewhat ambiguous

because the literature does not differentiate clearly between middle-rank and upper-rank (or bourgeois) members of the middle class. The financial resources required to hunt "big-game" would have placed most big-game hunters at the upper end of the middle class.

74. Roper and Tosh, "Historians and the Politics of Masculinity," 1.
75. For example, see the contributions on the subject of masculinity in two excellent collections on Canadian gender history: Parr and Rosenfeld, *Gender and History in Canada*; and Kathryn McPherson, Cecilia Morgan, and Nancy M. Forestell, eds., *Gendered Past: Historical Essays in Femininity and Masculinity in Canada* (Toronto: Oxford, 1999). The middle class that Andrew Holman, in *A Sense of Their Duty*, studies in the towns of Galt and Goderich would, in a larger city such as Toronto or Vancouver, have fit mostly into the middle ranks of society (and, hence, the middle class) rather than in the upper class (as did the Bell-Irvings in Vancouver).

Document 5.1
Ruby Cress

Letters from the 1950s

Writer Edna Staebler is an important part of the southwestern Ontario cultural scene. In *Haven't Any News: Ruby's Letters from the Fifties*, from which Document 5.1 is excerpted, she has gathered some of the many letters written in the 1950s to various family members by her younger sister, Ruby Cross. Ruby's letters detail day-to-day life with her husband and two children in Barrie, Ontario.

Issues to Consider
- What are the advantages to social historians of using private documents such as letters to probe private lives? In what ways are letters perhaps less advantageous in getting at "what life was really like"?
- What picture do the letters reveal of Ruby's everyday life? Do her own stories support the standard representation of 1950s housewives?

April 24/51

Dear Kay

They're singing on the radio Enjoy Yourself, it's later then you think. Guess they're playing that specially for me today — my 40th birthday. That song sure makes sence. I guess I'll just enjoy myself from now on. They say Life begins at 40 so maybe things might start happening to me. Fred sold a 5000 last nite, maybe he'll start getting breaks. A chap promised to phone him today and a man he picked up asked him to see him Friday about some insurance. Things look brighter.

I even think the sun's going to shine today, the paper said warmer. Thanks for the darling birthday card and the compact; I'd rather have had it then anything if you'd asked what I wanted and needed. It is a luxury to me cause I have only that very old wee one I had in collegiate. I love it and many many thanks. And for the card with the kitten in the hammock — wish we had a really one, don't you?

I must get at dresser drawers. I've been putting them off ever since house-cleaning talk has been going around. Was asked and refused to be a phone caller for Mission Band and for Federation group at church. I figured I'd be phoning all the time instead of getting my braided rug done this year. I'm at a dandy now: I wanted it navy and red but it's sort of rosy instead, for the bathroom. It's made out of Sally and the Smith and Rogers kids' navy and fawn wool stockings dyed. Nice to work with, soft and warm.

Thanks again for all you gave me. I like everything. I wear the slippers, use the compact, I wear your coat and I've worn your dress to four special occasions and got compliments for it. I wish you birds would visit us sometime, I met a dame who writes for radio and I'd like to have her in to talk to you, I think she'd enjoy it and you might get a kick out of it too but if I leave it go too long I may not have the nerve to invite her.

Source: Ruby Cress, *Haven't Any News: Ruby's Letters from the Fifties*, ed. Edna Staebler (Waterloo: Wilfrid Laurier University Press, 1995), 6–7, 11–12, 28–29.

Now I'd better hop along and get my work done. We haven't eaten in the dining room since Fred made me a table and bench in the kitchen and the old washing machine's been taken to the cellar, I love it here at the table where I can sit and watch what's going on outside on the road — a pleasure but a time waster.

Love, Ruby

April 26/51

Dear Mum

It's a really rainy day and all I can think about is fishworms. How can I grow them and get the kids interested in them? I think I could make a fortune selling wigglers if I only knew how to raise them. There'd be no end of sales of them here on the highway cause hundreds of tourists go by and if they're wanting worms we'd have first chance because we're out on the edge of town. There are worm places farther along; last year we tried to get some and had a terrible time because none of them had them in stock — they didn't really grow them they just caught them and hadn't enough. I think the trade would be good — the smell too, says Fred. Dead fishworms do kick up quite a stink but we won't let them die. I'd have to learn how to raise them and feed them etc. I was digging parsnips in the garden this morning before the rain came and I saw dozens of them. I'm keen and excited about it. Some woman out in B.C. is making a selling proposition out of them so why couldn't I? She grows them for top-soil, I want them for fish. If you should hear or read anything about raising them, let me know. I should be starting now to produce for the summer trade. The kids can catch them and sell them as well as me, it would sharpen them up and give them a hobby.

A Worm Farm. Gee it would be fun. I'd have a log book to write in where all my customers came from and what all they did. I bet we'd meet some interesting people.

I'll be a worm farmer. I'm anxious to get started, but beans — tomorrow I have to help clean someone else's house. A dame in our church group has to have an operation next week so the gang of women are going to her place to do her apartment so she can go and come from the hospital knowing it's clean. She's got something wrong with her neck gland — probably not much — she's a whiner and a bossy thing. Her husband died during an operation so I guess she's scared. He was a swell chap, a good church worker but henpecked. I don't know how I let the girls rope me into this thing but anyway I said I'd pitch in — wish I could talk them into helping me finish my housecleaning.

It sure is raining hard. Do you think I will worm farm? I keep shoving Fred, he needs pushes and so do I. If I could only keep enthused about life, I'd keep him up on his toes. Maybe the worms will do it.

Love, Ruby

July 24/51

Dear Kay

Mabel gave me this notepaper, she didn't like it cause it's pink. Can't say I'd buy it myself. She got it on sale but doesn't write letters and thought I could use it up on my family. I hope you don't mind.

I'm in bed and it's only 8 oclock. I've had a cold and I'm trying to get rid of it. I stayed in bed Thurs. Fri. and Sat. mostly but it didn't help. Fred made mustard plasters for me but no go. I phoned the doctor and he gave me medicine that's so terrible it makes me dizzy and I'm scared to take it.

I worked hard today. Maybe too hard for my own good. I washed 8 sheets, pillow cases and other regular stuff, refilled the machine with clean water and started over again. I picked 8 boxes of raspberries and Fred helped me preserve 12 quarts after dinner. We've 36 quarts now and 4 baskets of cherries canned with the pits in so kids can count how many they've eaten. This sure is the time for doing stuff. You should see our berries, big as my thumb; everyone says they've never seen the like. I'll be giving you some. Fred got up at 5 this morning and picked 2 six-quart baskets full. Tomorrow jelly and ironing is my skedule. We're eating things from our garden now — a 6 quart basket of beans on Sunday — Fred ate nothing but — I ate beets and carrots as well. We don't spend money on meat.

I must ask Chester behind us to come in for supper some day. He phoned to say Mabel was in hospital. High blood pressure. Soon as she's got something to go to or do she's OK, soon as she sits at home she's all tense with nerves.

I read Ethel Waters' story. Boy she sure had quite a life when young. I haven't a thing to write about, and what I wanted most to tell you I almost forgot. Thanks a million for the new slip. I love it and wear it for special. It sure is the nicest one I've ever owned. I hate to wear it under a dress it's so beautiful. You sure are good to me and I'll never be able to pay you back. Chester's in insurance too and he says business is getting harder and harder to find.

Love Ruby

Sept. 16/51

Dear Kay

I'm so excited about the coat you ordered for me. My first new coat since I've been married — 12 years. I've always wanted a Harris tweed and navy is just the color too cause most of my things are navy — least I've a navy hat and dress. And remember you're not paying for it. I am. I've exactly $74 in the bank so all I need extra is $1 and Fred can give me that.

Gee it's wonderful. I'm so thrilled cause I've kept thinking What will I wear this winter, I need a coat so badly. The grey one of yours you gave me is really too big, too long wasted and my coon that I've had since high school is as shabby as an old barn dog. But now, glory be, I'll be having a NEW one. When I get it and go to Western Alumnae dinner with Fred I won't feel ashamed. If only I had my B.A. too — how often I've wished I had that. I hope both my kids will one day get their's. I must tell them to concentrate hard and not let their minds run round in the cornfields like Mr. Muslin at London Collegiate said that mine did.

We've really been busy. I had the two school teachers in on Sunday for turkey and they gave us a pound of chocolates. Last nite Sally and I went to a mother and daughter banquet — she looked so cute in her middy. I washed this morning and baked 3 pies — wish you lived near us and I'd bring you one. This aft I made over slacks of mine for Sally and recovered her eider-down, this morning I cleaned, washed up the bathroom and kitchen and waxed floors. Now I'm tired and fat. Wish I were slim and figurey for my new coat.

Ethel Waters was a performer who sang and acted on New York stages.

Middy: A loose blouse with a square sailor collar worn by children, women and sailors.

I only hope it fits. But with measurements taken all round surely the salesgirl can tell the size I need — waist 28, chest 34, hip 37 (isn't that horrible?) sleeves 27, skirt length 43. I know a 16 is too big, even at my fattest I've never been a 16. A 14 should be just right, shouldn't it? I should be a 12.

Oh — I nearly forgot — the most important thing — Fred gets the cast off his broken ankel today. Beans, darn it, I wanted to take a picture of it but there's no sun and I've no film for the camera.

Love, Ruby

Jan. 10/53

Dear Jan

Gee whizz, kid, I sure was surprised to hear about your operation. I hope you're ok. Where was the lump and what happened? Nobody tells me anything. I've been having a tightness below my chest for ages and now for sure I'll go and have a checkup. I keep putting it off and now it's a little worse since I heard about you. I get terrible attacks of indigestion. Today I have the trots. I must get thinner, and I'll bet for sure I'll have to get specks cause my left eye twitches something awful. I'll let you know what the Dr. says. I've just made an appointment.

Haven't any news. I've been washing Sally's hair with proxide. I rinse it in vinegar, wash it in Vel. I'm trying everything to keep it fair. I'll only use proxide now and then, lemon once in awhile. It looks right pretty now. Her eyebrows are so shaped and her lashes are so black and curly, she looks kind of cute these days if I have to say so myself. She went skating with higher grades at school — skated with boys. And say, is she getting fussy — won't wear blue pants to match her dress any more cause the boys laugh and tease them should they happen to see their underpants. She'll be 12 next year. I guess I'll soon have to worry.

Billy came home today and said a kid was going to give him a puppy free when his dog had pups. Bill's so happy. Mary's a hound, brown and black, a gentle, sad-looking dog but very obedient. I don't know when the happy day will arrive. A dog — oh no — what will we do with a dog? I hope Mary's not pregnant.

The children go skating on the new rink behind the little store down the street it's a honey with two floodlights on it. They want to go at nite but we haven't let them. Maybe I'll go with them some nite, I haven't skated for years and will probably break my coxic.

Tonite is the Baby Band dance at the golf club — it should be fun but we're not going — $1.25 a person. It would be fun. The Rogers are going, Kath wants us to go, I haven't done anything but read and work for a long time. I read a story in Mabel's Ladies Home Journal — My Heart is in Hiding. It was good.

Love, Ruby

Feb. 2/53

Dear Kay

Glad you liked the pants I sent you, we'll celebrate your birthday by baking a cake for the joyful day, Sally wants to make it and I might let her.

There goes that Dickson dame with the high hips that knows you, she has on a green car coat, green shoes, red hat and Plad pants. Looks freeky.

Mother wrote us that you bought yourself a car. A pet. Is it really the smallest kind? Do you feel funny driving such a baby? Now you can come down to see us. We need a new one too, wish we could pick up a good second hand one. Fred's scouting around. I hope he hits a dandy like our old timer, she sure gave us little trouble but is using oil now and Fred's anxious to sell her. Wouldn't it be nifty to have a new car even if it's a second hand job? If only one can trust a car salesman — and they're such a price.

I'm having a bee this aft — 6 girls in to cut up rags for my rug. Fun, eh? They suggested it so I'm taking them up on it. Have to give them food but it will be well worth it to get rid of all the stuff I've got in bags upstairs. Must get going, their husbands are dropping them off here at 1 oclock.

I've written 5 letters this morning. I want to write to Over the Teacups in the Star to maybe win $25 but I don't know how to word it. I want to tell about a dame who was vaccuuming with her electrolux, had her budgie flying around the house and the first thing she knew the budgie was sucked up in the vacuum bag. She got him out, dusted him off and put him back in his cage no worse off. It's true. It happened right here in town. I'll split with you, dearie, if you write it up nifty. $25 would come in handy if we'd win.

Mother and Jan were both proud of Dave, both raved and sent clipping from the paper. I sent both back so mum could put them in her scrap book. I wish I could do something super to get into her scrap book — you and Dave sure get in plenty.

Sally's nuts about Anne of Green Gables and John loves Lassie that you gave them. They love reading, like you do. Maybe they'll do something famous and get in Mum's book even if I don't, eh?

Love, Ruby

Document 5.2
Claire Drainie Taylor

Swift Current

The voices of children are not often recorded. If they are recorded, they are seldom preserved, which makes the discovery of the first diary of seven-year-old Claire Brodbinger (later Drainie Taylor) a rare and special thing. Claire grew up in a middle-class Jewish-Canadian family in Regina, Saskatchewan, in the years after the Great War. She later worked as a radio/television actress and scriptwriter.

Issues to Consider

- What do we learn about a child's life in Western Canada during the tumultuous 1920s? Do we have any sense, through Claire's writing, of the larger world of her childhood? What sense do we get of her private world?
- How do we "see" her mother and father and their approach to their children through Claire's eyes? What more would we like to know about them that is not revealed in these excerpts?
- What do diaries and letters *not* tell us about private lives?

September 1924

Dear Diary: You are my frist one. My frend Minny Davidner gave you to me for my brithday. I am 7. My name is Claire Pearl Wodlinger. My muthr is Rose and my fathr is Hymy and my big bruthr is Jim and my litle one is David and my babe sisstr is Dorthy and that's all. I go to Centrl Scool. I am in grade 2. My best things I licke are speling, riting and reeding and not verry much arthmutic. My best thing at reecess is the maypol for swinging and if I haf muny for jah-brakrs. The dog of the candy stor lady has one blou eye and one is broun. If my best frend has a penny she givs me a jah-brakr. Her name is Mary Elen Hays. She has a litle bruthr to and he is Davids best frend. His name is Billy. Grampa Hays is very cross in the gardn. MaryElen issnt afrade of him but I am. Goodby.

September 1924

Dear Diary: My mothr sais you shood tell everthing to yore diary even if it is bad, And also if you think something. The bad thing I did was I toled Minny I was gowing to haf a party and she came but I didnt haf one and she brout me this diary and I took it withowt a party. And she had on a party dress. My mothr was mad wen I toled her but Minnys mothr sed I could keep the diary becus it was a mistaik and I rote in it anyway. And anyway Minny isnt my best frend. But I haf to taike her to a moving pitchr of Harld Loiyd and isecreem next Saterday for beeing bad. My other best pressant is a book The Tale of Henriette Hen. My Unkle David gave it to

Source: Claire Drainie Taylor, "Swift Current," in *The Surprise of My Life: An Autobiography* (Waterloo: Wilfrid Laurier University Press, 1998), 9–16.

me. I think I can reed most of it by myslef so it is my frist book. Yore suppost to rite all spechel things in a diary so if Im to bissy I dont haf to rite somthing. So some dais I wont. Mommy sais I can spell eny way I thinnk. Goodbye.

September 1924

Dear Diary: Dad got very mad at Jim today and a litl bit mad at me but David was to yung so Dad sed it wasnt his fawlt. What the trubble was we startd a fire on the grass on the mptee lot. Jim just wantd to start a litl fire but it went so fast in a big surcol and we got scard and ran for Dad. And he got the fire indjun becaus he culdnt stop it. The fireman sed the grass was so dry becaus no rain but Daddy spnked us for plaing with machs. My stumak aked becaus I was so scard and I fergot to pull my litl bruthr away from the fire. He ran away by hiself so I was lucky abowt that. I put this in here becaus it is speshel but I dont like it. I cant go to sleep becaus wen I close my eys I see the fire berning the grass and making it blak and are fense to. Jim and I wont play with machs any more in are liffe. Goodby.

October 1924

Dear Diary: If I think of speshuls from befor wen I didnt haf you can I put it in? Becaus my Daddy let me go to his stor and wasch him aftr scool and Saterdays. His store is for nales and cloth and kullard thred and strah hats and rubbr boots. And it has brumes and shuvels fly swatrs mowse traps candls pails and wurk overals and shurts and appels and flowr and a pile of othr stuff. I like to wasch him tye up the pakijes for peepl. The string coms down from on top but it starts at the cowntr and gose up frist. Som persons give Dad muny and som dont haf eny so Dad puts numbrs in a book. Somtims I see litl girls like me onlie they ware blak stokings and hie blak shoose. And hankkies on thare hedds and long skurts and sleevs even in sumer. And thare Mothrs to. Thare Fathrs have big blak hats and beerds. And the boys to but not eny beerds. They takkfuny to my Fathr but he takks the same to them. Daddy sais it is Jermin. It is anothr langwich. They are calld Mennunnites. They haf horses and buggees and the childern sit on a shelf on the bak. And they dont fall of. Goodby.

October 1924

Dear Diary: Daddy took Jim and me for a long wak all the way down Cenrtl Avenu to the stashun. We wasched the trane com in. The injun is verry big and blak and a mownten of steam. It made so mutch noys I hided behind Daddy but he wusnt afrade. Nobody got of. Daddy sais nobudy gets of in Swift Current they just get on. But we saw a trane man in a uniform and he was kullerd brown but he takkd to Daddy the way we do. He was a negrow. Daddy sed negrows dont live in Swift Current but they are just the same as peepl but thare skin is darkr. We were gettin cold so he took us to the Carlton Tea room for isecreem. Daddy sed we wont be abl to do that eny more this yeer becaus wintr is in the ayre. The Carlton has chares with thin wire legs and tabls to. And the seeling has tin flowrs in it. If you sit on a stul at the cownter if feels cold and smoothe. I like it most in Swift Current and the liberry. Goodby.

November 1924

Dear Diary: I fergot to tell you wen you wak down the hil on Centrl you come to the stors like my Daddys. And Coopers is the biggst and Levines is for mans close. And the Elite Cafe and the Canada cafe for eeting. Wigmores is for if you want to sew a dress or skurt and paterns and thred. 2 moving pitchrs called Lyruc and Eagle. And you go past Rooneys drug store and Erlys shoe store. Mummy takse me thare for blak pattant shoes and guloshis. They smell nice wen they are neiw. And Sykes music store and Beggs talors. And som more. Daddy and Mummy noe all those peepl. The sidewaks are sement whare the stors are but up the hill they are long peeces of wood with craks going down them. Wen you get up neer are howse you come to a mptee lot whare we had the fire and then us and then anothr mptee lot and one acros the street. And hier up is the convent. And then a farm howse but no farm. And then its the coollee. And if you want to wak some more its the sematary. Thats for ded peepl. o at Coopers store the muney gos in litl boxes that run arownd the stor and then com back agen. And the ladees close are in a mezzaneen. Goodby.

December 1924

Dear Diary: Mummy let me wasch her give a villin leson to a boy. If I kepped verry still and verry quite. His name is Oscar and he is 11. I like him. He is small and his hands to and his voiss but I like to hear him takk. But mostly he plays or Mum tells him things and then he plays some more. Like my pyano lesons onlie on the villin. My Mother is the best villin player in Swift Current and if they have a consert she plays on a stage and wares a pretty dress. And she plays for us after suppr somtimes only if we want to sing she plays sheet musick on are pyano. She even plays for dancis somtimes and Daddy stais home and wasches us. I think Mummy gets som muney for that. Becaus she gets us treets the next day. Are best treet so far was when she brot a choclot bar and we each got a scware. It was yummy. And one time chickletts which are gum. Goodby.

February 1925

Dear Diary: It was Valentine's day at our school. We make them in art. I made 14 for my frends but I onlie got 10. Mary Elen gave 18 and she got 20. But she is very nice. Now she thinks she should have sent 2 more. Enyway I dont have to wurry abowt that. We had a spelling bee and I came sekond. I got watch rong becaus it has a "t." Edith Muggelston came first. She is a good reeder and so am I. She is Sweedish so she has nice strate white hair and a very rownd voise. If we have vis-siters to our class Miss Hutchinson asks me to stand up and reed or eyether Edith. Goodbye.

July 1925

Dear Diary: Did you miss me? I broke my arm on a rock playing catch. So my arm was in a cast and I coudnt rite. It hurt a lot but I got to sleep in my mothers bed. I had to stop my pyano les-sons but I didn't mined that and enyway Daddy didnt have muney to pay for them. Then David broke his arm so I had to go back to my owne bed. One day I neerly got drounded becaus my arm was still in a sling and I was onlie suppost to go in the water to my nees so I was afrade to tell my Mom and Dad. You see I slipt in the mud and when I got upsidedown in the water I new I was drouning and I felt so sad. I rememberd all the lies I toled and beeng mean to David and Doro. I woke up on a bentch in the bath howse. I heurd one girl say were her eyes out of her head and sombody sed no but they were bullging. And a lady sed was she strugling and anuther girl sed no. They took of my wet bathing sute and put my dress on and I didnt have enything on underneeth. They wakked home with me but I sed I was fine so they woudnt come to are howse. I lied to my Mother and sed I lost my sute cause it got muddy by mistaik. I ate my supper and I went to bed erly. I didnt feel good Droudning is very scary. Goodbye.

September 1925

Dear Diary: Well I didnt have a party for my aith birthday but I got Grimms Fairy Tales and thats good. From my Unkle David. Mary Ellen my best frend has a diary to and she showd it to me so I showd her mine but maibe I wont agen. Its suppost to be privit if you want to say somthing if you dont want somebody to nowe abowt it. Mary Ellen puts in all day things and what time like 5.30 set the tabel. 6 o'clock ate diner but I think she means supper — dinner is on Sunday. 7 o'clock played hopscotch with Claire. My Mother sais Mary Ellen is verry orgenised like her Mother. Mommy sais Mrs. Hayes can do anything and her name is Ruth. She is Mothers best frend. So there are 3 best frends in there famly and also 3 in are famly. Isnt that funny. She can even drive thare car. It is a Star. They have a buntch of flowrs like sweet pees and bachler buttens becaus Mom sais Grampa Hayes lives in the gardn. My Grampas live in Selkurk. And my Grammas to. Mary Ellen has no Gramma but the best thing they have the books of Nowledje. I am aloud to look at them at thare howse but not to borro. 8 o'clock I'l go to bed now. I forgot to tell you wut I call my Grampas and Gramas Baba and Zada. Good night.

October 1925

Dear Diary: Heres a spechul thing but not verry nice. I had a tummy acke wen I was sleeping with Ant Gert and I went to the bathroom rite in bed and we both woke up and I gess she was mad at me. She kleened me up and made me sit on a chair in a blannkit and she changd the sheets but she didnt tok to me. I dont want her to tell my mothr but maibe she will. I didnt do it againe. Goodby. Sory.

December 1925

Dear Diary: We all got to go to a Honnica party. On top of Levines store. Us, Davidners Klings, Levines and some uthr famlys who go to Elmwould School. It was all dekrated blou and white and candls to. I got Anderson's Fairy Tales and I like them. For Crissmas I got skaits from Santa onlie thay are black with rust on them. And a Jap orange and nuts in my stoking. Mommy took me to the skaiting rinck and it was nice and cold and noysie and musick but I cept falling down and Mom cept holding me up but I coodnt skait. My Mother is a very good skaiter but not my fahter. It herts my ankels. Jim can skait and David on bob skaits. Daddy and I are the only ones. Goodbye. And Dorthy. Goodby agane.

March 1926

Dear Diary: We can't go to school or even outside. There is a teribble blisserd going on and some people get lost in the snow and then they freeze to deth. Our house is cold and Jim and I are to big for Docter Dentens sleepers so we sleep in our long underware and sox. And pijammas on top. Mom dosnt like it but she lets us. Doro and David can ware them cause thare small till they get to big. They have feet and they are soft and cosy and they smell nice. We have a bath on every Sat. night and then we get cleen underware. And I get a cleen vest with long garters for sholding up my stokings. They are very hard to put on over the underware and I always get bumps. But I'm lurning to do up the garters myself. For my cleen middy blows I have to butten on the navy bloue kollar and sometimes I get mad at it but then Mummy or Daddy helps me. My navy bloue skurt is pleetd with a vest on it that goes over my head sown on. It takes me a long time to dress in winter. And poor Mommy has to do a hole lot of washing or if we have a made they both do it. In a big coppr boyler on the stove and a long stick for mooving the close around. And blooing for making the close white. Isnt that funny? Goodbye. I forgot to tell you when you bring the close in of the line and they are frosen stiff I love the smell of them. I gess its the best smell in the world so far.

March 1926

Dear Diary: It got a little warmer so we tryed to go back to school but we had to come home agen. Here is why. I got stuck in the mud on the emtee lot and my foot came out of my galosh and I was balluncing on one foot and Jim was tring to get my gulosh on and he coodnt and we both fell over in the mudd and slush. It was so slippry and mukky we coold hardly get up. Mother was very mad at us because she toled us not to go throu the emtee lot even if it is a short cut. But I gess we lookd funny because after she got mad she started to lagh reely hard. So Jim and I got a xtra bath on a Wensday. The mudd is stikky as glu. So then we playd our new records. Mine is called Maid of the Mountain. It is so big you have to wind the victrola 2 and a half times. My Dad brout it to me from Winnipeg. And Valencia for Jim but its just one time winding and a cupple more turns. Mommy got a beutiful evning dress with beads and some tafeta lamp shades for there bedroom. And he brout some good things to eat. 1. corn beef. 2. rye bread. 3. hallva thats like fudje but not brown. 4. musslinnas there black salty ollivs. 5. Winnipeg gold eyes. Thats a good kind of fish. And we all got to taste everthing. We had fun like a picnick but in the dining room. Swift Current dosnt have those things. But Dad says Winnipeg has everthing. It is a city in Canada near Selkirk. But we have the same king and Queen. Bye now.

Topic 6

Regulating Sexuality:
The Moral, the "Normal," and the Deviant

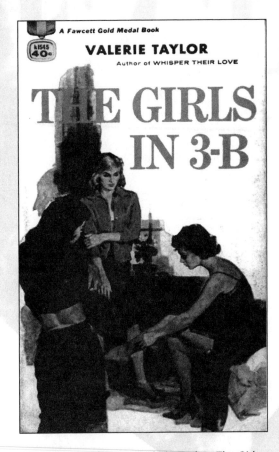

Paperback book cover, Valerie Taylor, *The Girls in 3-B* (Greenwich: Fawcett World Library Publications, 1959); Lesbian Pulp Fiction Collection, Mount Saint Vincent University Library, Halifax, Nova Scotia, www.msvu.ca/english/pulp/.

CONTEXT

The discussion of gender and family history leads into the history of sexuality: much of what defines prevailing gender ideals also constitutes the basis for the "norms" regarding human sexuality. The material in Topic 5 showed how attempts to regulate private relations, including reproduction, appealed to many reform groups, testifying to the depth of middle-class anxiety about the "crisis in the family" that appeared to be unfolding during the early 20th century. Building on its earlier temperance foundations, especially through the efforts of the Woman's Christian Temperance Union, the prohibition movement targeted "depraved" immigrant and working-class homes, encouraging facile correlations between class, race, and sexual immorality. Reformist interest in eugenics, a pseudo-science that distorted Darwinian theory and promoted "selective breeding" to ensure the survival of the fittest, also led to anti-contraception campaigns, since family limitation was perceived to be largely a practice of the "better stock," or precisely those who should be reproducing. Eugenicists supported crusades to restrict marriage by raising the legal age, requiring medical examinations, and tightening licensing; an avowedly pro-natalist infant welfare movement; and proposals for the segregation and sterilization of the "unfit." "Unfit" became a medical/moral classification applied to any number of people who were found to be morally deviant, largely because of alleged departures from the established middle-class moral code that made anything other than heterosexual relations, sanctified in legal marriage and primarily for the purposes of procreation, quite simply outside the norm.

If sexuality is still very much a subject in the inaugural stages of historical study in Canada, even more so is the study of same-sex relations. As Valerie Korinek points out in her essay in this section, much like historians of women, the working class, race and ethnicity, and so on, the early practitioners in this research area were motivated by the absence of their subjects in the historical literature. The recent politicization of gay rights movements has also generated a new attention to the history of homosexuality and lesbianism. Whichever aspect of sexuality is pursued historically, much of the literature on courtship, marriage, and sex in the past, in Canada as elsewhere, is concerned more with public expectations, regulatory campaigns, and social constructions of the normal than with actual practices. This is largely explained by the specific challenges that historians face in locating sources — especially behavioural evidence — about the most private of all social relations. Recent analytical trends in historical writing, as in other subject areas, have pointed the historical study of sexuality in the direction of discourse and representation more so than practice or behaviour. Discourse analysis focuses critical attention on the assumptions that are made, both by our historical actors and by historians themselves, regarding the universality, or "norm," of heterosexuality. The normative language that was used in advice manuals, in the journals and writings of professionals in medicine and psychology, and in the print media cannot be taken to describe existing practices so much as to promote the values of the dominant class, and to shape ideas and behaviour to meet its standards for the ideal Canadian citizen: in short, it was prescriptive rather than descriptive.

As noted in a number of previous topics, Michel Foucault's influence dominated the 1990s historiography on sexuality. By placing power at the centre of private as well as social relations, he turned attention to the formidable "heterosexual matrix" of class, race, gender, and sexuality that establishes and upholds the norm by means of regulation and disciplinary action, even if only through social disapproval — for many, a high enough price to pay for any "deviation." But historians are quick to point out that regulation was not simply "done to" a passive social group (whether women, immigrants, youth, or the working class) by those intent on enforcing their moral standards (whether reformers, state agencies, the police, or the new caste of modern "experts" in medicine, psychology, and social work). Given the intensely private nature of sexuality, there is much scope for resistance, modification, rejection, or even conscious and willing acceptance of those standards by the target group.

Early 20th-century constructions of normal sexuality inspired campaigns promoting "social purity," or "the white life for two." Social purity activists invoked the state's duty to enter the bedrooms of the nation in the interests of a regenerated society based on traditional family and gender relations, and especially on feminine morality, even while they criticized the double standard that turned a blind eye to male promiscuity. The Society for the Protection of Women and Children used such arguments to influence the 1892 amendments to the Criminal Code, which elaborated a comprehensive system of offences to protect the sexual innocence of women and enforce a stringent code of sexual behaviour. Abortion, contraception, and "seduction" were criminalized. Homosexual acts were now designated as "gross indecency." The law's protection from sexual violence and exploitation was clearly beneficial to women, but it was underwritten by unrelenting traditional notions about their biologically decreed moral superiority and maternal vocation. The overall result, therefore, was conservative and repressive, allowing very little scope for female sexuality.

Advice literature premised on social purity ideals was already circulating widely before World War I. The best-selling "Self and Sex" series was produced by doctors and Protestant clergy, with each of its eight volumes directed to specific age groups and one or the other sex exclusively. These advice manuals stressed the importance of restricting sexuality for the sake of personal health and healthy reproduction, hence "racial" or national health. Especially during the war years, much emphasis was placed on the prevention of venereal disease, doubly a scourge in that it was transmitted by indulgence in immoral activity and was also incurable and could be passed to the next generation. Ominous euphemisms such as "solitary vice" and "self-abuse" also equated masturbation with waste and corruption, at once sources and symptoms of moral and physical decay that would probably lead to dissipation, insanity, and early death. By this time as well, medical professionals and social critics were paying closer attention to the "evils" of "unnatural" same-sex relationships. The medical author of *What a Young Girl Ought to Know* warned that "fondling and gushing" among adolescent girls might lead to a "weakening of moral fibre" and the degeneration of friendship into "a species of self-abuse."

During the interwar years, similar types of advice literature were increasingly produced and disseminated by provincial and federal health departments, as the state became more involved in the "sex hygiene" of its citizens, especially the adolescents on their way to marriage and parenthood. While lectures and classroom talks were heard by thousands of young Canadians, school boards across the land were reluctant to place sex education in the regular curriculum until the 1950s. Even then, the "normal" remained as traditionally defined, with instruction focused on promoting marriage and postponing sex until that time. Homosexuality remained a "problem" that could scarcely be addressed, and certainly not directly. Not until the liberation of sexuality from reproduction with the advent of the Pill, and the emergence of new ideas and behaviour in the 1960s, would such rigid norms be challenged. Both contraception and homosexuality were finally removed from the Criminal Code in 1969.

REFERENCES/FURTHER READING

Adams, M. L. *The Trouble with Normal: Postwar Youth and the Making of Heterosexuality*. Toronto: University of Toronto Press, 1997.

Cassels, J. *The Secret Plague: Venereal Disease in Canada, 1838–1939*. Toronto: University of Toronto Press, 1987.

Dubinsky, K. *Improper Advances: Rape and Heterosexual Conflict in Ontario, 1880–1929.* Chicago: University of Chicago Press, 1993.

Foucault, M. *The History of Sexuality.* New York: Pantheon, 1984.

Kinsman, G. *The Regulation of Desire.* 2nd ed. Montreal: Black Rose Books, 1996.

Loo, T., and C. Strange. *Making Good: Law and Moral Regulation in Canada, 1867–1939.* Toronto: University of Toronto Press, 1997.

———. *True Crime, True North: The Golden Age of Canadian Pulp Magazines.* Vancouver: Raincoast Books, 2004.

McLaren, A., and A. Tigar McLaren. *The Bedroom and the State: The Changing Practices and Politics of Contraception and Abortion in Canada, 1880–1997.* Toronto: Oxford University Press, 1997.

Sangster, J. *Regulating Girls and Women: Sexuality, Family, and the Law in Ontario, 1920–1960.* Toronto: Oxford University Press, 2001.

Ward, P. *Courtship, Love and Marriage in Nineteenth-Century English Canada.* Montreal and Kingston: McGill-Queen's University Press, 1990.

Warner, Tom. *Never Going Back: A History of Queer Activism in Canada.* Toronto: University of Toronto Press, 2002.

ILLUSTRATION 6.1 (P. 227)

The history of "pulp fiction"— cheap, mass-produced, sensationalist novels adorned by lurid covers such as the one shown in Illustration 6.1 — dates back to the "penny dreadfuls" of the 19th century. By the 1950s, pulp fiction had established its market, and stories that adhered to a formulaic storyline were immensely popular. Written by both men and women, the lesbian series is simply a twist on the classic heterosexual "romance" novel. It is impossible to know the sexual orientation of the authors; nor can we assume that only lesbians read the books. In any case, they must have provided a rare source of identification for those readers during a time when heterosexual marriage and the ideal wife/mother were glorified.

Issue to Consider

- Pulp fiction covers are notoriously lurid. What gender and sexual images are evident in Illustration 6.1? How does this pulp fiction cover both reflect and subvert the "norm"?

ARTICLES

Both articles in this section employ a form of discourse analysis to uncover prevailing ideas/ideals about sexuality before and after marriage, about "normal" gender and sexual behaviour, and about the ways in which some women and men nonetheless managed to resist — even if only in small ways — their own regulation, while others conformed to social pressures. Catherine Gidney discusses the regulatory capacity of educational institutions in the past, including those (such as universities) whose subjects were an elite group of young adults in a transitional life stage that took many of them away from the watchful eye of parents, family, and community. Valerie Korinek considers how the leading Canadian women's magazine, the venerable *Chatelaine*, promoted the circulating ideals of womanhood, marriage, and family, but also, surprisingly, left a little space for more subversive elements that hinted at other possibilities for feminine social and sexual fulfillment.

Article 6.1

Catherine Gidney

Under the President's Gaze: Sexuality and Morality at a Canadian University During the Second World War

Issues to Consider

- Gidney frames her discussion around the story of one student, whose "indiscreet" private correspondence brought about the intervention of university administrators. How does his story represent the major issues underlying the larger subjects of youth, constructions of the "normal," sexuality, and regulation?
- As Gidney considers them, what were public expectations of Canadian youth during the World War II years, and more particularly of those in university? Why was there social anxiety about young people at this time?
- How does Gidney characterize the prevalent ideas regarding youth sexuality?
- What role did age play in influencing the universities' understanding of their relationship with their students? In what ways did age facilitate the methods that they devised to mould their "character," especially in regard to sexuality?
- How did educators of the time justify intrusive — or, as Gidney categorizes them, "coercive"— methods to ensure a certain standard of behaviour on campus?
- How does Gidney link psychology, citizenship, and Christianity within the context of concerns about the social development of youth during this time?

During the Second World War, Johann Schmidt, a young man recently released from an internment camp, entered one of Canada's many universities still holding denominational affiliation.[1] Alone in a new culture and living amid strangers, Schmidt wrote to a companion in the camp. Following their mandate, immigration officials vetted the correspondence of the friends. Schmidt's letter contained the usual chitchat: inquiries as to how his friend was doing and when he would be released from the camp. The letter also reported on Schmidt's experiences in residence, in particular the way in which college boys wasted their time, the immaturity of some students who had not been through what he had, and his delight at having an intelligent and friendly roommate. There were, however, two items in the letter which alarmed immigration officials. First, Schmidt's letter to his friend expressed a general appreciation for the male body. Second, having worked on a farm the summer before, as part of the war effort, Schmidt expressed his determination in the coming summer not to take a "steady job," but to work on successive farms as it suited him. Concerned about the moral fibre of the student, in terms of both his sexuality and his apparent laziness, the director of the Immigration Branch, F. C. Blair, wrote to the president of the university, and a secretive investigation into the student's character ensued.[2]

A number of historians have documented how Canadian universities have traditionally tried to regulate student behaviour and mores. In the nineteenth and early twentieth centuries, residences recreated the Christian home, university presidents and faculty expected Christian

Source: Catherine Gidney, "Under the President's Gaze: Sexuality and Morality at a Canadian University During the Second World War," *Canadian Historical Review* 82, no. 1 (2001): 36–54.

deportment, and chapel services and religious knowledge courses reinforced the role of religion on campus.[3] Little is known, however, of the extent to which Christian ideals shaped university students after the First World War.[4] Moreover, the work that has been done on the process of character formation and the creation of moral norms in modern Canada — a literature focusing on the family, motherhood, and sexuality — has tended to ignore the role of religion in shaping these concepts.[5] This article seeks to reveal the way in which, for many educators, religious imperatives continued to inform evolving conceptions about morality and sexuality well into the twentieth century.

While the Schmidt case provides an illustration of the use of direct coercion to maintain "proper" deportment on campus, it must be understood within the broader project of creating Christian citizens. The middle decades of the century were a particularly anxious time for Canadians because of the disruption of traditional social and moral norms. Students had been pushing the boundaries of acceptable behaviour through the interwar period. The trend from single-sex socialization to co-ed activities, and from the surveillance of parlour courtship to a more anonymous culture of dating, led to the notion of sex for pleasurable consumption and marked the development of a new heterosexual culture.[6] Fears about students' sexual purity merged with concerns during the Second World War about the increase of divorce rates, venereal disease, juvenile delinquency, and the growing number of women in the workforce, resulting in a general anxiety about the stability of the family and in calls for the moral regeneration of society.[7]

Universities were one site where social and cultural values could be moulded. Although universities were each shaped by their own set of traditions — in this particular case the university was a small, urban, Protestant institution — by the twentieth century they also promoted certain common ideals. University administrators, for example, believed their institutions had a central role to play in the moral guardianship and training of Canada's future leaders. Although expectations of comportment were rarely laid out clearly, glimpses may be seen in residence rules or the reaction to an occasional lapse in good behaviour. Explicit references to students' sexual behaviour are even more limited. Indeed, presidents' reports, university correspondence, and even student newspapers generally avoided discussing sexual conduct.

One exception to this silence was the 1941 Hazen Conference on religion and life. In the face of growing concern over the moral fibre of Canada's youth, faculty, presidents, and deans of women from across English Canada convened to determine how to secure the proper development of Canadian students. Offering one of the rare glimpses into the views of university administrators on sexuality, the conference provides context for the Schmidt case and suggests that universities generally attempted to educate students and mould their conduct. Only in rarer cases, when educational methods failed, did coercion ensue.[8]

In the context of increased societal fears over moral and sexual transgressions by Canadian youth, it is not surprising that, when the president was sent a copy of Schmidt's letter, he immediately became distraught. Two issues were of particular concern: Schmidt's sexual references to other men and his attitude towards work. In his letter, Schmidt reminded his friend of a mutual acquaintance whose body he particularly admired. He went on to say that, while he still liked this acquaintance, he no longer thought of him as an ideal. Since he had been released from the internment camp, he related, he had met a new boy whose body he admired. Yet he also worried over his reaction, feeling that he liked this boy's body "too much." As Schmidt wrote to his friend: "I was a bit afraid that my experiences and impressions in camp might have an influence on my sex life or rather attitude towards sex. However lately this trouble seems to disappear more and more, nevertheless I have to be a bit careful still in my thoughts and also my actions. Naturally nobody out here respects anything of that kind. It would be the last thing people think of. In the opposite, I am getting a reputation of being very interested in girls which by the way is quite true." Schmidt's letter suggests a young man attempting to understand and cope with his own sexuality. There is no explicit evidence of sexual relations, though certainly his writing is suggestive in its admiration for the male body. He was clearly worried about the effect of his camp experiences on his sexual conduct and believed that his feelings or experiences in the internment camp broke the moral or sexual codes of the university. Keeping his own activities in check would protect his reputation. So, too, would the fact that homosexuality was something few people knew about on campus. Ultimately, he believed, his reputation was secure through a genuine interest in girls.

Schmidt's letter raised further concerns because of his attitude towards summer work. Canadian students were being asked to work on farms as their part in the war effort, and the Immigration Branch felt that refugee students should be similarly employed. Attempting to remain in good standing with the branch, Schmidt had asked for permission to work on a farm. After spending a month with the university's Canadian Officers' Training Corps (COTC) contingent, he expected to perform farm work, as he had the previous year. However, in his letter to his friend he wrote: "This summer I shall probably be working on a farm again but it will be much nicer. I won't take a steady job but just work till I do not like it any more and then go on to another place. It will be different now that I have friends here."

When Blair learned about Schmidt's letter, he immediately sent it on to the president. In a covering letter, Blair spent little time discussing Schmidt's sexual proclivities. There was, it seems, an assumption that the president would immediately recognize Schmidt's sexual transgressions and that these did not need to be delineated. Instead, Blair focused on Schmidt's questionable work ethic. Since Schmidt had already asked to work on a farm, Blair was irritated by what he perceived to be a whimsical attitude towards work.

The university and the broader Canadian community expected students, who were privileged not to be at the war front, to be serious and upright members of the community in both their social activities and their military training. As a result, student activities such as sports, social functions, and initiations at universities across Canada were limited by the faculty and the students themselves.[9] Those recreational activities that were allowed were expected to be frugal, simple, and quiet.[10] When the war broke out in 1939, dormant units of the COTC quickly re-formed.[11] Military training was initially voluntary, but by the fall of 1940 it entailed six hours a week of compulsory military training during the academic year and two weeks at the end of the year at spring camp.[12] By mid-war, women were also compelled to participate in war work. Although some women volunteered for military drill through the university Canadian Red Cross Corps, most took classes such as child care, first aid, or auto mechanics, and engaged in practical work such as knitting socks for the troops overseas.[13] Having fulfilled their military training, male students who remained in good academic standing could continue to the end of their undergraduate program without being called up.[14] Students attempting to evade military training were threatened either with having their grades withheld or, more seriously, with conscription.[15] [...]

With students expected to take their academic activities and contributions to the war effort seriously, Blair felt offended by Schmidt's cavalier attitude to work. He had only one recommendation for Schmidt: if the president dismissed him, "we will return him to the refugee camp and keep him there until he can be sent back to where he came from." Blair's harshness towards Schmidt was not an isolated incident. Although the Immigration Branch fell under the jurisdiction of the Department of Mines and Resources, Blair, rather than the elderly minister, Thomas Crerar, made and enforced much of the immigration policy when the Liberals came into power after 1935. He reflected the anti-immigration policies of the times, but historians have also argued that he rigidly enforced, and indeed strengthened, these policies against "undesirable" immigrants.[16] Department of Immigration bureaucrats had traditionally "carried out a clandestine and illegal immigration selection process, and deported immigrants according to their own informal and extralegal system of justice."[17] As part of this system, and as a result of his personal sense of responsibility for preserving the character of Canada, Blair personally scrutinized the documents and qualities of every potential immigrant. Schmidt, then, was only one individual who fell under Blair's scrutiny.[18]

At first the president's reaction was the same as Blair's: Schmidt had failed "to appreciate either the moral standards or the obligations which he should have assumed after release" and should be dismissed. The president ascribed Schmidt's moral lapses to his European background. Implying that Europeans had lower sexual standards than North Americans, the president claimed that Schmidt had "to be judged by European rather than by Canadian standards." Yet, even so, the president felt he could not afford such lapses in college residence, especially since he believed that a homosexual could, as he phrased it, "turn others." Despite the fact that several weeks later he had still not talked to Schmidt, the president continued to believe that he was a "real Problem." Apparently the president did not want to interview the student until officials from the Immigration Branch were ready to pick the boy up because, on the advice of the local RCMP, he believed that "such an interview would almost certainly result in his leaving college and taking to the open road." Moreover, while the president had "found no evidence that he has spread vicious practices," he still felt that "the evidence being what it is, he cannot return to college here."

The president directly linked sexual transgression with a lack of general moral soundness and also felt that Schmidt's moral lapses explained the young man's reluctance to take steady work during the summer. Ironically, the president understood that Blair would be acting not on the grounds of the student's "moral turpitude," but on the basis of his "hypocrisy." At the beginning of the correspondence between the president and Blair, then, Schmidt was to be returned to the camp because of his laziness rather than any sexual transgression.

Yet the president was also worried about the effect that returning Schmidt to camp would have on him. While he believed that "such persons" should not be allowed to immigrate to Canada, he was concerned that the "return of the boy to camp may only increase the temptation to and the opportunities for the vices of which he boasts." Moreover, he contended that the student's letter indicated that he had the potential to recover from his moral lapse. He was anxious not to send Schmidt off without a kind word, fearing that the experience might destroy "all hope of his return to normal living." Despite his optimism for Schmidt's future moral rectitude, the president also believed he had a duty to protect the moral fibre of his students. Good character was needed both for participation in the university community and for citizenship, and it was the president's unofficial duty to foster it. Faulty character could not be tolerated and, indeed, justified deportation.

Surveillance of youth was not new to wartime. Students in residence traditionally faced a variety of rules that they often enforced themselves. Women, in particular, endured strict curfews, restrictions that were linked to the belief in the need to preserve their moral character and sexual purity.[19] Men, while given more freedom, were prohibited from gambling or drinking and were constantly reminded of standards of dress and comportment.[20] Still, moral and sexual restraints were loosening during the interwar years. As Paul Axelrod discovered for the 1930s, students attended a multitude of dances, holding them off campus if they were prohibited at denominational institutions.[21] Students also began discussing sexual issues and holding lectures on birth control and preparation for marriage.[22] Administrators' acceptance of such topics was not always forthcoming. In the late 1920s the Social Sciences Club at the University of British Columbia held a debate on birth control. Despite the fact that the club had engaged a local minister to give the proceedings a high moral tone, the Board of Governors gave the club a dressing down for having brought unfavourable publicity to the campus.[23]

The holding of dances as well as lectures on birth control attests to the fact that university students were beginning to take a more open approach towards heterosexual activity. Compared with their counterparts in the United States, however, Canadian students pushed gently at the boundaries of moral and sexual propriety. While American surveys of college students in the 1930s illustrate a high level of sexual experimentation, Axelrod has found in interviews with graduates that there was a greater degree of sexual restraint among Canadian students. He argues that this moderation was due at least in part to the continuing influence of denominational colleges.[24] Sexual and moral purity was expected of students at both denominational and non-denominational universities and was enforced in a number of ways, such as through residence rules and the censorship of club activities.

Expectations of a wholesome campus also extended to students' intellectual and political endeavours. For example, during the 1930s, when an editor of the University of Toronto *Varsity* described the campus as seething with atheism, the editor lost his job and the paper was suspended.[25] Such action on the part of the administration indicates, among other things, the continuing understanding of the university as a Christian institution.[26] Administrators were not the only ones concerned about the tone of campus activities. Through much of the twentieth century the RCMP kept an eye on the Student Christian Movement and other left-wing campus groups believed to be involved in radical activities and to have Communist ties.[27]

If surveillance addressed breaches of proper moral conduct, the task of educators was also to provide students with the tools to attain sexual and moral maturity. As Canadians grew concerned about the moral regeneration of their society, educators took the opportunity to attempt to understand the needs of Canada's youth and create strategies to ensure youth's proper development. The First Canadian Hazen Conference, which, in 1941, brought together educators who were not only involved in personal counselling but concerned about the place of religion in higher education, was one such attempt.[28] The conference drew a variety of English Canadian educators from both religious and secular universities. Deans of women such as Marion Grant of Acadia and Marion Ferguson of University College attended. Christian activists and senior scholars such as Gregory Vlastos and Martyn Estall of Queen's University and R. B. Y. Scott of McGill University, all active during the 1930s in the left-wing Fellowship for a Christian Social Order, were also there. Other professors had, as students, been involved in the Student Christian Movement: the psychologist J. Davidson Ketchum, for example, and Norman MacKenzie, the president of the University of New Brunswick and, later, of the University of British Columbia.

The conference report stated that, because students arrived at university in late adolescence, and not as fully formed adults, the purpose of liberal education should be to address the whole person — the social and physical side as well as the intellectual. Universities, it contended, needed to pay more attention to four aspects of students' development: emotional independence from their family, engagement in heterosexual relations, the discovery of a vocation, and acceptance of a philosophy of life.[29] Each element was important in and of itself, but all were necessary if the student was to become a well-adjusted adult.

This lengthy and detailed Hazen report makes explicit many of the assumptions in the correspondence between Blair and the president. The report began by placing much of the blame for students' emotional immaturity on their families. Most parents, it contended, had failed to wean their children fully before sending them to university. Children who had not been taught to be independent, who did not feel secure in the love of their parents, who had been overprotected, or who had either too much or not enough discipline became homesick and hysterical at university, or broadcast their insecurity and attempted to assert their independence by throwing "conventions to the winds" and trying "to be tough and wild."[30] The family, and then the schools, had a responsibility to create self-directed, self-controlled, and self-reliant children. Only by stimulating a critical mind, the report argued, could students become full members of society.[31]

The Hazen report reiterated beliefs common among Protestants. The family formed the basis of Christian society. Yet with young men and women away in the services or working in recently expanded war industries, with the increase of divorce and drinking, venereal disease and juvenile delinquency, as well as the continuing poor housing and health conditions in Canada, the stability of the family lay in question.[32] This crisis in family life, many believed, foretold the ruin of Canadian society. Such concerns during the war anticipated investigations in the postwar period, such as those by the Canadian Youth Commission, in which educators and civil servants explicitly linked family life to active citizenship, national stability, and the preservation of democracy. As one late 1940s report stated, "If democracy is to be a reality in community and national affairs, it obviously must begin in the home."[33] The family was increasingly perceived as the cradle of democracy, where a child's independence could be carefully nurtured or just as easily squashed by an authoritarian or neglectful parent.[34]

As the Hazen report forewarned in the early war years, parents could not always be counted upon to provide children with the necessary tools to participate fully in the community. Nor were Canadian universities providing adequate services for students with emotional problems. The Student Health Services of American universities should be adopted in Canada.[35] Dealing with students' emotional problems, the report stated, was part of the role of a liberal education, and guidance was needed "for the student to achieve personal values in any adequate fashion." It was the responsibility of the university to aid the student's development "as a person."[36]

Ensuring proper sexual development was, in the Hazen report, part of this responsibility. Drawing on Freudian terminology, the conference report saw the sexual development of youth as progressing through various stages, culminating in maturity through heterosexual union.[37] It stated that adjustment to the opposite sex was usually far from complete in boys and girls entering college and that, in fact, completion could only be reached in "a happy marriage." "If adolescents do not accept their characteristic sex role during the years of middle and late adolescence," the report went on, "they may never do so." The few students who arrived with no interest in the opposite sex were either exhibiting "delayed maturity" or had "deep-seated emotional problems" that could cripple their development. Yet those interested in the opposite sex also had problems to face. Dating, petting, masturbation, continence, selecting a mate, and adjusting to marriage were all issues that had to be faced. Few were equipped, the report continued, to handle "the psychological aspects of sex and marriage."[38] Clearly, the conference participants linked proper adjustment to family life, a connection that Schmidt's letter failed to embody. [...]

While the report's section on heterosexual relations used psychological language to understand proper sexual conduct, comments about sexual adjustment cannot be taken out of the broader context of the conference report. Historians have tended to describe the early twentieth century, especially within the university, as an era marked by a shift from moral concerns to social scientific ones.[39] But the use of psychological language took place within broader moral assumptions, particularly Christian ones. The Hazen Conference is a good example of the slippage between a continuing ideal of moral guardianship and the expertise of a trained set of professionals (psychiatrists, psychologists, health services) whom the university would increasingly come to rely upon.[40]

For the conference participants, sexuality was embedded in broader ideals about citizenship and Christianity. Students needed not only to reach sexual maturity but also to learn self-reliance, independence, discipline, and self-control.[41] Sexual development could be achieved through courses on sex and marriage, greater opportunities for healthy interaction between the sexes in, for example, student-run extracurricular activities, and a more progressive educational system that would encourage the critical thinking ideally begun within the home.[42] The end purpose of all this development in the university was an ethic of service. Students, educators argued, needed to become active participants in the community. Their technical or professional training was the tool that a liberal education could teach them to put to use in service to society. The concept of the socially minded citizen was, of course, a useful one for the state during a time of war, but one that also had a long history within the Christian tradition.

The conference participants clearly perceived the personal physiological and psychological needs and desires of adolescents to be part of the broader need to find purpose in life or universal principles they could follow. This search for a "philosophy of life" was presented as an open one, without ties to a particular religion,[43] though it was clearly rooted in Christian ideals. If the end of university development was service, this was, the conference report stated, also the cornerstone of Christianity.[44] "One of the chief reasons why university education is not a liberating process for students is that it often negates the New Testament verse — 'He that saveth his life shall lose it, and he that loseth his life shall save it.' No one can find full self-expression and full freedom except in so far as he freely gives himself in service for others. This is not preaching — it is merely good psychology."[45] For the Hazen Conference on religion and life, psychology and Christianity reinforced each other, at least on broad social values.

Such sentiments were generally expressed within Canadian universities. Increasingly during the twentieth century, administrators shared both purpose and rhetoric. As Patricia Jasen states, "by the interwar period, presidents and principals of most universities in English Canada had developed a common style of speech and policy-making which emphasized the service function of their institutions."[46] Such commonalities arose out of the predominance of two particular intellectual strands. During the first decades of the twentieth century, educators were influenced by social gospel ideals and philosophical idealism. The social gospel, with its imperative to create the Kingdom of God on earth, and the idealist emphasis on the interconnectedness of reality and life, gave credence to the notion that all should be active participants in the community. Indeed, before the First World War, this notion helped fuel the development of the social sciences out of which psychology emerged.[47] As the Hazen Conference indicates, psychology had an influence on religious thought.[48] Yet the notion of personality development also arose out of a more liberal theology. William McGuire King suggests that, in the American context, the concept of "personality" was central to the social gospel. "The fundamental claim of the social gospel," he contends, was the belief "... that religious self-realization manifests itself as a religious enthusiasm for humanity."[49]

Linking psychological language, philosophical idealism, and the ethic of service, Robert Falconer, the president of the University of Toronto in the 1930s, stated, "the University is at once a source of individual culture and of public service. It deepens and enriches personality, and through the enriched personality of its members it can be a servant of the whole nation."[50] This emphasis on the importance of social citizenship and service to the nation was heightened during the Second World War. Falconer's successor, H. J. Cody, reassured students in 1941 that their studies were part of their "preparation to serve the state in this time of grave national crisis" and that it was through the production of "trained and educated men and women" that the university served the country.[51] These prominent educators were drawing on liberal theology as well as on the language of the new social sciences in emphasizing their vision of the role of the student and the university in society.

For many administrators, then, the need to defend the nation was not simply a secular service. The roots of democracy, many argued, were Christian.[52] Students needed to enter the work world realizing that they had "duties to God and man as citizens of a democratic community."[53] Students in college were expected to search for both intellectual and spiritual values to ground their life in the eternal, for it was only as individuals recognized and incorporated the divine spirit into their lives that society could reach a higher level.[54] Indeed, their duty would continue in the postwar years. "The task of you and your generation," one commentator told graduating students in 1945, "is to re-establish a civilization based upon the supremacy of intellectual, moral and spiritual values. This is the task for which men of our nation, men of this college, and men of your year have given their lives. By the sacrifice of their lives they have increased your responsibility."[55]

The connection between Christianity, democracy, and service was also forcefully articulated within the Protestant press. Where educators focused on the role of students in Canadian society, commentators in the popular Christian press linked education to broader world issues. For them, improper education resulted in the "barbarism and brutality"[56] not only of Nazi Germany but also of Communist Russia, a theme that would become particularly prominent in the postwar period. Democracy could only be renewed through a strong spiritual life,[57] and many considered "the highest standards of democracy" to be "the standards of Christian living."[58] Only through a proper education melding faith and duty would students recognize their responsibility to use their abilities to ensure peace and liberty.[59] Thus private faith and public endeavour intertwined on the university campus. University students were envisioned as the natural leaders of the nation, and, as such, they were being prepared in the university not only for service to their country but for a Christian service. To become active participants in Canadian society, educators believed, university students should ideally be educated in "the home, the church, the school, [and] the university."[60] The home and church would provide the roots for healthy growth, and the university would allow the spirit to blossom so that students could enter the workforce, create a family of their own, and contribute to the prosperity of the country.

Yet not all students fit within this version of productive citizenship. A month after writing the letter to his friend, Johann Schmidt found himself charged with, as he stated, "the intention of violating rules by the Director of Immigration and also with an immoral behaviour, to be more explicit, with homosexuality." In an attempt to defend himself, Schmidt acknowledged that his letter showed him "in a very bad light," but maintained he was not guilty of the charges. He presented three main arguments in his defence. First, he contended it had not occurred to him that his statements about liking men could be understood in an ambiguous manner, as anything other than friendship. Second, he stated he had written the letter late at night, had been depressed, and had been reading an author who described "similar feelings" and explained them as "unconsciously sexual and as a development of the adolescent stage of boyhood." Thus, contradicting his first defence, Schmidt in some sense admitted to fearing he was sexually attracted to men. But he also contended that he had never been engaged sexually with a man; "that anybody could suspect me of such immorality," he said, "makes me blush." Finally, Schmidt argued that if inquiries into his moral conduct were made, he would be found to be an upright individual. He challenged his investigators to make inquiries of the men in the internment camp, his professors at the university, his roommate, and the women in the female residence. As he stated, "Girls appeal very much to me.... I only went steady with a girl in my first term and in my second term I took many girls out but did not go steady." Before the Second World War, casual dating was the norm and indicated popularity.[61] Schmidt, then, used the notion of a vigorous heterosexuality as proof of his good moral conduct.

Schmidt also explained what he had meant in reference to changing jobs. He considered himself a conscientious worker and argued that the farmers he had worked for had wanted him back. But he had not liked his work the summer before (he did not explain why) and was looking forward to changing farms as the fruit seasons changed, to regular hours, and to the chance, if the RCMP agreed, of a trip to James Bay with his roommate. Schmidt realized what was expected of him as a potential citizen and as a student during the war. Students at Canadian universities had been told clearly that they should be serious and upright members of the community. Those who did not perform well at mid-terms were hauled off to military authorities or, if not eligible for service, to their parents. But Schmidt argued that he was fulfilling all that was expected of him and more — eagerly entering the COTC, working on a farm, and even becoming a blood-donor. "I never intended to disregard any regulations," he stated. "In the opposite it was always my ambition to show my gratitude to this country."

After reading Schmidt's letter of defence, the president began to see the case in a new light, and, on making inquiries, he found that Schmidt's moral conduct was sound. He came to feel that most of the misunderstandings were due to the fact that English was Schmidt's second language. The president thus wrote to Blair stating, "if he is innocent, I certainly cannot be a party to driving him to despair and bitterness. He is too able a lad to be treated harshly." The student's fate was also determined by the president's own beliefs about homosexuality. As he observed:

> I may say further that what little experience I have had with the kind of pervert that we at first suspected him to be leads me to doubt his guilt. It would be almost practically impossible for a pervert, who can be as often a medical case as a purely moral problem, to live in a men's residence for a year without giving rise to some suspicions at least. My inquiries among responsible students have revealed no such suspicions, and I am coming to feel that this is strong presumptive evidence that we were misled by his unfortunate language. As I have said earlier, I am not yet prepared to make a final judgement, but I am definitely hesitant about taking any drastic action.

While Schmidt's language had initially condemned him, lack of proof of any physical activity with another man vindicated him. The president's belief that homosexuals could not hide their sexual desires proved to be Schmidt's ultimate defence.

[...] If the Hazen Conference rooted sexual transgressions in psychological terms, the president's description of Schmidt's sexuality as "moral turpitude" and "vicious practices," and the fear these qualities could be spread to others, suggest that the medical understanding of the homosexual as a particular personality type had still not become the dominant discourse. Gary Kinsman suggests that, in the 1950s, "psychiatric definitions of sex deviation and homosexuality became firmly established,"[62] but certainly in the early 1940s the language of social science and of morality continued to overlap.

Moral and medical discourses existed side by side for the president and for the authors of the Hazen Conference report, indicating that the medical language just being developed in this period could not be divorced from the Christian moral canvas on which it was inscribed. While psychologists saw homosexuality as a medical problem, many leaders within the Canadian universities and mainline churches of mid-century viewed it also as a moral one. This article reveals that, in wartime, university educators saw themselves as training the private individual for public service. As the head of a denominational university, the president understood himself to be playing an important public role. His college's involvement in such events as the Hazen Conference suggests that the university community perceived itself as engaged with other concerned Christians in the process of shaping future citizens.

If, in Gary Kinsman's phrase, sexuality and morality are "socially produced and regulated,"[63] it is evident that the university was one of the prime sites for such activity. The university helped construct, reinforce, and regulate the ideal of heterosexuality, seeing family as the outcome of proper relations between men and women. Its purpose was to recreate a particular type of citizen: industrious, Christian, heterosexual, capable of leadership — none of these elements could be missing from the whole, well-adjusted person. Mariana Valverde argues that moral regulation is not just about prevention but about having a vision of how people should pass their time.[64] Clearly, both aspects existed at the university. The president, faculty, and even the students envisioned and worked to produce a particular type of student. But when such methods did not work, the coercive arm of the university was never far afield, as the secretive investigation of Johann Schmidt illustrates.

NOTES

1. Neither the name of the student nor the identity of the university bears on the arguments I make in this article. For that reason, and to protect the anonymity of the student involved, I have chosen to disguise both. The two letters from the student that I am referring to or quoting from, along with the correspondence between Blair and the university president, are preserved in the university's archives.
2. Blair was the director of the Immigration Branch of the Department of Mines and Resources. In the 1930s, restrictions on immigration to Canada were so extensive that a separate Department of Immigration was deemed unnecessary. See Irving Abella and Harold Troper, *None Is Too Many: Canada and the Jews of Europe, 1933–1948* (Toronto: Lester and Orpen Dennys 1983), 5–7.
3. See, for example, Michael Gauvreau, *The Evangelical Century: College and Creed in English Canada from the Great Revival to the Great Depression* (Montreal and Kingston: McGill-Queen's University Press 1991); A. B. McKillop, *Matters of Mind: The University in Ontario, 1791–1951* (Toronto: University of Toronto Press 1994); Marguerite Van Die, *An Evangelical Mind: Nathanael Burwash and the Methodist Tradition in Canada, 1839–1919* (Montreal and Kingston: McGill-Queen's University Press 1989).
4. One exception is Paul Axelrod, *Making a Middle Class: Student Life in English Canada during the Thirties* (Montreal and Kingston: McGill-Queen's University Press 1990).
5. See, for example, Cynthia R. Comacchio, *"Nations Are Built of Babies": Saving Ontario's Mothers and Children, 1900–1940* (Montreal and Kingston: McGill-Queen's University Press 1993); Karen Dubinsky, *Improper Advances: Rape and Heterosexual Conflict in Ontario, 1880–1929* (Chicago: University of Chicago Press 1993); Mary Louise Adams, *The Trouble with Normal: Postwar Youth and the Making of Heterosexuality* (Toronto: University of Toronto Press 1997); Mona Gleason, *Normalizing the Ideal: Psychology, Schooling and the Family in Postwar Canada* (Toronto: University of Toronto Press 1999). Mariana Valverde connects religion and moral regulation to a greater extent in *The Age of Light, Soap, and Water: Moral Reform in English Canada, 1885–1925* (Toronto: McClelland & Stewart 1991).
6. See Alyson King, "Literature, Debates and Frolics: Women Students' Culture at McMaster University, 1900–1930," paper presented at the annual meeting of the Canadian Historical Association, June 1997; Beth L. Bailey, *From Front Porch to Back Seat: Courtship in Twentieth-Century America* (Baltimore and London: Johns Hopkins University Press 1988), 3, 13, 80; Jonathan Ned Katz, *The Invention of Heterosexuality* (New York: Dutton Books 1995), 61, 83. Katz argues that the terms "heterosexual" and "homosexual" were invented in the late nineteenth century and mark the public legitimation of a different-sex eroticism disconnected from reproduction. See especially pages 28, 181.
7. See Annalee Golz, "Family Matters: The Canadian Family and the State in the Postwar Period," *Left History* 1, 2 (1993): 9, 13; Ruth Roach Pierson, *"They're Still Women After All": The Second World War and Canadian Womanhood* (Toronto: McClelland & Stewart 1986), 20; Christabelle Sethna, "Wait Till Your Father Gets Home: Absent Fathers, Working Mothers and Delinquent Daughters in Ontario during World War Two," in Lori Chambers and Edgar-André Montigny, eds., *Family Matters: Papers in Post-Confederation Canadian Family History* (Toronto: Canadian Scholars' Press 1998), 22; John Costello, *Virtue under Fire: How World War Two Changed Our Social and Sexual Attitudes* (Boston: Little, Brown 1985), 258; Mona Gleason, "Psychology and the Construction of the 'Normal' Family in Postwar Canada, 1945–60," *Canadian Historical Review* 78, 3 (1997): 442–3.
8. This argument follows Valverde, *Age of Light, Soap, and Water*, 24, who has suggested that moral regulation involved as much the preservation of a certain type of personality as a system of punishment or repression.
9. "President Stresses Need for Balanced Outlook," *Varsity*, 25 Sept. 1941, 7; "Klinck Urges Students Curtail Frosh Rites," *Ubyssey*, 24 Sept. 1940, 1.
10. Frederick G. Gibson, *"To Serve and Yet Be Free": Queen's University, 1917–1961* (Montreal and Kingston: McGill-Queen's University Press 1983), 181.

11. Nancy Kiefer and Ruth Roach Pierson, "The War Effort and Women Students at the University of Toronto, 1939–45," in Paul Axelrod and John G. Reid, eds., *Youth, University and Canadian Society: Essays in the Social History of Higher Education* (Montreal and Kingston: McGill-Queen's University Press 1989), 162.

12. Gibson, *"To Serve and Yet Be Free,"* 185.

13. "Delta Gamma," *Dalhousie Alumni News*, April 1943, 18; Report of Dean of Women in the Annual Report of the President of the University of British Columbia, 1941–2, 40; Kiefer and Pierson, "The War Effort and Women Students," 162, 164, 175–6. For Ontario universities more generally, see McKillop, *Matters of Mind*, 523.

14. Kiefer and Pierson, "The War Effort and Women Students," 1.

15. University of British Columbia Archives, Klinck Papers, box 1, file 2, Address to Freshmen Students during Newcomers' Organizational Period, 18 Sept. 1942. In 1942 students who failed a course were reported to the government and subject to the draft. By 1943 those placing in the bottom half of their class faced conscription. See McKillop, *Matters of Mind*, 535–6.

16. Abella and Troper, *None Is Too Many*, 7.

17. Barbara Roberts, *Whence They Came: Deportation from Canada 1900–1935* (Ottawa: University of Ottawa Press 1988).

18. Abella and Troper, *None Is Too Many*, 7–9.

19. United Church of Canada/Victoria University Archives (UCA/VUA), Records of the President's Office, 89.130v, box 71-9, Residence Regulations 1945–6; University of King's College Archives, E.1.1.4, University of King's College Students' Handbook, 1940.

20. UCA/VUA, Burwash Hall and Men's Residence Committee, 87.195v, box 1-5, Burwash Hall, 1935; ibid., box 1-1, Victoria University Men's Residences, 1946–7; University of King's College Archives, Calendars 1930–1, 1939–40. Such moral requirements remained in effect well into the twentieth century. See Dalhousie University Archives, MS-1-3, A226, Dalhousie President's Office, Buildings – Men's Residence (Howe Hall), Dalhousie Men's Residence Handbook, c. 1959.

21. Axelrod, *Making a Middle Class*, 113.

22. Ibid., 116.

23. Samuel Leonard Simpson, "The Social Sciences Club — A Study in Sex and Censorship," in Philip A. Krigg et al., *The Way We Were: Anecdote - Antic - Absurdity at the UBC* (Vancouver: UBC Alumni Association 1987), 36.

24. Axelrod, *Making a Middle Class*, 115.

25. Ibid., 137.

26. Administrators were also motivated by fears that funding would be cut. See, for example, Michiel Horn, *Academic Freedom in Canada: A History* (Toronto: University of Toronto Press 1999), 66.

27. Catherine Gidney, "Poisoning the Student Mind? The Student Christian Movement at the University of Toronto, 1920–1965," *Journal of the Canadian Historical Association*, new series, 8 (1997): 150; S. R. Hewitt, "Spying 101: The RCMP's Secret Activities at the University of Saskatchewan, 1920–1971," *Saskatchewan History* (fall 1995): 24.

28. UCA/VUA, SCM, box 84-53, file First Hazen Conference 1941, "The Influence of the University in Canada on the Life of the Student," Account of First Canadian Hazen Conference, Chaffey's Locks, Ontario, June 23–29, 1941. The Edward W. Hazen Foundation was an American institution that commissioned leading scholars to write about religion in higher education and sponsored faculty conferences on the same topic. While these conferences had been going on periodically since 1929 in the United States, the first Canadian conference occurred in 1941. See Douglas Sloan, *Faith and Knowledge: Mainline Protestantism and American Higher Education* (Louisville, Ky: Westminister John Knox Press 1994), 36.

29. UCA/VUA, SCM, box 84-53, file First Hazen Conference 1941, "The Influence of the University in Canada on the Life of the Student," 9–14.

30. Ibid., 9.

31. Ibid.

32. Editorial, "The Spirit is Essential," *United Church Observer*, 15 Feb. 1943, 4; Editorial, "Christian Family Week," ibid., 1 May 1944, 4; Mrs Hugh MacMillan, "Reconstructing Family Life," ibid., 15.

33. Canadian Youth Commission, *Youth Speaks Out on Citizenship* (Toronto: Ryerson Press 1948), 53. Several of the educators involved in the Hazen report participated in the Canadian Youth Commission. For example, Martyn Estall, S. R. Laycock, Gregory Vlastos, and R. G. Riddell were all members of the citizenship committee, while S. N. F. Chant and N. A. M. Mackenzie were members of the broader Canadian Youth Commission. See ibid., iv–v.

34. Ibid., 104–5.
35. UCA/VUA, SCM, box 84-53, file First Hazen Conference 1941, "The Influence of the University in Canada on the Life of the Student," 10.
36. Ibid., 8.
37. For this interpretation of Freud, see Katz, *The Invention of Heterosexuality*, 73–4.
38. UCA/VUA, SCM, box 84-53, file First Hazen Conference 1941, "The Influence of the University in Canada on the Life of the Student," 10
39. See McKillop, *Matters of Mind*; Marlene Shore, *The Science of Social Redemption: McGill, the Chicago School, and the Origins of Social Research in Canada* (Toronto: University of Toronto Press 1987); Doug Owram, *The Government Generation: Canadian Intellectuals and the State, 1900–1945* (Toronto: University of Toronto Press 1986).
40. This division has been found for other contexts. Mariana Valverde has found that, in examining juvenile delinquency, some members of the Toronto Welfare Council committee continued to use traditional moral language while others used psychiatric language. All members, however, were concerned about familial instability and social disorder. See Valverde, "Building Anti-Delinquent Communities: Morality, Gender, and Generation in the City," in Joy Parr, ed., *A Diversity of Women: Ontario, 1945–1980* (Toronto: University of Toronto Press 1995), 31. Similarly, Sethna, in "Wait Till Your Father Gets Home," 19–37, has found that social hygienists were more concerned with public morality than public health in creating sex education courses.
41. UCA/VUA, SCM, box 84-53, file, First Hazen Conference 1941, "The Influence of the University in Canada on the Life of the Student," 9.
42. Ibid., 10–13.
43. Ibid., 14.
44. Ibid., 9.
45. Ibid., 12.
46. Patricia Jasen, "The English Canadian Liberal Arts Curriculum: An Intellectual History, 1880–1950" (PhD dissertation, University of Manitoba 1987), 203.
47. For the social gospel, see Richard Allen, *The Social Passion: Religion and Social Reform in Canada, 1914–28* (Toronto: University of Toronto Press 1971). For idealism and the rise of the social sciences, see A. B. McKillop, *A Disciplined Intelligence: Critical Inquiry and Canadian Thought in the Victorian Era* (Montreal and Kingston: McGill-Queen's University Press 1979).
48. Heather Warren argues that the shift in American Protestant thought from the language of character to that of personality occurred in the late 1930s and early 1940s as Christians attempted to come to terms with psychoanalysis. See Heather A. Warren, "The Shift from Character to Personality in Mainline Protestant Thought, 1935–1945," *Church History: Studies in Christianity and Culture* 67, 3 (1998): 537.
49. William McGuire King, "An Enthusiasm for Humanity: The Social Emphasis in Religion and Its Accommodation in Protestant Theology," in Michael J. Lacey, ed., *Religion and Twentieth-Century American Intellectual Life* (Cambridge: Woodrow Wilson International Center for Scholars and Cambridge University Press 1989), 53.
50. Robert Falconer. "The Place of the University in National Life," *University of Toronto Quarterly* 4, 3 (1934–5). See also Gibson, "*To Serve and Yet Be Free*," 202.
51. "President Stresses Need for Balanced Outlook," *Varsity*, 25 Sept. 1941, 1.
52. Falconer, "The Place of the University in National Life." For the link between Christianity and democracy, see also Dr Thomas Greenwood, "Why Britain Shall Win the War," *King's College Record*, Nov. 1940, 6; Gibson, "*To Serve and Yet Be Free*," 202.
53. Annual Report of the President of the University of Toronto, 1941–2, 17
54. UCA/VUA, Records of the President's Office, 89.130v, box 37-14, Baccalaureate Service by Walter T. Brown, Principal, Victoria College, 19 April 1942.
55. Ibid., Baccalaureate Service 1945, no author.
56. Principal J. G. Brown, Union College, "The Church's Present Educational Policy," *United Church Observer*, 15 Aug. 1942, 16
57. Editorial, "Education," ibid., 1 Nov. 1942, 4; George E. Levy, "Democracy and Religion," ibid., 15 July 1942, 15; Editorial, "Education for Life," ibid., 1 Nov. 1944, 4. For the postwar period, see Canadian Youth Commission, *Youth Speaks Out on Citizenship*.
58. Ruth Brownbridge, "Building Today for a Christian World," *United Church Observer*, 1 Jan. 1945, 10.
59. David B. Roe, King's College Record, Encaenia 1946, 22.

60. "The President Looks at the University," University of British Columbia Graduate Chronicle, Jan. 1945. For a similar comment in the Christian press, see "Christian Family Week," United Church Observer, 15 April 1942, 5.
61. Bailey, From Front Porch to Back Seat, 26.
62. Gary Kinsman, The Regulation of Desire: Sexuality in Canada (Montreal and New York: Black Rose Books 1987), 115.
63. Ibid., 15.
64. Valverde, The Age of Light, Soap, and Water, 33.

Article 6.2

Valerie J. Korinek

"Don't Let Your Girlfriends Ruin Your Marriage": Lesbian Imagery in *Chatelaine* Magazine, 1950–1969

Issues to Consider

- In this analysis, Korinek is effectively reading her material—*Chatelaine* magazine— against the grain, or in a manner that she calls "perverse reading." She is trying to uncover subtle references and images that go against the standard "happy housewife" portrayal of women in mass-circulation magazines. What does she discover by using this method? What other source materials can historians read in this manner in order to find buried or subversive references? What are the possible advantages and disadvantages of this type of reading of historical sources?

- Despite its mainstream status as a magazine, Korinek characterizes *Chatelaine* as "unconventional." How was *Chatelaine* unconventional throughout its history and especially during the 1950s and 1960s?

- How did the Cold War context of the 1950s affect matters of sexuality and constructions of the normal?

- How did the period's experts in psychology and medicine define the "deviate" and explain the causes of deviation? What new and controversial perspective did the Kinsey reports of 1948 and 1953 introduce into the expert discourses?

- What explains *Chatelaine*'s "new-found fascination with lesbianism" by the mid-1960s? Were there changes in how lesbians were "constructed" by comparison to a decade earlier?

- How does class fit into the magazine's discussions of female sexuality?

Middle-class women's magazines, as *Chatelaine* was and is, are supposed to entice their readers with affordable recipes, light fiction, articles on Hollywood entertainers and heavy doses of fashion, beauty and interior decorating features. Yet this Canadian women's magazine was, by American standards, very unconventional.[1] Throughout its history, the magazine's editors, associate editors and most of its editorial staff were women and from 1958 to 1977 the magazine was edited by an avowed and committed feminist named Doris Anderson. The magazine regularly published feminist editorial essays and articles along with romance fiction, departmental features and a hefty dose of brand-name advertising from North American corporations.[2] Any given copy of the magazine required readers to negotiate a variety of messages — from the liberal and often feminist messages of editorials, through the frequently unconventional article topics, to the more standard women's magazine fare of romance fiction and departmental features and, finally, at the other end of the spectrum, the most conservative component — the advertising — that glorified the comfortable world of suburban consumption.

During this era, *Chatelaine* had four different editors. The first, Byrne Hope Sanders, completed her 24-year tenure as editor in January 1952. Her successor, newspaper columnist Lotta

Source: Valerie J. Korinek, "'Don't Let Your Girlfriends Ruin Your Marriage': Lesbian Imagery in *Chatelaine* Magazine, 1950–1969," *Journal of Canadian Studies* 33, no. 3 (1998): 83–109.

Dempsey, edited the magazine for less than a year before she abandoned the periodical to return to writing. On short notice, Maclean Hunter installed *Maclean's* stalwart John Clare, the only male editor. Clare continued until a more willing and suitable candidate was located. Doris Anderson, a staff writer at *Chatelaine*, became editor with the September 1957 issue. Editorial turbulence and neglect was generally reflected in the product, a slim, old-fashioned and dowdy periodical. In 1958, partly as a business initiative and partly on Anderson's direction, the magazine was remodelled to make it more *au courant* and relevant for Canadian women. In the 1960s, editorial continuity and the remodelling served *Chatelaine* well as it attempted to reposition itself as a more trendy magazine, which would appeal to a younger audience. Circulation and advertising figures shot upwards, and Maclean Hunter knew that they had a hit on their hands regardless of what many of their corporate executives might personally think of the changes to the editorial content. Anderson's revamped *Chatelaine* was the premier Canadian women's magazine of the era and the only Canadian women's magazine to be published between 1957 and 1969.[3]

Chatelaine had a very large, broadly defined readership. Women (and some men) from all classes, regions, ages and ethnic groups purchased *Chatelaine*. In fact, despite its categorisation as a "women's magazine," *Chatelaine* had a larger circulation than the two "national" Canadian magazines. In 1969, its circulation was 909,453 whereas *Maclean's* (English language) had 666,406 readers and *Saturday Night* only 86,192 subscribers.[4] Despite the editorial bias in favour of married readers, 32 per cent of the readership was composed of single women.[5]

While I was determined to avoid the presumption that all readers were heterosexual, I did not expect to discover any self-identified lesbian readers or material that would appeal to them. The historiography confirms that presumption. Research on lesbian magazine fiction concluded that stories involving lesbian plots or characters were regularly published in American women's and general interest magazines until the 1920s.[6] According to Lillian Faderman, after 1920 the general populace was well aware of the medical and psychiatric pronouncements about such relationships, and thus these stories were abandoned. A previously acceptable genre was now regarded as morally suspect. Recent works about lesbian and gay history in the postwar era point to the importance of bar culture, house parties and friendship networks and, much less frequently, pulp novels of the era as the means by which lesbians and gay men discovered each other and forged identities.[7] American lesbian and gay periodicals were launched in the late 1950s but since their circulations were very small their impact was limited.[8] In 1964, two separate gay magazines were launched in Toronto — *Gay*, later renamed *Gay International*, and *Two* — but both proved very short-lived.[9] Sensationalistic stories of gay and lesbian misadventures were common in the tabloid presses of the era, but it was not until the 1960s that mainstream newspaper and newsmagazine articles began to explore the gay male lifestyle.[10] Historians have discovered only one article on lesbianism in mainstream American women's magazines during that era — *Cosmopolitan*'s 1968 article "The Lesbian Experience," by W. H. Manville.[11] Hence the assumption remained that women's magazines in the post-war era generally did not publish overtly lesbian material or articles about lesbians. But *Chatelaine* did.

In keeping with their mandate of delivering a wide variety of material, *Chatelaine* provided articles geared to all segments of its audience. The articles directed at single women, young women and mothers are particularly interesting because, in a number of instances, they contained references, both explicit and implicit, to lesbianism. "Don't Let Your Girlfriends Ruin Your Marriage" provides an analysis and overview of the explicit and implicit references to lesbians in Canada and provides a unique, alternative reading of a conventional Canadian women's history source.

Depending upon your perspective, this paper is either a piece of social history detective work, or to borrow Bonnie Zimmerman's term, a "perverse reading."[12] Gay and lesbian historians follow in the footsteps of social, labour and women's historians, for they share with these groups an agenda of reintegrating and reversing the historical neglect, misunderstanding and ignorance of those groups often written out of or ignored by conventional historical accounts. When historians have turned their attention to lesbianism the result has proved controversial as problems of definition continue to plague the process.[13] Lack of attention to issues of sexuality and the presumption of an a historical, universal heterosexuality, however, has prevented much historical discussion of the assumption of "normative" sexual mores. Judging by many of the articles in *Chatelaine*, many Canadian women did not find the transition from adolescence to heterosexual maturity as easy or as "natural" as one might suspect.[14] Furthermore, the lack of attention to the history of sexuality has effectively excluded the same-sex historical experience.

Within the realm of cultural studies, some theorists and literary critics have begun to question the primacy of the text and have started to focus their analysis on the act of reading. According to Zimmerman's definition, "a perverse reader is one highly conscious of her own agency, who takes an active role in shaping the text she reads in accordance with her perspective of the world."[15] Diana Fuss has explored the "homospectatorial look" in contemporary women's fashion magazines and contends that those periodicals "provide a socially sanctioned structure in which women are encouraged to consume ... the images of other women."[16] Thus Zimmerman, Fuss and others contend that, regardless of the overt or intended meanings of various pop cultural products, many readers will resist those readings. Instead they will focus on different issues, willfully misread the text or concentrate on subordinate themes in their attempts to make the text relevant to them. This paper combines these two perspectives as it details some of the overt and specific references to lesbians and lesbian imagery contained in the magazine during the era along with some "perverse readings" of material that, filtered through a lesbian perspective, appears much different than the writers or editors intended. Thus the paper illustrates how attention to issues of sexuality, along with analytical tools of race, class, gender, region and age, create a more accurate historical portrait. In addition, it calls into question assumptions about the audience and content of women's magazines and of *Chatelaine* in particular.

PLAYING IT STRAIGHT

The recriminations, paranoia and governmental purges of the Cold War affected Canadians as well as Americans.[17] Homosexuals, particularly men, were suspect; articles about homosexuals accentuated their pathological nature. Not surprisingly, given that climate, *Chatelaine*'s first explicit reference to lesbianism was found in an April 1956 article by Dr Samuel R. Laycock entitled "How to Protect Your Child from Sex Deviates,"[18] written in response to what appeared at the time to be an outbreak of sexual abuse against children. Although most articles were accompanied by photographs or illustrations, this piece did not have any accompanying graphic. The language and title were startling enough to grab the reader's attention. Likewise, the article was not printed on continuous pages at the front of the magazine, but rather skipped from page 11 to page 93. While it sought not to sensationalise the topic — indeed, it referred to the effects sensationalistic news stories had upon "deviates"— the author set out to explain clearly who deviates were and how parents could prevent such abuses from happening to their children. The opening paragraphs informed readers that this problem was as "old as civilization" and that "most sex deviations are an immature expression of the sex impulse."[19] Safely hidden in the middle of the article (and at the back of the magazine) was the author's disturbing thesis:

> In the background of most adult deviates is a history of unhappy childhoods, rejections, broken homes and unhealthy home attitudes toward sex or sex education. It is also a fact — for every parent to ponder — that these same conditions are frequently the background of the child who becomes willingly involved with a deviate.... With a sound attitude toward sex a child can experience a

chance encounter with a deviate with a minimum of mental anguish. And he is far less likely to become a willing partner. For the fact is most sex crimes are performed by people the child knows, and in many cases the child is willing to participate.[20]

Thus, the pathology of the deviate was established. He or she came from an unhappy home where unhealthy attitudes about sexuality were allowed to circulate. The deviate was also char-acterised as a rapacious individual quick to prey upon youngsters with whom he or she had a relationship. Laycock's fears, interestingly, are almost equally placed upon the predator and the child as "willing accomplice" in this criminal behaviour. The onus was placed upon parents to teach wholesome sex roles and to monitor their children in order to minimise any damage should they encounter a deviate.

The description of deviates was provided, presumably, so that parents could be on guard for individuals fitting these descriptions and alert to the danger signs in their children. Of partic-ular interest was Laycock's distinction between male sex deviates and "female homosexuals":

> Many male sex deviates are feminine in outlook and personality and many female homosexuals are masculine in their characteristics. For some reason, they were not able, as children, to accept their own sex roles as boys and girls.... In some homes boys either do not get on well with their father or are not encouraged to identify with his manly qualities. Sometimes they have an overpossessive mother who ties them too tightly to her apron strings. They become "mama's boys" and develop fem-inine characteristics. Some authorities think this is why some boys do not develop normally and why they become sex deviates although not necessarily sex criminals. In the same way a girl may not get along with her mother or she may receive little encouragement to identify with her mother's wom-anly qualities. She may be tied too tightly, emotionally, to her father as his companion or the son he wanted but didn't have; she may become a tomboy and develop many masculine characteristics. Her chances of growing up to be a womanly woman with a healthy sex life would be greatly lessened. Such a girl is more apt to become a female homosexual.[21]

Stereotypes of the effeminate gay male, or to use Laycock's terms the "sexual deviate," and the masculine or butch "female homosexual" were classic psychiatric definitions.

Those stereotypes were remarkably resilient, as they were initially advanced in the late-nineteenth and early-twentieth century by sexologists Richard Von Kraft Ebbing, Havelock Ellis and Sigmund Freud. According to Jennifer Terry, "homosexuals came to symbolise sterility, madness, and decadence."[22] The search for causation would continue into the twentieth cen-tury and took many forms — psychiatric analysis, genital observation and invasive exploratory procedures. Although it is beyond the scope of this paper to survey the literature on the med-icalisation of homosexuality, by the time these articles were appearing in *Chatelaine* there were two important and competing paradigms in the psycho-medical literature on homosexuals. The first, having failed to find a clear genetic or biological difference, claimed that homosexual individuals were sexually immature, easily influenced and in need of psychiatric assessment and treatment. This camp of experts advocated vigilant parenting and sex-role instruction as a pre-ventive measure and as a way to nip homosexuality in the bud. That particular viewpoint would reappear time and again in *Chatelaine* articles in the 1950s. The second, advanced by Alfred C. Kinsey, was that sexuality did not divide neatly into normative heterosexuality and deviant homosexuality, but deserved to be understood as a continuum of experience. There was an immediate backlash to Kinsey's reports (published in 1948 and 1953) and his *laissez-faire* sexual ethos. In keeping with the Cold War era's demands for conformity, the conservative sex-perts urged parents, educators, doctors and psychiatrists to search vigilantly for any signs of sexual confusion. When found, responsible professionals and parents were instructed to inculcate proper — namely heterosexual — modes of behaviour.

Ultimately, Laycock's article relied on the conservative psycho-medical view, which purported that poor gender role identification was to blame. Clearly, the portrait of homosexuality provided by this article was negative. Homosexuals, or sex deviates, were immature people who had failed to learn appropriate gender roles. The harshest criticism was reserved for male homosexuals whose predatory behaviour and search for willing children labeled them as deviant. There were, however, some ways in which the article could be read differently. With respect to gay men, Laycock was willing to admit that not all of them would become sex criminals. It would appear, similarly, given the use of the term "female homosexual" for women and not "female sex deviate," that women were not considered to be sexual predators. That they were abnormal was clear, that they were criminals was not made evident. Most important, articles such as this did provide a name for this phenomenon. For readers coming to terms with their sexual identity the article hints at a community, or at least a group, of other such "deviates." The inclusion of an article such as this in *Chatelaine* magazine was significant because it reached a very large national audience. In particular, for rural and isolated gays and lesbians to find such essays in an accessible and respectable periodical provided some information about themselves without fear of discovery.

In May 1960, the magazine published "Why Don't We Do Something About Sex Criminals?" by Elizabeth Donovan.[23] A grainy black-and-white photograph of a man peering through the school-yard fence at the children playing in the yard provided a frightening image for this gritty article about child sexual abuse. The overt message of the photograph plays upon fears of intruders in our midst and of the vulnerability of children, since the man depicted does not seem identifiably abnormal. Donovan's purpose, like Laycock's, was the protection of children from sexual abuse. Much of the same ground was trod again, except that this time a detailed list of deviations was provided. These included homosexuality, exhibitionism, voyeurism, fetishism, sadism and masochism. Donovan concluded that "the first four are usually committed by relatively harmless, unaggressive people and could be described as annoyances rather than menaces to society."[24] The connection between homosexuals (presumably men since no reference was made anywhere in the article to women) and criminal behaviour was broken. The article makes it abundantly clear that while homosexuality may be troubling or annoying, it did not necessarily follow that all homosexuals were pedophiles or sex criminals.

In 1962 the editors received an article proposal about lesbians from freelance writer John O'Keefe.[25] Unfortunately it is not included in the archival documents, but memos from Jean Yack (Associate Editor) and Keith A. Knowlton (Managing Editor) to Doris Anderson are extant. These memoranda provide insight into the behind-the-scenes editorial commentary about article selection and reveal the editors' presumptions about reader interests. Yack's analysis is fascinating both for its cynical, sarcastic tone, and for her assessment of why readers would not find an article about lesbians very interesting:

> Lesbians ... sure look at it on spec, but I doubt that the girls can have much worthwhile to offer especially as they are the "nasty practicing kind." We aren't going to say ... lesbianism is good for you, and I don't really think mothers, or women (separated from "male-female life" by business life) really worry all that much ... after all, sex with men is what worries moms because it often ends up showing.[26]

She obviously felt that the article lacked any interest for the magazine's core readership of mothers and careerists (she presumes that all working women are heterosexual), and she seemed disinclined to sensationalise the subject matter. Although she appeared unfazed by the proposed topic, that was not the case for Knowlton, who wrote: "This would be read and criticised by some, I'm sure. But I suspect you may think it too indelicate for this magazine. John [O'Keefe] says he's going to write it anyway, so, if you are at all interested, we could ask him to let us have a look."[27] The return memo from Anderson does not exist, but a letter from Knowlton to O'Keefe, written in December 1962, firmly declined the lesbian article, stating: "There seems to be no chance whatever of our using a piece on Lesbians," but encouraging O'Keefe to send the article in for a reading if he did write it.[28] It would be another four years before an article specifically devoted to lesbians would be published in *Chatelaine*.

When Anderson was interviewed about her experiences at the periodical, and more importantly queried about the process of editing and selecting material for *Chatelaine*, she claimed that ideas for articles came from a multitude of places — academic journals, staff members, readers' letters and occasionally from unsolicited articles submitted to the magazine. She did not volunteer any comment about lesbian material in the periodical, but did say that the reaction to the increased number of articles devoted to sexuality caught the eye of the corporate brass. "Back then — to talk about sex at all was something. I remember one of the more conservative Vice Presidents in the company came down and was practically weeping, saying 'We never used sex on the cover of *Chatelaine*,' he thought that was an unbearable thing to do. Well I thought, you have to talk about sex — it's important."[29] Sometimes, as Anderson herself remembered, their new-found mission to advance sexual knowledge went too far, and letters indicated that "people were offended."[30]

There are, however, many levels of censorship. In a candid and unprompted comment, journalist June Callwood mentioned her own role in self-censoring the material of Dr Marian Hilliard. Callwood worked as the ghost-writer for Hilliard, who would gain fame across the country for her series of medical articles (see below). According to Callwood:

> Hilliard was a fierce, strong-minded woman. I have thought a couple of times of re-doing them all [the articles] because I edited her and fierce and strong as she was there was one thing she wanted to get through and she told me she was a lesbian. She told me this several times, and said that it doesn't matter who you make love to, whether it's a man and another man or a man and woman the quality of the relationship is what mattered. Whenever she would say something like that, I would write it down but I wouldn't write it. I mean I would put it in my notes because we didn't have tape recorders but I wouldn't write it because I thought she couldn't mean what she was saying.[31]

Callwood cited *naïveté* as the reason for her refusal to include overt lesbian or homosexual comments in the Hilliard articles. It is equally likely, though, judging from Anderson's experiences in the 1960s, that any positive mention, or even use of the word "lesbian," might well have been excised from the articles by the editor for fears of the responses of executives and the readers or for fears of damaging Hilliard's reputation.

A topic that was so indelicate and unworthy of an article in 1962 was considered perfectly acceptable to list on the cover two years later. Undoubtedly one of the reasons for this change was the 1964 publication of a two-part series on homosexuality in *Maclean's* magazine, a general interest Canadian magazine and brother publication.[32] On *Chatelaine*'s October 1966 cover, buried under three other feature titles and to the left of the model's eye, was the terse title "What Turns Women to Lesbianism?"[33] *Chatelaine*'s new-found fascination with lesbianism mirrors the pattern described by John D'Emilio for the American mass media, although he did not report any coverage of lesbianism in *Good Housekeeping* or *Ladies Home Journal*.[34]

According to author Renate Wilson, "unlike male homosexuality, there is far less fact and more myth about the causes and frequency of this sexual deviation among females."[35] The opening paragraphs introduce us to Jane, "a slim, quiet spoken" 26-year-old salesgirl, and her partner, Teresa, a 31-year-old "somewhat stocky figure" who "drives a delivery truck." We learn that they have lived together for four years in their own apartment, that they love each other, "share the double bed" (*Chatelaine's* genteel euphemism for sex) and that they "look forward to spending the rest of their lives together." To make the situation perfectly clear, Wilson, as the expert, makes this authoritative statement:

> Jane and Teresa are lesbians — homosexual females. They are attracted only to women and find the idea of lovemaking with a man repulsive. On the surface this is all that distinguishes them from heterosexual, or normal, women. The real differences lie deep and concern both their evolution and evaluation of themselves as women.[36]

Heterosexuality was normal and lesbianism was abnormal. The rest of the article enumerated Wilson's research findings, her interviews with North American psychiatrists and Canadian religious groups, and her discussions with Teresa and Jane's friends from Vancouver. "Lesbianism" was not a sensationalistic exposé, but a balanced article that surveyed historical, medical and religious commentary juxtaposed with interviews of lesbians. The emphasis was on the causes of lesbianism and how it could be avoided or treated. Jane and Teresa's friends and the religious groups, ironically, advocated acceptance and thus both criticised and countered the omnipresent psychiatric angle of the piece.

Despite the incessant "Why?" which ran throughout the article, for lesbians, for those unsure of their sexuality, or for those interested in or titillated by the subject matter, the article was thorough and informative. This was Wilson's historical and contemporary definition of the term:

> The word lesbian is derived from the Greek island of Lesbos, where poetess Sappho enjoyed and sang the praises of such relationships with women. Lesbians come in all ages and nationalities, professions and social classes. They can be married, single, childless or mothers of several children. They can hang out on skid row or live respectively in suburbia. They may never advance their sexual longings beyond an affectionate hug and kiss, or they may take part with another woman in sexual activity leading to orgasm.[37]

Wilson's was an inclusive, if classist, definition of the lesbian. She hesitated to state unequivocally the sexual nature of the relationship, but she does admit that for many women lesbianism was more than passionate friendship. Her definition, which she must have gleaned from both her conversations with the lesbians she interviewed, and the medical and psychiatric experts, was a very broad one. Its key defining feature was not a sexual relation with women, but rather a disgust with heterosexual sex and an attraction (however actualised) to women. She quoted the statistical estimates of the American expert, Dr A. C. Kinsey, who, in his book *Sexual Behavior in the Human Female* (published in 1953), had estimated that "2 per cent of women were exclusively lesbian, and 15 per cent partially so."[38] While Wilson was aware of the terms used in the community and in psychiatric literature — "'gay,' 'deviant,' 'invert,' 'homophile,' 'butch,' or 'femme'" — her bias was evident when she wrote that the women she met in Teresa and Jane's apartment were not "distinguishable by appearance."[39] Except for one butch, she stressed their normality or their ability to pass as normal in society. At a time when the first lesbian organization in the United States, the Daughters of Bilitis, applauded lesbians who conformed to the dress codes of the day, it would be short-sighted to critique a general interest women's magazine for making the same conclusion.[40] Often forgotten, as the sartorial freedom of today has obscured the restrictions and social conventions of the 1950s and 1960s, was the importance women placed upon choosing jobs that enabled them to wear trousers or slacks:

> Of the dozen I met ... a few wore slacks, but only one was vehement against skirts. "I would feel ghastly all dolled up in frills — I hate wearing women's clothing," she told me. Some girls had chosen jobs such as chauffeuring, gardening, or working at a garage where they could wear slacks quite

happily. They would not have stood out in a group of housewives, office girls or nurses getting together to play bridge or discuss PTA or union affairs. What we did talk about, however, was the "gay" life.... "The girls you're meeting here," said Vera, a stoutish girl in slacks, "don't go to gay bars and hangouts. We look on the butch on skid row wearing men's clothing the way you do the rest of the skid row population. They're a minority. Just because we're gay, we don't run in a pack. There are groups of working class girls, of professional women, and middle class girls like us — and there's very little come-and-go among us."[41]

Class definitions, as in many *Chatelaine* articles, were of key importance to both the subjects interviewed and the writer. The emphasis on these women as "middle-class girls" and the corresponding adjectives of respectability (even in light of their sexual identity) stood in sharp contrast to the cross-dressing, bar-hopping, working-class lesbian or skid-row butch. Wilson's focus on their ability to pass in society was one of their concerns as well, as few of them were "out" to parents, close friends or at their place of employment. Ultimately, Wilson's foray into the world of real lesbians seems to have confused her. She remarked, "The women I spoke to seemed very average. Why had they — why does any woman — turn to lesbianism?"[42] [...]

In a provocative article entitled "How Couples Choose Their Friends" (April 1967) writer Dorothy Sangster probed psychiatric explanations for friendship, the differences between women and men's friendships and the thorny issue of female friends.[43] In her historical and analytical commentary about the changing nature of friendship, Sangster wrote: "Friendship is personal, private, values eccentricity, relishes a person for what he is. In the old Greek days, when morals were different, friendship between men was often based on a homosexual relationship."[44] Dr Fadiman, a Toronto psychiatrist, strengthened the link between homosexuality and friendship: "So much friendship is sublimated homosexuality that it's hard to know what to tell the public about friendship."[45] He identified "the public," that mass of gullible consumers of pop cultural products, as highly impressionable and susceptible. Did he imagine that readers would fear that developing strong friendships would lead to being classified as a homosexual? Sangster counter-posed the critical comments of writer Jessamyn West, thereby ridiculing and questioning Fadiman's homophobic assumptions. West archly commented:

> Friendship between women is discussed like the Loch Ness Monster — something that's interesting to speculate about, but probably doesn't exist. On the contrary there have always been female friendships — Charlotte Brönte and her friend Ellen Nussey, Vera Brittain and her friend Winnifred Holtby — but women have learned to hide them because they know men sneer at the very idea, deride their friends, make jokes, even suggest lesbianism as the basis for any enduring relationship between women.[46]

By giving a prominent position to West's comment, Sangster provided a corrective to the misogynistic interpretation that used the spectre of lesbianism to deride women in long-term friendships. It is interesting as well that the examples West provided of "female friendship" were both what historians would now categorise as "passionate friends" or "independent women."[47] Although the article does not elaborate on the Brittain–Holtby and Brönte–Nussey relationships it does offer them as positive role models of women's friendships. Lesbianism was not characterised as pathological and deviant; instead, it was portrayed as a form of female relationship. Negative images were attributed to misogynists and moralists who invoked them to prevent women from developing close friendships.

The only reference to lesbianism that was free of either moralising or medical pronouncements was a July 1969 editorial entitled "How real are reel-life [sic] women?"[48] Anderson's editorial applauded the representative and realistic images of women that were prevalent in film.

She wrote:

> Negro heroines are "in" and so are lesbians. So far Negro [sic] heroines are treated quite gently. Men fall in love with them, even marry them and there's scarcely a psycho or sadist to be found. Lesbians are a bad thing, of course, and pretty sad and ugly to boot. But the real encouraging fact to be taken from all this is that more real women are appearing on that big wide screen.[49]

Anderson favoured an ironic style of writing, so her criticism of lesbianism should be interpreted as a criticism of how lesbians were portrayed in the movies. As the letters to the magazine attested, however, undoubtedly many readers interpreted this statement literally. Anderson linked lesbian heroines and Black heroines with a growing trend towards film diversity. The editorial ended with this comment: "Women are growing up and becoming more realistic in the better, more serious films. Although it may be a less pretty picture than we've been used to, it does bring with it more truth and that's an encouraging step in the right direction."[50]

Explicit references to lesbianism were relatively few — two features, one editorial and one health column, plus two articles that mentioned homosexuality — yet these were important because they provided explicit definitions of the lesbian or the female homosexual. Descriptions of their behaviour, mode of dress and characteristics were often stereotypical but they did play a critical role in naming this phenomenon and providing information and education. All of the articles made specific references to groups of deviants, thus acknowledging that this was not a rare psychiatric phenomenon but one that affected a number of men and women. It was virtually impossible for articles on such a subject matter in this period to avoid sensationalism, but they strove to adopt a measured tone. They were firmly based on current research both with individual respondents and with experts, and were not merely gossipy attempts to shock or titillate readers. In this respect, the articles in *Chatelaine* were very different from those published in urban tabloid newspapers or pulp magazines.[51] This is largely explained by the differences in target audiences: *Chatelaine* editors and corporate executives strove to attract a national audience of middle-class women readers. They did so because these women, it was believed, would purchase the products of the advertisers on whose revenue the magazine depended. Another important difference was the manner in which the publications were purchased. *Chatelaine* was primarily sold by subscription whereas tabloids and novels were purchased at news-stands, variety stores and drugstores. Thus tabloids and pulp magazines relied far more on lurid headlines, titles and cover art to sell their products. They promised readers sensational stories and titillation, while *Chatelaine* promised information, "clean" entertainment and news about Canadian women.

SEXUAL PERVERSITY IN *CHATELAINE*

According to the authors of these articles, ultimately, lesbians were women who had no interest in relationships with men, but preferred instead the company of other women. No decisive link was made between lesbianism and sexual relationships. This provided readers with a very inclusive definition that encompassed all of the "perverse readings" that follow. Some readers undoubtedly made these connections because of their exposure to the "overt" material. Equally important, lesbian readers (who undoubtedly read *Chatelaine*, given the limited entertainment and reading material available to Canadian women) were more than capable of reading between the lines and providing an alternate ending, analysis or meaning to these ambiguous stories and articles.

In contrast to Faderman's conclusions that lesbian stories were absent in American women's magazines after the 1920s, *Chatelaine* did publish one "lesbian" story in January 1950 — Louise Dickenson Rich's "Vixen in the Snow."[52] If a perverse reading is employed, this story can easily be interpreted as a lesbian story or, at the very least, as one with a very intense female relationship and an indifferent female–male relationship. From the suggestive title and the story's opening teaser: "The story of an elfin girl and a love that knew neither time nor age," it is clear that this will not be a standard piece of romance fiction.[53] The accompanying blue-gray illustration depicts a fox and a bright-eyed young woman caught in a blinding snow storm, hence the double entendre in the title. "Vixen in the Snow" is a veritable treasure trove of suggestive imagery, because the author's choice of a fantasy or fairytale genre allows her great latitude in character development, plotting and motivation.

The isolated setting is Hazen's Hollow, seven miles from the village where the protagonist's family lives. This "queer place," as the Hollow is repeatedly identified, was long since abandoned by the Hazen family after attempts to eke a living from farming and milling had proved unsuccessful.[54] While it is inhospitable for farming, the place's ridge, hollow and swift stream teem with flora and fauna — wild roses, sweet-william, lilacs, spice pinks, deer and foxes. Largely abandoned by people, the Hollow has returned to its natural state — a rustic, edenic paradise. It is a fertile and enchanted place where weeds, wildflowers, animals and two young girls cavort amongst the tangle of shrubs, grasses, overgrown fruit trees — apples naturally — and abandoned cottages.

The story follows the friendship of Ivy Frazier and Mattie Hazen. Through the story, Ivy ages from 10 to 19, and the plot follows her weekly visits to her elderly Uncle Ira, the Hollow's only remaining resident. On her first solo journey she immediately falls in love with the Hollow and meets the mysterious Mattie Hazen:

> This morning, though, as I was passing the old Hazen cemetery, I caught a flash among the tipsy headstones … and turned to investigate it, I saw, stretched out in the sun on a fallen moss covered slate marker surrounded by patches of pink and white ground phlox, a mother fox. Her ears were alert, but her pointed face was placid and pleased … with infinite care I lowered myself until I lay flat on my stomach in the tall weeds and gave myself up to the pure pleasure of watching them play. They were so pretty and graceful and unconscious of being observed that I laughed aloud.… "Now you've done it," said a voice in my ear, and I turned my head quickly.… A little girl was lying prone beside me, her slanting yellowish eyes laughing at my discomfort.… She had a pointed little face, and her remarkable eyes were fringed with long black lashes, but her hair was the peculiar thing about her — reddish, with a queer dark gloss to it. It was the sort of hair you wanted to stroke. She said, "I'm Mattie Hazen. What shall we play?"[55]

And so the love that knew "neither time nor age" begins. Ivy and Mattie become fast friends, and their weekly rendezvous by the Hazen cemetery becomes the focus of the story.[56]

When Ivy returns to her uncle's, she is quick to tell him about her new friend; she "breathlessly" tells him that she "loves her."[57] Ira, the stereotypically laconic, unflappable farmer advises her to "keep your tongue between your teeth" and not to tell her family or friends. Ivy's visits continue, and throughout the summer she is able to spend more time in the Hollow than during the school year. While Mattie and Ivy's relationship blossoms easily and is a source of great joy to both of them, Ivy's relationships with other girls are an entirely different matter, as she explains:

> None of the other girls were like her, and their silly chatter and budding interest in the boys and bewildering habit of being Best Friends one day and Not Speaking the next left me uneasy and unhappy. There were times when I didn't see how I could possibly stand the days till I could … run the Hollow with Mattie.…[58]

The seamlessness of this story makes it difficult to keep track of Ivy's age, but at this point she is about 13 or 14.

Threats to Mattie and Ivy's relationship come from two fronts: teenage boys and Ivy's mother. Ivy's brother Paul wants to trap foxes to help pay for his college tuition, thus threatening the nature of the Hollow and removing the reason for Ivy's weekly visits. Paul proves to be no match for the supernatural world of the Hollow, however, as, on his first and only trip, he is scared away by Mattie, the foxes and mysterious happenings that he will not, or perhaps cannot, explain. Other teenage boys and young men meet the same fate when they venture into the Hollow to hunt, thus defining the place as one primarily for women — Ivy, Mattie, the mother fox and her whelps. Only the elderly Ira, who ekes out a harmonious existence in the Hollow, remains unscathed. The second, more troubling threat to Ivy and Mattie's relationship is Ivy's persistent suitor, Fred Ellis. Now that Ivy is 16, her mother comments on her unhealthy attachment to the Hollow and her misguided priorities:

> "I've just about reached the limit of my patience with you, Ivy," she announced. "And the first thing you know, Fred will stop asking you. He'll get as sick as I am of hearing nothing but the Hollow, the Hollow, the Hollow. You're going on 17 and it's time you grew up. You act like a child, always running to the Hollow to *play*!" Oh, the scorn she put into that word, and I suppose she was right. I'd been so wrapped up in the Hollow and Mattie for so many years that my emotional development hadn't kept pace with my age.[59]

That emotional immaturity is implied by the bond with a female as opposed to a male parallels the psychiatric descriptions of female homosexuals described earlier. The Hollow appears to be much more than just a geographical location. Its fecund and particularly female imagery easily invokes sex. Psychiatrists were quick to impress upon parents that masturbation was another form of juvenile or immature sexuality that required vigilance. Ivy's playing in the Hollow and her mother's concern about how much time she spends there could be a metaphor for masturbation just as easily as it could be for lesbianism or intense same-sex bonding. Her mother is not aware of the friendship with Mattie, but Ivy immediately makes the connection between her relationship with Mattie and her immaturity. Fred symbolises more than just marriage and the normal life: he is Ivy's future. If she spurns him she will jeopardise an ordered, comfortable life for a tenuous, insecure one.

Ivy's mother warns her that Ira ruined his life pining away for a young woman who had died of pneumonia. This is the climactic moment of the story, as the mother reveals the name of Ira's long lost love — Mattie Hazen. When her mother mentions that name, Ivy's face "went stiff and queer," and her father remarked that Mattie was a "queer looking girl."[60] In an attempt to rationalise the situation, Ivy decides that her Mattie must be the deceased woman's namesake. Shortly after this discussion she makes one last, tragic trip to the Hollow, where she discovers Uncle Ira dying of pneumonia. She races to find Mattie, but in a raging snowstorm, she trips over a headstone — Mattie's — and promptly passes out. Her family, and the ever loyal Fred, find her lying in the snow.

After weeks of bed rest she is finally able to tell Fred what happened, and the concluding paragraph explains the story for the readers as well:

> I told him a little of all this, because I thought he should know why I couldn't marry him. He refused to understand, or perhaps he couldn't. "Ivy, darling" he said, "you've been very sick. You had a terrible shock, finding your uncle dying, and then lying out there in the snow all that while until we found you. No wonder you're all mixed up and upset. That little girl you say you used to play with — all children go through that, you know…. You'll forget about it when you're stronger." I closed my eyes, pretending to be even more tired than I was, and after a while Fred went away. For just a moment I was sorry and a little lonely. But I'd get used to loneliness, I thought, as I began the long

wait for the kind of love that I knew now could exist — the kind of love that refused to surrender to death, the kind of love that I might never find, but for which I could never, now, accept a substitute.[61]

It is unreasonable to wish that Rich had defined "the kind of love" to which Ivy refers, but its imagery and intensity, coupled with the decisive dismissal of Fred, permits one to conclude that this "fairytale" is really about the "love that dare not speak its name." The ending of "Vixen in the Snow" is remarkably different from the conventions of the *Chatelaine* romance, where countless female and male characters marry and live happily ever after in suburbia. Likewise, few stories ever focused upon female friendships as the major plot devices; they were almost always secondary to the love-interest. Very few romances, and few fiction stories in general, included such open-ended resolutions. The reader can conclude Ivy's tale according to her perception of what the story had been about. Was the intense love Ira's for Mattie or was it Ivy's for Mattie? Readers who believe in an afterlife can imagine Ira and Mattie happily reunited, but there is no authoritative direction for that conclusion. Moreover, Ivy is the protagonist: her story occupies centre stage, and for her the outcome resists closure. Rich's use of the fantasy or fairytale genre, ultimately, permits two very different interpretations of this story. In one it is a mystical story of undying love between Mattie and Ira and of a passionate friendship between Ivy and Mattie; if readers follow the suggestive language, code words and metaphors for female sexuality, it is a love story between two teenage girls complete with an affirmative ending in which the remaining character expresses her determination to seek out that sort of love again.

Two other stories that did not contain lesbian plotlines did, however, offer suggestive artwork and titles alluding to homo-social behaviour. They seem calculated to entice readers into these stories with a hint of subversiveness, only to deliver variations on the traditional romance fiction themes. Neither of the illustrations would have appeared out of place on the cover of lesbian pulp novels. Both "Off Men" (July 1952) and "Let Della Do It" (January 1950) featured double-page illustrations of female characters involved in heated discussions. In the illustration for "Off Men" one figure, Midge, is clad in a respectable sweater, skirt and pumps while the other character, Amy, is sprawled in a chair, wearing jeans, a white shirt, bandanna and loafers.[62] The appropriation of a butch-femme pairing is particularly suggestive. The title and illustration immediately make the reader wonder, if the women are off men, what exactly are they on to? The story itself makes perfectly clear that Amy is taking a respite from dating men, but the title and illustration suggest other possible interpretations. "Let Della Do It" features an illustration of two women, one sitting facing the reader, the other standing with her back to the reader and thus facing the seated woman.[63] The character with her back to the reader is naked, except for a towel that she is rubbing provocatively along her back, thus displaying a completely naked body to the other character. This illustration was eye-catching and, in combination with the story's intriguing title, makes an arresting image. It is made clear very quickly, however, that Della and the nude character are sisters, which — supposedly — undercut the sexuality of the image.

The issue of homosexuality was addressed more explicitly in Sheila MacKay Russell's story "Mr Nightingale." Published in January 1968, "Mr Nightingale" differed considerably from "Vixen in the Snow." Here, the author uses the term "queer" deliberately, for the story explores the character and background of Leslie Norland, a male nurse: "A man nurse? Obviously, he had to be a weirdo, and obviously, Karen (another nurse) had to let him know it."[64] Russell utilises an androgynous name, a little ambiguity about his sexuality and appearance (he is slight and very attractive) and the adjective "queer" to get readers speculating about Norland's sexuality. Of course, he is not gay and the story turns into a case study about gender stereotypes and reverse discrimination. By the end, Norland and Karen have shared a kiss meant to demonstrate and prove his heterosexuality. Similarly, his life story has been fully revealed: previously employed as a hospital orderly, he lacked the money to finance a medical career and so he decided to study nursing in order to support his younger brothers and sisters. It all adds up to a rather saintly portrait of a misunderstood man.

Equally significant was the 1969 publication of a Jane Rule story entitled "The List."[65] Whenever a Canadian author was featured in *Chatelaine* (despite the overt nationalism of the periodical, most of the fiction was American), the editors provided the readers with a brief biography. Accordingly, the editors described Rule as a resident of Vancouver, an English professor at the University of British Columbia and a former American. They did not identify her as a lesbian. They did, however, mention that she had published a novel — *The Desert of the Heart* — and that she had contributed stories to *Redbook*, amongst other American magazines. Any *Chatelaine* readers who were inspired to seek out Rule's novel would discover that its topic — lesbian relationships in the 1950s — bore little resemblance to the story she had written for the magazine about young marriages.

As a general interest magazine for women, each issue of *Chatelaine* usually contained an article devoted to marriage or family issues. While most of these were overwhelmingly heterosexual, many concentrated on the differences between the sexes. Many articles, like the aptly named "I Learned to Live with a Man" (April 1950) or the more vehement "I Hate My Husband" (September 1964), included the thesis that men and women were completely different species.[66] According to *Chatelaine* writers and experts, for many women marriage proved to be a problematic adjustment — akin to life with an alien. Thus while heterosexual marriage and family were supposed to be the goals of all young single women, the magazine frequently acknowledged that this "natural" state required a considerable amount of adjustment, compromise and work. Numerous articles identified areas where husbands were supposed to compromise or be accommodating but most of the adaptation to marriage usually came from wives. A critical examination of six articles from this genre shows that, despite the presumption that heterosexuality was the norm, there was a persistent subtext of concern about intense female friendships and the damaging effect they could have upon a marriage or, in more severe cases, how they could prevent women from marrying in the first place.

A pair of articles from 1954 by Eileen Morris, "Don't Let Your Girlfriends Ruin Your Marriage" and "Why Some Women Never Marry," illustrate some of these fears about the power of female relationships.[67] "Girlfriends" cautioned "that the Other Woman in a marriage is too often the good friends with whom you discuss problems that should be worked out only with the man you married."[68] According to the experts (in this case psychiatrists, ministers and social workers) women who turned to their girlfriends were guilty of committing "an act of unfaithfulness, or infidelity, that amounts to running out on marriage."[69] While the experts feared verbal infidelities between the women friends they also criticised these relationships for their immaturity:

> In numerous cases where a wife turns to girl friends to an excessive extent, she is still an adolescent.... Incapable of a full-size adult relationship with her husband she turns to thick, girlish relationships that are normal for a teenager, but which should be part of the past in the life of an emotionally mature woman. Wives who are emotionally immature have no true understanding of the character of marriage — the most adult relationship we know.[70]

While this article depicts infidelity with another woman as an intense friendship carried on behind the husband's back, the references to immaturity and maladjustment utilise the same descriptive phrases and concerns as did articles on sex deviates and lesbians. The following description of the typical "Other Woman" contains very unsubtle references to lesbian relationships:

Some unmarried women, because of an unhealthy attitude, find the thought of marriage slightly disgusting, and display a lofty contempt for men. Others equally twisted in their emotional outlook flit from man to man and some from affair to affair. The playgirl, the drifter, the girl on the prowl, the maladjusted — these are often the very women the wife invites to share her hearth and her confidences, and whose extremely unsound advice she heeds....[71]

Morris reports that the problem is so severe that many men search for other "more truly feminine women or simply walk out" on their wives because husbands "want to be the center" of their wives' worlds.[72] This cautionary tale impressed upon the *Chatelaine* reader that female friendships were adolescent, not adult, and could put considerable strain on marriage. Women who required such homo-social crutches to make their marriages work were labeled maladjusted. Although never mentioned explicitly the lesbian is alluded to as a maladjusted, immature woman repelled by heterosexual sex. Her willingness to become an accomplice to marital infidelities, interestingly defined as verbal not sexual, provides a new wrinkle to her description.

In the companion article "Why Some Women Never Marry," Morris probed the phenomenon of "bachelor girls who secretly want to miss out on marriage."[73] Like the articles on lesbians and sex deviates discussed earlier, this article also stressed the importance of children learning healthy ideas about marriage and the opposite sex from their parents. Women who did not have adequate parental examples formed "distorted" views of men. In a lengthy list of possible neurotic parenting techniques that could turn women off men, most disastrous were the "women who as girls develop a strong hostility for their fathers" and who will later "show the same attitude toward all men."[74] Morris wrote: "If a girl's disagreement with her father is very great, her preparation for love and marriage may be hampered, and even physical attraction to the other sex may be blocked."[75] While no mention was made of a corresponding attraction to women the spectre of the maladjusted woman functioned in these articles as the apex of women's dysfunctional behaviour. Articles such as this could, and probably did, have multiple effects and readings. For unmarried heterosexual women, they created insecurity, for mothers they were educational and for lesbians they provided some representation in a popular magazine.

Keen public interest in articles written by or in consultation with psychologists or psychiatrists resulted in a regular column by Montreal psychologist Dr Reva Gerstein entitled "Learn to Live With Yourself." One column, "How to Share an Apartment," (January 1956) instructed women in the art of sharing an apartment either with their husband or a girlfriend.[76] Gerstein made clear that roommate life should be an interim arrangement: "When two or more girls move into an apartment, it's rarely a permanent arrangement and for this reason it is sometimes much harder to work out a satisfactory way of life. The first rule is not to become too entwined in one another's lives."[77] She cautioned readers about the effect this could have upon marital prospects: "There is also a danger of the arrangements becoming so comfortable that it might jeopardise any relationship with any men either girl meets. Two females, completely at home with one another, can be a pretty forbidding barrier to a shy unsophisticated suitor."[78] Gerstein implied that economising on rent could ultimately prove very costly and warned about the limits of such relationships. Women's easy interaction with each other should not prevent them from searching for Mr Right. Her solution to too much female bonding was to encourage the roommates to respect each other's privacy: "Make sure you have a bed of your own and preferably a room of your own."[79] From today's perspective such a comment seems strikingly naïve (although it does support Callwood's claim about her own *naïveté*) about why two roommates might share a bed but its inclusion opened the article to a different reading, and a different reader.

Another article, "Dr Marion Hilliard Talks to Single Women," (February 1956), also included a subtext of lesbian imagery in its discussion of the fulfilling life possible for unmarried women. Hilliard was the head of obstetrics and gynaecology at Toronto's Women's College

Hospital and *Chatelaine*'s most popular "freelancer" during the 1950s.[80] After her untimely death in 1958 the magazine published a series of biographical articles tracing Hilliard from her early years in a loving, but strict, Methodist family to her student days at the University of Toronto's medical school and her subsequent distinguished career. Rounding out the list of her academic and professional accomplishments were details of her love of sports (she had played ice hockey at the varsity level and numerous intramural sports), her hobbies, her love of the outdoors and fishing, her gregarious personality and her close female friendships.[81] Hilliard herself, notably, never married. Judging from her biography and her own personal comments she considered that she had lived a full and happy life but she regretted never having children. Although she wrote about her few love affairs with men after she graduated from university, she lived, at different times, with one of two close female friends. While she might have been open with certain friends and professional acquaintances, like June Callwood, given the era it is not surprising that she was not more outspoken and determined to state explicitly her sexual identity.[82] Clearly, Hilliard was able to write from a very authoritative position on "this great problem."[83] The majority of the article examined the misconceptions that married and unmarried women had about each other, but buried in its middle was a paragraph in which Hilliard advocated that an unmarried woman find a congenial friend with whom to live. Her advice contradicted Gerstein's and provided an alternate, positive image of "roommates":

> If the unmarried girl is fortunate enough to find another girl her own age with whom she can share her interest in art galleries or books, they are wise to consider sharing an apartment. Both girls, through their mutual respect and affection, can help one another through the lonely patches of their lives. The essential of such a relationship is that neither girl tries to dominate the other and that both are free to go on about their work unchanged. I've always considered it a dreadful wrong to impose your personality and opinions on any other person, in a friendship or a marriage. I was once asked for my definition of living in sin. It's this: two people living together while one dominates and tyrannises the other are, to me, living in sin.[84]

Although the rest of the article addressed issues of late marriages and affairs with married men, this short paragraph about life with a roommate, particularly as this was how Hilliard chose to live her life, was significant. It was clear that her version of roommate life was governed by choice, not by economics. She considered fortunate the single woman who found another woman with whom to share her interests — and her life. While subtle, the emphasis was on mutual respect and affection. Her intriguing definition of living in sin presented readers with a rather charmed, passionate friendship. Unlike the authors of the other articles, Hilliard did not distinguish between appropriate behaviour in a marriage and in a friendship. Friendship was not derided as an immature or less significant relationship. The classist interpretation of what makes a perfect roommate along with her stated dislike of domination (perhaps an allusion to butch-femme roles) makes compelling an interpretation of this part of the article as a rare depiction of a respectable (closeted) middle-class lesbian lifestyle.[85] Remember, the Vancouver lesbians quoted in Wilson's article were not out to family, friends or employers. [...]

CONCLUSION

The explicit and implicit images of lesbians or intense female relationships in *Chatelaine* at the very least attest to the magazine's variety. Not all of the material in the magazine featured white, heterosexual wives and mothers — immigrants, working-class women and families, rural Canadians, Black and Native Canadians and lesbians were also featured. Although they were not numerically overwhelming these images are important for a variety of reasons. First, they illustrate that information about lesbians, or female homosexuals, was widely disseminated in a very popular Canadian mass market women's magazine during the 1950s and 1960s. The portrait of lesbianism was usually negative. Only "Vixen in the Snow" and the Hilliard and Sangster articles depicted a friendly, comfortable world of intense relationships, compatibility and fun with other women. What was permissible in the world of fantasy or between "respectable" professional women was not as permissible in the real world depicted by the other articles and editorials. The lesbian, the female homosexual or the maladjusted woman was usually seen as neurotic and immature. One of her main purposes was to represent the apex of women's dysfunctional behaviour. The lesbian was dysfunctional primarily because of her negative attitude towards men and disgust with heterosexual sex — not for her attraction to women. While not characterised as predatory, she posed a threat to marriage by virtue of her ability to develop deep emotional bonds with other women, thus making marriage appear unattractive to the unmarried and creating fissures between husbands and wives. As well, she served as an object of interest or novelty that provided fodder for story illustrations or feature articles. Finally, in the late 1960s she appeared as a representative, like Black women, of the diversity of female experience.

The magazine's attention to sexuality, and homosexuality in particular, also reveals some of the stresses and strains within heterosexuality. Even a fairly straightforward reading of the problem-marriage articles would indicate that some women found adjustment to heterosexual sex roles and to marriage rather trying. Until well into the 1960s, adult heterosexual women were encouraged to sublimate their desires in favour of their husband's needs and the demands of child-raising. It is ironic that one of the most respected Canadian "experts" on sexuality and women's health issues was a closeted, middle-class, lesbian doctor. All of the issues of *Chatelaine* that featured Hilliard articles sold out, many within days. Hilliard was so popular (her articles and books are still part of the collective memory of that generation of Canadian women) because she was not afraid to champion women's rights — in the bedroom, the boardroom and the community. With the exception of her articles, however, the definitions and descriptions of female heterosexuality were often as narrow, rigid and "constructed" as were the definitions of lesbianism. Neither was unproblematic, but at the end of the day heterosexuality was defined as "normal" and lesbianism "abnormal."

Avoiding a heterosexist bias or employing a perverse reading permits a new perspective on a traditional source. It also acknowledges that although lesbian readers would definitely have been in the minority, many probably did read the magazine during the era. This was due to *Chatelaine*'s availability, wide-ranging topic matter, and the lack of other, more specifically lesbian magazines. In additional, all women interested in Canadian women's issues — employment prospects, fashions, prominent female politicians or celebrities, or women's legal or medical issues — read *Chatelaine*. Unlike American women, who could choose from a number of national, general interest women's magazines, Canadian women had only this one periodical. Fear of exposure and the very small circulations of lesbian and gay magazines severely restricted access to explicitly gay periodicals. For women who lived in rural or isolated areas of the country who were not able to participate regularly (if ever) in the bar culture available to women who lived in Toronto, Montreal and Vancouver, *Chatelaine*'s importance was amplified.[86] The wide availability of lesbian pulp novels combined with the exposure given to this issue in the magazine, however, provided even the most isolated reader with information. Thus lesbian readers could easily resist the preferred meanings of the material and opt for alternate interpretations that more aptly reflected their sense of themselves. Restoring the readers' agency and recognizing that reading is an active, not a passive process, also provides possible lesbian readings of articles and fiction. Without a search for lesbian imagery in the magazine, ultimately, many images might be written off as odd, when in reality they should be decoded as queer.

ACKNOWLEDGMENTS

The Lesbian and Gay History Discussion Group at the University of Toronto provided the impetus to write this paper along with a congenial atmosphere in which to present the first draft. My thanks to Paul Rutherford, Laurel MacDowell and Elsbeth Heaman for their comments on earlier drafts of this paper. In addition, I wish to thank the reviewers of the *Journal of Canadian Studies* for their perceptive and helpful commentary.

NOTES

1. For more detailed analysis of *Chatelaine* magazine in the 1950s and 1960s, see Valerie J. Korinek, *Roughing It in the Suburbs: Reading* Chatelaine *Magazine in the Fifties and Sixties* (Toronto: University of Toronto Press, 2000).

2. The composition of the magazine was consistent throughout the 1950s and 1960s, with the content split almost equally between editorial and advertising content. The exact breakdown for the 1960s was: advertising (53 per cent), articles (17 per cent), departments, which included editorial essays (21 per cent), and fiction (9 per cent). V. J. Korinek, "Roughing It in Suburbia: Reading *Chatelaine* Magazine in the Fifties and Sixties," PhD dissertation, University of Toronto, 1996.

3. In 1960, in response to fears that one of the American women's magazines would create a "Canadian edition" and engage in direct competition with *Chatelaine*, Maclean Hunter bought the French-Canadian magazine *Revue Moderne* and launched *Chatelaine La Revue Moderne*. Veteran editor Fernande Saint-Martin emphasized *Chatelaine*'s key selling feature — a French-Canadian identity. Produced in Montreal, *Chatelaine* employed French-Canadian journalists, novelists and fiction writers. Although the two sister periodicals often shared articles, the French-language version had, thanks to a different editor, writers and content, a different tone. Unless otherwise stated, this paper explores the English-language version of *Chatelaine*.

4. *Canada's Magazine Audience: A Study From the Magazine Advertising Bureau of Canada, Volume 1: Profile of Readers* (Originated by the Canadian Media Directors Council. Validated by the Canadian Advertising Research Foundation Conducted by ORC International Limited, 1969) 2.

5. Ibid. 20.

6. Lillian Faderman, "Lesbian Magazine Fiction in the Early Twentieth Century," *Journal of Popular Culture* 11.4 (1978): 800–17.

7. Much of the work on Canadian lesbian and gay history of the era is in progress. For the literature available in print, see Robert Champagne "Interview with Jim Egan," *The Challenge of Modernity*, ed. Ian McKay (Toronto: McGraw-Hill Ryerson, 1992) 431–38; Ross Higgins and Line Chamberland, "Mixed Messages: Gays and Lesbians in Montreal Yellow Papers in the 1950s," *The Challenge of Modernity* 422–31; Line Chamberland, "Remembering Lesbian Bars: Montreal, 1955–1975," *Journal of Homosexuality* 25.3 (1993): 231–69; Daniel J. Robinson and David Kimmel, "The Queer Career of Homosexual Security Vetting in Cold War Canada," *Canadian Historical Review* LXXV.3 (1994): 319–45; Becki L. Ross, *The House That JILL Built: A Lesbian Nation in Formation* (Toronto: University of Toronto Press, 1995); Becki L. Ross, "Destaining the (Tattooed) Delinquent Body: The Practices of Moral Regulation at Toronto's Street Haven, 1965–1969," *Journal of the History of Sexuality* 7.4 (1997): 565–94. For as-yet-unpublished work and conference papers, see Mary Louise Adams, "Lesbians as Obscenity, or Women's Barracks as a Threat to Girls," Out of the Archives Conference, Toronto, 13–15 January 1994; Elise Chenier, "Risks, Roles and Rounders: Lesbian Bar Culture in Toronto, 1950–1965," Out of the Archives Conference; David Stewart Churchill, "Gay Sites and Public Space: Toronto in the 1950s," Out of the Archives Conference; and Eric Setliff, "Sex Fiends or Swish Kids? Gay Men in Toronto Tabloids 1946–1956," Lesbian and Gay History Discussion Group, Toronto, 20 March 1995. Books published on American gay and lesbian history (1950s and 1960s) include: John D'Emilio, *Sexual Politics, Sexual Communities: The Making of a Homosexual Minority in the United States, 1940–1970* (Chicago: University of Chicago, 1983); Joan Nestle, *A Restricted Country: Essays and Short Stories* (Ithaca: Firebrand Books, 1987); Andrea Weiss and Greta Schiller, *Before Stonewall: The Making of a Gay and Lesbian Community* (New York: Niad, 1988); Leila Rupp, "Imagine My Surprise: Women's Relationships in Mid-Twentieth Century America," *Hidden From History*, eds. Martin Duberman, Martha Vicinus and George Chauncey Jr. (New York: Meridian, 1990); Lillian Faderman, *Odd Girls and Twilight Lovers: A History of Lesbian Life in Twentieth-Century America* (New York: Columbia University Press, 1991); John D'Emilio, *Making Trouble: Essays on Gay History Politics and the University* (New York: Routledge 1992); Elizabeth Lapovsky Kennedy and Madeline D. Davis, *Boots of Leather, Slippers of Gold: The History of a Lesbian Community* (New York: Routledge, Chapman and Hall, 1993).

8. D'Emilio, *Sexual Politics* 110.

9. Donald W. McLeod, *Lesbian and Gay Liberation in Canada: A Selected Annotated Chronology, 1964–1975* (Toronto: ECW Press, 1996) 3–5, 10.

10. D'Emilio, Champagne, Higgins and Chamberland, and Setliff all stress this point.

11. My thanks to the *Journal of Canadian Studies* reader for this information.

12. Bonnie Zimmerman, "Perverse Reading: The Lesbian Appropriation of Literature," *Sexual Practice/Textual Theory: Lesbian Cultural Criticism*, eds. Susan J. Wolfe and Julia Penelope (Cambridge: Blackwell, 1993) 135–49.

13. The "passionate friends/lesbian" dichotomy, questions of how we "define" lesbianism and analysis of the historiography is well covered elsewhere. See Sylia Martin, "'These Walls of Flesh': The Problem of the Body in the Romantic Friendship/Lesbianism Debate," *Historical Reflections/Reflections Historiques* 20.2 (1994): 243–66; Randolph Trumbach, "Review Essay: The Origin and Development of the Modern Lesbian Role in the Western Gender System: Northwestern Europe and the United States, 1750–1990," *Historical Reflections/Reflections Historiques* 20.2 (1994): 287–320; and Vicki L. Eaklor, "Introduction" and "Afterword: See Lesbians in Film and History," *Historical Reflections/Reflections Historiques* 20.2 (1994): 165–68, 321–33.

14. There is a growing body of scholarship which seeks to explore the history of heterosexuality. See Jonathan Ned Katz, *The Invention of Heterosexuality* (New York: Penguin, 1995); Gary Kinsman, *The Regulation of Desire: Homo and Hetero Sexualities*, 2nd ed. (Toronto: Black Rose Books, 1996); Karen Dubinsky, *Improper Advances: Rape and Heterosexual Conflict in Ontario, 1880–1929* (Chicago, University of Chicago Press, 1993); and Mary Louise Adams, *The Trouble with Normal: Postwar Youth and The Making of Heterosexuality* (Toronto: University of Toronto Press, 1997).

15. Zimmerman 139.

16. Diana Fuss, "Fashion and the Homospectatorial Look," *Critical Inquiry* 18 (Summer 1992): 713.

17. Robinson and Kimmel.

18. Dr Samuel R. Laycock, "How to Protect Your Child from Sex Deviates," *Chatelaine* (April 1956): 11.

19. Ibid.

20. Ibid. 93.

21. Ibid. 94.

22. For more detail on the psycho-medicalization of homosexuality and lesbianism, see Jennifer Terry, "Anxious Slippages between 'Us' and 'Them': A Brief History of the Scientific Search for Homosexual Bodies," *Deviant Bodies: Critical Perspectives on Difference in Science and Popular Culture*, eds. Jennifer Terry and Jacqueline Urla (Bloomington & Indianapolis: Indiana University Press, 1995) 132. In addition, Jennifer Terry, "Lesbians Under the Medical Gaze: Scientists Search for Remarkable Differences," *The Journal of Sex Research* 27.3 (1990): 317–39; Jennifer Terry, "The Seductive Power of Science in the Making of Deviant Subjectivity," *Posthuman Bodies*, eds. Judith Halberstam and Ira Livingston (Bloomington & Indianapolis: Indiana University Press, 1995) 135–61.

23. Elizabeth Donovan, "Why Don't We Do Something About Sex Criminals?" *Chatelaine* (May 1960) 33.

24. Ibid. 62.

25. Maclean Hunter did not systematically archive readers' letters, editorial memos or notes; all that remains are their own collection of bound periodicals. Maclean Hunter did, however, donate some documents to the Public Archives of Ontario. What pertains to *Chatelaine* in this era is limited to a smattering of records from 1958, 1961 and 1962. This is not an uncommon situation for cultural historians and is the major reason why it is so difficult to reconstruct behind-the-scenes editorial commentary about magazine design and production.

26. Public Archives of Ontario (PAO), Maclean Hunter Records Series (MHRS), F-4-4-b Box 445, Jean Yack to Doris Anderson, re: article suggestions from John O'Keefe; undated, yet must be from the 1962 correspondence.

27. PAO, MHRS, F-4-4-b Box 445, Keith A. Knowlton to Doris H. Anderson, re: John O'Keefe Proposal, 1962.

28. PAO, MHRS, F-4-4-b Box 445, Keith A. Knowlton to John O'Keefe, 21 December 1962.

29. Doris Anderson interview with the author, 30 June 1994.

30. Ibid.

31. June Callwood interview with the author, 23 May 1995.

32. Champagne, "Interview with Jim Egan."

33. Renate Wilson, "What Turns Women to Lesbianism?" *Chatelaine* (October 1966): 33.

34. D'Emilio, *Sexual Politics* 129.

35. Wilson 33.

36. Ibid.

37. Ibid. 130.

38. Ibid.

39. Ibid. 33, 130.
40. D'Emilio, *Sexual Politics* 106.
41. Wilson 130–31.
42. Ibid. 132.
43. Dorothy Sangster, "How Couples Choose Their Friends," *Chatelaine* (April 1967): 64.
44. Ibid. 120.
45. Ibid.
46. Ibid. 121.
47. See Martha Vicinus, *Independent Women: Work and Community for Single Women, 1850–1920* (Chicago: University of Chicago Press, 1985).
48. Doris Anderson, "How real are reel-life women?" *Chatelaine* (July 1969): 1.
49. Ibid.
50. Ibid.
51. See Becki L. Ross, "Destaining the (Tattooed) Delinquent Body," for a summary of this literature.
52. Louise Dickenson Rich, "Vixen in the Snow," *Chatelaine* (January 1950): 8.
53. Rich 8.
54. Rich's recurrent use of the word queer is worth mentioning, in contrast to its absence from most other works of fiction in *Chatelaine*. The other story that utilized the word —"Mr Nightingale" by S. M. Russell (below) — was about a presumably homosexual nurse, and thus Rich's use of "queer" could be understood as a code word for lesbian readers or those familiar with its multiple meanings.
55. Rich 30–31.
56. The imagery and the intense friendship between the two girls is reminiscent of Lucy Maud Montgomery's *Anne of Green Gables,* and given both the popularity of that work and the similarities between the texts, it would appear that Rich was familiar with Montgomery's work.
57. Rich 31.
58. Ibid.
59. Ibid. 34.
60. Ibid. 34–35.
61. Ibid. 50.
62. Isabel Langis, "Off Men," *Chatelaine* (July 1952): 14–15.
63. Rosalie F. Wilson, "Let Della Do It," *Chatelaine* (January 1950): 10.
64. Sheila MacKay Russell, "Mr Nightingale," *Chatelaine* (January 1968): 25.
65. Jane Rule, "The List," *Chatelaine* (April 1969): 30–31.
66. See Mary Jukes, "I Learned to Live with a Man," *Chatelaine* (April 1950): 5; and Phyllis Yates, "I Hate My Husband," *Chatelaine* (September 1964): 14.
67. Eileen Morris, "Don't Let Your Girlfriends Ruin Your Marriage," *Chatelaine* (October 1954): 26; Morris, "Why Some Women Never Marry," *Chatelaine* (November 1954): 20.
68. Morris, "Girlfriends" 26.
69. Ibid. 50.
70. Ibid. 51.
71. Ibid.
72. Ibid. 55.
73. Morris, "Why Some Women Never Marry" 20.
74. Ibid. 67.
75. Ibid.
76. Dr Reva Gerstein, "How to Share an Apartment," *Chatelaine* (January 1956): 4.
77. Ibid.
78. Ibid. 37.
79. Ibid.
80. These articles were ghost-written by June Callwood.
81. Marion O. Robinson, "The Story of Marion Hilliard," *Chatelaine* (September 1964): 32.
82. While it was clear from her conversations with Callwood and Callwood's interview with the author that Hilliard was a lesbian, her untimely death and the natural tendency of family members and friends to "protect" her reputation has obscured the truth of the situation. Current biographical work on Marion Hilliard, by Wendy Mitchinson, remains coy about her orientation. The editors of *Great Dames,* in which Mitchinson's biographical essay appears, are also uncomfortable about an explicit statement about Hilliard's orientation. See Elspeth

Cameron and Janice Dickin, eds., *Great Dames* (Toronto: University of Toronto Press, 1997). This is a controversial area of scholarship, but, given Callwood's comments about Hilliard's determination and relative openness, and the hints which remain in Hilliard's published articles and biographies, I have opted to make a clear, and accurate, statement about Hilliard's sexuality.

83. Dr Marion Hilliard, "Dr Marion Hilliard Talks to Single Women," *Chatelaine* (February 1956): 17.

84. Ibid. 49–50.

85. For a compelling peek into the closeted world of middle-class lesbians in the 1950s and 1960s, see Katie Gilmartin, "'We Weren't Bar People': Middle-Class Lesbian Identities and Cultural Spaces," *GLQ: A Journal of Lesbian and Gay Studies* 3.1 (1996): 1–51.

86. According to Gilmartin's article, "We Weren't Bar People," middle-class lesbians might not have participated in bar culture, even if they did have access to them or lived in urban areas, because they did not consider themselves "the sort" who frequented "those establishments." Issues of class and, more importantly, middle-class respectability were key.

Document 6.1
Percy E. Ryberg, MD

On Sex Education

Dr. Percy E. Ryberg was employed by the Ontario health department when *Health, Sex and Birth Control* was published in 1942. Wartime concerns — also present during World War I — about venereal disease, promiscuity, and juvenile delinquency made this book an important contribution to "sex hygiene," as sex education was called at the time.

Issues to Consider

- Why would a national emergency such as war increase public anxiety about morality?
- What is Dr. Ryberg's stand on sex education? How does he propose that it should be managed? What role does he suggest doctors and other "experts" play, either directly or implicitly, in dispelling sexual ignorance?

Practising doctors are not usually given to showing astonishment; yet one of the things that surprises us is the considerable amount of talk prevalent amongst people of all ages about the sexual organs and their functions, based on, really, a very small amount of accurate knowledge. This, in spite of the fact that sexual intercourse itself is not unknown to most of them.

The reasons for this ignorance are many. There are too few parents who are themselves sufficiently educated in matters of sex, having come upon such knowledge as they possess by the hard way of experience; they are not skilled in the technique of imparting information to others; they may still retain the belief that all sex is sinful and not to be spoken of by nice people; they may be embarrassed by the whole subject and afraid to talk of it to their usually very critical offspring; or, they may be plain lazy, and excuse this shortcoming by saying that they themselves had to pick it up, and look what wonderful people they became notwithstanding!

There is no excuse for any of these attitudes in view of the vast amount of medical and psychological knowledge that is available to them. They should regard it as their most important duty to tell the truth to their children as early as they are capable of grasping it, which is usually indicated by the child's questions. No purpose whatever is served by keeping them in ignorance. If they neglect their duty, then the children will somehow pick up the knowledge for themselves. And the "knowledge" so acquired will certainly be incomplete, and probably largely incorrect.

Every boy and girl is aware from an early age that he or she possesses certain organs the use of which is not too obvious to them. But at puberty (*pew'-berty*), which is the age when they begin to change into adults, certain external signs come into evidence accompanied by profound inner changes, and these cannot be ignored. This is an indication to the parents that their children's enlightenment is overdue.

Children should be gently prepared for these changes so that they may understand what is happening to them. If parents do not undertake this responsibility, they will most certainly find that they have been relieved of it by the older amongst their children's playmates. If, on the

Source: Percy E. Ryberg, MD, "On Sex Education," chap. 1 in *Health, Sex and Birth Control* (Toronto: T. H. Best, 1942), 1–4.

other hand, something happens which makes the parents realize that they should wait no longer, and if, without further ado, they try to teach their children the truth about these matters, they must be prepared for a lack of response and a certain attitude of doubt.

By this time the boy or girl will be more self-conscious than ever, especially if the necessary frankness and friendship between parents and children have not been built up from childhood. He or she will feel definitely ill at ease, and think their parents are just being fastidious over something that they believe they know well enough by now. Besides, self-relief or some form of sexual play will probably have been indulged in already, and the youngsters will be extremely mortified to learn that they have been doing something "evil," if the parents adopt this line of thought.

Therefore, wise parents will have won their children's confidence from an early age by trying to give a loving understanding to their problems, especially their sexual ones. They will make sure that they have told them two things: the nature of their sex organs, and their purpose — which will, of course, include the truth about "the stork" and "where babies come from."

It is not intended here to indicate just how they should be told, since this will depend largely upon the tact and understanding of the parents and the intelligence of their children. But the important facts must be conveyed to them in the best way possible. At the same time certain elementary facts of sex hygiene, for instance, the cleansing of the genital organs, should be included. This is particularly advisable in the case of the girl, and of the uncircumcised boy. [...]

Never let them think that they are asking things they should not. It can always be requested of children that these questions be asked only in private, suggesting that they are of a sacred nature. Parents, however, should not feel that with this knowledge their children will be safe. If they do find that they are indulging in self-relief or sexual play, they must act with great tact and draw attention away from such practices by suggesting other activities and interests. Above all they should not raise the slightest question as to whether such practices are right or wrong. They must accept in a realistic way the fact that self-relief will occur naturally, and trust that, with the knowledge given, apart from any spiritual guidance and development, moderation will be observed.

Obviously, therefore, a sound, though not necessarily minute, knowledge of the male and female organs is required, firstly by the parents, who will find it much simpler to explain these facts to their children in a pictorial or easily understood manner; and secondly, by the average individual as common knowledge. [...]

Document 6.2
Anglican Synod of Ontario

Recommendations Re the Protection of Girl Life

This 1932 report was produced for consideration by the Council on Child and Family Welfare. Its authors are a special investigative committee of the Anglican Synod of Ontario, who surveyed their own parishes and parish organizations in order to come up with "recommendations" regarding particular concerns about young women of the time.

Issues to Consider
- What inspired this study? What were adolescent girls in need of protection from?
- In the view of the investigators, what were the causes of "incorrigibility" and delinquency in young girls?
- Why did the investigators recommend for these girls "the development of personal service" over institutionalization, the traditional approach to their problems?

(Suggestions offered as a result of the study being made by a special committee appointed by the Synod of the Ecclesiastical Province of Ontario.)

The study began originally with the question of the necessity and possibility of arranging custodial care for wayward and incorrigible girls or unmarried mothers of the Anglican faith in the different dioceses that comprise the Ecclesiastical Province of Ontario. However, as soon as the study was put under way it immediately broadened into a field of much wider considerations. The final report will contain detailed statistics and summaries of the various aspects of the studies, but the following suggestions seemed to the committee in charge to warrant consideration as the outline of the programme in this field.

1. The committee recommends that a continuing committee on the problems of girl life be created advisory to the Synod and that the committee should include, in addition to representatives of the Synod, representative church women engaged in work in this field.
2. That as indicated in the whole study any programme undertaken in this field by the Church should place its major emphasis on the development of personal service rather than institutional facilities as the fundamental features of our programme. This would admittedly be pioneering away from the traditional institutional policy that has characterized so much of the programme in this field of many public authorities and of the Roman Catholic Church and to some degree of some of the Protestant Churches.
3. The programme must be visualized as of very broad scope. Beyond any doubt the questionnaires revealed a very strong opinion among the Clergy that the Church must endeavour to arouse a much greater sense of responsibility for character training and education in the fundamental relationships of life on the part of the parents. To the breakdown of parental relationship in this field in early childhood is attributed much of the difficulty, incorrigibility, etc., in the adolescent period. Many of the Clergy suggest that

Source: "Recommendations Re the Protection of Girl Life," Canadian Social Development Council Fonds, MG 28 I 14, v. 167, File 1-16, National Archives of Canada, May 1932, pp. 1–8.

through some medium, clergy and parents should be provided with literature that would be of value to parents in this connection and that the Church itself should endeavour to direct attention in every way to the necessity of more effective exercise of its responsibility by the home.

4. Many of the Clergy express their conviction that just as the home has failed to discharge as fully as possible its responsibilities in character and moral training so there is room for greater emphasis being placed by the Church itself on the fundamental attributes of moral integrity, simple morality, and chastity in the preparation of our boys and girls for confirmation and that were the Church to make available simply written literature which on the one hand could be directed to the Clergy and on the other hand could be placed in the hands of adolescent boys and girls that it would have a most decided effect in the whole problem in which we were interested.

5. In this broader field also the question of recreation came up in a very forceful aspect and seemed to sub-divide into three or four different lines of consideration:

   (a) Much appreciation was expressed of the Girl Guide movement, but it seemed evident that it failed to hold or appeal to many girls after the age of entering collegiate, generally around thirteen or fourteen years of age, and that there was the greatest need for some development in the Guide programme or for some similar recreational interest which would particularly appeal to the girl from about fourteen to eighteen years of age. It was pointed out that in scores of cases the girl would outgrow her Guide interests about this age and was then thrown on her own resources and neighbourhood to make up her new associations often with undesirable results. It was suggested that the committee should bring this matter to the attention of the Girl Guide Association and also to the women's organizations within the Church.

   The A.Y.P.A. (Anglican Young People's Association) movement was highly commended but the opinion was expressed that it would lose its strength with the youth and girl of eighteen to twenty-three or twenty-four were it to take in this younger group in its membership since the recreational interests of this different age group were not likely to be the same.

   (b) A very difficult problem was encountered in the mission charges in small parishes where it was pointed out that there might be only seven or eight young girls and an equal number of young men in the whole area. Many of the Clergy wrote quite pathetic summaries of the breakdown of morals and of other problems developing in such circumstances. It would seem that if some arrangement could be worked out for co-operative recreational interests with the young people of other faiths in these districts or of the provision of library, correspondence services and recreation within these homes that much of value would result. It is possible that by co-operation with the representatives of the Provincial Department of Agriculture certain developments might be worked out in this aspect of the problem.

   (c) The distressing fact that out of 215 unmarried mothers of the Anglican faith in the Ecclesiastical Province 83 only were of Canadian birth, seemed to indicate the necessity of a greater effort on the part of our Church for the organization of special recreational services for the young British girl especially entering housework in the Canadian community. Inquiry suggested that a great number of these girls in the last five years had come to Ontario, particularly to Ottawa, Hamilton, Toronto, and Windsor and in smaller numbers to London, Ontario. There was quite definite record of the formation of recreation groups among these girls in some cities, but too much of this work was of a spasmodic nature or not so organized or directed as to encourage their association in parish recreation activities. However, the really serious question in these centres seemed to be the lack of any facilities for these girls for entertainment of their friends, especially those of the opposite sex and for some social recreation on their "half day off" and on their Sundays. What is required does not seem to be anything elaborate in the way of a club house, etc., but merely the provision at some central place of a sitting room where these girls could go where they could write or read or sew, or entertain their friends of either sex. This should be provided in two or three of these centres. It would not cost much and its possibilities would be undoubted.

6. *Unmarried Parenthood.*

One of the questions of reference to the committee was that of the provision of custodial or institutional care for the unmarried mother of the Anglican faith. After careful inquiry into the age and distribution of these girls and on the other hand study of the institutional services existing in the province, the professional advisors to the committee were not in favour of the development of additional facilities in this line, but rather strongly emphasized that the Church of England should have the courage and foresight to pioneer in this field by an experiment in the provision of personal service for the unmarried mother and her child.

The legislation of the province provides that local Children's Aid Society agents are to be considered as local officers under the Unmarried Parenthood Act of the province. However, since in all centres but Ottawa, Hamilton, and Toronto, services are available only through the local offices of the Children's Aid Society, practically no social or case work services are offered, only legal and apprehension facilities being offered. This undoubtedly contributes towards the congregation of young unmarried mothers in three or four city centres where hospitalization and other services are offered. In many cases full maintenance costs would be paid if the service were only available for the mother and in addition social re-establishment of the mother and her child would be assured in a larger group. It is now the general impression in more advanced programmes and standards of work, that granted the mother is normal, her withdrawal from the realization and contacts of community life should be for as short a period as possible and that she should be adjusted back into the community as soon as possible. It is for this reason that we have ventured to suggest that the Church should pioneer in making available for the young unmarried mother of its faith, social and case work services rather than institutional care, arranging the latter through the former where necessary.

It is therefore proposed that instead of considering the erection or establishment of any additional institutions to care for the unmarried mother and her child, that we should attempt to evolve a personal service programme utilizing the existing agencies and services for that part of the work which can be entrusted to them, and the provincial office and the Deputy Provincial officers for legal and maintenance work, collaborating with them for case work also where they have women workers attached to their staffs. Where custodial care is required it would be provided through private boarding home care for the mother or the child, or both, and hospital services would be used for hospitalization.

It is therefore suggested that consideration should be given to provision, at the office of the Council for Social Service in Toronto, for one thoroughly experienced worker in the unmarried parenthood field as a case work secretary for this type of case in the Ecclesiastical Province with an assistant to be added as soon as possible, who with the worker in charge, would endeavour to carry on the field work of this service. It is proposed that the service should be made known to the Clergy and various church organizations throughout the Ecclesiastical Province with the thought in mind that any Clergyman or any family facing this problem in an individual case might apply to this secretary, who would in turn arrange directly or through co-operation with existing services, to have immediate contact with the girl, preferably in her own home, looking towards consideration of the case and decision as to whether she should be transferred to another community, where and what plan for her care and that of her child should be worked out. It is realized that especially in the smaller towns and villages the girl's chances at social re-establishment is greater if part of her problem can be dealt with in another community. [...]

7. *Custodial Care for the Incorrigible Girl.*
So far the study has seemed to develop contradictory evidence in this aspect. Social workers consulted state that the number of girl delinquents who are not mentally defective is very, very slight and not sufficient to justify special institutional facilities especially for the Church of England. The statistical analysis which has been made of committed girl delinquents would bear this out there being only an average of thirty in the entire province of Ontario in care at a given time. However, others were of the opinion that the question of the wayward and incorrigible girl beyond parental control is a serious one and that were well organized services available similar to those offered by St. Faith's in Toronto that they would be extensively used likely with complete maintenance provided by the parents in many cases. There was general agreement that such care should be under the direction of Church people in so far as the personal life and development of the girl was concerned. The Ontario government is erecting in Western Ontario a girls' school similar to the boys' school at Bowmanville, where girls who have not been committed in the courts will be given care on voluntary admission. As in the case of Bowmanville parents will meet maintenance if possible and if not, maintenance is to be paid by the province and municipality.

The suggestion is made that an approach should be made to the Ontario government asking that provision be made in the new property for one cottage which would be given a special name and in which Anglican girls of any age sent to the school would live under their own house mother, the Church of England in the Ecclesiastical Province undertaking to make a fair contribution towards the capital expenditure involved in the erection of the building. It is proposed that these girls should not have separate educational, recreational or other life apart from the school and the house mother in charge would be a member of the staff under the general superintendent. It is strongly urged however, that the girls in this cottage would, in respect of their home and Church life, be assured direction along the lines of their own faith. The situation would be that for all general subjects they would partake in the life of the school and practically return to their own home for their personal life with their own Chaplain serving their cottage. [...]

Document 6.3

Basic Education (Editorial in *Toronto Star*)

This editorial appeared in the *Toronto Star* (a local newspaper that nonetheless enjoyed a fairly broad readership in Southern Ontario) shortly after World War II ended. It is a supportive response to a Toronto Board of Education recommendation that sex education be incorporated in the standard health curriculum of the high school, a subject of heated debate since the Great War. At the time the editorial was written, only high schools in British Columbia offered regular sex education.

Issues to Consider
- Why does the author of "Basic Education" feel that sex education should be included in the high-school curriculum?
- What understandings of gender roles and human sexuality come through in this editorial?

It is hoped that the board of education will adopt the report sent forward by the management committee that instruction in sex hygiene be included in the curriculum for secondary school pupils. This was recommended by Dr. C. C. Goldring, director of education, with the proviso that such instruction be given by the school doctor and nurse and by physical education teachers as part of the general health education in the schools. Classes in this subject should be conducted separately for boys and girls.

The school system has for some time been under criticism for its avoidance of so basic a subject as sex relations. It has endeavored to prepare the children for almost everything but family life. Yet the foundations of a healthy society consist of well-adjusted parents capable of raising a healthy family.

It is questionable whether the fear of venereal disease should be the starting point for sex education. The topic should be approached from a positive, not negative viewpoint. And if it is to become part of the school's health instruction program, mental and spiritual as well as physical health requires to be stressed. Teachers on this subject should be persons who are skilled in the psychology of adolescence and of human relations as well as in physiology. Fear of disease is apparently not enough to deter young people from unhealthy sex relations, as statistics indicate. About 75 per cent of the cases of venereal disease are today found among young people under 30 years of age. A large percentage of these are among adolescent girls.

Sound education in this field is all the more needed now to protect the post-war generation from the troublesome, unsettling influences which follow a period of war. Such education is not solely the responsibility of the schools. It should be part of the general social attitude toward women. For example, the protection of and respect for motherhood is an essential part of "sex education."

Source: Editorial, "Basic Education," *Toronto Star*, October 28, 1945, 3.

Topic 7

Age Matters:
Youth and the Elderly

Monks giving shoes and clothes to elderly men, Montreal, circa 1930; McCord Museum, MP-1978.107.4.

CONTEXT

Closely connected to the subject of family history considered in Topic 5, that of age, including such related concepts as life stage and generation, has been drawing the attention of social historians over the past twenty years. Age is seen as an analytical category that operates in ways similar to that of class. As a fundamental element of social experience, and one that has become increasingly important as an identifying or classifying principle since the late 19th century, age denotes much more than merely the years counted since birth. It is a status marker and a source of power. Most societies are organized along a hierarchy of age as much as one of social class, gender, and race. Furthermore, the experience of being a certain age or belonging to a certain generation is historical: what it means to be a child, an adolescent, an adult, or an elder changes over time and in accordance with the social needs and goals of particular historical moments.

Although much criticized for his broad inferences made from a narrow and largely upper-class source base, French cultural historian Philippe Aries inspired an international scholarly interest in this subject in *Centuries of Childhood* (1962). In Canada, the first to take up the point that children have a history — that childhood is specific to time and place — were historians of education. Neil Sutherland's seminal *Children in English Canadian Society, 1880–1920* (1976) detailed how childhood was reconceptualized through reform campaigns and related state initiatives, demonstrating the growth of public support for a "modernized" childhood as the nation's best way forward. As much as its members' dedication to Christian service and civic duty, fear that an impoverished childhood would have negative effects for the future citizenry galvanized the multifaceted child welfare campaign that was integral to the social gospel movement considered in Topic 3. By 1900, the childhood experience was being modified in the wake of changes in industrial production that reduced the demand for child labour, the enactment of protective legislation restricting ages and hours of work, and the new ideas about children's socialization that were being disseminated throughout the Western world as the "Century of the Child" opened. With their future-oriented mandate that gave new social value to children as "national assets," child welfare reformers redefined childhood as a special stage of institutionalized dependence centred on careful nurturance at home, school attendance, and supervised play.

The 20th century also saw the emergence of a distinctive life stage between childhood and adulthood, a modern adolescence. This development was in many ways a logical extension of the new ideas about childhood, while reflecting also a changing economy that restricted work opportunities for the young and called for more schooling in preparation for the labour market. In addition, there were significant changes unfolding in ideals about family life, now emphasizing affective and "companionate" relations more than the material assistance and shared labour of its members as an economic unit. While increasingly a common experience that crossed other social boundary lines, much as did childhood and old age, this newly distinct life stage still depended primarily on the family's economic standing. Although the age of school-leaving was raised to fifteen or sixteen years in most provinces by 1930, it was only in the context of post–World War II affluence that teenagers' wages became less critical in the working-class family economy. Yet during the years between 1920 and 1950, youth labour increasingly took the form of part-time work, wages afforded adolescents all manner of new consumer options, and the primary occupation of youth became high school. These years also saw a recognizably modern "youth culture" take shape within the context of a technology-led and increasingly commercialized popular culture. Not by mere coincidence, these years were punctuated by periodic waves of moral panic about "the youth problem" inscribed in the modern ways of the "rising generation," and especially their "new morality" and seeming potential for delinquency. Worried Canadians took to insisting that citizenship training be part of every high-school curriculum and even incorporated into the extracurriculum and the activities of organized youth, as Linda Ambrose indicates in her contribution to this section.

The historical writing on life stages and their keynote experiences points to the fact that there are multiple sociocultural factors at work in how they are defined at any time, and how they are experienced within different social groups. As we have seen in Topic 3, reform-minded Canadians at the turn of the 20th century were enthusiastic about adopting the surveying, measuring, and categorizing methods of the emergent social sciences. By this time, old age was also becoming a distinct category in an increasingly categorical social order. Persons sixty and over represented just under 8 percent of Canada's population in 1901. No longer regarded as useful and active participants in an industrial society that lauded efficiency and productivity, the elderly haplessly joined the ranks of other "social problems." Demographic shifts and the marginal economic status of working-class families added to the problematic character of old age. With declining fertility, and as fewer women gave birth in their forties, more children had left home by the time their parents reached old age. Falling birth rates also lowered the ratio of elderly to adult children. It was now more likely for an adult child to have a surviving parent, but fewer siblings to share the burden of care. Elderly women were especially vulnerable to economic distress: slightly over 50 percent of Canadian women were widowed by ages seventy to seventy-nine.

As would transpire with so many of the other "social problems" of the time, the state was again called upon to assume the responsibility of providing for its elderly citizens. Even its direct intervention ultimately did little to improve their lot. Under pressure from independent Labour representatives in the House of Commons, most notably J. S. Woodsworth (see Topic 3), the federal government passed the Old Age Pensions Act of 1927. This was a shared-cost program, jointly financed by federal and provincial governments but administered by the provinces because the British North America Act placed social welfare under provincial jurisdiction. By 1930, only four provinces had enacted the pension act; the others would do so later in the Depression decade largely because it was a way to transfer some of their burgeoning relief costs back into federal hands. In any case, the provisions for support were so meagre that few elderly Canadians could have lived on the pension alone without some measure of deprivation. The pension paid a maximum of $20 per month, depending on other income and assets, and was available to British subjects seventy years of age and older with twenty years of residence in Canada. A strict means test determined the candidate's eligibility through careful examination of his or her financial condition. In today's dollars, the roughly $240 per year pension would translate to about $2,500, much less than the current average amount of state pension benefits. It was not until the passage of the Old Age Security Act of 1951, which provided a universal pension of $40 monthly for all Canadians over seventy years, and the employment-based Canada and Quebec Pension Plans of 1965, that progress was made in assuring the material welfare of Canada's older generation. By the end of the 20th century, with the aging of the general population, the major issues were health care and the continued viability of government pensions for an expanding social group.

REFERENCES/FURTHER READING

Aries, P. *Centuries of Childhood: A Social History of Family Life*. New York: Knopf, 1962.

Comacchio, C. R. *"Nations Are Built of Babies": Saving Ontario's Mothers and Children*. Montreal and Kingston: McGill-Queen's University Press, 1993.

Davies, M. J. *Into the House of Old: A History of Residential Care in British Columbia*. Montreal and Kingston: McGill-Queen's University Press, 2003.

Low, Brian. *NFB Kids: Portrayals of Children by the National Film Board of Canada, 1939–1989*. Waterloo: Wilfrid Laurier University Press, 2002.

McIntosh, Robert. *Boys in the Pits: Child Labour in Coal Mines*. Montreal and Kingston: McGill-Queen's University Press, 2000.

Montigny, E.-A. *Foisted upon the Government? State Responsibilities, Family Obligations, and the Care of the Dependent Aged in Late Nineteenth-Century Ontario*. Montreal and Kingston: McGill-Queen's University Press, 1997.

Owram, D. *Born at the Right Time: A History of the Baby Boom Generation*. Toronto: University of Toronto Press, 1996.

Richardson, T. R. *The Century of the Child: The Mental Hygiene Movement and Social Policy in the United States and Canada*. Albany, N.Y.: State University of New York Press, 1989.

Rooke, Patricia T., and R. L. Schnell. *Discarding the Asylum: From Child Rescue to the Welfare State in English Canada, 1800–1950*. Llanham, Md.: University Press of America, 1983.

Snell, J. *The Citizen's Wage: The State and the Elderly in Canada, 1900–1951*. Toronto: University of Toronto Press, 1996.

Sutherland, N. *Children in English Canadian Society, 1880–1920: Framing the Twentieth-Century Consensus*. Toronto: University of Toronto Press, 1976; reissued by Wilfrid Laurier University Press, 2000.

———. *Growing Up: Childhood in English Canada from the Great War to the Age of Television*. Toronto: University of Toronto Press, 1997.

ILLUSTRATION 7.1 (P. 273)

The Depression hit the elderly — many of whom were already living at the edges of poverty — with particular force, especially in situations where family members who might have looked after them were also affected by unemployment or wage cuts. Municipal relief was earmarked for male breadwinners; many elderly people became dependent on charity. In Quebec, the Catholic Church played a central role in social welfare matters.

Issue to Consider

- What impression does Illustration 7.1 — a photograph probably taken in a church hall or basement where the needy were usually attended to — communicate about the conditions of these men's lives?

ARTICLES

The articles and documents in this section consider two of the so-called social problems of modernity as defined by age and generation. Linda Ambrose discusses the efforts of government agencies, social scientists, and a rural social organization called the Junior Farmers to persuade rural youth that their best interests, and those of the nation, would be realized if they stayed on the farm. Megan Davies explores the new social meanings that were being ascribed to old age by the 1930s, and how the homes established for the elderly in British Columbia reflected those meanings in their spatial design and in their programs for residents.

Article 7.1

Linda Ambrose

Cartoons and Commissions: Advice to Junior Farmers in Postwar Ontario

Issues to Consider

- What was the mandate of the Junior Farmer clubs? What, according to Ambrose, were its participants also being taught through its various activities and projects?
- What was the state of rural society in Canada during this time? How did conditions affect the status of the young in those communities?
- Ambrose uses cartoons as historical documents to examine the messages that were given to the rural youth of the 1940s and 1950s. What can this kind of visual evidence tell us, and not tell us, about society at the time?
- What did the experts have to say about rural society and rural youth? Did their views support those presented in the cartoons?
- What was the outcome of the federal government's Canadian Youth Commission surveys of rural youth?
- Why were rural residents categorized, by their own representatives, according to their level of social activism?

"It was only really through the Junior Farmers' Association that young farm people had the opportunity to learn how to pull everything together; to prepare for choosing and managing a farm operation before being beset by mortgages and mistakes."[1] That is how Linda Biesenthal, the author of *Rural Legacy: The History of the Junior Farmers' Association of Ontario*, describes the important educational role of Ontario's largest postwar club for rural youth. Junior Farmer clubs were created and run by the provincial Department of Agriculture, and, just after the Second World War, there were almost 5,500 members.[2] Although best known for its "calf clubs" and fall fair competitions, the Junior Farmer curriculum evidently covered much more than animal husbandry and farm management. Not only were club members taught how to prepare for a career in farming,[3] they also learned about the division of labour in farm families and about ideal models for each sex. The Junior Farmers' Association offers a rich case study for analysing messages about gender roles, specifically the appropriate behaviour for men and women, that Ontario rural youth were expected to take up as adults in the 1950s. While city dwellers began to digest the gendered realities of postwar family life in suburbia,[4] teenagers and young adults throughout the Ontario countryside were also fed a steady diet of highly stereotyped ideas about sex roles. Junior Farmer clubs clearly acted as one avenue for socializing teenagers and young adults into their future careers and the business of farm life. Moreover, the advice that was given to rural youth was based on a particular perception of the problems that plagued the countryside in the years after the Second World War.

Source: Linda Ambrose, "Cartoons and Commissions: Advice to Junior Farmers in Postwar Ontario," *Ontario History* 93, no. 1 (Spring 2001): 57–80.

Various texts in the *Junior Farmer News*, the club magazine published by the Ontario Department of Agriculture, reveal that teaching gender roles was a strong, though unstated, theme and purpose of the group. At the same time, the youth organization gave rural strategists an important forum for communicating their concerns about rural stratification, farm management, and the future of agriculture. Despite the optimism of "country life ideology" at the turn of the century[5] and popular stereotypes about the advantages of rural life, the Ontario countryside was not a place of equal opportunity at mid-century. For example, data from the 1941 census confirm that most farm homes lacked amenities such as indoor plumbing and hydroelectricity that were common to urban dwellings by this time. While it is important to note that discrepancies existed between urban and rural families, one must be careful to avoid generalizations about rural life. One thing is clear: important differences existed between farmers too. Historians have grappled for a long time with the problem of how to measure stratification in rural society because the paradigm of social class cannot easily be transplanted to the rural setting. Parvin Ghorayshi concludes that "there is no general tendency of capitalist development applicable to all types of farming. Canadian agriculture is characterized both by the development of capitalist farms and persistence of viable petit bourgeois production."[6] Charles Johnson, who also takes up this question of social stratification among early-twentieth-century Ontario farmers, maintains that a wide diversity of social experiences and ranks existed.[7] To illustrate that rural society was indeed highly stratified, Kerry Badgley's recent study of the United Farmers of Ontario makes a useful foray into the quantification of economic diversity among farmers in three Ontario counties. Using assessment rolls, he considers the variables of age, acreage, land value, and so on and concludes that "a UFO farmer ... was as close to an average farmer as one could be."[8] At the same time, he finds that the leaders of the movement were slightly better off than the average.

Yet a more complete understanding of the kinds of hierarchies that characterized rural communities in the first half of the twentieth century seems to defy our grasp as historians. Paying closer attention to what rural experts in the postwar era said about stratification helps to clarify the ideology that framed the social realities of rural Ontario at mid-century.[9] Some of these hierarchies were based on economics, but others differentiated between the sexes, and still others between various levels of education. The theme of success, measured both in economic viability and in social influence, was central to expert thinking about postwar agriculture and rural society. Rural Ontario was most definitely a stratified place. Agricultural cartoons provide us with a window into the problem of stratification because they contain representations of the ideas that prevailed in the postwar period. Those who did research and made recommendations about rural Ontario subscribed to complex and sometimes contradictory ideas about why hierarchies existed, which ones should be endorsed, and which ones should be challenged.

This study examines the cartoons that appeared in *Junior Farmer News* throughout the 1950s.[10] Social scientists interested in gender studies and social stratification have begun to explore humour to understand how social constructions operated to reinforce prevalent ideologies.[11] Historians can make effective use of cartoons to explore the discourses that were implicit in this medium of popular culture. For example, Margaret Conrad used cartoons in her 1991 study dealing with nineteenth-century regional protest in the Maritimes.[12] More recently, Christina Burr's study on labour reform in Toronto illustrates that careful analysis of cartoons can enrich our understanding of social history because these sources unlock key ideas about gender and politics.[13] Scott Vokey has compared the 1930s editorial cartoons published in Toronto's *Evening Telegram* and the *Toronto Star* to see how the content of those sketches differed from those published in a labour newspaper, *The Worker*.[14]

In this article, I survey agricultural cartoons created for young readers to see what they may show about a variety of questions: What did Ontario rural teens learn from Junior Farmers about the nature of differences between successful and unsuccessful farmers? To what extent did this reflect the thinking of government authorities and academic researchers? How was the sexual division of labour in the countryside portrayed? Did this match reality? What did the cartoons teach youth about the roles they would fulfil as they became adults and took up the occupation of farming? What challenges were they taught to expect?

The person who created the sketches under scrutiny here was a cartoonist and commercial artist named Jack Cockburn. Even before he began to publish his cartoons in *Junior Farmer News*, Cockburn had an association with the Junior Farmers of Ontario because he became a member of a local club in the mid-1940s. By 1950, he had risen through the ranks to take office as president of the provincial Junior Farmers' Association. Cockburn described his teenage experiences in the early postwar years, saying, "Like many others, I had left school to help on the farm. I was young, shy, and generally confused about my future." Yet he attributed his later success as a commercial artist to the experiences he enjoyed in the Junior Farmer movement, where he honed both his artistic and his leadership abilities. "Many of the skills I've developed," he testified, "are the direct result of the experience I gained as a member of the Junior Farmers' Association."[15] Cockburn's cartoons enjoyed a long and successful run in the magazine, and that can only mean that their messages were more than just one idealistic young man's impressions about his favourite youth group. Indeed, these cartoons are not simply isolated sketches from the pen of an enthusiastic club alumnus. In Cockburn's "art," the Ontario Department of Agriculture found the communication tool it needed to convey its messages to young subscribers.[16] The experts hoped to exploit the cartoons fully in order to translate their academic findings and recommendations into a medium that youth would read and accept. Cockburn's humorous sketches reflect the thinking of postwar authorities about what was wrong with rural Ontario, how it could be fixed, and the role that rural youth would play in that transformation. Cartoons are meant to be funny, so what better medium could there be to capture the attention of such a young audience of would-be farmers? Once they were hooked by the format, Junior Farmer members would likely accept the cartoons' messages.

Cockburn drew attention to a variety of issues. Explicitly, he reminded club members about upcoming conferences, key projects, and program themes. Implicitly, he sketched much more. The cartoons under consideration here are taken from a six-year period in the mid-1950s when *Junior Farmer News* was published monthly. A total of fifty-seven cartoons forms the basis of this analysis. The settings of the cartoons varied, reflecting the many facets of the Junior Farmer program and aspects of members' lives, as Table 1 demonstrates.

If a conference was pending, readers were reminded to make arrangements to attend. It is significant that, in portraying the experiences of farm youth, only a total of ten cartoons were set either on the family farm or in the home. The focus of Junior Farmer clubs was clearly on peer-group activities, not on the family business or the domestic scene. This reflects the fact that, in Ontario at this time, a youth culture had emerged and extracurricular youth organizations were a large part of that social experience.[17] Moreover, this emphasis on life outside the family underscores the efforts of the provincial government to depict rural life as an attractive option for youth, more than just an incessant routine of drudgery and hard work.

Themes about gender begin to emerge as one analyses the cartoons for character composition. Counting the number of characters who appeared in the sketches produces the statistics shown in Table 2.

Table 1   Subject matter of cartoons

Type of Setting	No. of Cartoons
Regular club meeting	11
Competitions/exhibits	10
Club socials	9
Provincial conferences	8
Family farm	7
Team sporting event	4
Club members' home	3
Bus tour	1
Choir practice	1
Debate	1
Drama presentation	1
News item	1
TOTAL	57

Table 2   Characters portrayed in cartoons

Boys	353
Girls	213
Adult men	49
Adult women	17
Animals	39
Space creatures	9
TOTAL	680

The nine space creatures appearing in a total of three different cartoons serve to remind one of the historical context of the 1950s, marked by the beginnings of space exploration at the height of that phase of the Cold War. The themes in these sketches are all futuristic. In one, Junior Farmer members are shown as the first to land on Mars because they go there on a club-exchange visit. The suggestion was that Junior Farmers were progressive and forward-thinking, both in terms of their awareness of world affairs and in their agricultural practices. The animals in the cartoons (which incidentally outnumber the adult women by more than two to one) are mainly domestic animals, though in three cases wild animals are shown. The domestic animals are most commonly cattle, reflecting the fact that most Junior Farmer livestock clubs involved each member raising a calf and exhibiting it at the local fall fair.

Of the people in the cartoons, boys outnumber girls 353 to 213; 140 more boys than girls. There are several explanations for these figures. In part, the imbalance between the sexes reflects the reality that male club members outnumbered female ones. A 1946 report revealed that 5,482 young Ontarians were members of the Junior Farmers, and the same account estimated that these were "one-third girls and two-thirds boys."[18] Another explanation is that the cartoons reflect the widely held assumption that labour in farming communities was rigidly divided between the sexes. Of the adults in the cartoons, men outnumber women almost three to one (49 to 17). This ratio reinforced false perceptions about farm women by significantly underestimating their important economic and social roles on family farms and in rural organizations. Only three of the cartoons were set in the home (where women and girls would presumably be found in greater numbers). Perhaps even fewer females would have been portrayed were it not for the fact that romantic heterosexual themes and social events figured so largely. In any event, the message is clear that, through the male eyes of Jack Cockburn and his publisher, the Ontario Department of Agriculture, Junior Farmers, the provincial organization for rural youth, was a male-dominated group.

Beyond those messages about gender, the cartoons serve to illustrate some of the assumptions that sociologists and agricultural representatives[19] held about rural life in Ontario. Experts premised their views on particular biases and promoted their favourite solutions. Indeed, an effective analysis of these cartoons must begin with an understanding of the current academic opinions of the day. The cartoons reflect the discourse of agricultural experts — sociologists and agricultural representatives[20]— who gave careful attention to rural questions.

To explore the content of those academic ideas, this article relies on two kinds of sources. The first type is the reports and recommendations of the Canadian Youth Commission (CYC). During a series of postwar planning exercises in the 1940s, this non-government commission turned its attention to various social issues concerning Canadian young people.[21] Its findings are particularly useful for understanding what expert opinion had to say about rural youth in the period leading up to the 1950s. A second useful kind of source is the academic research of rural sociologists, both of those who informed the prescriptive social planning of the CYC before the war had ended, and of those who published their research in the late 1950s and early 1960s. Professor Helen Abell was one such postwar researcher. She concentrated on two themes: the situation of rural women, and the prospects of the small family-farm enterprise.

On the roles of women, Abell saw things differently from her male colleagues. "Whether he tells you so or not," she assured a group of rural Ontario women in 1960, "the farmer of today can not and would not want to operate our typical Canadian family farm without the feminine component of agriculture — you."[22] That assurance was not found often in farming circles, and it was certainly not offered during the 1950s by the Junior Farmers of Ontario. The way that women's roles were constructed is quite fascinating because the messages in the club magazine certainly do not bear out Abell's findings. Indeed, the role of rural women was diminished significantly in the cartoons' representation of reality. Yet the messages that the Junior Farmers communicated to young men are equally fascinating, and not only for the biases that favoured men over women. Jack Cockburn's cartoons illustrate that ideal constructions of masculinity were premised upon a generational tension and differentiation between fathers and sons. To obtain a more complete picture of the gender history, we shall consider how roles for the sexes were socially constructed for rural postwar teens in the pages of this youth magazine. The cartoons provide a set of texts that are rich with imagery about gender prescriptions. The fact that these images were historically specific to the period becomes clear when one considers the concerns that sociologists were expressing about the social and economic viability and future of the family farm from the 1940s onward.

The Canadian Youth Commission, like other postwar planning groups that functioned during the Second World War, worked on the supposition that if sufficient planning occurred before the end of the war, then the transition to peacetime would be smooth and trouble free. The CYC published a series of reports between 1944 and 1948 on such wide-ranging topics as employment, education, leisure, religion, and health.[23] Indeed, one would be hard pressed to think of a social issue that the CYC did not include within the scope of its inquiry. When it came to studying the particular problems of rural youth, the CYC turned to a group of academics who specialized in rural studies and to rural activists who formed the leadership for a variety of movements, including: farm parties (the United Farmers of Ontario [UFO] and the United Farmers of Alberta [UFA]); cooperative movements (United Co-operatives and the Wheat Pool); and adult education (the Canadian Association for Adult Education, the New Canada Movement, and the National Farm Forum). Because rural activists controlled the process of shaping the CYC's studies and interpreting the results, the commission's rural findings are more a manifesto of the rural experts' opinions than a representation of youths' perceptions. The experts formed a rural elite who were deemed the most qualified to interpret the problems of rural youth and to prescribe solutions. In particular, the CYC asked for advice from these experts on "the population drift of youth from the smaller communities to the larger centres of industry and population." Concerned by the trend, one correspondent pointed out that "we ought to think of how this will affect our National life in the future."[24] Rural depopulation had been under way for several decades from the beginning of the rapid growth of Canadian cities at the turn of the century. Yet the CYC was quick to point out that, in the 1940s, 45 per cent of the population of Canada was still rural.

The commission published its findings on rural youth and their employment prospects in 1945. The committee that did this study for the CYC worked with a model of rural social stratification widely known at the time as "the agricultural ladder." The ladder was a convenient metaphor to outline the various levels of farm jobs, but it assumed an implicit desire among rural people for vertical vocational mobility. The top of the ladder, the goal of aspiring agriculturalists, was the independent owner-operator. This rank, and the ones below it, produced the following model.

THE AGRICULTURAL LADDER
Owner-Operator
Tenant Farmer
Wage Labourer
Unpaid Labourer

Rural committee members freely admitted that the climb would not be an easy one, and in fact noted that "definite obstacles stand in the way of achieving farm ownership." Moreover, statistics showed that at least 20 per cent of the rural youth population would not even attempt the climb but would choose instead to migrate to urban centres.

Yet there was another scale of stratification at work. This second one was not an economic classification but an ideological one that categorized rural people according to their relative activism or apathy. The experts implicitly perceived themselves to be operating at the highest level of this configuration because of their acute awareness and self-declared understanding of rural problems. Their outlook can best be described according to a scale of social activism, where the views of the rural elite were paramount. At the lowest level of this scale was the apathetic and uninvolved farmer; somewhere in the middle were members of farm organizations, who were committed to the ideal of collective action. The scale can be presented as follows:

ACTIVISM SCALE
Rural Elite (the "experts")
Members of Rural Organizations
Apathetic, Uninvolved Farmers

Rating rural Canadians according to this scale, the experts were concerned with what they viewed as widespread apathy among Canadian farmers, and they made it their goal to elevate such people from the lowest levels of uninvolvement to new heights of rural activism. Progress would occur when and if they could convert the children of the apathetic to a life of activism. Their work on the CYC was an important part of that strategy.

Who were these so-called "experts?" Typically, they held institutional affiliations with schools that specialized in agricultural education: in Saskatoon at the University of Saskatchewan Extension Department, in Guelph at the Ontario Agricultural College, and in Montreal at Macdonald College. They were also closely affiliated with rural organizations that stressed adult education and collective action such as the cooperative movement, the UFO and UFA federations of agriculture both provincial and national, the New Canada Movement, and the rural wing of the Canadian Association for Adult Education. A faith in collective action was one of the main tenets of farm organizations. It comes as no surprise, then, that when members of this rural elite set out to poll rural youth, they turned to those who were younger versions of themselves.

The youth who cooperated with the CYC committees in Saskatchewan and Ontario also had close ties to rural organizations — groups like Boys and Girls Agricultural and Homecraft Clubs, Wheat Pool Junior Cooperators, 4-H clubs, and Junior Farmers. In Ontario, the CYC's rural-research team invited ten "carefully selected" youth delegates to participate in their inquiry. They were selected on the basis of their involvement in commodity-marketing boards, their participation as junior partners in family-farm operations, and their membership in the Junior Farmers' Association of Ontario. These young people were active in organizations, articulate about rural issues, and above average in their education and economic status. In short, they could be characterized as young protégés of the experts themselves.

The commissioners' work was premised clearly on the idea that a hierarchy or system of stratification existed among Canadian farmers; the CYC report referred specifically to the "agricultural ladder." While the most successful rural people were owner-operators, others worked only as tenant farmers or hired hands. Rural youth were relegated to the bottom of this ladder because they were most often in the category of "unpaid labourers," while they waited either to inherit family property holdings or to gather the means to begin an independent operation. Moreover, the CYC noted that, for a number of them, it seemed that "many of the steps were missing" from the ladder altogether, because there was a shortage of positive role models. In the minds of the experts who informed the commission's view, many small farmers in Canada operated under less than ideal conditions, whether because of economic criteria or because of social ones. This is where rural youth organizations entered the picture.[25] The CYC placed great faith in the ability of organizations and clubs to educate and to shape the values of Canadian youth.

Thus, the CYC promoted the activities of all sorts of associations, including those sponsored by the churches, the state, and the community. The Junior Farmers of Ontario had a lot to say to rural youth whether they aspired to a career in farming or not. Echoing the CYC's concerns, the Junior Farmers' message to members was clear: some Ontario farmers succeeded in their work, others only "muddled along." In a cartoon, published in June 1955,[26] the two frames clearly show the contrast between two farm families. "The McMuddles of FAGGEDOUT Farm," who "do their bookeeping [sic] on the kitchen calendar," live in a state of turmoil, stress, and disarray. Meanwhile, the Neighbours followed the model of the Elgin County Junior Farmers and implemented a "farm business center" which consisted of a desk space and a filing cabinet. They obviously run the more successful business enterprise. But there is much more to this cartoon than the simple message about business procedures.

The humour behind this cartoon lies partly in its depiction of the two sexes. Mr McMuddle, the stressed-out and disorganized farmer, rifles through a pile of papers, sweating over his self-imposed plight while trying to run his farm operation from the kitchen table. His wife looks on, wringing her hands helplessly because she cannot find the letter he needs or even remember the date in question. Altogether, they seem a hopeless example of incompetence. Meanwhile, next door, the Neighbours' home is depicted as a tidy place where clean-shaven Mr Neighbour easily locates the file he needs. Meanwhile, Mrs Neighbour competently works in her sphere, the kitchen, either arranging flowers or preparing Mr Neighbour's meal. She is the ideal postwar picture of female domesticity, though she is rather startled when her husband quips that he now needs "a cute little secretary" to go with his efficient business setup. Evidently, Mr Neighbour, with a twinkle in his eye, has learned to fend for himself in managing his farm operation, keeping his farm business out of the kitchen. What the cartoon fails to show is the statistical probability that Mrs Neighbour likely had something to do with bookkeeping for the operation because a 1960 study revealed that 42 per cent of Ontario farm women did that work.[27] Readers are reassured about Mr Neighbour's masculinity because his sexist remark underscores the fact that, although he benefits from the well-appointed filing system, office work is really for women, and if he could hire someone outside the family to assist him, she would be not only skilled but physically attractive.

The McMuddles versus the Neighbours cartoon not only raises questions about success and business procedures but also introduces a second theme: ideals about sexual division of labour in the farm home. According to the stereotypes, farm men and farm women lived in separate spheres. The cover illustration of *Junior Farmer News* in May 1954, commemorating the organization's tenth anniversary, clearly depicted this separation of work.[28] On the one side, the man is in the field driving his tractor and cultivating the soil. On the other, his wife is working in the garden near the house. Statistics from sociologist Helen Abell's 1960 study bear out the fact that 89 per cent of the Ontario farm women whom she polled indicated that they gardened. It would be a false assumption, however, to think that the kind of rigid division of labour between men and women suggested in the Junior Farmer magazine really existed. Abell's study also showed that women performed a wide range of other farm work. She found that 61 per cent of the farm women she polled either cleaned milkers or pails or helped with the milking or feeding of cattle. In addition, 53 per cent reported that they fed poultry and/or cleaned eggs. More than one-quarter (26 per cent) did some fieldwork and 13 per cent did some other type of farm work such as driving a tractor or some other machine.[29] Clearly, then, farm women engaged in a variety of farm tasks outside housework.

Readers of *Junior Farmer News*, however, were given a different message. In a cartoon published in October 1956, a young woman is depicted as a competitor in the annual Fall Plowing Match.[30] The all-male audience is completely astonished by her performance. All heads turn and all eyes are upon her as the men run from a distance, point at her, and gawk at the spectacle of a woman plowing her furrow. It is difficult to discern whether they were most fascinated by her skill at plowing or by her physical appearance. The sketch of the young woman is drawn with a highly exaggerated body shape — a tiny waist and voluptuous hips and thighs. The message to Junior Farmers was one that reinforced two accepted notions about sex roles. First, according to the cartoonist, it was highly unusual for a woman to drive a tractor with skill. Secondly, a rural woman entering into the male sphere was most likely to gain attention for her sexual attractiveness, and whether she was considered "sexy" or not, she could expect to be objectified and judged based on her body shape.

Of course, it is the very exaggeration of her body shape and the juxtaposition of roles that were intended to make readers laugh at the cartoon. Our concern here is to discover the message behind the cartoon, the implicit message about ideals. As Randall Harrison points out in

Jack Cockburn, *Junior Farmer News* 18, 10 (October 1956): 12. © Queen's Printer for Ontario 1956, reproduced by permission.

his study of the genre of humour, cartoons purposely deviate from reality by simplifying and exaggerating images in order to increase the impact.[31] Many different academic works have effectively explored humour using content-analysis techniques to illuminate different facets of gender studies.[32] Historians can usefully adopt these models by placing humorous texts back into their historical contexts, an approach that will help to explain how gender was operating as a factor in shaping the opinions of the time.

While women crossed over the divide to perform "men's work" on the farm during the postwar years, even if only occasionally, the reverse was apparently not true. At least men did not take up "women's work" with ease or comfort. One cartoon depicting a young male Junior Farmer at camp showed how much he struggled when faced with the simple task of making his bed and tidying up his cabin.[33] In the caption below that frame the cartoonist wrote, "He never had to do these menial tasks at home!!!" In the more than fifty-seven cartoons that form the basis of this article, there is only one other that shows a man doing any domestic or housework duty. In that frame, a young man dries dishes to impress the young woman he wants to date.[34] Otherwise, men in the cartoons did not appear in the kitchen, except to eat the food that the women had prepared (30 per cent of all the cartoons involve men and food in this way). There was one other scenario where three men came into a kitchen to catch a rat while the women looked on in fright.[35]

The message implicit in these samples of popular discourse was that while women might temporarily cross over into male territory to perform some farm work, or to "help" their husbands, the reverse was rarely true. Women, therefore, had a wider range of responsibilities on the farm, concentrating on housework and gardening but not being limited to these. Men, on the other hand, were either inept at household tasks or managed to avoid them completely except on rare occasions. The images in the cartoons serve to reinforce a rather rigid notion about gender roles that may have been true for men but certainly was not true for women.

Jack Cockburn, *Junior Farmer News* 18, 6 (June 1956): 8. © Queen's Printer for Ontario 1956, reproduced by permission.

The ideals that were held out to Ontario rural youth were firmly grounded in notions about what was "normal" for heterosexual couples.[36] Indeed, the Junior Farmers' Association referred to itself as a marriage bureau for rural youth. The monthly magazine ran a column called "Wedding Bells" that reported news of engagements and marriages between organization members.[37] Dating and heterosexual marriages were indeed a central theme of the magazine, and closer analysis of the messages implicit in Junior Farmer humour reveals a complex picture of gender ideals, where both men and women found instruction about how to select an ideal mate.

Cartoons, such as the one published in the June 1956 issue, illustrate that certain expectations existed for young women.[38] In the first frame, where a girls' softball tournament is under way, the young women play hard, one of them sliding into home plate while the opposing team's catcher reaches for the speeding ball. These athletes are strong, aggressive, and clearly competitive. As the cartoonist says, "To win is the thing — dust, dirt and sweat are all part of the business." These young women are far from frail or delicate. In the next frame, however, the cartoonist depicts a contrast between the afternoon game and a social function later that same night. The caption reads: "But come the evening dance, and the same girls can step out looking as if they've just popped from a fashion page! The transformation never ceases to amaze us." The boyfriends are clearly not only amazed but also appreciative of these fine female specimens in their revealing dresses and high-heeled shoes. Femininity in the pages of the *Junior Farmer News* was constructed through attention to beauty and fashion, though women sometimes operated outside those limitations — as they did when, in our example, they played sports.

Rural experts were concerned about young women, specifically about how to keep them from leaving the rural community altogether. While migration away from the farm was common for both sexes, the CYC found that it was more frequently the girls who left for the city than the boys. According to their calculations, the rate of leaving was "one girl in four, one boy in seven."[39] As the commissioners observed, this had implications for heterosexual unions because "on the farm each six young men find themselves left with only five eligible young ladies." Therefore, the CYC turned its attention to strategies designed to attract young women to rural life. The Saskatchewan rural committee of the CYC raised this issue in its question-naire, asking respondents, "Are there any unmarried women leaving your community? If so, what changes would you consider necessary to make the rural and small urban communities sat-isfactory places of employment and residence for young unmarried women?" A typical response came from a discussion group led by the local Baptist minister in Yorkton, Saskatchewan, whose list of suggestions included three specific measures: more modern homes and furnishings, various forms of recreation in the community, and young women's clubs.[40]

While the Baptists' list insisted that modern amenities and more leisure opportunities would appeal to rural women, other Saskatchewan groups seemed more aware of the fact that it was largely economic realities that drew women away from rural communities. These other groups suggested that a more diversified rural economy was the key to attracting and supporting young women.[41] Certainly, there were stark differences between the experience of rural and urban youth. For example, in the realm of education, the CYC's Saskatchewan committee reported "the startling fact that 65% of rural youth ... had not more than eight years of formal schooling, while for the same period only 30% of urban youth were found in this category."[42]

Indeed, the conditions that youth reported to the rural CYC committee painted a nega-tive picture of limited economic opportunities (some of which were gender-specific, others not), substandard housing, and inadequate facilities for education, recreation, and health serv-ices. Looking for the root causes of these social problems of family and community organiza-tion in rural Canada, the CYC cited, first, the absence of creative rural leadership. Because teachers, ministers, and youth group leaders were typically urban-trained or in some cases com-pletely untrained, they lacked an appreciation of rural life and did not understand the unique-ness of some aspects of rural culture and sociology. Second, the CYC cited the apparent apathy of rural people, especially those who lived at the lowest economic level. This is where rural youth organizations hoped to turn the tide. They would do so by focusing on the young men in rural communities.

Model young men were depicted in the Junior Farmer publication, but unlike the por-trayals of their sisters, the masculine ideal had less to do with appearance than with ability. To get to the top of the agricultural ladder that rural sociologists had discussed in the 1940s, young men who aspired to become farmers would have to change some things about how farms oper-ated. The experts shared a concern that there were too many small farming operations, where farmers failed to take advantage of the scientific advances in agriculture. A 1956 article by Helen Abell offered some explanations about why some farmers failed to prosper. In short, she traced the problem to the attitudes of farmers who said they were satisfied with their present way of life. "This satisfaction," she noted, "has social rather than economic foundations." More specifically, she identified three problems. First, many farmers failed to adopt new farming prac-tices which could increase their income; second, they were reluctant to take advantage of available credit to expand their farms; and third, farmers were opposed to their sons' obtaining sufficient education to enable them to become more skilled farmers.[43] Abell and other rural specialists hoped for major changes in attitude and social values when postwar youth reached adulthood.

Clearly, a great deal was riding on the next generation of men. The Junior Farmers of Ontario echoed Abell's findings. If the farm population was going to prosper, then young men needed to throw off their fathers' backward ways and take up the opportunities — educational, economic, and scientific — that their parents were reluctant to grasp. This idea of progressive sons as the bright hope for rural Ontario's future was depicted in the cartoons of *Junior Farmer News*. As early as 1953, the provincial conference of the organization took up the theme

Jack Cockburn, *Junior Farmer News* 15, 4 (April 1953): 14. © Queen's Printer for Ontario 1953, reproduced by permission.

"Yesterday, Today and Tomorrow" to try to inspire promising young men to adapt to new technologies and to dream about running farm operations in ways their fathers refused to consider. The bright young farmer of tomorrow would bring all the latest technologies to his farm and, according to the cartoonist, perhaps even operate his farm machinery by remote control.[44]

The fathers who were depicted in the Junior Farmer cartoons were not part of this futuristic thinking. They were hardly the types that one would aspire to emulate. Consider the April 1952 cartoon that depicts a group of young people departing for the provincial conference.[45] In the last moments before they leave, the young women fuss with their hair and make-up while Mother offers them yet another pair of high-heeled shoes to take along. The young men puzzle over how to fit the luggage into the trunk, and attach a pennant to the car aerial. Father, meanwhile, looks on. He is a dishevelled looking older man who smokes his pipe, tugs on his suspenders with one hand, and totes a pail of water with the other. He is stereotyped as the "clodhopper," or "country bumpkin," an old farmer who probably fit Abell's criteria as one who persisted in his small farm operation and outdated thinking. If there was to be a future for this family farm, it clearly rested with the young men, in suits and ties, who were off to an educational Junior Farmer convention for rural youth. The contrast between the two generations of men is stark.

The masculine ideal offered to Ontario rural youth in the postwar years consisted of a bright young lad who took up the educational opportunities offered to him, who participated in rural youth organizations, and who broke away from the limitations that his father's old-fashioned approach to farming would impose. This forward-looking farmer ideally would find an attractive wife with whom he would establish a new farming operation. Meanwhile, his potential partner, a female reader of the Junior Farmer magazine, was subtly being taught to identify the kind of young man who was a desirable mate and who had potential for future success in agriculture.

These ideal young couples were just the types that the Canadian Youth Commission had in mind in the 1940s when it concluded that one of the biggest obstacles for rural society was a crisis of leadership. This crisis was less concrete than the problems associated with economics or lack of facilities, but it was no less real in the minds of the experts. In highlighting this leadership crisis, the CYC commissioners added a psychological dimension to their analysis. This was a central theme in the work of R. Alex Sim, secretary of the adult-education service of

Macdonald College at McGill University, who wrote a background paper for the CYC in 1943. In that paper he argued that inferiority was commonly fostered in a rural person, based on the knowledge that "professional personnel in the [rural] community — his doctor, teacher, minister, lawyer, or even of all things his banker — in many cases remain there because they lack the qualifications, skill or experience to take command of higher salaries and the better living conditions those salaries would command at a larger centre."[46] To offset this psychological crisis among rural people, Sim and his fellow commissioners recommended an educational antidote.

Committed to the value of various adult-education measures, the CYC and the rural sociologists who informed its findings concluded that an exercise in consciousness-raising was in order. Recommending programs such as the Farm Radio Forum, or the New Canada Movement, these left-of-centre ideologues hoped that they could be instrumental in turning the tide for rural young people by encouraging them to become social activists. As Sim argued, "the [rural] man who has never had a dentist is more likely to blame the weather or his kidneys for his toothache than society in general, and is therefore not likely to fight for rural dental services, nor to overrule the dentists who presumably are organized to maintain the existing system ..."[47]

With great faith in the potential of adult-education schemes, the power of collectivism, and the appropriateness of self-determined solutions, the CYC recommended the establishment of more discussion groups for farm youth. This was a perfectly logical solution coming from a group of commissioners with a deep intellectual commitment to solving the problems of rural young people. The apathetic subsistence farmer and his offspring, however, were not willing converts. The idea of joining a local discussion group that urged one to "read, listen, and discuss" (the motto of the Farm Forum) was too academic an exercise for many rural people, especially considering the fact that their previous education had proved to be largely irrelevant and inadequate.[48] In short, the proposals of the elite held little appeal for rural people except those already committed to social activism. The proposals were particularly unappealing to individual young people who stood waiting at the bottom of the agricultural ladder, wondering whether or not to attempt the climb. It seems that rural Ontarians held tenaciously to their own values and practices despite the well-intentioned suggestions that were offered by their provincial Department of Agriculture and the academics and experts who hoped to remake the farm community in their own image through youth organizations. Indeed, it would be difficult to establish that the majority of members really looked to the Junior Farmers for anything more than a venue for socializing.

There is no doubt that the cartoonists' ideals oversimplified and exaggerated some aspects of rural youth culture in postwar Ontario. Indeed, oversimplification and exaggeration are tools that humorists deliberately employ in order to increase the impact of their messages.[49] Yet, for the gender historian versed in postwar debates about rural stratification, these cartoons are more than silly sketches to illustrate a youth newsletter. Indeed, the cartoons can be read as rich texts that reflect a rural youth culture full of complex messages for each sex about business success, the division of labour on the farm, and the choice of an ideal marriage partner.

The cartoons were teaching tools designed to communicate the messages of the rural sociologists. These authorities hoped to change the cultural landscape of rural Ontario by shaping the values of its youth. In the humorist's sketches, one finds the concerns of the academic elite translated into a popular culture genre. Something was definitely lost in the translation. While sociologists hoped to use their expertise to encourage youth to be instrumental in bringing about that change, the cartoonist's rendition of the rural situation was self-deprecating. The Canadian Youth Commission's 1940s informants were concerned with the agricultural ladder and the obstacles that faced youth standing at the bottom of that ladder. It is not clear, though, that rural youth were seriously considering the climb. Indeed, the trend of rural depopulation continued and even accelerated as young people had even greater access to post-secondary education in the 1960s and 1970s. Helen Abell's study echoed some of the same concerns, but she specifically criticized the intransigent subsistence farmer who refused to change his ways. Neither of these research reports was particularly optimistic about the prospects for rural youth. Both recognized that there were serious structural barriers for young people. But there were contradictions in their findings. For example, while the CYC concluded that concrete steps should be taken to make rural life more appealing for young women, Abell reported that amenities in rural homes lagged far behind those available to urban women. Moreover, while the editors of *Junior Farmer News* led readers to believe that men's and women's spheres of work on the farm were quite separate, Abell's findings contradicted that assumption. She found that women were directly involved in farm labour, a model of integration that the CYC recommended against when it suggested that in a bid to attract and retain young women, their lives should revolve around more domestic and leisure pursuits. In its popular discourses about women's roles, the *Junior Farmer News* pretended that the spectacle of a female driving a tractor or doing chores in the barn was rare because rural women were completely preoccupied with their beauty regime and fashion concerns. That message seriously misrepresented the economic contribution that women made on the family farm.

For the past several decades, repeated agricultural crises have captured public attention as rural-lobby groups organize to fight for the survival of the family farm. Continued calls for agricultural subsidies testify that the problems are ongoing.[50] This suggests that the bright young lads who were supposed to take over Ontario's family-farm operations in the postwar period did not succeed in making lasting change to the agriculture industry. It seems that they failed to climb successfully to the top of the agricultural ladder. Heavy debt loads for those who did attempt the climb, inherent problems associated with free trade, and the complex politics of commodity-marketing boards indicate that postwar proposals for the future were simplistic at best. The idealism of postwar commissions and cartoons was intended to inspire rural youth eager to take up the challenge of a career in farming. Unfortunately, those ideals and models were not equal to the task of overcoming the systemic hierarchies that blocked and defeated many an aspiring young farmer, whether male or female.

NOTES

The author wishes to thank *Ontario History*'s anonymous reviewers for their helpful comments and suggestions. Research for this article was funded in part by the Social Sciences and Humanities Research Council of Canada. An abbreviated version of the article was presented at the Ontario Historical Society's symposium, "Celebrating One Thousand Years of Ontario's History," in Willowdale on 16 April 2000.

1. Linda Biesenthal, *Rural Legacy: The History of the Junior Farmers Association of Ontario* (Toronto: Junior Farmers of Ontario, 1981), 112–13.
2. George Tuttle, *Youth Organizations in Canada: A Reference Manual* (Toronto: Ryerson Press, 1946), 77. In 1941 there were almost 150 Junior Farmer associations in more than 17 counties throughout Ontario. Ontario, *Sessional Papers*, Annual Report of the Minister of Agriculture, Sessional Paper 21, 1941, 50.
3. Formal academic education and practical training for aspiring farmers were available through the agricultural colleges, but youth clubs like Junior Farmers were reaching a larger audience than the privileged few who were exposed to formal post-secondary instruction. For institutional histories of two Ontario colleges (Guelph and Kemptville), see Alexander M. Ross and Terry Crowley, *The College on the Hill: A New History of the Ontario*

Agricultural College, 1874–1999 (Toronto: Dundurn Press, 1999); and Phyllis E. Dutchak, College with a Purpose: A History of the Kemptville College of Agricultural Technology, 1916–1973 (Belleville, Ont.: Mika Book Publishing, 1976).

4. Doug Owram, Born at the Right Time: A History of the Baby Boom Generation (Toronto: University of Toronto Press, 1996); Veronica Strong-Boag, "Home Dreams: Women and the Suburban Experiment in Canada, 1945–1960," Canadian Historical Review 72, 4 (December 1991): 504.

5. See, for example, David C. Jones, "'There Is Some Power about the Land'— the Western Agrarian Press and Country Life Ideology," Journal of Canadian Studies 17, 3 (Fall 1982): 96–108.

6. Parvin Ghorayshi, "Canadian Agriculture: Capitalist or petit bourgeois?" Canadian Review of Sociology and Anthropology 24, 3 (1987): 358–73.

7. Charles M. Johnson, "'A Motley Crowd': Diversity in the Ontario Countryside in the Early Twentieth Century," in Donald H. Akenson, ed., Canadian Papers in Rural History, vol. 8 (Gananoque, Ont.: Langdale Press, 1990).

8. Kerry Badgley, Ringing in the Common Love of Good: The United Farmers of Ontario, 1914–1926 (Montreal and Kingston: McGill-Queen's University Press, 2000), 50.

9. For a discussion of how the farm movement in Manitoba was shaped by prevailing expert ideology, see Jeffery Taylor, Fashioning Farmers: Ideology, Agricultural Knowledge, and the Manitoba Farm Movement, 1890–1925 (Regina: Canadian Plains Research Center, 1994).

10. The research is based on content analysis of seventy-two issues of Junior Farmer News during the six-year period between January 1952 and December 1957. I used the collection housed in the University of Guelph Library.

11. There are several precedents for using cartoons and humour to do this type of study. See, for example, Marlene Mackie, "Who Is Laughing Now? The Role of Humour in the Social Construction of Gender," Atlantis 15, 2 (Spring 1990): 11–26; Anthony J. Chapman and Nicholas J. Gadfield, "Is Sexual Humour Sexist?" Journal of Communications 26 (1976): 141–53; Deborah Chavez, "Perpetuation of Gender Inequality: A Content Analysis of Comic Strips," Sex Roles 13, 1-2 (1985): 93–102; Gail Dines-Levy and Gregory W. H. Smith, "Representations of Women and Men in Playboy Sex Cartoons," in Chris Powell and George E. C. Paton, eds., Humour in Society: Resistance and Control (London: Macmillan Press, 1988), 234–59; Jamie Snell, "Marriage Humour and Its Social Functions," Atlantis 11, 2 (Spring 1986): 70–85.

12. Margaret Conrad, "The Art of Regional Protest: The Political Cartoon," Acadiensis 21, 1 (Autumn 1991): 5–27.

13. Christina Burr, Spreading the Light: Work and Labour Reform in Late Nineteenth-Century Toronto (Toronto: University of Toronto Press, 1999). See especially chapter 4, "An Artist of Righteousness: J. W. Bengough's Comic Art and Labour and Working-Class Reform."

14. Scott Vokey, "Inspiration for Insurrection or Harmless Humour? Class and Politics in the Editorial Cartoons of Three Toronto Newspapers during the Early 1930s," Labour/Le Travail 45 (Spring 2000): 141–70.

15. Jack Cockburn, "My Alma Mater," in Biesenthal, Rural Legacy, 161, 165.

16. The agricultural press of the 1940s and 1950s is full of evidence that the provincial departments of agriculture adopted this deliberate strategy of shaping youth opinion. See, for example, "Progress through Junior Organization," Country Guide 60 (October 1941): 22–3. In that article, agricultural education is defined: "The modern version of the idea, as developed experimentally during the last 30 years, is to take the information to the younger as well as to the older generation. Now the method has proven itself beyond doubt, if one is to judge by the impressive number of junior calf clubs, baby beef clubs, grain clubs, foal clubs, poultry clubs, swine clubs … that are recorded annually" (22).

17. See the article by Cynthia Comacchio, "Inventing the Extracurriculum: High School Culture in Interwar Ontario," Ontario History 93, 1 (2001): 33–56; reprinted in this volume. For proof of the extensive web of youth organizations that were active by the middle of the century, see Tuttle, Youth Organizations in Canada, especially 73–81, where the clubs that existed for rural youth are listed.

18. Tuttle, Youth Organizations in Canada, 79.

19. Agricultural representatives were paid employees of the Department of Agriculture who were assigned to each county throughout the province to help educate farmers in the practice of scientific approaches to agriculture.

20. Part of the work of the Department of Agriculture's representatives was to encourage farmers to avail themselves of the information and programs provided by the department.

21. Linda M. Ambrose, "The Canadian Youth Commission: Planning for Youth in the Postwar Era," PhD thesis, University of Waterloo, 1992.

22. Helen C. Abell, "Future Role of Farm Women," Home and Country 27, 1 (Winter 1961): 16. The author wishes to thank Terry Crowley for an introduction to the work of Helen Abell, and Anne Moore for sharing her graduate research on Abell.

23. The CYC reports were: *Young Canada and Religion* (1945); *Youth Challenges the Educators* (1946); *Youth and Health* (1944); *Youth and Jobs in Canada* (1945); *Youth, Marriage and the Family* (1948); *Youth and Recreation: New Plans for New Times* (1946); *Youth Speaks Out on Citizenship* (1947); *Youth Speaks Its Mind* (1948). All were published by Ryerson Press of Toronto.

24. National Archives of Canada (NAC), CYC Papers, vol. 18, file 9, J. W. Smith, general secretary, Midland YMCA, to R. E. G. Davis, National Council YMCA, 12 March 1943.

25. Canadian Youth Commission, *Youth and Jobs* (Toronto: Ryerson Press, 1945), 190; Tuttle, *Youth Organizations in Canada*, especially chapter 10, "Rural Youth Organizations in Canada," 73–80.

26. *Junior Farmer News* 17, 6 (June 1955): 9.

27. Abell, "Future Role of Farm Women," 15.

28. *Junior Farmer News* 16, 5 (May 1954): 1.

29. Abell, "Future Role of Farm Women," 15.

30. *Junior Farmer News* 18, 10 (October 1956): 12.

31. Randall Harrison, *The Cartoon: Communication to the Quick* (Beverly Hills, Calif.: Sage Publications, 1981), 54.

32. Marlene Mackie, "Who Is Laughing Now?"; Joanne R. Cantor, "What Is Funny to Whom? The Role of Gender," *Journal of Communications* 26 (1976): 167–72; Chapman and Gadfield, "Is Sexual Humor Sexist?"; Chavez, "Perpetuation of Gender Inequality"; Dines-Levy and Smith, "Representations of Women and Men in *Playboy* Sex Cartoons"; Paul E. McGhee, "The Role of Laughter and Humor in Growing up Female," in Claire B. Kopp, ed., *Becoming Female: Perspectives on Development* (New York: Plenum Press, 1979), 183–206.

33. *Junior Farmer News* 16, 10 (October 1954): 13.

34. Ibid., 16, 9 (September 1954): 14.

35. Ibid., 19, 2 (February 1957): 8.

36. See, for example, Mona Gleason, *Normalizing the Ideal: Psychology, Schooling, and the Family in Postwar Canada* (Toronto: University of Toronto Press, 1999); and Mary Louise Adams, *The Trouble with Normal: Postwar Youth and the Making of Heterosexuality* (Toronto: University of Toronto Press, 1998).

37. Biesenthal, *Rural Legacy*, 16.

38. *Junior Farmer News* 18, 6 (June 1956): 8.

39. Canadian Youth Commission, *Youth Figured Out: A Statistical Study of Canadian Youth* (Ottawa: CYC, n.d.), 7.

40. NAC, CYC Papers, vol. 27, file 10, "Employment for Young Women."

41. This was the perspective of, for example, the Melville, Saskatchewan, group led by Mr Wass, high school principal; the Preeceville, Saskatchewan, group led by the Reverend G. E. Tate, Anglican minister; and the Buchanan, Saskatchewan, group led by W. D. Welykholowa, Wheat Pool elevator agent. Ibid., vol. 27, file 10.

42. "Rural Youth Speak," 5.

43. Helen Abell, "Some Reasons for the Persistence of Small Farms," *Economic Analyst*, October 1956, 120.

44. *Junior Farmer News* 15, 4 (April 1953): 14.

45. Ibid., 14, 4 (April 1952): 4.

46. NAC, CYC Papers, vol. 26, file 8, R. Alex Sim, "Economic Opportunity and Occupational Adjustment of Rural Youth," 3.

47. Ibid., 6.

48. Ibid., vol. 27, file 10, R. E. G. Davis to Marion Royce, 3 November 1944; Sim, "Economic Opportunity and Occupational Adjustment of Rural Youth," 3; author interview with R. Alex Sim, Guelph, Ontario, 16 October 1990.

49. Randall Harris, *The Cartoon*, 54.

50. For a discussion of contemporary rural issues from a sociological perspective, see Satadal Dasgupta, *Rural Canada: Structure and Change* (Lewiston, N.Y., and Queenston, Ont.: Edwin Mellen Press, 1988).

Article 7.2

Megan J. Davies

Renovating the Canadian Old Age Home: The Evolution of Residential Care Facilities in B.C., 1930–1960[1]

Issues to Consider

- Davies points out that the health and comfort aspects of institutions for elderly care, although important, were not the only elements influencing their development between 1930 and 1960. Why does she call this "the positivist period"? Why were Canadians paying close attention to residential facilities for the elderly? Did the reasons for their scrutiny change over the course of these years?
- What was the rationale behind giving these facilities a "homelike" appearance and function?
- What were the "poor law practices" of the earliest homes? Why were these practices established?
- What do changing architectural styles and approaches to interior decoration tell us about attitudes toward the aged and their welfare, according to Davies?
- Davies discusses the medicalization of old age, especially after World War II. What explains this process? Was it purely for "clinical" reasons that the medical model was increasingly adopted ?
- Why did women dominate among the new professionals employed in facilities for the elderly?
- How does the author describe the new, socially constructed ideal for the elderly? How did class and gender fit into this concept of the "well-adjusted" senior?

Canadian historians, like the rest of the populace, do not like the old age home.[2] [...] Ageism is also strong outside the shelter of the academy, where there is a similar reluctance to acknowledge the old age home. Part of the problem is the low status of this facility in our society. Residential care facilities for the elderly rank low on the institutional hierarchy, far below ones that serve the acutely ill, the young, or those with specialised medical conditions like cancer. Another factor is the social and physical marginalization of the inhabitants of the old age home: elderly residents are likely to be the very old, the most disabled, people in poor mental health, men without families and women living alone. The current focus on community-based care, while important, turns our gaze away from the institution and those who dwell within its walls.[3]

   Yet the old age home has not always been a second-rate institution. Public and political interest in residential accommodation for the elderly has waxed and waned over the course of the nineteenth and twentieth centuries. In this paper I look at one "positivist" period — that of the 1930s through to the 1950s, when there was a great growth of interest in old age.[4] Over

Source: Megan J. Davies, "Renovating the Canadian Old Age Home: The Evolution of Residential Care Facilities in B.C., 1930–1960," *Journal of the Canadian Historical Association* 12 (2001): 155–76.

these decades, pushed by public pressure and new professional concerns, efforts were made to sever the historical link between the old age home and the poorhouse and to reshape residential accommodation for the aged into middle-class medical institutions.[5] Canadian health and social welfare professionals scorned public institutions for the elderly for being too regimented, for having a "prison-like atmosphere," and for being irrelevant reminders of the antiquated Poor Law in the modern welfare state.[6] A 1946 statement by H. S. Farquhar, Nova Scotia's Director of Old Age Pensions, reflects the general opinion of professionals: "In many parts of our land, we find almost unchanged the old poor house where the aged are housed with the senile and sick. Endless idle days, dull monotony until death comes as a welcome release."[7] Framed in the ethos of post–World War II social regeneration, residential facilities for elderly public patients were no longer to be a punishment for a life of irresponsibility, but a respectable "home" for worthy Canadian citizens in their old age.

The ideal was an old age home where modernity meant medical professionalism and compassion, amidst middle-class comforts and surroundings. Health and social welfare professionals made the old age home part of their professional terrain, redefining inmates as patients in need of their expert attention. The ideological force of the middle class as a measuring stick for normalcy also made its mark on the old age home: facilities were meant to be "homelike," modelled on something midway between the post-war suburban family home and the modern hospital. The post–World War II cultural focus on the nuclear family added an emphasis on presenting this institution as "a home."

Using British Columbia as a case study, I consider the old age home as a cultural institution that embodied broader societal ideas about ageing, professionalism, and the place of institutional care in post-war policy formation. This is a period during which, I argue, the old age home evolved from an essentially "poor law" institution into a middle-class medical facility.[8] The process of reforming the old age home began earlier in B.C. than elsewhere, in the 1930s era of Liberal provincial health and welfare administrative and policy innovation, but the broad strokes of my picture hold true for the national scene as well.[9] I develop my main points by focusing on naming institutions, institutional architecture, interior decoration, medicalization, and institutional professionalism.

The first public and charitable facilities for aged British Columbians were built at the close of the nineteenth century, as a focus of civic pride and a reflection of the belief that elderly pioneers had earned the right to die in some comfort. The City of Victoria opened an Old Men's Home in 1892. A new, unimposing two-storey brick structure was completed on the edge of the city in 1906, set amongst spacious grounds with fruit trees, flowers, and vegetable gardens, and frequently visited by citizens bringing small comforts to the inmates. The Provincial Home for Aged Men, which was intended "To care for the old and infirm without suitable homes, particularly the pioneer miners, trappers, lumbermen, and others," was built in the interior town of Kamloops two years after the Victoria home was first established.[10] Its sweeping drive and substantial façade presented a message of state charity as a grand philanthropic enterprise. A small Chinese Hospital, primarily used by aged indigent men, opened in Victoria in 1884, later expanding to a two-storey brick building on Herald Street.[11] The Home for Aged and Infirm Ladies (Rose Manor), a middle-class philanthropic institution managed and run entirely by women, commenced operation in 1897. The gracious front façade of the building, with curved arches and a rooftop cupola, speaks to the genteel public image of what became a beloved Victoria institution.

The shifting status of the old age home and its residents is evident in early twentieth century institutional development. Vancouver did not establish its municipal Old People's Home until 1915; elderly people hated and feared this place and the facility was so poorly regarded that I was unable to find a single photographic image for analysis. In 1923, the Provincial

Home for Incurables was acquired by the province. The intention was to relocate this Vancouver institution, a former hotel located in the Marpole district of the city, but lack of funds and public interest halted this plan.

The Home for Incurables and the Chinese Hospital were the only state or charitable facilities specifically set up for the aged infirm in B.C. at the outset of the period. All the other buildings were constructed for a clientele that was relatively able-bodied and some institutions, like the Victoria Old Men's Home, did not permit ailing residents to enter in the early years of operation. Although my research indicates that public facilities for the aged poor in B.C. were more humane than those studied by Stormi Stewart, James Snell and James Struthers in central and eastern Canada, these old age homes also followed poor law practices.[12] Residents were expected to work for their keep, follow institutional codes of behaviour, and turn over any income or property to the state when they entered.[13]

While few institutions had the facilities necessary to adequately accommodate the frail elderly, the re-crafted old age home envisioned by health and social welfare professionals was in fact based on the reality of an evolving institutional clientele.[14] B.C.'s particular population of elderly working-class bachelors, whose presence had sparked the founding of a number of homes for old men, still remained an especially vulnerable group.[15] It is clear by the 1940s, however, that the old age pension had added a valuable card in their bid to remain outside the institution; residents of west coast facilities for the elderly were now noticeably more frail and less able to shift between the old age home and the community in seasonal or daily movements. In spite of this change, the statistics available indicate a rapid growth in B.C.'s residential populations of elderly people during the period covered by this article. In the early 1930s there were some three hundred men and women over the age of sixty-five in charitable and benevolent institutions in the province, and another three hundred beds in private hospitals that cared for adults.[16] By 1957, there were 1,750 beds in the latter category alone.[17]

NEW NAMES, NEW BUILDINGS, AND NEW DÉCOR

Institutional names were intended to make a strong public statement and thus are a useful way of "placing" residential facilities within a broader social and cultural milieu.[18] From the late 1930s there was a distinct shift in the names bestowed on B.C.'s old age homes, and many older institutions were renamed. Institutional titles discarded throughout the 1940s included the Provincial Home for Incurables, the Home for Aged and Infirm Ladies, the Old People's Home (Vancouver), and the Old Men's Home (Victoria). The only public old age home in the province that retained its original title, and the word "old," was the Provincial Home for Old Men in Kamloops. Typically, the names left behind in historical memory were those that made direct reference to the age or ill health of the institution's residents. New names shift the focus from the resident to the curative purpose of the institution, to the gardens that surround it, or to the politician who founded it. [...]

A second trend was to name an institution after a worthy public figure: a fact which was both an indication of the growing respectability of old age homes and of an aspiration for higher status in the public community. Thus, Vancouver's residence for aged men and women was renamed Taylor Manor in 1947, honouring a former mayor of the city. At Taylor Manor, the new title was part of a broader set of institutional reforms designed to make the facility more appealing to Vancouver's elderly.[19] In Kelowna, the new municipal home was also named after a popular local politician.

A third pattern was the adoption of names that presented the old age home as a place for recreation or as a quiet place for the last stage of life. In 1950 the Home for Aged and Infirm Ladies in Victoria was transformed into Rose Manor, a reference to the beautiful gardens surrounding the building rather than its elderly occupants. The new name might also have been a nod to the English country home, a not uncommon custom in Victoria, one of B.C.'s most "English" communities. When the Oliver and District Senior Citizens Society opened an old age home in 1957, the new facility was called "Sunnybank" after a favoured English location. At the same time, names with what British scholar Peter Townsend calls "a faint echo of gloomy foreboding" were also used, such as "Eventide" for the municipal home in Prince Rupert.[20]

Emerging architectural forms for the old age home echoed the messages of new institutional titles. Victoria's Mount Saint Mary's Hospital, built in partnership between the Sisters of Saint Ann and the provincial government in the early 1940s, was the first B.C. institution specifically designed and built for the infirm elderly. It was also the first old age home to be constructed in the province since the Vancouver Old People's Home was completed in 1916. The functional evolution of residential accommodation for the aged from welfare institution to health care facility was clearly evident in the new building. Located in a quiet semi-residential street across from the Anglican Cathedral, the Roman Catholic institution resembled a modern hospital, office block, or apartment building. The style of the building, coupled with its location away from Victoria's commercial and social clusters, discouraged interaction between elderly patients and the larger community. Residents of the new building were meant to be ill, not integrated members of the local neighbourhood. [...]

The dominant model for the new old age home was not, however, Mount Saint Mary's, but the new purpose-built municipal homes for aged British Columbians that had begun to open by the late 1940s. "Pioneer House" was established in Prince Rupert in 1946. Five years later Kelowna's new David Lloyd-Jones Home opened with space for twenty-eight old city residents. In 1954, the Dunsmuir residence was demolished to make way for a new, modern structure and Victoria Nursing Home was renamed "The Gorge Road Hospital." The cost of the nursing home was paid for in part by a grant from the provincial government.[21] Architecturally, these new facilities were somewhat different from Mount Saint Mary's, mixing features reminiscent of both "hospital" and "home," and attempting to convey a dualistic image of competent, scientific professionalism and homelike, family care. New, purpose-built old age homes, like the David Lloyd-Jones Home, were low-rise structures, created with nursing stations and other medical facilities. The design of these homes, with rooms facing toward an inner courtyard, emphasised the fact that the old age home was now regarded as separate from the larger community.

Victoria's Salvation Army Matson Lodge, opened in 1955, provides an excellent illustration of the new emphasis on the familial and middle-class comfort in institutional architecture for old age homes. The west coast firm of Wade, Stockdill and Armour provided plans for a new building with a view across Victoria Harbour to the Olympic Mountains beyond. The "guest rooms," as they were called in a 1962 *Royal Architectural Institute of Canada Journal* article, radiated out in two directions from a central "hub" corridor that contained the dining room, the lounge, a shop, a library, a television room, and a radio room. The centrality of these communal rooms in the overall design indicates a new emphasis on sociability in the old age home. As architectural theorist Thomas Markus notes, what is placed at the centre of a building is a critical indication of its central purpose.[22] In a very direct contrast to old age homes established earlier, comfort and sociability, rather than institutional efficiency, was the organising principle here. Again, as with Mount St. Mary and the David Lloyd-Jones Home, the emphasis within the building's design is away from the external community, toward either the magnificent view or the internal world of the old age home. The sweeping Y-shaped driveway up to the building, with large central flowerbeds, appears to have been designed with vehicle rather than pedestrian traffic in mind.[23]

The notion of "home" was of course an extremely powerful theme in the years following the disruption of the Second World War, when people were anxious to resume "normal" family life and Canadian families had to work so hard to find places to live.[24] As Elaine Tyler May makes clear in her work on American family during the Cold War era, the organisation and appearance of external and internal family dwellings provide an important insight into post-war society.[25] The same held true for old age homes. The goal was to extinguish the image of the old age home as a punitive place of last resort: the tall, gloomy workhouse of Dickensian mythology. The reformed old age home would be fit for the newly minted "senior citizen."[26] It would be a modern, single storey complex, decorated inside with light paint rather than dark stained wood. Communal areas would bring together residents for social events rather than merely for meals. All of this suggests a middle-class family home.

The theme of "home" occurs frequently in the literature calling for institutional rebirth. Social work student Dennis Guest detailed the reshaping of an unpopular institution into a respectable home for the aged in his 1952 study of Vancouver's Taylor Manor. In 1945, city officials sought to make the facility more attractive to elderly applicants by redefining it as a "home" rather than a public poorhouse. Guest described the process, placing particular emphasis on the word "home": "The most difficult task was trying to remove the stigma of an institution that had, during the depression, filled the role of that most odious of all institutions, the workhouse. Related to this was the job of converting the Old People's Home from an institution into a place that could really be called a *home* for the aged."[27]

The author of a 1944 report detailing the need for a new old age home in Victoria stressed the importance of a "cheerful and homelike" environment, arguing that this kind of atmosphere was in itself therapeutic.[28] The concept of creating a "home" out of an institution was in fact most clearly expressed in interior decoration, recreating the interior of such facilities to resemble respectable "homes" rather than harsh institutions. In long-established facilities, interior décor became even more critical in the drive to banish the image of the poorhouse. Redecorating schemes, it was felt, served to "modernise" old buildings, putting further distance between the poor law purpose for which the institution had been intended and the re-visioned nursing home. [...]

Other well-established facilities followed this same pattern. In 1939, the curtains on the cubicles and the tiny individual rooms at the Provincial Home were replaced with doors to give more privacy and each man was assigned a new bedside table, a freshly painted bed, and a chair.[29] Redecoration schemes were also underway at the Marpole branch of the Provincial Infirmary System (the former Home for Incurables) in the early 1940s. The auditorium, evidently meant to be the social nexus for the institution's patients, was transformed with new curtains, standard lamps, easy chairs, and sofas. "New red tops with monometal trimmings" were fixed onto the first floor tables. The fact that the institution's enthusiastic women's auxiliary had been responsible for donating all the new furnishings except for the drapes suggests that women, particularly middle-class volunteers, were key agents of this process.[30] The minute books of the Home for Aged and Infirm Ladies (Rose Manor) indicate that a similar process was underway at charitable homes for the elderly. In 1949, Miss Boulton, the matron, brought samples of china to show the committee and a rose pattern was selected.[31] Although the home committee had always taken a considerable interest in new linen, furnishings and wall coverings, the 1952 annual report noted that, "Many improvements have been made throughout the Home during the year — rooms and corridors painted, new linoleum laid, new drapes and covers added where necessary, all adding to the comforts of home surroundings."[32]

In descriptive passages relating to this transformation, images of colour and light are juxtaposed against the drabness and darkness of the past. There is an obvious parallel to what was taking place at the same time in Ontario and to Olive Matthew's British campaign to "bring more colour into the lives of old people in institutions," although there is no indication that [provincial policy analyst] Isobel Harvey and her colleagues were drawing directly on ideas from these places.[33] At the Vancouver Old People's Home woodwork and walls were painted in lighter colours.[34] At the Kamloops institution dark woodwork and drab colours were covered by plywood panelling and white paint and more lighting was added.[35] Grey blankets were replaced by rose-coloured throws on Marpole's women's wards. The installation of personal bedside lights was a feature of the period. Small bed lamps were donated by the Marpole Women's Auxiliary in 1941 and three years later extra electrical outlets were put in all the sleeping quarters to bring more light into the rooms.[36] Floor to ceiling windows and large modern table lamps dominated the circular lounge at the Salvation Army's Matson Lodge in Victoria.[37]

New names, new buildings, and new paint all comprised different ways in which the old age home was remodelled from the 1930s through the 1950s. Although the messages encoded in these various changes were somewhat complex and even contradictory, overall the bedside lamps, the pastel paint, and reconditioned names spoke of a familial, middle-class institution, and a compassionate place.

THE OLD AGE HOME AS A MEDICAL INSTITUTION

Administrative reforms and a reconceptualization of elderly inmates as patients were other elements of the transformation of the old age home, through which the older custodial institutions evolved into medical facilities. Here, the changes to residential care facilities for the elderly show some similarity to the earlier evolution of the hospital from poor law institution to a centre of medical technology. The provincial state played a key role in this process, with innovation centred on the Provincial Infirmary at Marpole. The reform of the old age home in B.C. was tightly linked to the growth of the provincial health and welfare state after the Liberal government came to power in 1933; new medical and administrative standards were adopted at the same time as closer regulation of residential facilities for the aged was enacted and a Hospital Clearances Program began to shift elderly people from acute care hospital beds to other facilities.[38]

Visiting the provincial Home for the Incurables in 1938, Assistant Provincial Health Officer Gregoire Amyot and Provincial Inspector of Hospitals Percy Ward made a number of recommendations designed to bring conditions in line with broader health and welfare reforms in the province.[39] Harry Cassidy, Provincial Director of Social Welfare, wrote a report on their findings that called for a new focus on the study and treatment of Marpole residents and the creation of hierarchical models of responsibility and authority and professionalism. [...]

The dual positions of Matron and Medical Superintendent, which had caused conflict in leadership within the Marpole branch of the Provincial Infirmary, were replaced by a single Superintendent directly responsible to the Deputy Provincial Secretary.[40] Doctors and social workers took over the role of provincial police, government agents, and relief officers as the "gatekeepers" of public facilities for the elderly in the province. By doing work that had previously been done by poor law officers and administrators, they transformed the task of "gatekeeping" from a purely administrative function to a psycho-medical exercise.[41]

Under the guidance of "expert" staff, the Marpole facility was to be run on a medical model, with new regularised procedures that would chart the physical and mental health of each patient. Dr. West was appointed visiting physician to the Provincial Infirmary and a medical survey of all patients was undertaken. A system of detailed medical and social patient records was created and physical examinations of residents became routine. A range of practices now underscored the medical function of the institution. New residents were given a thorough physical examination by a physician. The 1943 annual report of the institution noted that all residents were being given a blood test upon admission. A decade later, it had become routine practice for all incoming patients to be given a medical screening at either the Vancouver General Hospital or Saint Joseph's Hospital in Victoria: "The organized medical staff of these two institutions diagnose each case; advise on treatments; set our prognosis and generally assist the attending physician at each branch."[42]

Routine medical supervision of the institutionalised elderly now became the accepted standard, and its absence was commented upon. The 1949 annual report of the welfare institutions licensing board noted that the majority of state-licensed boarding homes now had a regular attending physician.[43] In a 1944 article for *Canadian Welfare*, Laura Holland, then advisor on social policy for the provincial government, held up the Soroptimist House in Vancouver as a model because it had a resident matron to provide medical supervision for the older women who lived there.[44]

A parallel process took place at the Marpole Infirmary in the field of social work. Following the 1938 survey, Zella M. Collins, a senior social worker and administrator with the provincial Welfare Field Service, was assigned to create a system of numerical files and patient case histories. Collins placed her own professional stamp on admission procedures at the provincial infirmary: henceforth, every application was to be accompanied by a social history of the individual. Workers from the provincial Welfare Field Service became adjunct workers and gatekeepers for the infirmary system, funnelling appropriate patients into the institution accompanied by well-documented case files.[45]

The use of social casework techniques and routine medical examinations as appropriate care for the institutionalised elderly now meant knowing them in a more systematic and intimate fashion. A 1943 memorandum written by Percy Ward, Provincial Inspector of Hospitals, stressed the importance of social work in dealing with infirmary residents: "To make satisfactory placements we must bring all relatives and interested parties into consideration and we must know all about these people, if we are to use good judgement in caring for the clients."[46] Individual cases and situations were now defined by medical and social work ideas about appropriate behaviour, care, and treatment of the aged. This professional perception of older people as "aged" is new, and is a clear illustration of the emergence of a patient/client group whose care and treatment becomes the remit of a range of socio-medical professionals.

With a new focus on the elderly as a unique category of clients, a notion of specialised care for older women and men in residential facilities took shape. This new way of ordering institutional care was evident in the hierarchy of care institutions for the aged that had evolved in B.C. by the late 1940s: boarding homes for the physically able and private hospitals and public chronic hospitals for those who required nursing care.[47] Professionals and administrators argued that the elderly should now be assessed by professionals to gauge their physical and mental health, and placed in an appropriate institution. A 1957 document, sent by F. Heaton, an administrator for the municipality of Saanich, to Donald Cox, Deputy Minister of Hospital Insurance, shows how systems of classification evolved. Heaton divided the elderly into four categories: the healthy, the infirm, the sick, and the psychiatric. With ongoing evaluation and therapeutic help, old people might move from one category to another. Appropriate residential accommodation was, of course, to be chosen in accordance with classification. Heaton recommended the establishment of geriatric assessment and research departments in general hospitals to stream elderly people into the correct institution.[48]

Professional interest grew in cataloguing the intimacies of the bodies, minds and personal histories of institutionalised old people. By the early 1960s, Dr. Doris Mackay, a specialist in rehabilitative medicine, was able to subdivide patients in private hospitals into six categories, based on the level of care that they required. Reviewing patient populations at thirteen facilities in Greater Vancouver and Victoria, Mackay gathered information on a set of criteria that ranged from financial solvency to bowel and bladder continence. The mental state of patients was also evaluated. Although Mackay's data provided strong evidence of patient improvement through wider use of physio- and occupational therapy, she cautioned against placing patients from different classifications alongside one another in old age homes.[49]

The creation of administrative hierarchies within the old age home was matched by new socio-medical categorization of old people. In both instances, the model was medical — the hospital and the patient — and the catalyst was the state of the professionals. Administratively, this gave impetus to the creation of detailed patient information systems and a set of coded entry procedures. Elderly people were not just recreated as patients, but as people whose place in the life cycle now indicated a specific medical agenda.

HEALTH PROFESSIONALS IN THE OLD AGE HOME

Positing themselves as the new "experts" in the emerging speciality of geriatric medicine, health and social welfare professionals were pivotal players in the transformation of the poor-house to the old age home. Doctors, nurses, social workers, and physio- and occupational therapists came to regard the elderly and old age homes as part of their professional jurisdiction. In an institutional setting, they maintained, aged men and women required the special skills of a variety of health and social welfare professionals to solve their problems.[50] Because professionalization in B.C.'s old age homes predated broader provincial academic and professional interest in the elderly, staff at residential care facilities and government bureaucracies that worked with institutions played an important role in the development of the field of geriatric specialization. Overall, social workers and nurses, rather than physicians, dominated professional discussion about old age and homes for the elderly in the western province.

In the reformed old age home, these professionals now had the power to make judgements concerning the diagnosis and treatment of elderly residents, a kind of cultural control that superintendents and staff of older poor law institutions had never had. In the professional mind, residents in these facilities were transformed from inmates into social work clients and medical patients. Professional authority became built into both the culture and the administrative structure of the old age home.[51] Thus, this growth of professional power was both structural and ideological, with the Marpole branch of B.C.'s Provincial Infirmary again acting as a flagship institution for change in the province.[52] Inside Marpole and other facilities, the work of core staff was now supplemented by a number of extra-institutional "experts" who included social workers, physio- and occupational therapists, and nutritionists.

Occupational therapy was the first new professional enterprise to enter the old age home. Work had always been standard poor law practice at the Provincial Home for Old Men and the Old People's Home in Vancouver. But occupational therapists working in old age homes transformed poor law labour into a therapeutic experience, creating an entirely new field of enterprise.

The Provincial Infirmary at Marpole was certainly the most dynamic institution in terms of physio- and occupational therapy. Somewhat ironically, the initial involvement of this group of extra-institutional practitioners owed their professional place inside the old age home to the crusading efforts of the voluntary women's auxiliary. Faced with bureaucratic intransigence, the powerful auxiliary went over the heads of provincial administrators to hire the first part-time occupational therapist in the late 1930s. By 1944, an occupational therapy program had been formally established at the Allco and Marpole branches of the Provincial Infirmary.[53] The women's auxiliary, highly organised and willing to use its power to push professionals into place at Marpole, was a very different kind of extra-institutional group than the charity workers who took Christmas fare to the Old Men's Home in Victoria. The Marpole Women's Auxiliary was clearly a pressure group, whose members, although not professionals themselves, were connected to the world of professionals by marriage and class alliances.

The story of physiotherapy is similar. Geriatric physiotherapy had begun in England during the 1930s with the development of exercise programs to increase the activity of stroke patients.[54] Interest in this field soon spread to Canada. Two years after the occupational therapy program had set down roots at Marpole, a part-time physiotherapist was added to the staff. Although there was less enthusiasm for such therapeutics among the Sisters of Saint Ann who ran Mount Saint Mary's in Victoria, the 1946 Report of the Provincial Infirmary noted that a part-time physiotherapist had joined the staff there as well.[55]

Nutritionists also became involved in old age homes during the 1940s. By 1942 Superintendent Motherwell at the Provincial Infirmary was lobbying for a separate "diet kitchen" at Marpole.[56] M. Baldwin, Nutritional Consultant with the Provincial Board of Health, visited the Provincial Home for Aged Men in 1945. Her report shows how Canada's Food Rules were applied to a clientele of institutionalised elderly people. Arguing that well-balanced meals were essential to the quality of life in old age, Baldwin recommended the use of tasty appetisers and seasoning to encourage reluctant elderly eaters, and advised against heavy meals at noon and full-fat milk, which would encourage constipation among the old men at the institution. "Our aim in the care of the aged," Baldwin concluded, "is to 'Add life to years rather than years to life.'"[57]

Women dominated the ranks of the new professionals now finding employment within the walls of the old age home, as social workers, nutritionists, physiotherapists, and occupational therapists.[58] Outside of social work, I found no men hired as professionals for these positions during the period. With their special nurturing qualities and their cultural connection with "the home," women were seen as essential in a modern compassionate institution for the aged. Professionals and government bureaucrats looked for maternal qualities in caregivers, implicitly suggesting that women were most suitable for aged patients.[59] Professional writing repeatedly stressed the "female" or "maternal" qualities of professionals in the old age home.

This maternalism had all the heavy-handed properties of traditional paternalism. An equation of the elderly with children is evident. The best kind of social worker or nurse, these authors maintained, was someone who would be sympathetic and understanding, make sure that their elderly patients or clients were dressed in appropriate clothing, and encourage interests and hobbies. A 1947 article in *Canadian Nurse* told its readers that old people "are forgetful, tend to reminisce and to fabricate. Therefore, the nurse caring for these people should be kind, understanding, and willing to take time to listen sympathetically to their stories."[60] Social workers were to act as intermediaries, taking on the female role as peace-maker to smooth over differences between patients, families, administrators, staff, and doctors.[61]

Under the earlier poor law model, a good inmate was one who conformed to the rules and regulations of the institution, worked hard and co-existed peacefully with other residents. Now, an "ideal" patient was required to be social, to be part of the institutional "family," and to be willing and able to participate in therapeutic and recreational activities. Such programs fostered new expectations of how aged men and women would perform in residential facilities, pathologising behaviours viewed as antisocial. Professional journals urged caregivers to encourage the elderly to keep up old hobbies or develop new interests.[62] Social work thinking of the period held that group work was both healthy and "normal." In the larger community, this meant regular church attendance and a close relationship with kin.[63] Inside the old age home, a "well-adjusted" elderly man or woman, social workers argued, should show an active interest in the home by participating in social and recreational events. Recent studies of old age homes have found that residents labelled "well-adjusted" by professionals are those who demonstrate the right combination of normative "group" behaviour and independence: knitting a tea-cosy for an exhibition and making their own way to the supper table, for example.[64] [...]

The new professional focus on treating chronic illness in old age also narrowed the medical definition of "ideal" patient. Aged men and women whose illnesses were not treatable, or whose health failed to improve following physio- or occupational therapy, did not fit the new professional paradigm. The interest of health care professionals, particularly medical personnel, became fixed on old people who would benefit from therapeutic intervention. As for the rest, they could be maintained in a custodial institution where they would receive compassionate care. In this fashion the issue of chronic illness in old age divided the elderly into two categories: the treatable, and those who could not be healed.

In her 1942 annual report, Marpole superintendent Motherwell proudly stated that, "The treatment of the aged is now being recognised as a special branch of Medicine."[65] This was a profound, if well-intentioned, overstatement. Mainstream medicine remained uninterested in the old and their illnesses. Without advanced analgesics, innovative surgical techniques and medical technologies could not yet be used for this group of patients. The continued absence of men from professional ranks within the old age home was another indication of the secondary status of these facilities and the ageist equation of the elderly with children. For the "female" professions of social work, nutrition, physio- and occupational therapy, however, the old age home was a fruitful site for professional colonization.

CONCLUSION

The changes I have outlined point to a re-visioned old age home, a compassionate place staffed by trained professionals, where the promise of post-war Canadian society could unfold. In fact, this was an imperfect process, with untenable contradictions at work within the new vision of residential care for Canada's senior citizens.

First, the old age home did not really become a *bona fide* medical institution. The enhanced role for a broader range of health and social welfare professionals within the old age home did indeed facilitate a shift from poor law to medical institution, yet this transformation was never really complete. Drawn into a new medico-socio paradigm where they were no longer inmates, residents of institutions for the elderly were re-conceptualised as patients in need of medical and social work attention. But beyond a hugely expanded role for pharmacology, which was only beginning to emerge in the 1950s and 1960s, the place of the "pure" medical professionals and innovative medical technologies in residential care facilities for the aged remained minimal. The professionals who did become involved with the old age home were non-elite professionals — nutritionists, social workers, physio- and occupational therapists — from fields dominated by women. Thus, even within the hierarchy of medical facilities, the old age home remained second-rank, staffed by women, the second sex.

Second, there is a strong statement about class and care here that should also be noted. Residential facilities for the elderly were no longer to be places of last resort for B.C.'s "surplus" population of impoverished old men on society's margins. Instead, it was anticipated that people drawn from across a broad social spectrum would receive professional care in a home-like setting. These were meant to be kinder places where residents would be treated in a more egalitarian fashion, living integrated lives in well-decorated surroundings. But this new "ideal" facility was not a classless institution. The notion of institutions as "homes" drew upon the culture of middle-class family, a place where many of the professionals working in the old age homes had begun their lives, but the majority of their patients had not. Thus, class and pro-fessionalism intersected as the old age home evolved into a medical institution. This was a par-allel process to what American medical historian Paul Starr calls the "moral assimilation" of the hospital, where a social organisation constructed for the poor was transformed into a respectable, middle-class institution.[66]

Third, the theme of "home" never really attached itself to these institutions in any real cul-tural sense, for "home" is supposedly the place where one chooses to live with people one loves, not a place apart from one's family, friends, and former life. New names, new paint, and soft sofas might add the ambiance of the middle-class family home, but they do not alter the insti-tutional reality. Indeed, I believe that these cosmetic changes served to facilitate a public and professional denial about the real purpose of institutions for the elderly.

The notion of "home" should also be set in a wider context of the local community so we can appreciate the shifting place of the old age home in its immediate neighbourhood. New architectural models for residential care facilities of the 1940s and 1950s, with their emphasis on the hospital, the inner courtyard, or the view, were concrete manifestations of a profound change. When the inmate population was healthy and a visible presence on nearby streets, in neighbourhood shops, and the local library, the division between the residential institution and community was not as sharp as it is today. Health and social welfare professionals of the post-war years worked hard to put a positive spin on the changing nature of residential accommo-dation for the elderly, but they were dealing with an institution that was essentially turning inward. In sum, the old age home came out the other side of the reforms of this period as an uneasy institution, resting uncomfortably between home and hospital: a place quite separate from the community, rather than a community institution.

NOTES

1. This paper is based on doctoral research funded by the Hannah Institute for the History of Medicine. I would like to thank the Institute for its support of my work, and Colin Coates, Dr. D. C. Barker, and the anonymous reviewers of this journal for their comments on previous drafts of the paper.

2. Among the few Canadian studies that address the old age home are the following: Sharon Cook, "'A Quiet Place … to Die': Ottawa's First Protestant Old Age Homes for Women and Men," *Ontario History* LXXXI/1 (March, 1989): 25–40; Stormi Stewart, "The Elderly Poor in Rural Ontario: Inmates of the Wellington County House of Industry, 1877–1907," *Journal of the Canadian Historical Association* (1992): 217–33; James Snell, *The Citizen's Wage: The State and the Elderly in Canada, 1900–1951* (Toronto: University of Toronto Press, 1996); James Struthers, *The Limits of Affluence: Welfare in Ontario, 1920–1970* (Toronto: University of Toronto Press, 1994); Edgar-André Montigny, *Foisted upon the Government? State Responsibilities, Family Obligations, and the Care of the Dependent Aged in Late Nineteenth-Century Ontario* (Montreal: McGill-Queen's University Press, 1997); Bettina Bradbury, "Elderly Inmates and Caregiving Sisters: Catholic Institutions for the Elderly in Nineteenth-Century Montreal," in *On the Case: Explorations in Social History*, eds. Franca Iacovetta and Wendy Mitchinson (Toronto: University of Toronto Press, 1998), 129–155.

3. The best discussion of these ideas that I have found is in Sheila Peace, Leonie Kellaher, and Dianne Willcocks, *Re-evaluating Residential Care* (Buckingham, England: Open University Press, 1997).

4. For an analysis of American developments, see W. Andrew Achenbaum, *Crossing Frontiers: Gerontology Emerges as Science* (Cambridge: Cambridge University Press, 1995). For an introduction to geriatric specialization with a British background, see Pat Thane, "Geriatrics," in *Companion Encyclopedia of the History of Medicine*, vol. 2, eds. W. F. Bynum and Roy Porter, (London and New York: Routledge, 1993), 1092–1115.

5. Canada followed a similar pattern to the United States, Britain, and Australia. For the U.S., see Carole Haber, *Beyond Sixty-Five: The Dilemma of Old Age in America's Past* (Cambridge: Cambridge University Press, 1983), chapter 5. For Australia, see R. A. Parker, *The Elderly and Residential Care: Australian Lessons for Britain* (Aldershot, Hants.: Gower Publishing Ltd., 1987), chapter 2. For Britain, the best source is Robin Means and Randall Smith, *From Poor Law to Community Care: The Development of Welfare Services for Elderly People, 1939–1971* (Bristol: The Policy Press, 1998).

6. For example, Margaret Wagner, "New Patterns for Old Age," *Proceedings of the 11th Biennial Meeting of the Canadian Conference on Social Work* (1948): 63–71.

7. H. S. Farquhar, "Services for the Aged," *Proceedings of the 10th Biennial Meeting of the Canadian Conference on Social Work* (1946): 109–12.

8. There is excellent literature dealing with this topic by British and American historians. See Anne Crowther, *The Workhouse System, 1834–1929: The History of an English Social Institution* (London: Batsford Academic and Educational Ltd., 1981); David Thomson, "Workhouse to Nursing Home: Residential Care of Elderly People in England since 1840," *Ageing and Society* 3/2 (1983): 43–69; and Michael B. Katz, "Poorhouses and the Origins of the Public Old Age Home," *Milbank Memorial Fund Quarterly* 62/1 (1984): 110–40.

9. I deal with this topic more fully in Megan J. Davies, "Competent Professionals and Modern Methods: State Medicine in British Columbia during the 1930s," *Bulletin of the History of Medicine* (76/1, Spring 2002): 56–83, and *Into the House of Old: A History of Residential Care in British Columbia* (Montreal: McGill-Queen's University Press, 2003).

10. Quoted in H. M. Cassidy, *Public Health and Welfare Reorganization: The Post-War Problem in the Canadian Provinces* (Toronto: Ryerson Press, 1945), 45.

11. David Chueyan Lai, "From Self-Segregation to Integration: The Vicissitudes of Victoria's Chinese Hospital," *BC Studies* 80 (Winter 1988–89): 52–68.

12. See Stewart, "The Elderly Poor"; Snell, *The Citizen's Wage*; and Struthers, *The Limits of Affluence*.

13. The Poor Law is both theory and praxis, and is essentially based on the principle of "less eligibility" which demands that state aid be as unattractive as possible, thereby forcing people to seek employment of any sort or help from elsewhere *before* they turn to the state. In this construct, state aid is intended to be demeaning and depersonalizing, whether given in the community or the institution. See Gertrude Himmelfarb, *The Idea of Poverty: England in the Early Industrial Age* (London: Faber and Faber, 1984); Geoffrey Finlayson, *Citizen, State and Social Welfare in Britain, 1830–1990* (Oxford: Clarendon Press, 1994); Michael B. Katz, *Poverty and Policy in American History* (New York: Academic Press, 1983); and James Struthers, *The Limits of Affluence*.

14. See Davies, *Into the House of Old*, chapters 1 and 4.

15. Megan J. Davies, "Old Age in B.C.: The Case of the 'Lonesome Prospector,'" *BC Studies* 118 (Summer 1998): 41–66.

16. The 1931 federal census found 308 people over 65 years of age in charitable and benevolent institutions in B.C. See *Canada Census, 1931*, vol. 9, table 9, 281. There were 290 beds in private hospitals (excluding maternity hospitals) in the province in 1934. See Province of British Columbia, Department of Provincial Secretary, *Hospital Services and Costs, 1934* (Victoria: King's Printer, 1935), 11.

17. Province of British Columbia, Department of Health and Welfare, *Report on Hospital Statistics and Administration of the "Hospital Act," 1957* (Victoria: Queen's Printer, 1958), 44–45.

18. Peter Townsend notes the same range of types of names for post-war old age homes in England and Wales that I found in B.C. but does not speculate as to their meaning. Peter Townsend, *The Last Refuge: A Survey of Residential Institutions for the Aged in England and Wales* (London: Routledge and Kegan Paul, 1964), 112.

19. Dennis Guest, "Taylor Manor — A Survey of the Facilities of Vancouver's Home for the Aged" (Master of Social Work thesis, University of British Columbia, 1952), 25.

20. Townsend, *The Last Refuge*, 112.

21. Gorge Road Hospital Collection, J. L. Gayton, "A Short History of Gorge Road Hospital," 2.

22. Thomas A. Markus, *Buildings and Power: Freedom and Control in the Origin of Modern Building Types* (London: Routledge, 1993), 129.

23. "The Salvation Army Matson Lodge," *Royal Architectural Institute of Canada Journal*, Series 444, 39/8 (August 1962): 35–37.

24. Veronica Strong-Boag. "Home Dreams: Women and the Suburban Experiment in Canada, 1945–60," *Canadian Historical Review* 72/4 (December 1991): 471–504.

25. Elaine Tyler May, *Homeward Bound: American Families in the Cold War Era* (New York: Basic Books, 1988), 172.

26. Snell discusses the development of the "senior citizen" in Canada. Snell, *The Citizen's Wage*, introduction.

27. Guest, "Taylor Manor," 25.

28. Local Council of Women, Victoria, Temporary Committee to the Mayor of Victoria and the Board of Aldermen, 26 June 1944, British Columbia Archives (hereafter BCA), Add. Mss. 2818, File 27. Norma Rudy sees this notion of "home" as the philosophical basis for Ontario's 1949 Homes for Aged Act. Norma Rudy, *For Such a Time as This: L. Earl Ludlow and a History of Homes for the Aged in Ontario, 1837–1961* (Toronto: Ontario Association of Homes for the Aged, 1987), 116, 153–54.

29. Noble to Walker, 16 July 1941, BCA, GR 496, Box 54, File 1.

30. "Annual Report of the Provincial Infirmary for the year ending March 31, 1942" and "Annual Report of the Provincial Infirmary for the year ending March 31, 1943," BCA, GR 496, Box 23, File 12.

31. Minute Book of the Aged Women's Home started 5 May 1936; Minutes of meeting, 1 December 1936, 2 February 1937 and 6 February 1937; Minute Book of the Aged Women's Home started May 1944; Minutes of meeting, 1 November 1949, Rose Manor Collection (hereafter RMC).

32. Minute Book of the Aged Women's Home started May 1944, 44th Annual Report, 6 May 1952, RMC.

33. Means and Smith, From Poor Law to Community Care, 18; Rudy, For Such a Time, 153.

34. Guest, "Taylor Manor," 20.

35. Annual Report, Provincial Home, 1 April 1950 to 31 March 1951, BCA, GR 131, Box 2, File 12.

36. Details from the provincial institutions were taken from Annual Report of the Provincial Infirmary for the year ending March 31, 1944," "Annual Report of the Provincial Infirmary for the year ending March 31, 1941," and "Annual Report for the Provincial Infirmary for the year ending March 31, 1943," BCA, GR 496, Box 23, File 12.

37. "The Salvation Army Matson Lodge," Royal Architectural Institute of Canada Journal, Series 444, 39/8 (August 1962): 35–37.

38. See Davies, Into the House of Old, chapter 5, for a full discussion of the Hospital Clearances Program and the Welfare Institutions Licensing Board.

39. Dr. Harry Cassidy submitted a report on the Home for Incurables to Weir, the Provincial Secretary, in October 1937. Based in part on observations of Amyot and Ward, this document advocated sweeping changes to the facility. The complete text of this report appears to have been lost. H. Cassidy, "Report on the Home for Incurables," 25 January 1938, BCA, GR 496, Box 47, File 8.

40. C. M. Motherwell, "Annual Report of the Provincial Infirmary for the year 1938–39," BCA, GR 496, Box 23, File 12.

41. I draw here on the ideas of Andrew Abbott concerning the cultural malleability of professional work. Abbott, The System of Professionals: An Essay on the Division of Expert Labor (Chicago: University of Chicago Press, 1988), especially chapter 2.

42. C. M. Motherwell, "Annual Report of the Provincial Infirmary for the year 1938–39," BCA, GR 496, Box 23, File 12; M. Law, "Annual Report of the Provincial Infirmary for the year ending March 31, 1943" File 12; M. Law, "Annual Report on Provincial Infirmaries, 1950," GR 277, Box 5, File 1.

43. "Annual Report of the Welfare Institutions Licensing Board, 1949," Session Papers (hereafter SP) B.C., vol. 2, (1951), R 105.

44. Laura Holland, "Our Senior Citizens," Canadian Welfare, xx/6 (1 December 1944): 26–27.

45. H. Cassidy, "Report on the Home for Incurables," 25 January 1938, BCA, GR 496, Box 47, File 8.

46. P. Ward to P. Walker, 25 May 1943, BCA, GR 496, Box 48, File 2.

47. Memo by James Mainguy details the administrative criteria of these different levels of care, 19 July 1956, BCA, GR 678, Box 1, File 6. The evolution of this system was closely linked to the Hospital Clearances Program and the work of the Welfare Institutions Licensing Board.

48. F. Heaton to D. Cox, January 1957, BCA, GR 678, Box 1, File 14.

49. Doris E. Mackay, "Survey of the Population of Private Hospitals in B.C.," completed in 1965, BCA, GR 678, Box 43, File 20.

50. "Annual Report of the Social Welfare Branch of the Department of Health and Welfare, 1950," SP, 1951, R-63-64. For a reference to training for work with aged in Britain, see Means and Smith, From Poor Law to Community Care, 195–96. Rehabilitative medicine, a medical specialty that expanded during the Second World War, emphasised a broad approach to healing and well-being. Psychiatry, physiotherapy, occupational and speech therapy, social service, guidance and testing, vocational and employment training, recreation, financial assistance, selective placement, and "careful follow-up" were all included under the rubric of rehabilitative medicine. Bruce McKenzie MacQuarrie, "The Care of an Ageing and Disabled Group in a Veterans Hospital: An Appraisal of the Domiciliary Care Programme Provided by the Department of Veterans' Affairs in Vancouver" (Master of Social Work thesis, University of British Columbia, 1950), 3.

51. I draw on the ideas of Paul Starr here, from The Social Transformation of American Medicine (New York: Basic Books, 1982), 13–21.

52. For an extended discussion of professionalism, see Harold Perkin, The Rise of Professional Society: England since 1880 (London: Routledge, 1989).

53. "Annual Report of the Provincial Infirmary for the year 1938–39," BCA, GR 496, Box 23, File 12; Office of the Inspector of Hospitals to P. Walker, 30 May 1944, Box 5, File 5. In 1948 McFarland noted that Marpole was the only institution in the province that could be classified as a chronic care hospital. William Donald McFarland, "The Care of the Chronically Ill: A Survey of the Existing Facilities and Needs of Vancouver" (Master of Social Work thesis, University of British Columbia, 1948), 15.

54. Thane, "Geriatrics."

55. "Report of the Provincial Infirmary for the year ending March 31, 1946," BCA, GR 496, Box 23, File 12.

56. "Annual Report of the Provincial Infirmary for the year ending March 31, 1942," in ibid.

57. M. Baldwin, "Report on Food Served and Feeding Facilities, Provincial Home, Kamloops," April 1945, in ibid., Box 12, File 2.

58. Women, who had a strong position within the field of social work, benefited from the fact that the new Pattullo administration was anxious to base their welfare programs on social work principles and that there was a shortage of trained social workers during the Depression years. The extreme reluctance of the B.C. government to bring in trained personnel from outside the province may also have worked to the advantage of women. Megan Davies, "Handmaidens of the State: Welfare Field Workers in Rural B.C. in the Interwar Years," unpublished research paper.

59. Looking at the British situation. Means and Smith tell us that, "Residential work with elderly people was seen as women's work in which the appropriate qualities of warmth, gentleness and good housekeeping would flow naturally from the right type of applicant with the minimum of instruction." Means and Smith, *From Poor Law to Community Care*, 195.

60. Edith Rowe, Jane LeWare, and Jessie Wilson, "The Care of the Chronically Ill," *Canadian Nurse* 43/8 (August 1947): 596–8. Also Dr. Lewellys Barker, "On the Care of the Aged," *Canadian Hospital* 18/4 (April 1941): 31, 38. Government officials also favoured these qualities in those who worked with the elderly. For example, "Report of the Social Assistance Branch, 1944–45," in SP, vol. II, (1946), R-44. Harvey's report also stressed the importance of a "pleasant personality" and "understanding and kindness" in caregivers, assuming this person would be female. British Columbia Legislative Library (hereafter BCLL), Isobel Harvey, "Study of Chronic Diseases in British Columbia," 1945, 9, 22.

61. Reporting a serious lack of communication between field staff, doctors, and infirmary administrators, Harvey argues that a medical social worker (always referred to as "she") would be able to act as an interpreter between the various parties involved. BCLL, Harvey, "Study of Chronic Diseases," 12. A 1952 report also sees the social worker as intermediary. A. Mann, "Report concerning a Social Worker for the Provincial Infirmary," 25 November 1952, BCA, GR 277, Box 7, File 4.

62. Rowe, LeWare, and Wilson, "The Care of the Chronically Ill," and Barker, "On the Care of the Aged." For a description of the ideal components of community recreation for seniors from a B.C. perspective, see Elizabeth Talker, "Services for Married Couples on Assistance and Pension: A Type Study of a Selected Group of Cases in Vancouver" (Master of Social Work thesis, University of British Columbia, 1956), 58–61.

63. William Graebner has a good analysis of group work theory and old age in "The Golden Age Clubs," *Social Service Review* 57/3 (September 1983): 416–28. Talker, in her thesis on married couples on social assistance, characterizes good adjustment as sociability, church attendance, and family connections. Talk, "Services for Married Couples," 26.

64. Roger Clough, *Old Age Homes* (London: George Allen, 1981), 158–59.

65. "Annual Report of the Provincial Infirmary for the year ending March 31, 1942," BCA, GR 496, Box 23, File 12.

66. Starr, *The Social Transformation*, 145.

Document 7.1

Speech of the Hon. Sir Richard Cartwright on Old Age Pensions

The first two of the following documents deal with the federal government's earliest provisions for the elderly. In the first, Senator Richard Cartwright, a wealthy Liberal businessman and former MP from Ontario, promotes the government's first such foray, a planned annuity that operates something like present-day registered retirement savings plans. At a specified age, the purchaser would receive a fixed annual benefit. The Canadian Government Annuities Act of 1908 was one of the earliest significant pieces of social legislation in Canada, but it hardly solved the problems of the elderly poor because many did not have the money for forced savings.

Issues to Consider

- Why does Cartwright maintain that the annuity plan before the government is preferable to a true pension, which would entail a government payout?
- Although enabling legislation would be passed the following year, it would have to get parliamentary approval before going back to the Senate. Why is Cartwright so intent on declaring his support? What view of the state's role in modern society does his speech convey?

[...] I have no doubt myself that within a comparatively short space of time this question of old age pensions, or a somewhat similar question, will most undoubtedly be engaging the attention of many legislatures, as indeed it has already in the mother country and in several of our sister colonies. I am free to admit that I have always regarded the case of honest, industrious men who have for many years led a life of toil, and at the end of their lives find themselves either by accident or misfortune or some other cause of a similar kind, thrown on the charity of their neighbours or their relatives, as pre-eminently deserving the compassion and consideration of everybody, and if it were possible to confine the question of old age pensions to that particular class I do not know that I, and I dare say that many other people would be of the same opinion, would object to introducing some such measure. But this is a subject to which I have given for a considerable space of time a good deal of attention. It is pre-eminently a question on which there are two sides. The one side is the side I have presented and the other side, which undoubtedly deserves our most serious consideration, is this — what would be the effect of a scheme of old age pensions on the community at large? How far would it discourage thrift? How far would it discourage self-reliance; and what is quite as important if such a scheme were adopted, how would it affect the working men themselves? My own impression is that, in a great many cases, such a scheme would be found to encourage extravagance, and the result would be that the thrifty, industrious working man would find himself compelled ultimately to bear the burden of his less industrious and possibly dissolute companion. [...]

Source: *Senate Debates*, 10th Parliament, 3rd Session, Speech of the Hon. Sir Richard Cartwright on Old Age Pensions, February 27, 1907, Ottawa, 1–5.

[...] Fortunately for us in Canada [...] there is very little risk of any hardworking, industrious, able-bodied man not being able to make an adequate provision for his old age, if only an opportunity were given to him. [...] I doubt extremely the expediency of having recourse to a system of old age pensions, but I do believe there is a real opportunity for the state to avail itself of the machinery at its disposal for the purpose of placing within the grasp of every industrious man in Canada the opportunity, at an easy rate, and at a very small cost to the state, of providing a reasonable annuity for his support at an advanced period of life. [...] I believe that some such scheme would attain an end of very great national importance and meet a great want which is felt and which will be more and more from time to time as we grow in wealth and importance, and as there are higher numbers of our people engaged in what may be called daily wage earning occupations. [...]

[...] no wage-earner of the ordinary kind desiring to make such an investment at an early age, could feel absolute certainty that an ordinary corporation, no matter how solvent it might be at that particular moment, would be equally solvent and equally well managed twenty, thirty, or forty years thereafter. As I said, these things can only be secured by the state. The working man can trust the state, and nobody else, and as a matter of fact I do not believe he would trust anybody else. [...] If any man chooses, when he comes of age, to put aside the wage of one or one and one-half hours per week, or one half day per month, I say that the state could afford when that man attained to the age of 60, to guarantee him an annuity of $120 a year. [...]

[...] I think it is also pretty well ascertained that, in the case of a great many wage-earners, the duration of life is considerably shorter than it is in the case of persons engaged in other occupations. [...] I admit that this is designed chiefly for the benefit of daily wage-earners; still it would necessarily be available for all citizens, farmers, tradesmen, professional men, or for their wives and children, and in short for all those who choose to avail themselves of it. [...]

[...] The chief advantage is what I have stated, that it would enable all wage-earners, by a moderate sacrifice, to make an effectual provision for their old age, and would guard them against the swindling projects by which many of them have been deluded into making sacrifices they could ill afford, only to wake up in their old age to find themselves destitute. [...]

Document 7.2

Minister Discusses Old-Age Pensions

Under the 1927 legislation, the federal labour minister, Peter Heenan, had final responsibility for old-age pensions. He was touring the provinces in an effort to sell the federal government's proposed pension plan when this article was written. The federal government at the time was Liberal, with Mackenzie King serving as prime minister; the government of Ontario, under the leadership of George Howard Ferguson, was Conservative.

Issues to Consider

- What is Heenan's position on the pension plan and the provincial government's lack of action in that regard?
- What does his address before the Ontario women's group indicate about attitudes toward women and social and familial obligations during this period?
- The article provides a rare glimpse of an elderly Canadian citizen's view on the pension issue. Given the general criticism at the time that the payout was too low to make a difference, how might you account for the man's seeming enthusiasm for the proposed plan?

Boys and girls yet unborn will be 70 years of age and in their graves before the Ontario Government concludes the survey of the needs of the Province for the old-age pensions, predicted Hon. Peter Heenan, federal Minister of Labor, in his address before the members of the Ontario Women's Liberal Association yesterday afternoon in the Prince George Hotel. If the survey was not dragged out quite as long as that, Mr. Heenan expressed his firm conviction that it would last at least until the event of the next election. In the meantime, he averred, older folk, many of whom have done real spade work in the province, are being denied the decencies of life in their last days.

"The women of this country could do no better than to get out and concentrate on that piece of legislation," declared Mr. Heenan. "See that it is not made a political football. Never mind what you would like, what you think it right to have; just accept what we have got and we'll amend it afterward."

"If you get it out of the hands of politicians you have saved it," Mr. Heenan told his audience. At the outset of his talk on the Old-Age Pension Act, Mr. Heenan said he had hoped that it would be one question so sacred to the people of Canada that it would have been kept out of politics. He said that it was his conviction that if the question had not gone into politics, there would be old-age pensions in every province.

No public man would dare to come out against old-age pensions, but in the opinion of the Labor Minister, they adopt strange and varied ways of blocking the bill. Misrepresentation, inconsistencies and unjust criticism — these were some of the blocking measures used by politicians cited by the speaker. But he declared that the possibilities of the system in Canada today were greater than in any other system in the world.

That $20 a month for a man or woman over 70 years of age is insufficient was one criticism which Mr. Heenan cited as coming from the Opposition. At the conclusion of the minister's talk a member of the audience, who stated that he would be 76 years on his next birthday, answered that criticism. He said: "If I could get $20 a month I would not want any more. I would not try to get any more. I could live on $20 a month, pay rent, and keep myself clean and nice." [...]

Source: *The Globe*, "Minister Discusses Old-Age Pensions: Federal Minister of Labor Urges Women to Concentrate on Needs of Aged," February 23, 1928.

Document 7.3

Toronto's First Teenage Club

The 1920s saw the beginnings of a concerted effort on the part of middle-class Canadians to organize young people as an alternative to their evident obsession with commercial entertainment in such questionable venues as dance halls, speakeasies, and even the cinema. Most of the organized groups were similar to the early 20th-century Scouting movements: they were based on middle-class Christian principles of personal morality, had a strong ethic of community service, and were gender-segregated. Although popular, they did not attract the lower-class "problem youth" who were their real object.

During the World War II years, a new phenomenon — the mixed-sex "teen canteen" or "teen club" movement — was launched. Intended to provide safe, healthy, upright recreation for the young, the teen club in practice resembled more an adolescent version of an adult social club. The article below describes Toronto's first such venture, a private initiative. The teen club model was eventually taken over by such service clubs as the YM/YWCA and the Rotary, who gave their support to the "teen town" phenomenon of the 1950s.

Issues to Consider

- Judging from the description of Mrs. Trevor's intentions and how the club was actually run, which class do you think would most likely provide its adolescent clientele? Why?
- Aside from keeping young people off the streets and in safe, chaperoned quarters, what are the other benefits that such clubs are supposed to provide?

Originator, planner, organizer and bulwark of Toronto's only teen-age club, Mrs. Trevor at year end took stock of the fact that single-handed she had got the club rolling along with a membership of over 100 enthusiastic high school students [...]

In the eccentric idiom of the high school, when she actualized her dream of a club for teenagers early in December, she was really "cooking with gas, not just slapping her gums." Here was an adult who was hep to the dirty boogie and the all-importance of the Saturday night rat race.

Describing her contribution to the field of youth recreation, Mrs. Trevor prefers less colorful modes of expression. "I have two teen-age girls myself and I just decided that something ought to be done about providing inexpensive fun for them. School children can't afford to buy entertainment in the same market with wage earners. For one thing, it's too hard on their parents' pocketbooks. [...] For another, it makes them feel inferior and dissatisfied to associate with wage earners, just at a time when they should be given every opportunity to feel important and independent. And to the young, a Saturday night dance is very important."

The club, membership in which is restricted to secondary school students and demands an entry fee of $2 a student, meets every Saturday night at Jesse Ketchum hall, where there is dancing, games, coffee and hot dogs, all for 25 cents.

Right now it operates in the red. Expenses run at approximately $50 for each Saturday night dance: rent, $5 to each member of the high school orchestra, $5 to the girls who attend the check room, payment to the woman who mans the kitchen and serves the food. Mrs. Trevor makes up the difference herself. [...]

Source: *Toronto Daily Star*, "Organizes Teenage Club," January 2, 1945.

The club has just two rules, one for members and one for parents, to whom a standing invitation to drop in is extended. The members' rule is "no smoking, no drinking." The parents' rule is "come as often as you please but don't stay too long."

"I know from my own experience that these boys and girls don't want to be chaperoned by their parents. They want to play at being grown-up and to feel that nobody's bossing them. The chaperones who regularly attend the gatherings are all instructed to stay in the background and only interfere if things aren't going as they should." […]

Mrs. Trevor, an amateur student of psychology, sees the club not only as a source of healthy and inexpensive fun, but as a means of developing youthful initiative. "These youngsters run the whole thing for themselves. It is good training for they are learning to be leaders, not followers. Nothing is done unless they indicate they want it by popular vote." […]

Topic 8

Modernizing Institutions:
Church and School

"Mr. James' class at work," Baker Lake, Northwest Territories, 1948; photograph by S. J. Bailey, Library and Archives Canada, PA-167663, http://www.collectionscanada.ca/inuit/054304-e.html.

CONTEXT

Both the history of education and that of religion in Canada have been primarily concerned with the exploration of three major themes: school and church as agents of moral regulation and nation-building; the public role of the Christian churches, most evident in the evolving Christian activism of the late 19th and early 20th centuries; and the changing relations of church, society, and state as Canada became a modern industrial nation. There is much overlap, consequently, between histories of schooling and those concerned with childhood, youth, public health, citizenship training, family change, reform movements, and state intervention, as there is also between histories of religion and all of these. Debates and commentaries about school, church, and their place and function in modern society have made up a significant portion of the ongoing public discourses about nation-building, Canadian identity, model citizenship, and ultimately the very nature of modernity. Many of the questions arising remain salient in our own times.

The discussion of youth in Topic 7 indicates how closely entwined were developments in the age-classification of society and the expansion of public schooling. Both childhood and adolescence owe much of their "modern" delineation to their growing association with schooling rather than labour. Beginning with Ontario in 1871, by 1905 all provinces except Quebec had laws requiring children between the ages of seven and fourteen years to go to school for certain minimum periods. Although most working-class and farm children continued to finish before their fourteenth birthdays, school was gradually replacing apprenticeship, domestic service, and other full-time wage labour for young adolescents. Canadian children were typically spending almost eight years in school by 1911. Only slightly more than 44 percent of all fifteen-year-olds, however, actually attended school in that year. Attendance continued to be shaped by the family's economic needs and the nature of the local labour market. The common experience was a moving in and out of the classroom, as parents kept children home to mind younger siblings, take on temporary employment, or assist with domestic or farm chores.

The school, it was theorized, would fill whatever void was created by the perceived flaws in family life, especially among the families of the recently arrived and those of the working class. The modernization process necessitated a certain "transfer of functions," as sociologists called it, out of such traditional socializing institutions as family, community, and church and into the public sphere, where the schools were located. By teaching citizenship and "Canadian ways"—much the same thing—alongside academic subjects, the schools would promote social order and shape ideal future citizens. Children of "foreign" and Aboriginal families would learn to speak English, be Christian (preferably Protestant), adopt middle-class standards of hygiene and family values, and acquire attitudes conducive to productivity and citizenship. The paradox of public schooling rests in the fact that, while offering educational opportunities to more children of different backgrounds than ever before, schools also taught young Canadians to accept and embrace social identities defined by class, gender, and race; in short, they were democratizing on one level, while maintaining traditional hierarchies on the other.

Influenced by American historiographical trends of the 1960s and 1970s, historians of education in Canada examined the relationships of socioeconomic and educational change, public schooling and state formation, underscoring the connections between school reform and the period's fundamentally class- and race-based social anxieties. "Nation-building" of a kind that would reproduce the values of those of Anglo-Protestant heritage was as much a force behind the "new education" movement of the early 20th century as were pedagogical developments, new ideas about childhood, and the reformist objectives encapsulated in the social gospel. The profound public faith in education was not diminished by war and depression. The mid-20th century witnessed a reinvigorated domesticity in their aftermath, its gender and family ideals reinforced by an economic prosperity that was placing more Canadians in a position to achieve the long-standing male-breadwinner family goal. Modern psychology entered the classrooms of the nation as medicine had done through systematic school inspection half a century earlier. The objectives and the outcome were roughly similar: through testing, "guidance," inspection, classroom teaching, and, as my essay in this section suggests, through an extracurriculum designed for that purpose, the "normal" was transmitted in the shape of certain expectations about gender roles, sexuality, family relations, and the all-important concept of citizenship.

The Christian churches constituted the core traditional institutions of preindustrial Canada, serving not only the spiritual but also the material needs of its inhabitants by attending to the welfare matters — orphanages, any number of charitable services, even schools — that were not yet within the aegis of the state. At the time of Confederation, religious influences, mainly Catholic and Protestant, and further defined as French- and English-speaking respectively, pervaded the public realm. A certain animosity between Catholics and Protestants came to the fore over the various "school questions" of the late 19th and early 20th centuries, in which the Confederation promise to safeguard the educational rights of Catholic minorities outside Quebec was gradually reneged. By the last quarter of the 19th century, the Catholic Church in Quebec had taken charge of virtually its entire social welfare and education systems. Until the Quiet Revolution of the 1960s, it would contribute enormously to the generational transmission of the conservative, agrarian, and messianic ideals integral to its nationalist ideology and leadership.

The mainstream churches were also compelled to undergo some modernization in order to adapt to the needs of an industrial urban society to which immigrants were bringing new customs of worship, although most remained within the Christian denominations. Fear of losing the urban working class led to a form of missionary activity in the cities, intended to take the message of Christian living, and consequently "Canadianization," directly to its members. This was often centred in a "mission," such as the famous Winnipeg All People's Mission in which J. S. Woodsworth figured strongly, as previously discussed. The settlement house movement, patterned after those of Great Britain and the United States, saw local social workers and volunteers, usually social work students such as those connected with the University of Toronto, take up residence in the midst of working-class and immigrant communities. As in the case of Woodsworth's mission, these outreach programs were usually affiliated with the social gospel movement considered in Topic 3.

Despite continued concerns about the secularizing trends of modern society, the churches remained strong both in public roles and in the private commitment of Canadians until at least the 1960s, when there was a decided turning away from formal church membership and attendance. This was most remarkable in Quebec, where the newly interventionist Liberal government of Jean Lesage broke through the Church's long-held authority in welfare and education, and the younger generation, as elsewhere in Canada, loosened its ties to organized religion. This trend would continue to the century's end: the 2001 census revealed that a record number of Canadians — 16 percent of the population, up from 12 percent in 1991, and only 1 percent in 1971 — reported that they have "no religion."

REFERENCES/FURTHER READING

Axelrod, Paul. *Making a Middle Class: Student Life in English Canada during the Thirties*. Montreal and Kingston: McGill-Queen's University Press, 1990.

———. *The Promise of Schooling: Education in Canada, 1800–1914*. Toronto: University of Toronto Press, 1997.

Choquette, Robert. *Canada's Religions: An Historical Introduction*. Ottawa: University of Ottawa Press, 2004.

Clarke, Brian P. *Piety and Nationalism: Lay Voluntary Associations and the Creation of an Irish-Catholic Community in Toronto, 1850–1895*. Montreal and Kingston: McGill-Queen's University Press, 1994.

Danylewycz, M. *Taking the Veil: An Alternative to Marriage, Motherhood, and Spinsterhood in Quebec, 1840–1920*. Toronto: McClelland and Stewart, 1987.

Fay, Terence J. *A History of Canadian Catholics*. Montreal and Kingston: McGill-Queen's University Press, 2002.

Gaffield, C. *Language, Schooling and Cultural Conflict: The Origins of the French Language Controversy in Ontario*. Montreal and Kingston: McGill-Queen's University Press, 1987.

Gidney, R. D., and W. Millar. *Inventing Secondary Education: The Rise of the High School in Nineteenth-Century Ontario*. Montreal and Kingston: McGill-Queen's University Press, 1990.

Gleason, Mona. *Normalizing the Ideal: Psychology, Schooling, and the Family in Postwar Canada*. Toronto: University of Toronto Press, 1999.

Marks, L. *Revivals and Roller Rinks: Religion, Leisure, and Identity in Late-Nineteenth-Century Small-Town Ontario*. Toronto: University of Toronto Press, 1996.

Moss, Mark. *Manliness and Militarism: Educating Young Boys in Ontario for War*. Toronto: University of Toronto Press, 2001.

Prentice, A. *The School Promoters: Education and Social Class in Mid-Nineteenth Century Upper Canada*. Toronto: University of Toronto Press, 1977.

Semple, Neil. *The Lord's Dominion: The History of Canadian Methodism*. Montreal and Kingston: McGill-Queen's University Press, 1996.

Westfall, W. *Two Worlds: The Protestant Culture of Nineteenth-Century Ontario*. Montreal and Kingston: McGill-Queen's University Press, 1989.

ILLUSTRATION 8.1 (P. 313)

Baker Lake, now known as Qamanittuaq, is a small Caribou Inuit community located to the west of Hudson Bay — at approximately the geographic centre of Canada — in the area that formed its own self-governing territory, Nunavut, in 1999. It underwent rapid development and exposure to the "southern" world just after World War II when it became a Canadian army base for a snowmobile expedition, although the traditional lifestyle of its residents, based on hunting and fishing, remained in place. Until the postwar years, schooling was provided largely in mission schools, often residential and located in the larger population centres.

Issue to Consider

• What does the setting of the school and the appearance of the children suggest about cultural influences?

ARTICLES

My contribution to this section focuses on an often-overlooked part of the educational agenda, the development of an extracurriculum in the expanding secondary schools that was intended to support and reinforce a specific notion of citizenship derived from traditional Euro-Canadian, Christian, middle-class values. Looking specifically at the Great Depression, Heidi Macdonald examines the remarkable range and scope of health and welfare services supplied by the Catholic sisters of Prince Edward Island. During a time of straitened municipal relief budgets, a continuing reluctance on the part of the federal government to take on these responsibilities, and the persistence of gender constructions that made women "the weaker sex," the needs of the Island's people were met by an organization that depended almost entirely on its members' will to serve and their resourcefulness.

Article 8.1

Cynthia Comacchio

Inventing the Extracurriculum: High School Culture in Interwar Ontario

Issues to Consider

- What was happening in Ontario during the 1920s, both socioeconomically and in terms of education, that effectively set the scene for the development of a particular kind of extracurriculum in the province's public high schools? What were the effects of the Great War?
- How did the experts in medicine and psychology theorize the modern adolescent experience? How did emergent theories about the nature of adolescence affect the development of high schools?
- Despite anxieties about the "youth problem," adults of the time were confident that it could be addressed by means of education. What explains this view?
- In a study of this kind, what is the value of such "internal" sources as yearbooks and high-school newspapers, school songs and school colours, and so on? What are their drawbacks as historical sources? What would be an ideal additional source?
- What were the objectives behind the introduction of technical, commercial, and domestic science subjects? Did they achieve the intended results?
- How did new access to high schools affect class and gender identities in the young?
- How did the extracurriculum make the high school a "laboratory" or test case for nation-building?

In many ways, the history of adolescence is a chronicle of the anxieties and preoccupations of adults. By the end of the Great War, Canadians were becoming increasingly uneasy about a so-called "youth problem" attributed to a litany of related causes: the disruptive impact of the war, particularly on families; the "hectic" qualities of modern life; and, most important, the waning influence of such traditional sources of sociocultural reproduction as family, church, school, community, and workplace. To worried observers, it also appeared that popular culture, more and more a youth culture, posed a special challenge to the existing order of things, including personal morality and the historic relations of authority derived from class, gender, "race," and age. Eager to be "modern," young people seemed dangerously close to rejecting all that was held to exemplify a young, ambitious nation, especially industry and self-discipline. As an Ontario high school inspector remarked in 1920, there was a "pretty general complaint among teachers" that, since the close of the war, their adolescent students had been "unsettled by the general spirit of unrest that is prevalent throughout the province." It was agreed that "the allurements of the automobile and the movies and the craze for dancing" had "seriously interfered" with their attention to their studies. The situation in some high schools had evidently deteriorated to the point that several principals had "protested publicly," feeling compelled to warn parents that "the moral fibre of the young is being weakened and their success in life endangered by their pursuit of pleasure."[1]

Source: Cynthia Comacchio, "Inventing the Extracurriculum: High School Culture in Interwar Ontario," *Ontario History* 93, no. 1 (Spring 2001): 33–56.

The invaluable "raw material" of a modern industrial democracy, adolescents represented the nation's potential in the wake of a war that had killed or maimed 60,000 Canadian men, a resource of leaders, fathers, workers, and soldiers that a sparsely populated country feared it could never replenish. In view of such concerns, the young came to constitute a "youth problem" that contributed significantly to the myriad "social problems" of the time which were demanding the attention of all right-minded Canadians.[2]

While the physical attributes of biological puberty manifest little change historically, its cultural traits are clearly subject to ongoing revision. Early twentieth-century theories and practices respecting adolescence were part of a larger process that was placing childhood social-ization in the hands of experts in pedagogy, medicine, and psychology, increasingly active par-ticipants in the modern family. Influenced by the seminal work of American psychologist G. Stanley Hall (1904), which shaped perceptions of adolescence for much of the century, the emergent body of experts helped to devise policies and programs — intended to contain and regulate — which were premised on institutionalized age segregation and subordination.[3] In their hands, adolescence was construed not so much as a passage to adult status and responsi-bility as a condition of physical and mental anarchy, fraught with nervous disorders and all their imagined ill-effects for both individual and society. Even if the desire for excitement was explained biologically as a "natural" youthful inclination, its possibly unnatural repercussions called for close supervision of all outlets for adolescent urges — especially those involving the commercial amusements which typified modernity, the cinema and dance hall representing the foremost choices of the young. Adult vigilance was required to protect and nurture them safely through this maelstrom, although this would have to be carried out cautiously, in that adoles-cents were "sensitive" and resented any hint of "interference" from the adults in their lives.[4] A balanced and regulated regimen of school, work, and play was the ultimate aim. As Hall him-self remonstrated, "we are progressively forgetting that for the complete apprenticeship to life, youth needs repose, leisure, art, legends, romance, idealization, and in a word, humanism, if it is to enter the kingdom of man well-equipped for man's highest work in the world."[5]

Although images of adolescence as a "dangerous time" characterized discussions of the "youth problem" during the interwar years, they were generally matched by more hopeful theo-ries hinging on the power of education. The "adventurous instinct" intrinsic to adolescence was proclaimed to be the same spirit "that grips the heart and soul in passionate devotion to the national ideal," the motive force so evident at Vimy Ridge, the Canadian wartime experience that came to memorialize that ideal. Wholesome recreation organized by "capable and inspiring leaders" and, above all, "constructive education in citizenship and the ideals of national and individual life" would see it channelled properly.[6] A prime objective of the period's broad-ranging campaign for social order, consequently, was to coax young Canadians away from the troubling new commercial amusements and into adult-sanctioned and supervised "educational" venues offering the sort of "character training" that they saw as the only viable solution to the pressing youth problem. And the most obvious starting point for the organization of youthful free time was the high school, increasingly central to the adolescent experience. If adolescents were being "made or marred, for the most part before they are sixteen years of age," they remained nonetheless susceptible to the positive influences of the school. The high school's pur-pose went far beyond training productive and efficient workers; equally important was its role in imparting "the training which is to produce the future character." Through the school, commu-nity spirit could be fostered "as it could never be through church, home or press," for the school would "fit [the young person] for future service and citizenship."[7]

If secondary schooling was a nineteenth-century invention, the high school's historical moment, manifesting in "the second great transformation" of Canadian education, arrived in the years immediately following the Great War.[8] Still largely unexplored in this context of educational expansion is the function of the extracurriculum. As high schools began to serve a wider community in the 1920s and 1930s, their socializing functions changed as much as their population and curriculum. This essay considers the development of school-based, out-of-class socialization for adolescents through an adult-supervised extracurriculum, in relation to public concerns about youth and citizenship in a modern Ontario determined to lead the nation to a prosperous, productive future. Borrowing from theories about the key role of educational institutions in the transmission of cultural capital, I argue that the extracurriculum taking distinctive shape in Ontario high schools during the interwar years was critical to the shaping of a modern adolescence. It reflected and projected the new social meanings ascribed to adolescence, and consequently to the high school as the key formative influence in the lives of young Canadians. A sampling of high school yearbooks suggests the degree to which the extracurriculum imparted convention and conformity. However much — or little — they reflect majority experience, these publications self-consciously promoted ideas, behaviour, and values representing the official institutional culture — as they could not help but do, seeing as they were not unmediated expressions of adolescent views. Despite their obvious limitations in disclosing the voices of youth, these student-generated sources uncover the normative culture, thus the measures that the young were meant to use to motivate themselves, and to assess their "progress," as they matured.

The historiography of Canadian secondary education has highlighted such vital developmental issues as the expansion of public schooling in the closing quarter of the nineteenth century, the growing importance of credentials in a modernizing society, and the design of a curriculum to meet public notions about adolescence as a preparatory phase for adult labour. It has been demonstrated that wider access to secondary schooling, along with new demands for occupational training, culminated in the introduction of class- and gender-delimited technical subjects, commercial studies, and domestic science. The outcome was not simply more relevant or practical education, however, but the reinforcement of gender, "race," and class inequalities which "deferred to the principle of mass schooling while maintaining rigid curricular distinctions in terms of status and cultural capital."[9] The growth of the high school was integral to the formation of a new middle class, itself part of a process of nation-building premised on Anglo-conformity. In the late nineteenth century, the high school still functioned primarily as the privileged enclave of the academically oriented middle class, a preparation for university or further professional training. By the start of the Second World War, it was a nearly universal experience for Canadian adolescents, the vast majority of whom were heading into the working world. During this transition, the entire meaning of the high school experience underwent fundamental change.[10]

In regard to the expansion of secondary education, Ontario, the most populous and industrialized province, took the lead. The Industrial Education Act of 1911 provided provincial funding for technical education for adolescents beyond the school-leaving age of fourteen years.[11] In 1919 the Conservative government of Howard Ferguson passed the Adolescent School Attendance Act, implemented in 1921, which fixed the age of school-leaving at sixteen years. The population of Ontario's high schools quadrupled during the 1920s, growing 325 percent in the twenty years between 1918 and 1938.[12] Every annual report of the province's Department of Education through the interwar years comments on the rising crest of enrolment across the province, including the rural areas serviced only by "continuation" schools. For the province's three high school inspectors, the growing numbers were not only the outcome of legislation: "undoubtedly the greatest cause," in their view, was a new public appreciation of the importance of education, as well as "a general desire among parents to have their children share in its benefits." Whatever the reason, it is clear that the high schools' influence was "being exercised over a much wider field than formerly." As Robert Stamp has effectively argued, however, the reasons probably had as much — or more — to do with the structural changes intensified by war and their concomitant sociocultural adaptations. Modern technology demanded more schooling at the same time that it provided fewer job opportunities for untrained adolescents, while the rise of a consumer economy also heightened youthful expectations for "something better" than the material conditions of life that their parents had known.[13]

As noteworthy as the numbers was the growing proportion of working-class adolescents now spending more time in the classroom than in the shop or factory. Although class patterns in attendance persisted well past World War II, secondary schooling was becoming an option for more young members of working-class families. The modern high school was idealistically proclaimed "the school of the common people," where "the rich and the poor, the high and the low, the Protestant and the Roman Catholic, mingle together and work together in the spirit of amity and equality, regardless of distinctions of class or creed." In the northern resource town of Timmins, the new high school opened in September 1923 was filled to capacity a year later; already plans were being made to enlarge it to accommodate new students, "many of them with foreign names but with loyal Canadian hearts."[14] In the industrial city of Hamilton, despite the strain on working-class family economies when the wages of teenaged children were forfeited, the high school population from this sector doubled in public academic schools, and exploded (from 206 in 1921 to over 1,400 in 1930) in the new technical schools. A similar process was at work in the expansion of London's secondary schools.[15] With the extension of secondary schooling, working-class youth were more likely than ever before to experience an adolescence closer to that enjoyed by their middle-class peers. For many young Canadians, modern adolescence was a newly configured stage of life, characterized by schooling and guided social and cultural activities rather than full-time wage labour, a historic modification in the very structures of adolescence.[16]

Class formation and gender identity are transmitted, and their associated values consolidated, as much through home and school as in community and workplace. They also depend on the acquisition of cultural capital as well as its material forms. In the settings of family and classroom, young people learn what is expected of them, both in their day-to-day behaviour and in terms of how they will make their way as adults, expectations shaped by socioeconomic and familial position as well as contemporary ideals about what constitutes "success" and full membership in adult society. These expectations are further developed through the kind of schooling that they receive, and, more to the point, through their experiences, individual and collective, in the wider institutional culture of the school. In his influential study of sociocultural reproduction through schooling, sociologist Pierre Bourdieu argues forcefully that the school functions "in the manner of a huge classificatory machine which inscribes changes within the purview of the structure," thereby helping "to make and to impose the legitimate exclusions and inclusions which form the basis of the social order." What his empirical research has shown is an altogether unsurprising "very close statistical relationship" between achievement and "ascription," the latter referring to social origins and birth. Thus, cloaked with the rhetoric of equality and merit, schools perpetuate and legitimate social hierarchies. The extracurriculum, an increasingly integral part of the "pedagogic action" pertaining to modern secondary education, plays a vital role in this selection process.[17] On one level, much like the expanded high school itself, the extracurriculum contributed to the "containment" of problem youth by providing "safe" alternatives to "dangerous" commercial, or otherwise unsupervised, leisure activities. More important, however, the newly structured extracurriculum reinforced lessons about citizenship that equated loyalty to the school with national pride and performance, lessons that helped to preserve and reproduce the class, gender, and "racial" identities of a "Canadian" middle class intent on stabilizing itself amidst jarring sociocultural change.

By the 1920s, then, unprecedented high school enrolments, increasingly regular attendance, and rising graduation rates allowed, for the first time, a significant age cohort which would make its way collectively through high school. This demographic watershed provided the basis for an institutionalized, teacher-supervised peer group culture which largely replaced the less formal tra-ditional framework of student clubs and teams by the 1930s.[18] With the attainment of sufficient numbers to support a complex network of peer group societies, the cultural system of the modern high school took more definite form in such mixed-sex activities as student government, clubs, journalism, and the newly important [though not new] expressions of identity signified by tradi-tional school colours, school songs and cheers, and gender-segregated athletic teams.[19]

Keeping young people in school longer, however, was seen as only a partial solution to the "youth problem," first construed as the problem of an urban subculture of working-class adoles-cents, primarily, but not exclusively, boys. It was hoped that the new commercial and technical streams would mitigate boredom and its attendant evils, while preparing them to become all-round productive adults in both work and play.[20] But the extracurriculum also featured strongly in the making of ideal male citizens. In Ontario, "a noticeable feature" of the high school student body was that girls outnumbered boys in the majority of schools. It was surmised that "through personal desire or for family reasons, the boys are impatient to be free to be out in the world, earning their own living." In all likelihood, the economic opportunities that continued to favour young men over young women were the primary reason for this disparity. The new attendance legislation and the revised course of study were important approaches to the problem, but it was also argued that "larger playgrounds" and "a more general encouragement" of games, sports, and other school-related, non-academic pastimes would be a strong incentive to boys to attend and to remain longer at school. "All work and no play" could not appeal to "the average boy," but "the chance of getting a place on the school's baseball, hockey or basketball team, or taking part in the school's literary society, dramatic or debating club," educators contended, would give him "an entirely different view of the high school."[21] Girls also participated actively in all these activities, but the leadership positions usually went to boys, particularly where student government and student publications were concerned. When girls did aspire to leadership positions, their ambitions were considered — by their peers — to be so unusual as to merit comment. At Kitchener Collegiate Institute, the first-ever female student council president was elected in 1931; the student newspaper editorialized that "undoubtedly a girl would have emerged victorious earlier had she succeeded in securing the votes of her own sex," among whom, in the view of this male commentator, "competition seems to be more vital … evidently they hesitate to concede victory to their own sex."[22]

This expanding roster of organized activities legitimized the peer group as a socializing agency, giving it a crucial role in the process of cultural transmission. It was believed that stu-dents benefited by learning from each other in this setting, though in fact they were mostly learning from their adult supervisors. What they learned were progressive middle-class goals encompassing both competition *and* teamwork, commitment to the community *and* individual leadership, as well as a personal success increasingly denoted as "popularity." Through the medium of adult-organized social, recreational, non-academic activities, young Canadians were exposed to ideals of adult behaviour that would help them define their own goals while sup-plying some of the requisite training for adult social success — at least as this was defined in middle-class circles.[23] Faculty were quick to correlate successful extracurricular programs with "exceptional capacity in achievement," and, significantly, with "the charm manifested in the personalities of the leaders," a feature of school culture thought to be "quite striking."[24]

For high school students, social participation and modern citizenship were encapsulated in the concept of "school spirit," the very premise of the extracurriculum. During the interwar years, "school spirit" became the rallying call and symbolic expression of Ontario's high school culture. Although representing "the fun and comradeship of school-days," the larger purposes of school spirit were noted by students themselves. School spirit instilled loyalty, cooperation, and fairness. During a time when Stanley Hall's theories about adolescent angst held sway, school spirit was held to "invariably cheer those pupils who are prone to pitch their tents on the north side of life," their "morbid outlook" conquered by "such enthusiasm, loyalty and friendliness." Special measures were taken during regular school hours in order to foster this spirit, which were then reinforced in publications, student government, clubs, and teams. At Ottawa Collegiate, as in many other high schools, an "assembly" was held each morning in the auditorium. Before the regular opening exercises, consisting of prayer, anthem singing, and announcements, the students engaged in a sing-song "under the baton of a competent conductor and to the accompaniment of the school orchestra," an exercise kept up for about ten minutes and constituting "a happy ushering in of the school day."[25] The auditorium was increasingly the "central feature" of the modern high school, home to these daily assemblies which did so much to nurture "a healthy school spirit, to train the pupils in public speaking, in self control, in orderly habits, in consideration for others and in respect for authority."[26] Moreover, school spirit could not be contained by school walls; as one young yearbook editor proclaimed, it gave "vivacity" to the entire community, and prepared students "for the greater field of activity than our school environment, the field where mistakes are not so kindly overlooked — life."[27]

As high schools integrated gyms and assembly halls into their functioning physical space, and strove to provide organized recreational programs under trained leadership, the trend was lauded as one of the "more progressive signs in modern education." A new understanding of adolescent education as preparation for a healthy, wholesome, balanced adulthood, in its every sense, meant a new emphasis on the balancing of intellectual achievement with the development of social and citizenship skills. High school was to be valued as much for the cultural experience that it provided through peer group activity as for its learning experiences. In fact, social activities would enhance both scholarship and mental and physical health by replenishing the energy expended in book study. As one high school principal pointed out, "It should not be forgotten that our young people are also preparing for future leisure ... and the mind well stored with interesting knowledge ... does not have to go abroad for entertainment. The entertainment of such a student is self-contained."[28]

Self-containment was also the implicit purpose of the extracurriculum. The larger "youth problem," which revolved around keeping adolescents out of danger once they headed home after all their school-related activities, saw much promotion of carefully directed youth clubs in close association with churches and schools. "Group work" advocates — social workers and educators foremost among them — argued that "the group system contributes much to the team play necessary to democracy and unselfish cooperative living." It also took advantage of the youthful "gang instinct" that would otherwise lead to anti-social, even criminal, activity. In properly supervised clubs, the peer group would be put to useful effect: "in common activity with his compeers, [the young person learns] the responsibilities of social living which no adult can teach him."[29] Student government, which "not only encourages students to take a greater interest in their school," but also "provides excellent training for their future lives," became an important new component of the high school experience in Ontario by 1930. In Toronto's Northern Vocational Institute, the city's largest vocational school, the student council was responsible for the management of social and athletic events, the morning assembly, and minor discipline problems such as smoking, bad language, and "unbecoming conduct" in the school's halls and washrooms. London South Collegiate Institute inaugurated its School Council in 1931; it was believed to "serve as a medium for encouraging student responsibility" as well as "regulating and supervising all student activities and organizations." School governments were not only mechanisms for self-policing, they were also meant to teach adolescents an appropriate code of conduct within an ethical context that could effectively utilize "peer pressure" to ensure conformity.[30]

High school athletics became increasingly institutionalized during these years, coming to represent, as never before, both the motive force of school spirit and its ultimate measure. Since "life itself is based on fair play, the knowledge of how to win and how to lose," it was obvious that "nothing in the world will develop a better, more noble character than sport."[31] In this manner, sports became instruments of socialization for the children of immigrants, promoting a "Canadianism" based on the physical discipline, fair play, and team work that were perceived to be lacking in other cultures. Even while "styles of play" changed historically, it was argued, the "gold standard" would ever be "the desirable citizen of the future." If the school and its playing fields were made "the centre and servant of a satisfying community life," youth would easily find an attractive alternative to the streets, the dance and billiard halls and speakeasies, and countless unhealthy and immoral pursuits in the name of fun. "Well-conducted" physical exercises, gymnastics, and games were not only means of keeping the body fit, but also of "training the characteristics essential to a virile manhood and womanhood." School boards were duly empowered by law to set aside annual funds "for the encouragement of athletics and to defray the expenses of school games."[32]

Records indicate that, by 1920, almost every high school had an athletic association. The 1928 Fort William High School yearbook declared that "athletic societies play a big part in school life. They have the most to do with extracurriculars."[33] "Inter-form" and inter-scholastic matches provided opportunities for healthy competition and camaraderie, even romance, all under the watchful eye of adult teachers and coaches. Operating at once as activity, spectacle, and ultimate manifestation of "school spirit," the modern sports regime also offered up a new set of adolescent heroes, and in a manner explicitly gender-defined. The muscular Christianity of the Victorian age, with its correlation of moral integrity and manly strength and endurance, was being eclipsed by an emphasis on physique as the measure of both manliness and the newly coined "sex appeal" that the period's advertisers sold alongside new consumer products. At London South Collegiate, a school serving the middle-class and affluent families near the city core, once again the benefits to (male) adult life were emphasized in the promotion of school sports: "This development of the body, so important to the player, will always stand in good stead in after life. No employer wants a man working for him who is on the sick list frequently. He will employ the man who is on the job in good physical condition."[34]

While never named explicitly in student publications, "sex appeal"— obliquely referred to as "it"— was certainly important to young people. The common scenario at matches was an all-boy game with a mixed audience featuring the newly organized and feminized extracurricular activity of cheer-leading, which was becoming both a sport in itself and an emblem of feminine social success. The school's "reputation" was considered to be upheld not by victory alone, but by the intensity of its members' support. In fact, the "rooters" themselves were part of the competition, school spirit being judged in regard to cheering, horn-blowing, "snake-walks," and, of course, the size of the crowd.[35] Annual "field days," even in small towns, could draw as many as 300 spectators. The Guelph Collegiate yearbook, in 1926, reported that "Everyone seems to be taking more interest in sports than hitherto, and many were eager to help in any way, even if they could not play the games themselves," with "the girls in particular showing more than their usual interest."[36]

In fact, the 1920s appear to have constituted a new peak for girls' sports in Ontario high schools, with extracurricular opportunities expanding and intramural leagues growing rapidly. Basketball, invented in 1891 by Ontario native James Naismith, was especially popular, as noted in the Renfrew Collegiate yearbook for 1922: "Every year basketball becomes more and more the real game among the collegiate girls and is played not only by the favoured few on the regular team but by nearly every girl in the school." At one infamous game between Guelph Collegiate and Galt Collegiate girls, as recalled by a male spectator, one of the players felt her bloomers slipping, at which point "in the extremity [sic], all the other girls of both teams formed a circle around her while repairs were made — we men all seated or standing around the hall, a few hundred of us, quite fascinated by this unforeseen development."[37] But girls' athletic clubs often served up more than sports activities, with yearbook references indicating that recitations, songs, and dancing demonstrations were common components of meetings. In Toronto, in the late 1920s, Jarvis,

Harbord, and Parkdale collegiates all chose to discontinue their girls' athletic associations in favour of the new Hi-Y Clubs, which were school-based but organized and supervised by the YWCA. The new clubs still featured sports, but also included drama and arts in their programs, in an effort to broaden their appeal and bring into the safety of the group the young women who were not athletically inclined.[38] Thus, sports prowess for both boys and girls, and personal connection to high school sports heroes for girls, provided an entry into the hierarchy of "popularity" within the age group — just as their absence could as readily spell social failure for some. All this physical energy and enthusiasm was just the sort of "pep" that 1920s popular culture applauded.

High schools also began to formalize their "identity markers," the colours, cheers, crests, mottoes, and songs that had traditionally signified exclusive private school membership. At Arnprior High School, A. H. D. Ross, appointed principal in 1919, made one of his first projects the "casting about for a suitable motto and crest" for the school. Upon consulting with his staff (but not students), it was decided that the motto should consist of "three or four simple Latin words which would be understood even by those who have only an elementary knowledge of that ancient language." After due consideration of 120 mottoes, "the choice fell upon *Hodie non cras*, which means 'today, not tomorrow,' and constantly holds before us the idea of making the best possible use of present opportunities." The crest, it was decided, "should be as elegant and chaste as possible," the chosen one featuring an hour glass to signify time, a "lamp of knowledge," and an open book. Finally, the principal, noting that "the outstanding characteristics of college and school yells which have stood the test of time are the frequent repetition of the name of the institution, the introduction of some startling foreign word or phrase, and the reiteration of an unalterable determination to overcome all opposition and finally achieve victory," composed the following school cheer: "Arnprior High School!! Rah, rah, rah!! On the field and in the class — *hodie non cras*!! Our colours are the red and white for which we'll fight with all our might!! Arnprior High School!! Rah, rah rah!!"[39] At Guelph Collegiate, the rallying cry was a simple and — it was hoped — infectious "Chee hee! Chee haw! Chee haw! Haw! Haw! Collegiate, Collegiate, Rah! Rah! Rah!"[40] Similar mottoes, crests, and cheers were devised across the province, reflecting both the new importance ascribed to the "school spirit" that they signified, and also the involvement of principals and staff in their creation. At times, students were actively encouraged to participate: at the Fergus High School, the school motto, *Per ardua ad astra* (Strive for the Stars), was the direct result of a student contest held in 1930.[41] Kitchener Collegiate, on the other hand, found its faculty-motivated campaign to replace the old school song ("O Fair Ontario") with a new student composition sadly "unconsummated" after several years' efforts, causing much lament among student leaders about the embarrassing lack of school spirit behind this failure.[42] In many ways, school spirit was an adult project, actively manufactured and disseminated through the relationship between faculty and a recognized student elite. Recognizing this, some students complained about the "feeble" character of student government. Its promised management of student affairs on behalf of students was "practically a dead issue," the reality being that the student council was "overrun by staff supervision."[43]

Perhaps most important, in their obvious appeal to the young and in their increasing frequency, were the "socials," commonly involving dancing, that modern high schools incorporated into their extracurricular activities, allowing young men and women opportunities to meet and get to know each other — a primary, if not the primary, purpose of adolescent socializing. As "dating" became the modern custom, often in peer group settings away from the home and the adult chaperone that signified old-fashioned courtship but also kept "danger" at bay, these school-supervised activities appeared a wise alternative to the public spaces where "spooning" might otherwise take place. Capitalizing on the "modern dance rage," school dances were especially important.[44] These were memorable events for many of their participants, as one man recalled: "They were great occasions. Much competition amongst the boys to invite the popular girls, the girls dressing in 'formals,' and the boys in their best suit, their 'Sunday' or 'Church' suit."[45] At Guelph Collegiate, "tea dances" were held between 4 and 6 in the afternoon in the school auditorium, and given "splendid" support by the lower-form students for whom they were specifically intended, with music often provided by school bands. Although the Depression limited the number of dances held under school auspices for lack of funds, the school's 1933 yearbook described the end-of-term festivities in a manner that suggests anything but austerity: the auditorium was decorated with streamers "stretching from the skylight to the balcony, and multicoloured balloons awning over the heads of the dancers; green Collegiate crests stood out in sharp relief upon each pillar; a background in futuristic design brought into prominence the orchestral stand at the front." Jean's Night-Hawks provided "all that could be desired in the way of dance rhythm." The varied program included a lucky balloon dance and a "Paul Jones," as well as what the yearbook described as "an extraordinary rose-dance" in which young men tossed rosebuds over the balcony and then danced with the young women who caught their particular rose, combining romance with competition and probably no small amount of disappointment for the less nimble. There was little sign of Depression restraint in Kitchener, either, where Kitchener Collegiate's Christmas dance in 1937 saw "young ladies and escorts" entering the gymnasium through a "snow-laden cottage."[46]

Even if such events were intended to be healthy substitutes for declining familial and community supervision of mixed-sex socializing, some critics wondered at the schools' place in encouraging these activities, with their propensity for "extremes." Toronto's Board of Education, echoed by other boards in the province, considered that more attention was being paid to such "frills" as dancing and swimming than to "really necessary studies."[47] Along these lines, the Ottawa Collegiate "scandal" of 1927 struck such nervous chords among parents, teachers, and other worried adults that a provincial Royal Commission was established to investigate the allegations of immorality levelled against the school. The scandal was precipitated by the *Ottawa Evening Citizen*'s front-page coverage of a Presbyterian minister's statement, under the sensationalist headline, "Charges Unspeakable Conditions at O.C.I. Dances."[48] The minister declared that he was not singling out one school: his statement was meant as a "blanket condemnation" of the entire coeducational high school system in the province of Ontario. As he saw it, modern high schools were the dangerous playgrounds of "children with the freedom and license of adults but lacking the experience and balance." They were made all the more dangerous because of the mixing of the sexes and the employment of young female teachers. His only supporting evidence, however, consisted of stories that parents had told him about "petting parties" and "drinking parties" in connection with school events, though not actually on school premises. A woman with a daughter and two sons attending the school testified that she never permitted them to go to any school dances, because of the "rumours" about "looseness of morality" involving "hip flasks and hasty marriages."[49] For the other side, a Collegiate student, having never missed a dance in the previous four years, maintained that he had seen "nothing he would classify as objectionable." The principal himself insisted that "insubordination did not exist as a general thing," and that boys and girls were kept strictly segregated in both playground and classroom arrangements. The commission concluded that there was "no reason to believe any of the conditions [the Reverend] alleged as rendering it unsafe for parents to send children to Ottawa Collegiate Institute exist at all."[50] Whatever adolescents were up to off the premises, official extracurricular activities were evidently above reproach. Yet one of the Ottawa commissioners "could not help" advising parental accompaniment for youth attending dances, especially girls, because "modern conditions are such that they have to be met in some such way." Despite the evidence, or its lack in this case, the unease of adults concerning "modern conditions" made for a generational suspicion that was itself an emergent modern cultural trait.

The Depression would have curiously mixed effects on the culture of the modern high school, in that financial straits confronted by school boards put a halt to some important extracurricular activities — student publications were among the first to be axed, as the community businesses that underwrote their costs through advertising often withdrew support — while reinforcing a common perception of the critical role of such programs in the lives of young people who now had even fewer alternatives for wholesome socializing. The crisis bore down especially hard on the young. Among youth between the ages of fourteen and twenty, even the unreliable statistics of the period indicate an unemployment rate far surpassing that of any other age category.[51] The Minister of Education consistently reported a "considerable increase" in "congestion" and "serious over-crowding" in high schools throughout the province because of "enforced economies" on the part of municipalities and, more specifically, because more young people were staying in school or returning due to unemployment.[52] Many were embarrassed and ashamed as their deteriorating family circumstances compelled them to attend in ever-shabbier attire at a moment in their lives when appearance counted for so much.[53] Other young people, less fortunate or perhaps less patient than these, took to the streets and to the rails, collectively embodying the archetypal "lost generation," having attained the threshold of adulthood in this time of international crisis.

In the midst of raging, and largely futile, debates over state responsibility for the suffering masses, the only palliative offered to youth, besides postponing the date of unemployment through extended schooling, was "to ensure to the young people participation in some definite activity." After some years of seeming progress in organizing them into purposeful clubs and pastimes, there were worrisome indications that adolescents left to their own devices were turning to less positive outlets than those preferred for them by adults. As funding for both school and community recreational programs dried up, the "gang" appeared to be "again developing into a contaminating source of infection."[54] By the late 1930s, the flourishing of various anti-democratic movements around the world made the young appear even more threatening to the social order, as these movements had "recognized and exploited the potential power for social change which youth possesses." Social workers argued the equal importance of vocational training and recreational opportunities, especially sports and games. Any recreational activity based on "a broad social view" would represent a step towards reintegration of alienated youth into the social mainstream.[55] Organized recreation was a form of "social education" that would demonstrate to the young "the idea of democracy involving unselfishness, his or her own worth, conventions with respect to sex, the worth of religion as a workable philosophy of life." Consequently, it was both "economical and safe to conserve a source of future good citizenship."[56] The "citizenship" arguments that justified the school's centrality in the adolescent world were reinforced by the crisis atmosphere of the Great Depression: "now, more than ever before, [the young person] is a social being, a citizen of the world, he must develop a social consciousness ... it is to make good citizens that the modern school must bend its energies."[57]

The Depression, some maintained, was delivering a necessary lesson to modern youth by teaching them the benefits of active participation and weaning them away from "the easier way of paying to be amused."[58] Recognizing the importance of keeping up morale under these historic circumstances, teachers were reportedly devoting much time to non-academic activities, with music given high priority. "Glee clubs," which featured chorus singing, often dominated by girls, were thought to be especially motivational, but the important point was the "advantage found in working together for a common end." The extracurriculum was also becoming even more organized and formalized with the creation, in "three or four sections of the province," of "leagues" to ensure "high standards of efficiency" in extracurricular activities, to foster "a fine sense of honour in interschool competitions," and to maintain, "as in athletics, a proper balance between the physical and the intellectual."[59] Yet, despite these efforts on the part of teachers and administrators, students themselves noted the overall "seriousness" of tone, the dampening of "school spirit," wrought by the Depression: "in fact, depression seems rampant in the school, as much in esprit de corps as in anything else." Participation in extracurricular activities dropped decidedly across the province. At Guelph Collegiate, a drama club production of *Julius Caesar* was "sadly handicapped" by students who either did not take appear at practices or withdrew the day before the play's opening. There was evidently difficulty in getting members of the school sports teams, especially the senior teams, out to practice.[60]

By the outbreak of World War II in 1939, compulsory school attendance to age sixteen had made high school a much more common adolescent occupation. It was not, however, a universal or uniform experience for those outside the Canadian-born middle class. The modern high school reinforced class, ethnic, and gender distinctions in significant ways, not only through particular types of schooling, but also by making more apparent the contrasts between high school culture and the outside lives of less-favoured students. The peer society at the basis of the extracurriculum contributed to the construction of a behavioural code, and disciplined, usually by exclusion, those who did not conform to recognized group standards. This allowed for a rigidly defined status hierarchy of "in and out," good and bad, increasingly expressed in the political terminology of "popular and unpopular." Those who did not, or could not, fit in, had three choices: reconstruct a group identity among others like themselves, suffer alone, or leave. Clearly, young people did not simply "take" whatever form of social activity that adults deemed was good for them. They were quite capable of subverting attempts to "train" them by setting up alternate, "secret" societies or by participating in existing clubs only to the degree, and in the measure, that they chose to, as well as by simply refusing any involvement.

Guelph Collegiate and Vocational Institute, girls' softball team, 1925; GCVI, *Acta Nostra*, 1926.

Even in public high schools exhibiting an unprecedented class, ethnic, and gender mix, and even with a new roster of academic and social opportunities, many young people could not measure up against the cultural capital inherited by their better-established peers.[61] Those from affluent families continued to enjoy certain advantages in shaping the clubs and their activities, and, in turn, derived special class-specific benefits through their participation. In effect, high school clubs became small-scale youthful replicas of the various organizations dear to the heart of white middle-class adults, mimicking their internal organization, platforms, regulations, fundraising, promotion, and activities. The customary gendered hierarchies were upheld: boys dominated student and associational governments as presidents and vice-presidents, and headed newspapers and yearbooks as editors in chief. Girls often filled secretarial or assistant or otherwise auxiliary positions.[62] It also appears that, in high school as in other institutional cultures, the axiom that "nothing succeeds like success" held true: the same student, usually male, often occupied several official extracurricular positions. At one high school, the 1928 valedictorian was also president of the Hi-Y Club, treasurer of the student council, secretary-treasurer of the badminton club, advertising manager of the school newspaper, manager of the basketball team, sergeant in the cadet corp, and, "in spite of all this," the student newspaper marvelled, "he has some time for sports."[63]

The socioeconomic transformations of the early twentieth century opened up new worlds to youth, prompting a reconfiguration of adolescence in ways that made it significantly different from the experience of previous generations. Adolescents came to identify, and to be identified, more with school and leisure than with paid labour. But even a stronger generational identification did not obliterate hierarchies within that generation, as suggested by the culture of the modern high school, newly institutionalized in the peer societies of the extracurriculum, with its status cliques and exclusionary divides. The high school also established the peer group as chief agent of adolescent socialization through promotion of its students' membership in, and identification with, the school. The intention was to universalize the high school experience and homogenize the newly diversified student body. In this respect, high school was a levelling element in the adolescent social environment. But it also made more apparent the contrasts between high school culture and the outside lives of less-fortunate students. Before public schooling, restricted admission ensured the reproduction of existing social relations. In the twentieth-century educational system, and especially in the modern high school, the schools themselves replicated the differentiating structures of the larger society.[64]

The extracurriculum is fundamental to the concept of the high school as a "container" for unruly youth. In co-opting the less objectionable aspects of popular culture and an increasingly commercialized youth culture by the 1920s, high schools attempted to supply safe alternatives under trained adult leadership. The expanding extracurriculum consequently also expanded the labour of teachers as well as the potential influence of extrafamilial adults on the lives, and lifestyles, of young people. Reporting on the importance of vocational guidance to high school students, the Minister of Education contended that "it is the duty of every teacher to give direction to those under his care — he probably knows his pupils better than the parents do."[65] The kin- and class-based, often work-based, cultures of working-class and immigrant youth were opened wider to middle-class example. If generational tensions were exacerbated by the culture clash inherent in the relationship between "old world" immigrant parents and their "Canadian" adolescent children, they could be made all the worse when the latter opted for the teacher's "modern" guidance over that of "old-fashioned" parents and other adult kin.[66]

An even more likely short-term outcome was a solidifying sense of difference among young people whose social success was measured in terms of "joining," "fitting in," and becoming "one of the gang." In many ways, those who could not, or would not, conform appeared all the more as "outsiders." Living in Toronto's working-class Cabbagetown neighbourhood, the young protagonist of Hugh Garner's autobiographical Depression-era novel attended the "Tech" in the hope that "somehow the school would release him from his shabby district and even shabbier home, and make him a belonging part of its friendliness and comradeship and happier life." He found, instead, that socioeconomic divisions "were of fine complexity but nevertheless clearly marked," given away by such things as after-school jobs and shabby clothes that prevented young people from participating in extracurricular socializing. The fictional hero, in common with many of his real historical counterparts, remained "an outsider from the cliques revolving around athletics, the school magazine, the auditorium stage, the possession of a Model T Ford."[67]

Its proponents argued that organized, school-supervised social activity allowed for a wider, more diversified participation across the customary social boundaries, opening doors to young people who might not otherwise have had access to clubs, sports, and wholesome cultural and intellectual activities. In reality, the extracurriculum, like the curriculum itself, continued to favour those economically better-positioned to begin with, boys over girls, and white Anglo-Celtic Canadians over all others. Social "tracking," in effect, crossed the boundary from curriculum to extracurriculum.[68] Reinforced by growing attendance, the apparently universal nature of the high school experience allowed an illusion of youth cohesion and reassuring uniformity at a time when a sense of national objectives and national identity were of tremendous importance. It was, ultimately, just as illusory as that historical brand of "national identity."

ACKNOWLEDGMENTS

I would like to acknowledge the Social Sciences and Humanities Research Council, whose funding for my ongoing research into the sociocultural history of English-Canadian adolescents during the first half of the twentieth century is much appreciated, and also the Research Office, Wilfrid Laurier University, for its heartening support. Thanks are also due to Erica Morant, who, as unpaid but dedicated archivist/librarian at Guelph Collegiate and Vocational Institute, did much to encourage my work when I started this project many years ago; likewise to Ms. M. Mulholland, GCVI librarian, who helped with illustrations; Susan Bellingham, archivist for the Dana Porter Rare Books Room and Archives, University of Waterloo; and Inge Sanmiya, who took time to find material on London high schools despite her own research agenda. This paper is for my daughter Stefanie, GCVI, class of 2001.

NOTES

1. Ontario, Department of Education, *Annual Report of the Inspectors of High Schools*, 1920, 49; also ibid., 1922, 45–6. The latter also notes the increase in juvenile delinquency since the war and comments on the "great need for moral training."

2. Contemporary commentaries include, for example, T. R. Robinson, "Youth and the Virtues," *Social Welfare*, October 1928, 9; H. Dobson, "Youth: Scapegrace or Scapegoat," *Social Welfare*, July 1929, 228; Editorial, "Hygiene of Recreation," *Canadian Practitioner*, June 1924, 309. On similar European developments regarding "modern youth," see K. Alaimo, "Shaping Adolescence in the Popular Milieu: Social Policy, Reformers, and French Youth, 1870–1920," *Journal of Family History* 17, 4 (1992): 420; W. S. Haine, "The Development of Leisure and the Transformation of Working-Class Adolescence in France," *Journal of Family History* 17, 4 (1992): 451. I explore these anxieties more fully in C. R. Comacchio, "Dancing to Perdition: Adolescence and Leisure in Interwar English Canada," *Journal of Canadian Studies* 32, 3 (Fall 1997): 5–27. Although used occasionally in the media during the interwar years, the term "teenager" does not seem to have come into popular usage until the 1950s; on post–World War II developments, see M. L. Adams, *The Trouble with Normal: Postwar Youth and the Making of Heterosexuality* (Toronto: University of Toronto Press, 1997).

3. Alaimo, "Shaping Adolescence," 419–21.

4. D. N. McLachlan, "The Spiritual and Ethical Development of the Child," *Social Welfare*, December 1929, 68.

5. G. Stanley Hall, *Adolescence: Its Psychology and Its Relation to Physiology, Anthropology, Sociology, Sex, Crime, Religion and Education*, vol. 1 (New York: D. Appleton and Company, 1904), xvi–xvii.

6. Ibid., 4.

7. Ontario, Department of Education, *Report of the Inspectors of High Schools*, 1919, 32–3; ibid., 1922, 45–6; R. Ueda, *Avenues to Adulthood: The Origins of the High School and Social Mobility in an American Suburb* (Cambridge: Cambridge University Press, 1987), 141.

8. On "the second great transformation" in American schools, see C. Goldink, L. F. Katz, "Human Capital and Social Capital: The Rise of Secondary Schooling in America, 1910–40," *Journal of Interdisciplinary History* 29, 4 (Spring 1999): 685–6.

9. I. F. Goodson and I. R. Dowbiggin, "Vocational Education and School Reform: The Case of the London Technical School, 1900–1930," *History of Education Review* 20, 1 (1991): 55. On vocational education, see also N. S. Jackson and J. S. Gaskell, "White Collar Vocationalism: The Rise of Commercial Education in Ontario and British Columbia, 1870–1920," in R. Heap and A. Prentice, eds., *Gender and Education in Ontario: An Historical Reader* (Toronto: Canadian Scholars Press, 1991), 165–94; T. A. Dunn, "Teaching the Meaning of Work: Vocational Education in British Columbia, 1900–29," in D. C. Jones, N. M. Sheehan, and R. M. Stamp, eds., *Shaping the Schools of the Canadian West* (Calgary: Detselig, 1979), 237–53. The classic works on the development of Canadian education include J. D. Wilson, R. Stamp, L-P. Audet, eds., *Canadian Education: A History* (Scarborough, Ont.: Prentice-Hall, 1970); R. Stamp, *The Schools of Ontario, 1876-1976*; A. Prentice and S. Houston, eds., *Family, School and Society in Nineteenth-Century Canada* (Toronto: University of Toronto Press,1975); N. Sutherland, *Children in English Canadian Society* (Toronto: University of Toronto Press, 1976; repr. Waterloo: Wilfrid Laurier University Press, 2000); R. D. Gidney and W. P. J. Millar, *Inventing Secondary Education: The Rise of the High School in Nineteenth-Century Ontario* (Toronto: University of Toronto Press, 1990). For an overview of recent writings, see P. Axelrod, "Historical Writing and Canadian Education from the 1970s to the 1990s," *History of Education Quarterly* 36, 1 (Spring 1996): 20–38.

10. P. Axelrod, *The Promise of Schooling: Education in Canada* (Toronto: University of Toronto Press, 1997), 68. See also J. Modell and J. Trent Alexander, "High School in Transition: Community, School, and Peer Group in Abilene, Kansas, 1939," *History of Education Quarterly* 37, 1 (Spring 1997): 1–2. P. Axelrod, *The Making of a Middle Class* (Montreal and Kingston: McGill-Queen's University Press, 1995), discusses the class, gender, and ethnic basis of the university population during the 1930s.

11. Ontario, *Statutes of the Province of Ontario*, 1911, An Act Respecting Education for Industrial Purposes. The federal government would follow suit in 1919 with its Technical Education Act; see Ontario, Department of Education, *Report of the Division of Industrial and Technical Education*, 1919, 13; Technical Education Act, *Statutes of the Dominion of Canada* 9–10, George V, c. 73, 7 July 1919.

12. Ontario, Department of Education, *Report of the Minister of Education*, 1919, 15; W. F. Dyde, *Public Secondary Education in Canada* (New York: Columbia University, 1929), 41; J. M. McCutcheon, *Public Education in Ontario* (Toronto: Best, 1941), 171; F. Johnson, *A Brief History of Canadian Education* (Toronto: McGraw-Hill, 1968), 142–3. See also Robert Stamp, "Canadian High Schools in the 1920s and 1930s," Canadian Historical Association, *Historical Papers*, 1978, 77–80; Sutherland, *Children in English Canadian Society*, 164.

13. Ontario, Department of Education, *Report of the Inspectors of High Schools*, 1922, 34. Stamp, "Canadian High Schools," 78–9; he develops this further in *High Schools of Ontario*. I discuss the rise of consumer society and its impact on family in *The Infinite Bonds of Family: Domesticity in Canada, 1850–1940* (Toronto: University of Toronto Press, 1999), 75–81.

14. Ontario, Department of Education, *Report of the Inspectors of High Schools*, 1920, 56, which notes that the yearly expansion of high schools is the "outstanding feature" of the system. These comments are repeated in every report through the decade. In 1929 there were 63 collegiate institutes and 142 high schools in the province; of the collegiates, only 7 of 63 had retained their original buildings, and of the high schools, more than half were in new buildings or expanded and modernized structures; see ibid., 1929, 38. The minister reported in 1923 that attendance had reached a "point never reached before" during the 1922 school year; enrolment was 60,395, an increase of 41.9 percent during the two years under the Adolescent Attendance Act; see *Report of the Minister of Education*, 1923, iii.

15. Sutherland, *Children in English Canadian Society*, 164. The Ontario population grew by 17 percent in the 1920s, but secondary school population quadrupled during that decade; Stamp, "Canadian High Schools," 79–80. On working-class attendance, see C. Heron, "The High School and the Household Economy in Working-Class Hamilton, 1890–1940," *Historical Studies in Education* 7, 2 (Fall 1995): 242, 246; see also the oral histories in J. Synge, "The Transition from School to Work: Growing up Working Class in Early 20th Century Hamilton, Ontario," in K. Ishwaran, ed., *Childhood and Adolescence in Canada* (Toronto: McGraw-Hill Ryerson, 1979), 249–69. On London, see Goodson, Dowbiggin, "Vocational Education and School Reform."

16. C. Campbell, "Family Strategy, Secondary Schooling and Making Adolescents: The Indian Summer of the Old Middle Class, 1945–60," *History of Education Review* 22, 2 (1993): 19, 38.

17. P. Bourdieu, *Reproduction in Education, Society and Culture*, 2nd ed. (London: Sage, 1990), ix–xi, 102, 158. Similar themes are explored for Australia by Campbell, "Family Strategy"; for the United States, see Goldin and Katz, "Human Capital and Social Capital."

18. Ueda, *Avenues to Adulthood*, 119.

19. Gutowski, "Student Initiative and the Origins of the High School Extracurriculum," 83–100.

20. *Statutes of the Dominion of Canada*, 9–10, George V, c. 73, 7 July 1919. The Royal Commission on Industrial Training and Technical Education was appointed in 1908 and reported in 1911; see also Sutherland, *Children in English Canadian Society*, especially chapters 12 and 13; see also R. Stamp, "Those Yankee Frills: The New Education in Ontario," in M. Piva, ed., *History of Ontario: Selected Readings* (Toronto: McClelland and Stewart, 1985).

21. *Report of the Inspectors of High Schools*, 1920, 49–50.

22. Editorial, Kitchener Collegiate Institute, *The Grumbler*, 1931, 18. *The Grumbler* began publication in 1907 as "a few mimeographed sheets" produced bi-weekly by the Literary Society. By 1931 it had become a hybrid newspaper/annual, published three times a year, with as many as 300 students involved; see ibid., "Principal's Message," 1938, 5. By 1938 there was also discussion of making it a monthly venture: "Shall We Change *The Grumbler?*" 1938, 4.

23. Ueda, *Avenues to Adulthood*, 150.

24. "Principal's Message," *The Grumbler*, 1937, 2.

25. *Report of the Inspectors of High Schools*, 1919, 39; the report notes similar events taking place at other Ontario schools.

26. *Report of the Minister of Education*, 1929, 14.

27. Guelph Collegiate and Vocational Institute, *Acta Nostra*, vol. 1, 1926, 90.

28. J. F. Ross, "Principal's Message," *Acta Nostra*, vol. 1, 1926, 11. This was the first edition of the yearbook of Guelph Collegiate and Vocational Institute. In 1879 the Guelph Grammar School became the Guelph High School, then the Collegiate Institute in 1886, when a gymnasium was added. A new school building was erected in 1923, with technical-education facilities. By the 1920s, it was the largest high school in Wellington District and served a combined rural/urban population of about 10,000; see G. Shutt, *The High Schools of Guelph* (Toronto: University of Toronto Press, 1961). The particularly rich and well-kept archives of GCVI have permitted me to use the school as a case study for my larger project on adolescence.

29. M. W. Beckleman, "The Group Worker in the Modern Scene," *A Canadian Welfare Summary*, July 1938, 64.

30. "The Advantages of Student Government," *The Grumbler*, 1924, 5. Kitchener Collegiate Institute was evidently one of the first Ontario high schools to establish a student council, consisting of an elected executive and representatives for each year under a teacher "advisory committee." This was accomplished in 1922, though the editorial cited argues that "in the future it will be a recognized organization" throughout Canada. C. E. Phillips, *The Development of Education in Canada* (Toronto: W. Gage, 1957), 534, describes student government as "accepted practice" in secondary schools across Canada by the 1930s.

31. D. G. Bell, "Teaching Young Canada to Play," *Maclean's*, 15 July 1926, 19.

32. Editorial, *Child Welfare News*, May 1927, 31; Rev. E. Thomas, "The Church of God and the Homes of His People," *Social Welfare*, November 1920, 48; *Report of the Minister of Education*, 1929, 14; on funding, see, for example, Ontario High Schools Act, *Revised Statutes of Ontario*, c. 360, 1937.

33. Quoted in H. Gurney, *Girls' Sports: A Century of Progress in Ontario High Schools* (Don Mills, Ont.: Ontario Federation of School Athletic Associations, 1979), 24.

34. "Athletics," *The Oracle*, 1932, 81.

35. "Athletics," *The Grumbler*, 1937, 85. Kitchener Collegiate Institute was proclaimed "second to none" for its enthusiasm, both in terms of participation and audience support for its teams.

36. Guelph Collegiate and Vocational Institute, *Acta Nostra*, vol. 1, 1926, 31–2; vol. 3, 1929, 15.

37. Guelph Public Library Archives, Shutt Family Papers, Item 7-1, letter to G. Shutt, undated [1960s], signed "A Happy Reader," from a former GCVI student who attended during the 1920s; on sports, see also Axelrod, *The Promise of Schooling*, 116.

38. The earliest record is the Girls Athletic Club at Jarvis Collegiate in 1897. Jarvis was also the first to affiliate with the YWCA in 1924, naming its new club ROAD to reflect the new emphasis on reading, outdoors, athletics, and dramatics; Oakwood Collegiate maintained the two as separate clubs. See Gurney, *Girls' Sports*, 24–6.

39. A. H. D. Ross, *A Short History of the Arnprior High School* (Ottawa: Popham, 1922), 53.

40. "The School Spirit," Guelph Collegiate and Vocational Institute, *Acta Nostra*, vol. 1, 1926, 91.

41. Fergus High School, *Vox Scholae*, vol. 1, 1930, 3.

42. Kitchener Collegiate Institute, *The Grumbler*, 1928, 21.

43. Ibid., 1931, 8.

44. Guelph Collegiate and Vocational Institute, *Acta Nostra*, vol. 2, 1927, 47–8.

45. Guelph Public Library Archives, Shutt Family Collection, Item 7-l, letter to G. Shutt, unsigned, undated [references to 1920s], 2.
46. Guelph Collegiate and Vocational Institute, *Acta Nostra*, vol. 8, 1933. The yearbook ceased publication with this issue, as advertising revenues from local businesses dwindled; it resumed publication only in 1942; Kitchener Collegiate Institute, *The Grumbler*, 1938, 77.
47. Editorial, "Avoid Extremes," *Toronto Star*, 13 January 1921.
48. Public Archives of Ontario, RG 18-88, Box l, B-72, Royal Commission: Ottawa Collegiate Institute Inquiry, 6 January 1927, Evidence, 2, 11–15.
49. Ibid., 22, 29.
50. Ibid., 72.
51. J. Struthers, *No Fault of Their Own: Unemployment and the Canadian Welfare State, 1914–1941* (Toronto: University of Toronto Press, 1983), 100, 132–5; R. Pierson, "Gender and the Unemployment Insurance Debates in Canada," *Labour/Le Travail* 25 (Spring 1990): 82–4.
52. *Report of the High School Inspectors*, 1932, 15; also *Report of the Minister of Education*, 1934, 3; ibid., 1939, viii. By 1939, there were 198 high schools in Ontario, including 58 collegiate institutes; there were also 217 continuation schools. Enrolment in the former was 53,400, with 9,654 in the latter.
53. See the letters to R. B. Bennett in M. Bliss and L. Grayson, eds. *The Wretched of Canada* (Toronto: University of Toronto Press, 1971); see also B. Broadfoot, *Ten Lost Years* (Toronto: Doubleday, 1977), and W. Johnson, "Keeping Children in School: The Response of the Montreal Catholic School Commission to the Depression of the 1930s," Canadian Historical Association, *Historical Papers*, 1985, 197.
54. F. T. Sharpe, "Stopping Before Starting," *Child Welfare News*, January 1934, 43–4. The classic contemporary survey is K. H. Rogers, *Street Gangs in Toronto: A Study of the Forgotten Boy* (Toronto: Ryerson Press, 1945).
55. Depression and Unemployment," *Child and Family Welfare*, November 1935, 15; E. Muncaster, "Strengthening Family Ties through Recreation," *Child and Family Welfare*, November 1933, 47; see also Canadian Council on Child and Family Welfare, Division on Leisure Time and Educative Activities, "Relief Is Not Enough: The Idle Time of Compulsorily Idle Canadians," *Bulletin No. 1*, 25 September 1933, 1–4; "Will Canada Have a Youth Movement?" *The Canadian Doctor*, January 1939, 17–18.
56. S. Brent, "Reinforcing Family Strengths by the Provision of Leisure Time Activities," *Child and Family Welfare*, September 1931, 53; W. R. Cook, "Getting Down to Brass Tacks in Community Planning for Leisure Time," *Child and Family Welfare*, March 1938, 10–11.
57. Department of Education, *Report on Vocational Guidance*, 1931, 4.
58. W. Bowie, "The Character of a Nation," *Social Welfare*, July 1931, 199.
59. *Report of the High School Inspectors*, 1932, 17; ibid., 1934, 3.
60. Guelph Collegiate and Vocational Institute, Editorial, *Acta Nostra*, vol. 8, 1933, 11; Gurney, *Girls' Sports*, notes that sports competitions and such groups as the Hi-Y seem to have "faded" by the mid-1930s.
61. On "secret societies," see W. Graebner, "Outlawing Teenage Populism: The Campaign against Secret Societies in the American High School, 1900–1960," *Journal of American History* 74 (September 1987): 412–5; Ueda, *Avenues to Adulthood*, 119–20.
62. Ueda, *Avenues to Adulthood*, 121.
63. St. John Vocational School, *The Challenger*, June 1940, 4.
64. Modell and Alexander, "High School in Transition," 23.
65. *Report of the Minister of Education*, 1931, 4.
66. Certainly this view of the immigrant family seemed to prevail among the period's social workers; see H. Atkinson, "Boys in Trouble," *Child and Family Welfare* 7, 6 (March 1932): 2. See also the oral testimony from Italian- and Ukrainian-Canadian youth recorded in C. M. Bayley, "The Social Structure of the Italian and Ukrainian Immigrant Communities in Montreal" (M.A. thesis, McGill University, 1939), especially 85–7 and 241–2. Between 1935 and 1937 Bayley, as a research fellow in sociology at McGill, spent fifteen months among Italians and seven months among Ukrainians in Montreal. P. Fass, *Outside In: Minorities and the Transformation of American Education* (New York: Oxford University Press, 1989), 108, found that, in practice, ethnic patterns in students' extracurricular choices within the newly diverse high schools of New York City during the 1930s revealed "a deeply divided social universe."
67. H. Garner, *Cabbagetown* (Richmond Hill, Ont.: Penguin, 1971), 12–13. Although written after the Depression, this is a semi-autobiographical story set in Toronto's notorious working-class district. According to the author (who grew up there), Cabbagetown was "a sociological phenomenon, the largest Anglo-Saxon slum in North America." See author's preface, i.
68. Ueda, *Avenues to Adulthood*, 119–20; Modell and Alexander, "High School in Transition," 12–18.

Article 8.2

Heidi Macdonald

Doing More with Less: The Sisters of St. Martha (PEI) Diminish the Impact of the Great Depression

Issues to Consider

- What explains the standard historical interpretation of Prince Edward Island's Depression experience? Why does Macdonald dispute it?
- Why does the author compare the Sisters' social welfare work to domestic labour?
- What explains the federal government's approach toward relief for the Island's unemployed during the Depression? What was the status of government and voluntary social service agencies at that time?
- How did the Church plan to "steer" the Islanders through the Depression? What role was intended for the Sisters?
- Why does Macdonald deem St. Vincent's Orphanage "a crucial institution" at that time in particular?
- The Sisters of St. Martha, as Macdonald demonstrates, did not fit the traditional gender construction of the time in regard to women's role, seeing as they were unmarried by choice and worked in the public sphere. At the same time, however, it is clear that they too were constrained by prevailing views of women. Discuss.

Prince Edward Island had the lowest per capita income in the country in the first half of the 20th century and fewer government-funded health and social services than most provinces.[1] Because of this ongoing poverty and lack of services, some historians have argued that the Great Depression was hardly noticed in PEI, while provinces such as Saskatchewan, whose economy really plummeted, suffered more severely.[2] Such arguments concerning the relative poverty of provinces obscure the more valuable question of how Prince Edward Islanders survived the Depression. A significant factor in Islanders' survival was the work of the Sisters of St. Martha in health and social services. This was true particularly for the 45 per cent of the PEI population who were Roman Catholic. During the Depression, this small congregation of sisters, who numbered 41 in 1930, cared for thousands of people. Although the Depression prevented many clients from paying the fees that supported their social institutions, the sisters continued providing the services that constituted most of the Roman Catholic social order: a 72-bed hospital, a 100-bed orphanage and a 75-bed geriatric facility.[3] In addition, they directly confronted the Depression by creating a social services department that served thousands of Roman Catholics annually, beginning in 1931. Contrary to John Taylor's contention that in the early 1930s "voluntary charity as a means of providing relief collapsed," the Sisters of St. Martha and other congregations of women religious provided relief throughout the decade in the form of social services.[4]

Source: Heidi Macdonald, "Doing More with Less: The Sisters of St. Martha (PEI) Diminish the Impact of the Great Depression," *Acadiensis* 33, no. 1 (Fall 2003): 21–46.

Useful comparisons can be made between the labour performed by women religious during the Depression and that of housewives. For example, Denyse Baillargeon argues that Montreal housewives absorbed the impact of the Great Depression by intensifying their existing efforts. The Sisters of St. Martha did the same. They worked harder. Moreover, this paper argues that women religious' labour has only reluctantly been accepted into the historical record for the same reasons that Baillargeon has argued for housewives: invisibility, lack of documentation and the underrated value of unwaged reproductive labour.[5]

As Carol Coburn and Martha Smith have noted of the United States, women religious are "one of the oldest and least analyzed of women's groups ... [largely] ignored by scholars of Catholic history and women's history."[6] Similarly, scholars of economic and labour history have not considered women religious' work in any depth, despite widespread acknowledgement that sisters' skilled and inexpensive labour was essential to the success of thousands of North American Roman Catholic schools, hospitals and other social institutions in the 19th and 20th centuries.[7] Mary J. Oates notes that although male religious (brothers) were the preferred workers in 19th-century American Catholic institutions, "sisters became key actors in all types of charity work because ... [b]rothers both expected and received much higher compensation than sisters for the same work."[8] This pay differential supports Alicja Muszinsky's argument that in secular society, the person who performs labour (i.e., men, women or children of the dominant or minority ethnicity) determines the wages paid for it. Just as Muszinsky insists that Marx's labour theory of value should consider patriarchy, which "cuts into and across ... capitalism,"[9] religious vocation must be taken into account when analyzing sisters' labour. Women religious were motivated by a desire to live out their faith.[10] They dedicated their labour to the glory of God and to the service of fellow human beings, and their vow of poverty mean that wages mattered less to them than to most workers. Religious vocation may be one reason why their labour has so rarely been considered by scholars.

This paper considers a congregation of sisters in a very specific time and place, Prince Edward Island during the Depression, yet, even in this context, political economists and religious historians have not addressed sisters' crucial contribution to health and social services. Ernest Forbes convincingly argues that the Maritime provinces received considerably less than other regions in federal relief. Forbes refers to the Antigonish Movement as the Roman Catholic Church's most significant response to the Depression.[11] Similarly, in *A History of Canadian Catholics*, Terence Fay focuses on the Antigonish Movement, the Catholic Social Order for Quebec and the Action libéral nationale, higher education, lay women and the Cooperative Commonwealth Federation in a chapter titled "Catholic Response to the Depression."[12] These grassroots organizations were all of major importance, and in the case of the Antigonish Movement, internationally implemented and respected.[13] What historians have yet to consider, however, is how groups that existed before 1929, including those within the Catholic Church, responded to the Depression. With the exception of contemplative congregations, of which there are relatively few in North America, congregations of women religious were founded to serve the poor, whether in schools, health care, social services or some combination of these fields.[14] By the 1930s, many congregations had more than a century of experience and, as Coburn and Smith note, were often in a better position to provide charity than Protestant women, who "usually had to balance these activities with their duties to their families. The sisters had to their advantage a centuries-old tradition of female collective living and activity, a large mobile workforce, disciplined and narrowly-focused goals and the ability to react quickly to the needs of a given situation."[15] These unique qualities often allowed congregations such as the Sisters of St. Martha of PEI to respond to the effects of the Depression more immediately and effectively than non-governmental or governmental organizations.

As in the rest of the country,[16] the Depression caught Prince Edward Island with little room to manoeuvre. According to John Taylor, in the post–First World War era, costly infrastructure pressed hard on the tax base, which stopped growing around 1919.[17] While the Maritimes did not experience the degree of economic growth that the rest of the country did in the 1920s, the Depression still caused dramatic falls in revenue.[18] PEI agricultural revenue and agricultural production had increased steadily in the latter half of the 1920s, with PEI's staple export, seed potatoes, fetching as much as $1.50 a bushel in 1929; two years later the price bottomed out at only $0.06 a bushel.[19] Because the fishery was less prosperous in the late 1920s and comprised only 6 per cent of the gross provincial product, the impact of a downturn in the fishery was less severe than the decline in agriculture.[20] The downturn in the fishery was, however, devastating to the Acadian Catholics who dominated the industry.[21]

While the Depression was misunderstood and misdiagnosed in its first years on Prince Edward Island, its severity was clear by 1932 when the gross value of production had fallen to half its value three years earlier — $15,943,467 compared to $32,807,542 in 1929 — and many traditional sources of relief were exhausted.[22] By this time, according to Dennis Guest, the Depression had become a significant force for making social policy the responsibility of the state. Guest uses the example of unemployment, which "was seen less as a result of personal inadequacy and more as a common and insurable threat to the livelihood of the average citizen."[23] Unfortunately, tax revenue had decreased markedly in the early 1930s, and very little money was available for civic or provincial public spending.[24] Moreover, as Ernest Forbes has explained, the federal government, rather than undertaking a per capita program for relief, undertook a matching grant scheme; consequently the most impoverished region of the country, the Maritimes, received only 3.3 per cent of federal funding, or one-third, per capita, of the national average. Island relief recipients in 1935 received an average of $1.93 a month, while Canadians outside the Maritimes received an average of $6.18 a month.[25]

Between 1930 and 1935, PEI received a total of $495,879 from the federal government under all forms of relief legislation. Nova Scotia, by comparison, received $4,248,084, Saskatchewan $20,970,948 and Ontario $47,479,062.[26] PEI received $65,985 in direct relief in the same five-year period; New Brunswick received the second lowest amount of direct relief with $633,156, which was almost 10 times what PEI received despite New Brunswick's population being only 4.6 times larger.[27] The four western provinces received between $5.3 and $9.4 million in direct relief, while Quebec and Ontario received $15.4 and $25.6 million respectively.[28] Clearly, Islanders could not depend on federal or provincial government funding to alleviate the effects of the Depression.

In addition to receiving less relief per capita from the federal government than other provinces, PEI also had fewer existing governmental and non-governmental services in place that could respond to the Depression. PEI was the only province, for example, in which the Victorian Order of Nurses (VON) did not serve.[29] Similarly, despite having the highest tuberculosis mortality rates in Canada, PEI was the only province without a sanatorium in the 1920s.[30] Like the other Maritime provinces, PEI did have a Children's Aid Society, but the society did not flourish as it did in Ontario, where it was more of an umbrella organization over Catholic, Protestant and Jewish orphanages as well as foster and adoptive programs. In PEI, children's social services were administered and funded by parallel Catholic and Protestant systems that included orphanages and geriatric facilities.[31] Secular organizations such as the Children's Aid Society contracted out to the denominational institutions and were weak in comparison.[32]

The Red Cross, on the other hand, was a significant force in PEI after the Second World War. With insufficient human and financial resources and no department of health, the provincial government contracted out some public health work to the Red Cross. The Red

Cross, in turn, focused on promoting community health through school programs. The Chief Nurse of the PEI Division of the Red Cross, Mona Wilson, and two assistant nurses, made great strides in the late 1920s, particularly in controlling tuberculosis. For a variety of reasons, however, the Red Cross was unable to confront the Depression in PEI effectively. Turnover was high among their own small staff and the organization's board was dominated by the elite of PEI Protestants; Roman Catholics avoided the Red Cross both as volunteers and clients.[33] The Red Cross did not create any programs to confront the needs of the Depression in PEI, although it did respond to individual families with particularly serious needs. If anything, the Red Cross may have been slightly less active than usual in the most severe years of the Depression because some of their regular volunteers were involved with other relief activities, including a soup kitchen in Charlottetown.[34]

The government of PEI had little social service infrastructure in place that could respond to the economic crisis of the Depression. The Department of Health was established only in 1931, although individual employees had previous experience in health care on the Island through the Red Cross. Rather than responding to the economic crisis of the early 1930s, the new Department was occupied in taking over the public health program established by the Red Cross, and in supervising tuberculosis care at the Dalton Sanatorium and mental health care at Falconwood Hospital, both of which had opened in 1931 thanks to federally funded construction initiatives. If health care services were slight, social services were even thinner. At no time during the Depression was the provincial government involved in social work. Not only was social work needed in its own regard, but, as Charlotte Whitton, Canada's early 20th-century social work expert, noted, its unavailability (beyond the services of the Sisters of St. Martha at the Charlottetown Hospital) negatively affected the work of the Island's three referral hospitals and other health services. In Whitton's words: "There seems little doubt that much of the good work of the hospitals, clinics, sanatorium and other health services are being impaired and hampered by the lack of adequately organized social work with families throughout the entire community."[35]

In short, in the early 1930s, the impoverished and ill of PEI had less hope of receiving direct relief of social services than people in other provinces. None of the 83 Canadian branches of the Victorian Order of Nurses were located in PEI and the Red Cross concentrated its limited resources on educating school children in public health. Not only was the provincial government unable to offer more than a small fraction of direct relief per capita compared to the national average, it was involved in health care in a very limited way — and only after 1931 — and avoided social work completely. The Roman Catholic Church, on the other hand, had many plans for confronting the Depression.

The Roman Catholic Church responded at several levels to the effects of the economic crisis of the 1930s. Upon issuing the encyclical *Rerum Novarum* in 1891, the papacy had moved away from merely encouraging Roman Catholics to help each other to urging them to work for more fundamental societal changes. In the same tone, *Quadragesimo Anno*, which translates as "Forty Years Having Passed" and refers to *Rerum Novarum*, addressed the effects of the Depression in 1931, rejecting both capitalism and socialism. As Terrence Fay noted, in *Quadragesimo Anno*, Pius XI recognized "the economic system for the average worker … was 'hard, cruel, and relentless,'"[36] and advised reconstructing the social order by encouraging self-determination.[37] Partly as an antidote to socialism, Pope Pius XI promoted *subsidiarity*, a theory based on the centrality of the human being which stated that all institutions, including governments, existed for the individual rather than for society. Furthermore, he argued, it was preferable that organizations function at the most basic and local level possible. In one Roman Catholic theologian's words: "Societies should not assume what individuals can do, nor should larger societies undertake what smaller associations can accomplish. Conversely the state has the responsibility to take up those tasks that neither individuals nor smaller societies can perform."[38] This principle of *subsidiarity*, combined with the encyclical's confirmation that it was the church's "right and duty ... to deal authoritatively with social and economic problems,"[39] fuelled the Roman Catholic Church's actions during the Depression. In addition to their recommendation for socio-economic change, the directives of *Rerum Novarum* and *Quadragesimo Anno* were a continuation of the church's commitment to serve the poor, the sick and the imprisoned, each of whom was *alter Christus*, or "the other Christ."

The Reverend Joseph O'Sullivan, who was consecrated Bishop of Charlottetown on 18 May 1931, firmly steered Island Roman Catholics through the Depression.[40] One of O'Sullivan's predecessors, Bishop Peter MacIntyre, had stabilized the Roman Catholic social order in PEI during his long episcopate in the late 19th century by building a slate of social institutions, including schools, a university and a hospital.[41] Roman Catholic social order determined that the church must continue to care for its own in these social institutions despite the increased financial difficulty of doing so. He ordered parishes to continue paying their annual assessments to keep up the properties and buildings required for Roman Catholic institutions.[42] His main plan for administering and staffing the institutions was to continue engaging the Sisters of St. Martha, who were responsible for the operational costs of the Roman Catholic social institutions and who could be trusted to enforce the principal of *subsidiarity*.[43] By 1930, the sisters' social institutions were frequented by at least 5,000 Island Roman Catholics annually.

The Sisters of St. Martha were a relatively new diocesan congregation, founded by Bishop Henry O'Leary in 1916 to serve the 45 per cent Roman Catholic population of Prince Edward Island in a variety of ways.[44] In their first decade, 97 per cent of the entrants were native Islanders, almost 80 per cent were Irish and most were uneducated beyond their district schools.[45] Although their first two assignments were in domestic service, in the tradition of their namesake, the Biblical "Martha," by the mid-1920s they had overcome a dearth of education, experience and human resources to administer the Charlottetown Hospital, St. Vincent's Orphanage and the Sacred Heart Home after the Sisters of Charity (Grey Nuns) left the diocese in 1925.[46] Although, by 1930, its resources were still stretched with only 41 members, the congregation was more stable than at any other point in its 15-year history and was involved in a variety of endeavours as outlined in Table 1.

The Depression marked the onset of another serious challenge for the Sisters of St. Martha. Although they had always served some people unable to pay, the Charlottetown Hospital, St. Vincent's Orphanage and St. Dunstan's University were all highly dependent on the payments of those families who used their various services, as was the custom before the development of the welfare state. In the cash-strapped days of the Depression, however, far fewer clients than before were able to pay. The economic crisis caused falling enrolments at St. Dunstan's University,[47] but the number of children at the orphanage remained relatively constant and the number of patients and patient days increased steadily at the Charlottetown Hospital. However, contributions fell so much at St. Vincent's Orphanage that expenditures in the 1935 budget had to be cut to one-third of those in the 1930 budget, and an average of 39 per cent of Charlottetown Hospital patients did not pay any part of their bill in the 1930s.[48]

Although the Depression threatened every Roman Catholic social institution, running a hospital was especially difficult. As David Gagan and Rosemary Gagan document, hospital operating costs rose greatly in the period after the First World War.[49] The Depression exacerbated the problem of collecting fees and led many would-be patients to avoid the hospital completely, because they knew they could not pay a hospital bill. Manitoba's hospitals experienced more than a sixfold increase in the costs of caring for indigents in the first year of the Depression, while 33 Saskatchewan hospitals were forced to shut down during the 1930s.[50]

Table 1   Sisters of St. Martha 1931 Work Assignments

Institutions (Founded)	No. of Sisters Assigned	No. of Total Members	Duties
St. Dunstan's University (1916)	9.0	22.0	Domestic service (including meals) for 170 university students and staff
Bishop's Palace (1916)	4.0	9.7	Domestic service, including organizing many banquets
Kinkora School (1921)	4.0	9.7	Three sister-teachers taught grades 1 to 10 in 3-room district school (1 sister-housekeeper for the convent)
Sacred Heart Home (1923)	5.0	12.0	24-hour care of approximately 100 geriatric patients
Charlottetown Hospital (1925)	8.5	21.0	Administration, nursing, dietary services, pharmacy, x-ray and clerical responsibilities for 1,599 patients (72 beds)
St. Vincent's Orphanage (1925)	5.0	12.0	Care for approximately 60 children including the operation of its own school
Social Services Bureau (1931)	2.5	6.1	Distribute relief and make home visits, providing both nursing and social work
Congregation Administration	3.0	7.3	Recruit and train new members and coordinate all aspects of sisters' education, work assignments and care
Sick	4.0	—	These 4 sisters are not included in the per cent of total members
Total	45	99.8	

Source: "Sisters' Ministries," series 3, sub-series 3, SSMA.

Roman Catholic diocesan officials involved in administering the Charlottetown Hospital tried to maintain business as usual during the Depression, but that business was getting tougher, and what was "usual" was a lack of cash. While hospital fees had been kept relatively low, the percentage of patients not paying any of their hospital bill rose to 38 per cent in 1932, 37 per cent in 1933, and 42 per cent in 1934.[51] [...]

The Charlottetown Hospital reacted to this lack of funds with a policy very different from public general hospitals: the financial problems caused by the Depression were passed on to the sisters who administered the Charlottetown Hospital. Although fewer than half the patients paid their fees, Bishop O'Sullivan blamed the Sisters of St. Martha, rather than non-paying patients and the wider economic slump, when an operating deficit started to mount in the early 1930s. The bishop criticized the sisters' administration and would not allow them to carry any debt. In 1933, he not only blamed the sisters for the hospital's debt, but condemned them for taking an allowance. He wrote to the mother general: "It seems to me incongruous that, when your Sisters cannot run the hospital without going into debt monthly, they still have collected their monthly salary."[52] At this time there were 13 sisters working at the hospital: one graduate nurse, four registered nurses, two nurses in training, two office staff, two kitchen staff and one seamstress.[53] The secular, paid personnel consisted of one orderly, one bookkeeper, one engineer, one general man, two laundry women, nine maids and 20 student nurses. For the year 1933, there were 1,340 patients, only 42 per cent of whom paid fully. Twenty-one per cent paid only part of their bills while 37 per cent paid nothing.[54] Nevertheless, the bishop demanded that the $4.66 a month average salary of the 14 sisters for the previous 10 months (since February) be returned to the hospital and that the mother general "have this matter adjusted in the hospital books so that it will be shown that your sisters are receiving absolutely no monetary recompense for their labours, and that they are really Sisters of Charity."[55] Needless to say, given the poverty in the province and in the congregation, the $652 in question was long spent. Mother M. Paula relayed this to the bishop, writing:

> In reply I may say it is impossible to do this as the money has been spent, and in great part for the wherewithal necessary of the sisters to carry on their work — for clothing, footwear, dentists' and opticians' bills ... Our community bank balance in current account today stands at $57.76. Though we cannot give what we have not, yet we are willing to forego all future salaries until such time as the hospital is in a position to cover the expenses of its sister-personnel.[56]

If the sisters had available the money that the bishop requested, they would have been required to give it back: the hospital was owned by the Episcopal corporation, and the vow of obedience dictated that sisters must act as the bishop directed.[57]

The Sisters of St. Martha who served at the hospital and represented about one-quarter of the whole congregation went without their allowance for a year. They also trimmed the budget in a variety of ways so that in the financial year of 1934, the hospital showed an operating deficit of only $49.70, a feat which the bishop praised: "They have conclusively shown that they know how to manage a hospital economically."[58] The sisters must have been extremely frugal because they had almost 400 more patient days in 1934 than in 1933 and had 7 per cent fewer fully paying patients. The annalist noted in 1934: "The years of the depression have been especially difficult for all hospitals which must have the equipment at whatever cost to carry on its work."[59] Finally, in 1935, the hospital sisters started receiving their $56-a-year salary again and they even received an increase in 1937 as the economy began to recover. Bishop O'Sullivan noted the economic value of the sisters' work:

> There is no comparison between the cost of our hospital and the cost of hospitals conducted entirely by lay help. If the remuneration received by the Sisters was according to the salaries paid in other institutions, our Hospital could not begin to carry on. This item of salary alone would soar to about $15,000 per year. But we know the Sisters are devoting their lives to the service of the church.[60]

In 1938 Bishop O'Sullivan again emphasized the sisters' economic contribution when he compared the wages at the Charlottetown Hospital to those at the Prince Edward Island Hospital, the Protestant referral hospital: "Comparisons are odious, but it may be pardonable to remind you that the total salaries and wages paid by our hospital last year amounted to only $7,436.80 while the Prince Edward Island Hospital reported $19,369.43. We can imagine what our deficit would be if we had to pay for the services of our Sisters."[61] Five years earlier, in 1933, the contrast in wage costs between the two hospitals had been almost as large — a contrast which the bishop was not adverse to pointing out as an illustration of the value of the sisters' work and their good management. [...]

The two hospitals were frequented by patients in numbers approximating the Protestant–Roman Catholic split in the provincial population. Both the Protestant and Roman Catholic hospitals received a small amount of government funding, $2,000 each from the province and $1,500 each from the city. More significantly, both hospitals were among the more than 200 Canadian hospitals that saved a great deal in labour costs by operating nursing schools, though without a medical school in the province, neither was able to cash in on student physicians.[62] Until the late 1950s, like almost all public hospitals in the country, these two PEI hospitals were highly dependent on user fees to cover their operating costs.[63]

While the Prince Edward Island Hospital undoubtedly struggled to serve Protestant patients during the Depression, it received more in patient fees and endowments than the Charlottetown Hospital. The percentage of non-paying and free patient days at the Charlottetown Hospital was 9.2 per cent higher than at the Prince Edward Island Hospital; the Charlottetown Hospital had 13 per cent fewer patients and 12.3 per cent fewer patient days than the Prince Edward Island Hospital in 1933. While the two hospitals had very similar totals for the cost of non-paying and free patients, these costs were calculated on such a basis that per diem costs at the Protestant hospital were 12.5 per cent higher than at the Charlottetown Hospital, $3.28 compared to $2.87. Several factors affected per diem costs at the two hospitals, including the amount of money paid in wages, which was much lower at the Charlottetown Hospital, especially when compared to the average Maritime rates of pay for the hospital jobs the sisters filled. There were six sisters at the Charlottetown hospital: one superintendent, one nurse/x-ray technician, three nurses and one lab technician. If they had been paid at the going rate for these positions, the staff pay would have totalled approximately $8,667 per annum.[64]

Instead, the sisters, who lived in a convent inside the hospital, were remunerated eight dollars a month in addition to room and board, all of which came out of the hospital budget. Some lay nurses at many Canadian hospitals were also boarders, less as a fringe benefit than as part of being on 24-hour duty; thus, it seems unreasonable to deduct the value of board from the sisters' salaries. If the pay of eight dollars a month is multiplied by six (the number of sister-nurses), and then multiplied by 12 months, the total remuneration is $576. This amount may be subtracted from the total value ($8,667) to show that the approximate unpaid value of the sisters' labour was $8,091 a year in the late 1920s. In other words, the Charlottetown Hospital saved $8,091 by employing sisters rather than lay employees, a source of savings that became especially significant during the Depression.

Proportionate to the number of patients, food, insurance, x-ray costs and light and power were no more than 10 per cent higher at the Protestant hospital than at the Roman Catholic hospital in 1933.[65] The differences in the costs of fuel, salaries, medicine and operating room, laundry and cleaning and telephone were far greater. With the exclusion of heating costs, which may indicate a poorer-quality building, all the above costs at the Charlottetown Hospital were only half of what they were at the Prince Edward Island Hospital, even adjusting for the Roman Catholic hospital's fewer patient days. Clearly, the sisters who administered the Charlottetown Hospital were experts in efficiency.

As the decade wore on, the difference in the budgets of the two general hospitals continued. In 1913, the Charlottetown Hospital received 71 per cent less in patient fees per patient day than the Prince Edward Island Hospital. In 1937, the Charlottetown Hospital still received 57 per cent less. [...]

Income from Roman Catholic Charlottetown Hospital patient fees decreased 16 per cent or $0.25 per patient day between 1933 and 1937, while income from Protestant Prince Edward Island Hospital patient fees increased by 5 per cent or $0.11. With no alternative, the Protestant hospital engaged the most common means of meeting increased hospital costs: increasing hospital fees for paying patients.[66] The Roman Catholic hospital consistently set lower patient fees, either realizing their clientele could not sustain any higher fees or passing on the savings generated by the hospital sisters' very inexpensive labour. Whatever the case, the fees collected at the Charlottetown Hospital amounted to a relatively small sum. With the Roman Catholic hospital unable to depend on patient fees, the sisters' virtually unpaid labour was crucial, as it was with virtually any Roman Catholic hospital in North America.[67] The Depression made it very difficult for the hospital to meet the health and safety standards of the American College of Surgeons, which was necessary to maintain accreditation for a "standardized" hospital.[68] The Sisters of St. Martha's frugal and skilled management offset decreasing financial resources and allowed the Charlottetown Hospital to remain open in the 1930s. As the bishop himself noted more than once during the Depression, the Charlottetown Hospital "could not begin to carry on" without the sisters' skilled and very inexpensive labour.[69] That labour was often taken for granted outside the church hierarchy and continues to be today in that it has not been recognized in the historical record.

Keeping the Charlottetown Hospital open was probably the Sisters of St. Martha's greatest challenge during the Depression, but it was certainly not their only one. St. Vincent's Orphanage, which opened in 1910 and came under the management of the Sisters of St. Martha in 1925, also suffered the effects of the Depression very keenly but maintained its usual services. The orphanage cared for an average of 55 children a day in the late 1930s. It was common to have more children in the winter and fewer in summer, when a great effort was made to place them in the temporary care of Roman Catholic rural families so the children could have the benefit of a country vacation.

Because St. Vincent's Orphanage provided short-term care for children whose families were experiencing financial crisis, it was a crucial institution during the Depression era. Like St. Alexis, the 19th-century Montreal Roman Catholic orphanage on which Bettina Bradbury has written,[70] as well as the Little Flower Institute, a Roman Catholic orphanage run by the Antigonish Sisters of St. Martha in Bras D'Or, Cape Breton, in the 1940s,[71] St. Vincent's Orphanage housed children from families in economic stress as well as parentless children.[72] In the period 1935 to 1939, for which the most complete Depression-era statistics are available, an average of 58 children resided in the orphanage as of January 31st of each year.[73] Over the five-year period, an average of 35.4 per cent of the children had two parents alive, 29.2 had one parent alive and 32 per cent were termed "illegitimate" and were not calculated into the sisters' statistics on the number of parents alive. It was very uncommon for both parents to be dead; never more than two children in a given year were reported to be true orphans, a statistic which works out to an average over four years of 1.3 children with both parents dead. Moreover, in the years 1935 to 1939, a significant number of children were returned to relatives, a category that included parents. Between 1936 and 1939, an average of 19.5 per cent of children who had been in the orphanage the previous year were returned to relatives. Bradbury found that 10 per cent of the approximately 1,000 girls who passed through St. Alexis Orphanage in Montreal between 1860 and 1889 stayed less than a month and another half stayed less than a year, a trend that became more common later in the 19th century. Moreover, some girls returned for a second or third stay at the orphanage, further illustrating the elastic supply and demand of the orphanage. According to Bradbury, "increasingly, parents seem to have used the orphanage to solve short-term rather than long-term family crises."[74] While case files for St. Vincent's Orphanage are not available for the 1930s, the aggregate data strongly suggests that St. Vincent's provided for short-term care for as many as one in five children who came to the orphanage. Of course, children were also accepted into more permanent arrangements; between 1935 and 1939, the sisters arranged an average of 10 adoptions per year.[75]

As with the hospital, St. Vincent's provision of 24-hour care was labour intensive. The nursery, which was home to between one-third and one-half of orphanage residents in the 1930s,[76] required a great deal from the staff. Among the older children, one sister was responsible for the "girls' side" and one for the "boys' side." One or two sisters were also engaged in teaching the children during regular school hours as the children remained inside the orphanage to attend school.

Even with the virtually unpaid labour provided by the sisters, meeting the operating costs of the orphanage was a great struggle. The provincial government paid the per diem fees of children who were officially wards of the state, but those children usually comprised under 10 per cent of the residents of the orphanage in the 1930s.[77] With no significant alternative funding for the other children, the church intended that St. Vincent's Orphanage, like the Charlottetown Hospital, be financed primarily through fees paid by the families of residents. Understandably, a significant number of the children's bills were not paid during the 1930s. And so the sisters continued to depend on local Roman Catholic business to donate food and other supplies for the orphanage and upon charitable groups and individuals to donate cash.[78] Even with the generous donation from the St. Elizabeth's Aid's hugely successful cookbook sale in 1930, the sisters noted a greater shortage of cash than in the previous five years. The bursar of the orphanage wrote:

> [I]t is with trepidation I think of how I am going to find the 850 loaves of bread we have to have every month, the 12 hundred dollar bills we have to pay for coal, not to mention anything else needed for housekeeping nor the little bits that make a muckle going out for lead pencils, shoe laces etc. We receive payment in part for only 11 of our 80 children so we look hopefully for a continuation of the charity always shown us.[79]

As the Depression continued, the sisters at the orphanage had to slash their budget. By 1935, contributions from Roman Catholic charities and children's board dropped, respectively, to one-half and one-fifth their 1930 amounts. Consequently, operating expenditures dropped two-thirds from $9,471.43 in 1930 to $3,500.33 in 1935. [...]

As with many religious congregations, the Sisters of St. Martha raised some revenue for the orphanage by begging.[80] The sisters' "bread collection" was first performed by their predecessors, the Sisters of Charity, in the late 19th century, with profits going to the Charlottetown Hospital; but, when the orphanage was founded in 1910, contributions were directed to it. Sometime in the early 20th century, probably because of the difficulty in transportation and the preference for cash, monetary donations — rather than bread — were requested, although the name of the collection stayed the same.[81] A Sister of St. Martha who participated in the bread collection recalled the process as follows:

> Two Sisters (one did not travel alone in those days but we did walk each side of the same street alone) [solicited donations]. The usual donation was 25 cents and if you happened to get a 50 cent piece you considered you were wealthy. There were between 250 and 300 calls on the list and it occupied the first two days of every month rain or shine snow or ice twelve months of the year — really the only cash we ever had.[82]

The bread collection could never garner much, given the poverty of the people who were canvassed, but it remained a steady source of income for the orphanage even during the Depression. The bread collection was also an uncomfortable, humbling task for the Sisters of St. Martha. As Smith and Coburn have noted, begging was the traditional fundraising method of European congregations, but some American-born sisters "abhorred the humiliating task."[83]

The other main fundraising method the Sisters of St. Martha used at the orphanage was farming. They not only produced food for the orphanage but also garnered income from selling some of the produce. The sisters were extremely frugal; the amount of money they spent on food dropped by 1935 to only 37 per cent of what it had been in 1930. Moreover, the sisters' income from sales of farm produce increased by 24.6 per cent between 1930 and 1935, a significant feat given the rate of deflation and a very competitive market in the agricultural province. Most of the farm labour was performed by a full-time "paid man" who was also a handyman at the orphanage, as well as by seasonal employees. Because the amount of money paid for salaries at the orphanage had decreased in 1935 to less than one-third of the amount paid out in 1930, it was likely that the sisters and older children at the orphanage performed much of the farm labour during the Depression.

The added difficulty of operating the orphanage during the early 1930s led the bishop to tighten the admissions policy. In 1938, Bishop O'Sullivan wrote a pastoral instruction regarding the orphanage and illegitimate infants in response to complaints; he stated that "the Orphanage was being made a 'dumping place' for these children ... [and] that no provision was made for the upkeep of these unfortunate little ones, except possibly an initial payment, and that some effort should be made to stop these abuses."[84] The sisters were instructed not to accept children at the orphanage unless "every other means of providing for the child had failed." Given how dependent the orphanage was on donated cash and goods, the bishop no doubt wished to assure potential donors, in particular, that the orphanage was meant to serve needy legitimate children. About one-third of the orphanage residents were classified as illegitimate, but public perception seems to have assumed the number was higher.

The moral outrage toward unmarried mothers was standard fare not only in Roman Catholic institutions but also in Protestant circles and the general society until at least the 1950s. Andrée Lévesque's analysis of the Hôpital de la Miséricorde, where approximately 20 per cent of illegitimate births in Quebec occurred from 1929 to 1939, explains that the sister-administrators tried to reform the unmarried mothers. Lévesque notes that the single mother "was considered weak and ignorant, strong-minded and wicked, or simple-minded."[85] This stigma led most provincial governments to exclude unmarried single mothers from mothers' allowances and some provinces to exclude them from relief during the Depression,[86] two pieces of legislation that no doubt increased the demand for orphanage space for children born outside marriage. The timing of the bishop's "instruction" regarding illegitimate children suggests that the financial crisis of the 1930s may have decreased PEI Roman Catholics' tolerance for what they perceived to be immoral behaviour. Like many other Canadians, they wanted to be able to define who was worthy of help. [...]

In addition to keeping their established institutions open during the Depression, in 1931 the Sisters of St. Martha also confronted the economic crisis by opening a social services department at the Charlottetown Hospital to serve impoverished Roman Catholics in a variety of practical ways.[87] Gagan and Gagan have explained the creation of outpatient clinics and social service departments as a means to direct impoverished patients away from expensive and possibly lengthy hospital care for which the hospital would never be remunerated.[88] The timing of the opening of the Charlottetown Hospital's social service department in 1931 and the fact that it was moved to a separate downtown building as soon as was possible suggests, instead, that it was more precisely a way to serve the poor with direct and indirect relief, spurred by a particularly serious economic crisis. Other congregations of women religious responded to the Depression with similar social work efforts. The Antigonish Sisters of St. Martha, for example, opened Catholic Charities offices in their hospitals in Sydney (1935) and Glace Bay (1938), and provided professionally trained sister–social workers for many parishes in Cape Breton.[89] More established congregations, including the Sisters of Charity of Halifax, founded in 1849, and the Sisters of St. Joseph in the Archdiocese of Toronto, founded in 1851, were already engaged in social work by the 1930s.[90]

The Sisters of St. Martha in PEI described the purpose of their new social service department in their congregation's newspaper, *Laudate*, in the following way: "to provide part–time nursing where required and to care for out-patients; follow-up work is done among the hospital's patients; the sick poor are attended; the down and out are assisted and encouraged to help themselves and where carelessness about duties to God is evident, efforts are made to remedy this."[91] The department was originally staffed by two women, a lay nurse who was a graduate of the Charlottetown Hospital School of Nursing, and a sister who concentrated on social work but stressed religion throughout. It strove "to combine what is best in recognized social service methods with the highest and holiest in religion."[92]

Bishop O'Sullivan saw an obvious need for social service in the economically depressed province, particularly in the 1930s, and the Sisters of St. Martha accepted the new assignment despite already being overburdened.[93] Bishop O'Sullivan used the department to fulfil the sisters' role in charitable service; the bishop quoted Pope Leo XIII's "affirmation of duty of charity" which stated: "People are not free to choose whether they will take up the cause of the poor or not: it is a matter of simple duty; what the weight of our obligation is we may discover from the superabundance of the good things we have received."[94]

In its first months of operation, the social service department carried out 1,250 home visits, clothed 62 children for school, cared for 10 bedridden patients and nine maternity cases and attended six dying people. The department was aided by three Roman Catholic women's groups — the St. Vincent de Paul sewing circle, the St. Charles Auxiliary and the Catholic Women's League — in distributing food and clothing to 51 families. At Christmas, 30 baskets were distributed and 160 Christmas stockings were given to children, the supplies for which came from Charlottetown Roman Catholic merchants.[95] Three thousand home visits were made in 1932, and that number remained steady for the remainder of the decade.[96] The social service department not only coordinated charity for Charlottetown Roman Catholic families, but also engaged in professional home nursing, serving as a Roman Catholic version of the Victorian Order of Nurses.[97]

During the Depression, the Sisters of St. Martha also continued their work at a district school in Kinkora, which they began to staff in 1921. Although staffed completely by sisters, the school was considered a public district school.[98] The school was not markedly more difficult for the congregation to run during the Depression than in earlier years because the sister-teachers were paid by the provincial government, although teachers' wages were cut by 10 per cent in the early 1930s.[99] The congregation still often had to pay for the sisters' training, however, as many were unprepared for a career in education when they entered the congregation. In addition, it became increasingly difficult to staff the school during the 1930s because of the increased demands of the Charlottetown Hospital. On the other hand, running the school in the 1930s was more crucial than in earlier years because the sisters' wages went into the congregation's general coffers and financed those aspects of the congregation, such as the novitiate and infirmary, that did not receive any funding.[100] The three sister-teachers, Jeanette Coady, Nellie MacDonald and Annie Walsh, held first, second and third class teachers' licences and received $411.50 (plus a $25 supplement), $247.50 and $140 respectively in 1931.[101]

While the Sisters of St. Martha responded to the Depression quite effectively, all of their social institutions suffered from a shortage of labour. One annalist recorded that "subjects are needed so badly for the houses now in existence and for the many other demands being constantly made upon the community. We will have to pray more and make greater sacrifices."[102] In 1932, Bishop O'Sullivan acknowledged the shortage of labour, writing "if we had 50 more nuns at the moment, our present institutions would be only properly staffed."[103] As entrants finished their novitiates, and special training if chosen, and became available for active ministry, they were readily and easily absorbed into the congregation's existing responsibilities. The number of sisters working at the hospital, for example, doubled over the decade, which is more of an indication of the under-staffing at the beginning of the decade than a comment on a large staff at the decade's end. Similarly, the number serving at the bishop's palace increased from four to seven. In this case, the workload expanded to include caring for the Basilica sacristy and taking on some clerical duties.

The congregation actively sought young Roman Catholic women to join them. A 1931 issue of *Laudate*, the congregation's newsletter, included a defiant appeal for vocations, delivered in a chastising tone:

> Do the young women of Prince Edward Island realize that in the Congregation of St. Martha ... there is unlimited scope for the utilization of every talent to the honour and glory of God? Throughout the length and breadth of North America and in foreign countries are found Sisters who were born and brought up in Prince Edward Island.... We even hope in the not too distant future their adopted lands will pay back the debt owing our Province by sending us useful subjects.... Dear Catholic girls, it depends on YOU. Are you interested?[104]

Even when young women joined the congregation, there was quite a high attrition rate as one annalist noted:

> Only one of the four aspirants who entered so hopefully last September persevered and we had a lone ceremony for Sister M. Annunciatta ... on March 25.[105]

> Some of our postulants did not receive the grace of perseverance and the only consolation we have is to remember the maxim: "Quality is better than quantity." How we would like to have quantity too.[106]

The labour shortage in the Sisters of St. Martha's institutions was exacerbated by the need to educate sisters for many of the jobs required by the congregation. Removing a sister from a specific work in order to train her meant losing a much-needed source of labour, the benefits of which were often not realized for several years depending on the course of study. The further burden of tuition and board, paid from the sisters' small salaries, was very difficult for the small community to support.

Despite the strain on human resources that professional training posed, the congregation paid for the further education of several members in the 1930s: Sister M. Dunstan and Sister M. Delores took a six-week course at Miss Farmer's cooking school in Boston in 1929; three sisters finished grade 10; Sister St. Hugh became a registered pharmacist after attending Dalhousie University; four sisters graduated from Prince of Wales College with teaching certificates; Mother Loyola obtained a B.Sc. in Home Economics from St. Francis Xavier; Sister M. Angela obtained a B.Sc. in Nursing from St. Francis Xavier; three sisters graduated from the Charlottetown Hospital School of Nursing and two sisters completed grade 12 at St. Dunstan's, the first two women to attend or graduate from the high school's program.[107] Because of the congregation's focus on education, even during the Depression, the sisters did not fall behind professionally and were able to maintain standards in their institutions during the Second World War and after.

The Depression threatened social institutions throughout Canada. In Prince Edward Island, the most impoverished province in the nation, Roman Catholic institutions were particularly threatened. The amount of money the Roman Catholic population could donate or pay in fees was finite and falling in the 1930s. The provincial and municipal governments were similarly able to make only small contributions and provided minimal administrative infrastructure in health care and none in social work. Finally, there were fewer non-governmental agencies in PEI than in most provinces. The Sisters of St. Martha managed to keep the province's slate of

Roman Catholic health and social institutions open by intensifying their economizing efforts, fundraising, keeping salaries very low, using their own labour almost exclusively and putting off repairs. In addition to keeping the Charlottetown Hospital, St. Vincent's Orphanage, Sacred Heart Home and a district school open in the 1930s, the sisters also provided a much-needed social services bureau that conducted 3,000 home visits annually. [...]

Women religious' invisibility is an important issue, particularly in socially isolated institutions such as homes for unmarried expectant women or orphanages, which clearly replicated the private or domestic sphere. The general population, and even the Roman Catholic population, would rarely see these sisters and thus would not recognize the value of their labour. Sisters working in hospitals and schools were "seen" by more people, and thus their labour was more likely to be recognized. It is not surprising, therefore, that the bulk of the historiography on North American women religious focuses on congregations who ran hospitals and schools. Sisters engaged in domestic service were the least visible and certainly their work was the most like that of housewives. For example, in a history of St. Dunstan's University, where the Sisters of St. Martha provided domestic service from 1916 until 1968, Edward MacDonald explained their work in terms that we might associate with mothers: "Together, they are cook, maid, laundress, gardener, seamstress, and nurse to the campus community.... Their duties are performed with such quiet circumspection that their sacrifices and privations go largely unnoticed."[108] This author would argue not only that invisibility has prevented historical recognition for sisters' labour, but also that there is a scale of invisibility within religious institutions. Just as women working in the domestic sphere are far less visible than their husbands who worked in the public sphere, so is the domestic labour of nuns less visible than professional occupations such as teaching and nursing. [...]

The greatest reason why sisters' work has been overlooked is because it is undervalued, much like the work of housewives. Since the 19th century in particular, housewives have been expected to perform reproductive labour without acknowledgement, much less remuneration. As Nancy Folbre has argued regarding British and American censuses, "the concept of the unproductive housewife was a by-product of a new definition of productive labor that valorized participation in the market and devalorized the nonmarket work central to many women's lives. The terminological shift formalized the assumptions of androcentric political economy."[109] The Sisters of St. Martha, as diocesan sisters, functioned under a particularly patriarchal structure in which they were created by, and completely responsible to, a diocesan bishop. Just as the census listed a man's occupation but indirectly suggested that "housewives" were unproductive and did not accomplish anything, sisters were often listed in the *Census of Canada* as "nuns" rather than by the occupation they performed. The lack of value placed on nuns' labour, at least partly because it was often not clearly remunerated, must, among other things, skew occupational statistics. There were approximately 30,000 women religious in Canada in 1931, yet the *Census of Canada* lists 8,260 "nuns" and enumerated the remainder into occupational groups.[110] Enumerating 8,260 women as nuns rather than by a more specific occupation recognizes them as unproductive in a way comparable to housewives; in the case of these nuns, the bishop may be considered the breadwinner in the relationship.

The Sisters of St. Martha succeeded in operating several social institutions during the Depression. Their contributions, motivated by their religious faith, explain in part how Prince Edward Islanders survived the Depression. Although the sisters worked within a very patriarchal system, the success was theirs alone. The contributions of women religious to the economy during the Depression need to be recognized in the same manner that feminist historians have begun to recognize the value of women's unwaged labour in the home.

NOTES

1. Although the Maritime economy received a boost from the First World War, by the end of that decade the region had returned to its low economic status. See Ian McKay, "The 1910s: The Stillborn Triumph of Progressive Reform," in E. R. Forbes and D. A. Muise, eds., *The Atlantic Provinces in Confederation* (Toronto and Fredericton, 1993), pp. 204–5, 228. An example of the province's lagging social infrastructure is the late establishment of the Department of Health in 1931. See Douglas Baldwin, *She Answered Every Call: The Life of Public Health Nurse, Mona Gordon Wilson, 1894–1981* (Charlottetown, 1997), p. 187. The population of PEI was 88,038 in 1931, down from a high of 109,078 in 1891. See Table 1a: Population of Canada, by counties or census divisions, 1851–1931, *Census of Canada*, 1931, vol. 1, p. 348. I would like to express my appreciation to T. W. Acheson, Gail G. Campbell, D. Gillian Thompson, Ruth Compton Brouwer, Marisa Ferraiuolo and the four anonymous *Acadiensis* reviewers who offered very useful comments on earlier drafts of this paper. I am also grateful for the financial support received from the University of Lethbridge Research Fund. Most notably, I wish to acknowledge the Sisters of St. Martha, Charlottetown, for their generosity in allowing me to study them.

2. The myth that the Maritimes suffered less from the Depression than other regions is discussed in E. R. Forbes, "Cutting the Pie into Smaller Pieces: Matching Grants and Relief in the Maritime Provinces During the 1930s," in E. R. Forbes, ed., *Challenging the Regional Stereotype: Essays on the 20th Century Maritimes* (Fredericton, 1989), pp. 149–50, and Edward MacDonald, *If You're Stronghearted: Prince Edward Island in the Twentieth Century* (Charlottetown, 2000), p. 159.

3. More precise utilization statistics are not available for 1930 but figures for 1935 can be found in note 43.

4. John H. Taylor, "Sources of Political Conflict in the Thirties: Welfare Policy and the Geography of Need," in Allan Muscovitch and Jim Albert, eds., *The "Benevolent" State: The Growth of Welfare in Canada* (Toronto, 1987), p. 150. Part of Taylor's argument in this very interesting article is that the collapse of voluntary relief required municipalities to become involved in relief work. This description of voluntary relief "collapsing," however, is rather overstated. The article would have been strengthened with an acknowledgement of the variety of relief distributed during the Depression, including cash dispersals, meals and clothing.

5. Denyse Baillargeon, *Making Do: Women, Family and Home in Montreal During the Great Depression*, trans. Yvonne Klein (Waterloo, 1999), p. 2.

6. Carol Coburn and Martha Smith, *Spirited Lives: How Nuns Shaped Catholic Culture and American Life, 1836–1920* (Chapel Hill, 1998), pp. 2–3.

7. Mary J. Oates, *The Catholic Philanthropic Tradition in America* (Bloomington, 1995), pp. 21, 87, 154.

8. Oates, *The Catholic Philanthropic Tradition*, p. 21. This point should not be overstated; it is impossible to prove that women religious predominated among the workers of Roman Catholic institutions in the same way secular teaching became feminized because there were so many more professional options available to men than women.

9. Alicja Muszinsky, *Cheap Wage Labour: Race and Gender in the Fisheries of British Columbia* (Montreal and Kingston, 1996), pp. 28, 62.

10. As Laurie Stanley writes regarding sisters' work in a lazaretto in Tracadie, New Brunswick, "The sisters firmly imbedded their faith in the scenes of their labour." See Laurie C. C. Stanley, "'So Many Crosses to Bear': The Religious Hospitallers of St. Joseph and the Tracadie Leper Hospital, 1868–1910," in Elizabeth Gillan Muir and Marilyn Färdig Whiteley, eds., *Changing Roles of Women within the Christian Church in Canada* (Toronto, 1995), pp. 22–3.

11. E. R. Forbes, "The 1930s: Depression and Retrenchment," in E. R. Forbes and D. A. Muise, eds., *The Atlantic Provinces in Confederation* (Fredericton and Toronto, 1993), p. 288. A recent biography of Moses Coady, the founder of the Antigonish Movement, describes the purpose and significance of the widespread, international movement — Michael R. Welton, *Little Mosie from the Margaree: A Biography of Moses Michael Coady* (Toronto, 2001).

12. Terence Fay, *A History of Canadian Catholics* (Montreal and Kingston, 2002), pp. 198–200.

13. Moses Coady's invitation to speak at the United Nations in 1949 is some indication of the international respect for the Antigonish Movement. See Fay, *A History of Canadian Catholics*, p. 201.

14. Congregations also served wealthier clientele, particularly in elite schools or by teaching extracurricular music lessons, with the understanding that their remuneration from that work could finance their work with the poor or pay their personal expenses if their salaries in parochial schools were especially low. See Coburn and Smith, *Spirited Lives*, pp. 52, 144–5.

15. Coburn and Smith, *Spirited Lives*, p. 206.

16. Canada was at least as vulnerable as other countries to the economic catastrophe of the 1930s, particularly because of heavy reliance on a few exports — forest, mineral and agricultural products — to two countries, the United States and Britain. Between 1929 and 1932, Canadian exports to the United States dropped 50 per cent while exports to Britain decreased by two-thirds. The unemployment rate in Canada peaked at almost 27 per cent in 1933. See Kenneth Norrie and Douglas Owram, *A History of the Canadian Economy*, 2nd ed. (Toronto, 1996), pp. 55–61, 157, 355.

17. Taylor, "Sources of Political Conflict," p. 147.

18. Dennis Guest, *The Emergence of Social Security in Canada*, 3rd ed. (Vancouver, 1999), p. 65.

19. MacDonald, *If You're Stronghearted*, p. 157.

20. Agricultural revenue increased from $16,840,000 in 1922 to $25,976,000 in 1929 and agricultural output increased 21.2 per cent between 1925 and 1929. See *Canada Year Book*, 1925, p. 204, and 1931, p. 215. The peak year for fishing production was 1923 ($1,754,980). Production dropped to $1,279,407 in 1928. See *Canada Year Book*, 1926, p. 308; *Guardian*, 18 February 1929.

21. In some cases Roman Catholics were more affected by the Depression than non-Catholics because particular ethno-religious groups congregated in certain occupations. The fishery, for example, was dominated by Acadian Roman Catholics for decades. Premier MacMillan stated that Acadians should find more lucrative means of financial support, specifically farming. In the 1920s and 1930s, the demand for herring was so low that fishers sold it to farmers at a "ridiculously" low price for fertilizer. Spurred by the desperation of the Depression as well as by the hope of the Antigonish Movement, fishing cooperatives were formed in the following Acadian Roman Catholic communities during the 1930s: Mont Carmel, 1931; Miminigash, 1935; North Rustico, 1936; Egmont Bay, 1938; and Skinner's Pond, 1939. See Georges Arsenault, *The Island Acadians, 1720–1980*, trans. Sally Ross (Charlottetown, 1989), p. 222. Although precise figures are unavailable, far more Roman Catholics than Protestants were engaged in this unstable occupation.

22. *Canada Year Book*, 1936, p. 208.

23. Guest, *The Emergence of Social Security*, p. 93.

24. Eric Hobsbawm, *Age of Extremes: The Short Twentieth Century* (London, 1994), p. 93. Canada was like other countries lacking public provisions for social security. In most of Europe, only one-quarter of unemployed workers were eligible for relief. See also Taylor, "Sources of Political Conflict," p. 148.

25. The Maritimes' cost of living was estimated to be 7.4 per cent lower than the national average, yet this does not account for the Maritimes' much lower rates of federal funding. See E. R. Forbes, "Cutting the Pie," pp. 149, 153. In 1933, the Island was the first of the Maritime provinces to implement Old Age Security payments. It did so only by limiting the program to fit revenues, and thus only 20 per cent of Islanders 70 years of age and over were eligible, and the monthly pension amounted to $15 instead of the $20 previously agreed upon. See Forbes, "Cutting the Pie," p. 155, and Forbes, "The 1930s," p. 281.

26. Small amounts of federal funding were also assigned to relief endeavours through departments such as Justice and Agriculture, as well as through the Canadian National Railway. See "Survey of Federal Relief Activities Since 1930," May 1935, p. 25, RG 21, series 3:1, file 91, Public Archives and Records Office [PARO] (Charlottetown).

27. In 1931, the population of PEI was 88,038 and the population of New Brunswick was 408,219. See Table 1a: Population of Canada, by counties or census divisions, 1851–1931, *Census of Canada*, 1931, vol. 1, p. 348.

28. "Survey of Federal Relief Activities Since 1930," May 1935, p. 25, PARO.

29. By 1933, the VON had 83 branches in Canada — none of them in PEI. In a general report on social services in PEI, sponsored by the Children's Aid Society of Prince Edward Island in 1933, Charlotte Whitton very strongly recommended that the VON be invited to open a branch in PEI. See "Child Welfare, PEI, 1933," Accession #4222, PARO, cross-referenced as "Child Welfare PEI, 1933," MG 28, 110, vol. 19, file 80, National Archives of Canada [NA]. It is likely that sufficient resources could not be provided to support the VON, and thus they may have never been asked or may have had to decline an invitation.

30. Charles Dalton donated a tuberculosis sanatorium to the province in 1913 and the province quickly passed on the operating costs to the War Hospitals Commission during the First World War. In 1922, the province refused to accept the expense of operating the sanatorium and closed it. A new sanatorium opened in 1931 through the major effort of the Canadian Life Insurance Officers Association who donated $75,000 over a five-year period for the operation of the sanatorium. See MacDonald, *If You're Stronghearted*, pp. 125–8, and Katherine McCuaig, *The Weariness, the Fever, and the Fret: The Campaign against Tuberculosis in Canada, 1900–1950* (Montreal and Kingston, 1999), p. 117.

31. The Roman Catholic Diocese founded St. Vincent's Orphanage in 1910 and Sacred Heart Home in 1925, while Protestants founded the Prince Edward Island Protestant Orphanage in 1908. Beech Grove Home was founded by both Protestants and Catholics in the early 1920s but it came to be known later as a Protestant

facility. I would like to thank Jill MacMicken-Wilson at the Public Archives and Records Office in Charlottetown for helping me with these details.

32. Gail Aitken, "Criteria of Adoptability in Ontario, 1945–1965: The Circumstances, Processes and Effects of Policy Change," Ph.D. diss., University of Toronto, 1985, pp. 88–126.

33. Douglas Baldwin, *She Answered Every Call*, pp. 163–181. Dr. W. J. P. MacMillan was a notable exception to the absence of Roman Catholics in the Red Cross. Premier of the province from 1933 to 1935 and a doctor at the Charlottetown Hospital for several decades, MacMillan was both a prominent Catholic and devoted member of the Red Cross. MacMillan received a medical degree from McGill in 1908 and was elected to the Legislature in 1923. He served as Minister of Education and Public Health before becoming leader of the Conservative Party and premier from 1933 until 1935, when the Conservatives fell victim to the Depression and lost the provincial election. See *Canada Who's Who*, 1925, p. 763. No evidence was found of any negotiations between the bishop and the premier, but D. MacMillan, as chief of staff at the Charlottetown Hospital and a devout Roman Catholic, inevitably brought an understanding of Catholicism to his office.

34. Hartwell Daley, *Volunteers in Action: The Prince Edward Island Division, Canadian Red Cross Society, 1907–1979* (Summerside, 1971), pp. 91–2.

35. "Child Welfare in PEI, 1933," p. 5, PARO.

36. Fay, *A History of Canadian Catholics*, p. 203.

37. Thomas C. Kohler, "Quadragesimo Anno," in George Weigel and Robert Royal, eds., *A Century of Catholic Social Thought: Essays on 'Rerum Novarum' and Nine Other Key Documents* (Washington, 1991), pp. 27–8; Brian Clarke, "English-Speaking Canada from 1854," in Terrence Murphy and Roberto Perin, eds., *A Concise History of Christianity in Canada* (Don Mills, 1996), p. 352.

38. Kohler, "Quadragesimo Anno," p. 30.

39. Kohler, "Quadragesimo Anno," p. 33.

40. G. Edward MacDonald, *The History of St. Dunstan's University, 1855–1956* (Charlottetown, 1989), pp. 325–6.

41. Heidi Macdonald, "Developing a Strong Roman Catholic Social Order in Late Nineteenth-Century Prince Edward Island," *Canadian Catholic Historical Association Historical Studies*, 69 (2003), pp. 34–51.

42. Bishop O'Sullivan. Circular to Island Clergy, 24 June 1932, p. 6, O'Sullivan box, Roman Catholic Diocesan Archives, [RCDA] (Charlottetown).

43. The estimated clientele of PEI Roman Catholic institutions in 1935, for example, was as follows: Kinkora School, 100 pupils; Sacred Heart Home, 74 residents; Charlottetown Hospital, 1,340 patients; St. Dunstan's University, 115 students; St. Vincent's Orphanage, 85 children; and social service department, 3,195 patrons. The sisters ministered to at least the same number again, less directly, including visitors to the Charlottetown Hospital and parents of school children. See Annals, 1930s, series 11, St. Stanislaus Convent, box 9, Sisters of St. Martha Archives [SSMA] (Charlottetown); "Diocese of Charlottetown Yearbook," 1935, RCDA; "Statistics and Financial Information Charlottetown Hospital," 1935, series 12, Charlottetown Hospital, box 1, #7, SSMA.

44. Bishop O'Leary engaged the Sisters of St. Martha of Antigonish (founded 1900) to train the new congregation. Although the two have always been completely separate congregations despite sharing a name, the Antigonish congregation did help the new Charlottetown congregation get established by sending four of its senior sisters to Charlottetown from 1915 to 1921, a generosity that was never forgotten. See James Cameron, *"And Martha Served": History of the Sisters of St. Martha, Antigonish, Nova Scotia* (Halifax, 2000), pp. 53–7.

45. Heidi Macdonald, "The Social Origins and Congregational Identity of the Founding Sisters of St. Martha, Charlottetown, PEI, 1915–1925," *Canadian Catholic Historical Association Historical Studies*, 70 (2004): 29–47.

46. Bishop Louis O'Leary (Bishop Henry O'Leary's successor) was very upset that the Sisters of Charity decided to leave and was very concerned about how he would replace them. Bishop Louis O'Leary to Sister Ste. Christine, Superior General, Hospice of the Sisters of Charity, Quebec, PQ, 19 June 1924, series 8, sub-series 2, #7, SSMA.

47. According to MacDonald, enrolment slumped the year of the "Great Crash," rallied to 170 students in 1931–32, but then slid to a low of 115 students in 1935–36. MacDonald, *History of St. Dunstan's*, p. 321.

48. No comparison is available regarding the number of paying and non-paying patients at the Charlottetown Hospital in the 1920s, but, overall, PEI had a large increase in non-paying patients in the early 1930s. See "Bed Occupancy in Canadian Hospitals During 1931," *The Canadian Hospital* (October, 1932), pp. 12–3, 30, as quoted in W. G. Godfrey, "Private and Government Funding: The Case of the Moncton Hospital, 1898–1953," *Acadiensis*, XXXI, 1 (Autumn 2001), p. 17.

49. David Gagan and Rosemary Gagan, *For Patients of Moderate Means: A Social History of the Voluntary Public General Hospital in Canada, 1890–1950* (Montreal and Kingston, 2002), p. 73. Increased costs were passed on to patients at an average increase of over 200 per cent between 1915 and 1930. In part, increases in patient fees were meant to cover the growing number of transient and elderly patients who were unable to pay their bills. See Gagan and Gagan, *For Patients of Moderate Means*, p. 75.

50. Gagan and Gagan, *For Patients of Moderate Means*, pp. 77–80.

51. The per diem patient fee at the Charlottetown Hospital was $2.87 in 1933. For comparison, the fee was $3.28 at the PEI Hospital in 1933 and $5.21 at the Moncton Hospital in 1934. See Godfrey, "Private and Government Funding," p. 17.

52. Bishop O'Sullivan to Mother M. Paula, 2 December 1933, series 8, sub-series 3(c), #1, SSMA.

53. "Sisters' Ministries," 1934, series 3, sub-series 4, #1, SSMA.

54. The 37 per cent is composed of 29 per cent non-paying patients and 8 per cent free patients. The free patients were those who were not charged, including diocesan priests, sisters and the very poor without family. See "Statistics and Financial Information, Charlottetown Hospital," series 12, box 1, #7, SSMA.

55. Bishop O'Sullivan to Mother M. Paula, 2 December 1933, series 8, sub-series 3(c), #1, SSMA.

56. Mother M. Paula to Bishop O'Sullivan, 11 December 1933, O'Sullivan box, RCDA.

57. Bishop O'Sullivan must have known that in the first 40 years of their existence — and particularly at the height of the Depression — the sisters probably never had that amount of money in their bank account.

58. Bishop O'Sullivan, Pastoral letter, 22 April 1935, O'Sullivan box, RCDA.

59. Annals, Charlottetown Hospital, 1934, series 12, box 1, #1, SSMA.

60. Bishop O'Sullivan to PEI clergy, 3 May 1937, O'Sullivan box, RCDA.

61. Bishop O'Sullivan to Island clergy, 30 March 1938, O'Sullivan box, RCDA. The $7,436.80 refers to wages for both sisters and secular staff. Certainly the bishop used the figures to illustrate his point, but there is no reason to think the figures are exaggerated. Records from the Prince Edward Island Hospital did not survive a fire in the 1940s. (Interview with Joann Edgecomb, Director of Medical Records, Queen Elizabeth Hospital, July 1995). While there are examples of public institutions that were secular but were referred to as Protestant because they were frequently mainly by Protestants, the PEI Hospital was a private institution that was accurately named a Protestant hospital. The PEI Hospital was governed by a Protestant board of directors and served Protestants, some of whom were defined more by not being Roman Catholic than by being actively Protestant. With the small exception of a few specialist doctors who obtained privileges at both hospitals in Charlottetown, all of the PEI Hospital's staff were Protestant. See MacDonald, *If You're Stronghearted*, p. 18.

62. Kathryn McPherson, *Bedside Matters: The Transformation of Canadian Nursing, 1900–1990* (Toronto, 1996), pp. 31–2; Gagan and Gagan, *For Patients of Moderate Means*, pp. 62–3. The Charlottetown Hospital opened a school of nursing in 1920. While annual enrolments are unavailable, a total of 554 students entered between 1920 and 1959, with 82 per cent of that number graduating from the three-year program. See Mary Irene McKinnon, "History of the Charlottetown Hospital School of Nursing, Charlottetown, Prince Edward Island, Canada, from 1920 to 1959," M.Sc. thesis, St. Louis University, 1959.

63. Gagan and Gagan note that from 1910 onward, patient fees accounted for up to 80 per cent of hospitals' operating costs. See Gagan and Gagan, *For Patients of Moderate Means*, pp. 61–2.

64. The annual average rates of pay for nursing staff in the Maritimes, for the fiscal year 1929–30, were as follows: Superintendent — $1,850; Nurse/x-ray technician — $1,600; Nurse — $1,339; Lab technician — $1,200. These figures are approximate and based on a nurse with x-ray training receiving more than a ward nurse and a lab technician receiving less than a nurse. See George Weir, *Survey of Nursing Education in Canada* (Toronto, 1932), p. 50, and the author's estimates using Peter Twohig, "'Local Girls' and 'Lab Boys': Gender, Skill and Medical Laboratories in Nova Scotia in the 1920s and 1930s," *Acadiensis*, XXXI, 1 (Autumn 2001), pp. 55–75. Twohig also notes the fluidity between nurses and lab technicians, arguing that nurses were expected to perform most hospital jobs, including lab work; the wages for nurses and lab technicians could have been very similar. See Twohig, "'Local Girls' and 'Lab Boys,'" pp. 62–3.

65. Food costs were 8.7 per cent higher, light and power was 0.02 per cent higher and insurance was 0.96 per cent higher at the PEI Hospital. The Charlottetown Hospital figures were multiplied by 1.13 to account for the 13 per cent more patients at the Prince Edward Island Hospital. See "Comparative Financial Statement Charlottetown Hospital and Prince Edward Hospital, 1933," O'Sullivan box, RCDA.

66. Gagan and Gagan, *For Patients of Moderate Means*, p. 61.

67. Oates, *The Catholic Philanthropic Tradition*, p. 29.

68. They passed this examination in June 1930. See Annals, Charlottetown Hospital, 1930, series 12, box 1, #1, SSMA.

69. Bishop O'Sullivan, Pastoral letter, 22 April 1935, and Bishop O'Sullivan to PEI clergy, 03 May 1937, O'Sullivan box, RCDA.

70. Bettina Bradbury, "The Fragmented Family: Family Strategies in the Face of Death, Illness and Poverty, Montreal 1860–1885," in Joy Parr, ed., Childhood and Family in Canadian History (Toronto, 1982), pp. 109–128.

71. Cameron, "And Martha Served," p. 149.

72. Although an American rather than Canadian example, a quotation from a Chicago priest explains why families chose to put their children in orphanages during difficult times: "These poor people try to put their children ... where they were able to see them frequently and bring them clothing and other necessities." See J. A. Charlebois to Archbishop J. E. Quigley, Chicago, Illinois, 1911, as quoted in Coburn and Smith, Spirited Lives, p. 207.

73. The sisters of St. Vincent's Orphanage kept statistics on the average number of children cared for per day as well as more detailed statistics on those children who resided at the orphanage as of 1 January each year. Admissions, adoptions and returning children to relatives lead to significant turnover at the orphanage.

74. Bradbury, "The Fragmented Family," p. 71.

75. Annual Reports of St. Vincent's Orphanage, 1935–1939, series 12, box 11, SSMA.

76. Thirty-eight of the 97 residents were in the nursery at the time of the Sisters of St. Martha's takeover in 1925. Annals, St. Vincent's Orphanage, 1925, series 12, box 11, #11, SSMA.

77. St. Vincent's Orphanage Financial Statements, 1930s, series 12, box 11, #3, SSMA.

78. Lay women's groups such as St. Elizabeth's Aid and the Catholic Women's League raised money for Roman Catholic institutions including the orphanage and hospital. See Annals, 1934, series 8, sub-series 4, SSMA.

79. Laudate, December 1931, p. 12, series 8, sub-series 5, SSMA. Laudate was a publication of the Sisters of St. Martha that ran from December 1929 to August 1933. It had 400 subscribers in its first year and 949 subscribers in its history. "[Laudate] Introduction and Historical Sketch," series 8, sub-series 4, SSMA.

80. Coburn and Smith, Spirited Lives, pp. 174, 212.

81. When the Sisters of Charity returned to Quebec in 1925, the bread collection was discontinued, but Bishop Louis O'Leary requested that the Sisters of St. Martha reinstate it in 1928 when the Sisters of St. Martha were more settled at the hospital. See Annals, 1928, series 8, sub-series 4, SSMA. Some accounts say the orphanage maintenance man and tallest boy at the orphanage performed the bread collection while other accounts say two sisters did it. Both accounts are probably true at different times.

82. Written recollection from unidentified Sister of St. Martha, series 12, box 12, #8, SSMA.

83. Smith and Coburn, Spirited Lives, p. 174.

84. O'Sullivan explained that if a child had to be placed at the orphanage, his/her provisions, about $100 annually, should be secured, if possible, by means which could include putting a lien against the father's real estate. See his "The Orphanage and Illegitimate Infants: A Pastoral Instruction by the Bishop," 1939, series 12, box 11, SSMA.

85. Andrée Lévesque, "Deviants Anonymous: Single Mothers at the Hôpital de la Miséricorde in Montreal, 1929–1939" in Veronica Strong-Boag and Anita Clair Fellman, eds., Rethinking Canada: The Promise of Women's History, 3rd ed. (Toronto, 1997), p. 327.

86. See Lévesque, "Deviants Anonymous," p. 332; Margaret Hillyard Little, "Claiming a Unique Place: The Introduction of Mothers' Pensions in British Columbia," in Rethinking Canada, p. 294; James Struthers, The Limits of Affluence: Welfare in Ontario, 1920–1970 (Toronto, 1994), p. 159.

87. The opening of this department marked the beginning of the sisters' foray into social work, which continues to this day.

88. Gagan and Gagan, For Patients of Moderate Means, pp. 58–9.

89. Cameron, "And Martha Served," pp. 141–5.

90. Sister Maura, The Sisters of Charity Halifax (Toronto, 1956), pp. 3, 13; Elizabeth Smyth, "Christian Perfection and Service to Neighbours: The Congregation of the Sisters of St. Joseph, Toronto, 1851–1920," in Elizabeth Gillan Muir and Marilyn Färdig Whiteley, eds., Changing Roles of Women within the Christian Church in Canada (Toronto, 1995), p. 40. Due to several redrawings of diocesan boundaries in Ontario between 1951 and 1936, six independent congregations of the Sisters of St. Joseph were eventually established in the Archdiocese of Toronto.

91. Laudate, December 1931, p. 11, series 8, sub-series 5, SSMA.

92. Laudate, December 1931, p. 11, series 8, sub-series 5, SSMA.

93. Costs for the new endeavour were kept low because the department was operated from within the hospital so a new building was not required and the sister–social worker(s) could live at the convent in the hospital. A secular nurse may have been employed because some of the work was in maternity care and post-partum care and

the Sisters of St. Martha were not usually engaged in this field. In addition, the sisters' skills and labour was already stretched beyond reasonable limits, so a secular nurse may have been necessary for human resource reasons.

94. *Laudate*, December 1931, p. 11, series 8, sub-series 5, SSMA.

95. *Laudate*, June 1932, p. 8, series 8, sub-series 5, SSMA.

96. *Laudate*, August 1933, p. 12, series 8, sub-series 5, SSMA.

97. The sisters often worked in conjunction with the City of Charlottetown in referring people for relief and monitoring those who received it. See *A History of the Catholic Family Services Bureau, 60th Anniversary* (Charlottetown, 1991), p. 8.

98. The founder of the Sisters of St. Martha, Bishop Henry O'Leary, noted that the congregation would become engaged in teaching in the rural schools. Because the congregation, however, took on the administration of the hospital and orphanage on short notice, and because these institutions were so demanding on human resources, plans to staff other rural schools in addition to Kinkora were postponed.

99. MacDonald, *If You're Stronghearted*, p. 160.

100. The instruction must have been a good quality; in 1930 five students passed grade 10 examinations and Dorothy Cullen, a 14-year-old, led the province, "being 30 marks ahead of the next one." The year before, another Kinkora student, Bernice Cullen, a future Sister of St. Martha, won a provincial award for her high marks. See Annals, 1929 and 1930, series 8, sub-series 4, SSMA.

101. These are the sisters' birth names as they appeared in the Department of Education Annual Report. The Congregation of Notre Dame also ran convent schools within the district school system. The Congregation of Notre Dame teachers received higher wages and presumably held higher licences than the Sisters of St. Martha, and all Congregation of Notre Dame sister-teachers received supplements in 1931. Furthermore, the Congregation of Notre Dame schools received higher scores on property evaluation. In 1925, the Tignish, Miscouche and Rustico convent schools received a full score of 250 while Kinkora lagged behind at 156. The higher-class teaching licences among the Congregation of Notre Dame teachers in Island schools, combined with their schools' perfect property evaluation, indicate that the Congregation of Notre Dame ran schools which were more elite than most Island schools, including the Kinkora school. See Department of Education, *Annual Report*, 1931, RG 10, PARO.

102. Annals, 1939, series 8, sub-series 4, SSMA.

103. Bishop O'Sullivan to all Priests of the Diocese, 24 June 1932, O'Sullivan box, RCDA. While in the 1930s there were sometimes more than 10 postulants annually, only about half that number stayed in the congregation permanently.

104. *Laudate*, June 1931, pp. 3, 15, series 8, sub-series 5, SSMA.

105. Annals, 1936, series 8, sub-series 4, SSMA.

106. Annals, 1937, series 8, sub-series 4, SSMA.

107. Annals, 1939, series 8, sub-series 4, SSMA.

108. MacDonald, *History of St. Dunstan's*, p. 363. Moreover, MacDonald notes that when the university closed — it amalgamated with a Protestant university to become the University of Prince Edward Island in 1968 — neither the diocese nor the college formally thanked the sisters, for "apparently they just packed up and left without so much as a handshake." Edward MacDonald, correspondence with author, 5 February 1999.

109. Nancy Folbre, "The Unproductive Housewife: Her Evolution in Nineteenth-Century American Thought," *Signs: Journal of Women in Culture and Society*, 16, 3 (1991), p. 481.

110. The "approximately 30,000" is compiled from "Communautés De Femmes" in *Canada Ecclesiastique, 1932* (Montreal, 1932), pp. 631–756. This lists the members of 102 women religious' institutes serving in Canada in 1931. All members of the institutes, including postulants, were included in the figure, which totalled 29,623. The number is only approximate, however, because 22 of the smaller institutes did not submit their membership figures and are thus not included in the total number. In addition, sisters serving in other countries were excluded when possible, but this was not always possible. I am grateful to Marisa Ferraiuolo for compiling these figures. Regarding the *Census of Canada*, over 20,000 women religious must have been enumerated into occupational groups, but there is no way to distinguish how many of the total number of graduate nurses in Canada (20,462) or female teachers (64,709) were also women religious. See "Table 40: Gainfully occupied, 10 years of Age and over, by occupation, age, and sex for Canada and the provinces, 1931," *Census of Canada*, 1931, vol. 7, p. 72.

Document 8.1
The Women's Canadian Club of St. John, N.B.

A Suggested Programme for Empire Day Celebration 1915 in the Schools of New Brunswick

Although not an official holiday, Empire Day was set aside to celebrate Canada's historical ties to Great Britain. By mid-century, this event was largely discarded in favour of a late May celebration of Queen Victoria's birthday.

Issue to Consider

- Judging by the schedule of events, what is the purpose of the school's involvement in Empire Day? What was the effect of Canada's participation in the war on the plans made for the celebration? How is the enemy side presented to the schoolchildren?

MOTTOES FOR BANNERS

or to Adorn School Walls or Blackboards.

"The Empire is my Country; Canada is my Home."

"Lives of great men all remind us
We can make our lives sublime,
And departing leave behind us
Footsteps on the sands of time."

"England expects that every man
This day will do his duty."

"Whose flag has braved a thousand years
The battle and the breeze."

"We are watchers of a beacon
Whose light must never die."

"Whose frail barques the ocean surge defied,
And trained the race that live upon the wave."

"We sowed the seed of Empire in the furrows of the sea."

"We've sailed wherever ships could sail
We've founded many a state."

"The seas but join the regions they divide."

FOR EMPIRE DAY

Empire Day is not a holiday, but it is desirable that the occasion be made as bright, interesting and inspiring to the children as is possible.

The morning session should be devoted to the Geography and History of the Empire, impressing upon the children its reality, growth, magnitude, essential unity and common purpose; and the privileges, responsibilities and duties of citizenship.

If possible have the whole school assembled out of doors. Open proceedings with THE LORD'S PRAYER, and, if desired, a Scripture Reading such as *Deuteronomy viii*, 6-11. If in the open air, have a flag staff in a space in the centre of the assembly upon which the Union Jack may now be run up. If this cannot be arranged, have the Flag displayed in some other way while all present sing:

"GOD SAVE THE KING"

followed by the recitation, by one of the pupils —

"THE OLD FLAG"
It is only a small bit of bunting,
It is only an old colored rag,
But thousands have died for its honor,
And shed their best blood for the Flag.

It is charged with the cross of St. Andrew,
Which of old, Scottish heroes had led,
It carries the cross of St. Patrick
For which Ireland's noblest have bled.

Joined to these is the old British Ensign,
St. George's red cross on white field,
Round which, from King Richard to Wolseley,
Britons conquer or die, but ne'er yield.

It flutters triumphant o'er ocean,
As free as the wind and the wave,
And the captive from shackles unloosen'd
'Neath its shadow no longer a slave.

We hoist it to show our devotion,
To our King, to our Country and Laws,
It's the outward and visible emblem,
Of advancement and liberty's cause.

You may call it a small bit of bunting,
You may say it's an old colored rag,
But freedom has made it majestic,
And time has ennobled the Flag.

An appointed Orator, an invited speaker or the teacher, will then say —

"Let us reverently remember that the British Empire stands out before the whole world as the fearless champion of freedom, fair play and equal rights; that its watchwords are Responsibility, Duty, Sympathy and Self-sacrifice, and that a special responsibility rests with you individually to be true to the traditions and to the mission of your race.

"I also want you to remember that one day Canada will become, if her people are faithful to their high British traditions, the most powerful of all the self-governing nations, not excluding the people of the United Kingdom, which make up the British Empire, and that it rests with each one of you, individually, to do your utmost by your own conduct and example to make Canada not only the most powerful, but the noblest of all the self-governing nations that are proud to owe allegiance to the King."

— *Earl Grey, Late Governor-General of Canada.*

Ceremony of Salutation of the Flag

All present make the Military Salute to the Flag, and while doing so say slowly and [...] in unison:

"Emblem of Liberty, Truth and Justice,
Flag of my country, to thee I bow."

(All bow.)

Doxology.
Praise God from whom all blessings flow,
Praise Him all creatures here below,
Praise Him above, ye heavenly host,
Praise Father, Son and Holy Ghost. Amen. [...]

THE WAR

(A Reading)

When we think of the wonderful opportunities of the great works of peace which are presented to all nations of the world today, and most of all within the far-flung boundaries of our great British Empire, our hearts are grieved and horrified to find that we have been called upon to take part in a war which for the members engaged in it, the territory over which it is waged, the destruction of life, property, and priceless treasure it is consuming, is by far the greatest war, and the most appalling calamity that has ever come upon the world.

It has come now because it had to come some time. [...]

Peace has been the high ambition of the Sovereigns and leaders of our Empire, but Germany has despised peace [...] When the opportunity came the German rulers threw away their cloak of civilization and Christian brotherhood [...]

And the German people readily went to war. [...]

Finding that others are manufacturing goods, others are conducting banks, others are building steamships, others are engaged in commerce and transportation — Germany has taken such commercial rivalries as personal affronts. Because of them, Germany has felt hemmed in and oppressed by outside powers. In other words the German nation has not been willing to be what is known as "a good sport," has not been willing to fight fairly on free fields of competition, and has felt that such competition is a personal insult, and in a manner a tyranny.

Most of all has she felt this towards the competition of the great British Empire, in whose peaceful aspirations she sees only weakness and decadence, and in whose far-flung territory she sees lost opportunity for the impositions upon many nations of the world her own ideas of force and efficiency.

But Germany has made the great mistake of underestimating her opponent — Great Britain did not yield to her dishonourable proposals to desert her friends and break her plighted word to them in the day of their distress, neither would she bow her head to the occupation of the friendly shores of her neighbour France by the greedy hordes of Germany — and her defences by land and sea have not crumpled up under Germany's attack. Side by side with her Allies, stands the British Empire to-day — bleeding from many wounds, but bravely facing the flood and fury of the enemy. Keeping their power and efficiency and diabolical devices of destruction in check, while from the ends of the earth her sons rush to support her.

The end is not yet. The enemy is strong and determined, the issues are enormous, inestimable. Let all our boys and girls acquaint themselves with the causes, conduct and issues of this great struggle, and lend their aid in some way or other with God's help to the righteous cause, whose overthrow will spell disaster for us all too horrible to contemplate.

Document 8.2

Excerpts from *Fact and Fancy*

Edited by Canadian educators and published in Canada, the *Fact and Fancy* readers were the standard language-skills textbooks of the upper-elementary grades in Ontario from about the late 1930s through much of the 1950s.

Issue to Consider

- Intended for grade 7 students, the following excerpts from *Fact and Fancy* represent typical elementary-school poetry, history, and civic lessons. As you read the excerpts, look closely at the language employed. What shared themes and messages are being communicated to Ontario schoolchildren?

My Land

She is a rich and rare land;
Oh, she's a fresh and fair land;
She is a dear and rare land —
This native land of mine.

No men than hers are braver;
Her women's hearts ne'er waver;
I'd freely die to save her,
And think my lot divine.

She's not a dull or cold land;
No! she's a warm and bold land;
Oh, she's a true and old land —
This native land of mine.

Could beauty ever guard her,
And virtue still reward her.
No foe would cross her border;
No friend within it pine!

Oh, she's a fresh and fair land;
Oh, she's a true and rare land;
Yes, she's a rare and fair land —
This native land of mine.

Thomas Osborne Davis

Source: *Fact and Fancy*, Grade Seven (Toronto: Toronto: Ginn and Company, 1942), 322–27.

PATRIOTISM AND RELIGION

Even as, on Creation day, God loved His work with a benevolent love because it was good, so we too imitate Him in our love and affection for our Empire and our own beautiful homeland from the headlands of Acadia down the majestic St. Lawrence, across the blue lakes of Ontario, through the gardens of the prairie to the western sea of valleys which is the playground of the world — a country bathed in the glamour of adventure and romance, glorying in the freedom of her institutions and government and promising before God a wondrous destiny, our own, our native land.

God, too, has taught us gratitude, and we love our country for the gifts she has given us. For many, it is the land of their birth; for others, the land of their adoption; for all, it is a land of boundless resources of mine, forest, and field, of commercial advantages, educational facilities, and religious freedom, of law and order under a government that borrows the best of British traditions and of American experiments.

Allow me to call to your attention the patriotism of a Catholic who is not a professional but a practical Catholic. The practical Catholic will always remember that he is a member of the Kingdom of God, as well as a citizen of his country. He is not only called upon to give to God the things that are God's, but also to give to Caesar the things that are Caesar's. He is taught that obedience to law and respect for public officers is not through fear of police, but for conscience' sake, "for those who are in power, are ordained by God."

Read the history of this, our country, from its earliest discovery down through the days of exploration and settlement linked, as they are, with the names of Cartier and Champlain; read of the evangelization of the great wide lands of the west and north and you will note that our country was sealed in its cradle with the Cross of Christ. Read the story of the magnificent example of mutual toleration given the world in the pact of Confederation and you will find there, too, Catholic Canadians in the forefront of the movement. Read again the story of the adjustment between the mother country and the new Republic to the south, and, in view of Chateauguay, Montgomery's fall, and the Glengarry Invincibles under the valiant first Bishop of Kingston, can their loyalty ever be questioned? Did we fail in the hour of danger in 1914?

Are we failing now? Ask the victor of the *Graf Spee*! Ask the victor of the *Weser*! Who was the first to win the coveted Victoria Cross in the army during this present war? The first to win the same in the Air Force? Who was the first to win the newly created George Cross? Who, but Catholics all!

The record of Catholic citizens on the pages of history of our country show gloriously how freely and gladly Catholics have responded, in peace and in war, to the country's call. Individually and collectively they have realized the duties and responsibilities that citizenship in this democratic country places on the shoulders of every loyal citizen. Our responsibility in the face of the danger at our gates is to give an example of Christian solidarity and toleration. No matter what our differences may be, let our hearts be one.

In unity and co-operation with all its citizens, at war or in peace, we shall work for Canada and our Empire, pray for Canada and our Empire, to the end that, when God's plans shall have been completed and Canada has filled gloriously the role assigned to her by the Creator, her children shall, on that other shore, in the land of hope and promise beyond the stars, be all united before the Great Throne of God under the sceptre of Christ the King.

Reverend S. B. Plunkett

ADD TO YOUR KNOWLEDGE

1. Recall the most important facts in connection with the work of Cartier, Champlain, and the first missionaries in Canada.
2. What is meant by "mutual toleration"? "the new Republic"?
3. Who was "the valiant first Bishop of Kingston"?
4. What are the duties and responsibilities of citizenship? Name some ways in which young Canadians can prove themselves worthy citizens of a country from which they receive so much.
5. Do you know to what brave persons the writer refers in the fifth paragraph? Here they are. Try to find out why these men have been thus honoured.
   a. Victor of the *Graf Spee*: Rear Admiral Sir Henry Harwood, O. B. E.
   b. Victor of the *Weser*: Commander Charles Taschereau Beard, R. N.
   c. First to win the V. C. in the army during the present war: Captain Harold E. Andrews.
   d. First to win the V. C. in the Air Force during the present war: Flying Officer Donald Garland, R. A. F.
   e. First to win the George Cross: Patrick King.

The Maple

All hail to the broad-leaved Maple!
With her fair and changeful dress —
A type of our youthful country
In its pride and loveliness;
Whether in Spring or Summer,
Or in the dreary Fall,
'Mid Nature's forest children,
She's fairest of them all.

Down sunny slopes and valleys
Her graceful form is seen,
Her wide, umbrageous branches
The sunburnt reaper screen;
'Mid the dark-browed firs and cedars
Her livelier colours shine,
Like the dawn of the brighter future
On the settler's hut of pine.

She crowns the pleasant hilltop,
Whispers on breezy downs,
And casts refreshing shadows
O'er the streets of our busy towns;
She gladdens the aching eyeball,
Shelters the weary head,
And scatters her crimson glories
On the graves of the silent dead.

When winter's frosts are yielding
To the sun's returning sway,

And merry groups are speeding
To sugar-woods away;
The sweet and welling juices,
Which form their welcome spoil,
Tell of the teeming plenty
Which here waits honest toil.

When sweet-toned Spring, soft-breathing,
Breaks Nature's icy sleep,
And the forest boughs are swaying
Like the green waves of the deep;
In her fair and budding beauty,
A fitting emblem, she,
Of this our land of promise,
Of hope, of liberty.

And when her leaves, all crimson,
Droop silently and fall,
Like drops of life-blood welling
From a warrior brave and tall;
They tell how fast and freely
Would her children's blood be shed,
Ere the soil of our faith and freedom
Should echo a foeman's tread.

Then hail to the broad-leaved Maple!
With her fair and changeful dress —
A type of our youthful country
In its pride and loveliness;
Whether in Spring or Summer,
Or in the dreary Fall,
'Mid Nature's forest children,
She's fairest of them all.

Reverend H. F. Darnell

The Arms of Canada

The honour of her heraldry,
The splendour of her soul,
Upon her shield — from sea to sea,
Shall Canada enroll.
The glory that was Yesterday,
To-day shall proudly borrow
To lend its light to show the way
To glorify To-morrow.

Blanche E. Holt Murison

Document 8.3

H. H. Draper

"My First Day of School" and "My Primary School Teacher"

Harold H. Draper was born in 1924, the youngest of four children, to English immigrants who had arrived in southwestern Manitoba in 1908. His father established a dairy farm near Lenore, Manitoba, where he grew up. This excerpt from his memoirs describes his primary-school experiences in a one-room rural school.

Issues to Consider

- What kind of schooling could children growing up in farm communities during the Depression expect to receive?
- Teachers were important figures in these isolated communities. What role did Draper's teacher play beyond the educational?

THE FIRST DAY OF SCHOOL

Before leaving for my first day of school my parents gave me the standard instructions: obey the teacher, respect my elders and keep quiet when they were talking. I left with more than the usual amount of intrepidation because I had little prior contact with the children in the community who were to become my classmates. I got aboard the horse-drawn summer van when it stopped in front of our house, clutching the Bee Hive Golden Corn Syrup pail that contained my lunch. The van had an arched canvas-covered roof that gave it the appearance of a lightweight American prairie schooner. There was a wooden bench down each side for sitting on and space underneath for putting our lunch pails and books. Otherwise, there wasn't a lot of furniture.

School began at 9:00 a.m. and ended at 4:00 p.m., with a fifteen-minute recess in the morning and afternoon and a one-hour break at noon. The children who lived in town went home for lunch whereas those who lived in the country brought their lunch from home and ate it at school. A few brought lunch in a designated lunch box with a thermos containing hot soup in the top. The significance of this symbol of social class was not lost on the other children. There were lunch box students and syrup pail students.

I don't remember much about my first morning at school, but I have a clear recollection of the afternoon. After eating my lunch at school I went downtown to buy some jawbreakers (large, round, black licorice-coated candies) with the nickel my mother had given me. When it came time to return to school I mistakenly took the familiar road that led to our previous farm. After getting a half mile into the countryside, by which time I realized that I was lost, a truck driver recognized me and took me home, not knowing (because I didn't tell him) that I

Source: H. H. Draper, *Growing up in Manitoba* (Regina: Canadian Plains Research Center, 1998), 20–22.

was supposed to be at school. I explained my three o'clock arrival at home by telling my mother that school had been let out early on the first day. That explanation lasted until she saw the school van going past the house at 4:30.

I successfully resisted going back to school until the matter finally was taken out of my hands. To make sure that I got there, my father and brother decided to take me in our Model T Ford. I did my best to elude them, but they cornered me in the farmyard, put me in the right front seat and locked the door. However, they neglected to lock the door on the driver's side, so I bolted out of it and took off again. They recaptured me with the help of a cousin who was visiting from England and I was deposited at the front door of the school. This episode conforms with my mother's definition of a hypocrite: a boy who goes to school with a smile on his face. From that point on my schooling went fairly smoothly. My father said that getting me started to school required an international effort but once I got started he couldn't get me stopped.

MY PRIMARY SCHOOL TEACHER

The school I attended for all but four of my school years was a square two-storey brick building consisting of a primary room on the first floor, a secondary and high school room on the second floor and two toilets, a furnace and a bare "recreation room" in the basement. The total enrollment of eighty to a hundred students was distributed fairly evenly among the four grades in the primary and secondary rooms and the three in the high school room. There was no grade twelve. Students who sought further education went either to grade twelve in a bigger school or directly to university. I was the second student in the history of the school to go on to university.

By the time I entered grade one my teacher was well into the second generation of pupils she had taught in the same room, and by the time she retired she had been employed continuously in the same position for over three decades. By contrast, most female teachers married and gave up teaching after two or three years. She taught all subjects to all four grades. Her teaching regimen would be an anathema to modern educators, but she managed to inculcate into most of us a phonetic approach to reading that enabled us to identify new words on our own, a foundation in arithmetic, spelling and grammar, and even the beginnings of an appreciation of the arts.

Parents assumed less responsibility for their children's education than they do now. Children weren't taught how to read or given any information about their cultural background or natural environment before they entered school. These responsibilities were assigned to the teachers to deal with at their own discretion. I thought of this devolution of responsibility for children's education fifteen years later when I listened to the President of the University of Manitoba ask my graduating class to remember that the most important educational institution in our society was not the university or the school but the home.

I share fond and appreciative memories of my primary room teacher with all her former students whose views I have ever heard expressed. Her effectiveness as a teacher was due as much to the interest she took in the personal lives of her pupils as to her formal instruction. They knew they could trust her with the confidential information they whispered to her before the start of classes in the morning, and over the years she came to know more about what went on within families in the community than anyone else. She kept this information to herself and, knowing this, parents didn't resent the fact that she was privy to it. By the time she finally retired she was already a local legend.

Document 8.4

Excerpts from *The Boy's Own Book*

The first National Committee on Boys' Work, comprising delegates from all Protestant denominations and the Young Men's Christian Association, was formed in 1912. The following year, the committee sponsored leaders' training camps and three boys' conferences. By 1917, there were Tuxis and Trail Ranger programs across Canada. Older Boys' Parliaments, conducted by the sixteen- to eighteen-year-old members in provincial legislative buildings, were held annually in the capital cities. Profoundly Christian in outlook, they passed earnest resolutions condemning the use of tobacco, alcohol, and drugs, and urging Sunday observance and active membership in their club. This excerpt from the Tuxis manual details the organization's goals and activities.

Issues to Consider

* What kind of boys would be likely to join the Trail Ranger or Tuxis programs?
* What was the group's mandate or mission?

His New Day

Last night I was a care-free boy,
My play was life, my life was play;
No future called; from day to day
I laughed, and romped, and lived — a boy.

But now another day I see,
A day to do with as I will;
Shall it be fraught with good or ill,
What message does it bring to me?

I catch its gleam! I breathe its air!
I hear its ringing call to me,
Its call to live, to serve, to be.
My beating heart finds voice in prayer —

In prayer that I may find the way,
The way that He in service went —
A life for others freely spent
To meet the torn world's need to-day.

To help the other boy who gropes
Along the road I just came through,
Storm-swept with feelings strange and new;
To help him realize his hopes.

Source: *The Boy's Own Book* (Toronto: Religious Education Council of Canada, 1929), 7, 9–14.

Life beckons me to eager quest:—
To love, to laugh, to work, to play,
To serve, to sacrifice, to pray;
He calls — and He shall have my best!

— *E. C. Foster.*

HISTORY OF THE TRAIL RANGER AND TUXIS PROGRAMMES

As Canada is a young country many of its important events are of comparatively recent occurrence. It was in 1912, just seventeen years ago, that the forerunning of our present Trail Ranger and Tuxis programmes was prepared and published. The group of men who laid the foundation of our present programmes was appointed by the National Council of the Young Men's Christian Association. The moving spirit in and through it all was Mr. Taylor Statten, then secretary of the Boys' Work Committee of the National Council Y.M.C.A.

The origin, however, goes back another five years, during which period Messrs. Taylor Statten and Wallace Forgie, as Boys' Work Secretaries of the Central Branch of the Y.M.C.A., in Toronto, were carrying on experiments which in 1912 were to blossom out into what were then called the Canadian Standard Efficiency Tests. It was in 1907 that Mr. Forgie got the idea of Luke 2:52, "And Jesus increased in wisdom and stature and in favour with God and man," as a basis for such a programme. It was about this time also that the idea of charting boys on a four-fold scale was first practiced. [...]

When Mr. Forgie returned to the front, Gordon Hignell, of Winnipeg, was set aside by the Association to complete the work of publication. This was his last task for on the completion of this strenuous work he was stricken with illness and passed to the Great Beyond. In his death the boys of Canada lost one who thought not of himself but of others.

Finally in October 1918, the work was complete. The name "Canadian Standard Efficiency Training" became a covering name for the two programmes — the Trail Ranger programme for boys twelve to fourteen, with its own emblems, crests, badges, and the Tuxis programme with somewhat similar yet distinctive features for boys from fifteen to seventeen. Separate manuals were issued for both Trail Ranger and Tuxis boys which have since been widely used. The Trail Ranger manual is still with us. The Tuxis manual, however, has been superseded by the Boy's Own book.

In 1918 an event took place similar to the formation of the Advisory Committee for Cooperation in Boys' Work, but wider in its scope. The Religious Education Council of Canada was organized for the purpose of giving leadership to all phases of Religious Education.

To harmonize with this larger development, the National Advisory Committee for Cooperation in Boys' Work changed its name and in 1920 became the National Boys' Work Board of the Religious Education Council of Canada. In this they were followed by the Provincial Advisory Committees which are now all known as the Boys' Work Boards of their respective provincial councils.

Such is the history of our programme and movement. From these modest beginnings we have today 2,287 registered groups in Canada at work in over 928 communities with an enrolment of 27,921 boys. The number of our summer camps for boys has increased from two or three in 1915 to 71 in 1928 when over 3,600 boys were helped to round out the training they had received during the fall and winter months. Instead of one provincial Older Boys' Parliament, we now have six, to which each year 450 boys are coming with a view to discovering what part they can play when they go back to work through the multitude of Trail Ranger and Tuxis boys who make up this fellowship.

Nor is the history finished. It is for you and those who follow after you to write the remaining chapters. Pretors and Premiers, Mentors and Camp Leaders, Sunday School Teachers and Ministers are needed if the cause is to flourish. To you who have experienced this fellowship, who during these getting ready days have learned what training for Christian living means, must we look for the leadership of to-morrow.

TUXIS INSIGNIA

Have you ever, while in a strange place and feeling somewhat lonesome, met a boy wearing the Tuxis pin? If you have, you know what it feels like unexpectedly to meet a friend. Or, have you attended a Tuxis Boys Conference or conclave where hundreds of boys were wearing the pin or crest and felt thrilled as you realized, possibly for the first time, that you were one of the 28,000 Tuxis and Trail Ranger Boys in Canada?

The Tuxis pin is the badge of your membership in the movement. It is an outward expression that you are striving to grow into something of the measure and the fullness of Christ. Further, it is an indication that you are a member in good standing of a registered Tuxis Square and consequently are entitled to use the Tuxis pin, crest or emblem.

The word "Tuxis" is made up of five letters, each having a very significant meaning. "T" stands for training, the last letter, "S" for Service —"Training for Service." "X" placed in the centre denotes the Greek letter "Chi," the first letter in the Greek word "Christos" meaning Christ, which is to indicate that the program is Christ-centred. The "U" and "I" suggest our social relationships, the attitude of brotherliness and unselfishness — the "Help the Other Fellow Spirit."

Document 8.5

"Students' Council Notes" from *En Avant*

En Avant (translated roughly as "going forward") was a yearly publication detailing the activities of the previous year and showing photographs of each school member by "form" or class, in the traditional format of the school yearbook or annual. It was produced by the student council of Alexandra High School in Medicine Hat, Alberta.

Issues to Consider

- The student council president mentions a number of activities proposed for the annual field day. What do the recommendations tell us about the significance of this event?
- Thinking in terms of who writes in them and who the intended audience is, what are some of the challenges of using high-school publications to get a sense of what went on there?

One of the topics, creating much discussion in the present Students' Council meetings, is the question of Field Day. May 30 has been submitted as the most practical day for our track meet. A list of recommendations was presented to the Council by the Athletic Committee, stating that:

1. A good school parade in the morning of May 20 would aid in the development of school spirit and also attract a larger crowd to the track meet.
2. Following the parade, the regular track meet would take place in the new "Ball Park" in the afternoon.
3. To top off everything, a "Field Day and Presentation Dance" should take place the same evening, where the awards for all athletic functions of the year would be presented to the winners.

Let's exert every effort to make this the best Field Day yet. If anyone has any further ideas, as to the betterment of our field day, these will be gratefully received by the room representatives or any member of the Athletic Committee. [...]

Source: Alfred Bennett, President, "Students' Council Notes," *En Avant* (Alexandra High School yearbook), March 1945.

Topic 9

Medium and Message: Popular Culture, Mass Media, and National Identity

Cover illustration, *Captain Canuck*, first issue, July 1975,
http://www.collectionscanada.ca/superheroes/
t3-210.04-e.html.

CONTEXT

Much of the history of popular culture in post–Confederation Canada is tied to that of youth, as noted in the preceding section, and as the essays by Neil Sutherland and Ryan Edwardson attest to in this one. Of all social groups, the young are considered the most inclined to embrace emergent cultural trends and the most attuned, as reflected in the early 20th-century public debates on the matter, to the technologies that transformed earlier, localized, traditional popular cultures into mass culture. Nonetheless, the "popular" clearly belongs to all, even if social groups participate in ways distinguished not only by age but also along the usual lines of demarcation: class, gender, race, region, religion, urban or rural location, sexual orientation, and any combination or permutation of these. Social historians are understandably interested in the subject, which concerns how culture is created, disseminated, and received on the level of ordinary everyday life, their particular playing field. The recent flourishing of cultural and communications studies has expanded the area enormously, while also ensuring that it is both interdisciplinary and transnational in approach and method. Borrowing from sociology, cultural anthropology, and media and literary studies, historians of Canada have been active participants in the study of popular culture.

Because much of what fits under the broad heading of popular culture is concerned with fun, it would be easy to see its history as a respite from more "serious" subjects. However its practitioners feel about their personal enjoyment of the work, such a view obscures the power relations that are the basis of what might too readily be dismissed as inconsequential because it is "popular." Most human beings experience these relations in their day-to-day social interactions, with other people or with the media that transmits popular culture and brings it within the grasp of the majority. Power relations are embedded in the activities, rites, rituals, and practices that make up popular culture, whether these take the form of a church hall gathering, listening to radio with family around the kitchen table, viewing the newest "talkie" on an after-school cinema date, buying the latest recording on the "top 10" list, indulging in pulp fiction or comic books or television sitcoms or video games.

Technology, as noted, is integral to modern popular culture. Access to technological innovations grew as mass production and prosperity made them more affordable to more Canadians, as well as more desirable, thanks to the expanding social power of advertising and what might be called a modern consumer ethos. These developments have made popular culture more a homogeneous "common" experience than ever before in history. Yet its universality can be overstated. In the options that are available and accessible, in the personal or group selection, in the nature, extent, and frequency of participation, we may share aspects of popular culture with others but we may also distinguish ourselves from them in some measure. The study of popular culture allows us a sense of how more discernible power relations — those hinging on economic and political issues, for example — are manifested, on the level of customs and practices, in the everyday culture of everyday people.

Networks of transportation and communications, in close relation with changing technologies, have been major formative influences in Canadian history since the days of early contact and imperial trade. The studies of such theorists as Harold Innis (1894–1952) and Marshall McLuhan (1911–1980) not only brought these connections to the fore within our own national context but also added much to an international body of knowledge on the larger subject. In a nation characterized by sparse population, harsh climate, difficult geography, and islands of population density that exert a metropolitan influence over surrounding "hinterlands," these networks were critical both for the obvious practical reasons and for the development of any sense of national identity. Paradoxically, the media also sustain regional identities: the Canadian Broadcasting Corporation (CBC), established in the 1930s, links all Canadians in an information network while also reflecting back to them certain regional cultures. At the same time, however, the CBC and such important cultural instruments as the Canada Council and the Canadian Radio-television and Telecommunications Commission (CRTC), were expressly created to defend and promote the "Canadianness" of our culture in the face of American proximity, cultural commonality, and media domination. By the end of the 1920s, Canada's fledgling feature film industry had been overtaken by Hollywood. American radio programming was being broadcast to, and enjoyed by, Canadian listeners across the land by the 1930s. The age of television that dawned in the 1950s was, in very short order, identified with American TV shows and "stars." The rock music that revolutionized 1960s popular culture was also, by and large, the music of *American Bandstand*.

Questions about national identity and cultural sovereignty, consequently our relations with our powerful southern neighbour, dominate our cultural history, especially that of popular culture where the borders are more permeable and the access and participation proportionately greater. This is particularly relevant in contemporary Canada, as the "global village" envisioned by McLuhan is realized through instantaneous Internet communication. The purportedly border-free World Wide Web carries a considerable proportion of American content, opening up the rest of the world to the kinds of "cultural domination" questions that have so long been part of the Canadian identity conundrum.

Ultimately, the historic forces shaping what Canadians have embraced as popular culture reveal a great deal about the changes and continuities in our perceptions of ourselves as citizens, as a society, and as a nation. The actual content and message of various components of popular culture, moreover, both reflect and actively contribute to social constructions that identify different groups and their status by conveying and repeating certain representations to the enormous audience that mass media create and serve. This is equally pertinent in our own time, with the proliferation of wireless, digital, and Internet technologies that transmit instantaneously and unremittingly around the world.

REFERENCES/FURTHER READING

Dawson, Michael. *The Mountie from Dime Novel to Disney*. Toronto: Between the Lines, 1998.

Francis, Daniel. *National Dreams: Myth, Memory and Canadian History*. Vancouver: Arsenal Pulp Press, 1997.

Innis, Harold Adams. 1951. *The Bias of Communication*. Toronto: University of Toronto Press, 1991.

———. 1950. *Empire and Communications*. Victoria, B.C.: Press Porcepic, 1986.

Kuffert, L. B. *A Great Duty: Canadian Responses to Modern Life and Mass Culture in Canada, 1939–1967*. Montreal and Kingston: McGill-Queen's University Press, 2003.

Litt, Paul. *The Muses, the Masseys and the Massey Commission*. Toronto: University of Toronto Press, 1992.

Magder, Ted. *Canada's Hollywood: The Canadian State and Feature Films*. Toronto: University of Toronto Press, 1993.

McLuhan, Marshall. *The Global Village: Transformations in World Life and Media in the 21st Century*. New York: Oxford University Press, 1989.

———. *The Medium Is the Massage*. New York: Bantam Books, 1967.

Morris, Peter. *Embattled Shadows: A History of Canadian Cinema, 1895–1939*. Montreal and Kingston: McGill-Queen's University Press, 1978.

Rutherford, Paul. *A Victorian Authority: The Daily Press in Late Nineteenth-Century Canada*. Toronto: University of Toronto Press, 1982.

———. *When Television Was Young: Prime Time Canada, 1952–1967*. Toronto: University of Toronto Press, 1990.

Tippett, Maria. *Making Culture: English-Canadian Institutions and the Arts before the Massey Commission*. Toronto: University of Toronto Press, 1990.

Vipond, Mary. *Listening In: The First Decade of Canadian Broadcasting, 1922–1932*. Montreal and Kingston: McGill-Queen's University Press, 1992.

ILLUSTRATION 9.1 (P. 369)

As Ryan Edwardson notes in Article 9.2, Captain Canuck was the creation of artist Richard Comely, with initial inspiration from Calgary teacher and cartoonist Ron Leishman.

Issue to Consider

- The issue that launched the Captain Canuck series in 1975 portrays the superhero in a manner that is obviously both "manly" and nationalistic. What impression does the representation on this cover illustration make? What are readers "seeing" here?

ARTICLES

The essays by Neil Sutherland and Ryan Edwardson demonstrate how such different components of popular culture as television, representing modern technology, and the comic book, in the more traditional format of print media (though the genre is of recent vintage, historically speaking, dating from the 1930s), share messages as well as audiences.

Article 9.1
Neil Sutherland

Popular Media in the Culture of English-Canadian Children in the Twentieth Century[1]

Issues to Consider

- Sutherland uses anecdotal evidence in the form of childhood memories, representing different times and different pastimes, to frame his discussion. What are the themes that are established through this narrative device?
- Why does the author describe this form of oral history as "scripts"? What does he see as their primary value to historians?
- Why does he contend that "the past, in entertainment, never goes away"?
- Sutherland's approach is child-centred, in that he attempts to provide the child's perspective rather than taking the top-down approach of using adult-generated evidence about children. What are some of the challenges of the child-centred approach?
- Sutherland concludes with the optimistic reflection that "none of the media has had anywhere nearly as much negative effect on the young" as critics have warned over the past century. What, then, explains the persistence of this concern and the ongoing attempts to regulate the relationship between children and the media?

I

In 1901, the Canadian naturalist writer Ernest Thompson Seton lectured in Toronto. A mother reported she "took my children to hear him but hear him we did not! They had allowed the Public School children in for ten cents (we had to pay 50cts) & they behaved so badly & made so much noise that we could not hear one word & what was more disgusting they spit on us from the gallery."[2]

* * *

In Winnipeg, just after the Great War, James H. Gray was "infected by my friend Gordon Main … He was, he said, building a wireless set on which he would be able to hear music being broadcast on Station KDKA in Pittsburgh, Pennsylvania. Within the hour I had absorbed all of Gordon's newly acquired expertise … With our homemade crystal sets we not only astounded our parents … but we also flabbergasted the neighbours with the snatches of music coaxed from our sets."[3]

Source: Neil Sutherland, "Popular Media in the Culture of English-Canadian Children in the Twentieth Century," *Historical Studies in Education/Revue d'histoire de l'éducation* 14, no. 1 (2002): 1–33.

* * *

In 1956, twelve-year-old Frank McEnaney was in grade six in a Toronto public school. He recounted that "one day my best friend … ran up to a bunch of us, more excited than we had ever seen him. He'd seen this guy on TV." When McEnaney's gang came to watch the newly discovered singer on television, "one thing was clear to every kid in that room: This was no crooner. This was something different entirely. This felt … *right*." As each of the singer's new records appeared, "We would … play it over and over and over again. Elvis! Elvis! Elvis! Each one seemed more amazing than the one before. Hound Dog, Blue Suede Shoes, Heartbreak Hotel, Don't Be Cruel, All Shook Up." Then, "Elvis was coming to Toronto! My father, in an act of generosity for which I will always be grateful, stopped off at Maple Leaf Gardens on his way to work and purchased two tickets. Elvis Presley was coming to town, and I — I and my best friend, Jerry — were going to get to see him."[4]

* * *

In January 1998, three "very angry girls"— Sherry Kennedy, Laura Gibbons, and Katie Gibbons — wrote to the *Vancouver Sun* that theatre staff "wouldn't let us in *Scream 2*, even with our parents' permission … We are 14, can't drive and have nothing to do but see movies to be entertained, and if we can't see movies that are good, what is there to do? … Young adults like us want thrills, and scary movies are as thrilling as we can get."[5]

* * *

As soon as the video version of *Star Wars Episode I: The Phantom Menace* appeared, Susan Mayes reported, she "discovered my 10-year-old daughter camped in front of the VCR. Scene by scene, Annie was freeze-framing her way through … to check rumours (false) of a walk-through" by the minor character Boba Flett, whom fans brought "back to life" and made a hero "in the alternate universe of novels and short stories that surround the film." Annie also wanted to read these spinoff stories.[6]

* * *

As these opening quotations demonstrate, from peep shows and Charlie Chaplin one-reelers at the nickelodeon to the Saturday cartoons on television and game sites and chat rooms on the Internet, children enthusiastically and actively welcomed the new. And if there was enormous change in the media themselves over the century, there was also considerable continuity in kids' response to them. Their "scripts" reveal a persistent pattern repeating itself from child to child and from year to year over most of the century. From their reading and re-reading and discussing such favourites as the Anne books, to their enthusiastic foot-pounding during chases in one-reelers, to their deconstruction (and reconstruction) of *Star Wars* in the myth-making around the character Boba Flett, children entered into an active relationship with what they heard and saw. And, as what follows will show, both their gender and their class affected their response, although in the case of gender, perhaps not to the degree popular notions might lead one to expect.

Children's relations with media were not isolated from their wider world. From classification schemes, censorship, and curfews, to the V-chip, parents, teachers, and other adults have tried to regulate and control their youngsters' enjoyment of all media. In their earliest years, the sounds youngsters heard and the images they saw were in the control of others. Over the years of childhood, however, children tried to establish an independent relationship with media and, on their own or in co-operation with siblings and peers, enter into the role that media played in the culture of childhood. Advertisers recognized the market potential in youthful interests. From newspaper advertisements for "you, too, can be a magician" kits, through "Quint" dolls, to the creation of such children's cartoons, centred around expensive toys, as "Pokemon" and the "Power Rangers," business has tied merchandise to children's entertainment.

And the past, in entertainment, never goes away. Children still read such classics as the Anne books and *Huckleberry Finn* and can watch television programs, such as the "Flintstones" and the "Three Stooges," and movies, such as *Bambi*, that captivated their parents and grandparents. Modern media are also increasingly self-referential. As Kenneth Tynan shrewdly observed, "Novels, plays, *and films* are filled with references to, quotations from, parodies of — old movies. They dominate the cultural subconscious because we absorb them in our formative years ... and we see them again on TV when we grow up."[7]

Although written in light of the considerable research in Canada and elsewhere on the supposed effects of media on children, and the supposed need for control and censorship of young people's access to them, this paper gives its attention to youngsters' own perception of both domestic and public media and their relationship to them.[8] Its data are the recollections of Canadians born in the period from the last years of the nineteenth century up to the final ones of the twentieth. I collected my data from taking oral histories, from interviews recorded in newspapers and magazines, and from memoirs, autobiographies, and biographies. I focus on the childhood years; that is, on those years from children's earliest memories to early adolescence.

One cannot rely on the exact factual details of such memories. One can, however, usually accept the emotional dimension embodied in them. We can, for example, believe that Frank McEnaney and his friends were, indeed, fascinated by Elvis Presley and that his warmly recalled gratitude to his father was deeply felt. On the other hand, much of what is written these days about memory by historians and others suggests there is an ironic distance amongst memory, the topic remembered, and those doing the remembering. Since most of those cited in this paper are not reflective professionals, irony is not amongst the historiographical problems they raise.[9] Even those now aware of the irony tend not to apply it to their own childhood experiences. Thus, Johanna Schneller wrote of her fascination with Julie Andrews as an "ideal mum." In her role as Maria, "for those of us who saw it when we were kids — un-ironic, non-judgemental —*The Sound of Music* got its hooks in, and held. We wanted to be Julie ... At the same time we wanted to be cared for by Julie ..."[10]

While the paper deals with the whole of the twentieth century, my conclusions are more tentative with regard to its later years than to the earlier ones. More data, and especially those recorded in as yet unwritten autobiographies and memoirs, will enable a later generation of historians to come to more certain conclusions.

II

Some media are as old as the race itself. From the moment they are born children are immersed in sound. Sounds, and especially speaking and singing voices, swirl around them, forming the context in which they begin to construct their growing sense of themselves. Some of this sound is aimed at them; they hear prayers, lullabies, songs, stories, and conversation directed at or about them. Over the century, recorded music and words, radios, televisions, and videos came to merge their sounds into the background cacophony to childhood experiences.

Since family culture is an oral culture, the sway of the human voice persists through childhood. From it, children took on the history and lore of their families, and heard myths, legends, and tall stories that often triggered their imaginations. They also acquired attitudes on gender, class, race, and nationality, and on local and national events. In her family's farmhouse home in Ontario before the Great War, Jessie Beattie "was never weary of hearing stories"; she drew her "small rocking chair to a half-hidden position between my father's armchair and the oval table centred by a large lamp and littered with papers and books" to listen to her parents talk with their visitors.[12] At about the same time, in the upper Fraser Valley near Hope, BC, self-described half-breed Henry Pennier related that "at night," his step-father's father "used to tell us long stories of the past. Especially in the long winter evenings with us sitting around the wood stove to stay warm we listened to him tell us about brave Indian warriors and spooky dead spirits and beautiful Indian maidens and I guess that was when I started to be proud I was a Indian or at least part of one."[13]

When he was about five or six towards the end of that war, Joe Zuken's family "spent many fascinating evenings in the winter time in the kitchen" of their North Winnipeg home "listening to these *landsleit* [people from the same village in Eastern Europe] reminisce about the things they had left behind and the struggles that some of them had gone through."[14] Growing up in the late 1930s and 1940s in the isolated Newfoundland fishing village of Arnold's Cove, Ray Guy recalled: "Night after night the old men sat around lamp-lit kitchens and repeated their repertoire of anecdotes, half of which they'd learned verbatim from their own fathers and grandfathers." On his first visit to St. John's in 1948, Guy expected to see Water Street as "an almost medieval nightmare of whipping posts, cat-o'-nine-tails, stocks, dunking stools, pirates, gallows and gibbets … And the Whirlygig, most terrible because I couldn't even imagine what it was 'they used to put young boys, your age, into for stealing a loaf of bread.'"[15]

Most children participated in family discourse. Some employed their own voices as weapons. Lee Maracle, born in 1950, reported that when she was "three years old I still didn't talk. My parents were worried about it and took me to see a doctor, several in fact … My folks were always arguing about me. I was often left with a woman … because dad kept beating up on me and mom didn't like it … My silence lasted another year. Then one day mom caught me talking to Roger [her brother who was eleven months older], with whom I was very close, and after that the jig was up. I started talking a little with my parents, but not very much. I didn't like big people. I thought they were interesting, but not people I wanted to talk to."[16]

The sound of music was central to the life of many families. "My mother loved music," reported Angus MacLean of his family in Prince Edward Island early in the twentieth century. "She sang in the church choir, and when she had a rare free moment, she used to play hymns and favourite songs in the parlour on her beloved reed organ, an instrument she had brought with her when she came to the house as a bride." MacLean and his sister Margaret played together "and sang together around the reed organ."[17] In the 1930s Helen (Masse) Sigurdson's Franco-Manitoba home contained a player piano, an organ, and a gramophone. She spent "many hours listening to the seventy-eight-inch records of the time. I enjoyed 'Rubber Dolly,' 'The Red River Valley,' the 'Yellow Rose of Texas,' and other favourites."[18] John Norris, who sang in school and church choirs in Nelson, BC, remembers "the extraordinary feeling of blessedness that sometimes overcame me on dark winter afternoons as we stood in the music room practising … carols."[19]

Even as phonograph records, radio, television, and other forms of recorded music brought professionally created music into the home, many families continued to perform their own. Although his grandfather first taught Stompin' Tom Connors to sing, his teenage "mother was my greatest musical influence. Names like Wilf Carter and Hank Snow were household words at our place, and my mother used to know the words to most of the songs ... I can still picture her standing in front of a mirror, wearing one of Grampy's old hats and singing 'I'm an Old Cowhand from the Rio Grande.' Pausing for a moment to reflect, she turned and went to the kitchen ... and now there was a more satisfactory performance. She was strumming on the broom!"[20] As did Connors himself, some families, including the Rankin children in Cape Breton and the McGarrigles of Montreal, turned family music-making into professional careers.

Music could leaven harsh upbringings. There is not much happiness in Rita MacNeil's account of her childhood. Her parents argued, sometimes fought each other, and occasionally drank heavily. She was sexually abused by a great-uncle, and, until she had corrective surgery, teased about her upper lip. Nonetheless, some lightness shows through when she discusses the role that music played in her life. "I was very fond of the old piano ... I discovered how much music meant to me then, bubbling up from deep inside ... I took up singing and poured my soul into it." MacNeil listened to the radio with her mother. On evenings in December they "listened to Christmas carols sung by a choir ... It is one of my most treasured memories, lying in bed with my mother as the choir sang 'O Holy Night.'" After the family moved from Big Pond, on Cape Breton, to Toronto, "I'd sit inside the dark apartment and listen to the radio ... singing along to an Elvis Presley song, like 'Love Me Tender,' or 'Blue Suede Shoes,' rocking back and forth on my parents' bed when they were at work."[21]

Children took special delight in letters that connected separated families. In Canada with her mother and brother during the Second World War, Marianne Hollanby considers letters from her father in England as amongst her "most treasured possessions."[22] In 1957, when she was seven years old, welfare workers sent Mary Lawrence and two of her siblings from their home on a reserve near Vernon, BC, to the residential school in Cranbrook. They often received a one-page letter from their aunt Yvonne "telling us that Grandma, Bill, James and she were all fine. She never mentioned Mom but ended her letter with 'Write soon, Always, Yvonne.' I never got a letter from Mom ... The letters I received from Yvonne I treasured. I can't recall what they said, probably just that everyone was fine. It wasn't so much what the letter said, it was just that someone had taken the time to write ... I had no idea when we would be able to go home."[23]

Reading was often an oral medium, especially for young children. Many parents regularly read or told their youngsters bedtime stories. People who grew up in the 1920s, '30s, and '40s recalled being read the Thornton W. Burgess stories that appeared in many daily newspapers. Others remember hearing parents or teachers reading "Hiawatha," *Robinson Crusoe, Beautiful Joe, The Water Babies, Westward Ho!, Noddy*, the novels of Sir Walter Scott, Charles Dickens, and Robert Munsch. Young children had favourites that they liked to hear again and again. One youngster in the 1930s loved to hear the stereotypical *Little Black Sambo* over and over again. Like many young children, he was never absolutely certain that the story would end just as it had on other readings and was always relieved when the tiger again turned into butter for the pancakes.

Children remember when they began to read for themselves. Many people fondly recall the adventures of Dick and Jane, not, obviously for the content but because they, themselves, read about them. Earl Baity grew up in a pioneering home in north central British Columbia. His rural school had no library but when his teacher, "an exceptionally good reader," started to read *Treasure Island* he found "it something of a surprise when I learned that reading could be fun." Baity had to quit school at about fourteen to look after, entirely on his own, the family horses kept at a remote location. His teacher, Jean McClarty, "managed to keep a trickle of books coming up to me. *Huckleberry Finn; Kidnapped; Oliver* Twist and *The Man From Glengarry* all found their way up that winding sleigh road and into that lonely cabin in the wilderness."[24]

Children wove what they read into games and pastimes. Huckleberry Finn prompted many children into building rafts on nearby bodies of water, although rarely to the extent taken by "Fee" Hellman. "If Huckleberry Finn and Tom Sawyer could do it," reported Hellman, "so could we." In the late 1920s, and after two attempts, one of which was nearly fatal, Hellman and a friend made a raft and rode it some miles down the Kootenay River, when the "fresh spring foliage was at its brightest and best, the light breeze loaded with fragrance." They grounded "our craft in a backwater, clambered to firm ground, and then faced the long journey home on foot."[25]

For some, reading became a practical skill, one to be employed at school, or to find information on topics that interested them. They read *Mechanix Illustrated*, *The Books of Knowledge*, encyclopaedias, books describing natural history topics such as the ever-popular dinosaurs, magazines and catalogues for details of the latest fashions, and stories about sport, film, and pop stars in movie, sports, and "teen" magazines. Indeed, many children did not go beyond using reading as practical skill, for use at school and later in the wider world. Certainly, whether for a lack of books or of interest, recreational reading was not a universal practice amongst Canadian youngsters. My informal survey of most of the Canadian biographies and autobiographies in the large popular biography section of the Vancouver Public Library found only about half of their authors or subjects mentioned reading, or favourite books of childhood.

Sensational newspaper stories attracted youthful attention. When he was nine, in 1922, Duke DeCoursey "became fascinated for the first time with the written word." A local murder was covered "in great detail" in the weekly *Free Press Prairie Farmer*. Each Saturday, DeCoursey "rode my saddle pony, Katy … six miles" to pick up the paper, "read the murder trial and hanging proceedings carefully, then returned home to contemplate the following week's edition."[26] In British Columbia in the 1940s, children followed and avidly discussed the widely reported trial of a rapist and murderer.[27]

Other children read mostly for their own pleasure. Once Phyllis Grosskurth "could read by myself, I developed strong likes and dislikes. I didn't like animal stories, but I devoured the whole Bobbsey Twins series … But generally I was addicted to stories of suffering orphans. There was Cedric, Little Lord Fauntleroy … Elsie Dinsmore was even more of a tearjerker … I skipped all the religious bits … in order to learn whether Elsie's father ever appreciated her true worth … My all-time favourite was handed to me on my tenth birthday by Mother; she had loved L. M. Montgomery's *The Story Girl* when she was young." None of Montgomery's other girl protagonists, such as Anne or Emily, "was a patch on the storytelling Sara Stanley, another orphan, who holds all the children on the farm transfixed with her tales … I must have read *The Story Girl* a hundred times."[28]

In Jackson's Arm, Newfoundland, Reg Sparks found "in those summer 'days that were as long as twenty days are now,' the magic that lay between the covers of a book dissolved all barriers of time and space and swept me away with the clouds to all the corners of the earth and far beyond. To the stars with Flammarion, into the lands of enchantment with the brothers Grimm and into the world of mythology with Bullfinch; but the greatest joy was to discover that there was no limit to the world of books."[29] Turn-of-the-new-century children have been captivated by the series of novels featuring teen-aged wizard Harry Potter. Nine-year-old Victorian Breanna Francis told a reporter that "I hadn't read much before but, at Christmas, my grandmother bought me the first book and I've been reading a lot." A twelve-year-old girl reported that she had read one of the series seven times.[30]

The number of widely read books for children increased enormously in the latter half of the century. Nonetheless, the popularity of certain classics persisted. The range was nicely revealed when, in one of many articles marking the publication of a new Harry Potter book, five Canadian writers of books for children described the favourite authors of their youth.

Marie-Louise Gay noted *Winnie the Pooh*, the *Chronicles of Narnia*, Tolkien's books, *Watership Down*, by Richard Adams, and "a lot of classic science fiction, including John Wyndham's *The Day of the Triffids*." Janet Lunn, who "loved fantasy and historical novels," listed the Bobbsey Twins, Nancy Drew, Louisa May Alcott, Lucy Maud Montgomery, Robert Louis Stevenson's *A Child's Garden of Verses*, and Edith Nesbit's *The Treasure Seekers*. Jean Little's "favourite was Frances Burnett's *The Secret Garden*, without question." She also liked Montgomery's books. Robert Munsch selected *The 500 Hats of Bartholomew Cubbins*, by Dr. Seuss. When Munsch "started reading it was *Lassie Come Home*. I was a nerd — I went to the library every day in the summer when everybody else was playing baseball." Richard Scrimger selected *Narnia*. His "hero was Freddy the Pig, a detective." Science fiction was "vital" to him. He "never read *Anne of Green Gables* or *Little Women*" but "liked the Hornblower series by C. S. Forester."[31]

For some children, reading provided a private place, or even a refuge to which they could escape from loneliness, illness, real or imagined wrongs, or even abuse. Gertrude Story was "crazy about *Anne of Green Gables* ... [because] Anne was as misfortunate as I was, and so we connected and were kindred spirits or anything else she wanted to say we were ..."[32] Takashima reported reading in her home in the New Denver internment camp. "The small candle casts an orange glow on my book. I am reading about Marco Polo again. My mind leaves our house ... I feel like a princess being rescued by a brave, dark Tartar."[33] When self-described gay activist Jim Egan was "around twelve to fourteen years old," in the early 1930s, he bought copies of his "favorite English boys' magazines," *The Magnet*, *The Gem*, and *The Boy's Own Annual*. "Although there was never a whisper of homosexuality in them, looking back now it seems that the stories ... were charged with homoerotic implications ... I read these stories religiously. The schoolboys who were depicted in them were probably sixteen or seventeen years old, and were shown in line drawings of idealized youthful beauty. I suppose I projected a degree of friendship that wasn't there ... [but] it seems to me that it would be easy to interpret the stories that way. And, believe me, my imagination went wild!"[34]

Daily and weekly newspapers sometimes catered to both the practical and imaginative characteristics of youthful readers. They ran daily and weekly comic strips — often called "the funnies"— which attracted a wide readership amongst adults as well as children. In the early 1930s, Harvey Kirck lived in the hamlet of Uno Park in northeastern Ontario. "Each weekend it was my job to pick up the [Toronto] *Star Weekly* and the first thing I'd do was check to make sure that the funnies were there, tucked into the glossy lithograph section: Tarzan the Ape Man, Maggie and Jiggs, Bronco Bill, Mandrake the Magician, Popeye, Dick Tracy, and Jimmy Frise and Greg Clark's 'Bird's Eye Centre.' What finer way is there for a young fellow to spend a Saturday afternoon than to sit with his father and mother reading the funnies?"[35]

Some newspapers also provided an outlet for those who wanted to express themselves in print. Norah Lewis' collection of children's letters drawn from weekly newspapers, most directed at rural audiences, demonstrates the breadth of youthful interests and the very considerable skill with which they described them.[36] Early in the century, Gilean Douglas contributed to the *Toronto News*. Much later, she wrote, "I can smell that newsprint now ... The day my letter was in, and a poem, I went flying down the walk to meet Daddy with the paper in my hand."[37] Claire Drainie Taylor wrote: "The *Regina Leader Post* may, or may not, have been a good newspaper, but it did feature a Saturday 'Torchbearers' page all written by children, which I loved. I read it religiously and ... got up the nerve to mail in a few poems and letters of my own ... and to my great delight the letter was published."[38]

Comics also appeared in the form of comic books. Mordecai Richler argued that, for his generation, "there was nothing quite like comic books."[39] And later cohorts agreed. When Paul Jay was in grade five, "the boys all wanted to be one hero: Wolverine ... a mutant superhero from Canada with acute animal senses, a nasty temper, and retractable, razor-sharp metal claws that he uses for gouging, slashing, and grappling with evildoers ... [M]y friends and I embraced Wolverine as our own. I worked with my brothers at fashioning Wolverine-style claws out of tinfoil. (The claws were, to our disappointment, more ornamental than utilitarian.) ... Wolverine represented how we wanted to see ourselves — not polite or retiring, but tough and not to be trifled with. His northern roots showed through when he was out of costume, quaffing beer or chopping wood in a plaid shirt, toque and mutton chopped ..."[40]

Contrary to gendered expectations and stereotypes, girls also employed comic books to envision themselves in active, adventurous roles. Poet Gwendolyn MacEwen loved comic books. She remembered "with a mixture of humour and terror" that a local druggist caught her stealing the latest issue of *Wonder Women* "and chased her through the icy streets of Winnipeg." MacEwen was also caught up by the Marvel family and knew "all the key words to utter to bring about the thundering transformation."[41] Marvel comics also stimulated in MacEwen dreams of flying: "You know you can fly, the way they do, straight out, with the arms forward and poised like upside-down divers ..."[42] "All one spring and summer," Helen Porter and her cousin Dot "had a running series of Flash Gordon adventures, during which we acted out the escapades of Flash and Dale ... We carefully watched the serials at the Capitol Theatre and read the comic books, adapting them all to the South Side. The big rope swing in Dot's garden was the place for this, for when we swung high it was not too difficult to imagine ourselves in a space ship."[43] Simone Blais, dressed as Superwoman, "was a hero ... I would take a running start towards the three stairs into our sunken living room, where I would take a flying leap. One day, however, I landed wrong, and ended up in the hospital emergency room with a broken arm ... No longer invincible, I watched her on TV, wishing I could fly."[44]

Particularly in the early years of the century, many youngsters found reading materials very hard to come by. Many families, even amongst those who could afford them, had no books other than a bible, a catechism, and other religious material. Jessie Mifflin, who grew up in Bonavista, Newfoundland, explained "books were regarded as a luxury," and quoted a neighbour's comment on the many books in her house: "it seemed an awful waste of money to buy them."[45] Those whose homes lacked books had to borrow from friends, or a school or public library. School and classroom libraries, such as the one noted above by Earle Baity, often depended on the generosity of teachers for their generally meagre collections. Denominational publications, such as weekly Sunday school papers and the United Church's popular magazines *Canadian Girl* and *Canadian Boy*, tried to provide wholesome reading for youngsters.

Even after the Second World War, there still weren't a lot of books available in country schools. Linda Turk reported, "I started Grade 1 in 1960, and still feel a thrill of excitement at the thought of the library truck, bringing us a new set of books to enjoy for two or three months. Fifty books and a painting; that was the allowance for a school with twenty-some students. I don't remember an encyclopedia at any of the three public schools I attended."[46]

Children in larger towns and cities often had children's collections in their public libraries. When Dorothy Jean Harris returned to Canada early in the Second World War, "there was the St. Catharine's Public Library, with a basement devoted entirely to children's books. What a treasure trove! I think it was reading *The Count of Monte Christo* non-stop that led to my first pair of glasses."[47] Mary Pratt's grandmother took her to the Legislative Library in Fredericton, and arranged for her to have a library card. There, the librarian "chirped directions as to what books were suitable for children. When she found Beth and me looking for the wicked bits in adult books, she'd haul us away from *Forever Amber* or *The Sheik* and lead us to the great volumes of Audubon lithographs. We were not only allowed but encouraged to turn the pages, using two hands under each page."[48]

Some parents controlled both what might be read and when reading might be done. Parents in the early years of the century were particularly concerned about the malign influence of "penny dreadfuls" and "dime novels."[49] In the early 1950s, publication in the United States of Dr. Fredric Wertham's *Seduction of the Innocent*,[50] an attack on so-called crime comics, prompted Senator Estes Kefauver of Tennessee to conduct Senate hearings on the topic. The fuss spilled over into Canada, where, as Mona Gleason has shown, Progressive Conservative Member of Parliament E. Davie Fulton campaigned successfully for legislation—still in place—controlling crime comics.[51] The strength of the furore here is indicated by the fact that Parliament passed a private member's bill introduced by a member of the opposition.

Over the whole of the century some people have tried to restrict the sorts of books available for children in school and public libraries. In the 1990s in British Columbia, some parents and the school board in the Surrey school district restricted the use of reading and school library materials dealing with families that differed from traditional ones.[52] Native Canadians have objected to how they have been portrayed as "savages" in school texts.[53]

Despite parental and other forms of social concern and controls, youngsters very often ignored or evaded restrictions. When he was seven, Farley Mowat claims, "I worked my way through a big, lavishly illustrated volume of Gargantua and Pantagruel and, though I must admit I did not understand much of the text, I certainly appreciated the marginal drawings of grotesque human beings engaged in things dear to the imagery of small boys, especially the representations of Rabelaisian farting and pissing."[54] Helen Sigurdson's father "haunted" auctions, bringing home what her mother described as "junk." One item of interest to his children was a magic lantern with a set of French postcards. "The last one showed the man's back with two distinct handprints of flour on his shoulders."[55]

Children secretly perused their parents' sex manuals and copies of "true confessions" magazines, and later such adult fare as *Playboy*. "In Grade 6," Shannon Stewart reported, "my best friend slipped me a copy of *The Happy Hooker*. I read the book as quickly as was humanly possible, in sheer terror that my parents might discover its hiding place. Xaviera Hollander's account of brothel life left me and a small group of suburban girls with enough knowledge of exotic and unlikely sexual acts that we would have been more interested in the *Kama Sutra* than the mandatory pink and blue pamphlets distributed in our Sex Ed classes."[56]

As well as reading, other forms of earlier media persisted from the nineteenth century into the twentieth. Children attended live theatre, vaudeville, church and Sunday school concerts, minstrel shows, and chautauqua sessions.[57] What were called "medicine shows" always attracted youthful audiences. Joseph Wilder recalled "Professor" Sutton's visit to Winnipeg early in the century. On a makeshift stage lighted by oil pressure torches, there was a "free show with minstrels, black face comedy and fancy ladies who danced." At its peak "the professor came onto the stage" and pointed to "his display of bottles filled with tapeworms. With a pair of forceps he drew out yards and yards of one ..." However, at a dollar a bottle, his "wonderful medicine will resist not only the ravages of tapeworm, but also cancer and fever."[58]

Even such prosaic, even solemn, occasions as prayer meetings provided entertainment. In her diary, thirteen-year-old Christina Young noted almost weekly attendance at a Methodist mid-week meeting. On 25 April 1897, she wrote, "Lucy Mason and I almost always sit together in prayer meeting, and when we sing we try to drown each other out. Lucy and I sing about the same, but Virginia soars far above us." On 1 May she set the wider stage for us. "Before the meeting the men talked about the weather and the price of things. And who was likely to go in at the next election ... After prayer meeting the young men hurried outside and stood waiting in the dark till the girls came out. Then each one that had a girl stepped up and asked to see her home."[59]

Live theatre, especially vaudeville combined with motion picture performances, persisted until after the Second World War. In the late 1930s, actor Al Waxman recalled that when "I was probably less than five, my parents took us to see Abbie's Irish Rose at the Royal Alexandra Theatre. We sat way up in the second balcony. So steep and up so high that it was scary, but I was on my daddy's lap, so I felt safe and excited. Mostly I remember being surrounded by laughter, and that my parents were happy."[60] Sandra Woolfrey remembers being taken, in the 1940s, "to two plays in the townhall. They were thrilling. One was a minstrel show. The novelty of the blackened faces and the banjo music was exciting. The other play featured a romantic looking young woman to whom a young man sang, 'Daisy, Daisy, give me your answer true.'"[61]

Cinema was the century's first new popular medium. From the very first motion pictures, Canadian children clearly valued them above all other forms of popular culture .[62] Angelo Branca recalled Vancouver's Bijou Theatre as it was before the Great War: "We used to pay a nickel to go in there, and with the nickel you got a ticket to go back next week, so you got in for two and a half cents, really."[63] A woman born at the turn of the century recalled viewing "Charlie Chaplin one-reelers. We even had skipping songs about him."[64]

Sometimes, "going to the picture shows" was family entertainment for many children, especially younger ones. It was "a big treat to go to the picture show with Mom and Dad."[65] For Harvey Kirck, growing up in northeastern Ontario, his first motion picture was shown by a temperance organization in the basement of the local United Church, "a faded print of a tear-jerker called Ten Nights in a Bar-room."[66] Many rural youngsters had to wait until the National Film Board's rural circuit, begun during the Second World War, to see their first motion picture.

Most often, however, children and adults attended at different times. For over half of the century, for children "the good day was Saturday" because of the afternoon matinee at the local cinema. While they clearly enjoyed the features, the serials, and the cartoons, children most of all enjoyed matinees as a social experience. By the early 1920s matinees arrived at a pattern that persisted until television, videos, and parental concerns brought them to an end: one or two adult features together with various short subjects.

As matinees came to follow a similar pattern all across the country, so too did the movie-going script of Canadian youngsters. "For several years," wrote John Norris of his Nelson, BC, childhood of the 1930s, "Saturday was a very special day for my brother and me, not only because we were free of school, but also because the whole day from noon until bedtime followed a pleasurable routine — a walk to the centre of Uptown for an afternoon at the picture show, a streetcar ride home to one of our favourite suppers."[67] In Sault Ste. Marie, in October 1935, wrote Morley Torgov, "It is Saturday, lunchtime ... the Saturday matinee at the Algoma Theatre begins in less than an hour. Burgess, my redheaded friend, will soon be knocking at the door. There will be a dime for the movie, a nickel for a chocolate bar, and a couple of hours of re-enacting with Burgess that day's episode of the Tarzan serial after the show is over and we are let out blinking in the late afternoon sun."[68]

If over these years the fare changed — silent films accompanied by organ, orchestra, or piano music gave way to the "talkies," colour replaced black and white, and the technology of cartoons improved greatly — the children's response to the Saturday matinee did not. In an atmosphere of what one described as "disorganized bedlam," "they stamped their feet, went on an endless procession to the bathroom," hissed scenes they didn't like, "threw stuff over the edge of the balcony and at each other," and otherwise "did all the things you couldn't do at school."

Movies sometimes frightened their youthful audiences, and might even bring on nightmares. Watching Son of Lassie, Jean Little "had both hands tightly pressed over my ears, and I kept shutting my eyes and then opening them a slit only to squeeze them shut again ... Suddenly one of the Germans raised his rifle and fired. With a spring, I was out of my front-row seat and under the stage, crouching among the litter of candy wrappers. Now, with both eyes and ears as closed as I could get them, I was moaning 'Tell me when it's over. Tell me when it's over.'"[69] "It was funny," noted "Candice," because "during cowboy movies when the guys died, my sister would always think they were dead so we had to sit through the movie again to make sure they weren't."[70] However, most children learned to know what to expect, looking forward, as one explained, to "the safe but delicious terror" brought on by certain movies. Sometimes they employed such mechanisms as closing, or partly closing, their eyes, covering their ears, or putting their heads down during the parts they both did and did not want to watch.

But there was sometimes a grim side to the matinee experience. "Anita" remembered, of a matinee in the late 1950s, "this creepy kind of man who sat beside me and kept putting his hand on my leg, just above the knee. I kept wriggling, trying to move further away. I was really afraid to yell out or even say a single word, except I started to cry. He said a really bad word, got out of his seat and disappeared into the dark."[71] As was the case with other sexual assaults, children's fears of what they often did not know, or fear of in some way of being blamed for what was happening, meant that many, perhaps most, such attacks passed unreported.

Even if they seemed to pay them little conscious attention, children absorbed something of history and current affairs from the wider world displayed in films and newsreels. Films and newsreels also taught or strengthened racial, gender, ethnic, national, and class stereotypes. Blacks, whether American or as "natives" located elsewhere, were never taken seriously but seen as figures of fun or fear.[72] Over the century films depicting wars at various times demonized native North Americans, Germans, Italians, Japanese, Russians, North Vietnamese, Chinese, Iranians, and Iraqis. In 1945, scenes of Nazi concentration and death camps, and of released prisoners-of-war who had been captured by the Japanese, deeply disturbed some youngsters.[73] Such westerns as Little Big Horn portrayed Indians as vicious savages, and such adventure films as The Siege implied that many Muslims were terrorists. Movies also reinforced gender stereotypes. From Snow White and the Seven Dwarfs (1937) through to Mulan (1998), the heroines of Disney cartoon features were destined for a happy-ever-after marriage.[74]

Girls and boys looked at films and later at television in different ways, and movies thus added another dimension to emerging gender identities. Boys identified themselves with the leading male characters, especially when they were involved in vigorous activities: fighting, shooting, riding horses, and so on. When the male lead turned to romance, boys jeered. In their fantasies, and later in their play, boys saw themselves in the hero's role as he dealt with the villain. Girls identified with female stars in a more romantic way. They enjoyed the tender moments between romantic leads, and sometimes wept during scenes that were sad. They carefully studied the hairstyles and clothing of attractive women. Girls disliked the noise made by boys during "love" scenes and tried to hush them. In their fantasies, girls saw themselves in a romantic relationship with the male lead.

During the years of strict movie censorship — from the late 1920s to the 1970s — movies were both less violent and less sexually explicit than later became the case. Daydreams then neither led to an explicit understanding of the grim realities of violent death nor, in male–female relationships, beyond dreams of hand-holding, embracing, kissing, and so on. The introductory vignettes dealing with Scream 2 and Star Wars suggest, however, that children have less difficulty with the subject matter of more recent films than adults have feared.

The social value of the Saturday matinee and other shared movie experiences carried over into childhood discourse and play. A woman noted we "would get together and retell the movie with much arguing over the sequence of events."[75] In the case of a particularly good movie, a number of women reported, they "would spend the whole week reconstructing it with an effort to get the dialogue correct and facial expressions described accurately."[76] Boys built much of their play around activities (and stereotypes) they had seen in films, especially in war movies and westerns. In fact, the stereotyping was so strong that, as Judge Albert Scow reported, at the Alert Bay residential school he attended, children often "re-enacted some of the more dramatic scenes of the movie and of course we played cowboys and Indians. Everyone wanted to be a cowboy; nobody wanted to be an Indian."[77] As the opening vignette featuring Annie Mayes suggested, the coming of videos that one could play over and over again intensified the possibilities for the imaginative employment of movie events.

Movies sometimes served as a sort of job training. When he was about nine years old, Sammy Luftspring's father took him to his first boxing match, where he "immediately fell in love with the sport." After watching the excitement, including a victory procession, Luftspring, who went on to be a championship boxer, reported: "That was the night I decided on my life goal. I, too, would take a shot at becoming a king." Luftspring started to box before he was ten. He then attended the movies on Saturday "to study the previous week's main eventer from Madison Square Garden," a regular feature of the newsreels of the day, often staying through three or even four performances of the program. "How fascinated, how hypnotized I could get ... seeing on that screen an arsenal of ring techniques ..."[78] When actor Al Waxman saw *The Jolson Story*, he "couldn't leave the theatre. I sat and watched the next showing and the next, until the last showing that day. And then I came back every Saturday with a lunch that I had packed so I wouldn't have to leave the theatre until the last showing was completed." In all, Waxman saw the film "twenty-seven times ... I bought all his records ... I began to imitate him ... that is, in front of a record player, playing his songs."[79]

Not all children went to the Saturday matinee. Some stayed away through choice; they found the noise, and the press of so many children confined in a small space, uncomfortable or even frightening. Some families took up all of their youngsters' non-school time with family chores. Other families objected to movies on religious, moral, or safety grounds, and forbade their children to attend them.[80] "John" noted that the "only time we went to the theatre was to see the Coronation of Queen Elizabeth II. The pastor of our church went to the school ... I guess he gave them permission to take the kids."[81] Nonetheless, most children made it their business to have at least a rough idea of what was going on in the world of the feature film, the cartoons, and the weekly serials.

Radio was the century's second great new medium. In the early 1920s, crystal set radios, listened to through earphones, served as a novelty item for children and adults alike. With the addition of amplifiers, radios became an exciting centre of family rather than individual entertainment. Of himself and his childhood friend Glenn Gould, Robert Fulford observed: "We were vehemently part of the first and last radio generation, the people for whom radio was a central medium of communication ... We were both born in 1932, just as the Americans and Canadians were clicking into the idea of national radio ... it became the center [sic] of our knowledge of the world." Fulford explained that a "large part of music came to Glenn through the radio ... for him it was radio and live performances, and records I think were in third place."[82]

Most radio stations devoted the lunch, supper, and early evening hours to programs directed to family audiences. Parents usually controlled the choice of station. Families, "everyone sitting around in the living room," listened to "Don Messer," "The Happy Gang," "Saturday Night Barn Dance," and to hockey and baseball games. Robert Thompson recalled "Sports broadcasts that held you riveted to the set included the Joe Louis fights ... and Hockey Night in Canada with Foster Hewitt."[83] Many other families joined the Waxmans in listening to such American shows as "'Lux Theater of the Air,' 'The Jack Benny Show,' 'Fibber McGee and Mollie,' 'Wayne and Shuster,' [and] all the serials: 'The Lone Ranger,' 'The Green Hornet,'

'Suspense,' 'Inner Sanctum.' So many trips into fun, fright and fantasy."[84] Family members listened as they went about their tasks. Thus radio and doing the dishes became part of the routines in many families as parents and children listened together as they did this pervasive chore.

In the late afternoon and on weekends, some radio stations carried programs for children; "Audrey" reported that two "radio programs that we could not miss were 'Maggie Muggins' and 'Just Mary.'"[85] "Little Orphan Annie," "Dick Tracy," "The Lone Ranger," and other children's programs on private stations had "clubs" that youngsters could join, usually in exchange for cereal boxtops or other proofs of purchase of the sponsor's product. In exchange, children received badges, secret codes, and other inexpensive paraphernalia, thus adding a new dimension to traditional youthful activities.

While many people, especially men, recall listening to championship boxing matches, especially those featuring the American Joe Louis, hockey was the most popular of radio sports. Harvey Kirck reported, "Our 'local' station was CJKL in Kirkland Lake, which carried CBC programs, including the Saturday night hockey games ... Is there a middle-aged man anywhere who did not collect Bee Hive Golden Syrup hockey photos in his youth? I had a collection a couple of inches high, and right on top were Syl Apps, Gordie Drillon, and Bob Davidson — all glorious action pictures, with the players cutting in front to the camera, sticks low and poised, skates sending up a shower of ice that seemed to leap right out at you."[86] A later generation collected hockey cards, initially distributed in bubble-gum packages.

While family radios became increasingly widespread in urban Canada through the late 1920s and 1930s, they were still rare in rural Canada. Battery radios were expensive and inconveniently took their power from "wet-cell" (or a combination of dry-cell and wet-cell) batteries. Since wet-cell batteries had to be recharged, involving either a windmill charger or a long trip to town, families rationed radio listening. Rural listening to distant stations also brought problems with static. Thus Roch Carrier's family radio "crackled like an egg that's cooking in a frying pan."[87] Nonetheless, rural listening patterns resembled their urban counterparts. In the 1930s, in the outport settlement of Ship Island, in Bonavista Bay on the northeast coast of Newfoundland, Walter Carter joined other local boys at his uncle's home to listen to "The Adventures of Superman."[88]

As small radio sets became widely available and increasingly inexpensive, especially after the development of transistors, older youngsters acquired their own. This change was accompanied by a rapid extension of commercial radio programming directly focused on the adolescent consumers. Although not the targeted audience, children joined teenagers in abandoning programs directed at wide audiences for those "hosted" by disc jockeys who played popular music, often in a "top 40s" format. In Toronto, radio station CHUM made a local star out of "Jungle" Jay Nelson, as did Vancouver's CJOR of "Red" Robinson, who in 1957 interviewed a visiting Elvis Presley for his audience. In Windsor, *the* station to listen to was CKLW and, in Montreal, CFCA.

Jeanne Beker recalled that her "palm-sized, bright orange and gold radio, with the brand 'Hollywood' emblazoned across the front, was one of the most fascinating and liberating things I'd ever owned. It transported me to worlds outside the confines of my safe, suburban bedroom, where cute deejays talked to you under the covers, late into the night ... I was 10 years old when I got that radio. By the time I was 12, I knew every pop song by heart. My six-transistor had become a constant companion, a valuable ticket to life beyond Grade 7."[89] Cynthia Good explained that through radio there was a "pre-Beatles me and a post-Beatles me."[90]

Prompted by their radio (and, later, television) listening, some youngsters, as well as their teen-aged siblings, also listened to their favourite singers on records, a practice made much more widespread with the introduction in the 1950s of inexpensive 45rpm records and record players. Youngsters quickly acquired their own records of current pop favourites such as Presley, the Beatles, through to the compact discs of rap stars of the 1990s. In August 1966, Shelley Fralic was "barely 13 … My best friend Debbie and I are sitting on my bedroom floor … On the table, a transistor radio turned up loud … It is everything. My connection. To the music, to the world, to the voices of my generation." Fralic won a ticket to go to Seattle to see the Beatles. "To be honest, I don't remember much else about the trip. (Except the screaming, of course … And to this day, my mother still can't believe that she and all those other parents let their tender baby girls get on a bus going to another country with a 20-year-old rock jock with a reputation)."[91]

In her study of women in her 1961 class at R. H. King Collegiate in Scarborough, Ontario, Maggie Siggins noted a central characteristic of popular music of her school years but one that also applies to much of the twentieth century. For youngsters of the 1950s and 1960s, she explains, their "music world, the beat we danced to in the gym Friday nights, was entirely a masculine phenomenon … That girls could be the originators, the creators of any type of music never entered our heads."[92] It was not until the 1970s that a significant number of women, including Connie Francis, Anne Murray, and Peggy Lee, began to appear amongst the higher rankings on the popular music charts.

In the 1950s television gradually replaced radio as the centre of family entertainment.[93] As television reception spread across Canada — often first from nearby stations in the United States — many families began to spend time, including mealtime, together in front of their black-and-white set. They watched the news, "Howdie Doodie," "Highway Patrol," "George Gobel," "wrestling," and, as the CBC network came to their community, the televised version of "Hockey Night in Canada." Together, families watched Elvis Presley and then the Beatles on the "Ed Sullivan Show." Television news programs took more children into the wider world than had other media. Watching supper hour news programs ended such sheltering from violence as movie censorship had tried to accomplish. Depictions of natural disasters, American civil rights marches, and political demonstrations in all parts of the world, and of wars in Vietnam, the Middle East, and Africa opened many youngsters' eyes to the brutality and violence that has always been a characteristic of human relations.

As it had been earlier with the Saturday matinee, it was essential to know what went on in the popular programs in order to take part in peer-group discourse. Those children without television visited those who did have it. The ingenious efforts made by others to watch testify as to the importance of knowing what went on. In the early 1950s, Murray McLauchlan's family did not have a television but neighbours across the street did. The McLauchlan children sat in their glassed-in sunporch, telephoned the neighbour's children, "and we'd all sit on the daybed listening to the sound on the telephone as we watched through the window."[94] In 1957, when she was about ten, Catherine Macleod's family emigrated from Scotland and settled first in a trailer park in Fruitland, near Hamilton, Ontario. She wrote that before "we got our own television, my brother and I would slip out on moist summer nights to perch ourselves on a neighbour's trailer hitch and watch" whatever the Turners were watching, all to the sounds of crickets. "If the neighbours knew our faces were pressed to their window they never let on."[95]

Some programs for children made life-long impressions on their youthful watchers. Every child who could do so watched the "Mickey Mouse Club" and "Captain Kangaroo," both now fondly recalled. Nick Finnamore, of Arthurette, NB, reported that, on reading the obituary of Robert Homme, "Childhood visions of the Friendly Giant in his suit, Jerome with his head in the window and Rusty in his bag passed through my mind. I could hear the Friendly Giant's gentle voice offering 'a little chair for one of you, an armchair for two or more of you to curl up in, and for someone who likes to rock, a rocking chair in the middle.'"[96] Of Ernie Coombs as

"Mr. Dressup," Karen Chee wrote, "He taught me English when I only knew how to speak the Cantonese of my parents. He taught me creativity and imagination ... Along with my parents and 'Sesame Street,' Mr. Dressup nurtured me into becoming a healthy, happy child. He represented stability in my world."[97]

A multiplicity of channels and the increasing numbers of families owning more than one television set gradually separated children and adults into separate audiences. Some programs, however, were so popular that both parents and children made a point of keeping up with what went on in them. They puzzled over the final couplet in the theme song of "All in the Family" ("Gee our old LaSalle ran great ...") and the various levels of meaning in "The Simpsons."

From the late 1950s onward, however, children's viewing was dominated by commercial television. Many stations began to schedule special cartoon programs for children, especially on Saturday mornings. By the end of the century children with access to cable television could find cartoons at virtually any time of the day, but especially before and after school. Increasingly, the most popular of these programs were tied to commercial products that they advertised aggressively.

In the latter years of the century, the appearance of video cassettes and the video cassette recorder would turn cinema into family entertainment analogous to the earlier days of radio and then television. Parents rented or bought tapes of movies deemed suitable for children, who then watched them over and over again. Saturday matinees virtually disappeared as younger children watched television cartoon programs and videos, alone or with friends. Their older siblings turned to "adult" films, especially those featuring "special effects" and considerable violence. Although adolescents often rented the latter, most preferred to see them on the large screen in the company of friends. By the end of the century, cinema permeated the lives of children more completely than ever before.

In the final years of the century, computers, and especially computer games, e-mail "chat" rooms, the Internet, and cellular telephones added themselves to the array of media enjoyed by the young. For some young people, and especially those who did not fit into a school hierarchy, the Internet provided an alternative social network. Chad Skelton explained that he "didn't have the school spirit to be on student council, the muscles to make the football team or the artistic flair to try out for the school play." He spent his time "with my two or three good friends ... [and] hours every week online." There, he "found people who shared my interests ... The online community became my circle of friends, a place where I fit in, an oasis from the intense stress and loneliness of high school. Once every few months a bunch of us would ... meet for dinner. In short, my online life made my high-school years bearable."[98]

In 2000 and 2001, a study funded by the federal government and conducted by the non-profit Media Awareness Network of Ottawa surveyed over a thousand Canadian families and, later, thousands of children and youth as to how the latter use the Internet. These surveys revealed a wide discrepancy between what parents believed about their children's use of the Internet and how the latter actually used it. The fact that many youngsters reported visiting pornographic sites and adult chat rooms alarmed at least some of those who examined the findings of the studies. Others were less concerned. Is the fact that boys are far more likely than girls to visit adult sites a matter of new concern, or but the most recent manifestation of the perennial interest that boys, even quite young ones, have always displayed in sex? This and other aspects of the topic are certainly worthy of study, and parents, teachers, researchers, and social commentators will undoubtedly return to it in the new century.[99]

III

My conclusions about the role played by the media in the culture of Canadian children in the twentieth century are tentative ones. Clearly, books, magazines, radio and television programs, the Internet, and, especially, movies played a major role in children's lives. Some roles were within the conscious or unconscious intentions of the adults who created and supervised the media. Although certain things children read may have undermined those gender, class, racial, ethnic, political, or national stereotypes that pervaded popular culture, most media ceaselessly reinforced them. Nonetheless, both on their own and as members of their peer group, children also employed media in ways of their own devising to meet needs arising out of youthful culture. In "cowboys and Indians" those playing the latter insisted on winning some of the time, and many a Barbie, imagined as a movie heroine, had simulated sexual intercourse with a star represented by Ken. Further, although youngsters valued these media mostly for their entertainment, willy-nilly they also informed them about the world in which they lived.

Second, this paper suggests some of the influence on children that flowed from the human voice. Since it was the medium of family, school, congregational, and playground discourse, what has been said here only hints at the importance of the spoken word in the lives of the young. It but touches on voices raised in song. Many of my informants told me that they could still hear the voices of parents, grandparents, and teachers both in their minds and in their dreams. Perhaps "the voices of childhood" deserve a separate investigation.

Finally, an observation triggered by the historian of colonial America, Bernard Bailyn. In an influential interpretive essay, Bailyn defined education "not only as formal pedagogy but as the entire process by which a culture transmits itself across the generations."[100] Like other historians of education, I enthusiastically quoted Bailyn's definition to students over the years. Also, like my colleagues, I made but limited use of Bailyn's formulation in my own research and writing. Although I have described here how some popular elements in the process of cultural transmission were looked upon by Canadian children, we really know little about how their outlook on their culture was actually affected by media.

Writer Joy Kogawa was born in Vancouver in the mid-1930s. In 1942, she with other Japanese Canadians was interned. "In Slocan I read the *Book of Knowledge* and also the *Book of Golden Deeds*. There was a poem in one of them by 'Author Anonymous' that somehow seemed to make things possible for me. I aspired to have one poem published before I died." In contrast to modern youngsters raised on Bugs Bunny and Road Runner, she "was lucky enough to have been exposed to both Japanese folk stories and Christian stories in the Anglican Church. I went to a whole range of Sunday schools. The Power Rangers teach that might is right. It makes me weep."[101]

Since they are widely shared, we have to take seriously the sorts of concerns embedded in Kogawa's comparison between her experience of the media and that of present-day children. While I'm not sure that weeping is in order, probably some vigilance is. Nonetheless, about the only firm judgment I will venture is that, so far, none of the media has had anywhere nearly as much negative effect on the young as was foretold in the warnings of their critics.

NOTES

1. I gave an earlier version of this paper to the European Social Science History Conference in Amsterdam in March 1998. Small portions of it have been drawn, much recast, from my *Growing Up: Childhood in English Canada from the Great War to the Age of Television* (Toronto: University of Toronto Press, 1997).

2. Winnifred Woolryche, Toronto, to Grace, 26 Mar. 1901. Letter in the possession of the writer.

3. James H. Gray, *The Boy from Winnipeg* (Toronto: Macmillan, 1970), 14–15. The first commercial radio broadcasts in Canada took place in 1919. Sandy Stewart, *A Pictorial History of Radio in Canada* (Toronto: Gage, 1975), 29–30.

4. Toronto *Globe and Mail*, 16 Aug. 1997, C1.

5. *Vancouver Sun*, 3 Jan. 1998, D2.

6. Susan Mayes, "The Tao of Boba Flett," *Vancouver Sun*, 3 June 2000, D13.

7. Kenneth Tynan's journals, 19 Oct. 1975, as quoted in *The New Yorker*, 14 Aug. 2000, 64.

8. Canadian research on media and young people is listed in Neil Sutherland, Jean Barman, and Linda L. Hale, eds., *History of Canadian Childhood and Youth: A Bibliography* (Westport, CN: Greenwood, 1993) and Sutherland, Barman, and Hale, eds., *Contemporary Canadian Childhood and Youth: A Bibliography* (Westport CT: Greenwood, 1993). The latter volume, for example, lists over 120 items under the heading "Media Impact." Recent psychological and social science research on children and television is summarized in Maire Messenger Davies, *'Dear BBC': Children, Television Storytelling and the Public Sphere* (Cambridge: Cambridge University Press, 2001).

9. I discuss the reliability and other aspects of memories of childhood in Sutherland, *Growing Up*, chap. 1.

10. Toronto *Globe and Mail*, 3 Feb. 2001, R1–2.

11. As later pages will show, most of the autobiographies and biographies of those born after mid-century that I consulted are of media "personalities." Their scripts may not always be representative of their cohort.

12. Jessie L. Beattie, *A Season Past: Reminiscences of a Rural Canadian Childhood* (Toronto: McClelland and Stewart, 1969), 50–51.

13. Henry Pennier, *Chiefly Indian: The Warm and Witty Story of a British Columbia Half Breed Logger*, ed. Herbert L. McDonald (West Vancouver: Graydonald, 1972), 17–18.

14. Doug Smith, *Joe Zuken: Citizen and Socialist* (Toronto: Lorimer, 1990), 12.

15. Ray Guy, "Water Street's ebb and flow," *Canadian Geographic*, 1999 Annual, 59.

16. Lee Maracle, *Bobbi Lee: Indian Rebel* (Toronto: Women's Press, 1990), 23.

17. J. Angus MacLean, *Making It Home: Memoirs of J. Angus MacLean* (Charlottetown: Ragweed, 1998).

18. Helen Sigurdson, *I Wanted You to Know* (Winnipeg: JP & Associates, 1994), 25.

19. John Norris, *Wo Lee Stories: Memories of a Childhood in Nelson, BC* (New Denver: Twa Corbies, 1997), 53.

20. Stompin' Tom Connors, *Stompin' Tom: Before the Fame* (Toronto: Penguin, 1995), 13.

21. Rita MacNeil, with Anne Simpson, *On a Personal Note* (Toronto: Key Porter, 1998), 19, 41, 60.

22. Marianne Burwood Hollanby, *I Remember in Colour* (London: M. B. Hollanby, 1999), facing p. 17.

23. Mary Lawrence, *My People, Myself* (Prince George, BC: Caitlin Press, 1996), 23–25.

24. Earl S. Baity, *I Remember Chilako* (Prince George, BC: Prince George Printers, 1978), 71–72.

25. Ernest F. "Fee" Hellman, *Kootenay Country: One Man's Life in the Canadian Rockies* (Bothwell, WA: Alaska Northwest Books, 1990), 9, 13.

26. Duke DeCoursey, *All in a Lifetime: Newspapering and Other Pioneer Adventures* (Squamish, BC: Parkview Publishing, n.d.), 32–33.

27. I did not understand oblique references to this case that came up in at least three interviews until I read Howard White, "Duchaume: Anatomy of a Legend," *Raincoast Chronicles* 9 (1979): 51–57.

28. Phyllis Grosskurth, *Elusive Subject: A Biographer's Life* (Toronto: Macfarlane, Walter & Ross, 1999), 20–21.

29. R. F. Sparkes, *The Winds Softly Sigh* (St. John's: Breakwater, 1981), 34–35.

30. *Victoria Times Colonist*, 7 July 2000, 5.

31. *National Post*, 8 July 2000, W12.

32. Gertrude Story, *The Last House on Main Street* (Saskatoon: Thistledown, 1998), 98.

33. Takashima, *A Child in a Prison Camp* (Montreal: Tundra 1971), chap. 3.

34. Jim Egan, *Challenging the Conspiracy of Silence: My Life as a Canadian Gay Activist*, comp. and ed. Donald W. McLeod (Toronto: Homewood Books, 1998), 18.

35. Harvey Kirck, with Wade Rowland, *Nobody Calls Me Mister Kirck* (Toronto: Collins, 1985), 7.

36. Norah L. Lewis, ed., *"I want to join your club": Letters from Rural Children, 1900–1920* (Waterloo: Wilfrid Laurier University Press, 1996).

37. Andrea Lebowitz and Gillian Milton, *Gilean Douglas: Writing Nature, Finding Home* (Victoria: Sono Nis, 1999), 21.

38. Claire Drainie Taylor, *The Surprise of My Life* (Waterloo: Wilfrid Laurier University Press, 1998). Lloyd Person also described the pleasure he derived from the same feature. See Lloyd H. Person, *No Foot in Heaven* (Saskatoon: Western Producer, 1978), 5–6.

39. Mordecai Richler, "The Great Comic Book Heroes," in *Hunting Tigers Under Glass: Essays and Reports* (London: Panther, 1971), 78–79.

40. Paul Jay, "Wolverine," *Saturday Night*, May 1999, 24. Wolverine comics began to appear in the early 1970s.

41. Rosemary Sullivan, *Shadow Maker: The Life of Gwendolyn MacEwen* (Toronto: HarperCollins, 1995), 37–41.

42. Ibid., 40.

43. Helen Porter, *Below the Bridge: Memories of the South Side of St. John's* (St. John's: Breakwater, 1979), 84.

44. *Vancouver Sun*, 1 May 1999, A22.

45. Jessie Mifflin, *A Collection of Memories by Jessie Mifflin* (St John's: Harry Cuff, 1989), 4.

46. Linda Turk, *Thunder Bay Chronicle-Journal*, 9 Jan. 2000, C1.

47. Dorothy Joan Harris, "Most people would find it hard to pinpoint their earliest memory," in *Too Young to Fight: Memories from Our Youth During World War II*, ed. Priscilla Galloway (Toronto: Stoddart, 1999), 51.

48. Mary Pratt, *A Personal Calligraphy* (Fredericton: Goose Lane, 2000), 51.

49. Turn-of-the-century concern about unsuitable books for children is discussed in Neil Sutherland, *Children in English-Canadian Society: Framing the Twentieth Century Consensus* (Reprint: Waterloo: Wilfrid Laurier University Press, 2000), 19–21.

50. New York: Kennikat Press, 1954.

51. Mona Gleason, "'They have a bad effect': Crime Comics, Parliament, and the Hegemony of the Middle Class in Postwar Canada," in *Pulp Demons: International Dimensions of the Postwar Anti-Comic Campaigns*, ed. John Lent (Madison, NJ: Fairleigh Dickinson University Press, 1999), 129–54.

52. Three books excluded from Surrey school classrooms are texts written for primary-grade youngsters: Rosamund Elwin and Michele Paulse, *Asha's Mums* (Toronto: Women's Press, 1990); Johnny Valentine, *One Dad, Two Dads, Brown Dads, Blue Dads* (Boston: Alyson, 1994); and Leslie Newman, *Belinda's Bouquet* (Boston: Alyson, 1991); see *Vancouver Sun*, 22 June 2000, B1, B4.

53. Mea culpa. First Nations are harshly described in my two 1960s high school texts. Neil Sutherland and Edith Deyell, *Making Canadian History*, v. 1 & 2 (Toronto: Gage, 1966; 1967).

54. Farley Mowat, *Born Naked* (Toronto: Key Porter, 1993), 51.

55. Sigurdson, *I Wanted You to Know*, 11.

56. *Vancouver Sun*, 4 March 2000, E11.

57. Church concerts, called "Times" in Newfoundland and elsewhere, are vividly evoked in R. F. Sparkes, *The Winds Softly Sigh* (St. John's: Breakwater, 1981), 99–102.

58. Joseph Wilder, *Read All About It: Reminiscences of an Immigrant Newsboy* (Winnipeg: Peguis Publishers, 1978), 64. In *O Time in Your Flight* (Madeira Park: Harbour, 1979), 116–22, Hubert Evans evokes the excitement aroused by the visit of a medicine show to a small Ontario town at the turn of the century.

59. Mary Mckenzie (pseudonym), *When I Was Thirteen* (Aylmer, ON: Aylmer Press, 1979), 37, 43.

60. Al Waxman, *That's What I Am* (Toronto: Malcolm Lester Books, 1999), 14.

61. Sandra Woolfrey, "Growing Up in Bloomfield: How I Got Culture in the 40's and 50's," *County Magazine: The Magazine of Prince Edward County* 18, no. 85 (Fall 1997): 21.

62. My subjective evaluation is confirmed, at least for American children, by an extensive investigation into the role of motion pictures in the lives of young people conducted by social scientists under the auspices of the Payne Foundation. The research, conducted between 1929 and 1933, is summarized in Henry James Forman, *Our Movie Made Children* (New York: Macmillan, 1933).

63. Daphne Marlatt and Carole Itter, eds., *Opening Doors: Vancouver's East End* (Victoria: Provincial Archives, 1979), 28.

64. See "Charlie Chaplin went to France …" in Edith Fowke, *Sally Go Round the Sun: 300 Songs, Rhymes and Games of Canadian Children* (Toronto: McClelland and Stewart, 1969), 60. See also "Charlie Chaplin," in *The Lore and Language of Schoolchildren*, ed. Iona and Peter Opie (Oxford: Oxford, 1959), 108–10, for the worldwide use of various versions of this rhyme.

65. Canadian Childhood History Project (CCHP) interview.

66. Kirck, *Nobody Calls Me Mister Kirck*, 22.

67. Norris, *Wo Lee Stories*, 75.

68. Morley Torgov, *A Good Place to Come From* (Toronto: Lester and Orpen, 1974), 39.

69. Jean Little, "I sat in Loews Theatre …" in *Too Young to Fight: Memories from Our Youth During World War II*, ed. Priscilla Galloway, (Toronto: Stoddart, 1999), 80.

70. Quoted in Lorraine Blashill, *Remembering the '50s: Growing Up in Western Canada* (Victoria: Orca, 1997), 107.

71. Quoted in ibid., 102.

72. Many of these caricatures are shown in clips in Spike Lee's film *Bamboozled* (2000).

73. See, for example, Joe Rosenblatt, *Escape from the Glue Factory: A Memoir of a Paranormal Toronto Childhood in the Late Forties* (Toronto: Exile Editions, 1985), 47–48.

74. See Kathi Maio, "Disney's Dolls," *New Internationalist* 309 (Dec. 1988): 12–14.

75. CCHP interview.

76. Ibid.

77. Quoted in J. R. Miller, *Shingwauk's Vision: A History of Native Residential Schools* (Toronto: University of Toronto Press, 1996), 281.

78. Sammy Luftspring, with Brian Swarbrick, *Call Me Sammy* (Scarborough: Prentice-Hall, 1975), 34–35, 43.

79. Waxman, *That's What I Am*, 35–36.

80. Seventy-six children died in a motion picture theatre fire in Montreal on 9 Jan. 1927. Toronto *Globe*, 10 Jan. 1927, 1, facsimile reprint, in Toronto *Globe and Mail*, 9 Jan. 1999, D9.

81. Quoted in Blashill, *Remembering the '50s*, 92.

82. Quoted in Peter F. Ostwald, *Glenn Gould: The Ecstasy and Tragedy of Genius* (New York: Norton, 1997), 64.

83. Robert H. Thompson, *Penny Candy, Bobskates and Frozen Roadapples: Growing Up in the Thirties and Forties* (Victoria: Orca, 1990), 69.

84. Waxman, *That's What I Am*, 14, 31.

85. Quoted in Blashill, *Remembering the '50s*, 87.

86. Kirck, *Nobody Calls Me Mister Kirck*, 19.

87. Roch Carrier, "I was eight years old on August 6, 1945 ..." in *Too Young to Fight*, ed. Galloway, 67.

88. Walter C. Carter, *Never a Dull Moment* (St. John's: Creative Book Publishing, 1998), 19–22.

89. *Vancouver Sun*, 26 Dec. 2000, F12.

90. On "Vinyl Café," CBC 2, 27 Jan. 2001.

91. The disc jockey who organized the contest and trip was Fred Latremouille. *Vancouver Sun*, 21 Nov. 1999, E5.

92. Maggie Siggins, *In Her Own Time: A Class Reunion Inspires a Cultural History of Women* (Toronto: HarperCollins, 2000), 558–59.

93. See Doug Owram, *Born at the Right Time: A History of the Baby Boom Generation* (Toronto: University of Toronto Press, 1996), 87–93, 152–55.

94. Murray McLauchlan, *Getting Out of Here Alive: The Ballad of Murray McLauchlan* (Toronto: Viking, 1998), 24.

95. Catherine Macleod, *Waking Up in the Men's Room: A Memoir* (Toronto: Between the Lines, 1998), 20.

96. *Maclean's Magazine*, 12 June 2000, 8.

97. *Vancouver Sun*, 21 Sept. 2001, A15; some adults who watched Coombs as children appear in "Ernie Coombs: Tales from the Tickle Trunk," a program in the CBC series "Life and Times."

98. *Vancouver Sun*, 29 May 1999, E5–6.

99. The study and comments about it are summarized in the Toronto *Globe and Mail*, 5 Jan. 2002, F6–7. The study itself can be found in Media Awareness Network, "Young Canadians in a Wired World," www.media-awareness.ca.

100. Bernard Bailyn, *Education in the Forming of American Society: Needs and Opportunities for Study* (New York: Vintage Books, 1960), 14.

101. Lisa Birnie Hobbs, "Joy Kogawa: Medieval Nun in Search of the Soul," *Western Lights: Fourteen Distinctive British Columbians* (Vancouver: Raincoast, 1996), 102–3.

Article 9.2

Ryan Edwardson

The Many Lives of Captain Canuck: Nationalism, Culture, and the Creation of a Canadian Comic Book Superhero

Issues to Consider

- Why does Edwardson see *Captain Canuck* as "a cultural artifact"? What purposes have been ascribed to this artifact, in terms of how the ideals and the imagery associated with the comic book's titular hero have been put to social and cultural uses?
- What connections does the author draw between popular culture, consumerism, and national identity?
- What made the premiere of *Captain Canuck* in 1975 "a milestone"? What was happening in Canada at the time that provided a favourable context for the comic book's launch?
- What was the public response to *Captain Canuck* in its various incarnations? What do its readers' views suggest about Canadian popular culture at the time?
- How does the history of the "made in Canada" comic book follow the path of similar attempts to establish uniquely Canadian radio programming, film, music and other forms of popular culture?

"Canada finally has her own honest-to-goodness comic magazine, with Canada's very own super-hero — Captain Canuck!" (C.C. 1).[1] *Captain Canuck*'s 1975 release was the first Canadian comic book success since the collapse of the Second World War comic book industry. Captain Canuck, clad in a red and white suit and maple leaf emblems, used his strength — derived from a healthy diet and fitness — to fight for Canadian "peace, order, and good government." He avoided violence when possible, prayed before missions, and dedicated himself to protecting Canada and the world from evildoers. Canadian readers enjoyed the familiarity of national images, symbols, and locations infused with the action-adventure format established by American comic books. Yet, despite its popularity, the comic collapsed several times due to the economics of publishing in Canada and the problem of American cultural "dumping."

Captain Canuck is more than a comic book relic, however; it is a cultural artifact, a key item in the construction of modern Canadian cultural identity and consciousness. While in print, the comic presented popular cultural characteristics, myths, symbols, and stereotypes that legitimized the national identity and reinforced the conception of Canada as a "peaceable kingdom." Following the comic's publication run, Captain Canuck was revived by the Canadian government and incorporated as a national icon valuable for fostering national awareness and pride. It is an example of perpetual nation-building, an item of popular culture

Source: Ryan Edwardson, "The Many Lives of Captain Canuck: Nationalism, Culture, and the Creation of a Canadian Comic Book Superhero," *Journal of Popular Culture* 37, no. 2: 184–201.

presenting national signifiers that, following its demise, was resurrected and recycled into a national signifier itself; it was fostered in a period of nationalism, empowered the national identity, and later was integrated into the national myth-symbol roster.

"Nationalism," according to Ernest Gellner, "is not the awakening of nations to self-consciousness: it invents nations where they do not exist" (169). Benedict Anderson has furthered this idea, arguing that nations are imagined into existence because "the members of even the smallest nation will never know most of their fellow-members, meet them, or even hear of them, yet in the minds of each lives the image of their communion" (6). Comic books, as a visual medium, engage this act of imagination, in turn facilitating the mental construction of the nation and national identity. It is an act that may be an essential part of being Canadian. Canadian cultural historian Daniel Francis has argued (perhaps too generally but a valid observation nonetheless) that "because we lack a common religion, language or ethnicity, because we are spread out so sparsely across such a huge piece of real estate, Canadians depend on this habit of 'consensual hallucination' more than any other people" (10).

National identity, it can be argued, is also consumed into existence. Commodities can embody and popularize social identities and lifestyles — such as Nike and "Just do it" or the Body Shop and environmentalism — which are in turn confirmed through the consumption of those products (Klein). Through the consumption of commodities proposing certain myths, symbols, and values, national identities can be popularized and validated. In the area of Japanese national identity, Kosaku Yoshino has made some interesting insights into "a 'market' process whereby ideas of cultural differences are 'produced,' 'reproduced' and 'consumed'" (9). By drawing on Jean Baudrillard's argument that consumption "is a whole system of values, with all that expression implies in terms of group integration and social control functions" (81), one can see how cultural consumption provides a basis for identity construction. The material consumed carries a series of meanings that are either accepted or rejected by the consumer. [...]

[...] Consequently, in mass culture one can find mass national identity. Captain Canuck's red and white costume adorned with maple leaves signified his Canadianness, while his moralism, natural strength, and self-sacrificing persona reinforced conceptions of Canadians as polite, kind, moral, heroic peacekeepers. Distinctively national comic books, then, are vessels for transmitting national myths, symbols, ideologies, and values. They popularize and perpetuate key elements of the national identity and ingrain them into their readers — especially, given the primary readership, younger generations experiencing elements of that identity for the first time.

ALL IN THE FAMILY: CAPTAIN CANUCK'S COMIC BOOK LINEAGE

Late nineteenth-century Canadian newspapers often explored social, political, and cultural issues through comical caricatures, not only to highlight the editor's view, but to use as an aid for those lacking reading abilities. In the tradition of Miss Britannia, Canada often was cast as Miss Canada, the young daughter of the British Empire, or joined other masculine characters — including Britain's John Bull and America's Uncle Sam — as a youthful and sprightly Johnny or Jack Canuck.[2] Political parties, for example, attacked each other through newspaper cartoons that depicted Miss Canada in jeopardy, her virginal Victorian morality threatened by the older, seedy Uncle Sam. Jack or Johnny Canuck, on the other hand, embodied the "youthful" national spirit, ready to take on the world or, more often, confront Uncle Sam over an issue of trade or natural resources.

Comic books first appeared in the early 1930s, bringing together collections of reprinted comic strips. By 1938, stimulated by the popularity of Superman and similar superhero figures, they often included full-length original stories.[3] From the very beginning, the lack of a

Canadian publishing industry and the cheap cost of American comic overruns ensured that the Canadian market was dominated by American comics. Stories of American heroes and villains supplied entertainment through exciting and spectacular figures, including Superman, the Flash, and Batman. They were a part of the American monomyth that "secularizes Judeo-Christian ideals by combining the selfless individual who sacrifices himself for others and the zealous crusader who destroys evil" (Land and Trimble 158). Yet Canadians share those "youthful, physically vigorous" and "morally upright" heroes, not only because their popular fiction is predominantly American in origin, but because their national, social, and economic developments have been similar. Thus, while the comics were of American origin, they engaged the imagination of Americans and Canadians by drawing on a shared North American monomyth of individualism, self-sacrifice, and personal humility. The fact that the superheroes existed in American cities like New York — or, at best, an undefined or imaginary "Anywhere, USA" metropolis — was a requisite part of reading comics in Canada.

In 1940, however, the American comics in Canada faced a challenge they were powerless to overcome: political policymaking. American comic book dominance was delivered a swift blow by Prime Minister William Lyon Mackenzie King's War Exchange Conservation Act, which limited the importation of "nonessentials"— including comic books — as a means of conserving American dollars for the war effort. Canadian companies, previously unable to compete against the "dumped" American comics, prospered in the protected market. Maple Leaf Publishing, Anglo-American, Hillborough Studios, and Bell Features and Publishing filled the Canadian demand for comic book entertainment. They produced superhero figures in mass quantities, relying on established American character types and war-inspired storylines. Out of the numerous heroes emerged Canada's first distinctly Canadian superhero, Nelvana of the North. The product of Hillborough Studios, Nelvana drew on the powers of the Aurora Borealis to fight super-powered Nazi agents. Nelvana's name came from an Inuit legend, but she was drawn as an Anglo-Saxon and clothed in a cape and miniskirt. In *Guardians of the North: The National Superhero in Canadian Comic-Book Art*, John Bell, Canada's foremost comic book historian, describes Nelvana as coming from the "same mold as the many white queens and goddesses that had appeared in popular fiction" (7). Nelvana was joined by Johnny Canuck in 1942, taking care of Nazis with his fast fists and solid jaw in adventure-packed (if slightly monotonous) comic book stories. Lacking superpowers but endowed with wit, charisma, and a strong right hook, Johnny Canuck traveled the world fighting Nazi tyranny. The war's end, however, brought the return of American comic books and the end of comic book Nazi antagonists. Canadian production quickly ended, once again unable to compete with the cheaper American material.

Until the 1970s, Canadians were limited to American comic books. There was little to ask for in the way of quality, as the comics supplied elaborate plot lines, skillful artistry, and exciting characters. The comics were very American, however, in their symbols, figures, myths, and locations, right down to advertisements and the spelling of words. In Bell's assessment,

> what all Canadian comic-book readers of the 1950–1970 period had in common was a sense of alienation. For English Canadians, comics had become an American medium: the heroes were American, the settings were largely American, and even the alluring comic-book ads for toy soldiers and sea monkeys were American. Like U.S. television, comics seemed to contain an implicit message: Canada was a backwater bereft of heroes, bereft of guardians. For French Canadians, the medium was also dominated by the European francophone publishing houses. (*Guardians of the North* 19)

Indeed, in *Canuck Comics*, Bell notes that "Life in America, we just knew, was more exciting. Superman might visit his Fortress of Solitude in our Arctic from time to time, but never Toronto or Montreal, let alone Halifax where I lived" (13). It was a common experience for many Canadians. Reflecting on his own experience, Francis has described how in the universe I inhabited as a boy, there were no Canadian stars. There was no room; the skies were filled with the super novas of American history, politics, and pop culture…. When I was looking for "role models" … I found them on American television or in the myths of the American West or the comic books about U.S. marines in World War II. (112)

American cultural dominance increasingly came under criticism in the late 1960s, as a Canadian nationalist boom sparked an intense interest in cultural identity and concern over the lack of domestic cultural products. While American comics utilized ideas of heroism and self-sacrifice common to both Americans and Canadians, the dominance of American symbols and references drew scorn. Nationalists were especially keen to distinguish between conceptions of the American melting pot, tarnished by race riots and Vietnam violence, and the Canadian mosaic, a "peaceable kingdom" and multicultural haven of pluralism and understanding.[4] They called for cultural products reflecting distinct Canadian values, myths, and symbols.[5] Where were the Canadian songs, movies, books, and even comic books? they asked.

"UP, UP, AND AWAY, EH?": THE BIRTH OF A CANADIAN SUPERHERO

Ron Leishman, a teacher and amateur cartoonist living in Winnipeg, Manitoba, first sketched a character he called Captain Canada in 1971. About a year later, Leishman met fellow comic book fan Richard Comely at a meeting of the Church of Jesus Christ of Latter Day Saints. They talked of creating a Canadian-themed comic book based on Leishman's Captain Canada, but the venture did not look promising. They were unable to get funding through government programs or loans, and in 1974 Leishman left to work in Alberta, followed by a two-year church mission in Belgium and France (Comely 2001).

Despite Leishman's absence, Comely did not give up on the plan. There were trademark problems with the name Captain Canada, so Comely changed it to Captain Canuck. The similarity to Johnny Canuck, however, was accidental; Comely was not aware of the national Nazi fighter until after the first issue of *Captain Canuck* was published (Comely 2001). "Canuck," the slang term for a Canadian, was distinctively national but not without its drawbacks. As one fan wrote in to the comic, "I thought it was some kind of a joke. Who would seriously think of naming a hero — even a comic book hero —'Captain Canuck'? Even if he is Canadian?" (12). The editor responded that "Canuck" was just "a casual term," and "like Yankee, it depends on how and when you say it." By placing the slang in a culturally positive context, Captain Canuck empowered the term, helping to popularize it as a valid nickname for a Canadian.

The first issue of *Captain Canuck* was published in 1975 with Comely as editor, artist, writer, publisher, production manager, and floor sweeper. Comely was, however, aided by Dave Abbott's "writing assistance," and he consulted Leishman on aspects of the comic. By the third issue, he was joined by George Freeman and Jean-Claude St. Aubin on penciling and coloring duties. Its release is regarded as the beginning of English Canada's "Silver Age" of comic book production (Bell, *Guardians of the North* 39). It was a milestone in Canadian comic book production. "Captain Canuck's very existence," Bell notes, "underscored the paucity of indigenous heroes that Canadian kids had experienced throughout the fifties and sixties" (*Canuck Comics* 39).

Captain Canuck was set in the future of the early 1990s, with Canada as the dominant world superpower — certainly a situation that could only occur in a comic book — facing evil forces seeking world domination. Tom Evans, a Mountie recruited into the Canadian International Security Organization, was of British descent, clean cut, strong and stocky, part "Indian blood,"[6] bilingual, and an ardent nationalist: a suitable candidate to protect Canada. As Captain Canuck, he literally embodied the Canadian flag, clad in a red and white costume adorned with maple leaves. Joined by the French Canadian agent "Kébec" and the super-Mountie "Redcoat," Captain Canuck was the first line of defense against supervillains seeking world domination. From futuristic Mounties to a maple-leaf-emblazoned snowmobile, Comely incorporated numerous Canadian references. Nelvana of the North may have fought superagents in the arctic while Johnny Canuck was overseas, but, in the first three issues alone, Captain Canuck's travels included dog sledding across the arctic, flying over "the magnificent Rockies," strolling "across the rooftops of scenic Montreal," and being abducted from "smog-ridden Sudbury" (Issues 1–3).[7]

Comely was "moved by the nationalism at the time" and proud of the comic's origin (Comely 2001). "We're 100% Canadian," the first issue announced, with the letters column in the third issue describing "national pride and patriotism [as] worthy attributes." *Captain Canuck* tapped into the nationalism of the period, and readers responded with great enthusiasm to having a distinctively Canadian comic: "as a Canadian I am proud to see our nation's greatness recognized," "here's to success in making *Captain Canuck* 100% Canadian," and "*Captain Canuck* has brought out the nationalistic spirit in all its readers, a pride this country now needs" (Issues 2, 3) are a few of the comments mailed in. He tried to make the comic as Canadian as possible, right down to the advertising. It was not easy, however. He contacted over 600 Canadian and 250 American companies, but had more success with the American advertisers. "Hopefully," Comely noted in the second issue, "it won't be too much longer before Canadian companies realize that it would be to their advantage to advertise in a 100% Canadian magazine like Captain Canuck." The lack of a Canadian publication industry posed problems, so distribution was handled by a U.S. company (*TIME* 1975, 10).

The myths and symbols were Canadian, but Comely's interest in conspiracy theories and his Mormon beliefs shaped the comic's content. "We're proud to say that there is nothing within that is degrading or offensive," the introduction to the first issue stated. Radical Communists bent on world domination were dealt with swiftly and with as little violence as necessary.[8] Captain Canuck prayed before missions and fought with God on his side. His abilities came from his moral character and natural health, a strong contrast to the supernatural powers of the American comic book characters. "Captain Canuck's tremendous strength and endurance come from a good wholesome diet and lots of exercise," Comely explained in the second issue. "His alertness and determination come from having a strong, clean mind." As the Canadian edition of *TIME* magazine noted in its 1975 review of the comic, "What distinguishes Captain Canuck from his American counterparts? Answer: The Canadian is polite and God-fearing and, although immensely strong, is not noted for his speed" (10). Concerned about the impact of excessive violence in society, in issue 2, Comely reprinted a four-page article on "How do movies and TV influence behaviour?" from a Mormon magazine. Comely was concerned with establishing a greater moral standard than existed in many mainstream comic books. He told *TIME* that "we need some moral fiber today and U.S. comics are tending more and more to violence and sexual innuendo … [Captain Canuck] will give thanks to God from time to time. [But] I don't want people to think I'm out to subvert them through a comic" (10).

At thirty-five cents, it was significantly more expensive than the popular twenty-five-cent American comics, yet Comely tried to provide plenty of value for the money. The early issues used a higher quality glossy paper and more complex coloring than their American counterparts. The issues contained a Captain Canuck story as well as a second feature story, often featuring two of Comely's other hero figures: "Jonn," a space commander stuck on a planet of iron-age warriors, or "Catman," a costume-clad vigilante. Occasionally there was "Beyond," a comical adventure series set in the Middle Ages. The early issues also included lessons on drawing and illustrating comic characters, a gallery for reader-submitted art, and small comic strip filler. With fewer ads, "at least 30% less than most super hero comics," issue 2 boasted, and a lower comic-to-ads ratio than the American comics, Comely offered a graphic-packed comic.

Captain Canuck was a source of inspiration for many Canadian comic book artists. Bell has noted that "the comic served to demystify the comic book business. Suddenly, the dream of creating Canadian superhero comics, which so many young artists and writers obviously harbored, became attainable" (Bell, *Canuck Comics* 39).[9] Yet *Captain Canuck* could not maintain production. Comely Comix, as the business was called, described itself as "a small struggling company with grand and lofty ideas" (C.C. 3) — an accurate claim for many Canadian publishing houses. Although "Canadian content" was fostered in television and radio through broadcasting regulations, and the arts community benefited from the Canada Council for the Arts, publishing had very little protection or domestic support.[10] The extensive coloring and higher quality paper added to the cost of production, but the biggest problem was the cost of producing a comic book in Canada. The market was small, funding sparse, distribution difficult, and printing expensive. As Comely explained to the readers in issue 2,

> I'm sure you're ... aware that C.C. cost [sic] slightly more than U.S. comics. Sure, the higher quality increases the cost, but this is not the main reason. The small print runs and the fact that printing costs of comics are higher in Canada, cause our magazine to cost more than twice as much to produce than the U.S. comic magazines. I'm trying my best to bring cost down. One of the ways is to increase sales by distributing through out the U.S. as well as Canada.

Besides funding problems, the comic suffered from rigid characters, poor detailing, and unsophisticated plots with little tension or hook. In its review of the first issue, *TIME* magazine criticized its "amateurish quality" and "often clumsy artwork and story line" ("Canuck to the Rescue," 10). Issue number 3 was released in 1975, leaving the reader hanging on as Captain Canuck, badly wounded, was abducted in an ambulance by evildoers. Unfortunately, Comely Comix folded, unable to bear the costs of publishing *Captain Canuck*. It was a storyline cliffhanger that lasted for four years.

In 1979, Comely and partners, as CKR Productions in Calgary, Alberta, restarted the series at issue number 4. Comely wrote the stories, Ken Ryan was the business manager, George Freeman did the artwork, and Jean-Claude St. Aubain took care of the inking and coloring. Although this allowed Comely to focus on improving storylines, it isolated him from the aesthetic side of the comic. As of issue 5, Freeman was editing the comic with Comely as editor-in-chief.

This next generation of *Captain Canuck* maintained the focus on Canadian content. When confronted with the possibility of a Canadian civil war, for example, Captain Canuck announced that it would be stopped by "the War Measures Act! Then the Army would be everywhere!" (C.C. 6). Issue 11, set in Quebec City, had characters speaking French without translation for much of the issue, to the delight of some readers. One fan told the comic that he had "been interested in Captain Canuck over these years because of its potential to voice Canadian traditions and attitudes but never, in all that time, did I ever expect you to venture into such a sensitive area as Canadian bilingualism, especially when your magazine is so dependent on popularity for its existence" (13). Captain Canuck traveled to Halifax dockyards, Labrador ice fields, and visited his brother on a western Canadian ranch, interspersed with trips to more exotic places, including a lost South America city of gold and a multinational space station. "It is nice to see some Canadian landmarks for a change," a reader remarked, "such as Ottawa and Halifax. It is better than seeing New York and Washington all the time" (C.C. 9).

Under the new team, however, the revamped series integrated aspects of the established American comic book genre while shedding the elements that gave Comely's first three issues a grassroots feel. The religious undertone disappeared, and the conspiracy-driven plot lines were replaced by superhero supernaturalism and space-oriented themes. Captain Canuck no longer derived his strength from diet and moral cleanliness; history was rewritten, making him the product of an alien ray-beam that doubled his strength and speed (C.C. 5). Although this moved *Captain Canuck* in line with the established superhero genre, one fan complained that the change "lowers him to the level of the American super-heroes" (9). In addition, Captain Canuck became a freelance operative, serving both the Canadian government and a science-fiction-style international antiterrorist organization called Earth Patrol. Along with hoods and crooks, the Captain increasingly fought supernatural creatures and space aliens. Finally, perhaps in an attempt to spark circulation among American readers, Captain Canuck was removed from the future of the 1990s and, like most other superheroes, was relocated into the contemporary timeline — by that point, the early 1980s (13). Business manager Ken Ryan told readers that the time shift was for the best, as "a whole new lifestyle has been opened up for Captain Canuck — one that was not possible in the confines of the semi-futuristic period of the mid 1990s" (13).

The revitalized *Captain Canuck* was quite successful. In Bell's assessment, "*Captain Canuck* was transformed into one of the most accomplished alternative superhero comics ever published" (*Canuck Comics* 41). One fan confessed that "at first I only bought the comic out of Canadian pride, but now, who can resist?" (Special Summer issue 1980). In 1979, it was the bestselling comic book in Canada (C.C. 7), even though, at fifty cents an issue, it was still more expensive than many forty-cent American comics. A year later, *Captain Canuck* was the first Canadian comic to be distributed coast to coast in both Canada and the United States (10). There was even a *Captain Canuck* comic strip in the *Winnipeg Tribune*. Yet in 1981, with thirteen issues completed, Comely left *Captain Canuck*, returning to freelance design. In 1982, he released a new comic book titled *Star Rider and the Peace Machine*, but it only lasted two issues. With Comely's departure, Freeman was to take over the writing duties. Captain Canuck's time shift and the impact of Comely's departure did not have a chance to come to fruition, however, as CKR Productions only produced one more issue before financial difficulties caused it to shut down; *Captain Canuck* once again came to an end.

If Captain Canuck proved his heroism by never giving in to defeat, it reflected Comely's personal dedication to producing a Canadian comic book. In 1993, Comely and a new production staff released *Captain Canuck Reborn*, a new series with a different cast of characters and a new origin for Captain Canuck. The comic provided Comely with the opportunity to return to his original conception of *Captain Canuck* — a national superhero of natural strength and health in a comic with plenty of Canadian references and conspiracy theories.

In the new series, Darren Oak, along with his Native Canadian friend Daniel Blackbird, uncovered an international conspiracy to take over the world, led by none other than Darren's brother, Nathan, and his New World Order conglomerate. As a *Captain Canuck Reborn* commemorative trading card, released in 1993, explained,

> In a desperate attempt to rally a nation against an international conspiracy, Darren Oak becomes Captain Canuck. His big brother, Nathan, is involved in a devious plan to ignite civil war. Canada is to be HQ [Head Quarters] for a New World Order, but first they must gain complete control of Canada's government. Darren, armed only with truth and tremendous courage, must conceal his identity while he exposes the conspiracy. Inspired by a comic book, he becomes Captain Canuck.

Aided by Blackbird and other pro-Canada freedom fighters, Captain Canuck fought the New World Order on Parliament Hill, infiltrated a white-supremacist group in Lucyville, Alberta, and recovered from wounds at his home in Ourtown, Northern Ontario (C.C.R. 0–3).

Comely's skills as an artist, storywriter, and businessman had matured in the two decades since he first released *Captain Canuck*. Unfortunately, Captain Canuck once again fell victim to an enemy he could not defeat: the problems of publishing a comic book in Canada. The new series lasted for only four issues, ending in 1996 and taking with it a *Captain Canuck* newspaper strip that had started to run in various newspapers.

Captain Canuck was not only comic book entertainment, it was part of Canadian consumer culture. From the very first issue, readers were offered a barrage of items, including T-shirts, posters, iron-on crests, pens, pins, and doodle posters. Issue 7 introduced a series of merchandise with "New Captain Canuck paraphernalia to please even the pickiest patron!" There was even a Captain Canuck fan club, including a membership card and special merchandise for members only. The sale of Captain Canuck merchandise eventually made its way from the comic book and into Eaton's department stores in western Canada (Comely 2001). This was a key part of keeping the comic book going. According to Comely, "Captain Canuck merchandising made more than the sale of comic books. Printing costs were too high. The C.C. club, T-shirt licensing deal and other merchandise kept us afloat" (Comely 2001).[11] CKR Productions even went so far as to offer shares in the company to the readers. "This share bonus is not a gimmick!" the advertisement stated. "We've consulted the appropriate representatives of the Government of the Province of Alberta and we've received their cooperation and approval for our proposal to let you, the readers, actually own a part of the company" (14). It may have been a last ditch attempt to keep the company afloat, however, given that the offer was in the last issue of *Captain Canuck* to make it to press. This Canuck commodification was supported by publicity campaigns. Comely drove around Winnipeg in a yellow AMC Pacer with *Captain Canuck* emblazed on the side. As well, a 210-pound, 6'3" karate expert was hired to dress in a Captain Canuck costume and make public appearances at shopping centers and special events. Comely thought the events were quite successful (9, 11).

POST–COMIC BOOK LIFE AND THE TRANSITION FROM NATIONAL DEFENDER TO NATIONAL ICON

Nations need heroes, even fictional ones.[12] Not surprisingly, governments that lay claim to popular heroes, instituting them as representatives and manifestations of national might, validate the national identity and add cultural depth to an institutional hegemonic agent. Embracing popular culture, the Canadian government created a public showing of its comic book superheroes. From February 13 to June 7, 1992, the National Archives of Canada held "Guardians of the North: The National Superhero in Canadian Comic-Book Art," exhibiting Canadian comic books and paraphernalia, and detailing the development of Canadian comic art and superheroes. Canadian superheroes, the exhibition explained, were the "embodiment of our national spirit and identity" (Bell, *Guardians of the North* 50). Captain Canuck's natural strength and abilities, for example, were cited by the exhibition's catalogue as Canadian characteristics:

> ... typifying Canadian reticence in so many things, some of these heroes possess no actual superpowers, relying rather on superior physical and intellectual skills to enable them to combat their enemies.... In a sense, Canuck was the appropriate superhero for a middle power that was somewhat distrustful of heroism and very much aware of the limits of power. (v, 25–26)

The exhibition claimed that comics were much more than adventure stories: they probed Canadian society and reflected the issues within a national context.

> Why superheroes? Why comics? These are not just entertaining fantasy figures. They are important to our history because they are symbols of the Canadian identity. Their creators were probing issues of great concern to the Canadians of the day — World War II, national identity, our relationship with the United States. (v)

There is certainly some truth to this. As Alphons Silbermann has noted, "comics mediate, even as pure entertainment, certain mental values. Since the fact is that entertainment and information do not exclude each other, comics are latently or overtly open to any ideology" (21).

The National Archives exhibition was followed by Canada Post's recognition of five Canadian comic book heroes, institutionalizing them as important cultural icons. On October 2, 1995, Canada Post issued a booklet of ten stamps containing the "Canadian crusaders" Superman, Nelvana of the North, Fleur de Lys (who appeared in the late 1980s comic *Northguard*), Johnny Canuck, and Captain Canuck. Ironically, the government that would not provide funding for Captain Canuck two decades earlier now provided a different form of investment: a symbolic one. The Captain Canuck stamp commoditized his image in a new way, as an official national commodity — forty-five cents of federal currency added to the hats, pins, and pens Comely sold to keep the comic afloat.

Canada Post's inclusion of Superman as a Canadian superhero reflects an interesting part of the Canadian cultural psyche. Striving to establish strong cultural mythologies and heroes, it associates the nation with an internationally recognized, culturally important icon. This has been supported by some cultural nationalists, including Marsha Boulton, who gives him a section and a predominant place on the cover of *Just a Minute: Glimpses of Our Great Canadian Heritage*. Superman co-creator Joe Shuster was born in Toronto, Ontario, in 1914, and that alone was sufficient for Superman to be deemed Canadian. Shuster left Canada for the United States when he was eight years old, and Superman was not created until a decade later with his friend Jerry Siegal. First a comic strip reflecting American New Deal politics and social consciousness, it was later reconfigured into a comic book action-adventure format. Let's not forget that Superman defended "Truth, Justice, and the American Way," not Canada's motto of "Peace, Order, and Good Government." Heritage Canada reaffirmed the government's claim to Superman through historical tampering, releasing a Superman "Heritage Moment" as part of its series of sixty-second television commercials that dramatize a moment in Canadian history. The spot showed a young Joe Shuster boarding a train, ranting about a new type of superhero he was creating, and passing a drawing of Superman to his friend "Lois" as she laughed about "you Canadian kids!" It was pure fabrication. And, as author Will Ferguson has slyly noted, Captain Canuck is from Canada, Superman is from Krypton (175).[13]

The image of Captain Canuck has become so associated with Canada that the nation itself has been placed in the costume. The April 28, 1997, Canadian edition of *TIME* magazine cast Captain Canuck on its cover, along with a banner declaring that "Canada is the new superhero of global trade (and even Superman is being produced in Winnipeg these days)."[14] Inside the issue, Canada — as Captain Canuck — lifted bar graphs and hurled pie charts detailing Canada's economic strength. In the context of *TIME*, Canada *became* Captain Canuck — Canada *was* strong and powerful. The magazine detached Captain Canuck's image from the comic book and resituated it in a new context and narrative, constructing a new denotative meaning that drew on the established connotation of heroism and strength.[15]

Soon after these developments, Captain Canuck was reconfigured yet again, his status as a national icon attracting the interest of the arts community. Featuring artwork from the *Captain Canuck Reborn* series, "Canada's Own Captain Canuck: Inked Drawings by Richard Comely" was exhibited at the Burlington Art Centre in Burlington, Ontario, during the summer of 1998. By exhibiting the artwork as individual pieces instead of as part of the comic book whole, the segmented, paneled aesthetics separated the artwork from the storylines. *Captain Canuck* was no longer just a comic book; it was now popular art and material for aesthetic critique and display, the images providing content for the exhibition.

Captain Canuck — comic book superhero and national protector, embodiment of Canadian values, forty-five-cent postage stamp, Canada's alter ego, and, finally, popular art — survived not only fictional supervillains, but, perhaps even more heroically, the dangers of the Canadian publishing industry. *Captain Canuck*'s history is a story of grassroots cultural production and a distinctly national superhero who became valuable to the government it fictionally protected. The comic's demise, however, may once again be temporary. In 1999, Mark Shainblum (writer and co-creator of popular 1980s Canadian comic book *Northguard*) and Sandy Carruthers, both contributors to the early 1990s *Captain Canuck* newspaper comic strip, attempted to bring back Tom Evans as Captain Canuck in *Captain Canuck: Utopia Moments*. Plans were made for a four-issue miniseries, but these have yet to come to fruition. An issue was compiled and released on a trial promotional run limited to one hundred copies, but has not progressed any further. Comely returned to the comic book scene in 2000 with a plan for yet another Captain Canuck. Establishing media contacts and setting up an Internet Web page, his project is still in the works. Things look hopeful, though. The Canadian publishing industry is not as weak now as it was twenty (even ten) years ago. Captain Canuck may again provide a generation of Canadian comic book fans with a sense of national identity in a cultural arena where New York overwhelms New Brunswick, and one rarely sees a maple leaf.

NOTES

1. Captain Canuck citations will be listed by issue number, not page number.
2. For examples, see J. W. Bengough, *A Caricature History of Canadian Politics*.
3. For a solid overview of the transition from comic strips to comic books, see Ian Gordon, *Comic Strips and Consumer Culture, 1890–1945*.
4. William Kilbourn popularized the term in Canada with the title of his edited collection of nationalist writing, *Canada: A Guide to the Peaceable Kingdom*.
5. Defining just what constituted "Canadian," however, was a more difficult task.
6. In issue 12, Captain Canuck slipped back in time and encountered a group of Micmac Native Canadians. In hopes of ingratiating himself with them, he pulled off his mask, showing them his "Indian blood," and was welcomed by them.
7. The location of issue 3 was identified in issue 4.
8. Interestingly, the Communist leader in issue 1 was drawn so similar to Lenin that a fourteen-year-old reader wrote into the comic about it in the second issue.
9. For an interesting look at comic books and fan mentality, see Matthew J. Pustz's *Comic Book Culture: Fanboys and True Believers*.
10. The 1972 Ontario Royal Commission on Book Publishing's *Canadian Publishers and Canadian Publishing* noted that there may have been "Canadian publishers," but that did not necessarily mean that there was "Canadian publishing" (60). "Commercial realism" and profitability prevented many Canadian publishers, foreign-owned or not, from publishing large quantities of distinctly Canadian content material (63).
11. Comely puts the number of C.C. club members at 1,200–1,500. The phenomenon of comic book commodification first took hold with Detective Comics's trademarking of *Superman* and the extensive merchandising of products during the 1940s, including a toy ray gun and wristwatch. Ian Gordon explains that "In the hands of a corporation, Superman was more important as a business asset than a fictional character" (134). Merchandising hit a high point in the 1990s — with the fusion of comic book characters and global media production — with characters such as Batman commoditized into billion-dollar industries. For more information, see Ian Gordon's *Comic Strips and Consumer Culture*, pp. 133–35 and 152–57.
12. Much can be said about the role of fiction in the stories of nonfictional heroes, of course. History is far from a precise science and, especially in the case of national history, is quite positive and supportive of its heroes. History, after all, is not only written by the victors but also by the heroes.

13. See Will Ferguson, *Why I Hate Canadians*, p. 175.
14. Part of the colorization process for *Superman* was handled in Canada.
15. Swiss linguist Ferdinand de Saussure's semiological work showed how a *signifier* (the communicative) is connected with a *signified* (mental concept, object, and so on) to construct a *sign* (the arbitrary signifying construct). Roland Barthes produced the most influential work on semiology and culture, first outlined in *Mythologies* (1957), *Elements of Semiology* (1964), and *The Fashion System* (1967). Extending Saussure's work on the denotative, Barthes explored the connotative, a subjective meaning produced by the meeting of the sign and the viewer. It is within the connotative that emotions, values, and so on are expressed.

WORKS CITED

Anderson, Benedict. *Imagined Communities*. London: Verso, 1991.

Baudrillard, Jean. *The Consumer Society: Myths and Structures*. London: Sage Publications, 1998.

Bell, John. *Canuck Comics*. Downsview, Ontario: Eden Press, 1986.

Bell, John. "Curator, National Archives of Canada." *Guardians of the North: The National Superhero in Canadian Comic-Book Art*. Ottawa: Minister of Supply and Services Canada, 1992.

Bengough, J. W. *A Caricature History of Canadian Politics*. Toronto: Peter Martin Associates, 1974.

Boulton, Marsha. *Just a Minute: Glimpses of Our Great Canadian Heritage*. Toronto: McArthur & Co., 1998.

Canada Post Corporation. Press release, 26 Sept. 1995.

Captain Canuck. Issues 1–3. Winnipeg, Manitoba: Comely Comix, 1975.

Captain Canuck. Issues 4–14. Calgary, Alberta: CKR Productions Ltd, 1979–1981.

Captain Canuck Reborn. Cambridge, Ontario: Comely Communications, 1993–1996.

Comely, Richard. Correspondence with author, summer 2001.

Ferguson, Will. *Why I Hate Canadians*. Vancouver: Douglas & McIntyre, 1997.

Francis, Daniel. *National Dreams: Myth, Memory, and Canadian History*. Vancouver: Arsenal Pulp Press, 1997.

Gellner, Ernest. *Thought and Change*. London: Weidenfeld and Nicolson, 1964.

Gordon, Ian. *Comic Strips and Consumer Culture, 1890–1945*. Washington, DC: Smithsonian Institution Press, 1998.

Klein, Naomi. *No Logo: Taking Aim at the Brand Bullies*. Toronto: Vintage Canada, 2000.

Land, Jeffrey, and Patrick Trimble. "Whatever Happened to the Man of Tomorrow? An Examination of the American Monomyth and the Comic Book Superhero." *Journal of Popular Culture* 2 (1988): 157–73.

Ontario Royal Commission on Book Publishing. *Canadian Publishers and Canadian Publishing*. Toronto: Queen's Printer and Publisher, 1992.

Pustz, Matthew J. *Comic Book Culture: Fanboys and True Believers*. Jackson: UP of Mississippi, 1999.

Silbermann, Alphons. "The Way Toward Visual Culture: Comics and Comic Films." *Comics and Visual Culture*. Ed. A. Silbermann and H. D. Dyroff. New York: K. G. Saur, 1986. 11–27.

TIME. "Canuck to the Rescue." Canadian edition, 9 June 1975: 10.

TIME. "Captain Exporter." Canadian edition, 28 Apr. 1997: Cover.

TIME. "Super Exporter." Canadian edition, 28 Apr. 1997: 34–40.

Yoshino, Kosaku. "Rethinking Theories of Nationalism: Japan's Nationalism in a Marketplace Perspective." *Consuming Ethnicity and Nationalism: Asian Experiences*. Ed. Yoshino Kosaku. Honolulu: U of Hawaii P, 1999.

Document 9.1
Harry J. Boyle

Excerpt from *With a Pinch of Sin*

Broadcaster, newspaper columnist, writer, and CBC personality Harry Boyle (1915–2005) was born in rural St. Augustine, Ontario. He worked as a farm broadcaster for CBC Toronto during World War II, and was one of the CBC's earliest regional program directors for both radio and television. Following is an excerpt from the first volume of his published memoirs.

Issues to Consider
- Boyle makes the ironic observation that the people in his small town did not "know very much about culture," then proceeds to detail a lively local cultural scene. What assumptions about the meaning of "culture" are suggested by his wry commentary?
- What eventually happened to this home-grown rural popular culture?

You might say Clover was a well-knit community when I was a boy. A few strangers, and there weren't many, slipped into the pattern of living without too much fuss.

But now and then one came along who fought the customs, and the results were sometimes tragic and often amusing.

Mrs. Henderson, a frothy-looking woman with piled-up hair, was determined to make over our place. She was a city girl, tolerated for the most part because her banker husband controlled a good deal of the credit in the township.

A week after she arrived, the Clover *Clarion* printed her picture in a cartwheel hat and said she looked forward to living in the village and hoped to encourage a cultural upsurge. She was interested in music, drama, and folk songs.

Grandfather threatened to call on her and recite some of his lumberjack ballads or invite her to a "wet" evening at the Smoke Hole in back of Olsen's Blacksmith Shop. But Mother threatened him in turn with all kinds of punishment.

We didn't know very much about culture, except the kind they talked about at the cheese factory. The item caused a lot of talk for a time, but it died down.

There was a concert after the fowl supper and we heard a piano player, a very loud female singer, a harmonica quartet, a fiddle player who didn't play a recognizable tune, and a man with a deep voice who sucked in a moth at one point and was considered the highlight of the affair.

They were from Handrich, the county town, and were hired because the Methodists didn't believe in having a dance and you couldn't just close up after the supper.

By the time we got around to the Christmas concerts at the various churches and schools that only varied in structure, content, and performance by the difference in the two Santa suits available, most people had forgotten about Mrs. Henderson. She was busy, however!

She persuaded Mr. McPherson, a dour Scots minister, to allow the Swiss Bell Ringers to put on a concert. It was a great success, and Mrs. Henderson made a speech in which she promised real cultural entertainment for Clover.

Source: Harry J. Boyle, *With a Pinch of Sin* (New York: Doubleday, 1966), 57–63.

We heard a lot of rumors. It was apparent that Mrs. Henderson was organizing something special. She ferreted out almost everybody in the township who ever had any musical training. Of course most of the best locals played by ear. She didn't want them, because it seems she had written some music. Somebody said she had sent it to Ernest MacMillan (that was before he was knighted), and he wrote back and said he had never seen a score like it before.

She had Agatha Simms, a retired singer with a mad passion for flying, and all the local music teachers to her house for afternoon tea.

She took over the Oddfellows Hall and borrowed Jake Deegan, the handyman who looked after the bank, to rig up a stage.

Mr. Henderson took to visiting the back room of the Commercial Hotel because his wife had turned his house into a rehearsal hall. Most of the regulars said that after a few belts of brew he was quite a likable fellow and quite different from the austere banker who questioned them so sharply when they wanted a loan.

Then one day a lean, sallow-faced man with long gray hair and dark pouches under his eyes came in on the afternoon train from Toronto. He wore a gray plug hat and a cape and carried a cane with silver knob. He registered at the Commercial and said he was Cecil Hubert Fotheringham, an actor.

He ate his meals, except breakfast, which he missed, at the banker's home and sent the bill for his room to Mrs. Henderson. George Warner wouldn't charge drinks in the back room, because of the Canada Temperance Act, I guess, but the actor didn't go shy because he evidently had a vast repertoire of bawdy verses which he found no difficulty in exchanging for the hospitality of the other visitors.

The *Clarion* ran an advertisement for "An Evening of Varied Cultural Entertainment," and handbills appeared in all the stores and the post office. There were to be ensembles, trios, and solo performances of readings and music. No one would admit that they were going, but everyone knew that the place was going to be packed.

Some people worried about it happening in Lent. Others thought seventy-five cents for adults and forty cents for children was a bit steep. It didn't hold down attendance, however, because the hall was packed.

There was a stage with a velvet curtain drawn across it, bearing the arm and hammer emblem of Clover, later identified as a trademark for washing soda. There were footlights made out of tin cans and gasoline lamps on both sides of the hall.

People kept poking their heads out between the folds of the curtain, and at one point it collapsed, sending about a dozen people on the stage scrambling into the wings.

It took some time to get the curtain back up on the wire, but finally Mrs. Henderson came out and made a speech. She had a long dress on that showed a lot of her top and made some of the women in the audience fidget and whisper. Then the curtains jerked apart and we saw what was supposed to be the ensemble.

"Chicken Jimmy" Wilks, who had flunked out of the second-year poultry course at Ontario Agricultural College, was waving a stick in front of them. It was the composition by Mrs. Henderson called "Clover Number One." Gramp said it was named after a grass seed. Jimmy Henderson, who was playing a thing called a bull fiddle, played for about a minute after everyone else finished.

Agatha Simms sang "Trees," which was well received, and besides, everybody liked her.

Then Cecil Hubert Fotheringham came out in a funny suit with long stockings and a feathered hat and carried a thin sword and went on and on reciting something that nobody knew, but he jumped around a lot and seemed to be fighting with something imaginary.

Mrs. Henderson sang what she called an aria which was pretty high and gave me a headache. A Swiss fellow from the cheese factory played the accordion and yodeled. The musical ensemble came back and played some more and it wasn't bad because you could almost recognize some of the tunes.

The actor recited some Shakespeare which was all about murder and sleep. "Chicken Jimmy" played a sad piece on the violin, and then Mrs. Henderson came out again.

She said it was a shame that folk songs were being neglected and that she had a treat for the audience. A local resident was going to sing some treasures in this field.

Grandfather sat up and opened his eyes, and out stepped "Sheep Willy" Jenks, the chieftain of a clan who lived in a ramshackle collection of rooms beside the village dump. He was dressed up in one of the banker's suits, and he even had a necktie on with the knot hanging in midair between his Adam's apple and his navel. His son Bert brought out a guitar and "Sheep Willy" brushed his whiskers and proceeded to sing "The Jam on Garry's Rocks."

It was pretty good, and when all that applause rolled in he bowed and started in to sing something called "Black-Eyed Tess."

That broke up the concert. Mothers started hauling their youngsters out. But "Sheep Willy" kept right on to the end.

The concert was the main topic of talk for a week. The next Saturday night when our folks were going to confession, Rosie Glynn came out smiling and announced in a loud whisper: "You don't have to tell about going to the concert in Lent. Father Morrison says it was no sin to listen to Sheep Willy's song. Just going to the concert was penance enough."

That about finished culture in Clover!

After that we went back to dances, especially in the township. There was a tacit agreement that the young people from the white-brick Methodist church would attend dances as long as there was a sprinkling of square dances to command the attention of the older people who came along ostensibly as chaperones. […]

It was strange, but Albert, [a local] who hated work, was the cause of the breakdown in our township hall dances. He introduced the radio to our valley and older folks started getting interested in listening. They would congregate at my uncle's store, where he had installed an extra speaker from the set in the kitchen. Soon quite a few had radios at home, and while this broke up some of the conversation parties at the general store, it had another and unexpected effect.

The younger members of the township families grew dissatisfied with the makeshift orchestra. They were hearing tunes on the radio that Red Sandy didn't know, and it became apparent that there wasn't a great deal of variety in his playing.

This was 1927, and change was in the air. Toronto had its new Union Station opened by the Prince of Wales. We heard on the radio about the collapse of George Young and the win by Vierkoetter in the Wrigley Swim.

The banker had paid over $900 for a Chrysler car. Grandfather was quite upset by the fact that when he was in Toronto with the drover to sell cattle they had paid over fifty cents apiece to see a movie with Dorothy Gish.

In the light of so much progress, it was bound to happen. The Young Farmers' Club hired an outside orchestra to play for a dance. […]

Document 9.2
Massey Commission

The National Gallery

The Royal Commission on National Development in the Arts, Letters and Sciences, named for its chair, Vincent Massey (then chancellor of the University of Toronto), was appointed by the federal government in 1949. Its purpose was to take stock of cultural activity across the nation. Its final report, from which the following excerpt is derived, proposed that the federal government fund a wide range of cultural activities, both at the community level and through the establishment of a national agency, the Canada Council, to support voluntary efforts in promoting Canadian art, literature, humanities, and social sciences. In 1952, Massey became the first Canadian-born governor general.

Issues to Consider
- What do the commissioners conclude about the Canadian art scene? What do their recommendations for the National Gallery aim to accomplish?
- Art can belong to the realms of both "high culture" and "popular culture." Discuss.

1. Of all the Federal Institutions dealt with in this section the National Gallery has perhaps the most universal appeal, and has certainly achieved the widest contacts with the Canadian public. Some seventy briefs discussed its work, many of them in considerable detail. There was much appreciation and helpful criticism which will be noticed later. We were particularly interested in the wide variety of purposes represented by the groups which came before us to discuss the services and the problems of the Gallery.

2. The National Gallery has been in temporary quarters for seventy years. It was founded in 1880 by the Marquess of Lorne, who selected the pictures which were then lodged with the Department of Public Works. In 1907 an Advisory Arts Council was appointed, first, to administer grants to the National Gallery and second, to advise the Minister of Public Works on purchases of or expenditures on any works of art, including monuments in Ottawa and elsewhere. In 1910 the pictures were moved to the east wing of the Victoria Memorial Museum building where they still are. The Gallery was incorporated by an Act of Parliament in 1913, under the control of a Board of Trustees. The Board was entrusted with the development and management of the National Gallery, and with the cultivation of Canadian interest in the fine arts.

3. The various functions of the Gallery have been described to us in some detail in the National Gallery brief. The National Gallery, we are informed, should not in any sense play a paternal role in relation to other institutions but should advise upon, stimulate and co-ordinate art activities in Canada which the Gallery believes are the better for being the result of local initiative. The relations between the National Gallery and art societies in Canada have been, we are told, most cordial and co-operative.

Source: Royal Commission on National Development in the Arts, Letters and Sciences, 1949–1951, *Report* (Ottawa 1951).

4. The first charge of the National Gallery is, as the brief states, the development and care of the national collections. The Gallery's collection of Canadian art is the most complete in existence, and the European collections, although not fully representative, are regarded as important by well-informed authorities in Canada and from abroad. Requests for the loan of important individual paintings in the collection for exhibitions in other countries are received from time to time. Each request is considered on its merits, in accordance with the importance of the occasion, the prestige and equipment of the receiving institution and the conditions of transportation. Such loans enhance the international recognition of the importance of the National Gallery collection, and the treasures of the Gallery become more widely known and studied by experts. Loans from the European collections in the National Gallery have been made to American and to British galleries. In 1949 a request was received for a Botticelli to be sent to a special exhibition in Florence.

5. The second important service of the Gallery is the arrangement of loans and exhibitions from abroad, or from its own holdings which are sent to galleries throughout the country. During the past twenty-five years exhibitions have been brought to Canada from some twenty other countries including Britain, France, the United States, Australia, Germany, Poland and Sweden. In addition, the Gallery sponsors exhibitions of Canadian painting which have increased in number from 31 in 1928–29 to 200 in 1947–48. These may be arranged by the chartered art societies, such as the Royal Canadian Academy of the Arts, the Canadian Group of Painters or the Canadian Society of Painters in Water Colour. The Gallery has arranged from time to time retrospective exhibitions of the work of Canadian artists, notably those of Morrice, of Emily Carr [www.tbc.gov.bc.ca/culture/schoolnet/carr/] and of Pegi Nicol.

6. There are, however, two major limiting factors, apart from the cost, in the extension of loan exhibitions. One is the absence in other Canadian cities of fireproof buildings in which to hang the pictures, and the other is the want of experienced staff in local galleries to take care of unpacking, display and repacking. There are only about six local art galleries in the country completely satisfactory in these respects.

7. Another very important function of the Gallery is its general extension work. In 1922 the present Director, on tour in Western Canada, discovered the need for reproductions of Canadian pictures. A year or two later a series of reproductions in large and in postcard sizes was begun. These were sent out to schools with lesson leaflets prepared by an expert in art education. This educational programme was carried further with the development of radio which made possible broadcasts from the Gallery over the national network. The National Gallery has also taken an active part in the production of films dealing with the work of Canadian artists. It has encouraged lecturers from abroad to come to Canada. The officials of the National Gallery consider that broadcasts and films on art undertaken at national expense are a legitimate and essential part of the Gallery's responsibilities. The production of large silk-screen prints of Canadian paintings was undertaken by the Gallery during the war. These reproductions have been displayed throughout Canada and in many places abroad. We were interested in a suggestion from British Columbia that they should be purchased for display in rural post offices in order to bring Canadian paintings to Canadians everywhere.

8. The National Gallery also undertakes to send exhibitions of Canadian art abroad. This work began in 1924 when the Gallery was put in charge of the Canadian Section of Fine Arts at the British Empire Exhibition in London. The event created great interest in Canadian art and has been followed by a series of Canadian exhibitions in various parts of the world for which the Gallery has been responsible. These include the first continental exhibition of Canadian art in Paris in 1927, and later exhibitions in the Argentine, South

Africa, Australia and New Zealand. The series culminated before the recent war with the "Century of Canadian Art" at the Tate Gallery in London in 1938. Since the war there have been other important exhibitions including the recent large and representative one in Washington.

9. The National Gallery states that it can only with difficulty carry on even its present services unless certain immediate needs are met. First of all, it asks that its present anomalous position in relation to the Department of Public Works be clarified and that it be established as a separate branch of government under a Board of Trustees, with a status similar to that of the Public Archives. It is further suggested that the general advisory functions of the former Advisory Arts Council be revived and re-assigned to the Board of Trustees of the National Gallery. It is considered important that some competent authority be responsible for advising the Government on such art matters as are properly a matter of public interest.

10. The second pressing need, according to the brief, is a new building. The present building is inconveniently situated, ill-arranged and badly lighted; it lacks proper facilities for the staff; it is overcrowded, and the temporary partitions together with the highly inflammable materials used in the basement workshops form a serious fire hazard. The very large collection of historical paintings of the First and Second World Wars is, for the most part, still in storage. The new Gallery should have adequate space for the display of pictures, prints and drawings, sculpture and loan exhibitions, a reference section, a library and proper office accommodation and an air conditioning plant. A photographic studio and a laboratory for the inspection and repair of works of art are also necessary. The present laboratory, which is completely inadequate, undertakes to serve all the public galleries in Canada.

11. A greatly increased staff is also needed immediately since the amount and the variety of work at present is quite beyond the power of the Director and of his three professional assistants. [...]

Document 9.3
Ontario Secondary School Teachers' Federation

Our Culture: Canadian or American?

The Ontario Secondary School Teachers' Federation was founded in 1919 and now represents over 50,000 anglophone and francophone educational employees in 139 bargaining units across the province. In the mid-1980s, it was recognized as a trade union by the Ontario Labour Relations Board. "Our Culture, Canadian or American?" is a commentary from the newsletter that the OSSTF publishes for its members.

Issues to Consider

- Why does the writer contend that the CRTC's point system for measuring Canadian content on television is insufficient? What would be preferable?
- More than a half-century after the publication of the Massey Report the difficulty of protecting Canadian culture from American domination has been complicated by the influx of non-Canadian content made available through satellite television and the Internet. Should Canadians accept the new universe of borderless popular culture or should the struggle for a home-grown culture continue?

More Canadian content on television was the primary request of the Canadian Labour Congress (CLC) in its brief to the Canadian Radio-television and Telecommunications Commission (CRTC) in July. The CRTC began hearings on the Canadian television system in Hull, Quebec, in September.

The CBC delivers lots of Canadian content but the private broad- and cable-casters primarily air American programming. In fact, the only way private television companies make the CRTC's requirement for 50 percent Canadian content for the prime-time evening slot is to include news broadcasts in the count. The CLC brief called for tighter content regulations and greater pressure on private companies to comply.

Television watching in Canada is the most popular voluntary activity. In fact, watching television is third behind sleeping and working, based on hours consumed per activity. The average Canadian 12-year-old spends as much time watching television as going to school.

Despite these statistics, English-speaking Canada is the only industrialized country in the world where domestic-content television is not the primary source of programs for viewers of all ages. A recent study by the Friends of Canadian Broadcasting found that Canadian television stations in Winnipeg broadcast *The Simpsons* 27 times per week, *Due South* twice and *This Hour Has 22 Minutes* once.

Source: Ontario Secondary School Teachers' Federation, "Our Culture: Canadian or American?" *Update* 26, no. 2 (September 22, 1998), http://www.osstf.on.ca/www/pub/update/vol26/2se/2seacbc.html.

Television is a powerful purveyor of values. The question is whose values. When we fail to place high-quality Canadian content before Canadian audiences, we are squandering the opportunity to strengthen our culture and celebrate our unique character. As it is now regulated, private prime-time television broadcasting is suffusing US culture into Canada.

The CLC brief requested that the CRTC change the definition of Canadian content. Presently, Canadian content is determined by a point system which gives more points to programs created by Canadians serving in senior capacities. This is good and necessary but insufficient. The point system should be applied to the actual content of the programs. Such a system could give points for characters, issues, and locations that are clearly identified as Canadian.

"To those who scream that there are no audiences for shows about Canadians, we answer that there are plenty of engaging and compelling Canadian stories and that Canadians will tune in when these stories are told well," stated Nancy Riche, CLC vice president. "Those who claim otherwise are simply lazy and uncreative."

Topic 10

The Playing Fields:
Sport and Recreation

Two girls with bicycle, Eastern Townships, Quebec, about 1900; McCord
Museum collection, MP-1987.3.2, http://www.-mccord-museum.qc.ca.

CONTEXT

Sport and recreation, as pastimes and leisure activities, definitely belong to the sphere of popular culture considered in Topic 9. As is true of that more-encompassing classification, their history also reveals much about the relations of power and how these are literally "played out": in their rules and regulations, in determining the popularity of certain activities and certain players, in identifying who is encouraged or even permitted to play and who constitutes the audience, in shaping the relations between players and team owners, players and fans, teams and communities, professionals and amateurs. The professionalization and commercialization of sport that have characterized its history since Confederation also underscore issues at the very heart of capitalist relations. What is the nature of the "ownership" of teams or athletes, since we are talking about physical skill rather than labour, bodies rather than commodities? How is profit distributed? Do the traditional principles governing ethics and behaviour — the importance of "how you play the game"— matter when winning, gate receipts, and player salaries become the driving force? Most historians of sport acknowledge that, as also discussed in the preceding section, sport tends to make such social distinctions as class and race appear less relevant, while at the same time serving to reinforce and uphold the status quo and the values that sustain it.

The early post-Confederation years witnessed a number of changes taking place in sport, as in the larger society. The cricket, golf, and rowing transplanted from Great Britain and Scotland remained popular, but newer activities, such as lacrosse (derived from the Aboriginal game of baggataway), as well as baseball and hockey, were drawing more participation and spectator interest. In the late 19th century, Canadians also contributed to the development of basketball and football in North America. Advances in transportation and communications affected sport, as they did popular culture in general. More nonparticipants could now take part in these activities, whether as spectators in the stands of an out-of-town match, or by reading the latest sporting news in the dailies, the growing number of mass-circulation family magazines, or even the new specialized sport press aimed at a male readership. After the Great War, radio brought games into Canadian homes. Legendary play-by-play announcer Foster Hewitt made the first hockey broadcast from a telephone in 1923; he would also call the first game played at Toronto's Maple Leaf Gardens when it opened in 1931.

Industrialization and urbanization gave new meaning to the social value of sport and recreation in the interests of public health and civic order. Factory teams became a means to advance good employee relations, while also, ironically, serving as vehicles for class consciousness and worker solidarity. The accompanying rapid, unplanned urbanization, with its resultant overcrowded housing and dirty streets, its diverse "evils" (real and imagined), also spurred reformers' interest in the health, citizenship training, and overall fitness benefits of organized sport and recreation. The social gospellers considered in Topic 3, among them medical professionals, city planners, and other civic leaders, rallied enthusiastically behind the cause. It was hoped that, in the hands of trained personnel, a worthy source of diversion would lure Canadians of all ages away from the less-worthy new commercial entertainments, mitigate class hostility, and promote a common "Canadian" identity among native-born and newly arrived alike. At the same time, as the essays by Michael Robidoux and Robert Kossuth and Kevin Wamsley demonstrate, a carefully constructed ideal of manliness was also part of the package delivered through such activities as lacrosse, hockey, and bicycling. When women participated, they did so always in much smaller numbers, with much cautionary advice about the possible threats to their physical health and, most important, future maternity, and also with much emphasis on how to play the game "like girls" in order to avoid subverting the roles and images appropriate to their own sex.

Organization, rationalization, standardization of regulations, and increasing professionalization among both athletes and trainers also affected sport and recreation, the changes intensifying with the new century. Established in 1881, the Montreal Amateur Athletic Association was the first umbrella group to bring together the city's many sport clubs. It served as a prototype for others to follow, and was the basis of the Amateur Athletic Association of Canada, the first such national organization. The distinction between amateurism and professional sport came to hinge on the issue of wages: professionals earned their livelihood by means of sport, while amateurs participated purely for health and recreational purposes. As amateur sport itself became more businesslike, often due to the influence of professionals and businessmen who volunteered their skills and training to the community, other distinctions — most notably exclusions based on class and race — became more significant. It was more and more the case, as Robidoux shows, that there were clubs for "gentlemen" and clubs for workers, and that colour and ethnic background led to segregated teams and matches, at times inflaming social conflict rather than preventing it.

The 20th century also brought the commercialization of sport as the mass media became its primary purveyor. Hockey took on iconic status as "the national game." Radio, and especially television, transformed Saturday night into "Hockey Night in Canada" in many Canadian homes, and the Stanley Cup playoffs became the culmination of the year's sporting calendar. So profound was the national identification with "the game" that the 1972 Summit Series, considered by Robidoux in Article 10.2, occasioned some soul-searching among Canadian fans when the presumed "easy victory" over the formidable Soviet team proved to be rather more complicated. Fandom rallied, however, and the "lifestyle advertising" that connected hockey ever more closely with youth, beer, and the meaning of Canadianism — as the wildly popular "I am Canadian" advertising campaign by Molson Breweries proved — made hockey "the coolest game on ice" for the late 20th-century generation. More of the players than ever before in the history of the sport are of other than Canadian origin, however.

Among the other popular sports, professional football, through the Canadian Football League, continues to draw a healthy audience, although its coaches and key players are now mostly American. The Toronto Blue Jays (est. 1977) became the first non-American team to win the World Series in 1993 and again in 1994, but the second of the two Canadian major league teams is the sole franchise left in the country after the demise of the Montreal Expos (est. 1969) in 2002. Thus the issue of national identity, with its central question of what makes us different than our southern neighbours, also persists on the playing fields. The correlation of sport and national health and prestige is seen in the 1961 Fitness and Amateur Sport Act, passed by the Conservative government of John Diefenbaker to provide an annual fund of $5 million for amateur sport and fitness activities. The program, now worth about $50 million annually, has brought considerable international success to Canadian amateur athletes in a wide variety of sport activities.

REFERENCES/FURTHER READING

Burstyn, Varda. *The Rites of Men: Manhood, Politics, and the Culture of Sport.* Toronto: University of Toronto Press, 1999.

Gruneau, R., and David Whitson. *Hockey Night in Canada: Sport, Identities and Cultural Politics.* Toronto: Garamond, 1993.

Gurney, Helen. *A Century to Remember, 1893–1993: Women's Sport at the University of Toronto.* Toronto: University of Toronto Press, 1993.

Hall, Anne, T. Slack, G. Smith, and D. Whitson. *Sport in Canadian Society.* Toronto: University of Toronto Press, 1991.

Howell, Colin D. *Blood, Sweat, and Cheers: Sport and the Making of Modern Canada*. Toronto: University of Toronto Press, 2001.

———. *Northern Sandlots: A Social History of Maritime Baseball*. Toronto: University of Toronto Press, 1995.

Humber, William. *Diamonds of the North: A Concise History of Baseball in Canada*. Toronto: Oxford University Press, 1995.

Kidd, Bruce. *The Struggle for Canadian Sport*. Toronto: University of Toronto Press, 1996.

Metcalfe, Alan. *Canada Learns to Play: The Emergence of Organized Sport, 1807–1914*. Toronto: McClelland and Stewart, 1987.

Morton, Suzanne. *At Odds: Gambling and Canadians, 1919–1969*. Toronto: University of Toronto Press, 2002.

Tillotson, Shirley. *The Public at Play: Gender and the Politics of Recreation in Post-War Ontario*. Toronto: University of Toronto Press, 2000.

Walden, Keith. *Becoming Modern in Toronto: The Industrial Exhibition and the Shaping of a Late Victorian Culture*. Toronto: University of Toronto Press, 1997.

Wetherell, Donald G., and Irene Kmet. *Useful Pleasures: the Shaping of Leisure in Alberta, 1896–1945*. Regina: Canadian Plains Research Center, 1990.

ILLUSTRATION 10.1 (P. 413)

The bicycle "craze" of the late 19th century brought women into active, public recreation more than ever before. While women's rights advocates supported their participation, many Canadians were scandalized by the appearance of young women who wore the new "split skirts," called "bloomers," while cycling on city streets and country roads and in parks.

Issue to Consider

• Note the age and appearance of the young women in this posed photograph. What "story" does this photograph suggest?

ARTICLES

In the essays that follow, Michael Robidoux discusses the historical connections between the two most "Canadian" of games — lacrosse and hockey — and the development of a national consciousness, within the context of the struggle between the traditional and the modern, the professional and the amateur, in the arena and on the fields. These themes also inform Robert Kossuth and Kevin Wamsley's consideration of the how bicycling came to be represented as a respectable "manly" form of urban recreation in London, Ontario, in the late 19th century.

Article 10.1

Robert S. Kossuth and Kevin B. Wamsley

Cycles of Manhood: Pedaling Respectability in Ontario's Forest City

Issues to Consider

- What were the main issues in the public debate about bicycling in Victorian Canada?
- How did the period's conventions about class, gender, and sexuality influence notions of respectability and the social roles of men and women?
- What were the "legitimizing strategies" put into practice by cycling clubs in order to make cycling at once respectable and manly?
- Why do the authors contend that "cyclists were met with some resistance" in late 19th-century London?
- What was the symbolic value of the club structure? What was its practical value?

A. T. Lane, riding through the streets of Montreal on 1 July 1874, on his plain-bearing, socket-steering, high wheeler, heralded the ominous arrival of the penny-farthing, or the ordinary bicycle, to Canadian social life.[1] For some, the arrival of the bicycle and its high riders shook the foundations of public decorum, rousing the citizenry against this newest form of public nuisance perpetrated by reckless individuals and rowdies. Initially an object of wonder to passersby, the increasing popularity and prevalence of the bicycle on town streets polarized public opinions about issues of safety and on the more controversial questions about the ritual parading of men's and later women's bodies on the roads and pathways of late-nineteenth-century urban Canada. Freedom of movement, sweat, vigor, and early-evening physical pleasures aside, the bicycle became a scourge to some respectable pedestrians and carriage drivers. Critics framed the debates over the issue in the context of appropriate and honorable manliness and woman-hood, underscored by the physiological dispositions supposedly stimulated by cycling, or structured such controversies more comfortably as technical attention toward public safety and traffic decorum. Implicit throughout the debates waged in the newspapers were the often-invoked notions that responsible men with honor showed concern for others, particularly women and children, and behaved as proper gentlemen in public. Responsible women were to be cognizant of social hierarchies and ladylike, with bodies disciplined by fashion and behavioral codes of Victorian morality.[2] Agitated city dwellers, thus, lobbied for bylaws to control the cyclists under the social guise of predominantly middle-class standards of the "respectable," an unequivocal position of argument that equated cyclists with the long-standing public nuisances of the tavern brawler, the brazen harlot, and the reckless carriage driver.

The weight of such arguments was not lost on the "respectable" young male cyclists in question, avid traders in social capital, who responded in kind by carefully positioning their emergent masculine attributes under the guise of physically active, but good, citizenship — the

Source: Robert S. Kossuth and Kevin B. Wamsley, "Cycles of Manhood: Pedaling Respectability in Ontario's Forest City," *Sport History Review* 34, no. 2 (2003): 169–89.

responsible but daring public man. These ideological invocations gained public legitimacy through the establishment of cycling clubs with members who advocated safe and organized rides, gentlemanly races, and cycling paths for members, both men and women. The legitimizing strategies undertaken by early Canadian cycling-club members,[3] specifically those of the Forest City Cycling Club of London, Ontario, secured some measure of respectability for these active young men and were indicative of their roles in the broader social agendas forwarded by various middle-class men over appropriate public masculinities and bodily dispositions.

MIDDLE-CLASS MEN, MASCULINITY, AND THE BICYCLE

The second half of the nineteenth century represented an era when gender roles and identities for men and women were subjected to a variety of challenges, many of which arose within the sphere of physical recreation.[4] Cycling was a visible form of physical activity that stimulated considerable public debate about acceptable public displays of men's and women's bodies. Literature examining the processes that influenced the physical and social emancipation of middle-class Victorian women has consistently pointed to recreational cycling during the 1890s as representing an arena in which women were able to gain greater control over their bodies.[5] This focus on cycling and its influence on women's lives has been drawn on to confirm the existence of rigid gender identities at that time, as well as the presence of reform-minded individuals who sought to challenge the existing gender order. Despite this focus on issues of cycling and femininity, however, little serious attention has been paid to the role of cycling, particularly during the 1880s and early 1890s in Canada, in constructing and reproducing masculine identities for middle-class men. While offering some comments about the social consequences of women's participation, this study examines some of the substantive and theoretical issues extant in men's cycling, late-nineteenth-century masculinities, and the current debates about gender relations in history.

Who were the men who initially participated in cycling? The men who made up the ranks of early cyclists in both Europe and North America were drawn almost exclusively from the wealthier middle classes. These mostly young men engaged in recreational and competitive cycling on a variety of machines ranging from the solid iron velocipede, or the "boneshaker," popular in the 1860s to the high wheeler, "ordinary," or penny-farthing bicycle popular in the 1870s and early 1880s.[6] Cycling and other physically active pursuits in the growing ranks of organized sport in Canada[7] offered alternatives to the more popular forms of entertainment situated in the local taverns or inns, where "measuring up" as a man and protecting personal honor often required that an individual participate in tests of physical strength and physical confrontations that included fist fights and brawls.[8] Part of the process of measuring up for men of the emerging middle classes entailed expressing physical masculinities in public places such as sporting fields, pitches, and, in the case of cycling, streets, which of course were more visible than the confines of the tavern. Public endorsement was integral to class identity and the process of legitimation; public rejection was problematic. For young professionals and businessmen, exemplars of the new industrial capitalist ethos, formal and informal demonstrations of rational, moral character were crucial to personal reputation and status. Some young men chose sport or physical feats in clearly defined contexts, in contradistinction to women and weaker men, to position themselves socially. Cycling, for example, invoked a measure of bravado and masculine daring, similar to that found on the rugby pitch, while the exclusivity of the enterprise ensured rank in the local social hierarchy. In this sense, cyclists could be manly yet respectful, conforming to acceptable and rational masculine behaviors that were expected of young gentlemen of the time.[9]

Current literature suggests that a number of forms of manhood or even disparate masculinities were extant in 1870s to 1890s Canada.[10] For the following examination of cycling in London, Ontario, the primary point of focus lies in the emerging middle class's notion of manhood that was particularly apparent in sport and physical recreation activities. In order to examine the role of physical activity in the complex process of making men, this study focuses on the Forest City Bicycle Club of London while also drawing on available information about other cycling clubs, organizations, and events in Canada, the United States, and Britain. Arguably, the appearance of the high-wheel bicycle signaled the first period of cycling interest in Canada, when male cyclists attempted to assign a degree of validity to the activity. During this era, through interactions with other cyclists and the general public, cycling moved from being an unregulated and often disruptive activity to one generally organized and controlled by formal cycling clubs and other sport organizations. The popularity of cycling began to grow within the structure of private clubs, sanctioned by rules and regulations, which provided a legitimizing influence within broader communities. In time, however, with the arrival and increasing availability of the safety bicycle, the private bicycle club's unique social position declined and the cycling male lost some of his luster.

CYCLING THE "ROUGH" ROAD: CONFLICT AND BACKPEDALING FOR RESPECTABILITY

In the late 1870s and early 1880s, cycling represented a socially exclusive pastime, limited primarily to upper middle-class men who could afford the rather significant investment of purchasing a bicycle and could meet the physical demands of the high wheeler that required one to be young and athletic. According to Glen Norcliffe, in the 1880s most high-wheel bicycle riders were either businessmen or professional men in their 20s and 30s, the young scions of the nation's leading families.[11] In his examination of cycling in Britain and North America, Seamus McGonagle argues that cycling in this era represented "a status symbol of the rich middle class."[12] In Canada at this time, bicycles were not widely accessible, primarily because of their cost. A catalogue produced by London's first bicycle importer, William Payne, presented and priced several lines of bicycles and tricycles for the 1883 model year. The most expensive of these was the British Challenge high-wheel bicycle, which cost $110 for the 56-inch-wheel model. Even the more modestly priced Royal Challenge model was listed at $78 for the 54-inch-wheel version.[13] At these prices, only the wealthiest Londoners would have been able to afford to purchase a bicycle strictly for recreational use. To provide some perspective of the relative worth of these machines, L. N. Bronson points out that the average wage for a worker at London's Morehead Furniture factory in the late 1870s ranged from $9 to $15 a week, and a male teacher working in a rural school in Middlesex County earned a maximum of $445 a year.[14] Thus, to purchase a bicycle for $80, $100, or more would have been exceedingly difficult for anyone but the upper middle-class men who adopted cycling as their avocation. For those who could afford it, however, the bicycle provided a unique status signaling both economic stature and a manly physical competence. At the same time, cyclists could also be viewed as public nuisances on streets and sidewalks, a concern evident in towns and cities in Britain and North America.

In Britain the ordinary, or high-wheel, bicycle replaced the cruder velocipede or boneshaker style of bicycle in the mid-1870s. In England, according to Andrew Ritchie, by 1875 the high-wheel represented the dominant bicycle design.[15] Credit for the invention of this new style of bicycle has been ceded to several individuals including M. Magee of Paris and W. F. Reynolds and J. A. Mays in England, all of whom developed similar machines in 1869.[16] Nonetheless, it was the "Ariel" bicycle patented by James Starley and William Hillman in 1870 that popularized the high-wheel bicycle in Britain.[17] The ordinary bicycle offered several improvements and advantages for the young men who rode them that had not been available in the earlier models. One such advantage suggested by John Woodforde was that "the bigger the wheel, the higher rose a young man's self-esteem."[18] Certainly the height of the bicycle provided visceral excitement while it simultaneously obtained as a metaphor for status, augmented by physical, social, and economic prominence. Even so, the bicycle's critics scoffed at this spatial imperative, particularly when cyclists frightened horses or splashed mud on pedestrians.

As the number of bicycles navigating urban thoroughfares increased, so did conflicts with pedestrians and horse-drawn vehicles. Occasionally this discord led to verbal and physical assaults. For example, derogatory terms used to describe cyclists included "cad" and "monkey on a wire," and those who harbored greater animosity went as far as thrusting sticks into unsuspecting cyclists' wheels or placing bricks and other objects in their paths so as to dislodge them from their bicycles.[19] One such incident occurred in London, Ontario, in 1890:

> Mr. Joe Knowles was severely hurt while training in Queen's Park.... On coming down the home stretch at a rapid rate, a small boy threw a stone almost as large as himself directly in front of our record breaker. Joe, not being accustomed to riding in hurdle races, took a "header." He was carried home unconscious, but we are pleased to see him around again, an eye draped in mourning being the only visible evidence of his fall.[20]

Despite the danger of these sorts of run-ins, it was incidents involving carriages, horses, and pedestrians that were more serious. As these conflicts became increasingly commonplace, bylaws were passed to regulate cyclists, and those who contravened the law risked facing legal action. Most often, cyclists were fined either for driving at excessive rates of speed or for reckless driving.[21]

In London, cyclists were met with some resistance. An editorial published in late July of 1881 by the *London Advertiser* newspaper outlined concerns about cycling and the behavior of cyclists on city streets:

> The number of young men who are fond of exercising on the altitudinous wheel are becoming more numerous in this city. Some of them forget that the sidewalk is not a proper place for exercising their skill, and in one or two cases children and elderly persons have had narrow escapes. The Chief of Police is determined to confine all bicycle riding to the road, and with this object in view has summoned a well-known hotel-keeper on a charge of breach of by-law.[22]

The Chatham *Planet* reported that a horse was startled by two cyclists and upset its carriage. When cyclist Alex Wood attempted to help the fallen carriage driver, he was beaten with the butt of his whip.[23] Another rider was told to move to the road on the Proof Line Sidewalk, outside of London's city limits. The wheelman refused, was knocked into the ditch, and, as a result of the ensuing fistfight, broke the gentleman's collarbone.[24] Such contempt for cycling compromised its legitimacy at times, particularly when it was identified as a public nuisance. Not coincidentally, attendance to public perceptions and the search for social legitimacy played a role in the formation of the Forest City Cycling Club in London the following year. In this era, the process of organizing clubs, institutions, and societies served to both standardize and legitimize myriad social and political relations, a strategy through which ascendant middle-class men actively asserted their authority. Organizational structures ostensibly lent weight, social and legal, to the values and meanings extant in cultural practices. The symbolic value of the club structure, alone, could deflect some of the public concerns about irresponsibility, enabling the group to advance its interests relatively unfettered.

THE FOREST CITY BICYCLE CLUB

The Forest City Bicycle Club, founded on 18 September 1882,[25] was one of the first cycling clubs to be formally organized in Canada.[26] Initially, this new club's members were young men in their 20s and 30s drawn primarily from London's elite merchant and manufacturing classes. Later, in the early 1890s, a small number of women also became members, a change similar to that which took place in clubs throughout Canada.[27] The club also played a role in the formation of the Canadian Wheelmen's Association, cycling's national organizing body.[28] Over the course of the 1880s, the Forest City Bicycle Club set about establishing and legitimizing cycling in London by organizing a variety of competitive and social/recreational events. These events focused on embracing and reinforcing ideas and values about how this new activity ought to be experienced. Exclusivity, of course, was paramount to establishing any social hierarchy. These men were drawn to the sport during the 1880s and early 1890s in part because of the activity's prestige, which was, in large part, based on the expense and corresponding exclusivity of the bicycle. Races and excursions sponsored by the club affirmed the logic of physical competitions, a hallmark of the kind of masculine identity encouraged through late-nineteenth-century sport,[29] and the physical ability required to cycle provided ample symbolic value for its translation to social capital.[30] Exclusionary practices extended beyond the economic and the physical, evidently, as club restrictions were viewed and reported quite seriously. It was noted in London that

> a certain young man of the Jewish extraction is in the habit of wearing a uniform and badge, like those worn by the members of the Forest City Bicycle Club, to which he is not entitled, and the club are about to take action to restrain him from appearing in such uniform and badge. He tried to join the club, but they would not have him in it under any circumstances.[31]

At another level, the contestation over urban space, fueled in part by the formation of bicycle clubs in Toronto, according to Christopher Armstrong and H. V. Nelles, was "to absorb the energies of enthusiasts and reduce speeding on city streets."[32] In London, the Forest City Bicycle Club claimed that cycling promoted positive social benefits for participants to placate local police and government officials and even organized a safety division within its club structure. To this end, and in order to advance interest in the activity among members of the city's social elite, the Forest City club actively promoted two forms of organized cycling during the 1880s and 1890s. It organized amateur and professional cycling races on long courses, usually between two towns or between outlying communities and London, and short-course meets or tournaments at local athletic parks including, for example, the Tecumseh and Queen's parks in London. The club also organized cycling "tours" or "excursions," which generally included greater numbers of riders, between London and adjacent communities. These social rides ranged from short evening and day trips to longer weekend tours of the outlying countryside. Such events provided positive publicity for the Forest City club and for the rival clubs to follow. They also served to normalize the conditions for rugged, if not daring, trained, physical masculinities to be appreciated. Spills, falls, and collisions were described by participants as humorous interludes and even as bouts of excitement for all but the scraped and bruised, as the following wheelman's entry suggested:

> He dropped to earth from off his wheel
> With a distressing sprawl.
> "Whate'er," said he, "the time may be,
> With me 'tis always fall."[33]

In newspaper reports, cycling accidents could be carefully positioned as exciting but not exceedingly hazardous: "Mullins took a very beautiful 'header' just this side of Exeter, his elastic body, however, suffering but slightly."[34]

The first races held under the auspices of the Forest City Bicycle Club were intraclub events held on city and county roads. One example of this type of road race was the club championship racing series held on a road course for the Irving Medal. This series of races was positioned as the local pinnacle of rugged and manly cycling competition over extended distances on rough country roads. The events of the 1890 race attest to multiple significations, inherent in codes of conduct, expectations, and symbolic posturing. The final race in the Irving Medal championship was held on 9 July 1890, beginning in the town of Lucan and finishing at the guns (cannons) in Victoria Park in London, a distance of roughly 18 miles. Mr. W. G. Owens bested Mr. S. E Lawrason, who finished in second place after recovering from an accident that left him with a broken handlebar and a bruised body. As a result of Owens's victory, he and Lawrason were left tied with 16 points each in the race series.[35] To determine a winner, it was decided at a 14 July meeting of the Forest City Bicycle Club to schedule a final race over the same course to be held the following week.[36]

When race day arrived to determine the winner of the Irving Medal, Mr. Lawrason complained that he could not ride as a result of a knee injury he had sustained in the race the previous week. The referee refused to postpone the race, however, because Lawrason had not provided sufficient warning of his inability to compete. As a result, all Owens had to do was complete the race on his own to win the Irving Medal outright. In response to the decision to run the race, and Owens's uncontested victory, Lawrason launched a public protest in the local newspaper:

> I, S. Fred Lawrason do hereby enter a protest against any decision given in the above named race, on grounds that I have not had sufficient time to recover from [my] accident in [the] race of July 9, which time was allowed me by the club at a meeting held on July 11. If necessary a doctors certificate can be produced that I am not in condition, owing to inflation having attacked my knee cap.[37]

When this protest did not elicit the response he sought, Lawrason pursued a new tact by directly challenging Owens to a road race for the championship of London. Understandably, Owens refused this challenge, asserting, "I would say the road championship of London for this year has been decided.... It is therefore unnecessary for me to ride again for the same."[38]

Like similar competitive challenges, from the tavern to the boxing ring and, in this case, a cycling road race, the sporting rhetoric always conflated honor with physical and moral integrity. A further exaggeration of the competitive manly posturing of this episode, the debate wore on in the papers. In response to Owens's outright dismissal of his challenge, Lawrason responded once again in a letter published on 30 July 1890 to the sporting editor of the London Advertiser, in which he elevated the personal nature of his challenge by suggesting that "either [Owens] does not understand my challenge or he is trying to evade it."[39] Lawrason pointed out in the same letter that Owens was not the holder of the London road championship but only the Forest City Bicycle Club road championship and that Owens knew fully that his offer of a race on or after 1 September 1890 was impossible because he would not be in London after August. Bravado, honor, and competitiveness were the hallmarks of identity for the sporting man of late-nineteenth-century Canada.[40]

Not to be outdone, the series of public challenges between Owens and Lawrason incited a response from two of the city's top cyclists, J. A. Tune and James Lamb, who expressed their indignation at being excluded from any race for the championship of London. Mr. Lamb admonished Lawrason for challenging the wrong man for the road championship of the city, arguing that he was the rightful holder of that title.[41] There is no record of Owens, Lawrason, or Lamb competing together in another road race that summer. Clearly, Mr. Lawrason did not receive any satisfaction in the matter. This series of events provides a degree of insight into the importance that these middle-class men placed on protecting their honor, particularly when it came to physical competition. In this case, Owens exhibited his gentlemanly character by remaining above the fray, adhering to the rules laid down by the club, and not being goaded into a rematch by Lawrason's challenges. It would seem that Lawrason came out of the conflict poorly in terms of protecting his honor and was likely viewed by his peers as an upstart who was unwilling to accept the rulings of the Forest City Bicycle Club.

Although the long-course road races, at times, generated a degree of local interest as evident in the case of the 1890 Irving Medal, short-track meets were generally more popular spectator-oriented events that served the financial interests of the club while also affording members the opportunity to compete before larger audiences.[42] The Forest City Bicycle Club's growing interest in short-track cycling led to an announcement in June of 1891 that "plans for a quarter-mile track [had been] prepared ... [but] the location of the new track [had] not been decided upon."[43] The rules governing who could participate in the short-track races were established by the event organizers under the direction of the sponsoring club, which in turn abided by Canadian Wheelmen's Association directives.[44] Most club-sponsored races were open only to club members, and others were specified to be open to professional riders.[45] This clear demarcation between club members and "others" remained a constant throughout the period during which club-sponsored events were staged. Because a gentleman club member could not race against a professional cyclist, divisions were created to provide a safe venue for members in which they could avoid competing against and likely losing to men of lower social and economic standing. Before 1896, the distinction between an amateur and a professional, according to Keith Lansley, fell under the jurisdiction of the Canadian Wheelmen's Association, an organization in which Forest City Bicycle Club members had played a founding role in 1882. The doctrine of amateurism held considerable currency for gentlemen club members, both at the personal level and in securing control over most significant organized sport competitions and championships.

The Canadian Wheelmen's Association placed cyclists into three divisions so as to differentiate between amateurs and professionals. Class A cyclists were strictly amateurs, Class B included cyclists who were employed by cycle firms and were not considered true professionals or amateurs, and Class C cyclists were considered professionals for whom racing prizes represented at least part of their livelihood.[46] Thus, bicycle-club members, who were all Class A cyclists, only competed against other amateurs, while the rest were separated into the two professional classes. On occasion, races were sponsored by bicycle retailers who restricted cyclists to using specific bicycle models in order to secure prizes while still adhering to the established class structure for their cycling meets.[47] Whatever the auspices under which these races were staged, bicycle-club members were assured of having to compete only against their peers, with no risk of being bested or tainted by a professional rider. This was particularly important considering the fact that respectable female spectators were likely to patronize these events.[48] The variety of cycling races held in London during the 1880s and early 1890s were primarily organized for bicycle-club members by the members themselves, although some accommodations were made for professionals for social entertainment. To this end, an important underlying concern for the members of the bicycle clubs was creating venues in which respectable middle-class men could exhibit their cycling abilities against their peers.

Unlike racing, which provided opportunities for nonmembers and professionals to participate in the events, cycling tours remained the preserve of club members and served to foster and reinforce both the social exclusivity of the bicycle club and the men's leadership roles therein. This primarily social form of cycling, which remained exclusively the preserve of bicycle clubs such as the Forest City Bicycle Club, included "tours" or "excursions" between London and its surrounding communities.[49] Clubs were able to maintain a degree of control over this form of cycling in the later decades of the nineteenth century by limiting participation exclusively to members and respectable guest cyclists from recognized bicycle clubs. An example of one such tour was the Forest City Bicycle Club's annual weekend excursion to Goderich, Ontario.[50] This represented one of the highlights of the cycling season for club members.[51] The Goderich excursion began on a Saturday afternoon, leaving London's Victoria Park at 2:30 p.m., stopping overnight in the town of Exeter en route to the Lake Huron community. The trip ended in Goderich on Sunday, and the cyclists then made their way back to London by train. The cyclists frequently used the local newspapers to create impressions of their physical stamina, conviviality, and good reputation. Evidently, they wanted note taken of their humorous antics, in addition to their masculine proclivities — attracting the attention of the "fair" sex in the town of Exeter, en route to Goderich, for example.[52] On one such trip, however, the group was chided by a citizen of the town of Exeter for parading through the streets singing and behaving like members of an "Aboriginal tribe," like an "African at the opening of melon season," as "though they had been let loose from the asylum." The letter in response from "One of the Aborigines" argued, "We behaved with the utmost respect and civility towards the people of Exeter" and "were complimented for our gentlemanly behavior with a noble effort."[53]

The relatively rigid organization of the Forest City Bicycle Club was legitimized through both the structure of the club's executive and the composition of the touring parties. Similar to other sport organizations, the Forest City club's executive organized itself along traditional

Cyclists preparing to race at the London Western Fair grounds, circa 1895, Tune Family Fonds, The University of Western Ontario Archives, RC-40417.

lines of command that included a president, vice president, financial secretary, and corresponding secretary.[54] This represented a typical executive organization for a sporting club of the day, structured to provide rational order for the operation of the club. Similarly, in order to signify a measure of rational conduct on the part of cyclists while on official club tours or representing the club at a meet, members of the Forest City Bicycle Club were assigned ranks based on the military model. These included an elected club captain, a first lieutenant, and a second lieutenant. The remaining members of a touring party were assigned the rank of private.[55] This regimented structure and organization provided a clear chain of command in the Forest City Bicycle Club both on and off the road. Charles E. Pratt, in his manual *The American Cycler*, provided a clear description of the type of man who ought to be elected captain of a late-nineteenth-century bicycle club. According to Pratt, "the captain ought to be the best rider, or one of the best, in the club, the winner in a race is not always that man; and, if he were, he would not necessarily have those other qualifications of good judgment, quick perception, courteous bearing and yet respecting authority, which are looked for in a commander or a leader."[56] As the choice of the captain suggests, the organizational structure of the club reflected the deep-seated understanding of the qualities of leadership that a man should possess in order to be chosen for such a position. In this case, physical ability on the bicycle was a prerequisite but was not sufficient to be trusted as the leader of the club on the road. Therefore, the strength of the club rested, in part, on the authority invested in its leaders through the implementation of approved social hierarchies that linked physical abilities with masculine honor. This organization was underscored by a distinct form of middle-class masculinity that paid homage to commonly held notions of honor, leadership, and responsibility to the club, indeed, to that class fragment. Members of the Forest City Bicycle Club even received a lesson on military drill after their monthly meeting. The cyclists were to lead the 7th Fusiliers in parade.[57]

One of the exemplars of gentlemanly honor, embodied in racing skill, bravado, good humor, and business reputation, was John Albert "Nip" Tune, prominent member and eventual captain of the club. Tune was one of London's best racers and a regular on club excursions and tours. For Tune, reputation went beyond cycling prowess: "He is a good strong rider and has made first rate showing in the three recent road races, and without much training. He has undoubtedly the strongest claims to being the dude of the club … and as a ladies' man he is right at home."[58] The "genial, whole-souled" Nip was identified as a "rising young business man and well respected," operating a bottled-water company in London.[59] A baseball and lacrosse player of note, Tune was active in building his own reputation through the public issuing of competitive challenges and accepting formidable tests himself. He and a cycling peer named Burns accepted a "dare" to ride from London to nearby St. Thomas and back, then to Ingersoll in time to catch the evening express train back home, a total distance of 60–70 miles. In what were identified as rainy, wet, and sloppy conditions, the two cyclists made the complete trip with an hour to spare, having attracted the interest of several farmers along the way and a "sympathetic housewife" who brought them cream and hot biscuits.[60] The combination of business acumen, gentlemanly antics, physical skill, racing performance, and of course the manly status of "dude" was a potent constellation of attributes for the ascendant middle-class male, who sought leadership positions in public organizations.

The organization and administration of the Forest City Bicycle Club originated from both national and international influences including the Canadian Wheelmen's Association and, most likely, the guide published by Charles Pratt that outlined the practical organization and structure for cycling clubs. Nonetheless, the impetus for forming the club arose locally, driven by issues that were present in other growing communities and the common strategy of establishing a respectable body to legitimize cycling in the city. This process of legitimization was clearly based on reproducing particular, although sometimes fragmented, middle-class masculine ideals that melded physical prowess with social responsibility. This club- and sport-building strategy was largely a successful endeavor, although by the middle of the 1890s the club began to lose control over cycling in London, ultimately leading to changes in how middle-class men were able to promote these masculine ideals within the setting of the bicycle club.

CYCLING FOR THE EVERYMAN/EVERYWOMAN

The Forest City Bicycle Club represented the sole organized cycling club in London from 1882 through the beginning of the 1890s. Despite this monopoly, the popularity of cycling among the general population of London increased rapidly during the 1890s.[61] The first club to represent a challenge to the Forest City Bicycle Club was the London Bicycle Club, which competed against it in head-to-head races as early as 1891.[62] Shortly thereafter, as bicycles became increasingly available and affordable, additional bicycle clubs formed and began to attract members.[63] Attempts by these clubs, including the Forest City Bicycle Club, to maintain their exclusive positions as the rightful organizers of cycling in London by restricting membership and the continued use of distinctive club uniforms were only partly successful.[64] As early as 1885, reports suggested that bicycle manufacturers were "contemplating a large reduction in the price of machines to retailers as trade [had been] falling off perceptibly and the large profits accruing the past few years [could] be easily cut and yet make handsome dividends for stockholders."[65] By 1890, according to Mark Cossarin, bicycles were increasingly being mass-produced and had become more affordable for many more people than during the 1880s.[66] As the availability of bicycles expanded along with the number of dealers in London, cycling became increasingly accessible to a wider range of London's population, including women.

The large-scale entry of women into cycling in Britain and North America is commonly linked to the development of the safety bicycle in the early 1890s.[67] Before this innovation, women's involvement in cycling was generally limited to tricycles or tandem bicycles that were much less difficult to operate and served to maintain and reinforce necessary fashion and social propriety that made the high wheeler unavailable to all but young, active men.[68] For example, when the Forest City Bicycle Club set off on its annual excursion to Goderich in 1890, the party included two women, Mrs. Lamb and Mrs. Payne, the wives of two prominent club members. Special note was made of Mr. and Mrs. Lamb, who "on their tandem 'cycle, led the party throughout the 150 miles covered, the lady's perseverance and strength surprising the male riders."[69] As in the case of other sports and events, the inclusion of women was sometimes perceived to add social and moral respectability. Evidently such respectability superseded one of the traditional pillars of competitive sport — sustaining gender polarities by positioning women as mere spectators to men's physical accomplishments. Other observers of tripping cyclists were less respectful and viewed the participation of women as being part of a general trend precipitated and supported by men of questionable conduct: "It was not a very edifying sight to see the ladies of the party spending the Sabbath in such a questionable way. Wonder if Jack the dude got any medicines from his ma and pa to give the Sabbath breaking crowd."[70]

By the mid-1890s, increasing numbers of female cyclists made their way to the city's roads, weathering the overt control of the cycling club and the once socially and gender-exclusive high-riding men. This shift in participation sent class- and gender-based codes of empowered physicality into flux; the bicycle club was forced to share its activity with women, and increasing numbers from the city's male population from the lower social and economic strata traveled the roads once occupied only by club members. The Petrolia *Advertiser* opined, "Why don't our young ladies try cycling and not let the London belles knock their eye out, which they did on Dominion Day. They looked quite charming"; furthermore, there was the "advantage you have in taking your mash right along with you on a double wheel, gliding imperceptibly through lovely country lanes, and breaking forth in impassioned eloquence. Women's rights."[71]

By the late 1890s, the bicycle had become an increasingly available choice of recreation and transportation in London, yet a vestige of the elite roots of the activity persisted. On one occasion in 1897, London's city council approved funds to organize the hosting of the Canadian Wheelmen's Association national meet. The following excerpt from the 1897 minutes describes the acceptance of a petition by local bicycle enthusiasts to secure financial and political support for hosting this event. Applying were

> John Mills and 400 other ratepayers, for [a] grant to assist in procuring for London the meet of the Canadian Wheelman's Association. A deputation present in the interest of the petitioners is, upon motion heard. Dr. Geo. Davis and Mr. Benjamin Nash thereupon address the council. Ald. Stevely, seconded Ald. Carrothers, moves that the prayer of the petition be granted, the Rule of Order suspended, and the sum of $300 be placed to the joint credit of His Worship the Mayor and the Chairman of Committee No. 1, to be expended in connection with the proposed bicycle meet as they may be advised and deem expedient, and that Ald. Hunt, Stevely, and Carrothers be appointed a committee from this council to act with the committee of the bicycle clubs. Carried on the following division: Yeas — Aldermen Rumball, Taylor, Douglass, Olmsted, Carrothers, Stevely, Hunt, Turner, Bennet, Nutkins, Parnell, McCallum and Gerry. Nays — Aldermen Johnston, O'Meara, Winnett and Dreaney. Total: Yeas —13; Nays — 4. Ald. Hunt, seconded by Ald. Cooper, thereupon moves that the Municipal Council of the Corporation of the City of London hereby extends to the Canadian Wheelmen's Association a cordial invitation to hold the Annual Meet for 1897 in this city, and the Council assures the Association that in the event of London being selected for the purpose everything in the power of the Council to do, will be done, to make the visit of the Wheelmen to the Forest City a memorable and enjoyable one. Carried.[72]

Support for the endeavor demonstrated both public legitimacy and a measure of city boosterism, particularly considering the fact that many of the Londoners who supported the petition likely had no association with the cycling clubs. Despite the obvious interest in attracting wealthy and influential cyclists from across the nation to London, this event suggests the residual influence of a private organization, adapting to the proliferation of cyclists on the streets from all classes. The level of support for cycling evident through this petition also suggests that the project of the Forest City Bicycle Club to legitimize cycling had been a success, so much so that the men of the club were no longer required to perform their earlier roles as promoters and practitioners of the activity.

The mid-1890s also represented a period of rapid change in terms of how cycling was regulated in London. In response to the increased number of cyclists, the London city council began to take a greater interest in the regulation of cycling in the city in lieu of the waning governance provided by bicycle-club members. City leaders were no longer able to rely on the Forest City Bicycle Club and the city's other private cycling organizations to enforce proper cycling etiquette and safety on the city's streets. This change did not represent a loss of respect for the men who administered the cycling clubs but, rather, was the result of the perceived lack of control over who participated in cycling. In June of 1894, the No. 2 committee of the London city council, responsible for works, parks, and exhibitions, made the following recommendation:

> Your Committee Begs to submit the letter of A. C. Graydon, City Engineer, re bicycles, and recommends the adoption of the suggestions contained therein, and that the speed of bicycles in Victoria Park be limited not to exceed the rate of five miles per hour, and that the necessary By-Law be prepared to enforce the same.[73]

The contents of the city engineer's report included suggestions to limit the right of way for bicycles and the use of bells and lanterns for night riding.[74] A related proposal by the same committee also suggested "that persons keeping bicycles for hire be charged an annual licence fee."[75] Again in 1896, Chief Williams of London's police department sought to regulate the speed of bicycles. This action led to the passing of bylaw No. 760, which resulted in the implementation of further regulations on cycling in the city.[76] This bylaw, however, as with those passed before 1896, did not fully satisfy individuals who sought to regain control over the use of bicycles on the city's streets. In December 1901 a recommendation to the city council sought to "regulate persons using bicycles in city streets."[77] The continued efforts on the part of the City of London to regulate the use of bicycles suggests that there had been at least a partial return to unregulated cycling that had existed in the period before the formation of the Forest City Bicycle Club in 1882. As more and more individuals became involved in cycling, there arose greater potential for conflicts between cycling and noncycling Londoners. This situation also provided a clear indication that the private bicycle clubs and the men who administered them were no longer considered the exemplars of respectable cycling in the city. Arguably, for the members, their perceived socially valued reputation — the exclusivity, the daring — had been diminished.

CONCLUSION

By the turn of the twentieth century, members of the Forest City Bicycle Club, along with London's other bicycle clubs, were no longer positioned as the city's daring but respectable young men, who could ensure the safety of pedestrians and riders; 1900 was the final year that the Forest City Bicycle Club appeared in the listings of the London City Directory,[78] although the YMCA Bicycle Club continued to be listed up to 1906.[79] According to Glen Norcliffe, by 1900, mass production had reduced the price of a "lower-grade" bicycle by two-thirds in just five years. This rapid change, Norcliffe argues, "destroyed the exclusivity of bicycling as new forms of manufacturing made cheaper bicycles available to a mass market."[80] The noticeable decline in the influence of the Forest City Bicycle Club during the late 1890s, despite the degree of respect it retained when it came to organized cycling events, foreshadowed the club's impending demise. The club, which during the 1880s had legitimated both the sport and the club's dominant role in its organization and practice, could by the turn of the twentieth century no longer boast a leadership position in London. Furthermore, unlike the sports of hockey and boxing, in which leagues and participants were permitted to police themselves,[81] the city assumed the role of regulating cyclists on London streets. Through the 1880s and early 1890s, the clubs had managed to regulate and even to a degree delimit participation in organized cycling events held on both public roads and private sports grounds. By the end of the century, however, the Forest City Bicycle Club's once exclusive hold over organized cycling in London had eroded not because of the formation of rival clubs but because the bicycle had become increasingly accessible to Londoners with interest and disposable income. Thus, the bicycle was used to a greater extent by members of the public for transportation and for vocational and recreational purposes.[82] The bicycle no longer served as a vehicle, literally, for a few elite young men to publicly reaffirm their risk-laden but honorable displays of manliness and physical prowess that were common signifiers in the broader elite organized sports movement. Risk, excitement, and masculine bravado were qualities that men, of certain class fragments, continued to invoke as signifiers of manhood through sport into the twentieth century, but for the Forest City club and others, an historically unique cycle of manhood had passed.

NOTES

1. Don Morrow, "Montreal: The Cradle of Organized Sport," in Don Morrow and Mary Keyes, eds., *A Concise History of Sport in Canada* (Toronto: Oxford Univ. Press, 1989), 15. The ordinary, or high-wheel, bicycle was not the first style of bicycle to be ridden in Canada. It was preceded by the velocipede, or boneshaker, which appeared as early as the late 1860s according to Glen Norcliffe, *The Ride to Modernity: The Bicycle in Canada, 1869–1900* (Toronto: Univ. of Toronto Press, 2001), 3–5.

2. See Helen Lenskyj, "Perfecting Womanhood Through Sport," in *Out of Bounds: Women, Sport & Sexuality* (Toronto: Women's Press, 1986), and Patricia Vertinsky, "The 30 Year Pilgrimage: Exercise in the Prime of Life," in *The Eternally Wounded Woman: Women, Doctors, and Exercise in the Late Nineteenth Century* (Manchester: Manchester Univ. Press, 1990).

3. Morrow, "The Cradle of Organized Sport," 15–17. The formation of the Montreal Bicycle Club in 1878 and the club's subsequent role in the formation of the Montreal Amateur Athletic Association in 1881 provides some evidence of the growing need for public legitimacy among cyclists during the infancy of the activity in Canada.

4. Kevin B. Wamsley, "The Public Importance of Men and the Importance of Public Men: Sport and Masculinities in Nineteenth-Century Canada," in Philip White and Kevin Young, eds., *Sport and Gender in Canada* (Toronto: Oxford Univ. Press, 1999), 24–39.

5. See, for example, Ann Hall, *The Girl and the Game: A History of Women's Sport in Canada* (Peterborough, Ontario: Broadview Press, 2002), 16–20; David Rubinstein, "Cycling in the 1890s," in *Victorian Studies* 21, no. 1 (1977): 61–62; Lenskyj, *Out of Bounds*, 59–61; Mary Keyes, "Women and Sport," in Don Morrow and Mary Keyes, eds., *A Concise History of Sport in Canada* (Toronto: Oxford Univ. Press, 1989), 231; and Ann Hall, "Creators of the Lost and Perfect Game? Gender, History, and Canadian Sport," in Philip White and Kevin Young, eds., *Sport and Gender in Canada* (Toronto: Oxford Univ. Press, 1999), 9–10. There is broad acceptance that in urban Canada, women's involvement in cycling grew rapidly beginning in the mid-1890s with the introduction of the safety bicycle. It is also widely recognized that despite opposition to women's participation, based primarily on the moral concerns of maintaining appropriate womanhood, it was also believed that cycling could improve a woman's overall health. These authors, to varying degrees, recognize that cycling led to a variety of positive social changes for some middle-class women, including popularizing of less restrictive clothing and providing greater freedom of movement without having to rely on men. This agreement is not universal, however. Anita Rush's "The Bicycle Boom of the Gay Nineties: A Reassessment," in *Material History Bulletin/Bulletin d'histoire de la culture matérielle*, Fall 1983: 3, suggests that the cycling might not have played as significant a role in popularizing the bloomer or bifurcated skirts and other forms of social freedom widely associated with cycling but was merely one of a number of changes that led to greater involvement of women in public life. Apart from this lone dissenting voice, the propensity of the evidence suggests that the bicycle did play an important role in the social emancipation of Canadian women.

6. Anita Rush, "The Bicycle Boom of the Gay Nineties," 2.

7. For an examination of the growth in organized sport in nineteenth-century Canada, see Alan Metcalf's *Canada Learns to Play: The Emergence of Organized Sport, 1807–1914* (Toronto: McClelland & Stewart, 1997).

8. Kevin B. Wamsley and Robert Kossuth, "Fighting It Out in Nineteenth-Century Upper Canada/Canada West: Masculinities and Physical Challenges in the Tavern," *Journal of Sport History* 27, no. 3 (2000): 418–419.

9. See David Whitson, "Sport in the Social Construction of Masculinity," in Michael A. Messner and Donald R. Sabo, eds., *Sport, Men, and the Gender Order: Critical Feminist Perspectives* (Champaign, Ill.: Human Kinetics, 1990), 21. Whitson argues that sport played an important role in constructing nineteenth-century masculinity. Specifically, he points to the role of elite English boys' public schools where participation in rough sports on the playing fields, tempered by Christian values, turned boys into men. This social movement is referred to as muscular Christianity.

10. Wamsley, "The Public Importance of Men and the Importance of Public Men," 27–30. It is suggested that the dichotomy of "bush" and "gentry" masculinities that had existed in the Canadas during the eighteenth and early nineteenth centuries became increasingly fractured by the late nineteenth century. The emergence of a middle-class notion of what it meant to be a man based in this group's dominant political and economic position in society was juxtaposed against that of the less respectable and often violent lives of urban working-class men.

11. Norcliffe, *The Ride to Modernity*, 182. The average cost for a high-wheel bicycle in the 1880s was about $100 Canadian, or roughly four months' wages for the average factory hand. The high-wheel bicycle was popular through the 1880s and early 1890s, but by the mid-1890s the equal-sized-wheel safety bicycle had become the popular style.

12. Seamus McGonagle, *The Bicycle in Life, Love, War, and Literature* (New York: A. S. Brunswick & Co., 1968). McGonagle divides the history of the bicycle into three stages: the very early period dominated by aristocratic

play (early 1800s), the years that the middle class employed the bicycle as a status symbol (1870s and 1880s), and finally the emancipation of the working class through access to a relatively inexpensive form of transportation (1890s and into the twentieth century). The focus of this study falls in the middle period, dominated by the middle class's involvement in the activity.

13. "The Challenge," catalogue prepared by William Payne, Bicycle Importer, P.O. Box 304, London, Ontario, circa 1883. Microfiche Collection, The D. B. Weldon Library, Univ. of Western Ontario.

14. L. N. Bronson, "Old Time Baseball," unpublished paper delivered to London-Middlesex Historical Society, February 15, 1972, 53.

15. Andrew Ritchie, "The Origins of Bicycle Racing in England: Technology, Entertainment, Sponsorship and Advertising in the Early History of Sport," *Journal of Sport History* 26, no. 3 (1999): 499.

16. McGonagle, *The Bicycle in Life, Love, War, and Literature*, 27–28.

17. John Woodforde, *The Story of the Bicycle* (New York: Universe Books, 1970), 40, and McGonagle, *The Bicycle in Life, Love, War, and Literature*, 28.

18. Woodforde, *The Story of the Bicycle*, 41.

19. Ibid., 49–50. Andrew Richie, "The Origins of Bicycle Racing in England," 501–502, provides similar descriptions of early English cyclists who faced stone-throwing rural residents who sought to upset the riders.

20. *London Free Press*, June 26, 1890. Although this incident occurred in 1890, it does provide evidence that similar acts of cyclist sabotage took place in Canada.

21. McGonagle, *The Bicycle in Life, Love, War, and Literature*, 42–48.

22. *London Advertiser*, July 26, 1881.

23. "Photographs and Scrapbook of the Tune Family, Soda Water Manufacturers, London, 1889–1893," 1889, J. J. Talman Regional Room, Univ. of Western Ontario, Box 4301. The scrapbook contains a collection of newspaper clippings, mostly related to J. A. "Nip" Tune's involvement in cycling and the Forest City club, although there are some materials relating to other social events, sports, and family affairs. The scrapbook is dated 1889, with some clippings dated as late as 1891.

24. Ibid.

25. *London Free Press*, September 19, 1882. The individuals present at the meeting that resulted in the formation of the Forest City Bicycle Club included R. Burns, elected president; C. M. Wallace, elected 1st lieutenant; W. M. Begg, elected 2nd lieutenant; C. E. Keenlyside, elected secretary-treasurer; George Burns, Jr.; C. H. Wallace; George Cameron; J. W. Simpson; W. Chisholm; R. Millar; J. Lamb; S. Williams; J. Dignam; and William Payne, a local bicycle importer. Payne was London's first bicycle importer; his business first appeared in the City of London Directory in 1881–82.

26. Don Morrow, "Montreal: The Cradle of Organized Sport," 15. The first bicycle club formed in Canada was the Montreal Bicycle Club, in 1878.

27. Norcliffe, *The Ride to Modernity*, 191. Norcliffe suggests that women first became active in Canadian cycling in 1890 and 1891. *London Free Press*, 19 August 1890. This account of the Forest City Bicycle Club's annual tour between London and Goderich made mention of Mr. and Mrs. Lamb on their tandem bicycle leading the party through the 150-mile trip. The reporter noted that "the lady's perseverance and strength surpris[ed] the male 'cyclers.' "

28. *London Free Press*, September 25, 1882. The Forest City Bicycle Club formed just before the staging of a large "bicycling tournament" held in St. Thomas, Ontario, on Friday, September 22, 1882. After the tournament, members from the participating clubs met to form the Canadian Wheelmen's Association. The election of the first executive of the association included men who were members of clubs from Toronto, Aylmer, Hamilton, London, Brantford, Simcoe, and Montreal. C. E. Keenlyside of London served as a member of the national body's committee of management in the club's first year.

29. Don Morrow, "Knights of the Snowshoe," *Journal of Sport History* 15, no. 1 (1988): 5–40. Morrow provides ample evidence of how masculine identities emerged from competition and club activities.

30. From Pierre Bourdieu's framework of physical and symbolic capital; see Pierre Bourdieu, "The Forms of Capital," in *Handbook of Theory and Research for the Sociology of Education*, J. Richardson, ed. (New York: Greenwood, 1986).

31. "Scrapbook of the Tune Family."

32. Christopher Armstrong and H. V. Nelles, *The Revenge of the Methodist Bicycle Company: Sunday Streetcars and Municipal Reform in Toronto, 1888–1897* (Toronto: Peter Martin, 1977), 170.

33. "Scrapbook of the Tune Family."

34. Ibid.

35. *London Advertiser*, July 10, 1890, and *London Free Press*, July 10, 1890.

36. *London Advertiser*, July 15, 1890, and *London Free Press*, July 15, 1890.

37. *London Advertiser*, July 24, 1890.

38. *London Advertiser*, July 29, 1890.

39. *London Advertiser*, July 30, 1890, and *London Free Press*, July 30, 1890.

40. For further discussion on the idea of the physical challenge and its association with sport and masculine identity, see Kevin B. Wamsley and David Whitson, "Celebrating Violent Masculinities: The Sporting Death of Luther McCarty," *Journal of Sport History* 25, no. 3 (1998): 419–431.

41. *London Free Press*, July 31, 1890.

42. Mark A. Crossarin, "Joyride: Manifestations of the 1890s Bicycle Craze in Toronto" (master's thesis, Univ. of Western Ontario, May 1993), 87–88. According to Crossarin, short-track bicycle racing in Toronto was more popular with spectators because they could watch the entire event unfold, while the clubs were able to profit from charging admission to the races.

43. *London Free Press*, June 24, 1891.

44. Crossarin, "Joyride," 88–92. Crossarin suggests that most track racing was organized by local clubs for members only. Rarely were events organized for professional riders, and if they were, these professional cycling races were organized by groups other than the cycling clubs.

45. London Bicycle Club advertisement for "Race Meet" held in London, August 17, 1896, in the Rick Wolfe Bicycling Collection, displayed at the London Regional Art and Historical Museum, summer 2000. This meet consisted of "3 Championships, 6 Amateur and 3 Professional Events."

46. Keith L. Lansley, "The Amateur Athletic Union of Canada and Changing Concepts of Amateurism" (Ph.D. diss., Univ. of Alberta, 1971), 48. In 1896 the Canadian Wheelmen's Association bowed to the pressure of the Amateur Athletic Association of Canada and collapsed the two professional classes into one group.

47. *London Free Press*, June 27, 1891. In this race, sponsored by bicycle retailer William Payne, Mr. F. White of the Forest City Bicycle Club did not receive a prize because he was not riding a "Singer" bicycle. As a result, the club took it upon themselves to remedy this oversight and presented him with their own prize.

48. Andrew Richie, "The Origins of Bicycle Racing in England," 514. Richie suggests that in England during the 1870s and 1880s women were regular spectators at cycling races. Moreover, Morrow's work on the snowshoe clubs confirms that such sporting events reproduced distinct gender polarities.

49. Charles E. Pratt, *The American Bicycler: A Manual for the Observer, the Learner, and the Expert*, 2nd ed. (Boston: Rockwell & Churchill, 1880), 175–180. Article XII of the "By-Laws, Rules, and Regulations" section of the manual outlined in great detail how these cycling excursions were to be run. These rules outlined the position of the captain in the company of riders, the whistle calls used to communicate to riders, how to pass horses, when and how to ride down hills, and even when it was acceptable to ride in the dark.

50. Goderich, Ontario, is a town located roughly 90 kilometers [approximately 56 miles] northwest of London on the shores of Lake Huron.

51. *London Free Press*, August 15, 18, and 19, 1890.

52. "Scrapbook of the Tune Family."

53. Ibid.

54. *The London City and Middlesex County Directory, 1891* (London: Might's Directory, 1891). The Forest City Cycling Club listing in the directory included the address 115 Carling St., and the executive members Alfred Morphy, president; James Lamb, vice president; R. M. Burns, financial secretary; and W. E. Mathews, corresponding secretary.

55. *London Free Press*, August 19, 1890. According to Norcliffe, *The Ride to Modernity*, 193, this military organization of bicycling clubs evolved in American bicycle clubs, many members of which were experienced with this type of organization based on their experiences in the American Civil War.

56. Pratt, *The American Bicycler*, 168.

57. "Scrapbook of the Tune Family."

58. Ibid.

59. Ibid.

60. Ibid.

61. *The London City and Middlesex County Directory, 1880–81* (London: R. L. Polk & Co., 1880). Over the decade of the 1880s there was only one bicycle importer in London, William Payne, located at 217 Wortley Rd. in London South. *Foster's London City and Middlesex County Directory, 1900* (Toronto: J. G. Foster & Co., 1900). In 1890, local sporting-goods merchant William Gurd, located at 185 Dundas St., also began to sell bicycles.

62. *London Free Press*, September 15, 1891.

63. *London Free Press*, June 15, 1892. This newspaper article discusses the YMCA Bicycle Club and its activities in London. *The London City and Middlesex County Directory, 1894* (London: Might Directory, 1894). The 1894 directory lists a new bicycle club, the Meteor Bicycle Club. In the same directory there were five bicycle dealers listed, three more than in 1890.

64. Morrow, "Montreal: The Cradle of Organized Sport," 15–16. According to Morrow, the Montreal Bicycle Club used uniforms to distinguish themselves in a manner similar to the Montreal Snow Shoe Club. For the same reasons, the Forest City Cycling Club members wore uniforms as a method of distinguishing members from "other" cyclists. According to Pratt's *The American Bicycler*, 182–183, a strict code of dress was essential for clubs.

65. *London Free Press*, July 14, 1885.

66. Crossarin, "Joyride," 4–5.

67. Rubinstein, "Cycling in the 1890s," 49; Lenskyj, *Out of Bounds*, 59–61; Keyes, "Women and Sport," 231; Hall, "Creators of the Lost and Perfect Game?" 9; Norcliffe, *The Ride to Modernity*, 35; and William Humber, *Freewheeling: The Story of Bicycling in Canada* (Erin, Ontario: Boston Mills Press, 1986), 35. This is a sample of authors who have reaffirmed the link between the safety bicycle and women's involvement in cycling starting in the mid-1890s.

68. Woodforde, *The Story of the Bicycle*, 122–123.

69. *London Free Press*, August 19, 1890.

70. "Scrapbook of the Tune Family."

71. Ibid.

72. Proceedings of London City Council, April 5, 1897.

73. Proceedings of London City Council, June 18, 1894.

74. Proceedings of London City Council, April 2 and May 7, 1894.

75. Proceedings of London City Council, June 18, 1894.

76. Proceedings of London City Council, June 1, 1896.

77. Proceedings of London City Council, December 2, 1901.

78. *Foster's London City and Middlesex County Directory, 1900* (Toronto: J. G. Foster & Co., 1900).

79. *Foster's London City and Middlesex County Directory, 1906* (Toronto: J. G. Foster & Co., 1906).

80. Norcliffe, *The Ride to Modernity*, 119.

81. See Kevin Young and Kevin Wamsley, "State Complicity in Sports Assault and the Gender Order in 20th Century Canada: Preliminary Observations," *AVANTE* 2, no. 2 (1996): 51–69.

82. Archibald Bremner, *City of London, Ontario, Canada: The Pioneer Period and the London of Today* (London: London Printing & Lithograph, 1900), 68. According to Bremer's chronicle of life in London, "the use of the wheel … has ceased to be solely a means of recreation, and it now plays an important part of locomotion for business purposes." Thus, by the turn of the twentieth century the role of the bicycle had expanded from its elite recreation roots.

Article 10.2

Michael A. Robidoux

Imagining a Canadian Identity through Sport: A Historical Interpretation of Lacrosse and Hockey

Issues to Consider

- What are the connections between class relations, gender constructions, ethnic values, national identity, and the late 19th-century rise of "controlled" sport in Canada?
- What evolution did the Native sport "baggataway" have to undergo to become Canada's first national sport? What does Robidoux contend was the nature of its appeal to Canadian men?
- What part did amateurism play in shaping Canadian sport?
- How did the strict adherence to the rules of amateurism in lacrosse inadvertently transfer Canadian sport enthusiasts' interests to hockey in the early 20th century?
- Why does Robidoux reject the "discourse of nature" in explaining the rise of hockey in Canada?
- How does he interpret the Summit Series of 1972 within the context of Canada's national identity and international position?

In *Imagined Communities*, Benedict Anderson convincingly reduces the concept of nationalism to an imagining — imagined "because members of even the smallest nation will never know most of their fellow-members, meet them, or even hear of them, yet in the minds of each lives the image of their communion" (1991:6). It is this notion of communion that motivates nations to define and articulate their amorphous existence. If Anderson is correct — which I believe to be the case — the task of defining a national identity is a creative process that requires constructing a shared history and mythology(ies) that best suit the identity *imagined* by those few responsible for responding to this task. For a nation as young as Canada (confederated in 1867), this constructive process is somewhat recent and largely incomplete, which is disconcerting for Canadians who have twice witnessed the threat of national separation.[1] As a result, what it means to be Canadian is often scrutinized, lamented, and at times even celebrated (most recently through a Molson Canadian Beer advertisement).[2] Yet through all of this there has been one expression of nationalism that has remained constant since Confederation, that being the game of ice hockey.[3]

Since World War II, Canadians have been internationally perceived more as peacekeepers and, perhaps, even as being unreasonably polite — both political constructions in themselves — which makes it difficult to comprehend why a game such as hockey, known for its ferocity, speed, and violence, would come to serve as Canada's primary national symbol. The mystery intensifies if we consider that the game of hockey was born out of a period of social reform in Canada, where popular pastimes that involved violence, gambling, and rowdiness were being replaced by more "civilized" pursuits imported from Europe. [...]

Source: Michael A. Robidoux, "Imagining a Canadian Identity through Sport: A Historical Interpretation of Lacrosse and Hockey," *Journal of American Folklore* 115, no. 456 (2002): 209–25.

[...] The question becomes, then, how did a game such as hockey not only take shape in Canada, but become "frequently cited as evidence that a Canadian culture exists" (Laba 1992:333)? Furthermore, to what extent does the game of hockey embody a Canadian collective sensibility, or is this *imagining* of Canadian identity without justification even at a symbolic level? In order to respond to these questions, it is necessary to explore early vernacular forms of sport in this nation and consider how these sensibilities have maintained themselves in a contemporary sporting context.

THE PROCESS OF MODERNIZATION

Sport historians and sociologists have documented extensively the development of physical activity from a traditional folk (vernacular) pastime to a modern organized event.[4] Much of this discourse, however, concerns itself with the impact of modernization on traditional physical activities without taking into account the influences of traditional sporting behavior and its role in shaping (at least from a Canadian perspective) a national sport identity. Colin Howell is critical of these prejudicial tendencies and writes:

> Modernization theory views history as a linear continuum in which any given circumstance or idea can be labeled "pre-modern" or traditional, and thus, can safely be ignored as something that the seemingly neutral process of "modernization" has rendered anachronistic. (1995:184)[5]

What needs to be understood is that the process of modernization is not, in fact, a linear progression, but rather a series of contested stages that maintain certain aspects of the past, while housing them in an entirely different framework. [...]

[...] It was not until later in the century that schools and churches began to take a more active role in introducing structured forms of physical activity to Canadians of various class and ethnic backgrounds. The intent of making sport and physical activity more socially democratic was threefold: to acquire levels of control over increased amounts of leisure time made possible by industrialization and a shorter workweek; to reduce class conflict by enabling male participants of various backgrounds to compete on an equal playing field; and to build a physically fit yet subordinate workforce, ensuring maximum levels of industrial production. In short, advocating for institutionalized sport served as an important means of reproducing a Victorian social order in Canada, where young men learned to be honorable and genteel gentlemen. As with any hegemonic process,[6] however, control was never absolute, and almost immediately emergent and residual cultures affected the desired outcome in unexpected ways.

RESISTING AN IMPORTED CANADIAN IDENTITY

The development of "controlled" sport took an important turn by the middle of the 19th century with a new emergent class — led by Montreal-born dentist George Beers — responding to impositions of British nationalism in Canada. Beers's role in Canadian sport history was that of a romantic nationalist, as his politics were comparable to Herder's romantic nationalism of 18th-century Germany. Like Herder, Beers understood that to construct a national identity, two things needed to occur. First, foreign influence needed to be eliminated — Herder contended with French influence; Beers contended with English imperialism. And second, a national history/mythology needed to be consciously constructed. Instead of turning to indigenous poetry and language as Herder did, Beers turned to indigenous sport as a means of portraying the soul of a nation. What better place to look, he surmised, than Canada's First

Peoples, whose game of *baggataway*—filled with speed, violence, and skill—appeared to best embody the harsh and grueling existence of Canadian natives as well as the trials of early Canadian settlers in this new and untamed land.

The game *baggataway*, renamed lacrosse by French settlers,[7] was played by many First Nations (Native Canadians) across North America prior to European contact, and it proved to be a game that both fascinated and repulsed early settlers (Eisen 1994:2). Some English Europeans were least sympathetic to First Nations' leisurely activities largely because of puritanical sensibilities that tended to perceive all forms of play as wasteful and unproductive. It is not surprising that English observations of lacrosse disparaged the violence; yet negative comments were often countered with admiration for First Nations players who exuded remarkable sportsmanship and respect for their opponents (Carver 1956:237). [...] For many young French males, the rough nature of the sport was appealing, and as a result, these men became enamoured with not only the game of lacrosse but with its participants as well. [...]

For a certain sector of French Canadian males — later known as *les Canadiens*— the First Nations male provided an alternative model of masculinity to what they had known in France, one where physicality, stoicism, and bravado were valued and celebrated, not repressed, as was the typical Christian model of masculinity:

> The young voyageurs struggled to copy the Indians' stoicism in the face of adversity and their endurance when confronted with hardship, deprivation, and pain. They also copied, to the extent that their employers and governors could not prevent, the autonomy that Indian society inculcated in its young. French males found the liberated sexual attitudes of young Indian women before matrimony as attractive as the missionaries found them repugnant. (Miller 2000:54)

Early French settlers began emulating First Nations males, and in doing so began sharing in their cultural practices. Occupational and survival-related pursuits such as canoeing, snowshoeing, and hunting were some of the obvious activities that were learned and performed. Native team sports such as lacrosse also proved to be of tremendous interest to *les Canadiens*, as these games gave both First Nations and French males the opportunity to prove their worth to one another as men. According to Joseph Oxendine, these white settlers did not fare very well, however, "because of the Indian's clear superiority of the game. Indians were frequently reported to have used fewer players in an effort to equalize the competition" (1988:48). First Nations proficiency at lacrosse was highly regarded by early sport enthusiasts, but these skills were also perceived by others to be violent and dangerous, a perception that began generating its own folklore among the early North American settlers. [...]

[...] It was the legendary status the sport commanded that made it the perfect vehicle for George Beers's nationalist agenda. The game ran counter to British bourgeois sensibilities that understood sport to be refined and gentlemanly, one that could ultimately serve as a breeding ground for proper British mores and values. Instead, lacrosse was a display of rugged, brutal, and aggressive behaviors that were said to embody what it meant to be a Canadian settler in this unforgiving northern territory. Thus, Beers called on Canadians to refrain from engaging in the imperial pursuit of cricket and take up lacrosse as the new national game, in effect ridding Canada of foreign influences and acquainting the new populations with the soul of the nation.

In order to make this fictious proposal possible, the native game needed to be claimed by the male settlers and then incorporated into a modern sporting climate. *Baggataway*, as First Nations peoples played it, was not merely a sport but a spiritual and religious occasion, often having healing or prophetic significance.[8] The game also had regional and tribal idiosyncrasies, which meant that there was no standard form of play, making Euro-Canadian adoption difficult. Thus, *baggataway* as a native vernacular entity needed to be transformed into lacrosse, which meant claiming the game and eliminating traits that were linked to First Nations culture. To achieve this transformation, it was necessary to standardize the rules to create a sense of uniformity. An important step was made, in fact, by George Beers, who published the first rules of lacrosse under the name "Goal-keeper" in a series of advertisements in the *Montreal Gazette* in 1860 (Cosentino 1998:15). These rules were later adopted by the Montreal Lacrosse Club and became the "official" rules of lacrosse, later republished in the *Montreal Gazette* in July of 1867 (Morrow 1989:47). Efforts to standardize the game not only eliminated regional variation, but also seemed to dictate how the game of lacrosse was to be played. All that was left, then, was to attract people to the game, and, again, in this Beers was instrumental.

Through various print forms (magazines and newspapers), Beers began to promote lacrosse as Canada's national game, and in the process deride cricket as foreign and irrelevant to Canadians. In an article that appeared in the *Montreal Gazette* in August of 1867, suitably entitled, "The National Game," Beers writes:

> As cricket, wherever played by Britons, is a link of loyalty to bind them to their home so may lacrosse be to Canadians. We may yet find it will do as much for our young Dominion as the Olympian games did for Greece or cricket for our Motherland.

Of course, Beers makes no apologies for appropriating an aboriginal game and promoting it as the national pastime. Instead, he sees appropriation as an accurate depiction of European presence in Canada and argues, "just as we claim as Canadian the rivers and lakes and land once owned exclusively by Indians, so we now claim their field game as the national field game of our dominion" (1867). Beer's proselytizing was enormously effective, to the extent that a National Lacrosse Association was formed — the first national sporting body in Canada — and lacrosse was being touted by many as Canada's official national game.[9]

These developments, which documented how a vernacular sporting pastime was transformed into a modern sport, were not as complete as scholars have suggested. Sports historian Don Morrow claims: "At first heralded in adoption, then transformed in nature, the Indian origins of the game were finally shunned by nineteenth-century white promoters and players" (1989:46). While ritual/sacred components and regional variations were erased from modern lacrosse competitions, there were native/vernacular elements of the game that remained, largely to the chagrin of elite sporting officials who were governing these developments. To begin, the popularization of lacrosse did not arise merely because of Beers's ideological ravings. It is incorrect to claim, as Morrow does, that the new national affinity of lacrosse was achieved through the word of George Beers. Crediting only one person simply does not allow for human agency, and while public consciousness can be influenced, it is not something that can be dictated. In other words, there needed to be some preexisting value in lacrosse that allowed it to be so willingly adopted by Canadian sport enthusiasts. It is here, then, that we can begin examining the cultural value of lacrosse (and later hockey) and its relationship to Canadian identity.

SPORT SENSIBILITIES IN CONFLICT

One of the primary reasons lacrosse served as a viable alternative to imported British sports such as cricket was its emphasis on physical aggression, volatility, and danger. The game appealed to males who identified with a more physically aggressive notion of masculinity rather than the reserved and civil expressions of masculinity exemplified in cricket. In essence, the attraction to lacrosse was an extension of early French Canadians' infatuation with First Nations masculinity, where the emphasis was on physical superiority, bodily awareness, and perseverance. Lacrosse provided males the opportunity to display these heralded qualities and challenge themselves through formal competitions. However, in the attempt to modernize lacrosse and market it to a broader audience, the game needed to become less violent and needed to be played in a manner more suitable for "gentlemen"; otherwise the game would not enter dominant sport culture. Efforts were in place to sanitize the game, but they were not entirely successful. In fact, those who were most successful at the sport were First Nations and working-class players who played the game as it was originally designed — aggressively and intensely. Attempts to turn the game into something else merely put those who engaged in it as "gentlemen" at a clear disadvantage to those who maintained its aggressive style of play. One team renowned for its aggressive play was the Montreal Shamrocks, who "were, without question, the most successful team prior to 1885.... The Shamrocks were out of place both socially and athletically. Social misfits on the middle-class playing fields, the Shamrocks were Irish, Roman Catholic, and working class" (Metcalfe 1987:196).

What is critical here is that the ideological and political value of lacrosse as advocated by those in power paled in relation to the actual meanings early participants experienced through playing it. Colin Howell, also a sports historian, correctly observes that lacrosse was "a relatively minor sport" that "was suddenly elevated to prominence because of the symbolic role that was associated with it at the time of Confederation" (Howell 1995:103). However, those elite officials who helped elevate the status of lacrosse understood the sport symbolically, not according to its literal value as a meaningful expression of Canadian consciousness. I do not wish to imply that this is a singular phenomenon, but there is evidence that lacrosse did have value for certain Canadian males as an identifiable articulation of who they were as men. In essence, lacrosse did signify class, gender, and ethnic values, but these values were generally unacknowledged by elite sporting officials who were suddenly threatened by their own ideological maneuverings. The official recourse was to prohibit the "people" from playing the game and to attempt to make it instead the game of an exclusive minority:

> The logical conclusion for lacrossists was that the incidence of disputes, violence, and undesirable conduct on the field of play could mean only one thing — some players were not gentlemen. The truth of this observation was given substance by the presence of Indians, who always played for money and, by race alone, could not be gentlemen, and of the working-class Shamrock team. (Metcalfe 1987:195)

This prohibition of undesirable participants eventually led to the introduction of amateurism.

Amateur athletics in Canada did not merely function as a means of ensuring that athletes engage in sport in a gentlemanly manner,[10] but served as a discriminatory system that prevented "undesirable" players from playing. Prior to 1909, the year when a national amateur athletic union was formed in Canada, national sporting bodies used the concept of amateurism to best suit their sport's needs. In the case of the National Lacrosse Association, league officials decided to make it an "amateur" association restricted to those players who fit under the definition of amateur. An amateur was conveniently defined by the Amateur Athletic Union of Canada as someone who had "never competed for a money prize, or staked bet with or against any professional for any prize," or one who "never taught, pursued, or assisted in the practice of athletic exercises as a means of obtaining a livelihood" (Metcalfe 1987:105–106). The stipulations were highly restrictive and deliberate in design.

First, the new requirements made working-class participation virtually impossible, in that wage earners were no longer able to receive financial compensation for taking time off from work to play. Keeping in mind that it was illegal to play sports on Sunday, and that the workweek ran from Monday to Saturday, working-class participation in sport was restricted generally to Saturday afternoons. As a result, players were not only prevented from receiving payment for time lost at work, but those players who at one time received compensation for their services were no longer eligible to play. The second aspect of the restrictions was equally effective because it denied access to individuals who at one time gambled on sport. During this period in Canadian history, gambling and sport were virtually inextricable: gambling made up part of the fabric of vernacular sporting pastimes. For First Nations cultures in particular, gambling in sport (by spectators and participants) was deeply ingrained in their traditions and at times even played a role in their overall economies (Oxendine 1988:31). Therefore, by these first two stipulations alone, most ethnic minorities and working-class players were considered ineligible and could no longer play amateur athletics. The final stipulation reinforced economic divisiveness further by making it clear that sport was not the property of the people but, rather, of men who "had the leisure, economic resources and social approval to explore intensive athletic training in a financially disinterested manner" (Burstyn 1999:224).

The restrictive measures imposed by the National Lacrosse Association did not go unchallenged, however. Teams tried to circumvent the rules by covertly using "professional" players to become more competitive, and in certain cases even paid players for their services. In response, the National Lacrosse Association was compelled to enforce disciplinary measures to contend with these dissident organizations. Teams caught cheating were brought before the Canadian Amateur Athletic Union to face arbitration and potential censuring.[11] As these arbitration cases grew in number, tremendous pressures were being placed on the National Lacrosse Association to retract its strictly amateur policy and permit both professionals and amateurs into the league. Despite this, the National Lacrosse Association remained steadfast in its position to prohibit professional players and was ultimately successful in maintaining itself as an amateur association; this success, however, proved to be its inevitable downfall.

By maintaining its exclusive membership, the National Lacrosse Association forced potential lacrosse players to pursue alternative sporting options. Other team-sport leagues (i.e., baseball, football, and hockey) were not as resistive to the influences of professionalism, and thus, they provided working-class and ethnic minority players alternatives to play in these sports, and be financially compensated at the same time. While baseball and football did attract many of the players, these sports did not possess the symbolic and literal value found in lacrosse. Instead, it was hockey that early Canadian sport enthusiasts embraced by the turn of century, for the same reasons they were attracted to lacrosse 20 years earlier. Unlike baseball or football, hockey was seen as uniquely Canadian in origin and character. An amalgam of modern and vernacular sporting pastimes, hockey resembled lacrosse in design and in the manner it was played. Play was aggressive and often violent, providing men the opportunity to display this emergent notion of masculinity. At a symbolic level, it was played on a frozen landscape, perfectly embodying what life as a Canadian colonialist was supposed to be like. Thus, hockey provided all that lacrosse entailed, but without the restrictions of amateurism. By the 1920s hockey had succeeded in becoming Canada's national sport pastime.

VIOLENCE, MASCULINITY, AND CANADIAN IDENTITY

It is here, then, that we return to the politics of identity and the manner in which hockey, a game notoriously aggressive and violent, serves as a potential symbol for national expression. Along with other social scientists,[12] I have been critical of popular discourse that tends to mythologize hockey and locate it as a unifying force in this nation. Gruneau and Whitson astutely observe:

> The myth of hockey as a "natural" adaptation to ice, snow, and open space is a particularly graphic example of what Barthes is alerting us to — about how history can be confused with nature.... This discourse of nature creates a kind of cultural amnesia about the social *struggles* and vested interests — between men and women, social classes, regions, races, and ethnic groups — that have always been part of hockey's history. (1993:132)

While these sentiments are certainly valid, it would be incorrect to say that hockey is without cultural or historical relevance in Canada. In fact, it is my contention that hockey is more than a mythological construct; it is a legitimate expression of Canadian national history and identity. Hockey *does* speak to issues of gender, race, ethnicity, and region in this nation, albeit not in an entirely positive manner. For this reason, hockey moves beyond symbol and becomes more of a metaphoric representation of Canadian identity.

First, hockey was born out of post-Confederation Canada,[13] in a period of political uncertainty and unrest. Canada was a disparate nation, divided in terms of language, region, and ethnicity — lacking in identity and national unity. Thus, while hockey was used ideologically to express national sentiment, its value as a vernacular entity was equal to, if not greater than, its symbolic value. From the outset, hockey's violent and aggressive style separated itself from other bourgeois (European) pastimes, including the increasingly popular game of baseball that was entering Canada from the United States. Early games often appalled certain sport writers and sport officials who saw the violence on the ice and in the stands as unfit for gentlemen. J. W. Fitsell provides two accounts of the first recorded game of hockey, which took place in 1875. The first, from *The Daily British Whig*, states that "Shins and heads were battered, benches smashed and the lady spectators fled in confusion" (Fitsell 1987:36). The other report from *The Montreal Witness* claimed that:

> Owing to some boys skating about during play an unfortunate disagreement arose: one little boy was struck across the head, and the man who did so was afterwards called to account, a regular fight taking place in which a bench was broken and other damages caused. (Fitsell 1987:36)

These accounts of violence are undoubtedly extreme, yet what is significant is that even in its earliest stages hockey was a sport perceived as excessively aggressive and violent within a modern European context.

It was largely because of this excessive violence that hockey became a sport Canadians could call their own, and they quickly began to showcase it in international contexts. By the mid-1890s, competitions were being staged between Canadian hockey teams and American ice-polo teams. The Canadian teams dominated these early competitions and revelled in the press they received. Newspapers did applaud their skill, but at the same time reports were critical of their rough play. *The Daily Mining Gazette* of Houghton, Michigan, described one game as "rush, slash and check continually.... Calumet were knocked off the puck by Portage Lakes 'any old way.' Many a man had to be carried to the dressing room" (Fitsell 1987:120). In a game in Sault Ste. Marie, Michigan, an incident occurred where "Stuart [an American player] was laid out by a board check from Jack Laviolette. He recovered and tangled with the same player, fans rushed on the ice and as Stuart bled from the facial cuts, police were called in" (Fitsell 1987:120). These accounts illustrate that within 20 years of organized existence, hockey was internationally known as being first, Canadian, and second, notoriously violent. [...]

The distinction hockey received as being a rough sport also served as a means for Canadians to display their proficiency in the clearly demarcated context of a sporting event, making hockey a valuable vehicle for expressing national identity. But it was not simply proficiency on the ice, it was physical proficiency within the masculinist tradition that was earlier identified in relation to lacrosse. Hockey displayed men who were perceived to be stoic, courageous, and physically dominant: precisely the same images of masculinity valued in First Nations culture, and later by early Canadian settlers. These historically pertinent attitudes attracted Canadians to hockey as the game provided Canadian males with an identifiable image outside of a British Victorian framework. Moreover, through hockey competitions, Canadians could exude superiority over Americans, illustrating for many a "victory for the industrious Canadian beaver over the mighty U.S. eagle" (Fitsell 1987:106). In essence, hockey became a vehicle of resistance against British and American hegemony, something that Canadians continue to call on in periods of political or national uncertainty.

The political implications went beyond resistance to British and American rivalries. One such occasion was the 1972 Summit Series in which Canadian professional hockey players engaged in an eight-game series against the Soviet Union national hockey team. The event was a debacle, yet it is considered by many to be the greatest Canadian story ever told. The series was described as East meets West — communism versus capitalism. So as the players rightfully admitted, it was no longer just about hockey. Reflecting on the series, Team Canada member Phil Espisito stated: "It wasn't a game anymore; it was society against society ... it wasn't fun. It was *not* fun" (*September 1972* 1997). The series was filled with incidents of extreme violence: one Canadian player (Bob Clarke), following instructions from a coach, broke a Soviet player's ankle with his stick. Other incidents involved a Soviet referee nearly being attacked by a Canadian player; throat-slitting gestures; kicking (with skates); fighting; and a *mêlée* with former NHL commissioner Alan Eagleson, the Soviet Guard, and the Canadian hockey team. The event, which was advertised as an expression of goodwill between nations, turned sour when the favored Canadians were defeated in the initial games and obviously outclassed in terms of skill and sportsmanship. Canadian players were simply unaware of the tremendous abilities of the Soviets and were hence humiliated both on the ice by the Soviets, and off the ice by an unforgiving Canadian public who lambasted them with jeers.

In response to their dire predicament, Canadian players resorted to bullying and intimidation tactics and literally fought their way back into contention. In a miraculous comeback, overcoming real and imagined barriers, the Canadian team proved victorious, winning the final game and the series. Their "heroism" became permanently etched into the memory of Canadians, despite actions that have recently been described by two American journalists as "hacking and clubbing the Soviet players like seal pups and bullying their way to a thrilling, remarkable comeback" (Klein and Reif 1998:31).While there have been critics of the series, the games in the Canadian collective consciousness remain as "an orgy of self-congratulation about the triumph of 'Canadian virtues'— individualism, flair, and most of all, character" (Gruneau and Whitson 1993:263). Historically speaking, these seemingly appalling behaviors are compatible with Canadian hockey in general, and for this reason are embraced, not denounced. The players performed in a manner consistent with Canadian play, illustrating a Canadian character that has yet to be defined in more concrete fashion. Therefore, despite Canadian behavior that was an assault on international hockey, and on international competition in general, this assault was distinctly Canadian, something which is invaluable for the construction of a national identity.

CONCLUSION

The connection I have made between hockey and Canadian nationalism is very real. I do not make the claim that Canadians are predisposed to violence or that they condone violent behavior. Rather, I argue that hockey enabled Canadians to display qualities that have been valued in patriarchal relations: stoicism, courage, perseverance, and proficiency. The singularity of the game and the manner in which it was played were critical for a young and disparate nation to have as its own as it faced encroaching social, political, and cultural interests from Europe and the United States. At a more pedestrian level, hockey was accessible to men of various ethnic and class backgrounds, and thus, to a greater degree than lacrosse, it became a game of the people. The fact that "people" here is specific only to males established hockey as a male preserve, making it a popular site for males to define their worth as men, drawing on notions of masculinity that date back to 17th-century Canada. In this sense, understanding hockey beyond its mythological rhetoric acknowledges the "social *struggles* and vested interests — between men and women, social classes, regions, races, and ethnic groups" and confirms that hockey was, as Gruneau and Whitson state, "all of these" (1993:132).

Finally, by linking hockey to Canadian nationalism I am not situating either as being positive. In fact, the Canadian penchant to understand itself through hockey repeats masculinist formulas of identification that reflect poorly the lives of Canadians. The physically dominant, heterosexist, and capitalist associations of this specific identity are certainly exclusionary, but for that matter, all nationalist expressions cannot suitably speak for the polyphony of a nation. Despite the obvious fallibility of nationalistic representation, the legitimacy of nationalistic expression remains. Canada's history is located firmly in patriarchy, heterosexism, and capitalism; thus, the use of hockey to promote national pride and unity was not random then, nor is it today. Playing hockey is a means of constructing an image of a nation in the manner in which dominant forces within it wish to be seen. With this, hockey does not merely symbolize the need to define a national identity, it offers insight into the actual imaginings of what this identity entails. Hockey provides Canada a means by which to be distinguished. As Benedict Anderson astutely observes, such distinction ought not to be characterized by the dichotomy of "falsity/genuineness, but by the style in which it is 'imagined'" (1991:6).

NOTES

1. The province of Quebec has twice voted on separating from Canada (1980 and 1995). The most recent referendum saw only 51 percent of Quebecers voting "no" to separation.

2. The television commercial gained national notoriety because of its pro-Canadian stance. It depicts an ordinary "Joe" pronouncing his Canadian identity in contrast to perceived stereotypes of Canadians. The following is "Joe's Rant":

    Hey. I'm not a lumberjack or a fur trader. And I don't live in an igloo, or eat blubber, or own a dogsled. And I don't know Jimmy, Sally, or Suzy from Canada, although I'm certain they're really, really nice. I have a Prime Minister, not a President.

    I speak English and French, not American. And I pronounce it "about," not "aboot."

    I can proudly sew my country's flag on my backpack. I believe in peace-keeping, not policing: diversity, not assimilation. And that the beaver is a truly proud and noble animal. A toque is a hat, a chesterfield is a couch, and it is pronounced "zed" not "zee."

    Canada is the second largest landmass, the first nation of hockey, and the best part of North America! My name is Joe, and I *am* Canadian!
    Thank you.

3. From this point forward ice hockey will be referred to as hockey.

4. See Gruneau 1983, 1988; Gruneau and Whitson 1993; Dunning 1975; Hargreaves 1986; Burstyn 1999; Metcalfe 1987; Morrow et al. 1989; Guttmann 1994; and Guay 1981.

5. Richard Gruneau in "Modernization or Hegemony" similarly recognizes the shortcomings of "overlooking, or misconstruing, the importance of social and cultural continuities in sport" (1988:19).

6. Guttmann expresses his dissatisfaction with the term *cultural imperialism* to describe sport diffusion. Instead, he prefers the term *cultural hegemony*, which better communicates the lively "contestation that has accompanied ludic diffusion" (1994:178).

7. It has been argued that the term *la crosse* was applied to the game because the sticks used by the participants resembled a bishop's crozier (Thwaites 1959:326). Maurice Jetté argues, however, that the name comes from "an old French game called 'la soule' which was played with a 'crosse' very similar to the Indian implement" that was also cross-like in shape (1975:14).

8. Jean de Brébeuf, a Jesuit priest, writes in 1636: "There is a poor sick man, fevered of body and almost dying, and a miserable Sorcerer [Shaman] will order for him, as a cooling remedy, a game of crosse. Or the sick man himself, sometimes, will have dreamed that he must die unless the whole country shall play crosse for his health" (Thwaites 1959:185).

9. Despite claims made in *The Story of Nineteenth-Century Canadian Sport* (1966) and the 1894 edition of the *Dictionnaire Canadien–Francais* that lacrosse was the national game of Canada, there are no official records that substantiate this claim (Morrow 1989:52–53).

10. Varda Burstyn writes, "For many of the founding sport associations of the late nineteenth century, 'amateur' athletics meant 'gentlemen' athletics" (1999:49).

11. The Amateur Athletic Association of Canada changed its name in 1898 to the Canadian Amateur Athletic Union in an attempt to strengthen its position as a national sport governing body (Metcalfe 1987:110).

12. See Robidoux (2001); Gruneau and Whitson (1993); and Laba (1992).

13. Canada became a confederation in 1867, and the first recorded game of hockey took place in 1875.

REFERENCES CITED

Anderson, Benedict. 1991 [1983]. *Imagined Communities: Reflections on the Origin and Spread of Nationalism*. New York: Verso.

Beers, W. G. 1867. "National Game." *Montreal Gazette*, August 8.

Bourdieu, Pierre. 1993. "How Can One Be a Sports Fan?" In *The Cultural Studies Reader*. Simon During, ed. Pp. 339–358. London: Routledge.

Burstyn, Varda. 1999. *The Rites of Men: Manhood, Politics, and the Culture of Sport*. Toronto: University of Toronto.

Carver, J. 1956 [1796]. *Travels through the Interior Parts of North America*. Minneapolis: Ross and Haines, Inc.

Cosentino, Frank. 1998. *Afros, Aboriginals and Amateur Sport in Pre–World War One Canada*. Ottawa: Canadian Historical Association.

Dunning, Eric. 1975. "Industrialization and the Incipient Modernization of Football," *Stadion* 1(1): 103–139.

Eisen, George. 1994. "Early European Attitudes toward Native American Sports and Pastimes." In *Ethnicity and Sport in North American History and Culture*. George Eisen and David K. Wiggins, eds. Pp. 1–18. Westport, CT: Greenwood Press.

Fitsell, J. Williams. 1987. *Hockey's Captains, Colonels, and Kings*. Erin, ON: The Boston Mills Press.

Gruneau, Richard. 1983. *Class, Sports, and Social Development*. Amherst: University of Massachusetts Press.

———. 1988. "Modernization or Hegemony: Two Views on Sport and Social Development." In *Not Just a Game: Essays in Canadian Sport Sociology*. Jean Harvey and Hart Cantelion, eds. Pp. 9–32. Ottawa: University of Ottawa Press.

Gruneau, Richard, and David Whitson. 1993. *Hockey Night in Canada: Sport, Identities and Cultural Politics*. Culture and Communication Series. Toronto: Garamond Press.

Guay, D. 1981. *L'Histoire de l'Education Physique au Quebec: Conceptions et Evenements (1830–1980)*. Chicoutimi: Gaetan Morin.

Guttman, Allen. 1994. *Games and Empires: Modern Sports and Cultural Imperialism*. New York: Columbia University Press.

Hargreaves, John. 1986. *Sport, Power and Culture: A Social and Historical Analysis of Popular Sports in Britain*. New York: St. Martin's Press.

Henry, Alexander. 1901 [1809]. *Travels and Adventures in Canada and the Indian Territories between the Years 1760 and 1776*. James Bain, ed. Toronto: G. N. Morang.

Howell, Colin D. 1995. *Northern Sandlots: A Social History of Maritime Baseball*. Toronto: University of Toronto Press.

Jarvie, Grant, and Joseph Maguire. 1994. *Sport and Leisure in Social Thought*. London: Routledge.

Jetté, Maurice. 1975. "Primitive Indian Lacrosse: Skill or Slaughter?" *Anthropological Journal of Canada* 13(1): 14–19.

Klein, Jeff Z., and Karl-Eric Reif. 1998. "Our Tarnished Past." *Saturday Night Magazine* 113(10): 30–33.

Laba, Martin. 1992. "Myths and Markets: Hockey as Popular Culture in Canada." In *Seeing Ourselves: Media Power and Policy in Canada*. Helen Holmes and David Taras, eds. Pp. 333–444. Toronto: Harcourt Brace Jovanovich Canada.

Metcalfe, Alan. 1987. *Canada Learns to Play: The Emergence of Organized Sport, 1807–1914*. Toronto: McClelland and Stewart.

Miller, J. R. 2000 [1989]. *Skyscrapers Hide the Heavens: A History of Indian–White Relations in Canada*. 3rd edition. Toronto: University of Toronto Press.

Morrow, Don. 1989. "Lacrosse as the National Game." In *A Concise History of Sport in Canada*. Don Morrow, Mary Keyes, Wayne Simpson, Frank Cosentino, and R. Lappage, eds. Pp. 45–68. Toronto: Oxford University Press.

Parkman, Francis. 1962. *The Conspiracy of Pontiac*. 10th edition. New York: Collier Books.

Perrot, Nicolas. 1973 [1864]. *Mémoire sur les Moeurs, Coustumes, er Relligion des Sauvages de l'Amérque Septentrionale*. Publie pour la premiere fois par J. Tailhan. Montréal: Éditions Élysée.

Oxendine, Joseph B. 1988. *American Indian Sports Heritage*. Champaign, IL: Human Kinetic Books.

Robidoux, Michael A. 2001. *Men at Play: A Working Understanding of Professional Hockey*. Montreal: McGill-Queen's University Press.

September 1972. 1997. By Ian Davey. August Schellenberg, narrator. Robert MacAskill, dir. Ian Davey and Robert MacAskill, producers. CTV.

Thwaites, Reuben G., ed. 1959. *The Jesuit Relations and Allied Documents: Travels and Explorations of the Jesuit Missionaries in New France, 1610–1791*, vol. 10. New York: Pageant Book Company.

Wheeler, Robert F. 1978. "Organized Sport and Organized Labour: The Workers' Sports Movement." *Journal of Contemporary History* 13: 191–210.

Document 10.1

Excerpts from *Freedom to Play*

The following excerpts from Lewis's collection of memories about childhood pastimes demonstrates some of the ways in which traditional and emerging or new elements of play can exist alongside each other.

Issues to Consider

- What are some of the common themes expressed in the three reminiscences? What might explain these shared, although private, memories?
- What questions arise for historians in using memory as evidence? What other sources might be used to investigate the mostly undocumented area of childhood recreation in the past?

SONGS TO SING, GAMES TO PLAY, AND PLACES TO EXPLORE

Peggy Sherman recalls Fort Saskatchewan, Alberta, as a wonderful place in which to grow up.

I had twin sisters who were eight years older than I. Their mother died just after they were born, so my father married her sister. The four of us were born with just a year and a half between. We admired and looked up to our older sisters, but the four of us were very close and we did a lot of things together. My father died when I was six.

In summer we went on picnics, and it didn't seem to matter where we went as long as we took something to eat. We picked berries. Always on Saturday we picked flowers for the house — tiger lilies, roses, etc., as they came along.

We played soft ball, "work-up" it was called. All you needed was a pitcher, catcher and batter. If there was a fourth you had a fielder. We often played on the corner lot just outside our yard, and you know how noisy we could be. Sunday evenings it used to upset Mother that we were out there making so much noise. She'd say, "Why don't you come in and we'll sing some nice hymns?" She'd play the piano and we'd have some kids come that never came to Sunday School. I remember singing "You in Your Small Corner and I in Mine." And after singing we would always have some cocoa or something.

We played marbles and jacks. Everybody had their tin of marbles, we called them alleys and they were made of glass. And there was hopscotch. We used pretty pieces of broken pottery for our toss for playing hopscotch.

Our house was just on the brow of a hill that went down to the river road and then on down to the river. In winter we had our choice of which of four hills we wanted to slide down. When we didn't want to wait for somebody to came back up with the sleigh, well, my father had a big box of shingles left over from shingling the roof — so we used those shingles to slide on down the hill. We went skating practically every night, home by nine o'clock. We played fox and goose and made angels in the snow.

Source: Norah L. Lewis, ed., *Freedom to Play: We Made Our Own Fun* (Waterloo: Wilfrid Laurier University Press, 2002), 55–56, 63–66.

I played with dolls. I can't remember for how long, but I had one beautiful baby doll that I just adored. We played house a lot too. We'd just take sticks and lay them out on the lawn. On rainy days we'd pull the dining room table apart, but we didn't put in a board. We'd stand up in the space and play store. We played rummy and other kinds of card games, crokinole, snakes and ladders, checkers, and parcheesi. We made our own valentines, and that was always a big deal. We read a lot. When we went home for lunch we'd read until the food was on the table. We were usually given books as Christmas and birthday presents.

I CAN'T RECALL A DULL MOMENT

Judy Wells, daughter of R. B. Green, lived her first eleven years at Gander Falls, Newfoundland.

Television wasn't in my vocabulary until my family moved to Ontario in 1955 and we would be invited to neighbours' homes to see "I Love Lucy" on Monday nights and cartoons and westerns on Saturday mornings.

I can't recall a dull moment "before television." Time was filled with reading (Bobbsey Twins, Nancy Drew, and the Hardy Boys, etc.) long after lights out by use of a flashlight under the covers. Other indoor activities might be making crafts, using suggestions from mom's old teacher's manual, playing madeup paper games, such as Consequences (several people sat around the table, each with a sheet of paper and pencil. First, one would write an adjective and then fold the paper over so no one could read the word and then pass the paper to the next person, who would write the name of a well-known male, either famous, a family member, or a local, fold and pass along. Next, another adjective — a well-known female name [oh yes, one should write the word met after the male name to make the story flow], then the setting where they met — what he said, what she said, and the final outcome. Eight times the paper would be passed and then opened.) What laughter would erupt when these mixed up stories were read out! My sisters and I so enjoyed this game that we played it over and over with our own families — especially when camping.

We also loved to get old catalogues and cut out people and make up stories using the cutouts. Often we would cut out other outfits from the catalogue and lick them to have them stick on the originals. What a treat it would be to be given a real cutout book where the outfits could be put on the figures with little tabs instead of having to lick them to stick!

I could go on and on about rainy day activities, playing house or doctor (we never played school as we had enough of that from 9–4), experimenting with the short wave band on our radio, or getting a blanket and sliding down the wooden staircase.

We loved playing outdoors and spent hours in our yard with neighbours involved in games such as hide and seek, statues (where a leader would fling the rest, one at a time, with all his strength in a circle until they broke off and landed in some strange position which they would maintain until the leader chose the best to be the next leader), or just climbing on dad's pile of birch logs not yet sawed up for fuel.

I once found a lovely soft wide round chunk of wood and spent a most enjoyable morning driving in nails in the warm sunshine. How was I to know that it was my father's chopping block!

Our favourite pastime was to make up plays and perform them for the rest of the neighbourhood children, 1 cent admittance. An old unused hen house in the yard made a grand theatre.

I spent hours on my bicycle, which I still have, going all over town, even to the next town, 10 miles away, with friends.

On hot summer days we set up a Freshie stand and sold drinks to the thirsty mill workers as they walked home from work. We had lots of family picnics just out of town by the big Exploits River where we could see logs floating by on their way to the paper mill in town. Dad made many attempts to try to teach us to swim.

In winter we did everything we could, to snow-shovelled paths for 10 cents, made tunnels, igloos, snow people, and horses, spent hours on our wooden sleighs with iron runners, and even ate the odd mouthful.

We would collect the neighbours' Christmas trees and make a teepee by tying them together at the top and putting branches on the floor. What a cosy hut this made.

Summer holidays were always something to look forward to. Mostly, we put our car on the train (the highway didn't go all the way) and went to our grandparents' homes in the Newfoundland outports. There was always a little boat which my sisters and our cousins were allowed to row in the cove. Often, the fishermen would let me go out squid-jigging with them in the early evening. One had to have a strong stomach for this activity as squid juice has an unpleasant odor. But it was worth it to be able to be in an open boat on the ocean waves.

All year round there were community and church activities to capture our interest — Brownies, concerts, choir, local baseball and hockey games, a Labour Day parade where I could decorate my bicycle and enter the parade, a skating carnival with prizes to be won for the best costumes.

To this day, I could live without television. The childhood lessons of self-entertainment have served me well.

THE EFFECTS OF A DISTANT WAR

Paul Barker recalls his Nova Scotia childhood.

In 1942 my parents moved to Yarmouth, N.S. It was during the war years and at that time Yarmouth was an exciting place. Members of the armed services were a common sight as well as planes, jeeps and other war vehicles. We were constantly glued to the radio to hear what was happening overseas. It was during that period that I became interested in radio episodes such as Captain Midnight, Jack Armstrong and the Lone Ranger. My parents were very fond of reading and every night before my brother and I went to bed they would read to us. As time went on I embraced this love of reading and I became an avid reader.

The war, radio programs and reading had a great effect on what I played. I possessed a good imagination and I would act out a lot of the things that I heard or read about. With my friends we played war games with our toy guns and grenades. I remember putting a wooden box on my wagon and on top of this a bushel basket. With a broom handle sticking out of the basket I had an army tank. The cover of a bushel basket was a shield and with a wooden sword I was a knight. I made a bow and some arrows and I became Robin Hood. I was able to fashion a cave in the back yard for the enactment of Aladdin and Ali Baba. My grandparents gave me an old phonograph and some records and with this I created a radio station. For Xmas one year I received a coping saw and a vise and I was thus enabled to create a lot of the props I needed. [...]

What I have described in detail is that period of my life between the age of six and eleven. In 1947 we moved to Stirling, Ontario, and there things changed dramatically. I became very involved in team sports, softball, soccer, football and hockey.

Document 10.2

Newspaper Coverage of Hockey

Sport became an increasingly newsworthy topic in the press toward the end of the 19th century, as news itself travelled more quickly and urbanization brought more newspapers into the market, and as sport became commercialized, hence publicized, for spectator enjoyment. As hockey captured the public imagination, at least among men, the coverage increased accordingly.

Issues to Consider

- How did the 1911 creation of a regional league, the Pacific Coast Hockey Association, affect the game both in the short and long term?
- How did world events affect the Stanley Cup playoffs in 1919? What connections are made between the game and the global crisis?
- What kind of response does radio broadcasting of hockey elicit?
- What is the tone and message delivered along with the news about the Summit Series of 1972?
- Overall, does the language employed to report on hockey capture the "manliness" of the game? Does it capture the national pride associated with it?

Document 10.2a

This *Montreal Gazette* item of March 4, 1875, is thought to be the earliest published account of an organized game of hockey at a stated time and place, between two identified teams and with a recorded score. The Victoria Skating Rink, 49 Drummond Street, Montréal, was the site of this historic match. Earlier published references to hockey and its forerunners were written in general terms.

At the Rink Last Night ... (*Montreal Gazette*, March 4, 1875)

At the Rink last night a very large audience gathered to witness a novel contest on the ice. The game of hockey, though much in vogue on the ice in New England and other parts of the United States, is not much known here, and in consequence the game of last evening was looked forward to with great interest. Hockey is played usually with a ball, but last night, in order that no accident should happen, a flat block of wood was used, so that it should slide along the ice without rising, and thus going among the spectators to their discomfort. The game is like Lacrosse in one sense — the block having to go through flags placed about 8 feet apart in the same manner as the rubber ball — but in the main the old country game of shinty

Source: "Backcheck: A Hockey Retrospective — Great Hockey Stories," Library and Archives Canada, http://www.collectionscanada.ca/hockey/024002-3000-e.html (updated August 19, 2004).

gives the best idea of hockey. The players last night were eighteen in number — nine on each side — and were as follows: — Messrs. Torrance (captain), Meagher, Potter, Goff, Barnston, Gardner, Griffin, Jarvis and Whiting. Creighton (captain), Campbell, Campbell, Esdaile, Joseph, Henshaw, Chapman, Powell and Clouston. The match was an interesting and well-contested affair, the efforts of the players exciting much merriment as they wheeled and dodged each other, and notwithstanding the brilliant play of Captain Torrance's team Captain Creighton's men carried the day, winning two games to the single of the Torrance nine. The game was concluded about half-past nine, and the spectators then adjourned well satisfied with the evening's entertainment.

Document 10.2b

This detailed account of an 1877 match in Montréal includes hockey's earliest written rules. Except for the use of the word "ice" in Rule 5, the rules were identical to those of field hockey.

Hockey on Ice (*Montreal Gazette*, February 27, 1877)

Yesterday afternoon eight gentlemen of the St. James' and eight of the Metropolitan Clubs took part in a Hockey match at the Victoria Skating Rink […]

THE RULES OF THE GAME

1. The game shall be commenced and renewed by a Bully in the centre of the ground. Goals shall be changed after each game.
2. When a player hits the ball, any one of the same side who at such a moment of hitting is nearer to the opponents' goal line is out of play and may not touch the ball himself, or in any way whatever prevent any other player from doing so, until the ball has been played. A player must always be on his own side of the ball.
3. The ball may be stopped, but not carried or knocked on by any part of the body. No player shall raise his stick above his shoulder. Charging from behind, tripping, collaring, kicking or shinning shall not be allowed.
4. When the ball is hit behind the goal line by the attacking side, it shall be brought out straight 15 yards, and started again by a Bully; but, if hit behind by any of the side whose goal line it is, a player of the opposite side shall hit out from within one yard of the nearest corner, no player of the attacking side at that time shall be within 20 yards of the goal line, and the defenders, with the exception of the goal-keeper, must be behind their goal line.
5. When the ball goes off at the side, a player of the opposite side to that which hit it out shall roll it out from the point on the boundary line at which it went off at right angles with the boundary line, and it shall not be in play until it has touched the ice, and the player rolling it in shall not play it until it has been played by another player, every player being then behind the ball.
6. On the infringement of any of the above rules, the ball shall be brought back and a Bully shall take place.
7. All disputes shall be settled by the Umpires, or in the event of their disagreement, by the Referee.

The Play

commenced at 4:30 and continued for three-quarters of an hour at a stretch, the total result of the games to be called at the termination of the second three-quarters of an hour. The ice was soft and the general condition of the rink was not favorable for good play. Probably in no game is there to be seen so much "bullying" as in this. Indeed, the "bully" is indispensable, for without, hockey is a thing of naught. However, the term, although not euphonious, is merely a technical one, with which every hockey player is familiar.

The St. James' men soon distinguished themselves through their captain, who turned a complete somersault, which, doubtless, under other circumstances, he would never have thought it possible he could achieve. Even a professional acrobat would have envied that well formed body describing a circle through space and alighting with an ominous thump on the wet and soft ice. Galt, on the same side, was the next to fall, and he fell nobly, while his stick got between another man's legs in the most extraordinary manner. And then came the fun. To an outsider the falls seemed to be an important part of the game. It was soon seen that the St. James' men were not sound on their legs, although the sound on their sticks could be heard all over the building. It was a good moral sight to see the disappointment which several shaky gentlemen experienced in failing to get at the ball. The interest soon became concentrated at the west end goals (the St. James'), and fruitless efforts were made to get the ball through, but thanks to the energy of the St. James' goal-keeper, and the length of his body, he kept it at a safe distance from the flags. Here Joseph made some fine play, and Whitehead distinguished himself by knocking the ball, and we were about to add a player too, almost out of time. Geddes soon came to the rescue, and toying with the ball in his peculiar and graceful way, succeeded in putting it through the goal and scoring the first game for the Metropolitans. Time, 15 minutes.

The Second Game

The St. James' men looked disappointed but hopeful, and went to work with a will. But their legs were "onreliable" and went under, leaving them deposited on the ice while the ball was — somewhere else. During several of these *mêlées*, Hart saved the game by his elongated stopping, but unfortunately for the St. James' men, Creighton made some admirable play into Geddes' hands, who put the ball through in a twinkling, thus scoring the second game for the Metropolitans. Time, 3 minutes.

The Third Game

Whitehead now changed places with Hart, and kept goal, the former playing forward. Gordon, of the St. James', here showed some good play, but alas for the frailty of the human understanding! down he went, and remained there for a minute. He got up and looked regretfully at the ball at the other end of the rink, and bided his time. David and Whitehead next got hold of it, but it again slipped through their fingers. Hart saved the goal several times and the contest became hot and keen, the St. James' men showing that they were on their metal, but the Metropolitans were too many for them, and Geddes again took the ball from their men and sent it through the goal for the third time, making the third game for his side. Time, 7 minutes.

The Fourth Game

was long and earnest. The goals were changed, and the St. James' men resolved either "to do or die." Hart proved to be the saviour of his side on half a dozen occasions, when by really clever playing he saved the ball passing the flag by purely physical exertion. "We haven't had a single chance of a goal yet," he remarked mournfully, and by way of reviving the energies of his side he issued stentorian instructions, but the energy of the St. James' men had become a thing of the past. Falls were frequent, and several unavoidable blows were exchanged instead of cards, with no other unpleasant results than a few bruises and much wet clothing. But fate seemed against the St. James' men and "time" was called at 6 o'clock when the Referee decided that the St. James' men had lost the match. In point of superiority the Metropolitans had decidedly the advantage as they were more active, better skaters, and played with some show of science. However, the next interesting point will be the dinner, which no doubt will be a good one and about which we presume there will not be two opinions.

Document 10.2c

On December 7, 1911, Frank and Lester Patrick announced the formation of the Pacific Coast Hockey Association. It was the beginning of professional hockey in British Columbia. To the dismay of the established National Hockey Association (NHA), the new league attracted many eastern stars, thus diminishing NHA talent and driving up salaries.

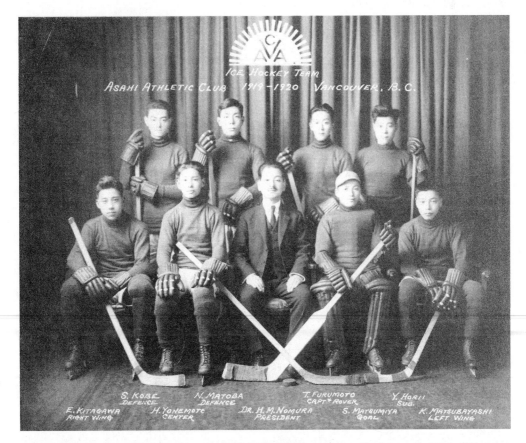

Vancouver's Asahi Athletic Club ice hockey team, 1919–1920. Professional hockey officially began in B.C. in 1911, but as this photo illustrates, hockey's appeal at the time spread throughout B.C. society.

Professional Hockey League Is Formally Organized
(*Vancouver Daily Province*, December 8, 1911)

Formal organization of the Pacific Coast Hockey Association was perfected at a meeting held at the Vancouver Hotel last evening when delegates from the newly-formed clubs in Vancouver, New Westminster and Victoria assembled and made all preparations for the first regularly organized ice hockey season on the lower mainland of British Columbia.

The championship season of the league will open on January 2 when New Westminster plays at Victoria. Vancouver will see its first game on January 5 when New Westminster will play here. This should really be New Westminster's home game but as the Royal City will not have a rink till next season all the games scheduled for there this year will be played in Vancouver. The season will close on March 15 the same time as the National Hockey Association in Eastern Canada and the winners of the British Columbia league will go straight down to Ottawa after the Stanley Cup, representing the hockey supremacy of the world. The delegates at last night's meeting were convinced that the proper place for the historic trophy was on the coast along with the Minto and Mann cups.

WILL PLAY SEVEN A SIDE

The association decided to stand by the old established rule of seven players in hockey and the Eastern amendment abolishing the position of rover was not accepted. In case the champions go after the Stanley Cup the question of whether six or seven players shall be used will come up for consideration but that will be up to the trustees to decide.

Frank Patrick was instructed to draft a constitution for the new league. In the main the constitution of the National Hockey Association will be followed and special attention will be paid to the eligibility of players. The eastern rule allows the players to shift clubs up to January 31 and the same rule will be adopted here. Thus should any of the three teams develop weaknesses after the start it will be possible to strengthen up for a period of one month.

Document 10.2d

The 1919 Stanley Cup final in Seattle was abandoned in mid-series when an outbreak of Spanish influenza decimated the Montreal Canadiens team. Each team had won two games, with one game tied. The Canadiens' "Bad" Joe Hall, an eleven-year professional hockey veteran, was one of the infected players. He died in a Seattle hospital on April 5th, four days after authorities had called off the series.

World's Hockey Series Cancelled: Seven of the Canadiens and Owner George Kennedy Stricken with "Flu" (*Montreal Gazette*, April 2, 1919)

Seattle, April 1.—Definite and final announcement was made by the Arena management at 2.30 p.m. that there will be no more world series games here this year. At noon today workmen started tearing up the Arena ice floor preparatory to converting the building into a roller skating rink.

The fact that the ice was being taken up settled all arguments as to whether or not the series would be continued if the visitors were able later to put enough men on the ice.

Lalonde, Berlanquette, Couture and Kennedy are reported only slightly ill. Last night the remaining four men came down, leaving only Pitre, Cleghorn and Vezina, who are not afflicted. It is believed here the Canadiens contracted the disease in Victoria, where the players of that team are just recovering from influenza, seven of them having been in bed at one time.

Not in the history of the Stanley Cup series has the world's hockey championship been so beset with hard luck as has this one. Of the 19 players engaged in it, hardly one of them has gone through without some bad luck. The Seattle team has been badly battered, Rowe, Foyston, Wilson, Murray and Walker all having had injuries. Corbeau, the great Canadien defence man, was hurt in the very first game and has not been able to do more than substitute since.

The great overtime games of the series have taxed the vitality of the players to such an extent that they are in poor shape indeed to fight off such a disease as influenza. However, the Canadiens are being given the very best of care, nurses and physicians being in attendance at all times on them and every other attention is being shown the stricken players.

Document 10.2e

The earliest play-by-play radio broadcast of a hockey game may have been this one from the Winnipeg Amphitheatre on February 22, 1923. Until then, the only way to get up-to-the-minute details of a game was to go to the office of the local newspaper, where telegraph reports sent directly from the rink were transcribed and posted in the window. Note how the *Free Press* places the story in a radio entertainment context, not a sporting one.

First Radio Broadcast Play-by-Play Game (*Manitoba Free Press*, February 23, 1923)

The first radio broadcast of play-by play description of a hockey game told from the side of the ice, was successfully transmitted last night by CJCG when thousands of radio fans listened to a running story of the Falcon–Port Arthur game at the Amphitheatre rink. Description of every play of the game reached the ears of listeners-in as fast as the plays were made. Many of the radio fans declared the broadcast was the first successful transmission from an outside source achieved by local stations.

The popularity of the service which enabled the many who were unable to attend the game to keep posted on the entire play as fast as it took place was shown in the enthusiastic reports from city and outside points from listeners-in who declared they heard every word of the bulletins perfectly. The transmission was effected by announcements made from the side of the ice which carried to the *Free Press* operating room by special wire, through the radio transmitter, and out to the world in direct transmission without relay.

A splendid midnight programme of dance music supplied by George Poot's orchestra completed the evening of radio entertainment. The popularity of recent midnight concerts was repeated last night, many of the radio audience expressing their enthusiastic approval of the playing of the orchestra. Composed of six individually talented musicians, the orchestra performed in finished manner, combining their efforts to excellent advantage. Incorporating in their interpretations of a repertoire of the latest dance music a thorough appreciation of the spirit of the popular numbers played, they delighted listeners-in with the programme presented.

As a musical organization the orchestra showed distinct merit. Members of the organization are George Poots, piano; Harry Gurney, banjo; George Woolley, saxophone; W. G. McPherson, cornet; George Cullison, trombone, and Mickey Werhan, traps.

Document 10.2f

Paul Henderson's last-minute goal to give Team Canada victory in the 1972 Summit Series with the Soviet Union was a defining moment in Canadian sports history. Hockey fans applauded the desperate determination of the Canadian players and marveled at the skill of the Soviets.

From Russia with Glory (*Globe and Mail*, September 29, 1972)

By DAN PROUDFOOT, *Globe and Mail* Reporter

MOSCOW — Paul Henderson's winning goal yesterday, with 34 seconds left in the game on which international hockey prestige was balanced, completed an incredible comeback by Team Canada and left the place of sports, Lenin Central Stadium, echoing to O Canada.

When the Canadian fans, more than 2,500 of them, finished their anthem, they started the chant, "We're number one." The final score was 6–5 for the Canadians, and a series victory of four wins, three losses and a tie.

Inside the Team Canada dressing room, there was a feeling of frantic pride. Not a lot of noise, no victory champagne, just a team of proud men making assertive statements.

"It was the biggest thrill of my career to be named to this team," said Henderson, the left-winger who has skated for four years with the Toronto Maple Leafs to modest reviews. "The next biggest thrill was to make the team."

"And now three winning goals in a row. Who can believe it?"

Henderson's arrival on the ice for the goal-front pass from Esposito that won the series remains a mystery to some extent.

The Leaf winger was on the bench when he saw the final minute ticking off on the Palace timeclock. "I don't know what it was, maybe a feeling, but I yelled to Harry (manager-coach Sinden) and asked him who was on the next shift. I as much as asked him to go. He said 'Ratelle.'

"And then he turned around and said, 'No, you go on.'"

"Peter Mahovlich was skating by and I said, 'Peter, how are you?' Peter just said, 'Get on,' and I did."

Henderson found himself in front of Russian goaltender Vladislav Tretiak and in a scramble he fell down. He got up, he got in front again, and Esposito's centring pass arrived.

"I let him on, "said Peter Mahovlich, "because he told me to get off, he was going to score a bleeping goal." Peter Mahovlich has a strong sense of humor.

Team Canada came to Moscow with a losing record of one win, two losses and a lie.

In the first game here, Team Canada blew a three-goal lead and lost 5–4. But the Canadians won the three final Moscow meetings to take the eight-game series, and each time Henderson scored the winner.

Last night Team Canada never led until it went ahead 6–5 in the final minute. Four times the Russians were ahead but the National Hockey League selects kept coming back. The Russians had the beautiful plays, the Canadians had the grim determination and the startling efforts of such individuals as Phil Esposito who scored twice and figured in all three goals of the third period comeback.

Henderson and Esposito complete the series as the top scorers with seven goals each.

At the end of the game Henderson's lawyer, Alan Eagleson, was yelling again as after the previous game at Leafs owner Harold Ballard.

"This has to be worth $25,000, Harold!" shouted Eagleson, who is seeking bonuses for both Henderson and his Leafs line-mate Ron Ellis on the basis of their play for Team Canada.

"Sure, let's give Henderson $50,000," said Ballard later, "or why not $150,000, make it three, make it a million, heh, heh?

"The guy who really started things in the third period was Esposito. He's the super of supers, I would say."

The impact of the goal on the fans was shared by Canadian goaltender Ken Dryden, who saw it clearly from the far end of the ice. "I saw the puck sitting there in front and I thought somehow, at the last second, someone would knock it away. Fortunately, nobody did."

Dryden skated the length of the ice to congratulate Henderson. He said he doesn't remember ever making such a long congratulatory skate. Nor does he remember a win meaning so much.

John Ferguson, assistant coach, said: "I've been through Stanley Cups but they were for Quebec, and this was for Canada." […]

Somebody asked where Bobby Orr had been. The best player of the NHL not only missed the series with a sore knee, he missed the final game completely. "I don't think B.O. was here," said Wayne Cashman, another Team Canada player sidelined by an injury. "He got too emotional watching the earlier games and I think he stayed at the hotel to watch this one on television."

Topic 11

Nature and Society: Tourism, Conservation, and Environmental Issues

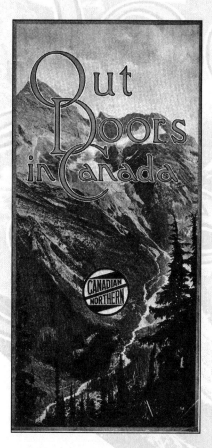

Travel brochure, Canadian Northern Railway, 1915; National Library and Archives Canada, http://www.collectionscanada.ca/trains/.

CONTEXT

The subject of tourism also comes under the broader heading of recreation, explored in the previous section with specific reference to sport history. In a nation so profoundly shaped by its geography, tourism has been closely associated with such environmental concerns as the preservation of wilderness and the conservation of natural resources. Both have motivated public campaigns as well as state involvement (see the discussion of reformism in Topic 3) toward the dual, and sometimes clashing, purposes of promoting the beauty of the Canadian landscape as a lucrative revenue source and protecting it for its own sake.

Recent analyses in the history of tourism owe much to the development of cultural studies. In particular, historians have fruitfully applied the concepts of social construction and representation to its examination. Inspired by Foucauldian theory, for example, the idea of the "tourist gaze" has brought about new insights into the ways in which "scenic attractions" are both presented and received. The spate of pre-Confederation travel writings, often illustrated by landscape paintings, that was published for an avid readership overseas demonstrates the early interest in "taking in the sights" of Canada. After Confederation, the Canadian Pacific Railway (completed in 1885), through its extensive and expanding rail and steamship services and hotels, and especially through its lavish promotional campaigns, set out to entice European and American tourists. The CPR and others in the tourism industry capitalized on the abundant natural beauty of the Canadian landscape, the Pacific, the Rockies, the spacious Prairies, the woods, rivers, lakes, and waterfalls of Ontario and Quebec, the rugged textures of the Atlantic coastline. The pre–World War I years saw the growth of this enterprise, but the expense and leisure time required to travel meant that it was confined to the more affluent social classes. Expanding prosperity, quicker and cheaper transportation, and especially the advent of the "family car" (and later the airplane) brought tourism within the reach of more Canadians than ever before by the interwar years, even if only in the form of a "Sunday drive," a family day trip, or a short road excursion. As Linda Jessup points out in her discussion of the Group of Seven's western tours, the 1920s gave rise to a mass tourism that relied increasingly on state support. Not surprisingly, thanks to its proximity, familiarity, and affordability, the United States has always accounted for the vast proportion of our tourism market (over 85 percent as the 21st century opens).

Environmental history is also a "hot" subject area in Canadian scholarship. Although a legitimate field of research in its own right, there are many ways in which its subject matter intersects with that of the history of tourism while also fitting within the larger field of social history. In essence, it is the history of humanity's relations with the natural environment, an enormous subject that attempts, as American historian Richard White succinctly summarizes its challenges, to integrate "natural history, social relations, technology and culture into unified explanations of social change." The type of questions posed fairly demands interdisciplinary and even multidisciplinary approaches. Historians working in this area apply to good advantage the conceptual frameworks and methods of their colleagues in historical geography and historical ecology, medical history and medical geography, history of science and technology, rural and urban history, and, as noted, cultural studies and the history of tourism.

The conservation impulse manifested itself soon after the achievement of Confederation, some of the necessary groundwork having predated the birth of the new nation-state. As both an ideal and a social movement, conservationism could draw on the careful knowledge base prepared by the Geological Survey of Canada. The Geological Survey was appointed by the legislature of Upper Canada in 1842 to map the land for its mineral resources, and, after 1867, to explore the enormous tracts acquired in the North and West. The Victorians related the "conquest of nature" to progress, as science and technology brought about the apparent victory of society and industry —"civilization"— over the natural world. But Canadians of the time also recognized that the vast wilderness, the diverse soil conditions, the great bodies of water and mountain ranges, and the plant and animal life contained in the nation's expanse "from sea to sea" demanded a committed stewardship. Before the close of the 19th century, a number of parks, forest and wildlife reserves, and bird sanctuaries had been created. The first national parks were established in the Rocky Mountains, at Banff in 1885, and Yoho and Glacier the following year. From their beginnings, an important objective was the federal revenue to be acquired by encouraging tourist travel.

The Liberal government of Sir Wilfrid Laurier set up the Commission of Conservation in 1909 to act as a scientific advisory board on the protection of natural resources. Laurier's energetic immigration minister, Clifford Sifton, a dedicated conservationist, would chair the commission until shortly before its demise. Although its research resulted in roughly two hundred reports and publications, policy was not as quick to follow. In 1911, the federal government inaugurated an official parks branch under an appointed Dominion Parks Commissioner, but state responsibility for the parks' preservation was not encoded until amendments were made to the National Parks Act in 1930. In the meantime, the Commission of Conservation came to an end in 1921, as other government agencies became more actively involved in resource management.

In the years after World War II, the expansion of national and provincial parks was again motivated primarily by recreational and tourism objectives. The 1960s, however, gave rise to the contemporary environmental movement. Larger numbers of Canadians than ever before, especially among the young who also spearheaded other activist campaigns of the decade, organized to lobby corporations and governments about the deleterious effects on nature of continued thoughtless exploitation. Inspired by the shocking findings of American conservationist Rachel Carson in *Silent Spring* (1962), groups such as Pollution Probe were formed. The National and Provincial Parks Association of Canada was established in 1963, the Canadian branch of the Sierra Club in 1970. That year also saw the founding of Greenpeace in Vancouver; instigated to protest nuclear testing, it quickly developed into a leading international environmental organization. Such was the political impact of these social movements that the decade also saw the establishment of a number of federal and provincial environment ministries and related agencies, as well as necessary protective legislation. As indicated by current debate on Canadian participation in the Kyoto Protocol to address the long-term environmental impact of chemical emissions, the so-called greenhouse effect, the cause remains important but the conflict between economic ambitions and conservation is still a forceful one.

REFERENCES/FURTHER READING

Baranowski, S., and E. Furlough, eds. *Being Elsewhere: Tourism, Consumer Culture, and Identity in Modern Europe and North America.* Ann Arbor, Mich.: University of Michigan Press, 2001.

Binnema, Theodore. *Common and Contested Ground: A Human and Environmental History of the Northwestern Plains.* Toronto: University of Toronto Press, 2004.

Dawson, Michael. *Selling British Columbia: Tourism and Consumer Culture, 1890–1970.* Vancouver: UBC Press, 2004.

Dubinsky, Karen. *The Second Greatest Disappointment: Honeymooning and Tourism at Niagara Falls.* Toronto: Between the Lines, 1999.

Foster, Janet. *Working for Wildlife: The Beginning of Preservation in Canada.* 2nd ed. Toronto: University of Toronto Press, 1998.

Hart, E. J. *The Selling of Canada: The CPR and the Beginnings of Canadian Tourism.* Banff, Alta.: Altitude Publishing, 1983.

Jasen, Patricia. *Wild Things: Nature, Culture, and Tourism in Ontario, 1790–1914.* Toronto: University of Toronto Press, 1995.

MacEachern, Alan. *Natural Selections: National Parks in Atlantic Canada, 1935–1970*. Montreal and Kingston: McGill-Queen's University Press, 2001.

Nicol, J. I. *The National Parks Movement in Canada*. Ottawa: National and Historic Parks Branch, 1969.

White, Richard. "Environmental History, Ecology and Meaning." *Journal of American History* 76, no. 4 (March 1990): 1111–16.

Zaslow, Morris. *The Northward Expansion of Canada, 1914–1967*. Toronto: McClelland and Stewart, 1988.

Zeller, Suzanne. *Inventing Canada: Early Victorian Science and the Idea of a Transcontinental Nation*. Toronto: University of Toronto Press, 1987.

ILLUSTRATION 11.1 (P. 457)

The travel brochure in Illustration 11.1, featuring a photograph of the Rocky Mountains, was distributed in the interests of promoting so-called wilderness tourism. At this early stage in the history of the West (Alberta and Saskatchewan were created in 1905), there were a number of luxury hotels and other travel accommodations to draw tourists, and it was simply practical as well as profitable to emphasize the "great outdoors" aspects to adventurous visitors.

Issue to Consider

• What immediate impression does the illustration on the brochure cover evoke? What do we make of the fact that the illustration, despite advertising the Canadian Northern Railway, does not include the image of a train?

ARTICLES

As Linda Jessup and John Sandlos discuss in their respective essays, the landscape was "sold" to Canadians and other potential tourist markets in representations that emphasized the visual beauty of its primeval "natural" state, either on canvas, as in the portrayals of the famous Group of Seven, or by emphasizing the sanctity of its resources and wildlife. At the same time, however, such images and discourses of pristine nature were intended to increase human traffic and, with it, the kind of interaction between society, nature, and the state that might well pose a serious threat to its continued enjoyment.

Article 11.1

Lynda Jessup

The Group of Seven and the Tourist Landscape in Western Canada, or The More Things Change …

Issues to Consider

- Why does Jessup contend that the nationalism of the Group of Seven, in the sense of reflecting back to Canadians a meaning of the nation with which the majority could identify, has been overplayed?
- What makes the Group's artistic perspective characteristic of urban Ontario?
- How did landscape and wilderness figure into a romantic reaction against modernism?
- What was the relationship between the railways and the artists?
- What was involved in the "commodification of the wilderness experience"?

Today, fifty years after the first Group of Seven exhibition of May 1920, [they] still remain the most famous, and to many people the only, "movement" in the history of Canadian art. In terms of considered critical opinion, as far as that can be said to have existed, the measure of their importance has fluctuated. However, in the eyes of the public at large, they have steadily ascended until now they occupy a position in the Canadian cultural pantheon shared only with a few hockey stars and a handful of beloved politicians.

Dennis Reid 1970

The post-colonial dilemma confronting inter-war Canadian nationalists was how to develop a powerful set of stories and symbols through which a British "Dominion" … could become a Canadian nation…. To meet this challenge, such cultural producers as the Group of Seven, new liberal and Laurentian historians, and political novelists … began to "narrate the nation" in ways which stressed the inevitability and goodness of Canada. There was little here that any student of twentieth-century nationalism would find surprising, except, perhaps, the fact that with the exception of a few areas and people, the new definitions did not really take hold. Canadian novels did not, by and large, set the framework within which a majority of Canadians "imagined" a new community; Canadian paintings, although frequently found on the walls of banks (as a "natural" part of standardized corporate iconostases) did not establish a consensus about the ultimate signifier of Canadianness. This failure to "naturalize" Canada makes the lavish Ontario celebrations of the Group of Seven in 1995 an ironic and melancholy exercise in nostalgia — a visual homage, one might almost say, to the official nationalism of the Former Canada.

Ian McKay 2001

Source: Lynda Jessup, "The Group of Seven and the Tourist Landscape in Western Canada, or The More Things Change …," *Journal of Canadian Studies* 37, no. 1 (2002): 144–79.

Things changed in the 25 years that separated the National Gallery of Canada's fiftieth anniversary celebration of the Group of Seven's formation and the gallery's 1995 extravaganza in honour of the Group's seventy-fifth anniversary. There was increasing awareness among historians of Canadian culture that the Group of Seven, and the ideas of nation advanced in and around their work, were never as fully embraced by the public at large as once assumed. The Group, and the cultural producers with whom they aligned themselves, Ian McKay points out, failed "to construct a truly hegemonic discourse of nation, founded on both cultural consent and state coercion, in which the disparate *ethnies*, territories, provinces, regions (not merely a self-selected central Canadian elite) could all recognize themselves" (McKay, "Handicrafts" 118). Rather, the Group's work and activities articulated an exclusive national identity based on an Anglo-Celtic ancestry, exclusive on the one hand of indigenous peoples, certainly, and on the other of the immigrant, that racialized concept occupied in Canada must conspicuously by Asians (beginning with the Japanese and Chinese immigrants of the nineteenth century) and by eastern and southern Europeans, who have also been distinguished historically from the Anglo-Celtic settler by what Matthew Frye Jacobson describes as "whiteness of a different colour."[1]

The Group's was also a Canadian nationalism that in its appearance of inclusiveness — its claim to speak for the nation as a whole — was characteristic of what has been defined more precisely as Ontario regionalism. The Group's success in articulating this regional identity was, and is, such that the lack of acceptance of their work and ideas in other regions of the country (even within the realm of high culture) has never been disputed. It has simply been reconfigured as a barrier to the rightful establishment of "a national art." Regional opposition became part of the conventional story of the Group as a downtrodden avant-garde that enjoyed hard-won victory over its opponents in the face of criticism and resistance. That the artists enjoyed the overwhelming support of the National Gallery of Canada and the then Art Gallery of Toronto had always been part of the story as well, the inherent contradiction between their status as struggling artists and the aggressive purchase and exhibition of their work by the two major cultural institutions having been recast by the National Gallery from the outset as evidence of its willingness to assertively exercise its mandate to support art in Canada (even as it reinterpreted that mandate to mean the support of a nationalist and, as such, "Canadian" art). Generating accusations of favouritism from artists in Montreal and resentment among artists in Vancouver at being told what Westerners should admire, the National Gallery advanced this regional perspective and, with it, a centralizing, nationalist approach to official culture that privileged Ontario to the detriment of what became by definition the eastern and western peripheries.[2] In so doing, it contributed to the sense of alienation from central Canada that has become a defining feature of regional identities elsewhere in the country, while the painting of Canada by members of the Toronto-based Group echoed in the realm of high culture the economic and political exploitation that had been felt to both east and west since the enactment of the National Policy in the late nineteenth century (see den Otter 208–38).

One of the reasons the Group's paintings of other parts of the country resonated most strongly, if not exclusively, with central Canadian audiences was the urban perspective reflected in the artists' work and activities, a perspective characteristic of Ontario regionalism. For Ontarian viewers, the landscape in paintings by the Group of Seven was not a place of productive labour, nor a permanent home, but rather a place of recreation — of scenic value and spiritual renewal. Much has been made recently of the fact that the Group's landscape paintings are uninhabited, that their landscape vision was tied to questions of territorialization and possession, all of them predicated on the erasure — in their case, pictorially — of the country's Aboriginal populations and, with them, Aboriginal claims to prior settlement, hereditary lands and resources (Bordo; Teitelbaum; Watson). As William Cronon points out, the removal of indigenous populations to create "uninhabited wilderness" was part of the transformation of the wilderness concept that began in North America in the late nineteenth century. Reconfigured under the dual influence of the romantic movement and a growing antimodernist backlash to the perceived ills and artificiality of contemporary life, wilderness emerged as a recuperative environment, and, increasingly, as the preferred landscape of elite, urban tourists hoping to return to what they saw as an elemental environment untainted by civilization. Among other ironies implicit in this cultural construction of wilderness as unaffected by the culture that constructed it, is the fact that the establishment of national parks followed quickly on the subjugation of Native populations "in which the prior inhabitants of these areas were rounded up and moved onto reservations." As Cronon puts it, "The myth of the wilderness as 'virgin,' uninhabited land had always been especially cruel when seen from the perspective of the Indians who had once called that land home. Now they were forced to move elsewhere, with the result that tourists could safely enjoy the illusion that they were seeing their nation in its pristine, original state, in the new morning of God's creation."[3]

In this sense, wilderness, whether in concept or in paintings of the Group of Seven, was empty as well of other tourists. It reflected a romantic notion of nature, which placed emphasis on solitude, privacy and an intimate, semi-spiritual relationship with undisturbed natural beauty; "nature, according to romanticism," writes J. A. Walter, "is where mankind isn't" (Walter 297; see also Cronon 72–76; Urry 1990, 45). Just as it does today, romanticism exalted a solitary experience of landscape conceived as scenery and views for visual consumption. This aesthetic experience of nature, of seeing the physical environment as landscape, is also at the root of modern sightseeing, which had taken shape as an aesthetic activity by the nineteenth century. It ushered in what John Frow describes as "a new discipline of connoisseurship for the eye, centering on the cultivation and display of 'taste'": the ability to judge and distinguish between different physical environments, as well as the social position necessary to engage in such activity in the first place. "Originating in the discriminating perusal of privately owned works of art and cabinets of curiosities," Frow explains, "its conception of the aesthetic later broadens to take in landscape and cityscape: not just pictures but the picturesque, now integrated into a more general economy of looking. It is this economy, the 'belief in the restorative effects of happily constituted scenes, and an increasingly romantic orientation to aesthetic sightseeing,' that forms the basis of modern tourism and of what John Urry describes as a generalized tourist gaze."[4] In this context, Urry notes, the "romantic gaze" is one of the primary modes of tourist consumption, distinguished from the collective, popular mode of tourist consumption — from convivial, anti-elitist forms of pleasure — by its emphasis on the solitary appreciation of outstanding scenery by those with the cultural capital necessary for the task.[5]

Of course, artists have had such cultural capital in the "general economy of looking" from the outset. Privileged players in the realm of the aesthetic, they are generally recognized as arbiters of taste and thus of picturesque scenery. This is why railway companies in Canada — specifically the Canadian Pacific and the Canadian National railways — provided Group members with free passage over their lines; they did this consistently throughout the 1920s as the artists expanded their sketching grounds from Algonquin Park and Algoma to other parts of the country.[6] In the west, the interests of the railways and the artists also converged on the national parks — on the "CPR Rockies," which embraced what are now Banff, Yoho and Kootenay national parks, and, to the north, on Jasper National Park on the line of the CNR through the Yellowhead Pass. Even A. Y. Jackson and Edwin Holgate's trip to the Skeena River, which they made in 1926, took place in the context of the area's development as a tourist attraction and its promotion for consideration as a national park. Jackson's awareness that their activities could "give the place some publicity" reflected the artists' easy understanding of their value to the railways.[7] Writing to request passage on the CNR to Edmonton in connection with his trip to Great Slave Lake in 1928, Jackson acknowledged this openly, arguing (unsuccessfully, it seems) that passes for his trip to Great Slave Lake would constitute a happy exception that proved the rule: "It is not tourist country," he contended, "but it is Can. Nat. country and the artist can help create an interest in it."[8]

It was not that the national parks were the object of railway interest in themselves; the fact was, both companies had been working in conjunction with the National Parks Branch of the Department of the Interior to develop these tourist areas specifically as destinations, in the case of the railways, not just to increase ticket sales, but also to feed their related facilities — whether the tourist accommodations and services they had established in the parks themselves, or the company hotels they had built along their lines further west. In this sense, their reason for supporting artists who wanted to sketch along their lines was much the same as it had been since the nineteenth century, as was the nature of their support. The government-run Intercolonial Railway, for instance, had issued passes to Toronto- and Montreal-based artists to travel east between Québec and New Brunswick almost immediately upon the completion of that railroad in 1876. Conceived as the eastern section of a transcontinental railway and built in connection with the federation of British North America in 1867, the Intercolonial had provided access to a newly articulated national landscape that artists had wanted to portray. They travelled out on the line, then returned with pictures of landmarks, scenery and salmon streams for the visual consumption of armchair travellers and elite tourists in central Canada whose participation, not only in the aesthetics of landscape but also in art patronage and collecting, deepened their claim to this landscape as their national aesthetic property (Jessup 1992, 99–146; see also Helsinger 103–25).

Many of these people had already travelled to the rivers of the lower St. Lawrence region and New Brunswick to fish for salmon; they were active participants as well in the "sportsmen's club movement" that swept central Canada and the northeastern United States in the mid-1870s. Reflecting contemporary notions of wilderness as a therapeutic environment, an antidote to the debilitating effects of urban-industrial civilization, the movement organized these elite tourists into private clubs for the pursuit of sport, which was conceptualized as a form of personal involvement in the rhythms of nature, and for the preservation of game, which they saw as threatened by the same urban-industrial capitalism that compelled their periodic retreat to wilderness.[9] One of the movement's chief advocates, *Forest and Stream* editor Charles Hallock, expressed this wilderness nostalgia in familiar terms when he incited his readers — the same men who benefited most from modern industrial capitalism — to work for the preservation of the natural environment in the hope that their efforts would ultimately "restore the original Eden which was made perfect for our first parents."[10] In this respect, the movement's members were reflective, as well, of British imperial culture at the end of the nineteenth century, which was imported to the club movement directly through its members' enthusiastic adoption of the British concept of sportsmanship, with its aristocratic overtones and sophisticated, ultimately exclusive, sportsman's code of conduct. Through it, they transformed the concept of hunting and fishing in North America into the dominant pursuit of the elite — in John MacKenzie's words, "an ethos to be respected and admired by subordinate social classes"— and then "set about the separation of the human and animal worlds to promote 'preservation' (later 'conservation') as a continuing justification for its monopoly."[11]

In Canada, as elsewhere, the resultant removal of Native rights to the animal world through the introduction of policies and laws restricting hunting and fishing technologies and access went hand in hand with the aesthetic appropriation of the environment as landscape. As John Reiger points out, "even when it came to basic guide books, hunting and angling locations were continually rated in terms of their picturesque qualities," and every angler and hunter not only had his own favourite microcosm of forest and stream but felt an attachment, as well, to the characteristic topography and picturesque features of the larger region he identified as "his territory."[12] Part of what prevented the Intercolonial from developing the tourist potential of this scenery in the years immediately following the completion of the railroad was the lack of related tourist facilities and services in the area. Despite the railway's enthusiastic promotion of the region's scenic grandeur, there was little accommodation for sightseers along the line and, aside from private club houses and Daniel Fraser's "quiet hostelry" at the confluence of the Matapedia and Restigouche rivers, none for what Hallock called "kid glove tourists" who wanted to fish for salmon in the immediate interior. The railway's success was also diminished in the comparison the CPR created a decade later when it began to develop the Rocky Mountains as a tourist destination by undertaking the construction of hotels and resort facilities to increase tourist revenue.[13]

The CPR benefited, as well, from the location of its facilities in the country's first nature reserves, which were established in the mountains by the Canadian government in the ten years following the completion of the railroad in 1885. Although often lauded as an act by the government to preserve the picturesque mountain scenery of the region from development, the establishment of the reserves was in keeping with the conservation efforts spearheaded by sportsmen during this period. So, while the reserves protected prized tracts of "uninhabited wilderness" from conventional development — from what the Dominion Land Acts described as "sale, settlement or squatting"— the protection of the natural environment was driven as much, if not more, by the desire to preserve fish and game in the region for sport hunting and angling (Wonders 30–31). The second phase in Canada of the international development of Western conservation practices, the creation of reserves, marked what MacKenzie has identified as "the progressive conversion of game from a direct economic resource ... into an indirect one, a means of raising revenue from 'sport' and tourism" (MacKenzie 201). In this context, Cronon points out, "one went to the wilderness not as a producer but as a consumer," hiring buggies or saddle horses to view the scenery, or "guides and other backcountry residents who could serve as romantic surrogates for the rough riders and hunters of the frontier."[14] By negotiating special leases with the government for land on the reserves, the CPR was able to capitalize on this, which it did from the outset, actively promoting the region both as an area of unrivalled scenery and as "a sportsman's Eden," where those kid-glove tourists could recuperate both under the stars in pursuit of blood sport and in the midst of sublime landscape in one of the railway's luxurious resort hotels. In other words, when the government created the reserves to protect these areas from development, it was from development other than that of tourism, to which the government gave the CPR almost exclusive rights.[15]

Otherwise, the early years of the CPR serve to establish the fact that the type of railway support for landscape painters offered by the Intercolonial became a convention in Canada. Just as the Intercolonial had done for eastward travel earlier, the company issued passes to Montreal- and Toronto-based painters to travel west, beginning in 1885, exploiting the artist's social authority as a judge of landscapes to promote the Rocky Mountains to what CPR general manager William Cornelius Van Horne referred to as "the class that travels."[16] Again, the idea was to establish the value of the region, not in the eyes of the traveller as such, but in the eyes of an urban elite that, like the artists it patronized, possessed the cultural capital necessary for discriminating between different landscapes. (As John Barrell explains, members of this class not only had the social standing required for this purpose, but also "had experience of more landscapes than one, in more geographical regions than one; and even if they did not travel much, they were accustomed, by their culture, to the notion of mobility, and could easily imagine other landscapes.") To facilitate such cultural legitimization, the railway avoided any perception that the company had a vested interest in the artists who travelled its route, eschewing direct purchase and use of paintings by the company in favour of the benefits reaped from the artists' success among those in the best position to make appropriate judgements in taste. This worked well for the CPR, as long as landscape painting was featured prominently in art exhibitions in central Canada, and as long as the most celebrated painters of the day sought to distinguish themselves with sensational paintings of the national landscape that was now linked to central Canada (Jessup 1992, 147–248). [...]

The Group of Seven's subsequent work and activities suggest something of the sustaining impact of this political economy; the urban perspective embodied in their work reflects both central Canadian urban-industrial dominance and the continuing vitality in Canada of a picturesque landscape tradition in which artists created views of outlying regions for consumption by this metropolitan market. What distinguishes the Group of Seven's work and activities from those of their predecessors in this regard is their relationship to the rise of middle-class tourism, which took shape in the context of what Bryan Palmer describes as "the first act of the theatre of mass culture," a commodification of leisure time that provided growing numbers of Canadians in the 1920s, most of them members of an increasingly affluent middle class, with the same possibility of momentary escape from the perceived effects of modern-industrial capitalism that had been available to the urban elite since the nineteenth century (Palmer 229). With it came the beginnings of state involvement in the organization of the tourist industry. "Until the 1920s," Ian McKay points out, "it had not been a permanent part of state policy either to attract tourists or to coordinate various aspects of local culture and society as part of the 'tourism plant.' After that decade, however, the state aggressively intervened in civil society to construct such a plant by paving highways, developing hotels, inventing new ethnic and sporting traditions, and monitoring the steady advance of the 'industry'" (McKay 1994, 33). In the development of the tourist economy, he explains, "this intervention did not mean undercutting the role of capital; rather, it meant that the state, acting not on behalf of a particular class but in the interests of the stability of the socio-economic system as a whole, served as capital's pioneer, exploring hitherto uncommodified areas of cultural life that could be turned into profitable activities" (34).

In the national parks, this took shape as active state involvement in the commodification of the wilderness experience. It could even be argued that the operation of the National Parks Branch of the Department of the Interior was predicated from the outset on the development of this commodity. Certainly, it occupied the attention of National Parks Commissioner James Bernard Harkin, who was appointed in 1911 when the Branch was established to administer the new Dominion (later National) parks, which were created at this time out of the earlier nature reserves. His Commissioner's Reports insistently stressed the recuperative value of what he saw as National Park wilderness; he argued that the importance of the parks lay both in the increasing revenue they generated from American and other international tourism and in what he repeatedly described as "the service they render to the people of Canada."[17] Conflating well-worn ideas of wilderness with a heightened sense of the parks as a national possession, Harkin consistently cast National Park wilderness as an originary environment within which humanity — in this case specifically Canadians — could temporarily escape the bureaucratic institutions and hectic work routines of everyday life in urban-industrial society to renew the "play spirit" Harkin saw as essential to the development of nationality. In doing so, he reconciled what otherwise seem to be the contradictory aims of national park policy during this period: the conservation of "unspoiled" wilderness from human influence on the one hand (which served to maintain the essential *idea* of wilderness, and thus its restorative value to contemporary society), and, on the other, the promotion of the parks as therapeutic "playgrounds," in this case both for Canadians and for international tourists (who, it was argued, generated the revenue necessary to pay for infrastructure to support increased domestic use of the parks).[18]

In other words, the commodification of wilderness experience involved celebrating the pre-modern, unspoiled "essence" of National Park wilderness while, paradoxically, looking for ways in which that essence could be commercialized in the creation of a modern tourism economy.[19] Although it might not be immediately apparent, the root of such thinking lay in the creation of national parks themselves, which was actually an extension of the idea of separate living spaces that until recently has characterized Western conservation practices internationally. As MacKenzie puts it, "reserves demarcated land use between human cultivators and fauna. They were designed to avoid, rather than promote interaction between them, each being subject to the control of an alien elite. National parks were designed for an urban society so that the denizens of the one could … visit the inhabitants of the other." He writes, "National parks were designed for an age of tourism."[20] This explains why the Branch promoted conservation even as it aggressively developed infrastructure to increase the accessibility of the parks, which, almost from the beginning of the Branch's existence, meant the construction of scenic roads throughout the national park system. In fact, Harkin's determination to advance road-building was such that, during the First World War, he initiated the establishment of park internment camps so that road-building could proceed using internment labour —"park prisoners" (as Bill Waiser calls them) consisting primarily of unemployed or destitute Ukrainian men who worked in what were even then regarded as appalling conditions in the mountain parks to lay the first in what amounted to 400 miles of scenic roads by 1930.[21] By then, one in every seven Canadians over the age of 14 owned an automobile, and the country was second only to the United States in per capita consumption of cars (Palmer 233; Davis 109).

Perhaps more important to national parks development in these years than the increasing consumption of automobiles alone was the attendant popularity and almost immediate commercialization of auto camping as a leisure activity among the more affluent members of the middle class. By the mid-1920s, when Harkin was reporting that more than half the record 104,000 visitors to Rocky Mountain (later Banff National) Park were entering by car, it had stimulated not only the building of the roads in the parks, but also the construction of related facilities, which, after the early years of auto camping as simple roadside squatting, had evolved into a range of commercial accommodations for motorists, including roadside reservations, campsites and cabins, all of them capitalizing on the assertion of individual freedom, informality and ascetic self-reliance then associated with automobile travel.[22] Ironically, at least in the context of Canada's mountain parks, North Americans had defined automobility in direct opposition to the perceived authority of the rail-hotel complex, which was thought, among other things, to channel movement along collective, monopolized lines at invariable speeds determined by rigid schedules and standardized time. "The train, not the car, represented modern times," Warren James Belasco writes. The car embodied a rejection of the values associated with the modern; camping, careening around the mountains, wearing old clothes and living according to one's own schedule was to defy the perceived formality of the hotel and the restrictions of train travel. If the railroad was the modern industrial establishment, he points out, "the car was the New Freedom. It promised a nostalgic return to a simpler age of benignly individualistic operators, an age before the beginnings of the Industrial Revolution, and thus, before the railroad" (Belasco 19, 20).

This is ironic because, in Canada's mountain parks, the Canadian Pacific and Canadian National railways worked closely with the National Parks Branch to encourage automobile-based tourism; because of their privileged, if not exclusive, situation in the parks, they stood to benefit most immediately from the state's efforts to develop the tourist economy in western Canada. The CPR was even committed to splitting the construction costs of the Banff-Windermere Highway through what is now Kootenay National Park with the British Columbia government, shouldering the total cost of this scenic highway with the National Parks Branch, which was financing the road's construction within the boundaries of Rocky Mountain Park.[23] In the early 1920s, the CPR also introduced "bungalow camps"— compounds consisting of small, homely cabins grouped around central dining halls — for motor tourists who sought lodgings that were comfortable yet economical. It operated these in the parks alongside the campgrounds and roadside motor parks the Branch had built to "accommodate motorists who desire to live under canvas," as Harkin put it (Canada, Department of the Interior 1926, 91). Such accommodations were expressive, as well, of a perceived shift in the physical experience of wilderness — a new primitivist intimacy that served to distinguish it from what had been defined as the more restricted, formal experience associated with Victorian resort hotels and rail travel. In keeping with this, the CNR used a similarly primitivist vocabulary of "peeled logs and native boulders" when, in 1923, it constructed its new resort hotel, Jasper Park Lodge, which consisted of a luxurious central structure surrounded by what it described as smaller, "bungalow style" log cabins.[24] By then it was also supplementing its celebrated "motor roads" with extensive hiking trails, as was the CPR, both railways developing them in conjunction with the riding trails the Branch was building to service increasing numbers of tourists in search of the wilderness experience.[25]

By 1924, when Lawren Harris and A. Y. Jackson painted in Jasper Park, hiking, saddle and packhorse trips were already an important part of the railways' promotional literature. Although belied by Jackson's later account of their sketching trips as uncharted treks into what he called Jasper's "big country," in reality their excursions to Medicine and Maligne lakes and to the Tonquin Valley were described in detail in that summer's "Jasper Park Lodge" brochure, which also provided a playful topographical map of each trip and a list of that season's rates for camping equipment, food, horses, and guides.[26] (The next year, they were described simply as Saddle Trips nos. 18 and 19.)[27] Like the development of infrastructure and other related facilities, the introduction of such services was part of the commodification of the wilderness experience, the restructuring of experience, as McKay puts it, "by the very modern capitalism from which it seemed to provide momentary and partial escape" (McKay 1994, 35). They served, alongside other developments, to organize the generalized tourist gaze to which John Urry refers, helping state and capital to construct the tourist's experience, which existed as a wilderness experience only insofar as it satisfied the romantic gaze — that particular type of tourist vision emphasizing the restorative, solitary consumption of landscape (if not by the individual, then by the couple, the family, or, at most, one's companions).[28] [...]

The Branch's interest in supporting the work of artists was also predicated on the understanding that cultural capital could accrue to the parks by association. In 1923, the Department of the Interior commissioned "A Choric Ode" to distribute as a souvenir in connection with the opening of the Banff-Windermere Highway; Harkin argued in an internal memo that "the tourist sees through the eyes of the poet and values [the landscape] more highly on that account." Casually conflating the tourist's gaze with that of the Canadian, he concluded as a result that such work "would add romance and the glamour of art to the mountains and so make them more valuable in the eyes of Canadians themselves."[29] The Branch also contributed handsomely towards the production costs of the CNR's 1927 deluxe booklet, *Jasper National Park*, an elaborate souvenir brochure featuring 21 black-and-white illustrations suggestive of charcoal drawings and six tipped-in colour reproductions of gouache paintings, most of them signed at the lower left or right — the drawings by Group of Seven members J. E. H. MacDonald, Frank Carmichael and A. J. Casson and the paintings by. A. Y. Jackson. Strictly a commercial production, it was designed to evoke values conventionally associated with works of fine art and the artist's response to the environment; in reality, all the illustrations were based on photographs, including the pictures by Jackson, who painted in gouache only when doing commercial work in any case.[30] (MacDonald, Carmichael and Casson have never even been to the park.) Drawing on their friendship and on the artists' experience as commercial designers, the commission would have come through Carmichael, who was then art director at the commercial art firm Sampson Matthews Ltd. in Toronto, where he was supervising production of a number of CNR brochures.[31]

In other words, despite its play on the values of fine art in the promotion of National Park wilderness, the project had more to do with the Group members' contacts within the field of commercial design than it did with recognition of their status as "bonefide artists," to use CNR president Henry Thornton's epithet.[32] An illustration by MacDonald in the 1928 CPR brochure, *Resorts in the Canadian Pacific Rockies*, in contrast, is a good example of a commercial production that acknowledged their standing as working artists. Following what was by then CPR convention, it is a colour reproduction of one of his sketches, a small work he probably gave to general tourist agent John Murray Gibbon as a gesture of gratitude for free passage over the railroad, which he enjoyed annually from 1924 to 1930.[33] In this brochure, his painting is one of several reproductions of works by artists who had sketched in the "CPR Rockies"; the other artists are lesser-known today than MacDonald.[34] At the time, however, their views would have worked seamlessly with his to suggest values generally associated with landscape art, the titles of their works having clearly been adapted by the railway to serve its immediate interests. The title of MacDonald's sketch, *Lake O'Hara — seen from the Bungalow Camp*, is a case in point. Even though both MacDonald and fellow Group member Arthur Lismer stayed in the company's Lake O'Hara bungalow camp (Lismer first visiting the mountains on a pass in 1928), the titles they assigned to the products of their sketching trips do not make such explicit references to the commercial aspects of their wilderness experience.[35] The titles of their paintings make general or specific references instead to geographical locations or physical features, a work such as MacDonald's related sketch, *Lake McArthur, Yoho Park*, underscoring the origins of the Group's work in the picturesque landscape tradition and the seemingly private experience of undisturbed natural beauty characteristic of the romantic gaze.

The reproduction of MacDonald's painting is an isolated example of the use of a Group member's work in a railway brochure in any case, and there is no evidence to suggest that the artists were specifically interested in generating commercial art commissions in connection with their trips west to the parks. They were there to advance their work as painters and, through it, their respective careers as artists, which, if anything, made them sensitive to the potential uses of fine art in the development of a tourism economy. Their various proposals for promotional decorative schemes and murals in railway hotels and stations have been documented, along with the one decorative work of this type completed by a Group member, the Jasper Tea Room at the CNR's Chateau Laurier Hotel in Ottawa, which was undertaken by Edwin Holgate in the late 1920s using motifs inspired by his 1926 trip with Jackson west of Jasper Park to the Skeena River region.[36] There is also evidence of the artists' interest in the production of souvenirs. According to Jackson, Harris had a long talk with Thornton about "the souvenir business," probably when the two artists returned from Jasper Park in 1924.[37] At that time, Lismer was also trying to advance the idea in collaboration with National Gallery director Eric Brown, who met with J. B. Harkin ("apropos the application of Canadian Art to economic matters") to discuss a proposal by Harkin's office that the Branch sell works by Canadian artists as souvenirs in the parks: "small pictures and sketches via colour prints; woodblocks, small figurines, wood carvings, pottery, metal work and many other things." In keeping with the nationalist imperative characteristic of the artist's work and activities, Brown argued that "this was the time for Canadian art to go forward." He suggested that the National Gallery help by exhibiting this souvenir art and by providing loans and exhibitions to the parks in turn. "The larger Parks might build a small and picturesque gallery," he suggested to Harkin, "where all such objects could be sold, where lectures and talks could be given and Canadian art could be featured to the tourist."[38]

Preliminary arrangements, which were made early the next year, included Harkin's commitment to gain the necessary approval of the scheme from the Department of the Interior, which he hoped to secure with the aid of a memorandum from Brown arguing (as Brown phrased it) "the artistic value of the enterprise as well as the commercial and nationalistic ones." He and Brown also devised a provisional advisory committee, which included Harkin and Brown, Group members Lismer and MacDonald and Group supporter and National Gallery trustee Vincent Massey. Working out of Toronto or Ottawa with start-up funds Harkin evidently anticipated along with department approval, they planned to discuss the organization and administration of the project, including sources of supplies, standards of excellence and designs and methods of production.[39] (Clearly inspired by the idea of a centralized, state-supervised "souvenir industry," Brown and Lismer had already discussed the possibility of working through the established art schools, using students such as those at the Ontario College of Art in Toronto, where both Lismer and MacDonald were teaching at the time; "if," Brown cautioned, "they could be organized into producing the right kind of stuff.")[40] As far as Brown was concerned, the souvenirs would need to be not only well designed and applicable to quantity production, but also reflective of what he described in his memo as the "Canadian nationality" seen in the art of the Group of Seven and their followers, which he characteristically conflated with Canadian art in general. "I can imagine nothing better calculated to stimulate Canadian art and to turn it towards the development of a national spirit," he argued, casting their plans for the touristic commercialization of fine art in terms consistent with the ideas of the Group.[41] Although he did not deal explicitly with the commercial value of the scheme in his memo, it is clear that he understood the potential market for this new commodity; he wrote to Massey at almost the same time that Harkin was sure the railways would support the scheme "both in hotels and probably on boats. Those, added to parks, ought to make a great demand when you think that about 60,000 souvenir buying visitors go to Banff Park alone each year."[42]

As it turned out, however, the scheme was not realized — good indication, perhaps, that departmental approval was not forthcoming. None the less, Harkin continued to express interest in the commercialization of fine art as souvenirs, the Branch's efforts to advance the scheme from the outset having been part of its larger involvement in the commodification of the wilderness experience and the development of a tourist industry.[43] Despite the fact that the authenticity they claimed to embody as souvenirs of the place would have been undermined by their supervised mass production in central Canada, clearly, to Harkin's mind, "artistic Canadian souvenirs" would serve as authentic mementos of the tourist's experience of National Park wilderness in so far as they appeared to embody the individual artistic expression of the Canadian artist whose essential Canadianness was understood in relationship to wilderness landscape. On another level, the scheme was part of his ongoing efforts to structure the tourist's gaze through identification of the parks with the values of fine art and what he described as its ability "to arouse the sort of ideas" he wanted Canadians to associate with the Rocky Mountains.[44] That Brown stood ready to use the National Gallery of Canada to help "in any way in the working out of this idea" was important; it indicates not only that Brown understood the role of the National Gallery in the processes of cultural legitimization at the root of Harkin's scheme, but also that he was willing to use the power of the National Gallery to facilitate it.[45] Ultimately, of course, the instrumentality of this cultural authority in promoting the work and ideas of the Group of Seven to the level of "official culture" also served to institutionalize the wilderness experience Harkin was trying to advance, bringing it into close association with the ideas of nationality in and around the work of the Group of Seven and, through the medium of elite culture, with notions of value understood in terms of cultural capital.

In this connection, it is important to remember that, in the end, the wilderness experience authorized — and nationalized — in the process was a function of the romantic gaze, with its emphasis on elitist — and solitary — consumption of undisturbed Nature. As such, the artists' expressions of this experience also work effectively to obscure what was, in the 1920s, its increasing availability for mass consumption as a commodity in the development of a tourism economy (a process that, in itself, facilitates the denial of mass accessibility essential to the tourist's experience). Even today, the artists' accounts of their sketching trips (and, thus, of their sketches) are still received at face value and accepted as chronicles of rugged engagement with an elemental, pre-modern environment, even as they are identified as a primary source for the romantic images of bushwhacker, pioneer and adventurer at the root of the Group's mythology.[46] While there is no reason to doubt the sincerity of the artists' reports (whether colourful or poetic), it is now evident that their accounts, activities and resulting works can also be seen in terms of the antimodern impulses at the heart of the middle-class wilderness experience and the willing suspension of disbelief required for the restorative, solitary experience of a "virgin," uninhabited landscape otherwise populated by other tourists [see Illustration 11.2]. In this context, their wilderness images can be resituated as products of a time when they used hiking and pony trails, stayed in bungalow camps or "lived under canvas" like other visitors to the parks, participating in the very tourist experience their work was helping to structure. Even Harris's treks to what have been seen through his paintings as increasingly remote locations in the mountains can be viewed in the context of modern tourism and the positional competition for landscape that seems to exist outside the very circuit of exchange values and commodity relations that make it accessible to the tourist. If they are, the spiritual exploration of the mountain landscape he undertook at the time takes on new meaning; among other things, it is informed by the fact that, in 1929, the year he was making sketches for his lonely *Isolation Park, Rocky Mountains*, the number of visitors to National Park wilderness reached almost half a million.[47]

As Jin-me Yoon suggests, this romantic tourist experience is central to the idea of nationality constructed in and around the work of the Group of Seven. The Vancouver-based artist's well-known work, *Souvenirs of the Self*, is richly allusive in this respect, a product of her interests (as she puts it) in "the naturalization of Canadian identity and its social, cultural and historical construction through representation," both in images and in the contexts within which images are viewed (Gagnon, "Other Conundrums," 49, 57; Lafleur 218–27). When shown in 1993 at the Mendel Art Gallery in Saskatoon, it took shape as an installation consisting of three large photographs of an Asian woman at various tourist sites in Banff installed adjacent to an untitled Lawren Harris painting of the Rocky Mountains drawn from the gallery's collection of the Group's work.[48] For this reason, many readers initially read the piece as suggestive of various disjunctions between the identity of the person in the photographs — understood primarily in terms of race, gender and relationship to place — and the idea of Canadianness constructed around the landscape paintings of the Group of Seven.[49] The relationship between Yoon's large "tourist photographs" and the painting alludes, as well, to the ways in which constructions of identity are disseminated — some, like the work of art in the public institution, as more legitimate, more exclusive or perhaps more "official" than others, among them the personal "snapshot" taken at the tourist site by one of the crowd with camera in hand who identifies with the collective experience of the place through "*the* activity which has in a way become emblematic of the tourist: the democratized taking of photographs" (Urry 1990, 138). Ironically, the effect, as well, is to suggest the degree to which the Group's nationalist images are also those of the tourist; as Hyun Yi Kang points out, "presuming that 'tourist' and 'Canadian' are mutually exclusive identifications denies the full contestatory force of this piece, which operates more effectively only against the possibility that this female figure can be seen as coterminously Canadian and tourist" (Kang 32).

Canadian National Railways Magazine 18:8 (August 1932), back cover. Photo: National Library of Canada (neg. no. NL22457).

What is not immediately apparent, however, is the fact that her work also operates within the realm of high culture, even while challenging its authority and the ideas of nationality advanced through its institutions. It could even be argued that the work can operate effectively only within this realm, that its critique has been premised on what both the artist and the work assert to be a naturalized Canadian identity — which is a false premise, but which also has been mobilized in an environment where its accuracy is reasserted by students of high culture, who read the work through the established history of Canadian art and the hegemonic position within it of the Group's notions of nationality. Key to this misreading is acceptance of the idea that the so-called "naturalized Canadian identity" represented through the Group's work is at least historically (and thus socially and culturally) real, an act of acceptance that reaffirms the conventional story that the Ontario-based Group was "a national art movement," despite the lack of acceptance of their work and ideas in other regions of the country, even within the realm of high culture. (It is ironic, of course, that Yoon's critique, which is intended as well to address the institutional construction of this identity, should be based on acceptance of a story that has been most aggressively advanced by the National Gallery of Canada.) In reality, however, this misreading exists as such only if it is acknowledged that in the work and activities of the Group of Seven the nationalist and the tourist are the urban Ontarian. Otherwise, Yoon's work ultimately serves as testament to the fact that the tourist landscapes of the Group of Seven are not the ultimate signifier of Canadianness through which the majority of Canadians have imagined community, but rather, the well-worn mascot of an "official culture" that still locates itself firmly in the realm of high culture, and in a centralizing, nationalist identity characteristic of Ontario regionalism.

ACKNOWLEDGMENTS

I am grateful to Alan MacEachern and Jeffrey Brison for the helpful comments and suggestions they provided in the preparation of this paper.

NOTES

1. Matthew Frye Jacobson, *Whiteness of a Different Color: European Immigrants and the Alchemy of Race* (Cambridge, Mass: Harvard University Press, 1998). The recent revisionist work dealing with the Group of Seven and Tom Thomson includes McKay, "Handicrafts"; Lynda Jessup, "Bushwhackers in the Gallery: Antimodernism and the Group of Seven," in *Antimodernism and Artistic Experience*, 130–52; Ross D. Cameron, "Tom Thomson, Antimodernism, and the Ideal of Manhood," *Journal of the Canadian Historical Association*, new series 10 (1999): 185–208; Lynda Jessup, "Prospectors, Bushwhackers, Painters: Antimodernism and the Group of Seven," *International Journal of Canadian Studies* 17 (Spring 1998): 193–214; Jonathan Bordo, "The *Terra Nullius* of Wilderness — Colonialist Landscape Art (Canada & Australia) and the So-called Claim to American Exception," *International Journal of Canadian Studies* 15 (Spring 1997): 13–36; Lynda Jessup, "Art for a Nation?" *Fuse* (Summer 1996): 11–14; Robert Linsley, "Landscapes in Motion: Lawren Harris, Emily Carr and the Heterogenous Modern Nation," *Oxford Art Journal* 19 (1996): 80–95; Scott Watson, "Race, Wilderness, Territory and the Origins of Modern Canadian Landscape Painting," *Semiotext(e)* 6 (1994): 93–104; Jonathan Bordo, "Jack Pine — Wilderness Sublime or the Erasure of the Aboriginal Presence from the Landscape," *Journal of Canadian Studies* 27 (Winter 1992–1993): 98–128; Scott Watson, "Disfigured Nature: The Origins of the Modern Canadian Landscape," in *Eye of Nature* (Banff, Alta: Walter Phillips Gallery, 1991), 103–12; Matthew Teitelbaum, "Sighting the Single Tree, Sighting the New Found Land," in *Eye of Nature*, 71–88; Paul H. Walton, "The Group of Seven and Northern Development," *Revues des arts canadiens/Canadian Art Review* 17 (1990): 171–79. Consideration of the Group of Seven has also arisen in connection with the recent work of Vancouver-based artist Jin-me Yoon. See Adrienne Lai, "Renegotiating the Terms of Inclusion: Institutional Space, (Dis)location and A *Group of Sixty-Seven*," *Fuse* 23 (April 2000): 15–20; Monika Kin Gagnon in conversation with Jin-me Yoon, "Other Conundrums," in *Jin-me Yoon: Between Departure and Arrival* (Vancouver: Western Front, 1997), 49, 57; Hyun Yi Kang, "The Autobiographical Stagings of Jin-me Yoon," in *Jin-me Yoon: Between Departure and Arrival*, 22–42; Grant Arnold, "Purism, Heterogeneity and A *Group of Sixty-Seven*," *Collapse* 3 (1997): 147–53; Monika Kin Gagnon, "Jin-me Yoon's A *Group of Sixty-Seven*," *Backflash* 15 (Spring 1997): 9–12; Brenda Lafleur, " 'Resting' in History: Translating the Art of Jin-me Yoon," in *Generations & Geographies in the Visual Arts: Feminist Readings*, ed. Griselda Pollock (London & New York: Routledge, 1996), 218–27; Grant Arnold, "Shared Terrain/Contested Spaces: New Work by Fifteen B.C. Artists," in Grant Arnold, Monika Kin Gagnon and Doreen Jensen, *Topographies: Aspects of Recent B.C. Art* (Vancouver: Douglas and McIntyre, 1996), 1–44.

2. See Jessup, "Bushwhackers in the Gallery." The story of the Group of Seven advanced by the National Gallery is provided in Reid, *Group of Seven* (Ottawa: National Gallery of Canada, 1970), and Charles Hill, *The Group of Seven: Art for a Nation* (Toronto and Ottawa: National Gallery of Canada and McClelland & Stewart, 1995), which also provide a history of the National Gallery's advancement of the Group and of regional opposition to this support. For their recognition of the Toronto-based popularity of the artists and their documentation of

regional opposition to the Group's advancement, see, for example, Reid, 198–99, 202–03 (especially n. 43); Hill, 139, which is dealt with in Jessup, 139–40. See also Charles Hill, "The National Gallery, A National Art, Critical Judgement and the State," in *The True North: Canadian Landscape Painting, 1896–1939*, ed. Michael Tooby (London: Lund Humphries with the Barbicon Art Gallery, 1991), 64–83. A detailed analysis of the Group's critical reception in the Montreal Francophone press and its identification of the Seven as a Toronto-based, regional movement is provided by Esther Trépanier, "Nationalisme et Modernité: Le réception critique du Groupe des Sept dans la presse montréalaise francophone des années vingt," *Journal of Canadian Art History* 17 (1996): 29–57.

3. "The Trouble with Wilderness; or, Getting Back to the Wrong Nature," in *Uncommon Ground: Toward Reinventing Nature*, ed. William Cronon (New York: W. W. Norton & Co., 1995), 79, 72–81. Although Cronon's North American case study is the United States, his arguments are equally applicable to Canada. Canada's prototype of a national park (now Banff National Park) was established in 1885 following the model established by Yellowstone National Park, which had been created in the United States only fourteen years earlier. For a discussion of North American national park histories, see Alan MacEachern, *Natural Selections: National Parks in Atlantic Canada, 1935–1970* (Montreal: McGill-Queen's University Press, 2001), 9–14.

4. John Frow, "Tourism and the Semiotics of Nostalgia," *October 57* (Summer 1991): 143, citing Judith Adler, "Origins of Sightseeing," *Annals of Tourism Research* 16 (1989): 23; John Urry, *Consuming Places* (New York: Routledge, 1994), 174–75; Ning Wang, *Tourism and Modernity: A Sociological Analysis* (Amsterdam: Pergamon, 2000), 72–90. See also Elizabeth Helsinger, "Turner and the Representation of England," in *Landscape and Power*, ed. W. J. T. Mitchell (Chicago: University of Chicago Press, 1994), 120, n. 5, for the distinction between the use of the word *picturesque* in a broad sense to describe "land presented as a picture, an implicitly framed view from a single, fixed perspective, directed at a spectator external to it," and theories of the sublime and the picturesque as they were set out in the late eighteenth century by such writers as Uvedale Price, Richard Payne-Knight and William Gilpin.

5. Urry, *Tourist Gaze*, 40–47; *Consuming Places*, 174–76. The qualities and experiences characteristic of the collective gaze are examined, for example, in John F. Kasson, *Amusing the Millions: Coney Island at the Turn of the Century* (New York: Hill and Wang, 1978).

6. National Gallery of Canada Library and Archives (hereafter NGC), NGC fonds, 7.1 J, "A. Y. Jackson," Jackson to Marius Barbeau, 19 April (1927); 7.1 V, "F. Varley," Varley to Eric Brown, 10 August 1926 and Varley to Brown, 11 August 1926; 7.1 L, "A. Lismer," Henry Thornton to Brown, 25 July 1927; Canadian Museum of Civilization (hereafter CMC), Information Management Services (hereafter IMS), Marius Barbeau correspondence, B197, f.: 19, "Gibbon, J. Murray (1919, 1922–1926)," Gibbon to Barbeau, 20 August 1925 and 28 April 1927; B205, f.: 23, "Jackson, Alex. Y.," Barbeau to Jackson (February 1926); Jackson to Barbeau, (May 1926, early June 1926 and mid-June 1928); B204, f.: 70, "Howard, C. K.," Barbeau to Howard, 15 February 1927; B242, f.: 90, "Thompson, Walter," Barbeau to Thompson, 4 February 1929.

7. CMC, IMS, Barbeau correspondence, B205, f.: 23, "Jackson, Alex Y.," Jackson to Barbeau, 9 February 1927. Jackson published an article about the Skeena River region in *Maclean's* June travel number that year; see A. Y. Jackson, "Rescuing Our Tottering Totems," *Maclean's* 40 (15 December 1927): 23, 37. For the development of the Skeena River region as a tourist area and the proposal to make it a national park, see Douglas Cole, *Captured Heritage: The Scramble for Northwest Coast Artifacts* (Vancouver: Douglas and McIntyre, 1985), 270–78; CMC, IMS, Barbeau correspondence, B202, f.: 22, "Harkin, J. B. (1916–1934)," memorandum, Barbeau and M. B. Williams to Harkin, "National Park at Hazelton, British Columbia," 1924; National Archives of Canada (hereafter NAC), RG84, Canadian Parks Service, vol. 1981, file U2-19-1-1; "Report re: Totem Pole Villages and Proposed National Park near Hazelton, B.C.," 29 April 1924, and, for related correspondence, vol. 1981, file U2-19-4, part 1, and vol. 184, file U2-19-4, part 1.

8. CMC, IMS, Barbeau correspondence, B205, f.: 23, "Jackson, Alex Y.," Jackson to Barbeau, 21 May (1928); Jackson to Barbeau (mid-June 1928).

9. The sportsmen's club movement is dealt with in John F. Reiger, *American Sportsmen and the Origins of Conservation* (New York: Winchester Press, 1975). For discussion of the activities of fishing tourists in Atlantic Canada, see Bill Parenteau, "'Care, Control and Supervision': Native People in the Canadian Atlantic Salmon Fishery, 1867–1900," *Canadian Historical Review* 79 (1998): 1–35; Gary Hughes, "The Lure of the River: Sport Fishing in New Brunswick," in "Lifelines: Canada's East Coast Fisheries," text of the exhibition "Lifelines: Canada's East Coast Fisheries," Canadian Museum of Civilization, Hull, 8 April 2001 to 24 February 2002 (http://www.civilization.ca/hist/lifelines/licollae.html). See also Bill Parenteau, "Angling, Hunting and the Development of Tourism in Late Nineteenth Century Canada: A Glimpse at the Documentary Record," *Archivist* no. 117 (1998): 10–19.

10. Charles Hallock, "A New Gospel of Aesthetics," *Forest and Stream* 7 (24 August 1876): 40.

11. John M. MacKenzie, *The Empire of Nature: Hunting, Conservation, and British Imperialism* (Manchester: Manchester University Press, 1988), 23, 22; Reiger. *American Sportsmen*, 25–49; Cronon, "The Trouble with Wilderness," 71–80. For the relationship of the sportsmen's club movement to art and art patronage in Canada, see Jessup, "Artists, Railways, the State," 121–47.

12. Reiger, *American Sportsmen*, 35. See also W. J. T. Mitchell, "Imperial Landscape," in *Landscape and Power*, 5–34, and MacKenzie, *Empire of Nature*. In eastern Canada, the restriction of Aboriginal access to salmon, for instance, was enacted not only in the commercial fishery, but also in relation to Aboriginal subsistence fishing, which was limited when regulations enabling the leasing of salmon streams to sport fishermen prevented salmon fishing in local waters. In the late 1870s, when this colonization of the environment had been fully conceptualized in terms of conservation and "guardianship," the Aboriginal practice of spear fishing was also declared illegal, rendering many Aboriginal people dependent on employment by sport fishermen as guides and on the charity of the "Indian Fund" sport fishermen maintained as paternalistic compensation for this loss of Aboriginal fishing rights. (See Parenteau, "'Care, Control and Supervision,'" 1–35. The nature and operation of the "Indian Fund" is outlined in NAC, MG29 B1, Sir Sandford Fleming Papers, vol. 41, f.: 292, "Restigouche Salmon Fishing, Mr. Fleming's Waters," 28 May 1878.)

13. Charles Hallock, *The Salmon Fisher* (New York: The Harris Publishing Company, 1890), 69. See also *Guide Book to the Intercolonial Railway. Sketches of Scenery and a General Description of the Principal Points of Interest Along the Route* (Montreal, 1877); Fred J. Hamilton, *A Trip Over the Intercolonial* (Montreal: "Gazette" Printing House, 1876), 23–26. The degree to which the CPR's activities in tourism development have eclipsed those of the Intercolonial is reflected in the title and thesis of E. J. Hart, *The Selling of Canada: The CPR and the Beginnings of Canadian Tourism* (Banff, Alta.: Altitude Publishing Ltd., 1983).

14. See Cronon, "Trouble with Wilderness," 78.

15. An account of the land grants, leases and special arrangements made by the Canadian government to accommodate early CPR tourist development is provided in Lothian, *History of Canada's National Parks*, vol. 3 (see, for example, 12–13, 27–8, 36). For the early promotion of the region, see Wonders, "Sportsman's Eden," 30–7; Hart; *Selling of Canada*; Jessup, "Artists, Railways, the State," 147–248. The conventional history of the CPR's involvement in the mountain parks is part of the larger body of literature upholding what Andy den Otter calls the "CPR nation-building theme." (See, for example, Hart, *Selling of Canada*; W. F. Lothian, *A History of Canada's National Parks*, 4 vols. [Ottawa: Parks Canada, 1977–81].) As den Otter points out, this literature posits the inherent goodness of the CPR project, presupposes a conjunction of interests between the CPR and the Canadian government and "bolsters the notion that the earning of profits was but an incidental objective" (8); see den Otter, *Philosophy of Railways*, 2–12. It should be noted, as well, that although development was permitted within the boundaries of Rocky Mountain Park from the outset, it was controlled by the government in order to exploit the park's "usefulness," which, as MacEachern points out, "referred specifically to making Banff a resort" (17); see MacEachern, *Natural Selections*, 14–19, 35.

16. The company's London agent, Alexander Begg, referred to them more precisely perhaps as "the better class of people such as tourists and others of that character" (NAC, Records of the Canadian Government Exhibition Commission, vol. 42, f.: 1129/1886-1143/1886, no. 1233, Begg to C. C. Chipman, 7 June 1886).

17. Canada, Department of the Interior, *Annual Report of the Commissioner of National Parks of Canada* (1914), 1. Harkin distinguished between the benefits of artificial city parks and what he saw as the greater potential benefits of the National Park wilderness beginning with his first report in 1912.

18. See, in particular, Canada, Department of the Interior, *Annual Report of the Commissioner of National Parks of Canada* (1911–20). MacEachern, *Natural Selections*, 25–33, also argues for revision of the idea that Harkin was an ardent conservationist who only advanced the economic benefits of tourism as a strategy in defence of National Park wilderness. For more conventional assessments of Harkin's position, see, for example, Gavin Henderson, "James Bernard Harkin: The Father of Canadian National Parks," *Borealis* 5 (Fall 1994): 28–33; J. I. Nicol, "The National Parks Movement in Canada," *Canadian Parks in Perspective*, eds. J. G. Nelson and R. C. Scace (Montreal: Harvest House Ltd., 1970), 22–23; Janet Foster, *Working for Wildlife: The Beginning of Preservation in Canada* (Toronto: University of Toronto Press, 1978), 13–15, 220–3; Lothian, *History of Canada's National Parks*; vol. 2, 13–15.

19. McKay, *Quest of the Folk*, 35, makes this observation about the commercialization of the seemingly uncommercial, pre-modern "essence" of the Folk in his discussion of twentieth-century tourism in Nova Scotia. See also Frow, "Tourism and the Semiotics of Nostalgia," 129.

20. MacKenzie, *Empire of Nature*, 265, 264. See also Cronon, "Trouble with Wilderness," which deals with the concept of separate living spaces in relation to the twentieth-century conservation and environmental movements.

21. Bill Waiser, *Park Prisoners: The Untold Story of Western Canada's National Parks, 1915–1946* (Saskatoon: Fifth House Publishers, 1995), 3–47. Having come to Canada as part of a temporary industrial workforce in the years immediately before war, and then having been interned as prisoners of war at its outbreak, many of these men found themselves in the Yellowhead Pass building roads, ironically enough, by pulling up railroad tracks along the transcontinental railway they had helped to lay in the years immediately before the war. See Lucy Alderson and John Marsh, "J. B. Harkin, National Parks and Roads," *Park News* 15 (Summer 1979): 12, Table 1, for the mileage of road construction to 1930.

22. Canada, Department of the Interior, *Annual Report of the Commissioner of National Parks of Canada* (1924–25), 90–91. In the 1927–28 fiscal year there were 260,000 visitors to the mountain parks, three-quarters of them entering by car. The next year, when there were 370,000 visitors, most of them arrived by car. (Department of the Interior, *Annual Report*, Report of the Commissioner of National Parks [1927–28; 1928–29] 76–77, 99–100, respectively.) The history of auto camping and its development in the United States is provided in Warren James Belasco, *Americans on the Road: From Autocamp to Motel, 1910–1945*, Johns Hopkins paperbacks ed. (Baltimore: Johns Hopkins University Press, 1997). For the development of auto camping facilities in Canadian national parks, see Alderson and Marsh, "J. B. Harkin, National Parks and Roads"; Department of the Interior, *Annual Report of the Commissioner of National Parks of Canada* (1920–30); Lothian, *History of Canada's National Parks*, vol. 1, 38, 40–1, 54, 57, 73, and vol. 3, 24–25, 63, 79, 111.

23. NAC, RG84, Canadian Parks Service, vol. 169, file U109-25, Director of Publicity, National Parks Branch, Department of the Interior to W. S. Tempest, c/o *The Motorist*, 9 January 1923; Deborah Wightman and Geoffrey Wall, "The Spa Experience at Radium Hot Springs," *Annals of Tourism Research* 12 (1985): 401–07. Construction began in British Columbia under this agreement in 1911 but was interrupted by the war. In 1919, the National Parks Branch of the Department of the Interior took over the construction of the uncompleted section of road in British Columbia in return for a five-mile strip of land on each side of the proposed road (of about 53 miles in length). The area involved some 587 square miles, which then became Kootenay National Park.

24. NAC, Canadian National Railways, MG30/34, vol. 12535, Item 645, CNR, *Jasper Park Lodge: Canadian Rockies* (1925), n.p.; CNR, *Jasper Park Lodge on Lac Beauvert* (1923), n.p. For the development of Jasper Park Lodge, see also I. S. MacLaren, "Cultured Wilderness in Jasper National Park," *Journal of Canadian Studies* 34 (Fall 1999): 25–31. Belasco, *Americans on the Road*, 40–92, identifies the perceived shift in the experience of wilderness at this time, which he connects to the rise of automobile tourism. For the expression of this connection with the national parks, including the development of bungalow-style accommodations, see Canadian Pacific Railway Archives (hereafter CPRA), *Lake Wapta Bungalow Camp: Canadian Pacific Rockies* (1921); CPR, *Lake Windermere Camp in the Canadian Pacific Rockies* (1922, 1923, 1925); CPR, *Emerald Lake by Madge MacBeth* (1925); CPR, *Lake O'Hara Bungalow Camp* (1925, 1928); CPR, *Moraine Lake Bungalow Camp: Canadian Pacific Rockies* (1928); CPR, *Bungalow Camps in the Canadian Pacific Rockies* (1928), and CPR, *Resorts in the Canadian Pacific Rockies* (1927, 1928, 1929); National Library of Canada, CPR, *Bungalow Camps in Canada* (1923), and CPR, *Resorts in the Canadian Pacific Rockies* (1924, 1925); NAC, MG30/34, vol. 12535, Item 645, CNR, *Jasper Park Lodge on Lac Beauvert* (1923); CNR, *Jasper Park Lodge: Canadian Rockies* (1925); CNR, *Jasper National Park and the Triangle Tour* (1924); CNR, *The Triangle Tour of British Columbia through the Canadian Rockies, Jasper National Park* (1925); CNR, *The Triangle Tour of British Columbia* (1926); CNR, *Jasper National Park: The Canadian Rockies* (1927). See also Lothian, *History of Canada's National Parks*, vol. 1, 40–41, 54, 63, and vol. 3, 24, 79; Alderson and Marsh, "J. B. Harkin, National Parks and Roads," 14.

25. Lothian, *History of Canada's National Parks*, vol. 4, 76; Canada, Department of the Interior, *Annual Report of the Commissioner of National Parks of Canada* (1920–30). The pony trails were developed by the National Parks Branch for use in fire patrol as well as tourism. They were promoted exclusively as scenic trails by the two railway companies, however, the CPR sponsoring the formation of the Trail Riders of the Canadian Rockies in 1924 especially to encourage horseback riding in the mountains. Similarly, to promote hiking, "walking tour camps" and walking tours were instituted in the 1920s; A. O. Wheeler, director of the Alpine Club of Canada, organized them with the support of the Branch and the railways. By the end of the 1920s, there were 2,000 miles of trails in the mountain parks. (Canada, Department of the Interior, *Annual Report*, Report of the Commissioner of National Parks [1928–1929] 103.) Development of individual hiking and pony trails in the parks during the 1920s is dealt with in detail in railway brochures of the period; for a selection of relevant brochures, see note 24.

26. NAC, Canadian National Railways, MG30/34, vol. 12535, Item 645, CNR, *Jasper Park Lodge on Lac Beauvert* (1923), n.p. An updated version of this brochure was issued annually until 1925, at which time a second brochure, entitled *Jasper Park Lodge: Canadian Rockies*, was also issued. A. Y. Jackson, *A Painter's Country: The Autobiography of A. Y. Jackson* (Toronto: Clarke, Irwin, 1958; memorial ed. 1976), 106–09.

27. By this time, the trail through the MacCarib Pass the artists had taken the year before had been replaced by what was described at the time as "the new Portal Creek trail"; see NAC, MG30/34, vol. 12535, Item 645, CNR, *Jasper Park Lodge: Canadian Rockies* (1925).

28. The conceptualization of "solitary" to include limited companionship in the consumption of Nature has been identified by Walter, "Social Limits to Tourism," 297. The degree to which the artists' experiences of the mountains were themselves framed by the tourist gaze is evidenced by Harris, as well, whose description of the experience recalls the type of visitor testimonial often used in promotional literature. Giving expression to the conventional idea that the best tourist landscapes defy description, he states, "When I first saw the mountains, [and] travelled through them, I was discouraged. Nowhere did they measure up to the advertising folders, or to the conception these had formed in my mind's eye. But after I became better acquainted with the mountains, camped and tramped and lived among them, I found a power and a majesty and a wealth of experience at nature's summit which no travel-folder ever expressed." (Quoted in Bess Harris and R. G. P. Colgrove, *Lawren Harris* [Toronto: Macmillan, 1969], 62.)

29. NAC, RG84, vol. 169; file U109-23, memorandum from Harkin to W. W. Cory, 8 June 1923.

30. NAC, RG84, vol. 146, J-113-200 (vol. 2), W. K. Crighton to Harkin, 26 January 1928. Crighton, assistant manager of the CNR's Advertising Bureau, uses the word "handsomely" to describe how the Branch contributed to the production of the brochure. The publication was distributed, at least in part, to those attending the second annual conference of the Canadian Chamber of Commerce in 1927; an additional cover to the booklet consistent in border design with the main cover and titled *Canadian Chamber of Commerce Second Annual Convention, 1927* can be found in NAC, RG30/34, vol. 12507, Item 383, CNR, *Jasper National Park*, 1927.

31. The artists' background in the commercial art field is well known, MacDonald, Lismer, Varley, Carmichael and Casson all working professionally in the field at some point in their careers, Jackson occasionally throughout. For other CNR brochure covers by Carmichael, see, for example, NAC, RG30/34, vol. 12534, Item 645, CNR, *The Triangle Tour, British Columbia Canada* (1928); vol. 12535, Item 645, CNR, *Jasper National Park: Canadian Rockies* (1928); NAC, Franklin Carmichael Paper, MG30, D293, vol. 1, Item 4, CNR, *Alaska and the Yukon* (1928); McMichael Canadian Art Collection Library, Mary Mastin Donation, Item 3, CNR, *The Canadian Rockies: The Triangle Tour* (1926), with attached note: "Cover designed by Franklin Carmichael — authenticated by CAG Matthews." The colour plates produced for the 1927 brochure were used again later on the covers of *Canadian National Railways Magazine*, a lavish magazine the company began to develop in 1920 when it redesigned *Canadian National Railways Employees Magazine* (formerly *Canadian Government Railways Employees Magazine*). By the end of the 1920s, *Canadian National Railways Magazine* had a monthly circulation of 92,750. See, for example, vol. 18 (September 1932): cover, for "Amethyst Lake and the Ramparts, Jasper National Park, from a painting by A. Y. Jackson," which appears in CNR, *Jasper National Park*, 18, as "Amethyst Lake" (NAC, RG30/34, vol. 12507, Item 383).

32. NGC, NGC fonds, 7.1 L, "Arthur Lismer," Thornton to Eric Brown, 25 July 1927.

33. CPRA, CPR, *Resorts in the Canadian Pacific Rockies* (1928), opposite page 18. (The 1927 version of CPR, *Resorts in the Canadian Pacific Rockies*, which is also in the Canadian Pacific Railway Archives, does not contain a reproduction of MacDonald's sketch.) Unsolicited presentation of a sketch or painting to the company in gratitude for free passage was not unusual, and the works were sometimes reproduced in the railway's brochures. This type of exchange should be distinguished from the commission and reproduction of paintings by the CPR, which was unusual, but which took place in the 1890s when paintings of landscape along the railroad lost prominence both in the art scene in central Canada and in international exhibitions. At that time, the CPR was forced to commission landscape paintings and to exhibit them itself, which it did in its own display at the 1893 World's Columbian Exhibition in Chicago, reproducing the works in portfolios for tourists, entitled *Glimpses Along the Line of the Canadian Pacific Railway*. (See Jessup, "Artists, Railways, the State," 227–48.) The CNR's only effort in this area occurred in 1927, when it agreed to cover the cost of the colour illustrations for *The Downfall of Temlaham*, a book by National Museum of Canada ethnologist Marius Barbeau popularizing the mythology of the Tsimshian of the Skeena River region; having paid for their production, the company intended to retain the plates for use in what was described in related correspondence as a "C.N.R. album." The paintings reproduced in the book, which included works by A. Y. Jackson, Edwin Holgate, Anne Savage, Emily Carr and American artist Langdon Kihn, were selected from the National Gallery of Canada, "Exhibition of Canadian West Coast Art, Native and Modern," an exhibition that enjoyed the support of both railway companies, which saw it as an opportunity to publicize their western lines. Although the album has not come to light, some of the plates were used later by the CNR in promotional contexts; reproductions of Langdon Kihn's *Totems at Kitwinkul* (now *Gitwinlkool Totem Poles*, National Gallery of Canada) and Emily Carr's *The Totem Pole of the Bear and the Moon* (private collection) appear in NAC, RG30/34, vol. 12535, Item 645, CNR, *Jasper National Park: The Canadian*

Rockies (1929), 10 and 11, respectively, and in *Canadian National Railway Magazine* 17 (February 1931): inside back cover, "Visit the Land of the Mystic Totem … magnificent British Columbia," while reproductions of Kihn's *A Feast Among the Skeena River People* and Edwin Holgate's *The Totem Poles of Git-Segyukla* (now *Totem Poles of Gitsegiuklas*, National Gallery of Canada) appear in Pegi Nicol, "Where Forgotten Gods Sleep," *Canadian National Railways Magazine* 17 (March 1931): 25. (See Barbeau, *Downfall of Temlaham* [Toronto, Macmillan, 1928]; CMC, IMS, Barbeau correspondence, B197, f.: 21, "Gibbon, J. Murray [1927]," Barbeau to Gibbon, 12 November 1927; B242, f.: 90, "Thompson, Walter," Barbeau to Thompson, 30 December 1927; B205, f.: 23, "Jackson, Alex Y.," Barbeau to Jackson, 19 January 1928 and 23 January 1928; Jackson to Barbeau, 30 January 1928; NGC, NGC fonds, 5.5 W, "West Coast Art, Native and Modern Exhibition 1927–28," Barbeau to H. S. Eayrs, 23 January 1928.)

34. The other illustrations in the brochure are reproductions of pastels by Leonard Richmond and paintings by Carl Rungius and Hal Ross Perrigard.

35. NGC, NGC fonds, 7.1 L, "Arthur Lismer," Lismer to H. O. McCurry, 22 August 1928.

36. In keeping with the railway's promotion of the west, the tea room was named after Jasper Park even as it featured totem pole decorations referencing the Skeena River region; this served to highlight the park as a holiday destination while promoting anticipated attractions farther west on the line of the CNR. In this sense, the "confusion of Jasper with totem poles" (which MacLaren identifies) was deliberate. In fact, railway officials were aware of the incongruity of using totem poles in connection with the park, choosing to ignore it in order to exploit the recognized tourist value of the totem pole. (MacLaren, "Cultured Wilderness in Jasper," 27, 48, n. 33; CMC, IMS, Edward Sapir correspondence [I-A-236M], 624; f.: 2, "Harkin, J. B. [1929–1925]," "Harkin to Sapir, 22 July 1924.) For both Holgate's work and proposals for similar decorations, see Dennis Reid, *Edwin Holgate* (Ottawa: National Gallery of Canada, 1976), 14–16; Hill, *Group of Seven*, 243–44; Jackson, *Painter's Country*, 108; CMC, IMS, Barbeau correspondence, B205, f.: 23, "Jackson, Alex Y.," Jackson to Barbeau (early May 1928); Barbeau to Jackson, 11 May 1928; B168, f.: 27, "Beatty, E. W.," Barbeau to Beatty, 9 May 1928; B243, f.: 4, "Thornton, Henry Worth (Sir)," Barbeau to Thornton, 9 May 1928 and 30 June 1928.

37. CMC, IMS, Barbeau correspondence, B205, f.: 23, "Jackson, Alex Y.," Jackson to Barbeau (1935); Jackson, *Painter's Country*, 108.

38. NGC, NGC fonds, 7.1 L, "Arthur Lismer," Brown to Lismer, 31 October 1924. See also CMC, IMS, Barbeau correspondence, B205, f.: 23, "Jackson, Alex Y.," Jackson to Barbeau (1935). Harkin's assistant, Mabel B. Williams, is credited with the idea of selling such souvenirs in the parks; see NGC, NGC fonds, 7.4 C, "Canadian National Parks Branch 1925 (Outside Activities/Organizations)," Brown to Vincent Massey, 22 January 1925.

39. NGC, NGC fonds, 7.3 C, "Canadian National Park Branch 1925 (Outside Activities/Organizations)," Brown to Massey, 22 January 1925. The memorandum from Brown that Harkin requested was written in the form of a letter. (NGC, NGC fonds, 7.4 C, "Canadian National Park Branch 1925 [Outside Activities/Organizations]," Brown to Harkin, 23 January 1925.) Brown submitted the letter to Harkin the day after his letter to Massey in which he outlines his and Harkin's plans, including Harkin's request for the memorandum. The proposed committee also included Arthur Haming, a Toronto artist and early associate of the Group members, who promoted himself as a painter of "wilderness life." Although Brown considered including a French Canadian on the committee, he dismissed the idea quickly, writing to Massey, "I cannot think of any French Canadian who might be of interest in such things that would make him a valuable on the committee, can you?" (See also NGC, NGC fonds, 7.4 H, "Arthur Heming," Brown to Heming, 5 August 1925; Heming to Brown, 24 May 1925 and 31 July 1925.)

40. NGC, MGC fonds, 7.1 L, "Arthur Lismer," Brown to Lismer, 31 October 1924.

41. NGC, NGC fonds, 7.4 C, "Canadian National Park Branch 1925 (Outside Activities/Organizations)," Brown to Harkin, 23 January 1925. See also NGC, NGC fonds, 7.1 L, "Arthur Lismer," Brown to Lismer, 31 October 1924.

42. NGC, NGC fonds, 7.4 C, "Canadian National Park Branch 1925 (Outside Activities/Organizations)," Brown to Massey, 22 January 1925.

43. CMC, IMS, Barbeau correspondence, B241, f.: 41, "Lismer, Arthur (1925–1928)," Barbeau to Lismer, 10 June 1927.

44. NAC, RG84, vol. 169, file U109-23, memorandum from Harkin to W. W. Cory, 8 June 1923.

45. NGC, NGC fonds, 7.4 C, "Canadian National Park Branch 1925 (Outside Activities/Organizations)," Brown to Harkin, 23 January 1925.

46. This acceptance of the artists' writing is pervasive in treatments of the Group members and their work and can be found, as well, in revisionist studies, where it operates alongside identification of a Group of Seven mythology. See, for example, Teitelbaum, "Sighting the Single Tree."

47. Canada, Department of the Interior, *Annual Report of the Commissioner of National Parks of Canada* (1929–30), 99. For treatments of Lawren Harris's mountain landscapes, see Peter Larisey, *Light for a Cold Land: Lawren Harris's Work and Life— An Appreciation* (Toronto and Oxford: Dundurn Press, 1993), 99–105; Ann Davis, *The Logic of Ecstasy: Canadian Mystical Painting, 1920–1940* (Toronto: University of Toronto Press, 1992), 65–69; Christopher Jackson, *Lawren Harris: North by West: The Arctic and Rocky Mountain Paintings of Lawren Harris, 1924–1931* (Calgary: Glenbow Museum, 1991).

48. The representative Group of Seven painting included in the installation changed from one venue to the next as the installation toured. In Edmonton, for instance, the work installed adjacent to Yoon's photomurals was Lawren Harris's 1924 painting, *Athabaska Valley, Jasper Park*, which was drawn from the collection of the Edmonton Art Gallery (Lafleur, " 'Resting' in History," 220–21.)

49. See Kang, "Autobiographical Stagings"; Gagnon, "Other Conundrums." A similar reading was effected by Yoon's now well-known work, *A Group of Sixty-Seven*, and many of the observations made in connection with that work can be applied here. See, for example, Arnold, "Shared Terrain/Contested Spaces"; Arnold, "Purism, Heterogeneity and *A Group of Sixty-Seven*"; Gagnon, "Other Conundrums"; Gagnon, "Jin-me Yoon's *A Group of Sixty-Seven*"; Lai, "Renegotiating the Terms of Inclusion."

WORKS CITED

Alder, Judith. "Origins of Sightseeing." *Annals of Tourism Research* 16 (1989): 7–29.

Alderson, Lucy and John Marsh. "J. B. Harkin, National Parks and Roads." *Park News* 15 (Summer 1979): 9–16.

Arnold, Grant. "Purism, Heterogeneity and *A Group of Sixty-Seven*." *Collapse* 3 (1997): 147–53.

———. "Shared Terrain/Contested Spaces: New Work by Fifteen B.C. Artists." In *Topographies: Aspects of Recent B.C. Art*. Eds. Grant Arnold, Monika Kin Gagnon and Doreen Jensen. Vancouver: Douglas and McIntyre, 1996.

Barrell, John. *The Idea of Landscape and the Sense of Place, 1730–1840*. Cambridge: Cambridge University Press, 1972.

Belasco, Warren James. *Americans on the Road: From Autocamp to Motel, 1910–1945*. Johns Hopkins paperbacks ed. Baltimore: Johns Hopkins University Press, 1997.

Bordo, Jonathan. "Jack Pine — Wilderness Sublime or the Erasure of the Aboriginal Presence from the Landscape." *Journal of Canadian Studies* 27 (Winter 1992–93): 98–128.

———. "The *Terra Nullius* of Wilderness — Colonialist Landscape Art (Canada & Australia) and the So-called Claim to American Exception." *Journal of Canadian Studies* 15 (Spring 1997): 13–36.

Cameron, Ross D. "Tom Thomson, Antimodernism, and the Ideal of Manhood." *Journal of the Canadian Historical Association*, new series 10 (1999): 185–208.

Canada, Department of the Interior. *Annual Report of the Commissioner of National Parks of Canada* (1911–20).

Canada, Department of the Interior. *Annual Report of the Commission of National Parks of Canada* (1914).

Canada, Department of the Interior. *Annual Report of the Commissioner of National Parks of Canada* (1924–25).

Canada, Department of the Interior. *Annual Report of the Commissioner of National Parks of Canada* (1926–27).

Cole, Douglas. *Captured Heritage: The Scramble for Northwest Coast Artifacts*. Vancouver: Douglas and McIntyre, 1985.

Cronon, William. "The Trouble with Wilderness: or, Getting Back to the Wrong Nature." In *Uncommon Ground: Toward Reinventing Nature*. Ed. William Cronon. New York: W. W. Norton and Co., 1995.

Davis, Ann. *The Logic of Ecstasy: Canadian Mystical Painting, 1920–1940*. Toronto: University of Toronto Press, 1992.

Davis, Donald E. "Dependant Motorization: Canada and the Automobile to the 1930s." *Journal of Canadian Studies* 21 (Fall 1986): 109.

den Otter, A. A. *The Philosophy of Railways: The Transcontinental Railway Idea in British North America*. Toronto: University of Toronto Press, 1997.

Foster, Janet. *Working for Wildlife: The Beginning of Preservation in Canada*. Toronto: University of Toronto Press, 1978.

Frow, John. "Tourism and the Semiotics of Nostalgia." *October* 57 (Summer 1991): 123–51.

Gagnon, Monika Kin. "Jin-me Yoon's *A Group of Sixty-Seven*." *Backflash* 15 (Spring 1997a): 9–12.

———. In conversation with Jin-me-Yoon, "Other Conundrums." *Jin-me-Yoon: Between Departure and Arrival*. Vancouver: Western Front, 1997b, 45–71.

Guide Book to the Intercolonial Railway. Sketches of Scenery and a General Description of the Principal Points of Interest Along the Route. Montreal, 1877.

Hallock, Charles. "A New Gospel of Aesthetics." *Forest and Stream* 7 (24 August 1876): 40.

———. *The Salmon Fisher*. New York: The Harris Publishing Company, 1890.

Hamilton, Fred J. *A Trip Over the Intercolonial.* Montreal: "Gazette" Printing House, 1876.

Harris, Bess, and R. G. P. Cosgrove. *Lawren Harris.* Toronto: Macmillan, 1969.

Hart, E. J. *The Selling of Canada: The CPR and the Beginnings of Canadian Tourism.* Banff, Alta.: Altitude Publishing Ltd., 1983.

Helsinger, Elizabeth. "Turner and the Representation of England." In *Landscape and Power.* Ed. W. J. T. Mitchell. Chicago: University of Chicago Press, 1994.

Henderson, Gavin. "James Bernard Harkin: The Father of Canadian National Parks." *Borealis* 5 (Fall 1994): 28–33.

Hill, Charles. *The Group of Seven: Art for a Nation.* Toronto and Ottawa: National Gallery of Canada and McClelland & Stewart, 1995.

———. "The National Gallery, A National Art, Critical Judgement and the State." In *The True North: Canadian Landscape Painting, 1896–1939.* Ed. Michael Tooby. London: Lund Humphries with the Barbicon Art Gallery, 1991. 65–83.

Hughes, Gary. "The Lure of the River: Sport Fishing in New Brunswick." In "Lifelines: Canada's East Coast Fisheries," text of the exhibition "Lifelines: Canada's East Coast Fisheries." Canadian Museum of Civilization, Hull, 8 April 2001–24 February 2002 (http://www.civilization.ca/hist/lifelines/licollae.html).

Jackson, A. Y. *A Painter's Country: The Autobiography of A. Y. Jackson.* Toronto: Clarke, Irwin, 1958. Memorial ed. 1976.

———. "Rescuing Our Tottering Totems." *Maclean's* 40 (15 December 1927): 23, 37.

Jackson, Christopher. *Lawren Harris: North by West: The Arctic and Rocky Mountain Paintings of Lawren Harris, 1924–1931.* Calgary: Glenbow Museum, 1991.

Jacobson, Matthew Frye. *Whiteness of a Different Color: European Immigrants and the Alchemy of Race.* Cambridge, Mass: Harvard University Press, 1998.

Jessup, Lynda. "Bushwhackers in the Gallery: Antimodernism and the Group of Seven." In *Antimodernism and Artistic Experience: Policing the Boundaries of Modernity.* Ed. Lynda Jessup. Toronto: University of Toronto Press, 2001. 130–52.

———. "Prospectors, Bushwhackers, Painters: Antimodernism and the Group of Seven." *International Journal of Canadian Studies* 17 (Spring 1998): 193–214.

———. "Art for a Nation?" *Fuse* (Summer, 1996): 11–14.

———. "Artists, Railways, the State, and 'The Business of Becoming a Nation.'" PhD thesis, University of Toronto, 1992.

Kang, Hyun Yi. "The Autobiographical Stagings of Jin-me Yoon." *Jin-me Yoon: Between Departure and Arrival.* Vancouver: Western Front, 1997. 22–42.

Kasson, John F. *Amusing the Millions: Coney Island at the Turn of the Century.* New York: Hill and Wang, 1978.

Lafleur, Brenda. "'Resting' in History: Translating the Art of Jin-me Yoon." *Generations & Geographies in the Visual Arts: Feminist Readings.* Ed. Griselda Pollock. London & New York: Routledge, 1996. 218–27.

Lai, Adrienne. "Renegotiating the Terms of Inclusion: Institutional Space, (Dis)location and A Group of Sixty-Seven." *Fuse* 23 (April 2000): 15–20.

Larisey, Peter. *Light for a Cold Land: Lawren Harris's Work and Life—An Appreciation.* Toronto and Oxford: Dundurn Press, 1993.

Linsley, Robert. "Landscapes in Motion: Lawren Harris, Emily Carr and the Heterogenous Modern Nation." *Oxford Art Journal* 19 (1996): 80–95.

Lothian, W. F. *A History of Canada's National Parks.* 4 vols. Ottawa: Parks Canada, 1977.

MacEachern, Alan. *Natural Selections: National Parks in Atlantic Canada, 1935–1970.* Montreal and Kingston: McGill-Queen's University Press, 2001.

MacKenzie, John M. *The Empire of Nature: Hunting, Conservation, and British Imperialism.* Manchester: Manchester University Press, 1988.

MacLaren, I. S. "Cultured Wilderness in Jasper National Park." *Journal of Canadian Studies* 34 (Fall 1999): 7–58.

McKay, Ian. "Handicrafts and the Logic of 'Commercial Antimodernism': The Nova Scotia Case." In *Antimodernism and Artistic Experience: Policing the Boundaries of Modernity.* Ed. Lynda Jessup. Toronto: University of Toronto Press, 2001. 117–29.

———. *The Quest of the Folk: Antimodernism and Cultural Selection in Twentieth-Century Nova Scotia.* Montreal and Kingston: McGill-Queen's University Press, 1994.

Mitchell, W. J. T. "Imperial Landscape." In *Landscape and Power.* Ed. W. J. T. Mitchell. Chicago: University of Chicago Press, 1994. 5–34.

Nicol, J. I. "The National Parks Movement in Canada." In *Canadian Parks in Perspective.* Eds. J. G. Nelson and R. C. Scace. Montreal: Harvest House Ltd., 1970. 19–34.

Nicol, Pegi. "Where Forgotten Gods Sleep." *Canadian National Railways Magazine* 17 (March 1931): 25, 52.

Palmer, Bryan D. *Working-Class Experience: Rethinking the History of Canadian Labour, 1880–1991.* Second ed. Toronto: McClelland & Stewart, 1992.

Parenteau, Bill. "Angling, Hunting and the Development of Tourism in Late Nineteenth Century Canada: A Glimpse at the Documentary Record." *Archivist* no. 117 (1998a): 10–19.

———. " 'Care, Control and Supervision': Native People in the Canadian Atlantic Salmon Fishery, 1867–1900." *Canadian Historical Review* 79 (1998b): 1–35.

Reid, Dennis. *Edwin Holgate.* Ottawa: National Gallery of Canada, 1976.

———. *The Group of Seven/Le Groupe des Sept.* Ottawa: National Gallery of Canada, 1970.

Reiger, John F. *American Sportsmen and the Origins of Conservation.* New York: Winchester Press, 1975.

Teitelbaujm, Matthew. "Sighting the Single Tree, Sighting the New Found Land." In *Eye of Nature.* Ed. Dana Augaitas. Banff, Alta.: Walter Phillips Gallery, 1991. 71–88.

Trépanier, Esther. "Nationalisme et Modernité: Le réception critique du Groupe des Sept dans la presse montréalaise francophone des années vingt." *Journal of Canadian Art History* 17 (1996): 29–57.

Urry, John. *Consuming Places.* New York: Routledge, 1994.

———. *The Tourist Gaze: Leisure and Travel in Contemporary Societies.* London: Sage Publications, 1990.

Waiser, Bill. *Park Prisoners: The Untold Story of Western Canada's National Parks, 1915–1946.* Saskatoon: Fifth House Publishers, 1995.

Walter, J. A. "Social Limits to Tourism." *Leisure Studies* 1 (1982): 295–304.

Walton, Paul H. "The Group of Seven and Northern Development." *Revues des arts canadiens/Canadian Art Review* 17 (1990): 171–79.

Wang, Ning. *Tourism and Modernity: A Sociological Analysis.* Amsterdam: Pergamon, 2000.

Watson, Scott. "Race, Wilderness, Territory and the Origins of Modern Canadian Landscape Painting." *Semiotext(e)* 6 (1994): 93–104.

———. "Disfigured Nature: The Origins of the Modern Canadian Landscape." In *Eye of Nature.* Ed. Dana Augaitas. Banff, Alta.: Walter Phillips Gallery, 1991. 103–12.

Wightman, Deborah and Geoffrey Wall. "The Spa Experience at Radium Hot Springs." *Annals of Tourism Research* 12 (1985): 393–416.

Wonders, Karen. "A Sportsman's Eden." *Beaver* 79 (December 1999–January 2000): 30–37.

Article 11.2
John Sandlos

From the Outside Looking In: Aesthetics, Politics, and Wildlife Conservation in the Canadian North

Issues to Consider

- What, in Sandlos's view, was the "basic tenet" of the Canadian conservation movement in the early 20th century?
- How did the North come to be associated with the formation of Canadian identity?
- Both Jessup and Sandlos make reference to the Group of Seven and the idea/ideal of a national art premised on the beauty of the Canadian landscape. What does Sandlos have to say about Lawren Harris and the North? Does he find the artist's work "exclusive," as Jessup does in discussing the Group and its western forays?
- Why does the author contend that the wildlife policy that the federal government devised for the North was "a product of the imagined North"? What place was ascribed to the Aboriginal peoples who also inhabited the territory?
- How does Sandlos counter the standard view, written into northern wildlife policy, that the Natives of the North were "wantonly destructive" in their traditional hunting customs? How did the cultural clash over this issue manifest itself in the caribou crisis of the 1950s?

When Dominion government entomologist and pioneering conservationist C. Gordon Hewitt wrote in 1921 that "it rests with us to prove that the advance of civilization in the more remote sections of Canada does not imply the total destruction of the wild life [sic], but that civilization in its true sense signifies the elimination of the spirit of barbarism and the introduction of an enlightened attitude," he confirmed a basic tenet of the early wildlife conservation movement in Canada: conservation was not a politically neutral and principled effort to preserve living things but was intimately associated with the civilizing ideology of the late colonial period in Canada.[1] The attempt to preserve northern herds of big game animals such as wood bison, musk-oxen, and caribou in the early to middle parts of the twentieth century represented an extension of intellectual and political sovereignty over the North, an attempt to replace traditional Dene and Inuit social relationships to animals and each other with an *idea* of landscape as aesthetic and technical and thus antisocial and nonrelational. Colonial expansion in the North was not always characterized by a direct conflict between parallel material ecologies, a choice between "two human ways of living," or "two ways of belonging to an ecosystem," as William Cronon has argued for the early contact period in New England.[2] There was often no direct physical colonizer apart from a few trappers and traders in many remote areas of northern Canada. No parallel community of non-indigenous settlers waited to directly appropriate the land base of northern aboriginal people.[3] Rather, the early process of colonization in the North proceeded almost entirely as an ideological and institutional project. The full weight of state

Source: John Sandlos, "From the Outside Looking In: Aesthetics, Politics, and Wildlife Conservation in the Canadian North" *Environmental History* 6, no. 1 (2001): 6–31.

power was used through such management tools as wildlife conservation to impose an aesthetic and technical idea of landscape as a wilderness, as resource producing factory, and as elemental North on local Dene and Inuit people.

AESTHETIC IDEOLOGY IN THE CANADIAN NORTH

Canadian art, literature, and letters have traditionally mythologized the North. The historian Daniel Francis writes: "to a Canadian, North is an idea, not a location; a myth, a promise, a destiny."[4] The eighteenth- and nineteenth-century exploration narratives of Alexander Mackenzie, Samuel Hearne, and especially John Franklin founded a well-documented tradition of imagining the North as a harsh, ominous, and challenging landscape where travel is uncomfortable and survival always tenuous.[5] The mysterious disappearance of and ensuing search for the third Franklin expedition (1845–48), combined with later revelations of cannibalism and murder on the first expedition, gave birth to an entire tradition of northern "intrigue narratives." Stories regarding strange human behaviour in the less-than-civilized arctic landscape, best exemplified by the gold rush narratives of Robert Service and the many renditions of the mad trapper Albert Johnson's story, created an image of the North as a dangerous oppositional force to the domesticating influence of civilization.[6]

A lesser known but equally pervasive aesthetic counterpoint to the "howling arctic" metaphor was the image of the North as a wilderness sublime. British colonial painters such as W. H. J. Browne, J. Coventry, and S. G. Cresswell, who recorded the arctic landscape during the mid-nineteenth-century search for Franklin, imported many of the conventions of Wordsworthean and particularly Burkean conceptions of the sublime. Huge expanses of cliff walls and wide horizon combined with picturesque conventions such as bright sunrises and large, dramatic depictions of the sky are common in the paintings. In many cases, human beings are completely overwhelmed by the landscape. There is no suggestion as to how one might participate in such a vast wilderness. I. S. MacLaren has argued that the choice of a picturesque locale for Fort Enterprise — one set high on a hill with a view resembling the Lake District of the English countryside — was a key to the ensuing starvation of Franklin's party on their return from the arctic coast. Weak from their journey, few men had the strength to walk to the surrounding lakes to fish, and "aesthetics had precluded saving themselves."[7] In the end, the overimagining of the North and the maintenance of aesthetic distance precluded a practical, social, and ecological relationship with the landscape. Aesthetic distance replaced the basic ecology of survival, and as MacLaren suggests, "fanciful pictures of the arctic produce graves."[8]

The aestheticization of the North as a vital wilderness had somewhat less dramatic consequences for those who viewed it from afar. Once the process of idealizing of the North was removed from its physical context and its primary reference point became merely a system of abstract ideas, the northern landscape could, without consequence, take on any significance deemed necessary by the architects of an emerging Canadian culture.[9] R. G. Haliburton, a founding member of the nationalist Canada First movement, broke the British imaginative hegemony over the North and wrote of Canadian identity as an essentially Nordic phenomenon:

> As long as the north wind blows, and the snow and the sleet drive over the forests and field, we may be poor, but we must be a hardy, a virtuous, a daring, and if we are worthy of our ancestors, a dominant race.
>
> Let us then, should we ever become a nation, never forget the land that we live in, and the race from which we have sprung. Let us revive the grand old name of Norland, "the Land of the North"; We are the Northmen of the New World. We must claim the name and render ourselves worthy of it.[10]

The basic content of Haliburton's remarks became commonplace in the next eighty years of northern discourse: the physical North was essential to the formation of a Canadian identity, Canada's national destiny was intimately associated with the North, and the northern character of Anglo-Canadian people was part of a natural and social evolutionary pattern that affirmed their racial and cultural superiority.

The homage to the North was repeated time and time again by Canadian artists, intellectuals, and policymakers during the early decades of the twentieth century. Lawren Harris, a member of the famous Group of Seven painters that emerged in the 1920s, wanted to "permit the [northern] country to dictate the way it should be painted," but his professed desire to paint a perfect reflection of the northern landscape was tempered by a "pure" social metaphor very similar to Haliburton's:

> We in Canada are in different circumstances [than the United States].... Our population is sparse, the psychic atmosphere is comparatively clean, whereas the States fill up and the heavy masses crowd a heavy psychic blanket over nearly all the land. We are on the fringe of the great North and its living whiteness, its loneliness and replenishment, its resignation and release, its call and answer — its cleansing rhythms. It seems that the top of the continent is a source of spiritual flow that will ever shed clarity into the growing race of America, and we Canadians being closest to this source seem destined to produce an art somewhat different from our Southern fellows — an art more spacious, of a greater living quiet, perhaps of a more certain conviction of eternal values.[11]

At no point in Harris's equation of Canadian nationalism with the northern wilderness did he acknowledge the presence of the North's aboriginal inhabitants. Indeed, the cultural critic Jonathan Bordo has argued that the artistic efforts of Harris and his colleagues in the Group of Seven created an iconic image of a dehumanized northern wilderness — characterized by lonely pine trees, windswept shorelines, and the desolate grey rock of the Canadian Shield — that effectively erased aboriginal people from southern conceptions of the northern wilderness.[12]

Political interest in Canada's North grew out of the aesthetic obsession with a Nordic national destiny. The publication of senate hearings into the future of the unexplored territories in 1907 inaugurated an entire tradition of official speculation on how to develop the North to the best advantage of the nation. The results of the hearings, published as *Canada's Fertile Northland*, appear as a series of government-sponsored exploration narratives. None of the witnesses are local northerners. All were sent by the government to gauge the resourceful potential of the Northwest Territories, and all dutifully provided extensive catalogues of the timber, minerals, oil and gas deposits, and agricultural lands that were available for exploitation. In the introduction to the report, editor Ernest J. Chambers again echoed the theme of the North as a promised land: "After a few more years inflow at the present rate, Canada's future expansion as an agricultural, lumbering, mining and industrial country will depend upon the exploitation of the natural resources of the Dominion's vast, unexplored northland."[13] For the general reader, Vilhjalmur Stefansson's *The Northward Course of Empire* (1922) and Lewis R. Freeman's *The Nearing North* (1928) further extolled the latent resource potential of the northern landscape, and cemented the image of an inhabitable, pastoral, and exploitable North in the public imagination.[14]

The equation of the North with Canada's national character and destiny spilled over from the worlds of politics and art to various fields of academic research as prominent Canadian intellectuals such as Harold Innis and Griffith Taylor took a keen interest in the region. In 1945, Innis organized the Arctic Survey, a Rockefeller Foundation and Canadian Social Science Research Council–funded series of research projects that tacitly supported the extension of federal government bureaucratic power and development policy in the "New

Northwest."[15] Taylor further developed the idea of Nordic destiny, inaugurating a tradition of environmental determinism related to cool environments that influenced a generation of Canadian geographers and historians.[16] In just one example of Taylor's pervasive influence, the historian W. L. Morton writes, "because of this separate origin in the northern frontier, economy, and approach, Canadian life to this day is marked by a northern quality, the strong seasonal rhythm which still governs even academic sessions.... The line which marks off the frontier from the farmstead, the wilderness from the baseland, the hinterland from the metropolis, runs through every Canadian psyche."[17]

To a large extent, as Douglas West argued, Anglo-Canadian southerners have, through their research and writing, "Nordicized" the North — made it a categorical reflection of themselves and their creative desires — much in the same way that Edward Said argued that Western researchers created the ideology of Orientalism in response to their experience of the Orient.[18] In either case, an image of a physical and cultural landscape becomes an object that is defined by the researcher for particular material and ideological purposes. As West suggests, "in the field of human geography it has long been recognized that one's perception of an area or region will influence one's desired use for that space."[19] Perceptions of the North as a wilderness sublime, a "pure" landscape, a source of the nation's destiny, and as a natural resource frontier ascribed the center — society's definitions to the northern landscape prior to the process of physical colonization. Rather than attempt to understand the cultural landscape of local Dene and Inuit inhabitants, Canadian artists and intellectuals created an idea of North that would, for them, become the North. Their effort to extend imaginative and intellectual sovereignty over the North ensured that the legitimate basis for social and political action in the "unexplored territories" would always be understood in southern terms. John Moss, in his own recent effort to deconstruct arctic exploration narratives, has written that "government policies on the north are made in consequence of how outsiders imagine it to be. Legislation affecting land claims, ecology, and human welfare is enacted on the basis of an arctic written into the imagination of legislators whose own experience of the north is often limited to, and always shaped by, what others write about it."[20]

WILDLIFE POLICY AT THE MARGINS

Wildlife management in the New Northwest was no less a product of the imagined North than any of the federal policy initiatives that emerged in the early to middle years of the twentieth century. The effort to conserve northern wildlife proceeded more as a matter of national idealism than a response to local circumstances; as more of an idealized aesthetic reaction to the northern "wilderness" than a disinterested scientific effort to manage a wild game population in the interests of the local population. The attempt by southern federal officials and scientists to manage certain species of northern wildlife was intimately associated with the larger effort to extend aesthetic, political, and intellectual control over the North in a manner that effectively erased the cultural and political institutions of northern Native people.

The earliest examples of the tendency to display aboriginal concepts of wildlife with idealized conceptions of the northern wilderness can be found in late-nineteenth- and early-twentieth-century travel and exploration narratives. The British author/explorer Warburton Pike, who traveled and hunted widely in northern Canada, initiated a tradition of disdain for the "wasteful" nature of aboriginal hunting practices. Pike's immensely popular travel narratives such as *The Barren Ground of Northern Canada* (1892) and *Through the Subarctic Forest* (1896) revealed an attitude toward wildlife that was typical of the Victorian era: a strong attachment to a hunting code of ethics that abhorred the wanton slaughter of the abattoir and favored the more sporting pursuit of a nimble quarry. Central to the pleasure of this Victorian hunt was the lively exercise, the natural history of exotic locales, and the strange cultures of alien people. In addition, for many imperial travelers such as Pike, the abundant wildlife herds of the Canadian Northwest provided a hunter's paradise, one of the last opportunities to hunt large game in a sporting manner.[21]

What a surprise it must have been for Pike to discover that many of the large animals of the barren-grounds do not give chase at the sight of human hunters. Caribou do not run at the first sign of human beings or wolves, and the musk-oxen, which were the object of Pike's quest, will actually form a defensive circle and stand their ground against high-powered rifles. Unable to reconcile the idea of gentlemanly sport with local subsistence hunting practices, Pike describes the killing of eighteen animals by himself and his Dene guides as a "sickening slaughter, without the least pretense of sport to recommend it," but still describes his own first individual kill of a musk-ox in almost Arcadian terms: "The shaggy head was carried high, and when he finally pulled up at sight of us, within forty yards, with his neck slightly arched and a gleam of sunshine lighting up the huge white boss formed by the junction of the horns, he presented a most formidable appearance. His fate was no longer in doubt, as my first shot settled him, and the main object of my trip was accomplished; whatever might happen after this, I could congratulate myself on having killed a musk-ox."[22]

Pike's contrast between Native hunting practices and his own "clean" kill presages an entire tradition of critical commentary concerning the "needless slaughter" and "reckless" hunting practices of Native people in the North. He continually accuses his guides of imprudence when they feast on their kills instead of saving for tomorrow, and describes the traditional practice of spearing large numbers of migrating caribou at river crossings with a revulsion that will resurface again and again in southern descriptions of northern hunting: "a large band had been seen to start from the opposite bank, and was soon surrounded by seven hunting-canoes; the spears were going as long as there was life to take, with the result that three hundred and twenty-six carcasses were hauled ashore, and fully two hundred of these left to rot in shallow water."[23] Foreshadowing the concerns of later conservationists, Pike muses: "only four days before there had been one of those big slaughters, which one would think could not fail in a short time to exterminate the caribou."[24] Pike assures his readers in a passage suggestive of the later conservation practice of relocating human communities to preserve wildlife that the caribou will survive because "the Indians themselves are surely dying out year by year."[25] Pike's allusion to an erasure of human presence in the North allows him to satisfy the aesthetic desire of his urban English countrymen for an untouched wilderness landscape: "But surely we carry this civilization too far, and are in danger of warping our natural instincts by too close observance of the rules that some mysterious force obliges us to follow when we herd together in big cities…. A dweller in cities is too wrapped up in the works of man to have much respect for the works of God, and to him the loneliness of forest and mountain, lake and river, must ever appear but a weary desolation. But there are many sportsmen who *love to be alone with Nature and far from their fellow-men*."[26] Pike's idealization of the wilderness North is a self-conscious intellectual appropriation of a living landscape for recreational and spiritual purposes that excludes all other forms of human occupation. The contrived quality of Pike's "wilderness" is readily apparent to the attentive reader: Pike never was alone on the arctic tundra. He depended almost entirely on local people for guidance and food during his journey, but he still must remove local people from his final image of the North to make his encounter with the exotic wilderness believable to his readers. As William Cronon suggests, the exotic wilderness idea that Pike extols in his writing tells us nothing about a landscape that is "*home*, the place where we actually live."[27] Pike's wilderness leaves no room for local conceptions of the landscape, no place for local methods of hunting and food production, and no space figuratively and literally for an idea of the North as a homeland for Native people.

Pike's notion of the northern wilderness was not unique to the British imperial imagination. By the turn of the twentieth century, the American cult of wilderness had begun to influence the Canadian imagination, accounting for the rise of the Woodcraft Movement, a precursor of the Boy Scouts, an increased interest in outdoor recreation, and the immense popularity of the animal stories crafted by Charles G. D. Roberts and Ernest Thompson Seton.[28] Canadian civil servants were also deeply influenced by the sometimes conflicting American examples of conservationist and preservationist policy. Senior federal civil servants such as Hewitt, Howard Douglas, Robert Campbell, and James Harkin were all impressed by American efforts to create and protect wildlife in national parks such as Yellowstone, and by the extension of rational state control over the production and conservation of natural resources such as forests, fish, and wildlife.[29]

The new idealism resulted in the creation of several national parks in the Canadian West, beginning with Rocky Mountain (present-day Banff) in 1885. It also produced the first legislative attempt by the Canadian government to control northern wildlife harvesting in the Unorganized Territories Game Preservation Act of 1894, which prohibited the killing of buffalo and established closed seasons for many other wildlife species. The 1917 revisions to this act, authored by Hewitt, who was then a member of the Commission of Conservation and the Advisory Board on Wild Life Protection, established protective measures for yearling caribou and bison, a licensing system for northern hunters, and restrictions on exporting the skins of musk-ox, caribou, and arctic fox. A year later, the Migratory Birds Convention Act, a law that effectively denied Native northerners legal access to many species of game birds, was passed through Parliament without the input of northern Native people. In a further step, the federal government established Wood Buffalo National Park in 1922 to protect the remaining wood bison herds of the Slave-Athabasca region.[30]

The policy decisions of Hewitt, the Conservation Commission, and the federal government were not based on any hard scientific evidence, systematic wildlife surveys, or a cultural understanding of traditional Dene hunting practices. Rather, the image of the Indian as "wantonly destructive" emerged from the "eyewitness" accounts, often only rumors, contained in government reports and popular narratives on the North. In his testimony to the 1907 senate hearings on the North, Fred G. Durnford concluded without citing any firsthand evidence that "a very sad fact in connection with these caribou is that the Indians think the more they kill of them the more there will be. The result is that they slaughter them indiscriminately."[31] Ernest Thompson Seton's government-sponsored exploration narrative, *The Arctic Prairies* (1911), exonerated the wolf and blamed Native people for declining wood bison numbers in the Fort Smith region as a result of the comments of a single Northwest Mounted Police officer, Major Jarvis, who suggested that "the Wolves are indeed playing havoc with the Buffalo, and the ravenous leaders of the pack are called Sousi, Kiya, Kirma, and Squirrel [four local Chipewyan people]."[32] In his investigation of northern caribou and bison populations, Seton noted that "the mania for killing that is seen in many white men is evidently a relic of savagery, for all of these Indians and half-breeds are full of it." He lamented that, for Native people, "it is nothing but kill, kill, kill every living thing they meet."[33]

Narrative descriptions of Native people as naturally destructive in their relationship to wildlife were jarring for bureaucrats concerned with wilderness and wildlife in the emerging federal government conservation bureaucracy. They were used to "prove" that the local culture and social structures of Dene and Inuit communities were completely inadequate to the task of wildlife conservation. In his seminal volume on wildlife conservation, Hewitt presents an anthropology of Inuit spiritual beliefs without citing a reputable source for his information. He argues that "some of the Eskimo tribes entertain a belief that the caribou are sent to them by the spirit world to kill, and that unless they kill every caribou they meet, whether they require it or not for food or clothing, the spirit world will not send them any more." Though Hewitt was sympathetic to the "necessity of a native food supply in northern Canada," he also believed such supply could only be assured through the guiding light of colonial assimilation: "such a belief [that the caribou are sent for Inuit to kill] naturally leads to wasteful slaughter on the part of the Eskimos, and it is to be hoped that missionaries and others will endeavor to dispel such a pernicious idea."[34] Failing that, Hewitt was forthright with his call for a system of vigorous "educational propaganda" as part of an "individual community effort in the conservation of wild life."[35] Hewitt took the patronizing position that a plentiful supply of game animals in the North could not be assured through the self-directed efforts of local people, but only by the rational planning hand of the federal government.

The policy direction that grew out of the federal government's colonial stance produced a double bind for many Native people: in order to maintain access to wildlife they had to be denied access to it. In order to continue a traditional hunting and trapping existence, the traditional structures of Dene and Inuit social life had to be ignored. Hewitt *does* argue at one point that "the Indian, when unspoiled by white men, is traditionally a conserver of wildlife." Whether he is being inconsistent, singling out the Inuit, or exposing his own ambivalent relationship to northern Native people is difficult to discern. Regardless, Hewitt's idealization of pre-contact relationships to wildlife imposed impossible "traditional" standards for contemporary behaviour and threatened to abrogate traditional hunting rights when those standards could not be maintained.[36]

The misrepresentation of tradition is more than a mere misunderstanding. By extending a degree of intellectual ownership over traditional Native sources of legitimacy and by appealing to a romantic ideal of the Native hunter whose only legitimacy lies in a dimly remembered past, federal bureaucrats could now define the northern landscape completely in accordance with their own political, social, and economic goals. The federal government's effort to preserve a wilderness sublime for the last remnants of the large buffalo herds necessitated a parallel effort to legislate Native people, their culture, and their values out of the wild northern landscape. The civil servant Maxwell Graham, chief of the Animal Division for the Parks Branch of the Department of the Interior, advocated the complete removal of Native people around Wood Buffalo National Park. In a clear declaration of state authority over the northern "wilderness," Graham wrote Parks Commissioner James Harkin that "it is now generally conceded that the local inhabitants do not have the divine right to pollute streams with sawdust, or destroy forests with axe and fire, or slaughter every living thing; for game and forests belong to all the nation." The Indians of the Athabasca, Graham concluded, must be persuaded to leave the proposed area and a national park be reserved at once for the protection of all wildlife in the North.[37]

Graham did not achieve this perfect, dehumanized wilderness with the creation of Wood Buffalo National Park in 1922. Except for the strict restrictions on buffalo, Native people retained their right to hunt and trap in the park.[38] Nonetheless, the creation of a partially exclusive political boundary in the South Slave region was linked to the almost wholly exclusionary aesthetic boundaries that had been imposed on the North since the earliest exploration. The written record of Ernest Thompson Seton's journey north to assess the condition of the Fort Smith wood buffalo herds and the barren-ground caribou is rife with romantic descriptions of the northern wilderness and wildlife. Seton's ideas of the North would not be taken lightly by policymakers and the reading public. He was critical of Native hunting practices and was also obsessed with romanticizing and "visualizing" the northern landscape and its wildlife. Seton prevents his Native guide Sousi from shooting at a buffalo herd so that it is possible to take photographs. At the moment that he transforms Sousi's potential source of livelihood into a visual aesthetic object, Seton waxes sentimental: "All at once it came to me. Now, indeed, was fulfilled the long-deferred dream of my youth, for in the shelter of those flowers of my youth, I was gazing on a herd of wild Buffalo."[39] There is an anterior quality to Seton's narrative. For him, viewing buffalo herds is "like tipping back the sands of time," and his journey allows him "to roll backward the scroll of time for five decades and live that year in the romantic bygone days of the Wild West."[40] Such nostalgia allows Seton to erase the past in his northern narrative, the "flight from history" that Cronon speaks of in relations to a wilderness landscape. In turn, Seton's camera and visual narrative allows him to fix and control the present, freezing the image of the last buffalo herds in the public imagination. In the absence of any clear historical relationship between the buffalo and Native people, Seton's official recommendation is to fully restrict buffalo hunting with cash compensation for the affected communities.[41] Seton's landscape begins as an aesthetic, ahistorical panorama and ends by 1922 as a legislated and non-participatory government park. Nowhere in this projection of an image onto a policy is a long history of aboriginal presence acknowledged. The act of imagining wildlife as part of the landscape "backdrop" becomes, for Seton and other conservationists, a way of establishing control, of naming and appropriating the very thing they seek to protect. Seton's conclusion to *The Arctic Prairies*— where he asks, "have I not found for myself a kingdom?"— may be a mere rhetorical flourish, but it also confirms the basic ideological commitment of the early Canadian wildlife conservation movement: to establish an exotic, highly aestheticized wilderness landscape in the North as an act of sovereignty in spite of the day-to-day subsistence needs of local Native communities.[42]

MANAGING THE LIVING LANDSCAPE

The greatest contradiction attached to increased regulation of the northern landscape by the federal government in the early part of the century was the simultaneous desire for a preservation of a wilderness primeval and the exploitation of a developed landscape containing untold riches. On a very basic level, the conflict between Native and non-Native political visions of the landscape — one as a frontier to be simultaneously exploited and conserved to generate profits and the other as a homeland to be exploited for a livelihood — are fundamental to the historical dispute over land tenure within the region. When claimstaking began in the South Great Slave Lake region during the 1898 gold rush, the federal government quickly established a negotiating team to present a treaty to the surrounding local communities. The written versions of Treaty 8 and Treaty 11, which cover most Dene groups living in the South Slave region and Mackenzie Valley, stipulated a surrender of land title in the region in return for services such as health and education, supplies, and cash payments. Native negotiators sought repeated assurances that their freedom to hunt and trap would not be interrupted, and could not imagine any notion of land tenure existing separately from these basic rights. Native leaders maintain that the oral version of the treaties were merely a peace agreement that contained no mention of land surrenders, and that title to their homeland remained intact. Federal officials, by contrast, established in Treaties 8 and 11 what they perceived to be huge tracts of uninhabited crown land that could be exploited and conserved to meet the needs of the central society.[43]

On a more fundamental level than politics and legislation, the idea of a centrally managed, legislated, and abstracted landscape also conflicted with Dene and Inuit conceptions of the land. Dene and Inuit aesthetic traditions, as captured in oral narratives, exhibit a profoundly intimate and participatory vision of landscape. The visual distancing process that has governed western representations of the North — the landscape that MacLaren suggests "produces dead bodies"— is anathema to northern Native people who must live *within the landscape*. Hunting cultures in the North are not at liberty to view large herds of animals as a distanced aesthetic object as did southern hunter-naturalists. Traditional Dene narratives exhibit a relationship to game species that is profoundly social and contractual in nature. In one Colville Lake (K'ahbamitue) story, a "caribou person" named Cheely consults other caribou in the moments before his death and transformation into a human being: "'I want to make a deal with you,' he told them. 'Even if I become a human being in my next life, I want us to agree that we will always help each other.'"[44] In another Dene narrative, a hunter receives the terms of his relationship with the caribou from a member of the herds: "The caribou said [to the hunter], 'We are just traveling north to a special place where our babies will be born. I came over to help you. Here, take my pipe and keep it all of your life. If you are hungry and can't get caribou, fill your pipe and think hard that you want to see me. I will come, but not every time. I will control the meetings we have, if necessary.'"[45] An Inuit shaman, Orpingalik, is recorded to have used song to "coax" the caribou to his people:

> Wild caribou, land louse, long-legs,
> With the great ears,
> And the rough hairs on your neck,
> Flee not from me.
>
> Here I bring skins for soles,
> Here I bring moss for wicks,
> Just come gladly
> Hither to me, hither to me.[46]

These narratives demonstrate that non-technical and non-professional conservation mechanisms do exist in northern Native cultures. Inuit and Dene people have not historically hunted blindly, with no consideration for the health of certain wildlife species. Large slaughters of caribou are common in the North, but they are also the only hunting strategy with which communities on the migration routes, which are only active for short periods in the spring and fall, may be assured adequate supplies of wild meat. There may also be historical and contemporary examples of wastage during such hunts, but these do not necessarily indicate a breakdown in community-level systems of conservation. Rather, the overwhelming anthropological evidence suggests that conservation methods based on family and kinship groups existed throughout the North. Such mechanisms may have changed in response to new social conditions, but they are active, if somewhat muted by the power of territorial and federal wildlife managers, in many northern Native communities.[47] George Wenzel, an anthropologist who has worked in the North for decades, argues that the Clyde Inuit hunting system reveals a complex set of ecological relationships. The Inuit do not hunt without restraint, but make collective decisions about where, when, and how much to hunt according to the best available ecological information. Wenzel argues that Inuit subsistence strategies are governed by rules, social traditions, and standards of conduct associated with particular kinship groups, rather than the relative availability of technological artifacts such as guns and snowmobiles. His work suggests that Inuit approaches to subsistence and conservation are derived from a series of culturally instituted rights and responsibilities, rather than a desire to hunt as much as opportunity permits. In addition, the ecological management systems of the Inuit are not based on the distancing mechanisms of the wildlife technician or of the strict preservationist. As Peter

Usher points out, traditional conservation in the North is based on ecological intimacy with hunted animals and the living landscape. Wildlife management and harvesting are not separate activities for Native northerners. The activities associated with harvesting — checking traps, travelling, hunting, searching, and butchering — produce an intimate knowledge of wildlife health and abundance that is immediately shared among members of the household and family. Moreover, this knowledge circulates through the wider society in the form of oral narratives that are passed down from generation to generation.[48]

The testimony of Dene and Inuit elders before the Berger inquiry confirms Usher's analysis. Many of the elders suggest that their love of the land comes from its status as a source of food. For Norah Ruben of Paulatuk, land is more than just "the view": "As the sea is laying there, we look at it, we feed from it and we are really part of it." Others refer to the land as a "bank," a source of security against permanent deprivation. Still others suggest that the land is "our blood" and "our flesh," a primary connection to place that is confirmed by the hunting and eating of wild animals. An important theme emerging from this commentary was a common Dene and Inuit view of themselves as custodians of land and wildlife. Speaking through an interpreter, Frank Cockney of Tuktoyaktuk described the careful consideration that governed Dene and Inuit land use: "At one time the Eskimos used to get together in Aklavik after ratting and just before it was whaling season time.... He said he was big enough to understand, and that was the first time he saw the Indians there. And the Indians and the Inuit used to mix together, and that was the first time that he found out there were chiefs.... He said he used to wonder how they always got together, but later he found out they were making plans about their land.... They always planned how they would look after their land, so he said now, after he grew up, he knew it's nothing new that people plan about their land and how they look after it. It was done a long time ago also." With a similar idea in mind, Louis Caeser of Fort Good Hope testified simply that "we worry about our land because we make our living off the land."[49]

It would be naive to suggest that such views of the land represent the practice of a perfect natural form of wildlife conservation. Traditional sources of understanding do not always translate into a perfect human ecology. They are contingent and subject to error and influence like any other form of knowledge. Native northerners have shown a historical capacity for depleting wildlife populations. Large caribou herds were largely destroyed on both sides of the Mackenzie Delta in the 1920s to provide meat and skins to traders and whaling ships.[50]

Such examples may be important for a complete understanding of Dene and Inuit material relationships to wildlife, but they do not invalidate community-based systems of conservation. Rather, the stories and comments of Dene and Inuit people all suggest that their philosophical orientation, their concept of community, and their consequent practical interest in the land are all very different, but no less valid than the scientific practices of the modern resource manager. Nonetheless, government bureaucrats and scientists did not merely disagree with the specifics of Dene and Inuit philosophies of wildlife management. They refused even to acknowledge their existence. As a consequence, the image of the northern Native as wantonly destructive began to intensify in the middle decades of the twentieth century as the federal wildlife bureaucracy extended its absolute sovereignty over northern wildlife during the so-called caribou crisis of the 1950s.

MANAGING FOR SCARCITY: THE CARIBOU CRISIS, 1948–1970

After the initial surveys of northern resources, wildlife, and people in the early part of the century, the Canadian federal government largely turned its attention away from the North and toward the two wars and the Depression that engulfed the globe for the next thirty years.

Interest in the territorial North did grow in the years following World War II, partly out of the perceived need to build continental defense systems and assert Canadian sovereignty, but also out of concern for the welfare of the Native population in the face of a global collapse in fur prices. Federal government policy proceeded on the assumption that the traditional trapping and hunting economy was no longer viable, and that Native people had no choice but to accept poverty or the southern ways associated with wage employment and industrial development.[51]

It is not coincidence that the emergence of a caribou crisis occurred simultaneously with the advancement of industrial and military infrastructure in the North. Increased construction of roads and airports allowed government biologists greater access to the remote herds of caribou than ever before. Previous estimates of caribou numbers had been high. Seton combined anecdotal information with the cattle density data for Illinois to produce a highly questionable estimate of thirty million caribou between the Mackenzie River and Hudson Bay. The biologist C. D. H. Clarke based his 1940 estimate of three million animals on an assessment of the tundra's carrying capacity using aerial photographs, but with little other evidence to support his claim.[52] It came as a shock when the first formal aerial survey of the caribou, conducted in 1948–49 by A. W. F. Banfield of the newly established Canadian Wildlife Survey (CWS), revealed a startlingly "low" estimate of 670,000 caribou for the ranges within northern Alberta, Saskatchewan, Manitoba, and the Northwest Territories. Banfield estimated that the annual calf crop of 145,000 animals was less than the combined mortality caused by predation, human hunting, accidents, weather, and changing range conditions resulting from fire. Using the only previous population estimates, Banfield appraised the "primitive" carrying capacity of the caribou range at close to three million animals, and used his present estimate of a 5 percent annual herd decrease to suggest a long-term decline in the caribou population. Banfield's report recommended conservation education to reduce waste and inefficiency among hunters, an expansion of predator control operations, and increased fire protection.[53]

Despite Banfield's claims, research from 1950 to 1953 revealed no dramatic declines in the herd numbers. Government scientists did discover that herd movements were more erratic than anticipated, and extremely large herds of caribou showed signs of drifting in and out of the main study areas.[54] The next comprehensive caribou survey, conducted by CWS biologists J. P. Kelsall and A. G. Laughrey in 1955, touched off a storm of controversy with an estimate of only 278,900 animals. A caribou crisis was declared in the government circles, and Banfield raised the public profile of the issue with an article in *The Beaver*. The article does mention the drift theory but does not suggest any fundamental methodological problems in Kelsall and Laughrey's study. Even more disturbing, Banfield admits to insufficient data on the impact of human hunting, but prints a photograph revealing "a scene of carnage where swimming caribou have been speared from canoes" on the first page of the article.[55] Such conscious manipulation of the issue using disturbing visual images was perhaps somewhat crude for a biologist such as Banfield, but he did at least recognize the cultural importance of the caribou to Dene and Inuit people by proposing hunting restrictions only for non-resident northerners. In addition, he also acknowledged co-factors such as disease, weather, the impact of forest fires, poor calf production, and wolf predation that contributed to the decline in the caribou population.[56]

Several of Banfield's colleagues were not as sympathetic to the concerns of northern Native people. Kelsall published research results in 1960 indicating further herd reductions to only 200,000 animals. Ignoring his own previous discussion of erratic herd movements, Kelsall placed the blame for the further decline solely on Native hunting, suggesting that the human kill rate alone had exceeded annual calf production in the last years of the 1950s despite a huge improvement in the calf increment to more than 20 percent in 1968–60.[57] CWS biologist John S. Tener quickly interpreted the results for the public in the *Canadian Geographical*

Journal. Using the somewhat flimsy logic that the good calf numbers suggested a reduction in natural mortality factors and proved that human hunting was the constant factor causing the decline, Tener suggests that "the evidence gathered since 1948 leads one to one inescapable conclusion. The human kill of caribou alone is sufficient to exterminate the caribou. Unless immediate and effective control is instituted, this once prolific and valuable Arctic resource will be gone."[58]

Following the 1960 survey, consensus in the scientific community began to collapse. In 1966, R. G. Ruttan identified a miraculous recovery in the maintained herds to 700,000 animals mostly as a result of changed conditions in winter habitat, and suggested that a new caribou crisis would result from too many animals trying to survive on a limited range.[59] CWS biologist Gerry R. Parker questioned the conclusions from the 1955 and 1960 surveys. Using the analytical standards of a 1967 aerial survey, Parker actually adjusted the numbers for the 1955 survey, which had originally produced the caribou crisis, to 390,000 animals, a figure slightly larger than the 1967 survey that revealed an estimated herd of 385,500 caribou. Parker suggested that the total number of caribou in northern Canada changed only slightly between 1955 and 1967, but paradoxically warned against liberalized access to the caribou because the low numbers of the 1955 survey could no longer be used as a baseline from which to judge herd increase.[60] Parker's detailed study of the Kaminuriak (eastern arctic) herd from 1966–68 estimated that the population had increased from a low of 50,000 animals to 63,000 at the end of the study period. He also noted that the herd numbers varied greatly on a seasonal basis depending on calf survival rates, and that the population of the herd was subject to "extreme fluctuations" as a result of immigration from other herds and unusually high rates of calf survival. Scientific uncertainty and a generally healthy herd were not enough to deflect criticism of Native hunting practices. Parker singled out Native hunting as the primary factor preventing an increase in the Kaminuriak population in spite of his own data suggesting a slow increase in the number of caribou. In addition, Parker recorded only one instance of deliberate wastage by a Native hunter during the entire length of his study — noting that in all other cases the entire animal had been used by the hunter — but still quoted extensively from Warburton Pike to argue that although "many people are under the impression that the primitive Indian was a dedicated conservationist," in reality, "nothing could be further from the truth."[61]

Parker's adherence to the orthodoxy of scarcity among the caribou despite the emergence of contradictory data was typical of CWS biologists. The image of the wantonly destructive Native person did not fade quickly in the face of scientific uncertainty. As late as 1968, Kelsall was calling for severe restrictions on Native hunting:

> The position of the Treaty Indians is legally sound, but in many ways it appears morally indefensible. There is no valid reason, other than the Treaty terms, why they as a group should be permitted privilege in resource use beyond that afforded to other aboriginal groups having equal need of the resource. The privilege would be of little importance if the Treaty Indians exercised restraint and conservation in using the resource, but they do not. *There is no major instance on record where Treaty Indians have shown restraint in caribou hunting unless it has been imposed on them, often illegally, by authorities concerned with the welfare of the caribou.*[62]

In his large volume summarizing his research on the barren-ground caribou, Kelsall provided little data or cultural analysis beyond the exploration narratives and anecdotal reports that had been circulating since the beginning of the caribou crisis to prove his point. In a section titled "The Abuse of Caribou by Man," Kelsall cites examples of large slaughters of caribou with no discussion of how this practice might contribute to the subsistence cycle. Kelsall attacked aspects of Dene and Inuit cultures he found distasteful and impractical. He writes: "Hearne

(1795), Mackenzie (1801), and Pike (1892) all commented on the Indian practice of killing pregnant females to secure 'the favourite dish of all, the unborn young caribou cut from its dead mother.' No practice seems more out of keeping with rational resource use, but it is still encountered."[63] Kelsall also refers to the "uncivilized" Inuit practice of taking only the fatty parts of summer kills to complete their diet and suggests that the time has come for Inuit people to obtain food from other sources.[64]

Kelsall's comments place him firmly in the narrative tradition of "nordicizing" and imposing sovereignty over the North in a manner that literally and figuratively displaced local cultural traditions. The front of his book contains several picturesque photographs of caribou herds, moves to several pictures of Native people hunting and skinning caribou, and then follows with the now famous picture of the massacre at Duck Lake, Manitoba, the same photograph that Banfield used in his article. The symbolic message could not be more clear: the cultural practices of Native people and the picturesque living herds of barren-ground caribou are incompatible. In the end, Native people produce dead caribou. Kelsall goes on to quote Manitoba Game Branch Officer J. D. Robertson's eyewitness account of the "carnage" at Duck Lake, one that describes "caribou lying scattered over the barrens, some bloated and rotten, others eaten (all but the bones) by ravens. The sight was terrible."[65]

The sight may have been jarring to Robertson, but it did not support wildlife management by horror story, with no consequent understanding of the human communities affected by policy decisions. Consider the very different perspective of the Dene historian Ila Bussidor, who was born in Duck Lake the same year as "the slaughter": "The scientists were pointing to the carcasses left on the shores of Duck Lake as evidence of wastage, yet the Dene had been following their centuries-old method of survival. For them, leaving carcasses to be buried under the winter snow was a time-honored, reasonable way of storing some meat, in a land where people could never be sure of enough food for their families.... Conservation Committee reports show that government officials talked about educating the Dene. But there's no record of anyone ever asking the Sayisi Dene why they killed so many caribou carcasses at one time and left the carcasses on the shores."[66]

One year later, in 1956, the Sayisi Dene community was relocated to an area just outside Churchill, Manitoba. Although the move was connected to the wider government policy of pulling northern Native people toward large communities with the promise of better services, Bussidor provides a quote from the elder John Solomon, a description of a meeting between the Sayisi Dene and R. D. Ragan of Indian Affairs regarding the proposed relocation, that draws clear connections between the caribou crisis and the proposed removal of the community: "The people from the Department of Natural Resources started coming around and they implied we were slaughtering the caribou. When we had Treaty Days in July, 1956, there was a meeting in a tent.... Artie Cheekie, who was chief at that time, spoke at that meeting. He said, 'Our people are here because the caribou come. There are plenty of fish on these connecting lakes and that's why this trading post was built here, to be near us. What is there for us to live on in Churchill?'"[67] Cheekie's analysis of the situation proved prophetic. In the absence of traditional occupations associated with the caribou and other wildlife, the Sayisi Dene community at Churchill descended into a world of alcohol, violence, and sexual abuse.[68] Kelsall's only comment in 1968 was to blandly note that "a comparable situation [of large caribou slaughters near trading posts] prevailed at Duck Lake in northern Manitoba until that post was closed and the resident Chipewyan Indians moved to Fort Churchill in 1956." Despite the failed social experiment in Churchill, Kelsall suggested, "through both voluntary and government-aided withdrawal of substantial portions of the human population, the annual kill will fall consistently below deficit populations."[69]

No more direct articulation of the colonial implications of wildlife conservation in the North than Kelsall's statement exists. In fact, the colonial policy of resettling northern Native people into larger centralized communities may have as much to do with "push" factors associated with the caribou policies as it did with the well-known "pull" factors of government services and wage employment.[70] The physical removal of people from their land and resources in the name of protecting wild species was the only logical outcome for a state bureaucracy that had assumed the responsibility for managing a wildlife "crisis" they had only begun to understand. It represented a final victory of the technical and bureaucratic conception of landscape versus the social idea of the land. As Carl Berger argues, the wildlife conservation movement was not merely a benign effort to protect wild species but was "indicative of a broader change involving the extension of bureaucratic method, with its faith in disinterested scientific expertise, rationality, and centralization. In this sense the conservationist had much in common with the city planners and other reformers who endeavoured to destroy the influence of localist and ignorant interests."[71]

If the use of stark photographs and vivid prose is any indication, the conservation movement was also part of a larger historical process of rewriting the North in terms of southern aesthetic and social values. Indeed, by the time of the caribou crisis the image of vast caribou herds roaming across the icy northern tundra had become an iconic image of Canadian culture. Seton and Pike are only two of the more prominent examples of caribou narratives. Another example, A. Radclyffe Dugmore's *The Romance of the Newfoundland Caribou* (1913), contains intensely picturesque photographs and paintings by the author and speaks in almost pastoral terms of the passing herds of caribou: "There is something indescribably beautiful in watching wild animals that, free from all suspicion, are behaving in a purely natural way, following their habits with no disturbing condition to influence their behaviour. There is something so peaceful and satisfying in it, that it makes a life-long impression on anyone that has been fortunate enough to have the opportunity of observing the animals under such conditions, and one cannot help wondering why some people who are really fond of outdoor life do not more freely indulge in this form of pastime."[72] Even the poet Florence Miller provided her readers with an ode accompanied by sheet music to the north country of the caribou:

In Caribou Land the north wind blows
With whistle of storm and swirl of snow,
And the frost king works his will a while
On seas that bluster and lakes that smile.
While skates are flashing, and, to and fro
The sleds are dashing and snowshoes go.
Our hearts go out to the landscape grand
That winter paints in Caribou Land.[73]

Caribou herds, when understood as an iconic image of the North, could not be left to die on the shores of such remote places as Duck Lake. They were and are part of "our" original wilderness heritage, a sentiment that was thoroughly exploited by CWS biologists in their popular articles, books, and public addresses. Fraser Symington's *Tuktu* (1965), a popular narrative that explains the government's caribou conservation program to the broader public, is perhaps the most poetic of all the CWS publications on the caribou. Symington does not restrict himself to technical aspects of caribou conservation but makes a determined aesthetic argument for their preservation. He describes the arctic tundra as "a land of awesome, naked distance, where the grandeur of the empty land dilutes the mind's ability to comprehend." He also describes the reactions of a research team as they encountered a herd of 5,000 caribou on a frozen lake in

April 1949: "the biologists were struck by the perfect co-ordination among the animals of the galloping herd when it stampeded: each caribou racing in perfect control in the close-packed formation."[74] In a similar narrative describing caribou research in the Keewatin region conducted in 1947, the American biologist Francis Harper describes a caribou herd sighted on the summit of a rocky hill as "a subject for a Millais." For Harper, "the glory of the scene was enhanced by picking out with the naked eye, at a distance of a couple of miles, two separate bands of 12 to 15 caribou making their way toward the broad, plateau-like summit." Francis also refers to the "Garden-of-Eden trustfulness" of the caribou, highlighting an important theme in many of the popular caribou narratives: the strong sense that the observation of large herds of caribou somehow ties one to an Edenic past that slowly slipping away.[75] As Banfield explained it in his *Beaver* article, "the Bison has long since vanished from its plains habitat ... but the caribou still occurs in numbers suggestive of those that greeted the first explorers."[76] Ian McTaggart Cowan, a biologist with the University of British Columbia, further elaborated on this theme at the 1975 International Caribou Symposium:

> Most of us who are engaged in trying to find facts about the caribou populations have found more than what we were looking for over the years. I think I will be understood if I say that a great many of us here are devoted to positions that are not only practical but sometimes impractical. To me there is a certain majesty in the biological world which we are inescapably related to — the great sweep of hundreds of thousands of geese going over in the spring, the inconceivable noises from a great herd of caribou on the move.... We are trying to keep some of the majesty of life that all of us enjoy and we hope that our children can enjoy too.[77]

In order to preserve the romantic and "impractical" attachment to wildlife that McTaggart Cowan espouses, the legitimate interests of the *practical* users of the northern wildlife had to be undermined by biologists writing about the caribou. Symington wanted to preserve the "'feel' of the caribou country," which "exerts a strange romantic attraction on many men who know it," by blaming the human kill of caribou entirely for the declines in herd numbers throughout the 1950s. His writings celebrated the relocation of the Keewatin Inuit in the late 1950s from the interior tundra regions to the marine environments surrounding Baker Lake and Rankin Inlet. According to Symington, Native people could not be trusted to live near the caribou because "their lifestyle did not encourage the conservation of game."[78]

The political and cultural sovereignty of northern aboriginal people were effectively erased by such statements. Images of the vast herds of caribou and the icy northern landscape had now been defined entirely in terms of the southern imagination. As the similarity between the writings of naturalists, biologists, artists, and poets concerned with the North demonstrates, the restrictive wildlife policy regime that emerged in the region was reinforced as much by an appeal to the aesthetic of a pure and uninhabited nature as it was by a scientific demonstration of objective circumstances. Indeed, the obvious shortcomings of the early biological work on caribou and wood bison populations left biologists with little choice but to construct a crisis in their prose and photographs by juxtaposing images of Native "slaughter" of wildlife with those of undefiled bison and caribou herds that could only be saved by the rational hand of state management. In the end, what was being "saved" was as much the appearance of a benevolent state acting in the interests of a pristine nature as a viable population of herd animals. The association of federal wildlife policy in the North with an uncorrupted and inviolate nature thus provided the necessary moral impetus for the extension of bureaucratic control and scientific management within the region. Despite the lack of a widespread interest in settlement on the part of the colonizer other than the few towns that grew around mineral and/or oil and gas deposits, northern people were colonized and at times physically excluded from the northern landscape by wildlife policies that imposed the southern aesthetic of the empty wilderness on the subsistence-oriented material cultures of Dene and Inuit people.

The process continues. While hunting rights to caribou and community-based co-management systems have been widely recognized in recent decades, and the mainland caribou herds of the North now number close to two million animals, controversy between animal rights activists and Inuit sealers in the late 1980s confirms that the southern desire to legislate the reality of North repeats itself again and again.[79] During the height of the controversy, animal rights activist Stephen Best is quoted, in a familiar effort to invalidate the traditional nature of contemporary Inuit cultures, as saying, "I own the Native culture. I bought it with my taxes. I own about two-thirds of it."[80] In another more recent high profile attack on the traditional basis for environmental knowledge in the North, Frances Widdowson and Albert Howard repeated in Canada's national newspaper many of the earlier arguments used to justify early colonial conservation policy in the North. For these two authors, "aboriginal people have not lost their spiritual relationship to the land because they never had one," and in another familiar argument, "the fact that aboriginal organizations now have the capacity to destroy the environment, and are motivated by profit rather than subsistence, requires that they be subject to the same regulations as other resource users."[81] The historical resonance of such statements would not be lost for the Dene or Inuit people who remember losing a degree of self-reliance as southern Canada extended its political and imaginative ownership over the North in the postwar period. Nor would its ominous significance be lost for those who experienced an impact on their lives and livelihoods as a result of the particular southern institution of wildlife conservation.

NOTES

1. C. Gordon Hewitt, *The Conservation of Wild Life in Canada* (New York: Charles Scribner's Sons, 1921), 1–2.
2. William Cronon, *Changes in the Land: Indians, Colonists, and the Ecology of New England* (New York: Hill and Wang, 1983), 12.
3. Indeed, it can be argued that the unique aspect of colonialism in the North is that, except for some non-Native settlement in subarctic areas and a number of resource extraction projects, Native northerners have never, in physical terms, lost their land base.
4. Daniel Francis, *National Dreams: Myth, Memory and Canadian History* (Vancouver, B.C.: Arsenal, 1997), 152.
5. See John Franklin, *Narrative of a Journey to the Shores of the Polar Sea in the Years 1819, 1820, 2821, and 1822* (Edmonton: Hurtig, 1969); Samuel Hearne, *A Journey from Prince of Wales's Fort, in Hudson's Bay in the Northern Ocean in the Years 1769, 1770, 1771, 1772* (London: Strahan and Cadell, 1795); Alexander Mackenzie, *Voyages from Montreal on the River St. Lawrence Through the Continent of North America to the Frozen Pacific Oceans in the Years 1789 and 1793* (London: Cadell, 1801).
6. For a good overview of the howling arctic motif, see Margaret Atwood's *Strange Things: The Malevolent North in Canadian Literature* (Oxford: Clarendon, 1995); see Chapter 1 in particular for an overview of the "haunting presence" of Franklin in Canadian literature. For a fictional rendition of the Johnson story, see Rudy Wiebe, *The Mad Trapper* (Toronto: McClelland and Stewart, 1908); for a further discussion of Johnson's life, see Rudy Wiebe, *Playing Dead: A Contemplation Concerning the Arctic* (Edmonton: NeWest, 1989), 50–77. For a good sampling of Service's poetry, including the immortal Klondike narrative "The Cremation of Sam McGee," see *The Complete Poems of Robert Service* (New York: Dodd Mead, 1945). For a discussion of Service's pervasive influence on the Canadian conceptions of the hostile North, see Atwood, op. cit., 17–19.
7. I. S. MacLaren, "The Aesthetic Map of the Canadian North, 1845–1859," in *Interpreting Canada's North: Selected Readings*, ed. Kenneth S. Coates and William R. Morrison (Toronto: Copp Clark, 1989), 22.
8. Ibid, 45. MacLaren is paraphrasing the record of George McDougall's journey into the Arctic. For a further discussion of the non-participatory nature of the perspectivist landscape, see Neil Evernden, *The Natural Alien: Humankind and Environment*, 2d ed. (Toronto: University of Toronto Press, 1996).

9. It is difficult to ascribe historical ideas of the Canadian North to a specific geographical location. The North may refer to Canadian Shield country only slightly removed from Toronto (i.e., Georgian Bay and Algonquin Park), or it may refer to the High Arctic. For the most part, this essay considers the practical consequences of the idea of North in the subarctic and arctic regions of the present-day Northwest Territories and Nunavut. Some reference will be made to northern wildlife policy in the present-day provinces of Alberta, Saskatchewan, and Manitoba.

10. R. G. Haliburton, "On Northern Culture," excerpted from "The Men of the North and Their Place in History," in *The Search for English-Canadian Literature: An Anthology of Critical Articles from the Nineteenth and Early Twentieth Centuries*, ed. Carl Ballstadt (Toronto: University of Toronto Press, 1975).

11. Lawren Harris, "Revelation in Canadian Art," *Canadian Theosophist* 7, no. 5 (15 July 1926): 85–86. Quoted in Roald Nasgaard, *The Mystic North: Symbolist and Landscape Paintings in Northern Europe and North America, 1890–1940* (Toronto: Art Gallery of Ontario, 1984), 167.

12. See Jonathan Bordo, "Jack Pine — Wilderness Sublime or the Erasure of Aboriginal Presence from the Landscape," *Journal of Canadian Studies* 27, no. 4 (winter 1992–93): 98–128.

13. Ernest J. Chambers, ed., *Canada's Fertile Northland: A Glimpse of the Enormous Resources of Part of the Unexplored Regions of the Dominion* (Ottawa: Government Printing Bureau, 1907), 1.

14. See Vilhjalmur Stefansson, *The Northward Course of Empire* (New York: Harcourt Brace and Company, 1922). Stefansson writes chapters on "The Livable North" and "The Fruitful Arctic." He also suggests domesticating musk-oxen (*ovibos*) and "reindeer" as a way to create a meat industry in the North. Lewis R. Freeman's *The Nearing North* (New York: Dodd, Mead and Company, 1928) is in many ways a straightforward travel narrative (he follows the Peace-Athabasca-Slave-Mackenzie route in the first part of the book, and the Saskatchewan River system to Churchill, Manitoba, in the second), but he also celebrates the agricultural potential of the North and the Hudson Bay railroad and shipping route proposal.

15. See C. A. Dawson, ed., *The New Northwest* (Toronto: University of Toronto Press, 1947). For an excellent analysis of the Arctic Survey, see Matthew Evenden, "Harold Innis, the Arctic Survey, and the Politics of Social Science During the Second World War," *Canadian Historical Review* 79, no. 1 (March 1998): 36–67.

16. In Taylor's work, this view led to an overt racism: he argues that the supposedly "poor mental and physical accomplishments" of India are due to an overly warm climate, and he has a "'hunch' that the broad-headed Alpines are slowly 'inheriting the earth.'" See Griffith Taylor, *Canada: A Study of Cool Continental Environments and Their Effect on British and French Settlement* (Methuen: London, 1947), 490, 503. The tradition perhaps reaches its height with L. E. Hamelin's development of a nordicity index used to measure the degree of northerness in remote Canadian communities. See L. E. Hamelin, *Canadian Nordicity, It's Your North Too* (Montreal: Harvest House, 1979). For an overview of the tradition, see L. Anders Sandberg and Joel Sloggett, "Geography in the Canadian North, c. 1945–1988," *Geographiska Annaler* 71 B (1989): 125–33.

17. W. L. Morton, *The Canadian Identity* (Madison: University of Wisconsin Press, 1961), 93.

18. See Douglas A. West, "Re-Searching the North in Canada: An Introduction to the Canadian Northern Discourse," *Journal of Canadian Studies* 26, no. 2 (summer 1991): 108–119.

19. Ibid., 109.

20. John Moss, *Enduring Dreams: An Exploration of Arctic Landscape* (Toronto: Anansi, 1994). The image of the North as an empty landscape that could be "written" according to the needs of southern values was not unique to Canada. Lisa Bloom has written extensively on the "emptiness" of the polar region providing a pure landscape for American exploration near the turn of the century. Bloom argues that "the absence of land, peoples, or wildlife to conquer gave polar exploration an aesthetic dimension that allowed the discovering of the North Pole to appear above political and commercial concerns." See Lisa Bloom, *Gender on Ice: American Ideologies of Polar Expeditions* (Minneapolis: University of Minnesota Press, 1993), 2–3.

21. For more on the British view of Canada as a hunting paradise, see R. G. Moyles and Doug Owram, *Imperial Dreams and Colonial Realities: British Views of Canada 1880–1914* (Toronto: University of Toronto Press, 1988), 61–86.

22. Warburton, Pike, *The Barren Ground of Northern Canada* (New York: Macmillan, 1892), 64–65, 108.

23. Ibid, 204.

24. Ibid.

25. Ibid., 47.

26. Ibid., 274. Emphasis mine.

27. William Cronon, "The Trouble with Wilderness: or, Getting Back to the Wrong Nature," in *Uncommon Ground: Rethinking the Human Place in Nature*, ed. Cronon (New York: W. W. Norton, 1986), 87.

28. See George Altmeyer, "Three Ideas of Nature in Canada, 1893–1914," in *Consuming Canada: Readings in Canadian Environmental History*, ed. Chad and Pam Gaffield (Toronto: Copp Clark, 1995), 96–118.

29. The split between preservationists who wanted to preserve nature for its intrinsic values, and conservationists who adopted the more utilitarian stance of maintaining a long-term supply of natural resources was never as extreme in Canada as in the United States. Canadian civil servants tended to admire both John Muir's idealism and Gifford Pinchot's pragmatism, combining elements of both men's ideas in their policies. For a discussion, see Janet Foster, *Working for Wildlife: The Beginnings of Preservation in Canada*, 2d ed. (Toronto: University of Toronto Press, 1998), 3–16. For the classic account of American preservationism, see Roderick Nash, *Wilderness and the American Mind*, 3d ed. (New Haven, Conn.: Yale University Press, 1982). For an account of the early conservation movement in the United States, see Samuel Hays, *Conservation and the Gospel of Efficiency: The Progressive Conservation Movement, 1890–1920* (New York: Atheneum, 1959). For the role of sport hunters in the early conservation movement, see James Trefethen, *An American Crusade for Wildlife* (New York: The Boone and Crockett Club, 1975) and John Reiger, *American Sportsmen and the Origins of Conservation* (Norman: University of Oklahoma Press, 1975).

30. See Dan Gottesman, "Native Hunting and the Migratory Birds Convention Act: Historical, Political and Ideological Perspectives," *Journal of Canadian Studies* 13, no. 3 (fall 1983): 78–79.

31. Chambers, *The Fertile Northland*, 33. Dissenting opinions in some parts of the evidence suggest the exact opposite of "wanton slaughter" in the North. Henry Anthony Conroy testified that "you do not need to enforce the law to protect the buffalo. The Indians will not kill them. They want to preserve them as much as anybody else…. The Indians think if the buffalo are gone they will have nothing left," 77.

32. Ernest Thompson Seton, *The Arctic Prairies* (New York: Harper and Row, 1911), 39. The federal government had little evidence of declining wood bison numbers because of Native hunting. The wood bison population of the Slave-Athabasca region is a distinct subspecies of the plains bison that was never commercially hunted or subject to the intense depredations of the large bison herds in the Midwest. A systematic survey of this population is physically impossible without aircraft because of their affinity for forest cover and the vast marshlands of the Slave-Athabasca Delta. There was therefore little baseline data with which to judge herd sizes other than some journals and explorations narratives describing a decline in wood bison range and numbers in the mid-nineteenth century due to an unusual series of harsh winters. The irony of the entire effort to preserve wood bison from Native hunters was the government's decision to transport one of the last herds of plains bison to Wood Buffalo National Park for protection after the closing of Buffalo National Park in Wainwright, Alberta, in 1935. Government officials were fully aware that the Wainwright herd was infected with brucellosis and tuberculosis (even Harkin supported the proposal), and the result has been the hybridization and infection of the Slave-Athabasca wood bison herds. Brucellosis and tuberculosis remain the fundamental conservation problem in the park. For an overview, see Foster, *Working for Wildlife*, 104–106, 221. My observations here are also based on extensive conversations with Wood Buffalo National Park staff carried out during several visits to the park in 1997–98.

33. Seton, *The Arctic Prairies*, 20, 179.

34. Hewitt, *The Conservation of Wild Life in Canada*, 12, 66.

35. Ibid., 286.

36. Ibid., 12. Contemporary anthropologists adopt a much wider view of traditional hunting than Hewitt. The narrow analysis of an Edenic pre-contact life that was interrupted by the introduction of "high-powered" European artifacts such as guns, snowmobiles, and outboard engines ignores the capacity of Native people to adapt new technologies to traditional lifestyles. As George Wenzel suggests, "anthropology today tends to see hunting as an active system of environmental relations dependent on harvester decision-making rather than technology itself. Consistent with that, we have already seen that the key dynamic in Inuit sealing is the choice that hunters make about where, when, what, and how much to harvest." See George Wenzel, *Animal Rights, Human Rights: Ecology, Economy and Ideology in the Canadian North* (Toronto: University of Toronto Press, 1991), 94. See also George Wenzel, *Clyde Inuit Adaptation and Ecology: The Organization of Subsistence* (Ottawa: National Museum of Canada, 1981); Hugh Brody, *Maps and Dreams: Indians and the British Columbia Frontier* (Vancouver: Douglas and McIntyre, 1981), 23–26, 247; and Hugh Brody, *Living Arctic: Hunters of the Canadian North* (Vancouver: Douglas and McIntyre, 1987), 76–85.

37. Public Archives of Canada, Records, Department of Northern Affairs and Natural Resources, RG 85, Vol. 664, Maxwell Graham to James Harkin, 30 June 1912. Quoted in Foster, *Working for Wildlife*, 112.

38. Local Native people were never allowed to determine for themselves the terms for traditional usage, and a debate rages to this day concerning who should have user rights in the park. Fort Resolution, a community outside the northeast boundary of the park, continues to press for access to traditional traplines in the park (I lived in the community in 1997–98). Furthermore, there were many convictions brought against Native people for

hunting buffalo in the park. Fumoleau cites the "many" records of convictions in the Public Archives of Canada, and mentions the case of John Gladu, who was expelled permanently from the park (where he was born and raised) for hunting bison. At the same time, the Victorian hunting ethos was alive and well in government circles, and officials mused at the possibility of enticing wealthy big game hunters to pay a thousand dollars for the privilege of hunting a buffalo. See René Fumoleau, *As Long as This Land Shall Last: A History of Treaty 8 and Treaty 11, 1870–1939* (Toronto: McClelland and Stewart, 1977), 257.

39. Seton, *The Arctic Prairies*, 48. Much the same thing happens later in the book, when Seton's guides Weeso and Billy are astonished that they cannot shoot caribou because Seton wants to take pictures. See p. 208.

40. Ibid, xi, 43.

41. The recommendation is contained in Appendix B of Seton, *The Arctic Prairies*, 320. In the following paragraph, Seton almost flippantly observes that "since this is written (1907) I learn that the Mounted Police have demonstrated the existence of a much greater number of Buffalo than I supposed."

42. Ibid., 308.

43. The Treaty 8 group is now pursing a land claim with the federal government. For a comprehensive treatment of Treaty 8 negotiations, see Fumoleau, *As Long as This Land Shall Last*. For Treaty 11, see George Blondin, *Yamoria, the Lawmaker: Stories of the Dene* (Edmonton: NeWest, 1997), 224–26.

   A curious "hybrid" initiative that combined both the "homeland" and resource frontier mentality was the effort of the federal government to import a herd of domestic reindeer from Alaska to the Mackenzie Delta region in 1929 to provide meat to the local population following the collapse of local caribou herds in the early whaling era. The federal government was particularly attracted to the idea of turning the Inuit into sedentary agriculturists who had a reliable food source. One of the challenges of the project was to keep track of the wide-ranging reindeer herds so that they could form the basis of an efficient agricultural industry in the North. See John Rutherford, James McLean, and James Harkin, *Report of the Royal Commission to Investigate the Possibilities of the Reindeer and Musk-Ox Industries in the Arctic and Sub-Arctic Regions of Canada* (Ottawa: The King's Printer, 1922); A. E. Porsild, "Reindeer and Caribou Grazing in Northern Canada," *Transactions of the North American Wildlife Conference* 7 (1942): 381–91; and C. D. H. Clarke, *Report on Development of the Reindeer Industry—Mackenzie District* (NWT Lands, Parks and Forests Branch, Department of Mines and Forests), mimeographed unpublished report, 17 pp.

44. Blondin, *Yamoria*, 116–17.

45. Ibid., 187.

46. Orpingalik's songs are contained in Penny Petrone, ed., *Northern Voices: Inuit Writings in English* (Toronto: University of Toronto Press, 1992), 23–27.

47. The anthropological literature on this subject is vast and varied according to the cultural group being considered. Good introductions to the field include Peter Usher, *The Devolution of Wildlife Management and the Prospects for Conservation in the Northwest Territories* (Ottawa: Canadian Arctic Resources Committee, 1986), particularly 79–116; "Indigenous Management Systems and the Conservation of Wildlife in the Canadian North," *Alternatives* 14 (1987): 3–9; *Property, the Basis of Inuit Hunting Rights, A New Approach* (Ottawa: Inuit Committee on National Issues, 1986); and *The Bankslanders: Ecology and Economy of a Frontier Trapping Community*, vols. 1–3 (Ottawa: Information Canada, 1970). See also F. Berkes, "Fishery Resource Use in a Subartic Community," *Human Ecology* 5 (1977): 289-307; H. Feit, "North American Native Hunting and Management of Moose Populations: A Paper Presented to the Second International Moose Symposium, Uppsala, Sweden 1985"; A. Gunn, G. Arlooktoo, and D. Kaomayak, "The Contribution of Ecological Knowledge of Inuit to Wildlife Management in the Northwest Territories," in *Traditional Knowledge and Renewable Resource Management*, ed. M. M. R. Freeman and L. M. Carbyn (Edmonton: Boreal Institute for Northern Studies, Occasional Publication no. 23, 1988); Martha Johnson, ed., *Lore: Capturing Traditional Environmental Knowledge* (Ottawa: Dene Cultural Institute and International Research Centre, 1992), 35–68; Miriam McDonald Fleming, "Reindeer Management in Canada's Belcher Islands: Documenting and Using Traditional Environmental Knowledge," in *Lore: Capturing Traditional Environmental Knowledge*, ed. Martha Johnson, 70–87; Takashi Irimoto, *Chipewyan Ecology: Group Structure and Caribou Hunting System* (Osaka: National Museum of Ethnology, 1981); Kerry Abel, *Drum Songs: Glimpses of Dene History* (Montreal: McGill-Queen's University Press, 1993), 28, 218–22; Michael A. D. Ferguson, Roberts P. Williamson, and Francois Messier, "Inuit Knowledge of Long Term Changes in a Population of Arctic Tundra Caribou," *Arctic* 51, no. 3 (September 1998): 201–219; and Michael A. D. Ferguson and Francois Messier, "Collection and Analysis of Traditional Ecological Knowledge About a Population of Arctic Tundra Caribou," *Arctic* 50, no. 1 (1997): 17–28. See also Body's *Living Arctic* and *Maps and Dreams*, and also Wenzel's *Animal Rights, Human Rights* and *Clyde Inuit Adaptation and Ecology*.

48. Usher, "Indigenous Management Systems," 6–7.
49. Thomas Berger, *Northern Frontier, Northern Homeland: The Report of the Mackenzie Valley Pipeline Inquiry*, vol. 1 (Toronto: James Lorimer and Co., 1977), 94–98. For an excellent analysis, see Paul Sabin, "Voices from the Hydrocarbon Frontier: Canada's Mackenzie Valley Pipeline (1974–1977)," *Environmental History Review* 19, no. 1 (1995): 17–48. Michael Asch has used the connection between wildlife, land, and human hunters as a basis for arguing exclusive Dene hunting and management rights in traditional lands. See Michael Asch, "Wildlife: Defining the Animals the Dene Hunt and the Settlement of Aboriginal Rights Claims," *Canadian Public Policy* 15, no. 2 (1989): 205–219.
50. Most Native depletions of wildlife populations were the result of market-driven responses to colonial economic activity in the North and the entry of large numbers of non-Natives such as the Arctic coast whaling fleet. Few (if any) serious depletions have resulted from the subsistence use of wildlife by Native northerners. For a discussion, see Wenzel, *Animal Rights, Human Rights*, 94–95 and Brody, *Living Arctic*, 71–85. See also Peter Clancy, *Native Hunters and the State* (Studies in National and International Development Occasional Paper, Queen's University, No. 87–101), and Usher, "Indigenous Systems," 8, where he suggests that traditional Dene systems of self-regulation may be "weaker" than those of the Cree due to imperfect knowledge of each community's impact on a single migrating caribou herd.
51. Berger, *Northern Frontier, Northern Homeland*, 87.
52. Of course, these estimates of caribou numbers were nothing more than mere guesses: See Seton, *The Arctic Prairies*, 260, and C. D. H. Clarke, *A Biological Investigation of the Thelon Game Sanctuary* (Ottawa: National Museum of Canada, 1940), 103.
53. A. W. F. Banfield, *Preliminary Investigation of the Barren-Ground Caribou*, Canadian Wildlife Service Wildlife Management Bulletin, Series 1, No. 10, 1954.
54. See J. P. Kelsall, *Continued Barren-Ground Caribou Studies*, Wildlife Management Bulletin, Series 1, No. 12 (Ottawa: Minister of Northern Affairs and Natural Resources, 1957), 7–22.
55. A. W. F. Banfield, "The Caribou Crisis," *The Beaver* Outfit 286 (Spring 1956): 7.
56. Ibid., 6–9.
57. J. P. Kelsall, *Co-operative Studies of Barren-Ground Caribou, 1957–58*, Canadian Wildlife Service Wildlife Management Bulletin Service 1, no. 15. The discussion of human utilization as "the most important single factor" in the caribou decline is on pp. 80–92.
58. John S. Tener, "The Present Status of the Barren-Ground Caribou," *Canadian Geographical Journal* 60, no. 3 (1960): 98–105. Tener erroneously cites Banfield as suggesting that human predation is the key factor causing the decline. Banfield only suggests that this factor is the most easily "controlled." He also cites the change in technology to rifles as a factor in the decline, but guns had been introduced to the North a century and a half earlier.
59. R. A. Ruttan, "New Crisis for the Barren-Ground Caribou," *Country Guide* 85, no. 11 (November 1966): 24–25.
60. Gerry R. Parker, *Trends in the Population of Barren-Ground Caribou of Mainland Canada Over the Last Two Decades: A Re-evaluation of the Evidence*, Canadian Wildlife Service Occasional Paper 10 (Ottawa: The Queen's Printer, 1972): 5. Parker presents no alternative baseline with which to judge the "health" of the herds. Presumably he is alluding to Banfield's reference to an archaic carrying capacity of three million animals.
61. G. R. Parker, *Biology of the Kaminuriak Population of Barren-Ground Caribou, Part 2*, Canadian Wildlife Service Report Series No. 20 (Ottawa: Information Canada, 1972), 74. A similar analysis of the Bluenose, Bathurst, and Beverly herds was produced by Donald C. Thomas. He estimated that the total population of the herds had increased from 200,000 to 387,000 animals from 1958 to 1967, a rate of change that would require either the "extremely high" recruitment rate of 17.6 percent or would indicate that "the 1958 population was larger than 200,000." See Donald C. Thomas, *Population Estimates of Barren-Ground Caribou, March to May, 1967*, Canadian Wildlife Service Report Series No. 9 (Ottawa: The Queen's Printer, 1969), 42.
62. Kelsall, *The Migratory Barren-Ground Caribou of Northern Canada*, 286. Italics mine.
63. Ibid., 216. One could interpret the consumption of fetuses as a cultural practice that prevents waste, given the necessity of late winter and early spring hunting.
64. Ibid., 211.
65. J. D. Robertson, *Caribou Slaughter—Duck Lake* (Manitoba Game Branch Officer's Report, 1955). Quoted in Kelsall, *The Migratory Barren-Ground Caribou of Northern Canada*, 219.
66. Ila Bussidor and Üstün Bilgen-Reinhart, *Night Spirits: The Story of the Relocation of the Sayisi Dene* (Winnipeg: University of Manitoba Press, 1997).
67. Ibid., 45.

68. The story of social breakdown in the community after the relocations is chilling; see Bussidor and Bilgen-Reinhart, *Night Spirits*, 55–119.
69. Kelsall, *The Migratory Barren-Ground Caribou of Northern Canada*, 227, 288.
70. Clancy, "Native Hunters and the State," 30.
71. Carl Berger, "Review of Janet Foster's *Working for Wildlife*," *Canadian Historical Review* 60, no. 1 (1979): 85–86.
72. A. Radclyffe Dugmore, *The Romance of the Newfoundland Caribou: An Intimate Account of the Life of the Reindeer of North America* (London: William Heineman, 1913), 83.
73. Florence Miller, *In Caribou Land* (Toronto: Ryerson Press, 1929), 11.
74. Fraser Symington, *Tuktu: The Caribou of the Northern Mainland* (Ottawa: The Queen's Printer, 1965), 24–25, 31.
75. Francis Harper, *The Barren Ground Caribou of Keewatin* (Lawrence: University Press of Kansas, 1955), 15, 5.
76. Banfield, "The Caribou Crisis," 4.
77. From transcripts of the discussants' responses to the plenary session, *Proceedings of the First International Reindeer and Caribou Symposium*, ed. Jack Luick et al., Biological Papers of the University of Alaska, Special Report Number 1, September 1975, 32.
78. Symington, *Tuktu*, 52–69.
79. For more detail on co-management systems, see the Berger Report and Peter Usher's works cited earlier. See also Martha Johnson, "Documenting Dene Traditional Environmental Knowledge," *Akwekon Journal* (Summer 1992): 72–79; Martha Johnson, ed., *Lore: Capturing Traditional Environmental Knowledge*; and A. Gunn, G. Arlooktoo, and D. Kaomayak, "The Contribution of Ecological Knowledge of Inuit to Wildlife Management in the Northwest Territories," in *Traditional Knowledge and Renewable Resource Management*, ed. M. M. R. Freeman and L. N. Carbyn. The caribou numbers in the Northwest Territories are thought to be close to one million animals, and the spectacular irruption of the George River herd in Labrador has added one million more animals to the mainland population. See Don Russell, "Knowing More with Less: Research Planning for Large Migratory Caribou Herds," unpublished address to the international workshop on "The Human Role in Reindeer/Caribou Systems: Coping with Threats to Environmental Security in Northern Landscapes," February 10–14, The Arctic Centre, Robanieni, Finland. See also the preface to the first paperback edition of George Calef's *Caribou and the Barren-Lands* (Toronto: Firefly Books, 1995), 13–14. Originally published in 1981, the preface to the new edition is a fascinating reassessment of the original viewpoint of the first edition. Calef has been a prominent CWS caribou biologist, and is also an avid wildlife photographer who published this popular book to stimulate interest in the "plight" of the caribou. He includes a long section in the original edition that condemns Native hunting practices and their impact on the caribou herds. His reassessment in the 1995 preface celebrates the recovery and health of the caribou herds, the new co-management regimes that have been instituted in the Northwest Territories, and suggests that "it is unclear why such dramatic, simultaneous increases should occur across huge areas where climatic factors, predators, and hunting pressures presumably vary considerably. Perhaps caribou and reindeer experience population cycles like those of voles, lemmings, and snowshoe hares, except on a time measured in decades rather than in years" (p. 13).
80. Quoted in George Wenzel, *Animal Rights, Human Rights*, 167.
81. Frances Widdowson and Albert Howard, "Natural Stewards or Profit-Makers?" *The Globe and Mail* (Toronto), 2 May 1997, A10.

Document 11.1
James White

The Work of the Commission of Conservation

James White (1863–1928) was a Fellow of the Royal Geographical Society of Canada, the secretary of the Commission of Conservation, and the author of a number of books on geography, conservation, and Native society in Canada. The following is a partial transcript of a public lecture he delivered at an elite men's club. As the speech indicates, the commission's work was well publicized and of considerable interest to the public, even though, ultimately, it brought about little in the way of protective legislation.

Issues to Consider

- Who were the members of the Commission of Conservation? What was the basis of their selection?
- What were the "definite basic principles" governing the work of the commission? What do these tell us about the perspective and the assumptions shaping its mandate?

The Canadian Commission of Conservation was formed in 1910 in response to a strong and growing public demand for a saner system of national economy with respect to the development of Canada's natural resources. In describing the work which it has undertaken, it is obviously impossible for me to give a detailed and extended account of the progress made in each of its numerous branches of activity during the past five years. I wish merely to place before you the salient facts with regard to the status and functions of the Commission, to indicate the basic principles to which it has endeavored to adhere in performing those functions, and to refer briefly to the chief results that have been attained.

In composition, the Commission is strictly non-partisan, and the greatest care has also been taken to ensure that its personnel shall be truly representative of the entire Dominion. It consists of twenty appointed members in addition to the ex-officio membership, the latter including the federal ministers of Agriculture, Mines and the Interior, and the minister in each provincial government whose department has charge of the administration of natural resources. It is worthy of note that no member receives any fee or emolument for his services and that opportunities for a list of office holders are totally lacking. A second feature, meriting attention, is the clause of the act, under which the Commission is constituted, requiring that at least one of the appointed members from each province be a member of the faculty of a university in that province. It may well be said, therefore, that, in addition to obtaining a membership of thoroughly representative character, Parliament has legislated with the object of securing upon the Commission a high degree of scholarship, of scientific knowledge and of administrative experience.

The functions of the Commission and the scope of its efforts have been clearly defined. Its practical work and general policy must conform to certain definite basic principles. First in importance among these is the fact that the Commission is essentially and purely an advisory body; it shall undertake no administrative work. Its success depends largely upon the manner

Source: Excerpted from an address delivered before the Canadian Club of Hamilton, June 4, 1915.

in which it recognizes and observes this limitation of its duties. Any overstepping of its proper bounds, especially encroachment on the field of executive government, would serve only to defeat the Commission's purpose and alienate the support of those bodies through whom alone those purposes can be achieved. The Commission's function, stated in the terms of the act, is "to take into consideration all questions relating to the conservation and the better utilization of the natural resources of Canada, to make such inventories, collect and disseminate such information, conduct such investigations inside and outside of Canada as may seem conducive to the accomplishment of that end." By proceeding along these lines, by acquiring detailed, accurate knowledge, and by thus qualifying itself to offer sound advice, it aims to secure, through co-operation with federal, provincial and municipal governments, the wisest management of our national domain.

This policy naturally involves, as a second basic principle, the attainment of the maximum of result for the minimum of expenditure. The outlay of the Commission is confined almost entirely to the maintenance of a staff of trained experts to investigate the extent, character and administration of our resources, and to the publication of the information so obtained. The sources of waste are exposed, the extent of resources ascertained, and the remedies suggested at the minimum cost and with no duplication of executive work.

Where waste and improvidence are apparent, it becomes the duty of the Commission to urge upon the proper executive authority feasible means of conserving the resources in question. The problems that arise and the methods of solution differ greatly. The means of checking waste, or rehabilitating depleted resources, and of utilizing those that have been left undeveloped must be pointed out. The difficulties encountered are numerous and diverse, including deficiencies in organic law, looseness of administration, ignorance and negligence, or, very often, simply greedy exploitation. All causes of national waste and efficiency command the Commission's study and attention. In its advisory capacity, it must take up desirable measures, whether legislative, administrative or educational, and urge their adoption. Sensational action is carefully avoided. While it is not always possible to secure prompt action, the most satisfactory results are the outcome of steady pressure backed up by accurate knowledge and conclusive evidence in support of the action desired. It is self-evident that the Commission's success in enlisting the co-operation of executive departments depends on the merits of its own work. To command confidence and acceptance, its recommendations must be soundly based and absolutely free from prejudice and ulterior motives.

A final word with regard to the work in general. The Commission's appropriation is small. Its investigatory tasks are large and, when conducted simultaneously in several branches, the funds available for each undertaking are very limited. To overcome this difficulty, we have adopted the plan of devoting a greater amount each year to some special investigation. The method is applied in turn to a different branch of work and, in this manner, we are enabled to make faster progress, to complete investigations and publish the results more quickly than would otherwise be the case. At the inaugural meeting, the Commission was divided, for more effective work, into seven committees dealing, respectively, with Lands, Forests, Waters and Water Powers, Mines, Fish, Game and Fur-Bearing Animals, Public Health, Press and Co-operating Associations. The activities of each may be briefly reviewed in turn.

To the Committee on Lands has fallen the task of studying and attempting to improve farming methods throughout the Dominion. Her fertile land comprises Canada's most valuable natural resource and successful agriculture incomparably the greatest factor in her progress and prosperity. Soil fertility, however, is destructible and can be conserved only through the practice of scientific agriculture. The Committee, at the outset, had to face the fact that Canadian agriculture, except in scattered sections, is far from being scientific, that great areas of rich lands were rapidly being robbed of their fertility and that crop yields were decreasing instead of increasing. The first step toward improvement was to investigate actual conditions thoroughly, and, for this purpose, an agricultural survey of representative farming sections in the various provinces was undertaken. Reliable information relating to every phase and problem of practical agriculture was collected. During the first year, a cursory survey of 985 farms revealed startling conditions. Of the farms surveyed, not more than nine per cent employed a systematic rotation of crops; weed conditions were bad; the care of wood lots, with a view to future fuel supply, received insufficient attention; water supplies were frequently impure and only ten per cent of the homes had running water. On the whole, the information secured demonstrated that the introduction of better farming methods would double the value of Canada's field crops in twenty years. As a means of gaining accurate knowledge of prevailing conditions and of the chief evils to be combatted, the survey work proved most effective. The Committee, however, recognized that such studies are of value only in so far as they afford a basis for constructive measures, and, in 1912, decided to supplement the survey by practical demonstrations of the benefits to be derived from more scientific agriculture. For this purpose an illustration farm was selected and conducted in each of the groups visited in connection with the survey. Under the supervision of the Commission's travelling instructors, thorough cultivation, careful seed selection, systematic crop rotation and other features of scientific farming were introduced. The results were highly gratifying, especially the marked improvement in the farming methods of the entire surrounding districts and the deep interest of the community in the success of the methods practised in the demonstration farms. Mere advice seldom induces a farmer to change his methods, but an actual test will find him as ready as the next man to adopt a system that means extra profits. Having been thoroughly organized and its immense practical value proven, the illustration farm work has been turned over to the federal Department of Agriculture to be continued on a larger scale, as the Commission's objects in initiating it have been fully achieved. [...]

The work of the Committee on Forests may also be divided into several branches. There has been, first, the task of securing as reliable an estimate as possible of the total extent of Canada's timber resources. As pointed out before, the taking of an inventory has been one of the Commission's primary objects with respect to each natural resource. It is particularly important in the case of our forests, regarding the extent of which the Canadian people have entertained very exaggerated notions. For many years, our forest policy was the acme of extravagance. It was the attitude of ignorance, based on the patently false assumption that our timber resources were boundless. A little exact knowledge of their actual extent and of the rate at which they are being exhausted has finally given the correct perspective. Forest conservation has been taken up energetically by federal and provincial governments. Our timber resources have been very much overestimated; just to what degree it is will remain unknown until a complete survey has been made. The Committee on Forests has this work well under way. Excellent progress has been made in British Columbia and Saskatchewan, while Nova Scotia conditions have already been dealt with in a comprehensive report.

As a result of the realization that Canada's supply of merchantable timber is strictly limited, a national forestry policy, calculated to remedy past and avoid future errors, has been entered upon. The initial step has been to check the enormous annual waste due to forest fires. The yearly loss from this cause has been almost inestimable. [...]

Document 11.2
William Clark Bethune

Conservation of Game

Canada's Western Northland is the second of two volumes William Clark Bethune wrote for the Lands, Northwest Territories, and Yukon Branch of the Department of the Interior. The earlier volume, published in 1935, dealt with the eastern Arctic.

Issues to Consider

- Although predating the caribou crisis described by Sandlos by more than a decade, Bethune's discussion of the situation in 1937 is ominous. What does he consider to be the nature of the crisis, its causes, and its remedy?
- What perspective does Bethune offer on the Native peoples of the North and their relationship to the land and the animals?

It is only within comparatively recent years that the problem of conserving the game resources of the Northwest Territories has become a matter requiring the serious attention of those responsible for the Government and administration of the Territories. The slow development of a crisis was undoubtedly due to the sparse human population scattered over an immense area and to the abounding wild life. Fortunately investigation was commenced and a measure of control effected in time, otherwise the story of the plains buffalo might have been repeated in the barren ground caribou, as it was to a large degree in the musk-ox, which are now reduced on the mainland to a few small herds within or comparatively close to the Thelon Game Sanctuary.

The need for control measures was brought about through the introduction of modern firearms by explorers, traders and trappers, and the change in the natives' views as to what constituted the necessities of life. In the normal course of events what happened was bound to happen, and for the purpose of this report it is considered sufficient to refer to the facts without discussing the reasons therefor.

To all intents and purposes the Indians and Eskimos of the Northwest Territories are still altogether dependent on game for their livelihood and the serious depletion of the wild life resources of the country would be a disaster from their standpoint. By nature and environment these natives must continue indefinitely as hunters and trappers. However, the matter is not important only to the natives. The fur trade of the Territories constitutes a not unimportant part of the Dominion's domestic and export trade, it is the base of supply of raw material for many Canadian industries, and it contributes considerable revenue to the federal treasury.

While appreciating the desirability of providing for the harvesting of the northern fur crop in an economic manner, the belief that the welfare of the native population is of paramount importance is reflected in many sections of the Northwest Game Regulations. The number of white trappers is restricted by a clause which limits eligibility for licences to British subjects who have resided in the Territories for at least four years. The quantity of game that may be

Source: William Clark Bethune, "Conservation of Game," in *Canada's Western Northland: Its History, Resources, Population, and Administration* (Ottawa: King's Printer, 1937), 82–83. Also available online at http://www.ourroots.ca/e/viewpage.asp?ID=268595&size=2.

taken is controlled by the regulation of the open and closed seasons and in one case, that of beaver, by the fixing of a bag limit. Aircraft may not be used to enable the operation of trap-lines in different districts by one individual. Many large areas have been set side as native game preserves and game sanctuaries. Trading may be carried on only at permanent establishments approved by the Administration.

Except in the case of those Indians whose superstitions disincline them to kill wolves, all hunters and trappers kill these predators whenever opportunity presents itself. It is expected that, in time, the superstitions of those Indian bands which hold this taboo will be removed through education. When wolf skins are fashionable the prices of the pelts are usually sufficient inducement for trappers to make a special effort to trap or shoot the animals during the winter season. However, to encourage their destruction the Government pays a bounty on all wolves killed in the Northwest Territories.

The part played by wolves in the maintenance of nature's balance of wild life is realized, also the fact that when one of the factors controlling that balance is removed other influences are likely to be brought to bear to replace that which has been taken away. Under these cir-cumstances it naturally follows that there is a limit beyond which it is difficult to secure ben-eficial results from the killing of wolves. However, even though the wolf population of the Northwest Territories can be kept only slightly below what is its normal level, that slight dif-ference is of value because it costs a great deal in other game for even one wolf to maintain itself throughout the year. What is killed by wolves is of course not available to man, and more-over the destruction of game in traps by wolves means a further loss.

To keep abreast of game conditions in the Northwest Territories advantage is taken of all available sources of information. The collection of a tax on all pelts exported from the Territories enables a fairly accurate compilation to be made of the number and kinds of fur-bearing animals killed each year. This statement, considered in conjunction with the reports of previous years which indicate the cycles of abundance and scarcity, portrays the status of the species. The local detachments of the Royal Canadian Mounted Police in the Northwest Territories supply reports periodically on game conditions in their respective districts. These reports are of great value. Questionnaires sent from time to time to trappers, traders and others tap other sources of information. When occasion warrants, special investigations are conducted by representatives of the Government.

Topic 12

Postmodern Canada:

Contemporary Social Issues

Tim Dolighan, political cartoon, July 2004, http://www.mapleleafweb.com;
http://www.dolighan.com.

CONTEXT

Since the field of social history, broadly construed, was inspired by the quest for "relevance" by the 1960s generation of students and scholars, it seems only fitting that some thought be given to the historical context and current relevance of themes and issues that have been, in some form, in process since Confederation. This collection concludes, therefore, with a discussion of some of the issues that predominated in Canadian society as "Canada's Century" wound to its close.

Both the condition of postmodernity and contemporary history are usually taken to signify historical developments since the close of World War II. The postwar years ushered in a "brave new world" in myriad ways. Internationally, the war in the Pacific gave way to the atomic age, the Cold War commenced as the Iron Curtain descended, the age of television dawned, and the space race was launched with the Soviet satellite Sputnik in 1957. On the domestic scene, Canadians were laying the foundation blocks of the modern welfare state through such programs as family allowances, hospital insurance, and old age security. As these programs were built upon during the heady 1960s, especially with the advent of state medicine, they would gradually come to be regarded as cornerstones of Canadian society and identity. Fuelled by an enthusiastic consumerism after the deprivations of war and depression, Canadians enjoyed a prosperity that, while not evenly distributed across class, region, race, and gender lines, was more widespread than ever before. Also characterizing these years were the baby boom, the expansion of suburbia, the second great wave of immigration, an intensified industrialization and urbanization, technological advances that would signal the microchip revolution, the rise of neonationalism in Quebec, and the subsequent Quiet Revolution in that province. In the Western industrial capitalist world, information technology was slowly beginning to work its effects on life and labour, transforming the modern into the postmodern in gradual but discernible steps.

Contemporary history is a slippery concept in that what defines "contemporary" is, by definition, itself subject to the passage of time: it does not denote a specific, time-bound era. Initially understood to mean "post-1945," we are now looking at a period of more than half a century, so the "contemporary" stretches with each passing year. In addition, this has been a rough half-century of rapid and intensive change as never before in recorded history, and the pace of change itself continues to accelerate. The years since 1945 have commanded new attention from Canadian historians in the past decade, although much of the work remains preliminary, in article or dissertation form. At the moment, a large proportion of the published analyses on the final quarter of the 20th century is not to be found in history itself but in related disciplines, especially sociology, political science, and such interdisciplinary fields as Canadian studies, cultural and communications studies, literary studies, and women's studies.

Part of the explanation lies in the historian's traditional wariness about writing history without the benefit of knowing "what comes next," a sort of history of the present that benefits from a wealth of documentation — at times, too much to be manageable — but little in the way of necessary perspective or a sense of change over time, much less what we might call historical trends. While historians may focus on short periods, the wider context is crucial to making viable generalizations from our research findings. The selections in Topic 12 are not by trained historians, but by a sociologist (Li) and a cultural analyst (Straw), both of whom work on Canadian subjects and use historical context to inform their work.

To consider the Canada of the last thirty years or so, even very briefly and selectively, is to understand quickly what is meant by intense and accelerated change, the sense that history itself has picked up speed. To begin, Canada's population increased from 23.4 million in 1971 to 30.8 million in 2000. Forty percent of this increase was due to immigration. More to the point, the countries of origin of this latest cohort showed significant change from that of barely a half-century earlier. While only 4 percent of all immigrants arriving during the years 1945 to 1962 originated from outside Great Britain and the United States, now 75 percent came from non-British, non-American sources, the majority of these from the Asian continent. By 1996, the nation's metropolitan centres were home to four million members of visible minorities, constituting 11.2 percent of the total Canadian population. This population has fostered the nation's ongoing urbanization and, most especially, its suburbanization, as well as the long-standing metropolitan–hinterland relationship between city and surrounding town, country-side and region. By 2000, twenty-five metropolitan census areas contained three out of five Canadians.

These years saw a historic surge of organization, politicization, and militancy among Aboriginal groups, including the Inuit and the Métis people. As Canada approached the mil-lennium, the condition of its Native communities had improved scarcely at all since the Indian Act of 1876. It is testimony to the pride and persistence of these communities that they man-aged to carry on despite endemic poverty, low life expectancy, high suicide rates, and a host of related social, familial, and health problems. The principal issues were the settlement of land claims outstanding since the treaties of the 1870s, the right to self-government, and control over education. In 1992, the Inuit of the eastern Arctic came to terms with the federal gov-ernment to create a separate, self-administered territory to be called Nunavut ("the people's land" in Inuktikut); this was achieved in 1999. The Royal Commission on Aboriginal Peoples (1991–96) produced a comprehensive survey of conditions and prospects, with a number of rec-ommendations about land, self-government, education, and health care, but few of these, to date, have been realized. The last of the despised residential schools was closed in 1996; the federal government issued a formal apology for the historical mistreatment of Native children, and a promise of financial reparations, in 1998, as did a number of the churches involved. Private lawsuits, mostly against the churches, keep the matter before the courts and in the public consciousness.

Economically, the picture was decidedly mixed. After the fairly consistent economic health of the 1950s and 1960s, the 1970s brought the shocks caused by the tenuous situation among the oil-producing nations of the Middle East. "Stagflation," or high inflation with stag-nant growth, became the catchword of the day. Unemployment rose to double digits for the first time since the Great Depression, with the national average approaching 14 percent during the 1982 recession. Although recovery would slowly come about, the years of government infu-sion into the welfare state gave way to cutbacks, deficit-slashing, and elimination of programs; many commentators labelled this period a "jobless recovery." The 1989 Free Trade Agreement with the United States, expanded in 1994 (through the inclusion of Mexico) to become the North American Free Trade Agreement, did little to improve the lot of unemployed Canadians. A disproportionate number of the unemployed were the young, a cohort popularized as Generation X in Vancouver writer Douglas Coupland's 1991 novel of the same name. Globalization was another word in the news, as Canadians were urged to position themselves within this new transnational and so-called borderless world system that was supposedly leading to the demise of the nation-state in favour of the multinational corporation. The much-touted information highway of the 1990s was routed through many Canadian homes by 2000, as wireless and digital communications networks became the new connections linking virtual communities within national boundaries as well as across them.

Canadian families carried on their traditional role of gauging social change. In 1967, the famous statement of then-justice-minister Pierre Trudeau about the state having "no place in the bedrooms of the nation" anticipated the liberalization of divorce laws, the decriminaliza-tion of contraception and homosexuality, and wider access to abortion. There was an upsurge in divorces (affecting approximately one in three marriages by the 1980s) and common-law unions, with the latter especially significant in Quebec. The fertility rate continued to decline: by 1976, it was below the 2.1 children per woman required to sustain population levels, with no signs of upward motion as the century ended. The second-wave feminism of the 1970s, heralded by the 1967 Royal Commission on the Status of Women, and culminating organizationally in the National Action Committee on the Status of Women (NAC) in 1972, worked to improve gender equity before the law and in education and employment. By 1995, women made up nearly half the adult workforce, but earned only 72 percent of the wages of working men. At century's end, there were more married women with children working for wages and more women working in nontraditional areas than ever before, but women remain underrepresented in some professions and at the upper ranks of the corporate and political worlds. Female undergraduates outnumbered men on university campuses by 1996, yet they continue to be concentrated in the arts and social sciences. The gay rights movement has also made tremendous strides insofar as discrimination is concerned, but the issue of same-sex marriage is one of the most controversial of present-day developments.

Finally, but not surprisingly, the cultural question at the heart of Canadian identity since Confederation was anything but resolved as the century closed. Despite the Canadian Radio-television and Telecommunications Commission's 1970 regulation that 30 percent of music on the airways must be Canadian, a full 89 percent of the recording market in Canada in 1984 was in the hands of twelve foreign-controlled firms. The most popular television shows were American. The CBC floundered, a victim of downsizing and federal government cutbacks. The Canadian feature film industry began to recover (especially in Quebec, where its audience is guaranteed), but it posed absolutely no threat to Hollywood dominance. Since the 1980s, the number of Canadian-born hockey players in the NHL has been declining apace; two of the Canadian expansion teams, the Winnipeg Jets and the Quebec Nordiques, left for the United States in the mid-1990s. But there was little letup in the popular understanding of hockey as "Canada's game," and the passionate embrace of "Joe's Rant" (reproduced in Document 12.2) suggests that sport and popular culture continue to be important instruments of personal and national identity. Perhaps when economic and political borders melt away, they become even more so.

REFERENCES/FURTHER READING

Corse, Sarah. *Nationalism and Literature: The Politics of Culture in Canada and the United States*. Cambridge: Cambridge University Press, 1997.

Day, Richard J. F. *Multiculturalism and the History of Canadian Diversity*. Toronto: University of Toronto Press, 2000.

Gaffield, Chad, and Karen Gould, eds. *The Canadian Distinctiveness into the XXIst Century*. Ottawa: University of Ottawa Press, 2003.

Gidney, R. D. *From Hope to Harris: The Reshaping of Ontario's Schools*. Toronto: University of Toronto Press, 1999.

Fleras, Augie. *Social Problems in Canada: Conditions, Constructions, and Challenges*. 4th ed. Toronto: Pearson Education Canada, 2005.

Li, Peter S. *The Making of Post-War Canada*. Toronto: Oxford University Press, 1996.

Long, David A., and Olive P. Dickason, eds. *Visions of the Heart: Canadian Aboriginal Issues*. 2nd ed. Toronto: Harcourt Canada, 2000.

Mackey, Eva. *The House of Difference: Cultural Politics and National Identity in Canada*. Toronto: University of Toronto Press, 2002.

Porter, Anne. *Gendered States: Women, Unemployment Insurance, and the Political Economy of the Welfare State in Canada, 1945–1997*. Toronto: University of Toronto Press 2003.

Rutherford, Paul. *Endless Propaganda: The Advertising of Public Goods*. Toronto: University of Toronto Press, 2000.

Watson, William. *Globalization and the Meaning of Canadian Life*. Toronto: University of Toronto Press, 1998.

Wright, Robert A. *Virtual Sovereignty: Nationalism, Culture and the Canadian Question.* Toronto: Canadian Scholars' Press, 2004.

ILLUSTRATION 12.1 (P. 509)

Public debates and parliamentary discussions have made the legalization of marijuana and same-sex marriage topical issues in early 21st-century Canada. Our American neighbours, ruled by a very conservative Republican president and Congress, have also given some media attention to these "Canadian" matters.

Issues to Consider

- What is the cartoonist getting across in this depiction of the American response?
- What national and historical images does Illustration 12.1 draw upon in portraying the Canada–U.S. relationship?

ARTICLES

The articles in this section explore two burning issues in contemporary Canadian society. Peter Li's essay examines immigration and multiculturalism, while Will Straw's piece deals with the "Canadianness" of Canadian popular music. There are countless other issues that could be touched upon to demonstrate both the changes and the continuities that have taken place within the various topic headings considered in this collection. What is important is that a look back at the preceding eleven topics will immediately indicate just how relevant they each remain to the 21st-century society that is our Canada.

Article 12.1
Peter Li

The Place of Immigrants: The Politics of Difference in Territorial and Social Space

Issues to Consider

- Difference is the central concept of Li's examination of contemporary immigration policy and reality. What does he mean by the expression "the politics of difference"?
- How does Li differentiate between territorial and symbolic/social/cultural space?
- How are immigrants "symbolic representations"?
- Why was the point system made the basis of the 1967 immigration regulations? What effects did its implementation have?
- How has contemporary anxiety about national security affected public discourse on immigration?
- In Li's view, the diversity that has long been a point of pride for Canadians is increasingly being viewed as a problem. Discuss.

INTRODUCTION

Canada's public immigration discourse tends to treat immigrants as the object of inquiry, focusing on who they are, how they perform in Canada, and whether they bring economic and social value. Rarely is the discourse itself scrutinized. This paper examines the cultural framework by which the understanding of immigrants has been shaped, focusing on the historical continuity and contemporary relevance of "race" or "racialized others." The focus is on the representation of desirable and undesirable immigrants in the construction, maintenance, and safe-keeping of Canada's actual and virtual boundaries. The place of immigrants in territorial and social space indicates not only the nature and quality of immigrants, but also the ideological and discursive grounds by which "insiders" represent "outsiders" and by which those who have successfully secured legitimacy and power racialize others deemed to be fundamentally different. Thus, the discursive mapping of immigrants in Canada's territorial and social terrains is an extension of politics of difference.

IDEOLOGICAL FRAMEWORK AND IMMIGRATION

Gramsci (1973) and Hall (1996a, 1996b) stressed the importance of cultural frameworks in giving meaning to different classes to enable them to make sense of the world around them, and that in doing so, cultural frameworks assume a life of their own, capable of changing the material and political world and thus contributing to reproducing it. In other words, the objectified

Source: Peter Li, "The Place of Immigrants: The Politics of Difference in Territorial and Social Space," *Canadian Ethnic Studies* 35, no. 2 (2003): 1–13.

social world is represented through ideas, language, symbols, and culture, and in turn, the representation provides the meaning of the social world. As Hall (1996c) put it, "regimes of representation in a culture do play a *constitutive*, and not merely a reflexive, after-the-event, role." In this way, contestations in the social world — whether based on class, gender, or race — necessarily involve contestations in the symbolic order of representation. The study of frames of representation incorporates many facets, including what Hall (1996c:442) called "relations of representation" such as the "contestation of the marginality," as well as how "a set of ideas comes to dominate the social thinking of a historical bloc" (Hall, 1996a:27). In short, unequal relations in the social world are both reflected and constituted by unequal relations of representation.

Immigrants are not only latecomers to Canada's geographical space, but also symbolic representations in ideas, norms, and language, and even in a system of understanding. In other words, immigrants are actual people born outside the country who have been admitted to Canada, as well as symbolic representations of those who, in the eyes of the resident population, should be given or denied entry to Canada. This system of understanding (or cultural framework) is used by Canada's resident population to evaluate immigrants and to pass judgments on their merits and shortcomings. This cultural framework is influenced and shaped by relations in society, but in turn, it also provides meanings to old-timers and affects how they relate to latecomers.

International migration involves individuals and families being uprooted from a country of origin, crossing the physical boundary of another nation, and venturing into the social boundary of the destination society. No doubt, the outcome of immigration is contingent upon the self-effort of immigrants in overcoming the hardship of boundary crossing, both geographical and social, but it also depends on how much the resident population is prepared to open the door to welcome the outsiders at the gate. The "warmth of the welcome," as Reitz (1998) calls it, depends on the institutional features of the receiving society, including educational opportunities, welfare accessibility, and labour market arrangements. However, it also depends on the representational frame with which those who see themselves as old-timers evaluate newcomers at the border.

Much of this representational frame is shaped by ideas, concepts, and norms which old-timers inherit and develop in their understanding of "others," that is, those who are deemed to be different by virtue of their birthplace, race, language, and other cultural idiosyncrasies. Historically, Canada has maintained a racialized cultural framework to judge those being excluded or included as immigrants within its national borders. That cultural framework continues to influence the way Canada sees the security of its territorial boundary as well as the integrity of its social boundary. Thus to understand the warmth of the welcome also involves studying insiders' cultural representation of "outsiders" and how the discursive frame enables insiders to maintain and safeguard the physical and symbolic boundary of the nation.

Like other discourses, the immigration discourse is guided by a normative framework, an ideological road map, and a linguistic coherence. Naturally, there are diversities in the way the discourse is articulated, but the discourse has coherence and has in common certain ideas, concepts, and terminologies regarding how "outsiders" are to be represented. The representation revolves around demarcating the national boundary in terms of two types of space: territorial space and symbolic/social/cultural space.

RADICALIZING CANADA'S BORDER

Canada's immigration discourse has been framed from the vantage point of self-interest, as defined by old-timers' predisposition of the type of newcomers to Canada that would advance or harm its national interests. From such a vantage point, the interests of immigrant-sending countries and of global inequality and redistribution are seldom considered (Li, 2003a).

Historically, the immigration discourse has racialized the territorial boundary of Canada in upholding the value of European immigrants, notably those from Britain, northern Europe, and the United States, and discounting the contribution of non-white immigrants, particularly those from Asia. In other words, Canada's territorial security and interest were expressed in clear racial terms, with an unequivocal understanding that the value of non-European races to Canada was questionable. This discursive framework has been influenced by Canada's long-standing racial ideology which saw Asian immigrants as racially, morally, and culturally inferior to the Occidental tradition of Canada (Anderson, 1991; Roy, 1989; Ward, 1978). Hence, the historical restriction and exclusion of Asian immigrants to Canada were equated with safeguarding Canada's borders and its European tradition from what was seen as the "yellow peril."

Even during the period of the wheat boom (at the turn of the nineteenth century when Canada adopted the immigration expansionist policy of Clifford Sifton, Minister of the Interior), the official discourse made a clear distinction between the European settlers and the questionable Asian workers (Hoerder, 1999; Kelly and Trebilcock, 1998; Li, 1998). It was an open door period for Europeans, and three million of them came between 1896 and 1914 as settlers in the prairies and workers in urban Canada (Li, 2003a:19). But the same period also saw the enactment of the Chinese Immigration Act in 1900 to raise the Chinese Head Tax to $100, another act in 1903 to further raise the Chinese Head Tax to $500, and the "continuous journey" act in 1908 to discourage the sailing of East Indians from India to Canada (Li, 1998). These legislative measures were deemed necessary to protect Canada as a nation of Europeans from the racial and social contamination of Asians. "Racial" distinction was deeply engraved in Canada's ideological framework of nation-building and was effectively used as an instrument of settlement, population growth, and border control.

The need to safeguard Canada's border from racially undesirable immigrants was reaffirmed by Mackenzie King in 1947, in his famous statement to reject what he called "large-scale immigration from the orient" because of its potential harmful effects at a time when Canada was planning to expand immigration. Throughout the 1950s, Canada restricted Chinese immigration on the grounds that it could become what J. W. Pickersgill, Minister of Citizenship and Immigration from 1954 to 1957, called "an avenue for the back door infiltration of communist agents" (Canada, House of Commons, 9 June 1960:4715–4716). Indeed, during the period of the Cold War, Canada's concerns of national and border security were guided by its anti-communist stance that interpreted communist regimes as a threat to Canada and western democracy. Since Chinese immigrants originated from China, a communist state, Chinese immigrants were seen as posing a potential security threat to Canada (Li, 1998:93). No doubt, the historical image of the Chinese as morally questionable, culturally inferior, and socially unassimilable could only contribute to the stereotypical perception that they were untrustworthy.

If communist China was an enemy of the West, then anti-communist elements could only advance the national interests of Canada as a democratic state. Undoubtedly, the mentality of the Cold War prompted Canada to accept, between 1956 and 1958, about 38,000 of the 190,000 refugees who fled Hungary following the Soviet suppression of the 1956 anti-communist uprising (see Hawkins, 1988:114).

The "point system" of selecting immigrants introduced by the 1967 Immigration Regulations was often cherished as marking the end of the racialization of immigration. In 1979 and 1980, Canada showed the same generosity to the Vietnamese refugees as it did to the Hungarians by accepting 60,000 "boat people" from Vietnam after the fall of Saigon (Li, 1998:95). The admission of Vietnamese boat people in the late 1970s served a political purpose of the time: It reinforced the image of Canada as a humanitarian and democratic nation in contrast to the horror of a communist regime even though it succeeded in uniting North and

South Vietnam. But Canada was reluctant to continue to admit large numbers of Vietnamese from refugee camps in Southeast Asia in the 1980s because the Vietnamese refugees had outlived their political value to Canada and had become an international burden.

By the time several boatloads of Chinese migrants came to the west shore of Canada in 1999 to claim refugee status, Canada was more interested in trading with countries behind the "iron curtain" than in using those who fled the country to undermine the regime. The 599 Chinese who landed illegally on the west coast in 1999 were seen as a threat to Canada's security because the migrants were pauperized and because more were suspected to follow. Canada reacted with panic and took extraordinary steps to incarcerate them. The public, too, was unsympathetic to the Chinese despite their hazardous journey. A 1999 public poll found 70 percent of Canadian respondents rejected the idea of automatically granting the Chinese boat people a claim to be political refugees (The Globe and Mail, 1999). A minister referred to the migrants as "law-breakers" who abused Canada's generosity, and as a result stirred up an anti-immigration backlash (National Post, 1999). By 2000, of the 599 Chinese migrants who came by boat in 1999, only 16 were granted refugee status, but the government spent $36 million in processing and incarcerating them (The Globe and Mail, 2000). In their analysis of the media reporting of the Chinese arrival, Hier and Greenberg (2002) argued that a racialized moral panic was created in Canada, with a large part of the public and the new media viewing the refugee system and the "illegal Chinese" as a threat to national security. In particular, the news media highlighted the potential threat of Chinese migrants in bringing infectious diseases to Canada, increasing organized crime, and using Canada as a conduit of illegal immigration to the U.S. (Hier and Greenberg, 2002). The moral panic toward the undocumented migrants created in the print media was out of proportion, and Hier and Greenberg (2002) attributed it to a racial backlash against the Chinese.

The threat of racialized populations to the security of Canada is also articulated in concerns over organized crime and violence. The idea of Asian immigrants bringing a higher level of organized crime and violence to Canada has periodically surfaced in the media. As early as 1991, Maclean's magazine ran a feature article entitled "Terror in the streets: Ruthless Asian gangs bring a new wave of violence to Canadian cities" (Maclean's, 1991). Based on several incidents, mostly in Toronto, the article said the killings have established a "new threshold in a surge of Asian violence sweeping the country" (Maclean's, 1991). In her book entitled Immigration: The Economic Case, Diane Francis described the growth of the Tamil community in Canada under the heading of Tamil terrorists, and quoted a source to refer to Tamil Tigers and their accomplices as having been "involved in a wide range of criminal activities in this country" (Francis, 2002:145). In their analysis of news reports of crimes committed by Asians in Canada, Henry and Tator (2002:201) pointed out that the media often made stereotypic assumptions of Asian immigrant communities as violent and gang-infected, and elevated crimes committed by individuals to the level of collective features of the communities.

The 9/11 disaster brought a new round of security concerns for Canada to safeguard the border. American allegations that Canada's border was lax and that terrorists could infiltrate it easily created added pressure to tighten security, targeting in particular those from the Middle East and Islamic countries. Immigration critics such as Daniel Stoffman seized the opportunity to attack immigration. He described what he called the "root causes of Canada's vulnerability to terrorism" as follows: "an immigration program that lets in more people than is consistent with public safety, and a refugee system that allows known criminals and terrorists and unidentified people from all over the world to roam freely in Canada" (Stoffman, 2002:53). In the aftermath of 9/11, the need to manage immigration and to keep racialized elements suspected of being prone to terrorism from entering became a priority security issue. The 9/11 attacks provided the grounds for the general public to condone vigilance and suspicion toward certain racial groups. A poll conducted by Environics in August of 2002 indicated that 43 percent of respondents said Canada accepts too many immigrants from Arab countries (*Ottawa Citizen*, 2002). Raja Khoury, president of the Canadian-Arab Federation, said that the Arab community suffered increased negative stereotyping and prejudice since September 11, 2001, and that "there is a continuous association between Islam and terrorism in the media, while there is nothing to balance the image" (*The Gazette*, 2003). In the post 9/11 period, there is wide acceptance by the Canadian government and the public that draconian measures toward those from Arab and Islamic countries are necessary to protect the borders of Canada and to safeguard its national security.

In addition to recent concerns of terrorism from those of Islamic origin, Canada also associated certain origins with potential health hazards. For example, in a 2002 article entitled "Immigration fuels soaring TB rate," the *Times Colonist* (Victoria) reported: "… most of the immigrants who come to B.C. arrive from countries where TB is rampant — India, China, the Philippines and Vietnam" (*Times Colonist*, 2002). The paper also printed the comment of Dr. Kevin Elwood, director of TB control for the B.C. Centre for Disease Control, as follows: "The Chinese immigrants are particularly not interested in preventive drugs" (*Times Colonist*, 2002). During the outbreak of SARS earlier this year, the Chinese-Canadian community in Toronto reported experiencing hostility and discrimination from the general public, as the Chinese were being blamed for having brought the disease to the city and devastating its economy (*Ming Pao*, 2003; *The Globe and Mail*, 2003). However, concerns over Britain's mad cow disease were not translated into blaming immigrants originating from Britain.

These examples demonstrate that a racialized ideological framework has influenced Canada's ideas of nation-building. Even though the groups being racialized have changed, a racialized framework continues to influence Canada's representation of, and discourse about, outside threats to national security.

SAFEGUARDING CANADA'S SOCIAL SPACE

Much of Canada's immigration discourse has to do with keeping the wrong people out and safeguarding its territorial space from intruders who are often depicted with a racial overtone. Canada also uses a cultural framework in guarding its social boundary from "undesirable" immigrants, including those who have been admitted to Canada. In other words, Canada maintains a normative standard to differentiate different kinds of immigrants being admitted based on how much immigrants are deemed to enrich or undermine the social boundary of Canada as a nation.

In their highly sensational attack on Canada's immigration system, critics such as Diane Francis (2002), Daniel Stoffman (2002), and Martin Collacott (2002) advocate a substantial reduction in immigration on the grounds that the types of immigrants Canada admits do not contribute very much, and indeed may be harmful, to the economic, social, demographic, and fiscal well-being of the nation. Besides using selective evidence and fallacious arguments, these authors dwell on a harsh utilitarian dictum: immigrants not obviously enriching Canada are useless to Canada. Indeed, it is precisely based on this principle that Collacott attacked priorities given to family-class sponsorship as having what he called "the most negative impact," on the presumed grounds that these immigrants do not bring human capital and that they take resources from Canada (Collacott, 2002:19).

The ideological premise upon which immigration critics construct their arguments is in fact not far from the official stance. Canada has maintained a *de facto* dual policy regarding immigration: the selection of economic immigrants and the admission of "unchosen" or "self-selected" family members and asylum seekers (Li, 2003a). Much attention to immigration policy development is directed toward selecting immigrants of high human capital capacity, and restricting and managing the sponsorship of family members and asylum seekers. The official discourse consistently attributes a greater value to economic immigrants and blames the so-called self-selected immigrants — family class and refugees — for squeezing out the economic stream (Employment and Immigration Canada, 1993:2,7). The 1996 annual report to Parliament by the Minister of Citizenship and Immigration stated: "Research shows that economic immigration is the component that benefits Canada and Canadians most quickly and to the greater extent" (Citizenship and Immigration Canada, 1996:7). It was this mentality which prompted the recent changes in immigration policy in allotting a greater proportion of landed immigrants to the economic class. Since 2000, the economic class has made up 60 percent or more of the total landed immigrants to Canada every year (Citizenship and Immigration Canada, 2003).

Immigration discourse periodically dwells on the extended familism of other cultures as a challenge to managing the "unchosen" family-class immigration. A 1994 report of Citizenship and Immigration Canada entitled *Into the 21st Century: A Strategy for Immigration and Citizenship* outlined the problem as follows:

> In Canada, the traditional definition of family has been changing. Single parent families are now common. Family is also defined differently in other cultures. The traditional family unit, i.e., father, mother, and independent children, has long been at the heart of Canadian society. However, in other countries close ties frequently exist with extended family members. These are some of the factors which need to be considered in Canada's approach to family immigration (Citizenship and Immigration Canada, 1994a:11).

The subtext is clear: immigrants from cultures foreign to Canada uphold extended familism and maintain a large family network that is contrary to the Canadian concept of family. There is a strong overtone regarding the need to reconceptualize the family reunification program based on the nuclear family of Canada and not the extended family of Asia or Africa. Several academic studies have attributed the declining earnings of immigrants in the 1980s relative to earlier arrivals to the increase in the family immigration stream and the disproportional distribution of Asian immigrants across the admission classes (Bloom, Grenier, and Gunderson, 1995; Miller, 1992). Taken together, the discourse portrays an urgency to control the family-class stream of immigration used more often by non-European immigrants in order to uphold Canada's living standard and to reserve immigration allotments to those more deserving, "selected" immigrants.

It is on the subject of immigrant diversity that the ideological framework used to maintain Canada's social boundary can be more fully understood. It is a widely accepted conclusion that, as a result of changes in immigration regulations in 1967, there has been an increase in the "diversity" of Canada, brought about by an increasing number of immigrants from "non-traditional" source countries (Li, 2003b). As early as 1989, a report by Employment and Immigration Canada (1989:8–9) had this to say:

> Canada's immigration is coming increasingly from "non-traditional" parts of the world. Thirty years ago, more than 80 percent of Canada's immigrants came from Europe or countries of European heritage, whereas 70 percent now come from Asia alone ... As a result, many Canadians are concerned that the country is in danger of losing a sense of national identity.

The notion of "diversity" in the immigration discourse has become a standard term used to refer to "non-white," and sometimes to the problem of having too many "non-whites." For example, under the heading "Immigration and Diversity," a 1994 CIC report (Citizenship and

Immigration Canada, 1994b) discussed how Canadians' concerns about immigration were triggered by increasingly large numbers coming from Asia (Li, 2001). Another CIC report of the same year talked about how Canadians were concerned about the impact of immigration on "values and traditions that form the foundation of Canadian society," and worried about their country being fragmented and becoming "a loose collection of parts" (CIC, 1994a:10). Throughout the 1990s, the immigration debate reiterated the idea that the rapid upsurge in immigration from Asia and Africa was changing urban Canada too radically (Li, 2001). Thus, too much diversity from non-white immigrants is seen as undermining Canada's traditional values, changing its social fabric, and weakening its cohesiveness.

The immigration discourse also depicts Canada as a demographic and open society that supports multiculturalism and allows immigrants to integrate without requiring them to abandon their cultures. The contradiction of endorsing multiculturalism on the one hand and questioning immigrants' diversity on the other is resolved by adopting a rhetoric that upholds the ideological value of multiculturalism but dismisses the merit of cultural specificities. For example, official statements often repeat the following message regarding integration: "In Canada, integration is a two-way process of accommodation between newcomers and Canadians: It encourages immigrants to adapt to Canadian society without requiring them to abandon their cultures" (Dorais, 2002:4). However, when it comes to the value of cultural specificities such as the immigrant enclaves, an official report has this to say:

> Ethnic enclaves can play a positive role in easing the shock of adjustment to a new culture ... To the degree that ethnic enclaves restrict their members and shield them from alternative norms, values, and behaviours, they can discourage immigrants from full participation in society and perpetuate segregation ... Ideally, in an integrated society, immigrants move through the ethnic enclave, using its resources in order to enter the mainstream society (Employment and Immigration Canada, 1993:4–5).

Thus, the underlying normative frame upholds a social boundary of Canada within which newcomers are expected to conform, and within which institutionalized cultural differences are seen as promoting segregation, hindering integration, and acting against the interest of "mainstream society."

Immigration critics tend to be more blatant in their condemnation of essentialized cultural differences. Stoffman (2002:16), for example, referred to multiculturalism as "divisive ... because different cultures have irreconcilable values ... [and] because Canada is built ... around a shared belief in the values of democracy and individual freedom." In short, people from different cultures are described as having "irreconcilable values," encouraged by official multiculturalism, that threaten Canada's democracy and freedom. Collacott (2002:29–30) made a similar point when he blamed family-class immigration and modern communication technology for assisting immigrant enclave development in urban Canada, thus slowing immigrant integration.

Breton (1984) has argued that the racial and ethnic tensions of the late 1970s and 1980s reflected the process of restructuring a symbolic order and status hierarchy in which the cultural dominance and complacency of British-origin Canadians were being challenged. Indeed, the tensions that underlie the reactions of some old-timers to many social challenges in Canada reflect a prevailing normative representation to essentialize superficial racial differences. Over time, as immigrants' racial differences are associated with undesirable changes in normative representation, diversity becomes incompatible with the demographic tradition and core values of Canada, or a threat to Canada's romanticized social space. The battle over the so-called Chinese "monster homes" in Vancouver in the late 1980s and early 1990s (Li, 1994), the attempt to restrict the Asianization of suburban malls in Markham in the 1990s (Li, 1998:146–148), and the general blaming of non-white immigrants for crowding the city and changing the urban landscape and indeed altering the Canadian way of life reflect a racialized normative standard which some old-timers use to territorialize Canada's urban and social space.

CONCLUSION

The place of immigrants in Canada is influenced by the cultural representation of "outsiders" used by those who have successfully secured and legitimized their territorial claim to safeguard the physical and symbolic boundary. As Stuart Hall (1996a) reminds us, cultural representation has its central place because it is in representation that categories and relations are to be understood and shaped.

Cultural representation relies on the use of codes as conveyed in language, symbols, texts, and subtexts, which have a history and a pre-existing understanding. The notion of race survives in a democratic country like Canada as a meaningful social code because its symbolic meaning has been reshaped and transformed to suit the time. Part of the transformation is to distil the ugly aspects associated with overt racism [and] to retain other aspects of race that make them palatable to people, as though they are not concerned with race and are indeed against racism. Thus, the new representation of race can appear as rational, public-minded (as opposed to self-serving), and even liberal-minded.

Much of Canada's assessment of immigrants has to do with its representation of racialized new immigrants as diversity problems for Canada: crowding major cities; contributing to urban crime, environmental degradation, and travel congestion; overburdening the educational, social, health, welfare, and infrastructural services; adding pressures to the job and housing markets; and altering the social fabric of Canada. In short, the immigration problem is represented as a problem of too much diversity, and racialized new immigrants are represented as endless intruders to urban and social space.

Racialized immigrants are also being represented as "newcomers" from "non-traditional" sources despite their long history in Canada. This representation reflects how racialized immigrants have been marginalized throughout Canada's history as foreign workers and not as deserving permanent citizens.

Racialized new immigrants are also represented as multicultural objects, and not subjects, of multiculturalism. As multicultural objects, they only bring superficial novelties and add quantity to Canada's diverse population. As objects, they are to make Canada look better as a tolerant society, but not to demand that Canada change for their sake.

This representation positions racialized new immigrants at the margin, as objects of evaluation, and not subjects whose values, aspirations, and wishes are to be taken into account. This is an extension of the normative, historical representation of non-whites in Canada, and it reflects their marginality in Canada's discursive space (see Hall, 1996b). The marginalized representation of racialized immigrants is justified on the grounds that old-timers have a right to decide who should be admitted as newcomers and citizens, and on the grounds that immigrants are not in a position to demand changes in Canada because they have made the choice to come to a pre-existing social order. In short, the representation successfully silences the voice of new immigrants and denies them a place in the representational space of the normative and symbolic order. The representation shapes the politics of difference and becomes in itself the politics of difference. Many relations and factors may have influenced the cultural representation of newcomers, but it is in the representation itself that social relations and social categories are given meaning in people's life. In short, the representation provides concrete meanings and contours to the symbolic and geographic space of a nation.

NOTE

This paper is a revised version of a keynote speech delivered at the Canadian Ethnic Studies Association's Seventeenth Biennial Conference, "Ethnicity: Space and Place," held at Banff, Alberta, October 2–5, 2003.

REFERENCES

Anderson, Kay J. 1991. *Vancouver's Chinatown.* Montreal/Kingston: McGill-Queen's University Press.

Bloom, David E., Gilles Grenier, and Morley Gunderson. 1995. "The changing labour market position of Canadian immigrants." *Canadian Journal of Economics* 28(4b): 987–1005.

Breton, Raymond. 1984. "The production and allocation of symbolic resources: An analysis of the linguistic and ethnocultural fields in Canada." *Canadian Review of Sociology and Anthropology* 21(2): 123–144.

Citizenship and Immigration Canada. 2003. *Facts and Figures 2002.* Ottawa: Minister of Public Works and Government Services Canada.

———. 1996. *A Broader Vision: Immigration Plan, 1996 Annual Report to Parliament.* Catalogue Cil-1996. Ottawa: Minister of Supply and Services Canada.

———. 1994a. *Into the 21st Century: A Strategy for Immigration and Citizenship.* Ottawa: Minister of Supply and Services Canada.

———. 1994b. *Canada and Immigration: A Discussion Paper.* Ottawa: Citizenship and Immigration Canada.

Collacott, Martin. 2002. *Canada's Immigration Policy: The Need for Major Reform.* Vancouver: The Fraser Institute.

Dorais, M. 2002. "Immigration and integration through a social cohesion perspective." *Horizons* 5(2): 4–5.

Employment and Immigration Canada. 1993. *Strategies for Immigrant Integration.* Ottawa: Public Affairs, Employment and Immigration Canada.

———. 1989. *Immigration to Canada: Issues for Discussion.* IM 061/11/89. Ottawa: Employment and Immigration Canada.

Francis, Diane. 2002. *Immigration: The Economic Case.* Toronto: Key Porter.

Globe and Mail, The. 2003. "Illness spawns some shunning of Asians." 03 April, p. A9.

———. 2000. "The boat people's big gamble." 22 July, p. A7.

———. 1999. "Migrants not owed free ride, poll says: Sympathy for newcomers lowest in B.C.; Public split on need for refugee hearings." 31 August, p.1.

Gramsci, Antonio. 1973. *Selections from the Prison Notebooks of Antonio Gramsci.* Edited and translated by Quintin Hoare and Geoffrey Nowell Smith. London: Lawrence and Wishart.

Hall, Stuart. 1996a. "The problem of ideology: Marxism without guarantees." In *Critical Dialogues in Cultural Studies,* edited by David Morley and Kuan-Hsing Chen, pp. 25–46. London/New York: Routledge.

———. 1996b. "Cultural studies and its theoretical legacies." In *Critical Dialogues in Cultural Studies,* edited by David Morley and Kuan-Hsing Chen, pp. 262–275. London/New York: Routledge.

———. 1996c. "New ethnicities." In *Critical Dialogues in Cultural Studies,* edited by David Morley and Kuan-Hsing Chen, pp. 441–449. London/New York: Routledge.

Hawkins, Freda. 1988. *Canada and Immigration: Public Policy and Public Concern.* Second Edition. Montreal/Kingston: McGill-Queen's University Press.

Henry, Frances, and Carol Tator. 2002. *Discourses of Domination: Racial Bias in the Canadian English-Language Press.* Toronto: University of Toronto Press.

Hier, Sean, and Joshua Greenberg. 2002. "News discourse and the problematization of Chinese migration to Canada." In *Discourses of Domination: Racial Bias in the Canadian English-Language Press,* edited by Frances Henry and Carol Tator, pp. 138–162. Toronto: University of Toronto Press.

Hoerder, Dirk. 1999. *Creating Societies: Immigrant Lives in Canada.* Montreal/Kingston: McGill-Queen's University Press.

Kelly, Ninette, and Michael Trebilcock. 1998. *The Making of the Mosaic: A History of Canadian Immigration Policy.* Toronto: University of Toronto Press.

Li, Peter S. 2003a. *Destination Canada: Immigration Debates and Issues.* Toronto: Oxford University Press.

———. 2003b. "Visible Minorities in Canadian Society: Challenges of Racial Diversity." In *Social Differentiation: Patterns and Processes,* edited by Danielle Juteau, pp. 117–153. Toronto: University of Toronto Press.

———. 2001. "The racial subtext in Canada's immigration discourse." *Journal of International Migration and Integration* 2(1): 77–97.

————. 1998. *The Chinese in Canada*. Second Edition. Toronto: Oxford University Press.

————. 1994. "Unneighbourly houses or unwelcome Chinese: The social construction of race in the battle over 'monster homes' in Vancouver, Canada." *International Journal of Comparative Race and Ethnic Studies* 1(1): 47–66.

Maclean's. 1991. "Terror in the streets: Ruthless Asian gangs bring a new wave of violence to Canadian cities." 25 March, pp. 18–21.

Miller, Paul W. 1992. "The earnings of Asian male immigrants in the Canadian labor market." *International Migration Review* 26(3–4): 1222–1247.

Ming Pao. 2003. "SARS ying fa Duolunduo qi shi gu lu [SARS causes worries of discrimination in Toronto]." 04 April.

Montreal Gazette, The. 2003. "Canadians seen as intolerant: People see prejudice in others, but find themselves tolerant." 22 April.

National Post. 1999. "Minister condemns smuggling of humans." 03 September, p. A10.

Ottawa Citizen, The. 2002. "Asian, Arab immigrants least favoured, poll finds: Canadians more open to accepting newcomers from Europe, Latin America and Africa." 12 September.

Reitz, Jeffrey G. 1998. *Warmth of the Welcome: The Social Causes of Economic Success for Immigrants in Different Nations and Cities*. Boulder, CO: Westview Press.

Roy, Patricia E. 1989. *A White Man's Province: British Columbia Politicians and Chinese and Japanese Immigrants, 1858–1914*. Vancouver: University of British Columbia Press.

Stoffman, Daniel. 2002. *Who Gets In: What's Wrong with Canada's Immigration Program — and How to Fix It*. Toronto: Macfarlane Walter and Ross.

Times Colonist, The. 2002. "Immigration fuels soaring TB rate: Disease increases 35 percent in B.C. to nearly twice the rate across Canada." 21 November.

Ward, W. Peter. 1978. *White Canada Forever: Popular Attitudes and Public Policy Toward Orientals in British Columbia*. Montreal/Kingston: McGill-Queen's University Press.

Article 12.2
Will Straw

In and Around Canadian Music

As Will Straw argues, the success of bands such as The Tragically Hip "works to paper over the fractures that more and more ... disrupt notions of a singular Canadian popular music tradition." What does the audience response in this concert photo suggest? http://thehip.com/web/setlists/ 2003_10_01_archive.php.

Issues to Consider

- Straw discusses the paradoxical social function of popular music. How does he describe its role in shaping a nation's "sentiments of collective belonging"? How does popular music create a "powerful force" that helps to distinguish between societies and cultures?
- What does the author mean by "a social history of listening"? How would historians go about putting together such a history? What would we most like to know, and what kinds of evidence would we — ideally — have at our disposal?
- What does the "music policy discourse" that has evolved since the regulatory government initiative of the past thirty years suggest about the relationship between national culture and music?
- What does Straw present as the chief differences between the musical culture of Quebec and that of English Canada? What does he see as the results of these differences?
- What is the significance of the 1999 launch of The Song Corporation?

Source: Will Straw, "In and Around Canadian Music," *Journal of Canadian Studies* 35, no. 3 (Fall 2000): 173–83.

What might we say about music as a national, popular cultural form? Musical events have long been seen as nodal points around which sentiments of collective belonging take shape. Music is embedded in the ceremonies of military display and civic pomp, bound up with the most official of national rituals. Indeed, prior to the twentieth century, military and religious institutions were principal sites of musical training and composition. In its folk forms, music is heard as the guarantee of historical, cultural continuities, of the persistence of traditions in the face of forces that threaten to disrupt these traditions or leave them behind. Music often seems among the most stable and slowly changing of cultural forms, the most effective in asserting a fundamental and long-term relationship between culture and place. Unlike film or television, music offers the fantasy of a cultural practice which, even when caught up in highly commercial structures of promotion or distribution, is at some level artisanal, even pre-capitalist. For all these reasons, music might claim a privileged role in nourishing sentiments of national belonging. One recent document on Quebec music policy argued that the chanson is the best expression of a people's soul (Groupe de travail sur la chanson).

At the same time, however, in our everyday experiences of culture and place, music is one of the most forceful, unavoidable markers of difference and change. This is, in part, an effect of its mobility. Music moves, not simply because of its much vaunted (and dubious) ethereality, but because the material forms in which it is embedded travel, more easily than most other cultural commodities, across the world. Radio signals, cassettes carried in the suitcases of immigrants or backpackers, rituals of night-life transported or reinvented with the passage of people from one country to another — all of these make music a powerful force in the differentiation of space and population. This differentiation shapes our sense of space and locality, casting nightclubs as morally upright or suspicious, or clarifying the demographic content of neighbourhoods. Indeed, while music is a forceful marker of social solidarity, it is, as well, one of the most effective forces in asserting social difference. Our own music, and that of others, intrudes upon public space in ways that make it impossible to overlook differences of taste and background. Music is important in such conflicts in part because it compels us to judge the pleasure of others. The music of others regularly comes across as excessively repetitive or chaotic, loud or innocuous, boring or disruptive. Either side of these oppositions will fuel the perception that the emotional life of others is distorted relative to a norm. These perceptions play a prominent role in the stereotyping of generation, race and ethnicity. Through them, music works to fracture the fantasies of a unitary national culture.

In his study of the audiences for opera and classical music in pre- and post-revolutionary France, James H. Johnson traces a shift in the nature of concert-going as it moved from an experience of collective solidarity to one of individualist, middle-class contemplation. Music, in this context, offered a laboratory in which new modes of citizenship took shape and were given concrete expression. Over the period of two or three decades, concerts ceased being the pretext and backdrop for an elite's staging of its social games and rituals. They became events in which an emergent middle class, now reliant on the guidance of journalistic critics and socially sanctioned experts, engaged in the activity of polite self-improvement. Johnson's "social history of listening" offers one model for examining music within the context of Canadian studies.

A long-standing feature of that history for anglophone Canadians has been the supplement of affect (or the fantasy of intimate connection) that comes with the knowledge that this or that performer, working within internationally disseminated musical idioms, is Canadian (The Band, Men Without Hats, Sarah McLachlan and so on). More recently, to listen to music as an anglophone Canadian may mean attendance at events in which the sprawling bigness of the rock concert nourishes the raucous pop nationalism of The Tragically Hip, in contexts that link band, venue and audience to the national, commercial iconography of breweries, sports franchises and Canadian-owned cellular phone companies. At the same time, to listen to jazz or Brazilian music in Canada is to do so, increasingly, in the context of outdoor festivals, events that fuel both a sense of civic belonging and the feeling that one is a tourist in one's own city. These events form part of a social history of listening, a history in which forms of cultural citizenship are mobilized within the social and spatial contexts of musical consumption.

Central to that history are the regulations governing noise levels, night-time economic activity and drinking ages in towns or cities; the patterns of sociality that lead particular groups to congregate in public places, such as ethnic social clubs, or in private homes; and the recent emergence of new sites of musical performance, such as restaurants with disc jockeys or the ascendant home concert movement (in which artists perform live for several dozen fans, and sizeable fees, in the living rooms of promoters' homes). A social history of listening is, at some level, a history of affective and aesthetic connections to music, but it is also a history of the fracturing and coalescing of social affinities. Music may be the cause, pretext or backdrop to such processes; its principal social effect is here, in the making and unmaking of social solidarities.

Music becomes meaningful, James Johnson suggests, paraphrasing Hans-Georg Gadamer, when sound meets prejudice (2). The prejudices are often those that strain to pin (or reduce) music to its origins, to the specific places or social groups the music is taken to represent. Jacques Attali, winding his way around similar issues, argues that music evokes within its listeners the "quest for lost differences," a yearning for those specificities of place or community that have been lost in the standardized, serial production of music as a capitalist commodity (5). The rowdy nationalism that now marks concerts by Sloan, The Tragically Hip or the reconstituted Guess Who works to paper over the fractures that more and more (amidst the Canadian explosions of club music, Canto-pop, bhangra and hip-hop) disrupt notions of a singular Canadian popular music tradition. At the same time, this nationalism depends on its own assertion of lost differences, those features of the listening event that might make an essentially Canadian experience of rock music somehow different from one transpiring in the US or elsewhere. Music is also, arguably, the cultural realm in which Canadian policy, over some 20 or 30 years, has seemed most successful. Canadian Content requirements for radio music programmers have been studied around the world by countries seeking to devise policies to protect and nourish local music industries. (In Canada, they are widely regarded as a major factor in the growth of a national recording industry.) For much of the past decade, Céline Dion, Bryan Adams, Shania Twain and Alanis Morissette have figured among the world's very biggest popular music stars. MuchMusic and MusiquePlus have come to play a promotional role vis-à-vis a Canadian cultural industry far exceeding that of television programmes devised to build audiences for Canadian cinema or literature. The music industries in Canada are represented by professional trade associations, supported by ongoing public funding programmes and engaged in building integrated conglomerates whose structures resemble those of major multinational companies.

The meaning and pertinence of these developments, on the other hand, remains obscure. This is not simply because Canadians are uncertain of the extent to which Neil Young remains "Canadian" or unclear as to whether Céline Dion's success tells us anything at all about our national music industries. The "health" of Canadian music, as the object of public policy and intervention, resists diagnosis in large measure because the place of music within the discourses of national cultural identity remains vague and elusive. Policies to support Canadian news media are typically justified in terms that invoke the need for a national conversation, or for information that reflects the distinct concerns of Canadians. The platitudes of film and television policy often speak of these media's role in offering the dramaturgical mirrors from which a national imagery is meant to take sustenance. Policy statements about music, in contrast, rarely express more than the desire for a "healthy and competitive environment within which

Canadian musical talent can flourish" (Canadian Heritage website, http://www.pch.gc.ca/mindep/misc/culture/htm/4.htm). There is an ongoing reluctance in music policy discourse — outside Quebec, where music's status as a practice of language makes it the bearer of greater cultural weight — to make significant claims about the cultural effectiveness of music itself.

The lack of a more substantial role for music within policy discourse reflects, in part, a well-known problem in musical analysis — that of determining how socio-cultural contexts embed themselves within music and speak through it. Few would venture to argue that Canadian music, like Canadian films, should "tell Canadians about themselves" in any kind of literal way, but on what other bases might one claim a cultural role for Canadian music? If musical styles crystallize particular complexes of regional and ethno-cultural tradition, their cultural value is more easily grasped, but an emphasis on tradition elides the mobility, commodification, transformation and appropriation that have always marked popular musical history. Music, more than cinema, television or even literature, forces us to confront the problematic status of tradition and continuity in efforts to imagine or devise a national culture. The enshrining of jazz as "classical music" of the United States — an act as messy, in its claim of unitary national ownership of the form, as it is noble — represents one way of confronting such questions. In other national contexts, these questions are often elided through a valorization of music's busy but unspecified creativity. In the United Kingdom, in recent policy documents, music is embraced as the paradigm case of successful "small business" development (DCMS 2000).

Like literary writing, music is almost never the focus of cultural policy because of a perception that it is scarce. In this, it is unlike domestic feature films or television series, whose very existence has seemed to require forms of public support and intervention. Radio station programmers, after the introduction of Canadian Content regulations in the 1970s, complained regularly about a lack of Canadian recordings, but the shortages to which they referred involved recordings of a specified technical standard, rather than musical activity in a broader sense. Musical culture is almost always marked by an extraordinary abundance of activity, informally organized in fine gradations from amateurism through all possible levels of professionalism. The continued existence of all such levels is necessary, not only for the apprenticeship and competition on which significant musical accomplishment is based, but for the value systems in which popular music is typically embedded. The significant forms of twentieth-century Western popular music (jazz, rock, club music and so on) have all seemed to rest on informally organized bohemian "scenes" as much as on industrial structures, and a sense that such scenes continue to provide their foundations is central to the critical judgement of popular music. As Jon Stratton has argued, the success of the music industries depends, in part, on the public perception that their operations are non-rational, that their products are the result of processes (of public evaluation and selection) occurring outside their own institutional walls (1983). Policies intended to professionalize popular music culture, however well intended, will always run up against the conviction that, in doing so, they are interfering in processes best left untouched.

INDUSTRY STRUCTURES

A common problem of music industry policies is that attempts to build a stable industry infrastructure of solid companies and durable careers risk creating the conditions in which a national industry will stagnate. In Quebec in recent years, controversy over the music industries has centred on the extent to which such industries successfully satisfy an increasingly heterogeneous social demand for music. In a report to the Société générale des entreprises culturelles du Québec, Marc Menard suggested that a key factor determining the sales of

Québécois music in Quebec might be the diversity of supply. Echoing comments by journalist Alain Brunet, Menard warned of a possible gap between public tastes, which were becoming increasingly diverse, and the continued homogeneity of popular music released by established music companies. In particular, Brunet had complained of too strong an emphasis on pop-rock and solo singers, and of the continued domination of the music industries by an aging establishment. If the Québécois music industries were to meet ascendant public demand for hip-hop, electronica and a myriad of other forms successfully, Menard suggested, a reorganization of industry structure to cater effectively to that demand might be desirable.

This diagnosis convincingly acknowledged a problem with long-term implications, and at the same time offered a misguided solution. The significant success of the Quebec music industries over the past decade has much to do with high levels of corporate integration, with the emergence of an efficient system through which music is recorded, promoted, given public exposure and distributed to stores. The best example of this integration is the complex of firms associated with the record label Audiogram. Audiogram's ownership overlaps with that of the concert promotion and production company Spectra-scene, the Archambault record store chain, the recording facility Le Studio, the Montreal Festival du jazz, the gala de l'ADISQ (the Association québécoise de l'industrie du disque, du spectacle et de la video) television programme and the record distribution companies Select and MusicCor. The Groupe Archambault is owned by media conglomerate Quebecor, publisher of the Sun newspapers and *Le Journal de Montréal*. More generally, the various components of the music industries are more tightly integrated in Quebec than elsewhere in Canada. This integrated structure, however, does not simply offer a channel through which a newly diversified "supply" of music might be delivered. Its very structure incorporates a bias towards solo singers, professional songwriters and back-up musicians and favours the use of television and live concerts as primary means of promotion. These are appropriate to the long-standing traditions of the chanson, through which the Quebec industry has acquired solidity and left behind a record of fertile creativity. An industrial structure appropriate to other musical forms (club music or hip-hop, for example), however, would require more than a new set of inputs. It would presume new relationships between music and the spaces in which music is typically consumed, new sorts of scenes in which creative relationships are established, new forms of small-scale entrepreneurship.

The Canadian music industries outside Quebec are marked by a much lower level of integration between different firms and functions. Indeed, the English-Canadian industry has long suffered from a high level of fragmentation, with a myriad of small firms each involved in complex ways with the music industries outside Canada. As a result, the English-Canadian industry has been regularly buffeted by shifts in the degree to which multinational firms are interested and involved in Canadian musical culture. In Quebec, the development of an effective, locally owned distribution system has absolved the Québécois music industry of an ongoing reliance on multinational firms. Outside Quebec, the absence of a comprehensive and domestically owned distribution system has left large Canadian record companies dependent on multinational majors. For 30 years, this situation has offered a reversal of Maurice Charland's well-known model of technological nationalism. While, for Charland, Canadians have typically built technologically based infrastructures (the railway and television broadcasting system, for example) through which American goods came to dominate our markets, international record companies operating in Canada devised the distribution systems on which a generation of Canadian-owned record companies came to depend for national distribution (cf. Straw, 1996).

One of the most revealing events in the history of the Canadian music industries transpired in 1999, to little notice outside the business sections of Canadian newspapers. In July of that year, Allan Gregg (media pundit, music talent manager and ex-pollster) announced the formation of The Song Corporation, a new music company based in Toronto. The Song

Corporation is a fully integrated company: its recording division was established through the purchase of Attic Records, and its music publishing arm through the purchase, from Alliance Atlantis, of The Music Publisher. Oasis Entertainment, a new company, would serve as The Song Corporation's distribution subsidiary.

The demise of Attic Records as an independent entity signalled the conclusion of a significant historical thread within Canadian popular music, one that led from the Yorkville folk scene of the late 1960s through the growth of Canada's largest independently owned record company. The launch of Song suggested that the long-standing model of development for Canadian music companies was, perhaps, no longer a good one. For 30 years, as suggested above, most Canadian record companies operating within the English-language market had stayed out of the distribution side of the music business, confining themselves to signing and recording artists. Typically, these companies affiliated themselves with multinational firms, such as Warner or Sony; often, as was the case with Attic, they changed such affiliations regularly, to seek more advantageous terms or in the face of declining support from their distributor. Attic, Anthem and the other great Canadian music companies of the post-1970 era had survived both long- and short-term alliances with multinational firms for almost 30 years.

The Song Corporation absorbed Attic Records and announced that its new distribution arm, Oasis Entertainment, would provide Canadian distribution for Attic and a host of other domestic and international companies. This development stood as the clearest proof yet that the two-tiered system of the previous 25 years had broken down. One feature of this system was the reliance by multinational firms on Canadian companies to do the preliminary work in seeking out Canadian performers with the potential for career development. By the late 1990s, however, the high international sales levels of acts such as Bare Naked Ladies and Céline Dion led multinational firms to sign talent directly to their American headquarters, rather than relying on Canadian independent companies to serve as intermediaries. With so many Canadian artists successful in other markets, Canadian-owned companies could no longer compete with international firms in offering advances or international distribution. The globalization of the music industries appeared to offer more opportunities to Canadian artists, but it risked transforming Canada into a talent pool, with few benefits trickling down to its own music companies.

At the same time, by 2000 a wave of mergers and buy-outs had left only four real "major" companies in the world (AOL-Time/Warner, Universal, BMG and Sony). As these four companies consolidated their operations within Canada, they cut the number of Canadian firms with whom they were affiliated. The Song Corporation's entry into music distribution was, in part, a response to this consolidation. With major companies trimming their rosters of affiliated labels, large numbers of such labels became available to smaller firms who offered to distribute them in the Canadian marketplace. The launch of Song also suggested that the English-Canadian music industry might be developing along American models, through the establishment of fully integrated firms involved in a variety of subsidiary industries. Like the recently formed Alliance Atlantis Communications company, the new company presented itself as a fully integrated, scaled-down version of a multinational major.

Arguably, the launch of The Song Corporation had much to do with changes in the economic logic of the music industries. Revisions to the Canadian Copyright Act in 1997 had instituted a performance right under which musicians and record companies (and not merely composers and music publishers) would benefit from the playing of music on radio and other media. The Song Corporation's acquisition of significant music publishing inventories, and of the back catalogues of Attic and other recording companies, converged with one important new direction in the music industries: the stockpiling of resources from the past so as to benefit from their role in delivery technologies of the future. In 2000, an evaluation of the federal government's Sound Recording Development Program noted that the successful Canadian music companies were typically those that had established back catalogues as steady, dependable sources of revenue (Études économique conseil, 2000). Just as, in spring of 2000, the Quebec music charts had been dominated by compilations of Québécois hits from the 1960s, The Song Corporation's acquisition of scattered pieces of Canada's recent musical heritage signalled the importance of the past to an industry facing profound uncertainty over its future.

CONCLUSION: MODELS OF A NATIONAL MUSIC

In historical discussions of Canadian popular music, scattered and fragmentary as these are, two models of national music may be distinguished. In one, music works to nourish and transform collective, public discourse, creating or renewing forms of language and tradition. The canonical popular music of the late 1960s (in its English-Canadian language versions, as with Gordon Lightfoot, or in the Québécois music of Harmonium or Beau Dommage) has assumed historical importance within such a model. Here, the institutional and economic dimensions of musical production are significant only in terms of the musical practices they bring to the public sphere or leave as their residues. If multinational record companies invested in the new traditionalism of the late 1960s, finding value in its integrity or authenticity, these links to international capital could be dismissed as incidental when set alongside the music's obvious rootedness in a local culture. National musical history thus stands as a series of milestones, in which the unfolding of individual careers produces the broader contours of a national tradition. Industry strategy works to confirm this sense of a tradition through its ongoing marketing of back catalogue materials as dependable, classic commodities that are reissued with each shift of sound carrier technology.

In another model, music is primarily a token of social and economic exchange — the pretext for small-scale commerce, regularized social interaction and new connections between actors in a wide range of industries and institutions. Here, the most obviously borrowed, short-lived and forgotten of musical practices might, nevertheless, create the thick webs of interconnection through which a national culture acquires solidity. What has counted in Canadian punk, Toronto techno or the Québécois ye-ye of the early 1960s, it might be argued, are the new forms and sites of social interaction that resulted, the networks and personal trajectories that drew new lines of movement and intersection across the map of a national culture. A common paradox in such examples is the discrepancy between their cosmopolitanism (or blatant imitation) and the grassroots localism through which they are commodified. In debates over musical value, the long-standing importance attached to the "local" has often obscured attention to the fact that all music "lands" somewhere, in one or many localities. Those styles that most obviously arrive from somewhere else — jungle, disco, ska — are often those that come to be most deeply rooted in the local, small-scale micro-economies of clubs, independent stores and part-time employment. These styles are important less for the professional careers they enable than for the subcultural careers, which, in their unfolding, join together certain kinds of activity. Twenty years ago, a characteristic subcultural career might have linked playing in a post-punk band to study in an art school; this year, it might draw lines of connection between the defence of raves and involvement in mobilization against the World Trade Organization. In this model, music is less an expressive form (articulating and updating a sense of place and community) than a mediating moment (the point of connection and division between different activities and the populations who engage in them).

Public policy may enhance music's ability to fulfil the first of these roles by subsidizing career development plans, management expertise and the awards shows through which a national musical culture may glimpse its scale and success. Music's more elusive, mediating function is shaped by policies that are rarely considered cultural in nature: by the regulation of alcohol consumption and nightclub closing hours, neighbourhood gentrification, work-study schemes and student loans. More and more, the resources that nourish musical consumption and creation in Canada depend on what Justin O'Connor has termed, following Jonathan Raban, "city knowledges"— acute sensitivities to shifts of style or taste, a grasping of the complex relationships and limits within which events may be organized or commodities set in circulation.

REFERENCES

Attali, Jacques. *Noise: The Political Economy of Music*. Translated by Brian Massumi. Minneapolis: University of Minnesota Press, 1985.

Bouw, Brenda. "Music industry veterans target independent artists[;] Oasis formed to compete with the giant record labels." *The National Post* (web edition), 1 July 1999.

Charland, Michael. "Technological Nationalism." *Canadian Journal of Political and Social Theory* 10.1–2 (1986).

DCMS. *Consumers Call the Tune: The Impact of New Technologies on the Music Industry*. London: Department for Culture, Media and Support, 2000.

Études économique conseil. *Evaluation of the Sound Recording Development Program* (SRDP/PADES). Hull: Department of Canadian Heritage, 2000.

Groupe de travail sur la chanson québécoise. "Puisque dans ce pays la parole est musique …" Proposition d'une stratégie de développement de la chanson québécoise. Montréal: La société de développement des entreprises culturelles, 1998.

Johnson, James H. *Listening in Paris: A Cultural History*. Berkeley: University of California Press, 1995.

Menard, M., avec la coll. de Saint-Jean, U. et Noll, I. L'industrie du spectacle de chanson au Québec — Portrait économique. Etude réalisée pour le Groupe de travail sur la chanson. Montréal: La société de développement des entreprises culturelles, 1998.

O'Connor, Justin. Untitled presentation. "Cultures of the City" Conference. Berlin Technical University, Berlin, Germany, July 2000.

Stratton, Jon. "What is 'Popular Music'?" *Sociological Review* 22.2 (May 1983): 293–309.

Straw, Will. "Sound Recording." *The Cultural Industries in Canada*. Ed. Michael Dorland. Toronto: James Lorimer and Company, 1996. 95–117.

Weisbard, Eric. "Over & Out: Indie Rock Values in the Age of Alternative Million Sellers." *The Village Voice Rock and Roll Quarterly* (Summer 1994): 15–19.

Document 12.1
Secrétariat à la politique linguistique

Living in French in Quebec

The historical tendency of immigrants to join the anglophone community in Quebec has made immigration to the province a complex matter for both the host society and the newcomers. In particular, Quebec's language laws of the past thirty years, which have restricted English-language schooling, advertising, and signing of all kinds, have necessitated the clarification of what "living in French in Quebec" means for immigrants.

Issue to Consider

• What is the image of Quebec society that this material promotes? As much as an official government publication can reveal, is it important for contemporary Quebec to attract immigrants?

INTRODUCTION

Québec, located in northeastern North America, has a population of more than seven million. It is also home to Canada's largest francophone population, with 81.4% of its inhabitants speaking French as their first language. Close to 86% of all francophones in Canada live in Québec.

Nevertheless, francophones form a minority in Canada and North America. During the last 50 years, the proportion of francophones in the Canadian population has steadily fallen, dropping from 29% in 1951 to 22.9% in 2001. And the French-speaking population outside of Québec accounted for just 4.4% of the Canadian population in 2001. Looking at the linguistic figures for all of North America, we see that francophones make up only 2% of the continent's population. Surrounded by 300 million anglophones, they are confronted by linguistically driven social and economic forces in Canada and the United States that give predominance to English. The position of French in North America is precarious, and it must be carefully and constantly monitored. That is why, beginning in the 1960s, successive Québec governments have enacted measures to provide Québec with a language policy.

The cornerstone of this language policy is the *Charter of the French Language*, which was adopted by the National Assembly of Québec on August 26, 1977. The *Charter*, with a scope greater than that of previous language legislation, reaffirms the determination of Québécois to make French the normal, everyday language of Québec's public life, and the language for expressing its social, cultural, intellectual, and economic vitality.

The *Charter of the French Language* is supplemented by close to a dozen regulations and a government framework policy concerning the use and the quality of the French language in the civil administration. To further ensure the sustainability and visibility of francophone society and institutions in Québec, other government policies have been adopted for sectors of equally strategic linguistic importance (e.g., education, culture, immigration, information and communication technologies, etc.). All these measures taken together make up Québec's language policy, the objective of which is to promote the French language and help it flourish in the context of North America.

Source: Excerpted from Secrétariat à la politique linguistique, *Living in French in Quebec* [online brochure], http://www.spl.gouv.qc.ca/publications/brochures/vivre/anghtml/vivre_anglais.html.

Québec's efforts to preserve its identity and promote its culture and language have been accompanied by an opening up to the world, which over the past several decades has been greater than ever before. One important illustration of this openness is seen in the growing size of Québec's exports, which now account for 60% of its GDP. Québec is also home to the most bilingual and multilingual workforce in North America. Because of its particular geopolitical situation, European heritage, and determination to live in French within a North American context, Québec has become a strong proponent of cultural and linguistic diversity. […]

PROGRESS MADE SINCE THE ADOPTION OF THE *CHARTER OF THE FRENCH LANGUAGE*

Québec's language policy was instituted to offset the growing power of attraction of English, which was perceptible primarily in Montréal and in the regions of Québec where French came into daily contact with English. Twenty-five years after the adoption of the *Charter of the French Language*, the use of French has visibly progressed in Québec:

- Public and commercial signs have, in part, recovered a French character, particularly in Montréal.
- Francophone consumers receive more services in their language.
- French is used to a greater extent among workers and in the day-to-day activities of enterprises.
- Increasing numbers of young immigrants are attending French-speaking schools, meaning they are integrating more easily into Québec society, which is mostly francophone.
- Gaps in terms of income and status, which previously worked to the disadvantage of francophones, have narrowed.

Despite these advances, a great deal more progress must be made so that French can become and remain the normal, everyday language of public communication in Québec. The French language is still confronted by pressures on a daily basis, especially in the context of the global economy and the rapid proliferation of information and communication technologies. Québec's language policy is therefore as fully relevant today as it has been in the past. […]

FRENCH: THE LANGUAGE OF A DYNAMIC CULTURAL LIFE OPEN TO THE WORLD

More than a social convention or a simple means of communication, the French language is for Québécois the very foundation of their identity and thus an intrinsic part of their culture. It is not surprising, then, that the Politique culturelle du Québec, adopted in 1992, begins by stressing the importance of promoting French as the vehicle of culture in Québec.

French as a Language of Creation

French is the language used in Québec for most forms of artistic expression involving the spoken and the written word. French-language works from Québec in music, theatre, literature and cinema have gained an influence and an audience not only in francophone countries but around the world.

Québec has at times had to develop original approaches to foster the dissemination of French-speaking cultural products in a marketplace dominated by American culture. For example, since the mid-1980s, the *Cinema Act* has worked to ensure that French versions of movies are seen in Québec. And for all areas of cultural activity, the Québec ministère de la Culture et des Communications has implemented measures to support the creation, emergence, and production of French-language content in the arts and culture.

In Canada, the federal government has jurisdiction over radio and television broadcasting. To respect the francophone character of Québec's music industry, quotas for songs in French were imposed on French-language radio stations beginning in the 1970s — a model that governments elsewhere have since imitated. More recently, at the request of Québec, specific regulations have facilitated the emergence of specialized French-language television channels in a context where cable and satellite broadcasting have made it easier to access an ever-increasing number of English-language channels.

Openness to Other Cultures

Québec's culture also draws part of its vigour and diversity from the contribution of anglophones, Aboriginal nations, and the cultural communities of immigrants. These groups express their cultural vitality in their own artistic activities, and at the same time are showing greater openness towards and participation in francophone culture.

In the very same way, the francophones of Québec, although profoundly attached to their own cultural life and achievements, take a keen and active interest in other cultures.

Québec's cultural life is thus marked by its openness to culture and art coming from all horizons. At the same time that it affirms its feeling of belonging to a French-speaking culture, Québec actively promotes cultural exchanges of all kinds and makes full room for the cultural and artistic expression of other societies.

The people of Québec enjoy culture in all its diversity, due in large part to their strong cultural affinities with Europe, the huge impact and success of their many cultural events, and the rich cultural contributions made by successive waves of immigration.

IMMIGRATION AND FRANCIZATION

Under the Canadian constitution, jurisdiction over immigration in Québec is shared by the Québec government and the Canadian government. Québec's main responsibilities include recruiting and selecting candidates for immigration, and providing orientation and integration services to newly arrived immigrants.

Every year, Québec takes in close to 40,000 immigrants from around the world. Between 1997 and 2001, 43% of newcomers already spoke French on their arrival. The Québec government is hoping to raise that proportion to 50%.

The Québec government offers French courses to newly arrived immigrants who do not speak French. These courses, intended to ease their integration into Québec society, are available through a number of means, which include full-time or part-time programs at carrefours d'intégrations ("integration hubs" for immigrant services) and educational institutions, community programs, and workplace initiatives.

Document 12.2

I Am Canadian (Joe's Rant)

The "I Am Canadian" advertising campaign not only proved lucrative for Molson Breweries, but also became a social phenomenon as Canadians of all ages found resonance in Joe's plea, ostensibly aimed at Americans, for an understanding of what makes us different from them; in that sense, it represents a traditional conceptualization of the Canadian identity. Document 12.3 outlines the explicit motivation behind, and objectives of, the advertising campaign.

Issues to Consider

- What familiar images does Joe draw upon to get his point across about what it means to be Canadian?
- What is appealing about Joe's Rant? Is it a credible definition of Canadian identity in the late 20th century? Why do Canadians identify with the points he makes?
- It is easy to forget, as many viewers seem to have done, that Joe's Rant was not so much a public statement of nationalism as it was a commercial designed to sell beer and increase Molson's share of the youth market. Read the marketers' explanation in Document 12.3 and consider whether or not a commercial can "sell" nationalism. What is happening in contemporary society that makes this at least a possibility?

Hey. I'm not a lumberjack or a fur trader. And I don't live in an igloo, or eat blubber, or own a dogsled. And I don't know Jimmy, Sally, or Suzy from Canada, although I'm certain they're really, really nice.

I have a Prime Minister, not a President.

I speak English and French, not American. And I pronounce it "about," not "aboot."

I can proudly sew my country's flag on my backpack. I believe in peace-keeping, not policing: diversity, not assimilation. And that the beaver is a truly proud and noble animal. A toque is a hat, a chesterfield is a couch, and it is pronounced "zed" not "zee."

Canada is the second largest landmass, the first nation of hockey, and the best part of North America!

My name is Joe, and I *am* Canadian!

Thank you.

Source: "I Am Canadian" (Joe's Rant), Molson Breweries televised commercial (released February 2000), http://www.adcritic.com.

Document 12.3

A Rant for the Record Books

In the summer of 2000, Molson Breweries and Thornley Fallis Communications wrote a new chapter into Canadian history. Together, they created an ad that generated 485 million impressions and became a Canadian cultural icon. Oh, they also took home the coveted IABC Gold Quill Award for their amazing achievements. [...]

THE BUSINESS NEED AND OPPORTUNITY

Between 1998 and the beginning of 2000, Molson Canadian, the top-selling lager in Canada and Molson's flagship brand, had been under significant competitive pressure from other brands and breweries. Molson was considered by beer drinkers and the media to be a conservative company who had not had any advertising or marketing breakthroughs in a number of years.

A new advertising agency was brought on board (Bensimon Byrne D'Arcy) and recommended that Molson do the unthinkable — resurrect its famous "I AM Canadian" tag-line with an updated, edgy, youth-relevant spin. A new focus was brought to Molson Canadian's brand image: "Be the only brand that can stand for and celebrate Canadian pride." [...]

The public relations opportunity arose out of the first Molson Canadian broadcast advertisement, which was scheduled to run beginning in mid-March. Entitled "The Rant," the 60-second spot featured a lone Canadian named "Joe" in front of a movie-screen of flashing Canadian images as he explained what it meant to be Canadian. His dialogue started off humble and meek, but quickly built to a crescendo of pride and emotion, until Joe passionately screams: "My name is Joe! And I Am Canadian!"

INTENDED AUDIENCE

Molson Canadian is the brewery's flagship brand and the national top-seller among the core market of legal drinking age (18/19) to 24 year olds, the primary audience for the brand's message of Canadian pride.

GOALS/OBJECTIVES

- Maximize exposure for the Molson Canadian brand, its "I AM Canadian" slogan and "Joe Canadian," the star of its new ad
- Generate extensive local, national and international news coverage that conveyed the brand's youthful, fun, energetic, irreverent and Canadian pride imagery
- Ensure "I AM Canadian" experience is universal in Canada. Break out of Toronto market and ensure brand messages and imagery are experienced in key cities from coast-to-coast

Source: "A Rant for the Record Books," *Strategy*, May 28, 2001, excerpted from the IABC Gold Quill submission coordinated by Nicolle Balen, http://www.prcanada.ca/STRATEGY/RANTP.HTM.

- Take control over share-of-mind during summer and most importantly Canada Day long weekend
- Steal share-of-mind from competitor during NHL playoffs. Become more associated with Canadian hockey than the official beer sponsor during this crucial period
- Position Molson as a relevant, creative company that makes world-class products that are marketed in a world-class way
- Create an environment that would take a creative image and turn it into a living breathing entity

SOLUTION OVERVIEW

The solution was to create a momentum-building six-month public relations plan. Once established, a program of appearances with "Joe Canadian" would be scheduled throughout the country, along with leveraging the interactive component of Molson's IAM.ca website, to continue building awareness and notoriety for "The Rant."

The program would culminate in a marathon tour of the country with Joe Canadian making appearances at Canada Day festivities from coast-to-coast in a 28-hour period. Each activity would be designed to personally connect with beer drinkers, while also being extremely newsworthy and suitable for media coverage. With Canadians screaming "I AM Canadian" from coast-to-coast.

Ultimately, we intended to make "The Rant," "Joe Canadian" and the "I AM Canadian" phrase a part of Canadian pop culture vernacular. [...]

Joe Canadian became a sensation during the summer of 2000. He appeared on the front page of 17 newspapers; was a featured guest on every major Canadian morning talk show; at least 25 spoofs were created by those honoring their own cultural heritage; Canada's Heritage Minister took a copy of the commercial and showed it to a US business audience as a light-hearted way to introduce Canadian culture

After the ad's initial airing and subsequent publicity, a special "post your own rant" section was created to leverage the Molson's IAM.ca website. More than 60,400 individual submissions were received by visitors to the website during the March to July period.

"The Rant" phenomenon was covered by influential news media in the US with significant spill into Canada, including *USA Today*, the *Today Show*, CBC *This Morning*, *The Boston Globe* and *The New York Times* as well as a full page article of Joe Canada in *People Magazine*. The ad also received a prestigious Bronze Lion Award at the International Advertising Awards in Cannes, France.

"The Rant" received extensive media coverage throughout the entire campaign. In total to-date, media results for the Molson Canadian "I AM Canadian" Rant are as follows:

total number of stories = 1,711

1. total circulation/audience reach = 191,423,575
2. total impressions = 484,690,845 as well as coverage from England, New Zealand and other areas that span the globe.

MEDIA PRAISE:

"A 60-second television ad that takes on American misconceptions about Canada has beer drinkers and hockey fans ... in the Great White North feeling good about themselves." – *The National Post*

"The building exploded. It was hard to make out the words, but it didn't matter. Everybody knew the words." – *The Halifax Daily News*

"More than a beer ad, it was a cultural phenomenon that was mimicked endlessly, parodied repeatedly and copied shamelessly around the world until we were all so sick of Joe, we wished he would climb back into his igloo." – *The Globe and Mail*

"Strangely, in a country known for its aversion to the sort of rah-rah jingoism associated with its southern neighbors, this nationalist tirade has become an overnight sensation: taped and shown in bars, filling mega screens at hockey games, performed live in movie theatres." – *The Boston Globe* [...]

CANADIAN HISTORY WEBSITES

Aboriginal Canada Portal:
http://www.aboriginalcanada.gc.ca/

Archives Canada (gateway to Canadian archival resources):
http://www.archivescanada.ca/

The Beaver Magazine Online (Canada's National History Society):
http://www.historysociety.ca/

British Columbia Archives:
http://www.bcarchives.gov.bc.ca/

The British Columbia History Internet/Web Site:
http://victoria.tc.ca/Resources/bchistory.html

British Columbia History Portal:
http://bchistoryportal.tc.ca/

Canada: A People's History:
http://cbc.ca/history/

Canada Science and Technology Museum:
http://imagescn.technomuses.ca/

Canada's Digital Collections:
http://collections.ic.gc.ca/

The Canadian Encyclopedia:
http://www.canadianencyclopedia.ca/

Canadian Heritage Gallery:
http://www.canadianheritage.ca/

Canadian Heritage Information Network:
http://www.chin.gc.ca/

Canadian Historical Association:
http://www.cha-shc.ca

Canadian Labour History Bibliography (Memorial University of Newfoundland):
http://www.library.mun.ca/qeii/labour/index.php

Canadian Military History Gateway:
http://www.cmhg.gc.ca/

Canadian Museum of Civilization: Online Resources for Canadian Heritage:
http://www.civilization.ca/

City of Toronto Archives:
http://www.city.toronto.on.ca/archives/

Early Canadiana Online:
http://www.canadiana.org/eco/index.html

H-Canada: Canadian History and Studies:
http://www.h-net.org/~canada/

Historica:
http://www.histori.ca/

History Television:
http://www.historytelevision.ca/

International Council for Canadian Studies: A Guide to the Sources:
http://www.iccs-ciec.ca/

Library and Archives Canada:
http://www.collectionscanada.ca/index-e.html

McCord Museum:
http://www.mccord-museum.qc.ca/

Our Future, Our Past (Alberta Heritage Digitization Project)
http://www.ourfutureourpast.ca/

Parks Canada: This Week in History:
http://www.pc.gc.ca/apps/cseh-twih/index_E.asp

Pier 21 (National Historic Site):
http://www.pier21.ca/

Quebec History:
http://www.histoirequebec.com/

Statistics Canada: Historical Statistics of Canada:
http://www.statscan.ca/

Virtual Museum of Canada:
http://www.virtualmuseum.ca/

COPYRIGHT ACKNOWLEDGMENTS

Text Credits

Article 1.1: N. St-Onge, "Memories of Métis Women of Saint-Eustache, Manitoba, 1910–1980," *Oral History Forum*, 1999–2000 (19–20): 90–111.

Article 1.2: Hugh Shewell, "'Bitterness Behind Every Smiling Face': Community Development and Canada's First Nations, 1954–1968," *Canadian Historical Review*, 2002 83(1): 58–84.

Document 1.1: Saskatchewan Indian Cultural Centre, Oral Histories of Cree Elders: Saskatchewan Indian Elders, 1976.

Document 1.2: Margeret Ecker Francis, "Strange Women in Our Midst: The First Canadians," *Chatelaine* 20, 8 (August 1947), pp. 24–25, 51.

Article 2.1: Jeremy L. Stein, "Dislocations: Changing Experiences of Time and Space in an Industrialising Nineteenth-Century Ontario Town." *British Journal of Canadian Studies* 14, 1 (1999): 115–130.

Article 2.2: Miriam Wright, "Young Men and Technology: Government Attempts to Create a 'Modern' Fisheries Workforce in Newfoundland, 1949–70," *Labour/La Travail*, 1998 (42): 143–159.

Document 2.1: [University of New Brunswick Library] Report of Commissioners Appointed to Enquire into and Investigate as to the Necessity of a Factory Act in the Province of New Brunswick, New Brunswick, 1905.

Document 2.2: Excerpt from D. Read, ed., *The Great War and Canadian Society: An Oral History* (Toronto: New Hogtown Press, 1978): 168.

Document 2.3: "The Canadian UAW-CIO Win the Peace Plan," UAW-CIO Meeting of October 28–29, 1944, King Edward Hotel, Toronto.

Article 3.1: Alan Hunt, "Measuring Morals: The Beginnings of the Social Survey Movement in Canada, 1913–1917." *Histoire sociale/Social History* 35 (69) (2002): 171–94.

Article 3.2: S. Purdy, "Industrial Efficiency, Social Order and Moral Purity: Housing Reform Thought in English Canada, 1900–1950." *Urban History Review* 1997 25(2): 30–40.

Document 3.1: Chapter 8, "The Seamy Side of Social Pathology," from J. S. Woodsworth, *My Neighbour*, originally published 1911; reprint, University of Toronto Press, 1972, 131–153. Reprinted with permission of the publisher.

Document 3.2: "Drink" *Calgary Eye Opener*, 1 July 1922, p. 3.

Document 3.3: A Juvenile Court Probation Officer, "As the Twig Is Bent: What Are We Doing to Keep Children from the Reformatory?" *Chatelaine*, March 1928, pp. 3–6.

Article 4.1: Elizabeth Beaton, "An African-American Community in Cape Breton, 1901–1904," *Acadiensis* 1995 24(2): 65–97.

Article 4.2: Kerry Badgley, "'As Long as He Is an Immigrant from the United Kingdom': Deception, Ethnic Bias and Milestone Commemoration in the Department of Citizenship and Immigration, 1953–1965," *Journal of Canadian Studies* 33(3) (1998): 130–144.

Document 4.1: J. T. M. Anderson, ch. 2, "Immigrant Communities," from Anderson, *The Education of the New Canadian*, Toronto: J. M. Dent and Sons, 1918, pp. 26–38.

Document 4.2: Editorials, July 21, 1923; August 4, 1923; September 1, 1923; in *The Dawn of Tomorrow*.

Article 5.1: Magda Fahrni, "The Romance of Reunion: Montreal War Veterans Return to Family Life, 1944–1949," *Journal of the CHA/Revue de la SHC* 1998, New Series, vol. 9, pages 187–208.

Article 5.2: Robert A. J. McDonald, "'He Thought He Was the Boss of Everything': Masculinity and Power in a Vancouver Family," *BC Studies* 2001–02 (132): 5–30.

Document 5.1: Excerpts from E. Staebler, ed., *"Haven't Any News": Ruby's Letters from the '50s* (Waterloo: Wilfrid Laurier University Press, 1995); pp. 6–7, 11–13, 20–21, 29.

Document 5.2: Claire Drainie Taylor, "Swift Current," from Drainie Taylor, *The Surprise of My Life: An Autobiography* (Waterloo: Wilfrid Laurier University Press, 1998): 9–16.

Article 6.1: Catherine Gidney, "Under the President's Gaze: Sexuality and Morality at a Canadian University During the Second World War," *Canadian Historical Review* 82(1) (2001): 36–54. Reprinted by permission of University of Toronto Press Incorporated (www.utpjournals.com).

Article 6.2: Valerie J. Korinek, "Don't Let Your Girlfriends Ruin Your Marriage: Lesbian Imagery in *Chatelaine* Magazine, 1950–1969," *Journal of Canadian Studies* 33(3), Fall 1998: 83–109.

Document 6.1: Percy E. Ryberg, M.D., "On Sex Education," in Ryberg, *Health, Sex and Birth Control* (Toronto: The Anchor Press, 1942), 1–4.

Document 6.2: Canadian Social Development Council Fonds, MG 28 I14, v. 167, File 1-16, National Archives of Canada, "Recommendations Re: The Protection of Girl Life," May 1932, pp. 1–8.

Document 6.3: Editorial: "Basic Education," *Toronto Star*, 28 October 1945.

Article 7.1: Linda Ambrose, "Cartoons and Commissions: Advice to Junior Farmers in Postwar Ontario," in *Ontario History*, XCIII, 1, Spring 2001, 57–80.

Article 7.2: Megan Davies, "Renovating the Canadian Old Age Home: The Evolution of Residential Care Facilities in B.C., 1930–1960," *Journal of the CHA/Revue de la SHC* 2001, New Series, vol. 12, pages 155–175.

Document 7.1: Senate Debates, Third Session, Tenth Parliament, Speech of the Honourable Sir Richard Cartwright on Old Age Pensions, Thursday, 28 February 1907, pp. 1–4.

Document 7.2: "Minister Discusses Old-Age Pensions: Federal Minister of Labour Urges Women to Concentrate on Needs of Aged," *The Globe*, 23 February 1928.

Document 7.3: "Organizes Teenage Club," *Toronto Daily Star*, 2 January 1945.

Article 8.1: Cynthia Comacchio, "Inventing the Extracurriculum: High School Culture in Interwar Ontario," first published in *Ontario History*, vol. 93, no. 1 (Spring 2002): 33–56, and reprinted here by permission of The Ontario Historical Society.

Article 8.2: Heidi Macdonald, "Doing More with Less: The Sisters of St. Martha (PEI) Diminish the Impact of the Great Depression," *Acadiensis* 33 (1) (Fall 2003): 21–46.

Document 8.1: The Women's Canadian Club of St. John, N.B., "A Suggested Programme for Empire Day Celebration 1915 in the Schools of New Brunswick."

Document 8.2: "My Land," "Patriotism and Religion," "The Maple," and "The Arms of Canada," in *Fact and Fancy* (Toronto: Ginn and Company, 1942).

Document 8.3: H. H. Draper, *Growing Up in Manitoba* (Regina: Canadian Plains Research Center, 1998), 20–22.

Illustration Credits

INDEX

Aboriginals
    agriculture and, 3, 8–11, 13, 17–18, 38
    community development, self-government and,
        20–34
    conservation movement and, 483–84, 488
    education and, 4, 11–13, 22, 25
    French Canadians and, 16–17
    Group of Seven paintings and, 463–64, 485
    lacrosse and, 436–37, 439
    land claims and, 490
    marriage and, 4, 15
    militancy and, 512
    Native rights and, 465, 490
    social policy and, 20–43
    wildlife policy and, 486–90
advertising. *See under* media
African-Americans
    Canadian armed services and, 176–77
    in Cape Breton, 139–52
    education and, 149–50, 174–75
    immigration and, 136
    recruitment of, 142–46
ageism, 294, 303
agriculture, 6–7
    Aboriginals and, 3, 8–11, 13, 17–18, 38
    Commission of Conservation and, 505–6
    cooperative movement and, 281, 284
    farming as business enterprise and, 284–85,
        288–89
    immigration and, 135
    industrialization and, 47
    institutions offering courses in, 284
    Junior Farmer clubs and, 278–91
    labour/ownership hierarchies and, 6–7, 283–84
    revenues and, 336
    women and, 282, 285–88
alcohol
    in Calgary, 129
    "Joe Canadian" and, 536, 537–39
    prohibition and, 129
    social reform and, 94, 96
Ambrose, Linda, 278
Anderson, Doris, 245, 246, 249, 250, 253
Anderson, J. T. M., 170
Anglican Synod of Ontario, 267
animal rights activists, 498

armed services
    African-Americans and, 176–77
    anti-conscription and, 193
    enlistment, privacy and, 186–89
    high-status families and, 205
    homecoming veterans and, 184–94
    memories of childhood and, 447
    military training, universities and, 234
    parents of soldiers in, 192–94
Asians
    immigration and, 135, 136, 202–3, 517–18
    stereotypes and, 518
assimilation. *See* Canadianization
automobile manufacturing, 79–82

baby boom, 181, 183
Badgley, Kerry, 158
baggataway, 436
Banfield, A. W. F., 493
Bell-Irving, Henry and Bella, 200–211
Bethune, William Clark, 507
bicycling, 418–29
    clubs, 422–27
    clubs, organization and structure of, 425–27
    cost of, 420
    popularity of, 427–29
    public attitudes toward, 421, 425, 427–29
    regulation of, 428–29
birth control, 230, 235
birth rates, 183
bison. *See* buffalo
Blacks. *See* African-Americans
Boyle, Harry J., 404
The Boy's Own Book, 364
buffalo, 488, 489–90

Calgary Eye Opener, 129
Callwood, June, 250, 258
Canadianization, 96
    housing and, 110, 112–13
    immigration and, 135–37, 170–73
    sports and, 415
Canadian North, 483–98
Canadian Radio-television and Telecommunications
    Commission, 410–11, 513
Canadian Wildlife Survey, 493–94, 496

Canadian Youth Commission, 282–84, 287–91
Captain Canuck, 393, 396–402
caribou, 487, 488–89, 491, 492–98
    crisis of 1948–1970, 492–98
cartoons and comics, 376, 380–81, 382
    American, 395, 396
    Canadian, 393, 395–402
    crime comics, 382
    junior farmers and, 279–82, 284–90
    merchandising and, 400, 401
    nationalism, culture and, 393–402
Cartwright, Richard, 308
censorship
    children's reading and, 382
    media and, 376
    movies and, 384
    sexuality and, 250
Charter of the French Language, 533–34
Chatelaine magazine, 245–60
children. *See also* families; youth
    of Aboriginals, 4
    of African-Americans, 174–75
    books, reading and, 378–82
    censorship and, 382, 384
    diaries of, 221–25
    education and (*see* education)
    fairy tales and, 379
    family violence, wartime soldiers and, 191–92
    housing and, 112
    "illegitimate" wartime, 186–87, 189
    juvenile delinquency and, 130, 191
    of Métis, 10–13
    movies and, 375, 382–85
    newspapers and, 379, 380
    oral history and, 377
    orphanages and, 334, 336, 338, 339, 342–44
    pastimes of, 445–47
    popular culture, media and, 374–89
    radio and, 385–86
    reformatories and, 130–31
    religion, entertainment and, 382
    sex education and, 265–66
    sexual abuse of, 247, 249, 377, 378, 384
    sexual publications and, 382
    slums and, 126–28
    social history and, 275
    sound and, 376–78
    television and, 387–88
    theatre and, 382, 383
    wartime soldiers and, 191–92
citizenship. *See also* patriotism
    ethnicity and, 112, 160
    schools, Empire Day and, 354–57

youth, education and, 276, 315, 316, 317, 322, 324, 327
class
    bicycling and, 419–20, 422, 427, 429
    education and, 204–5, 317, 320, 321, 322, 328–30
    high-status families and, 200–211
    housing and, 106–9, 111–12
    industrialization and, 47–48
    lacrosse and, 438–39
    lesbians and, 252
    schools and, 362–63
    social reform and, 85–86
    teenage clubs and, 311–12
    tourism and, 465, 466, 467
Cockburn, Jack, 280, 282
Cold War
    homosexuals and, 247, 248
    immigration and, 517
Comacchio, Cynthia, 318
comics. *See* cartoons and comics
Commission of Conservation, 504–6
communications, 51–52. *See also* media
    children's diaries, history and, 221–25
    gender, labour and, 65
    popular culture and, 371–72
    private letters, history and, 216–20, 378
    transportation and (*see* transportation)
    wartime, 186
communism, 517
conservation, 459–60
    aesthetic ideology in Canadian North and, 484–86, 496–98
    commission of, 504–6
    environmental groups and, 460
    Geological Survey of Canada and, 459
    land, wildlife, Aboriginals and, 490–92
    literature, paintings and, 484–86, 488
    movement, motives for, 483–84
    national parks and, 460, 488
    natural resources and, 485, 488, 490, 504–6
    tourism and, 459, 465, 466
    wildlife and, 483–84, 507–8
    wildlife policy and, 486–90, 495–98
    wildlife slaughter and, 487, 488–89, 492, 494, 495
contraception, 230, 235
Cornwall, Ontario, 51–60
Cress, Ruby, 216
crime, 89, 90, 94
    African-American workers and, 147–49
    comics and, 382
    family violence, wartime soldiers and, 191–92

homosexuality as, 230
immigration and, 522
reformatories and, 130–31
sexual deviants and, 248, 249
terrorism and, 518–19
urbanization and, 106–9
in Winnipeg, 124–25, 127–28
culture
American dominance of, 396, 410–11, 528
art as souvenirs and, 470, 471
Canadian identity and, 472, 473, 513, 536
Canadian North, literature, paintings and, 484–86
children, theatre and, 382, 383
education, social values and, 320–30
French language and, 534–35
Group of Seven and, 463–74, 485
mass, 394
Massey Commission and, 407–9
multiculturalism and, 521
music and (*see* music)
National Gallery and, 407–9, 463, 470, 471, 472
"official," 471
popular, 325, 371–89 (*see also* media)
popular, sports and, 415
small-town, 404–6
sportsmanship and, 465
tourism and (*see* tourism)

Dene
caribou crisis and, 493–98
treaties with, 490
wildlife and, 487, 488–92
Depression
education, youth and, 326–28
in P.E.I., 334–47
Doukhobors, 172
Draper, H. H., 362

education
Aboriginals, Métis and, 4, 11–13, 22, 25
African-Americans and, 149–50, 174–75
agricultural institutions and, 284
availability of books and, 381
children, schools and, 362–63
children's books, reading and, 378–82
class and, 204–5, 317, 320, 321
culture, social values and, 320–30, 371–72
extracurriculum in secondary schools and, 312–30
families and, 362–63
fisheries and, 67–69, 71

foreign teachers and, 171, 173
high-school socials and, 325–26
immigrants and, 170–73
Junior Farmer clubs and, 278–91
language skills and, 358
movies and, 384, 385
orphanages and, 341
patriotism and, 354–61
professional training and, 346
religion and, 315–16, 345, 364–66
school enrollments and, 320, 327, 363
school-leaving age and, 275, 320, 328
schools, Empire Day and, 354–57
school teachers and, 363
sexual-advice literature and, 230, 382
sexuality and (*see* sex education; sexuality)
sexual regulations, ethics and, 232–41
student councils and, 323, 325, 367
Edwardson, Ryan, 393
elderly, 276
health care, housing and, 294–304, 334
as "ideal" patients, 303
pensions and, 276, 308–10
Empire Day, 354–57
employment. *See* labour
employment insurance, 66–67
En Avant, 367
environmental issues. *See* conservation
ethnicity
citizenship and, 112, 160
class and, 7, 48
crime statistics and, 124–25
housing and, 113
immigration and, 135–37, 159
race co-operation and, 175–76
slums and, 136
eugenics, 112, 229

Fact and Fancy, 358
Fahrni, Magda, 184
families
African-American workers and, 146, 147
age, generations and, 275–76
children's books and, 382
children's diaries, history and, 221–25
children's emotional maturity and, 236–37
children's pastimes and, 445–47
housing and, 107–13
immigration and, 520
lifestyle of, in 1950s, 216–20
men's roles and, 66–67, 182, 183, 200–211
movies and, 383, 385
music and, 377–78

old age homes and, 297–98, 304
oral history and, 377
orphanages and, 342
personal letters and, 378
radio and, 385–87
rivalries in high-status, 205–6
sexuality and (see sexuality)
"sexual revolution" and, 181
social policy, racism and, 181
social reform and, 85–86
television and, 387–88
wartime and postwar domesticity and, 185–94
women's roles in, 182
farming. See agriculture
fertility rates, 183
fire engines, 57–59
First Nations. See Aboriginals
fisheries, 63–73
education and, 67–69, 71
gender and, 63–69, 72
income and, 66–67, 70, 72, 336
tourism and, 465, 466
unions and, 72
Forest City Bicycle Club, 422–27
forests, 506
Foucault, Michel, 85–86, 101, 181, 229
Francis, Margaret Ecker, 41
Franklin expedition, 484
Freedom to Play, 445
friendships
homosexuals, lesbians and, 252
marriage and, 258

gay rights. See homosexuals
gender
comic books and, 381
education and, 320, 321, 328–29
families and, 275
fisheries and, 63–69, 72
high-school activities and, 321–22
income and, 513
industrialization and, 47–48
men's roles and, 66–67, 182, 183, 193,
    200–211, 324
movies and, 384
narrative roles in military and, 193
physical recreation and, 418–19, 427 (see also
    sports)
public roles, private power and, 203–4, 207–8
roles in rural society and, 278–91
sexuality and (see sexuality)
stereotypes and (see stereotypes)
women's roles (see under women)

Gerstein, Reva, 258, 259
Gidney, Catherine, 232
globalization, 512
gold rush, 490
Gramsci, Antonio, 85, 107

Halpenny, Jill, 78
head tax, 136, 517
health
    elderly and, 294, 299–304
    hospital funding and, 338–42
    hospitals in P.E.I., Depression and, 337–47
    housing and, 107, 109–13
    immigration and, 519
    influenza, hockey playoffs and, 452–53
    religion, social services and, 334–35, 337–38
    services in P.E.I. and, 334–47
    sex education and, 265–66, 271
    sexuality and, 230, 236–37
    slums and (see slums)
    social surveys and, 95
    venereal disease and, 97, 112, 230
    vice and, 108
Hilliard, Marion, 258–59, 260
history
    Canadian websites and, 541–42
    children's diaries and, 221–25
    contemporary, 511–13
    gay, 246–47
    memory and, 376
    oral, 3, 374–76, 377, 490, 491, 492
    private letters and, 216–20, 378
    social, cartoons and, 279–80
hockey
    influenza, playoffs and, 452–53
    modernization and, 435
    nationalism and, 434–35, 439–42, 513
    newspaper coverage of, 448–51
    radio and, 416, 453–54
    rules of, 449, 452
    Stanley Cup and, 452
    Summit Series (1972), 441, 454–55
    symbolic values of, 440
homosexuals
    in armed services, 193
    books, reading and, 380
    Cold War and, 247, 248
    Criminal Code and, 230
    as deviants, 247–49
    gay rights and, 229
    "gross indecency" and, 230
    heterosexual matrix and, 229
    social justice and, 512

stereotypes of, 248, 256
terms used for, 251
theories about, 248
universities and, 232–35, 239–40
women (*see* lesbians)
hospitals, elderly and, 299–300
housing
    African-American workers and, 146–47, 150
    Canadianization and, 110, 112–13
    capitalism, profits and, 114, 115
    elderly and, 294–304
    families and, 107–13
    health and (*see* health)
    high-status families and, 208–9
    immigration and, 135
    in industrial towns, 142
    landlords and, 108
    manufacturers and, 108
    mortality rates and, 109
    partnership schemes and, 111, 114
    slums and (*see* slums)
    social reform and, 106–18
    social surveys and, 94
    state intervention and, 110–18
    in Toronto, 126–27
    town planning and, 110–12, 115, 116, 117
    war brides and, 190
    workers' homes and, 106–7
Hunt, Alan, 88
hunting, 39
    Aboriginals and, 488–92, 493, 507–8
    conservation and, 507–8
    tourism and, 465
    wildlife policy and, 486–90

"I AM Canadian" rant, 536, 537–39
idleness, 96
immigration, 47, 515–22
    African-Americans and, 136–52
    of African-Americans to U.S., 176
    Asians and, 135, 136, 202–3, 517–18
    Canada's borders and, 516–19
    Canada's population and, 511–12
    Canadian government and, 158–66, 234–35
    Canadianization and, 96, 135–37
    chain migration and (*see* migration)
    cultural framework and, 515–16
    Danish and, 165
    deception, ethnic bias and, 158–66
    "diversity" and, 520–21
    dual policy for, 519–20
    Dutch and, 162, 163
    education and (*see* education)

    housing and, 110, 112, 142, 146–47
    Hungarian refugees and, 517
    immigrant communities and, 170–73
    Irish and, 161–62
    Jews and, 136, 159
    media and, 159–66
    national security and, 518–19
    point system and, 517
    pro-British, 159–66
    public opinion and, 158, 166
    Quebec and, 535
    race and, 517
    racism and (*see* racism)
    refugees and, 159
    settlement houses and, 135
    sexuality, investigations and, 232, 234–35
    social policy and, 159
    social reform and, 88, 93, 94, 96
    social space and, 519–22
    Vietnamese refugees and, 517–18
income
    Aboriginals and, 24, 28, 39
    African-American workers and, 150–51
    during Depression, welfare and, 336
    education, labour and, 315, 345
    employment insurance and, 66–67
    fisheries and, 66–67, 70, 72
    gender and, 513
    hospital workers and, 340, 341
    housing and, 115
    industrialization and, 47–48, 53, 82
    labour, ethnicity and, 335
    Métis and, 11–18
    mothers' allowances and, 344
    parents of soldiers and, 192–93
    pensions and, 276, 308–10
    per capita in P.E.I., 334
    of steel makers, 143, 144–45
    of teachers, 150
    tourism revenues and, 466
    wartime allowances and, 186–87
Indian Act (1876), 3, 20
Indian Act (1951), 21
Indian-Eskimo Association, 22, 23
industrialization, 47–60
    bicycles and, 427, 429
    building industry and, 115
    caribou crisis and, 493
    "efficiency" and, 111, 145
    fisheries and (*see* fisheries)
    legislation and, 75–77
    social reform and (*see* social reform)
    sports and, 415, 435

state intervention and, 110
steel making (*see* steel making)
unions and, 79–82
women and, 78
Inuit
seal hunting and, 498
wildlife and, 488–98

Japanese-Canadians, 136
Jenkins, James, 174
Jessup, Lynda, 462
Jews, 136, 159
anti-Semitism and, 422
children's diaries and, 221–25
"Joe Canadian," 536, 537–39
Johnny Canuck, 394, 395
Johnston, Solomon, 38
Junior Farmers' Association, 278–91
Juvenile Delinquents Act (1908), 130

Kinsey, Alfred C., 248, 251
Korinek, Valerie J., 245
Kossuth, Robert S., 418
Kyoto Protocol, 460

labour
Aboriginals and, 38–39
accidents and, 56
agriculture and, 6–7, 283–86
birth rates and, 108
children, youth and, 275
education and, 321, 329–30, 345–46
efficiency and, 111, 145
employment during Depression, 336
employment insurance and, 66–67
fisheries and (*see* fisheries)
gender and (*see* gender)
hours of, 53, 55–56
housing and (*see* housing)
immigration and (*see* immigration; migration)
income and (*see* income)
industrialization and, 47–48, 78
Junior Farmer clubs and, 278–91
legislation and, 75–77
Métis women and, 10–16
racism and (*see* racism)
religious orders, recruitment and, 345–46
strikes, 150
Ukrainians and, 468
unemployment and, 327, 512
unions and (*see* unions)
women's, invisibility of, 347
work ethic and, 232, 234, 235

lacrosse, 436–39
amateurism, professionalism and, 438–39
rules of, 437
League for Social Reconstruction, 114–15
lesbians, 245–61. *See also* homosexuals
definitions of, 251, 252
dress codes of, 251–52
heterosexuality and, 251
male sex deviants and, 248
misogyny and, 252
sexual deviants and, 249
stereotypes of, 248
terms used for, 251
Lewis, Norah L., 445
liquor. *See* alcohol
London, Ontario, 419–29

Macdonald, Heidi, 334
marriage, 183
Aboriginals, Métis and, 4, 15–16
armed service personnel and, 185–89
divorce, separation and, 189
divorce, social justice and, 512–13
infidelity in wartime and, 186–89
media and, 257
restrictions to, 229
rural youth and, 287
war brides and, 189–91
Massey Commission, 407–9
McDonald, Robert A. J., 200
media
advertising, children and, 376
advertising, consumption and, 394
advertising, hockey and, 416
advertising, nationalism and, 434, 536, 537–39
advertising, sex appeal and, 324
American, 372
American dominance of, 410–11
American publications and, 395, 397
availability of books, 381
building radios and, 374
cartoons and comics (*see* cartoons and comics)
censorship and (*see* censorship)
children's books, reading and, 378–82
children's books and, 376, 378–82
computers, the Internet and, 388
immigration and, 159–66
"Joe Canadian" and, 536, 537–39
marriage and, 257
mass, sports and, 415
movies, children and, 382–85
movies, teenagers and, 375

music and, 386–87
music, families and, 377–78
newspaper coverage of hockey and, 448–51,
    454–55
newspapers, caricatures and, 394
newspapers, children and, 379, 380
parental control and, 376
personal letters and, 216–20, 378
popular culture and, 371–72
popular singers and, 375
pulp fiction and, 231
radio and, 385–87
radio, dance music and, 453–54
radio, hockey and, 416, 453–54
self-referencing in, 376
sexual advice and, 230
sexuality and, 245–61
sexual perversity and, 253–59
sound and, 376–78
sports, radio and, 386
stereotypes and, 384, 385, 389
student publications, 327, 367
television programs and, 371–72, 375–76, 387–88
vice, newspapers and, 129
videos and, 375, 388
war brides and, 190
war veterans and, 184
men. See also gender; labour
    domestic chores and, 286
    homecoming war veterans and, 184–94
    leadership training for boys, 364–66
    masculinity and (see under sports)
    role of, 66–67, 182, 183, 193, 200–211
Mennonites, 172
Métis, 6–17. See also Aboriginals
migration
    African-Americans and, 141, 150–51, 152
    immigration and, 136
    international, 516
    labour and, 47, 71, 152
military. See armed services
moral reform. See social reform
movies. See under media
multiculturalism, 135, 137, 521
music
    American domination of, 529, 530
    anglophone Canadians and, 526–27
    Canadian, 525–32
    Canadian content and, 527
    concerts and, 526, 527
    families and, 377–78
    industry structures and, 528–31

media and, 386–87
national, 531–32
noise levels and, 527
prejudices and, 527
in Quebec, 528–29, 531, 535
radio and, 453–54
National Hockey Association, 451, 452
national security, 518–19
nation-building/national identity
    Aboriginals and, 3–4, 20–34
    academic research and, 485–86
    Canadianization and (see Canadianization)
    Canadian North and, 485–86
    comics and, 393–402
    culture and, 463, 472, 473, 513, 536
    Group of Seven and, 463–71, 485
    hockey and, 434–35, 439–42
    housing and, 111–12
    lacrosse and, 436–39
    music and, 526–28, 531–32
    social reform and, 85–86
    wildlife policy and, 486–90
Newfoundland, 63–73
9/11, 518

old age. See elderly
Ontario Secondary School Teachers' Association, 410
orphanages
    education and, 343
    families and, 342, 343
    funding of, 343–44
    labour and, 342–43
    in P.E.I., 334, 336, 338, 339

Pacific Coast Hockey League, 451, 452
pastoral power. See social surveys
patriotism, 360–61 (see also citizenship)
    Empire Day, schools and, 354–57
    religion and, 359
pensions, 276, 308–10
population, 511–12
    of Quebec, 533
poverty
    during the Depression, 334
    housing and, 106–8, 109
    social surveys and, 95–96, 101, 102
    in Toronto, 126–27
Presley, Elvis, 375, 376, 378, 386, 387
Prince Edward Island, 334–47
prohibition. See under alcohol
prostitution, 89, 91, 95, 98, 99
    African-American workers and, 148–49

public opinion, immigration and, 158, 166
public policy. *See* social policy
Purdy, Sean, 106

Quebec
    French language and, 533–35
    immigration and, 535
    music and, 528–29, 531, 535
    population of, 533

racism, 135–37, 202–3
    Aboriginals and, 20–34, 41–43
    African-Americans and, 136, 140–52
    bicycle clubs and, 422
    immigration and, 110, 158–66, 517, 522
    social policy, families and, 181
    steel making and, 140–52
railways, 51–54
    tourism and, 459, 464–70, 471
recreation
    African-American workers and, 149
    athletics, gender and, 287, 324–25
    children's pastimes and, 445–47
    education, youth and, 318–19, 322–30
    Group of Seven's paintings and, 463
    media and (*see* media)
    social surveys and, 94
    sports and (*see* sports)
    teenage clubs and, 311–12
    tourism and (*see* tourism)
Red Cross, 336–37
religion
    Aboriginals and, 20
    African-American workers and, 149
    children, entertainment and, 382
    child welfare and, 275
    education and, 315–16, 345, 364–66
    education, immigration and, 170–71
    education, universities and, 236, 237
    movies and, 385
    protection of girls and, 267–70
    schools, Empire Day and, 355–56
    slums and, 127–28
    social reform and (*see* social reform)
    social services and, 334–35, 337–38
    universities and, 232–33
Riel, Louis, 4, 40
Robidoux, Michael A., 434
Rule, Jane, 257
rural life, 278–91 (*see also* agriculture)
    women and, 282, 285–88
Ryberg, Percy E., 265

Sandlos, John, 483
scandals, high-school socials and, 326
Seton, Ernest Thompson, 488, 489–90, 493
sex appeal, 324
sex education, 265–66, 271
    literature about, 230
    media and, 250
sexual abuse, 247, 249, 377, 378, 384
sexual deviants, 229–61
    crime and, 248, 249
sexuality
    advice literature and, 230, 382
    armed services and, 185–89, 193
    behaviour codes and, 230
    censorship and, 250
    education and (*see* sex education)
    European standards and, 233
    families and, 229–30, 247–48
    gay media and, 246
    Hazen Conference on, 233, 236, 237, 238,
      240
    homo- (*see* homosexuals; lesbians)
    masturbation and, 255
    in the military, 193
    norms, deviance, morals and, 229–61
    perversity, media and, 253–59
    psychiatric definitions and, 240
    pulp fiction and, 231
    regulation by universities, 232–41
    sexual development and, 237–38
    social justice and, 512
    social surveys and, 89, 90, 91, 95, 96, 98–99
"sexual revolution," 181
Shewell, Hugh, 20
Sisters of St. Martha (P.E.I.), 334–47
slums, 115, 116, 126–28
    defined, 126
    ethnicity and, 136
social policy
    Aboriginals and, 20–43, 488–96
    economic and, 512
    elderly and, 294–96
    housing and, 110–18
    immigration and (*see* immigration)
    industrialization and, 47–48
    multiculturalism and, 135, 137
    pensions and (*see* pensions)
    social justice and, 512–13
    social reform and, 85–86
    social scientists and, 114–18
    welfare and (*see* welfare)
social purity, 230

social reform, 85–86. *See also* social surveys
    families and, 85–86
    hockey and, 434
    housing and (*see* housing)
    League for Social Reconstruction and, 114–15
    public exhibitions and, 91, 97
    religion and, 88–92, 94, 96, 100, 238–39,
        337–38
    urbanization and, 88, 89
social services
    health, religion and, 334–35, 337–38, 344–45
    women, labour and, 335
social surveys, 88–102. *See also* social reform
    data used in, 96–98
    methods in, 92–95
    in Montreal, 92
    motivation for, 95–96
    pastoral power and, 88, 99–102
    in Pittsburgh, 90–91
    poverty and (*see* poverty)
    "social problems" and, 95–96, 101, 276
    sociology and, 90, 97
    in Toronto, 90, 91, 97, 98–99
The Song Corporation, 529–31
sports
    amateurism, professionalism and, 416, 424,
        438–39
    bicycling, 418–29
    class and (*see* class)
    commercialization of, 415, 416
    control and organization of, 428–29, 435–37
    foreign influences and, 435–37
    hockey, 434–42
    lacrosse, 436–39
    masculinity and, 418–21, 422, 426, 429,
        436–37, 439–42
    radio and, 386
    recreation and, 415–16
    school, gender and, 324–25
    speed, violence, skill and, 434, 436, 437–38,
        439–42
    women and, 287, 415, 445
steel making
    income and, 143
    racism and, 140–52
Stein, Jeremy, 50
stereotypes
    Arab community and, 519
    Asians and, 518
    gender, movies and, 384, 385
    of homosexuals, 248, 256
    media and, 389

    of older farmers, 289
    of women, 245–47, 252–53, 282, 285–88, 291
St-Onge, Nicole, 6
subsidiarity, 337–38
Sutherland, Neil, 374

Taylor, Claire Drainie, 221
technology
    education and, 320–21
    electricity and, 56–57
    fisheries and (*see* fisheries)
    industrialization, social change and, 50–51, 52,
        56–59
    popular culture and, 371–72
    steam and, 57–59
textile industry, 53–60
time, 53–54
tourism, 459–60
    auto camping and, 468
    Canadian landscape and, 459, 464–67
    conservation and, 459, 465, 466, 468
    facilities, services and, 466, 468–69
    Group of Seven and, 462–74
    hotels and, 466
    hunting, fishing and, 465, 466
    national parks and, 460, 464–70
    railways and, 459, 464–70, 471
    wilderness and, 463–67, 469, 472
Trail Ranger program, 365–66
transportation, 60
    African-American workers and, 144–46
    bicycles (*see* bicycling)
    car ownership and, 468
    railways, 51–54, 459, 464–70, 471
    road-building, tourism and, 468
    to schools, 362
    tourism and, 459, 464–70
travel. *See* tourism
Tuxis program, 365–66

unemployment insurance. *See* employment insur-
    ance
unions, 47–48
    fisheries and, 72
    immigration policy and, 159
    industrialization and, 79–82
    social surveys and, 93–94
    strikes and, 150, 202
urbanization, 51
    housing and, 106–18
    services and, 57–59
    social reform and, 88, 89

sports and, 415
town planning and, 110–12

venereal disease, 97, 112, 230
vice. *See also* alcohol; crime; prostitution
    education, universities and, 235
    health and, 108
    high-school socials and, 326
    newspapers and, 129
    sexuality and (*see* sexuality)

Wamsley, Kevin B., 418
war brides, 189–91
    French Canadians and, 190
    return to Britain of, 190–91
welfare
    Aboriginals and, 23–24, 26, 28, 33
    children, religion and, 275
    Depression in P.E.I. and, 334–47
    elderly and, 295, 296, 299–300
    girls, unmarried women and, 267–70
    mothers' allowances and, 344
    pensions and (*see* pensions)
    religion and, 316, 334
    social policy and, 181, 276
    wartime allowances and, 186–87
welfare state, 88, 181
West Indians, 141, 142
White, James, 504
white slavery, 90, 98
wildlife. *See under* conservation
With a Pinch of Sin, 404
wolves, 508
women
    Aboriginal, 41–43
    African-American workers and, 146, 147,
        148–49
    agriculture, rural life and, 282, 285–88
    bicycling and, 418, 427–28
    cheerleading in schools and, 324
    comic books and, 381
    families and (*see* families)
    feminism and, 182, 513
    as high-school teachers, 326
    homecoming war veterans and, 184–91
    housing and, 112–14, 116–17
    industrialization and, 78, 108
    invisibility of labour and, 347
    labour, social services and, 335
    labour legislation and, 76–77
    lesbian (*see* lesbians)
    media and, 245–47, 252–53
    Métis, 6–18

    military training, universities and, 234
    private letters, history and, 216–20, 378
    as professional caregivers, 302
    prostitution and (*see* prostitution)
    role of, 99, 108, 182, 281–88
    single, friendships and, 258–59
    sports and, 287, 324–25, 415, 445
    as unmarried mothers, 267–70, 344
Women's Canadian Club of St. John, N.B., 354
Woodsworth, J. S., 123, 276, 316

youth. *See also* children
    culture, public concerns and, 320–30, 371–72
    dating and, 325
    education and (*see* education)
    gangs and, 327
    Junior Farmer clubs and, 278–91
    media and (*see* media)
    Métis, 11–14
    rural vs. urban, 288
    school-leaving age and, 320
    teenage clubs and, 311–12